Principles *of*
Corporate Finance

THE MCGRAW-HILL/IRWIN SERIES IN FINANCE, INSURANCE, AND REAL ESTATE

Financial Management

Block, Hirt, and Danielsen
Foundations of Financial Management
Seventeenth Edition

Brealey, Myers, and Allen
Principles of Corporate Finance
Thirteenth Edition

Brealey, Myers, and Allen
Principles of Corporate Finance, Concise
Second Edition

Brealey, Myers, and Marcus
Fundamentals of Corporate Finance
Ninth Edition

Brooks
FinGame Online 5.0

Bruner
Case Studies in Finance: Managing for Corporate Value Creation
Eighth Edition

Cornett, Adair, and Nofsinger
Finance: Applications and Theory
Fourth Edition

Cornett, Adair, and Nofsinger
M: Finance
Fourth Edition

DeMello
Cases in Finance
Second Edition

Grinblatt (editor)
Stephen A. Ross, Mentor: Influence through Generations

Grinblatt and Titman
Financial Markets and Corporate Strategy
Second Edition

Higgins
Analysis for Financial Management
Twelfth Edition

Ross, Westerfield, Jaffe, and Jordan
Corporate Finance
Twelfth Edition

Ross, Westerfield, Jaffe, and Jordan
Corporate Finance: Core Principles and Applications
Fifth Edition

Ross, Westerfield, and Jordan
Essentials of Corporate Finance
Ninth Edition

Ross, Westerfield, and Jordan
Fundamentals of Corporate Finance
Twelfth Edition

Shefrin
Behavioral Corporate Finance: Decisions that Create Value
Second Edition

Investments

Bodie, Kane, and Marcus
Essentials of Investments
Eleventh Edition

Bodie, Kane, and Marcus
Investments
Eleventh Edition

Hirt and Block
Fundamentals of Investment Management
Tenth Edition

Jordan and Miller
Fundamentals of Investments: Valuation and Management
Eighth Edition

Stewart, Piros, and Heisler
Running Money: Professional Portfolio Management

Sundaram and Das
Derivatives: Principles and Practice
Second Edition

Financial Institutions and Markets

Rose and Hudgins
Bank Management and Financial Services
Tenth Edition

Rose and Marquis
Financial Institutions and Markets
Eleventh Edition

Saunders and Cornett
Financial Institutions Management: A Risk Management Approach
Ninth Edition

Saunders and Cornett
Financial Markets and Institutions
Seventh Edition

International Finance

Eun and Resnick
International Financial Management
Eighth Edition

Real Estate

Brueggeman and Fisher
Real Estate Finance and Investments
Sixteenth Edition

Ling and Archer
Real Estate Principles: A Value Approach
Fifth Edition

Financial Planning and Insurance

Allen, Melone, Rosenbloom, and Mahoney
Retirement Plans: 401(k)s, IRAs, and Other Deferred Compensation Approaches
Twelfth Edition

Altfest
Personal Financial Planning
Second Edition

Kapoor, Dlabay, and Hughes
Focus on Personal Finance: An Active Approach to Help You Develop Successful Financial Skills
Sixth Edition

Kapoor, Dlabay, and Hughes
Personal Finance
Twelfth Edition

Walker and Walker
Personal Finance: Building Your Future
Second Edition

Principles *of*
Corporate Finance

THIRTEENTH EDITION

Richard A. Brealey
Professor of Finance
London Business School

Stewart C. Myers
Professor of Financial Economics
Sloan School of Management Massachusetts
Institute of Technology

Franklin Allen
Professor of Finance and Economics
Imperial College London

PRINCIPLES OF CORPORATE FINANCE, THIRTEENTH EDITION

Published by McGraw-Hill Education, 2 Penn Plaza, New York, NY 10121. Copyright © 2020 by McGraw-Hill Education. All rights reserved. Printed in the United States of America. Previous editions © 2017, 2014, and 2011. No part of this publication may be reproduced or distributed in any form or by any means, or stored in a database or retrieval system, without the prior written consent of McGraw-Hill Education, including, but not limited to, in any network or other electronic storage or transmission, or broadcast for distance learning.

Some ancillaries, including electronic and print components, may not be available to customers outside the United States.

This book is printed on acid-free paper.

4 5 6 7 8 9 LKV 22

ISBN 978-1-260-01390-0
MHID 1-260-01390-1

Portfolio Manager: *Charles Synovec*
Product Developer: *Noelle Bathurst*
Marketing Manager: *Allison McCabe-Carroll*
Content Project Managers: *Fran Simon and Jamie Koch*
Buyer: *Laura Fuller*
Design: *Matt Diamond*
Content Licensing Specialist: *Ann Marie Jannette*
Cover Image: *Emily Tolan/Shutterstock*
Compositor: *SPi Global*
All credits appearing on page or at the end of the book are considered to be an extension of the copyright page.

Library of Congress Cataloging-in-Publication Data

Names: Brealey, Richard A., author. | Myers, Stewart C., author. | Allen,
     Franklin, 1956- author.
Title: Principles of corporate finance / Richard A. Brealey, Professor of
     Finance, London Business School, Stewart C. Myers, Robert C. Merton (1970)
     Professor of Finance, Sloan School of Management, Massachusetts Institute
     of Technology, Franklin Allen, Professor of Finance and Economics,
     Imperial College London.
Description: Thirteenth edition. | New York, NY : McGraw-Hill Education, [2020]
Identifiers: LCCN 2018040697 | ISBN 9781260013900 (alk. paper)
Subjects: LCSH: Corporations—Finance.
Classification: LCC HG4026 .B667 2020 | DDC 658.15—dc23
LC record available at https://lccn.loc.gov/2018040697

The Internet addresses listed in the text were accurate at the time of publication. The inclusion of a website does not indicate an endorsement by the authors or McGraw-Hill Education, and McGraw-Hill Education does not guarantee the accuracy of the information presented at these sites.

mheducation.com/highered

Dedication

To our parents.

About the Authors

❱ Richard A. Brealey

Professor of Finance at the London Business School. He is the former president of the European Finance Association and a former director of the American Finance Association. He is a fellow of the British Academy and has served as a special adviser to the Governor of the Bank of England and director of a number of financial institutions. Books written by Professor Brealey include *Introduction to Risk and Return from Common Stocks.*

❱ Stewart C. Myers

Professor of Financial Economics at MIT's Sloan School of Management. He is past president of the American Finance Association, a research associate at the National Bureau of Economic Research, a principal of the Brattle Group Inc., and a retired director of Entergy Corporation. His research is primarily concerned with the valuation of real and financial assets, corporate financial policy, and financial aspects of government regulation of business. He is the author of influential research papers on many topics, including adjusted present value, rate of return regulation, pricing and capital allocation in insurance, real options, and moral hazard and information issues in capital structure decisions.

❱ Franklin Allen

Professor of Finance and Economics, Imperial College London, and Emeritus Nippon Life Professor of Finance at the Wharton School of the University of Pennsylvania. He is past president of the American Finance Association, Western Finance Association, Society for Financial Studies, Financial Intermediation Research Society, Financial Management Association, and a fellow of the Econometric Society and the British Academy. His research has focused on financial innovation, asset price bubbles, comparing financial systems, and financial crises. He is Director of the Brevan Howard Centre for Financial Analysis at Imperial College Business School.

This book describes the theory and practice of corporate finance. We hardly need to explain why financial managers have to master the practical aspects of their job, but we should spell out why down-to-earth managers need to bother with theory.

Managers learn from experience how to cope with routine problems. But the best managers are also able to respond to change. To do so you need more than time-honored rules of thumb; you must understand why companies and financial markets behave the way they do. In other words, you need a *theory* of finance.

Does that sound intimidating? It shouldn't. Good theory helps you to grasp what is going on in the world around you. It helps you to ask the right questions when times change and new problems need to be analyzed. It also tells you which things you do *not* need to worry about. Throughout this book, we show how managers use financial theory to solve practical problems.

Of course, the theory presented in this book is not perfect and complete—no theory is. There are some famous controversies where financial economists cannot agree. We have not glossed over these disagreements. We set out the arguments for each side and tell you where we stand.

Much of this book is concerned with understanding what financial managers do and why. But we also say what financial managers *should* do to increase company value. Where theory suggests that financial managers are making mistakes, we say so, while admitting that there may be hidden reasons for their actions. In brief, we have tried to be fair but to pull no punches.

This book may be your first view of the world of modern finance. If so, you will read first for new ideas, for an understanding of how finance theory translates into practice, and occasionally, we hope, for entertainment. But eventually you will be in a position to make financial decisions, not just study them. At that point, you can turn to this book as a reference and guide.

Changes in the Thirteenth Edition

We are proud of the success of previous editions of *Principles,* and we have done our best to make the thirteenth edition even better.

Some of the biggest changes in this edition were prompted by the tax changes enacted in the U.S. Tax Cuts and Jobs Act passed in December 2017. One of the chapters most affected was Chapter 6, which is concerned with calculating the present value of capital projects. We describe the major tax changes in that chapter, and we work through an example of a capital budgeting problem with 100% bonus depreciation and a 21% corporate tax rate. But the U.S. system of immediate expensing of capital expenditures is almost unique. So we also set out examples of the more common systems of straight-line depreciation and double-declining-balance, which is essentially identical to the former U.S. MACRS depreciation.

Another 2017 tax change was the limit imposed on interest tax shields. For companies that are caught by this change, it may no longer make sense to discount cash flows by the weighted average cost of capital. We discuss the implications for company debt policy in Chapter 18. In Chapter 19, we show how adjusted present value can be used in these cases to value companies and projects. Similarly, the cap on interest tax shields complicates the valuation of leases. In Chapter 25, we show that when the cap is operative, leases need to be valued by constructing an equivalent loan. Finally, in Chapter 32, we consider the possible effect on the private-equity market.

The third important change was the switch by the United States to a territorial tax system. This has major implications for tax strategies, which we largely discuss in the chapters on working capital management (Chapter 30) and mergers (Chapter 31).

U.S. financial managers work in a global environment and need to understand the financial systems of other countries. Also, many of the text's readers come from countries other than the United States. Therefore, in recent editions we have progressively introduced more international material, including information about the major developing economies, such as China and India. In the current edition, we have continued to augment the international content. We hope that an understanding of practices in other countries will also lead to a better understanding of the characteristics of one's own financial system.

Users of previous editions of this book will not find dramatic changes in coverage or in the ordering of topics. However, there are a number of chapters that have been thoroughly rewritten. For example, the material on agency issues in Chapter 12 has been substantially revised. Chapter 13 on market efficiency and behavioral finance is now fresher and more up to date. Chapter 23 on credit risk focuses more on the practical issues of forecasting default probabilities.

Throughout, we have tried to make the book more up-to-date and easier to read. In many cases, the changes consist of some updated data here and a new example there. Often, these additions reflect some recent development in the financial markets or company practice.

In the 11th edition, we added digital extensions through our Beyond the Page features, or "apps" as we call them. This extra material can allow us to escape from some of the constraints of the printed page by providing more explanation for readers who need it and additional material for those who would like to dig deeper. The Beyond the Page features include extra examples and spreadsheet programs, as well as some interesting anecdotes.

There are now more than 150 of these apps. They are all seamlessly available with a click on the e-versions of the book, but they are also readily accessible from the traditional hard copy of the text through the shortcut URLs. Check out **mhhe.com/brealey13e** to learn more. Examples of these applications include:

- **Chapter 1** In Chapter 1, we refer to Bernard Madoff's ponzi scheme. But this scam pales into insignificance compared with the great Albanian ponzi scheme, which is described in an app.
- **Chapter 2** Do you need to learn how to use a financial calculator? The Beyond the Page financial calculator application shows how to do so.
- **Chapter 3** Would you like to calculate a bond's duration, see how it predicts the effect of small interest rate changes on bond price, calculate the duration of a common stock, or learn how to measure convexity? The duration application for Figure 3.2 allows you to do so.
- **Chapter 5** Want more practice in valuing annuities? There is an application that provides worked examples and hands-on practice.
- **Chapter 9** How about measuring the betas of the Fama–French three-factor model for U.S. stocks? The Beyond the Page beta estimation application does this.
- **Chapter 14** Ever wonder why Google split its stock into A and C shares? An app provides the answer.
- **Chapter 15** Want to now how companies can raise capital by an initial coin offering? There is an app on the topic.
- **Chapter 19** The text briefly describes the flow-to-equity method for valuing businesses, but using the method can be tricky. We provide an application that guides you step by step.
- **Chapter 20** The Black–Scholes Beyond the Page application provides an option calculator. It also shows

how to estimate the option's sensitivity to changes in the inputs and how to measure an option's risk.
- **Chapter 28** Would you like to view the most recent financial statements for different U.S. companies and calculate their financial ratios? There is an application that will do this for you.

We believe that the apps offer an opportunity to widen the types of material that can be made available and help the reader to decide how deeply he or she wishes to explore a topic.

We have added end-of-chapter questions, merged what was becoming a false distinction between basic and intermediate questions, and reordered the questions to follow better the same sequence as the chapter.

❯ Making Learning Easier

Each chapter of the book includes an introductory preview, a summary, and an annotated list of suggested further reading. The list of possible candidates for further reading is now voluminous. Rather than trying to include every important article, we largely list survey articles or general books. We give more specific references in footnotes.

Each chapter is followed by a set of problems on both numerical and conceptual topics and a few challenge problems. Answers to the starred problems appear in the Appendix at the end of the book.

We included a Finance on the Web section in chapters where it makes sense to do so. This section now houses a number of Web Projects, along with new Data Analysis problems. These exercises seek to familiarize the reader with some useful websites and to explain how to download and process data from the web.

The book also contains 13 end-of-chapter Mini-Cases. These include specific questions to guide the case analyses. Answers to the mini-cases are available to instructors on the book's website.

Spreadsheet programs such as Excel are tailor-made for many financial calculations. Several chapters include boxes that introduce the most useful financial functions and provide some short practice questions. We show how to use the Excel function key to locate the function and then enter the data. We think that this approach is much simpler than trying to remember the formula for each function.

We conclude the book with a glossary of financial terms.

The 34 chapters in this book are divided into 11 parts. Parts 1, 2, and 3 cover valuation and capital investment decisions, including portfolio theory, asset pricing models, and the cost of capital. Parts 4 through 8 cover payout policy, capital structure, options (including real options), corporate debt, and risk management. Part 9 covers financial analysis, planning, and working-capital management. Part 10 covers mergers and acquisitions, corporate restructuring, and corporate governance around the world. Part 11 concludes.

We realize that instructors will wish to select topics and may prefer a different sequence. We have therefore written chapters so that topics can be introduced in several logical orders. For example, there should be no difficulty in reading the chapters on financial analysis and planning before the chapters on valuation and capital investment.

❭ Acknowledgments

We have a long list of people to thank for their helpful criticism of earlier editions and for assistance in preparing this one. They include Faiza Arshad, Aleijda de Cazenove Balsan, Kedran Garrison, Robert Pindyck, Donna Cheung, and Gretchen Slemmons at MIT; Elroy Dimson, Paul Marsh, Mike Staunton, and Stefania Uccheddu at London Business School; Lynda Borucki, Marjorie Fischer, Larry Kolbe, Michael Vilbert, Bente Villadsen, and Fiona Wang at The Brattle Group Inc.; Alex Triantis at the University of Maryland; Adam Kolasinski at Texas A&M University; Simon Gervais at Duke University; Michael Chui at Bank for International Settlements; Pedro Matos at the University of Southern California; Yupana Wiwattanakantang at National University of Singapore; Nickolay Gantchev at the Southern Methodist University; Tina Horowitz, and Lin Shen, at the University of Pennsylvania; Darien Huang at Tudor Investment; Julie Wulf at Harvard University; Jinghua Yan at SAC Capital; Bennett Stewart at EVA Dimensions; and Mobeen Iqbal and Antoine Uettwiller at Imperial College London. We are grateful to Cyrus Brealey for his suggestions.

We would also like to thank the dedicated experts who have helped with updates to the instructor materials and online content in Connect and LearnSmart, including Kay Johnson, Blaise Roncagli, Deb Bauer, Mishal Rawaf, Marc-Anthony Isaacs, Frank Ryan, Peter Crabb, Victoria Mahan, Nicholas Racculia, Angela Treinen, and Kent Ragan.

We want to express our appreciation to those instructors whose insightful comments and suggestions were invaluable to us during the revision process:

Ibrahim Affaneh *Indiana University of Pennsylvania*
Neyaz Ahmed *University of Maryland*
Alexander Amati *Rutgers University, New Brunswick*
Anne Anderson *Lehigh University*
Noyan Arsen *Koc University*
Anders Axvarn *Gothenburg University*
John Banko *University of Florida, Gainesville*
Michael Barry *Boston College*
Jan Bartholdy *ASB, Denmark*
Penny Belk *Loughborough University*
Omar Benkato *Ball State University*
Eric Benrud *University of Baltimore*
Ronald Benson *University of Maryland, University College*
Peter Berman *University of New Haven*
Tom Boulton *Miami University of Ohio*
Edward Boyer *Temple University*
Alon Brav *Duke University*
Jean Canil *University of Adelaide*
Robert Carlson *Bethany College*
Chuck Chahyadi *Eastern Illinois University*
Fan Chen *University of Mississippi*
Celtin Ciner *University of North Carolina, Wilmington*
John Cooney *Texas Tech University*
Charles Cuny *Washington University, St. Louis*
John Davenport *Regent University*
Ray DeGennaro *University of Tennessee, Knoxville*
Adri DeRidder *Gotland University*
William Dimovski *Deakin University, Melbourne*
David Ding *Nanyang Technological University*
Robert Duvic *University of Texas at Austin*
Alex Edmans *London Business School*
Susan Edwards *Grand Valley State University*
Riza Emekter *Robert Morris University*
Robert Everett *Johns Hopkins University*
Dave Fehr *Southern New Hampshire University*
Donald Flagg *University of Tampa*
Frank Flanegin *Robert Morris University*
Zsuzanna Fluck *Michigan State University*
Connel Fullenkamp *Duke University*
Mark Garmaise *University of California, Los Angeles*
Sharon Garrison *University of Arizona*
Christopher Geczy *University of Pennsylvania*
George Geis *University of Virginia*
Stuart Gillan *University of Delaware*
Felix Goltz *Edhec Business School*
Ning Gong *Melbourne Business School*
Levon Goukasian *Pepperdine University*
Gary Gray *Pennsylvania State University*
C. J. Green *Loughborough University*
Mark Griffiths *Thunderbird, American School of International Management*
Re-Jin Guo *University of Illinois, Chicago*
Ann Hackert *Idaho State University*
Winfried Hallerbach *Erasmus University, Rotterdam*
Milton Harris *University of Chicago*
Mary Hartman *Bentley College*
Glenn Henderson *University of Cincinnati*
Donna Hitscherich *Columbia University*
Ronald Hoffmeister *Arizona State University*
James Howard *University of Maryland, College Park*
George Jabbour *George Washington University*

Ravi Jagannathan *Northwestern University*
Abu Jalal *Suffolk University*
Nancy Jay *Mercer University*
Thadavillil (Nathan) Jithendranathan *University of Saint Thomas*
Kathleen Kahle *University of Arizona*
Jarl Kallberg *NYU, Stern School of Business*
Ron Kaniel *University of Rochester*
Steve Kaplan *University of Chicago*
Eric Kelley *University of Arizona*
Arif Khurshed *Manchester Business School*
Ken Kim *University of Wisconsin, Milwaukee*
Jiro Eduoard Kondo *Northwestern University Kellogg School of Management*
C. R. Krishnaswamy *Western Michigan University*
George Kutner *Marquette University*
Dirk Laschanzky *University of Iowa*
Scott Lee *Texas A&M University*
Bob Lightner *San Diego Christian College*
David Lins *University of Illinois, Urbana*
Brandon Lockhart *University of Nebraska, Lincoln*
David Lovatt *University of East Anglia*
Greg Lucado *University of the Sciences in Philadelphia*
Debbie Lucas *Northwestern University*
Brian Lucey *Trinity College, Dublin*
Suren Mansinghka *University of California, Irvine*
Ernst Maug *Mannheim University*
George McCabe *University of Nebraska*
Eric McLaughlin *California State University, Pomona*
Joe Messina *San Francisco State University*
Tim Michael *University of Houston, Clear Lake*
Dag Michalsen *Bl, Oslo*
Franklin Michello *Middle Tennessee State University*
Peter Moles *University of Edinburgh*
Katherine Morgan *Columbia University*
James Nelson *East Carolina University*
James Owens *West Texas A&M University*
Darshana Palkar *Minnesota State University, Mankato*
Claus Parum *Copenhagen Business School*
Dilip Patro *Rutgers University*
John Percival *University of Pennsylvania*
Birsel Pirim *University of Illinois, Urbana*
Latha Ramchand *University of Houston*
Narendar V. Rao *Northeastern University*
Rathin Rathinasamy *Ball State University*
Raghavendra Rau *Purdue University*
Joshua Raugh *University of Chicago*
Charu Reheja *Wake Forest University*
Thomas Rhee *California State University, Long Beach*
Tom Rietz *University of Iowa*
Robert Ritchey *Texas Tech University*
Michael Roberts *University of Pennsylvania*
Mo Rodriguez *Texas Christian University*
John Rozycki *Drake University*
Frank Ryan *San Diego State University*
Marc Schauten *Eramus University*

Brad Scott *Webster University*
Nejat Seyhun *University of Michigan*
Jay Shanken *Emory University*
Chander Shekhar *University of Melbourne*
Hamid Shomali *Golden Gate University*
Richard Simonds *Michigan State University*
Bernell Stone *Brigham Young University*
John Strong *College of William & Mary*
Avanidhar Subrahmanyam *University of California, Los Angeles*
Tim Sullivan *Bentley College*
Shrinivasan Sundaram *Ball State University*
Chu-Sheng Tai *Texas Southern University*
Tom Tallerico *Dowling College*
Stephen Todd *Loyola University, Chicago*
Walter Torous *University of California, Los Angeles*
Emery Trahan *Northeastern University*
Gary Tripp *Southern New Hampshire University*
Ilias Tsiakas *University of Warwick*
David Vang *St. Thomas University*
Steve Venti *Dartmouth College*
Joseph Vu *DePaul University*
John Wald *Rutgers University*
Chong Wang *Naval Postgraduate School*
Faye Wang *University of Illinois, Chicago*
Kelly Welch *University of Kansas*
Jill Wetmore *Saginaw Valley State University*
Patrick Wilkie *University of Virginia*
Matt Will *University of Indianapolis*
David Williams *Texas A&M University, Commerce*
Art Wilson *George Washington University*
Shee Wong *University of Minnesota, Duluth*
Bob Wood *Tennessee Tech University*
Fei Xie *George Mason University*
Minhua Yang *University of Central Florida*
David Zalewski *Providence College*
Chenying Zhang *University of Pennsylvania*

This list is surely incomplete. We know how much we owe to our colleagues at the London Business School, MIT's Sloan School of Management, Imperial College London, and the University of Pennsylvania's Wharton School. In many cases, the ideas that appear in this book are as much their ideas as ours.

We would also like to thank all those at McGraw-Hill Education who worked on the book, including Chuck Synovec, Executive Brand Manager; Allison McCabe-Carroll, Senior Product Developer; Trina Mauer, Executive Marketing Manager; Dave O'Donnell, Marketing Specialist; Fran Simon, Project Manager; Matt Diamond, Designer; and Angela Norris, Digital Product Analyst.

Richard A. Brealey
Stewart C. Myers
Franklin Allen

Pedagogical Features

❯ Chapter Overview

Each chapter begins with a brief narrative and outline to explain the concepts that will be covered in
more depth. Useful websites related to material for
each Part are provided in the Connect library.

❯ Finance in Practice Boxes

Relevant news articles, often from financial pub-
lications, appear in various chapters throughout
the text. Aimed at bringing real-world flavor into
the classroom, these boxes provide insight into the
business world today.

❯ Numbered Examples

Numbered and titled examples are called out
within chapters to further illustrate concepts.
Students can learn how to solve specific problems
step-by-step and apply key principles to answer
concrete questions and scenarios.

❯ Beyond the Page Interactive Content and Applications

Additional resources and hands-on applications
are just a click away. Students can use the web
address or click on the icon in the eBook to learn
more about key concepts and try out calculations,
tables, and figures when they go Beyond the Page.

Excel

❭ Spreadsheet Functions Boxes

These boxes provide detailed examples of how to use Excel spreadsheets when applying financial concepts. Questions that apply to the spreadsheet follow for additional practice.

USEFUL SPREADSHEET FUNCTIONS

Discounting Cash Flows

❭ Spreadsheet programs such as Excel provide built-in functions to solve discounted cash flow (DCF) problems. You can find these functions by pressing *fx* on the Excel toolbar. If you then click on the function that you wish to use, Excel asks you for the inputs that it needs. At the bottom left of the function box there is a Help facility with an example of how the function is used.

Here is a list of useful functions for DCF problems and some points to remember when entering data:

- **FV:** Future value of single investment or annuity.
- **PV:** Present value of single future cash flow or annuity.
- **RATE:** Interest rate (or rate of return) needed to produce given future value or annuity.
- **NPER:** Number of periods (e.g., years) that it takes an investment to reach a given future value or series of future cash flows.
- **PMT:** Amount of annuity payment with a given present or future value.
- **NPV:** Calculates the value of a stream of negative and positive cash flows. (When using this function, note the warning below.)
- **EFFECT:** The effective annual interest rate, given the quoted rate (APR) and number of interest payments in a year.
- **NOMINAL:** The quoted interest rate (APR) given the effective annual interest rate.

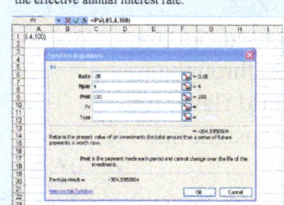

All the inputs in these functions can be entered directly as numbers or as the addresses of cells that contain the numbers.

Three warnings:

1. PV is the amount that needs to be invested today

be entered as a negative number. Entering both PV and FV with the same sign when solving for RATE results in an error message.

2. Always enter the interest or discount rate as a decimal value (for example, .05 rather than 5%).

3. Use the NPV function with care. Better still, don't use it at all. It gives the value of the cash flows one period *before* the first cash flow and not the value at the date of the first cash flow.

Spreadsheet Questions

The following questions provide opportunities to practice each of the Excel functions.

1. (FV) In 1880, five aboriginal trackers were each promised the equivalent of 100 Australian dollars for helping to capture the notorious outlaw Ned Kelly. One hundred and thirteen years later, the granddaughters of two of the trackers claimed that this reward had not been paid. If the interest rate over this period averaged about 4.5%, how much would the A$100 have accumulated to?

2. (PV) Your adviser has produced revised figures for your office building. It is forecasted to produce a cash flow of $40,000 in year 1, but only $850,000 in year 2, when you come to sell it. If the cost of capital is 12%, what is the value of the building?

3. (PV) Your company can lease a truck for $10,000 a year (paid at the end of the year) for six years, or it can buy the truck today for $50,000. At the end of the six years the truck will be worthless. If the interest rate is 6%, what is the present value of the lease payments? Is the lease worthwhile?

4. (RATE) Ford Motor stock was one of the victims of the 2008 credit crisis. In June 2007, Ford stock price stood at $9.42. Eighteen months later it was $2.72. What was the annual rate of return over this period to an investor in Ford stock?

5. (NPER) An investment adviser has promised to double your money. If the interest rate is 7% a year, how many years will she take to do so?

6. (PMT) You need to take out a home mortgage for $200,000. If payments are made annually over 30 years and the interest rate is 8%, what is the amount of the annual payment?

❭ Excel Exhibits

Select tables are set as spreadsheets, and the corresponding Excel files are also available in Connect and through the Beyond the Page features.

	(1)	(2)	(3)	(4)	(5)	(6)	(7)
							Product of
				Deviation	Deviation	Squared	Deviations
				from	from Average	Deviation	from Average
		Market	Anchovy Q	Average	Anchovy Q	from Average	Returns
Month	Return	Return	Market Return	Return	Market Return	(cols 4 × 5)
1	−8%	−11%	−10	−13	100	130
2	4	8	2	6	4	12
3	12	19	10	17	100	170
4	−6	−13	−8	−15	64	120
5	2	3	0	1	0	0
6	8	6	6	4	36	24
Average	2	2		Total	304	456
			Variance = σ_m^2 = 304/6 = 50.67			
			Covariance = σ_{im} = 456/6 = 76			
			Beta (β) = σ_{im}/σ_m^2 = 76/50.67 = 1.5			

❭ **TABLE 7.7**
Calculating the variance of the market returns and the covariance between the returns on the market and those of Anchovy Queen. Beta is the ratio of the covariance to the variance (i. e., $\beta = \sigma_{im}/\sigma_m^2$).

End-of-Chapter Features

❯ Problem Sets

For the 13th edition, we continue to use topic labels for each end-of-chapter problem to help instructors create assignments and to provide reinforcement for students. These end-of-chapter problems give students hands-on practice with key concepts and applications. Answers to select problems marked with * are included at the back of the book.

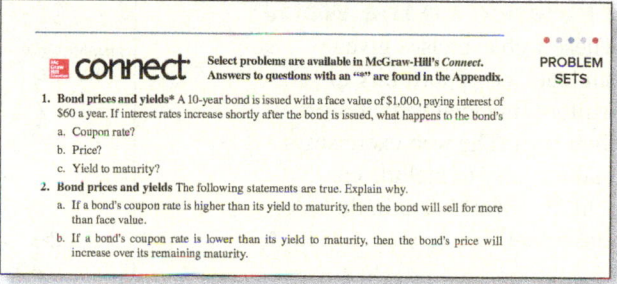

connect Select problems are available in McGraw-Hill's *Connect*. Answers to questions with an "°" are found in the Appendix.

PROBLEM SETS

1. **Bond prices and yields**° A 10-year bond is issued with a face value of $1,000, paying interest of $60 a year. If interest rates increase shortly after the bond is issued, what happens to the bond's
   a. Coupon rate?
   b. Price?
   c. Yield to maturity?
2. **Bond prices and yields** The following statements are true. Explain why.
   a. If a bond's coupon rate is higher than its yield to maturity, then the bond will sell for more than face value.
   b. If a bond's coupon rate is lower than its yield to maturity, then the bond's price will increase over its remaining maturity.

CHALLENGE

32. **Bond prices and yields** Write a spreadsheet program to construct a series of bond tables that show the present value of a bond given the coupon rate, maturity, and yield to maturity. Assume that coupon payments are semiannual and yields are compounded semiannually.
33. **Price and spot interest rates** Find the arbitrage opportunity(ies). Assume for simplicity that coupons are paid annually. In each case, the face value of the bond is $1,000.

Bond	Maturity (years)	Coupon ($)	Price ($)
A	3	0	751.30
B	4	50	842.30
C	4	120	1,065.28
D	4	100	980.57
E	3	140	1,120.12
F	3	70	1,001.62
G	2	0	834.00

❯ Excel Problems

Most chapters contain problems, denoted by an icon, specifically linked to Excel spreadsheets that are available in Connect and through the Beyond the Page features.

Questions 14 to 17 all refer to Greymare's bus lease. To answer them you may find it helpful to use the Beyond the Page live Excel spreadsheets in Connect.

BEYOND THE PAGE

Try it! Leasing spreadsheets

mhhe.com/brealey13e

13. **Valuing financial leases** Look again at the bus lease described in Table 25.2.
   a. What is the value of the lease if Greymare's marginal tax rate is $T_c = .30$?
   b. What would the lease value be if the tax rate is 21%, but for tax purposes, the initial investment had to be written off in equal amounts over years 1 through 5?

❭ Finance on the Web

These web exercises give students the opportunity to explore financial websites on their own. The web exercises make it easy to include current, real-world data in the classroom.

FINANCE ON THE WEB

You can download data for the following questions from **finance.yahoo.com.**

1. Look at the companies listed in Table 8.2. Calculate monthly rates of return for two successive five-year periods. Calculate betas for each subperiod using the Excel SLOPE function. How stable was each company's beta? Suppose that you had used these betas to estimate expected rates of return from the CAPM. Would your estimates have changed significantly from period to period?

2. Identify a sample of food companies. For example, you could try Campbell Soup (CPB), General Mills (GIS), Kellogg (K), Mondelez International (MDLZ), and Tyson Foods (TSN).

   a. Estimate beta and R^2 for each company, using five years of monthly returns and Excel functions SLOPE and RSQ.

   b. Average the returns for each month to give the return on an equally weighted portfolio of the stocks. Then calculate the industry beta using these portfolio returns. How does the R^2 of this portfolio compare with the average R^2 of the individual stocks?

   c. Use the CAPM to calculate an average cost of equity (r_{equity}) for the food industry. Use current interest rates—take a look at the end of Section 9-2—and a reasonable estimate of the market risk premium.

❭ Mini-Cases

Mini-cases are included in select chapters so students can apply their knowledge to real-world scenarios.

MINI-CASE ● ● ● ●

The Jones Family Incorporated

The Scene: It is early evening in the summer of 2018, in an ordinary family room in Manhattan. Modern furniture, with old copies of *The Wall Street Journal* and the *Financial Times* scattered around. Autographed photos of Jerome Powell and George Soros are prominently displayed. A picture window reveals a distant view of lights on the Hudson River. John Jones sits at a computer terminal, glumly sipping a glass of chardonnay and putting on a carry trade in Japanese yen over the Internet. His wife Marsha enters.

Marsha: Hi, honey. Glad to be home. Lousy day on the trading floor, though. Dullsville. No volume. But I did manage to hedge next year's production from our copper mine. I couldn't get a good quote on the right package of futures contracts, so I arranged a commodity swap.

John doesn't reply.

Supplements

> In this edition, we have gone to great lengths to ensure that our supplements are equal in quality and authority to the text itself.

MCGRAW-HILL'S *CONNECT*

Less Managing. More Teaching. Greater Learning.

McGraw-Hill's *Connect* is an online assignment and assessment solution that connects students with the tools and resources they'll need to achieve success.

McGraw-Hill's *Connect* helps prepare students for their future by enabling faster learning, more efficient studying, and higher retention of knowledge.

McGraw-Hill's *Connect* Features

 *Connect* offers a number of powerful tools and features to make managing assignments easier, so faculty can spend more time teaching. With *Connect,* students can engage with their coursework anytime and anywhere, making the learning process more accessible and efficient. *Connect* offers the features described here.

Simple Assignment Management

With *Connect,* creating assignments is easier than ever, so instructors can spend more time teaching and less time managing. The assignment management function enables the instructor to:

- Create and deliver assignments easily from end-of-chapter questions and test bank items.
- Streamline lesson planning, student progress reporting, and assignment grading to make classroom management more efficient than ever.
- Go paperless with the eBook and online submission and grading of student assignments.

Automatic Grading

When it comes to studying, time is precious. *Connect* helps students learn more efficiently by providing feedback and practice material when they need it, where they need it. When it comes to teaching, the instructor's time is also precious. The grading function enables the instructor to:

- Score assignments automatically, giving students immediate feedback on their work and side-by-side comparisons with correct answers.
- Access and review each response, manually change grades, or leave comments for students to review.
- Reinforce classroom concepts with practice tests and instant quizzes.

Instructor Library

The *Connect* Instructor Library provides additional resources to improve student engagement in and out of class. This library contains information about the book and the authors, as well as all of the instructor supplements, including:

- **Instructor's Manual** The Instructor's Manual was extensively revised and updated by Leslie Rush of the University of Hawaii, West Oahu. It contains an overview of each chapter, teaching tips, learning objectives, challenge areas, key terms, and an annotated outline that provides references to the PowerPoint slides.
- **Solutions Manual** The Solutions Manual, carefully revised by Mishal Rawaf, contains solutions to all basic, intermediate, and challenge problems found at the end of each chapter.
- **Test Bank** The Test Bank, revised by Deb Bauer of the University of Oregon, contains hundreds of multiple-choice and short answer/discussion questions, updated based on the revisions of the authors. The level of difficulty varies, as indicated by the easy, medium, or difficult labels.
- **PowerPoint Presentations** Leslie Rush also prepared the PowerPoint presentations, which contain exhibits, outlines, key points, and summaries in a visually stimulating collection of slides. The instructor can edit, print, or rearrange the slides to fit the needs of his or her course.
- **Beyond the Page** The authors have created a wealth of additional examples, explanations, and applications, available for quick access by instructors and students. Each Beyond the Page feature is called out in the text with an icon that links directly to the content.

- **Excel Solutions and Templates** There are templates for select exhibits, as well as various end-of-chapter problems that have been set as Excel spreadsheets—all denoted by an icon. They correlate with specific concepts in the text and allow students to work through financial problems and gain experience using spreadsheets. Useful Spreadsheet Functions Boxes are sprinkled throughout the text to provide helpful prompts on working in Excel.

Diagnostic and Adaptive Learning of Concepts: LearnSmart and SmartBook

LEARNSMART® Students want to make the best use of their study time. The LearnSmart adaptive self-study technology within *Connect* provides students with a seamless combination of practice, assessment, and remediation for every concept in the textbook. LearnSmart's intelligent software adapts to every student response and automatically delivers concepts that advance students' understanding, while reducing time devoted to the concepts already mastered. The result for every student is the fastest path to mastery of the chapter concepts. LearnSmart:

- Applies an intelligent concept engine to identify the relationships between concepts and to serve new concepts to each student only when he or she is ready.
- Adapts automatically to each student, so students spend less time on the topics they understand and practice more those they have yet to master.
- Provides continual reinforcement and remediation but gives only as much guidance as students need.
- Integrates diagnostics as part of the learning experience.
- Enables the instructor to assess which concepts students have efficiently learned on their own, thus freeing class time for more applications and discussion.

SMARTBOOK® SmartBook®, powered by LearnSmart, is the first and only adaptive reading experience designed to change the way students read and learn. It creates a personalized reading experience by highlighting the most important concepts a student needs to learn at each moment in time. As a student engages with Smart-Book, the reading experience continuously adapts by highlighting content based on what the student knows and doesn't know. This ensures that the focus is on the content he or she needs to learn, while simultaneously promoting long-term retention of material. Use SmartBook's real-time reports to quickly identify the concepts that require more attention from individual students—or the entire class. The end result? Students are more engaged with course content, can better prioritize their time, and come to class ready to participate.

Student Study Center

The Connect Student Study Center is the place for students to access additional resources. The Student Study Center:

- Offers students quick access to the Beyond the Page features, Excel files and templates, lectures, practice materials, eBooks, and more.
- Provides instant practice material and study questions, easily accessible on-the-go.

Student Progress Tracking

Connect keeps instructors informed about how each student, section, and class is performing, allowing for more productive use of lecture and office hours. The progress-tracking function enables you to

- View scored work immediately and track individual or group performance with assignment and grade reports.
- Access an instant view of student or class performance relative to learning objectives.

Lecture Capture through Tegrity Campus

For an additional charge Lecture Capture offers new ways for students to focus on the in-class discussion, knowing they can revisit important topics later. This can be delivered through *Connect* or separately. See below for more details.

TEGRITY CAMPUS: LECTURES 24/7

 Tegrity Campus is a service that makes class time available 24/7 by automatically capturing every lecture in a searchable format for students to review when they study and complete assignments. With a simple one-click start-and-stop process, you capture all computer screens and corresponding audio. Students can replay any part

of any class with easy-to-use browser-based viewing on a PC or Mac.

Educators know that the more students can see, hear, and experience class resources, the better they learn. In fact, studies prove it. With Tegrity Campus, students quickly recall key moments by using Tegrity Campus's unique search feature. This search helps students efficiently find what they need, when they need it, across an entire semester of class recordings. Help turn all your students' study time into learning moments immediately supported by your lecture.

To learn more about Tegrity, watch a two-minute Flash demo at **http://tegritycampus.mhhe.com**.

MCGRAW-HILL CUSTOMER CARE CONTACT INFORMATION

At McGraw-Hill, we understand that getting the most from new technology can be challenging. That's why our services don't stop after you purchase our products. You can e-mail our Product Specialists 24 hours a day to get product-training online. Or you can search our knowledge bank of Frequently Asked Questions on our support website.

For Customer Support, call 800-331-5094 or visit **www.mhhe.com/support**. One of our Technical Support Analysts will be able to assist you in a timely fashion.

 **Connect®**

Students—study more efficiently, retain more and achieve better outcomes. Instructors—focus on what you love—teaching.

SUCCESSFUL SEMESTERS INCLUDE CONNECT

FOR INSTRUCTORS

You're in the driver's seat.

Want to build your own course? No problem. Prefer to use our turnkey, prebuilt course? Easy. Want to make changes throughout the semester? Sure. And you'll save time with Connect's auto-grading too.

65%

Less Time Grading

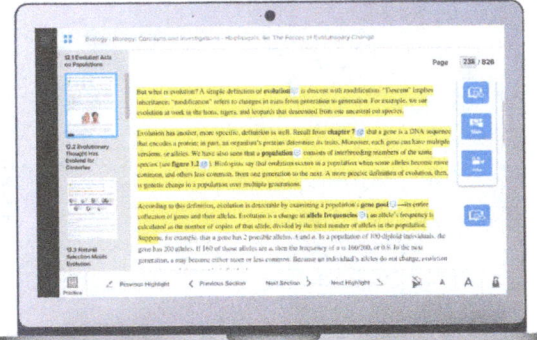

They'll thank you for it.

Adaptive study resources like SmartBook® help your students be better prepared in less time. You can transform your class time from dull definitions to dynamic debates. Hear from your peers about the benefits of Connect at **www.mheducation.com/highered/connect**

Make it simple, make it affordable.

Connect makes it easy with seamless integration using any of the major Learning Management Systems—Blackboard®, Canvas, and D2L, among others—to let you organize your course in one convenient location. Give your students access to digital materials at a discount with our inclusive access program. Ask your McGraw-Hill representative for more information.

©Hill Street Studios/Tobin Rogers/Blend Images LLC

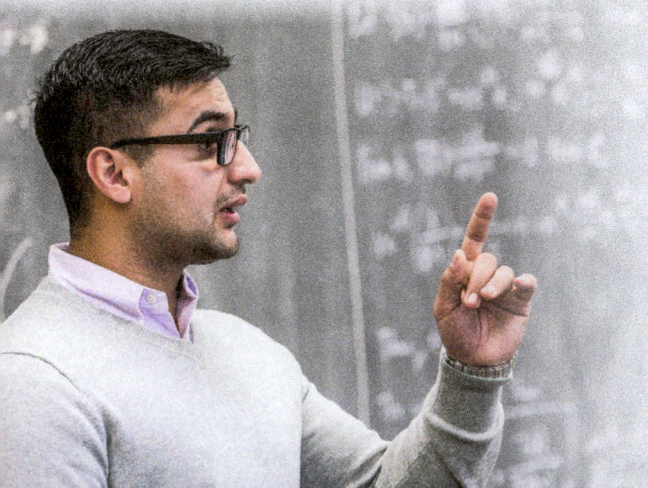

Solutions for your challenges.

A product isn't a solution. Real solutions are affordable, reliable, and come with training and ongoing support when you need it and how you want it. Our Customer Experience Group can also help you troubleshoot tech problems—although Connect's 99% uptime means you might not need to call them. See for yourself at **status.mheducation.com**

Effective, efficient studying.

Connect helps you be more productive with your study time and get better grades using tools like SmartBook, which highlights key concepts and creates a personalized study plan. Connect sets you up for success, so you walk into class with confidence and walk out with better grades.

©Shutterstock/wavebreakmedia

> " I really liked this app—it made it easy to study when you don't have your text-book in front of you. "
>
> - Jordan Cunningham,
> Eastern Washington University

Study anytime, anywhere.

Download the free ReadAnywhere app and access your online eBook when it's convenient, even if you're offline. And since the app automatically syncs with your eBook in Connect, all of your notes are available every time you open it. Find out more at **www.mheducation.com/readanywhere**

No surprises.

The Connect Calendar and Reports tools keep you on track with the work you need to get done and your assignment scores. Life gets busy; Connect tools help you keep learning through it all.

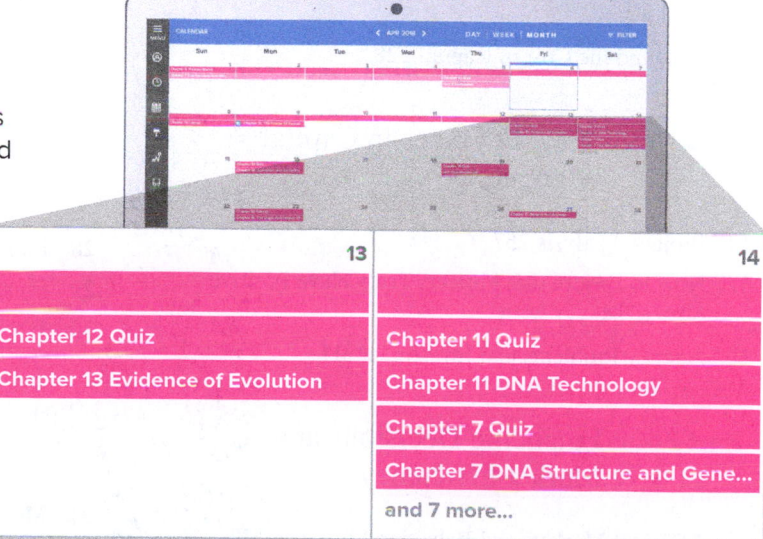

Learning for everyone.

McGraw-Hill works directly with Accessibility Services Departments and faculty to meet the learning needs of all students. Please contact your Accessibility Services office and ask them to email accessibility@mheducation.com, or visit **www.mheducation.com/about/accessibility.html** for more information.

Brief Contents

Preface vii

Part One: Value

1 Introduction to Corporate Finance 1
2 How to Calculate Present Values 20
3 Valuing Bonds 46
4 The Value of Common Stocks 77
5 Net Present Value and Other Investment Criteria 108
6 Making Investment Decisions with the Net Present Value Rule 135

Part Two: Risk

7 Introduction to Risk and Return 167
8 Portfolio Theory and the Capital Asset Pricing Model 198
9 Risk and the Cost of Capital 228

Part Three: Best Practices in Capital Budgeting

10 Project Analysis 257
11 How to Ensure that Projects Truly Have Positive NPVs 284
12 Agency Problems and Investment 311

Part Four: Financing Decisions and Market Efficiency

13 Efficient Markets and Behavioral Finance 337
14 An Overview of Corporate Financing 365
15 How Corporations Issue Securities 391

Part Five: Payout Policy and Capital Structure

16 Payout Policy 425
17 Does Debt Policy Matter? 451

18 How Much Should a Corporation Borrow? 475
19 Financing and Valuation 507

Part Six: Options

20 Understanding Options 542
21 Valuing Options 563
22 Real Options 590

Part Seven: Debt Financing

23 Credit Risk and the Value of Corporate Debt 614
24 The Many Different Kinds of Debt 631
25 Leasing 663

Part Eight: Risk Management

26 Managing Risk 683
27 Managing International Risks 717

Part Nine: Financial Planning and Working Capital Management

28 Financial Analysis 743
29 Financial Planning 770
30 Working Capital Management 801

Part Ten: Mergers, Corporate Control, and Governance

31 Mergers 830
32 Corporate Restructuring 863
33 Governance and Corporate Control around the World 888

Part Eleven: Conclusion

34 Conclusion: What We Do and Do Not Know about Finance 909

Contents

Preface vii

I Part One: Value

1 Introduction to Corporate Finance 1

1-1 Corporate Investment and Financing Decisions *2*
Investment Decisions/Financing Decisions/What Is a Corporation?/The Role of the Financial Manager

1-2 The Financial Goal of the Corporation *7*
Shareholders Want Managers to Maximize Market Value/A Fundamental Result/The Investment Trade-Off/Should Managers Look After the Interests of Their Shareholders?/Agency Problems and Corporate Governance

1-3 Preview of Coming Attractions *13*

Summary 15 · Problem Sets 15 · Appendix: Why Maximizing Shareholder Value Makes Sense 18

2 How to Calculate Present Values 20

2-1 Future Values and Present Values *20*
Calculating Future Values/Calculating Present Values/Valuing an Investment Opportunity/Net Present Value/Risk and Present Value/Present Values and Rates of Return/Calculating Present Values When There Are Multiple Cash Flows/The Opportunity Cost of Capital

2-2 Looking for Shortcuts—Perpetuities and Annuities *28*
How to Value Perpetuities/How to Value Annuities/Valuing Annuities Due/Calculating Annual Payments/Future Value of an Annuity

2-3 More Shortcuts—Growing Perpetuities and Annuities *34*
Growing Perpetuities/Growing Annuities

2-4 How Interest Is Paid and Quoted *36*
Continuous Compounding

Summary 39 · Problem Sets 40 · Finance on the Web 45

3 Valuing Bonds 46

3-1 Using the Present Value Formula to Value Bonds *47*
A Short Trip to Paris to Value a Government Bond/Back to the United States: Semiannual Coupons and Bond Prices

3-2 How Bond Prices Vary with Interest Rates *50*
Duration and Volatility

3-3 The Term Structure of Interest Rates *56*
Spot Rates, Bond Prices, and the Law of One Price/Measuring the Term Structure/Why the Discount Factor Declines as Futurity Increases—and a Digression on Money Machines

3-4 Explaining the Term Structure *60*
Expectations Theory of the Term Structure/Introducing Risk/Inflation and Term Structure

3-5 Real and Nominal Rates of Interest *62*
Indexed Bonds and the Real Rate of Interest/What Determines the Real Rate of Interest?/Inflation and Nominal Interest Rates

3-6 The Risk of Default *67*
Corporate Bonds and Default Risk/Sovereign Bonds and Default Risk

Summary 70 · Further Reading 71 · Problem Sets 71 Finance on the Web 76

4 The Value of Common Stocks 77

4-1 How Common Stocks Are Traded *78*
Trading Results for Boeing

4-2 How Common Stocks Are Valued *80*
Valuation by Comparables/Stock Prices and Dividends

4-3   Estimating the Cost of Equity Capital   *87*
*Using the DCF Model to Set Water, Gas, and
Electricity Prices/Dangers Lurk in Constant-
Growth Formulas*

4-4   The Link between Stock Price and Earnings
per Share   *92*
*Calculating the Present Value of Growth
Opportunities for Fledgling Electronics*

4-5   Valuing a Business by Discounted Cash Flow   *95*
*Valuing the Concatenator Business/Valuation
Format/Estimating Horizon Value/Free Cash Flow,
Dividends, and Repurchases*

Summary 100 · Problem Sets 101 · Finance on the
Web 106 · Mini-Case: Reeby Sports 106

5   **Net Present Value and Other
Investment Criteria   108**

5-1   A Review of the Basics   *108*
*Net Present Value's Competitors/Three Points to
Remember about NPV*

5-2   Book Rate of Return and Payback   *111*
Book Rate of Return /Payback/Discounted Payback

5-3   Internal (or Discounted Cash Flow) Rate of
Return   *114*
*Calculating the IRR/The IRR Rule/Pitfall 1—
Lending or Borrowing?/Pitfall 2—Multiple Rates of
Return/Pitfall 3—Mutually Exclusive Projects/Pitfall
4—What Happens When There Is More Than One
Opportunity Cost of Capital/The Verdict on IRR*

5-4   Choosing Capital Investments When Resources
Are Limited   *122*
*An Easy Problem in Capital Rationing/Uses of
Capital Rationing Models*

Summary 126 · Further Reading 127 · Problem Sets
127 · Mini-Case: Vegetron's CFO Calls Again 132

6   **Making Investment Decisions with
the Net Present Value Rule   135**

6-1   Applying the Net Present Value Rule   *135*
*Rule 1: Discount Cash Flows, Not Profits/Rule 2:
Discount Incremental Cash Flows /Rule 3: Treat*

*Inflation Consistently/Rule 4: Separate Investment
and Financing Decisions/Rule 5: Remember to
Deduct Taxes*

6-2   Corporate Income Taxes   *142*
U.S. Corporate Income Tax Reform

6-3   Example—IM&C's Fertilizer Project   *144*
*The Three Elements of Project Cash Flows/
Forecasting the Fertilizer Project's Cash Flows/
Accelerated Depreciation and First-Year
Expensing/Final Comments on Taxes/Project
Analysis/Calculating NPV in Other Countries and
Currencies*

6-4   Using the NPV Rule to Choose among
Projects   *151*
*Problem 1: The Investment Timing Decision/
Problem 2: The Choice between Long- and Short-
Lived Equipment/Problem 3: When to Replace an
Old Machine/Problem 4: Cost of Excess Capacity*

Summary 156 · Further Reading 157 · Problem Sets
157 · Mini-Case: New Economy Transport (A)
165 · New Economy Transport (B) 166

I Part Two: Risk

7   **Introduction to Risk and
Return   167**

7-1   Over a Century of Capital Market History in
One Easy Lesson   *167*
*Arithmetic Averages and Compound Annual
Returns/Using Historical Evidence to Evaluate
Today's Cost of Capital*

7-2   Diversification and Portfolio Risk   *174*
*Variance and Standard Deviation/Measuring
Variability/How Diversification Reduces Risk*

7-3   Calculating Portfolio Risk   *181*
*General Formula for Computing Portfolio Risk/Do
I Really Have to Add up 36 Million Boxes?*

7-4   How Individual Securities Affect Portfolio
Risk   *185*
*Market Risk Is Measured by Beta/Why Security
Betas Determine Portfolio Risk*

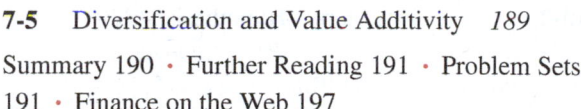

7-5   Diversification and Value Additivity   *189*

Summary 190 · Further Reading 191 · Problem Sets 191 · Finance on the Web 197

8   Portfolio Theory and the Capital Asset Pricing Model   198

8-1   Harry Markowitz and the Birth of Portfolio Theory   *198*
Combining Stocks into Portfolios/We Introduce Borrowing and Lending

8-2   The Relationship between Risk and Return   *205*
Some Estimates of Expected Returns/Review of the Capital Asset Pricing Model/What If a Stock Did Not Lie on the Security Market Line?

8-3   Validity and Role of the Capital Asset Pricing Model   *208*
Tests of the Capital Asset Pricing Model/Assumptions behind the Capital Asset Pricing Model

8-4   Some Alternative Theories   *213*
Arbitrage Pricing Theory/A Comparison of the Capital Asset Pricing Model and Arbitrage Pricing Theory/The Three-Factor Model

Summary 217 · Further Reading 218 · Problem Sets 219 · Finance on the Web 225 · Mini-Case: John and Marsha on Portfolio Selection 225

9   Risk and the Cost of Capital   228

9-1   Company and Project Costs of Capital   *229*
Perfect Pitch and the Cost of Capital/Debt and the Company Cost of Capital

9-2   Measuring the Cost of Equity   *232*
Estimating Beta/The Expected Return on CSX's Common Stock/CSX's After-Tax Weighted-Average Cost of Capital/CSX's Asset Beta

9-3   Analyzing Project Risk   *236*
What Determines Asset Betas?/Don't Be Fooled by Diversifiable Risk/Avoid Fudge Factors in Discount Rates/Discount Rates for International Projects

9-4   Certainty Equivalents—Another Way to Adjust for Risk   *242*
Valuation by Certainty Equivalents/When to Use a Single Risk-Adjusted Discount Rate for Long-Lived Assets/A Common Mistake/When You Cannot Use a Single Risk-Adjusted Discount Rate for Long-Lived Assets

Summary 248 · Further Reading 249 · Problem Sets 249 · Finance on the Web 254 · Mini-Case: The Jones Family Incorporated 254

Part Three: Best Practices in Capital Budgeting

10   Project Analysis   257

10-1   Sensitivity and Scenario Analysis   *258*
Value of Information/Limits to Sensitivity Analysis/Scenario Analysis

10-2   Break-Even Analysis and Operating Leverage   *262*
Break-Even Analysis/Operating Leverage and the Break-Even Point

10-3   Monte Carlo Simulation   *264*
Simulating the Electric Scooter Project

10-4   Real Options and Decision Trees   *266*
The Option to Expand/The Option to Abandon/Production Options/Timing Options/More on Decision Trees/Pro and Con Decision Trees

Summary 274 · Further Reading 275 · Problem Sets 275 · Mini-Case: Waldo County 282

11   How to Ensure That Projects Truly Have Positive NPVs   284

11-1   How Firms Organize the Investment Process   *284*
The Capital Budget/Project Authorizations—and the Problem of Biased Forecasts/Postaudits

11-2   Look First to Market Values   *287*
The BMW and Your Sporting Idol

11-3   Economic Rents and Competitive Advantage   *292*

11-4 Marvin Enterprises Decides to Exploit a New Technology—an Example *295*
Forecasting Prices of Gargle Blasters/The Value of Marvin's New Expansion/Alternative Expansion Plans/The Value of Marvin Stock/The Lessons of Marvin Enterprises

Summary 303 · Further Reading 303 · Problem Sets 303 · Mini-Case: Ecsy-Cola 309

12 Agency Problems and Investment 311

12-1 What Agency Problems Should You Watch Out For? *311*
Agency Problems Don't Stop at the Top/Risk Taking

12-2 Monitoring *314*
Boards of Directors /Auditors/Lenders/ Shareholders/Takeovers

12-3 Management Compensation *316*
Compensation Facts and Controversies/The Economics of Incentive Compensation/The Specter of Short-Termism

12-4 Measuring and Rewarding Performance: Residual Income and EVA *323*
Residual Income or Economic Value Added (EVA®)/Pros and Cons of EVA

12-5 Biases in Accounting Measures of Performance *326*
Example: Measuring the Profitability of the Nodhead Supermarket/Measuring Economic Profitability/Do the Biases Wash Out in the Long Run?/What Can We Do about Biases in Accounting Profitability Measures?

Summary 331 · Further Reading 332 · Problem Sets 332

Part Four: Financing Decisions and Market Efficiency

13 Efficient Markets and Behavioral Finance 337

13-1 Differences between Investment and Financing Decisions *338*
We Always Come Back to NPV

13-2 The Efficient Market Hypothesis *340*
A Startling Discovery: Price Changes Are Random/Random Walks: The Evidence/Semistrong Market Efficiency: The Evidence/Strong Market Efficiency: The Evidence

13-3 Bubbles and Market Efficiency *348*

13-4 Behavioral Finance *349*
Sentiment/Limits to Arbitrage/Incentive Problems and the Financial Crisis of 2008–2009

13-5 The Five Lessons of Market Efficiency *354*
Lesson 1: Markets Have No Memory/Lesson 2: Trust Market Prices/Lesson 3: Read the Entrails/ Lesson 4: The Do-It-Yourself Alternative/Lesson 5: Seen One Stock, Seen Them All/What If Markets Are Not Efficient? Implications for the Financial Manager

Summary 359 · Further Reading 360 · Problem Sets 361 · Finance on the Web 364

14 An Overview of Corporate Financing 365

14-1 Patterns of Corporate Financing *365*
Do Firms Rely Too Much on Internal Funds?/How Much Do Firms Borrow?

14-2 Common Stock *369*
Ownership of the Corporation/Voting Procedures/ Dual-Class Shares and Private Benefits/Equity in Disguise/Preferred Stock

14-3 Debt *374*
Debt Comes in Many Forms/A Debt by Any Other Name/Variety's the Very Spice of Life

14-4 Financial Markets and Intermediaries *377*
Financial Markets/Financial Intermediaries/ Investment Funds/Financial Institutions

14-5 The Role of Financial Markets and Intermediaries *382*
The Payment Mechanism/Borrowing and Lending/ Pooling Risk/Information Provided by Financial Markets/The Financial Crisis of 2007–2009

Summary 386 · Further Reading 387 · Problem Sets 388 · Finance on the Web 390

15 How Corporations Issue Securities 391

15-1 Venture Capital *391*
The Venture Capital Market

15-2 The Initial Public Offering *396*
*The Public-Private Choice/Arranging an Initial
Public Offering/The Sale of Marvin Stock/The
Underwriters/Costs of a New Issue/Underpricing
of IPOs/Hot New-Issue Periods/The Long-Run
Performance of IPO Stocks*

15-3 Alternative Issue Procedures for IPOs *406*
Types of Auction: A Digression

15-4 Security Sales by Public Companies *408*
*General Cash Offers/International Security
Issues/The Costs of a General Cash Offer/Market
Reaction to Stock Issues/Rights Issues*

15-5 Private Placements and Public Issues *413*

Summary 413 · Further Reading 414

Problem Sets 415 · Finance on the Web 420

Appendix: Marvin's New-Issue Prospectus 421

Part Five: Payout Policy and Capital Structure

16 Payout Policy 425

16-1 Facts about Payout *426*
*How Firms Pay Dividends/How Firms Repurchase
Stock*

16-2 The Information Content of Dividends and
Repurchases *428*
*The Information Content of Share
Repurchases*

16-3 Dividends or Repurchases? The Payout
Controversy *431*
*Payout Policy Is Irrelevant in Perfect Capital
Markets/Dividends or Repurchases? An Example/
Stock Repurchases and DCF Models of Share
Price/Dividends and Share Issues*

16-4 The Rightists *436*
*Payout Policy, Investment Policy, and Management
Incentives*

16-5 Taxes and the Radical Left *437*
*Empirical Evidence on Dividends and Taxes/
Alternative Tax Systems*

16-6 Payout Policy and the Life Cycle of the Firm *441*
Payout and Corporate Governance

Summary 443 · Further Reading 444 · Problem Sets 445

17 Does Debt Policy Matter? 451

17-1 The Effect of Financial Leverage in a
Competitive Tax-Free Economy *452*
*Enter Modigliani and Miller/The Law of
Conservation of Value/An Example of Proposition 1*

17-2 Financial Risk and Expected Returns *457*
*Proposition 2/Leverage and the Cost of Equity/
How Changing Capital Structure Affects Beta/
Watch Out for Hidden Leverage*

17-3 No Magic in Financial Leverage *464*
*Today's Unsatisfied Clienteles Are Probably
Interested in Exotic Securities/Imperfections and
Opportunities*

17-4 A Final Word on the After-Tax Weighted-
Average Cost of Capital *467*

Summary 468 · Further Reading 469 · Problem
Sets 470 · Mini-Case: Claxton Drywall Comes to the
Rescue 474

18 How Much Should a Corporation Borrow? 475

18-1 Corporate Taxes *476*
*How Do Interest Tax Shields Contribute to the
Value of Stockholders' Equity?/Recasting Johnson
& Johnson's Capital Structure/MM and Taxes*

18-2 Corporate and Personal Taxes *480*

18-3 Costs of Financial Distress *482*
*Bankruptcy Costs/Evidence on Bankruptcy Costs/
Direct versus Indirect Costs of Bankruptcy/
Financial Distress without Bankruptcy/Debt and
Incentives/Risk Shifting: The First Game/Refusing
to Contribute Equity Capital: The Second Game/
And Three More Games, Briefly/What the Games
Cost/Costs of Distress Vary with Type of Asset/The
Trade-Off Theory of Capital Structure*

18-4 The Pecking Order of Financing Choices *495*
*Debt and Equity Issues with Asymmetric
Information/Implications of the Pecking Order/The
Trade-Off Theory vs. the Pecking-Order Theory—
Some Evidence/The Bright Side and the Dark Side
of Financial Slack/Is There a Theory of Optimal
Capital Structure?*

Summary 501 · Further Reading 502 · Problem Sets
503 · Finance on the Web 506

19 Financing and Valuation 507

19-1 The After-Tax Weighted-Average Cost of
Capital *508*
*Review of Assumptions/Mistakes People Make in
Using the Weighted-Average Formula*

19-2 Valuing Businesses *512*
*Valuing Rio Corporation/Estimating Horizon
Value/WACC vs. the Flow-to-Equity Method*

19-3 Using WACC in Practice *517*
*Some Tricks of the Trade/Adjusting WACC When
Debt Ratios and Business Risks Differ/Unlevering
and Relevering Betas/The Importance of
Rebalancing/The Modigliani–Miller Formula, Plus
Some Final Advice*

19-4 Adjusted Present Value *524*
*APV for the Perpetual Crusher/Other Financing
Side Effects/APV for Entire Businesses/APV
and Limits on Interest Deductions/APV for
International Investments*

19-5 Your Questions Answered *529*

Summary 531 · Further Reading 532 · Problem
Sets 532 · Finance on the Web 537 · Appendix:
Discounting Safe, Nominal Cash Flows 538

Part Six: Options

20 Understanding Options 542

20-1 Calls, Puts, and Shares *543*
*Call Options and Position Diagrams/Put Options/
Selling Calls and Puts/Position Diagrams Are Not
Profit Diagrams*

20-2 Financial Alchemy with Options *547*
Spotting the Option

20-3 What Determines Option Values? *552*
Risk and Option Values

Summary 557 · Further Reading 558
Problem Sets 558 · Finance on the Web 562

21 Valuing Options 563

21-1 A Simple Option-Valuation Model *564*
*Why Discounted Cash Flow Won't Work for
Options/Constructing Option Equivalents from
Common Stocks and Borrowing/Valuing the
Amazon Put Option*

21-2 The Binomial Method for Valuing Options *568*
*Example: The Two-Step Binomial Method/The
General Binomial Method/The Binomial Method
and Decision Trees*

21-3 The Black–Scholes Formula *573*
*Using the Black–Scholes Formula/The Risk of
an Option/The Black–Scholes Formula and the
Binomial Method*

21-4 Black–Scholes in Action *577*
*Executive Stock Options/Warrants/Portfolio
Insurance/Calculating Implied Volatilities*

21-5 Option Values at a Glance *580*

21-6 The Option Menagerie *582*

Summary 582 · Further Reading 583 · Problem Sets
583 · Finance on the Web 588 · Mini-Case: Bruce
Honiball's Invention 588

22 Real Options 590

22-1 The Value of Follow-On Investment
Opportunities *590*
*Questions and Answers about Blitzen's Mark II/
Other Expansion Options*

22-2 The Timing Option *594*
*Valuing the Malted Herring Option/Optimal
Timing for Real Estate Development*

22-3 The Abandonment Option *597*
*Bad News for the Perpetual Crusher/Abandonment
Value and Project Life/Temporary Abandonment*

22-4 Flexible Production and Procurement *600*
Aircraft Purchase Options

22-5 Investment in Pharmaceutical R&D *604*

22-6 Valuing Real Options *606*
*A Conceptual Problem?/What about Taxes?/
Practical Challenges*

Summary 608 · Further Reading 609
Problem Sets 609

I Part Seven: Debt Financing

23 Credit Risk and the Value of Corporate Debt 614

23-1 Yields on Corporate Debt *614*
What Determines the Yield Spread?

23-2 Valuing the Option to Default *618*
*The Value of Corporate Equity/A Digression:
Valuing Government Financial Guarantees*

23-3 Bond Ratings and the Probability of
Default *622*

23-4 Predicting the Probability of Default *624*
*Statistical Models of Default/Structural Models
of Default*

Summary 628 · Further Reading 628 · Problem
Sets 629 · Finance on the Web 630

24 The Many Different Kinds of Debt 631

24-1 Long-Term Bonds *632*
*Bond Terms/Security and Seniority/Asset-Backed
Securities/Call Provisions/Sinking Funds/Bond
Covenants/Privately Placed Bonds/Foreign Bonds
and Eurobonds*

24-2 Convertible Securities and Some Unusual
Bonds *641*
*The Value of a Convertible at Maturity/
Forcing Conversion/Why Do Companies Issue
Convertibles?/Valuing Convertible Bonds/A
Variation on Convertible Bonds: The Bond–
Warrant Package/Innovation in the Bond Market*

24-3 Bank Loans *647*
*Commitment/Maturity/Rate of Interest/Syndicated
Loans/Security/Loan Covenants*

24-4 Commercial Paper and Medium-Term Notes *650*
Commercial Paper/Medium-Term Notes

Summary 652 · Further Reading 653 · Problem
Sets 653 · Mini-Case: The Shocking Demise of
Mr. Thorndike 658 · Appendix: Project Finance 660
Appendix Further Reading 662

25 Leasing 663

25-1 What Is a Lease? *663*

25-2 Why Lease? *664*
*Sensible Reasons for Leasing/Some Dubious
Reasons for Leasing*

25-3 Operating Leases *667*
Example of an Operating Lease/Lease or Buy?

25-4 Valuing Financial Leases *669*
*Example of a Financial Lease/Who Really Owns
the Leased Asset?/Leasing and the Internal
Revenue Service/A First Pass at Valuing a Lease
Contract/The Story So Far/Financial Leases When
There Is No Interest Tax Shield*

25-5 When Do Financial Leases Pay? *675*
Leasing around the World

25-6 Leveraged Leases *676*

Summary 677 · Further Reading 678 · Problem Sets 678

I Part Eight: Risk Management

26 Managing Risk 683

26-1 Why Manage Risk? *684*
*Reducing the Risk of Cash Shortfalls or Financial
Distress/Agency Costs May Be Mitigated by Risk
Management/The Evidence on Risk Management*

26-2 Insurance *687*

26-3 Reducing Risk with Options *689*

26-4 Forward and Futures Contracts *690*
*A Simple Forward Contract/Futures Exchanges/
The Mechanics of Futures Trading/Trading and*

Pricing Financial Futures Contracts/Spot and Futures Prices—Commodities/More about Forward Contracts/Homemade Forward Rate Contracts

26-5 Swaps   *697*
Interest Rate Swaps/Currency Swaps/Some Other Swaps

26-6 How to Set Up a Hedge   *702*
Hedging Interest Rate Risk/Hedge Ratios and Basis Risk

26-7 Is "Derivative" a Four-Letter Word?   *705*

Summary 707 · Further Reading 708 · Problem Sets 708 · Finance on the Web 714 · Mini-Case: Rensselaer Advisers 714

27 Managing International Risks   717

27-1 The Foreign Exchange Market   *717*
27-2 Some Basic Relationships   *719*
Interest Rates and Exchange Rates/The Forward Premium and Changes in Spot Rates/Changes in the Exchange Rate and Inflation Rates/Interest Rates and Inflation Rates/Is Life Really That Simple?

27-3 Hedging Currency Risk   *728*
Transaction Exposure and Economic Exposure

27-4 Exchange Risk and International Investment Decisions   *731*
The Cost of Capital for International Investments

27-5 Political Risk   *734*

Summary 736 · Further Reading 737 · Problem Sets 738 · Finance on the Web 741 · Mini-Case: Exacta, S.a. 742

I Part Nine: Financial Planning and Working Capital Management

28 Financial Analysis   743

28-1 Financial Ratios   *743*
28-2 Financial Statements   *744*
28-3 Home Depot's Financial Statements   *745*
The Balance Sheet/The Income Statement

28-4 Measuring Home Depot's Performance   *748*
Economic Value Added/Accounting Rates of Return/Problems with EVA and Accounting Rates of Return

28-5 Measuring Efficiency   *752*
28-6 Analyzing the Return on Assets: The Du Pont System   *754*
The Du Pont System

28-7 Measuring Leverage   *756*
Leverage and the Return on Equity

28-8 Measuring Liquidity   *758*
28-9 Interpreting Financial Ratios   *760*

Summary 763 · Further Reading 763 · Problem Sets 763 · Finance on the Web 769

29 Financial Planning   770

29-1 Links between Short-Term and Long-Term Financing Decisions   *770*
29-2 Tracing Changes in Cash   *773*
The Cash Cycle

29-3 Cash Budgeting   *778*
29-4 Dynamic's Short-Term Financial Plan   *780*
Dynamic Mattress's Financing Plan/Evaluating the Plan/A Note on Short-Term Financial Planning Models

29-5 Long-Term Financial Planning   *784*
Why Build Financial Plans?/A Long-Term Financial Planning Model for Dynamic Mattress/Pitfalls in Model Design/Choosing a Plan

29-6 Growth and External Financing   *789*

Summary 791 · Further Reading 791 · Problem Sets 792 · Finance on the Web 800

30 Working Capital Management   801

30-1 The Composition of Working Capital   *802*
30-2 Inventories   *804*
30-3 Credit Management   *806*

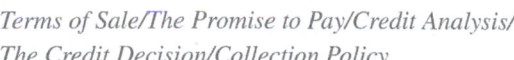

Terms of Sale/The Promise to Pay/Credit Analysis/
The Credit Decision/Collection Policy

30-4 Cash   *812*
*How Purchases Are Paid For/Speeding Up Check
Collections/International Cash Management/
Paying for Bank Services*

30-5 Marketable Securities   *816*
*Tax Strategies/Investment Choices/Calculating
the Yield on Money Market Investments/Returns
on Money Market Investments/The International
Money Market/Money Market Instruments*

Summary 822 · Further Reading 823 · Problem Sets
824 · Finance on the Web 829

**I Part Ten: Mergers, Corporate Control,
and Governance**

31 Mergers   830

31-1 Sensible Motives for Mergers   *831*
*Economies of Scale/Economies of Vertical
Integration/Complementary Resources/Surplus Funds/
Eliminating Inefficiencies/Industry Consolidation*

31-2 Some Dubious Reasons for Mergers   *836*
*Diversification/Increasing Earnings per Share:
The Bootstrap Game/Lower Financing Costs*

31-3 Estimating Merger Gains and Costs   *839*
*Right and Wrong Ways to Estimate the Benefits
of Mergers/More on Estimating Costs—What If
the Target's Stock Price Anticipates the Merger?/
Estimating Cost When the Merger Is Financed by
Stock/Asymmetric Information*

31-4 The Mechanics of a Merger   *844*
*Mergers, Antitrust Law, and Popular Opposition/
The Form of Acquisition/Merger Accounting/Some
Tax Considerations/Cross-Border Mergers and Tax
Inversion*

31-5 Proxy Fights, Takeovers, and the Market for
Corporate Control   *847*
*Proxy Contests/Takeovers/Valeant Bids for Allergan/
Takeover Defenses/Who Gains Most in Mergers?*

31-6 Merger Waves and Merger Profitability   *853*
*Merger Waves/Merger Announcements and the
Stock Price/Merger Profitability/Do Mergers
Generate Net Benefits?*

Summary 855 · Further Reading 856 · Problem
Sets 856 · Appendix: Conglomerate Mergers and
Value Additivity 861

32 Corporate Restructuring   863

32-1 Leveraged Buyouts   *863*
*The RJR Nabisco LBO/Barbarians at the Gate?/
Leveraged Restructurings/LBOs and Leveraged
Restructurings*

32-2 The Private-Equity Market   *868*
*Private-Equity Partnerships/Are Private-Equity
Funds Today's Conglomerates?*

32-3 Fusion and Fission in Corporate Finance   *873*
*Spin-Offs/Carve-Outs/Asset Sales/Privatization
and Nationalization*

32-4 Bankruptcy   *878*
*Is Chapter 11 Efficient?/Workouts/Alternative
Bankruptcy Procedures*

Summary 883 · Further Reading 884 · Problem Sets 885

**33 Governance and Corporate Control
around the World   888**

33-1 Financial Markets and Institutions   *888*
*Investor Protection and the Development of
Financial Markets*

33-2 Ownership, Control, and Governance   *892*
*Ownership and Control in Japan/Ownership and
Control in Germany/European Boards of Directors/
Shareholders versus Stakeholders/Ownership and
Control in Other Countries/Conglomerates Revisited*

33-3 Do These Differences Matter?   *902*
*Risk and Short-Termism/Growth Industries and
Declining Industries/Transparency and Governance*

Summary 905 · Further Reading 906
Problem Sets 907

I Part Eleven: Conclusion

34 Conclusion: What We Do and Do Not Know about Finance   909

34-1 What We Do Know: The Seven Most Important Ideas in Finance   *909*
1. Net Present Value/2. The Capital Asset Pricing Model/3. Efficient Capital Markets/4. Value Additivity and the Law of Conservation of Value/ 5. Capital Structure Theory/6. Option Theory/ 7. Agency Theory

34-2 What We Do Not Know: 10 Unsolved Problems in Finance   *912*
1. What Determines Project Risk and Present Value?/2. Risk and Return—What Have We Missed?/3. How Important Are the Exceptions to the Efficient-Market Theory?/4. Is Management an Off-Balance-Sheet Liability?/5. How Can We Explain the Success of New Securities and New Markets?/6. How Can We Resolve the Payout Controversy?/7. What Risks Should a Firm Take?/8. What Is the Value of Liquidity?/9. How Can We Explain Merger Waves?/10. Why Are Financial Systems So Prone to Crisis?

34-3 A Final Word   *918*

APPENDIX A-1

GLOSSARY G-1

INDEX I-1

Note: Present value tables are available in Connect.

Introduction to Corporate Finance

This book is about how corporations make financial decisions. We start by explaining what these decisions are and what they are intended to accomplish.

Corporations invest in real assets, which generate income. Some of these assets, such as plant and machinery, are tangible; others, such as brand names and patents, are intangible. Corporations finance their investments by borrowing, by retaining and reinvesting cash flow, and by selling additional shares of stock to the corporation's shareholders. Thus, the financial manager faces two broad financial questions: First, what investments should the corporation make? Second, how should it pay for those investments? The investment decision involves spending money; the financing decision involves raising it.

A large corporation may have hundreds of thousands of shareholders. These shareholders differ in many ways, including their wealth, risk tolerance, and investment horizon. Yet we shall see that they usually share the same financial objective. They want the financial manager to increase the value of the corporation and its current stock price.

Thus, the secret of success in financial management is to increase value. That is easy to say but not very helpful. Instructing the financial manager to increase value is like advising an investor in the stock market to "buy low, sell high." The problem is how to do it.

There may be a few activities in which one can read a textbook and then just "do it," but financial management is not one of them. That is why finance is worth studying. Who wants to work in a field where there is no room for judgment, experience, creativity, and a pinch of luck? Although this book cannot guarantee any of these things, it does cover the concepts that govern good financial decisions, and it shows you how to use the tools of the trade of modern finance.

This chapter begins with specific examples of recent investment and financing decisions made by well-known corporations. The middle of the chapter covers what a corporation is and what its financial managers do. We conclude by explaining why increasing the market value of the corporation is a sensible financial goal.

Financial managers increase value whenever the corporation earns a higher return than shareholders can earn for themselves. The shareholders' investment opportunities *outside* the corporation set the standard for investments *inside* the corporation. Financial managers, therefore, refer to the *opportunity cost* of the capital contributed by shareholders.

Managers are, of course, human beings with their own interests and circumstances; they are not always the perfect servants of shareholders. Therefore, corporations must combine governance rules and procedures with appropriate incentives to make sure that all managers and employees—not just the financial managers—pull together to increase value.

Good governance and appropriate incentives also help block out temptations to increase stock price by illegal or unethical means. Thoughtful shareholders do not want the maximum possible stock price. They want the maximum honest stock price.

This chapter introduces five themes that occur again and again throughout the book:

1. Corporate finance is all about maximizing value.

2. The opportunity cost of capital sets the standard for investment decisions.

3. A safe dollar is worth more than a risky dollar.

4. Smart investment decisions create more value than smart financing decisions.

5. Good governance matters.

To carry on business, a corporation needs an almost endless variety of **real assets.** These do not drop free from a blue sky; they need to be paid for. The corporation pays for its real assets by selling claims on them and on the cash flow that they will generate. These claims are called **financial assets** or **securities.** Take a bank loan as an example. The bank provides the corporation with cash in exchange for a financial asset, which is the corporation's promise to repay the loan with interest. An ordinary bank loan is not a security, however, because it is held by the bank and is not traded in financial markets.

Take a corporate bond as a second example. The corporation sells the bond to investors in exchange for the promise to pay interest on the bond and to pay off the bond at its maturity. The bond is a financial asset, and also a security, because it can be held and traded by many investors in financial markets. Securities include bonds, shares of stock, and a dizzying variety of specialized instruments. We describe bonds in Chapter 3, stocks in Chapter 4, and other securities in later chapters.

This suggests the following definitions:

$$\text{Investment decision} = \text{purchase of real assets}$$
$$\text{Financing decision} = \text{sale of securities and other financial assets}$$

But these equations are too simple. The investment decision also involves managing assets already in place and deciding when to shut down and dispose of assets when they are no longer profitable. The corporation also has to manage and control the risks of its investments. The financing decision includes not just raising cash today but also meeting its obligations to banks, bondholders, and stockholders that have contributed financing in the past. For example, the corporation has to repay its debts when they become due. If it cannot do so, it ends up insolvent and bankrupt. Sooner or later the corporation will also want to pay out cash to its shareholders.[1]

Let's go to more specific examples. Table 1.1 lists 10 corporations from all over the world. We have chosen very large public corporations that you are probably already familiar with. You may have used Facebook to chat with your friends, eaten at McDonald's, or used Crest toothpaste.

Investment Decisions

The second column of Table 1.1 shows an important recent investment decision for each corporation. These investment decisions are often referred to as **capital budgeting** or **capital expenditure (CAPEX)** decisions because most large corporations prepare an annual **capital budget** listing the major projects approved for investment. Some of the investments in Table 1.1, such as ExxonMobil's new oil field or Lenovo's factory, involve the purchase of tangible assets—assets that you can touch and kick. However, corporations also need to invest in intangible assets, such as research and development (R&D), advertising, and computer software. For example, GlaxoSmithKline and other major pharmaceutical companies invest billions every year on R&D for new drugs. Similarly, consumer goods companies such as Procter & Gamble invest huge sums in advertising and marketing their products. These outlays are investments because they build know-how, brand recognition, and reputation for the long run.

Today's capital investments generate future cash returns. Sometimes the cash inflows last for decades. For example, many U.S. nuclear power plants, which were initially licensed by

---

[1]We have referred to the corporation's owners as "shareholders" and "stockholders." The two terms mean exactly the same thing and are used interchangeably. Corporations are also referred to casually as "companies," "firms," or "businesses." We also use these terms interchangeably.

Company	Recent Investment Decisions	Recent Financing Decisions
Ahold Delhaize (Netherlands)	Invests €1.4 billion in supermarkets in the U.S. and Europe.	Announces a €1 billion share repurchase program.
ExxonMobil (U.S.)	Announces decision to proceed with development of a huge offshore oil discovery in Guyana.	Reinvests $8.5 billion of the cash that it generates from operations.
Facebook (U.S.)	Acquires Two Big Ears, a British virtual reality audio company.	Leases large new office building in San Francisco.
Fiat Chrysler (Italy)	Spins off its Ferrari luxury car unit.	Repays $1.8 billion of bank debt.
GlaxoSmithKline (U.K.)	Spends $3.6 billion on research and development for new drugs.	Issues additional short-term euro debt.
Lenovo (China)	Announces plans to build a new manufacturing facility in India to produce PCs and smartphones.	Issues $850 million of 5-year dollar bonds.
McDonald's (U.S.)	Announces plans to sell 2,000 restaurants in China.	Issues C$1 billion of Canadian dollar bonds.
Procter & Gamble (U.S.)	Spends over $7 billion on advertising.	Buys back $4.6 billion of stock and pays a $7.2 billion dividend.
Tesla Motors (U.S.)	Starts battery cell production at its new Gigafactory in Nevada.	Raises about $250 million by the sale of new shares.
Vale (Brazil)	Loads first shipment from its new $14.3 billion iron-ore mine in the Amazon rainforest.	Lines up a 5-year revolving credit facility, allowing it to borrow up to $2 billion from a group of international banks.

❭TABLE 1.1   Examples of recent investment and financing decisions by major public corporations

the Nuclear Regulatory Commission to operate for 40 years, are now being re-licensed for 20 more years and may be able to operate efficiently for 80 years overall.

Of course, not all investments have such distant payoffs. For example, Walmart spends about $50 billion each year to stock up its stores and warehouses before the holiday season. The company's return on this investment comes within months as the inventory is drawn down and the goods are sold.

In addition, financial managers know (or quickly learn) that cash returns are not guaranteed. An investment could be a smashing success or a dismal failure. For example, the Iridium communications satellite system, which offered instant telephone connections worldwide, soaked up $5 billion of investment before it started operations in 1998. It needed 400,000 subscribers to break even, but attracted only a small fraction of that number. Iridium defaulted on its debt and filed for bankruptcy in 1999. The Iridium system was sold a year later for just $25 million. (Iridium has recovered and is now profitable, however.)[2]

Among the contenders for the all-time worst investment was Hewlett-Packard's (HP) purchase of the British software company Autonomy. HP paid $11.1 billion for Autonomy. Just 13 months later, it wrote down the value of this investment by $8.8 billion. HP claimed that it was misled by improper accounting at Autonomy. Nevertheless, the acquisition was a disastrous investment, and HP's CEO was fired in short order.

In some cases, the costs and risks of an investment can be huge. For example, the cost of developing the Gorgon natural gas field in Australia has been estimated at more than

---

[2]The private investors who bought the bankrupt system concentrated on aviation, maritime, and defense markets rather than retail customers. In 2010 the company arranged $1.8 billion in new financing to replace and upgrade its satellite system. The first launches of a fleet of 66 new satellites took place in 2017.

$40 billion. But do not think of the financial manager as making such large investments on a daily basis. Most investment decisions are smaller and simpler, such as the purchase of a truck, machine tool, or computer system. Corporations make thousands of these smaller investment decisions every year. The cumulative amount of small investments can be just as large as that of the occasional big investments.

Also, financial managers do not make major investment decisions in solitary confinement. They may work as part of a team of engineers and managers from manufacturing, marketing, and other business functions.

Financing Decisions

The third column of Table 1.1 lists a recent financing decision by each corporation. A corporation can raise money from lenders or from shareholders. If it borrows, the lenders contribute the cash, and the corporation promises to pay back the debt plus a fixed rate of interest. If the shareholders put up the cash, they do not get a fixed return, but they hold shares of stock and therefore get a fraction of future profits and cash flow. The shareholders are *equity investors,* who contribute *equity financing.* The choice between debt and equity financing is called the **capital structure** decision. *Capital* refers to the firm's sources of long-term financing.

The financing choices available to large corporations seem almost endless. Suppose the firm decides to borrow. Should it borrow from a bank or borrow by issuing bonds that can be traded by investors? Should it borrow for 1 year or 20 years? If it borrows for 20 years, should it reserve the right to pay off the debt early? Should it borrow in Paris, receiving and promising to repay euros, or should it borrow dollars in New York?

Corporations raise equity financing in two ways. First, they can issue new shares of stock. The investors who buy the new shares put up cash in exchange for a fraction of the corporation's future cash flow and profits. Second, the corporation can take the cash flow generated by its existing assets and reinvest that cash in new assets. In this case the corporation is reinvesting on behalf of existing stockholders. No new shares are issued.

What happens when a corporation does not reinvest all of the cash flow generated by its existing assets? It may hold the cash in reserve for future investment, or it may pay the cash back to its shareholders. Table 1.1 shows that Procter & Gamble paid back $4.6 billion to its stockholders by repurchasing shares. This was in addition to $7.2 billion paid out as cash dividends. The decision to pay dividends or repurchase shares is called the *payout decision.* We cover payout decisions in Chapter 16.

In some ways, financing decisions are less important than investment decisions. Financial managers say that "value comes mainly from the asset side of the balance sheet." In fact, the most successful corporations sometimes have the simplest financing strategies. Take Microsoft as an example. It is one of the world's most valuable corporations. In December 2017, Microsoft shares traded for about $88 each. There were 7.7 billion shares outstanding. Therefore Microsoft's overall market value—its *market capitalization* or *market cap*—was $88 × 7.7 = $680 billion. Where did this market value come from? It came from Microsoft's product development, from its brand name and worldwide customer base, from its research and development, and from its ability to make profitable future investments. The value did *not* come from sophisticated financing. Microsoft's financing strategy is very simple: It carries no debt to speak of and finances almost all investment by retaining and reinvesting cash flow.

Financing decisions may not add much value, compared with good investment decisions, but they can destroy value if they are stupid or if they are ambushed by bad news. For example, after a consortium of investment companies bought the energy giant TXU in 2007, the company took on an additional $50 billion of debt. This may not have been a stupid decision, but it did prove nearly fatal. The consortium did not foresee the expansion of shale gas production and the resulting sharp fall in natural gas and electricity prices. In 2014, the company (renamed Energy Future Holdings) was no longer able to service its debts and filed for bankruptcy.

Business is inherently risky. The financial manager needs to identify the risks and make sure they are managed properly. For example, debt has its advantages, but too much debt can land the company in bankruptcy, as the buyers of TXU discovered. Companies can also be knocked off course by recessions, by changes in commodity prices, interest rates and exchange rates, or by adverse political developments. Some of these risks can be hedged or insured, however, as we explain in Chapters 26 and 27.

What Is a Corporation?

We have been referring to "corporations." Before going too far or too fast, we need to offer some basic definitions. Details follow in later chapters.

A **corporation** is a legal entity. In the view of the law, it is a legal *person* that is owned by its shareholders. As a legal person, the corporation can make contracts, carry on a business, borrow or lend money, and sue or be sued. One corporation can make a takeover bid for another and then merge the two businesses. Corporations pay taxes—but cannot vote!

In the United States, corporations are formed under state law, based on *articles of incorporation* that set out the purpose of the business and how it is to be governed and operated.[3] For example, the articles of incorporation specify the composition and role of the *board of directors*.[4] A corporation's directors are elected by the shareholders. They choose and advise top management and must sign off on important corporate actions, such as mergers and the payment of dividends to shareholders.

BEYOND THE PAGE

Zipcar's articles

mhhe.com/brealey13e

A corporation is owned by its shareholders but is legally distinct from them. Therefore the shareholders have **limited liability,** which means that they cannot be held personally responsible for the corporation's debts. When the U.S. financial corporation Lehman Brothers failed in 2008, no one demanded that its stockholders put up more money to cover Lehman's massive debts. Shareholders can lose their entire investment in a corporation, but no more.

When a corporation is first established, its shares may be privately held by a small group of investors, such as the company's managers and a few backers. In this case, the shares are not publicly traded and the company is *closely held*. Eventually, when the firm grows and new shares are issued to raise additional capital, its shares are traded in public markets such as the New York Stock Exchange. These corporations are known as *public companies*. Most well-known corporations in the U.S. are public companies with widely dispersed shareholdings. In other countries, it is more common for large corporations to remain in private hands, and many public companies may be controlled by just a handful of investors. The latter category includes such well-known names as Volkswagen (Germany), Alibaba (China), Softbank (Japan), and the Swatch Group (Switzerland).

A large public corporation may have hundreds of thousands of shareholders, who own the business but cannot possibly manage or control it directly. This *separation of ownership and control* gives corporations permanence. Even if managers quit or are dismissed and

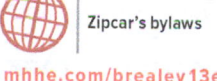

BEYOND THE PAGE

Zipcar's bylaws

mhhe.com/brealey13e

---

[3]In the U.S., corporations are identified by the label "Corporation," "Incorporated," or "Inc.," as in Iridium Communications Inc. The U.K. identifies public corporations by "plc" (short for "Public Limited Corporation"). French corporations have the suffix "SA" ("Société Anonyme"). The corresponding labels in Germany are "GmbH" ("Gesellschaft mit beschränkter Haftung") or "AG" ("Aktiengesellschaft").

[4]The corporation's bylaws set out in more detail the duties of the board of directors and how the firm should conduct its business.

Other Forms of Business Organization

❯ Corporations do not have to be prominent, multinational businesses such as those listed in Table 1.1. You can organize a local plumbing contractor or barber shop as a corporation if you want to take the trouble. But most corporations are larger businesses or businesses that aspire to grow. Small "mom-and-pop" businesses are usually organized as sole proprietorships.

What about the middle ground? What about businesses that grow too large for sole proprietorships but don't want to reorganize as corporations? For example, suppose you wish to pool money and expertise with some friends or business associates. The solution is to form a *partnership* and enter into a partnership agreement that sets out how decisions are to be made and how profits are to be split up. Partners, like sole proprietors, face unlimited liability. If the business runs into difficulties, each partner can be held responsible for *all* the business's debts.

Partnerships have a tax advantage. Partnerships, unlike corporations, do not have to pay income taxes. The partners simply pay personal income taxes on their shares of the profits.

Some businesses are hybrids that combine the tax advantage of a partnership with the limited liability advantage of a corporation. In a *limited partnership,* partners are classified as general or limited. General partners manage the business and have unlimited personal liability for its debts. Limited partners are liable only for the money they invest and do not participate in management.

Many states allow *limited liability partnerships (LLPs)* or, equivalently, *limited liability companies (LLCs).* These are partnerships in which all partners have limited liability.

Another variation on the theme is the *professional corporation (PC)* or *professional limited liability company (PLCC),* which is commonly used by doctors, lawyers, and accountants. In this case, the business has limited liability, but the professionals can still be sued personally—for example, for malpractice.

Most large investment banks such as Morgan Stanley and Goldman Sachs started life as partnerships. But eventually these companies and their financing requirements grew too large for them to continue as partnerships, and they reorganized as corporations. The partnership form of organization does not work well when ownership is widespread and separation of ownership and management is essential.

---

replaced, the corporation survives. Today's stockholders can sell all their shares to new investors without disrupting the operations of the business. Corporations can, in principle, live forever, and in practice, they may survive many human lifetimes. One of the oldest corporations is the Hudson's Bay Company, which was formed in 1670 to profit from the fur trade between northern Canada and England. The company still operates as one of Canada's leading retail chains.

The separation of ownership and control can also have a downside, for it can open the door for managers and directors to act in their own interests rather than in the stockholders' interest. We return to this problem later in the chapter.

There are other disadvantages to being a corporation. One is the cost, in both time and money, of managing the corporation's legal machinery. These costs are particularly burdensome for small businesses. There is also an important tax drawback to corporations in the United States. Because the corporation is a separate legal entity, it is taxed separately. So corporations pay tax on their profits, and shareholders are taxed again when they receive dividends from the company or sell their shares at a profit. By contrast, income generated by businesses that are not incorporated is taxed just once as personal income.

Almost all large and medium-sized businesses are corporations, but the nearby box describes how smaller businesses may be organized.

BEYOND THE PAGE

S-corporations

mhhe.com/brealey13e

BEYOND THE PAGE

The financial managers

mhhe.com/brealey13e

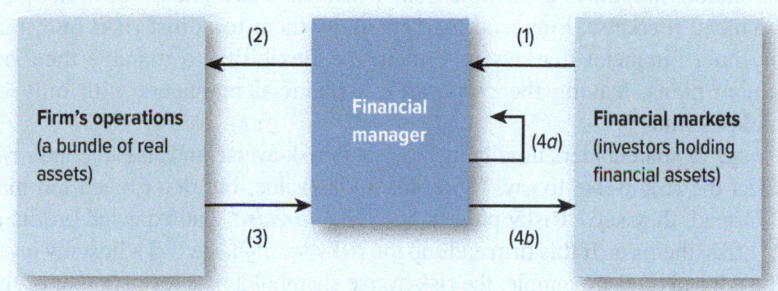

The Role of the Financial Manager

What is the essential role of the financial manager? Figure 1.1 gives one answer. The figure traces how money flows from investors to the corporation and back to investors again. The flow starts when cash is raised from investors (arrow 1 in the figure). The cash could come from banks or from securities sold to investors in financial markets. The cash is then used to pay for the real assets (capital investment projects) needed for the corporation's business (arrow 2). Later, as the business operates, the assets produce cash inflows (arrow 3). That cash is either reinvested (arrow 4a) or returned to the investors who furnished the money in the first place (arrow 4b). Of course, the choice between arrows 4a and 4b is constrained by the promises made when cash was raised at arrow 1. For example, if the firm borrows money from a bank at arrow 1, it must repay this money plus interest at arrow 4b.

You can see examples of arrows 4a and 4b in Table 1.1. ExxonMobil financed its new projects by reinvesting earnings (arrow 4a). Procter & Gamble decided to return cash to shareholders by paying cash dividends and by buying back its stock (arrow 4b).

Notice how the financial manager stands between the firm and outside investors. On the one hand, the financial manager helps manage the firm's operations, particularly by helping to make good investment decisions. On the other hand, the financial manager deals with investors—not just with shareholders but also with financial institutions such as banks and with financial markets such as the New York Stock Exchange.

1-2   **The Financial Goal of the Corporation**

Shareholders Want Managers to Maximize Market Value

Major corporations may have hundreds of thousands of shareholders. There is no way that these shareholders can be actively involved in management; it would be like trying to run New York City by town meetings. Authority has to be delegated to professional managers. But how can the company's managers make decisions that satisfy all the shareholders? No two shareholders are exactly the same. Some may plan to cash in their investments next year; others may be investing for a distant old age. Some may be wary of taking much risk; others may be more venturesome. Delegating the operation of the firm to professional managers can work only if these shareholders have a common objective. Fortunately, there is a natural financial objective on which almost all shareholders agree: Maximize the current market value of shareholders' investment in the firm.

A smart and effective manager makes decisions that increase the current value of the company's shares and the wealth of its stockholders. This increased wealth can then be put to whatever purposes the shareholders want. They can give their money to charity or spend it in glitzy nightclubs; they can save it or spend it now. Whatever their personal tastes or objectives, they can all do more when their shares are worth more.

Maximizing shareholder wealth is a sensible goal when the shareholders have access to well-functioning financial markets.[5] Financial markets allow them to adjust risks and transport savings across time. Financial markets give them the flexibility to manage their own savings and investment plans, leaving the corporation's financial managers with only one task: to increase market value.

A corporation's roster of shareholders usually includes both risk-averse and risk-tolerant investors. You might expect the risk-averse to say, "Sure, maximize value, but don't touch too many high-risk projects." Instead, they say, "Risky projects are OK, *provided* that expected profits are more than enough to offset the risks. If this firm ends up too risky for my taste, I'll adjust my investment portfolio to make it safer." For example, the risk-averse shareholders can shift more of their investment to safer assets, such as U.S. government bonds. They can also just say good-bye, selling shares of the risky firm and buying shares in a safer one. If the risky investments increase market value, the departing shareholders are better off than if the risky investments were turned down.

A Fundamental Result

The goal of maximizing shareholder value is widely accepted in both theory and practice. It's important to understand why. Let's walk through the argument step by step, assuming that the financial manager should act in the interests of the firm's owners, its stockholders.

1. Each stockholder wants three things:
   a. To be as rich as possible, that is, to maximize his or her current wealth.
   b. To transform that wealth into the most desirable time pattern of consumption either by borrowing to spend now or investing to spend later.
   c. To manage the risk characteristics of that consumption plan.

2. But stockholders do not need the financial manager's help to achieve the best time pattern of consumption. They can do that on their own, provided they have free access to competitive financial markets. They can also choose the risk characteristics of their consumption plan by investing in more- or less-risky securities.

3. How then can the financial manager help the firm's stockholders? There is only one way: by increasing their wealth. That means increasing the market value of the firm and the current price of its shares.

Economists have proved this value-maximization principle with great rigor and generality. After you have absorbed this chapter, take a look at the Appendix, which contains a further example. The example, though simple, illustrates how the principle of value maximization follows from formal economic reasoning.

We have suggested that shareholders want to be richer rather than poorer. But sometimes you hear managers speak as if shareholders have different goals. For example, managers may say that their job is to "maximize profits." That sounds reasonable. After all, don't shareholders want their company to be profitable? But taken literally, profit maximization is not a well-defined financial objective for at least two reasons:

1. Maximize profits? Which year's profits? A corporation may be able to increase current profits by cutting back on outlays for maintenance or staff training, but that may result in lower profits in the future. Shareholders will not welcome higher short-term profits if long-term profits are damaged.

---

[5]Here we use "financial markets" as shorthand for the financial sector of the economy. Strictly speaking, we should say "access to well-functioning financial markets and institutions." Many investors deal mostly with financial institutions, for example, banks, insurance companies, or mutual funds. The financial institutions in turn engage in financial markets, including the stock and bond markets. The institutions act as financial intermediaries on behalf of individual investors.

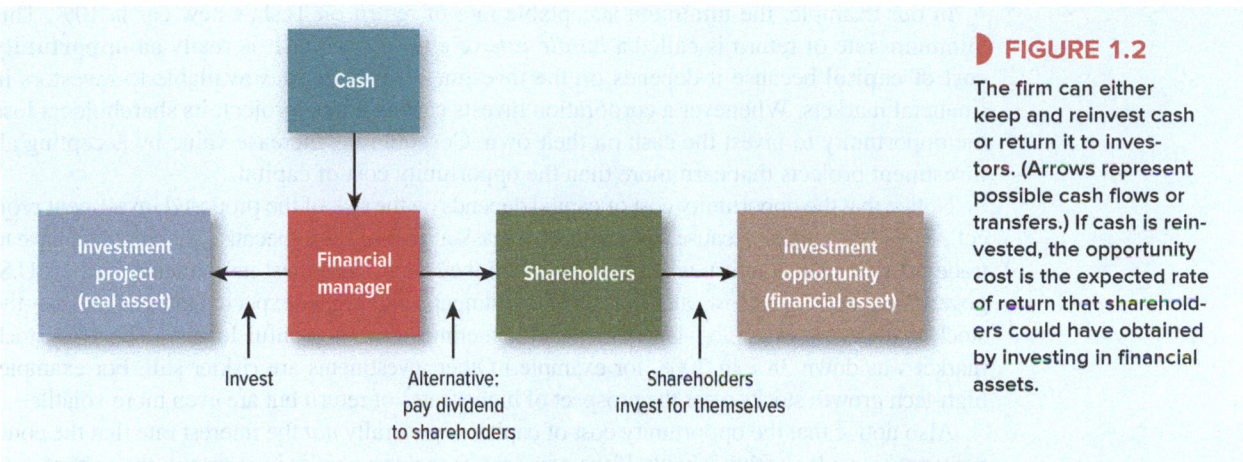

▶ **FIGURE 1.2**

The firm can either keep and reinvest cash or return it to investors. (Arrows represent possible cash flows or transfers.) If cash is reinvested, the opportunity cost is the expected rate of return that shareholders could have obtained by investing in financial assets.

2. A company may be able to increase future profits by cutting this year's dividend and investing the freed-up cash in the firm. That is not in the shareholders' best interest if the company earns only a modest return on the money.

The Investment Trade-Off

OK, let's take the objective as maximizing market value. But why do some investments increase market value, while others reduce it? The answer is given by Figure 1.2, which sets out the fundamental trade-off for corporate investment decisions. Suppose the corporation has a proposed investment in a real asset and enough cash on hand to finance the investment. If the corporation does not invest, it can instead pay out the cash to shareholders—say, as an extra dividend. How does the financial manager decide whether to go ahead with the project or to pay out the cash? (The investment and dividend arrows in Figure 1.2 are arrows 2 and 4b in Figure 1.1.)

Assume that the financial manager is acting in the interests of the corporation's owners, its stockholders. What do these stockholders want the financial manager to do? The answer depends on the project's rate of return and on the rate of return that the stockholders can earn by investing in financial markets. If the return offered by the investment project is higher than shareholders can get by investing on their own, then the shareholders would vote for the investment project. If the investment project offers a lower return than shareholders can achieve on their own, they would vote to cancel the project and take the cash instead.

Perhaps the investment project in Figure 1.2 is a proposal for Tesla to launch a new electric car. Suppose Tesla has set aside cash to launch the new model in 2020. It could go ahead with the launch, or it could choose to cancel the investment and instead pay the cash out to its stockholders. If it pays out the cash, the stockholders can then invest for themselves.

Suppose that Tesla's new project is just about as risky as the U.S. stock market and that investment in the stock market offers a 10% expected rate of return. If the project offers a superior rate of return—say, 20%—then Tesla's stockholders would be happy for the company to keep the cash and invest it in the new model. If the project offers only a 5% return, then the stockholders are better off with the cash and without the new model; in that case, the financial manager should turn down the project.

As long as a corporation's proposed investments offer higher rates of return than its shareholders can earn for themselves in the stock market (or in other financial markets), its shareholders will applaud the investments, and its stock price will increase. But if the company earns an inferior return, shareholders boo, stock price falls, and stockholders demand their money back so that they can invest on their own.

In our example, the minimum acceptable rate of return on Tesla's new car is 10%. This minimum rate of return is called a *hurdle rate* or *cost of capital.* It is really an **opportunity cost of capital** because it depends on the investment *opportunities* available to investors in financial markets. Whenever a corporation invests cash in a new project, its shareholders lose the opportunity to invest the cash on their own. Corporations increase value by accepting all investment projects that earn more than the opportunity cost of capital.

Notice that the opportunity cost of capital depends on the risk of the proposed investment project. Why? It's not just because shareholders are risk-averse. It's also because shareholders have to trade off risk against return when they invest on their own. The safest investments, such as U.S. government debt, offer low rates of return. Investments with higher expected rates of return—the stock market, for example—are riskier and sometimes deliver painful losses. (The U.S. stock market was down 38% in 2008, for example.) Other investments are riskier still. For example, high-tech growth stocks offer the prospect of higher rates of return but are even more volatile.

Also notice that the opportunity cost of capital is generally *not* the interest rate that the company pays on a loan from a bank. If the company is making a risky investment, the opportunity cost is the expected return that investors can achieve in financial markets *at the same level of risk.* The expected return on risky securities is well above the interest rate on a bank loan.

Managers look to the financial markets to measure the opportunity cost of capital for the firm's investment projects. They can observe the opportunity cost of capital for safe investments by looking up current interest rates on safe debt securities. For risky investments, the opportunity cost of capital has to be estimated. We start to tackle this task in Chapter 7.

Should Managers Look After the Interests of Their Shareholders?

So far we have assumed that financial managers should act on behalf of shareholders by trying to maximize their wealth. But perhaps this begs the questions: Is it *desirable* for managers to act in the selfish interests of their shareholders? Does a focus on enriching the shareholders mean that managers must act as greedy mercenaries riding roughshod over the weak and helpless?

Most of this book is devoted to financial policies that increase value. None of these policies requires gallops over the weak and helpless. In most instances, little conflict arises between doing well (maximizing value) and doing good. Profitable firms are those with satisfied customers and loyal employees; firms with dissatisfied customers and a disgruntled workforce will probably end up with declining profits and a low stock price.

Most established corporations can add value by building long-term relationships with their customers and establishing a reputation for fair dealing and financial integrity. When something happens to undermine that reputation, the costs can be enormous.

So, when we say that the objective of the firm is to maximize shareholder wealth, we do not mean that anything goes. The law deters managers from making blatantly dishonest decisions, but most managers should not be simply concerned with observing the letter of the law or with keeping to written contracts. In business and finance, as in other day-to-day affairs, there are unwritten rules of behavior. These rules make routine financial transactions feasible because each party to the transaction has to trust the other to keep to his or her side of the bargain.[6]

When something happens to damage that trust, the costs can be enormous. Volkswagen (VW) is a case in point. VW had installed secret software that cut back pollution from its diesel cars, but only when the cars were tested. Discovery of the software in 2015 caused a tidal wave of opprobrium. VW's stock price dropped by 35%. Its CEO was fired. VW diesel vehicles piled up unsold in car dealers' lots. In the United States alone, the scandal is likely to cost the company more than $20 billion in fines and compensation payments.

---

[6]See L. Guiso, P. Sapienza, and L. Zingales, "Trusting the Stock Market," *Journal of Finance* 63 (December 2008), pp. 2557–2600. The authors show that an individual's lack of trust is a significant impediment to participation in the stock market. "Lack of trust" means a subjective fear of being cheated.

Ethical Disputes in Finance

Short-Selling

Investors who take short positions are betting that securities will fall in price. Usually they do this by borrowing the security, selling it for cash, and then waiting in the hope that they will be able to buy it back cheaply.* In 2007, hedge fund manager John Paulson took a huge short position in mortgage-backed securities. The bet paid off, and that year Paulson's trade made a profit of $1 billion for his fund.[†]

Was Paulson's trade unethical? Some believe that he was not only profiting from the misery that resulted from the crash in mortgage-backed securities, but that his short trades accentuated the collapse. It is certainly true that short-sellers have never been popular. For example, following the crash of 1929, one commentator compared short-selling to the ghoulishness of "creatures who, at all great earthquakes and fires, spring up to rob broken homes and injured and dead humans."

Investors who sell their shares are often described as doing the Wall Street Walk. Short-selling is the Wall Street Walk on steroids. Not only do short-sellers sell all the shares they may have previously owned, they borrow more shares and sell them too, hoping to buy them back for less when the stock price falls. Poorly performing companies are natural targets for short-sellers, and the companies' incumbent managers naturally complain, often bitterly. Governments sometimes listen to such complaints. For example, in 2008 the U.S. government temporarily banned short sales of financial stocks in an attempt to halt their decline.

But defendants of short-selling argue that to sell securities that one believes are overpriced is no less legitimate than buying those that appear underpriced. The object of a well-functioning market is to set the correct stock prices, not always higher prices. Why impede short-selling if it conveys truly bad news, puts pressure on poor performers, and helps corporate governance work?

Corporate Raiders

In the movie *Pretty Woman*, Richard Gere plays the role of an asset stripper, Edward Lewis. He buys companies, takes them apart, and sells the bits for more than he paid for the total package. In the movie *Wall Street*, Gordon Gekko buys a failing airline, Blue Star, in order to break it up and sell the bits. Real corporate raiders may not be as ruthless as Edward Lewis or Gordon

Gekko, but they do target companies whose assets can be profitably split up and redeployed.

This has led many to complain that raiders seek to carve up established companies, often leaving them with heavy debt burdens, basically in order to get rich quick. One German politician has likened them to "swarms of locusts that fall on companies, devour all they can, and then move on."

But sometimes raids can enhance shareholder value. For example, in 2012 and 2013, Relational Investors teamed up with the California State Teachers' Retirement System (CSTRS, a pension fund) to try to force Timken Co. to split into two separate companies, one for its steel business and one for its industrial bearings business. Relational and CSTRS believed that Timken's combination of unrelated businesses was unfocused and inefficient. Timken management responded that the breakup would "deprive our shareholders of long-run value—all in an attempt to create illusory short-term gains through financial engineering." But Timken's stock price rose at the prospect of a breakup, and a nonbinding shareholder vote on Relational's proposal attracted a 53% majority.

How do you draw the ethical line in such examples? Was Relational Investors a "raider" (sounds bad) or an "activist investor" (sounds good)? Breaking up a portfolio of businesses can create difficult adjustments and job losses. Some stakeholders, such as the company's employees, may lose. But shareholders and the overall economy can gain if businesses are managed more efficiently.

Tax Avoidance

In 2012, it was revealed that during the 14 years that Starbucks had operated in the U.K., it paid hardly any taxes. Public outrage led to a boycott of Starbucks shops, and the company responded by promising that it would voluntarily pay to the taxman about $16 million more than it was required to pay by law. Several months later, a U.S. Senate committee investigating tax

---

*We need not go into the mechanics of short sales here, but note that the seller is obligated to buy back the security, even if its price skyrockets far above what he or she sold it for. As the saying goes, "He who sells what isn't his'n, buys it back or goes to prison."

[†]The story of Paulson's trade is told in G. Zuckerman, *The Greatest Trade Ever*, Broadway Business, 2009. The trade was controversial for reasons beyond short-selling. See the nearby Beyond the Page feature "Goldman Sachs causes a ruckus."

avoidance by U.S. technology firms reported that Apple had used a "highly questionable" web of offshore entities to avoid billions of dollars of U.S. taxes.

Multinational companies, such as Starbucks and Apple, have reduced their tax bills using legal techniques with exotic names such as the "Dutch Sandwich," "Double Irish," and "Check-the-Box." But the public outcry over these revelations suggested that many believed that their use, though legal, was unethical. If they were unethical, that leaves an awkward question: How do companies decide which tax schemes are ethical and which are not?

BEYOND THE PAGE

The great Albanian Ponzi scheme

mhhe.com/brealey13e

BEYOND THE PAGE

Goldman Sachs causes a ruckus

mhhe.com/brealey13e

BEYOND THE PAGE

Business culture and unethical behavior

mhhe.com/brealey13e

Charlatans and swindlers are often able to hide behind booming markets. It is only "when the tide goes out that you learn who's been swimming naked."[7] The tide went out in 2008, and a number of frauds were exposed. One notorious example was the Ponzi scheme run by the New York financier Bernard Madoff.[8] Individuals and institutions put about $65 billion in the scheme before it collapsed in 2008. (It's not clear what Madoff did with all this money, but much of it was apparently paid out to early investors in the scheme to create an impression of superior investment performance.) With hindsight, the investors should not have trusted Madoff or the financial advisers who steered money to Madoff.

Madoff's Ponzi scheme was (we hope) a once-in-a-lifetime event.[9] It was astonishingly unethical, illegal, and bound to end in tears. That much is obvious. The difficult ethical problems for financial managers lurk in the grey areas. Look, for example, at the nearby Finance in Practice box that presents three ethical problems. Think about where you stand on these issues and where you would draw the ethical red line.

What is the underlying source of unethical business behavior? Sometimes it is simply because an employee is dishonest. But frequently the behavior stems from a culture in the firm that encourages high-pressure selling or unscrupulous dealing. In this case, the root of the problem lies with top management that promotes such values. (Click on the nearby Beyond the Page feature for an interesting demonstration of this in the banking industry.)

Agency Problems and Corporate Governance

We have emphasized the *separation of ownership and control* in public corporations. The owners (shareholders) cannot control what the managers do, except indirectly through the board of directors. This separation is necessary but also dangerous. You can see the risks. Managers may be tempted to buy sumptuous corporate jets or to schedule business meetings at tony resorts. They may shy away from attractive but risky projects because they are worried more about the safety of their jobs than about maximizing shareholder value. They may work just to maximize their own bonuses, and therefore redouble their efforts to make and resell flawed subprime mortgages.

Conflicts between shareholders' and managers' objectives create *agency problems*. Agency problems arise when *agents* work for *principals*. The shareholders are the principals; the managers are their agents. **Agency costs** are incurred when (1) managers do not attempt to maximize firm value and (2) shareholders incur costs to monitor the managers and constrain their actions.

Agency problems can sometimes lead to outrageous behavior. For example, when Dennis Kozlowski, the CEO of Tyco, threw a $2 million 40th birthday bash for his wife, he charged half of the cost to the company. This of course was an extreme conflict of interest, as well as illegal. But more subtle and moderate agency problems arise whenever managers think just a little less hard about spending money when it is not their own.

---

[7]The quotation is from Warren Buffett's annual letter to the shareholders of Berkshire Hathaway, March 2008.
[8]Ponzi schemes are named after Charles Ponzi who founded an investment company in 1920 that promised investors unbelievably high returns. He was soon deluged with funds from investors in New England, taking in $1 million during one three-hour period. Ponzi invested only about $30 of the money that he raised, but used part of the cash provided by later investors to pay generous dividends to the original investors. Within months, the scheme collapsed, and Ponzi started a five-year prison sentence.
[9]Ponzi schemes pop up frequently, but few have approached the scope and duration of Madoff's.

Later in the book we will look at how good systems of governance ensure that shareholders' pockets are close to the managers' hearts. This means well-designed incentives for managers, standards for accounting and disclosure to investors, requirements for boards of directors, and legal sanctions for self-dealing by management. When scandals happen, we say that corporate governance has broken down. When corporations compete effectively and ethically to deliver value to shareholders, we are comforted that governance is working properly.

1-3   Preview of Coming Attractions

Figure 1.2 illustrates how the financial manager can add value for the firm and its shareholders. He or she searches for investments that offer rates of return higher than the opportunity cost of capital. But that search opens up a treasure chest of follow-up questions.

- *How do I calculate the rate of return?* The rate of return is calculated from the cash inflows and outflows generated by the investment project. See Chapters 2 and 5.

- *Is a higher rate of return on investment always better?* Not always, for two reasons. First, a lower-but-safer return can be better than a higher-but-riskier return. Second, an investment with a higher percentage return can generate less value than a lower-return investment that is larger or lasts longer. In Chapter 2, we show how to calculate the present value (PV) of the stream of cash flows from an investment. Present value is a workhorse concept of corporate finance that shows up in almost every chapter.

- *What determines value in financial markets?* We cover valuation of bonds and common stocks in Chapters 3 and 4. We will return to valuation principles again and again in later chapters. Sometimes the financial manager may be lucky, and may find an almost identical asset whose value is already known.[10] But there is no identical asset to ExxonMobil's offshore oil field in Guyana or Facebook's new investment in virtual reality. For most major financial decisions, the manager needs some fundamental principles to help him to determine value.

- *What are the cash flows?* The future cash flows from an investment project should be the sum of all cash inflows and outflows caused by the decision to invest. Cash flows are calculated after corporate taxes are paid. They are the free cash flows that can be paid out to shareholders or reinvested on their behalf. Chapter 6 explains free cash flows in detail.

- *How does the financial manager judge whether cash-flow forecasts are realistic?* As Niels Bohr, the 1922 Nobel Laureate in Physics, observed, "Prediction is difficult, especially if it's about the future." But good financial managers take care to assemble relevant information and to purge forecasts of bias and thoughtless optimism. See Chapters 6 and 9 through 11.

- *How do we measure risk?* We look to the risks borne by shareholders, recognizing that investors can dilute or eliminate some risks by holding diversified portfolios (Chapters 7 and 8).

- *How does risk affect the opportunity cost of capital?* Here we need a theory of risk and return in financial markets. The most widely used theory is the Capital Asset Pricing Model (Chapters 8 and 9).

- *Where does financing come from?* Broadly speaking, from borrowing or from cash invested or reinvested by stockholders. But financing can get complicated when you get down to specifics. Chapter 14 gives an overview of financing. Chapters 23 through 25 cover sources of debt financing, including financial leases, which are debt in disguise.

---

[10]The idea that identical assets must have the same value is sometimes called the *law of one price* or the *no-arbitrage condition.*

Fintech and the Changing World of Finance*

❯ The financial world is continually changing. A number of markets that barely existed a few decades ago are now trillion-dollar businesses. In some cases, the innovation may be nothing more than someone spotting an untapped demand; in others, it may stem from new economic ideas. But change may also be a result of technological advances. The application of technology to financial markets is commonly known as *fintech*. Here are four ways that fintech is changing financial practice.

Payment Systems Not that many years ago, cash or checks were the principal way to pay for purchases, but in many countries, cash is fast disappearing. For example, in Sweden cash transactions make up barely 2% of the value of all payments. You can't use cash to buy a bus ticket or a ticket on the Stockholm metro, and retailers are not legally obliged to accept coins and notes. The majority of Sweden's bank branches no longer keep cash on hand or take cash deposits—and many branches no longer have ATMs. Instead of cash, Swedes use either a card or a mobile phone app to transfer money from one bank account to another in real time.

Peer-to-Peer (P2P) Lending Peer-to-peer lending platforms directly link individuals willing to lend money with people seeking to borrow. For example, in the United States would-be borrowers can apply to Lending Club for a personal loan of up to $40,000 or a business loan of up to $300,000. The company then assigns a credit score to that customer, and on the basis of this score, potential investors can choose whether to participate in the loan. Thus, Lending Club cuts banks out of the lending equation entirely. It does not lend itself; instead, it verifies the identity of borrowers and lenders, uses the credit score to set the interest rate for the loan, and services the loan.

Robo Advice Providing investment advice to individuals and tailoring portfolios to their particular needs can be a costly business. Robo advisers seek to reduce these costs by automating the process. You will first need to complete an online questionnaire describing your personal situation and your risk tolerance. The robo adviser will then recommend a portfolio, usually a basket of low-cost funds. Then, once you deposit money in the account, the robo adviser will buy the investments and rebalance your portfolio to maintain your ideal mix of assets.

Blockchains A blockchain consists of a network of computers that simultaneously update a ledger of transactions or other data. This ledger doesn't exist in one place but is distributed across many participants in the network. Many believe that the technology offers a major advance in the speed and security of financial record-keeping. Stock exchanges around the world have begun to experiment with blockchains as a method for companies to list and trade their shares, and to ballot their shareholders. The effect should be lower costs of trading, faster transfers of ownership, and more accurate records.

---

*The Winter 2015 issue of the *Journal of Financial Perspectives* contains a collection of articles on fintech.

- *Debt or equity? Does it matter?* Not in a world of perfect financial markets. But in the real world, the choice between debt and equity does matter for many possible reasons, including taxes, the risks of bankruptcy, information differences, and incentives. See Chapters 17 and 18.

That's enough questions to start, but you can see certain themes emerging. For example, corporate finance is "all about valuation," not only for the reasons just listed, but because value maximization is the natural financial goal of the corporation. Another theme is the importance of the opportunity cost of capital, which is established in financial markets. The financial manager is an intermediary, who has to understand financial markets as well as the operations and investments of the corporation.

● ● ● ● ●

Corporations face two principal financial decisions. First, what investments should the corporation make? Second, how should it pay for the investments? The first decision is the investment decision; the second is the financing decision.

The stockholders who own the corporation want its managers to maximize its overall value and the current price of its shares. The stockholders can all agree on the goal of value maximization, so long as financial markets give them the flexibility to manage their own savings and investment plans. Of course, the objective of wealth maximization does not justify unethical behavior. Shareholders do not want the maximum possible stock price. They want the maximum honest share price.

How can financial managers increase the value of the firm? Mostly by making good investment decisions. Financing decisions can also add value, and they can surely destroy value if you screw them up. But it's usually the profitability of corporate investments that separates value winners from the rest of the pack.

Investment decisions involve a trade-off. The firm can either invest cash or return it to shareholders, for example, as an extra dividend. When the firm invests cash rather than paying it out, shareholders forgo the opportunity to invest it for themselves in financial markets. The return that they are giving up is therefore called the opportunity cost of capital. If the firm's investments can earn a higher return than the opportunity cost of capital, stock price increases. If the firm invests at a return lower than the opportunity cost of capital, stock price falls.

Managers are not endowed with a special value-maximizing gene. They will be tempted to consider their own personal interests, which may create a conflict of interest with outside shareholders. This conflict is called a principal–agent problem. Any loss of value that results is called an agency cost.

Investors will not entrust the firm with their savings unless they are confident that management will act ethically on their behalf. Successful firms have governance systems that help to align managers' and shareholders' interests.

Remember the following five themes, for you will see them again and again throughout this book:

1. Corporate finance is all about maximizing value.

2. The opportunity cost of capital sets the standard for investment decisions.

3. A safe dollar is worth more than a risky dollar.

4. Smart investment decisions create more value than smart financing decisions.

5. Good governance matters.

SUMMARY

● ● ● ● ●

PROBLEM SETS

McGraw Hill Education **connect®**

Select problems are available in McGraw-Hill's *Connect*. Answers to questions with an "*" are found in the Appendix.

1. **Investment and financing decisions** Read the following passage: "Companies usually buy (a) assets. These include both tangible assets such as (b) and intangible assets such as (c). To pay for these assets, they sell (d) assets such as (e). The decision about which assets to buy is usually termed the (f) or (g) decision. The decision about how to raise the money is usually termed the (h) decision."

    Now fit each of the following terms into the most appropriate space: *financing, real, bonds, investment, executive airplanes, financial, capital budgeting, brand names.*

2. **Investment and financing decisions*** Which of the following are real assets, and which are financial?

    a. A share of stock.

    b. A personal IOU.

    c. A trademark.

    d. A factory.

    e. Undeveloped land.

    f. The balance in the firm's checking account.

    g. An experienced and hardworking sales force.

    h. A corporate bond.

3. **Investment and financing decisions** Vocabulary test. Explain the differences between:

    a. Real and financial assets.

    b. Capital budgeting and financing decisions.

    c. Closely held and public corporations.

    d. Limited and unlimited liability.

4. **Corporations*** Which of the following statements always apply to corporations?

    a. Unlimited liability.

    b. Limited life.

    c. Ownership can be transferred without affecting operations.

    d. Managers can be fired with no effect on ownership.

5. **Separation of ownership** In most large corporations, ownership and management are separated. What are the main implications of this separation?

6. **Corporate goals*** We can imagine the financial manager doing several things on behalf of the firm's stockholders. For example, the manager might:

    a. Make shareholders as wealthy as possible by investing in real assets.

    b. Modify the firm's investment plan to help shareholders achieve a particular time pattern of consumption.

    c. Choose high- or low-risk assets to match shareholders' risk preferences.

    d. Help balance shareholders' checkbooks.

    But in well-functioning capital markets, shareholders will vote for only one of these goals. Which one? Why?

7. **Maximizing shareholder value** Ms. Espinoza is retired and depends on her investments for her income. Mr. Liu is a young executive who wants to save for the future. Both are stockholders in Scaled Composites LLC, which is building SpaceShipOne to take commercial passengers into space. This investment's payoff is many years away. Assume it has a positive NPV for Mr. Liu. Explain why this investment also makes sense for Ms. Espinoza.

8. **Opportunity cost of capital** F&H Corp. continues to invest heavily in a declining industry. Here is an excerpt from a recent speech by F&H's CFO:

> We at F&H have of course noted the complaints of a few spineless investors and uninformed security analysts about the slow growth of profits and dividends. Unlike those confirmed doubters, we have confidence in the long-run demand for mechanical encabulators, despite competing digital products. We are therefore determined to invest to maintain our share of the overall encabulator market. F&H has a rigorous CAPEX approval process, and we are confident of returns around 8% on investment. That's a far better return than F&H earns on its cash holdings. The CFO went on

to explain that F&H invested excess cash in short-term U.S. government securities, which are almost entirely risk-free but offered only a 4% rate of return.

a. Is a forecasted 8% return in the encabulator business necessarily better than a 4% safe return on short-term U.S. government securities? Why or why not?

b. Is F&H's opportunity cost of capital 4%? How in principle should the CFO determine the cost of capital?

9. **Ethical issues** The Beyond the Page feature, "Goldman Sachs causes a ruckus," describes the controversial involvement of Goldman Sachs in a mortgage-backed securities deal in 2006. When this involvement was revealed, the market value of Goldman Sachs' common stock fell overnight by $10 billion. This was far more than any fine that might have been imposed. Explain.

10. **Ethical issues** Most managers have no difficulty avoiding blatantly dishonest actions. But sometimes there are gray areas, where it is debatable whether an action is unethical and unacceptable. Suggest an important ethical dilemma that companies may face. What principles should guide their decision?

11. **Ethical issues** The Finance in Practice box in Section 1-2 describes three corporate practices that have been criticized as unethical. Select one of these and discuss at what point (if any) does the practice slide into unethical behavior.

12. **Agency issues** Why might one expect managers to act in shareholders' interests? Give some reasons.

13. **Agency issues** Many firms have devised defenses that make it more difficult or costly for other firms to take them over. How might such defenses affect the firm's agency problems? Are managers of firms with formidable takeover defenses more or less likely to act in the shareholders' interests rather than their own? What would you expect to happen to the share price when management proposes to institute such defenses?

APPENDIX • • •

Why Maximizing Shareholder Value Makes Sense

We have suggested that well-functioning financial markets allow different investors to agree on the objective of maximizing value. This idea is sufficiently important that we need to pause and examine it more carefully.

BEYOND THE PAGE

Foundations
of NPV

mhhe.com/brealey13e

How Financial Markets Reconcile Preferences for Current vs. Future Consumption

Suppose that there are two possible investors with entirely different preferences. Think of A as an ant, who wishes to save for the future, and of G as a grasshopper, who would prefer to spend all his wealth on some ephemeral frolic, taking no heed of tomorrow. Suppose that each has a nest egg of exactly $100,000 in cash. G chooses to spend all of it today, while A prefers to invest it in the financial market. If the interest rate is 10%, A would then have $1.10 \times \$100,000 = \$110,000$ to spend a year from now. Of course, there are many possible intermediate strategies. For example, A or G could choose to split the difference, spending $50,000 now and putting the remaining $50,000 to work at 10% to provide $1.10 \times \$50,000 = \$55,000$ next year. The entire range of possibilities is shown by the green line in Figure 1A.1.

In our example, A used the financial market to postpone consumption. But the market can also be used to bring consumption forward in time. Let's illustrate by assuming that instead of having cash on hand of $100,000, our two friends are due to receive $110,000 each at the end of the year. In this case, A will be happy to wait and spend the income when it arrives. G will prefer to borrow against his future income and party it away today. With an interest rate of 10%, G can borrow and spend $110,000/1.10 = $100,000. Thus the financial market provides a kind of time machine that allows people to separate the timing of their income from that of their spending. Notice that with an interest rate of 10%, A and G are equally happy with cash on hand of $100,000 or an income of $110,000 at the end of the year. They do not care about the timing of the cash flow; they just prefer the cash flow that has the highest value today ($100,000 in our example).

▶ **FIGURE 1A.1**

The green line shows the possible spending patterns for the ant and grasshopper if they invest **$100,000** in the capital market. The maroon line shows the possible spending patterns if they invest in their friend's business. Both are better off by investing in the business as long as the grasshopper can borrow against the future income.

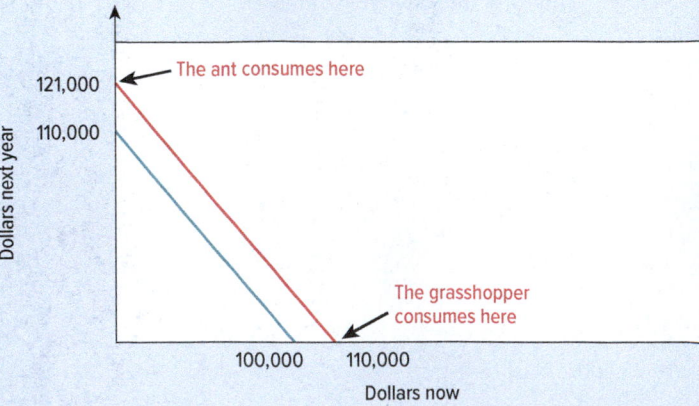

Investing in Real Assets

In practice, individuals are not limited to investing in financial markets; they may also acquire plant, machinery, and other real assets. For example, suppose that A and G are offered the opportunity to invest their $100,000 in a new business that a friend is founding. This will produce a one-off surefire payment of $121,000 next year. A would clearly be happy to invest in the business. It will provide her with $121,000 to spend at the end of the year, rather than the $110,000 that she gets by investing her $100,000 in the financial market. But what about G, who wants money now, not in one year's time? He too is happy to invest, as long as he can borrow against the future payoff of the investment project. At an interest rate of 10%, G can borrow $110,000 and so will have an extra $10,000 to spend today. Both A and G are better off investing in their friend's venture. The investment increases their wealth. It moves them up from the green to the maroon line in Figure 1A.1.

Why can both A and G spend more by investing $100,000 in their friend's business? Because the business provides a return of $21,000, or 21%, whereas they would earn only $10,000, or 10%, by investing their money in the capital market.

A Crucial Assumption

The key condition that allows A and G to agree to invest in the new venture is that both have access to a well-functioning, competitive financial market, in which they can borrow and lend at the same rate. Whenever the corporation's shareholders have equal access to competitive financial markets, the goal of maximizing market value makes sense.

It is easy to see how this rule would be damaged if we did *not* have such a well-functioning financial market. For example, suppose that G could not easily borrow against future income. In that case he might well prefer to spend his cash today rather than invest it in the new venture. If A and G were shareholders in the same enterprise, A would be happy for the firm to invest, while G would be clamoring for higher current dividends.

No one believes unreservedly that financial markets function perfectly. Later in this book we discuss several cases in which differences in taxation, transaction costs, and other imperfections must be taken into account in financial decision making. However, we also discuss research indicating that, in general, financial markets function fairly well. In this case maximizing shareholder value is a sensible corporate objective. But for now, having glimpsed the problems of imperfect markets, we shall, like an economist in a shipwreck, simply *assume* our life jacket and swim safely to shore.

QUESTIONS

1. **Maximizing shareholder value** Look back to the numerical example graphed in Figure 1A.1. Suppose the interest rate is 20%. What would the ant (A) and grasshopper (G) do if they both start with $100,000? Would they invest in their friend's business? Would they borrow or lend? How much and when would each consume?

2. **Maximizing shareholder value** Answer this question by drawing graphs like Figure 1A.1. Casper Milktoast has $200,000 on hand to support consumption in periods 0 (now) and 1 (next year). He wants to consume *exactly* the same amount in each period. The interest rate is 8%. There is no risk.

   a. How much should he invest, and how much can he consume in each period?

   b. Suppose Casper is given an opportunity to invest up to $200,000 at 10% risk-free. The interest rate stays at 8%. What should he do, and how much can he consume in each period?

CHAPTER

2

How to Calculate Present Values

Companies invest in lots of things. Some are *tangible assets*—that is, assets you can kick, like factories, machinery, and offices. Others are *intangible assets,* such as patents or trademarks. In each case, the company lays out some money now in the hope of receiving even more money later.

Individuals also make investments. For example, your college education may cost you $40,000 per year. That is an investment you hope will pay off in the form of a higher salary later in life. You are sowing now and expecting to reap later.

Companies pay for their investments by raising money and, in the process, assuming liabilities. For example, they may borrow money from a bank and promise to repay it with interest later. You also may have financed your investment in a college education by borrowing money that you plan to pay back in the future out of that fat salary.

All these financial decisions require comparisons of cash payments at different dates. Will your future salary be sufficient to justify the current expenditure on college tuition? How much will you have to repay the bank if you borrow to finance your degree?

In this chapter, we take the first steps toward understanding the relationship between the values of dollars today and dollars in the future. We start by looking at how money invested at a specific interest rate will grow over time. We next ask how much you would need to invest today to produce a specified future sum of money, and we describe some shortcuts for working out the value of a series of cash payments.

The term *interest rate* sounds straightforward enough, but rates can be quoted in different ways. We, therefore, conclude the chapter by explaining the difference between the quoted rate and the true or effective interest rate.

Once you have learned how to value cash flows that occur at different points in time, we can move on in the next two chapters to look at how bonds and stocks are valued. After that, we will tackle capital investment decisions at a practical level of detail.

For simplicity, every problem in this chapter is set out in dollars, but the concepts and calculations are identical in euros, Japanese yen, or Mongolian tugrik.

2-1 **Future Values and Present Values**

Calculating Future Values

Money can be invested to earn interest. So, if you are offered the choice between $100 today and $100 next year, you naturally take the money now to get a year's interest. Financial managers make the same point when they say that money has a *time value* or when they quote the most basic principle of finance: *A dollar today is worth more than a dollar tomorrow.*

Suppose you invest $100 in a bank account that pays interest of $r = 7\%$ a year. In the first year, you will earn interest of .07 × $100 = $7 and the value of your investment will grow to $107:

$$\text{Value of investment after 1 year} = \$100 \times (1 + r) = 100 \times 1.07 = \$107$$

By investing, you give up the opportunity to spend $100 today, but you gain the chance to spend $107 next year.

If you leave your money in the bank for a second year, you earn interest of .07 × $107 = $7.49 and your investment will grow to $114.49:

$$\text{Value of investment after 2 years} = \$107 \times 1.07 = \$100 \times 1.07^2 = \$114.49$$

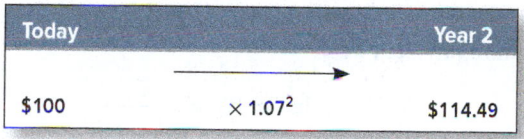

Notice that in the second year you earn interest on both your initial investment ($100) and the previous year's interest ($7). Thus your wealth grows at a *compound rate* and the interest that you earn is called **compound interest.**

If you invest your $100 for t years, your investment will continue to grow at a 7% compound rate to $100 × (1.07)^t$. For any interest rate r, the future value of your $100 investment will be

$$\text{Future value of } \$100 = \$100 \times (1 + r)^t$$

The higher the interest rate, the faster your savings will grow. Figure 2.1 shows that a few percentage points added to the interest rate can do wonders for your future wealth. For example, by the end of 20 years, $100 invested at 10% will grow to $100 × (1.10)^{20} = 672.75. If it is invested at 5%, it will grow to only $100 × (1.05)^{20} = 265.33.

Calculating Present Values

We have seen that $100 invested for two years at 7% will grow to a future value of $100 × 1.07^2 = 114.49. Let's turn this around and ask how much you need to invest *today* to

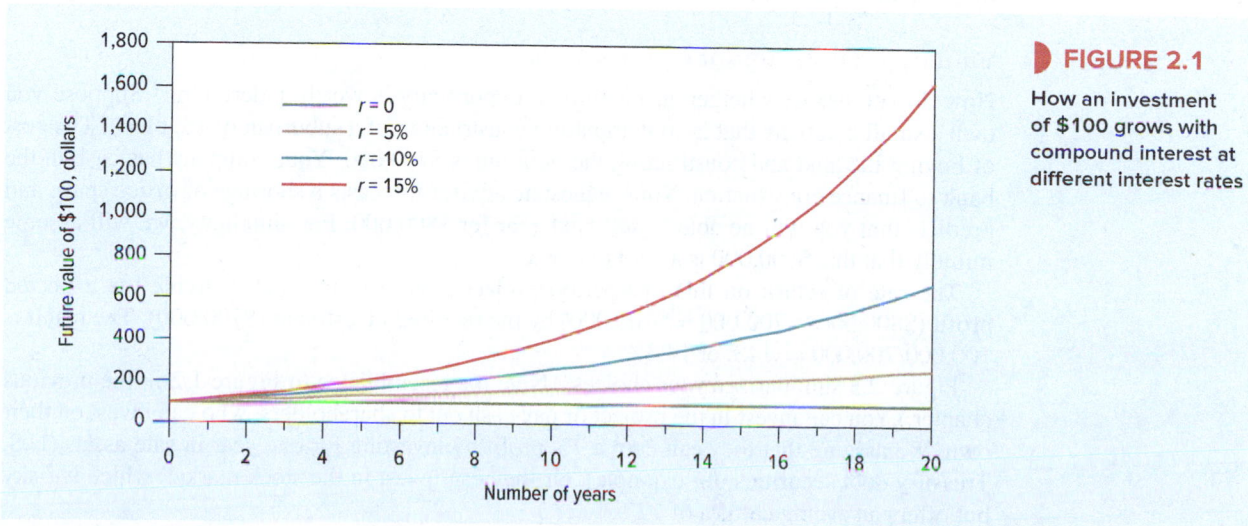

FIGURE 2.1

How an investment of $100 grows with compound interest at different interest rates produce \$114.49 at the end of the second year. In other words, what is the **present value (PV)** of the \$114.49 payoff?

You already know that the answer is \$100. But, if you didn't know or you forgot, you can just run the future value calculation in reverse and divide the future payoff by $(1.07)^2$:

$$\text{Present value} = \text{PV} = \frac{\$114.49}{(1.07)^2} = \$100$$

Today		Year 2
$100	$\div 1.07^2$	$114.49

In general, suppose that you will receive a cash flow of C_t dollars at the end of year t. The present value of this future payment is

$$\text{Present value} = \text{PV} = \frac{C_t}{(1 + r)^t}$$

The rate, r, in the formula is called the discount rate, and the present value is the discounted value of the cash flow, C_t. You sometimes see this present value formula written differently. Instead of dividing the future payment by $(1 + r)^t$, you can equally well multiply the payment by $1/(1 + r)^t$. The expression $1/(1 + r)^t$ is called the **discount factor.** It measures the present value of one dollar received in year t. For example, with an interest rate of 7% the two-year discount factor is

$$\text{DF}_2 = 1/(1.07)^2 = .8734$$

Investors are willing to pay \$.8734 today for delivery of \$1 at the end of two years. If each dollar received in year 2 is worth \$.8734 today, then the present value of your payment of \$114.49 in year 2 must be

$$\text{Present value} = \text{DF}_2 \times C_2 = .8734 \times 114.49 = \$100$$

The longer you have to wait for your money, the lower its present value. This is illustrated in Figure 2.2. Notice how small variations in the interest rate can have a powerful effect on the present value of distant cash flows. At an interest rate of 5%, a payment of \$100 in year 20 is worth \$37.69 today. If the interest rate increases to 10%, the value of the future payment falls by about 60% to \$14.86.

Valuing an Investment Opportunity

How do you decide whether an investment opportunity is worth undertaking? Suppose you own a small company that is contemplating construction of a suburban office block. The cost of buying the land and constructing the building is \$700,000. Your company has cash in the bank to finance construction. Your real estate adviser forecasts a shortage of office space and predicts that you will be able to sell next year for \$800,000. For simplicity, we will assume initially that this \$800,000 is a sure thing.

The rate of return on this one-period project is easy to calculate. Divide the expected profit (\$800,000 − 700,000 = \$100,000) by the required investment (\$700,000). The result is 100,000/700,000 = .143, or 14.3%.

Figure 2.3 summarizes your choices. (Note the resemblance to Figure 1.2 in the previous chapter.) You can invest in the project or pay cash out to shareholders, who can invest on their own. We assume that they can earn a 7% profit by investing for one year in safe assets (U.S. Treasury debt securities, for example). Or they can invest in the stock market, which is risky but offers an average return of 12%.

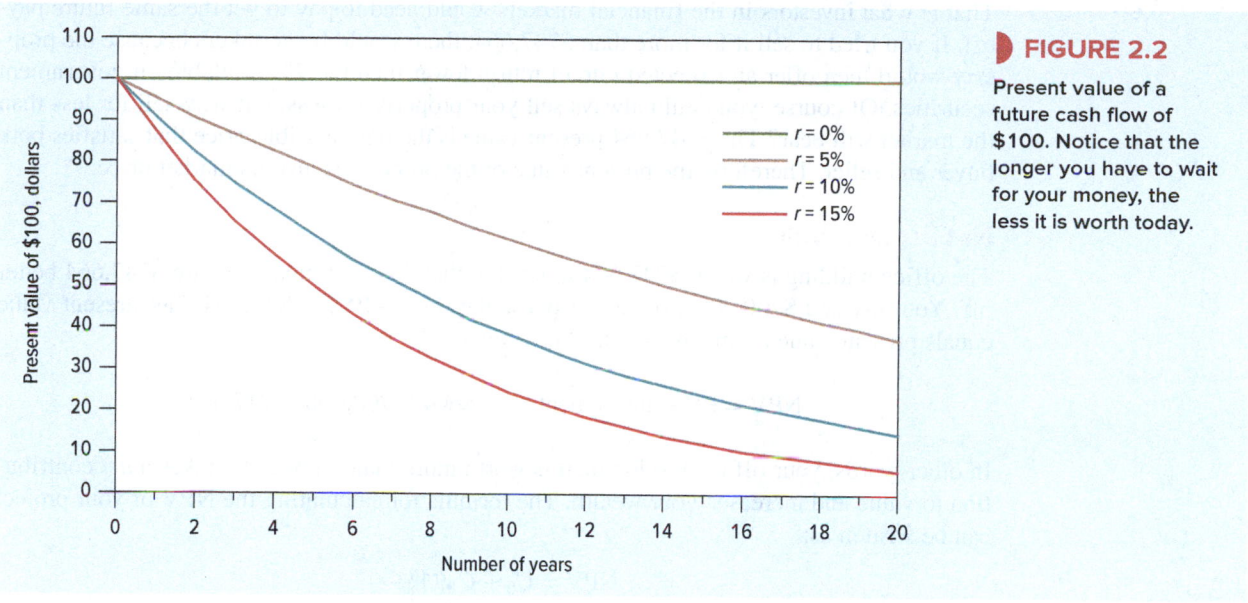

FIGURE 2.2

Present value of a future cash flow of $100. Notice that the longer you have to wait for your money, the less it is worth today.

What is the opportunity cost of capital, 7% or 12%? The answer is 7%: That's the rate of return that your company's shareholders could get by investing on their own at the same level of risk as the proposed project. Here the level of risk is zero. (Remember, we are assuming for now that the future value of the office block is known with certainty.) Your shareholders would vote unanimously for the investment project because the project offers a safe return of 14% versus a safe return of only 7% in financial markets.

The office-block project is therefore a "go," but how much is it worth and how much will the investment add to your wealth? The project produces a cash flow at the end of one year. To find its present value we discount that cash flow by the opportunity cost of capital:

$$\text{Present value} = \text{PV} = \frac{C_1}{1 + r} = \frac{800{,}000}{1.07} = \$747{,}664$$

Suppose that as soon as you have bought the land and paid for the construction, you decide to sell your project. How much could you sell it for? That is an easy question. If the venture will return a surefire $800,000, then your property ought to be worth its PV of $747,664 today.

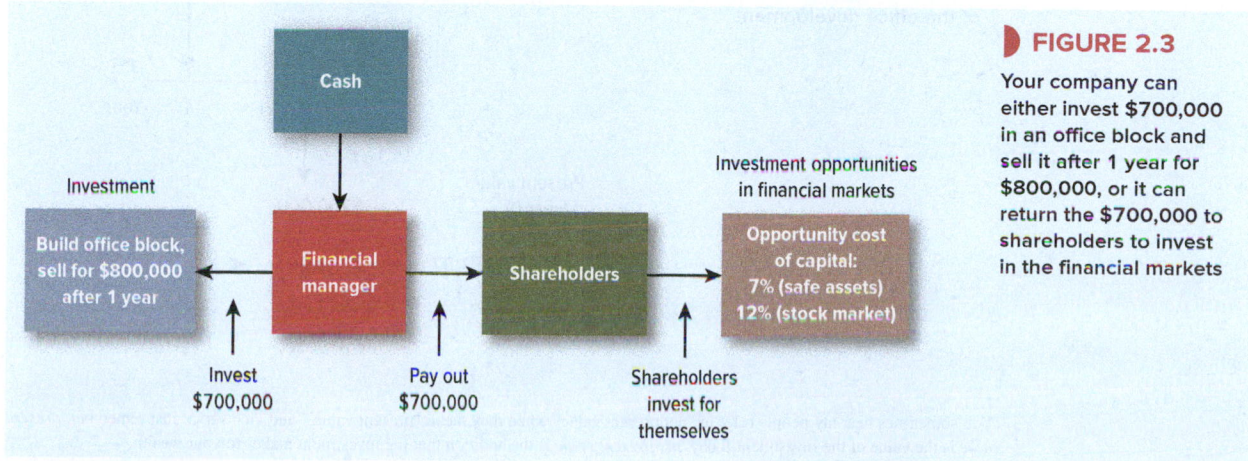

FIGURE 2.3

Your company can either invest $700,000 in an office block and sell it after 1 year for $800,000, or it can return the $700,000 to shareholders to invest in the financial markets

That is what investors in the financial markets would need to pay to get the same future pay-off. If you tried to sell it for more than $747,664, there would be no takers because the property would then offer an expected rate of return lower than the 7% available on government securities. Of course, you could always sell your property for less, but why sell for less than the market will bear? The $747,664 present value is the only feasible price that satisfies both buyer and seller. Therefore, the present value of the property is also its market price.

Net Present Value

The office building is worth $747,664 today, but that does not mean you are $747,664 better off. You invested $700,000, so the **net present value (NPV)** is $47,664. Net present value equals present value minus the required investment:

$$NPV = PV - investment = 747,664 - 700,000 = \$47,664$$

In other words, your office development is worth more than it costs. It makes a *net* contribution to value and increases your wealth. The formula for calculating the NPV of your project can be written as:

$$NPV = C_0 + C_1/(1 + r)$$

Remember that C_0, the cash flow at time 0 (that is, today) is usually a negative number. In other words, C_0 is an investment and therefore a cash outflow. In our example, $C_0 = -\$700,000$.

When cash flows occur at different points in time, it is often helpful to draw a timeline showing the date and value of each cash flow. Figure 2.4 shows a timeline for your office development. It sets out the net present value calculation assuming that the discount rate r is 7%.[1]

Risk and Present Value

We made one unrealistic assumption in our discussion of the office development: Your real estate adviser cannot be certain about the profitability of an office building. Those future cash flows represent the best forecast, but they are not a sure thing.

If the cash flows are uncertain, your calculation of NPV is wrong. Investors could achieve those cash flows with certainty by buying $747,664 worth of U.S. government securities, so

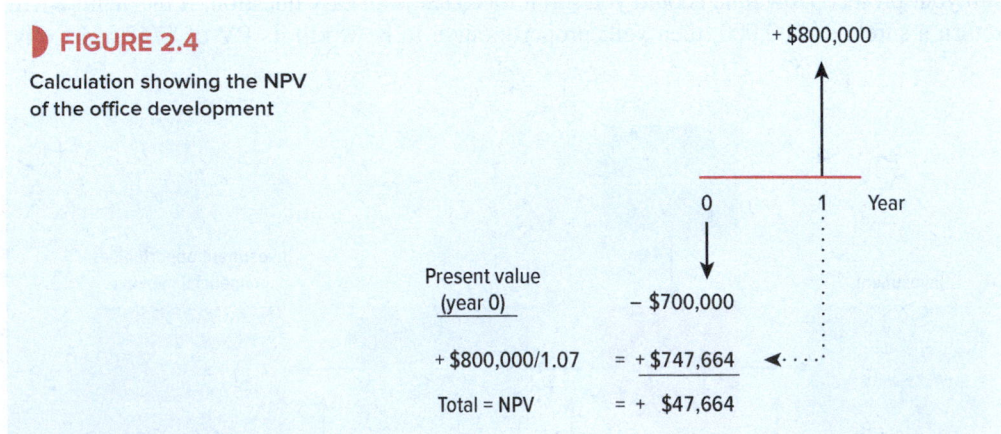

> **FIGURE 2.4**
>
> Calculation showing the NPV of the office development

+ $800,000

0   1   Year

Present value
(year 0)   – $700,000

+ $800,000/1.07   = + $747,664

Total = NPV   = + $47,664

---

[1]You sometimes hear lay people refer to "net present value" when they mean "present value," and vice versa. Just remember, *present value* is the value of the investment today; *net present value* is the addition that the investment makes to your wealth.

they would not buy your building for that amount. You would have to cut your asking price to attract investors' interest.

Here we can invoke a second basic financial principle: *A safe dollar is worth more than a risky dollar.* Most investors dislike risky ventures and won't invest in them unless they see the prospect of a higher return. However, the concepts of present value and the opportunity cost of capital still make sense for risky investments. It is still proper to discount the payoff by the rate of return offered by a risk-equivalent investment in financial markets. But we have to think of *expected* payoffs and the *expected* rates of return on other investments.[2]

Not all investments are equally risky. The office development is more risky than a government security but less risky than a start-up biotech venture. Suppose you believe the project is as risky as investment in the stock market and that stocks are expected to provide a 12% return. Then 12% is the opportunity cost of capital for your project. That is what you are giving up by investing in the office building and *not* investing in equally risky securities.

Now recompute NPV with $r = .12$:

$$PV = \frac{800,000}{1.12} = \$741,286$$

$$NPV = PV - 700,000 = \$14,286$$

The office building still makes a net contribution to value, but the increase in your wealth is smaller than in our first calculation, which assumed that the cash flows from the project were risk-free.

The value of the office building depends, therefore, on the timing of the cash flows and their risk. The $800,000 payoff would be worth just that if you could get it today. If the office building is as risk-free as government securities, the delay in the cash flow reduces value by $52,336 to $747,664. If the building is as risky as investment in the stock market, then the risk further reduces value by $33,378 to $714,286.

Unfortunately, adjusting asset values for both time and risk is often more complicated than our example suggests. Therefore, we take the two effects separately. For the most part, we dodge the problem of risk in Chapters 2 through 6, either by treating all cash flows as if they were known with certainty or by talking about expected cash flows and expected rates of return without worrying how risk is defined or measured. Then in Chapter 7 we turn to the problem of understanding how financial markets cope with risk.

Present Values and Rates of Return

We have decided that constructing the office building is a smart thing to do since it is worth more than it costs. To discover how much it is worth, we asked how much you would need to invest directly in securities to achieve the same payoff. That is why we discounted the project's future payoff by the rate of return offered by these equivalent-risk securities—the overall stock market in our example.

We can state our decision rule in another way: Your real estate venture is worth undertaking because its rate of return exceeds the opportunity cost of capital. The rate of return is simply the profit as a proportion of the initial outlay:

$$\text{Return} = \frac{\text{profit}}{\text{investment}} = \frac{800,000 - 700,000}{700,000} = .143, \text{ or } 14.3\%$$

The cost of capital is once again the return foregone by *not* investing in financial markets. If the office building is as risky as investing in the stock market, the return foregone is 12%.

---

[2]We define "expected" more carefully in Chapter 9. For now think of expected payoff as a realistic forecast, neither optimistic nor pessimistic. Forecasts of expected payoffs are correct on average.

Since the 14.3% return on the office building exceeds the 12% opportunity cost, you should go ahead with the project.

Building the office block is a smart thing to do, even if the payoff is just as risky as the stock market. We can justify the investment by either one of the following two rules:[3]

- *Net present value rule.* Accept investments that have positive net present values.
- *Rate of return rule.* Accept investments that offer rates of return in excess of their opportunity costs of capital.

Properly applied, both rules give the same answer, although we will encounter some cases in Chapter 5 where the rate of return rule is easily misused. In those cases, it is safest to use the net present value rule.

Calculating Present Values When There Are Multiple Cash Flows

One of the nice things about present values is that they are all expressed in current dollars—so you can add them up. In other words, the present value of cash flow (A + B) is equal to the present value of cash flow A plus the present value of cash flow B.

Suppose that you wish to value a stream of cash flows extending over a number of years. Our rule for adding present values tells us that the *total* present value is:

$$PV = \frac{C_1}{(1+r)} + \frac{C_2}{(1+r)^2} + \frac{C_3}{(1+r)^3} + \cdots + \frac{C_T}{(1+r)^T}$$

This is called the **discounted cash flow** (or **DCF**) formula. A shorthand way to write it is

$$PV = \sum_{t=1}^{T} \frac{C_t}{(1+r)^t}$$

where Σ refers to the sum of the series of discounted cash flows. To find the *net* present value (NPV) we add the (usually negative) initial cash flow:

$$NPV = C_0 + PV = C_0 + \sum_{t=1}^{T} \frac{C_t}{(1+r)^t}$$

EXAMPLE 2.1 ● Present Values with Multiple Cash Flows

Your real estate adviser has come back with some revised forecasts. He suggests that you rent out the building for two years at $30,000 a year, and predicts that at the end of that time you will be able to sell the building for $840,000. Thus there are now two future cash flows—a cash flow of $C_1 = \$30,000$ at the end of one year and a further cash flow of $C_2 = (30,000 + 840,000) = \$870,000$ at the end of the second year.

The present value of your property development is equal to the present value of C_1 plus the present value of C_2. Figure 2.5 shows that the value of the first year's cash flow is $C_1/(1+r) = 30,000/1.12 = \$26,786$ and the value of the second year's flow is $C_2/(1+r)^2 = 870,000/1.12^2 = \$693,559$. Therefore our rule for adding present values tells us that the *total* present value of your investment is:

$$PV = \frac{C_1}{1+r} + \frac{C_2}{(1+r)^2} = \frac{30,000}{1.12} + \frac{870,000}{1.12^2} = 26,786 + 69,559 = \$720,344$$

---

[3]You might check for yourself that these are equivalent rules. In other words, if the return of $100,000/$700,000 is greater than r, then the net present value −$700,000 + [$800,000/(1 + r)] *must* be greater than 0.

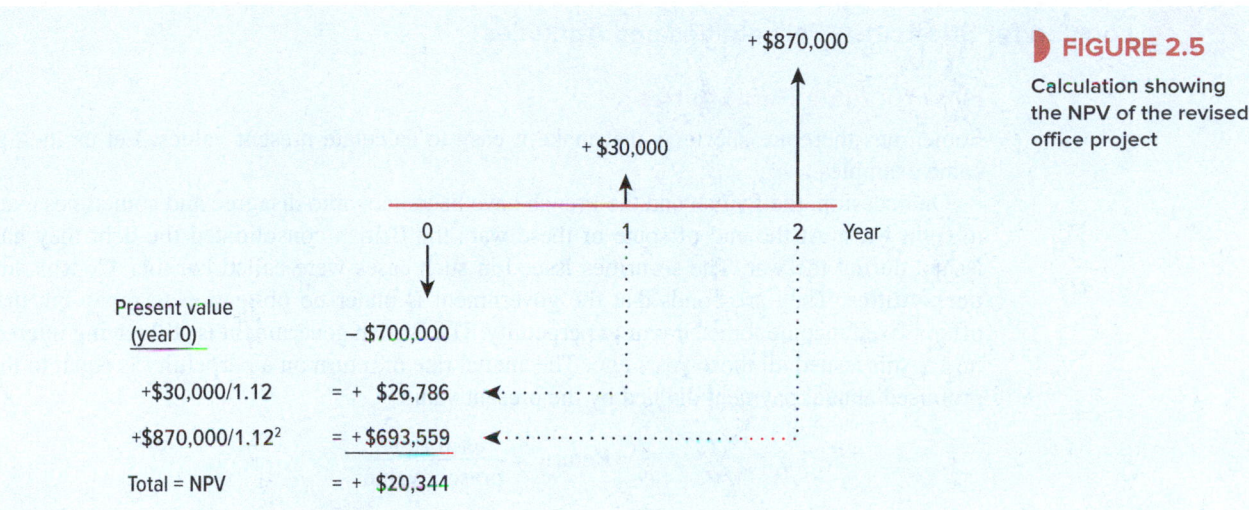

FIGURE 2.5

Calculation showing the NPV of the revised office project

It looks as if you should take your adviser's suggestion. NPV is higher than if you sell in year 1:

$$NPV = \$720,344 - \$700,000 = \$20,344$$

Your two-period calculations in Example 2.1 required just a few keystrokes on a calculator. Real problems can be much more complicated, so financial managers usually turn to financial calculators especially programmed for present value calculations or to computer spreadsheet programs. A box near the end of the chapter introduces you to some useful Excel functions that can be used to solve discounting problems.

BEYOND THE PAGE

Introduction to financial calculators

mhhe.com/brealey13e

The Opportunity Cost of Capital

By investing in the office building you are giving up the opportunity to earn an expected return of 12% in the stock market. The opportunity cost of capital is therefore 12%. When you discount the expected cash flows by the opportunity cost of capital, you are asking how much investors in the financial markets are prepared to pay for a security that produces a similar stream of future cash flows. Your calculations showed that these investors would need to pay $720,344 for an investment that produces cash flows of $30,000 at year 1 and $870,000 at year 2. Therefore, they won't pay any more than that for your office building.

BEYOND THE PAGE

Introduction to Excel

mhhe.com/brealey13e

Confusion sometimes sneaks into discussions of the cost of capital. Suppose a banker approaches. "Your company is a fine and safe business with few debts," she says. "My bank will lend you the $700,000 that you need for the office block at 8%." Does this mean that the cost of capital is 8%? If so, the project would be even more worthwhile. At an 8% cost of capital, PV would be $30,000/1.08 + 870,000/1.08^2 = \$773,663$ and NPV = $773,663 − $700,000 = +$73,663.

But that can't be right. First, the interest rate on the loan has nothing to do with the risk of the project: it reflects the good health of your existing business. Second, whether you take the loan or not, you still face the choice between the office building and an equally risky investment in the stock market. A financial manager who borrows $700,000 at 8% and invests in an office building is not smart, but stupid, if the company or its shareholders can borrow at 8% and make an equally risky investment in the stock market offering an even higher return. That is why the 12% expected return on the stock market is the opportunity cost of capital for your project.

2-2   Looking for Shortcuts—Perpetuities and Annuities

How to Value Perpetuities

Sometimes there are shortcuts that make it easy to calculate present values. Let us look at some examples.

On occasion, the British and the French have been known to disagree and sometimes even to fight wars. At the end of some of these wars the British consolidated the debt they had issued during the war. The securities issued in such cases were called consols. Consols are **perpetuities.** They are bonds that the government is under no obligation to repay but that offer a fixed income for each year to perpetuity. The British government is still paying interest on consols issued all those years ago. The annual rate of return on a perpetuity is equal to the promised annual payment divided by the present value:

$$\text{Return} = \frac{\text{cash flow}}{\text{present value}}$$

$$r = \frac{C}{\text{PV}}$$

We can obviously twist this around and find the present value of a perpetuity given the discount rate r and the cash payment C:[4]

$$\text{PV} = \frac{C}{r}$$

The year is 2030. You have been fabulously successful and are now a billionaire many times over. It was fortunate indeed that you took that finance course all those years ago. You have decided to follow in the footsteps of two of your philanthropic heroes, Bill Gates and Warren Buffett. Malaria is still a scourge and you want to help eradicate it and other infectious diseases by endowing a foundation to combat these diseases. You aim to provide $1 billion a year in perpetuity, starting next year. So, if the interest rate is 10%, you need to write a check today for

$$\text{Present value of perpetuity} = \frac{C}{r} = \frac{\$1 \text{ billion}}{.1} = \$10 \text{ billion}$$

Two warnings about the perpetuity formula. First, at a quick glance, you can easily confuse the formula with the present value of a single payment. A payment of $1 at the end of one year has a present value of $1/(1 + r)$. The perpetuity has a value of $1/r$. These are quite different.

Second, the perpetuity formula tells us the value of a regular stream of payments starting one period from now. Thus your $10 billion endowment would provide the foundation with its first payment in one year's time. If you also want to provide an up-front sum, you will need to lay out an extra $1 billion.

---

[4]You can check this by writing down the present value formula

$$\text{PV} = \frac{C}{1+r} + \frac{C}{(1+r)^2} + \frac{C}{(1+r)^3} + \cdots$$

Now let $C/(1 + r) = a$ and $1/(1 + r) = x$. Then we have (1) PV = $a(1 + x + x^2 + \cdots)$. Multiplying both sides by x, we have (2) PV$x = a(x + x^2 + \cdots)$. Subtracting (2) from (1) gives us PV$(1 - x) = a$. Therefore, substituting for a and x,

$$\text{PV}\left(1 - \frac{1}{1+r}\right) = \frac{C}{1+r}$$

Multiplying both sides by $(1 + r)$ and rearranging gives

$$\text{PV} = \frac{C}{r}$$

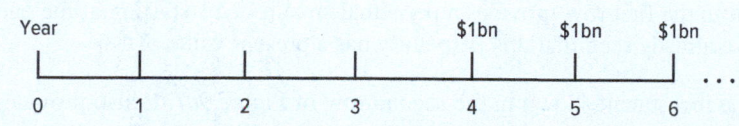

Year $1bn $1bn $1bn

0   1   2   3   4   5   6   · · ·

This perpetuity makes a series of payments of $1 billion a year starting in year 4

Sometimes you may need to calculate the value of a perpetuity that does not start to make payments for several years. For example, suppose that you decide to provide $1 billion a year with the first payment four years from now. Figure 2.6 provides a timeline of these payments. Think first about how much they will be worth in year 3. At that point the endowment will be an ordinary perpetuity with the first payment due at the end of the year. So our perpetuity formula tells us that in year 3 the endowment will be worth $1/r = $1/.1 = 10 billion. But it is not worth that much now. To find *today's* value we need to multiply by the three-year discount factor $1/(1 + r)^3 = 1/(1.1)^3 = .751$. Thus, the "delayed" perpetuity is worth $10 billion × .751 = 7.51 billion. The full calculation is:

$$\text{PV} = \$1 \text{ billion} \times \frac{1}{r} \times \frac{1}{(1+r)^3} = \$1 \text{ billion} \times \frac{1}{.10} \times \frac{1}{(1.10)^3} = \$7.51 \text{ billion}$$

How to Value Annuities

An **annuity** is an asset that pays a fixed sum each year for a specified number of years. The equal-payment house mortgage or installment credit agreement are common examples of annuities. So are interest payments on most bonds, as we shall see in the next chapter.

You can always value an annuity by calculating the value of each cash flow and finding the total. However, it is often quicker to use a simple formula that states that if the interest rate is r, then the present value of an annuity that pays C a period for each of t periods is:

$$\text{Present value of } t\text{-year annuity} = C \left[\frac{1}{r} - \frac{1}{r(1+r)^t} \right]$$

The expression in brackets shows the present value of $1 a year for each of t years. It is generally known as the t-year **annuity factor.**

If you are wondering where this formula comes from, look at Figure 2.7. It shows the payments and values of three investments.

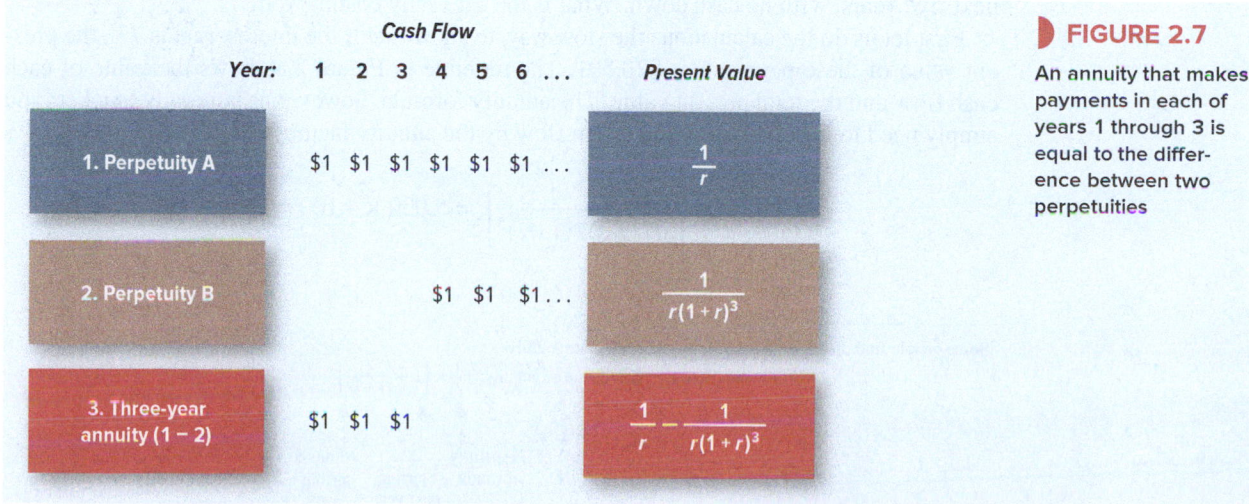

	Cash Flow	Present Value

FIGURE 2.7

An annuity that makes payments in each of years 1 through 3 is equal to the difference between two perpetuities

Row 1   The investment in the first row provides a perpetual stream of $1 starting at the end of the first year. We have already seen that this perpetuity has a present value of $1/r$.

Row 2   Now look at the investment shown in the second row of Figure 2.7. It also provides a perpetual stream of $1 payments, but these payments don't start until year 4. This stream of payments is identical to the payments in row 1, except that they are delayed for an additional three years. In year 3, the investment will be an ordinary perpetuity with payments starting in one year and will therefore be worth $1/r$ in year 3. To find the value *today,* we simply multiply this figure by the three-year discount factor. Thus, as we saw earlier

$$PV = \frac{1}{r} \times \frac{1}{(1+r)^3}$$

Row 3   Finally, look at the investment shown in the third row of Figure 2.7. This provides a level payment of $1 a year for each of three years. In other words, it is a three-year annuity. You can also see that, taken together, the investments in rows 2 and 3 provide exactly the same cash payments as the investment in row 1. Thus the value of our annuity (row 3) must be equal to the value of the row 1 perpetuity less the value of the delayed row 2 perpetuity:

$$\text{Present value of a 3-year annuity of \$1 a year} = \frac{1}{r} - \frac{1}{r(1+r)^3}$$

Remembering formulas is about as difficult as remembering other people's birthdays. But as long as you bear in mind that an annuity is equivalent to the difference between an immediate and a delayed perpetuity, you shouldn't have any difficulty.[5]

EXAMPLE 2.2 • Costing an Installment Plan

Most installment plans call for level streams of payments. Suppose that Tiburon Autos offers an "easy payment" scheme on a new Toyota of $5,000 a year, paid at the end of each of the next five years, with no cash down. What is the car really costing you?

First let us do the calculations the slow way, to show that if the interest rate is 7%, the present value of these payments is $20,501. The timeline in Figure 2.8 shows the value of each cash flow and the total present value. The annuity formula, however, is generally quicker; you simply need to multiply the $5,000 cash flow by the annuity factor:

$$PV = 5,000 \left[\frac{1}{.07} - \frac{1}{.07(1.07)^5} \right] = 5,000 \times 4.100 = \$20,501$$

---

[5]Some people find the following equivalent formula more intuitive:

$$\text{Present value of annuity} = \frac{1}{r} \times \left[1 - \frac{1}{(1+r)^t} \right]$$

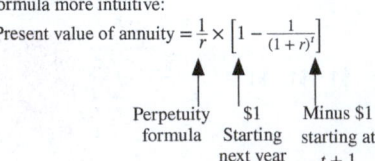

Perpetuity $1   Minus $1
formula   Starting   starting at
           next year $t+1$

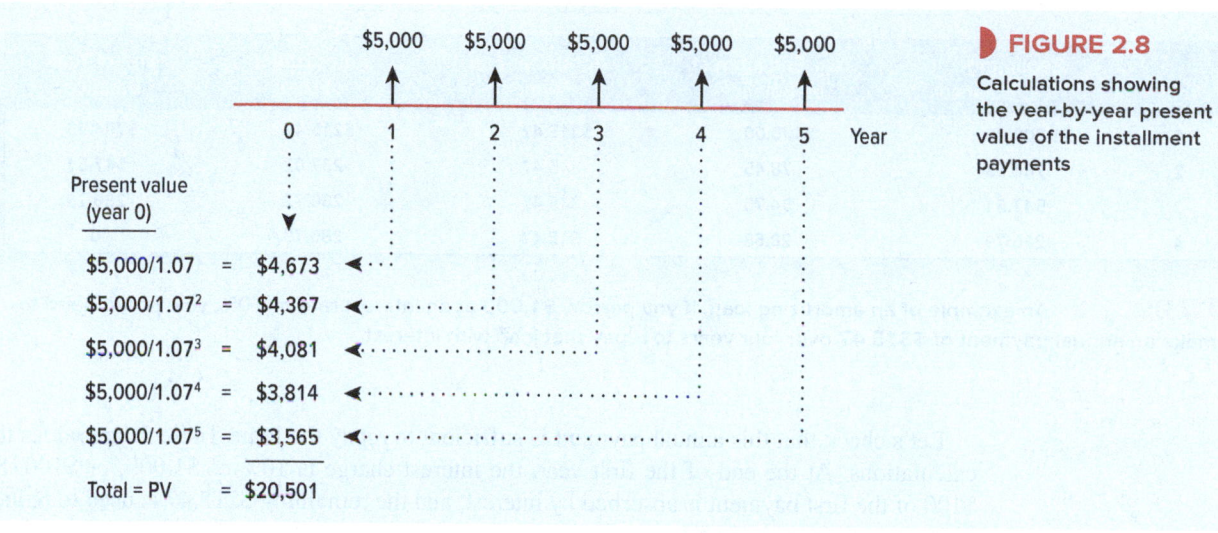

▶ **FIGURE 2.8**

Calculations showing the year-by-year present value of the installment payments

Valuing Annuities Due

When we costed the installment plan we assumed that the first payment was made at the end of the year. Suppose instead that the first of the five yearly payments is due immediately. How does this change the cost of the car?

If we discount each cash flow by one less year, the present value is increased by the multiple $(1 + r)$. In the case of the car purchase the present value of the payments becomes $20,501 \times (1 + r) = 20,501 \times 1.07 = \$21,936$.

A level stream of payments starting immediately is called an **annuity due.** An annuity due is worth $(1 + r)$ times the value of an ordinary annuity.

BEYOND THE PAGE

 Try It! More on annuities

mhhe.com/brealey13e

Calculating Annual Payments

Annuity problems can be confusing on first acquaintance, but you will find that with practice they are generally straightforward. For example, here is a case where you need to use the annuity formula to find the amount of the payment *given* the present value.

EXAMPLE 2.3 ● Paying Off a Bank Loan

Bank loans are paid off in equal installments. Suppose that you take out a four-year loan of $1,000. The bank requires you to repay the loan evenly over the four years. It must therefore set the four annual payments so that they have a present value of $1,000. Thus,

$$PV = \text{annual loan payment} \times \text{4-year annuity factor} = \$1,000$$

$$\text{Annual loan payment} = \$1,000/\text{4-year annuity factor}$$

Suppose that the interest rate is 10% a year. Then

$$\text{4-year annuity factor} = \left[\frac{1}{.10} - \frac{1}{.10(1.10)^4}\right] = 3.170$$

and

$$\text{Annual loan payment} = 1,000/3.170 = \$315.47$$

Year	Beginning-of-Year Balance	Year-End Interest on Balance	Total Year-End Payment	Amortization of Loan	End-of-Year Balance
1	$1,000.00	$100.00	$315.47	$215.47	$784.53
2	784.53	78.45	315.47	237.02	547.51
3	547.51	54.75	315.47	260.72	286.79
4	286.79	28.68	315.47	286.79	0

❭**TABLE 2.1**   An example of an amortizing loan. If you borrow **$1,000** at an interest rate of 10%, you would need to make an annual payment of **$315.47** over four years to repay that loan with interest.

Let's check that this annual payment is sufficient to repay the loan. Table 2.1 provides the calculations. At the end of the first year, the interest charge is 10% of $1,000, or $100. So $100 of the first payment is absorbed by interest, and the remaining $215.47 is used to reduce the loan balance to $784.53.

Next year, the outstanding balance is lower, so the interest charge is only $78.45. Therefore $315.47 − $78.45 = $237.02 can be applied to paying off the loan. Because the loan is progressively paid off, the fraction of each payment devoted to interest steadily falls over time, while the fraction used to reduce the loan increases. By the end of year 4, the amortization is just enough to reduce the balance of the loan to zero.

Loans that involve a series of level payments are known as *amortizing loans.* "Amortizing" means that part of the regular payment is used to pay interest on the loan and part is used to pay off or *amortize* the loan.

• • • • •

EXAMPLE 2.4 • Calculating Mortgage Payments

Most mortgages are amortizing loans. For example, suppose that you take out a $250,000 house mortgage from your local savings bank when the interest rate is 12%. The bank requires you to repay the mortgage in equal annual installments over the next 30 years. Thus,

$$\text{Annual mortgage payment} = \$250,000/30\text{-year annuity factor}$$

$$30\text{-year annuity factor} = \left[\frac{1}{.12} - \frac{1}{.12\,(1.12)^{30}}\right] = 8.055$$

and

$$\text{Annual mortgage payment} = 250,000/8.055 = \$31,036$$

Figure 2.9 shows that in the early years, almost all of the mortgage payment is eaten up by interest and only a small fraction is used to reduce the amount of the loan. Even after 15 years, the bulk of the annual payment goes to pay the interest on the loan. From then on, the amount of the loan begins to decline rapidly.

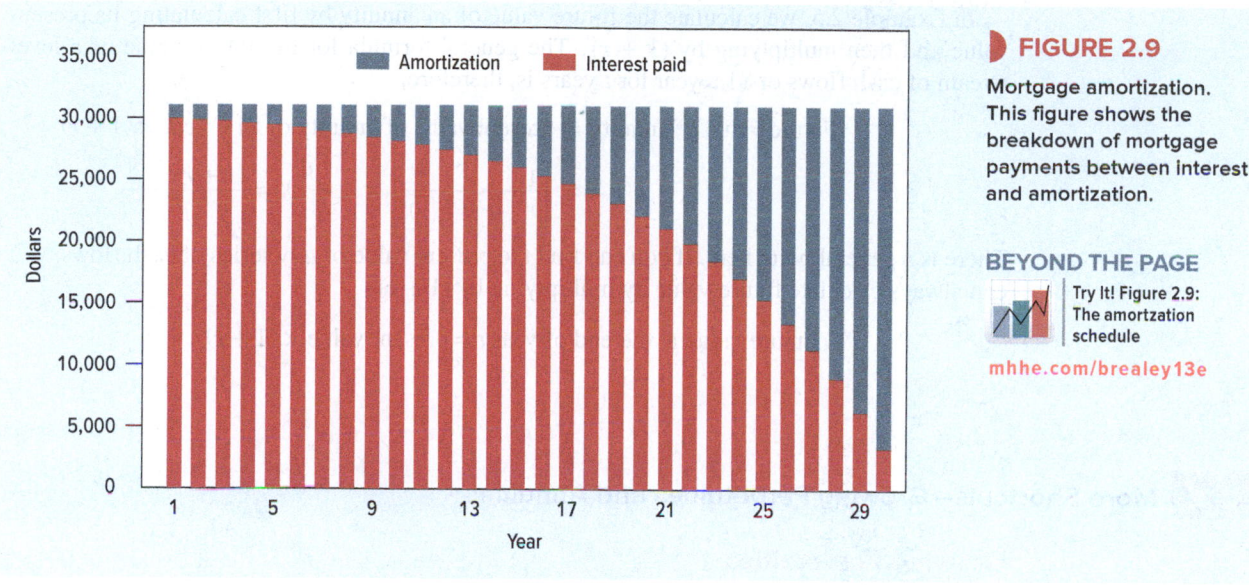

FIGURE 2.9

Mortgage amortization. This figure shows the breakdown of mortgage payments between interest and amortization.

BEYOND THE PAGE

Try It! Figure 2.9: The amortzation schedule

mhhe.com/brealey13e

Future Value of an Annuity

Sometimes you need to calculate the *future* value of a level stream of payments.

EXAMPLE 2.5 • Saving to Buy a Sailboat

Perhaps your ambition is to buy a sailboat; something like a 40-foot Beneteau would fit the bill very well. But that means some serious saving. You estimate that, once you start work, you could save $20,000 a year out of your income and earn a return of 8% on these savings. How much will you be able to spend after five years?

We are looking here at a level stream of cash flows—an annuity. We have seen that there is a shortcut formula to calculate the *present* value of an annuity. So there ought to be a similar formula for calculating the *future* value of a level stream of cash flows.

Think first how much your savings are worth today. You will set aside $20,000 in each of the next five years. The present value of this five-year annuity is therefore equal to

$$PV = \$20,000 \times 5\text{-year annuity factor}$$

$$= \$20,000 \times \left[\frac{1}{.08} - \frac{1}{.08(1.08)^5} \right] = \$79,854$$

Once you know today's value of the stream of cash flows, it is easy to work out its value in the future. Just multiply by $(1.08)^5$:

$$\text{Value at end of year 5} = \$79,854 \times 1.08^5 = \$117,332$$

You should be able to buy yourself a nice boat for $117,000.

In Example 2.5, we calculate the future value of an annuity by first calculating its present value and then multiplying by $(1 + r)^t$. The general formula for the future value of a level stream of cash flows of \$1 a year for t years is, therefore,

$$\text{Future value of annuity} = \text{present value of annuity of \$1 a year} \times (1 + r)^t$$

$$= \left[\frac{1}{r} - \frac{1}{r(1+r)^t} \right] \times (1 + r)^t = \frac{(1+r)^t - 1}{r}$$

There is a general point here. If you can find the present value of *any* series of cash flows, you can always calculate future value by multiplying by $(1 + r)^t$:

$$\text{Future value at the end of year } t = \text{present value} \times (1 + r)^t$$

2-3   More Shortcuts—Growing Perpetuities and Annuities

Growing Perpetuities

You now know how to value level streams of cash flows, but you often need to value a stream of cash flows that grows at a constant rate. For example, think back to your plans to donate \$10 billion to fight malaria and other infectious diseases. Unfortunately, you made no allowance for the growth in salaries and other costs, which will probably average about 4% a year starting in year 1. Therefore, instead of providing \$1 billion a year in perpetuity, you must provide \$1 billion in year 1, $1.04 \times \$1$ billion in year 2, and so on. If we call the growth rate in costs g, we can write down the present value of this stream of cash flows as follows:

$$\text{PV} = \frac{C_1}{1+r} + \frac{C_2}{(1+r)^2} + \frac{C_3}{(1+r)^3} + \cdots$$

$$= \frac{C_1}{1+r} + \frac{C_1(1+g)}{(1+r)^2} + \frac{C_1(1+g)^2}{(1+r)^3} + \cdots$$

Fortunately, there is a simple formula for the sum of this geometric series.[6] If we assume that r is greater than g, our clumsy-looking calculation simplifies to

$$\text{Present value of growing perpetuity} = \frac{C_1}{r-g}$$

Therefore, if you want to provide a perpetual stream of income that keeps pace with the growth rate in costs, the amount that you must set aside today is

$$\text{PV} = \frac{C_1}{r-g} = \frac{\$1 \text{ billion}}{.10 - .04} = \$16.667 \text{ billion}$$

You will meet this perpetual-growth formula again in Chapter 4, where we use it to value the stocks of mature, slowly growing companies.

---

[6]We need to calculate the sum of an infinite geometric series $\text{PV} = a(1 + x + x^2 + \cdots)$ where $a = C_1/(1 + r)$ and $x = (1 + g)/(1 + r)$. In footnote 4 we showed that the sum of such a series is $a/(1 - x)$. Substituting for a and x in this formula,

$$\text{PV} = \frac{C_1}{(r-g)}$$

Growing Annuities

EXAMPLE 2.6 • Winning Big at the Lottery

In August 2017, a Massachusetts woman invested in a Powerball lottery ticket and won a record $758.7 million. We suspect that she received unsolicited congratulations, good wishes, and requests for money from dozens of more or less worthy charities, relations, and newly devoted friends. In response, she could fairly point out that the prize wasn't really worth $758.7 million. That sum was to be paid in 30 annual installments. The payment in the first year was only $11.42 million, but it then increased each year by 5% so that the final payment was $47.00 million. The total amount paid out was $758.7 million, but the winner had to wait to get it.

If the interest rate was 2.7%, what was that $758.7 prize really worth? Suppose that the first payment occurs at the end of year 1, so that $C_1 = \$11.42$ million. If the payments then grow at the rate of $g = .05$ each year, the payment in year 2 is 11.42×1.05, and in year 3 it is 11.42×1.05^2. Of course, you could calculate each of the 30 cash flows and discount them at 2.7%. The alternative is to use the following formula for the present value of a growing annuity:[7]

$$\text{PV of growing annuity} = C \times \frac{1}{r-g}\left[1 - \frac{(1+g)^t}{(1+r)^t}\right]$$

In the case of our lottery, the present value of the growing stream of payments is

$$\text{PV} = 11.42 \times \left[1 - \frac{(1.05)^{30}}{(1.027)^{30}}\right]\frac{1}{.027-.05} = 11.42 \times 41.02 = \$468 \ million$$

Thus, the present value of a growing stream of payments starting at the end of the first year is $468 million. In practice, the news is not quite that bad because the lottery winner receives the first payment immediately (in year 0) and the last one is received in year 29 rather than in year 30. Therefore, we need to increase our estimate of present value by $1 + r$. So the present value of the prize is $468 \times 1.027 = \$481$ million.

If the total Powerball prize money was paid out immediately, it would be worth $757.8 million. Paying out this money over the next 29 years reduces the value of the prize to $481 million, much below the well-trumpeted prize but still not a bad day's haul.

For winners with big spending plans, lottery operators generally make arrangements so that they may take an equivalent lump sum. In our example, the winner could either take the $758.7 million spread over 30 years or receive $481 million up front. Both arrangements had the same present value.

---

[7]We can derive the formula for a growing annuity by taking advantage of our earlier trick of finding the difference between the values of two perpetuities. Imagine three investments (A, B, and C) that make the following dollar payments:

Year	1	2	3	4	5	6	...
A	$1	$(1+g)$	$(1+g)^2$	$(1+g)^3$	$(1+g)^4$	$(1+g)^5$	etc.
B				$(1+g)^3$	$(1+g)^4$	$(1+g)^5$	etc.
C	$1	$(1+g)$	$(1+g)^2$				

Investments A and B are growing perpetuities; A makes its first payment of $1 in year 1, while B makes its first payment of $(1+g)^3$ in year 4. C is a three-year growing annuity; its cash flows are equal to the difference between the cash flows of A and B. You know how to value growing perpetuities such as A and B. So you should be able to derive the formula for the value of growing annuities such as C:

$$\text{PV(A)} = \frac{1}{(r-g)}$$

So

$$\text{PV(B)} = \frac{(1+g)^3}{(r-g)} \times \frac{1}{(1+r)^3}$$

$$\text{PV(C)} = \text{PV(A)} - \text{PV(B)} = \frac{1}{(r-g)} - \frac{(1+g)^3}{(r-g)} \times \frac{1}{(1+r)^3} = \frac{1}{r-g}\left[1 - \frac{(1+g)^3}{(1+r)^3}\right]$$

If $r = g$, then the formula blows up. In that case, the cash flows grow at the same rate as the amount by which they are discounted. Therefore, each cash flow has a present value of $C/(1+r)$ and the total present value of the annuity equals $t \times C/(1+r)$. If $r < g$, then this particular formula remains valid, though still treacherous.

Too many formulas are bad for the digestions. So we will stop at this point and spare you any more of them. The formulas discussed so far appear in Table 2.2.

Year:	0	1	2 . . .	. . . $t-1$	t	$t+1$ . . .	Present Value
Perpetuity		1	1 . . .	1	1	1 . . .	$\dfrac{1}{r}$
t-period annuity		1	1 . . .	1	1		$\dfrac{1}{r} - \dfrac{1}{r(1+r)^t}$
t-period annuity due	1	1	1 . . .	1			$(1+r)\left(\dfrac{1}{r} - \dfrac{1}{r(1+r)^t}\right)$
Growing perpetuity		1	$1 \times (1+g)$ . . .	$1 \times (1+g)^{t-2}$	$1 \times (1+g)^{t-1}$	$1 \times (1+g)^{t \cdot \cdot}$	$\dfrac{1}{r-g}$
t-period growing annuity		1	$1 \times (1+g)$ . . .	$1 \times (1+g)^{t-2}$	$1 \times (1+g)^{t-1}$		$\dfrac{1}{r-g}\left[1 - \dfrac{(1+g)^t}{(1+r)^t}\right]$

❯TABLE 2.2 Some useful shortcut formulas

Note: a. The growing perpetuity formula works only if the discount rate r is greater than the growth rate g.
　　　 b. The growing annuity formula blows up if $r = g$. In this case, the value of the growing annuity is $C \times t/(1+r)$.

2-4 How Interest Is Paid and Quoted

In our examples we have assumed that cash flows occur only at the end of each year. This is sometimes the case. For example, in France and Germany, the government pays interest on its bonds annually. However, in the United States and Britain, government bonds pay interest semiannually. So if a U.S. government bond promises to pay interest of 10% a year, the investor in practice receives interest of 5% every six months.

If the first interest payment is made at the end of six months, you can earn an additional six months' interest on this payment. For example, if you invest $100 in a bond that pays interest of 10% compounded semiannually, your wealth will grow to $1.05 \times \$100 = \$105$ by the end of six months and to $1.05 \times \$105 = \$110.25$ by the end of the year. In other words, an interest rate of 10% compounded semiannually is equivalent to 10.25% compounded annually. The *effective annual interest rate* on the bond is 10.25%.

Let's take another example. Suppose a bank offers you an automobile loan at an **annual percentage rate, or APR,** of 12% with interest to be paid monthly. By this the bank means that each month you need to pay one-twelfth of the annual rate, that is, 12/12 = 1% a month. Thus the bank is *quoting* a rate of 12%, but the effective annual interest rate on your loan is $1.01^{12} - 1 = .1268$ or 12.68%.[8]

Our examples illustrate that you need to distinguish between the *quoted* annual interest rate and the *effective* annual rate. The quoted annual rate is usually calculated as the total annual payment divided by the number of payments in the year. When interest is paid once a year, the quoted and effective rates are the same. When interest is paid more frequently, the effective interest rate is higher than the quoted rate.

In general, if you invest $1 at a rate of r per year compounded m times a year, your investment at the end of the year will be worth $[1 + (r/m)]^m$ and the effective interest rate is

---

[8]In the U.S., truth-in-lending laws oblige the company to quote an APR that is calculated by multiplying the payment each period by the number of payments in the year. APRs are calculated differently in other countries. For example, in the European Union, APRs must be expressed as annually compounded rates, so consumers know the effective interest rate that they are paying.

$[1 + (r/m)]^m - 1$. In our automobile loan example $r = .12$ and $m = 12$. So the effective annual interest rate was $[1 + .12/12]^{12} - 1 = .1268$, or 12.68%.

Continuous Compounding

Instead of compounding interest monthly or semiannually, the rate could be compounded weekly ($m = 52$) or daily ($m = 365$). In fact, there is no limit to how frequently interest could be paid. One can imagine a situation where the payments are spread evenly and continuously throughout the year, so the interest rate is continuously compounded.[9] In this case m is infinite.

It turns out that there are many occasions in finance when continuous compounding is useful. For example, one important application is in option pricing models, such as the Black–Scholes model that we introduce in Chapter 21. These are continuous time models. So you will find that most computer programs for calculating option values ask for the continuously compounded interest rate.

It may seem that a lot of calculations would be needed to find a continuously compounded interest rate. However, think back to your high school algebra. You may recall that as m approaches infinity $[1 + (r/m)]^m$ approaches $(2.718)^r$. The figure 2.718—or e, as it is called—is the base for natural logarithms. Therefore, $1 invested at a continuously compounded rate of r will grow to $e^r = (2.718)^r$ by the end of the first year. By the end of t years it will grow to $e^{rt} = (2.718)^{rt}$.

Example 1   Suppose you invest $1 at a continuously compounded rate of 11% ($r = .11$) for one year ($t = 1$). The end-year value is $e^{.11}$, or $1.116. In other words, investing at 11% a year *continuously* compounded is exactly the same as investing at 11.6% a year *annually* compounded.

Example 2   Suppose you invest $1 at a continuously compounded rate of 11% ($r = .11$) for two years ($t = 2$). The final value of the investment is $e^{rt} = e^{.22}$, or $1.246.

Sometimes it may be more reasonable to assume that the cash flows from a project are spread evenly over the year rather than occurring at the year's end. It is easy to adapt our previous formulas to handle this. For example, suppose that we wish to compute the present value of a perpetuity of C dollars a year. We already know that if the payment is made at the end of the year, we divide the payment by the *annually* compounded rate of r:

$$PV = \frac{C}{r}$$

If the same total payment is made in an even stream throughout the year, we use the same formula but substitute the *continuously* compounded rate.

Suppose the annually compounded rate is 18.5%. The present value of a $100 perpetuity, with each cash flow received at the end of the year, is $100/.185 = $540.54. If the cash flow is received continuously, we must divide $100 by 17%, because 17% continuously compounded is equivalent to 18.5% annually compounded ($e^{.17} = 1.185$). The present value of the continuous cash flow stream is $100/.17 = $588.24. Investors are prepared to pay more for the continuous cash payments because the cash starts to flow in immediately.

Example 3   After you have retired, you plan to spend $200,000 a year for 20 years. The annually compounded interest rate is 10%. How much must you save by the time you retire to support this spending plan?

---

[9]When we talk about *continuous* payments, we are pretending that money can be dispensed in a continuous stream like water out of a faucet. One can never quite do this. For example, instead of paying out $1 billion every year to combat malaria, you could pay out about $1 million every 8 3/4 hours or $10,000 every 5 1/4 minutes or $10 every 3 1/6 seconds but you could not pay it out *continuously*. Financial managers *pretend* that payments are continuous rather than hourly, daily, or weekly because (1) it simplifies the calculations and (2) it gives a very close approximation to the NPV of frequent payments.

Discounting Cash Flows

❯Spreadsheet programs such as Excel provide built-in functions to solve discounted cash flow (DCF) problems. You can find these functions by pressing *fx* on the Excel toolbar. If you then click on the function that you wish to use, Excel asks you for the inputs that it needs. At the bottom left of the function box there is a Help facility with an example of how the function is used.

Here is a list of useful functions for DCF problems and some points to remember when entering data:

- **FV:** Future value of single investment or annuity.
- **PV:** Present value of single future cash flow or annuity.
- **RATE:** Interest rate (or rate of return) needed to produce given future value or annuity.
- **NPER:** Number of periods (e.g., years) that it takes an investment to reach a given future value.
- **PMT:** Amount of annuity payment with a given present or future value.
- **NPV:** Calculates the value of a stream of negative and positive cash flows. (When using this function, note the warning below.)
- **EFFECT:** The effective annual interest rate, given the quoted rate (APR) and number of interest payments in a year.
- **NOMINAL:** The quoted interest rate (APR) given the effective annual interest rate.

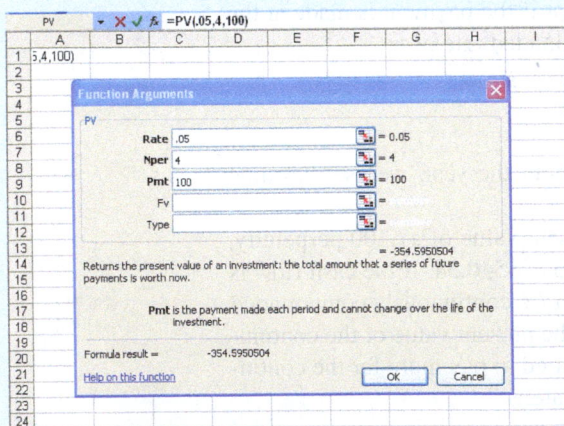

All the inputs in these functions can be entered directly as numbers or as the addresses of cells that contain the numbers.

Three warnings:

1. PV is the amount that needs to be invested today to produce a given future value. It should therefore be entered as a negative number. Entering both PV and FV with the same sign when solving for RATE results in an error message.

2. Always enter the interest or discount rate as a decimal value (for example, .05 rather than 5%).

3. Use the NPV function with care. Better still, don't use it at all. It gives the value of the cash flows one period *before* the first cash flow and not the value at the date of the first cash flow.

Spreadsheet Questions

The following questions provide opportunities to practice each of the Excel functions.

1. (FV) In 1880, five aboriginal trackers were each promised the equivalent of 100 Australian dollars for helping to capture the notorious outlaw Ned Kelly. One hundred and thirteen years later, the granddaughters of two of the trackers claimed that this reward had not been paid. If the interest rate over this period averaged about 4.5%, how much would the A$100 have accumulated to?

2. (PV) Your adviser has produced revised figures for your office building. It is forecasted to produce a cash flow of $40,000 in year 1, but only $850,000 in year 2, when you come to sell it. If the cost of capital is 12%, what is the value of the building?

3. (PV) Your company can lease a truck for $10,000 a year (paid at the end of the year) for six years, or it can buy the truck today for $50,000. At the end of the six years the truck will be worthless. If the interest rate is 6%, what is the present value of the lease payments? Is the lease worthwhile?

4. (RATE) Ford Motor stock was one of the victims of the 2008 credit crisis. In June 2007, Ford stock price stood at $9.42. Eighteen months later it was $2.72. What was the annual rate of return over this period to an investor in Ford stock?

5. (NPER) An investment adviser has promised to double your money. If the interest rate is 7% a year, how many years will she take to do so?

6. (PMT) You need to take out a home mortgage for $200,000. If payments are made annually over 30 years and the interest rate is 8%, what is the amount of the annual payment?

7. (EFFECT) First National Bank pays 6.2% interest compounded annually. Second National Bank pays 6% interest compounded monthly. Which bank offers the higher effective annual interest rate?

8. (NOMINAL) What monthly compounded interest rate would Second National Bank need to pay on savings deposits to provide an effective rate of 6.2%?

Let us first do the calculations assuming that you spend the cash at the end of each year. In this case we can use the simple annuity formula that we derived earlier:

$$PV = C\left(\frac{1}{r} - \frac{1}{r(1+r)^t}\right)$$

$$= \$200,000\left(\frac{1}{.10} - \frac{1}{.10(1.10)^{20}}\right) = \$200,000 \times 8.514 = \$1,702,800$$

Thus, you will need to have saved $1.7 million by the time you retire.

Instead of waiting until the end of each year before you spend any cash, it is more reasonable to assume that your expenditure will be spread evenly over the year. In this case, instead of using the annually compounded rate of 10%, we must use the continuously compounded rate of $r = 9.53\%$ ($e^{.0953} = 1.10$). Therefore, to cover a steady stream of expenditure, you need to set aside the following sum:[10]

$$PV = C\left(\frac{1}{r} - \frac{1}{r} \times \frac{1}{e^{rt}}\right)$$

$$= \$200,000\left(\frac{1}{.0953} - \frac{1}{.0953} \times \frac{1}{6.727}\right) = \$200,000 \times 8.932 = \$1,786,400$$

To support a steady stream of outgoings, you must save an additional $83,600.

Often in finance you need only a ballpark estimate of present value. An error of 5% in a present value calculation may be perfectly acceptable. In such cases it doesn't usually matter whether you assume that cash flows occur at the end of the year or in a continuous stream. At other times precision matters, and you do need to worry about the exact frequency of the cash flows.

---

[10]Remember that an annuity is simply the difference between a perpetuity received today and a perpetuity received in year t. A continuous stream of C dollars a year in perpetuity is worth C/r, where r is the continuously compounded rate. Our annuity, then, is worth

$$PV = \frac{C}{r} - \text{Present value of } \frac{C}{r} \text{ received in year } t$$

Since r is the continuously compounded rate, C/r received in year t is worth $(C/r) \times (1/e^{rt})$ today. Our annuity formula is therefore

$$PV = \frac{C}{r} - \frac{C}{r} \times \frac{1}{e^{rt}}$$

sometimes written as

$$\frac{C}{r}(1 - e^{-rt})$$

Firms can best help their shareholders by accepting all projects that are worth more than they cost. In other words, they need to seek out projects with positive net present values. To find net present value we first calculate present value. Just discount future cash flows by an appropriate rate r, usually called the *discount rate, hurdle rate,* or *opportunity cost of capital:*

SUMMARY

$$\text{Present value (PV)} = \frac{C_1}{(1+r)} + \frac{C_2}{(1+r)^2} + \frac{C_3}{(1+r)^3} + \cdots$$

Net present value is present value plus any immediate cash flow:

$$\text{Net present value (NPV)} = C_0 + PV$$

Remember that C_0 is negative if the immediate cash flow is an investment, that is, if it is a cash outflow.

The discount rate r is determined by rates of return prevailing in financial markets. If the future cash flow is absolutely safe, then the discount rate is the interest rate on safe securities such as U.S. government debt. If the future cash flow is uncertain, then the expected cash flow should be discounted at the expected rate of return offered by equivalent-risk securities. (We talk more about risk and the cost of capital in Chapters 7 to 9.)

Cash flows are discounted for two simple reasons: because (1) a dollar today is worth more than a dollar tomorrow and (2) a safe dollar is worth more than a risky one. Formulas for PV and NPV are numerical expressions of these ideas.

Financial markets, including the bond and stock markets, are the markets where safe and risky future cash flows are traded and valued. That is why we look to rates of return prevailing in the financial markets to determine how much to discount for time and risk. By calculating the present value of an asset, we are estimating how much people will pay for it if they have the alternative of investing in the financial markets.

You can always work out any present value using the basic formula, but shortcut formulas can reduce the tedium. We showed how to value an investment that makes a level stream of cash flows forever (a *perpetuity*) and one that produces a level stream for a limited period (an *annuity*). We also showed how to value investments that produce growing streams of cash flows.

When someone offers to lend you a dollar at a quoted interest rate, you should always check how frequently the interest is to be paid. For example, suppose that a $100 loan requires six monthly payments of $3. The total yearly interest payment is $6 and the interest will be quoted as a rate of 6% compounded semiannually. The equivalent *annually compounded rate* is $(1.03)^2 - 1 = .06$ or 6.1%. Sometimes it is convenient to assume that interest is paid evenly over the year so that interest is quoted as a continuously compounded rate.

PROBLEM SETS

Select problems are available in McGraw-Hill's *Connect*.
Answers to questions with an "*" are found in the Appendix.

1. **Opportunity cost of capital** Which of the following statements are true? The opportunity cost of capital:

    a. Equals the interest rate at which the company can borrow.

    b. Depends on the risk of the cash flows to be valued.

    c. Depends on the rates of return that shareholders can expect to earn by investing on their own.

    d. Equals zero if the firm has excess cash in its bank account and the bank account pays no interest.

2. **Opportunity cost of capital** Explain why we refer to the *opportunity* cost of capital, instead of just "cost of capital" or "discount rate." While you're at it, also explain the following statement: "The opportunity cost of capital depends on the proposed use of cash, not the source of financing."

3. **Compound interest** Old Time Savings Bank pays 4% interest on its savings account. If you deposit $1,000 in the bank and leave it there:

    a. How much interest will you earn in the first year?

    b. How much interest will you earn in the second year?

    c. How much interest will you earn in the tenth year?

4. **Compound interest** New Savings Bank pays 4% interest on deposits. If you deposit $1,000 in the bank and leave it there, will it take more or less than 25 years for your investment to double? You should be able to answer this without a calculator.

5. **Compound interest** In 2017, Leonardo da Vinci's painting *Salvator Mundi* sold for a record $450.3 million. In 1958, it sold for $125, equivalent in purchasing power to about $1,060 at

2017 prices. The painting was originally commissioned by King Louis XII of France in about 1500. *The Wall Street Journal* guesstimated that the king may have paid Leonardo the equivalent of $575,000 in 1519.[11]

    a. What was the annual rate of appreciation in the price of the painting between 1958 and 2017 adjusted for inflation?

    b. What was the annual estimated rate of appreciation in the price of the painting between 1519 and 2017 adjusted for inflation.

6. **Future values** If you invest $100 at an interest rate of 15%, how much will you have at the end of eight years?

7. **Future values*** Compute the future value of a $100 investment for the following combinations of rates and times.

    a. $r = 6\%, t = 10$ years

    b. $r = 6\%, t = 20$ years

    c. $r = 4\%, t = 10$ years

    d. $r = 4\%, t = 20$ years

8. **Future values** In the five years preceding the end of 2016, the price of Amazon shares rose by 34% a year. If you had invested $100 in Amazon at the beginning of this period, how much would you have by the end of the period?

9. **Discount factors**

    a. If the present value of $139 is $125, what is the discount factor?

    b. If that $139 is received in year 5, what is the interest rate?

10. **Present values** If the cost of capital is 9%, what is the PV of $374 paid in year 9?

11. **Present values** A project produces a cash flow of $432 in year 1, $137 in year 2, and $797 in year 3. If the cost of capital is 15%, what is the project's PV? If the project requires an investment of $1,200, what is its NPV?

12. **Present values** What is the PV of $100 received in:

    a. Year 10 (at a discount rate of 1%)?

    b. Year 10 (at a discount rate of 13%)?

    c. Year 15 (at a discount rate of 25%)?

    d. Each of years 1 through 3 (at a discount rate of 12%)?

13. **Present values*** Lofting Snodbury is considering investing in a new boring machine. It costs $380,000 and is expected to produce the following cash flows:

Year:	1	2	3	4	5	6	7	8	9	10
Cash flow ($000s)	50	57	75	80	85	92	92	80	68	50

If the cost of capital is 12%, what is the machine's NPV?

14. **Present values** A factory costs $800,000. You reckon that it will produce an inflow after operating costs of $170,000 a year for 10 years. If the opportunity cost of capital is 14%, what is the net present value of the factory? What will the factory be worth at the end of five years?

15. **Present values** Recalculate the NPV of the office building venture in Example 2.1 at interest rates of 5, 10, and 15%. Plot the points on a graph with NPV on the vertical axis and the discount rates on the horizontal axis. At what discount rate (approximately) would the project have zero NPV? Check your answer.

---

16. **Present values and opportunity cost of capital** Halcyon Lines is considering the purchase of a new bulk carrier for $8 million. The forecasted revenues are $5 million a year and operating costs are $4 million. A major refit costing $2 million will be required after both the fifth and tenth years. After 15 years, the ship is expected to be sold for scrap at $1.5 million.

    a. What is the NPV if the opportunity cost of capital is 8%?

    b. Halcyon could finance the ship by borrowing the entire investment at an interest rate of 4.5%. How does this borrowing opportunity affect your calculation of NPV?

17. **Perpetuities*** An investment costs $1,548 and pays $138 in perpetuity. If the interest rate is 9%, what is the NPV?

18. **Perpetuities** You have just read an advertisement stating, "Pay us $100 a year for 10 years and we will pay you $100 a year thereafter in perpetuity." If this is a fair deal, what is the rate of interest?

19. **Growing perpetuities** A common stock will pay a cash dividend of $4 next year. After that, the dividends are expected to increase indefinitely at 4% per year. If the discount rate is 14%, what is the PV of the stream of dividend payments?

20. **Perpetuities and annuities** The interest rate is 10%.

    a. What is the PV of an asset that pays $1 a year in perpetuity?

    b. The value of an asset that appreciates at 10% per annum approximately doubles in seven years. What is the approximate PV of an asset that pays $1 a year in perpetuity beginning in year 8?

    c. What is the approximate PV of an asset that pays $1 a year for each of the next seven years?

    d. A piece of land produces an income that grows by 5% per annum. If the first year's income is $10,000, what is the value of the land?

21. **Discount factors and annuity factors***

    a. If the one-year discount factor is .905, what is the one-year interest rate?

    b. If the two-year interest rate is 10.5%, what is the two-year discount factor?

    c. Given these one- and two-year discount factors, calculate the two-year annuity factor.

    d. If the PV of $10 a year for three years is $24.65, what is the three-year annuity factor?

    e. From your answers to parts (c) and (d), calculate the three-year discount factor.

22. **Annuities*** Kangaroo Autos is offering free credit on a new $10,000 car. You pay $1,000 down and then $300 a month for the next 30 months. Turtle Motors next door does not offer free credit but will give you $1,000 off the list price. If the rate of interest is .83% a month, which company is offering the better deal?

23. **Annuities** David and Helen Zhang are saving to buy a boat at the end of five years. If the boat costs $20,000 and they can earn 10% a year on their savings, how much do they need to put aside at the end of years 1 through 5?

24. **Annuities** Siegfried Basset is 65 years of age and has a life expectancy of 12 more years. He wishes to invest $20,000 in an annuity that will make a level payment at the end of each year until his death. If the interest rate is 8%, what income can Mr. Basset expect to receive each year?

25. **Annuities** Several years ago, *The Wall Street Journal* reported that the winner of the Massachusetts State Lottery prize had the misfortune to be both bankrupt and in prison for fraud. The prize was $9,420,713, to be paid in 19 equal annual installments. (There were 20 installments, but the winner had already received the first payment.) The bankruptcy court judge ruled that the prize should be sold off to the highest bidder and the proceeds used to pay off the creditors.

    a. If the interest rate was 8%, how much would you have been prepared to bid for the prize?

    b. Enhance Reinsurance Company was reported to have offered $4.2 million. Use Excel to find the return that the company was looking for.

26. **Annuities** The *annually* compounded discount rate is 5.5%. You are asked to calculate the present value of a 12-year annuity with payments of $50,000 per year. Calculate PV for each of the following cases.

    a. The annuity payments arrive at one-year intervals. The first payment arrives one year from now.

    b. The first payment arrives in six months. Following payments arrive at one-year intervals (i.e., at 18 months, 30 months, etc.).

27. **Annuities**   Dear Financial Adviser,

    My spouse and I are each 62 and hope to retire in three years. After retirement we will receive $7,500 per month after taxes from our employers' pension plans and $1,500 per month after taxes from Social Security. Unfortunately our monthly living expenses are $15,000. Our social obligations preclude further economies.

    We have $1,000,000 invested in a high-grade, tax-free municipal-bond mutual fund. The return on the fund is 3.5% per year. We plan to make annual withdrawals from the mutual fund to cover the difference between our pension and Social Security income and our living expenses. How many years before we run out of money?

    Sincerely,

    Luxury Challenged

    Marblehead, MA

    You can assume that the withdrawals (one per year) will sit in a checking account (no interest) until spent. The couple will use the account to cover the monthly shortfalls.

28. **Perpetuities and annuities** Refer to Sections 2-3 and 2-4. If the rate of interest is 8% rather than 10%, how much would you need to set aside to provide each of the following?

    a. $1 billion at the end of each year in perpetuity.

    b. A perpetuity that pays $1 billion at the end of the first year and that grows at 4% a year.

    c. $1 billion at the end of each year for 20 years.

    d. $1 billion a year spread evenly over 20 years.

29. **Annuities due** The $40 million lottery prize that you have just won actually pays out $2 million a year for 20 years. The interest rate is 8%.

    a. If the first payment comes after 1 year, what is the present value of your winnings?

    b. What is the present value if the first payment comes immediately?

30. **Annuities due** A store offers two payment plans. Under the installment plan, you pay 25% down and 25% of the purchase price in each of the next 3 years. If you pay the entire bill immediately, you can take a 10% discount from the purchase price.

    a. Which is the better deal if the interest rate is 5%?

    b. How will your answer change if the four payments on the installments do not start until the end of the year?

31. **Amortizing loans*** A bank loan requires you to pay $70,000 at the end of each of the next eight years. The interest rate is 8%.

    a. What is the present value of these payments?

    b. Calculate for each year the loan balance that remains outstanding, the interest payment on the loan, and the reduction in the loan balance.

32. **Amortizing loans** Suppose that you take out a $200,000, 20-year mortgage loan to buy a condo. The interest rate on the loan is 6%, and payments on the loan are made annually at the end of each year.

    a. What is your annual payment on the loan?

    b. Construct a mortgage amortization table in Excel similar to Table 2.1, showing the interest payment, the amortization of the loan, and the loan balance for each year.

    c. What fraction of your initial loan payment is interest? What about the last payment? What fraction of the loan has been paid off after 10 years? Why is the fraction less than half?

33. **Future values and annuities**

a. The cost of a new automobile is $10,000. If the interest rate is 5%, how much would you have to set aside now to provide this sum in five years?

b. You have to pay $12,000 a year in school fees at the end of each of the next six years. If the interest rate is 8%, how much do you need to set aside today to cover these bills?

c. You have invested $60,476 at 8%. After paying the above school fees, how much would remain at the end of the six years?

34. **Growing annuities** You estimate that by the time you retire in 35 years, you will have accumulated savings of $2 million. If the interest rate is 8% and you live 15 years after retirement, what annual level of expenditure will those savings support?

Unfortunately, inflation will eat into the value of your retirement income. Assume a 4% inflation rate and work out a spending program for your $2 million in retirement savings that will allow you to increase your expenditure in line with inflation.

35. **Growing annuities** You are contemplating membership in the St. Swithin's and Ancient Golf Club. The annual membership fee for the coming year is $5,000, but you can make a single payment today of $12,750, which will provide you with membership for the next three years. Suppose that the annual fee is payable at the end of each year and is expected to increase by 6% a year. The discount rate is 10%. Which is the better deal?

36. **Growing perpetuities and annuities**

As winner of a breakfast cereal competition, you can choose one of the following prizes:

a. $100,000 now.

b. $180,000 at the end of five years.

c. $11,400 a year forever.

d. $19,000 for each of 10 years.

e. $6,500 next year and increasing thereafter by 5% a year forever.

If the interest rate is 12%, which is the most valuable prize?

37. **Growing perpetuities and annuities** Your firm's geologists have discovered a small oil field in New York's Westchester County. The field is forecasted to produce a cash flow of $C_1 = \$2$ million in the first year. You estimate that you could earn a return of $r = 12\%$ from investing in stocks with a similar degree of risk to your oil field. Therefore, 12% is the opportunity cost of capital. What is the present value? The answer, of course, depends on what happens to the cash flows after the first year. Calculate present value for the following cases: a. The cash flows are forecasted to continue forever, with no expected growth or decline. b. The cash flows are forecasted to continue for 20 years only, with no expected growth or decline during that period. c. The cash flows are forecasted to continue forever, increasing by 3% per year because of inflation. d. The cash flows are forecasted to continue for 20 years only, increasing by 3% per year because of inflation.

38. **Compounding intervals** A leasing contract calls for an immediate payment of $100,000 and nine subsequent $100,000 semiannual payments at six-month intervals. What is the PV of these payments if the *annual* discount rate is 8%?

39. **Compounding intervals*** Which would you prefer?

a. An investment paying interest of 12% compounded annually.

b. An investment paying interest of 11.7% compounded semiannually.

c. An investment paying 11.5% compounded continuously.

Work out the value of each of these investments after 1, 5, and 20 years.

40. **Compounding intervals** You are quoted an interest rate of 6% on an investment of $10 million. What is the value of your investment after four years if interest is compounded:

a. Annually?

b. Monthly?

c. Continuously?

41. **Perpetuities and continuous compounding** If the interest rate is 7% compounded annually, what is the value of the following three investments?

   a. An investment that offers you $100 a year in perpetuity with the payment at the *end* of each year.

   b. A similar investment with the payment at the *beginning* of each year.

   c. A similar investment with the payment spread evenly over each year.

42. **Continuous compounding** How much will you have at the end of 20 years if you invest $100 today at 15% *annually* compounded? How much will you have if you invest at 15% *continuously* compounded?

43. **Continuous compounding** The continuously compounded interest rate is 12%.

   a. You invest $1,000 at this rate. What is the investment worth after five years?

   b. What is the PV of $5 million to be received in eight years?

   c. What is the PV of a continuous stream of cash flows, amounting to $2,000 per year, starting immediately and continuing for 15 years?

CHALLENGE PROBLEMS

44. **Future values and continuous compounding** Here are two useful rules of thumb. The "Rule of 72" says that with discrete compounding the time it takes for an investment to double in value is roughly 72/interest rate (in percent). The "Rule of 69" says that with continuous compounding the time that it takes to double is exactly 69.3/interest rate (in percent).

   a. If the annually compounded interest rate is 12%, use the Rule of 72 to calculate roughly how long it takes before your money doubles. Now work it out exactly.

   b. Can you prove the Rule of 69?

45. **Annuities** Use Excel to construct your own set of annuity tables showing the annuity factor for a selection of interest rates and years.

46. **Declining perpetuities and annuities** You own an oil pipeline that will generate a $2 million cash return over the coming year. The pipeline's operating costs are negligible, and it is expected to last for a very long time. Unfortunately, the volume of oil shipped is declining, and cash flows are expected to decline by 4% per year. The discount rate is 10%.

   a. What is the PV of the pipeline's cash flows if its cash flows are assumed to last forever?

   b. What is the PV of the cash flows if the pipeline is scrapped after 20 years?

FINANCE ON THE WEB

Finance.yahoo.com is a marvelous source of stock price data. You should get used to using it.

1. Go to **finance.yahoo.com** and look up "Analyst Estimates" for Apple (AAPL). You should find earnings per share (EPS) for the current year, the percentage annual growth rate of EPS for the past five years, and also a five-year EPS growth-rate forecast. What will be Apple's EPS after five years if EPS grows at the five-year historical average rate? What will EPS be if it grows at the analysts' forecasted rate? Try the same exercise for other stocks, for example Microsoft (MSFT), Merck (MRK), or the railroad CSX (CSX).

2. You need to have accumulated savings of $2 million by the time that you retire in 20 years. You currently have savings of $200,000. How much do you need to save each year to meet your goal if your savings earn a return of 10%? Find the savings calculator on **www.msn. com/en-us/money/tools/retirementplanner** to check your answer.

CHAPTER

3

Valuing Bonds

Investment in new plant and equipment requires money—often a lot of money. Sometimes firms can retain and accumulate earnings to cover the cost of investment, but often they need to raise extra cash from investors. If they choose not to sell additional shares of stock, the cash has to come from borrowing. If cash is needed for only a short while, firms may borrow from a bank. If they need cash for long-term investments, they generally issue bonds, which are simply long-term loans.

Companies are not the only bond issuers. Municipalities also raise money by selling bonds. So do national governments. We start our analysis of the bond market by looking at the valuation of government bonds and at the interest rate that the government pays when it borrows. Do not confuse this interest rate with the cost of capital for a corporation. The projects that companies undertake are almost invariably risky, and investors demand higher prospective returns from these projects than from safe government bonds. (In Chapter 7, we start to look at the additional returns that investors demand from risky assets.)

The markets for government bonds are huge. At the start of 2018, investors held $14.8 trillion of U.S. government securities, and U.S. government agencies held a further $5.7 trillion. The bond markets are also sophisticated. Professional bond traders make massive trades that are often motivated by tiny price discrepancies. This book is not for them, but if you are to be involved in managing the company's debt, you will need to get beyond the simple mechanics

of bond valuation. Qualified financial managers understand the bond pages in the financial press and know what bond dealers mean when they quote spot rates or yields to maturity. They realize why short-term rates are usually lower (but sometimes higher) than long-term rates and why the longest-term bond prices are most sensitive to fluctuations in interest rates. They can distinguish real (inflation-adjusted) interest rates and nominal (money) rates and anticipate how future inflation can affect interest rates. We cover all these topics in this chapter.

Companies can't borrow at the same low interest rates as governments. The interest rates on government bonds are benchmarks for all interest rates, however. When government interest rates go up or down, corporate rates follow more or less proportionally. Therefore, financial managers had better understand how the government rates are determined and what happens when they change.

Corporate bonds are more complex securities than government bonds. It is more likely that a corporation may be unable to come up with the money to pay its debts, so investors have to worry about default risk. Corporate bonds are also less liquid than government bonds: They are not as easy to buy or sell, particularly in large quantities or on short notice. These complications affect the "spread" of corporate bond rates over interest rates on government bonds of similar maturities.

This chapter only introduces corporate debt. We take a more detailed look in Chapters 23 and 24.

3-1   Using the Present Value Formula to Value Bonds

If you own a bond, you are entitled to a fixed set of cash payoffs. Every year until the bond matures, you collect regular interest payments. At maturity, when you get the final interest payment, you also get back the **face value** of the bond, which is called the bond's **principal.**

A Short Trip to Paris to Value a Government Bond

Why are we going to Paris, apart from the cafés, restaurants, and sophisticated nightlife? Because we want to start with the simplest type of bond, one that makes payments just once a year.

French government bonds, known as OATs (short for Obligations Assimilables du Trésor), pay interest and principal in euros (€). Suppose that in October 2017 you decide to buy €100 face value of the 6.00% OAT maturing in October 2025. Each year until the bond matures, you are entitled to an interest payment of .06 × 100 = €6.00. This amount is the bond's **coupon.**[1] When the bond matures in 2025, the government pays you the final €6.00 interest, plus the principal payment of €100. Your first coupon payment is in one year's time, in October 2018. So the cash payments from the bond are as follows:

Cash Payments (€)							
2018	2019	2020	2021	2022	2023	2024	2025
6.00	6.00	6.00	6.00	6.00	6.00	6.00	106.00

What is the present value of these payments? It depends on the opportunity cost of capital, which in this case equals the rate of return offered by other government debt issues denominated in euros. In October 2017, other medium-term French government bonds offered a return of just .3%. That is what you were giving up when you bought the 6.00% OATs. Therefore, to value the 6.00% OATs, you must discount the cash flows at .3%:

$$PV = €\frac{6.00}{1.003} + \frac{6.00}{1.003^2} + \frac{6.00}{1.003^3} + \frac{6.00}{1.003^4} + \frac{6.00}{1.003^5} + \frac{6.00}{1.003^6} + \frac{6.00}{1.003^7} + \frac{106.00}{1.003^8} = €144.99$$

Bond prices are usually expressed as a percentage of face value. Thus the price of your 6.00% OAT was quoted as 144.99%.

You may have noticed a shortcut way to value this bond. Your OAT amounts to a package of two investments. The first investment gets the eight annual coupon payments of €6.00 each. The second gets the €100 face value at maturity. You can use the annuity formula from Chapter 2 to value the coupon payments and then add on the present value of the final payment.

$$PV(\text{bond}) = PV(\text{annuity of coupon payments}) + PV(\text{final payment of principal})$$
$$= (\text{coupon} \times 8 - \text{year annuity factor}) + (\text{final payment} \times \text{discount factor})$$
$$= 6.00\left[\frac{1}{.003} - \frac{1}{.003(1.003)^8}\right] + \frac{100}{1.003^8} = 47.36 + 97.63 = €144.99$$

---

[1]Bonds used to come with a coupon attached which had to be clipped off and presented to the issuer to obtain the interest payments. This is still the case with *bearer bonds,* where the only evidence of ownership is the bond certificate. In many parts of the world, bearer bonds are still issued and are popular with investors who would rather remain anonymous. The alternative is *registered bonds,* where the identity of the bond's owner is recorded and the coupon payments are sent automatically. OATS are registered bonds.

Thus, the bond can be valued as a package of an annuity (the coupon payments) and a single, final payment (the repayment of principal).[2]

We just used the .3% interest rate to calculate the present value of the OAT. Now we turn the valuation around: If the price of the OAT is 144.99%, what is the interest rate? What return do investors get if they buy the bond and hold it to maturity? To answer this question, you need to find the value of the variable y that solves the following equation:

$$144.99 = \frac{6.00}{1+y} + \frac{6.00}{(1+y)^2} + \frac{6.00}{(1+y)^3} + \frac{6.00}{(1+y)^4} + \frac{6.00}{(1+y)^5} + \frac{6.00}{(1+y)^6} + \frac{6.00}{(1+y)^7} + \frac{106.00}{(1+y)^8}$$

The rate of return y is called the bond's **yield to maturity.** In this case, we already know that the present value of the bond is 144.99% at a .3% discount rate, so the yield to maturity must be .3%. If you buy the bond at 144.99% and hold it to maturity, you will earn a return of .3% per year.

Why is the yield to maturity less than the 6.00% coupon payment? Because you are paying €144.99 for a bond with a face value of only €100. You lose the difference of €44.99 if you hold the bond to maturity. On the other hand, you get eight annual cash payments of €6.00. (The immediate, *current yield* on your investment is 6.00/144.99 = .0414, or 4.14%.) The yield to maturity blends the return from the coupon payments with the declining value of the bond over its remaining life.

BEYOND THE PAGE

Try It! Bond prices and approaching maturity

mhhe.com/brealey13e

Let's generalize. A bond, such as our OAT, that is priced above its face value is said to sell at a *premium.* Investors who buy a bond at a premium face a capital loss over the life of the bond, so the yield to maturity on these bonds is always *less* than the current yield. A bond that is priced below face value sells at a *discount.* Investors in discount bonds look forward to a capital *gain* over the life of the bond, so the yield to maturity on a discount bond is *greater* than the current yield.

The only general procedure for calculating the yield to maturity is trial and error. You guess at an interest rate and calculate the present value of the bond's payments. If the present value is greater than the actual price, your discount rate must have been too low, and you need to try a higher rate. The more practical solution is to use a spreadsheet program or a specially programmed calculator to calculate the yield. At the end of this chapter, you will find a box that lists the Excel function for calculating yield to maturity plus several other useful functions for bond analysts.

Back to the United States: Semiannual Coupons and Bond Prices

Just like the French government, the U.S. Treasury raises money by regular auctions of new bond issues. Some of these issues do not mature for 20 or 30 years; others, known as *notes,* mature in 10 years or less. The Treasury also issues short-term debt maturing in a year or less. These short-term securities are known as *Treasury bills.* Treasury bonds, notes, and bills are traded in the *fixed-income market.*

Let's look at an example of a U.S. government bond. In 1991, the Treasury issued 8.00% bonds maturing in 2021. These bonds are called "the 8s of 2021." Treasury bonds and notes have face values of $1,000, so if you own the 8s of 2021, the Treasury will give you back $1,000 at maturity. You can also look forward to a regular coupon, but in contrast to our French bond, coupons on Treasury bonds and notes are paid *semiannually.*[3] Thus, the 8s of 2021 provide a coupon payment of 8/2 = 4% of face value every six months.

---

[2]You could also value a seven-year annuity of €6.00 plus a final payment of €106.00.

[3]The frequency of interest payments varies from country to country. For example, most bonds issued by eurozone governments pay interest annually (Italy and Malta are exceptions), while most bonds in the U.K., Canada, and Japan pay interest semiannually.

Maturity	Coupon	Asked Price (%)	Yield to Maturity (%)
November 2020	2.625	102.38	1.807
November 2021	8.00	123.41	1.893
November 2022	1.625	98.05	2.036
November 2023	2.75	103.48	2.128
November 2024	7.50	134.46	2.166
November 2025	2.25	99.80	2.278
November 2026	6.50	134.28	2.267
November 2027	6.125	133.99	2.300
November 2028	5.25	128.58	2.344

❭ **TABLE 3.1**   Treasury bond quotes, November 2017

Source: *The Wall Street Journal* website, www.wsj.com.

You can't buy Treasury bonds, notes, or bills on the stock exchange. They are traded by a network of bond dealers, who quote prices at which they are prepared to buy and sell. For example, suppose that you decide to buy the 8s of 2021. You phone a broker, who checks the current price on her screen. If you are happy to go ahead with the purchase, your broker contacts a bond dealer and the trade is done.

The prices at which you can buy or sell Treasury notes and bonds are shown each day in the financial press and on the web. In November 2017, there were 310 different Treasury notes and bonds. Table 3.1 shows the prices of just a small sample of them. Look at the entry for our 8.00s of 2021. The **asked price,** 123.41, is the price you need to pay to buy the bond from a dealer. This means that the 8.00% bond costs 123.41% of face value. The face value of the bond is $1,000, so each bond costs $1,234.10.[4]

The final column in the table shows the yield to maturity. Because interest is semiannual, annual yields on U.S. bonds are usually quoted as twice the semiannual yields. Thus, if you buy the 8.00% bond at the asked price and hold it to maturity, every six months you earn a return of 1.893/2 = .947%.

You can now repeat the present value calculations that we did for the French government bond. You just need to recognize that bonds in the U.S. have a face value of $1,000, that their coupons are paid semiannually, and that the quoted yield is a semiannually compounded rate.

Here are the cash payments for the 8.00s of 2021:

Cash Payments							
May 2018	Nov. 2018	May 2019	Nov. 2019	May 2020	Nov. 2020	May 2021	Nov. 2021
$40.00	$40.00	$40.00	$40.00	$40.00	$40.00	$40.00	$1,040

[4]The quoted bond price is known as the *flat* (or *clean*) price. The price that the bond buyer actually pays (sometimes called the *full* or *dirty* price) is equal to the flat price *plus* the interest that the seller has already earned on the bond since the last interest payment. The precise method for calculating this *accrued interest* varies from one type of bond to another. Always use the flat price to calculate the yield.

If investors demand a return of .947% every six months, then the present value of these cash flows is

$$PV = \frac{40}{1.00947} + \frac{40}{1.00947^2} + \frac{40}{1.00947^3} + \cdots + \frac{40}{1.00947^6} + \frac{40}{1.00947^7} + \frac{1,040}{1.00947^8} = \$1,234.10$$

Each bond is worth $1,234.10, or 123.41% of face value.

Again we could turn the valuation around: Given the price, what's the yield to maturity? Try it, and you'll find (no surprise) that the semiannual rate of return that you can earn over the eight remaining half-year periods is .00947. Take care to remember that the *yield* is reported as an annual rate, calculated as $2 \times .00947 = .01893$, or 1.893%. If you see a reported yield to maturity of $R\%$, you have to remember to use $y = R/2\%$ as the semiannual rate for discounting cash flows received every six months.

3-2   How Bond Prices Vary with Interest Rates

Figure 3.1 plots the yield to maturity on 10-year U.S. Treasury bonds[5] from 1900 to 2017. Notice how much the rate fluctuates. For example, interest rates climbed sharply after 1979 when Paul Volcker, the new chairman of the Fed, instituted a policy of tight money to rein in inflation. Within two years the interest rate on 10-year government bonds rose from 9% to a midyear peak of 15.8%. Contrast this with the summer of 2016, when long-term Treasury bonds offered a measly 1.4% rate of interest.

 **FIGURE 3.1**

The interest rate on 10-year U.S. Treasury bonds

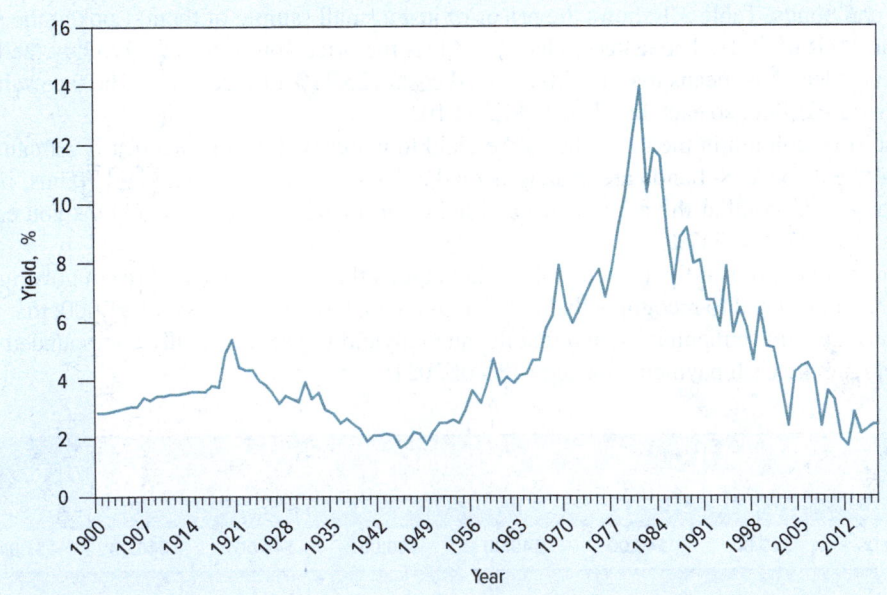

[5] From this point forward, we will just say "bonds" and not distinguish notes from bonds unless we are referring to a specific security. Note also that bonds with long maturities end up with short maturities when they approach the final payment date. Thus, you will encounter 30-year bonds trading 20 years later at the same prices as new 10-year notes (assuming equal coupons).

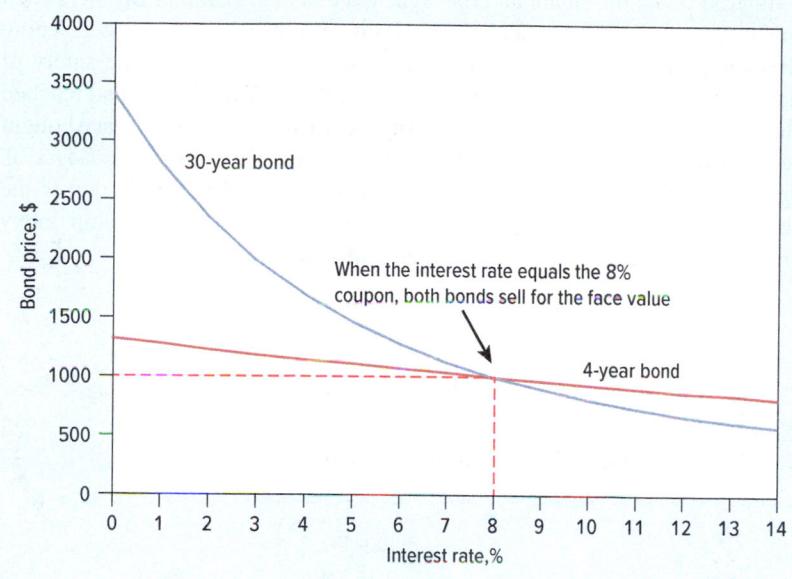

▶ **FIGURE 3.2**

Plot of bond prices as a function of the interest rate. The price of long-term bonds is more sensitive to changes in the interest rate than is the price of short-term bonds.

As interest rates change, so do bond prices. For example, suppose that investors demanded a semiannual return of 2% on the 8s of 2021, rather than the .947% semiannual return we used previously. In that case the price would be

$$PV = \frac{40}{1.02} + \frac{40}{1.02^2} + \frac{40}{1.02^3} + \cdots + \frac{40}{1.02^6} + \frac{40}{1.02^7} + \frac{40}{1.02^8} = \$1,146.51$$

The higher interest rate results in a lower price.

Bond prices and interest rates *must* move in opposite directions. The yield to maturity, our measure of the interest rate on a bond, is *defined* as the discount rate that explains the bond price. When bond prices fall, interest rates (i.e., yields to maturity) must rise. When interest rates rise, bond prices must fall. We recall a hapless TV pundit who intoned, "The recent decline in long-term interest rates suggests that long-term bond prices may rise over the next week or two." Of course, the bond prices had already gone up. We are confident that you won't make the pundit's mistake.

The brown line in Figure 3.2 shows the value of our 8% bond for different interest rates. As the yield to maturity falls, the bond price increases. When the annual yield is equal to the bond's annual coupon rate (8%), the bond sells for exactly its face value. When the yield is higher than 8%, the bond sells at a discount to face value. When the yield is lower than 8%, the bond sells at a premium.

Bond investors cross their fingers that market interest rates will fall so that the price of their securities will rise. If they are unlucky and interest rates jump up, the value of their investment declines.

EXAMPLE 3.1 • **Changes in Interest Rates and Bond Returns**

On May 15, 2008, the U.S. Treasury sold $9 billion of 4.375% bonds maturing in February 2038. The bonds were issued at a price of 96.38% and offered a yield to maturity of 4.60%. This was the return to anyone buying at the issue price and holding the bonds to maturity.

In the months following the issue, the financial crisis reached its peak. Lehman Brothers filed for bankruptcy with assets of $691 billion, and the government poured money into rescuing Fannie Mae, Freddie Mac, AIG, and a host of banks. As investors rushed to the safety of Treasury bonds, prices soared. By mid-December, the price of the 4.375s of 2038 had reached 138.05% of face value, and the yield had fallen to 2.5%. Anyone fortunate enough to have bought the bond at the issue price would have made a capital gain of $1,380.50 − $963.80 = $416.70. In addition, on August 15 the bond made its first coupon payment of $21.875 (this is the semiannual payment on the 4.375% coupon bond with a face value of $1,000). Our lucky investor would, therefore, have earned a seven-month **rate of return** of 45.5%:

$$\text{Rate of return} = \frac{\text{coupon income} + \text{price change}}{\text{investment}}$$

$$= \frac{\$21.875 + 416.70}{\$963.80} = .455, \text{ or } 45.5\%$$

Suddenly, government bonds did not seem quite so boring as before.

BEYOND THE PAGE

Try It! Figure 3.2: How changes in interest rates affect long- and short-term bonds

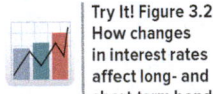

mhhe.com/brealey13e

A change in interest rates has only a modest impact on the value of near-term cash flows but a much greater impact on the value of distant cash flows. Thus the price of long-term bonds is affected more by changing interest rates than the price of short-term bonds. For example, compare the two curves in Figure 3.2. The brown line shows how the price of the four-year 8% bond varies with the interest rate. The blue line shows how the price of a 30-year 8% bond varies. You can see that the 30-year bond is much more sensitive to interest rate fluctuations than the four-year bond.

Duration and Volatility

Changes in interest rates have a greater impact on the prices of long-term bonds than on those of short-term bonds. But what do we mean by "long term" and "short term"? A coupon bond that matures in year 30 makes payments in *each* of years 1 through 30. It's misleading to describe the bond as a 30-year bond; the average time to each cash payment is less than 30 years.

EXAMPLE 3.2 • Which Is the Longer-Term Bond?

Table 3.2 calculates the prices of two seven-year bonds. We assume annual coupon payments and a yield to maturity of 4% per year. Take a look at the time pattern of each bond's cash payments and review how the prices are calculated:

Which of these two bonds is the longer-term investment? They both have the same final maturity, of course. But the *timing* of the bonds' cash payments is not the same. In the case of the 3s, the *average* time to each cash flow is longer, because a higher proportion of the cash flows occurs at maturity, when the face value is paid off.

Suppose now that the yield to maturity on each bond falls to 3%. Which bond would you most like to own? The 3s, of course. Since they have the longer effective life, they should benefit most from a fall in yields. Table 3.3 confirms that this is indeed the case:.

The 9s have the shorter average life and therefore a shift in interest rates has a more muted effect on the price. That much is clear. However, it would be useful to have a precise

		Cash Payments ($)			
Coupon	Price ($)	Year 1	Year 2 . . .	Year 6	Year 7
3%	$ 939.98	$30	$30	$30	$1,030
9%	1,300.10	90	90	90	1,090

❭TABLE 3.2   A comparison of the cash flows and prices of two bonds. Price is calculated assuming annual coupon payments and a yield to maturity of 4%.

Note: Both securities mature at the end of year 7.

	Yield = 4%	Yield = 3%	
Coupon	Price ($)	Price ($)	Change in Price (%)
3%	$ 939.98	$1,000.00	+6.4%
9%	1,300.10	1,373.82	+5.7

❭TABLE 3.3   The effect of a 1% fall in yield on the prices of two seven-year bonds

measure of the average life, one that could be used to predict the exposure of each bond's price to fluctuations in interest rates. There is such a measure, and it is called **duration** or **Macaulay duration** after its founder.

Duration is the weighted average of the times to each of the cash payments. The times are the future years 1, 2, 3, etc., extending to the final maturity date, which we call T. The weight for each year is the present value of the cash flow received at that time divided by the total present value of the bond.

$$\text{Duration} = \frac{1 \times \text{PV}(C_1)}{\text{PV}} + \frac{2 \times \text{PV}(C_2)}{\text{PV}} + \frac{3 \times \text{PV}(C_3)}{\text{PV}} + \cdots + \frac{T \times \text{PV}(C_T)}{\text{PV}}$$

Table 3.4 shows how to compute duration for the 9% seven-year bonds, assuming annual payments. First, we value each of the coupon payments of $90 and the final payment of coupon plus face value of $1,090. Of course, the present values of these payments add up to

				Year (*t*)				
	1	2	3	4	5	6	7	
Payment	$90	$90	$90	$90	$90	$90	$1,090	
PV(C_t) at 4%	$86.54	$83.21	$80.01	$76.93	$73.97	$71.13	$ 828.31	PV = $1,300.10
Fraction of total value [PV(C_t)/PV]	0.0666	0.0640	0.0615	0.0592	0.0569	0.0547	0.6371	
Year × fraction of total value [t × PV(C_t)/PV]	0.0666	0.1280	0.1846	0.2367	0.2845	0.3283	4.4598	Total = duration = 5.69 years

❭TABLE 3.4   Calculating the duration of the 9% seven-year bonds. The yield to maturity is 4% a year.

Years to Maturity	Coupon	Yield to Maturity (%)	Duration (years)
3	2.625	1.807	2.906
4	8.00	1.893	3.559
5	1.625	2.036	4.820
6	2.75	2.128	5.581
7	7.50	2.166	5.797
8	2.25	2.278	7.365
9	6.50	2.267	7.274
10	6.125	2.300	7.993
11	5.25	2.344	8.831

❭ **TABLE 3.5**   The duration in November 2017 of the Treasury bonds shown in Table 3.1. Duration calculations recognize that coupon payments are semiannual.

the bond price of $1,300.10. Then we calculate the fraction of the price accounted for by each cash flow and multiply each fraction by the year of the cash flow. The results sum across to a duration of 5.69 years.

We leave it to you to calculate durations for the 3% bonds in Table 3.2. You will find that duration increases to 6.40 years.

Table 3.5 shows the duration in November 2017 of the sample of U.S. Treasury bonds set out in Table 3.1. Notice that, in all cases, the duration is shorter than the number of years to maturity and that the difference is most marked in the case of high coupon bonds.

We mentioned that investors and financial managers track duration because it measures how bond prices change when interest rates change. For this purpose, it's best to use *modified duration* or *volatility,* which is just duration divided by one plus the yield to maturity:

$$\text{Modified duration} = \text{volatility}(\%) = \frac{\text{duration}}{1 + \text{yield}}$$

Modified duration measures the percentage change in bond price for a 1 percentage-point change in yield.[6] Let's try out this formula for our seven-year 9% bond in Table 3.3. The bond's modified duration is duration/(1 + yield) = 5.69/1.04 = 5.47. This means that a 1% change in the yield to maturity should change the bond price by 5.47%.

Let's check that prediction. Suppose the yield to maturity either increases or declines by .5%:

Yield to Maturity (%)	Price ($)	Change (%)
4.5%	$1265.17	−2.687%
4.0	1300.10	—
3.5	1336.30	+2.784

---

[6]In other words, the derivative of the bond price with respect to a change in yield to maturity is dPV/dy = −duration/(1 + y) = −modified duration.

Valuing Bonds

❯ Spreadsheet programs such as Excel provide built-in functions to solve for a variety of bond valuation problems. You can find these functions by pressing *fx* on the Excel toolbar. If you then click on the function that you wish to use, Excel will ask you for the inputs that it needs. At the bottom left of the function box, there is a Help facility with an example of how the function is used.

Here is a list of useful functions for valuing bonds, together with some points to remember when entering data:

- **PRICE:** The price of a bond given its yield to maturity.
- **YLD:** The yield to maturity of a bond given its price.
- **DURATION:** The duration of a bond.
- **MDURATION:** The modified duration (or volatility) of a bond.

  Note:

- You can enter all the inputs in these functions directly as numbers or as the addresses of cells that contain the numbers.

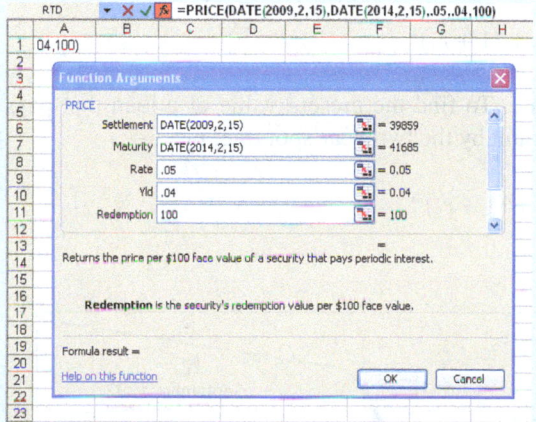

Source: Microsoft Excel.

- You must enter the yield and coupon as decimal values, for example, for 3% you would enter .03.
- Settlement is the date that payment for the security is made. Maturity is the maturity date. You can enter these dates directly using the Excel date function; for example, you would enter 15 Feb 2009 as DATE(2009,02,15). Alternatively, you can enter these dates in a cell and then enter the cell address in the function.
- In the functions for PRICE and YLD you need to scroll down in the function box to enter the frequency of coupon payments. Enter 1 for annual payments or 2 for semiannual.
- The functions for PRICE and YLD ask for an entry for "basis." We suggest you leave this blank. (See the Help facility for an explanation.)

Spreadsheet Questions

The following questions provide an opportunity to practice each of these functions.

1. (PRICE) In February 2009, Treasury 8.5s of 2020 yielded 3.2976%. What was their price? If the yield rose to 4%, what would happen to the price?

2. (YLD) On the same day, Treasury 3.5s of 2018 were priced at 107.46875%. What was their yield to maturity? Suppose that the price was 110.0%. What would happen to the yield?

3. (DURATION) What was the duration of the Treasury 8.5s? How would duration change if the yield rose to 4%? Can you explain why?

4. (MDURATION) What was the modified duration of the Treasury 8.5s? How would modified duration differ if the coupon were only 7.5%?

The total percentage difference between price at yields of 4.5% and 3.5% is 2.687 + 2.784 = 5.47%. Thus, a 1% change in interest rates means a 5.47% change in bond price, just as predicted.[7]

BEYOND THE PAGE

Try It! More on duration

mhhe.com/brealey13e

---

[7] If you look back at Figure 3.2, you will see that the plot of price against yield is not a straight line. This means that modified duration is a good predictor of the effect of interest rate changes only for small moves in interest rates.

The modified duration for the 3% bond in Table 3.3 is $6.40/1.04 = 6.15\%$. In other words, a 1% change in yield to maturity results in a 6.15% change in the bond's price.

You can see why duration (or modified duration) is a handy measure of interest-rate risk.[8] For example, the mini-case at the end of Chapter 26 looks at how financial managers can use the measure to protect the pension plan against unexpected changes in interest rates.

When we explained in Chapter 2 how to calculate present values, we used the same discount rate to calculate the value of each period's cash flow. This discount rate was the bond's yield to maturity y. For many purposes, using a single discount rate is a perfectly acceptable approximation, but there are also occasions when you need to recognize that short-term interest rates may be different from long-term rates. In this case, it may be worth discounting each cash flow at a different rate.

The relationship between short- and long-term interest rates is called the **term structure of interest rates.** Look, for example, at Figure 3.3, which shows the term structure in two different years. Notice that in the later year, the term structure sloped downward; long-term interest rates were lower than short-term rates. In the earlier year, the pattern was reversed and long-term bonds offered a much higher interest rate than short-term bonds. You now need to learn how to measure the term structure and understand why long- and short-term rates often differ.

Consider a simple loan that pays $1 at the end of one year. To find the present value of this loan you need to discount the cash flow by the one-year rate of interest, r_1:

$$PV = 1/(1 + r_1)$$

This rate, r_1, is called the one-year **spot rate.** To find the present value of a loan that pays $1 at the end of two years, you need to discount by the two-year spot rate, r_2:

$$PV = 1/(1 + r_2)^2$$

▶ **FIGURE 3.3**

Short- and long-term interest rates do not always move in parallel. Between September 1992 and April 2000, U.S. short-term rates rose sharply while long-term rates declined.

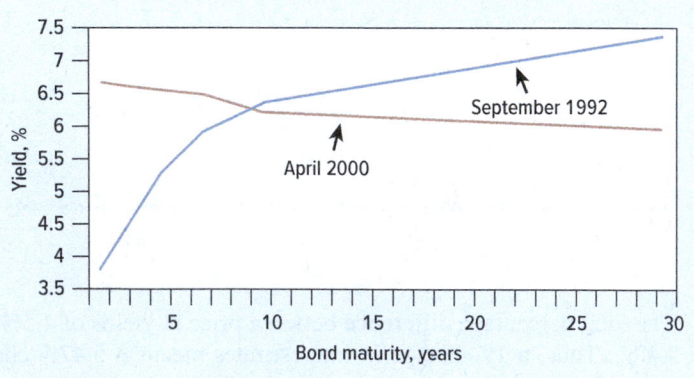

_____

[8]For simplicity, we assumed that the two Treasury bonds paid annual coupons. Calculating Macaulay duration for a bond with semiannual coupons is no different except that there are twice as many cash flows. To calculate modified duration with semiannual coupons you need to divide Macaulay duration by the semiannual yield to maturity.

The first year's cash flow is discounted at today's one-year spot rate, and the second year's flow is discounted at today's two-year spot rate. The series of spot rates $r_1, r_2, \ldots, r_t, \ldots$ traces out the term structure of interest rates.

Now suppose you have to value $1 paid at the end of years 1 *and* 2. If the spot rates are different—say, $r_1 = 3\%$ and $r_2 = 4\%$—then we need two discount rates to calculate present value:

$$PV = \frac{1}{1.03} + \frac{1}{1.04^2} = 1.895$$

Once we know that PV = 1.895, we can go on to calculate a single discount rate that would give the same answer. That is, we could calculate the yield to maturity by solving for y in the following equation:

$$PV = 1.895 = \frac{1}{(1+y)} + \frac{1}{(1+y)^2}$$

This gives a yield to maturity of 3.66%. Once we have the yield, we could use it to value other two-year annuities. But we can't get the yield to maturity until we know the price. The price is determined by the spot interest rates for dates 1 and 2. Spot rates come first. Yields to maturity come later, after bond prices are set. That is why professionals often identify spot interest rates and discount each cash flow at the spot rate for the date when the cash flow is received.

Spot Rates, Bond Prices, and the Law of One Price

The *law of one price* states that the same commodity must sell at the same price in a well-functioning market. Therefore, all safe cash payments delivered on the same date must be discounted at the same spot rate.

Table 3.6 illustrates how the law of one price applies to government bonds. It lists three government bonds, which we assume make annual coupon payments. All the bonds have the same coupon but they have different maturities. The shortest (bond A) matures in two years and the longest (bond C) in four.

	Year (t)					
	1	2	3	4	Bond Price (PV)	Yield to Maturity (y, %)
Spot rates	0.03	0.04	0.05	0.06		
Discount factors	0.9709	0.9246	0.8638	0.7921		
Bond A (8% coupon)						
Payment (C_t)	$80.00	1,080.00				
PV (C_t)	$77.67	998.52			$1,076.19	3.96
Bond B (8% coupon)						
Payment (C_t)	$80.00	80.00	1,080.00			
PV (C_t)	$77.67	73.96	932.94		$1,084.58	4.90
Bond C (8% coupon)						
Payment (C_t)	$80.00	80.00	80.00	1,080.00		
PV (C_t)	$77.67	73.96	69.11	855.46	$1,076.20	5.81

❯ TABLE 3.6   The law of one price applied to government bonds

Spot rates and discount factors are given at the top of each column. The law of one price says that investors place the same value on a risk-free dollar regardless of whether it is provided by bond A, B, or C. You can check that the law holds in the table.

Each bond is priced by adding the present values of each of its cash flows. Once total PV is calculated, we have the bond price. Only then can the yield to maturity be calculated.

Notice how the yield to maturity increases as bond maturity increases. The yields increase with maturity because the term structure of spot rates is upward-sloping. Yields to maturity are complex averages of spot rates. For example, you can see that the yield on the four-year bond (5.81%) lies between the one- and four-year spot rates (3% and 6%).

Financial managers who want a quick, summary measure of interest rates bypass spot interest rates and look in the financial press at yields to maturity. They may refer to the *yield curve,* which plots yields to maturity, instead of referring to the term structure, which plots spot rates. They may use the yield to maturity on one bond to value another bond with roughly the same coupon and maturity. They may speak with a broad brush and say, "Ampersand Bank will charge us 6% on a three-year loan," referring to a 6% yield to maturity.

Throughout this text, we too use the yield to maturity to summarize the return required by bond investors. But you also need to understand the measure's limitations when spot rates are not equal.

Measuring the Term Structure

You can think of the spot rate, r_t, as the rate of interest on a bond that makes a single payment at time t. Such simple bonds do exist. They are known as **stripped bonds,** or **strips.** On request the U.S. Treasury will split a normal coupon bond into a package of mini-bonds, each of which makes just one cash payment. Our 8% bonds of 2021 could be exchanged for eight semiannual coupon strips, each paying $40, and a principal strip paying $1,000. In November 2017, this package of coupon strips would have cost $307.58 and the principal strip would have cost $927.53, making a total cost of $1,235.11, just a little more than it cost to buy one 8% bond. The similarity should be no surprise. Because the two investments provide identical cash payments, they must sell for very close to the same price.

We can use the prices of strips to measure the term structure of interest rates. For example, in November 2017, a 10-year strip cost $793.37. In return, investors could look forward to a single payment of $1,000 in November 2027. Thus, investors were prepared to pay $.79337 for the promise of $1 at the end of 10 years. The 10-year discount factor was $DF_{10} = 1/(1 + r_{10})^{10} = .79337$, and the 10-year spot rate was $r_{10} = (1/.79337)^{.10} - 1 = .0234$, or 2.34%. In Figure 3.4, we use the prices of strips with different maturities to plot the term structure of spot rates from 1 to 25 years. You can see that in 2017 investors required a higher interest rate for lending for 25 years rather than for 1.

Why the Discount Factor Declines as Futurity Increases—and a Digression on Money Machines

In Chapter 2, we saw that the longer you have to wait for your money, the less is its present value. In other words, the two-year discount factor $DF_2 = 1/(1 + r_2)^2$ is less than the one-year discount factor $DF_1 = 1/(1 + r_1)$. But is this *necessarily* the case when there can be a different spot interest rate for each period?

Suppose that the one-year spot rate of interest is $r_1 = 20\%$ and the two-year spot rate is $r_2 = 7\%$. In this case, the one-year discount factor is $DF_1 = 1/1.20 = .833$ and the two-year discount factor is $DF_2 = 1/1.07^2 = .873$. Apparently, a dollar received the day after tomorrow is not necessarily worth less than a dollar received tomorrow.

But there is something wrong with this example. Anyone who could borrow and invest at these interest rates could become a millionaire overnight. Let us see how such a "money machine" would work. Suppose the first person to spot the opportunity is Hermione Kraft.

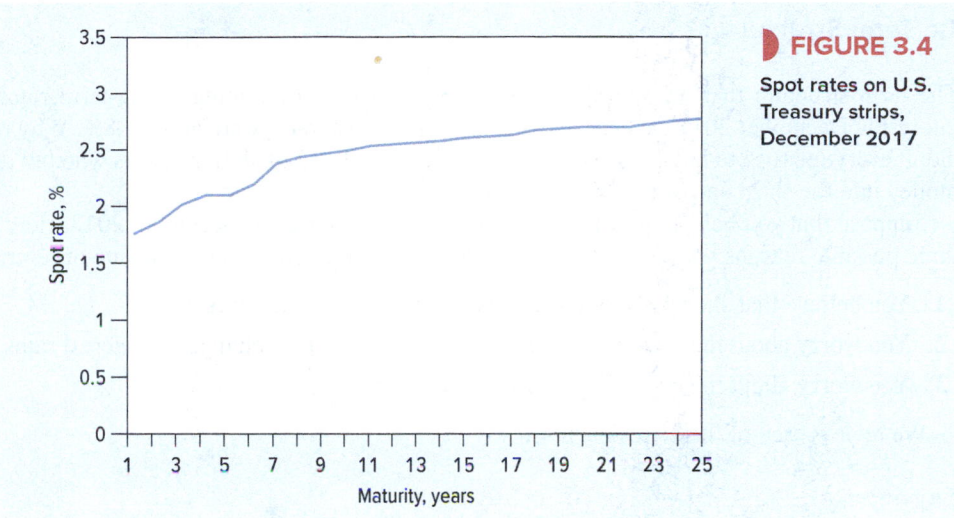

▶ **FIGURE 3.4**

Spot rates on U.S. Treasury strips, December 2017

Ms. Kraft first buys a one-year Treasury strip for $.833 \times \$1,000 = \$833$. Now she notices that there is a way to earn an *immediate* surefire profit on this investment. She reasons as follows. Next year the strip will pay off $1,000 that can be reinvested for a further year. Although she does not know what interest rates will be at that time, she does know that she can always put the money in a checking account and be certain of having $1,000 at the end of year 2. Her next step, therefore, is to go to her bank and borrow the present value of this $1,000. At 7% interest the present value is $PV = 1000/(1.07)^2 = \$873$.

So Ms. Kraft borrows $873, invests $830, and walks away with a profit of $43. If that does not sound like very much, notice that by borrowing more and investing more she can make much larger profits. For example, if she borrows $21,778,584 and invests $20,778,584, she would become a millionaire.[9]

Of course this story is completely fanciful. Such an opportunity would not last long in well-functioning capital markets. Any bank that allowed you to borrow for two years at 7% when the one-year interest rate was 20% would soon be wiped out by a rush of small investors hoping to become millionaires and a rush of millionaires hoping to become billionaires. There are, however, two lessons to our story. The first is that a dollar tomorrow *cannot* be worth less than a dollar the day after tomorrow. In other words, the value of a dollar received at the end of one year (DF_1) cannot be less than the value of a dollar received at the end of two years (DF_2). There must be some extra gain from lending for two periods rather than one: $(1 + r_2)^2$ cannot be less than $1 + r_1$.

Our second lesson is a more general one and can be summed up by this precept: "There is no such thing as a surefire money machine." The technical term for money machine is **arbitrage.** In well-functioning markets, where the costs of buying and selling are low, arbitrage opportunities are eliminated almost instantaneously by investors who try to take advantage of them.

Later in the book we invoke the *absence* of arbitrage opportunities to prove several useful properties about security prices. That is, we make statements like, "The prices of securities X and Y must be in the following relationship—otherwise there would be potential arbitrage profits and capital markets would not be in equilibrium."

---

[9]We exaggerate Ms. Kraft's profits. There are always costs to financial transactions, though they may be very small. For example, Ms. Kraft could use her investment in the one-year strip as security for the bank loan, but the bank would need to charge more than 7% on the loan to cover its costs.

The term structure that we showed in Figure 3.4 was upward-sloping. Long-term rates of interest in December 2017 were more than 2.5%; short-term rates were about 1.8%. Why then didn't everyone rush to buy long-term bonds? Who were the (foolish?) investors who put their money into the short end of the term structure?

Suppose that you held a portfolio of one-year U.S. Treasuries in December 2017. Here are three possible reasons you might decide to hold on to them, despite their low rate of return:

1. You believe that short-term interest rates will be higher in the future.
2. You worry about the greater exposure of long-term bonds to changes in interest rates.
3. You worry about the risk of higher future inflation.

We review each of these reasons now.

Expectations Theory of the Term Structure

Recall that you own a portfolio of one-year Treasuries. A year from now, when these Treasuries mature, you can reinvest the proceeds for another one-year period and enjoy whatever interest rate the bond market offers then. The interest rate for the second year may be high enough to offset a low return in the first year. You often see an upward-sloping term structure when future interest rates are expected to rise.

EXAMPLE 3.3 • Expectations and the Term Structure

Suppose that the one-year interest rate, r_1, is 5%, and the two-year rate, r_2, is 7%. If you invest $100 for one year, your investment grows to $100 \times 1.05 = \$105$; if you invest for two years, it grows to $100 \times 1.07^2 = \$114.49$. The extra return that you earn for that second year is $1.07^2/1.05 - 1 = .090$, or 9.0%.[10]

Would you be happy to earn that extra 9% for investing for two years rather than one? The answer depends on how you expect interest rates to change over the coming year. If you are confident that in 12 months' time one-year bonds will yield more than 9.0%, you would do better to invest in a one-year bond and, when that matured, reinvest the cash for the next year at the higher rate. If you forecast that the future one-year rate is exactly 9.0%, then you will be indifferent between buying a two-year bond or investing for one year and then rolling the investment forward at next year's short-term interest rate.

If everyone is thinking as you just did, then the two-year interest rate has to adjust so that everyone is equally happy to invest for one year or two. Thus the two-year rate will incorporate both today's one-year rate and the consensus forecast of next year's one-year rate.

• • • • •

We have just illustrated (in Example 3.3) the **expectations theory** of the term structure. It states that in well-functioning bond markets investment in a series of short-maturity bonds must offer the same expected return as an investment in a single long-maturity bond. Only if that is the case would investors be prepared to hold both short- and long-maturity bonds.

The expectations theory implies that the *only* reason for an upward-sloping term structure is that investors expect short-term interest rates to rise; the *only* reason for a declining term structure is that investors expect short-term rates to fall.

---

[10]The extra return for lending for one more year is termed the *forward rate of interest*. In our example, the forward rate is 9.0%. In Ms. Kraft's arbitrage example, the forward interest rate was negative. In real life, forward interest rates can't be negative. At the lowest they are zero.

If short-term interest rates are significantly lower than long-term rates, it is tempting to borrow short term rather than long term. The expectations theory implies that such naïve strategies won't work. If short-term rates are lower than long-term rates, then investors must be expecting interest rates to rise. When the term structure is upward-sloping, you are likely to make money by borrowing short only if investors are *overestimating* future increases in interest rates.

Even at a casual glance, the expectations theory does not seem to be the complete explanation of term structure. For example, if we look back over the period 1900–2017, we find that the return on long-term U.S. Treasury bonds was on average 1.5 percentage points higher than the return on short-term Treasury bills. Perhaps short-term interest rates stayed lower than investors expected, but it seems more likely that investors wanted some extra return for holding long bonds and that on average they got it. If so, the expectations theory is only a first step.

These days, the expectations theory has few strict adherents. Nevertheless, most economists believe that expectations about future interest rates have an important effect on the term structure. For example, you often hear market commentators remark that since the six-month interest rate is higher than the three-month rate, the market must be expecting the Federal Reserve Board to raise interest rates.

Introducing Risk

What does the expectations theory leave out? The most obvious answer is "risk." If you are confident about the future level of interest rates, you will simply choose the strategy that offers the highest return. But, if you are not sure of your forecasts, you may well opt for a less risky strategy even if it means giving up some return.

Remember that the prices of long-duration bonds are more volatile than prices of short-duration bonds. A sharp increase in interest rates can knock 30% or 40% off the price of long-term bonds.

For some investors, this extra volatility of long-duration bonds may not be a concern. For example, pension funds and life insurance companies have fixed long-term liabilities and may prefer to lock in future returns by investing in long-term bonds. However, the volatility of long-term bonds *does* create extra risk for investors who do not have such long-term obligations. These investors will be prepared to hold long bonds only if they offer the compensation of a higher return. In this case, the term structure will be upward-sloping more often than not. Of course, if interest rates are expected to fall, the term structure could be downward-sloping and still reward investors for lending long. But the additional reward for risk offered by long bonds would result in a less dramatic downward slope.

BEYOND THE PAGE

Arbitrage models
of term structure

mhhe.com/brealey13e

Inflation and Term Structure

Suppose you are saving for your retirement 20 years from now. Which of the following strategies is more risky? Invest in a succession of one-year Treasuries, rolled over annually, or invest once in 20-year strips? The answer depends on how confident you are about future inflation.

If you buy the 20-year strips, you know exactly how much money you will have at year 20, but you don't know what that money will buy. Inflation may seem benign now, but who knows what it will be in 10 or 15 years? This uncertainty about inflation may make it uncomfortably risky for you to lock in one 20-year interest rate by buying the strips.

You can reduce exposure to inflation risk by investing short-term and rolling over the investment. You do not know future short-term interest rates, but you do know that future interest rates will adapt to inflation. If inflation takes off, you will probably be able to roll over your investment at higher interest rates.

If inflation is an important source of risk for long-term investors, borrowers must offer some extra incentive if they want investors to lend long. That is why we often see a steeply upward-sloping term structure when inflation is particularly uncertain.

It is now time to review more carefully the relation between inflation and interest rates. Suppose you invest $1,000 in a one-year bond that makes a single payment of $1,100 at the end of the year. Your cash flow is certain, but the government makes no promises about what that money will buy. If the prices of goods and services increase by more than 10%, you will lose ground in terms of purchasing power.

BEYOND THE PAGE

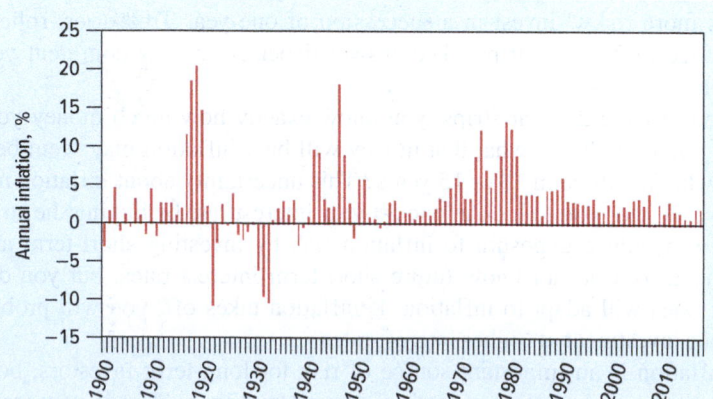

The German
hyperinflation

mhhe.com/brealey13e

Several indexes are used to track the general level of prices. The best known is the consumer price index (CPI), which measures the number of dollars that it takes to pay for a typical family's purchases. The change in the CPI from one year to the next measures the rate of inflation.

Figure 3.5 shows the rate of inflation in the U.S. since 1900. Inflation touched a peak at the end of World War I, when it reached 21%. However, this figure pales into insignificance compared with the hyperinflation in Zimbabwe in 2008. Prices there rose so fast that a Z$50 trillion bill was barely enough to buy a loaf of bread.

Prices can fall as well as rise. The U.S. experienced severe *deflation* in the Great Depression, when prices fell by 24% in three years. In Japan, which has experienced persistent deflation, prices in 2017 were only marginally higher than they had been 20 years earlier.

The *average* U.S. inflation rate from 1900 to 2017 was 3.0%. As you can see from Figure 3.6, among major economies, the United States has been almost top of the class in holding inflation in check. Countries torn by war have generally experienced much higher inflation. For example, in Italy and Japan, inflation since 1900 has averaged around 10% a year.

Economists and financial managers refer to current, or *nominal,* dollars versus constant, or *real,* dollars. For example, the nominal cash flow from your one-year bond is $1,100. But if prices rise over the year by 6%, then each dollar will buy you 6% less next year than it does today. So at the end of the year, $1,100 has the same purchasing power as 1,100/1.06 = $1,037.74 today. The nominal payoff on the bond is $1,100, but the real payoff is only $1,037.74.

The formula for converting nominal cash flows in a future period *t* to real cash flows today is

$$\text{Real cash flow at date } t = \frac{\text{nominal cash flow at date } t}{(1 + \text{inflation rate})^t}$$

For example, suppose you invest in a 20-year Treasury strip, but prices over that period grow by 6% per year. The strip pays $1,000 in year 20, but the real value of that payoff is only $1,000/1.06^{20} = \$311.80$. In this example, the purchasing power of $1 today declines to just over $.31 after 20 years.

▶ **FIGURE 3.5**

Annual rates of inflation in the United States from 1900–2017

Source: E. Dimson, P. R. Marsh, and M. Staunton, *Triumph of the Optimists: 101 Years of Investment Returns* (Princeton, NJ: Princeton University Press, 2002), with updates provided by the authors.

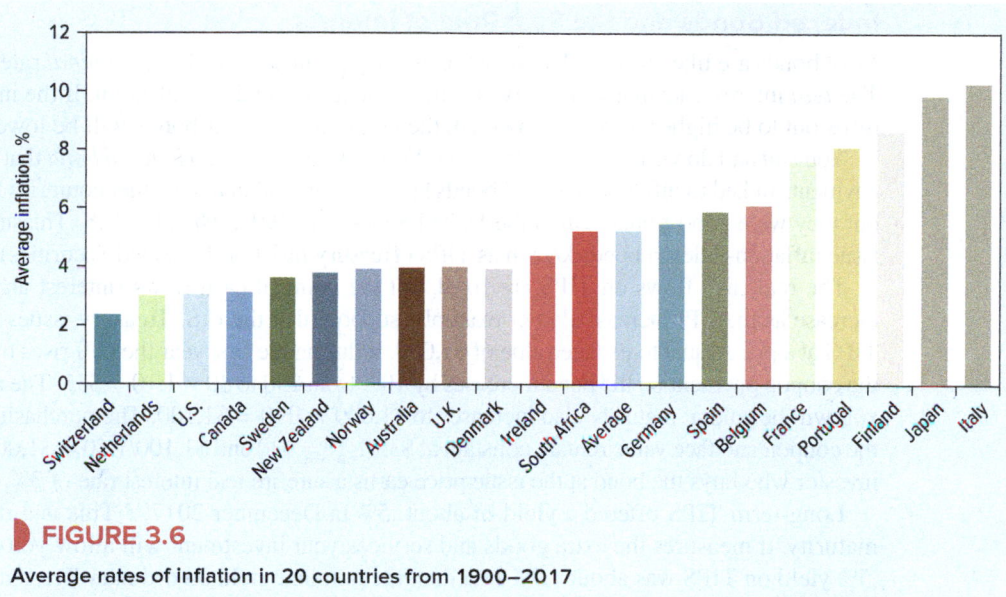

▶ **FIGURE 3.6**

Average rates of inflation in 20 countries from 1900–2017

Source: E. Dimson, P. R. Marsh, and M. Staunton, *Triumph of the Optimists: 101 Years of Investment Returns* (Princeton, NJ: Princeton University Press, 2002), with updates provided by the authors.

These examples show you how to get from nominal to real cash flows. The journey from nominal to real interest rates is similar. When a bond dealer says that your bond yields 10%, she is quoting a nominal interest rate. That rate tells you how rapidly your money will grow—say, over one year:

Invest Current Dollars	Receive Dollars in Year 1	Result
$1,000 →	$1,100	10% *nominal rate of return*

However, with an expected inflation rate of 6%, you are only 3.774% better off at the end of the year than at the start:

Invest Current Dollars	Expected Real Value of Dollars in Year 1	Result
$1,000 →	$1,037.74 (=1,100/1.06)	3.774% expected *real* rate of return

Thus, we could say, "The bond offers a 10% nominal rate of return," or "It offers a 3.774% expected real rate of return."

The formula for calculating the real rate of return is:

$$1 + r_{real} = (1 + r_{nominal})/(1 + \text{inflation rate})$$

In our example, $1 + r_{real} = 1.10/1.06 = 1.03774$. A common rule of thumb states that $r_{real} = r_{nominal} - \text{inflation rate}$. In our example, this gives $r_{real} = .10 - .06 = .04$, or 4%. This is not a bad approximation to the true real interest rate of 3.774%. But when inflation is high, it pays to use the full formula.

Indexed Bonds and the Real Rate of Interest

Most bonds are like our U.S. Treasury bonds; they promise you a fixed *nominal* rate of interest. The *real* interest rate that you receive is uncertain and depends on inflation. If the inflation rate turns out to be higher than you expected, the real return on your bonds will be lower.

You *can* nail down a real return, however. You do so by buying an *indexed bond* that makes cash payments linked to inflation. Indexed bonds have been around in many other countries for decades, but they were almost unknown in the United States until 1997, when the U.S. Treasury began to issue inflation-indexed bonds known as TIPS (Treasury Inflation-Protected Securities).[11]

The real cash flows on TIPS are fixed, but the nominal cash flows (interest and principal) increase as the CPI increases.[12] For example, suppose that the U.S. Treasury issues 3% 20-year TIPS at a price equal to its face value of $1,000. If during the first year the CPI rises by 10%, then the coupon payment on the bond increases by 10% from $30 to $30 \times 1.10 = \$33$. The amount that you will be paid at maturity also increases to $1,000 \times 1.10 = \$1,100$. The purchasing power of the coupon and face value remain constant at $33/1.10 = \$30$ and $1,100/1.10 = \$1,000$. Thus, an investor who buys the bond at the issue price earns a surefire real interest rate of 3%.

Long-term TIPS offered a yield of about .5% in December 2017.[13] This is a *real* yield to maturity. It measures the extra goods and services your investment will allow you to buy. The .5% yield on TIPS was about 1.9% less than the nominal yield on ordinary Treasury bonds. If the annual inflation rate turns out to be higher than 1.9%, investors will earn a higher return by holding long-term TIPS; if the inflation rate turns out to be less than 1.9%, they would have been better off with nominal bonds.

What Determines the Real Rate of Interest?

The real rate of interest depends on people's willingness to save (the supply of capital)[14] and the opportunities for productive investment by governments and businesses (the demand for capital). For example, suppose that investment opportunities generally improve. Firms have more good projects, so they are willing to invest more than previously at the current real interest rate. Therefore, the rate has to rise to induce individuals to save the additional amount that firms want to invest.[15] Conversely, if investment opportunities deteriorate, there will be a fall in the real interest rate.

Short- and medium-term real interest rates are affected by the monetary policy of central banks. For example, sometimes central banks keep short-term nominal interest rates low despite significant inflation. The resulting real rates can be negative. However, *nominal* interest rates cannot be negative except in fairly rare circumstances because investors can simply hold cash. Cash always pays zero interest, which is better than negative interest.

For many years, real interest rates were much more stable than nominal rates, but as you can see from Figure 3.7, both nominal and real interest rates have plummeted since the financial crash.

BEYOND THE PAGE

How to make a certain loss

mhhe.com/brealey13e

---

[11]Indexed bonds were not completely unknown in the United States before 1997. For example, in 1780 American Revolutionary soldiers were compensated with indexed bonds that paid the value of "five bushels of corn, 68 pounds and four-seventh parts of a pound of beef, ten pounds of sheep's wool, and sixteen pounds of sole leather."

[12]The reverse happens if there is deflation. In this case, the coupon payment and principal amount are adjusted downward. However, the U.S. government guarantees that when the bond matures, it will not pay less than its original nominal face value.

[13]In 2012, the yield on short-term TIPs was negative. You were actually *losing* in real terms.

[14]Some of this saving is done indirectly. For example, if you hold 100 shares of IBM stock, and IBM retains and reinvests earnings of $1.00 a share, IBM is saving $100 on your behalf. The government may also oblige you to save by raising taxes to invest in roads, hospitals, etc.

[15]We assume that investors save more as interest rates rise. It doesn't have to be that way. Suppose that 20 years hence you will need $50,000 in today's dollars for your children's college tuition. How much will you have to set aside today to cover this obligation? The answer is the present value of a real expenditure of $50,000 after 20 years, or $50,000/(1 + \text{real interest rate})^{20}$. The higher the real interest rate, the lower the present value and the less you have to set aside.

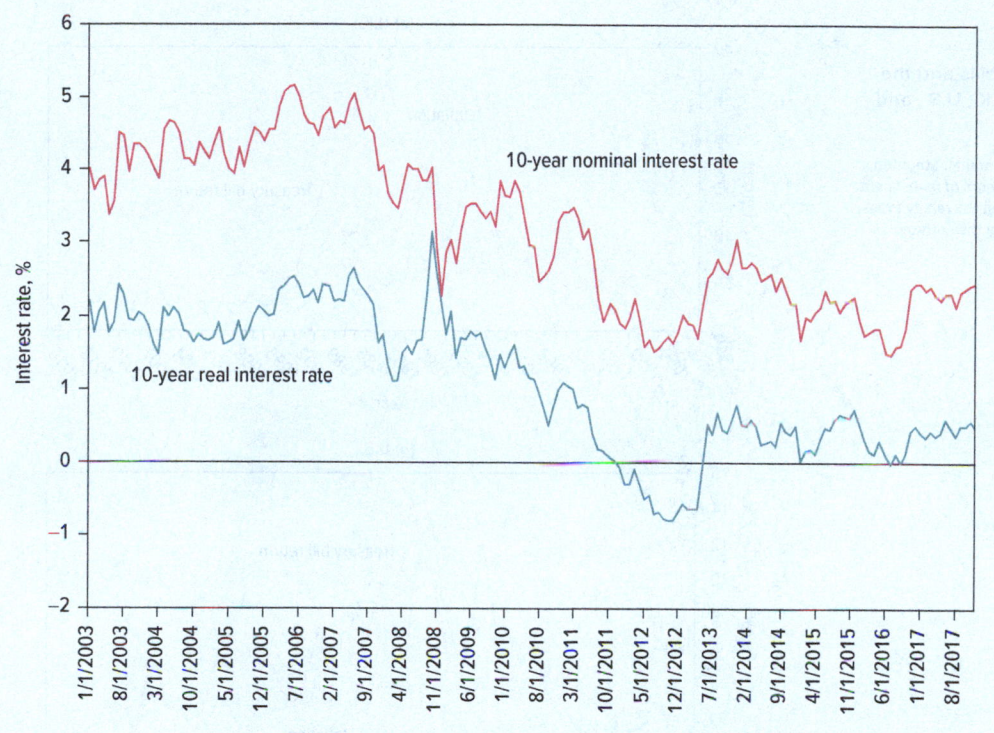

▶ **FIGURE 3.7**

The green line shows the real yield on long-term TIPS issued by the U.S. government. The brown line shows the yield on long-term nominal bonds.

Inflation and Nominal Interest Rates

How does the inflation outlook affect the nominal rate of interest? Here is how economist Irving Fisher answered the question. Suppose that consumers are equally happy with 100 apples today or 103 apples in a year's time. In this case, the real or "apple" interest rate is 3%. If the price of apples is constant at (say) $1 each, then we will be equally happy to receive $100 today or $103 at the end of the year. That extra $3 will allow us to buy 3% more apples at the end of the year than we could buy today.

But suppose now that the apple price is expected to increase by 5% to $1.05 each. In that case, we would *not* be happy to give up $100 today for the promise of $103 next year. To buy 103 apples in a year's time, we will need to receive 1.05 × $103 = $108.15. In other words, the nominal rate of interest must increase by the expected rate of inflation to 8.15%.

This is Fisher's theory: A change in the expected inflation rate causes the same proportionate change in the *nominal* interest rate; it has no effect on the required real interest rate. The formula relating the nominal interest rate and expected inflation is

$$1 + r_{nominal} = (1 + r_{real})(1 + i)$$

where r_{real} is the real interest rate that consumers require and i is the expected inflation rate. In our example, the prospect of inflation causes $1 + r_{nominal}$ to rise to 1.03 × 1.05 = 1.0815.

Not all economists would agree with Fisher that the real rate of interest is unaffected by the inflation rate. For example, if changes in prices are associated with changes in the level of industrial activity, then in inflationary conditions I might want more or less than 103 apples in a year's time to compensate me for the loss of 100 today.

We wish we could show you the past behavior of interest rates and *expected* inflation. Instead, we have done the next best thing and plotted in Figure 3.8 the return on Treasury

BEYOND THE PAGE

The yield on TIPs

mhhe.com/brealey13e

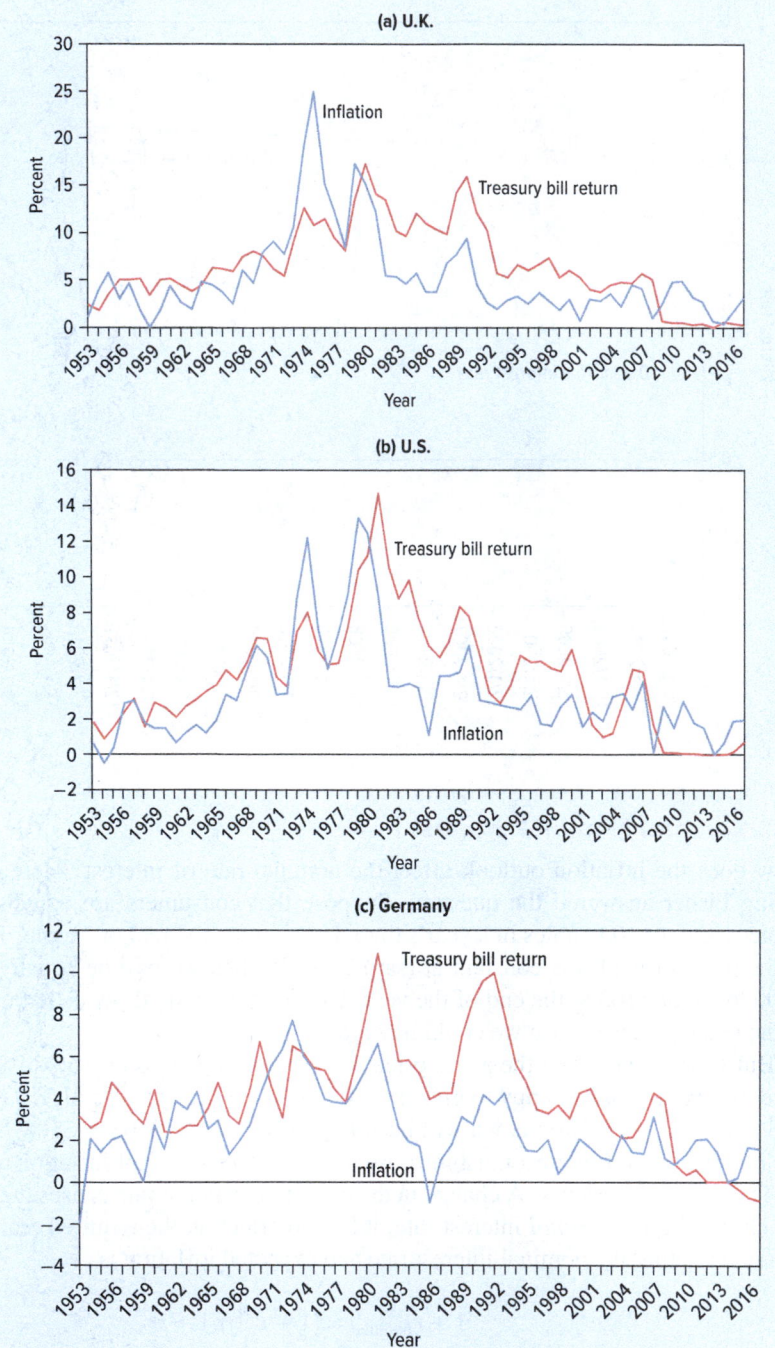

▶ **FIGURE 3.8**

The return on Treasury bills and the rate of inflation in the U.K., U.S., and Germany, 1953–2017

Source: E. Dimson, P. R. Marsh, and M. Staunton, *Triumph of the Optimists: 101 Years of Investment Returns* (Princeton, NJ: Princeton University Press, 2002), with updates provided by the authors.

bills (short-term government debt) against *actual* inflation for the United States, U.K., and Germany. Notice that since 1953, the return on Treasury bills has generally been a little above the rate of inflation. Investors in each country earned an average real return of between 1% and 2% during this period.

Look now at the relationship between the rate of inflation and the Treasury bill rate. Figure 3.8 shows that investors have for the most part demanded a higher rate of interest when inflation was high. So it looks as if Fisher's theory provides a useful rule of thumb for financial managers. If the expected inflation rate changes, it is a good bet that there will be a corresponding change in the nominal interest rate. In other words, a strategy of rolling over short-term investments affords some protection against uncertain inflation.

3-6 The Risk of Default

Corporate Bonds and Default Risk

Look at Table 3.7, which shows the yields to maturity on a sample of corporate bonds. Notice that the bonds all mature in 2023, but their yields to maturity differ dramatically. With a yield of 13.0%, the bonds of Quorum Health appeared to offer a mouth-watering rate of return. However, the company had been operating at a loss and had substantial debts. Investors foresaw that there was a good chance that the company would default and that they would not get their money back. Thus, the payments promised to the bondholders represent a best-case scenario: The firm will never pay more than the promised cash flows, but in hard times, it may pay less. This risk applies in some measure to all corporate bonds, but investors were much more confident that Johnson & Johnson would be able to service its debt and this is reflected in the low yield on its bonds.

The safety of most corporate bonds can be judged from bond ratings provided by Moody's, Standard & Poor's (S&P), and Fitch. Table 3.8 lists the possible bond ratings in declining order of quality. For example, the bonds that receive the highest Standard & Poor's rating are known as AAA (or "triple A") bonds. Then come AA (double A), A, BBB bonds, and so on. Bonds rated BBB and above are called investment grade, while those with a rating of BB or below are referred to as speculative grade, high-yield, or junk bonds. Notice that the bonds in the first four rows of Table 3.7 are all investment-grade bonds; the rest are junk bonds.

It is rare for highly rated bonds to default. However, when an investment-grade bond does go under, the shock waves are felt in all major financial centers. For example, in May 2001, World-Com sold $11.8 billion of bonds with an investment-grade rating. About one year later, WorldCom filed for bankruptcy, and its bondholders lost more than 80% of their investment. For these bond-holders, the agencies that had assigned investment-grade ratings were not the flavor of the month.

Because of the risk of default, yields on corporate bonds are higher than those of government bonds. For example, Figure 3.9 shows the yield spread of corporate bonds against U.S. Treasuries. Notice that the spreads widen as safety falls off. Notice also how spreads vary

BEYOND THE PAGE

Bond rating definitions

mhhe.com/brealey13e

Issuer Name	Coupon (%)	Maturity	S&P Rating	Price (%)	Yield (%)
Johnson & Johnson	6.73	2023	AAA	125.05	2.30
Walmart	6.75	2023	AA	122.95	2.62
Alabama Power	3.55	2023	A	104.74	2.71
PSEG	4.3	2023	BBB	105.65	3.23
Freeport-McMoRan	3.875	2023	BB	117.44	4.41
NGL Energy	7.5	2023	B	99.50	7.60
Quorum Health	11.625	2023	CCC	94.50	13.05

❭ TABLE 3.7   Prices and yields of a sample of corporate bonds

Source: Bond transactions reported on FINRA's TRACE service: http://finra-markets.morningstar.com/BondCenter/Screener.jsp.

❭**TABLE 3.8**   Key to bond ratings. The highest-quality bonds rated Baa/BBB or above are investment grade.

Moody's	Standard & Poor's and Fitch
Investment-grade bonds	
Aaa	AAA
Aa	AA
A	A
Baa	BBB
Junk bonds	
Ba	BB
B	B
Caa	CCC
Ca	CC
C	C

❭ **FIGURE 3.9**

Yield spreads between corporate and 10-year Treasury bonds, January 1953–January 2018

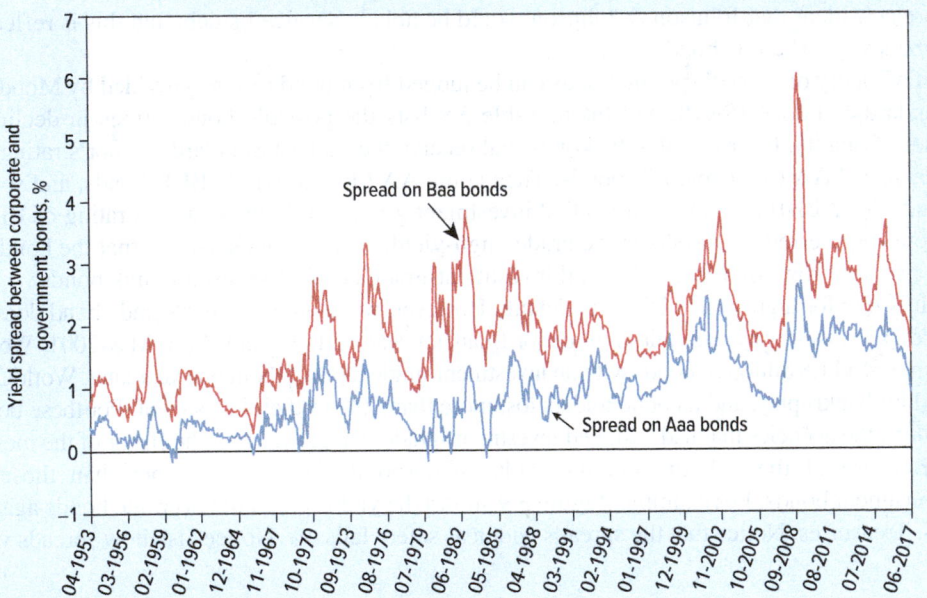

over time. On average, the spread on Baa bonds has been about 2%, but it widened to more than 6% during the credit crunch of 2007 to 2009.[16]

Sovereign Bonds and Default Risk

When investors buy corporate bonds or a bank lends to a company, they worry about the possibility of default and spend considerable time and effort assessing differences in credit risk. By contrast, when the U.S. government issues dollar bonds, investors can generally be

---

[16]Corporate bonds are also less liquid than Treasuries: They are more difficult and expensive to trade, particularly in large quantities or on short notice. Many investors value liquidity and will demand a higher interest rate on a less liquid bond. Lack of liquidity accounts for some of the spread between yields on corporate and Treasury bonds.

A Game of Political Chicken

❯In 2010, the U.S. Congress set a ceiling of $14.3 trillion on the amount that the federal government could borrow. However, government spending was fast outrunning revenues, and unless Congress voted to increase the debt ceiling, the U.S. government forecasted that by August 2, 2011, it would run out of cash to pay its bills. It would then face a stark choice between drastic cuts in government spending or defaulting on its debt. Treasury Secretary Tim Geithner warned that "failure to raise the limit would precipitate a default by the United States. Default would effectively impose a significant and long-lasting tax on all Americans and all American businesses and could lead to the loss of millions of American jobs. Even a very short-term or limited default would have catastrophic economic consequences that would last for decades."

Although there was general agreement that any increase in the debt ceiling should be accompanied by a deal to reduce the deficit, there was little meeting of minds as to how this should be achieved. Few observers believed that the United States would actually default on its debt, but as the dispute dragged on, the unthinkable became thinkable. Negotiations went down to the wire. On August 2, the day that the country was forecasted to run out of borrowing power, President Obama finally signed the Budget Control Act that increased the debt ceiling by $900 billion. Two days later, Standard & Poor's downgraded the long-term credit rating of the U.S. government from AAA to AA.

Source: "Secretary Geithner Sends Debt Limit Letter to Congress," U.S. Department of the Treasury, January 6, 2011. **http://www.treasury.gov/connect/blog/Pages/letter.aspx.**

confident that those bonds will be repaid in full and on time. Of course, bondholders don't know what that money will be worth. Governments have a nasty habit of reducing the real value of their debts by inflationary policies.

Although sovereign debt is generally less risky than corporate debt, we should not leave you with the impression that it is *always* safe even in money terms. Indeed, as the nearby Finance in Practice box explains, even in the United States investors in government bonds have had their slightly scary moments. Countries do occasionally default on their debts and, when they do so, the effects can be catastrophic. We will look briefly at three circumstances in which countries may default.

Foreign Currency Debt Most government bond defaults have occurred when a foreign government borrows dollars. In these cases investors worry that in some future crisis the government may run out of taxing capacity and may not be able to come up with enough dollars to repay the debt. This worry shows up in bond prices and yields to maturity. For example, in 2001 the Argentinian government defaulted on $82 billion of debt. As the prospect of default loomed, the price of Argentinian bonds slumped, and the promised yield climbed to more than 40 percentage points above the yield on U.S. Treasuries. Argentina has plenty of company. Since 1970, there have been more than 100 occasions that sovereign governments have defaulted on their foreign currency bonds.[17]

Own Currency Debt If a government borrows in its own currency, there is less likelihood of default. After all, the government can always print the money needed to repay the bonds. Very occasionally, governments have chosen to default on their domestic debt rather than create the money to pay it off. That was the case in Russia in the summer of 1998, when political

---

[17]Occasionally, defaults have been a case of "won't pay" rather than "can't pay." For example, in 2008 Ecuador's president announced that his country would disavow $3.9 billion of "illegal" debts contracted by earlier regimes. In dealing with international lenders, he said, "We are up against real monsters."

instability combined with a slump in oil prices, declining government revenues, and pressure on the exchange rate. By August yields on government ruble bonds had reached 200% and it no longer made sense for Russia to create the money to service its debt. That month the government devalued the ruble and defaulted on its domestic ruble debt.

Eurozone Debt   The 19 countries in the eurozone do not even have the option of printing money to service their domestic debts; they have given up control over their own money supply to the European Central Bank. This was to pose a major problem for the Greek government, which had amassed a massive €330 billion (or about $440 billion) of debt. In May 2010, other eurozone governments and the International Monetary Fund (IMF) rushed to Greece's aid, but investors were unconvinced that their assistance would be sufficient, and the yield on 10-year Greek government debt climbed to nearly 27%. In 2012, in return for a further bailout package, investors in Greek bonds were obliged to accept a write-down of some $100 billion in the value of their bonds. It was the largest ever sovereign default. However, the difficulties for Greece were by no means over. The rescue package required it to adopt an austerity policy that resulted in a sharp fall in national income and considerable hardship for the Greek people. The country was also unable to escape from its large debt burden. It missed a payment on its debt to the IMF in 2015, and two years later, despite a further bailout, was back in crisis mode.

The sovereign debt crisis in Europe was not confined to Greece. Cyprus also delayed repayment of its bonds, and the Irish and Portuguese government debt was down-rated to junk level. Investors joked that, instead of offering a risk-free return, eurozone government bonds just offered a return-free risk.

⬤ ⬤ ⬤ ⬤ ⬤

SUMMARY   Bonds are simply long-term loans. If you own a bond, you are entitled to a regular interest (or *coupon*) payment and at maturity you get back the bond's face value (or *principal*). In the U.S., coupons are normally paid every six months, but in other countries they may be paid annually.

The value of any bond is equal to its cash payments discounted at the spot rates of interest. For example, the present value of a 10-year bond with a 5% coupon paid annually equals

$$\text{PV (\% of face value)} = \frac{5}{(1+r_1)} + \frac{5}{(1+r_2)^2} + \cdots + \frac{105}{(1+r_{10})^{10}}$$

This calculation uses a different spot rate of interest for each period. A plot of spot rates by maturity shows the term structure of interest rates.

Spot interest rates are most conveniently calculated from the prices of strips, which are bonds that make a single payment of face value at maturity, with zero coupons along the way. The price of a strip maturing at a future date t reveals the discount factor and spot rate for cash flows at that date. All other safe cash payments on that date are valued at that same spot rate.

Investors and financial managers use the yield to maturity on a bond to summarize its prospective return. To calculate the yield to maturity on the 10-year 5s, you need to solve for y in the following equation:

$$\text{PV (\% of face value)} = \frac{5}{(1+y)} + \frac{5}{(1+y)^2} + \cdots + \frac{105}{(1+y)^{10}}$$

The yield to maturity discounts all cash payments at the same rate, even if spot rates differ. It is, therefore, rather like an average of the different spot rates.

A bond's maturity tells you the date of its final payment, but it is also useful to know the *average* time to each payment. This is called the bond's *duration*. Duration is important because there is a direct relationship between the duration of a bond and the exposure of its price to changes in interest rates. A change in interest rates has a greater effect on the price of long-duration bonds.

The term structure of interest rates is upward-sloping more often than not. This means that long-term spot rates are higher than short-term spot rates. But it does *not* mean that investing long is more profitable than investing short. The *expectations theory* of the term structure tells us that bonds are priced so that an investor who holds a succession of short bonds can expect the same return as another investor who holds a long bond. The expectations theory predicts an upward-sloping term structure only when future short-term interest rates are expected to rise.

The expectations theory cannot be a complete explanation of term structure if investors are worried about risk. Long bonds may be a safe haven for investors with long-term fixed liabilities, but other investors may not like the extra volatility of long-term bonds or may be concerned that a sudden burst of inflation may largely wipe out the real value of these bonds. These investors will be prepared to hold long-term bonds only if they offer the compensation of a higher rate of interest.

Bonds promise fixed nominal cash payments, but the *real* interest rate that they provide depends on inflation. The best-known theory about the effect of inflation on interest rates was suggested by Irving Fisher. He argued that the nominal, or money, rate of interest is equal to the required real rate plus the expected rate of inflation. If the expected inflation rate increases by 1%, so too will the money rate of interest. During the past 50 years, Fisher's simple theory has not done a bad job of explaining changes in short-term interest rates.

When you buy a U.S. Treasury bond, you can be fairly confident that you will get your money back. When you lend to a company, you face the risk that it will go belly-up and will not be able to repay its bonds. Defaults are rare for companies with investment-grade bond ratings, but investors worry nevertheless. Companies need to compensate investors for default risk by promising to pay higher rates of interest.

FURTHER READING

Some good general texts on fixed income markets are:

F. J. Fabozzi and S. V. Mann, *Handbook of Fixed Income Securities,* 8th ed. (New York: McGraw-Hill, 2012).

S. Sundaresan, *Fixed Income Markets and Their Derivatives,* 4th ed. (San Diego, CA: Academic Press, 2014).

B. Tuckman, *Fixed Income Securities: Tools for Today's Markets*(New York: Wiley, 2002).

P. Veronesi, *Fixed Income Securities: Valuation, Risk, and Risk Management* (New York: Wiley, 2010).

PROBLEM SETS

Select problems are available in McGraw-Hill's *Connect*. Answers to questions with an "*" are found in the Appendix.

1. **Bond prices and yields*** A 10-year bond is issued with a face value of $1,000, paying interest of $60 a year. If interest rates increase shortly after the bond is issued, what happens to the bond's
   a. Coupon rate?
   b. Price?
   c. Yield to maturity?

2. **Bond prices and yields** The following statements are true. Explain why.
   a. If a bond's coupon rate is higher than its yield to maturity, then the bond will sell for more than face value.
   b. If a bond's coupon rate is lower than its yield to maturity, then the bond's price will increase over its remaining maturity.

3. **Bond prices and yields** Construct some simple examples to illustrate your answers to the following:

   a. If interest rates rise, do bond prices rise or fall?

   b. If the bond yield to maturity is greater than the coupon, is the price of the bond greater or less than 100?

   c. If the price of a bond exceeds 100, is the yield to maturity greater or less than the coupon?

   d. Do high-coupon bonds sell at higher or lower prices than low-coupon bonds?

   e. If interest rates change, do the prices of high-coupon bonds change proportionately more than that of low-coupon bonds?

4. **Bond prices and yields*** A 10-year German government bond (bund) has a face value of €100 and a coupon rate of 5% paid annually. Assume that the interest rate (in euros) is equal to 6% per year. What is the bond's PV?

5. **Bond prices and yields** In November 2017, Treasury 4¾s of 2041 offered a semiannually compounded yield to maturity of 2.6%. Recognizing that coupons are paid semiannually, calculate the bond's price.

6. **Bond prices and yields** A 10-year U.S. Treasury bond with a face value of $1,000 pays a coupon of 5.5% (2.75% of face value every six months). The reported yield to maturity is 5.2% (a six-month discount rate of 5.2/2 = 2.6%).

   a. What is the present value of the bond?

   b. Generate a graph or table showing how the bond's present value changes for semiannually compounded interest rates between 1% and 15%.

7. **Bond prices and yields** Choose 10 U.S. Treasury bonds with different coupons and different maturities. Calculate how their prices would change if their yields to maturity increased by 1 percentage point. Are long- or short-term bonds most affected by the change in yields? Are high- or low-coupon bonds most affected? (Assume annual coupon payments.)

8. **Bond returns** If a bond's yield to maturity does not change, the return on the bond each year will be equal to the yield to maturity. Confirm this with a simple example of a four-year bond selling at a premium to face value. Now do the same for a four-year bond selling at a discount. For convenience, assume annual coupon payments.

9. **Bond returns***

   a. An 8%, five-year bond yields 6%. If this yield to maturity remains unchanged, what will be its price one year hence? Assume annual coupon payments and a face value of $1,000.

   b. What is the total return to an investor who held the bond over this year?

   c. What can you deduce about the relationship between the bond return over a particular period and the yields to maturity at the start and end of that period?

10. **Bond returns** A six-year government bond makes annual coupon payments of 5% and offers a yield of 3% annually compounded. Suppose that one year later the bond still yields 3%. What return has the bondholder earned over the 12-month period? Now suppose that the bond yields 2% at the end of the year. What return did the bondholder earn in this case?

11. **Duration*** True or false? Explain.

    a. Longer-maturity bonds necessarily have longer durations.

    b. The longer a bond's duration, the lower its volatility.

    c. Other things equal, the lower the bond coupon, the higher its volatility.

    d. If interest rates rise, bond durations rise also.

12. **Duration** Here are the prices of three bonds with 10-year maturities:

Bond Coupon (%)	Price (%)
2%	81.62%
4	98.39
8	133.42

If coupons are paid annually, which bond offered the highest yield to maturity? Which had the lowest? Which bonds had the longest and shortest durations?

13. **Duration** Calculate the durations and volatilities of securities A, B, and C. Their cash flows are shown below. The interest rate is 8%.

	Period 1	Period 2	Period 3
A	40	40	40
B	20	20	120
C	10	10	110

14. **Duration** Calculate durations and modified durations for the 3% bonds in Table 3.2. You can follow the procedure set out in Table 3.4 for the 9% coupon bonds. Confirm that modified duration closely predicts the impact of a 1% change in interest rates on the bond prices.

15. **Duration** Find the spreadsheet for Table 3.4 in Connect. Show how duration and volatility change if (a) the bond's coupon is 8% of face value and (b) the bond's yield is 6%. Explain your finding.

16. **Duration** The formula for the duration of a perpetual bond that makes an equal payment each year in perpetuity is (1 + yield)/yield. If each bond yields 5%, which has the longer duration—a perpetual bond or a 15-year zero-coupon bond? What if the yield is 10%?

17. **Spot interest rates and yields** Which comes first in the market for U.S. Treasury bonds:

    a. Spot interest rates or yields to maturity?

    b. Bond prices or yields to maturity?

18. **Spot interest rates and yields** Look again at Table 3.6. Suppose that spot interest rates all change to 4%—a "flat" term structure of interest rates.

    a. What is the new yield to maturity for each bond in the table?

    b. Recalculate the price of bond A.

19. **Spot interest rates and yields** Look again at Table 3.6. Suppose the spot interest rates change to the following *downward-sloping* term structure: r_1 = 4.6%, r_2 = 4.4%, r_3 = 4.2%, and r_4 = 4.0%. Recalculate discount factors, bond prices, and yields to maturity for each of the bonds listed in the table.

20. **Spot interest rates and yields** Look at the spot interest rates shown in Problem 19. Suppose that someone told you that the five-year spot interest rate was 2.5%. Why would you not believe him? How could you make money if he was right? What is the minimum sensible value for the five-year spot rate?

21. **Spot interest rates and yields** Assume annual coupons.

    a. What is the formula for the value of a two-year, 5% bond in terms of spot rates?

    b. What is the formula for its value in terms of yield to maturity?

    c. If the two-year spot rate is higher than the one-year rate, is the yield to maturity greater or less than the two-year spot rate?

22. **Spot interest rates and yields** A 6% six-year bond yields 12% and a 10% six-year bond yields 8%. Calculate the six-year spot rate. Assume annual coupon payments. (*Hint:* What would be your cash flows if you bought 1.2 10% bonds?)

23. **Spot interest rates and yields** Is the yield on high-coupon bonds more likely to be higher than that on low-coupon bonds when the term structure is upward-sloping or when it is downward-sloping? Explain.

24. **Spot interest rates and yields*** You have estimated spot rates as follows:

    $r_1 = 5.00\%$, $r_2 = 5.40\%$, $r_3 = 5.70\%$, $r_4 = 5.90\%$, $r_5 = 6.00\%$.

    a. What are the discount factors for each date (that is, the present value of $1 paid in year t)?

    b. Calculate the PV of the following bonds assuming annual coupons and face values of $1,000: (i) 5%, two-year bond; (ii) 5%, five-year bond; and (iii) 10%, five-year bond.

25. Look again at the bonds in part (b) of Problem 24.

    a. Explain intuitively why the yield to maturity on the 10% bond is less than that on the 5% bond.

    b. What should be the yield to maturity on a five-year zero-coupon bond?

    c. Show that the correct yield to maturity on a five-year annuity is 5.75%.

    d. Explain intuitively why the yield on the five-year bonds described in part (b) of Problem 24 must lie between the yield on a five-year zero-coupon bond and a five-year annuity.

26. **Measuring term structure*** The following table shows the prices of a sample of Narnian Treasury strips in December 2018. Each strip makes a single payment of $1,000 at maturity.

    a. Calculate the annually compounded, spot interest rate for each year.

    b. Is the term structure upward- or downward-sloping or flat?

    c. Would you expect the yield on a coupon bond maturing in December 2023 to be higher or lower than the yield on the 2020 strip?

Maturity	Price (%)
December 2020	90.703%
December 2021	85.892
December 2022	81.491
December 2023	77.243

27. **Term-structure theories** The one-year spot interest rate is $r_1 = 5\%$ and the two-year rate is $r_2 = 6\%$. If the expectations theory is correct, what is the expected one-year interest rate in one year's time?

28. **Term-structure theories** Look again at the spot interest rates shown in Problem 24. What can you deduce about the one-year spot interest rate in three years if:

    a. The expectations theory of term structure is right?

    b. Investing in long-term bonds carries additional risks?

29. **Real interest rates** The two-year interest rate is 10% and the expected annual inflation rate is 5%.

    a. What is the expected real interest rate?

    b. If the expected rate of inflation suddenly rises to 7%, what does Fisher's theory say about how the real interest rate will change? What about the nominal rate?

30. **Nominal and real returns*** Suppose that you buy a two-year 8% bond at its face value.

   a. What will be your *total* nominal return over the two years if inflation is 3% in the first year and 5% in the second? What will be your *total* real return?

   b. Now suppose that the bond is a TIPS. What will be your *total* two-year real and nominal returns?

31. **Bond ratings** A bond's credit rating provides a guide to its price. In the fall of 2017 Aaa bonds yielded 3.6% and Baa bonds yielded 4.3%. If some bad news causes a 10% five-year bond to be unexpectedly downrated from Aaa to Baa, what would be the effect on the bond price? (Assume annual coupons.)

CHALLENGE

32. **Bond prices and yields** Write a spreadsheet program to construct a series of bond tables that show the present value of a bond given the coupon rate, maturity, and yield to maturity. Assume that coupon payments are semiannual and yields are compounded semiannually.

33. **Price and spot interest rates** Find the arbitrage opportunity(ies). Assume for simplicity that coupons are paid annually. In each case, the face value of the bond is $1,000.

Bond	Maturity (years)	Coupon ($)	Price ($)
A	3	0	751.30
B	4	50	842.30
C	4	120	1,065.28
D	4	100	980.57
E	3	140	1,120.12
F	3	70	1,001.62
G	2	0	834.00

34. **Duration** The duration of a bond that makes an equal payment each year in perpetuity is (1 + yield)/yield. Prove it.

35. **Prices and spot interest rates** What spot interest rates are implied by the following Treasury bonds? Assume for simplicity that the bonds pay annual coupons. The price of a one-year strip is 97.56%, and the price of a four-year strip is 87.48%.

Maturity (years)	Coupon	Price (%)
5	2	92.89
5	3	97.43
3	5	105.42

36. **Prices and spot interest rates** Look one more time at Table 3.6.

   a. Suppose you knew the bond prices but not the spot interest rates. Explain how you would calculate the spot rates. (*Hint:* You have four unknown spot rates, so you need four equations.)

   b. Suppose that you could buy bond C in large quantities at $1,040 rather than at its equilibrium price of $1,076.20. Show how you could make a zillion dollars without taking on any risk.

The websites of *The Wall Street Journal* (**www.wsj.com**) and the *Financial Times* (**www.ft.com**) are wonderful sources of market data. You should become familiar with them.

1. Use **www.wsj.com** to answer the following questions:

   a. Find the prices of coupon strips. Use these prices to plot the term structure. If the expectations theory is correct, what is the expected one-year interest rate three years hence?

   b. Find a three- or four-year bond and construct a package of coupon and principal strips that provides the same cash flows. The law of one price predicts that the cost of the package should be very close to that of the bond. Is it?

   c. Find a long-term Treasury bond with a low coupon and calculate its duration. Now find another bond with a similar maturity and a higher coupon. Which has the longer duration?

   d. Look up the yields on 10-year nominal Treasury bonds and on TIPS. If you are confident that inflation will average 2% a year, which bond will provide the higher real return?

2. Bond transactions are reported on FINRA's TRACE service, which was the source of the data for Table 3.7. Use the Advanced Search facility in TRACE to find bond prices for Johnson & Johnson (JNJ), Walmart (WMT), Disney (DIS), SunTrust Banks (STI), and U.S. Steel (X). If possible, exclude callable issues that the company can buy back. What has happened to the yields of these companies' bonds? (You will find that bonds issued by the same company may have very different yields, so you will need to use your best judgment to answer this question.)

The Value of Common Stocks

We should warn you that being a financial expert has its occupational hazards. One is being cornered at cocktail parties by people who are eager to explain their system for making creamy profits by investing in common stocks. One of the few good things about a financial crisis is that these bores tend to disappear, at least temporarily.

We may exaggerate the perils of the trade. The point is that there is no easy way to ensure superior investment performance. Therefore, when in this chapter we use present value calculations to value common stocks, we are not providing a key to investment success nor attempting to turn you into a cocktail-party bore. We are just explaining the fundamental reasons some stocks are more valuable than others.

Why should you care about fundamentals? If you want to know what a stock is worth, why can't you just look up the price on the Internet?

There are at least three reasons you should care. First, changes in the price of a public company's shares reveal how well the company is doing financially, at least in the eyes of investors, and usually determine a large fraction of top management's compensation. If your company is going to use its stock price to assess performance, you had better understand what determines the price.

Second, many companies are not public. A private company may want to understand what its stock is worth or what it would be worth if it were traded.

Third, a firm that acts in it shareholders' interest should accept capital investments that increase the value of their stake in the firm. In order to do this, the financial manager needs to understand what determines the value of the firm's shares.

We begin with a look at how stocks are traded. Then we explain the basic principles of share valuation and the use of discounted-cash-flow (DCF) models to estimate expected rates of return. Later in the chapter, we show how these DCF models can be used to value entire businesses rather than individual shares.

We will also explain the fundamental difference between growth and income stocks. A growth stock doesn't just grow; its future investments are also expected to earn rates of return that are higher than the cost of capital. It's the *combination* of growth and superior returns that generates high price–earnings ratios for growth stocks.

Still another warning: Everybody knows that common stocks are risky and that some are more risky than others. Therefore, investors will not commit their hard-earned cash to stocks unless the expected rates of return are commensurate with the risks. But we say next to nothing in this chapter about the linkages between risk and expected return. A more careful treatment of risk starts in Chapter 7.

4-1 How Common Stocks Are Traded

Boeing has 596 million shares outstanding. Shareholders include large pension funds and insurance companies that each own millions of shares, as well as individuals who own a handful. If you owned one Boeing share, you would own .0000002% of the company and have a claim on the same tiny fraction of its profits. Of course, the more shares you own, the larger your "share" of the company.

If Boeing wishes to raise new capital, it can do so either by borrowing or by selling new shares to investors. Sales of shares to raise new capital are said to occur in the *primary market.* But most trades in Boeing take place on the stock exchange, where investors buy and sell existing Boeing shares. Stock exchanges are really markets for secondhand shares, but they prefer to describe themselves as *secondary markets,* which sounds more important.

BEYOND THE PAGE

Major world stock exchanges

mhhe.com/brealey13e

The two principal U.S. stock exchanges are the New York Stock Exchange and Nasdaq. Both compete vigorously for business and just as vigorously tout the advantages of their trading systems. In addition to the NYSE and Nasdaq, there are *electronic communication networks (ECNs)* that connect traders with each other. Large U.S. companies may also arrange for their shares to be traded on foreign exchanges, such as the London exchange or the Euronext exchange in Paris. At the same time, many foreign companies are listed on the U.S. exchanges. For example, the NYSE trades shares in Sony, Royal Dutch Shell, Canadian Pacific, Tata Motors, Deutsche Bank, Telefonica Brasil, China Eastern Airlines, and more than 500 other companies.

Suppose that Ms. Jones, a long-time Boeing shareholder, no longer wishes to hold her shares. She can sell them via the stock exchange to Mr. Brown, who wants to increase his stake in the firm. The transaction merely transfers partial ownership of the firm from one investor to another. No new shares are created, and Boeing will neither care nor know that the trade has taken place.

Ms. Jones and Mr. Brown do not trade the Boeing shares themselves. Instead, their orders must go through a brokerage firm. Ms. Jones, who is anxious to sell, might give her broker a *market order* to sell stock at the best available price. On the other hand, Mr. Brown might state a price limit at which he is willing to buy Boeing stock. If his *limit order* cannot be executed immediately, it is recorded in the exchange's limit order book until it can be executed.

Table 4.1 shows a portion of the limit order book for Boeing from the BATS Exchange, one of the largest electronic markets. The bid prices on the left are the prices (and number of shares) at which investors are currently willing to buy. The ask prices on the right are those at which investors are prepared to sell. The prices are arranged from best to worst, so the highest bids and lowest asks are at the top of the list. The broker might electronically enter Ms. Jones's market order to sell 100 shares on the BATS Exchange, where it would be

Bid		Ask	
Price	Shares	Price	Shares
263.76	1,100	264.07	200
263.73	100	264.12	1
263.67	100	264.13	100
263.61	100	264.18	200

❭**TABLE 4.1**   A portion of the limit order book for Boeing on the BATS BZX Exchange, November 20, 2017, at 09:51:03

matched with the best offer to buy, which at that moment was $263.76 a share. A market order to buy would be matched with the best ask price, $264.07. The bid-ask spread at that moment was, therefore, 31 cents per share.

When they transact on the NYSE or one of the electronic markets, Brown and Jones are participating in a huge auction market in which the exchange matches up the orders of thousands of investors. Most major exchanges around the world, including the Tokyo, Shanghai, London stock exchanges and the Deutsche Börse, are also auction markets, but the auctioneer in these cases is a computer.[1] This means that there is no stock exchange floor to show on the evening news and no one needs to ring a bell to start trading.

Nasdaq is not an auction market. All trades on Nasdaq take place between the investor and one of a group of professional dealers who are prepared to buy and sell stock. Dealer markets are common for other financial instruments. For example, most bonds are traded in dealer markets.

Trading Results for Boeing

You can track trades in Boeing or other public corporations on the Internet. For example, if you go to **finance.yahoo.com** and enter the ticker symbol BA under "Quote Lookup," you will see results like the table below.[2] We will focus here on some of the more important entries.

Boeing's closing price on November 20, 2017, was $264.63, up $2.37, or .90% from the previous day's close. Boeing had 595.58 million shares outstanding, so its market cap (shorthand for *market capitalization*) was 595.58 × $264.63 = $157.61 billion.

Boeing Common Stock (NYSE)			
264.63 +2.37 (+0.90%) Nov 20 4:00PM EST			
Previous close	262.26	Market cap	157.61B
Open	263.00	Beta	1.31
Day's range	262.76-265.62	P/E ratio (TTM)	23.2
52-week range	146.52-267.62	EPS (TTM)	11.41
Volume	2,404,762	Forward dividend	5.68
Average volume	3,187,640	Dividend yield	2.17%

Source: finance.yahoo.com.

Boeing's earnings per share (EPS) over the previous 12 months were $11.41 ("TTM" stands for "trailing 12 months"). The ratio of stock price to EPS (the P/E ratio) was 23.2. Notice that this P/E ratio uses past EPS. P/E ratios using forecasted EPS are generally more useful. Security analysts forecasted an increase in Boeing's EPS to 11.68 per share for 2018, which gives a *forward* P/E of 22.7.[3]

Boeing paid a cash dividend of $5.68 per share per year, so its *dividend yield* (the ratio of dividend to price) was 2.17%.

---

[1] Trades are still made face to face on the floor of the NYSE, but computerized trading is taking over. In 2006, the NYSE merged with Archipelago, an electronic trading system, and transformed itself into a public corporation. The following year, it merged with Euronext, an electronic trading system in Europe. It is now owned by Intercontinental Exchange Inc., a U.S.-based network of exchanges and clearing houses.

[2] Other good sources of trading data are **moneycentral.msn.com, finance.google.com,** or the online edition of *The Wall Street Journal* at **www.wsj.com** (look for the "Market" and then "Market Data" tabs).

[3] Yahoo! Finance provides extensive information and statistics on traded companies, including summaries of analyst forecasts. For example, you can click on "Statistics" or "Analyst Estimates."

Boeing's beta of 1.31 measures the market risk of Boeing's stock. We explain betas in Chapter 7.

Boeing stock was a wonderful investment in 2017: Its price was up 81% in the 12 months previous to the quotes summarized here. Buying stocks is a risky occupation, however. Take GE as an example. GE used to be one of the most powerful and admired U.S. companies. But GE stock fell by 40% over the 12 months ending on November 16, 2017—a period in which the S&P 500 market index gained 18.5%. The stock fell by 23% in the last month of that period when its new CEO cut GE's dividend in half and announced a plan for drastic restructuring. There weren't many GE stockholders piping up at cocktail parties over the 2017 holiday season; they either kept quiet or were not invited.

Most of the trading on the NYSE and Nasdaq is in ordinary common stocks, but other securities are traded also, including preferred shares, which we cover in Chapter 14, and warrants, which we cover in Chapter 21. Investors can also choose from hundreds of *exchange-traded funds (ETFs),* which are portfolios of stocks that can be bought or sold in a single trade. With a few exceptions ETFs are not actively managed. Many simply aim to track a well-known market index such as the Dow Jones Industrial Average or the S&P 500. Others track specific industries or commodities. (We discuss ETFs more fully in Chapter 14.) You can also buy shares in closed-end mutual funds[4] that invest in portfolios of securities. These include country funds, for example, the Mexico and India funds, that invest in portfolios of stocks in specific countries. Unlike ETFs, most closed-end funds are actively managed and seek to "beat the market."

4-2   How Common Stocks Are Valued

Finding the value of the stock of Boeing or GE may sound like a simple problem. Public companies publish quarterly and annual balance sheets, which list the value of the company's assets and liabilities. For example, at the end of September 2017, the *book value* of all GE's assets—plant and machinery, inventories of materials, cash in the bank, and so on—was $378 billion. GE's liabilities—money that it owes the banks, taxes that are due to be paid, and the like—amounted to $298.5 billion. The difference between the value of the assets and the liabilities was just over $79.5 billion. This was the book value of GE's equity.[5]

Book value is a reassuringly definite number. Each year KPMG, one of America's largest accounting firms, gives its opinion that GE's financial statements present fairly in all material respects the company's financial position, in conformity with U.S. generally accepted accounting principles (commonly called GAAP). However, the book value of GE's assets measures only their original (or "historical") cost less an allowance for depreciation. This may not be a good guide to what those assets are worth today.

One can go on and on about the deficiencies of book value as a measure of market value. Book values are historical costs that do not incorporate inflation. (Countries with high or volatile inflation often require inflation-adjusted book values, however.) Book values usually exclude intangible assets such as trademarks and patents. Also accountants simply add up the book values of individual assets, and thus do not capture *going-concern value.* Going-concern value is created when a collection of assets is organized into a healthy operating business.

---

[4]*Closed-end* mutual funds issue shares that are traded on stock exchanges. *Open-end* funds are not traded on exchanges. Investors in open-end funds transact directly with the fund. The fund issues new shares to investors and redeems shares from investors who want to withdraw money from the fund.

[5]GE's equity accounts included $3.4 billion for "Misc. stocks options warrants." The book value of GE's common stock was $79.5 − 3.4 = $76.1 billion.

Book values can nevertheless be a useful benchmark. Suppose, for example, that the aggregate value of all of Holstein Oil's shares is $900 million. Its book value of equity is $450 million. A financial analyst might say, "Holstein sells for two times book value. It has doubled shareholders' cumulative past investment in the company." She might also say, "Holstein's market value added is $900 – 450 = $450 million. (There is more on *market value added* in Chapter 28.)

Book values may also be useful clues about *liquidation value*. Liquidation value is what investors get when a failed company is shut down and its assets are sold off. Book values of "hard" assets like land, buildings, vehicles, and machinery can indicate possible liquidation values.

Intangible "soft" assets can be important even in liquidation, however. Eastman Kodak provides a good example. Kodak, which was one of the Nifty Fifty growth stocks of the 1960s, suffered a long decline and finally filed for bankruptcy in January 2012. What was one of its most valuable assets in bankruptcy? Its portfolio of 79,000 patents, which was subsequently sold for $525 million.

Valuation by Comparables

When financial analysts need to value a business, they often start by identifying a sample of similar firms as potential *comparables*. They then examine how much investors in the comparable companies are prepared to pay per dollar of earnings or book assets. They see what the business would be worth if it traded at the comparables' price–earnings or price-to-book-value ratios. This valuation approach is called *valuation by comparables*.

Table 4.2 tries out this valuation method for three companies and industries. Let's start with Union Pacific (UNP). In November 2017, UNP's stock was trading around $117. Security

Company	Stock Price	P/E	P/B	Comparable	P/E	P/B
Union Pacific (railroad)	$117	17.85	4.73	Canadian Pacific	16.66	5.37
				CSX	18.10	4.05
				Kansas City Southern	17.39	2.58
				Norfolk Southern	17.79	2.88
				Average	17.49	3.72
Johnson & Johnson (health care and pharmaceuticals)	$139	17.76	5.20	Astra Zeneca	20.03	6.20
				Merck	13.44	3.80
				Novartis	15.67	2.77
				Pfizer	12.87	3.61
				Average	15.50	4.10
Devon Energy (oil and gas)	$38	17.27	2.90	Apache	93.45	2.27
				Anadarko	–75.79	2.30
				Marathon	–78.39	1.02
				EOG Resources	58.41	4.22
				Average	–0.58	2.45

❭ **TABLE 4.2**   Stock price, price–earnings (P/E), and market-book (P/B) in November 2017 for three companies and potential comparables

Source: finance.yahoo.com.

analysts were forecasting earnings per share (EPS) for 2018 at $6.55, giving a "forward" price–earnings ratio of P/E = 17.85.[6] UNP's market–book ratio (price divided by book value per share) was P/B = 4.73.

P/Es and P/Bs for several of UNP's competitors are reported on the right-hand side of the table. Notice that UNP's P/E is close to the P/Es of these comparables. If you didn't know UNP's stock price, you could get an estimate by multiplying UNP's forecasted EPS of $6.55 by 17.49, the average P/E for the comparables. The resulting estimate of $114.56 would be almost spot on. On the other hand, UNP's P/B is higher than all the comparables' P/Bs except for that of Canadian Pacific. If you had used the average price-to-book ratio for the comparables to value UNP, you would have come up with an underestimate of UNP's actual share price.

Look now at Johnson & Johnson (J&J) and its four comparables in Table 4.2. In this case, the P/B ratio for J&J is higher than for the comparables (5.2 versus an average of 4.1). The average P/E for J&J is also higher (17.8 versus 15.5). An estimate of the value of J&J based on the comparables' P/Es and P/Bs would be too low. Comparing the estimate to J&J's actual stock price could still be worthwhile, however, if it leads you to ask *why* J&J was more attractive to investors.

The ratios for Devon Energy in Table 4.2 illustrate the potential difficulties with valuation by comparables. There is a huge variation in the P/E ratios of the comparables. Anadarko and Marathon had *negative* P/E ratios; their stock prices were of course positive, but their operations had been battered by a sudden fall in oil prices, and their forecasted earnings for the next year were negative. The average P/E of –.58 for the comparables is meaningless.[7] The comparables' average P/B is more informative.

The P/E ratios for the oil companies in Table 4.2 illustrate what can go wrong with the ratios in hard times when firms makes losses. P/E ratios are also almost useless as a guide to the value of new start-ups, most of which do not have any earnings to compare.

Such difficulties do not invalidate the use of comparables to value businesses. Maybe Table 4.2 doesn't show the companies most closely similar to Devon. A financial manager or analyst would need to dig deeper to understand Devon's industry and its competitors. Also, the method might work better with different ratios.[8]

Of course, investors did not need valuation by comparables to value Devon Energy or the other companies in Table 4.2. They are all public companies with actively traded shares. But you may find valuation by comparables useful when you *don't* have a stock price. For example, in August 2017 the mining giant, BHP Billiton, announced plans to sell its U.S. shale business. Preliminary estimates put the business's value at $8 to $10 billion. It's a safe bet that BHP and its advisers were burning the midnight oil and doing their best to identify the best comparables and check what the assets would be worth if they traded at the comparables' P/E and P/B ratios.

But BHP would need to be cautious. As Table 4.2 shows, these ratios can vary widely even within the same industry. To understand why this is so, we need to look more carefully at what determines a stock's market value. We start by connecting stock prices to the cash flows that stockholders receive from the company in the form of cash dividends. This will lead us to a discounted-cash-flow (DCF) model of stock prices.

---

[6]UNP's EPS for the most recent, or "trailing" 12 months were $5.51, so its trailing P/E was 117/5.51 = 21.15. Trailing P/Es are often quoted, but forward P/Es are more useful if good forecasts are available. Investors learn from the past but are mostly interested in the future.

[7]The P/E ratios for Devon's comparables stand as a warning to be extra careful when averaging P/Es. Watch out for companies with earnings close to zero or negative. One company with zero earnings and, therefore, an infinite P/E generates an infinite average P/E. Often, it's safer to use median P/Es than averages.

[8]Financial analysts often use ratios of EBIT (earnings before interest and taxes) or EBITDA (earnings before interest, taxes, depreciation, and amortization) to enterprise value (the sum of outstanding debt and the market cap of equity). EBIT or EBITDA ratios are less sensitive than P/E ratios to differences in financing. In Chapter 19, we cover valuation when financing comes from a mix of debt and equity. We discuss other ratios in Chapter 28.

Stock Prices and Dividends

Not all companies pay dividends. Rapidly growing companies typically reinvest earnings instead of paying out cash. But most mature, profitable companies do pay regular cash dividends.

Think back to Chapter 3, where we explained how bonds are valued. The market value of a bond equals the discounted present value (PV) of the cash flows (interest and principal payments) that the bond will pay out over its lifetime. Let's import and apply this idea to common stocks. The future cash flows to the owner of a share of common stock are the future dividends per share that the company will pay out. Thus, the logic of discounted cash flow suggests

$$PV(\text{share of stock}) = PV(\text{expected future dividends per share})$$

At first glance, this statement may seem surprising. Investors hope for capital gains as well as dividends. That is, they hope to sell stocks for more than they paid for them. Why doesn't the PV of a stock depend on capital gains? As we now explain, there is no inconsistency.

Today's Price   If you own a share of common stock, your cash payoff comes in two forms: (1) cash dividends and (2) capital gains or losses. Suppose that the current price of a share is P_0, that the expected price at the end of a year is P_1, and that the expected dividend per share is DIV_1. The rate of return that investors expect from this share over the next year is defined as the expected dividend per share DIV_1 plus the expected price appreciation per share $P_1 - P_0$, all divided by the price at the start of the year P_0:

$$\text{Expected return} = r = \frac{DIV_1 + P_1 - P_0}{P_0}$$

Suppose Fledgling Electronics stock is selling for $100 a share ($P_0 = 100$). Investors expect a $5 cash dividend over the next year ($DIV_1 = 5$). They also expect the stock to sell for $110 a year, hence ($P_1 = 110$). Then the expected return to the stockholders is 15%:

$$r = \frac{5 + 110 - 100}{100} = .15, \text{ or } 15\%$$

On the other hand, if you are given investors' forecasts of dividend and price and the expected return offered by other equally risky stocks, you can predict today's price:

$$\text{Price} = P_0 = \frac{DIV_1 + P_1}{1 + r}$$

For Fledgling Electronics, $DIV_1 = 5$ and $P_1 = 110$. If r, the expected return for Fledgling is 15%, then today's price should be $100:

$$P_0 = \frac{5 + 110}{1.15} = \$100$$

What exactly is the discount rate, r, in this calculation? It's called the **market capitalization rate** or **cost of equity capital,** which are just alternative names for the opportunity cost of capital, defined as the expected return on other securities with the same risks as Fledgling shares.

Many stocks will be safer than Fledgling and many riskier. But among the thousands of traded stocks, there will be a group with essentially the same risks. Call this group Fledgling's *risk class.* Then all stocks in this risk class have to be priced to offer the same expected rate of return.

Let's suppose that the other securities in Fledgling's risk class all offer the same 15% expected return. Then $100 per share has to be the right price for Fledgling stock. In fact, it is the only possible price. What if Fledgling's price were above $P_0 = \$100$? In this case, the expected return would be less than 15%. Investors would shift their capital to the other securities and, in the process, would force down the price of Fledgling stock. If P_0 were less than \$100, the process would reverse. Investors would rush to buy, forcing the price up to \$100. Therefore, at each point in time, *all securities in an equivalent risk class are priced to offer the same expected return*. This is a condition for equilibrium in well-functioning capital markets. It is also common sense.

Next Year's Price?   We have managed to explain today's stock price P_0 in terms of the dividend DIV_1 and the expected price next year P_1. Future stock prices are not easy things to forecast directly. But think about what determines next year's price. If our price formula holds now, it ought to hold then as well:

$$P_1 = \frac{DIV_2 + P_2}{1 + r}$$

That is, a year from now, investors will be looking out at dividends in year 2 and price at the end of year 2. Thus, we can forecast P_1 by forecasting DIV_2 and P_2, and we can express P_0 in terms of DIV_1, DIV_2, and P_2:

$$P_0 = \frac{1}{1 + r}(DIV_1 + P_1) = \frac{1}{1 + r}\left(DIV_1 + \frac{DIV_2 + P_2}{1 + r}\right) = \frac{DIV_1}{1 + r} + \frac{DIV_2 + P_2}{(1 + r)^2}$$

Take Fledgling Electronics. A plausible explanation for why investors expect its stock price to rise by the end of the first year is that they expect higher dividends and still more capital gains in the second. For example, suppose that they are looking today for dividends of \$5.50 in year 2 and a subsequent price of \$121. That implies a price at the end of year 1 of

$$P_1 = \frac{5.50 + 121}{1.15} = \$110$$

Today's price can then be computed either from our original formula

$$P_0 = \frac{DIV_1 + P_1}{1 + r} = \frac{5.00 + 110}{1.15} = \$100$$

or from our expanded formula

$$P_0 = \frac{DIV_1}{1 + r} + \frac{DIV_2 + P_2}{(1 + r)^2} = \frac{5.00}{1.15} + \frac{5.50 + 121}{(1.15)^2} = \$100$$

We have succeeded in relating today's price to the forecasted dividends for two years (DIV_1 and DIV_2) plus the forecasted price at the end of the *second* year (P_2). You will not be surprised to learn that we could go on to replace P_2 by $(DIV_3 + P_3)/(1 + r)$ and relate today's price to the forecasted dividends for three years (DIV_1, DIV_2, and DIV_3) plus the forecasted price at the end of the third year (P_3). In fact, we can look as far out into the future as we like, removing Ps as we go. Let us call this final period H. This gives us a general stock price formula:

$$P_0 = \frac{DIV_1}{1 + r} + \frac{DIV_2}{(1 + r)^2} + \cdots + \frac{DIV_H + P_H}{(1 + r)^H}$$

$$= \sum_{t=1}^{H} \frac{DIV_t}{(1 + r)^t} + \frac{P_H}{(1 + r)^H}$$

The expression $\sum_{t=1}^{H}$ indicates the sum of the discounted dividends from year 1 to year H.

	Expected Future Values		Present Values		
Horizon Period (*H*)	Dividend (DIV$_t$)	Price (*P$_t$*)	Cumulative Dividends	Future Price	Total
0	—	100	—	—	100
1	5.00	110	4.35	95.65	100
2	5.50	121	8.51	91.49	100
3	6.05	133.10	12.48	87.52	100
4	6.66	146.41	16.29	83.71	100
10	11.79	259.37	35.89	64.11	100
20	30.58	672.75	58.89	41.11	100
50	533.59	11,739.09	89.17	10.83	100
100	62,639.15	1,378,061.23	98.83	1.17	100

❭**TABLE 4.3**   Applying the stock valuation formula to Fledgling Electronics

Assumptions:
1. Dividends increase at 10% per year, compounded.
2. Discount rate (cost of equity or market capitalization rate) is 15%.

Table 4.3 continues the Fledgling Electronics example for various time horizons, assuming that the dividends are expected to increase at a steady 10% compound rate. The expected price *Pt* increases at the same rate each year. Each line in the table represents an application of our general formula for a different value of *H*. Figure 4.1 is a graph of the table. Each column shows the present value of the dividends up to the time horizon and the present value of the price at the horizon. As the horizon recedes, the dividend stream accounts for an increasing proportion of present value, but the *total* present value of dividends plus terminal price always equals $100.

How far out could we look? In principle, the horizon period *H* could be infinitely distant. Common stocks do not expire of old age. Barring such corporate hazards as bankruptcy or acquisition, they are immortal. As *H* approaches infinity, the present value of the terminal price ought to approach zero, as it does in the final column of Figure 4.1. We can, therefore, forget about the terminal price entirely and express today's price as the present value of a perpetual stream of cash dividends. This is usually written as

$$P_0 = \sum_{t=1}^{\infty} \frac{\text{DIV}_t}{(1+r)^t}$$

where ∞ indicates infinity. This formula is the **DCF** or **dividend discount model** of stock prices. It's another present value formula.[9] We discount the cash flows—in this case, the dividend stream—by the return that can be earned in the capital market on securities of equivalent risk. Some find the DCF formula implausible because it seems to ignore capital gains. But we know that the formula was *derived* from the assumption that price in any period is determined by expected dividends *and* capital gains over the next period.

Notice that it is *not* correct to say that the value of a share is equal to the sum of the discounted stream of *earnings* per share. Earnings are generally larger than dividends because part of those earnings is reinvested in new plant, equipment, and working capital. Discounting

---

[9]Notice that this DCF formula uses a single discount rate for all future cash flows. This implicitly assumes that the company is all-equity-financed or that the fractions of debt and equity will stay constant. Chapters 17 through 19 discuss how the cost of equity changes when debt ratios change.

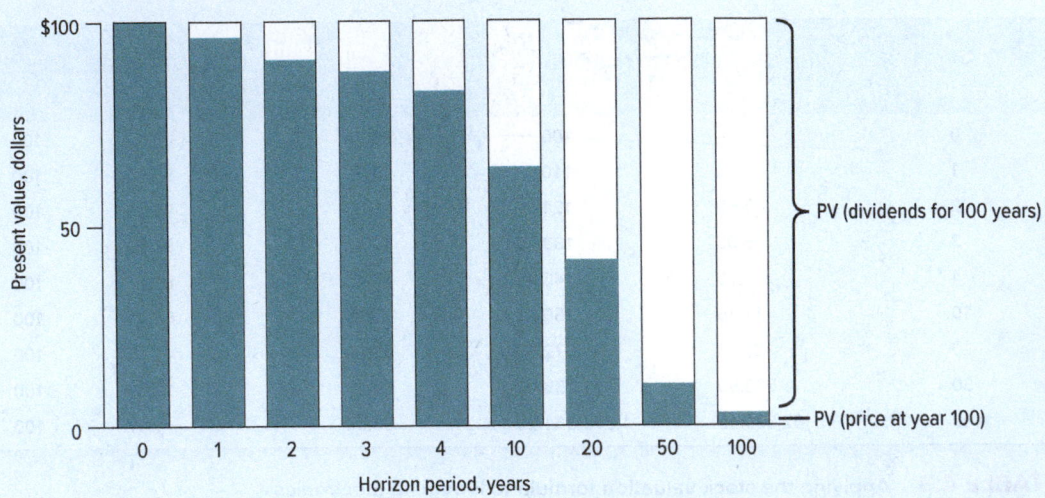

FIGURE 4.1

As your horizon recedes, the present value of the future price (shaded area) declines but the present value of the stream of dividends (unshaded area) increases. The total present value (future price and dividends) remains the same.

earnings would recognize the rewards of that investment (higher *future* earnings and dividends) but not the sacrifice (a lower dividend *today*). The correct formulation states that share value is equal to the discounted stream of dividends per share. Share price is connected to future earnings per share, but by a different formula, which we cover later in this chapter.

Although mature companies generally pay cash dividends, thousands of companies do not. For example, Amazon has never paid a dividend, yet it is a successful company with a market capitalization in January 2018 of $620 billion. Why would a successful company decide *not* to pay cash dividends? There are at least two reasons. First, a growing company may maximize value by investing all its earnings rather than paying out a dividend. The shareholders are better off with this policy, provided that the investments offer an expected rate of return higher than shareholders could get by investing on their own. In other words, shareholder value is maximized if the firm invests in projects that can earn more than the opportunity cost of capital. If such projects are plentiful, shareholders will be prepared to forgo immediate dividends. They will be happy to wait and receive deferred dividends.[10]

The dividend discount model is still logically correct for growth companies, but difficult to use when cash dividends are far in the future. In this case, most analysts switch to valuation by comparables or to earnings-based formulas, which we cover in Section 4-4.

Second, a company may pay out cash not as dividends but by repurchasing shares from stockholders. We cover the choice between dividends and repurchases in Chapter 16, where we also explain why repurchases do not invalidate the dividend discount model.[11]

---

[10]The deferred payout may come all at once if the company is taken over by another. The selling price per share is equivalent to a bumper dividend.

[11]Notice that we have derived the dividend discount model using *dividends per share*. Paying out cash for repurchases rather than cash dividends reduces the number of shares outstanding and increases future earnings and dividends per share. The more shares repurchased, the faster the growth of earnings and dividends per shares. Thus, repurchases benefit shareholders who do not sell as well as those who do sell. We show some examples in Chapter 16.

Nevertheless, the dividend discount model can be difficult to deploy if repurchases are irregular and unpredictable. In these cases, it can be better to start by calculating the present value of the total free cash flow available for dividends and repurchases. Discounting free cash flow gives the present value of the company as a whole. Dividing by the current number of shares outstanding gives present value per share. We cover this valuation method in Section 4-5.

The next section considers simplified versions of the dividend discount model.

4-3   Estimating the Cost of Equity Capital

In Chapter 2, we encountered some simplified versions of the basic present value formula. Let us see whether they offer any insights into stock values. Suppose, for example, that we forecast a constant growth rate for a company's dividends. This does not preclude year-to-year deviations from the forecast: It means only that *expected* dividends grow at a constant rate. Such an investment would be just another example of the growing perpetuity that we valued in Chapter 2. To find its present value we must divide the first year's cash payment by the difference between the discount rate and the growth rate:

$$P_0 = \frac{DIV_1}{r - g}$$

Remember that we can use this formula only when g, the anticipated growth rate, is less than r, the discount rate. As g approaches r, the stock price becomes infinite. Obviously, r must be greater than g if growth really is perpetual.

Our growing perpetuity formula explains P_0 in terms of next year's expected dividend DIV_1, the projected growth trend g, and the expected rate of return on other securities of comparable risk r. Alternatively, the formula can be turned around to obtain an estimate of r from DIV_1, P_0, and g:

$$r = \frac{DIV_1}{P_0} + g$$

The expected return equals the **dividend yield** (DIV_1/P_0) plus the expected rate of growth in dividends (g).

These two formulas are much easier to work with than the general statement that "price equals the present value of expected future dividends."[12] Here is a practical example.

Using the DCF Model to Set Water, Gas, and Electricity Prices

In the United States, the prices charged by local water, electric, and gas utilities are regulated by state commissions. The regulators try to keep consumer prices down but are supposed to allow the utilities to earn a fair rate of return. But what is fair? It is usually interpreted as r, the market capitalization rate for the firm's common stock. In other words, the fair rate of return on equity for a public utility ought to be the cost of equity—that is, the rate offered by securities that have the same risk as the utility's common stock.[13]

---

[12]These formulas were first developed in 1938 by Williams and were rediscovered by Gordon and Shapiro. See J. B. Williams, *The Theory of Investment Value* (Cambridge, MA: Harvard University Press, 1938); and M. J. Gordon and E. Shapiro, "Capital Equipment Analysis: The Required Rate of Profit," *Management Science* 3 (October 1956), pp. 102–110.

[13]This is the accepted interpretation of the U.S. Supreme Court's directive in 1944 that "the returns to the equity owner [of a regulated business] should be commensurate with returns on investments in other enterprises having corresponding risks." *Federal Power Commission v. Hope Natural Gas Company*, 302 U.S. 591 at 603.

Small variations in estimates of this return can have large effects on the prices charged to the customers and on the firm's profits. So both the firms' managers and regulators work hard to estimate the cost of equity. They've noticed that most utilities are mature, stable companies that pay regular dividends. Such companies should be tailor-made for application of the constant-growth DCF formula.

Suppose you wished to estimate the cost of equity for Aqua America, a local water distribution company. Aqua's stock (ticker symbol WTR) was selling for $33.62 per share at the end of September 2017. Dividend payments for the next year were expected to be $1.18 a share. Thus, it was a simple matter to calculate the first half of the DCF formula:

$$\text{Dividend yield} = \frac{DIV_1}{P_0} = \frac{1.18}{33.62} = .035 \; or \; 3.5\%$$

The hard part is estimating g, the expected rate of dividend growth. One option is to consult the views of security analysts who study the prospects for each company. Analysts are rarely prepared to stick their necks out by forecasting dividends to kingdom come, but they often forecast growth rates over the next five years, and these estimates may provide an indication of the expected long-run growth path. In the case of Aqua, analysts in 2017 were forecasting an annual growth of 6.6%.[14] This, together with the dividend yield, gave an estimate of the cost of equity capital:

$$r = \frac{DIV_1}{P_0} + g = .035 + .066 = .101 \; or \; 10.1\%$$

An alternative approach to estimating long-run growth starts with the **payout ratio,** the ratio of dividends to earnings per share (EPS). For Aqua, this ratio has averaged about 60%. In other words, each year the company was plowing back into the business about 40% of earnings per share:

$$\text{Plowback ratio} = 1 - \text{payout ratio} = 1 - \frac{DIV}{EPS} = 1 - .60 = .40$$

Also, Aqua's ratio of earnings per share to book equity per share has averaged about 12.6%. This is its **return on equity,** or **ROE:**

$$\text{Return on equity} = ROE = \frac{EPS}{\text{book equity per share}} = .126$$

If Aqua earns 12.6% on book equity and reinvests 40% of earnings, then book equity will increase by $.40 \times .126 = .05$, or 5%. Earnings and dividends per share will also increase by 5%:

$$\text{Dividend growth rate} = g = \text{plowback ratio} \times ROE = .40 \times .126 = .05$$

That gives a second estimate of the market capitalization rate:

$$r = \frac{DIV_1}{P_0} + g = .035 + .05 = .085 \; or \; 8.5\%$$

Although these estimates of Aqua's cost of equity seem reasonable, there are obvious dangers in analyzing any single firm's stock with the constant-growth DCF formula. First, the underlying assumption of regular future growth is at best an approximation. Second, even if it is an acceptable approximation, errors inevitably creep into the estimate of g.

---

[14]In this calculation, we're assuming that earnings and dividends are forecasted to grow forever at the same rate g. We show how to relax this assumption later in this chapter. The growth rate was based on the average earnings growth forecasted by Value Line and IBES. IBES compiles and averages forecasts made by security analysts. Value Line publishes its own analysts' forecasts.

	Stock Price	Dividend[a]	Dividend Yield	Long-Term Growth Rate[a]	DCF Cost of Equity[b]	Multistage DCF Cost of Equity[c]
American States Water	$49.84	$1.57	3.2%	6.2%	9.3%	6.6%
American Water Works	81.20	3.24	4.0%	7.8%	11.8%	6.8%
Aqua America	33.62	1.18	3.5%	6.6%	10.1%	7.1%
California Water	38.25	1.01	2.6%	7.1%	9.8%	6.5%
Connecticut Water	56.15	1.92	3.4%	4.8%	8.2%	6.4%
Middlesex Water	38.48	1.24	3.2%	8.1%	11.4%	7.1%
SJW Corp.	54.73	1.27	2.3%	5.7%	8.1%	6.0%
York Water Co.	33.73	0.87	2.6%	8.0%	10.6%	6.7%
				Average	9.9%	6.6%

❭**TABLE 4.4**   Cost-of-equity estimates for water companies in September 2017. The long-term growth rate is based on security analysts' forecasts. In the multistage DCF model, growth after five years is assumed to adjust gradually to the estimated long-term growth rate of gross domestic product (GDP).

[a] Dividend and analysts' long-term growth-rate forecasts at the end of September 2017.
[b] Sum of dividend yield and long-term growth rate. This column contains some small rounding differences.
[c] Long-term growth rate of GDP was forecasted at 4.1% by Blue-Chip Economic Indicators.

Source: The Brattle Group, Inc.

Remember, Aqua's cost of equity is not its personal property. In well-functioning capital markets, investors capitalize the dividends of all securities in Aqua's risk class at exactly the same rate. But any estimate of r for a single common stock is "noisy" and subject to error. Good practice does not put too much weight on single-company estimates of the cost of equity. It collects samples of similar companies, estimates r for each, and takes an average. The average gives a more reliable benchmark for decision making.

The next-to-last column of Table 4.4 gives DCF cost-of-equity estimates for Aqua and seven other water companies. These are all stable, mature companies for which the constant-growth DCF formula *ought* to work. Notice the variation in the cost-of-equity estimates. Some of the variation may reflect differences in the risk, but some is just noise. The average estimate is 9.9%.

Estimates of this kind are only as good as the long-term forecasts on which they are based. For example, several studies have observed that security analysts are subject to behavioral biases and their forecasts tend to be overoptimistic. If so, such DCF estimates of the cost of equity should be regarded as upper estimates of the true figure.

Dangers Lurk in Constant-Growth Formulas

The simple constant-growth DCF formula is an extremely useful rule of thumb, but no more than that. Naive trust in the formula has led many financial analysts to silly conclusions.

We have stressed the difficulty of estimating r by analysis of one stock only. Try to use a large sample of equivalent-risk securities. Even that may not work, but at least it gives the analyst a fighting chance because the inevitable errors in estimating r for a single security tend to balance out across a broad sample.

Also, resist the temptation to apply the formula to firms having high current rates of growth. Such growth can rarely be sustained indefinitely, but the constant-growth DCF formula assumes it can. This erroneous assumption leads to an overestimate of r.

Example   The U.S. Surface Transportation Board (STB) tracks the "revenue adequacy" of U.S. railroads by comparing the railroads' returns on book equity with estimates of their costs of equity. To estimate the cost of equity, the STB traditionally used the constant-growth formula. It measured g by stock analysts' forecasts of long-term earnings growth. The formula assumes that earnings and dividends grow at a constant rate forever, but the analysts' "long-term" forecasts looked out five years at most. As the railroads' profitability improved, the analysts became more and more optimistic. By 2009, their forecasts for growth averaged 12.5% per year. The average dividend yield was 2.6%, so the constant-growth model estimated the industry-average cost of capital at $2.6 + 12.5 = 15.1\%$.

So the STB said, in effect, "Wait a minute: Railroad earnings and dividends can't grow at 12.5% forever. The constant-growth formula no longer works for railroads. We've got to find a more accurate method." The STB now uses a multistage growth model.[15] Let us look at an example of such a model.

DCF Models with Two or More Stages of Growth   Consider Growth-Tech Inc., a firm with $DIV_1 = \$.50$ and $P_0 = \$50$. The firm has plowed back 80% of earnings and has had a return on equity (ROE) of 25%. This means that *in the past*

$$\text{Dividend growth rate} = \text{plowback ratio} \times \text{ROE} = .80 \times .25 = .20$$

The temptation is to assume that the future long-term growth rate g also equals .20. This would imply

$$r = \frac{.50}{50.00} + .20 = .21$$

But this is silly. No firm can continue growing at 20% per year forever, except possibly under extreme inflationary conditions. Eventually, profitability will fall and the firm will respond by investing less.

In real life, the return on equity will decline gradually over time, but for simplicity, let's assume it suddenly drops to 16% at year 3 and the firm responds by plowing back only 50% of earnings. Then g drops to $.50 \times .16 = .08$.

Table 4.5 shows what's going on. Growth-Tech starts year 1 with book equity of $10.00 per share. It earns $2.50, pays out 50 cents as dividends, and plows back $2. Thus, it starts

	Year			
	1	**2**	**3**	**4**
Book equity at start of year	10.00	12.00	14.40	15.55
Earnings per share (EPS)	2.50	3.00	2.30	2.48
Return on equity (ROE)	0.25	0.25	0.16	0.16
Payout ratio	0.20	0.20	0.50	0.50
Dividends per share (DIV)	0.50	0.60	1.15	1.24
Growth rate of dividends (%)	—	20	92	8

❭**TABLE 4.5**   Forecasted earnings and dividends for Growth-Tech. Note the changes in year 3: ROE and earnings drop, but payout ratio increases, causing a big jump in dividends. However, subsequent growth in earnings and dividends falls to 8% per year. Note that the increase in equity equals the earnings not paid out as dividends.

[15]The STB makes two estimates of the cost of equity. One is based on a three-stage DCF model, and the other uses the capital asset pricing model, which we describe in Chapter 8. The STB averages the two estimates.

year 2 with book equity of $10 + 2 = $12. After another year at the same ROE and payout, it starts year 3 with equity of $14.40. However, ROE drops to .16, and the firm earns only $2.30. Dividends go up to $1.15 because the payout ratio increases, but the firm has only $1.15 to plow back. Therefore, subsequent growth in earnings and dividends drops to 8%.

Now we can use our general DCF formula:

$$P_0 = \frac{DIV_1}{1+r} + \frac{DIV_2}{(1+r)^2} + \frac{DIV_3 + P_3}{(1+r)^3}$$

Investors in year 3 will view Growth-Tech as offering 8% per year dividend growth. So we can use the constant-growth formula to calculate P_3:

BEYOND THE PAGE

Try it! Table 4.5: Valuing Growth-Tech

mhhe.com/brealey13e

$$P_3 = \frac{DIV_4}{r - .08}$$

$$P_0 = \frac{DIV_1}{1+r} + \frac{DIV_2}{(1+r)^2} + \frac{DIV_3}{(1+r)^3} + \frac{1}{(1+r)^3} \times \frac{DIV_4}{r - .08}$$

$$= \frac{.50}{1+r} + \frac{.60}{(1+r)^2} + \frac{1.15}{(1+r)^3} + \frac{1}{(1+r)^3} \times \frac{1.24}{r - .08}$$

We have to use trial and error to find the value of r that makes P_0 equal $50. It turns out that the r implicit in these more realistic forecasts is just over .099, quite a difference from our "constant-growth" estimate of .21.

Our present value calculations for Growth-Tech used a *two-stage* DCF valuation model. In the first stage (years 1 and 2), Growth-Tech is highly profitable (ROE = 25%), and it plows back 80% of earnings. Book equity, earnings, and dividends increase by 20% per year. In the second stage, starting in year 3, profitability and plowback decline, and earnings settle into long-term growth at 8%. Dividends jump up to $1.15 in year 3, and then also grow at 8%.

Growth rates can vary for many reasons. Sometimes, growth is high in the short run not because the firm is unusually profitable, but because it is recovering from an episode of *low* profitability. Table 4.6 displays projected earnings and dividends for Phoenix Corp., which is gradually regaining financial health after a near meltdown. The company's equity is growing at a moderate 4%. ROE in year 1 is only 4%, however, so Phoenix has to reinvest all its earnings, leaving no cash for dividends. As profitability increases in years 2 and 3, an increasing dividend can be paid. Finally, starting in year 4, Phoenix settles into steady-state growth, with equity, earnings, and dividends all increasing at 4% per year.

	Year			
	1	**2**	**3**	**4**
Book equity at start of year	10.00	10.40	10.82	11.25
Earnings per share (EPS)	0.40	0.73	1.08	1.12
Return on equity (ROE)	0.04	0.07	0.10	0.10
Dividends per share (DIV)	0	0.31	0.65	0.67
Growth rate of dividends (%)	—	—	110	4

❯TABLE 4.6 Forecasted earnings and dividends for Phoenix Corp. The company can initiate and increase dividends as profitability (ROE) recovers. Note that the increase in book equity equals the earnings not paid out as dividends.

Assume the cost of equity is 10%. Then Phoenix shares should be worth $9.13 per share:

$$P_0 = \underbrace{\frac{0}{1.1} + \frac{.31}{(1.1)^2} + \frac{.65}{(1.1)^3}}_{\text{PV (first-stage dividends)}} + \underbrace{\frac{1}{(1.1)^3} \times \frac{.67}{(.10 - .04)}}_{\text{PV (second-stage dividends)}} = \$9.13$$

You could go on to valuation models with three or more stages. For example, the far right column of Table 4.4 presents multistage DCF estimates of the cost of equity for our local water companies. In this case the long-term growth rates reported in the table do not continue forever. After five years, each company's growth rate gradually adjusts down to an estimated long-term 4.1% growth rate for gross domestic product (GDP). The reduced growth rate cuts the average cost of equity to 6.6%.

We must leave you with two more warnings about DCF formulas for valuing common stocks or estimating the cost of equity. First, it's almost always worthwhile to lay out a simple spreadsheet, like Table 4.5 or 4.6, to ensure that your dividend projections are consistent with the company's earnings and required investments. Second, be careful about using DCF valuation formulas to test whether the market is correct in its assessment of a stock's value. If your estimate of the value is different from the market value, it is probably because you have used poor dividend forecasts. Remember what we said at the beginning of this chapter about simple ways of making money on the stock market: There aren't any.

4-4   The Link between Stock Price and Earnings per Share

Investors separate *growth stocks* from *income stocks*. They buy growth stocks primarily for the expectation of capital gains, and they are interested in the future growth of earnings rather than in next year's dividends. They buy income stocks primarily for the cash dividends. Let us see whether these distinctions make sense.

Imagine first the case of a company that does not grow at all. It does not plow back any earnings and simply produces a constant stream of dividends. Its stock would resemble the perpetual bond described in Chapter 2. Remember that the return on a perpetuity is equal to the yearly cash flow divided by the present value. So the expected return on our share would be equal to the yearly dividend divided by the share price (i.e., the dividend yield). Since all the earnings are paid out as dividends, the expected return is also equal to the earnings per share divided by the share price (i.e., the earnings–price ratio). For example, if the dividend is $10 a share and the stock price is $100, we have[16]

$$\text{Expected return} = \text{dividend yield} = \text{earnings-price ratio}$$

$$= \frac{\text{DIV}_1}{P_0} \qquad = \frac{\text{EPS}_1}{P_0}$$

$$= \frac{10.00}{100} \qquad = .10$$

The price equals

$$P_0 = \frac{\text{DIV}_1}{r} = \frac{\text{EPS}_1}{r} = \frac{10.00}{.10} = 100$$

---

[16]Notice that we use next year's EPS for E/P and P/E ratios. Thus we are using forward, not trailing, P/E.

The expected return for *growing* firms can also equal the earnings–price ratio. The key is whether earnings are reinvested to provide a return equal to the market capitalization rate. For example, suppose our monotonous company suddenly hears of an opportunity to invest $10 a share next year. This would mean no dividend at $t = 1$. However, the company expects that in each subsequent year the project would earn $1 per share, and therefore the dividend could be increased to $11 a share.

Let us assume that this investment opportunity has about the same risk as the existing business. Then we can discount its cash flow at the 10% rate to find its net present value at year 1:

$$\text{Net present value per share at year 1} = -10 + \frac{1}{.10} = 0$$

Thus, the investment opportunity will make no contribution to the company's value. Its prospective return is equal to the opportunity cost of capital.

What effect will the decision to undertake the project have on the company's share price? Clearly none. The reduction in value caused by the nil dividend in year 1 is exactly offset by the increase in value caused by the extra dividends in later years. Therefore, once again the market capitalization rate equals the earnings–price ratio:

$$r = \frac{\text{EPS}_1}{P_0} = \frac{10}{100} = .10$$

Table 4.7 repeats our example for different assumptions about the cash flow generated by the new project. Note that the earnings–price ratio, measured in terms of EPS_1, next year's expected earnings, equals the market capitalization rate (r) only when the new project's NPV = 0. This is an extremely important point—managers can make poor financial decisions because they confuse earnings–price ratios with the market capitalization rate.

In general, we can think of stock price as the capitalized value of average earnings under a no-growth policy, plus **PVGO,** the **net present value of growth opportunities:**

$$P_0 = \frac{\text{EPS}_1}{r} + \text{PVGO}$$

The earnings–price ratio, therefore, equals

$$\frac{\text{EPS}}{P_0} = r\left(1 - \frac{\text{PVGO}}{P_0}\right)$$

Project Rate of Return	Incremental Cash Flow (C)	Project NPV in Year 1[a]	Project's Impact on Share Price in Year 0[b]	Share Price in Year 0 (P_0)	$\dfrac{\text{EPS}_1}{P_0}$	r
0.05	$0.50	−$5.00	−$4.55	$ 95.45	0.105	0.10
0.10	1.00	0	0	100.00	0.10	0.10
0.15	1.50	+$5.00	+4.55	104.55	0.096	0.10
0.20	2.00	+10.00	+9.09	109.09	0.092	0.10

❯ **TABLE 4.7**   Effect on stock price of investing an additional $10 in year 1 at different rates of return. Notice that the earnings–price ratio overestimates r when the project has negative NPV and underestimates it when the project has positive NPV.

[a]Project costs $10.00 ($\text{EPS}_1$). NPV $= -10 + C/r$, where $r = .10$.
[b]NPV is calculated at year 1. To find the impact on P_0, discount for one year at $r = .10$.

It will underestimate r if PVGO is positive and overestimate it if PVGO is negative. The latter case is less likely, since firms are rarely forced to take projects with negative net present values.

Calculating the Present Value of Growth Opportunities for Fledgling Electronics

In our last example, both dividends and earnings were expected to grow, but this growth made no net contribution to the stock price. The stock was, in this sense, an "income stock." Be careful not to equate firm performance with the growth in earnings per share. A company that reinvests earnings at below the market capitalization rate r may increase earnings but will certainly reduce the share value.

Now let us turn to that well-known growth stock, Fledgling Electronics. You may remember that Fledgling's market capitalization rate, r, is 15%. The company is expected to pay a dividend of $5 in the first year, and thereafter, the dividend is predicted to increase indefinitely by 10% a year. We can use the simplified constant-growth formula to work out Fledgling's price:

$$P_0 = \frac{DIV_1}{r - g} = \frac{5}{.15 - .10} = \$100$$

Suppose that Fledgling has earnings per share of $EPS_1 = \$8.33$. Its payout ratio is then

$$\text{Payout ratio} = \frac{DIV_1}{EPS_1} = \frac{5.00}{8.33} = .6$$

In other words, the company is plowing back $1 - .6$, or 40% of earnings. Suppose also that Fledgling's ratio of earnings to book equity is ROE = .25. This explains the growth rate of 10%:

$$\text{Growth rate} = g = \text{plowback ratio} \times \text{ROE} = .4 \times .25 = .10$$

The capitalized value of Fledgling's earnings per share if it had a no-growth policy would be

$$\frac{EPS_1}{r} = \frac{8.33}{.15} = \$55.56$$

But we know that the value of Fledgling stock is $100. The difference of $44.44 must be the amount that investors are paying for growth opportunities. Let's see if we can explain that figure.

Each year Fledgling plows back 40% of its earnings into new assets. In the first year, Fledgling invests $3.33 at a permanent 25% return on equity. Thus, the cash generated by this investment is $.25 \times 3.33 = \$.83$ per year starting at $t = 2$. The net present value of the investment as of $t = 1$ is

$$NPV_1 = -3.33 + \frac{.83}{.15} = \$2.22$$

Everything is the same in year 2 except that Fledgling will invest $3.67, 10% more than in year 1 (remember $g = .10$). Therefore, at $t = 2$, an investment is made with a net present value of

$$NPV_2 = -3.67 + \frac{.83 \times 1.10}{.15} = \$2.44$$

Thus, the payoff to the owners of Fledgling Electronics stock can be represented as the sum of (1) a level stream of earnings, which could be paid out as cash dividends if the firm did not grow, and (2) a set of tickets, one for each future year, representing the opportunity to make investments having positive NPVs. We know that the first component of the value of the share is

$$\text{Present value of level stream of earnings} = \frac{\text{EPS}_1}{r} = \frac{8.33}{.15} = \$55.56$$

The first ticket is worth $2.22 in $t = 1$; the second is worth $2.22 \times 1.10 = \$2.44$ in $t = 2$; the third is worth $2.44 \times 1.10 = \$2.69$ in $t = 3$. These are the forecasted cash values of the tickets. We know how to value a stream of future cash values that grows at 10% per year: Use the constant-growth DCF formula, replacing the forecasted dividends with forecasted ticket values:

$$\text{Present value of growth opportunities} = \text{PVGO} = \frac{\text{NPV}_1}{r - g} = \frac{2.22}{.15 - .10} = \$44.44$$

Now everything checks:

$$\begin{aligned}
\text{Share price} &= \text{present value of level stream of earnings} \\
&\quad + \text{present value of growth opportunities} \\
&= \frac{\text{EPS}_1}{r} + \text{PVGO} \\
&= \$55.56 + \$44.44 \\
&= \$100
\end{aligned}$$

Why is Fledgling Electronics a growth stock? Not because it is expanding at 10% per year. It is a growth stock because the net present value of its future investments accounts for a significant fraction (about 44%) of the stock's price.

Today's stock price reflects investor expectations about the earning power of the firm's current and *future* assets. For example, take Alphabet, the parent company of Google. Alphabet has never paid a dividend. It plows back all its earnings into its business. In early 2018, its stock sold for $1,130 per share at a forward P/E of about 27. EPS forecasted for 2018 were $41.54.

Suppose that Alphabet did not grow and that future EPS were expected to stay constant at $41.54. In this case, Alphabet could pay a constant dividend of $41.54 per share. If the cost of equity is, say, 8%, market value would be PV = 41.54/.08 = $519.25 per share, about $611 less than the actual stock price of $1,130. So it appears that investors were valuing Alphabet's future investment opportunities at $611 per share, about half of the stock price. Alphabet is a growth stock because that large fraction of its market value comes from the expected NPV of its future investments.

BEYOND THE PAGE

Valuing Alphabet

mhhe.com/brealey13e

4-5 ## Valuing a Business by Discounted Cash Flow

Investors buy or sell shares of common stock. Companies often buy or sell entire businesses or major stakes in businesses. For example, we have noted BHP Billiton's plans to sell its U.S. shale business. Both BHP and potential bidders were doing their best to value that business by discounted cash flow.

DCF models work just as well for entire businesses as for shares of common stock. It doesn't matter whether you forecast dividends per share or the total free cash flow of a business. Value today always equals future cash flow discounted at the opportunity cost of capital.

Valuing the Concatenator Business

Rumor has it that Establishment Industries is interested in buying your company's concatenator manufacturing operation. Your company is willing to sell if it can get the full value of this rapidly growing business. The problem is to figure out what its true present value is.

Table 4.8 gives a forecast of **free cash flow (FCF)** for the concatenator business. Free cash flow is the amount of cash that a firm can pay out to investors after paying for all investments necessary for growth. As we will see, free cash flow can be negative for rapidly growing businesses.

Table 4.8 is similar to Table 4.5, which forecasted earnings and dividends per share for Growth-Tech, based on assumptions about Growth-Tech's equity per share, return on equity, and the growth of its business. For the concatenator business, we also have assumptions about assets, profitability—in this case, after-tax operating earnings relative to assets—and growth. Growth starts out at a rapid 12% per year, then falls in two steps to a moderate 6% rate for the long run. The growth rate determines the net additional investment required to expand assets, and the profitability rate determines the earnings thrown off by the business.

Free cash flow, the fourth line in Table 4.8, is equal to the firm's earnings less any new investment expenditures. Free cash flow is zero in years 1 to 3, even though the parent company is investing over $4 million during this period.

Are the early zeros for free cash flow a bad sign? No: Free cash flow is zero because the business is growing rapidly, not because it is unprofitable. Rapid growth is good news, not bad, because the business is earning 12%, 2 percentage points over the 10% cost of capital. If the business could grow at 20%, Establishment Industries and its stockholders would be happier still, although growth at 20% would mean still higher investment and negative free cash flow.

Valuation Format

The value of a business is usually computed as the discounted value of free cash flows out to a *valuation horizon (H),* plus the forecasted value of the business at the horizon, also discounted back to present value. That is,

$$PV = \underbrace{\frac{FCF_1}{1+r} + \frac{FCF_2}{(1+r)^2} + \cdots + \frac{FCF_H}{(1+r)^H}}_{PV(\text{free cash flow})} + \underbrace{\frac{PV_H}{(1+r)^H}}_{PV(\text{horizon value})}$$

	1	2	3	4	5	6	7	8	9	10
Asset value, start of year	10.00	11.20	12.54	14.05	15.31	16.69	18.19	19.29	20.44	21.67
Earnings	1.20	1.34	1.51	1.69	1.84	2.00	2.18	2.31	2.45	2.60
Investment	1.20	1.34	1.51	1.26	1.38	1.50	1.09	1.16	1.23	1.30
Free cash flow (FCF)	0.00	0.00	0.00	0.42	0.46	0.50	1.09	1.16	1.23	1.30
Asset value, end of year	11.20	12.54	14.05	15.31	16.69	18.19	19.29	20.44	21.67	22.97
Return on assets (ROA)	0.12	0.12	0.12	0.12	0.12	0.12	0.12	0.12	0.12	0.12
Asset growth rate	0.12	0.12	0.12	0.09	0.09	0.09	0.06	0.06	0.06	0.06
Earnings growth rate, from previous year		0.12	0.12	0.12	0.09	0.09	0.09	0.06	0.06	0.06

❯TABLE 4.8   Forecasts of free cash flow in $ millions for the concatenator division. Free cash flow is zero for periods 1 to 3 because investment absorbs all of net income. Free cash flow turns positive when growth slows down after period 3. Inputs required for the table's calculations are in bold type.

Notes:
1. Starting asset value is $10 million. Assets grow at 12% to start, then at 9%, and finally at 6% in perpetuity. Profitability is assumed constant at 12%.
2. Free cash flow equals earnings minus net investment. Net investment equals total capital outlays minus depreciation. We assume that investment for replacement of existing assets is covered by depreciation and that net investment is devoted to growth. Earnings are also net of depreciation.

Of course, the concatenator business will continue after the horizon, but it's not practical to forecast free cash flow year by year to infinity. PV_H stands in for free cash flow in periods $H + 1, H + 2$, and so on.

Valuation horizons are often chosen arbitrarily. Sometimes the boss tells everybody to use 10 years because that's a round number. We will try year 6, because growth of the concatenator business seems to settle down to a long-run trend after year 7.

BEYOND THE PAGE

Try It! Table 4.8: Valuing the concatenator division

mhhe.com/brealey13e

Estimating Horizon Value

There are two common approaches to estimating horizon value. One uses valuation by comparables, based on P/E, market-to-book, or other ratios. The other uses DCF. We will start with valuation by comparables.

Horizon Value Based on P/E Ratios   Suppose you can observe stock prices for good comparables, that is, for mature manufacturing companies whose scale, risk, and growth prospects today roughly match those projected for the concatenator business in year 6.[17] Suppose further that these companies tend to sell at price–earnings ratios of about 11. Then you could reasonably guess that the price–earnings ratio of a mature concatenator operation will likewise be 11. That implies:

$$PV(\text{horizon value}) = \frac{1}{(1.1)^6}(11 \times 2.18) = 13.5$$

The present value of the business up to the horizon is $.9 million. Therefore

$$PV(\text{business}) = .9 + 13.5 = \$14.4 \text{ million}$$

Horizon Value Based on Market–Book Ratios   Suppose also that the market–book ratios of the sample of mature manufacturing companies tend to cluster around 1.5. If the concatenator business market–book ratio is 1.5 in year 6,

$$PV(\text{horizon value}) = \frac{1}{(1.1)^6}(1.5 \times 16.69) = 14.1$$

$$PV(\text{business}) = .9 + 14.1 = \$15.0 \text{ million}$$

It's easy to poke holes in these last two calculations. Book value, for example, is often a poor measure of the true value of a company's assets. It can fall far behind actual asset values when there is rapid inflation, and it often entirely misses important intangible assets, such as your patents for concatenator design. Earnings may also be biased by inflation and a long list of arbitrary accounting choices. Finally, you never know when you have found a sample of truly similar companies to use as comparables.

But remember, the purpose of discounted cash flow is to estimate market value—to estimate what investors would pay for a stock or business. When you can *observe* what they actually pay for similar companies, that's valuable evidence. Try to figure out a way to use it. One way to use it is through valuation by comparables, based on price–earnings or market–book ratios. Valuation rules of thumb, artfully employed, sometimes beat a complex discounted-cash-flow calculation hands down.

Horizon Value Based on DCF   Now let us try the constant-growth DCF formula. This requires free cash flow for year 7, which we have at $1.09 million from Table 4.8; a long-run

---

[17]We have not asked how the concatenator business is financed. We are implicitly assuming 100% equity and zero debt. Therefore the comparables should also have little or no debt. If they do have debt, EBIT or EBITDA ratios would be better than P/E ratios. See footnote 8 and the examples in Section 19-2.

growth rate, which appears to be 6%; and a discount rate, which some high-priced consultant has told us is 10%. Therefore,

$$\text{Horizon value (PV looking forward from period 6)} = \text{PV}_H = \frac{1.09}{.10 - .06} = \$27.3 \text{ million}$$

$$\text{Horizon value (discounted back to PV in period 0)} = \frac{27.3}{(1.1)^6} = \$15.4 \text{ million}$$

The PV of the near-term free cash flows is $.9 million. Thus the present value of the concatenator division is

$$\text{PV (business)} = \text{PV(free cash flow)} + \text{PV(horizon value)}$$
$$= .9 + 15.4$$
$$= \$16.3 \text{ million}$$

Now, are we done? Well, the mechanics of this calculation are perfect. But doesn't it make you just a little nervous to find that 94% of the value of the business rests on the horizon value? Moreover, a little checking shows that horizon value can change dramatically in response to small changes in the assumed long-term growth rate.

Suppose the growth rate is 7% instead of 6%. That means that asset value has to grow by an extra 1% per year, requiring extra investment of $.18 million in period 7, which reduces FCF_7 to $.91 million. Horizon value increases to $\text{PV}_H = \$30.3$ million in year 6 and to $17.1 million discounted to year zero. The PV of the concatenator business increases from $16 .3 million to $.9 + 17.1 = \$18.0$ million.

Warning 1: When you use the constant-growth DCF formula to calculate horizon value, always remember that faster growth requires increased investment, which reduces free cash flow. Slower growth requires less investment, which increases free cash flow.

So 7% instead of 6% growth increases PV by $18.0 – 16.3 = $1.7 million. Why? We did not ignore warning 1: We accounted for the increased investment required for faster growth. Therefore the additional investment in periods 7 and beyond must have generated additional positive NPV. In other words, we must have assumed expanded growth opportunities and added more PVGO to the value of the business.

Notice in Table 4.8 that the return on assets (ROA) is forecasted at 12% forever, 2 percentage points higher than the assumed discount rate of 10%. Thus, every dollar invested in period 7 and beyond generates positive NPV and adds to horizon value and the PV of the business.

But is it realistic to assume that any business can keep on growing and making positive-NPV investments forever? Sooner or later you and your competitors will be on an equal footing. You may still be earning a superior return on past investments, but you will find that introductions of new products or attempts to expand profits from existing products trigger vigorous resistance from competitors who are just as smart and efficient as you are. When that time comes, the NPV of subsequent investments will average out to zero. After all, PVGO is positive only when investments can be expected to earn more than the cost of capital.

Warning 2: Always check to see whether horizon value includes post-horizon PVGO. You can check on warning 2 by changing the assumed long-term growth rate. If a higher growth rate increases horizon value—after you have taken care to respect warning 1—then you are assuming post-horizon PVGO. Is it realistic to assume that the firm can earn more than the cost of capital in perpetuity? If not, adjust your forecasts accordingly.

There is an easy way to calculate horizon value if post-horizon PVGO is zero. Recall that PV equals the capitalized value of next period's earnings plus PVGO:

$$\text{PV}_t = \frac{\text{earnings}_{t+1}}{r} + \text{PVGO}$$

If PVGO = 0 at the horizon period *H,* then,

$$PV_H = \frac{\text{earnings}_{H+1}}{r}$$

In other words, when the competition catches up and the firm can only earn its cost of equity on new investment, the price–earnings ratio will equal $1/r$, because PVGO disappears.

This latest formula for PV_H is still DCF. We are valuing the business *as if* assets and earnings will not grow after the horizon date.[18] (The business probably will grow, but the growth can be ignored, because it will add no net value if PVGO goes to zero.) With no growth, there is no net investment,[19] and all of earnings ends up as free cash flow.

Therefore, we can calculate the horizon value at period 6 as the present value of a level stream of earnings starting in period 7 and continuing indefinitely. The resulting value for the concatenator business is:

$$PV(\text{horizon value}) = \frac{1}{(1+r)^6}\left(\frac{\text{earnings in period 7}}{r}\right)$$

$$= \frac{1}{(1.1)^6}\left(\frac{2.18}{.10}\right)$$

$$= \$12.3 \text{ million}$$

$$PV(\text{business}) = .9 + 12.3 = \$13.2 \text{ million}$$

A Value Range for the Concatenator Business   We now have four estimates of what Establishment Industries ought to pay for the concatenator business. The estimates reflect four different methods of estimating horizon value. There is no best method, although we like the last method, which forces managers to remember that sooner or later competition catches up.

Our calculated values for the concatenator business range from $13.2 to $16.3 million, a difference of about $3 million. The width of the range may be disquieting, but it is not unusual. Discounted-cash-flow formulas only estimate market value, and the estimates change as forecasts and assumptions change. Managers cannot know market value for sure until an actual transaction takes place.

Free Cash Flow, Dividends, and Repurchases

We assumed that the concatenator business was a division of your company, not a freestanding corporation. But suppose it was a separate corporation with 1 million shares outstanding. How would we calculate price per share? Simple: Calculate the PV of the business and divide by 1 million. If we decide that the business is worth $16.3 million, the price per share is $16.30.

If the concatenator business were a public Concatenator Corp., with no other assets and operations, it could pay out its free cash flow as dividends. Dividends per share would be the free cash flow shown in Table 4.8 divided by 1 million shares: zero in periods 1 to 3, then $.42 per share in period 4, $.46 per share in period 5, etc.

---

[18]But what does "no growth" mean? Suppose that the concatenator business maintains its assets and earnings in real (inflation-adjusted) terms. Then nominal earnings will grow at the inflation rate. This takes us back to the constant-growth formula: Earnings in period $H + 1$ should be valued by dividing by $r - g$, where g in this case equals the inflation rate.

We have simplified the concatenator example. In real-life valuations, with big bucks involved, be careful to track growth from inflation as well as growth from investment. For guidance see M. Bradley and G. Jarrell, "Expected Inflation and the ConstantGrowth Valuation Model," *Journal of Applied Corporate Finance* 20 (Spring 2008), pp. 66–78.

[19]The business must invest enough to maintain its assets, even in the no-growth case. We have assumed that a base level of investment equal to depreciation is sufficient to maintain assets. Note that earnings are calculated after depreciation—that is, after paying for the base investment. Depreciation and this investment are not broken out in Table 4.7.

We mentioned stock repurchases as an alternative to cash dividends. If repurchases are important, it's often simpler to value total free cash flow than dividends per share. Suppose Concatenator Corp. decides not to pay cash dividends. Instead, it will pay out all free cash flow by repurchasing shares. The market capitalization of the company should not change because shareholders as a group will still receive all free cash flow.

Perhaps the following intuition will help. Suppose you own all of the 1 million Concatenator shares. Do you care whether you get free cash flow as dividends or by selling shares back to the firm? Your cash flows in each future period will always equal the free cash flows shown in Table 4.8. Your DCF valuation of the company will, therefore, depend on the free cash flows, not on how they are distributed.

Chapter 16 covers the choice between cash dividends and repurchases (including tax issues and other complications). But you can see why it's attractive to value a company as a whole by forecasting and discounting free cash flow. You don't have to ask how free cash flow will be paid out. You don't have to forecast repurchases.

● ● ● ● ●

SUMMARY

In this chapter, we have used our newfound knowledge of present values to examine the market price of common stocks. The value of a stock is equal to the stream of cash payments discounted at the rate of return that investors expect to receive on other securities with equivalent risks.

Common stocks do not have a fixed maturity; their cash payments consist of an indefinite stream of dividends. Therefore, the present value of a share of common stock is

$$PV = \sum_{t=1}^{\infty} \frac{DIV_t}{(1+r)^t}$$

However, we did not just *assume* that investors purchase common stocks solely for dividends. In fact, we began with the assumption that investors have relatively short horizons and invest for both dividends and capital gains. Our fundamental valuation formula is, therefore,

$$P_0 = \frac{DIV_1 + P_1}{1+r}$$

This is a condition of market equilibrium. If it did not hold, the share would be overpriced or underpriced, and investors would rush to sell or buy it. The flood of sellers or buyers would force the price to adjust so that the fundamental valuation formula holds.

We also made use of the formula for a growing perpetuity presented in Chapter 2. If dividends are expected to grow forever at a constant rate of g, then

$$P_0 = \frac{DIV_1}{r-g}$$

It is often helpful to twist this formula around and use it to estimate the market capitalization rate r, given P_0 and estimates of DIV_1 and g:

$$r = \frac{DIV_1}{P_0} + g$$

Remember, however, that this formula rests on a *very* strict assumption: constant dividend growth in perpetuity. This may be an acceptable assumption for mature, low-risk firms, but for many firms, near-term growth is unsustainably high. In that case, you may wish to use a *two-stage* DCF formula, where near-term dividends are forecasted and valued, and the constant-growth DCF formula is used to forecast the value of the shares at the start of the long run. The near-term dividends and the future share value are then discounted to present value.

The general DCF formula can be transformed into a statement about earnings and growth opportunities:

$$P_0 = \frac{EPS_1}{r} + PVGO$$

The ratio EPS_1/r is the present value of the earnings per share that the firm would generate under a no-growth policy. PVGO is the net present value of the investments that the firm will make in order to grow. A growth stock is one for which PVGO is large relative to the present value of EPS if the firm did not grow. Most growth stocks are stocks of rapidly expanding firms, but expansion alone does not create a high PVGO. What matters is the profitability of the new investments.

The same formulas that we used to value common shares can also be used to value entire businesses. In that case, we discount not dividends per share but the entire free cash flow generated by the business. Usually, a two-stage DCF model is deployed. Free cash flows are forecasted out to a horizon and discounted to present value. Then a horizon value is forecasted, discounted, and added to the value of the free cash flows. The sum is the value of the business.

Valuing a business is simple in principle but not so easy in practice. Forecasting reasonable horizon values is particularly difficult. The usual assumption is moderate long-run growth after the horizon, which allows use of the growing-perpetuity DCF formula at the horizon. Horizon values can also be calculated by the valuation-by-comparables method, for example by assuming normal price–earnings or market-to-book ratios at the horizon date.

The dividend discount models derived in this chapter work best for mature firms that pay regular cash dividends. The models also work when companies pay out cash by share repurchases as well as dividends. That said, it is also true that the dividend discount model is difficult to use if the company pays no dividends at all or if the split of payout between cash dividends and repurchases is unpredictable. In the latter case, it is easier to get price per share by forecasting and valuing the company's total free cash flow and then dividing by the current number of shares outstanding.

 Select problems are available in McGraw-Hill's *Connect*.
Answers to questions with an "*" are found in the Appendix.

PROBLEM SETS

1. **Stock markets** True or false?

   a. The bid price is always greater than the ask price.

   b. An investor who wants to sell his stock immediately should enter a limit order.

   c. The sale of shares by a large investor usually takes place in the primary market.

   d. Electronic Communications Network refers to the automated ticker tape on the New York Stock Exchange.

2. **Stock quotes**

   a. "I would like to sell 1000 shares of Walmart at best."

   b. "I would like to buy 500 shares of Hattersley at $50 or better."

   Which of these is a limit order and which is a market order? If the price of Walmart is $50 and the price of Hattersley is $60, which, if any, of these orders will be executed?

3. **Stock quotes*** Here is a small part of the order book for Mesquite Foods:

Bid		Ask	
Price	Size	Price	Size
103	100	103.5	200
102.5	200	103.8	200
101	400	104	300
99.8	300	104.5	400

   a. Georgina Sloberg submits a market order to sell 100 shares. What price will she receive?

   b. Norman Pilbarra submits a market order to buy 400 shares. What is the maximum price that he will pay?

   c. Carlos Ramirez submits a limit bid order at 105. Will it execute immediately?

4. **Stock quotes** Go to **finance.yahoo.com** and get trading quotes for IBM.

   a. What is the latest IBM stock price and market cap?

   b. What is IBM's dividend payment and dividend yield?

   c. What is IBM's trailing P/E ratio?

   d. Calculate IBM's forward P/E ratio using the EPS forecasted by analysts for the next year.

   e. What is IBM's price–book (P/B) ratio?

5. **Valuation by comparables** Look up P/E and P/B ratios for Entergy (ticker symbol ETR), using Yahoo! Finance or another Internet source. Calculate the same ratios for the following potential comparables: American Electric Power (AEP), CenterPoint Energy (CNP), and Southern Company (SO). Set out the ratios in the same format as Table 4.2. Are the ratios for these electric companies tightly grouped or scattered? If you didn't know Entergy's stock price, would the comparables give a good estimate?

6. **Dividend discount model** True or false?

   a. All stocks in an equivalent-risk class are priced to offer the same expected rate of return.

   b. The value of a share equals the PV of future dividends per share.

   c. The value of a share equals the PV of earnings per share assuming the firm does not grow, plus the NPV of future growth opportunities.

7. **Dividend discount model** Respond briefly to the following statement:

   "You say stock price equals the present value of future dividends? That's crazy! All the investors I know are looking for capital gains."

8. **Dividend discount model*** Company X is expected to pay an end-of-year dividend of $5 a share. After the dividend, its stock is expected to sell at $110. If the market capitalization rate is 8%, what is the current stock price?

9. **Dividend discount model** Company Y does not plow back any earnings and is expected to produce a level dividend stream of $5 a share. If the current stock price is $40, what is the market capitalization rate?

10. **Constant-growth DCF model*** Company Z's earnings and dividends per share are expected to grow indefinitely by 5% a year. If next year's dividend is $10 and the market capitalization rate is 8%, what is the current stock price?

11. **Constant-growth DCF model** Consider three investors:

    a. Mr. Single invests for one year.

    b. Ms. Double invests for two years.

    c. Mrs. Triple invests for three years.

    Assume each invests in company Z (see Problem 10). Show that each expects to earn a rate of return of 8% per year.

12. **Constant-growth DCF model** Pharmecology just paid an annual dividend of $1.35 per share. It's a mature company, but future EPS and dividends are expected to grow with inflation, which is forecasted at 2.75% per year.

    a. What is Pharmecology's current stock price? The nominal cost of capital is 9.5%.

    b. Redo part (a) using forecasted real dividends and a real discount rate.

13. **Constant-growth DCF model***

    Here are forecasts for next year for two stocks:

	Stock A	Stock B
Return on equity	15%	10%
Earnings per share	$2.00	$1.50
Dividends per share	$1.00	$1.00

    a. What are the dividend payout ratios for each firm?

    b. What are the expected dividend growth rates for each stock?

    c. If investors require a return of 15% on each stock, what are their values?

14. **Constant-growth DCF model** Look up General Mills (GIS), Kellogg (K), Campbell Soup (CPB), and Seneca Foods (SENEA).

    a. What are the current P/E and P/B ratios for these food companies? What are the dividend and dividend yield for each company?

    b. What are the growth rates of EPS and dividends for each company over the last five years? What EPS growth rates are forecasted by analysts? Do these growth rates appear to be on a steady trend that could be projected for the long run?

    c. Would you be confident in applying the constant-growth DCF model to measure these companies' costs of equity? Why or why not?

15. **Cost of equity capital** Under what conditions does r, a stock's market capitalization rate, equal its earnings–price ratio EPS_1/P_0?

16. **Cost of equity capital** Each of the following formulas for determining shareholders' required rate of return can be right or wrong depending on the circumstances:

    a. $r = DIV_1 / P_0 + g$

    b. $r = EPS_1 / P_0$

    For each formula, construct a simple numerical example showing that the formula can give wrong answers and explain why the error occurs. Then construct another simple numerical example for which the formula gives the right answer.

17. **Two-stage DCF model** Company Z-prime is like Z in Problem 10 in all respects save one: Its growth will stop after year 4. In year 5 and afterward, it will pay out all earnings as dividends. What is Z-prime's stock price? Assume next year's EPS is $15.

18. **Two-stage DCF model*** Consider the following three stocks:

    a. Stock A is expected to provide a dividend of $10 a share forever.

    b. Stock B is expected to pay a dividend of $5 next year. Thereafter, dividend growth is expected to be 4% a year forever.

    c. Stock C is expected to pay a dividend of $5 next year. Thereafter, dividend growth is expected to be 20% a year for five years (i.e., years 2 through 6) and zero thereafter.

    If the market capitalization rate for each stock is 10%, which stock is the most valuable? What if the capitalization rate is 7%?

19. **Two-stage DCF model** Company Q's current return on equity (ROE) is 14%. It pays out one half of earnings as cash dividends (payout ratio = .5). Current book value per share is $50. Book value per share will grow as Q reinvests earnings. Assume that the ROE and payout ratio stay constant for the next four years. After that, competition forces ROE down to 11.5% and the payout ratio increases to 0.8. The cost of capital is 11.5%.

    a. What are Q's EPS and dividends next year? How will EPS and dividends grow in years 2, 3, 4, 5, and subsequent years?

    b. What is Q's stock worth per share? How does that value depend on the payout ratio and growth rate after year 4?

20. **Two-stage DCF model** Compost Science Inc. (CSI) is in the business of converting Boston's sewage sludge into fertilizer. The business is not in itself very profitable. However, to induce CSI to remain in business, the Metropolitan District Commission (MDC) has agreed to pay whatever amount is necessary to yield CSI a 10% book return on equity. At the end of the year, CSI is expected to pay a $4 dividend. It has been reinvesting 40% of earnings and growing at 4% a year.

    a. Suppose CSI continues on this growth trend. What is the expected long-run rate of return from purchasing the stock at $100? What part of the $100 price is attributable to the present value of growth opportunities?

    b. Now the MDC announces a plan for CSI to treat Cambridge sewage. CSI's plant will, therefore, be expanded gradually over five years. This means that CSI will have to reinvest 80% of its earnings for five years. Starting in year 6, however, it will again be able to pay out 60% of earnings. What will be CSI's stock price once this announcement is made and its consequences for CSI are known?

21. **Growth opportunities** If company Z (see Problem 10) were to distribute all its earnings, it could maintain a level dividend stream of $15 a share. How much is the market actually paying per share for growth opportunities?

22. **Growth opportunities** Look up Intel (INTC), Oracle (ORCL), and HP (HPQ) on **finance .yahoo.com**. Rank the companies' forward P/E ratios from highest to lowest. What are the possible reasons for the different ratios? Which of these companies appears to have the most valuable growth opportunities?

23. **Growth opportunities** Alpha Corp's earnings and dividends are growing at 15% per year. Beta Corp's earnings and dividends are growing at 8% per year. The companies' assets, earnings, and dividends per share are now (at date 0) exactly the same. Yet PVGO accounts for a greater fraction of Beta Corp's stock price. How is this possible? (*Hint:* There is more than one possible explanation.)

24. **Growth opportunities** Look again at the financial forecasts for Growth-Tech given in Table 4.5. This time assume you know that the opportunity cost of capital is $r = .12$ (discard the .099 figure calculated in the text). Assume you do not know Growth-Tech's stock value. Otherwise follow the assumptions given in the text.

    a. Calculate the value of Growth-Tech stock.

    b. What part of that value reflects the discounted value of P_3, the price forecasted for year 3?

    c. What part of P_3 reflects the present value of growth opportunities (PVGO) after year 3?

d. Suppose that competition will catch up with Growth-Tech by year 4 so that it can earn only its cost of capital on any investments made in year 4 or subsequently. What is GrowthTech stock worth now under this assumption? (Make additional assumptions if necessary.)

25. **Free cash flow** What do financial managers mean by "free cash flow"? How is free cash flow calculated? Briefly explain.

26. **Horizon value** What is meant by the "horizon value" of a business? How can it be estimated?

27. **Horizon value** Suppose the horizon date is set at a time when the firm will run out of positive-NPV investment opportunities. How would you calculate the horizon value? (*Hint:* What is the *P*/EPS ratio when PVGO = 0?)

28. **Valuing a business** Permian Partners (PP) produces from aging oil fields in west Texas. Production is 1.8 million barrels per year in 2018, but production is declining at 7% per year for the foreseeable future. Costs of production, transportation, and administration add up to $25 per barrel. The average oil price was $65 per barrel in 2018. PP has 7 million shares outstanding. The cost of capital is 9%. All of PP's net income is distributed as dividends. For simplicity, assume that the company will stay in business forever and that costs per barrel are constant at $25. Also, ignore taxes.

    a. What is the ending 2018 value of one PP share? Assume that oil prices are expected to fall to $60 per barrel in 2019, $55 per barrel in 2020, and $50 per barrel in 2021. After 2021, assume a long-term trend of oil-price increases at 5% per year.

    b. What is PP's EPS/*P* ratio, and why is it not equal to the 9% cost of capital?

29. **Valuing a business** Construct a new version of Table 4.8, assuming that competition drives down profitability (on existing assets as well as new investment) to 11.5% in year 6, 11% in year 7, 10.5% in year 8, and 8% in year 9 and all later years. What is the value of the concatenator business?

30. **Valuing a business** Mexican Motors' market cap is 200 billion pesos. Next year's free cash flow is 8.5 billion pesos. Security analysts are forecasting that free cash flow will grow by 7.5% per year for the next five years.

    a. Assume that the 7.5% growth rate is expected to continue forever. What rate of return are investors expecting?

    b. Mexican Motors has generally earned about 12% on book equity (ROE = 12%) and reinvested 50% of earnings. The remaining 50% of earnings has gone to free cash flow. Suppose the company maintains the same ROE and investment rate for the long run. What is the implication for the growth rate of earnings and free cash flow? For the cost of equity? Should you revise your answer to part (a) of this question?

31. **Valuing a business*** Phoenix Corp. faltered in the recent recession but is recovering. Free cash flow has grown rapidly. Forecasts made in 2019 are as follows:

($ millions)	2020	2021	2022	2023	2024
Net income	1.0	2.0	3.2	3.7	4.0
Investment	1.0	1.0	1.2	1.4	1.4
Free cash flow	0	1.0	2.0	2.3	2.6

Phoenix's recovery will be complete by 2024, and there will be no further growth in net income or free cash flow.

a. Calculate the PV of free cash flow, assuming a cost of equity of 9%.

b. Assume that Phoenix has 12 million shares outstanding. What is the price per share?

c. Confirm that the expected rate of return on Phoenix stock is exactly 9% in each of the years from 2020 to 2024.

CHALLENGE

32. **Constant-growth DCF formula** The constant-growth DCF formula:

$$P_0 = \frac{DIV_1}{r - g}$$

is sometimes written as:

$$P_0 = \frac{ROE(1 - b)BVPS}{r - bROE}$$

where BVPS is book equity value per share, b is the plowback ratio, and ROE is the ratio of earnings per share to BVPS. Use this equation to show how the price-to-book ratio varies as ROE changes. What is price-to-book when ROE $= r$?

33. **DCF valuation** Portfolio managers are frequently paid a proportion of the funds under management. Suppose you manage a $100 million equity portfolio offering a dividend yield (DIV_1/P_0) of 5%. Dividends and portfolio value are expected to grow at a constant rate. Your annual fee for managing this portfolio is .5% of portfolio value and is calculated at the end of each year. Assuming that you will continue to manage the portfolio from now to eternity, what is the present value of the management contract? How would the contract value change if you invested in stocks with a 4% yield?

34. **Valuing a business** Construct a new version of Table 4.8, assuming that the concatenator division grows at 20%, 12%, and 6%, instead of 12%, 9%, and 6%. You will get negative early free cash flows.

    a. Recalculate the PV of free cash flow. What does your revised PV say about the division's PVGO?

    b. Suppose the division is the public corporation Concatenator Corp, with no other resources. Thus it will have to issue stock to cover the negative free cash flows. Does the need to issue shares change your valuation? Explain. (*Hint:* Suppose first that Concatenator's existing stockholders buy all of the newly issued shares. What is the value of the company to these stockholders? Now suppose instead that all the shares are issued to new stockholders, so that existing stockholders don't have to contribute any cash. Does the value of the company to the existing stockholders change, assuming that the new shares are sold at a fair price?)

FINANCE ON THE WEB

The major stock exchanges have wonderful websites. Start with the NYSE (**www.nyse.com**) and Nasdaq (**www.nasdaq.com**). Make sure you know how trading takes place on these exchanges.

MINI-CASE ● ● ● ● ●

Reeby Sports

Ten years ago, in 2010, George Reeby founded a small mail-order company selling high-quality sports equipment. Since those early days, Reeby Sports has grown steadily and been consistently profitable. The company has issued 2 million shares, all of which are owned by George Reeby and his five children.

For some months, George has been wondering whether the time has come to take the company public. This would allow him to cash in on part of his investment and would make it easier for the firm to raise capital should it wish to expand in the future.

But how much are the shares worth? George's first instinct is to look at the firm's balance sheet, which shows that the book value of the equity is $26.34 million, or $13.17 per share. A share price of $13.17 would put the stock on a P/E ratio of 6.6. That is quite a bit lower than the 13.1 P/E ratio of Reeby's larger rival, Molly Sports.

George suspects that book value is not necessarily a good guide to a share's market value. He thinks of his daughter Jenny, who works in an investment bank. She would undoubtedly know what the shares are worth. He decides to phone her after she finishes work that evening at 9 o'clock or before she starts the next day at 6.00 a.m.

Before phoning, George jots down some basic data on the company's profitability. After recovering from its early losses, the company has earned a return that is higher than its estimated 10% cost of capital. George is fairly confident that the company could continue to grow fairly steadily for the next six to eight years. In fact, he feels that the company's growth has been somewhat held back in the last few years by the demands from two of the children for the company to make large dividend payments. Perhaps, if the company went public, it could hold back on dividends and plow more money back into the business.

There are some clouds on the horizon. Competition is increasing and only that morning Molly Sports announced plans to form a mail-order division. George is worried that beyond the next six or so years it might become difficult to find worthwhile investment opportunities.

George realizes that Jenny will need to know much more about the prospects for the business before she can put a final figure on the value of Reeby Sports, but he hopes that the information is sufficient for her to give a preliminary indication of the value of the shares.

	2011	2012	2013	2014	2015	2016	2017	2018	2019	2020E
Earnings per share ($)	−2.10	−0.70	0.23	0.81	1.10	1.30	1.52	1.64	2.00	2.03
Dividend ($)	0.00	0.00	0.00	0.20	0.20	0.30	0.30	0.60	0.60	0.80
Book value per share ($)	9.80	7.70	7.00	7.61	8.51	9.51	10.73	11.77	13.17	14.40
ROE (%)	−27.10	−7.1	3.0	11.6	14.5	15.3	16.0	15.3	17.0	15.4

QUESTIONS

1. Help Jenny to forecast dividend payments for Reeby Sports and to estimate the value of the stock. You do not need to provide a single figure. For example, you may wish to calculate two figures, one on the assumption that the opportunity for further profitable investment disappears after six years and another assuming it disappears after eight years.

2. How much of your estimate of the value of Reeby's stock comes from the present value of growth opportunities?

5

Net Present Value and Other Investment Criteria

A company's shareholders prefer to be rich rather than poor. Therefore, they want the firm to invest in every project that is worth more than it costs. The difference between a project's value and its cost is its *net present value (NPV)*. Companies can best help their shareholders by investing in all projects with a positive NPV and rejecting those with a negative NPV.

We start this chapter with a review of the net present value rule. We then turn to some other measures that companies may look at when making investment decisions. The first two of these measures, the project's payback period and its book rate of return, are little better than rules of thumb, easy to calculate and easy to communicate. Although there is a place for rules of thumb in this world, an engineer needs something more accurate when designing a 100-story building, and a financial manager needs more than a rule of thumb when making a substantial capital investment decision.

Instead of calculating a project's NPV, companies often compare the expected rate of return from investing in the project with the return that shareholders could earn on equivalent-risk investments in the financial markets. The company accepts those projects that provide a higher return than shareholders could earn for themselves. If used correctly, this rate of return rule should always identify projects that increase firm value. However, we shall see that the rule sets several traps for the unwary.

We conclude the chapter by showing how to cope with situations when the firm has only limited capital. This raises two problems. One is computational. In simple cases, we just choose those projects that give the highest NPV per dollar invested, but more elaborate techniques are sometimes needed to sort through the possible alternatives. The other problem is to decide whether capital rationing really exists and whether it invalidates the net present value rule. Guess what? NPV, properly interpreted, wins out in the end.

5-1 A Review of the Basics

Vegetron's chief financial officer (CFO) is wondering how to analyze a proposed $1 million investment in a new venture code-named project X. He asks what you think.

Your response should be as follows: "First, forecast the cash flows generated by project X over its economic life. Second, determine the appropriate opportunity cost of capital (r). This should reflect both the time value of money and the risk involved in project X. Third, use this opportunity cost of capital to discount the project's future cash flows. The sum of the discounted cash flows is called present value (PV). Fourth, calculate *net* present value (NPV) by subtracting the $1 million investment from PV. If we call the cash flows C_0, C_1, and so on, then

$$\text{NPV} = C_0 + \frac{C_1}{1+r} + \frac{C_2}{(1+r)^2} + \cdots$$

where $C_0 = -\$1$ million. We should invest in project X if its NPV is greater than zero."

However, Vegetron's CFO is unmoved by your sagacity. He asks why NPV is so important.

You: Let us look at what is best for Vegetron stockholders. They want you to make their Vegetron shares as valuable as possible.

Right now Vegetron's total market value (price per share times the number of shares outstanding) is $10 million. That includes $1 million cash, which we can invest in project X. The value of Vegetron's other assets and opportunities must therefore be $9 million. We have to decide whether it is better to keep the $1 million cash and reject project X or to spend the cash and accept the project. Let us call the value of the new project PV. Then the choice is as follows:

	Market Value ($ millions)	
Asset	**Reject Project X**	**Accept Project X**
Cash	1	0
Other assets	9	9
Project X	0	PV
	10	9 + PV

Clearly project X is worthwhile if its present value (PV) is greater than $1 million, that is, if net present value is positive.

CFO: How do I know that the PV of project X will actually show up in Vegetron's market value?

You: Suppose we set up a new, independent firm X, whose only asset is project X. What would be the market value of firm X?

Investors would forecast the dividends that firm X would pay and discount those dividends by the expected rate of return of securities having similar risks. We know that stock prices are equal to the present value of forecasted dividends.

Since project X is the only asset, the dividend payments we would expect firm X to pay are exactly the cash flows we have forecasted for project X. Moreover, the rate that investors would use to discount firm X's dividends is exactly the rate we should use to discount project X's cash flows.

I agree that firm X is hypothetical. But if project X is accepted, investors holding Vegetron stock will really hold a portfolio of project X and the firm's other assets. We know the other assets are worth $9 million considered as a separate venture. Since asset values add up, we can easily figure out the portfolio value once we calculate the value of project X as a separate venture.

By calculating the present value of project X, we are replicating the process by which the common stock of firm X would be valued in the financial markets.

CFO: The one thing I don't understand is where the discount rate comes from.

You: I agree that the discount rate is difficult to measure precisely. But it is easy to see what we are *trying* to measure. The discount rate is the opportunity cost of investing in the project rather than in the financial markets. In other words, instead of accepting a project, the firm can always return the cash to the shareholders and let them invest it in financial assets.

You can see the trade-off (Figure 5.1). The opportunity cost of taking the project is the return shareholders could have earned had they invested the money on their own. When we discount the project's cash flows by the expected rate of return on financial assets, we are measuring how much investors would be prepared to pay for your project.

CFO: But which financial assets? The fact that investors expect only 12% on IBM stock does not mean that we should purchase Fly-by-Night Electronics if it offers 13%.

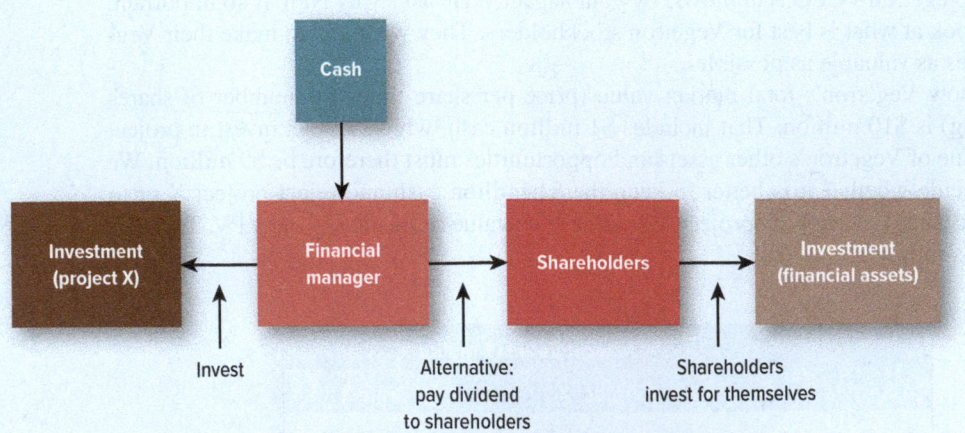

▶ **FIGURE 5.1**   The firm can either keep and reinvest cash or return it to investors. (Arrows represent possible cash flows or transfers.) If cash is reinvested, the opportunity cost is the expected rate of return that shareholders could have obtained by investing in financial assets.

You: The opportunity-cost concept makes sense only if assets of equivalent risk are compared. In general, you should identify financial assets that have the same risk as your project, estimate the expected rate of return on these assets, and use this rate as the opportunity cost.

Net Present Value's Competitors

When you advised the CFO to calculate the project's NPV, you were in good company. These days, 75% of firms always, or almost always, calculate net present value when deciding on investment projects. However, as you can see from Figure 5.2, NPV is not the only investment criterion that companies use, and firms often look at more than one measure of a project's attractiveness.

About three-quarters of firms calculate the project's internal rate of return (or IRR); that is roughly the same proportion as use NPV. The IRR rule is a close relative of NPV and, when used properly, it will give the same answer. You therefore need to understand the IRR rule and how to take care when using it.

A large part of this chapter is concerned with explaining the IRR rule, but first we look at two other measures of a project's attractiveness—the project's payback and its book rate of return. As we will explain, both measures have obvious defects. Few companies rely on them to make their investment decisions, but they do use them as supplementary measures that may help to distinguish the marginal project from the no-brainer.

Later in the chapter we also come across one further investment measure, the profitability index. Figure 5.2 shows that it is not often used, but you will find that there are circumstances in which this measure has some special advantages.

Three Points to Remember about NPV

As we look at these alternative criteria, it is worth keeping in mind the following key features of the net present value rule. First, the NPV rule recognizes that *a dollar today is worth more than a dollar tomorrow* because the dollar today can be invested to start earning interest immediately. Any investment rule that does not recognize the *time value of money* cannot be sensible. Second, net present value depends solely on the *forecasted cash flows* from the project and the *opportunity cost of capital.* Any investment rule that is affected by the manager's tastes, the company's choice of accounting method, the profitability of the company's existing business, or the profitability of other independent projects will lead to inferior decisions. Third,

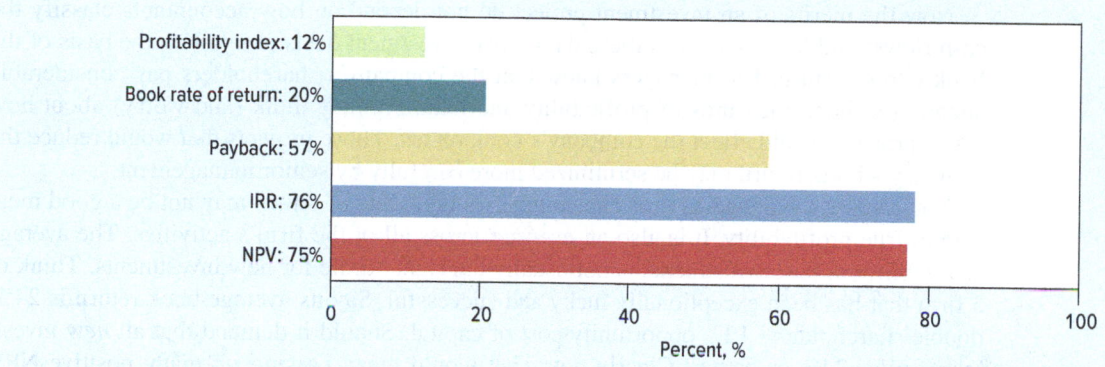

> **FIGURE 5.2**   **Survey evidence on the percentage of CFOs who always, or almost always, use a particular technique for evaluating investment projects**

Source: J. R. Graham and C. R. Harvey, "The Theory and Practice of Corporate Finance: Evidence from the Field," *Journal of Financial Economics* 60 (2001), pp. 187–243.

because present values are all measured in today's dollars, you can add them up. Therefore, if you have two projects A and B, the net present value of the combined investment is

$$NPV(A + B) = NPV(A) + NPV(B)$$

This adding-up property has important implications. Suppose project B has a negative NPV. If you tack it onto project A, the joint project (A + B) must have a lower NPV than A on its own. Therefore, you are unlikely to be misled into accepting a poor project (B) just because it is packaged with a good one (A). As we shall see, the alternative measures do not have this property. If you are not careful, you may be tricked into deciding that a package of a good and a bad project is better than the good project on its own.

5-2   Book Rate of Return and Payback

Book Rate of Return

Net present value depends only on the project's cash flows and the opportunity cost of capital. But when companies report to shareholders, they do not simply show the cash flows. They also report book—that is, accounting—income and book assets.

Financial managers sometimes use these numbers to calculate a book (or accounting) rate of return on a proposed investment. In other words, they look at the prospective book income from the investment as a proportion of the book value of the assets that the firm is proposing to acquire:

$$\text{Book rate of return} = \frac{\text{book income}}{\text{book assets}}$$

They typically compare this figure with the book rate of return that the company is currently earning.

Cash flows and book income are often very different. For example, the accountant labels some cash outflows as *capital investments* and others as *operating expenses.* The operating expenses are, of course, deducted immediately from each year's income. The capital expenditures are put on the firm's balance sheet and then depreciated. The annual depreciation charge is deducted from each year's income. Thus the book rate of return depends on which items the accountant treats as capital investments and how rapidly they are depreciated.[1]

---

[1]This chapter's mini-case contains simple illustrations of how book rates of return are calculated and of the difference between accounting income and project cash flow. Read the case if you wish to refresh your understanding of these topics. Better still, do the case calculations.

Now the merits of an investment project do not depend on how accountants classify the cash flows[2] and few companies these days make investment decisions just on the basis of the book rate of return. But managers know that the company's shareholders pay considerable attention to book measures of profitability and naturally they think (and worry) about how major projects would affect the company's book return. Those projects that would reduce the company's book return may be scrutinized more carefully by senior management.

You can see the dangers here. The company's book rate of return may not be a good measure of true profitability. It is also an *average* across all of the firm's activities. The average profitability of past investments is not usually the right hurdle for new investments. Think of a firm that has been exceptionally lucky and successful. Say its average book return is 24%, double shareholders' 12% opportunity cost of capital. Should it demand that all *new* investments offer 24% or better? Clearly not: That would mean passing up many positive-NPV opportunities with rates of return between 12 and 24%.

We will come back to the book rate of return in Chapters 12 and 28, when we look more closely at accounting measures of financial performance.

Payback

We suspect that you have often heard conversations that go something like this: "We are spending $6 a week, or around $300 a year, at the laundromat. If we bought a washing machine for $800, it would pay for itself within three years. That's well worth it." You have just encountered the payback rule.

A project's **payback period** is found by counting the number of years it takes before the cumulative cash flow equals the initial investment. For the washing machine the payback period was just under three years. The **payback rule** states that a project should be accepted if its payback period is less than some specified cutoff period. For example, if the cutoff period is four years, the washing machine makes the grade; if the cutoff is two years, it doesn't.

We have no quarrel with those who use payback as a descriptive statistic. It is perfectly fine to say that the washing machine has a three-year payback. But payback should never be a *rule*.

EXAMPLE 5.1 ● The Payback Rule

Consider the following three projects:

| Project | Cash Flows ($) | | | | Payback Period (years) | NPV at 10% |
	C_0	C_1	C_2	C_3		
A	−2,000	500	500	5,000	3	+2,624
B	−2,000	500	1,800	0	2	−58
C	−2,000	1,800	500	0	2	−50

Project A involves an initial investment of $2,000 ($C_0 = -2,000$) followed by cash inflows during the next three years. Suppose the opportunity cost of capital is 10%. Then project A has an NPV of +$2,624:

$$\text{NPV(A)} = -2,000 + \frac{500}{1.10} + \frac{500}{1.10^2} + \frac{5,000}{1.10^3} = +\$2,624$$

---

[2]Of course, the depreciation method used for tax purposes does have cash consequences that should be taken into account in calculating NPV. We cover depreciation and taxes in the next chapter.

Project B also requires an initial investment of $2,000 but produces a cash inflow of $500 in year 1 and $1,800 in year 2. At a 10% opportunity cost of capital project B has an NPV of −$58:

$$NPV(B) = -2,000 + \frac{500}{1.10} + \frac{1,800}{1.10^2} = -\$58$$

The third project, C, involves the same initial outlay as the other two projects but its first-period cash flow is larger. It has an NPV of +$50:

$$NPV(C) = -2,000 + \frac{1,800}{1.10} + \frac{500}{1.10^2} = +\$50$$

The net present value rule tells us to accept projects A and C but to reject project B.

Now look at how rapidly each project pays back its initial investment. With project A, you take three years to recover the $2,000 investment; with projects B and C, you take only two years. If the firm used the *payback rule* with a cutoff period of two years, it would accept only projects B and C; if it used the payback rule with a cutoff period of three or more years, it would accept all three projects. Therefore, regardless of the choice of cutoff period, the payback rule gives different answers from the net present value rule.

You can see why payback can give misleading answers:

1. *The payback rule ignores all cash flows after the cutoff date.* If the cutoff date is two years, the payback rule rejects project A regardless of the size of the cash inflow in year 3.

2. *The payback rule gives equal weight to all cash flows before the cutoff date.* The payback rule says that projects B and C are equally attractive, but because C's cash inflows occur earlier, C has the higher net present value at any positive discount rate.

To use the payback rule, a firm must decide on an appropriate cutoff date. If it uses the same cutoff regardless of project life, it will tend to accept many poor short-lived projects and reject many good long-lived ones.

We have had little good to say about payback. So why do many companies continue to use it? Senior managers don't truly believe that all cash flows after the payback period are irrelevant. We suggest three explanations. First, payback may be used because it is the simplest way to *communicate* an idea of project profitability. Investment decisions require discussion and negotiation among people from all parts of the firm, and it is important to have a measure that everyone can understand. Second, managers of larger corporations may opt for projects with short paybacks because they believe that quicker profits mean quicker promotion. That takes us back to Chapter 1, where we discussed the need to align the objectives of managers with those of shareholders. Finally, owners of small public firms with limited access to capital may worry about their future ability to raise capital. These worries may lead them to favor rapid payback projects even though a longer-term venture may have a higher NPV.

Discounted Payback

Occasionally companies discount the cash flows before they compute the payback period. The discounted cash flows for our three projects are as follows:

		Discounted Cash Flows ($)			Discounted Payback Period (years)	NPV at 10%
Project	C_0	C_1	C_2	C_3		
A	−2,000	$500/1.10 =$ 455	$500/1.10^2 =$ 413	$5,000/1.10^3 =$ 3,757	3	+2,624
B	−2,000	$500/1.10 =$ 455	$1,800/1.10^2 =$ 1,488		—	−58
C	−2,000	$1,800/1.10 =$ 1,636	$500/1.10^2 =$ 413		2	+50

The *discounted payback measure* asks, How many years does the project have to last in order for it to make sense in terms of net present value? You can see that the value of the cash inflows from project B never exceeds the initial outlay and would always be rejected under the discounted payback rule. Thus a discounted payback rule will never accept a negative-NPV project. On the other hand, it still takes no account of cash flows after the cutoff date, so that good long-term projects such as A continue to risk rejection.

Rather than automatically rejecting any project with a long discounted payback period, many managers simply use the measure as a warning signal. These managers don't unthinkingly reject a project with a long discounted payback period. Instead they check that the proposer is not unduly optimistic about the project's ability to generate cash flows into the distant future. They satisfy themselves that the equipment has a long life and that competitors will not enter the market and eat into the project's cash flows.

5-3   Internal (or Discounted Cash Flow) Rate of Return

Whereas payback and return on book are ad hoc measures, internal rate of return has a much more respectable ancestry and is recommended in many finance texts. If we dwell more on its deficiencies, it is not because they are more numerous but because they are less obvious.

In Chapter 2, we noted that the net present value rule could also be expressed in terms of rate of return, which would lead to the following rule: "Accept investment opportunities offering rates of return in excess of their opportunity costs of capital." That statement, properly interpreted, is absolutely correct. However, interpretation is not always easy for long-lived investment projects.

There is no ambiguity in defining the true rate of return of an investment that generates a single payoff after one period:

$$\text{Rate of return} = \frac{\text{payoff}}{\text{investment}} - 1$$

Alternatively, we could write down the NPV of the investment and find the discount rate that makes NPV = 0.

$$\text{NPV} = C_0 + \frac{C_1}{1 + \text{discount rate}} = 0$$

implies

$$\text{Discount rate} = \frac{C_1}{-C_0} - 1$$

Of course C_1 is the payoff and $-C_0$ is the required investment, and so our two equations say exactly the same thing. *The discount rate that makes NPV = 0 is also the rate of return.*

How do we calculate return when the project produces cash flows in several periods? Answer: We use the same definition that we just developed for one-period projects—*the project rate of return is the discount rate that gives a zero NPV*. This discount rate is known as the **discounted cash flow (DCF) rate of return** or **internal rate of return (IRR).** The internal rate of return is used frequently in finance. It can be a handy measure, but, as we shall see, it can also be a misleading measure. You should, therefore, know how to calculate it and how to use it properly.

Calculating the IRR

The internal rate of return is defined as the rate of discount that makes NPV = 0. So to find the IRR for an investment project lasting T years, we must solve for IRR in the following expression:

$$\text{NPV} = C_0 + \frac{C_1}{1 + \text{IRR}} + \frac{C_2}{(1 + \text{IRR})^2} + \cdots + \frac{C_T}{(1 + \text{IRR})^T} = 0$$

Actual calculation of IRR usually involves trial and error. For example, consider a project that produces the following flows:

Cash Flows ($)		
C_0	C_1	C_2
−4,000	+2,000	+4,000

The internal rate of return is IRR in the equation

$$\text{NPV} = -4,000 + \frac{2,000}{1 + \text{IRR}} + \frac{4,000}{(1 + \text{IRR})^2} = 0$$

Let us arbitrarily try a zero discount rate. In this case, NPV is not zero but +$2,000:

$$\text{NPV} = -4,000 + \frac{2,000}{1.0} + \frac{4,000}{(1.0)^2} = +\$2,000$$

The NPV is positive; therefore, the IRR must be greater than zero. The next step might be to try a discount rate of 50%. In this case, net present value is −$889:

$$\text{NPV} = -4,000 + \frac{2,000}{1.50} + \frac{4,000}{(1.50)^2} = -\$889$$

The NPV is negative; therefore, the IRR must be less than 50%. In Figure 5.3, we have plotted the net present values implied by a range of discount rates. From this, we can see that a discount rate of 28.08% gives the desired net present value of zero. Therefore, IRR is 28.08%. (We carry the IRR calculation to two decimal places to avoid confusion from rounding. In practice, no one would worry about the .08%.)[3]

You can always find the IRR by plotting an NPV profile, as in Figure 5.3, but it is quicker and more accurate to let a spreadsheet or specially programmed calculator do the trial and error for you. The Useful Spreadsheet Functions box near the end of the chapter shows how to use the Excel function to calculate an IRR.

Some people confuse the internal rate of return and the opportunity cost of capital because both appear as discount rates in the NPV formula. The internal rate of return is a *profitability measure* that depends solely on the amount and timing of the project cash flows. The

BEYOND THE PAGE

Calculating the IRR

mhhe.com/brealey13e

---

[3]The IRR is a first cousin to the yield to maturity on a bond. Recall from Chapter 3 that the yield to maturity is the discount rate that makes the present value of future interest and principal payments equal to the bond's price. If you buy the bond at that market price and hold it to maturity, the yield to maturity is your IRR on the bond investment.

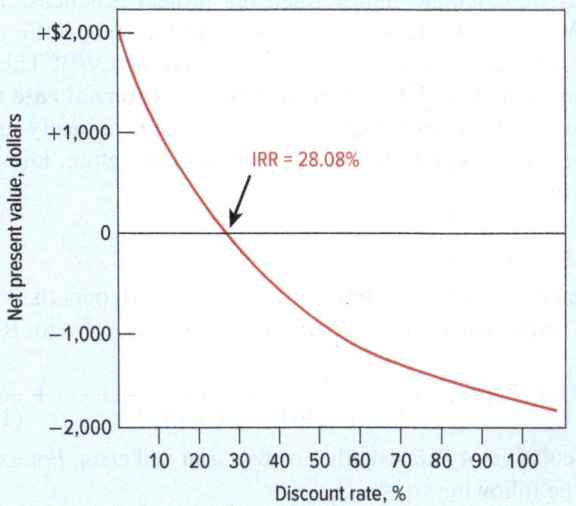

FIGURE 5.3

This project costs $4,000 and then produces cash inflows of $2,000 in year 1 and $4,000 in year 2. Its internal rate of return (IRR) is 28.08%, the rate of discount at which NPV is zero.

opportunity cost of capital is a *standard of profitability* that we use to calculate how much the project is worth. The opportunity cost of capital is established in the financial markets. It is the expected rate of return offered by other assets with the same risk as the project being evaluated.

The IRR Rule

BEYOND THE PAGE

Interpreting the IRR

mhhe.com/brealey13e

The internal rate of return rule states that the firm should accept an investment project if the opportunity cost of capital is less than the internal rate of return. You can see the reasoning behind this idea if you look again at Figure 5.3. If the opportunity cost of capital is less than the 28.08% IRR, then the project has a *positive* NPV when discounted at the opportunity cost of capital. If it is equal to the IRR, the project has a *zero* NPV. And if it is greater than the IRR, the project has a *negative* NPV. Therefore, when we compare the opportunity cost of capital with the IRR on our project, we are effectively asking whether our project has a positive NPV. This is true not only for our example. The rule will give the same answer as the net present value rule *whenever the NPV of a project is a steadily declining function of the discount rate.*

The 28.08% internal rate of return on our project tells us how high the opportunity cost of capital must be before the project should be rejected. Although we might not be able to put a precise number on the project's cost of capital, we might nevertheless be confident that it was less than 28.08% and that we can safely go ahead with the project. You can understand, therefore, why a manager may find it helpful to know the project's IRR. Our worries concern those managers who use the internal rate of return as a criterion *in preference to net present value.* Although, properly stated, the two criteria are formally equivalent, the internal rate of return rule contains several pitfalls.

Pitfall 1—Lending or Borrowing?

Not all cash-flow streams have NPVs that decline as the discount rate increases. Consider the following projects A and B:

Cash Flows ($)				
Project	C_0	C_1	IRR	NPV at 10%
A	−1,000	+1,500	+50%	+364
B	+1,000	−1,500	+50%	−364

Each project has an IRR of 50%. (In other words, $-1,000 + 1,500/1.50 = 0$ and $+1,000 - 1,500/1.50 = 0$.)

Does this mean that they are equally attractive? Clearly not, for in the case of A, where we are initially paying out $1,000, we are *lending* money at 50%; in the case of B, where we are initially receiving $1,000, we are *borrowing* money at 50%. When we lend money, we want a *high* rate of return; when we borrow money, we want a *low* rate of return.

If you plot a graph like Figure 5.3 for project B, you will find that NPV increases as the discount rate increases. Obviously the internal rate of return rule, as we stated it above, won't work in this case; we have to look for an IRR *less* than the opportunity cost of capital.

Pitfall 2—Multiple Rates of Return

Helmsley Iron is proposing to develop a new strip mine in Western Australia. The mine involves an initial investment of A$30 billion and is expected to produce a cash inflow of A$10 billion a year for the next nine years. At the end of that time, the company will incur A$65 billion of cleanup costs. Thus, the cash flows from the project are:

Cash Flows (billions of Australian dollars)				
C_0	C_1	$\cdots$	C_9	C_{10}
−30	10		10	−65

Helmsley calculates the project's IRR and its NPV as follows:

IRR (%)	NPV at 10%
+3.50 *and* 19.54	$A2.53 billion

Note that there are *two* discount rates that make NPV = 0. That is, *each* of the following statements holds:

$$NPV = -30 + \frac{10}{1.035} + \frac{10}{1.035^2} + \cdots + \frac{10}{1.035^9} - \frac{65}{1.035^{10}} = 0$$

$$NPV = -30 + \frac{10}{1.1954} + \frac{10}{1.1954^2} + \cdots + \frac{10}{1.1954^9} - \frac{65}{1.1954^{10}} = 0$$

In other words, the investment has an IRR of both 3.50% *and* 19.54%. Figure 5.4 shows how this comes about. As the discount rate increases, NPV initially rises and then declines. The reason for this is the double change in the sign of the cash-flow stream. There can be as many internal rates of return for a project as there are changes in the sign of the cash flows.[4]

Decommissioning and clean-up costs can sometimes lead to huge negative cash flows at the end of a project. The cost of decommissioning oil platforms in the British North Sea has been estimated at $75 billion. It can cost more than $500 million to decommission a nuclear power plant. These are obvious instances where cash flows go from positive to negative, but you can probably think of a number of other cases where the company needs to plan for later expenditures. Ships periodically need to go into dry dock for a refit, hotels may receive a major face-lift, machine parts may need replacement, and so on.

BEYOND THE PAGE

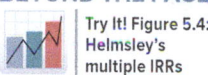 Try It! Figure 5.4: Helmsley's multiple IRRs

mhhe.com/brealey13e

---

[4]By Descartes's "rule of signs" there can be as many different solutions to a polynomial as there are changes of sign.

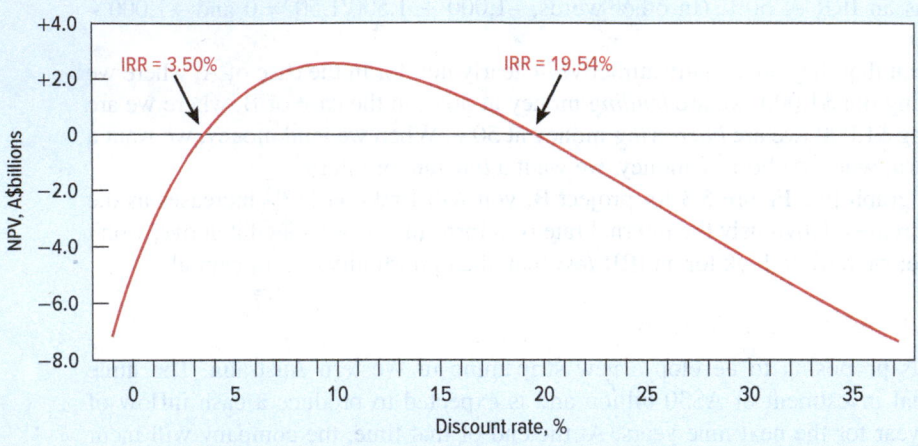

> **FIGURE 5.4**   Helmsley Iron's mine has two internal rates of return. NPV = 0 when the discount rate is +3.50% and when it is +19.54%.

Whenever the cash-flow stream is expected to change sign more than once, the company typically sees more than one IRR.

As if this is not difficult enough, there are also cases in which *no* internal rate of return exists. For example, project C has a positive net present value at all discount rates:

BEYOND THE PAGE

A project with no IRR

mhhe.com/brealey13e

	Cash Flows ($)				
Project	C_0	C_1	C_2	**IRR (%)**	**NPV at 10%**
C	+1,000	−3,000	+2,500	None	+339

A number of adaptations of the IRR rule have been devised for such cases. Not only are they inadequate, but they also are unnecessary, for the simple solution is to use net present value.[5]

Pitfall 3—Mutually Exclusive Projects

BEYOND THE PAGE

Try It! Calculate the MIRR

mhhe.com/brealey13e

Firms often have to choose between several alternative ways of doing the same job or using the same facility. In other words, they need to choose between **mutually exclusive projects.** Here, too, the IRR rule can be misleading.

---

[5]Companies sometimes get around the problem of multiple rates of return by discounting the later cash flows back at the cost of capital until there remains only one change in the sign of the cash flows. A modified internal rate of return (MIRR) can then be calculated on this revised series. In our example, the MIRR is calculated as follows:

1. Calculate the present value in year 5 of all the subsequent cash flows:

$$\text{PV in year 5} = 10/1.1 + 10/1.1^2 + 10/1.1^3 + 10/1.1^4 - 65/1.1^5 = -8.66$$

2. Add to the year 5 cash flow the present value of subsequent cash flows:

$$C_5 + \text{PV(subsequent cash flows)} = 10 - 8.66 = 1.34$$

3. Since there is now only one change in the sign of the cash flows, the revised series has a unique rate of return, which is 13.7%:

$$\text{NPV} = -30 + 10/1.137 + 10/1.137^2 + 10/1.137^3 + 10/1.137^4 + 1.34/1.137^5 = 0$$

Since the MIRR of 13.7% is greater than the cost of capital (and the initial cash flow is negative), the project has a positive NPV when valued at the cost of capital.

Of course, it would be much easier in such cases to abandon the IRR rule and just calculate project NPV.

Consider projects D and E:

	Cash Flows ($)			
Project	C_0	C_1	IRR (%)	NPV at 10%
D	−10,000	+20,000	100	+8,182
E	−20,000	+35,000	75	+11,818

Perhaps project D is a manually controlled machine tool and project E is the same tool with the addition of computer control. Both are good investments, but E has the higher NPV and is, therefore, better. However, the IRR rule seems to indicate that if you have to choose, you should go for D because it has the higher IRR. If you follow the IRR rule, you have the satisfaction of earning a 100% rate of return; if you follow the NPV rule, you are $11,818 richer.

You can salvage the IRR rule in these cases by looking at the internal rate of return on the *incremental* flows. Here is how to do it: First, consider the smaller project (D in our example). It has an IRR of 100%, which is well in excess of the 10% opportunity cost of capital. You know, therefore, that D is acceptable. You now ask yourself whether it is worth making the additional $10,000 investment in E. The incremental flows from undertaking E rather than D are as follows:

	Cash Flows ($)			
Project	C_0	C_1	IRR (%)	NPV at 10%
E − D	−10,000	+15,000	50	+3,636

The IRR on the incremental investment is 50%. While that is not as good as D's IRR, it is well in excess of the 10% opportunity cost of capital. So you should prefer project E to project D.[6]

Unless you look at the incremental expenditure, IRR is unreliable in ranking projects of different scale. It is also unreliable in ranking projects with different patterns of cash flow over time. For example, sometimes it can be worth taking a project that offers a good rate of return for a long period rather than one that offers an even higher rate for just a few years. To illustrate, suppose the firm can take project F or project G but not both:

	Cash Flows ($)										
Project	C_0	C_1	C_2	C_3	C_4	C_5	C_6	C_7	C_8	IRR (%)	NPV at 10%
F	−10,000	+6,000	+6,000	+6,000	0	0	0	0	0	36.3	4,921
G	−10,000	+3,000	+3,000	+3,000	+3,000	+3,000	3,000	3,000	3,000	25.0	6,005

The short-lived project, F, offers the higher IRR, but at a 10% cost of capital, project G has the higher NPV and would therefore make shareholders wealthier.

Figure 5.5 shows how the choice between these two projects depends on the discount rate. Notice that, if investors require a relatively low rate of return (less than 13.9%), they will pay a higher price for project G with its longer life. The short-lived project F is superior only if investors demand a very high rate of return (greater than 13.9%) and therefore place a low

---

[6]When you examine incremental cash flows, you may find that you have jumped out of the frying pan into the fire. The series of incremental cash flows may involve several changes in sign. In this case there are likely to be multiple IRRs and you will be forced to use the NPV rule after all.

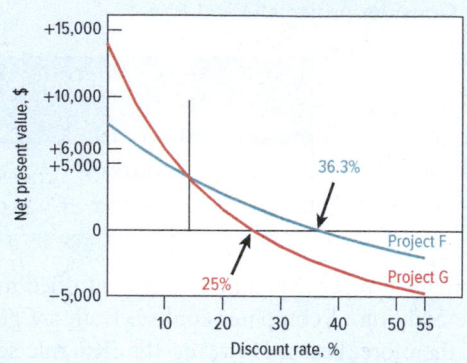

▶ FIGURE 5.5

The IRR of project F exceeds that of project G, but the NPV of project F is higher only if the discount rate is greater than 13.9%.

value on the more distant cash flows. This is not something you could discover by comparing the project IRRs.[7]

The simplest way to choose between projects F and G is to compare their net present values. But if your heart is set on the IRR rule, you can use it as long as you look at the return on the incremental cash flows. The procedure is exactly the same as we showed earlier. First you check that project F has a satisfactory IRR. Then you look at the return on the *incremental* cash flows from G.

The IRR on the incremental cash flows from G is 13.9%. Since this is greater than the opportunity cost of capital, you should undertake G rather than F:[8]

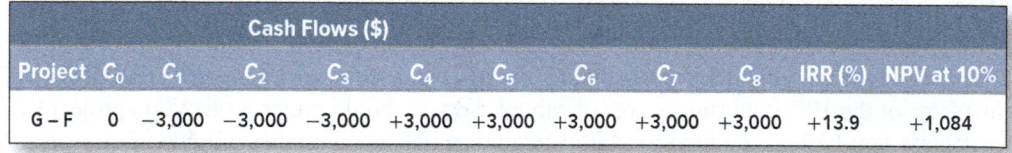

	Cash Flows ($)										
Project	C_0	C_1	C_2	C_3	C_4	C_5	C_6	C_7	C_8	IRR (%)	NPV at 10%
G – F	0	−3,000	−3,000	−3,000	+3,000	+3,000	+3,000	+3,000	+3,000	+13.9	+1,084

Pitfall 4—What Happens When There Is More Than One Opportunity Cost of Capital

We have simplified our discussion of capital budgeting by assuming that the opportunity cost of capital is the same for all the cash flows, C_1, C_2, C_3, and so on. Remember our most general formula for calculating net present value:

$$\text{NPV} = C_0 + \frac{C_1}{1 + r_1} + \frac{C_2}{(1 + r_2)^2} + \frac{C_3}{(1 + r_3)^3} + \cdots$$

In other words, we discount C_1 at the opportunity cost of capital for one year, C_2 at the opportunity cost of capital for two years, and so on. The IRR rule tells us to accept a project if the IRR is greater than the opportunity cost of capital. But what do we do when we have several

---

[7]It is often suggested that the choice between the net present value rule and the internal rate of return rule should depend on the probable reinvestment rate. This is wrong. The prospective return on another independent investment should not be allowed to influence the investment decision.

[8]Because F and G had the same 10% cost of capital, we can choose between the two projects by asking whether the IRR on the incremental cash flows is greater or less than 10%. But suppose that F and G had different risks and, therefore, different costs of capital. In that case, there would be no simple yardstick for assessing whether the IRR on the incremental cash flows was adequate.

opportunity costs? Do we compare IRR with $r_1, r_2, r_3, \ldots$? Actually we would have to compute a complex weighted average of these rates to obtain a number comparable to IRR.

The differences between short- and long-term discount rates can be important when the term structure of interest rates is not "flat." In 2017, for example, long-term U.S. Treasury bonds yielded almost 2% more than short-term Treasury bills. Suppose a financial manager was evaluating leases for new office space. Assume the lease payments were fixed obligations. The manager would not use the same discount rate for a 1-year lease as for a 15-year lease.

But the extra precision from building the term structure of discount rates into discount rates for risky capital investment projects is rarely worth the trouble. The gains from accurately forecasting project cash flows far outweigh the gains from more precise discounting. Thus, the IRR usually survives, even when the term structure is not flat.

The Verdict on IRR

We have given four examples of things that can go wrong with IRR. We spent much less space on payback or return on book. Does this mean that IRR is worse than the other two measures? Quite the contrary. There is little point in dwelling on the deficiencies of payback or return on book. They are clearly ad hoc measures that often lead to silly conclusions. The IRR rule has a much more respectable ancestry. It is less easy to use than NPV, but, used properly, it gives the same answer.

Nowadays, few large corporations use the payback period or return on book as their primary measure of project attractiveness. Most use discounted cash flow (or DCF), and for many companies, DCF means IRR, not NPV. For "normal" investment projects with an initial cash outflow followed by a series of cash inflows, there is no difficulty in using the internal rate of return to make a simple accept/reject decision. However, we think that the financial managers who like to use IRRs need to worry more about pitfall 3. Financial managers never see all possible projects. Most projects are proposed by operating managers. A company that instructs nonfinancial managers to look first at project IRRs prompts a search for those projects with the highest IRRs rather than the highest NPVs. It also encourages managers to *modify* projects so that their IRRs are higher. Where do you typically find the highest IRRs? In short-lived projects requiring little up-front investment. Such projects may not add much to the value of the firm.

We don't know why so many companies pay such close attention to the internal rate of return, but we suspect that it may reflect the fact that management does not trust the forecasts it receives. Suppose that two plant managers approach you with proposals for two new investments. Both have a positive NPV of $1,400 at the company's 8% cost of capital, but you nevertheless decide to accept project A and reject B. Are you being irrational?

The cash flows for the two projects and their NPVs are set out in the accompanying table. You can see that although both proposals have the same NPV, project A involves an investment of $9,000, while B requires an investment of $9 million. Investing $9,000 to make $1,400 is clearly an attractive proposition, and this shows up in A's IRR of nearly 16%. Investing $9 million to make $1,400 might also be worth doing if you could be *sure* of the plant manager's forecasts, but there is almost no room for error in project B. You could spend time and money checking the cash-flow forecasts, but is it really worth the effort? Most managers

	Cash Flows ($ thousands)					
Project	C_0	C_1	C_2	C_3	NPV at 8%	IRR (%)
A	−9.0	2.9	4.0	5.4	1.4	15.58
B	−9,000	2,560	3,540	4,530	1.4	8.01

Internal Rate of Return

❯Spreadsheet programs such as Excel provide built-in functions to solve for internal rates of return. You can find these functions by pressing *fx* on the Excel toolbar. If you then click on the function that you wish to use, Excel will guide you through the inputs that are required. At the bottom left of the function box there is a Help facility with an example of how the function is used.

Here is a list of useful functions for calculating internal rates of return, together with some points to remember when entering data:

- **IRR:** Internal rate of return on a series of regularly spaced cash flows.

- **XIRR:** The same as IRR, but for irregularly spaced flows.

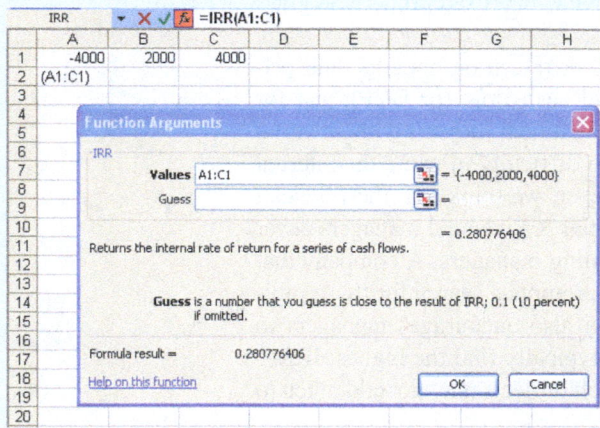

Source: Microsoft Excel.

Note the following:

- For these functions, you must enter the addresses of the cells that contain the input values.

- The IRR functions calculate (at most) only one IRR even when there are multiple IRRs.

Spreadsheet Questions

The following questions provide an opportunity to practice each of the above functions:

1. (IRR) Check the IRRs for project F in Section 5-3.

2. (IRR) What is the IRR of a project with the following cash flows:

C_0	C_1	C_2	C_3
−\$5,000	+\$2,200	+\$4,650	+\$3,330

3. (XIRR) What is the IRR of a project with the following cash flows:

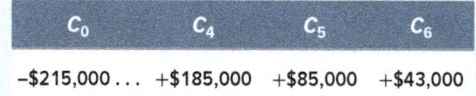

C_0	C_4	C_5	C_6
−\$215,000 ...	+\$185,000	+\$85,000	+\$43,000

(All other cash flows are 0.)

---

would look at the IRR and decide that if the cost of capital is 8%, a project that offers a return of 8.01% is not worth the worrying time.

Alternatively, management may conclude that project A is a clear winner that is worth undertaking right away, but in the case of project B, it may make sense to wait and see whether the decision looks more clear-cut in a year's time.[9] That is why managers will often postpone the decision on projects such as B by setting a hurdle rate for the IRR that is higher than the cost of capital.

5-4   Choosing Capital Investments When Resources Are Limited

Our entire discussion of methods of capital budgeting has rested on the proposition that the wealth of a firm's shareholders is highest if the firm accepts *every* project that has a positive net present value. Suppose, however, that there are limitations on the investment program that

---

[9]In Chapter 22, we discuss when it may pay a company to delay undertaking a positive-NPV project. We will see that when projects are "deep-in-the-money" (project A), it generally pays to invest right away and capture the cash flows. However, in the case of projects that are "close-to-the-money" (project B), it makes more sense to wait and see.

prevent the company from undertaking all such projects. Economists call this *capital ration-ing*. When capital is rationed, we need a method of selecting the package of projects that is within the company's resources yet gives the highest possible net present value.

An Easy Problem in Capital Rationing

Let us start with a simple example. The opportunity cost of capital is 10%, and our company has the following opportunities:

	Cash Flows ($ millions)			
Project	C_0	C_1	C_2	NPV at 10%
A	−10	+30	+5	21
B	−5	+5	+20	16
C	−5	+5	+15	12

All three projects are attractive, but suppose that the firm is limited to spending $10 million. In that case, it can invest *either* in project A *or* in projects B and C, but it cannot invest in all three. Although individually B and C have lower net present values than project A, when taken together they have the higher net present value. Here we cannot choose between projects solely on the basis of net present values. When money is limited, we need to concentrate on getting the biggest bang for our buck. In other words, we must pick the projects that offer the highest net present value per dollar of initial outlay. This ratio is known as the **profitability index:**[10]

$$\text{Profitability index} = \frac{\text{net present value}}{\text{investment}}$$

For our three projects the profitability index is calculated as follows:[11]

Project	Investment ($ millions)	NPV ($ millions)	Profitability Index
A	10	21	2.1
B	5	16	3.2
C	5	12	2.4

Project B has the highest profitability index and C has the next highest. Therefore, if our bud-get limit is $10 million, we should accept these two projects.[12]

Unfortunately, there are some limitations to this simple ranking method. One of the most serious is that it breaks down whenever more than one resource is rationed.[13] For

---

[10]If a project requires outlays in two or more periods, the denominator should be the present value of the outlays. A few companies do not discount the benefits or costs before calculating the profitability index. The less said about these companies the better.

[11]Sometimes the profitability index is defined as the ratio of the present value to initial outlay—that is, as PV/investment. This mea-sure is also known as the *benefit–cost ratio*. To calculate the benefit–cost ratio, simply add 1.0 to each profitability index. Project rankings are unchanged.

[12]If a project has a positive profitability index, it must also have a positive NPV. Therefore, firms sometimes use the profitability index to select projects when capital is *not* limited. However, like the IRR, the profitability index can be misleading when used to choose between mutually exclusive projects. For example, suppose you were forced to choose between (1) investing $100 in a project whose payoffs have a present value of $200 or (2) investing $1 million in a project whose payoffs have a present value of $1.5 million. The first investment has the higher profitability index; the second makes you richer.

[13]It may also break down if it causes some money to be left over. It might be better to spend all the available cash even if this involves accepting a project with a slightly lower profitability index.

example, suppose that the firm can raise only $10 million for investment in *each* of years 0 and 1 and that the menu of possible projects is expanded to include an investment next year in project D:

	Cash Flows ($ millions)				
Project	C_0	C_1	C_2	NPV at 10%	Profitability Index
A	−10	+30	+ 5	21	2.1
B	− 5	+ 5	+20	16	3.2
C	− 5	+ 5	+15	12	2.4
D	0	−40	+60	13	0.4

One strategy is to accept projects B and C; however, if we do this, we cannot also accept D, which costs more than our budget limit for period 1. An alternative is to accept project A in period 0. Although this has a lower net present value than the combination of B and C, it provides a $30 million positive cash flow in period 1. When this is added to the $10 million budget, we can also afford to undertake D next year. A and D have *lower* profitability indexes than B and C, but they have a *higher* total net present value.

The reason that ranking on the profitability index fails in this example is that resources are constrained in each of two periods. In fact, this ranking method is inadequate whenever there is *any* other constraint on the choice of projects. This means that it cannot cope with cases in which two projects are mutually exclusive or in which one project is dependent on another.

For example, suppose that you have a long menu of possible projects starting this year and next. There is a limit on how much you can invest in each year. Perhaps also you can't undertake both project alpha and beta (they both require the same piece of land), and you can't invest in project gamma unless you also invest in delta (gamma is simply an add-on to delta). You need to find the package of projects that satisfies all these constraints and gives the highest NPV.

One way to tackle such a problem is to work through all possible combinations of projects. For each combination you first check whether the projects satisfy the constraints and then calculate the net present value. But it is smarter to recognize that linear programming (LP) techniques are specially designed to search through such possible combinations.

Uses of Capital Rationing Models

BEYOND THE PAGE

Capital rationing
models

mhhe.com/brealey13e

Linear programming models seem tailor-made for solving capital budgeting problems when resources are limited. Why then are they not universally accepted either in theory or in practice? One reason is that these models can turn out to be very complex. Second, as with any sophisticated long-range planning tool, there is the general problem of getting good data. It is just not worth applying costly, sophisticated methods to poor data. Furthermore, these models are based on the assumption that all future investment opportunities are known. In reality, the discovery of investment ideas is an unfolding process.

Our misgivings center in part on the basic assumption that capital is limited. This may often be the case in countries such as China and India with financial markets that are not as fully developed as those in the United States, Europe, and Japan, but, when we come to discuss company financing, we shall see that large corporations in the latter economies do not face capital rationing and can raise large sums of money on fair terms. Why then do many company presidents in these countries tell their subordinates that capital is limited? If they are right, the financial markets are seriously imperfect. What then are they doing maximizing

NPV?[14] We might be tempted to suppose that if capital is not rationed, they do not *need* to use linear programming and, if it is rationed, then surely they *ought* not to use it. But that would be too quick a judgment. Let us look at this problem more deliberately.

Soft Rationing   Many firms' capital constraints are "soft." They reflect no imperfections in financial markets. Instead they are provisional limits adopted by management as an aid to financial control.

Some ambitious divisional managers habitually overstate their investment opportunities. Rather than trying to distinguish which projects really are worthwhile, headquarters may find it simpler to impose an upper limit on divisional expenditures and thereby force the divisions to set their own priorities. In such instances, budget limits are a rough but effective way of dealing with biased cash-flow forecasts. In other cases, management may believe that very rapid corporate growth could impose intolerable strains on management and the organization. Since it is difficult to quantify such constraints explicitly, the budget limit may be used as a proxy.

Because such budget limits have nothing to do with any inefficiency in the financial market, there is no contradiction in using an LP model in the division to maximize net present value subject to the budget constraint. On the other hand, there is not much point in elaborate selection procedures if the cash-flow forecasts of the division are seriously biased.

Even if capital is not rationed, other resources may be. The availability of management time, skilled labor, or even other capital equipment often constitutes an important constraint on a company's growth. In such cases also there is no contradiction in using an LP model to select the package of projects that maximizes NPV.

Hard Rationing   Soft rationing should never cost the firm anything. If capital constraints become tight enough to hurt—in the sense that projects with significant positive NPVs are passed up—then the firm raises more money and loosens the constraint. But what if it *can't* raise more money—what if it faces *hard* rationing?

Hard rationing implies market imperfections, but that does not necessarily mean we have to throw away net present value as a criterion for capital budgeting. It depends on the nature of the imperfection.

Arizona Aquaculture Inc. (AAI) borrows as much as the banks will lend it, yet it still has good investment opportunities. This is not hard rationing so long as AAI can issue stock. But perhaps it can't. Perhaps the founder and majority shareholder vetoes the idea from fear of losing control of the firm. Perhaps a stock issue would bring costly red tape or legal complications.[15]

This does not invalidate the NPV rule. AAI's *shareholders* can borrow or lend, sell their shares, or buy more. They have free access to security markets. The type of portfolio they hold is independent of AAI's financing or investment decisions. The only way AAI can help its shareholders is to make them richer. Thus, AAI should invest its available cash in the package of projects having the largest aggregate net present value.

A barrier between the firm and financial markets does not undermine net present value so long as the barrier is the *only* market imperfection. The important thing is that the firm's *shareholders* have free access to well-functioning financial markets.

The net present value rule *is* undermined when imperfections restrict shareholders' portfolio choice. Suppose that Nevada Aquaculture Inc. (NAI) is solely owned by its founder,

---

[14]Don't forget that in the Appendix to Chapter 1 we had to assume perfect financial markets to derive the NPV rule.

[15]A majority owner who is "locked in" and has much personal wealth tied up in AAI may be effectively cut off from financial markets. The NPV rule may not make sense to such an owner, though it will to the other shareholders.

Alexander Turbot. Mr. Turbot has no cash or credit remaining, but he is convinced that expansion of his operation is a high-NPV investment. He has tried to sell stock but has found that prospective investors, skeptical of prospects for fish farming in the desert, offer him much less than he thinks his firm is worth. For Mr. Turbot, financial markets hardly exist. It makes little sense for him to discount prospective cash flows at a market opportunity cost of capital.

SUMMARY

If you are going to persuade your company to use the net present value rule, you must be prepared to explain why other rules may *not* lead to correct decisions. That is why we have examined three alternative investment criteria in this chapter.

Some firms look at the book rate of return on the project. In this case, the company decides which cash payments are capital expenditures and picks the appropriate rate to depreciate these expenditures. It then calculates the ratio of book income to the book value of the investment. Few companies nowadays base their investment decision simply on the book rate of return, but shareholders pay attention to book measures of firm profitability, and some managers therefore look with a jaundiced eye on projects that would damage the company's book rate of return.

A few companies use the payback rule to make investment decisions. In other words, they accept only those projects that recover their initial investment within some specified period. Payback is an ad hoc rule. It ignores the timing of cash flows within the payback period, and it ignores subsequent cash flows entirely. It therefore takes no account of the opportunity cost of capital.

The internal rate of return (IRR) is defined as the rate of discount at which a project would have zero NPV. It is a handy measure and widely used in finance; you should therefore know how to calculate it. The IRR rule states that companies should accept any investment offering an IRR in excess of the opportunity cost of capital. Like net present value, the IRR rule is a technique based on discounted cash flows. It will therefore give the correct answer if properly used. The problem is that it is easily misapplied. There are four things to look out for:

1. *Lending or borrowing?* If a project offers positive cash flows followed by negative flows, NPV can *rise* as the discount rate is increased. You should accept such projects if their IRR is *less* than the opportunity cost of capital.

2. *Multiple rates of return.* If there is more than one change in the sign of the cash flows, the project may have several IRRs or no IRR at all.

3. *Mutually exclusive projects.* The IRR rule may give the wrong ranking of mutually exclusive projects that differ in economic life or in the scale of required investment. If you insist on using IRR to rank mutually exclusive projects, you must examine the IRR on each incremental investment.

4. *The cost of capital for near-term cash flows may be different from the cost for distant cash flows.* The IRR rule requires you to compare the project's IRR with the opportunity cost of capital. But sometimes there is more than one opportunity cost of capital. For example, if the term structure of interest rates is steeply upward-sloping, the financial manager may decide to use a lower discount rate for near than for distant cash flows. In these cases there is no simple yardstick for evaluating the IRR of a project.

In developing the NPV rule, we assumed that the company can maximize shareholder wealth by accepting every project that is worth more than it costs. But, if capital is strictly limited, then it may not be possible to take every project with a positive NPV. If capital is rationed in only one period, then the firm should follow a simple rule: Calculate each project's profitability index, which is the project's net present value per dollar of investment. Then pick the projects with the highest profitability indexes until you run out of capital. Unfortunately, this procedure fails when capital is rationed in more than one period or when there are other constraints on project choice. The only general solution is linear programming.

Hard capital rationing always reflects a market imperfection—a barrier between the firm and financial markets. If that barrier also implies that the firm's shareholders lack free access to a well-functioning financial market, the very foundations of net present value crumble. Fortunately, hard rationing is rare for corporations in the United States. Many firms do use soft capital rationing, however. That is, they set up self-imposed limits as a means of financial planning and control.

For a survey of capital budgeting procedures, see:

J. Graham and C. Harvey, "How Do CFOs Make Capital Budgeting and Capital Structure Decisions?" *Journal of Applied Corporate Finance* 15 (Spring 2002), pp. 8–23.

FURTHER READING

 Select problems are available in McGraw-Hill's *Connect.* Answers to questions with an "*" are found in the Appendix.

PROBLEM SETS

1. **Payback***

   a. What is the payback period on each of the following projects?

	Cash Flows ($)				
Project	C_0	C_1	C_2	C_3	C_4
A	−5,000	+1,000	+1,000	+3,000	0
B	−1,000	0	+1,000	+2,000	+3,000
C	−5,000	+1,000	+1,000	+3,000	+5,000

   b. Given that you wish to use the payback rule with a cutoff period of two years, which projects would you accept?

   c. If you use a cutoff period of three years, which projects would you accept?

   d. If the opportunity cost of capital is 10%, which projects have positive NPVs?

   e. "If a firm uses a single cutoff period for all projects, it is likely to accept too many short-lived projects." True or false?

   f. If the firm uses the discounted-payback rule, will it accept any negative-NPV projects? Will it turn down any positive-NPV projects?

2. **Payback** Consider the following projects:

	Cash Flows ($)					
Project	C_0	C_1	C_2	C_3	C_4	C_5
A	−1,000	+1,000	0	0	0	0
B	−2,000	+1,000	+1,000	+4,000	+1,000	+1,000
C	−3,000	+1,000	+1,000	0	+1,000	+1,000

   a. If the opportunity cost of capital is 10%, which projects have a positive NPV?

   b. Calculate the payback period for each project.

   c. Which project(s) would a firm using the payback rule accept if the cutoff period is three years?

   d. Calculate the discounted payback period for each project.

   e. Which project(s) would a firm using the discounted payback rule accept if the cutoff period is three years?

3. **Payback and IRR rules** Respond to the following comments:

   a. "I like the IRR rule. I can use it to rank projects without having to specify a discount rate."

   b. "I like the payback rule. As long as the minimum payback period is short, the rule makes sure that the company takes no borderline projects. That reduces risk."

4. **IRR** Write down the equation defining a project's internal rate of return (IRR). In practice how is IRR calculated?

5. **IRR***

   a. Calculate the net present value of the following project for discount rates of 0, 50, and 100%:

Cash Flows ($)		
C_0	C_1	C_2
−6,750	+4,500	+18,000

   b. What is the IRR of the project?

6. **IRR** Calculate the IRR (or IRRs) for the following project:

C_0	C_1	C_0	C_0
−3,000	+3,500	+4,000	−4,000

For what range of discount rates does the project have a positive NPV?

7. **IRR rule** You have the chance to participate in a project that produces the following cash flows:

Cash Flows ($)		
C_0	C_1	C_2
+5,000	+4,000	−11,000

The internal rate of return is 13%. If the opportunity cost of capital is 10%, would you accept the offer?

8. **IRR rule*** Consider a project with the following cash flows:

Cash Flows ($)		
C_0	C_1	C_2
−100	+200	−75

   a. How many internal rates of return does this project have?

   b. Which of the following numbers is the project IRR: (i) −50%; (ii) −12%; (iii) +5%; (iv) +50%?

   c. The opportunity cost of capital is 20%. Is this an attractive project? Briefly explain.

9. **IRR rule*** Consider projects Alpha and Beta:

	Cash Flows ($)			
Project	C_0	C_1	C_2	IRR (%)
Alpha	−400,000	+241,000	+293,000	21
Beta	−200,000	+131,000	+172,000	31

The opportunity cost of capital is 8%. Suppose you can undertake Alpha or Beta, but not both. Use the IRR rule to make the choice. (*Hint:* What's the incremental investment in Alpha?)

10. **IRR rule** Consider the following two mutually exclusive projects:

	Cash flows ($)			
Project	C_0	C_1	C_2	C_3
A	−100	+60	+60	0
B	−100	0	0	+140

a. Calculate the NPV of each project for discount rates of 0%, 10%, and 20%. Plot these on a graph with NPV on the vertical axis and discount rate on the horizontal axis.

b. What is the approximate IRR for each project?

c. In what circumstances should the company accept project A?

d. Calculate the NPV of the incremental investment (B − A) for discount rates of 0%, 10%, and 20%. Plot these on your graph. Show that the circumstances in which you would accept A are also those in which the IRR on the incremental investment is less than the opportunity cost of capital.

11. **IRR rule** Mr. Cyrus Clops, the president of Giant Enterprises, has to make a choice between two possible investments:

	Cash Flows ($ thousands)			
Project	C_0	C_1	C_2	IRR (%)
A	−400	+250	+300	23
B	−200	+140	+179	36

The opportunity cost of capital is 9%. Mr. Clops is tempted to take B, which has the higher IRR.

a. Explain to Mr. Clops why this is not the correct procedure.

b. Show him how to adapt the IRR rule to choose the best project.

c. Show him that this project also has the higher NPV.

12. **IRR rule** The Titanic Shipbuilding Company has a noncancelable contract to build a small cargo vessel. Construction involves a cash outlay of $250,000 at the end of each of the next two years. At the end of the third year the company will receive payment of $650,000. The company can speed up construction by working an extra shift. In this case there will be a cash outlay of $550,000 at the end of the first year followed by a cash payment of $650,000 at the end of the second year. Use the IRR rule to show the (approximate) range of opportunity costs of capital at which the company should work the extra shift.

13. **IRR rule** Plot the NPVs for the following projects for discount rates from 0% to 30%:

Project	C_0	C_1	C_2
A	− 100	20	100
B	−1,000	2260	−1,270
C	100	−50	−80
D	−1,080	2510	−1,500

a. Which one of these projects has no IRR?

b. One of the projects has two IRRs. Which is this project and what are the IRRs?

c. What are the IRRs of the other two projects?

d. Suppose projects A and C are mutually exclusive. If the cost of capital is 6%, which one would you accept?

e. If the cost of capital is very high, would you accept project C? Why or why not?

14. **Investment criteria** Consider the following two projects:

Cash flows	Project A	Project B
C_0	−$200	−$200
C_1	80	100
C_2	80	100
C_3	80	100
C_4	80	

a. If the opportunity cost of capital is 11%, which of these two projects would you accept (A, B, or both)?

b. Suppose that you can choose only one of these two projects. Which would you choose? The discount rate is still 11%.

c. Which one would you choose if the cost of capital is 16%?

d. What is the payback period of each project?

e. Is the project with the shortest payback period also the one with the highest NPV?

f. What are the internal rates of return on the two projects?

g. Does the IRR rule in this case give the same answer as NPV?

h. If the opportunity cost of capital is 11%, what is the profitability index for each project? Is the project with the highest profitability index also the one with the highest NPV? Which measure should you use to choose between the projects?

15. **Profitability index** Look again at projects D and E in Section 5-3. Assume that the projects are mutually exclusive and that the opportunity cost of capital is 10%.

a. Calculate the profitability index for each project.

b. Show how the profitability-index rule can be used to select the superior project.

16. **Capital rationing*** Suppose you have the following investment opportunities, but only $90,000 available for investment. Which projects should you take?

Project	NPV ($)	Investment ($)
1	5,000	10,000
2	5,000	5,000
3	10,000	90,000
4	15,000	60,000
5	15,000	75,000
6	3,000	15,000

17. **Capital rationing** Borgia Pharmaceuticals has $1 million allocated for capital expenditures. Which of the following projects should the company accept to stay within the $1 million budget? How much does the budget limit cost the company in terms of its market value? The opportunity cost of capital for each project is 11%.

Project	Investment ($ thousand)	NPV ($ thousand)	IRR (%)
1	300	66	17.2
2	200	−4	10.7
3	250	43	16.6
4	100	14	12.1
5	100	7	11.8
6	350	63	18.0
7	400	48	13.0

CHALLENGE PROBLEMS

18. **NPV and IRR rules** Some people believe firmly, even passionately, that ranking projects on IRR is OK if each project's cash flows can be reinvested at the project's IRR. They also say that the NPV rule "assumes that cash flows are reinvested at the opportunity cost of capital." Think carefully about these statements. Are they true? Are they helpful?

19. **Modified IRR** Look again at the project cash flows in Problem 6. Calculate the modified IRR as defined in footnote 5 in Section 5-3. Assume the cost of capital is 12%.

    Now try the following variation on the MIRR concept. Figure out the fraction x such that x times C_1 and C_2 has the same present value as (minus) C_3.

$$xC_1 + \frac{xC_2}{1.12} = -\frac{C_3}{1.12^2}$$

Define the modified project IRR as the solution of

$$C_0 + \frac{(1-x)C_1}{1+\text{IRR}} + \frac{(1-x)C_2}{(1+\text{IRR})^2} = 0$$

Now you have two MIRRs. Which is more meaningful? If you can't decide, what do you conclude about the usefulness of MIRRs?

20. **Capital rationing** Consider the following capital rationing problem:

    Set up this problem as a linear program and solve it.

You can allow partial investments, that is, $0 \leq x \leq 1$. Calculate and interpret the shadow prices[16] on the capital constraints.

Project	C_0	C_1	C_2	NPV
W	−10,000	−10,000	0	+6,700
X	0	−20,000	+5,000	+9,000
Y	−10,000	+ 5,000	+5,000	+0
Z	−15,000	+ 5,000	+4,000	−1,500
Financing available	20,000	20,000	20,000	

MINI-CASE ● ● ● ● ●

Vegetron's CFO Calls Again

(The first episode of this story was presented in Section 5-1.)

Later that afternoon, Vegetron's CFO bursts into your office in a state of anxious confusion. The problem, he explains, is a last-minute proposal for a change in the design of the fermentation tanks that Vegetron will build to extract hydrated zirconium from a stockpile of powdered ore. The CFO has brought a printout (Table 5.1) of the forecasted revenues, costs, income, and book rates of return for the standard, low-temperature design. Vegetron's engineers have just proposed an alternative high-temperature design that will extract most of the hydrated zirconium over a shorter period, five instead of seven years. The forecasts for the high-temperature method are given in Table 5.2.[17]

CFO: Why do these engineers always have a bright idea at the last minute? But you've got to admit the high-temperature process looks good. We'll get a faster payback, and the rate of return beats Vegetron's 9% cost of capital in every year except the first. Let's see, income is $30,000 per year. Average investment is half the $400,000 capital outlay, or $200,000, so the average rate of return is 30,000/200,000, or 15%—a lot better than the 9% hurdle rate. The average rate of return for the low-temperature process is not that good, only 28,000/200,000, or 14%. Of course, we might get a higher rate of return for the low-temperature proposal if we depreciated the investment faster—do you think we should try that?

You: Let's not fixate on book accounting numbers. Book income is not the same as cash flow to Vegetron or its investors. Book rates of return don't measure the true rate of return.

CFO: But people use accounting numbers all the time. We have to publish them in our annual report to investors.

You: Accounting numbers have many valid uses, but they're not a sound basis for capital investment decisions. Accounting changes can have big effects on book income or rate of return, even when cash flows are unchanged.

Here's an example. Suppose the accountant depreciates the capital investment for the low-temperature process over six years rather than seven. Then income for years 1 to 6 goes down because depreciation is higher. Income for year 7 goes up because the depreciation for that

---

[16] A shadow price is the marginal change in the objective for a marginal change in the constraint.
[17] For simplicity we have ignored taxes. There will be plenty about taxes in Chapter 6.

	Year						
	1	2	3	4	5	6	7
1. Revenue	140	140	140	140	140	140	140
2. Operating costs	55	55	55	55	55	55	55
3. Depreciation[a]	57	57	57	57	57	57	57
4. Net income	28	28	28	28	28	28	28
5. Start-of-year book value[b]	400	343	286	229	171	114	57
6. Book rate of return (4 ÷ 5)	7%	8.2%	9.8%	12.2%	16.4%	24.6%	49.1%

〉TABLE 5.1   Income statement and book rates of return for low-temperature extraction of hydrated zirconium ($ thousands)

[a] Rounded. Straight-line depreciation over seven years is 400/7 = 57.14, or $57,140 per year.
[b] Capital investment is $400,000 in year 0.

	Year				
	1	2	3	4	5
1. Revenue	180	180	180	180	180
2. Operating costs	70	70	70	70	70
3. Depreciation[a]	80	80	80	80	80
4. Net income	30	30	30	30	30
5. Start-of-year book value[b]	400	320	240	160	80
6. Book rate of return (4 ÷ 5)	7.5%	9.4%	12.5%	18.75%	37.5%

〉TABLE 5.2   Income statement and book rates of return for high-temperature extraction of hydrated zirconium ($ thousands)

[a] Straight-line depreciation over five years is 400/5 = 80, or $80,000 per year.
[b] Capital investment is $400,000 in year 0.

year becomes zero. But there is no effect on year-to-year cash flows because depreciation is not a cash outlay. It is simply the accountant's device for spreading out the "recovery" of the up-front capital outlay over the life of the project.

CFO: So how do we get cash flows?

You: In these cases, it's easy. Depreciation is the only noncash entry in your spreadsheets (Tables 5.1 and 5.2), so we can just leave it out of the calculation. Cash flow equals revenue minus operating costs. For the high-temperature process, annual cash flow is:

Cash flow = revenue − operating cost = 180 − 70 = 110, or $110,000

CFO: In effect you're adding back depreciation because depreciation is a noncash accounting expense.

You: Right. You could also do it that way:

Cash flow = net income + depreciation = 30 + 80 = 110, or $110,000

CFO: Of course. I remember all this now, but book returns seem important when someone shoves them in front of your nose.

You: It's not clear which project is better. The high-temperature process appears to be less efficient. It has higher operating costs and generates less total revenue over the life of the project, but of course, it generates more cash flow in years 1 to 5.

CFO: Maybe the processes are equally good from a financial point of view. If so, we'll stick with the low-temperature process rather than switching at the last minute.

You: We'll have to lay out the cash flows and calculate NPV for each process.

CFO: OK, do that. I'll be back in a half hour—and I also want to see each project's true, DCF rate of return.

QUESTIONS

1. Are the book rates of return reported in Tables 5.1 and 5.2 useful inputs for the capital investment decision?

2. Calculate NPV and IRR for each process. What is your recommendation? Be ready to explain to the CFO.

Making Investment Decisions with the Net Present Value Rule

In 2017, Intel announced plans to invest over $7 billion to produce 7-nanometer chips in its Chandler, Arizona, facility. How does a company such as Intel decide to go ahead with such a massive investment? We know the answer in principle. The company needs to forecast the project's cash flows and discount them at the opportunity cost of capital to arrive at the project's NPV. A project with a positive NPV increases shareholder value.

But those cash flow forecasts do not arrive on a silver platter. For example, Intel's managers would have needed answers to several basic questions. How soon can the new plant be brought into operation? How many semiconductor chips are likely to be sold each year and at what price? How much does the firm need to invest in the new facilities, and what is the likely production cost? How long will the chips stay in production, and what happens to the plant and equipment at the end of that time?

These predictions need to be pulled together to produce a single set of cash-flow forecasts. That requires careful tracking of taxes; changes in working capital; inflation; and the end-of-project salvage values of plant, property, and equipment. The financial manager must also ferret out hidden cash flows and take care to reject accounting entries that look like cash flows but truly are not.

Our first task in this chapter is to look at how to develop a set of project cash flows. We set out several rules of good financial practice. Later in the chapter, we work through a realistic and comprehensive example of a capital investment analysis.

This is the first chapter in which we grapple with the complexities of taxes. Therefore, we have added a section that includes an overview of corporate income taxes and the dramatic recent changes in the U.S. tax code.

We conclude the chapter by looking at how the financial manager should apply the present value rule when choosing between investment in plant and equipment with different economic lives. For example, suppose you must decide between machine Y with a 5-year useful life and a similar machine Z with a 10-year life. The present value of Y's lifetime investment and operating costs is naturally less than Z's because Z will last twice as long. Does that necessarily make Y the better choice? Of course not. You will find that when you are faced with this type of problem, the trick is to transform the present value of the cash flow into an *equivalent annual* flow—that is, the total cash per year from buying and operating the asset.

6-1 Applying the Net Present Value Rule

Many projects require a heavy initial outlay on new production facilities. But often the largest investments involve the acquisition of intangible assets. For example, U.S. banks invest huge sums annually in new information technology (IT) projects. Much of this expenditure goes to intangibles such as system design, programming, testing, and training. Think also of the huge expenditure by pharmaceutical companies on research and development (R&D). Merck, one of the largest pharmaceutical companies, spends more than $7 billion a year on R&D. The R&D cost of bringing *one* new prescription drug to market has been estimated at more than $2 billion.

Expenditures on intangible assets such as IT and R&D are investments just like expenditures on new plant and equipment. In each case, the company is spending money today in the expectation that it will generate a stream of future profits. Ideally, firms should apply the same criteria to all capital investments, regardless of whether they involve a tangible or intangible asset.

We have seen that an investment in any asset creates wealth if the discounted value of the future cash flows exceeds the up-front cost. Up to this point, however, we have glossed over the problem of *what* to discount. When you are faced with this problem, you should stick to five general rules:

1. Discount cash flows, not profits.
2. Discount *incremental* cash flows.
3. Treat inflation consistently.
4. Separate investment and financing decisions.
5. Forecast and deduct taxes.

We discuss each of these rules in turn.

Rule 1: Discount Cash Flows, Not Profits

The first and most important point: Net present value depends on the expected future cash flow. Cash flow is simply the difference between cash received and cash paid out. Many people nevertheless confuse cash flow with accounting income. Accounting income is intended to show how well the company is performing. Therefore, accountants *start* with "dollars in" and "dollars out," but to obtain accounting income, they adjust these inputs in two principal ways.

Capital Expenses When calculating expenditures, the accountant deducts *current* expenses but does not deduct *capital* expenses. There is a good reason for this. If the firm lays out a large amount of money on a big capital project, you do not conclude that the firm is performing poorly, even though a lot of cash is going out the door. Therefore, instead of deducting capital expenditure as it occurs, the accountant depreciates the outlay over several years.

That makes sense when judging firm performance, but it will get you into trouble when working out net present value. For example, suppose that you are analyzing an investment proposal. It costs $2,000 and is expected to provide a cash flow of $1,500 in the first year and $500 in the second. If the accountant depreciates the capital expenditure straight line over the two years, accounting income is $500 in year 1 and −$500 in year 2:

	Year 1	Year 2
Cash inflow	+$1,500	+$ 500
Less depreciation	− 1,000	− 1,000
Accounting income	+$ 500	−$ 500

Suppose you were given this forecast income and naïvely discounted it at 10%. NPV would appear positive:

$$\text{Apparent NPV} = \frac{\$500}{1.10} + \frac{-\$500}{1.10^2} = \$41.32$$

This has to be nonsense. The project is obviously a loser. You are laying out $2,000 today and simply getting it back later. At any positive discount rate the project has a negative NPV.

The message is clear: When calculating NPV, state capital expenditures when they occur, not later when they show up as depreciation. To go from accounting income to cash flow, you need to add back depreciation (which is not a cash outflow) and subtract capital expenditure (which is a cash outflow).

Working Capital   When measuring income, accountants try to show profit as it is *earned,* rather than when the company and its customers get around to paying their bills.

For example, consider a company that spends $60 to produce goods in period 1. It sells these goods in period 2 for $100, but its customers do not pay their bills until period 3. The following diagram shows the firm's cash flows. In period 1 there is a cash *outflow* of $60. Then, when customers pay their bills in period 3, there is an *inflow* of $100.

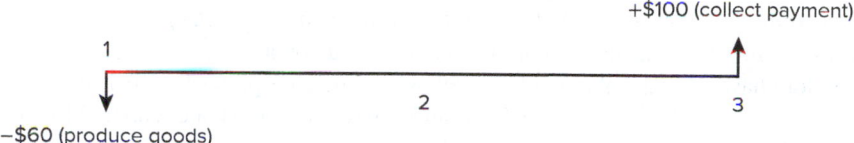

It would be misleading to say that the firm was running at a loss in period 1 (when cash flow was negative) or that it was extremely profitable in period 3 (when cash flow was positive). Therefore, the accountant looks at when the sale was made (period 2 in our example) and gathers together all the revenues and expenses associated with that sale. In the case of our company, the accountant would show for period 2.

Revenue	$100
Less cost of goods sold	− 60
Income	$ 40

Of course, the accountant cannot ignore the actual timing of the cash expenditures and payments. So the $60 cash outlay in the first period will be treated not as an expense but as an *investment* in inventories. Subsequently, in period 2, when the goods are taken out of inventory and sold, the accountant shows a $60 *reduction* in inventories.

The accountant also does not ignore the fact that the firm has to wait to collect on its bills. When the sale is made in period 2, the accountant will record accounts receivable of $100 to show that the company's customers owe $100 in unpaid bills. Later, when the customers pay those bills in period 3, accounts receivable are reduced by that $100.

To go from the figure for income to the actual cash flows, you need to add back these changes in inventories and receivables:

	Period		
	1	**2**	**3**
Accounting income	0	+40	0
− Investment in inventories	−60	+60	0
− Investment in receivables	0	−100	+100
= Cash flow	−60	0	+100

Net working capital (often referred to simply as *working capital*) is the difference between a company's short-term assets and liabilities. Accounts receivable and inventories of raw materials, work in progress, and finished goods are the principal short-term assets. The principal short-term liabilities are accounts payable (bills that *you* have not paid) and taxes that have been incurred but not yet paid.[1]

Most projects entail an investment in working capital. Each period's change in working capital should be recognized in your cash-flow forecasts.[2] By the same token, when the project comes to an end, you can usually recover some of the investment. This results in a cash inflow. (In our simple example the company made an investment in working capital of $60 in period 1 and $40 in period 2. It made a *disinvestment* of $100 in period 3, when the customers paid their bills.)

Working capital is a common source of confusion in capital investment calculations. Here are the most common mistakes:

1. *Forgetting about working capital entirely.* We hope that you do not fall into that trap.

2. *Forgetting that working capital may change during the life of the project.* Imagine that you sell $100,000 of goods a year and customers pay on average six months late. You therefore have $50,000 of unpaid bills. Now you increase prices by 10%, so revenues increase to $110,000. If customers continue to pay six months late, unpaid bills increase to $55,000, and so you need to make an *additional* investment in working capital of $5,000.

3. *Forgetting that working capital is recovered at the end of the project.* When the project comes to an end, inventories are run down, any unpaid bills are (you hope) paid off, and you recover your investment in working capital. This generates a cash *inflow*.

Rule 2: Discount Incremental Cash Flows

The value of a project depends on *all* the additional cash flows that follow from project acceptance. Here are some things to watch for when you are deciding which cash flows to include.

Include All Incidental Effects   It is important to consider a project's effects on the remainder of the firm's business. For example, suppose Sony proposes to launch PlayStation X, a new version of its videogame console. Demand for the new product will almost certainly cut into sales of Sony's existing consoles. This incidental effect needs to be factored into the incremental cash flows. Of course, Sony may reason that it needs to go ahead with the new product because its existing product line is likely to come under increasing threat from competitors. So, even if it decides not to produce the new PlayStation, there is no guarantee that sales of the existing consoles will continue at their present level. Sooner or later, they will decline.

Sometimes a new project will *help* the firm's existing business. Suppose that you are the financial manager of an airline that is considering opening a new short-haul route from Harrisburg, Pennsylvania, to Chicago's O'Hare Airport. When considered in isolation, the new route may have a negative NPV. But once you allow for the additional business that the new route brings to your other traffic out of O'Hare, it may be a very worthwhile investment.

Do Not Confuse Average with Incremental Payoffs   Most managers naturally hesitate to throw good money after bad. For example, they are reluctant to invest more money in a losing division. But occasionally you will encounter turnaround opportunities in which the *incremental* NPV from investing in a loser is strongly positive.

Conversely, it does not always make sense to throw good money after good. A division with an outstanding past profitability record may have run out of good opportunities. You would not pay a large sum for a 20-year-old horse, sentiment aside, regardless of how many races that horse had won or how many champions it had sired.

---

[1] If you delay paying *your* bills, your investment in net working capital is reduced. When you finally pay up, it is increased.

[2] Holdings of cash and marketable securities are also short-term assets and debt due within a year is a short-term liability. These are *not* relevant to your capital budgeting calculations.

Here is another example illustrating the difference between average and incremental returns: Suppose that a railroad bridge is in urgent need of repair. With the bridge the railroad can continue to operate; without the bridge it can't. In this case, the payoff from the repair work consists of all the benefits of operating the railroad. The incremental NPV of such an investment may be enormous. Of course, these benefits should be net of all other costs and all subsequent repairs; otherwise, the company may be misled into rebuilding an unprofitable railroad piece by piece.

Forecast Product Sales but also Recognize After-Sales Cash Flows   Financial managers should forecast all incremental cash flows generated by an investment. Sometimes these incremental cash flows last for decades. When GE commits to the design and production of a new jet engine, the cash inflows come first from the sale of engines and then from service and spare parts. A jet engine will be in use for 30 years. Over that period revenues from service and spare parts will be roughly seven times the engine's purchase price.

Many other manufacturing companies depend on the revenues that come *after* their products are sold. For example, the consulting firm Accenture estimates that services and parts typically account for about 25% of revenues and 50% of profits for auto companies.[3]

Include Opportunity Costs   The cost of a resource may be relevant to the investment decision even when no cash changes hands. For example, suppose a new manufacturing operation uses land that could otherwise be sold for $100,000. This resource is not free: It has an opportunity cost, which is the cash it could generate for the company if the project were rejected and the resource were sold or put to some other productive use.

This example prompts us to warn you against judging projects on the basis of "before versus after." The proper comparison is "with or without." A manager comparing before versus after might not assign any value to the land because the firm owns it both before and after:

Before	Take Project	After	Cash Flow, Before versus After
Firm owns land	→	Firm still owns land	0

The proper comparison, with or without, is as follows:

With	Take Project	After	Cash Flow, with Project
Firm owns land	→	Firm still owns land	0

Without	Do Not Take Project	After	Cash Flow, without Project
	→	Firm sells land for $100,000	$100,000

Comparing the two possible "afters," we see that the firm gives up $100,000 by undertaking the project. This reasoning still holds if the land will not be sold but is worth $100,000 to the firm in some other use.

Sometimes opportunity costs may be very difficult to estimate; however, where the resource can be freely traded, its opportunity cost is simply equal to the market price. Consider a widely used aircraft such as the Boeing 737. Secondhand 737s are regularly traded, and their prices

---

[3] Accenture, "Refocusing on the After-Sales Market," 2010.

are quoted on the web. So, if an airline needs to know the opportunity cost of continuing to use one of its 737s, it just needs to look up the market price of a similar plane. The opportunity cost of using the plane is equal to the cost of buying an equivalent aircraft to replace it.

Forget Sunk Costs   Sunk costs are like spilled milk: They are past and irreversible outflows. Because sunk costs are bygones, they cannot be affected by the decision to accept or reject the project, and so they should be ignored.

Take the case of the James Webb Space Telescope. It was originally supposed to launch in 2011 and cost $1.6 billion. But the project became progressively more expensive and further behind schedule. Latest estimates put the cost at $8.8 billion and a launch date of 2019. When Congress debated whether to cancel the program, supporters of the project argued that it would be foolish to abandon a project on which so much had already been spent. Others countered that it would be even more foolish to continue with a project that had proved so costly. Both groups were guilty of the *sunk-cost fallacy;* the money that had already been spent by NASA was irrecoverable and, therefore, irrelevant to the decision to terminate the project.

Beware of Allocated Overhead Costs   We have already mentioned that the accountant's objective is not always the same as the investment analyst's. A case in point is the allocation of overhead costs. Overheads include such items as supervisory salaries, rent, heat, and light. These overheads may not be related to any particular project, but they have to be paid for somehow. Therefore, when the accountant assigns costs to the firm's projects, a charge for overhead is usually made. Now our principle of incremental cash flows says that in investment appraisal we should include only the *extra* expenses that would result from the project. A project may generate extra overhead expenses; then again, it may not. We should be cautious about assuming that the accountant's allocation of overheads represents the true extra expenses that would be incurred.

Remember Salvage Value   When the project comes to an end, you may be able to sell the plant and equipment or redeploy the assets elsewhere in the business. If the equipment is sold, you must pay tax on the difference between the sale price and the book value of the asset. The salvage value (net of any taxes) represents a positive cash flow to the firm.

Some projects have significant shutdown costs, in which case the final cash flows may be *negative.* For example, the mining company, FCX, has earmarked $451 million to cover the future reclamation and closure costs of its New Mexico mines.

Rule 3: Treat Inflation Consistently

As we pointed out in Chapter 3, interest rates are usually quoted in *nominal* rather than *real* terms. For example, if you buy an 8% Treasury bond, the government promises to pay you $80 interest each year, but it does not promise what that $80 will buy. Investors take inflation into account when they decide what is an acceptable rate of interest.

If the discount rate is stated in nominal terms, then consistency requires that cash flows should also be estimated in nominal terms, taking account of trends in selling price, labor and materials costs, and so on. This calls for more than simply applying a single assumed inflation rate to all components of cash flow. Labor costs per hour of work, for example, normally increase at a faster rate than the consumer price index because of improvements in productivity. Tax savings from depreciation do *not* increase with inflation; they are constant in nominal terms because tax law in most countries allows only the original cost of assets to be depreciated.

Of course, there is nothing wrong with discounting real cash flows at a real discount rate. In fact, this is standard procedure in countries with high and volatile inflation. Here is a simple example showing that real and nominal discounting, properly applied, always give the same present value.

Suppose your firm usually forecasts cash flows in nominal terms and discounts at a 15% nominal rate. In this particular case, however, you are given project cash flows in real terms, that is, current dollars:

Real Cash Flows ($ thousands)			
C_0	1	C_2	C_3
−100	+35	+50	+30

It would be inconsistent to discount these real cash flows at the 15% nominal rate. You have two alternatives: Either restate the cash flows in nominal terms and discount at 15%, or restate the discount rate in real terms and use it to discount the real cash flows.

Assume that inflation is projected at 10% a year. Then the cash flow for year 1, which is $35,000 in current dollars, will be $35,000 \times 1.10 = \$38,500$ in year-1 dollars. Similarly, the cash flow for year 2 will be $50,000 \times (1.10)^2 = \$60,500$ in year-2 dollars, and so on. If we discount these nominal cash flows at the 15% nominal discount rate, we have

$$NPV = -100 + \frac{38.5}{1.15} + \frac{60.5}{(1.15)^2} + \frac{39.9}{(1.15)^3} = 5.5, \text{ or } \$5,500$$

Instead of converting the cash-flow forecasts into nominal terms, we could convert the discount rate into real terms by using the following relationship:

$$\text{Real discount rate} = \frac{1 + \text{nominal discount rate}}{1 + \text{inflation rate}} - 1$$

In our example, this gives

$$\text{Real discount rate} = \frac{1.15}{1.10} - 1 = .045, \text{ or } 4.5\%$$

If we now discount the real cash flows by the real discount rate, we have an NPV of $5,500, just as before:

$$NPV = -100 + \frac{35}{1.045} + \frac{50}{(1.045)^2} + \frac{30}{(1.045)^3} = 5.5, \text{ or } \$5,500$$

The message of all this is quite simple. Discount nominal cash flows at a nominal discount rate. Discount real cash flows at a real rate. *Never* mix real cash flows with nominal discount rates or nominal flows with real rates.

Rule 4: Separate Investment and Financing Decisions

Suppose you finance a project partly with debt. How should you treat the proceeds from the debt issue and the interest and principal payments on the debt? Answer: You should *neither* subtract the debt proceeds from the required investment *nor* recognize the interest and principal payments on the debt as cash outflows. Regardless of the actual financing, you should view the project as if it were all-equity-financed, treating all cash outflows required for the project as coming from stockholders and all cash inflows as going to them.

This procedure focuses exclusively on the *project* cash flows, not the cash flows associated with alternative financing schemes. It, therefore, allows you to separate the analysis of the investment decision from that of the financing decision. We explain how to recognize the effect of financing choices on project values in Chapter 19.

Rule 5: Remember to Deduct Taxes

Taxes are an expense just like wages and raw materials. Therefore, cash flows should be estimated on an after-tax basis. Subtract cash outflows for taxes from pretax cash flows and discount the net amount.

Some firms do not deduct tax payments. They try to offset this mistake by discounting the pretax cash flows at a rate that is higher than the cost of capital. Unfortunately, there is no reliable formula for making such adjustments to the discount rate.

Be careful to subtract cash taxes. Cash taxes paid are usually different from the taxes reported on the income statement provided to shareholders. For example, the shareholder accounts typically assume straight-line depreciation instead of the accelerated depreciation allowed by the U.S. tax code. We will highlight the differences between straight-line and accelerated depreciation later in this chapter.

The next section takes a broader look at corporate income taxes and the recent changes in the U.S. tax code.

6-2 Corporate Income Taxes

Look at Table 6.1, which shows corporate income tax rates in 11 countries. These are the tax rates imposed by the national governments, but corporations may also need to pay tax to a regional government. For example, in Canada, the provincial governments levy an additional tax of between 11% and 16%. In the United States, states and some municipalities also impose an extra layer of corporate tax that averages around 4%. To complicate matters further, in many countries, the first tranche of income may be taxed at a lower rate, or special arrangements may apply to some types of business.

Tax rates change over time, sometimes dramatically. For example, the U.K. has cut its corporate tax rate from 30% in 1998 to 19% today. The U.S. reduced its rate from 35% to 21% starting in 2018. This rate reduction was one of several important changes in U.S. corporate income taxes. We summarize the changes now.

Country	Corporate Tax Rate (%)
Australia	30
Brazil	34
Canada	15
China	25
France	33
Germany	16
India	30
Ireland	13
Japan	34
United Kingdom	19
United States	21

❭**TABLE 6.1** National corporate tax rates

Source: PWC, Worldwide Tax Summaries: Corporate Taxes, 2017/2018, www.pwc.com/taxsummaries.

U.S. Corporate Income Tax Reform

The U.S. Tax Cuts and Jobs Act was passed in December 2017 and implemented immediately in 2018. Suddenly, the corporate tax rate dropped from 35% to 21%. But there were several other important changes.[4]

Depreciation Before 2018, when calculating taxable income, U.S. corporations were allowed to deduct an immediate bonus depreciation of 50% of the asset's cost. The fraction of the investment not covered by this bonus depreciation was then depreciated over the following years using the modified accelerated cost recovery system (MACRS), a form of accelerated depreciation. ("Accelerated" means that depreciation is front-loaded: higher in the early years of an asset's life but lower as the asset ages. Straight-line depreciation is the same in all years.) But the new tax law allows companies to take bonus depreciation sufficient to write off 100% of investment immediately—the ultimate in accelerated depreciation. With 100% bonus depreciation, the firm can treat investments in plant and equipment as immediate expenses.

Bonus depreciation is a temporary provision, however. It is scheduled for phase-out starting in 2023. By 2027, it will be gone. We will have to wait and see what depreciation schedules apply to investments not covered by 100% bonus depreciation. Perhaps it will be that old standby MACRS. We discuss MACRS and other forms of accelerated depreciation in the next section.

Investment in real estate does not qualify for bonus or accelerated depreciation. It is depreciated straight-line over periods of 15 years or more.

Amortization of Research Expenses U.S. companies can now could write off most outlays for R&D as immediate expenses. Starting in 2022, most R&D investments must be amortized (depreciated) over a five-year period. Many observers were puzzled by this change. If investments in plant and equipment now (2018–2022) qualify for immediate expensing, why must investments in R&D, which used to be expensed, be put on the balance sheet and amortized?

Tax Carry-Forwards When a corporation makes a profit, it pays tax. But what happens when it suffers a loss? In 2017 and earlier, U.S. corporations could carry back losses to recover taxes paid on the prior two years' income. Starting in 2018, carry-backs are no longer allowed. But corporations can carry forward losses indefinitely, using the losses to offset up to 80% of future years' income. Suppose, for example, that a manufacturer of gargle blasters loses $100,000 in 2018 but earns $100,000 in 2019 and 2020. It pays no tax in 2018, but carries forward the loss. In 2019, it uses $80,000 of the loss to offset income, paying tax of $4,200 (21% of $20,000). In 2020, it uses the remaining $20,000 carried forward, paying tax of $16,800 (21% of $80,000).

Limits on Interest Deductions U.S. tax law treats interest on debt as a tax-deductible expense. In Chapters 17 and 18, we will show that the resulting *interest tax shields* favor debt over equity financing. But interest deductions are now (2018–2021) limited to 30% of taxable income before depreciation and amortization, though unused deductions can be carried forward and used in later years. From 2022 on, interest deductions are limited to 30% of taxable income *after* depreciation and amortization. (There are exceptions for small businesses, car dealerships, farmers, and some other taxpayers.) In other words, the limit from 2018–2021 is 30% of taxable EBITDA (earnings before interest, taxes, depreciation, and amortization); from 2022, it is 30% of taxable EBIT (earnings before interest and taxes). EBIT is smaller than EBITDA, so the restriction on interest deductions is tighter post-2021.

It appears that most large U.S. corporations will be safely below the 30% limits. But those corporations that do hit the limits may have to rethink their valuation methods and financing strategies. We cover these issues in Chapters 18, 19, and 25.

---

[4] The Tax Cuts and Jobs Act is much more extensive and complicated than the changes that we outline here. For example, we say nothing about changes in personal income taxes. We are not offering comprehensive tax advice, just noting the most important changes for corporate finance.

Territorial versus Worldwide Taxation   Most countries have *territorial* corporate income taxes: They tax income earned in their own countries but not outside their borders. The United States switched over to a territorial system in 2018.

Before the switch, the United States taxed U.S. corporations' *worldwide* income, which had some unfortunate consequences. To see why it mattered, think of a U.S. and a Canadian company, both operating in the United States and in Canada before the U.S. tax reform. Both companies paid U.S. taxes at 35% on their U.S. income and Canadian taxes at 15% on their Canadian income. But the U.S company owed an additional 20% in U.S. taxes when its Canadian income was repatriated. Thus, the U.S. company's total tax rate on its Canadian profits added up to 35%, far in excess of the 15% rate paid by the Canadian company on its Canadian profits.

The U.S. company could defer payment of the 20% additional U.S. tax by refusing to bring its Canadian profits home. That is exactly what U.S. corporations did. As we will see in Chapter 30, Apple, Microsoft, Alphabet, and several large pharmaceutical companies stored up mountains of cash in low-tax foreign jurisdictions. Once the U.S. switched to a territorial tax in 2018, these companies had no incentive to make their cash mountains higher. They were, however, subject to a one-time tax of 15.5% on overseas profits accumulated through the end of 2017. For example, Apple announced that it would pay a tax of $38 billion to repatriate cumulative foreign profits of $252 billion.

U.S. taxation of worldwide income also affected mergers and acquisitions. Suppose the U.S. company in our example bought the Canadian company before 2018, when the United States moved to the territorial system. The Canadian company's home operations would then be owned by the U.S. company and subject to the U.S. worldwide tax. But if the Canadian company bought the U.S. company, the profits from the Canadian operations that the U.S. company used to own would escape the worldwide tax. Only the Canadian tax of 15% is paid. If there were a merger, it was clearly better for the Canadian company to be the buyer.

Thus, worldwide taxation rewarded foreign acquisitions of U.S. companies. Some U.S. companies arranged *inversions,* which were takeovers designed so that the foreign party was treated as the buyer. For example, Pfizer's proposed 2016 merger with the smaller Irish company Allergen was designed to move the combined company's headquarters to Ireland, where the corporate tax rate was only 13%. The deal was abandoned after stubborn resistance by the U.S. Treasury. But if the Pfizer-Allergen deal resurfaced today, there would be no tax motive to move the headquarters to Ireland because the United States no longer taxes Pfizer's foreign profits.

6-3   Example—IM&C's Fertilizer Project

The Three Elements of Project Cash Flows

You can think of an investment project's cash flow as composed of three elements:

$$\text{Total cash flow} = \text{cash flow from capital investment}$$
$$+ \text{operating cash flow}$$
$$+ \text{cash flow from changes in working capital}$$

Capital Investment   To get a project off the ground, a company typically makes an up-front investment in plant, equipment, research, start-up costs, and diverse other outlays. This expenditure is a negative cash flow—negative because cash goes out the door.

When the project comes to an end, the company can either sell the plant and equipment or redeploy it elsewhere in its business. This salvage value (net of any taxes if the plant and equipment is sold) is a positive cash flow. However, remember our earlier comment that final cash flows can be negative if there are significant shutdown costs.

Operating Cash Flow   Operating cash flow consists of the net increase in sales revenue brought about by the new project less outlays for production, marketing, distribution, and other incremental costs. Incremental taxes are likewise subtracted.

$$\text{Operating cash flow} = \text{revenues} - \text{expenses} - \text{taxes}$$

Many investments do not produce any additional revenues; they are simply designed to reduce the costs of the company's existing operations. Such projects also contribute to the firm's operating cash flow. The after-tax cost saving is a positive addition to the cash flow.

Don't forget that the depreciation charge is not a cash flow. It affects the tax that the company pays, but the company does not send anyone a check for depreciation, and it should not be deducted when calculating operating cash flow.

Investment in Working Capital   When a company builds up inventories of raw materials or finished products, this investment in inventories requires cash. Cash is also absorbed when customers are slow to pay their bills; in this case the firm makes an investment in accounts receivable. On the other hand, cash is preserved when the firm can delay paying its bills. Accounts payable are in a way a source of financing.

Investment in working capital, just like investment in plant and equipment, represents a negative cash flow. On the other hand, later in the project's life, as inventories are sold and accounts receivable are collected, working capital is reduced and the firm enjoys a positive cash flow.

Forecasting the Fertilizer Project's Cash Flows

As the newly appointed financial manager of International Mulch and Compost Company (IM&C), you are about to analyze a proposal for marketing guano as a garden fertilizer. (IM&C's planned advertising campaign features a rustic gentleman who steps out of a vegetable patch singing, "All my troubles have guano way.")[5]

Table 6.2 shows the forecasted cash flows from the project. All the entries in the table are nominal. In other words, the forecasts that you have been given take into account the likely effect of inflation on revenues and costs. We assume initially that for tax purposes the company uses straight-line depreciation. In other words, when it calculates each year's taxable income, it deducts one-sixth of the initial investment.

The calculation in panel B of profit after tax is similar to the calculation in IM&C's financial statements. There is one important difference. When calculating the depreciation figure in the published income statement, IM&C may choose to depreciate the plant and equipment to its likely salvage value. By contrast, IRS rules for calculating the company's tax liability always assume that the plant and equipment has a salvage value of zero.

Capital Investment   Rows 1 through 4 of Table 6.2 show the cash flows from the investment in fixed assets. The project requires an investment of $12 million in plant and machinery. IM&C expects to sell the equipment in year 7 for $1.949 million. Any difference between this figure and the book value of the equipment is a taxable gain. By year 7, IM&C has fully depreciated the equipment, so the company will be taxed on a capital gain of $1.949 million. If the tax rate is 21%, the company will pay tax of $.21 \times 1.949 = \$0.409$ million, and the net cash flow from the sale of equipment will be $1.949 - 0.409 = \$1.540$ million. This is shown in rows 2 and 3 of the table.

Operating Cash Flow   Panel B of Table 6.2 show the calculation of the operating cash flow from the guano project. Operating cash flow consists of revenues from the sale of guano less

BEYOND THE PAGE

Try It! The guano spreadsheets

mhhe.com/brealey13e

---

[5]Sorry.

	Year:	0	1	2	3	4	5	6	7
Panel A Capital Investment									
1 Cash flow from investment in fixed assets		−12,000							
2 Sale of fixed assets									1,949
3 Less tax on sale									409[a]
4 Cash flow from capital investment (1 + 2 − 3)		−12,000							1,540
Panel B Operating Cash Flow									
5 Revenues			523	12,887	32,610	48,901	35,834	19,717	
6 Cost of goods sold			837	7,729	19,552	29,345	21,492	11,830	
7 Other costs[b]		4,000	2,200	1,210	1,331	1,464	1,611	1,772	
8 Depreciation[c]			2,000	2,000	2,000	2,000	2,000	2,000	
9 Pretax profit (5 − (6 + 7) − 8)		−4,000	−4,514	1,948	9,727	16,092	10,731	4,115	
10 Tax (.21 × 9)		−840[d]	−948	409	2,043	3,379	2,254	864	
11 Profit after tax (9 − 10)		−3,160	−3,566	1,539	7,684	12,713	8,477	3,251	
12 Operating cash flow (11 + 8)		−3,160	−1,566	3,539	9,684	14,713	10,477	5,251	
Panel C Investment in Working Capital									
13 Working capital			550	1,289	3,261	4,890	3,583	2,002	0
14 Change in working capital			550	739	1,972	1,629	−1,307	−1,581	−2,002
15 Cash flow from investment in working capital (−14)			−550	−739	−1,972	−1,629	1,307	1,581	2,002
Panel D Project Valuation									
16 Total project cash flow (4 + 12 + 15)		−15,160	−2,116	2,800	7,712	13,084	11,784	6,832	3,542
17 Discount factor at 20%		1.0	0.833	0.694	0.579	0.482	0.402	0.335	0.279
18 Discounted cash flows (16 × 17)		−15,160	−1,763	1,944	4,463	6,310	4,736	2,288	988
19 NPV		+3,806							

❭**TABLE 6.2** Calculating the cash flows and net present value of IM&C's guano project assuming straight-line depreciation ($ thousands)

[a] The asset has been entirely depreciated for tax purposes and the entire sales price is subject to tax.
[b] Start-up costs in years 0 and 1, and general and administrative costs in years 1–6.
[c] Depreciation is calculated straight line on the initial investment of $12 million.
[d] A negative tax payment means a cash inflow, assuming that IM&C can use the tax loss on the guano project to shield income from the rest of its business.

the cash expenses of production and any taxes. Taxes are calculated on profits net of depreciation. Thus, if the tax rate is 21%,

$$\text{Tax} = .21 \times (\text{sales} - \text{cash expenses} - \text{depreciation})$$

We assume in this first-pass table that the company uses straight-line depreciation. This means that, if the depreciable life of the equipment is six years, IM&C can deduct from profits one-sixth of the initial $12 million investment. Thus, row 8 shows that straight-line depreciation in each year is

$$\text{Annual depreciation} = (1/6 \times 12.0) = \$2.0 \text{ million}$$

Pretax profits and taxes are shown in rows 9 and 10. For example, in year 2

$$\text{Pretax profit} = 12.887 - (7.729 + 1.210) - 2.000 = \$1.948 \text{ million}$$

$$\text{Tax} = .21 \times 1.948 = \$0.409 \text{ million}$$

Once we have calculated taxes, it is a simple matter to calculate operating cash flow. Thus,

$$\text{Operating cash flow in year 2} = \text{revenues} - \text{cash expenses} - \text{taxes}$$

$$= 12.887 - (7.729 + 1.210) - 0.409 = \$3.539 \text{ million}^6$$

Notice that, when calculating operating cash flow, we ignored the possibility that the project may be partly financed by debt. Following our earlier Rule 4, we did not deduct any debt proceeds from the original investment, and we did not deduct interest payments from the cash inflows. Standard practice forecasts cash flows as if the project is all-equity financed. Any additional value resulting from financing decisions is considered separately.

Investment in Working Capital   You can see from Table 6.2 that working capital increases in the early and middle years of the project. Why is this? There are several possible reasons:

1. Sales recorded on the income statement overstate actual cash receipts from guano shipments because sales are increasing and customers are slow to pay their bills. Therefore, accounts receivable increase.

2. It takes several months for processed guano to age properly. Thus, as projected sales increase, larger inventories have to be held in the aging sheds.

3. An offsetting effect occurs if payments for materials and services used in guano production are delayed. In this case accounts payable will increase.

Thus, the additional investment in working capital can be calculated as:

$$\begin{matrix} \text{Additional} \\ \text{investment in} \\ \text{working capital} \end{matrix} = \begin{matrix} \text{increase in} \\ \text{inventory} \end{matrix} + \begin{matrix} \text{increase in} \\ \text{accounts} \\ \text{receivable} \end{matrix} - \begin{matrix} \text{increase in} \\ \text{accounts} \\ \text{payable} \end{matrix}$$

There is an alternative to worrying about changes in working capital. You can estimate cash flow directly by counting the dollars coming in from customers and deducting the dollars going out to suppliers. You would also deduct all cash spent on production, including cash spent for goods held in inventory. In other words,

1. If you replace each year's sales with that year's cash payments received from customers, you don't have to worry about accounts receivable.

2. If you replace cost of goods sold with cash payments for labor, materials, and other costs of production, you don't have to keep track of inventory or accounts payable.

However, you would still have to construct a projected income statement to estimate taxes.

---

[6]There are several alternative ways to calculate operating cash flow. For example, you can add depreciation back to the after-tax profit:

$$\text{Operating cash flow} = \text{after-tax profit} + \text{depreciation}$$

Thus, in year 2 of the guano project:

$$\text{Operating cash flow} = 1.539 + 2.000 = \$3.539 \text{ million}$$

Another alternative is to calculate after-tax profit assuming *no* depreciation, and then to add back the tax saving provided by the depreciation allowance:

$$\text{Operating cash flow} = (\text{revenues} - \text{expenses}) \times (1 - \text{tax rate}) + (\text{depreciation} \times \text{tax rate})$$

Thus, in year 2 of the guano project:

$$\text{Operating cash flow} = (12.887 - 7.729 - 1.210) \times (1 - .21) + (2.000 \times .21) = \$3.539 \text{ million}.$$

Project Valuation   Rows 16 to 19 of Table 6.2 show the calculation of project NPV. Row 16 shows the total cash flow from IM&C's project as the sum of the capital investment, operating cash flow, and investment in working capital. IM&C estimates the opportunity cost of capital for projects of this type as 20%.

Remember that to calculate the present value of a cash flow in year t you can either divide the cash flow by $(1 + r)^t$ or you can multiply by a discount factor that is equal to $1/(1 + r)^t$. Row 17 shows the discount factors for a 20% discount rate, and Row 18 multiplies the discount factor by the cash flow to give each flow's present value. When all the cash flows are discounted and added up, the project is seen to offer a net present value of $3.806 million.

Accelerated Depreciation and First-Year Expensing

Depreciation is a noncash expense; it is important only because it reduces taxable income. It provides an annual *tax shield* equal to the product of depreciation and the marginal tax rate. In the case of IM&C:

$$\text{Annual tax shield} = \text{depreciation} \times \text{tax rate} = 2{,}000 \times .21 = 420.0, \text{ or } \$420{,}000.$$

The present value of these tax shields ($420,000 for six years) is $1,397,000 at a 20% discount rate.

In Table 6.2 we assumed that IM&C was required to use straight-line depreciation, which allowed it to write off a fixed proportion of the initial investment each year. This is the most common method of depreciation, but some countries, including the United States, permit firms to depreciate their investments more rapidly.

There are several different methods of accelerated depreciation. For example, firms may be allowed to use the double-declining-balance method. Suppose that IM&C is permitted to use double-declining-balance depreciation. In this case, it can deduct not one-sixth, but $2 \times 1/6 = 1/3$ of the remaining book value of the investment in each year.[7] Therefore, in year 1, it deducts depreciation of $12/3 = \$4$ million, and the written-down value of the equipment falls to $12 - 4 = \$8$ million. In year 2, IM&C deducts depreciation of $8/3 = \$2.7$ million, and the written-down value is further reduced to $8 - 2.7 = \$5.3$ million. In year 5, IM&C observes that depreciation would be higher if it could switch to straight-line depreciation and write off the balance of $2.4 million over the remaining two years of the equipment's life. If this is permitted, IM&C's depreciation allowance each year would be as follows:

	Year					
	1	2	3	4	5	6
Written-down value, start of year ($ millions)	12	8	5.3	3.6	2.4	1.2
Depreciation ($ millions)	12/3 = 4	8/3 = 2.7	5.3/3 = 1.8	3.6/3 = 1.2	2.4/2 = 1.2	1.2
Written-down value, end of year ($ millions)	12 − 4 = 8	8 − 2.7 = 5.3	5.3 − 1.8 = 3.6	3.6 − 1.2 = 2.4	2.4 − 1.2 = 1.2	1.2 − 1.2 = 0

The present value of the tax shields with double-declining-balance depreciation is $1.608 million, $212,000 million higher than if IM&C was restricted to straight-line depreciation.

---

[7]IM&C's new plant and equipment has a life of six years. Therefore, with double-declining-balance, it can depreciate each year $2 \times (1/6) = 1/3$ of the asset's written-down value. If, for example, IM&C was allowed only 150% declining balance, it would be able to depreciate each year $1.5 \times (1/6) = 1/4$ of the written-down value.

From 1986 to the end of 2017, U.S. companies used a slight variation of the double-declining balance method, called the modified accelerated cost recovery system (MACRS).[8] But the 2017 Tax Cuts and Jobs Act offered companies bonus depreciation sufficient to write off 100% of their investment expenditures in the year that they come on line. Table 6.3 recalculates the NPV of the guano project, assuming that the full $12 million investment can be depreciated immediately.

We initially assumed that the guano project could be depreciated straight-line over six years. This resulted in an NPV of $3.806 million. We then calculated that if IM&C could use the double-declining-balance method, NPV would increase by $212,000 to $4.018 million. Finally, Table 6.3 shows that full first-year expensing introduced in the 2017 tax reform would increase NPV further to $4.929 million.

BEYOND THE PAGE

MACRS depreciation system

mhhe.com/brealey13e

				Period				
		0	**1**	**2**	**3**	**4**	**5**	**6**	**7**
	Panel A Capital Investment								
1	Investment in fixed assets	−12,000							
2	Sale of fixed assets								1,949
3	Less tax on sale								409
4	Cash flow from capital investment (1 + 2 + 3)	−12,000							1,540
	Panel B Operating Cash Flow								
5	Revenues	0	523	12,887	32,610	48,901	35,834	19,717	
6	Cost of goods sold	0	837	7,729	19,552	29,345	21,492	11,830	
7	Other costs	4,000	2,200	1,210	1,331	1,464	1,611	1,772	
8	Depreciation	12,000	0	0	0	0	0	0	
9	Pretax profit (5 − 6 − 7 − 8)	−16,000	−2,514	3,948	11,727	18,092	12,731	6,115	
10	Tax (.21 × 9)	−3,360	−528	829	2,463	3,799	2,674	1,284	
11	Profit after tax (9 − 10)	−12,640	−1,986	3,119	9,264	14,293	10,057	4,831	
12	Operating cash flow (8 + 11)	−640	−1,986	3,119	9,264	14,293	10,057	4,831	
	Panel C Investment in Working Capital								
13	Working capital		550	1,289	3,261	4,890	3,583	2,002	0
14	Change in working capital		550	739	1,972	1,629	−1,307	−1,581	−2,002
15	Cash flow from investment in working capital (−14)		−550	−739	−1,972	−1,629	1,307	1,581	2,002
	Panel D Project Valuation								
16	Total project cash flow (4 + 12 + 15)	−12,640	−2,536	2,380	7,292	12,664	11,364	6,412	3,542
17	Discount factor	1.000	0.833	0.694	0.579	0.482	0.402	0.335	0.279
18	Discounted cash flows (16 × 17)	−12,640	−2.113	1,653	4,220	6,107	4,567	2,147	988
19	NPV	4,929							

❯**TABLE 6.3**   IM&C's guano project. Revised analysis with immediate expensing of investment expenditures.

---

[8]The only difference between MACRS and our example of double-declining-balance is that MACRS assumes that the investment is made halfway through the year and, therefore, receives only half the allowance in the first year.

Final Comments on Taxes

Two final comments. First, note that all of the guano project's $12 million capital investment is in plant and equipment, which, under current U.S. tax law, can be expensed immediately. But suppose the project also requires an up-front R&D outlay of $500,000. Under the Tax Cuts and Jobs Act, R&D expenditures after 2021 cannot be expensed but must be written off over five years.

Second, all large U.S. corporations keep two separate sets of books, one for stockholders and one for the Internal Revenue Service (IRS). It is common to use straight-line depreciation on the stockholder books and accelerated depreciation on the tax books. The IRS doesn't object to this, and it makes the firm's reported earnings higher than if accelerated depreciation were used everywhere. There are many other differences between tax books and shareholder books.[9]

The financial analyst must be careful to remember which set of books he or she is look-ing at. In capital budgeting only the tax books are relevant, but to an outside analyst only the shareholder books are available.

Project Analysis

Let us review. Earlier in this section, you embarked on an analysis of IM&C's guano project. You drew up a series of cash-flow forecasts assuming straight-line depreciation. Then you remembered accelerated depreciation and recalculated cash flows and NPV. Finally, you rec-ognized that under the Tax Cuts and Jobs Act, IM&C could write off the capital expenditure in the year that it was incurred.

You were lucky to get away with just three NPV calculations. In real situations, it often takes several tries to purge all inconsistencies and mistakes. Then you may want to analyze some alternatives. For example, should you go for a larger or smaller project? Would it be better to market the fertilizer through wholesalers or directly to the consumer? Should you build 90,000-square-foot aging sheds for the guano in northern South Dakota rather than the planned 100,000-square-foot sheds in southern North Dakota? In each case, your choice should be the one offering the highest NPV. Sometimes the alternatives are not immediately obvious. For example, perhaps the plan calls for two costly, high-speed packing lines. But, if demand for guano is seasonal, it may pay to install just one high-speed line to cope with the base demand and two slower but cheaper lines simply to cope with the summer rush. You won't know the answer until you have compared NPVs.

You will also need to ask some "what if clear" questions. How would NPV be affected if inflation rages out of control? What if technical problems delay start-up? What if gardeners prefer chemical fertilizers to your natural product? Managers employ a variety of techniques to develop a better understanding of how such unpleasant surprises could damage NPV. For example, they might undertake a *sensitivity analysis,* in which they look at how far the project could be knocked off course by bad news about one of the variables. Or they might construct different *scenarios* and estimate the effect of each on NPV. Another technique, known as *break-even analysis,* is to explore how far sales could fall short of forecast before the project goes into the red.

In Chapter 10, we practice using each of these "what if clear" techniques. You will find that project analysis is much more than one or two NPV calculations.[10]

---

[9]This separation of tax accounts from shareholder accounts is not found worldwide. In Japan, for example, taxes reported to sharehold-ers must equal taxes paid to the government; ditto for France and many other European countries.

[10]In the meantime, you might like to get ahead of the game by viewing the spreadsheets for the guano project and seeing how NPV would change with a shortfall in sales or an unexpected rise in costs.

Calculating NPV in Other Countries and Currencies

Our guano project was undertaken in the United States by a U.S. company. But the principles of capital investment are the same worldwide. For example, suppose that you are the financial manager of the German company, K.G.R. Ökologische Naturdüngemittel GmbH (KGR), that is faced with a similar opportunity to make a €10 million investment in Germany. What changes?

1. KGR must also produce a set of cash-flow forecasts, but in this case the project cash flows are stated in euros, the eurozone currency.

2. In developing these forecasts, the company needs to recognize that prices and costs will be influenced by the German inflation rate.

3. Profits from KGR's project are liable to the German rate of corporate tax, which is currently 15.8% plus a large municipal trade tax.

4. KGR must use the German system of depreciation allowances. In common with many other countries, Germany requires firms to use the straight-line system. KGR, therefore, writes off one-sixth of the capital outlay each year.

5. Finally, KGR discounts the project's euro cash flows at the German cost of capital measured in euros.

Now suppose you are the financial manager of a U.S. company considering the same investment in Germany. You would go through exactly the same steps as KGR. You would not have to worry about U.S. taxes on your company's German profits because the United States now has a territorial corporate income tax. You would probably convert the project NPV from euros to U.S. dollars, however, and you might use a different cost of capital. We discuss cross-border capital investment decisions in Chapter 27.

6-4 Using the NPV Rule to Choose among Projects

Almost all real-world investment decisions entail either-or choices. Such choices are said to be *mutually exclusive*. We came across an example of mutually exclusive investments in Chapter 2. There we looked at whether it was better to build an office block for immediate sale or to rent it out and sell it at the end of two years. To decide between these alternatives, we calculated the NPV of each and chose the one with the higher NPV.

That is the correct procedure as long as the choice between the two projects does not affect any future decisions that you might wish to make. But sometimes the choices that you make today *will* have an impact on future opportunities. When that is so, choosing between competing projects is trickier. Here are four important, but often challenging, problems:

- *The investment timing problem.* Should you invest now or wait and think about it again next year? (Here, today's investment is competing with possible future investments.)

- *The choice between long- and short-lived equipment.* Should the company save money today by choosing cheaper machinery that will not last as long? (Here, today's decision would accelerate a later investment in machine replacement.)

- *The replacement problem.* When should existing machinery be replaced? (Using it another year could delay investment in more modern equipment.)

- *The cost of excess capacity.* What is the cost of using equipment that is temporarily not being used? (Increasing use of the equipment may bring forward the date at which additional capacity is required.)

We will look at each of these problems in turn.

Problem 1: The Investment Timing Decision

The fact that a project has a positive NPV does not mean that it is best undertaken now. It might be even more valuable if undertaken in the future. The question of optimal timing is not difficult when the cash flows are certain. You must first examine alternative start dates (t) for the investment and calculate the net *future* value at each of these dates. Then, to find which of the alternatives would add most to the firm's *current* value, you must discount these net future values back to the present:

$$\text{Net present value of investment if undertaken at date } t = \frac{\text{net future value at date } t}{(1 + r)^t}$$

For example, suppose you own a large tract of inaccessible timber. To harvest it, you need to invest a substantial amount in access roads and other facilities. The longer you wait, the higher the investment required. On the other hand, lumber prices may rise as you wait, and the trees will keep growing, although at a gradually decreasing rate.

Let us suppose that the net present value of the harvest at different *future* dates is as follows:

	Year of Harvest					
	0	1	2	3	4	5
Net *future* value ($ thousands)	50	64.4	77.5	89.4	100	109.4
Change in value from previous year (%)		+ 28.8	+20.3	+15.4	+11.9	+9.4

As you can see, the longer you defer cutting the timber, the more money you will make. However, your concern is with the date that maximizes the net *present* value of your investment, that is, its contribution to the value of your firm *today*. You therefore need to discount the net future value of the harvest back to the present. Suppose the appropriate discount rate is 10%. Then, if you harvest the timber in year 1, it has a net *present* value of $58,500:

$$\text{NPV if harvested in year } 1 = \frac{64.4}{1.10} = 58.5, \text{ or } \$58,500$$

The net present value for other harvest dates is as follows:

	Year of Harvest					
	0	1	2	3	4	5
Net present value ($ thousands)	50	58.5	64.0	67.2	68.3	67.9

The optimal point to harvest the timber is year 4 because this is the point that maximizes NPV.

Notice that before year 4, the net future value of the timber increases by more than 10% a year: The gain in value is greater than the cost of the capital tied up in the project. After year 4, the gain in value is still positive but less than the required return. So delaying the harvest further just reduces shareholder wealth.[11]

---

[11]Our timber-cutting example conveys the right idea about investment timing, but it misses an important practical point: The sooner you cut the first crop of trees, the sooner the second crop can start growing. Thus, the value of the second crop depends on when you cut the first. This more complex and realistic problem can be solved in one of two ways:

1. Find the cutting dates that maximize the present value of a series of harvests, taking into account the different growth rates of young and old trees.
2. Repeat our calculations, counting the future market value of cut-over land as part of the payoff to the first harvest. The value of cut-over land includes the present value of all subsequent harvests.

The second solution is far simpler if you can figure out what cut-over land will be worth.

The investment timing problem is much more complicated when you are unsure about future cash flows. We return to the problem of investment timing under uncertainty in Chapters 10 and 22.

Problem 2: The Choice between Long- and Short-Lived Equipment

An advertising agency needs to choose between two digital presses. Let's call them machines A and B. The two machines are designed differently but have identical capacity and do exactly the same job. Machine A costs $15,000 and will last three years. It costs $5,000 per year to run. Machine B is an "economy" model, costing only $10,000, but it will last only two years and costs $6,000 per year to run.

The only way to choose between these two machines is on the basis of cost. The present value of each machine's cost is as follows:

		Costs ($ thousands)			
Year:	0	1	2	3	PV at 6% ($ thousands)
Machine A	15	5	5	5	$28.37
Machine B	10	6	6	—	21.00

Should the agency take machine B, the one with the lower present value of costs? Not necessarily. All we have shown is that machine B offers two years of service for a lower total cost than three years of service from machine A. But is the *annual* cost of using B lower than that of A?

Suppose the financial manager agrees to buy machine A and pay for its operating costs out of her budget. She then charges the annual amount for use of the machine. There will be three equal payments starting in year 1. The financial manager has to make sure that the present value of these payments equals the present value of the costs of each machine.

When the discount rate is 6%, the payment stream with such a present value turns out to be $10,610 a year. In other words, the cost of buying and operating machine A over its three-year life is equivalent to an annual charge of $10,610 a year for three years.

		Costs ($ thousands)			
Year:	0	1	2	3	PV at 6% ($ thousands)
Machine A	15	5	5	5	28.37
Equivalent annual cost		10.61	10.61	10.61	28.37

We calculated this *equivalent annual cost* by finding the three-year annuity with the same present value as A's lifetime costs.

$$\text{PV of annuity} = \text{PV of A's costs} = 28.37$$
$$= \text{annuity payment} \times \text{3-year annuity factor}$$

At a 6% cost of capital, the annuity factor is 2.673 for three years, so

$$\text{Annuity payment} = \frac{28.37}{2.673} = 10.61$$

BEYOND THE PAGE

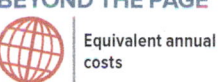

Investment timing decisions

mhhe.com/brealey13e

BEYOND THE PAGE

Equivalent annual costs

mhhe.com/brealey13e

A similar calculation for machine B gives an equivalent annual cost of $11,450:

	Costs ($ thousands)			
Year:	0	1	2	PV at 6% ($ thousands)
Machine B	10	6	6	21.00
Equivalent annual cost		11.45	11.45	21.00

Machine A is better because its equivalent annual cost is less ($10,610 versus $11,450 for machine B).

Equivalent Annual Cash Flow, Inflation, and Technological Change   When we calculated the equivalent annual costs of machines A and B, we implicitly assumed that inflation is zero. But, in practice, the cost of buying and operating the machines is likely to rise with inflation. If so, the *nominal* costs of operating the machines will rise, while the *real* costs will be constant. Therefore, when you compare the equivalent annual costs of two machines, we strongly recommend doing the calculations in real terms. Do *not* calculate equivalent annual cash flows as level *nominal* annuities. This procedure can give incorrect rankings of true equivalent annual flows at high inflation rates. See Challenge Problem 37 at the end of this chapter for an example.[12]

There will also be circumstances in which even the real cash flows of buying and operating the two machines are not expected to be constant. For example, suppose that thanks to technological improvements, new machines cost 20% less each year in *real* terms to buy and operate. In this case, future owners of brand-new, lower-cost machines will be able to cut their (real) rental cost by 20%, and owners of old machines will be forced to match this reduction. Thus, we now need to ask: If the real level of rents declines by 20% a year, how much will it cost to rent each machine?

If the real rent for year 1 is $rent_1$, then the real rent for year 2 is $rent_2 = 0.8 \times rent_1$. $Rent_3$ is $0.8 \times rent_2$, or $0.64 \times rent_1$. The owner of each machine must set the real rents sufficiently high to recover the present value of the costs. If the real cost of capital is 6%:

$$\text{PV of renting machine A} = \frac{rent_1}{1.06} + \frac{rent_2}{1.06^2} + \frac{rent_3}{1.06^3} = 28.37$$

$$= \frac{rent_1}{1.06} + \frac{0.8(rent_1)}{1.06^2} + \frac{0.64(rent_1)}{1.06^3} = 28.37$$

$rent_1 = 12.94$, or $12,940

For machine B:

$$\text{PV of renting machine B} = \frac{rent_1}{1.06} + \frac{0.8(rent_1)}{1.06^2} = 21.00$$

$rent_1 = 12.69$, or $12,690

The merits of the two machines are now reversed. Once we recognize that technology is expected to reduce the real costs of new machines, then it pays to buy the shorter-lived machine B rather than become locked into an aging technology with machine A in year 3.

---

[12]If you actually rent out the machine to the plant manager, or anyone else, be careful to specify that the rental payments be "indexed" to inflation. If inflation runs on at 5% per year and rental payments do not increase proportionally, then the real value of the rental payments must decline and will not cover the full cost of buying and operating the machine.

You can imagine other complications. Perhaps machine C will arrive in year 1 with an even lower equivalent annual cost. You would then need to consider scrapping or selling machine B at year 1 (more on this decision follows). The financial manager could not choose between machines A and B in year 0 without taking a detailed look at what each machine could be replaced with.

Comparing equivalent annual cash flows should never be a mechanical exercise; always think about the assumptions that are implicit in the comparison. Finally, remember why equivalent annual cash flows are necessary in the first place. It is because A and B will be replaced at different future dates. The choice between them therefore affects future investment decisions. If subsequent decisions are not affected by the initial choice (e.g., because neither machine will be replaced), then we do *not need to take future decisions into account.*[13]

Equivalent Annual Cash Flow and Taxes   We have not mentioned taxes. But you surely realized that machine A and B's lifetime costs should be calculated after-tax, recognizing that operating costs are tax-deductible and that capital investment generates depreciation tax shields.

Problem 3: When to Replace an Old Machine

Our earlier comparison of machines A and B took the life of each machine as fixed. In practice, the point at which equipment is replaced reflects economics, not physical collapse. *We must decide when to replace. The machine will rarely decide for us.*

Here is a common problem. You are operating an elderly machine that is expected to produce a net cash *inflow* of $4,000 in the coming year and $4,000 next year. After that it will give up the ghost. You can replace it now with a new machine, which costs $15,000 but is much more efficient and will provide a cash inflow of $8,000 a year for three years. You want to know whether you should replace your equipment now or wait a year.

We can calculate the NPV of the new machine and also its *equivalent annual cash flow—* that is, the three-year annuity that has the same net present value:

	Cash Flows ($ thousands)				
	C_0	C_1	C_2	C_3	NPV at 6% ($ thousands)
New machine	−15	+8	+8	+8	6.38
Equivalent annual cash flow		+2.387	+2.387	+2.387	6.38

In other words, the cash flows of the new machine are equivalent to an annuity of $2,387 per year. So we can equally well ask at what point we would want to replace our old machine with a new one producing $2,387 a year. When the question is put this way, the answer is obvious. As long as your old machine can generate a cash flow of $4,000 a year, who wants to put in its place a new one that generates only $2,387 a year?

It is a simple matter to incorporate salvage values into this calculation. Suppose that the current salvage value is $8,000 and next year's value is $7,000. Let us see where you come out next year if you wait and then sell. On one hand, you gain $7,000, but you lose today's salvage value *plus* a year's return on that money. That is $8,000 \times 1.06 = \$8,480$. Your net loss is $8,480 - 7,000 = \$1,480$, which only partly offsets the operating gain. You should not replace yet.

Remember that the logic of such comparisons requires that the new machine be the best of the available alternatives and that it in turn be replaced at the optimal point.

---

[13]However, if neither machine will be replaced, then we have to consider the extra revenue generated by machine A in its third year, when it will be operating but B will not.

Problem 4: Cost of Excess Capacity

Any firm with a centralized information system (computer servers, storage, software, and telecommunication links) encounters many proposals for using it. Recently installed systems tend to have excess capacity, and since the immediate marginal costs of using them seem to be negligible, management often encourages new uses. Sooner or later, however, the load on a system increases to the point at which management must either terminate the uses it originally encouraged or invest in another system several years earlier than it had planned. Such problems can be avoided if a proper charge is made for the use of spare capacity.

Suppose we have a new investment project that requires heavy use of an existing information system. The effect of adopting the project is to bring the purchase date of a new, more capable system forward from year 4 to year 3. This new system has a life of five years, and at a discount rate of 6%, the present value of the cost of buying and operating it is $500,000.

We begin by converting the $500,000 present value of the cost of the new system to an equivalent annual cost of $118,700 for each of five years.[14] Of course, when the new system in turn wears out, we will replace it with another. So we face the prospect of future information-system expenses of $118,700 a year. If we undertake the new project, the series of expenses begins in year 4; if we do not undertake it, the series begins in year 5. The new project, therefore, results in an *additional* cost of $118,700 in year 4. This has a present value of $118,700/(1.06)^4, or about $94,000. This cost is properly charged against the new project.

When we recognize it, the NPV of the project may prove to be negative. If so, we still need to check whether it is worthwhile undertaking the project now and abandoning it later, when the excess capacity of the present system disappears.

---

[14]The present value of $118,700 a year for five years discounted at 6% is $500,000.

SUMMARY

By now present value calculations should be a matter of routine. However, forecasting project cash flows will never be routine. Here is a checklist that will help you to avoid mistakes:

1. Discount cash flows, not profits.
   a. Remember that depreciation is not a cash flow (though it affects tax payments).
   b. Remember to track investment in working capital. As sales increase, the firm will probably make additional investments in working capital, and as the project comes to an end, it will recover those investments.
   c. Beware of allocated overhead charges. These may not reflect the incremental costs of the project.
2. Estimate the project's *incremental* cash flows—that is, the difference between the cash flows with the project and those without the project.
   a. Include all indirect effects of the project, such as its impact on the sales of the firm's other products.
   b. Forget sunk costs.
   c. Include *opportunity costs,* such as the value of land that you would otherwise sell.
3. Treat inflation consistently.
   a. If cash flows are forecasted in nominal terms, use a nominal discount rate.
   b. Discount real cash flows at a real rate.
4. Forecast cash flows as if the project is all-equity-financed. Thus, project cash flows should exclude debt interest or the cost of repaying any loans. This enables you to separate the investment from the financing decision.

5. Concentrate on cash flows after taxes. Stay alert for differences between tax depreciation and depreciation used in reports to shareholders.

The U.S. Tax Cuts and Jobs Act of 2017 changed corporate income taxes in several important ways:

1. The tax rate was cut from 35% to 21%.

2. Most investments in plant and equipment can be expensed—that is, completely depreciated—in their first year of operation. This expensing provision will phase out starting in 2023.

3. Starting in 2022, most investments in research and development (R&D) must be amortized (depreciated) over a five-year period.

4. Losses can no longer be carried back to recover past taxes. But losses can be carried forward to offset up to 80% of future income.

5. Interest expense exceeding 30% of taxable income is no longer tax deductible.

6. The United States moved to a territorial tax system. It no longer attempts to tax U.S. corporations' worldwide income.

The principles of valuing capital investments are the same worldwide, but inputs and assumptions vary by country and currency. For example, cash flows from a project in Germany would be in euros, not dollars, and would be forecasted after German taxes.

When we assessed the guano project, we transformed the series of future cash flows into a single measure of their present value. Sometimes it is useful to reverse this calculation and to convert the present value into a stream of annual cash flows. For example, when choosing between two machines with unequal lives, you need to compare equivalent annual cash flows. Remember, though, to calculate equivalent annual cash flows in real terms and adjust for technological change if necessary.

For a valuable summary of tax rules in different countries, see

PWC, *Worldwide Tax Summaries, Corporate Taxes 2017/18*, www.pwc.com/taxsummaries.

● ● ● ● ●

FURTHER READING

● ● ● ● ●

PROBLEM SETS

 **Select problems are available in McGraw-Hill's *Connect*. Please see the preface for more information.**

1. **Cash flows*** Which of the following should be treated as incremental cash flows when deciding whether to invest in a new manufacturing plant? The site is already owned by the company, but existing buildings would need to be demolished.

   a. The market value of the site and existing buildings.

   b. Demolition costs and site clearance.

   c. The cost of a new access road put in last year.

   d. Lost earnings on other products due to executive time spent on the new facility.

   e. A proportion of the cost of leasing the president's jet airplane.

   f. Future depreciation of the new plant.

   g. The reduction in the corporation's tax bill resulting from tax depreciation of the new plant.

   h. The initial investment in inventories of raw materials.

   i. Money already spent on engineering design of the new plant.

2. **Cash flows** Reliable Electric, a major Ruritanian producer of electrical products, is considering a proposal to manufacture a new type of industrial electric motor that would replace most of its existing product line. A research breakthrough has given Reliable a two-year lead on its competitors. The project proposal is summarized in Table 6.4.

   a. Read the notes to the table carefully. Which entries make sense? Which do not? Why or why not?

   b. What additional information would you need to construct a version of Table 6.4 that makes sense?

      Construct such a table and recalculate NPV. Make additional assumptions as necessary.

	2018	2019	2020	2021–2028
1. Capital expenditure	−10,400			
2. Research and development	−2,000			
3. Working capital	4,000			
4. Revenue		8,000	16,000	40,000
5. Operating costs		−4,000	−8,000	−20,000
6. Overhead		−800	−1,600	−4,000
7. Depreciation		−1,040	−1,040	−1,040
8. Interest		−2,160	−2,160	−2,160
9. Income	−2,000	0	3,200	12,800
10. Tax @ 30%	0	0	360	3,840
11. Net cash flow	−16,400	0	2,840	8,960
12. Net present value =	+16,149			

❯**TABLE 6.4**   Cash flows and present value of Reliable Electric's proposed investment ($ thousands). See Problem 2.

Notes:
1. *Capital expenditure:* $8 million for new machinery and $2.4 million for a warehouse extension. The full cost of the extension has been charged to this project, although only about half of the space is currently needed. Since the new machinery will be housed in an existing factory building, no charge has been made for land and building.
2. *Research and development:* $1.82 million spent in 2017. This figure was corrected for 10% inflation from the time of expenditure to date. Thus $1.82 \times 1.1 = \$2$ million.
3. *Working capital:* Initial investment in inventories.
4. *Revenue:* These figures assume sales of 2,000 motors in 2019, 4,000 in 2020, and 10,000 per year from 2021 through 2028. The initial unit price of $4,000 is forecasted to remain constant in real terms.
5. *Operating costs:* These include all direct and indirect costs. Indirect costs (heat, light, power, fringe benefits, etc.) are assumed to be 200% of direct labor costs. Operating costs per unit are forecasted to remain constant in real terms at $2,000.
6. *Overhead:* Marketing and administrative costs, assumed equal to 10% of revenue.
7. *Depreciation:* Straight-line for 10 years.
8. *Interest:* Charged on capital expenditure and working capital at Reliable's current borrowing rate of 15%.
9. *Income:* Revenue less the sum of research and development, operating costs, overhead, depreciation, and interest.
10. *Tax:* 30% of income. However, income is negative in 2018. This loss is carried forward and deducted from taxable income in 2020.
11. *Net cash flow:* Assumed equal to income less tax.
12. *Net present value:* NPV of net cash flow at a 15% discount rate.

3. **Cash flows*** True or false?

   a. Project cash flows should take account of interest paid on any borrowing undertaken to finance the project.

   b. In the United States, income reported to the tax authorities must equal income reported to shareholders.

   c. Accelerated depreciation reduces near-term project cash flows and therefore reduces project NPV.

4. **Cash flows** In 1898, Simon North announced plans to construct a funeral home on land he owned and rented out as a storage area for railway carts. (A local newspaper commended Mr. North for not putting the cart before the hearse.) Rental income from the site barely covered real estate taxes, but the site was valued at $45,000. However, Mr. North had refused several offers for the land and planned to continue renting it out if, for some reason, the funeral home was not built. Therefore, he did not include the value of the land as an outlay in his NPV analysis of the funeral home. Was this the correct procedure? Explain.

5. **Real and nominal flows** Mr. Art Deco will be paid $100,000 one year hence. This is a nominal flow, which he discounts at an 8% nominal discount rate:

$$PV = \frac{100,000}{1.08} = \$92,593$$

The inflation rate is 4%.

Calculate the PV of Mr. Deco's payment using the equivalent real cash flow and real discount rate. (You should get exactly the same answer as he did.)

6. **Real and nominal flows** Restate the net cash flows in Table 6.2 in real terms. Discount the restated cash flows at a real discount rate. Assume a 20% nominal rate and 10% expected inflation. NPV should be unchanged at +3,806, or $3,806,000.

7. **Real and nominal flows** Guandong Machinery is evaluating a new project to produce encapsulators. The initial investment in plant and equipment is RMB 500,000.[15] Sales of encapsulators in year 1 are forecasted at RMB 200,000 and costs at RMB 100,000. Both are expected to increase by 10% a year in line with inflation. Profits are taxed at 25%. Working capital in each year consists of inventories of raw materials and is forecasted at 20% of sales in the following year. The project will last five years and the equipment at the end of this period will have no further value. For tax purposes the equipment can be depreciated straight-line over these five years. If the nominal discount rate is 15%, show that the net present value of the project is the same whether calculated using real cash flows or nominal flows.

8. **Working capital** Each of the following statements is true. Use an example to explain why they are consistent.

   a. When a company introduces a new product, or expands production of an existing product, investment in net working capital is usually an important cash outflow.

   b. Forecasting changes in net working capital is not necessary if the timing of all cash inflows and outflows is carefully specified.

9. **Working capital*** The following table tracks the main components of working capital over the life of a four-year project.

	2019	2020	2021	2022	2023
Accounts receivable	0	150,000	225,000	190,000	0
Inventory	75,000	130,000	130,000	95,000	0
Accounts payable	25,000	50,000	50,000	35,000	0

Calculate net working capital and the cash inflows and outflows due to investment in working capital.

10. **Project NPV*** Better Mousetrap's research laboratories have developed a new trap. The project requires an initial investment in plant and equipment of $6 million. This investment will be depreciated straight-line over five years to a value of zero, but when the project comes to an end at the end of five years, the equipment will, in fact, be sold for $500,000. The firm believes that working capital at each date must be maintained at 10% of next year's forecasted

---

[15] The renminbi (RMB) is the Chinese currency.

sales starting immediately. Production costs are estimated at 25% of revenues. (There are no marketing expenses.) Sales forecasts are given in the following table. The firm pays tax at 25% and the required return on the project is 12%. What is the NPV?

Year	0	1	2	3	4	5
Sales (millions of dollars)	0	2.0	2.4	4.0	4.0	2.4

11. **Project NPV** A widget manufacturer currently produces 200,000 units a year. It buys widget lids from an outside supplier at a price of $2 a lid. The plant manager believes that it would be cheaper to make these lids rather than buy them. Direct production costs are estimated to be only $1.50 a lid. The necessary machinery would cost $150,000 and would last 10 years. This investment could be written off immediately for tax purposes. The plant manager estimates that the operation would require additional working capital of $30,000 but argues that this sum can be ignored since it is recoverable at the end of the 10 years. If the company pays tax at a rate of 21% and the opportunity cost of capital is 15%, would you support the plant manager's proposal? State clearly any additional assumptions that you need to make.

12. **Project NPV** Marsha Jones has bought a used Mercedes horse transporter for her Connecticut estate. It cost $35,000. The object is to save on horse transporter rentals. Marsha had been renting a transporter every other week for $200 per day plus $1.00 per mile. Most of the trips are 80 or 100 miles in total. Marsha usually gives the driver, Joe Laminitis, a $40 tip. With the new transporter she will only have to pay for diesel fuel and maintenance, at about $.45 per mile. Insurance costs for Marsha's transporter are $1,200 per year.

The transporter will probably be worth $15,000 (in real terms) after eight years, when Marsha's horse Spike, will be ready to retire. Is the transporter a positive-NPV investment? Assume a nominal discount rate of 9% and a 3% forecasted inflation rate. Marsha's transporter is a personal outlay, not a business or financial investment, so taxes can be ignored.

13. **Project NPV** United Pigpen is considering a proposal to manufacture high-protein hog feed. The project would make use of an existing warehouse, which is currently rented out to a neighboring firm. The next year's rental charge on the warehouse is $100,000, and thereafter the rent is expected to grow in line with inflation at 4% a year. In addition to using the warehouse, the proposal envisages an investment in plant and equipment of $1.2 million. This could be depreciated for tax purposes over 10 years. However, Pigpen expects to terminate the project at the end of eight years and to resell the plant and equipment in year 8 for $400,000. Finally, the project requires an initial investment in working capital of $350,000. Thereafter, working capital is forecasted to be 10% of sales in each of years 1 through 7. Year 1 sales of hog feed are expected to be $4.2 million, and thereafter sales are forecasted to grow by 5% a year, slightly faster than the inflation rate. Manufacturing costs are expected to be 90% of sales, and profits are subject to tax at 25%. The cost of capital is 12%. What is the NPV of Pigpen's project?

14. **Project NPV** Imperial Motors is considering producing its popular Rooster model in China. This will involve an initial investment of RMB 4 billion. The plant will start production after one year. It is expected to last for five years and have a salvage value at the end of this period of RMB 500 million in real terms. The plant will produce 100,000 cars a year. The firm anticipates that in the first year, it will be able to sell each car for RMB 65,000, and thereafter the price is expected to increase by 4% a year. Raw materials for each car are forecasted to cost RMB 18,000 in the first year, and these costs are predicted to increase by 3% annually. Total labor costs for the plant are expected to be RMB 1.1 billion in the first year and thereafter will increase by 7% a year. The land on which the plant is built can be rented for five years at a fixed cost of RMB 300 million a year payable at the beginning of each year. Imperial's discount rate for this type of project is 12% (nominal). The expected rate of inflation is 5%. The plant can be depreciated straight-line over the five-year period, and profits will be taxed

at 25%. Assume all cash flows occur at the end of each year except where otherwise stated. What is the NPV of the project plant?

15. **Project NPV and IRR** A project requires an initial investment of $100,000 and is expected to produce a cash inflow before tax of $26,000 per year for five years. Company A has substantial accumulated tax losses and is unlikely to pay taxes in the foreseeable future. Company B pays corporate taxes at a rate of 21% and can claim 100% bonus depreciation on the investment. Suppose the opportunity cost of capital is 8%. Ignore inflation.

    a. Calculate project NPV for each company.

    b. What is the IRR of the after-tax cash flows for each company? Why are the IRRs for A and B the same?

16. **Project analysis** Go to the Excel spreadsheet versions of Table 6.2 and answer the following questions.

    a. New engineering estimates raise the possibility that capital investment will be more than $12 million, perhaps as much as $15 million. On the other hand, you believe that the 20% cost of capital is unrealistically high and that the true cost of capital is about 11%. Is the project still attractive under these alternative assumptions?

    b. Continue with the assumed $15 million capital investment and the 11% cost of capital. What if sales, cost of goods sold, and net working capital are all 10% higher in each year? Recalculate NPV. (*Note:* Enter the revised sales, cost, and working-capital forecasts in the spreadsheet for Table 6.2.)

17. **Taxes and project NPV** In the International Mulch and Compost example (Section 6-3), we assumed that early losses on the project could be used to offset taxable profits elsewhere in the corporation. Suppose that the losses had to be carried forward and offset against future taxable profits from the project. How would the project NPV change? What is the value of the company's ability to use the tax deductions immediately?

18. **Depreciation and project NPV** Suppose that Sudbury Mechanical Drifters is proposing to invest $10 million in a new factory. It can depreciate this investment straight-line over 10 years. The tax rate is 40%, and the discount rate is 10%.

    a. What is the present value of Sudbury's depreciation tax shields?

    b. Suppose that the government allows companies to use double-declining-balance depreciation with the option to switch at any point to straight-line. Now what is the present value of the depreciation tax shields?

    c. What would be the present value of the tax shield if the government allowed Sudbury to write-off the factory immediately?

19. **Depreciation and project NPV** Ms. T. Potts, the treasurer of Ideal China, has a problem. The company has just ordered a new kiln for $400,000. Of this sum, $50,000 is described by the supplier as an installation cost. Ms. Potts does not know whether the company will need to treat this cost as a tax-deductible current expense or as a capital investment. In the latter case, the company could depreciate the $50,000 straight-line over five years. How will the tax authority's decision affect the after-tax cost of the kiln? The tax rate is 25%, and the opportunity cost of capital is 5%.

20. **Equivalent annual cash flow** When appraising mutually exclusive investments in plant and equipment, financial managers calculate the investments' equivalent annual cash flows and rank the investments on this basis. Why is this necessary? Why not just compare the investments' NPVs? Explain briefly.

21. **Equivalent annual cash flow*** Air conditioning for a college dormitory will cost $1.5 million to install and $200,000 per year to operate at current prices. The system should last 25 years. The real cost of capital is 5%, and the college pays no taxes. What is the equivalent annual cost?

22. **Equivalent annual cash flow** In 2022, the California Air Resources Board (CARB) started planning its "Phase 3" requirements for reformulated gasoline (RFG). RFG is gasoline blended to tight specifications designed to reduce pollution from motor vehicles. CARB consulted with refiners, environmentalists, and other interested parties to design these specifications. As the outline for the Phase 3 requirements emerged, refiners realized that substantial capital investments would be required to upgrade California refineries. Assume a refiner is contemplating an investment of $400 million to upgrade its California plant. The investment lasts for 25 years and does not change raw material and operating costs. The real (inflation-adjusted) cost of capital is 7%. How much extra revenue would be needed each year to recover that cost?

23. **Equivalent annual cash flow** Look at Problem 22 where you calculated the equivalent annual cost of producing reformulated gasoline in California. Capital investment was $400 million. Suppose this amount can be depreciated immediately for tax purposes. The marginal tax rate, including California taxes, is 25%, the cost of capital is 7%, and there is no inflation. The refinery improvements have an economic life of 25 years.

    a. Calculate the after-tax equivalent annual cost.

    b. How much extra would retail gasoline customers have to pay to cover this equivalent annual cost? (*Note:* Extra income from higher retail prices would be taxed.)

24. **Equivalent annual cash flow** Deutsche Transport can lease a truck for four years at a cost of €30,000 annually. It can instead buy a truck at a cost of €80,000, with annual maintenance expenses of €10,000. The truck will be sold at the end of four years for €20,000. Ignore taxes.

    a. What is the equivalent annual cost of buying and maintaining the truck if the discount rate is 10%?

    b. Which is the better option: leasing or buying?

25. **Investment timing** You can purchase an optical scanner today for $400. The scanner provides benefits worth $60 a year. The expected life of the scanner is 10 years. Scanners are expected to decrease in price by 20% per year. Suppose the discount rate is 10%.

    1. Should you purchase the scanner today or wait to purchase?

    2. When is the best purchase time?

26. **Mutually exclusive investments and project lives** The Borstal Company has to choose between two machines that do the same job but have different lives. The two machines have the following costs:

Year	Machine A	Machine B
0	$40,000	$50,000
1	10,000	8,000
2	10,000	8,000
3	10,000 + replace	8,000
4		8,000 + replace

These costs are expressed in real terms.

    a. Suppose you are Borstal's financial manager. If you had to buy one or the other machine and rent it to the production manager for that machine's economic life, what annual rental payment would you have to charge? Assume a 6% real discount rate and ignore taxes.

    b. Which machine should Borstal buy?

    c. Usually the rental payments you derived in part (a) are just hypothetical—a way of calculating and interpreting equivalent annual cost. Suppose you actually do buy one of the machines and rent it to the production manager. How much would you actually have to charge in each future year if there is steady 8% per year inflation? [*Note:* The rental payments calculated in part (a) are real cash flows. You would have to mark up those payments to cover inflation.]

27. **Mutually exclusive investments and project lives** Look again at your calculations for Problem 26. Suppose that technological change is expected to reduce costs by 10% per year. There will be new machines in year 1 that cost 10% less to buy and operate than A and B. In year 2, there will be a second crop of new machines incorporating a further 10% reduction, and so on. How does this change the equivalent annual costs of machines A and B?

28. **Mutually exclusive investments and project lives.** Econo-Cool air conditioners cost $300 to purchase, result in electricity bills of $150 per year, and last for five years. Luxury Air models cost $500, result in electricity bills of $100 per year, and last for eight years. The discount rate is 21%.

    a. What is the equivalent annual cost of the Econo-Cool model?

    b. What is the equivalent annual cost of the Luxury Air model?

    c. Which model is more cost-effective?

    d. Now you remember that the inflation rate is expected to be 10% per year for the foreseeable future. Redo parts (a) and (b).

29. **Mutually exclusive investments and project lives*** As a result of improvements in product engineering, United Automation is able to sell one of its two milling machines. Both machines perform the same function but differ in age. The newer machine could be sold today for $50,000. Its operating costs are $20,000 a year, but at the end of five years, the machine will require a $20,000 overhaul (which is tax deductible). Thereafter, operating costs will be $30,000 until the machine is finally sold in year 10 for $5,000. The older machine could be sold today for $25,000. If it is kept, it will need an immediate $20,000 (tax-deductible) overhaul. Thereafter, operating costs will be $30,000 a year until the machine is finally sold in year 5 for $5,000. Both machines are fully depreciated for tax purposes. The company pays tax at 21%. Cash flows have been forecasted in real terms. The real cost of capital is 12%. Which machine should United Automation sell? Explain the assumptions underlying your answer.

30. **Mutually exclusive investments and project lives** Machines A and B are mutually exclusive and are expected to produce the following real cash flows:

	Cash Flows ($ thousands)			
Machine	C_0	C_1	C_2	C_3
A	−100	+110	+121	
B	−120	+110	+121	+133

The real opportunity cost of capital is 10%.

    a. Calculate the NPV of each machine.

    b. Calculate the equivalent annual cash flow from each machine.

    c. Which machine should you buy?

31. **Replacement decisions** Machine C was purchased five years ago for $200,000 and produces an annual real cash flow of $80,000. It has no salvage value but is expected to last another five years. The company can replace machine C with machine B (see Problem 30) either now or at the end of five years. Which should it do?

32. **Replacement decisions** Hayden Inc. has a number of copiers that were bought four years ago for $20,000. Currently maintenance costs $2,000 a year, but the maintenance agreement expires at the end of two years, and thereafter, the annual maintenance charge will rise to $8,000. The machines have a current resale value of $8,000, but at the end of

year 2, their value will have fallen to $3,500. By the end of year 6, the machines will be value-less and would be scrapped. Hayden is considering replacing the copiers with new machines that would do essentially the same job. These machines cost $25,000, and the company can take out an eight-year maintenance contract for $1,000 a year. The machines would have no value by the end of the eight years and would be scrapped. Both machines are depreciated using seven-year straight-line depreciation, and the tax rate is 39%. Assume for simplicity that the inflation rate is zero. The real cost of capital is 7%. When should Hayden replace its copiers?

33. **Replacement decisions.** You are operating an old machine that is expected to produce a cash inflow of $5,000 in each of the next three years before it fails. You can replace it now with a new machine that costs $20,000 but is much more efficient and will provide a cash flow of $10,000 a year for four years. Should you replace your equipment now? The discount rate is 15%.

34. **Replacement decisions.** A forklift will last for only two more years. It costs $5,000 a year to maintain. For $20,000 you can buy a new forklift that can last for 10 years and should require maintenance costs of only $2,000 a year.

    a. If the discount rate is 4% per year, should you replace the forklift?

    b. What if the discount rate is 12% per year?

35. **The cost of excess capacity** The president's executive jet is not fully utilized. You judge that its use by other officers would increase direct operating costs by only $20,000 a year and would save $100,000 a year in airline bills. On the other hand, you believe that with the increased use the company will need to replace the jet at the end of three years rather than four. A new jet costs $1.1 million and (at its current low rate of use) has a life of six years. Assume that the company does not pay taxes. All cash flows are forecasted in real terms. The real opportunity cost of capital is 8%. Should you try to persuade the president to allow other officers to use the plane?

CHALLENGE

36. **Effective tax rates** One measure of the effective tax rate is the difference between the IRRs of pretax and after-tax cash flows, divided by the pretax IRR. Consider, for example, an investment I generating a perpetual stream of pretax cash flows C. The pretax IRR is C/I, and the after-tax IRR is $C(1 - T_C)/I$, where T_C is the statutory tax rate. The effective rate, call it T_E, is

$$T_E = \frac{C/I - C(1 - T_C)/I}{C/I} = T_C$$

    In this case, the effective rate equals the statutory rate.

    a. Calculate the effective tax rate for the guano project in Section 6-3.

    b. How does the effective rate depend on the tax depreciation schedule? On the inflation rate?

    c. Consider a project where all of the up-front investment is treated as an expense for tax purposes. Does this definition of the effective tax rate make sense for such a project?

37. **Equivalent annual costs** We warned that equivalent annual costs should be calculated in real terms. We did not fully explain why. This problem will show you.

    Look back to the cash flows for machines A and B (in "The Choice between Long- and Short-Lived Equipment"). The present values of purchase and operating costs are 28.37 (over three years for A) and 21.00 (over two years for B). The real discount rate is 6% and the inflation rate is 5%.

    a. Calculate the three- and two-year *level nominal* annuities which have present values of 28.37 and 21.00. Explain why these annuities are *not* realistic estimates of equivalent annual costs. (*Hint:* In real life machinery rentals increase with inflation.)

    b. Suppose the inflation rate increases to 25%. The real interest rate stays at 6%. Recalculate the level nominal annuities. Note that the *ranking* of machines A and B appears to change. Why?

MINI-CASE ● ● ● ● ●

New Economy Transport (A)

The New Economy Transport Company (NETCO) was formed in 1959 to carry cargo and passengers between ports in the Pacific Northwest and Alaska. By 2018, its fleet had grown to four vessels, including a small dry-cargo vessel, the *Vital Spark*.

The *Vital Spark* is 25 years old and badly in need of an overhaul. Peter Handy, the finance director, has just been presented with a proposal that would require the following expenditures:

Overhaul engine and generators	$340,000
Replace radar and other electronic equipment	75,000
Repairs to hull and superstructure	310,000
Painting and other repairs	95,000
	$820,000

Mr. Handy believes that all these outlays could be written off immediately for tax purposes. NETCO's chief engineer, McPhail, estimates the postoverhaul operating costs as follows:

Fuel	$ 450,000
Labor and benefits	480,000
Maintenance	141,000
Other	110,000
	$1,181,000

These costs generally increase with inflation, which is forecasted at 2.5% a year.

The *Vital Spark* is carried on NETCO's books at a net depreciated value of only $100,000, but could probably be sold "as is," along with an extensive inventory of spare parts, for $200,000. The book value of the spare parts inventory is $40,000. Sale of the *Vital Spark* would generate an immediate tax liability on the difference between sale price and book value.

The chief engineer also suggests installation of a brand-new engine and control system, which would cost an extra $600,000.[16] This additional equipment would not substantially improve the *Vital Spark*'s performance, but would result in the following reduced annual fuel, labor, and maintenance costs:

Fuel	$ 400,000
Labor and benefits	405,000
Maintenance	105,000
Other	110,000
	$1,020,000

Overhaul of the *Vital Spark* would take it out of service for several months. The overhauled vessel would resume commercial service next year. Based on past experience, Mr. Handy believes that it would generate revenues of about $1.4 million next year, increasing with inflation thereafter.

---

[16] This additional outlay would also qualify for an immediate 100% bonus depreciation.

But the *Vital Spark* cannot continue forever. Even if overhauled, its useful life is probably no more than 10 years, 12 years at the most. Its salvage value when finally taken out of service will be trivial.

NETCO is a conservatively financed firm in a mature business. It normally evaluates capital investments using an 11% cost of capital. This is a nominal, not a real, rate. NETCO's tax rate is 21%.

QUESTION

1. Calculate the NPV of the proposed overhaul of the *Vital Spark,* with and without the new engine and control system. To do the calculation, you will have to prepare a spreadsheet table showing all costs after taxes over the vessel's remaining economic life. Take special care with your assumptions about depreciation tax shields and inflation.

New Economy Transport (B)

There is no question that the *Vital Spark* needs an overhaul soon. However, Mr. Handy feels it unwise to proceed without also considering the purchase of a new vessel. Cohn and Doyle Inc., a Wisconsin shipyard, has approached NETCO with a design incorporating a Kort nozzle, extensively automated navigation and power control systems, and much more comfortable accommodations for the crew. Estimated annual operating costs of the new vessel are:

Fuel	$380,000
Labor and benefits	330,000
Maintenance	70,000
Other	105,000
	$885,000

The crew would require additional training to handle the new vessel's more complex and sophisticated equipment. Training would probably cost $50,000 next year.

The estimated operating costs for the new vessel assume that it would be operated in the same way as the *Vital Spark.* However, the new vessel should be able to handle a larger load on some routes, which could generate additional revenues, net of additional out-of-pocket costs, of as much as $100,000 per year. Moreover, a new vessel would have a useful service life of 20 years or more.

Cohn and Doyle offered the new vessel for a fixed price of $3,000,000, payable half immediately and half on delivery next year.

Mr. Handy stepped out on the foredeck of the *Vital Spark* as she chugged down the Cook Inlet. "A rusty old tub," he muttered, "but she's never let us down. I'll bet we could keep her going until next year while Cohn and Doyle are building her replacement. We could use up the spare parts to keep her going. We might even be able to sell or scrap her for book value when her replacement arrives.

"But how do I compare the NPV of a new ship with the old *Vital Spark*? Sure, I could run a 20-year NPV spreadsheet, but I don't have a clue how the replacement will be used by the end of that time. Maybe I could compare the overall *cost* of overhauling and operating the *Vital Spark* to the cost of buying and operating the proposed replacement."

QUESTIONS

1. Calculate and compare the equivalent annual costs of (a) overhauling and operating the *Vital Spark* for 12 more years, and (b) buying and operating the proposed replacement vessel for 20 years. What should Mr. Handy do if the replacement's annual costs are the same or lower?

2. Suppose the replacement's equivalent annual costs are higher than the *Vital Spark*'s. What additional information should Mr. Handy seek in this case?

7

Introduction to Risk and Return

We have managed to go through six chapters without directly addressing the problem of risk, but now the jig is up. We can no longer be satisfied with vague statements like "The opportunity cost of capital depends on the risk of the project." We need to know how risk is defined, what the links are between risk and the opportunity cost of capital, and how the financial manager can cope with risk in practical situations.

In this chapter, we concentrate on the first of these issues and leave the other two to Chapters 8 and 9. We start by summarizing more than 100 years of evidence on rates of return in capital markets. Then we take a first look at investment risks and show how they can be reduced by portfolio diversification. We introduce you to beta, the standard risk measure for individual securities.

The themes of this chapter, then, are portfolio risk, security risk, and diversification. For the most part, we take the view of the individual investor. But at the end of the chapter, we turn the problem around and ask whether diversification makes sense as a corporate objective.

7-1   Over a Century of Capital Market History in One Easy Lesson

Financial analysts are blessed with an enormous quantity of data. There are comprehensive databases of the prices of U.S. stocks, bonds, options, and commodities, as well as huge amounts of data for securities in other countries. We focus on a study by Dimson, Marsh, and Staunton that measures the historical performance of three portfolios of U.S. securities:[1]

1. A portfolio of Treasury bills, that is, U.S. government debt securities maturing in less than one year.[2]

2. A portfolio of U.S. government bonds.

3. A portfolio of U.S. common stocks.

These investments offer different degrees of risk. Treasury bills are about as safe an investment as you can make. There is no risk of default, and their short maturity means that the

---

[1]See E. Dimson, P. R. Marsh, and M. Staunton, *Triumph of the Optimists: 101 Years of Global Investment Returns* (Princeton, NJ: Princeton University Press, 2002).

[2]Treasury bills were not issued before 1919. Before that date, the interest rate used is the commercial paper rate.

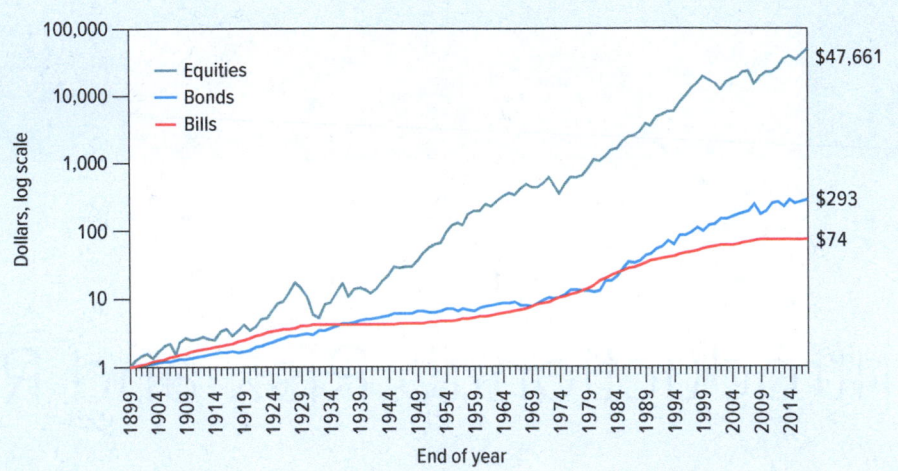

> **FIGURE 7.1**
>
> How an investment of $1 at the end of 1899 would have grown by the end of 2017, assuming reinvestment of all dividend and interest payments
>
> *Source:* E. Dimson, P. R. Marsh, and M. Staunton, *Triumph of the Optimists: 101 Years of Global Investment Returns* (Princeton, NJ: Princeton University Press, 2002), with updates provided by the authors.

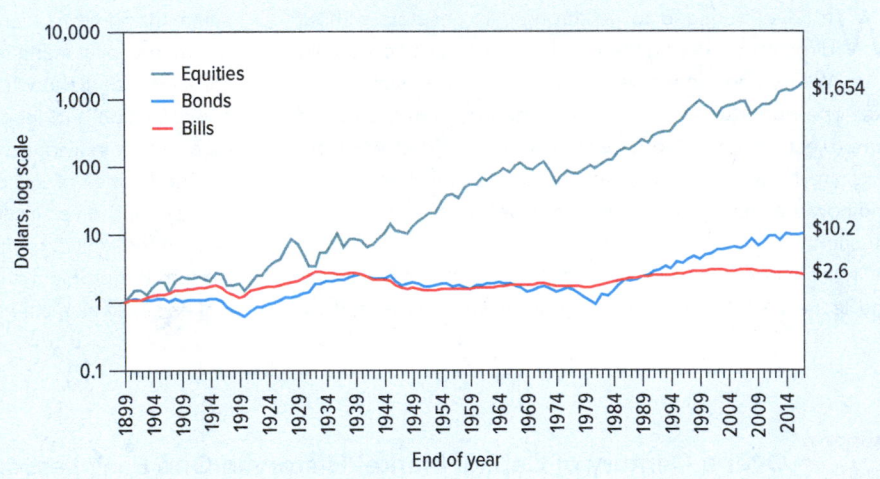

> **FIGURE 7.2**
>
> How an investment of $1 at the end of 1899 would have grown *in real terms* by the end of 2017, assuming reinvestment of all dividend and interest payments. Compare this plot with Figure 7.1, and note how inflation has eroded the purchasing power of returns to investors.
>
> *Source:* E. Dimson, P. R. Marsh, and M. Staunton, *Triumph of the Optimists: 101 Years of Global Investment Returns* (Princeton, NJ: Princeton University Press, 2002), with updates provided by the authors.

prices of Treasury bills are relatively stable. In fact, an investor who wishes to lend money for, say, three months can achieve a perfectly certain payoff by purchasing a Treasury bill maturing in three months. However, the investor cannot lock in a *real* rate of return: There is still some uncertainty about inflation.

By switching to long-term government bonds, the investor acquires an asset whose price fluctuates as interest rates vary. (Bond prices fall when interest rates rise and rise when interest rates fall.) An investor who shifts from bonds to common stocks shares in all the ups and downs of the issuing companies.

Figure 7.1 shows how your money would have grown if you had invested $1 at the end of 1899 and reinvested all dividend or interest income in each of the three portfolios.[3] Figure 7.2 is identical except that it depicts the growth in the *real* value of the portfolio. We focus here on nominal values.

---

[3]Portfolio values are plotted on a log scale. If they were not, the ending values for the common stock portfolio would run off the top of the page.

Average Annual Rate of Return			
	Nominal	**Real**	**Average Risk Premium (Extra Return versus Treasury Bills)**
Treasury bills	3.8	0.9	0
Government bonds	5.3	2.5	1.5
Common stocks	11.5	8.4	7.7

❭ **TABLE 7.1**   Average rates of return on U.S. Treasury bills, government bonds, and common stocks, 1900–2017 (figures in % per year).

Source: E. Dimson, P. R. Marsh, and M. Staunton, *Triumph of the Optimists: 101 Years of Global Investment Returns,* (Princeton, NJ: Princeton University Press, 2002), with updates provided by the authors.

Investment performance coincides with our intuitive risk ranking. A dollar invested in the safest investment, Treasury bills, would have grown to $74 by the end of 2017, barely enough to keep up with inflation. An investment in long-term Treasury bonds would have produced $293. Common stocks were in a class by themselves. An investor who placed a dollar in the stocks of large U.S. firms would have received $47,661.

We can also calculate the rate of return from these portfolios for each year from 1900 to 2017. This rate of return reflects both cash receipts—dividends or interest—and the capital gains or losses realized during the year. Averages of the 118 annual rates of return for each portfolio are shown in Table 7.1.

Over this period, Treasury bills have provided the lowest average return—3.8% per year in *nominal* terms and 0.9% in *real* terms. In other words, the average rate of inflation over this period was about 3% per year. Common stocks were again the winners. Stocks of major corporations provided an average nominal return of 11.5%. By taking on the risk of common stocks, investors earned a *risk premium* of 11.5 − 3.8 = 7.7% over the return on Treasury bills.

You may ask why we look back over such a long period to measure average rates of return. The reason is that annual rates of return for common stocks fluctuate so much that averages taken over short periods are meaningless. Our only hope of gaining insights from historical rates of return is to look at a very long period.[4]

Arithmetic Averages and Compound Annual Returns

Notice that the average returns shown in Table 7.1 are arithmetic averages. In other words, we simply added the 118 annual returns and divided by 118. The arithmetic average is higher than the compound annual return over the period. The 118-year compound annual return for common stocks was 9.6%.[5]

The proper uses of arithmetic and compound rates of return from past investments are often misunderstood. Therefore, we call a brief time-out for a clarifying example.

Suppose that the price of Big Oil's common stock is $100. There is an equal chance that at the end of the year the stock will be worth $90, $110, or $130. Therefore, the return could be −10%, +10%, or +30% (we assume that Big Oil does not pay a dividend). The *expected* return is ⅓ (−10 + 10 + 30) = +10%.

---

[4] We cannot be sure that this period is truly representative and that the average is not distorted by a few unusually high or low returns. The reliability of an estimate of the average is usually measured by its *standard error.* For example, the standard error of our estimate of the average risk premium on common stocks is 1.9%. There is a 95% chance that the *true* average is within plus or minus 2 standard errors of the 7.7% estimate. In other words, if you said that the true average was between 3.9% and 11.5%, you would have a 95% chance of being right. *Technical note:* The standard error of the average is equal to the standard deviation divided by the square root of the number of observations. In our case the standard deviation of the risk premium is 20.2%, and therefore the standard error is $19.7/\sqrt{118} = 1.9\%$

[5] This was calculated from $(1 + r)^{118} = 47,661$, which implies $r = .096$. *Technical note:* For log normally distributed returns the annual compound return is equal to the arithmetic average return minus half the variance. For example, the annual standard deviation of returns on the U.S. market was about .20, or 20%. Variance was therefore $.20^2$, or .04. The compound annual return is about $.04/2 = .02$, or 2 percentage points less than the arithmetic average.

If we run the process in reverse and discount the expected cash flow by the expected rate of return, we obtain the value of Big Oil's stock:

$$PV = \frac{110}{1.10} = \$100$$

The expected return of 10% is therefore the correct rate at which to discount the expected cash flow from Big Oil's stock. It is also the opportunity cost of capital for investments that have the same degree of risk as Big Oil.

Now suppose that we observe the returns on Big Oil stock over a large number of years. If the odds are unchanged, the return will be −10% in a third of the years, +10% in a further third, and +30% in the remaining years. The arithmetic average of these yearly returns is

$$\frac{-10 + 10 + 30}{3} = +10\%$$

Thus, the arithmetic average of the returns correctly measures the opportunity cost of capital for investments of similar risk to Big Oil stock.[6]

The average compound annual return[7] on Big Oil stock would be

$$(.9 \times 1.1 \times 1.3)^{1/3} - 1 = .088, \text{ or } 8.8\%$$

which is *less* than the opportunity cost of capital. Investors would not be willing to invest in a project that offered an 8.8% expected return if they could get an expected return of 10% in the capital markets. The net present value of such a project would be

$$NPV = -100 + \frac{108.8}{1.1} = -1.1$$

Moral: If the cost of capital is estimated from historical returns or risk premiums, use arithmetic averages, not compound annual rates of return.[8]

Using Historical Evidence to Evaluate Today's Cost of Capital

Suppose there is an investment project that you *know*—don't ask how—has the same risk as Standard and Poor's Composite Index. We will say that it has the same degree of risk as the *market portfolio,* although this is speaking somewhat loosely, because the index does not include all risky investments. What rate should you use to discount this project's forecasted cash flows?

Clearly you should use the currently expected rate of return on the market portfolio; that is, the return investors would forgo by investing in the proposed project. Let us call this market return r_m. One way to estimate r_m is to assume that the future will be like the past and that today's investors expect to receive the same "normal" rates of return revealed by the averages shown in Table 7.1. In this case, you would set r_m at 11.5%, the average of past market returns.

---

[6]You sometimes hear that the arithmetic average correctly measures the opportunity cost of capital for one-year cash flows, but not for more distant ones. Let us check. Suppose that you expect to receive a cash flow of $121 in year 2. We know that one year hence investors will value that cash flow by discounting at 10% (the arithmetic average of possible returns). In other words, at the end of the year they will be willing to pay PV1 = 121/1.10 = $110 for the expected cash flow. But we already know how to value an asset that pays off $110 in year 1—just discount at the 10% opportunity cost of capital. Thus PV0 = PV1/1.10 = 110/1.1 = $100. Our example demonstrates that the arithmetic average (10% in our example) provides a correct measure of the opportunity cost of capital regardless of the timing of the cash flow.

[7]The compound annual return is often referred to as the geometric average return.

[8]Our discussion assumed that we *knew* that the returns of −10, +10, and +30% were equally likely. For an analysis of the effect of uncertainty about the expected return see I. A. Cooper, "Arithmetic Versus Geometric Mean Estimators: Setting Discount Rates for Capital Budgeting," *European Financial Management* 2 (July 1996), pp. 157–167; and E. Jacquier, A. Kane, and A. J. Marcus, "Optimal Estimation of the Risk Premium for the Long Run and Asset Allocation: A Case of Compounded Estimation Risk," *Journal of Financial Econometrics* 3 (2005), pp. 37–55. When future returns are forecasted to distant horizons, the historical arithmetic means are upward-biased. This bias would be small in most corporate-finance applications, however.

Unfortunately, this is *not* the way to do it; r_m is not likely to be stable over time. Remember that it is the sum of the risk-free interest rate r_f and a premium for risk. We know that r_f varies. For example, in 1981 the interest rate on Treasury bills was about 15%. It is difficult to believe that investors in that year were content to hold common stocks offering an expected return of only 11.5%.

If you need to estimate the return that investors expect to receive, a more sensible procedure is to take the interest rate on Treasury bills and add 7.7%, the average *risk premium* shown in Table 7.1. For example, suppose that the current interest rate on Treasury bills is 2%. Adding on the average risk premium gives

$$r_m = r_f + \text{normal risk premium}$$
$$= .02 + .077 = .097, \text{ or } 9.7\%$$

The crucial assumption here is that there is a normal, stable risk premium on the market portfolio, so that the expected *future* risk premium can be measured by the average past risk premium.

Even with more than 100 years of data, we can't estimate the market risk premium exactly; nor can we be sure that investors today are demanding the same reward for risk that they were 50 or 100 years ago. All this leaves plenty of room for argument about what the risk premium really is.[9]

Many financial managers and economists believe that long-run historical returns are the best measure available. Others have a gut instinct that investors don't need such a large risk premium to persuade them to hold common stocks.[10] For example, surveys of businesspeople and academics commonly suggest that they expect a market risk premium that is somewhat below the historical average.[11]

If you believe that the expected market risk premium is less than the historical average, you probably also believe that history has been unexpectedly kind to investors in the United States and that this good luck is unlikely to be repeated. Here are two reasons that history may overstate the risk premium that investors demand today.

Reason 1   Since 1900, the United States has been among the world's most prosperous countries. Other economies have languished or been wracked by war or civil unrest. By focusing on equity returns in the United States, we may obtain a biased view of what investors *expected*. Perhaps the historical averages miss the possibility that the United States could have turned out to be one of those less-fortunate countries.[12]

Figure 7.3 sheds some light on this issue. It is taken from a comprehensive study by Dimson, Marsh, and Staunton of market returns in 20 countries and shows the average risk

BEYOND THE PAGE

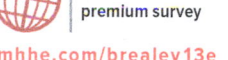

Market risk premium survey

mhhe.com/brealey13e

---

[9]Some of the disagreements simply reflect the fact that the risk premium is sometimes defined in different ways. Some measure the average difference between stock returns and the returns (or yields) on long-term bonds. Others measure the difference between compound rate of return on stocks and the interest rate. As we explained earlier, this is not an appropriate measure of the cost of capital.

[10]There is some theory behind this instinct. The high risk premium earned in the market seems to imply that investors are extremely risk-averse. If that is true, investors ought to cut back their consumption when stock prices fall and wealth decreases. But the evidence suggests that when stock prices fall, investors spend at nearly the same rate. This is difficult to reconcile with high risk aversion and a high market risk premium. There is an active research literature on this "equity premium puzzle." See R. Mehra, "The Equity Premium Puzzle: A Review," *Foundations and Trends in Finance* 2 (2006), pp. 11–81; and R. Mehra, ed., *Handbook of the Equity Risk Premium* (Amsterdam: Elsevier Handbooks in Finance Series, 2008).

[11]For example, a survey of U.S. CFOs in December 2017 produced an average forecast risk premium of 5.7% over the three-month bill rate. A parallel 2017 survey of academics, analysts, and managers likewise found that the average estimate of the required market risk premium for the United States was 5.4%, though this figure seems to represent the premium over a long-term bond rate. See, respectively, Duke/*CFO Magazine,* "Global Business Outlook Survey," Fourth Quarter 2017, **http://www.cfosurvey.org/**; and P. Fernandez, V. Pershin, and I. Fernández Acín, "Market Risk Premium and Risk-free Rate Used for 59 Countries in 2018: A Survey," April 4, 2018. Available at SSRN: **https://ssrn.com/abstract=3155709**.

[12]This possibility was suggested in P. Jorion and W. N. Goetzmann, "Global Stock Markets in the Twentieth Century," *Journal of Finance* 54 (June 1999), pp. 953–980.

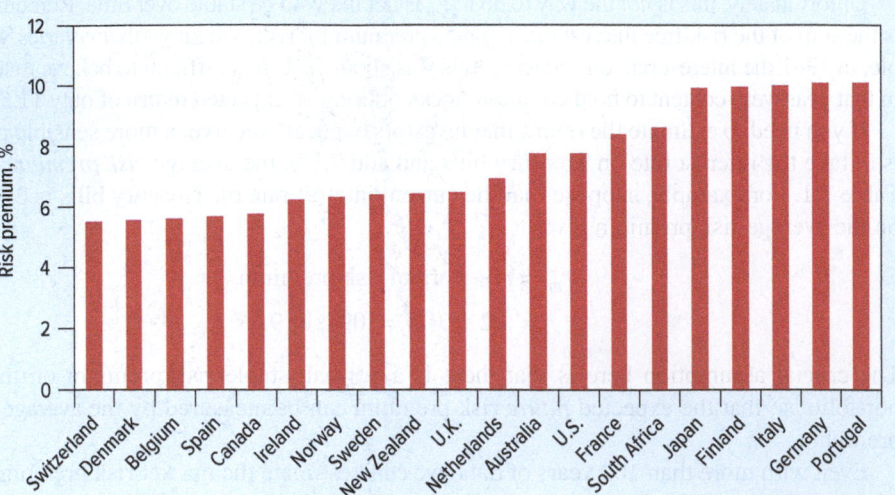

► FIGURE 7.3

Average market risk premiums (nominal return on stocks minus nominal return on bills), 1900–2017

Source: E. Dimson, P. R. Marsh, and M. Staunton, *Triumph of the Optimists: 101 Years of Global Investment Returns* (Princeton, NJ: Princeton University Press, 2002), with updates provided by the authors.

premium in each country between 1900 and 2017. There is no evidence here that U.S. investors have been particularly fortunate; the United States was just about average in terms of the risk premium.

In Figure 7.3, Swiss stocks come bottom of the league; the average risk premium in Switzerland was only 5.5%. The clear winner was Portugal, with a premium of 10.0%. Some of these differences between countries may reflect differences in risk. But remember how difficult it is to make precise estimates of what investors expected. You probably would not be too far out if you concluded that the *expected* risk premium was the same in each country.[13]

Reason 2   Economists who believe that history may overstate the return that investors expect often point to the fact that stock prices in the United States have for some years outpaced the growth in company dividends or earnings.

Figure 7.4 plots dividend yields in the United States from 1900 to 2017. At the start of the period, the yield was 4.4%. By 1917, it had risen to just over 10.0%, but from then onward, there was a clear, long-term decline. By 2017, yields had fallen to 1.9%. It seems unlikely that investors expected this decline in yields, in which case, some part of the actual return during this period was unexpected.[14]

How should we interpret the decline in yields? Suppose that investors expect a steady growth (g) in a stock's dividend. Then its value is $PV = DIV_1/(r - g)$, and its dividend yield is $DIV_1/PV = r - g$. In this case, the dividend yield measures the difference between the discount rate and the expected growth rate. So, if we observe that dividend yields decline, it could either be because investors have increased their forecast of future growth or because they are content with a lower expected return.

What's the answer? Have investors raised their forecast of future dividend growth? One possibility is that they now anticipate a forthcoming golden age of prosperity and surging profits. But a simpler (and more plausible) argument is that companies have increasingly

---

[13]We are concerned here with the difference between the nominal market return and the nominal interest rate. Sometimes you will see *real* risk premiums quoted—that is, the difference between the *real* market return and the *real* interest rate. If the inflation rate is i, then the real risk premium is $(r_m - r_f)/(1 + i)$. For countries such as Italy that have experienced a high degree of inflation, this real risk premium may be significantly lower than the nominal premium.

[14]This argument is made by Fama and French in E. F. Fama and K. R. French, "The Equity Premium," *Journal of Finance* 57 (April 2002), pp. 637–659.

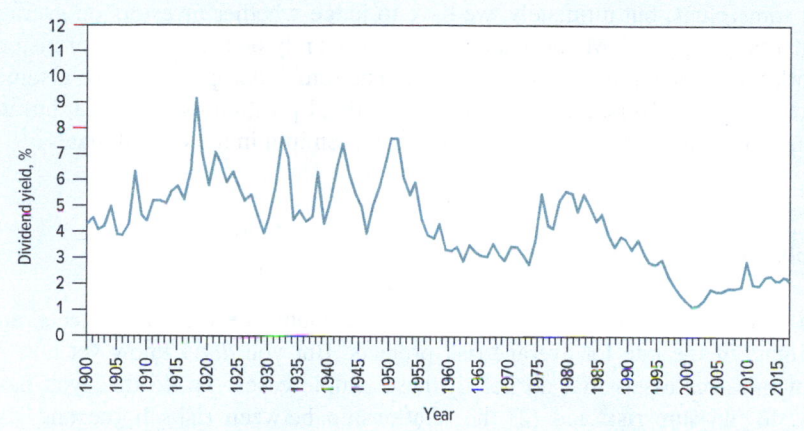

▶ **FIGURE 7.4**

Dividend yields in the United States 1900–2017

Source: Federal Reserve Bank of St. Louis, Economic Data.

preferred to distribute cash by stock repurchase. As we explain in Chapter 16, the effect of using cash to buy back stock is to reduce the current dividend yield and to increase the future rate of dividend growth. The dividend yield is lower but the expected return is unchanged.

What about the second possibility? Could a decline in risk have caused investors to be satisfied with a lower rate of return? A few years ago, you would likely hear people say that improvements in economic management have made investment in the stock market less risky than it used to be. Since the financial crisis of 2007–2009, investors are less sure that this is the case. But perhaps the growth in mutual funds has made it easier for individuals to diversify away part of their risk, or perhaps pension funds and other financial institutions have found that they also could reduce their risk by investing part of their funds overseas. If these investors can eliminate more of their risk than in the past, they may be content with a lower risk premium.

The effect of any decline in the expected market risk premium is to increase the *realized* rate of return. Suppose that the stocks in the Standard & Poor's Index pay an aggregate dividend of $400 billion ($DIV_1 = 400$) and that this dividend is expected to grow indefinitely at 6% per year ($g = .06$). If the yield on these stocks is 2%, the expected total rate of return is $r = 6 + 2 = 8\%$. If we plug these numbers into the constant-growth dividend-discount model, then the value of the market portfolio is $PV = DIV_1/(r - g) = 400/(.08 - .06) = \$20,000$ billion, approximately its actual total value in 2017.

The required return of 8%, of course, includes a risk premium. For example, if the risk-free interest rate is 1%, the risk premium is 7%. Suppose that investors now see the stock market as a safer investment than before. Therefore, they revise their required risk premium downward from 7% to 6.5% and the required return from 8% to 7.5%. As a result the value of the market portfolio increases to $PV = DIV_1/(r - g) = 400/(.075 - .06) = \$26,667$ billion, and the dividend yield falls to $DIV_1/PV = 400/26,667 = .015$ or 1.5%.

Thus a fall of 0.5 percentage point in the risk premium that investors demand would cause a 33% rise in market value, from $20,000 to $26,667 billion. The total return to investors when this happens, including the 2% dividend yield, is $2 + 33 = 35\%$. With a 1% interest rate, the risk premium earned is $35 - 1 = 34\%$, much greater than investors expected. If and when this 34% risk premium enters our sample of past risk premiums, we may be led to a double mistake. First, we will overestimate the risk premium that investors required in the past. Second, we will fail to recognize that investors require a lower expected risk premium when they look to the future.

Out of this debate only one firm conclusion emerges: Trying to pin down an exact number for the market risk premium is about as hopeless as eating spaghetti with a one-pronged fork.

History contains some clues, but ultimately, we have to judge whether investors on average have received what they expected. Many financial economists rely on the evidence of history and therefore work with a risk premium of about 7%. The remainder generally use a somewhat lower figure. Brealey, Myers, and Allen have no official position on the issue, but we believe that a range of 5% to 8% is reasonable for the risk premium in the United States.

7-2 Diversification and Portfolio Risk

You now have a couple of benchmarks. You know the discount rate for safe projects, and you have an estimate of the rate for average-risk projects. But you *don't* know yet how to estimate discount rates for assets that do not fit these simple cases. To do that, you have to learn (1) how to measure risk and (2) the relationship between risks borne and risk premiums demanded.

Figure 7.5 shows the 118 annual rates of return for U.S. common stocks. The fluctuations in year-to-year returns are remarkably wide. The highest annual return was 57.6% in 1933—a partial rebound from the stock market crash of 1929–1932. However, there were losses exceeding 25% in six years, the worst being the –43.9% return in 1931.

Another way to present these data is by a histogram or frequency distribution. This is done in Figure 7.6, where the variability of year-to-year returns shows up in the wide "spread" of outcomes.

Variance and Standard Deviation

The standard statistical measures of spread are **variance** and **standard deviation.** The variance of the market return is the expected squared deviation from the expected return. In other words,

$$\text{Variance } (\tilde{r}_m) = \text{the expected value of } (\tilde{r}_m - r_m)^2$$

where $\tilde{r}_m$ is the actual return and r_m is the expected return.[15] The standard deviation is simply the square root of the variance:

$$\text{Standard deviation of } \tilde{r}_m = \sqrt{\text{variance}(\tilde{r}_m)}$$

Standard deviation is often denoted by σ and variance by σ^2.

Here is a very simple example showing how variance and standard deviation are calculated. Suppose that you are offered the chance to play the following game. You start by investing $100. Then two coins are flipped. For each head that comes up, you get back your starting balance *plus* 20%, and for each tail that comes up, you get back your starting balance *less* 10%. Clearly there are four equally likely outcomes:

- Head + head: You gain 40%.
- Head + tail: You gain 10%.
- Tail + head: You gain 10%.
- Tail + tail: You lose 20%.

---

[15] One more technical point. When variance is estimated from a sample of *observed* returns, we add the squared deviations and divide by $N-1$, where N is the number of observations. We divide by $N-1$ rather than N to correct for what is called *the loss of a degree of freedom*. The formula is

$$\text{Variance}(\tilde{r}_m) = \frac{1}{N-1}\sum_{t=1}^{N}(\tilde{r}_m - r_m)^2$$

where $\tilde{r}_{mt}$ is the market return in period t and r_m is the mean of the values of $\tilde{r}_{mt}$.

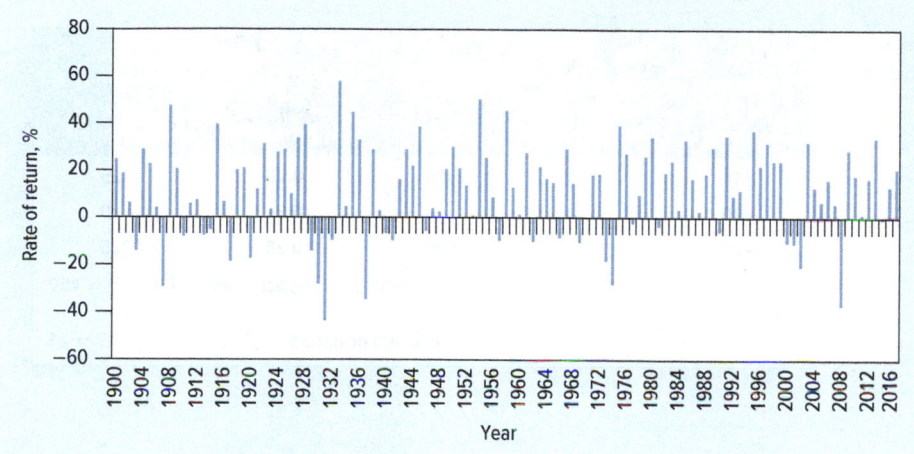

▶ **FIGURE 7.5**

The stock market has been a profitable but variable investment

Source: E. Dimson, P. R. Marsh, and M. Staunton, *Triumph of the Optimists: 101 Years of Global Investment Returns* (Princeton, NJ: Princeton University Press, 2002), with updates provided by the authors.

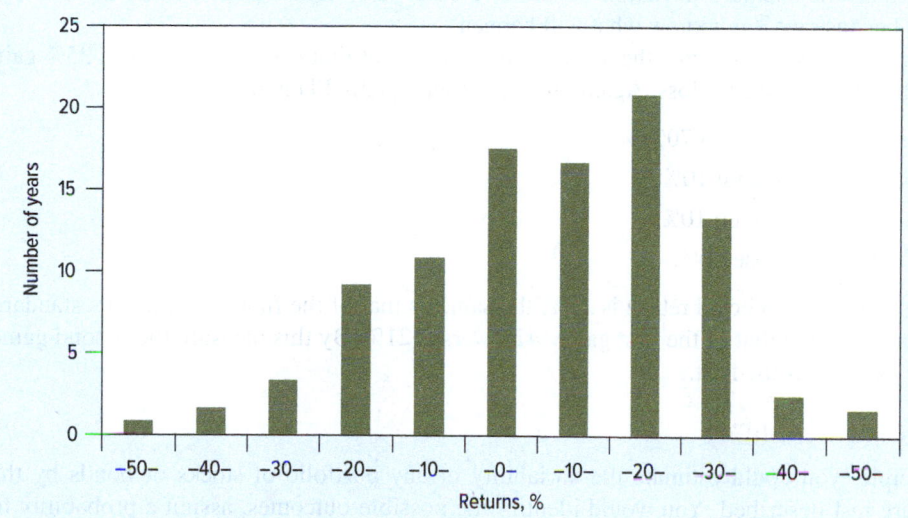

▶ **FIGURE 7.6**

Histogram of the annual rates of return from the stock market in the United States, 1900–2017, showing the wide spread of returns from investment in common stocks

Source: E. Dimson, P. R. Marsh, and M. Staunton, *Triumph of the Optimists: 101 Years of Global Investment Returns,* (Princeton, NJ: Princeton University Press, 2002), with updates provided by the authors.

There is a chance of 1 in 4, or .25, that you will make 40%; a chance of 2 in 4, or .5, that you will make 10%; and a chance of 1 in 4, or .25, that you will lose 20%. The game's expected return is, therefore, a weighted average of the possible outcomes:

$$\text{Expected return} = (.25 \times 40) + (.5 \times 10) + (.25 \times -20) = +10\%$$

Table 7.2 shows that the variance of the percentage returns is 450. Standard deviation is the square root of 450, or 21. This figure is in the same units as the rate of return, so we can say that the game's variability is 21%.

If outcomes are uncertain, then more things can happen than will happen. The risk of an asset can be completely expressed, as we did for the coin-tossing game, by writing all possible outcomes and the probability of each. In practice, this is cumbersome and often impossible. Therefore, we use variance or standard deviation to summarize the spread of possible outcomes.[16]

---

[16]Which of the two we use is solely a matter of convenience. Since standard deviation is in the same units as the rate of return, it is generally more convenient to use standard deviation. However, when we are talking about the *proportion* of risk that is due to some factor, it is less confusing to work in terms of the variance.

> **TABLE 7.2** The coin-tossing game: calculating variance and standard deviation

(1) Percent Rate of Return ($\tilde{r}$)	(2) Deviation from Expected Return ($\tilde{r} - r$)	(3) Squared Deviation ($\tilde{r} - r)^2$	(4) Probability	(5) Probability × Squared Deviation
+40	+30	900	0.25	225
+10	0	0	0.5	0
−20	−30	900	0.25	225

Variance = expected value of $(\tilde{r} - r)^2 = 450$

Standard deviation = $\sqrt{\text{variance}} = \sqrt{450} = 21$

These measures are natural indexes of risk.[17] If the outcome of the coin-tossing game had been certain, the standard deviation would have been zero. The actual standard deviation is positive because we *don't* know what will happen.

Or think of a second game, the same as the first except that each head means a 35% gain and each tail means a 25% loss. Again, there are four equally likely outcomes:

- Head + head: You gain 70%.
- Head + tail: You gain 10%.
- Tail + head: You gain 10%.
- Tail + tail: You lose 50%.

For this game the expected return is 10%, the same as that of the first game. But its standard deviation is double that of the first game, 42% versus 21%. By this measure the second game is twice as risky as the first.

Measuring Variability

In principle, you could estimate the variability of any portfolio of stocks or bonds by the procedure just described. You would identify the possible outcomes, assign a probability to each outcome, and grind through the calculations. But where do the probabilities come from? You can't look them up in the newspaper; newspapers seem to go out of their way to avoid definite statements about prospects for securities. We once saw an article headlined "Bond Prices Possibly Set to Move Sharply Either Way." Stockbrokers are much the same. Yours may respond to your query about possible market outcomes with a statement like this:

> The market currently appears to be undergoing a period of consolidation. For the intermediate term, we would take a constructive view, provided economic recovery continues. The market could be up 20% a year from now, perhaps more if inflation continues low. On the other hand, . . .

The Delphic oracle gave advice, but no probabilities.

Most financial analysts start by observing past variability. Of course, there is no risk in hindsight, but it is reasonable to assume that portfolios with histories of high variability also have the least predictable future performance.

BEYOND THE PAGE

How to calculate variance and standard deviation

mhhe.com/brealey13e

---

[17]As we explain in Chapter 8, standard deviation and variance are the correct measures of risk if the returns are normally distributed.

The annual standard deviations and variances observed for our three portfolios over the period 1900–2017 were:[18]

Portfolio	Standard Deviation (σ)	Variance (σ^2)
Treasury bills	2.9	8.1
Government bonds	9.0	80.6
Common stocks	19.7	388.7

As expected, Treasury bills were the least variable security, and common stocks were the most variable. Government bonds hold the middle ground.

You may find it interesting to compare the coin-tossing game and the stock market as alternative investments. The stock market generated an average annual return of 11.5% with a standard deviation of 19.7%. The game offers 10% and 21%, respectively—slightly lower return and about the same variability. Your gambling friends may have come up with a crude representation of the stock market.

Figure 7.7 compares the standard deviation of stock market returns in 20 countries over the same 118-year period. Portugal occupies high field with a standard deviation of 38.8%, but most of the other countries cluster together with percentage standard deviations in the low 20s.

Of course, there is no reason to suppose that the market's variability should stay the same over more than a century. For example, Germany, Italy, and Japan now have much more stable economies and markets than they did in the years leading up to and including the Second World War.

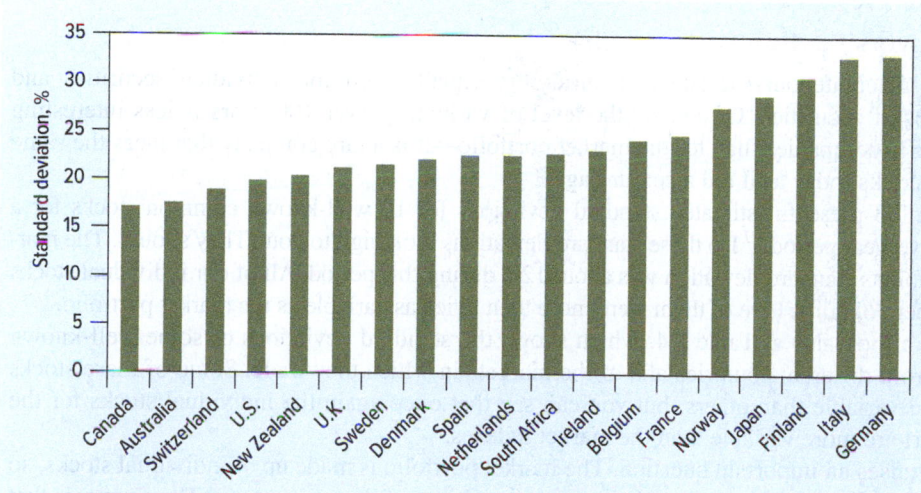

▶ **FIGURE 7.7**

The risk (standard deviation of annual returns) of markets around the world, 1900–2017

Source: E. Dimson, P. R. Marsh, and M. Staunton, *Triumph of the Optimists: 101 Years of Global Investment Returns* (Princeton, NJ: Princeton University Press, 2002), with updates provided by the authors.

---

[18]In discussing the riskiness of *bonds*, be careful to specify the time period and whether you are speaking in real or nominal terms. The *nominal* return on a long-term government bond is absolutely certain to an investor who holds on until maturity; in other words, it is risk-free if you forget about inflation. After all, the U.S. government can always print money to pay off its debts. However, the real return on Treasury securities is uncertain because no one knows how much each future dollar will buy.

The bond returns used to construct this table were measured annually. The returns reflect year-to-year changes in bond prices as well as interest received. The *one-year* returns on long-term bonds are risky in *both* real and nominal terms.

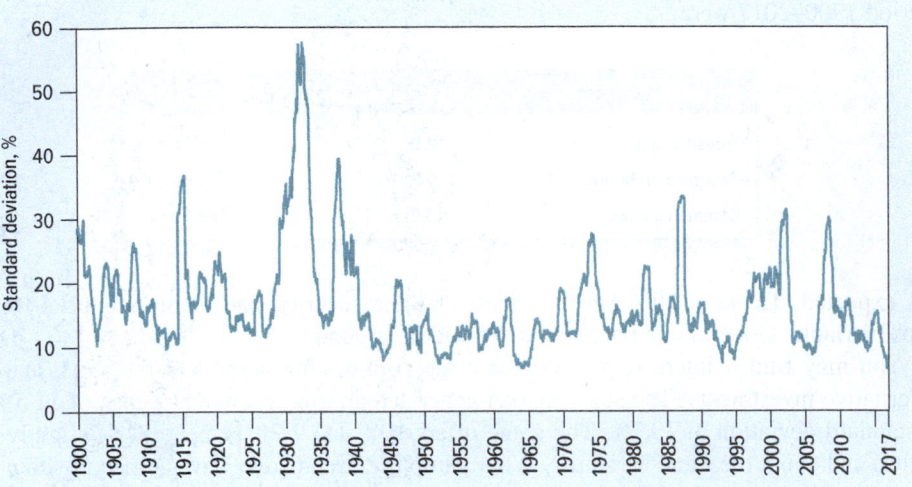

FIGURE 7.8

Annualized standard deviation of the preceding 52 weekly returns on the Dow Jones Industrial Average, January 1900 to December 2017

Figure 7.8 does not suggest a long-term upward or downward trend in the volatility of the U.S. stock market.[19] Instead there have been periods of both calm and turbulence. In 1995, an unusually tranquil year, the standard deviation of returns was less than 8%. Later, in the financial crisis, the standard deviation spiked at over 40%. By 2017, it had dropped back to its level in 1995.

Market turbulence over shorter daily, weekly, or monthly periods can be amazingly high. On Black Monday, October 19, 1987, the U.S. market fell by 23% *on a single day.* The market standard deviation for the week surrounding Black Monday was equivalent to 89% per year. Fortunately, volatility reverted to normal levels within a few weeks after the crash.

How Diversification Reduces Risk

We can calculate our measures of variability equally well for individual securities and portfolios of securities. Of course, the level of variability over 100 years is less interesting for specific companies than for the market portfolio—it is a rare company that faces the same business risks today as it did a century ago.

Table 7.3 presents estimated standard deviations for 10 well-known common stocks for a recent five-year period.[20] Do these standard deviations look high to you? They should. The market portfolio's standard deviation was about 12% during this period. All of our individual stocks had higher volatility. Five of them were more than twice as variable as the market portfolio.

Take a look also at Table 7.4, which shows the standard deviations of some well-known stocks from different countries and of the markets in which they trade. Some of these stocks are more variable than others, but you can see that once again the individual stocks for the most part are more variable than the market indexes.

This raises an important question: The market portfolio is made up of individual stocks, so why doesn't its variability reflect the average variability of its components? The answer is that *diversification reduces variability.*

---

[19]These estimates are derived from *weekly* rates of return. The weekly variance is converted to an annual variance by multiplying by the number of weeks in the year. That is, the variance of the annual return is 52 times the weekly variance. The longer you hold a security or portfolio, the more risk you have to bear.

This conversion assumes that successive weekly returns are statistically independent. This is, in fact, a good assumption, as we will show in Chapter 13.

Because variance is approximately proportional to the length of time interval over which a security or portfolio return is measured, standard deviation is proportional to the square root of the interval.

[20]These standard deviations are estimated from monthly data.

Stock	Standard Deviation σ	Stock	Standard Deviation σ
United States Steel	73.0	Consolidated Edison	16.6
Tesla	57.2	The Travelers Companies	16.4
Newmont	42.2	ExxonMobil	14.0
Southwest Airlines	27.9	Johnson & Johnson	12.8
Amazon	26.6	Coca-Cola	12.6

❱**TABLE 7.3**   Standard deviations for selected U.S. common stocks, January 2013–December 2017 (figures in percent per year)

	Standard Deviation (σ)			Standard Deviation (σ)	
	Stock	Market		Stock	Market
BHP Billiton (Australia)	26.1	11.8	LVMH (France)	21.4	13.2
BP (U.K.)	21.6	10.1	Nestlé (Switzerland)	12.8	10.9
Siemens (Germany)	18.9	14.8	Sony (Japan)	46.7	16.7
Samsung (Korea)	26.5	8.8	Toronto Dominion Bank (Canada)	15.7	7.6
Agricultural Bank (China)	18.5	25.2	Tata Motors (India)	35.2	14.1

❱**TABLE 7.4**   Standard deviations for selected foreign stocks and market indexes, July 2012–June 2017 (figures in percent per year)

Selling umbrellas is a risky business; you may make a killing when it rains, but you are likely to lose your shirt in a heat wave. Selling ice cream is not safe; you do well in the heat wave, but business is poor in the rain. Suppose, however, that you invest in both an umbrella shop and an ice cream shop. By diversifying your business across two businesses, you make an average level of profit come rain or shine.

For investors, even a little diversification can provide a substantial reduction in variability. Suppose you calculate and compare the standard deviations between 2007 and 2017 of one-stock portfolios, two-stock portfolios, five-stock portfolios, and so forth. You can see from Figure 7.9 that diversification can cut the variability of returns by about a third. Notice also that you can get most of this benefit with relatively few stocks: The improvement is much smaller when the number of securities is increased beyond, say, 20 or 30.

Diversification works because prices of different stocks do not move exactly together. Statisticians make the same point when they say that stock price changes are less than perfectly

BEYOND THE PAGE

Try It! Risk and increasing diversification

mhhe.com/brealey13e

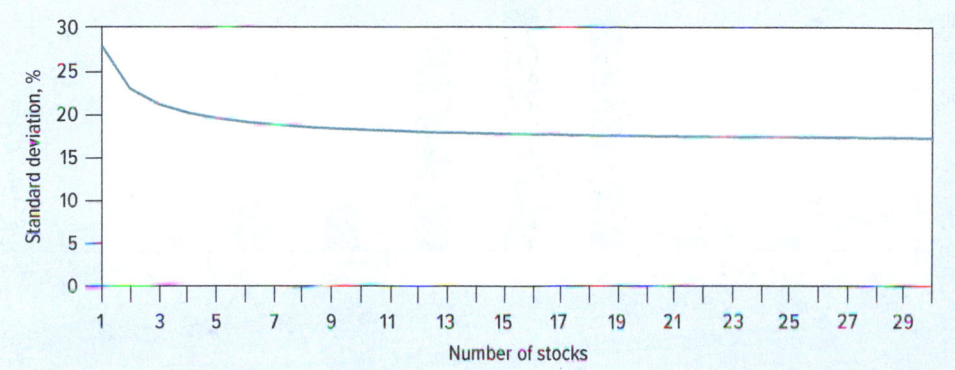

❱ **FIGURE 7.9**

Average risk (standard deviation) of portfolios containing different numbers of stocks. The stocks were selected randomly from stocks traded on the New York Exchange from 2007 through 2017. Notice that diversification reduces risk rapidly at first, then more slowly.

▶ FIGURE 7.10

Diversification reduces risk. Panels (*a*) and (*b*) show histograms of the monthly returns on the stocks of Southwest Airlines and Amazon between January 2013 and December 2017. Panel (*c*) shows a comparable histogram of the returns on a portfolio that was evenly divided between the two stocks. The spread of the portfolio's returns is markedly less than that of the individual stocks.

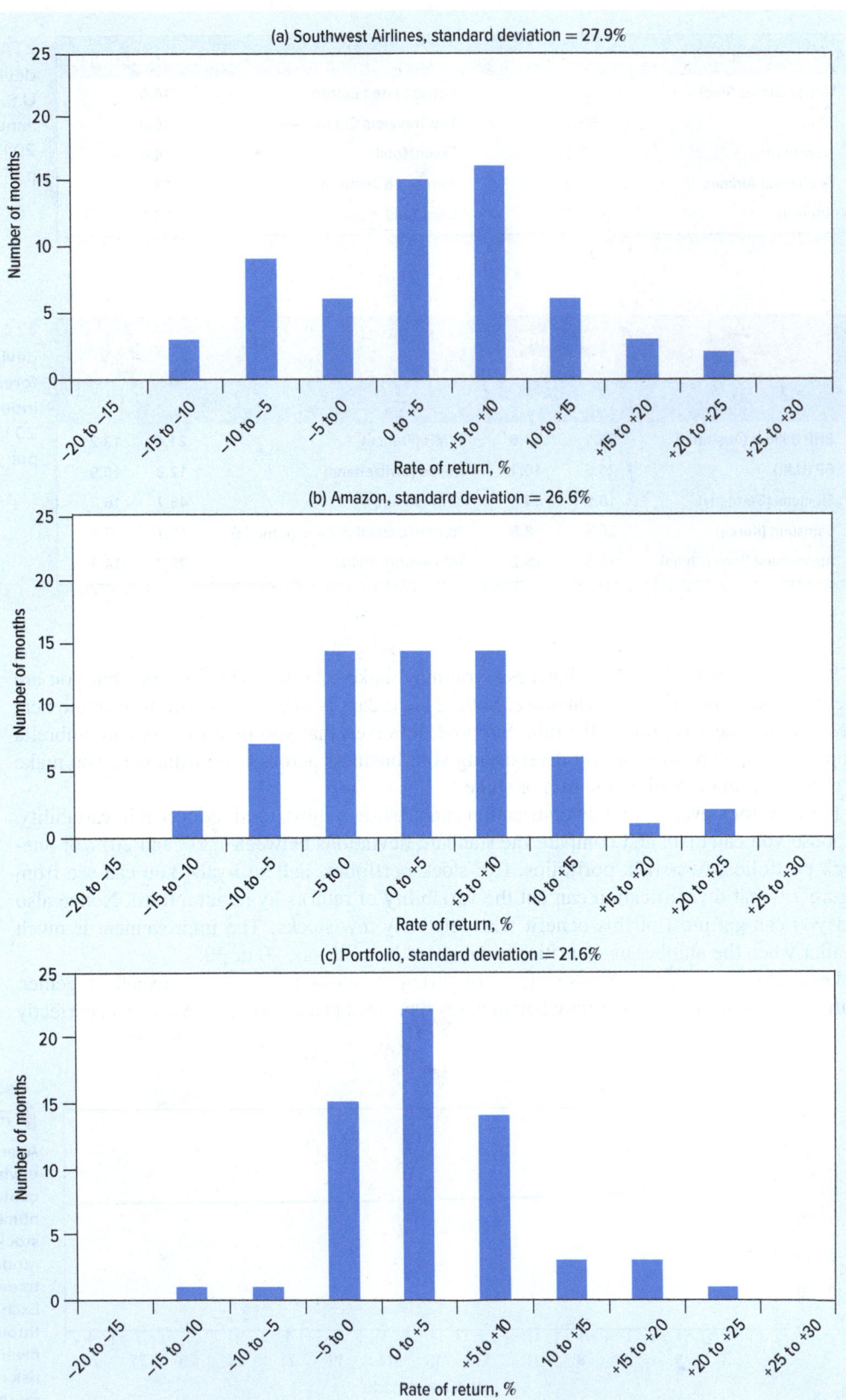

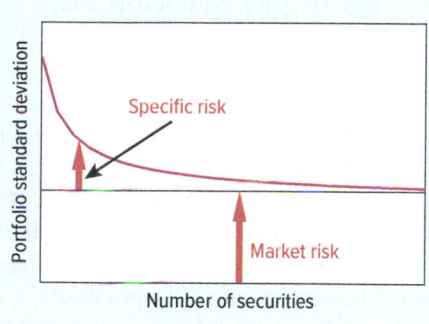

> **FIGURE 7.11**
>
> Diversification eliminates specific risk. But there is some risk that diversification cannot eliminate. This is called *market risk*.

correlated. Look, for example, at Figure 7.10. Panels (*a*) and (*b*) show the spread of monthly returns on the stocks of Southwest Airlines and Amazon. Although the two stocks enjoyed a fairly bumpy ride, they did not move in exact lockstep. Often a decline in the value of one stock was offset by a rise in the price of the other.[21] So, if you had split your portfolio evenly between the two stocks, you could have reduced the monthly fluctuations in the value of your investment. You can see this from panel (*c*), which shows that if your portfolio had been evenly divided between the two stocks, there would have been many more months when the return was just middling and far fewer cases of extreme returns.

The risk that potentially can be eliminated by diversification is called **specific risk.**[22] Specific risk stems from the fact that many of the perils that surround an individual company are peculiar to that company and perhaps its immediate competitors. But there is also some risk that you can't avoid, regardless of how much you diversify. This risk is generally known as **market risk.**[23] Market risk stems from the fact that there are other economywide perils that threaten all businesses. That is why stocks have a tendency to move together. And that is why investors are exposed to market uncertainties, no matter how many stocks they hold.

In Figure 7.11, we have divided risk into its two parts—specific risk and market risk. If you have only a single stock, specific risk is very important; but once you have a portfolio of 20 or more stocks, diversification has done the bulk of its work. For a reasonably well-diversified portfolio, only market risk matters. Therefore, the predominant source of uncertainty for a diversified investor is that the market will rise or plummet, carrying the investor's portfolio with it.

7-3   Calculating Portfolio Risk

We have given you an intuitive idea of how diversification reduces risk, but to understand fully the effect of diversification, you need to know how the risk of a portfolio depends on the risk of the individual shares.

Suppose that 60% of your portfolio is invested in Southwest Airlines and the remainder is invested in Amazon. You expect that over the coming year, Amazon will give a return of

---

[21] Over this period, the correlation between the returns on the two stocks was .26.
[22] Specific risk may be called *unsystematic risk, residual risk, unique risk,* or *diversifiable risk.*
[23] Market risk may be called *systematic risk* or *undiversifiable risk.*

10.0% and Southwest 15.0%. The expected return on your portfolio is simply a weighted average of the expected returns on the individual stocks:[24]

$$\text{Expected portfolio return} = (.60 \times 15) + (.40 \times 10) = 13\%$$

Calculating the expected portfolio return is easy. The hard part is to work out the risk of your portfolio. In the past, the standard deviation of returns was 26.6% for Amazon and 27.9% for Southwest Airlines. You believe that these figures are a good representation of the spread of possible *future* outcomes. At first you may be inclined to assume that the standard deviation of the portfolio is a weighted average of the standard deviations of the two stocks—that is, $(.40 \times 26.6) + (.60 \times 27.9) = 27.4\%$. That would be correct *only* if the prices of the two stocks moved in perfect lockstep. In any other case, diversification reduces the risk below this figure.

The exact procedure for calculating the risk of a two-stock portfolio is given in Figure 7.12. You need to fill in four boxes. To complete the top-left box, you weight the variance of the returns on stock $1(\sigma_1^2)$ by the *square* of the proportion invested in it (x_1^2). Similarly, to complete the bottom-right box, you weight the variance of the returns on stock $2(\sigma_2^2)$ by the *square* of the proportion invested in stock $2(x_2^2)$.

BEYOND THE PAGE

How to calculate correlation coefficients

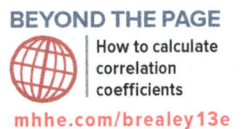

mhhe.com/brealey13e

The entries in these diagonal boxes depend on the variances of stocks 1 and 2; the entries in the other two boxes depend on their **covariance.** As you might guess, the covariance is a measure of the degree to which the two stocks "covary." The covariance can be expressed as the product of the correlation coefficient ρ_{12} and the two standard deviations:[25]

$$\text{Covariance between stocks 1 and 2} = \sigma_{12} = \rho_{12}\,\sigma_1\,\sigma_2$$

For the most part stocks tend to move together. In this case the correlation coefficient ρ_{12} is positive, and therefore the covariance σ_{12} is also positive. If the prospects of the stocks were wholly unrelated, both the correlation coefficient and the covariance would be zero; and if

▶ **FIGURE 7.12**

The variance of a two-stock portfolio is the sum of these four boxes. $x_1, x_2 =$ proportions invested in stocks 1 and 2; $\sigma_1^2, \sigma_2^2 =$ variance of stock returns; $\sigma_{12} =$ covariance of returns $(\rho_{12}\,\sigma_1\,\sigma_2)$; $\rho_{12} =$ correlation between returns on stocks 1 and 2.

	Stock 1	Stock 2
Stock 1	$x_1^2 \sigma_1^2$	$x_1 x_2 \sigma_{12}$ $= x_1 x_2 \rho_{12} \sigma_1 \sigma_2$
Stock 2	$x_1 x_2 \sigma_{12}$ $= x_1 x_2 \rho_{12} \sigma_1 \sigma_2$	$x_2^2 \sigma_2^2$

---

[24]Let's check this. Suppose you invest $40 in Amazon and $60 in Southwest Airlines. The expected dollar return on your Amazon holding is $.10 \times 40 = \$4.00$, and on Southwest it is $.15 \times 60 = \$9.00$. The expected dollar return on your portfolio is $4.00 + 9.00 = \$13.00$. The portfolio *rate* of return is $13.00/100 = .130$, or 13.0%.

[25]Another way to define the covariance is as follows:
Covariance between stocks 1 and 2 $= \sigma_{12} =$ expected value of $(\tilde{r}_1 - r_1) \times (\tilde{r}_2 - r_2)$
Note that any security's covariance with itself is just its variance:

$$\sigma_{11} = \text{expected value of } (\tilde{r}_1 - r_1) \times (\tilde{r}_1 - r_1)$$
$$= \text{expected value of } (\tilde{r}_1 - r_1)^2 = \text{variance of stock } 1 = \sigma_1^2$$

the stocks tended to move in opposite directions, the correlation coefficient and the covariance would be negative. Just as you weighted the variances by the square of the proportion invested, so you must weight the covariance by the *product* of the two proportionate holdings x_1 and x_2.

Once you have completed these four boxes, you simply add the entries to obtain the portfolio variance:

$$\text{Portfolio variance} = x_1^2\sigma_1^2 + x_2^2\sigma_2^2 + 2(x_1x_2\rho_{12}\sigma_1\sigma_2)$$

The portfolio standard deviation is, of course, the square root of the variance.

Now you can try putting in some figures for Southwest Airlines (LUV) and Amazon (AMZN). We said earlier that if the two stocks were perfectly correlated, the standard deviation of the portfolio would lie 40% of the way between the standard deviations of the two stocks. Let us check this out by filling in the boxes with $\rho_{12} = +1$.

The variance of your portfolio is the sum of these entries:

$$\text{Portfolio variance} = \left[(.6)^2 \times (27.9)^2\right] + \left[(.4)^2 \times (26.6)^2\right] + 2(.6 \times .4 \times 1 \times 27.9 \times 26.6)$$
$$= 749.7$$

The standard deviation is $\sqrt{749.7} = 27.4\%$ or 60% of the way between 26.6 and 27.9.

Southwest Airlines and Amazon do not move in perfect lockstep. If recent experience is any guide, the correlation between the two stocks is .26. If we go through the same exercise again with $\rho_{12} = .26$, we find

$$\text{Portfolio variance} = \left[(.6)^2 \times (27.9)^2\right] + \left[(.4)^2 \times (26.6)^2\right]$$
$$+ 2(.6 \times .4 \times .26 \times 27.9 \times 26.6) = 486.1$$

The standard deviation is $\sqrt{486.1} = 22.0\%$. The risk is now less than 60% of the way between 26.6 and 27.9. In fact, it is almost a fifth less than investing in just one of the two stocks.

The greatest payoff to diversification comes when the two stocks are negatively correlated. Unfortunately, this almost never occurs with real stocks, but just for illustration, let us assume it for Amazon and Southwest Airlines. And as long as we are being unrealistic, we might as well go whole hog and assume perfect negative correlation ($\rho_{12} = -1$). In this case,

$$\text{Portfolio variance} = \left[(.6)^2 \times (27.9)^2\right] + \left[(.4)^2 \times (26.6)^2\right]$$
$$+ 2[.6 \times .4 \times (-1) \times 27.9 \times 26.6] = 37.2$$

The standard deviation is $\sqrt{37.2} = 6.1\%$. Risk is almost eliminated. But you can still do better in terms of risk by putting 51.2% of your investment in Amazon and 48.8% in Southwest Airlines.[26] In that case, the standard deviation is almost exactly zero. (Check the calculation yourself.)

When there is perfect negative correlation, there is always a portfolio strategy (represented by a particular set of portfolio weights) that will completely eliminate risk. It's too bad perfect negative correlation doesn't really occur between common stocks.

General Formula for Computing Portfolio Risk

The method for calculating portfolio risk can easily be extended to portfolios of three or more securities. We just have to fill in a larger number of boxes. Each of those down the diagonal—the red boxes in Figure 7.13—contains the variance weighted by the square of the proportion

---

[26] The standard deviation of Southwest is $27.9/26.6 = 1.049$ times the standard deviation of Amazon. Therefore, you have to invest 1.049 times more in Amazon than in Southwest to eliminate all risk in a two-stock portfolio. The portfolio weights that exactly eliminate risk are .512 for Amazon and .488 for Southwest.

▶ **FIGURE 7.13**

To find the variance of an *N*-stock portfolio, we must add the entries in a matrix like this. The diagonal cells contain variance terms ($x^2\sigma^2$) and the off-diagonal cells contain covariance terms ($x_i x_j \sigma_{ij}$).

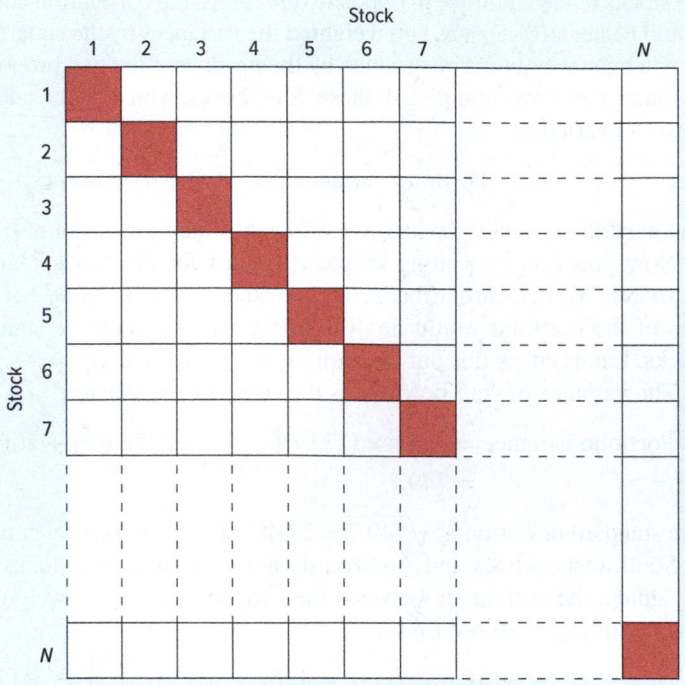

invested. Each of the other boxes contains the covariance between that pair of securities, weighted by the product of the proportions invested.[27]

EXAMPLE 7.1 • Limits to Diversification

Did you notice in Figure 7.13 how much more important the covariances become as we add more securities to the portfolio? When there are just two securities, there are equal numbers of variance boxes and of covariance boxes. When there are many securities, the number of covariances is much larger than the number of variances. Thus the variability of a well-diversified portfolio reflects mainly the covariances.

Suppose we are dealing with portfolios in which equal investments are made in each of *N* stocks. The proportion invested in each stock is, therefore, $1/N$. So in each variance box we have $(1/N)^2$ times the variance, and in each covariance box we have $(1/N)^2$ times the covariance. There are *N* variance boxes and $N^2 - N$ covariance boxes. Therefore,

$$\text{Portfolio variance} = N\left(\frac{1}{N}\right)^2 \times \text{average variance}$$

$$+ (N^2 - N)\left(\frac{1}{N}\right)^2 \times \text{average covariance}$$

$$= \frac{1}{N} \times \text{average variance} + \left(1 - \frac{1}{N}\right) \times \text{average covariance}$$

---

[27]The formal equivalent to "add up all the boxes" is

$$\text{Portfolio variance} = \sum_{i=1}^{N}\sum_{j=1}^{N} x_i x_j \sigma_{ij}$$

Notice that when $i = j$, σ_{ij} is just the variance of stock *i*.

Notice that as *N* increases, the portfolio variance steadily approaches the average covariance. If the average covariance were zero, it would be possible to eliminate *all* risk by holding a sufficient number of securities. Unfortunately common stocks move together, not independently. Thus most of the stocks that the investor can actually buy are tied together in a web of positive covariances that set the limit to the benefits of diversification. Now we can understand the precise meaning of the market risk portrayed in Figure 7.11. It is the average covariance that constitutes the bedrock of risk remaining after diversification has done its work.

BEYOND THE PAGE

Correlations between markets

mhhe.com/brealey13e

Do I Really Have to Add up 36 Million Boxes?

"Adding up the boxes" in Figure 7.13 sounds simple enough, until you remember that there are nearly 6,000 companies listed on the New York and NASDAQ stock exchanges. A portfolio manager who tried to include every one of those companies' stocks would have to fill up about 6,000 × 6,000 = 36,000,000 boxes! Of course, the boxes above the diagonal line of red boxes in Figure 7.13 match the boxes below. Nevertheless, getting accurate estimates of about 18,000,000 covariances is just impossible. Getting unbiased forecasts of rates of return for about 6,000 stocks is likewise impossible.

Smart investors don't try. They don't attempt to forecast portfolio risk or return by "adding up the boxes" for thousands of stocks. But they do understand how portfolio risk is determined by the covariances across securities. (See Example 7.1.) They appreciate the power of diversification, and they want more of it. They want a well-diversified portfolio. Often, they end up holding the entire stock market, as represented by a market index.

You can "buy the market" by purchasing shares in an *index fund:* a mutual fund or exchange-traded fund (ETF) that invests in the market index that you want to track. Well-run index funds track the market almost exactly and charge very low management fees, often less than 0.1% per year. The most widely used U.S. index is the Standard & Poor's Composite, which includes 500 of the largest stocks. Index funds have attracted about $5 trillion from investors.

If you have no special information about any of the stocks in the index, it makes sense to be an *indexer*—that is, to buy the market as a passive rather than active investor. In that case, there is only one box to add up. Just think of the market portfolio as occupying the top-left box in Figure 7.13.

If you want to try out as an active investor, you are well-advised to (1) start with a widely diversified portfolio, for example, a market index fund, and then (2) concentrate on a few stocks as possible additions. You may decide to trade off some investment in the stocks that you are especially fond of against the resulting loss of diversification. In this case, the market index fund occupies the top-left box, and the possible additions occupy a few adjacent boxes.

But our main takeaway so far is this: *Smart and serious investors hold widely diversified portfolios; their starting portfolio is often the market itself.* How then should such investors assess the risk of individual stocks? Clearly they have to ask how much risk each stock contributes to the risk of a diversified portfolio.

7-4   How Individual Securities Affect Portfolio Risk

This brings us to our next major takeaway: *The risk of a well-diversified portfolio depends on the market risk of the securities included in the portfolio.* Tattoo that statement on your forehead if you can't remember it any other way. It is one of the most important ideas in this book.

Market Risk Is Measured by Beta

If you want to know the contribution of an individual security to the risk of a well-diversified portfolio, it is no good thinking about how risky that security is if held in isolation—you need to measure its *market risk,* and that boils down to measuring how sensitive it is to market movements. This sensitivity is called **beta** (β).

Stocks with betas greater than 1.0 tend to amplify the overall movements of the market. Stocks with betas between 0 and 1.0 tend to move in the same direction as the market, but not as far. Of course, the market is the portfolio of all stocks, so the "average" stock has a beta of 1.0. Table 7.5 reports betas for the 10 well-known common stocks we referred to earlier.

Over the five years from January 2013 to December 2017, Amazon had a beta of 1.47. If the future resembles the past, this means that *on average,* when the market rises an extra 1%, Amazon's stock price will rise by an extra 1.47%. When the market falls an extra 2%, Amazon's stock price will fall, *on average,* an extra $2 \times 1.47 = 2.94\%$. Thus, a line fitted to a plot of Amazon's returns versus market returns has a slope of 1.47. See Figure 7.14.

Of course, Amazon's stock returns are not perfectly correlated with market returns. The company is also subject to specific risk, so the actual returns will be scattered about the line in Figure 7.14. Sometimes, Amazon will head south while the market goes north, and vice versa.

Of the 10 stocks in Table 7.5, U.S. Steel has the highest beta. Newmont Mining is at the other extreme. A line fitted to a plot of Newmont's returns versus market returns would be less steep: Its slope would be only .10. Notice that many of the stocks that have high standard deviations also have high betas. But that is not always so. For example, Newmont, which has a relatively high standard deviation, is a leading member of the low-beta club in the right-hand column of Table 7.5. It seems that while Newmont is a risky investment if held on its own, it does not contribute to the risk of a diversified portfolio.

Just as we can measure how the returns of a U.S. stock are affected by fluctuations in the U.S. market, so we can measure how stocks in other countries are affected by movements in *their* markets. Table 7.6 shows the betas for the sample of stocks from other countries.

Why Security Betas Determine Portfolio Risk

Let us review the two crucial points about security risk and portfolio risk:

- Market risk accounts for most of the risk of a well-diversified portfolio.
- The beta of an individual security measures its sensitivity to market movements.

It is easy to see where we are headed: In a portfolio context, a security's risk is measured by beta. Perhaps we could just jump to that conclusion, but we would rather explain it. Here is an intuitive explanation. We provide a more technical one in footnote 29.

Where's Bedrock?   Look again at Figure 7.11, which shows how the standard deviation of portfolio return depends on the number of securities in the portfolio. With more securities,

〉TABLE 7.5
Estimated betas for selected U.S. common stocks, January 2013– December 2017

Stock	Beta (β)	Stock	Beta (β)
United States Steel	3.01	ExxonMobil	0.82
Amazon	1.47	Johnson & Johnson	0.81
Southwest Airlines	1.35	Coca-Cola	0.70
The Travelers Companies	1.26	Consolidated Edison	0.11
Tesla	0.94	Newmont	0.10

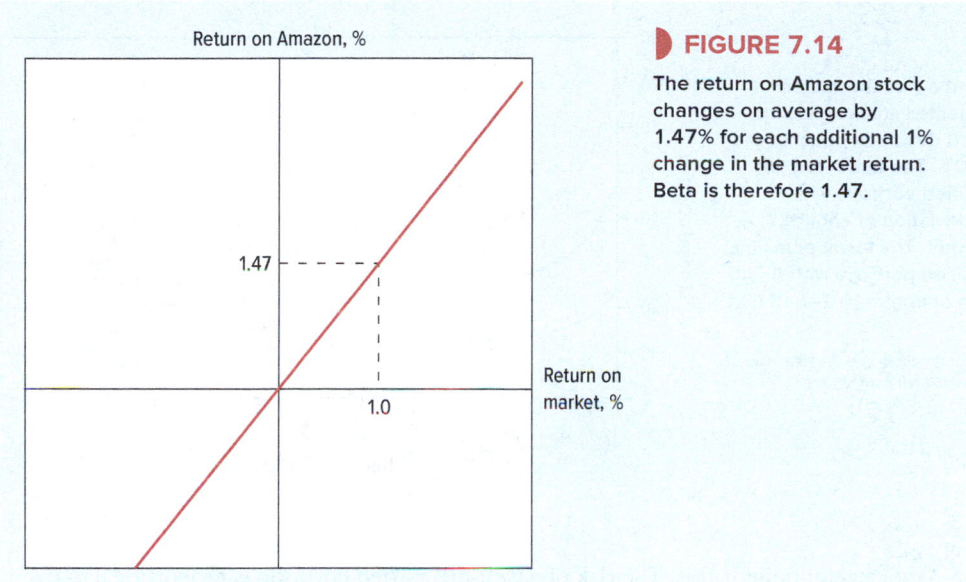

Return on Amazon, %

1.47

1.0

Return on market, %

FIGURE 7.14

The return on Amazon stock changes on average by 1.47% for each additional 1% change in the market return. Beta is therefore 1.47.

Stock	Beta (β)	Stock	Beta (β)
Tata Motors (India)	1.47	Toronto Dominion Bank (Canada)	1.05
Samsung (Korea)	1.33	Siemens (Germany)	1.01
BP (U.K.)	1.28	Heineken (Netherlands)	0.82
LVMH (France)	1.19	Nestlé (Switzerland)	0.76
Sony (Japan)	1.08	Industrial and Commercial Bank (China)	0.56

TABLE 7.6

Betas for selected foreign stocks, July 2012–June 2017 (beta is measured relative to the stock's home market)

and therefore better diversification, portfolio risk declines until all specific risk is eliminated and only the bedrock of market risk remains.

Where's bedrock? It depends on the average beta of the securities selected.

Suppose we constructed a portfolio containing a large number of stocks—500, say—drawn randomly from the whole market. What would we get? The market itself, or a portfolio *very* close to it. The portfolio beta would be 1.0, and the correlation with the market would be 1.0. If the standard deviation of the market were 20% (roughly its average for 1900–2017), then the portfolio standard deviation would also be 20%. This is shown by the green line in Figure 7.15.

But suppose we constructed the portfolio from a large group of stocks with an average beta of 1.5. Again we would end up with a 500-stock portfolio with virtually no specific risk—a portfolio that moves almost in lockstep with the market. However, *this* portfolio's standard deviation would be 30%, 1.5 times that of the market.[28] A well-diversified portfolio with a beta of 1.5 will amplify every market move by 50% and end up with 150% of the market's risk. The upper red line in Figure 7.15 shows this case.

Of course, we could repeat the same experiment with stocks with a beta of .5 and end up with a well-diversified portfolio half as risky as the market. You can see this also in Figure 7.15.

---

[28] A 500-stock portfolio with β = 1.5 would still have some specific risk. Its actual standard deviation would be a bit higher than 30%. If that worries you, relax; we will show you in Chapter 8 how you can construct a fully diversified portfolio with a beta of 1.5 by borrowing and investing in the market portfolio.

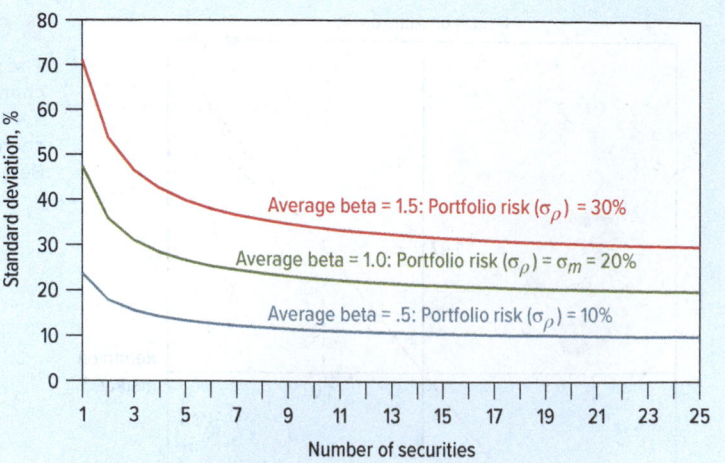

▶ **FIGURE 7.15**

The green line shows that a well diversified portfolio of randomly selected stocks ends up with β = 1 and a standard deviation equal to the market's—in this case 20%. The upper red line shows that a well diversified portfolio with β = 1.5 has a standard deviation of about 30%—1.5 times that of the market. The lower blue line shows that a well-diversified portfolio with β = .5 has a standard deviation of about 10%—half that of the market.

Note: In this figure we assume for simplicity that the total risks of individual stocks are proportional to their market risks.

The general point is this: The risk of a well-diversified portfolio is proportional to the portfolio beta, which equals the average beta of the securities included in the portfolio. This shows you how portfolio risk is driven by security betas.

Calculating Beta   A statistician would define the beta of stock i as

$$\beta_i = \sigma_{im}/\sigma_m^2$$

where σ_{im} is the *covariance* between the stock returns and the market returns and σ_m^2 is the variance of the returns on the market. It turns out that this ratio of covariance to variance measures a stock's contribution to portfolio risk.[29]

Here is a simple example of how to do the calculations. Columns 2 and 3 in Table 7.7 show the returns over a particular six-month period on the market and the stock of the Anchovy Queen restaurant chain. You can see that, although both investments provided an average return of 2%, Anchovy Queen's stock was particularly sensitive to market movements, rising more when the market rises and falling more when the market falls.

Columns 4 and 5 show the deviations of each month's return from the average. To calculate the market variance, we need to average the squared deviations of the market returns (column 6). And to calculate the covariance between the stock returns and the market, we need to average the product of the two deviations (column 7). Beta is the ratio of the covariance to the market variance, or 76/50.67 = 1.50. A diversified portfolio of stocks with the same beta as Anchovy Queen would be one-and-a-half times as volatile as the market.

BEYOND THE PAGE

Try It! Table 7.7: Calculating Anchovy Queen's beta

mhhe.com/brealey13e

---

[29]To understand why, skip back to Figure 7.13. Each row of boxes in Figure 7.13 represents the contribution of that particular security to the portfolio's risk. For example, the contribution of stock 1 is

$$x_1 x_1 \sigma_{11} + x_1 x_2 \sigma_{12} + \cdots = x_1(x_1 \sigma_{11} + x_2 \sigma_{12} + \cdots)$$

where x_i is the proportion invested in stock i, and σ_{ij} is the covariance between stocks i and j (note: σ_{ii} is equal to the variance of stock i). In other words, the contribution of stock 1 to portfolio risk is equal to the relative size of the holding (x_1) times the average covariance between stock 1 and all the stocks in the portfolio. We can write this more concisely by saying that the contribution of stock 1 to portfolio risk is equal to the holding size (x_1) times the covariance between stock 1 and the entire portfolio (σ_{1p}).

To find stock 1's *relative* contribution to risk we simply divide by the portfolio variance to give $x_1 (\sigma_{1p}/\sigma_p^2)$. In other words, it is equal to the holding size (x_1) times the beta of stock 1 relative to the portfolio (σ_{1p}/σ_p^2).

We can calculate the beta of a stock relative to *any* portfolio by simply taking its covariance with the portfolio and dividing by the portfolio's variance. If we wish to find a stock's beta *relative to the market portfolio* we just calculate its covariance with the market portfolio and divide by the variance of the market:

$$\text{Beta relative to market portfolio (or, more simply, beta)} = \frac{\text{covariance with the market}}{\text{variance of market}} = \frac{\sigma_{im}}{\sigma_m^2}$$

(1)	(2)	(3)	(4)	(5)	(6)	(7)
						Product of
			Deviation	Deviation	Squared	Deviations
			from	from Average	Deviation	from Average
	Market	Anchovy Q	Average	Anchovy Q	from Average	Returns
Month	Return	Return	Market Return	Return	Market Return	(cols 4 × 5)
1	−8%	−11%	−10	−13	100	130
2	4	8	2	6	4	12
3	12	19	10	17	100	170
4	−6	−13	−8	−15	64	120
5	2	3	0	1	0	0
6	8	6	6	4	36	24
Average	2	2		Total	304	456

Variance $= \sigma_m^2 = 304/6 = 50.67$

Covariance $= \sigma_{im} = 456/6 = 76$

Beta $(\beta) = \sigma_{im}/\sigma_m^2 = 76/50.67 = 1.5$

〉TABLE 7.7
Calculating the variance of the market returns and the covariance between the returns on the market and those of Anchovy Queen. Beta is the ratio of the covariance to the variance (i. e., $\beta = \sigma_{im}/\sigma_m^2$)

7-5 Diversification and Value Additivity

We have seen that diversification reduces risk and, therefore, makes sense for investors. But does it also make sense for the firm? Is a diversified firm more attractive to investors than an undiversified one? If it is, we have an *extremely* disturbing result. If diversification is an appropriate corporate objective, each project has to be analyzed as a potential addition to the firm's portfolio of assets. The value of the diversified package would be greater than the sum of the parts. So present values would no longer add.

Diversification is undoubtedly a good thing, but that does not mean that firms should practice it. If investors were *not* able to hold a large number of securities, then they might want firms to diversify for them. But investors *can* diversify. In many ways they can do so more easily than firms. Individuals can invest in the steel industry this week and pull out next week. A firm cannot do that. To be sure, the individual would have to pay brokerage fees on the purchase and sale of steel company shares, but think of the time and expense for a firm to acquire a steel company or to start up a new steel-making operation.

You can probably see where we are heading. If investors can diversify on their own account, they will not pay any *extra* for firms that diversify. And if they have a sufficiently wide choice of securities, they will not pay any *less* because they are unable to invest separately in each factory. Therefore, in countries like the United States, which have large and competitive capital markets, diversification does not add to a firm's value or subtract from it. The total value is the sum of its parts.

This conclusion is important for corporate finance, because it justifies adding present values. The concept of *value additivity* is so important that we will give a formal definition of it. If the capital market establishes a value PV(A) for asset A and PV(B) for B, the market value of a firm that holds only these two assets is

$$PV(AB) = PV(A) + PV(B)$$

A three-asset firm combining assets A, B, and C would be worth PV(ABC) = PV(A) + PV(B) + PV(C), and so on for any number of assets.

We have relied on intuitive arguments for value additivity. But the concept is a general one that can be proved formally by several different routes.[30] The concept seems to be widely accepted, for thousands of managers add thousands of present values daily, usually without thinking about it.

---

[30]You may wish to refer to the Appendix to Chapter 31, which discusses diversification and value additivity in the context of mergers.

SUMMARY

Our review of capital market history showed that the returns to investors have varied according to the risks they have borne. At one extreme, very safe securities like U.S. Treasury bills have provided an average return over 118 years of only 3.8% a year. The riskiest securities that we looked at were common stocks. The stock market provided an average return of 11.5%, a premium of 7.7% over the safe rate of interest.

This gives us two benchmarks for the opportunity cost of capital. If we are evaluating a safe project, we discount at the current risk-free rate of interest. If we are evaluating a project of average risk, we discount at the expected return on the average common stock. Historical evidence suggests that this return is 7.7% above the risk-free rate, but many financial managers and economists opt for a lower figure. That still leaves us with a lot of assets that don't fit these simple cases. Before we can deal with them, we need to learn how to measure risk.

Risk is best judged in a portfolio context. Most investors do not put all their eggs into one basket: They diversify. Thus, the effective risk of any security cannot be judged by an examination of that security alone. Part of the uncertainty about the security's return is diversified away when the security is grouped with others in a portfolio.

Risk in investment means that future returns are unpredictable. This spread of possible outcomes is usually measured by standard deviation. The standard deviation of the *market portfolio*, as represented by the Standard and Poor's Composite Index, has averaged around 20% a year.

Most individual stocks have higher standard deviations than this, but much of their variability represents *specific* risk that can be eliminated by diversification. Diversification cannot eliminate *market* risk. Diversified portfolios are exposed to variation in the general level of the market.

A security's contribution to the risk of a well-diversified portfolio depends on how the security is liable to be affected by a general market decline. This sensitivity to market movements is known as *beta* (β). Beta measures the amount that investors expect the stock price to change for each additional 1% change in the market. The average beta of all stocks is 1.0. A stock with a beta greater than 1 is unusually sensitive to market movements; a stock with a beta below 1 is unusually insensitive to market movements. The standard deviation of a well-diversified portfolio is proportional to its beta. Thus a diversified portfolio invested in stocks with a beta of 2.0 will have twice the risk of a diversified portfolio with a beta of 1.0.

One theme of this chapter is that diversification is a good thing *for the investor*. This does not imply that *firms* should diversify. Corporate diversification is redundant if investors can diversify on their own account. Since diversification does not affect the value of the firm, present values add even when risk is explicitly considered. Thanks to *value additivity,* the net present value rule for capital budgeting works even under uncertainty.

In this chapter, we have introduced you to a number of formulas. They are reproduced in the endpapers to the book. You should take a look and check that you understand them.

Near the end of Chapter 9, we list some Excel functions that are useful for measuring the risk of stocks and portfolios.

For international evidence on market returns since 1900, see:

E. Dimson, P. R. Marsh, and M. Staunton, *Triumph of the Optimists: 101 Years of Global Investment Returns* (Princeton, NJ: Princeton University Press, 2002). More recent data are available in the *Credit Suisse Global Investment Returns Yearbook* at **https://www.credit-suisse.com/media/assets/corporate/docs/about-us/media/media-release/2018/02/giry-summary-2018.pdf**.

The Ibbotson Yearbook is a valuable record of the performance of U.S. securities since 1926:

R. Ibbotson, R. J. Grabowski, J. P. Harrington, and C. Nunes, *2017 Stocks, Bonds, Bills, and Inflation SBBI Yearbook* (New York: Wiley, 2017).

Useful books and reviews on the equity risk premium include:

P. Fernandez, V. Pershin, and I. Fernandez Acín, "Market Risk Premium and Risk-free Rate Used for 59 Countries in 2018: A Survey," April 3, 2018. Available at SSRN: **https://ssrn.com/abstract=3155709**.

W. Goetzmann and R. Ibbotson, *The Equity Risk Premium: Essays and Explorations* (Oxford, U.K.: Oxford University Press, 2006).

R. Mehra (ed.), *Handbook of the Equity Risk Premium* (Amsterdam: North-Holland, 2007).

R. Mehra and E. C. Prescott, "The Equity Risk Premium in Retrospect," in *Handbook of the Economics of Finance,* eds. G. M. Constantinides, M. Harris, and R. M. Stulz (Amsterdam: North-Holland, 2003) Vol. 1, Part 2, pp. 889–938.

FURTHER READING

PROBLEM SETS

 **Select problems are available in McGraw-Hill's *Connect*. Please see the preface for more information.**

1. **Rate of return** The level of the Syldavia market index is 21,000 at the start of the year and 25,500 at the end. The dividend yield on the index is 4.2%.

   a. What is the return on the index over the year?

   b. If the interest rate is 6%, what is the risk premium over the year?

   c. If the inflation rate is 8%, what is the *real* return on the index over the year?

2. **Real versus nominal returns** The Costaguana stock market provided a rate of return of 95%. The inflation rate in Costaguana during the year was 80%. In Ruritania the stock market return was 12%, but the inflation rate was only 2%. Which country's stock market provided the higher real rate of return?

3. **Arithmetic average and compound returns*** Integrated Potato Chips (IPC) does not pay a dividend. Its current stock price is $150 and there is an equal probability that the return over the coming year will be –10%, +20%, or +50%.

   a. What is the *expected* price at year-end?

   b. If the probabilities of future returns remain unchanged and you could observe the returns of IPC over a large number of years, what would be the (arithmetic) average return?

   c. If you were to discount IPC's expected price at year-end from part (a) by this number, would you underestimate, overestimate, or correctly estimate the stock's present value?

   d. If you could observe the returns of IPC over a large number of years, what would be the compound (geometric average) rate of return?

   e. If you were to discount IPC's expected price at year-end from part (a) by this number, would you underestimate, overestimate, or correctly estimate the stock's present value?

4. **Risk premiums*** Here are inflation rates and U.S. stock market and Treasury bill returns between 1929 and 1933:

Year	Inflation, %	Stock Market Return, %	T-Bill Return, %
1929	−0.2	−14.5	4.8
1930	−6.0	−28.3	2.4
1931	−9.5	−43.9	1.1
1932	−10.3	−9.9	1.0
1933	0.5	57.3	0.3

a. What was the real return on the stock market in each year?

b. What was the average real return?

c. What was the risk premium in each year?

d. What was the average risk premium?

5. **Risk Premium** Suppose that in year 2030, investors become much more willing than before to bear risk. As a result, they require a return of 8% to invest in common stocks rather than the 10% that they had required in the past. This shift in risk aversion causes a 15% change in the value of the market portfolio.

a. Do stock prices rise by 15% or fall?

b. If you now use past returns to estimate the expected risk premium, will the inclusion of data for 2030 cause you to underestimate or overestimate the return that investors required in the past?

c. Will the inclusion of data for 2030 cause you to underestimate or overestimate the return that investors require in the future?

6. **Stocks vs. bonds** Each of the following statements is dangerous or misleading. Explain why.

a. A long-term U.S. government bond is always absolutely safe.

b. All investors should prefer stocks to bonds because stocks offer higher long-run rates of return.

c. The best practical forecast of future rates of return on the stock market is a 5- or 10-year average of historical returns.

7. **Expected return and standard deviation** A game of chance offers the following odds and payoffs. Each play of the game costs $100, so the net profit per play is the payoff less $100.

Probability	Payoff	Net Profit
0.10	$500	$400
0.50	100	0
0.40	0	−100

What are the expected cash payoff and expected rate of return? Calculate the variance and standard deviation of this rate of return. (Do not make the adjustment for degrees of freedom described in footnote 15.)

8. **Standard deviation of returns** The following table shows the nominal returns on Brazilian stocks and the rate of inflation.

a. What was the standard deviation of the market returns? (Do not make the adjustment for degrees of freedom described in footnote 15.)

b. Calculate the average *real* return.

Year	Nominal Return (%)	Inflation (%)
2012	0.1	5.8
2013	−16.0	5.9
2014	−14.0	6.4
2015	−41.4	10.7
2016	66.2	6.3
2017	26.9	2.9

9. **Average returns and standard deviation** During the boom years of 2010–2014, ace mutual fund manager Diana Sauros produced the following percentage rates of return. Rates of return on the market are given for comparison.

	2010	2011	2012	2013	2014
Ms. Sauros	+24.9	−0.9	+18.6	+42.1	+15.2
S&P 500	+17.2	+1.0	+16.1	+33.1	+12.7

Calculate the average return and standard deviation of Ms. Sauros's mutual fund. Did she do better or worse than the market by these measures?

10. **Risk and diversification** Hippique s.a., which owns a stable of racehorses, has just invested in a mysterious black stallion with great form but disputed bloodlines. Some experts in horse-flesh predict the horse will win the coveted Prix de Bidet; others argue that it should be put out to grass. Is this a risky investment for Hippique shareholders? Explain.

11. **Risk and diversification** Lonesome Gulch Mines has a standard deviation of 42% per year and a beta of +.10. Amalgamated Copper has a standard deviation of 31% a year and a beta of +.66. Explain why Lonesome Gulch is the safer investment for a diversified investor.

12. **Diversification*** Here are the percentage returns on two stocks.

    a. Calculate the monthly variance and standard deviation of each stock. Which stock is the riskier if held on its own?

    b. Now calculate the variance and standard deviation of the returns on a portfolio that invests an equal amount each month in the two stocks.

    c. Is the variance more or less than half way between the variance of the two individual stocks?

Month	Digital Cheese	Executive Fruit
January	+15%	+7%
February	−3	+1
March	+5	+4
April	+7	+13
May	−4	+2
June	+3	+5
July	−2	−3
August	−8	−2

13. **Risk and diversification** In which of the following situations would you get the largest reduction in risk by spreading your investment across two stocks?

    a. The two shares are perfectly correlated.

    b. There is no correlation.

    c. There is modest negative correlation.

    d. There is perfect negative correlation

14. **Portfolio risk*** True or false?

    a. Investors prefer diversified companies because they are less risky.

    b. If stocks were perfectly positively correlated, diversification would not reduce risk.

    c. Diversification over a large number of assets completely eliminates risk.

    d. Diversification works only when assets are uncorrelated.

    e. Diversification reduces the portfolio beta.

    f. A portfolio of stocks, each with a beta of 1.0, will have a beta of less than 1.0 unless the returns are perfectly correlated.

    g. A stock with a low standard deviation always contributes less to portfolio risk than a stock with a higher standard deviation.

    h. The contribution of a stock to the risk of a well-diversified portfolio depends on its market risk.

    i. A well-diversified portfolio with a beta of 2.0 is twice as risky as the market portfolio.

    j. An undiversified portfolio with a beta of 2.0 is less than twice as risky as the market portfolio.

15. **Portfolio risk** To calculate the variance of a three-stock portfolio, you need to add nine boxes:

    Use the same symbols that we used in this chapter; for example, x_1 = proportion invested in stock 1 and σ_{12} = covariance between stocks 1 and 2. Now complete the nine boxes.

16. **Portfolio risk**

    a. How many variance terms and how many different covariance terms do you need to calculate the risk of a 100-share portfolio?

    b. Suppose all stocks had a standard deviation of 30% and a correlation with each other of .4. What is the standard deviation of the returns on a portfolio that has equal holdings in 50 stocks?

    c. What is the standard deviation of a fully diversified portfolio of such stocks?

17. **Portfolio risk** Suppose that the standard deviation of returns from a typical share is about .40 (or 40%) a year. The correlation between the returns of each pair of shares is about .3.

    a. Calculate the variance and standard deviation of the returns on a portfolio that has equal investments in 2 shares, 3 shares, and so on, up to 10 shares.

    b. Use your estimates to draw a graph like Figure 7.11. How large is the underlying market variance that cannot be diversified away?

    c. Now repeat the problem, assuming that the correlation between each pair of stocks is zero.

	BHP Billiton	Siemens	Nestlé	LVMH	Toronto Dominion Bank	Samsung	BP
BHP Billiton	1.00	0.19	−0.11	0.22	0.40	0.32	0.29
Siemens		1.00	0.32	0.52	0.42	0.25	0.20
Nestlé			1.00	0.24	0.10	0.21	0.25
LVMH				1.00	0.07	0.21	0.13
Toronto Dominion Bank					1.00	0.19	0.15
Samsung						1.00	0.31
BP							1.00
Standard deviation, %	26.1	18.9	12.8	21.4	15.7	26.5	21.6

〉TABLE 7.8 Standard deviations of returns and correlation coefficients for a sample of seven stocks

Note: Correlations and standard deviations were calculated using returns in each country's own currency. In other words, they assume that the investor is protected against exchange risk.

18. **Portfolio risk** Table 7.8 shows standard deviations and correlation coefficients for seven stocks from different countries. Calculate the variance of a portfolio with equal investments in each stock.

19. **Portfolio risk** Your eccentric Aunt Claudia has left you $50,000 in BP shares plus $50,000 cash. Unfortunately, her will requires that the BP stock not be sold for one year and the $50,000 cash must be entirely invested in one of the stocks shown in Table 7.8. What is the safest attainable portfolio under these restrictions?

20. **Portfolio risk*** Hyacinth Macaw invests 60% of her funds in stock I and the balance in stock J. The standard deviation of returns on I is 10%, and on J it is 20%. Calculate the variance and standard deviation of portfolio returns, assuming

   a. The correlation between the returns is 1.0.

   b. The correlation is .5.

   c. The correlation is 0.

21. **Stock betas*** What is the beta of each of the stocks shown in Table 7.9?

22. **Stock betas** There are few, if any, real companies with negative betas. But suppose you found one with $\beta = -.25$.

   a. How would you expect this stock's rate of return to change if the overall market rose by an extra 5%? What if the market fell by an extra 5%?

	Stock Return if Market Return Is:	
Stock	−10%	+10%
A	0	+20
B	−20	+20
C	−30	0
D	+15	+15
E	+10	−10

〉TABLE 7.9 Stock betas. See Problem 21.

b. You have $1 million invested in a well-diversified portfolio of stocks. Now you receive an additional $20,000 bequest. Which of the following actions will yield the safest overall portfolio return?

    i. Invest $20,000 in Treasury bills (which have $\beta = 0$).

    ii. Invest $20,000 in stocks with $\beta = 1$.

    iii. Invest $20,000 in the stock with $\beta = -.25$.

    Explain your answer.

23. **Portfolio betas** A portfolio contains equal investments in 10 stocks. Five have a beta of 1.2; the remainder have a beta of 1.4. What is the portfolio beta?

    a. 1.3.

    b. Greater than 1.3 because the portfolio is not completely diversified.

    c. Less than 1.3 because diversification reduces beta.

24. **Portfolio betas** Suppose the standard deviation of the market return is 20%.

    a. What is the standard deviation of returns on a well-diversified portfolio with a beta of 1.3?

    b. What is the standard deviation of returns on a well-diversified portfolio with a beta of 0?

    c. A well-diversified portfolio has a standard deviation of 15%. What is its beta?

    d. A poorly diversified portfolio has a standard deviation of 20%. What can you say about its beta?

CHALLENGE

25. **Portfolio risk** Here are some historical data on the risk characteristics of Ford and Harley Davidson:

	Ford	Harley Davidson
β (beta)	1.26	0.96
Yearly standard deviation of return (%)	18.9	23.1

Assume the standard deviation of the return on the market was 9.5%.

    a. The correlation coefficient of Ford's return versus Harley Davidson is 0.30. What is the standard deviation of a portfolio invested half in each share?

    b. What is the standard deviation of a portfolio invested one-third in Ford, one-third in Harley Davidson, and one-third in risk-free Treasury bills?

    c. What is the standard deviation if the portfolio is split evenly between Ford and Harley Davidson and is financed at 50% margin, that is, the investor puts up only 50% of the total amount and borrows the balance from the broker?

    d. What is the *approximate* standard deviation of a portfolio composed of 100 stocks with betas of 1.26 like Ford? How about 100 stocks like Harley Davidson? [*Hint:* Part (d) should not require anything but the simplest arithmetic to answer.]

26. **Portfolio risk** Suppose that Treasury bills offer a return of about 6% and the expected market risk premium is 8.5%. The standard deviation of Treasury-bill returns is zero and the standard deviation of market returns is 20%. Use the formula for portfolio risk to calculate the standard deviation of portfolios with different proportions in Treasury bills and the market. (*Note:* The covariance of two rates of return must be zero when the standard deviation of one return is zero.) Graph the expected returns and standard deviations.

27. **Beta** Calculate the beta of each of the stocks in Table 7.8 relative to a portfolio with equal investments in each stock.

You can download data for questions 1 and 2 from **finance.yahoo.com.** Refer to the Useful Spreadsheet Functions box near the end of Chapter 9 for information on Excel functions.

1. Download to a spreadsheet the last three years of monthly adjusted stock prices for Coca-Cola (KO), Citigroup (C), and Pfizer (PFE).

    a. Calculate the monthly returns.

    b. Calculate the monthly standard deviation of those returns (see Section 7-2). Use the Excel function STDEVP to check your answer. Find the annualized standard deviation by multiplying by the square root of 12.

    c. Use the Excel function CORREL to calculate the correlation coefficient between the monthly returns for each pair of stocks. Which pair provides the greatest gain from diversification?

    d. Calculate the standard deviation of returns for a portfolio with equal investments in the three stocks.

2. Download to a spreadsheet the last five years of monthly adjusted stock prices for each of the companies in Table 7.5 and for the Standard & Poor's Composite Index (S&P 500).

    a. Calculate the monthly returns.

    b. Calculate beta for each stock using the Excel function SLOPE, where the "y" range refers to the stock return (the dependent variable) and the "x" range is the market return (the independent variable).

    c. How have the betas changed from those reported in Table 7.5?

3. A large mutual fund group such as Fidelity offers a variety of funds. They include *sector funds* that specialize in particular industries and *index funds* that simply invest in the market index. Log on to **www.fidelity.com** and find first the standard deviation of returns on the Fidelity Spartan 500 Index Fund, which replicates the S&P 500. Now find the standard deviations for different sector funds. Are they larger or smaller than the figure for the index fund? How do you interpret your findings?

CHAPTER

8

Portfolio Theory and the Capital Asset Pricing Model

In Chapter 7, we began to come to grips with the problem of measuring risk. Here is the story so far.

The stock market is risky because there is a spread of possible outcomes. The usual measure of this spread is the standard deviation or variance. The risk of any stock can be broken down into two parts. There is the *specific* or *diversifiable risk* that is peculiar to that stock, and there is the *market risk* that is associated with marketwide variations. Investors can eliminate specific risk by holding a well-diversified portfolio, but they cannot eliminate market risk. *All* the risk of a fully diversified portfolio is market risk.

A stock's contribution to the risk of a fully diversified portfolio depends on its sensitivity to market changes. This sensitivity is generally known as *beta*. A security with a beta of 1.0 has average market risk—a well-diversified portfolio of such securities has the same standard deviation as the market

index. A security with a beta of .5 has below-average market risk—a well-diversified portfolio of these securities tends to move half as far as the market moves and has half the market's standard deviation.

In this chapter, we build on this newfound knowledge. We present leading theories linking risk and return in a competitive economy, and we show how financial managers use these theories to estimate the returns required by investors in different stock market investments. We start with the most widely used theory, the capital asset pricing model, which builds directly on the ideas developed in the last chapter. We will also look at another class of models, known as arbitrage pricing or factor models. Then in Chapter 9, we show how these ideas can help the financial manager cope with risk in practical capital budgeting situations.

8-1   Harry Markowitz and the Birth of Portfolio Theory

Most of the ideas in Chapter 7 date back to an article written in 1952 by Harry Markowitz.[1] Markowitz drew attention to the common practice of portfolio diversification and showed exactly how an investor can reduce the standard deviation of portfolio returns by choosing stocks that do not move exactly together. But Markowitz did not stop there; he went on to work out the basic principles of portfolio construction. These principles are the foundation for much of what has been written about the relationship between risk and return.

We begin with Figure 8.1, which shows a histogram of the daily returns on IBM stock from 1997 to 2017. On this histogram we have superimposed a bell-shaped normal distribution.

---

[1]H. M. Markowitz, "Portfolio Selection," *Journal of Finance* 7 (March 1952), pp. 77–91.

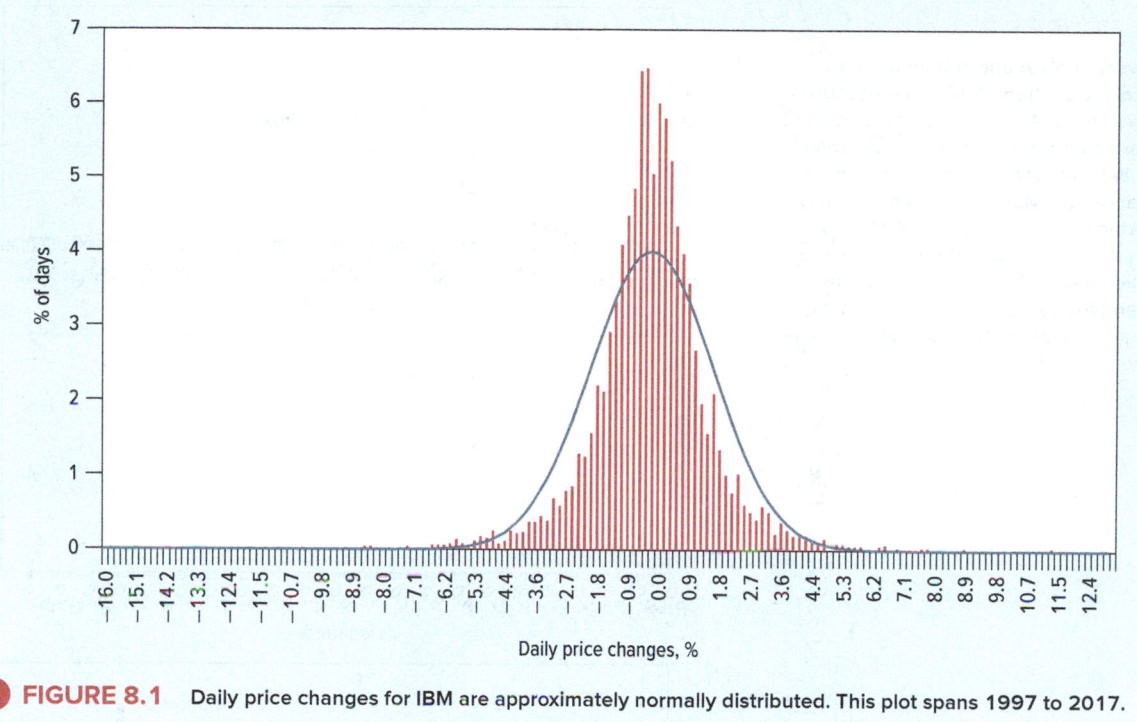

FIGURE 8.1   Daily price changes for IBM are approximately normally distributed. This plot spans 1997 to 2017.

The result is typical: When measured over a short interval, the past rates of return on any stock conform fairly closely to a normal distribution.[2]

Normal distributions can be completely defined by two numbers. One is the average or expected value; the other is the variance or standard deviation. Now you can see why we discussed the calculation of expected return and standard deviation in Chapter 7. They are not just arbitrary measures: If returns are normally distributed, expected return and standard deviation are the *only* two measures that an investor need consider.

Figure 8.2 pictures the distribution of possible returns from three investments. Investments A and B offer an expected return of 10%, but A has the much wider spread of possible outcomes. Its standard deviation is 15%; the standard deviation of B is 7.5%. Most investors dislike uncertainty and would therefore prefer B to A.

Now compare investments B and C. This time both have the *same* standard deviation, but the expected return is 20% from stock C and only 10% from stock B. Most investors like high expected return and would therefore prefer C to B.

BEYOND THE PAGE

 Utility theory

mhhe.com/brealey13e

Combining Stocks into Portfolios

Think back to Section 7-3, where you were wondering whether to invest 60% of your savings in the shares of Southwest Airlines and 40% in those of Amazon. You decided that Southwest Airlines offered an expected return of 15.0% and Amazon offered an expected return of

---

[2]If you were to measure returns over *long* intervals, the distribution would be skewed. For example, you would encounter returns greater than 100% but none less than −100%. The distribution of returns over periods of, say, one year would be better approximated by a *lognormal* distribution. The lognormal distribution, like the normal, is completely specified by its mean and standard deviation. You would also find that the distribution of price changes has a longer tail than the normal and lognormal distributions. Extreme events or "black swans" crop up with alarming frequency.

FIGURE 8.2

Investments A and B both have an *expected* return of 10%, but because investment A has the greater spread of *possible* returns, it is more risky than B. We can measure this spread by the standard deviation. Investment A has a standard deviation of 15%; B, 7.5%. Most investors would prefer B to A. Investments B and C both have the same standard deviation, but C offers a higher expected return. Most investors would prefer C to B.

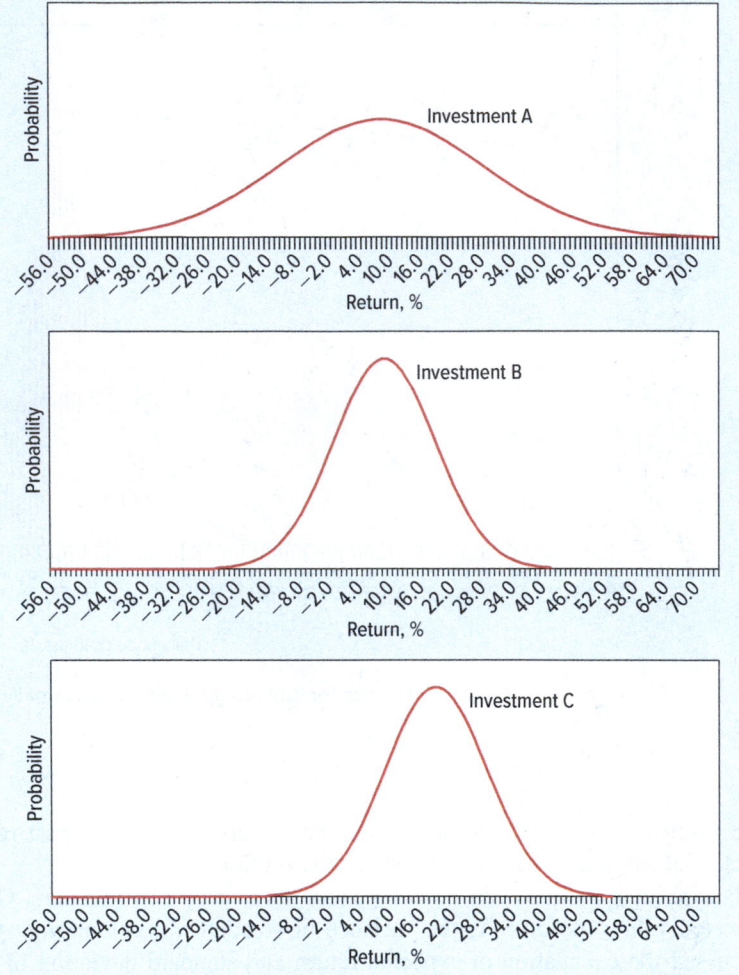

10.0%. After looking back at the past variability of the two stocks, you also decided that the standard deviation of returns was 27.9% for Southwest and 26.6% for Amazon.

The expected return on this portfolio is 13%, simply a weighted average of the expected returns on the two holdings. What about the risk of such a portfolio? We know that thanks to diversification the portfolio risk is less than the average of the risks of the separate stocks. In fact, on the basis of past experience the standard deviation of this portfolio is 22.0%, well below that of either stock.[3]

The curved blue line in Figure 8.3 shows the expected return and risk that you could achieve by different combinations of the two stocks. Which of these combinations is best

---

[3]We pointed out in Section 7-3 that the correlation between Southwest Airlines and Amazon has been .26. The variance of a portfolio that is invested 60% in Southwest and 40% in Amazon is

$$\text{Variance} = x_1^2\sigma_1^2 + x_2^2\sigma_2^2 + 2x_1x_2\rho_{12}\sigma_1\sigma_2$$

$$= \left[(.6)^2 \times (27.9)^2\right] + \left[(.4)^2 \times (26.6)^2\right] + 2(.6 \times .4 \times .26 \times 27.9 \times 26.6)$$

$$= 486.1$$

The portfolio standard deviation is $\sqrt{486.1} = 22.0\%$

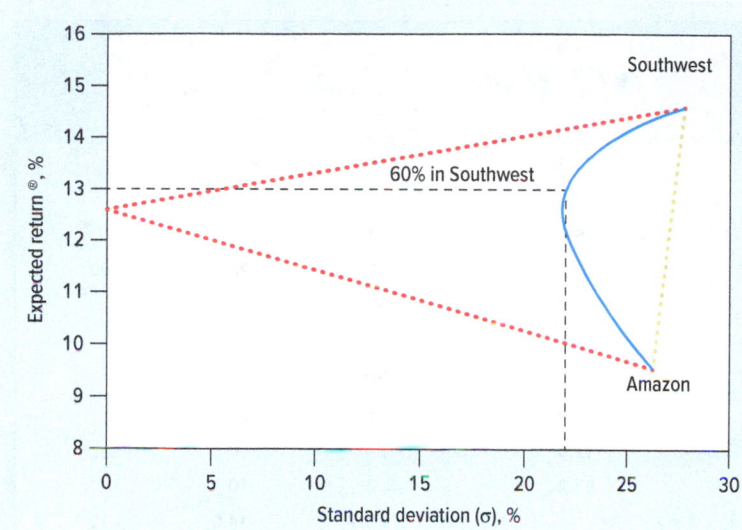

▶ **FIGURE 8.3**

The curved line illustrates how expected return and standard deviation change as you hold different combinations of two stocks. For example, if you invest 60% of your money in Southwest Airlines and the remainder in Amazon, your expected return is 13%, which is 60% of the way between the expected returns on the two stocks. The standard deviation is 22.0%, which is less than that of either stock. This is because diversification reduces risk.

depends on your stomach. If you want to stake all on getting rich quickly, you should put all your money in Southwest Airlines. If you want a more peaceful life, you should split your money between the two stocks.[4]

We saw in Chapter 7 that the gain from diversification depends on how highly the stocks are correlated. Fortunately, on past experience, there is only a modest correlation between the returns of Southwest Airlines and Amazon ($\rho = +.26$). If their stocks moved in exact lockstep ($\rho = +1$), there would be no gains at all from diversification. You can see this by the gold dotted line in Figure 8.3. The red dotted line in the figure shows a second extreme (and equally unrealistic) case in which the returns on the two stocks are perfectly *negatively* correlated ($\rho = -1$). If this were so, there is a combination of the two stocks that would have no risk.[5]

In practice, you are not limited to investing in just two stocks. For example, you could decide to choose a portfolio from the 10 stocks listed in the first column of Table 8.1. After analyzing the prospects for each firm and talking to your stockbroker, you come up with forecasts of their returns. You are most optimistic about the outlook for Newmont and forecast that it will provide a return of 18.1%. At the other extreme, you predict a return of only 8% for Johnson & Johnson. You use data for the past five years to estimate the risk of each stock and the correlation between the returns on each pair of stocks.[6]

Now look at Figure 8.4. Each dot marks the combination of risk and return offered by a different individual security.

By holding different proportions of the 10 securities, you can obtain an even wider selection of risk and return, but which combination is best? Well, what is your goal? Which direction do you want to go? The answer should be obvious: You want to go up (to increase expected return) and to the left (to reduce risk). Go as far as you can, and you will end up with

BEYOND THE PAGE

Try It! Markowitz portfolio program

mhhe.com/brealey13e

---

[4]The portfolio with the minimum risk has just over 53% in Amazon. We assume in Figure 8.3 that you may not take negative positions in either stock; that is, we rule out short sales.

[5]The ratio of the standard deviation of Amazon to that of Southwest Airlines is 26.6/27.9 = .953. To achieve zero risk your investment in Southwest should be 0.953 times your investment in Amazon.

[6]There are 45 different correlation coefficients, so we have not listed them in Table 8.1.

	Expected Return (%)	Standard Deviation (%)	Three Efficient Portfolios—Percentages Allocated to Each Stock (%)		
			A	B	C
United States Steel	17.2	73.0	0	0	
The Travelers Companies	12.5	16.4	0	30	
Amazon	10.0	26.6	1	0	
Newmont	18.1	42.2	2	20	100
Johnson & Johnson	8.0	12.8	14	0	
Consolidated Edison	11.8	16.6	20	18	
ExxonMobil	10.3	14.0	30	0	
Southwest Airlines	15.0	27.9	5	21	
Coca-Cola	9.4	12.6	24	0	
Tesla	16.7	57.2	4	10	
Expected portfolio return			10.7	14.0	18.1
Portfolio standard deviation			9.3	12.1	72.8

❯ **TABLE 8.1**   Examples of efficient portfolios chosen from 10 stocks

Note: Standard deviations and the correlations between stock returns were estimated from monthly returns, January 2013–December 2017. Efficient portfolios are calculated assuming that short sales are prohibited.

❯ **FIGURE 8.4**

Each dot shows the expected return and standard deviation of stocks in Table 8.1 (we omit two stocks with standard deviations greater than 50%). There are many possible combinations of expected return and standard deviation from investing in a *mixture* of these stocks. If you like high expected returns and dislike high standard deviations, you will prefer portfolios along the red line. These are *efficient* portfolios. We have marked the three efficient portfolios described in Table 8.1 (A, B, and C).

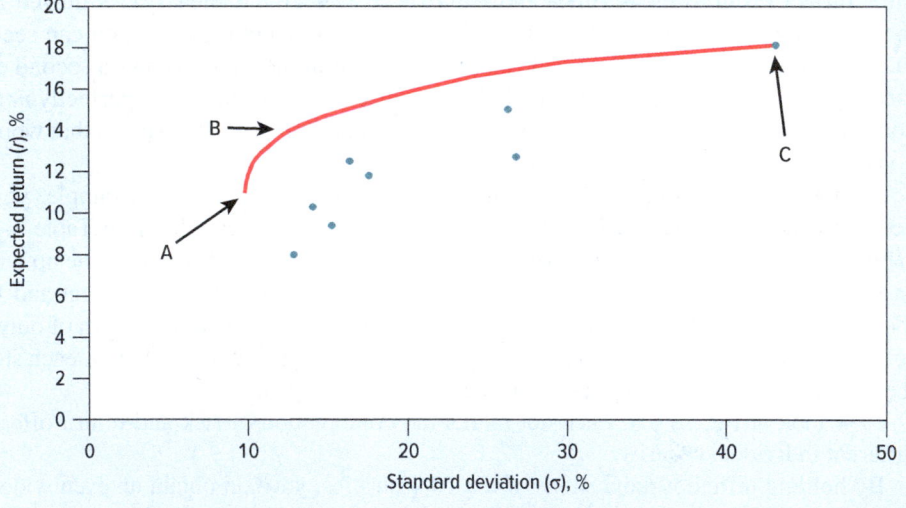

one of the portfolios that lies along the red line. Markowitz called them **efficient portfolios.** They offer the highest expected return for any level of risk.

We will not calculate the entire set of efficient portfolios here, but you may be interested in how to do it. Think back to the capital rationing problem in Section 5-4. There we wanted to deploy a limited amount of capital investment in a mixture of projects to give the highest NPV. Here we want to deploy an investor's funds to give the highest expected return for a given standard deviation. In principle, both problems can be solved by hunting and pecking—but only in principle. To solve the capital rationing problem, we can employ linear programming; to solve the portfolio problem, we would turn to a variant of linear programming known as *quadratic programming*. Given the expected return and standard deviation for each stock, as well as the correlation between each pair of stocks, we could use a standard quadratic computer program to search out the set of efficient portfolios.

Three of these efficient portfolios are marked in Figure 8.4. Their compositions are summarized in Table 8.1. Portfolio C offers the highest expected return: It is invested entirely in one stock, Newmont. Portfolio A offers the minimum risk; you can see from Table 8.1 that it has large holdings in ExxonMobil, Consolidated Edison, Coca-Cola, and Johnson & Johnson, which have the lowest standard deviations. However, the portfolio also has a small holding in Tesla even though it is individually risky. The reason? On past evidence, Tesla's fortunes are almost uncorrelated with those of other stocks and so provide additional diversification.

Table 8.1 also shows the composition of a third efficient portfolio with intermediate levels of risk and expected return.

Of course, large investment funds can choose from thousands of stocks and thereby achieve a wider choice of risk and return. This choice is represented in Figure 8.5 by the shaded, broken-egg-shaped area. The set of efficient portfolios is again marked by the red curved line.

We Introduce Borrowing and Lending

Now we introduce yet another possibility. Suppose that you can also lend or borrow money at some risk-free rate of interest r_f. If you invest some of your money in Treasury bills (i.e., lend money) and place the remainder in common stock portfolio S, you can obtain any combination of expected return and risk along the straight line joining r_f and S in Figure 8.5. Since borrowing is merely negative lending, you can extend the range of possibilities to the right of S by borrowing funds at an interest rate of r_f and investing them as well as your own money in portfolio S.

Let us put some numbers on this. Suppose that portfolio S has an expected return of 15% and a standard deviation of 16%. Treasury bills offer an interest rate (r_f) of 5% and are risk-free (i.e., their standard deviation is zero). If you invest half your money in portfolio S and

BEYOND THE PAGE

Portfolio selection
in practice

mhhe.com/brealey13e

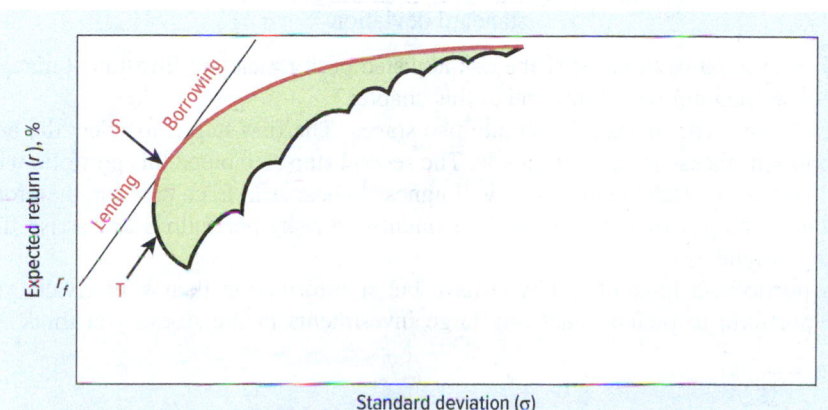

Standard deviation (σ)

▶ **FIGURE 8.5**

Lending and borrowing extend the range of investment possibilities. If you invest in portfolio S and lend or borrow at the risk-free interest rate, r_f, you can achieve any point along the straight line from r_f through S. This gives you the highest expected return for any level of risk. There is no point in investing in a portfolio like T.

lend the remainder at 5%, the expected return on your investment is likewise halfway between the expected return on S and the interest rate on Treasury bills:

$$r = \left(\frac{1}{2} \times \text{expected return on S}\right) + \left(\frac{1}{2} \times \text{interest rate}\right)$$

$$= 10\%$$

And the standard deviation is halfway between the standard deviation of S and the standard deviation of Treasury bills:[7]

$$\sigma = \left(\frac{1}{2} \times \text{standard deviation of S}\right) + \left(\frac{1}{2} \times \text{standard deviation of bills}\right)$$

$$= 8\%$$

Or suppose that you decide to go for the big time: You borrow at the Treasury bill rate an amount equal to your initial wealth, and you invest everything in portfolio S. You have twice your own money invested in S, but you have to *pay* interest on the loan. Therefore your expected return is

$$r = (2 \times \text{expected return on S}) - (1 \times \text{interest rate})$$

$$= 25\%$$

And the standard deviation of your investment is

$$\sigma = (2 \times \text{standard deviation of S}) - (1 \times \text{standard deviation of bills})$$

$$= 32\%$$

You can see from Figure 8.5 that when you lend a portion of your money, you end up partway between r_f and S; if you can borrow money at the risk-free rate, you can extend your possibilities beyond S. You can also see that regardless of the level of risk you choose, you can get the highest expected return by a mixture of portfolio S and borrowing or lending. S is the *best* efficient portfolio. There is no reason ever to hold, say, portfolio T.

If you have a graph of efficient portfolios, as in Figure 8.5, finding this best efficient portfolio is easy. Start on the vertical axis at r_f, and draw the steepest line you can to the curved red line of efficient portfolios. That line will be tangent to the red line. The efficient portfolio at the tangency point is better than all the others. Notice that it offers the highest *ratio* of risk premium to standard deviation. This ratio of the risk premium to the standard deviation is called the *Sharpe ratio*:

$$\text{Sharpe ratio} = \frac{\text{Risk premium}}{\text{standard deviation}} = \frac{r - r_f}{\sigma}$$

Investors track Sharpe ratios to measure the risk-adjusted performance of investment managers. (Take a look at the mini-case at the end of this chapter.)

We can now separate the investor's job into two stages. The first step is to select the best portfolio of common stocks—S in our example. The second step is to blend this portfolio with borrowing or lending to match the investor's willingness to bear risk. Each investor, therefore, should put money into just two benchmark investments—a risky portfolio S and a risk-free loan (borrowing or lending).

What does portfolio S look like? If you have better information than your rivals, you will want the portfolio to include relatively large investments in the stocks you think are

---

[7]If you want to check this, write down the formula for the standard deviation of a two-stock portfolio: Standard deviation = $\sqrt{x_1^2\sigma_1^2 + x_2^2\sigma_2^2 + 2x_1x_2\rho_{12}\sigma_1\sigma_2}$. Now see what happens when security 2 is riskless, that is, when $\sigma_2 = 0$.

undervalued. But in a competitive market, you are unlikely to have a monopoly of good ideas. In that case, there is no reason to hold a different portfolio of common stocks from anybody else. In other words, you might just as well hold the market portfolio. That is why many professional investors invest in a market-index portfolio and why most others hold well-diversified portfolios.

8-2   The Relationship between Risk and Return

In Chapter 7, we looked at the returns on selected investments. The least risky investment was U.S. Treasury bills. Since the return on Treasury bills is fixed, it is unaffected by what happens to the market. In other words, Treasury bills have a beta of 0. We also considered a much riskier investment, the market portfolio of common stocks. This has average market risk: Its beta is 1.0.

Wise investors don't take risks just for fun. They are playing with real money. Therefore, they require a higher return from the market portfolio than from Treasury bills. The difference between the return on the market and the interest rate is termed the *market risk premium*. Since 1900, the market risk premium ($r_m - r_f$) has averaged 7.7% a year.

In Figure 8.6, we have plotted the risk and expected return from Treasury bills and the market portfolio. You can see that Treasury bills have a beta of 0 and a risk premium of 0.[8] The market portfolio has a beta of 1 and a risk premium of $r_m - r_f$. This gives us two benchmarks for an investment's expected risk premium. But what risk premium can one look forward to when beta is not 0 or 1?

In the mid-1960s three economists—William Sharpe, John Lintner, and Jack Treynor—produced an answer to this question.[9] Their answer is known as the **capital asset pricing model,**

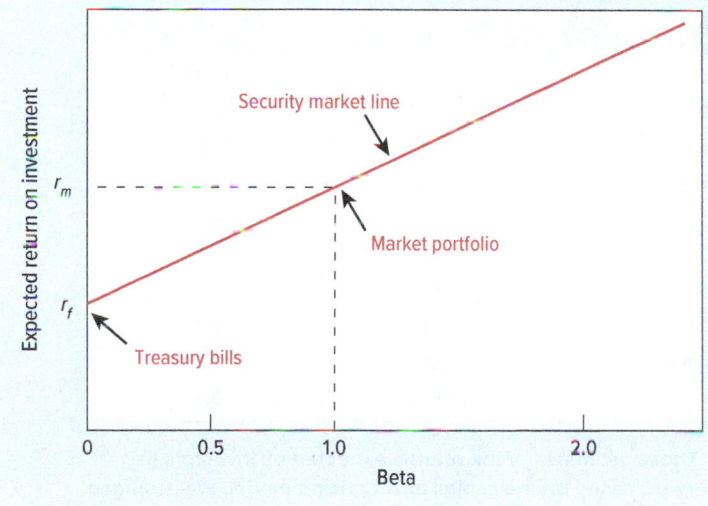

▶ **FIGURE 8.6**

The capital asset pricing model states that the expected risk premium on each investment is proportional to its beta. This means that each investment should lie on the sloping security market line connecting Treasury bills and the market portfolio.

---

[8]Remember that the risk premium is the difference between the investment's expected return and the risk-free rate. For Treasury bills, the difference is zero.

[9]W. F. Sharpe, "Capital Asset Prices: A Theory of Market Equilibrium under Conditions of Risk," *Journal of Finance* 19 (September 1964), pp. 425–442; and J. Lintner, "The Valuation of Risk Assets and the Selection of Risky Investments in Stock Portfolios and Capital Budgets," *Review of Economics and Statistics* 47 (February 1965), pp. 13–37. Treynor's article has not been published.

or **CAPM.** The model's message is both startling and simple. In a competitive market, the expected risk premium varies in direct proportion to beta. This means that in Figure 8.6 all investments must plot along the sloping line, known as the **security market line.** The expected risk premium on an investment with a beta of .5 is, therefore, *half* the expected risk premium on the market; the expected risk premium on an investment with a beta of 2 is *twice* the expected risk premium on the market. We can write this relationship as

Expected risk premium on stock = beta × expected risk premium on market

$$r - r_f = \beta(r_m - r_f)$$

Some Estimates of Expected Returns

Before we tell you where the formula comes from, let us use it to figure out what returns investors are looking for from particular stocks. To do this, we need three numbers: β, r_f, and $r_m - r_f$. We gave estimates of the betas of 10 stocks in Table 7.5. We will suppose that the interest rate on Treasury bills is about 2%.[10]

Table 8.2 puts these numbers together to give an estimate of the expected return on each stock. The stock with the highest beta in our sample is U.S. Steel. Our estimate of the expected return from U.S. Steel is 22.3%. The stock with the lowest beta is Newmont. Our estimate of its expected return is just 2.7%. Notice that these expected returns are not the same as the hypothetical forecasts of return that we assumed in Table 8.1 to generate the efficient frontier. They are the returns that investors can expect if the stocks are fairly priced.

Stock	Beta (β)	Expected Return $r_f = \beta(r_m - r_f)$
United States Steel	3.01	23.1
Amazon	1.47	12.3
Southwest Airlines	1.35	11.5
The Travelers Companies	1.26	10.8
Tesla	0.94	8.6
ExxonMobil	0.82	7.7
Johnson & Johnson	0.81	7.7
Coca-Cola	0.70	6.9
Consolidated Edison	0.11	2.8
Newmont	0.10	2.7

❯**TABLE 8.2**   These estimates of the returns expected by investors in December 2017 were based on the capital asset pricing model. We assumed 2% for the interest rate r_f and 7% for the expected risk premium $r_m - r_f$.

---

[10]Notice that it is the current interest rate that is relevant. The level of interest rates in the past has nothing to do with the returns that investors expect today.

You can also use the capital asset pricing model to find the discount rate for a new capital investment. For example, suppose that you are analyzing a proposal by Coca-Cola to expand its business. At what rate should you discount the forecasted cash flows? According to Table 8.2, investors are looking for a return of 6.9% from businesses with the risk of Coca-Cola. So the cost of capital for a further investment in the same business is 6.9%.[11]

In practice, choosing a discount rate is seldom so easy. (After all, you can't expect to be paid a fat salary just for plugging numbers into a formula.) For example, you must learn how to adjust the expected return to remove the extra risk caused by company borrowing. Also you need to consider the difference between short- and long-term interest rates. As we write this in February 2018, the interest rate on Treasury bills is well below long-term rates. It is possible that investors were content with the prospect of quite modest equity returns in the short run, but they almost certainly required higher long-run returns. If that is so, a cost of capital based on short-term rates may be inappropriate for long-term capital investments. In Table 8.2, we largely sidestepped the issue by arbitrarily assuming an interest rate of 2%. We will return later to some of these refinements.

Review of the Capital Asset Pricing Model

Let us review the basic principles of portfolio selection:

1. Investors like high expected return and low standard deviation. Common stock portfolios that offer the highest expected return for a given standard deviation are known as *efficient portfolios*.

2. If the investor can lend or borrow at the risk-free rate of interest, one efficient portfolio is better than all the others: the portfolio that offers the highest ratio of risk premium to standard deviation (i.e., portfolio S in Figure 8.5). A risk-averse investor will put part of his money in this efficient portfolio and part in the risk-free asset. A risk-tolerant investor may put all her money in this portfolio or she may borrow and put in even more.

3. The composition of this best efficient portfolio depends on the investor's assessments of expected returns, standard deviations, and correlations. But suppose everybody has the same information and the same assessments. If no one has any superior information, each investor should hold the same portfolio as everybody else; in other words, everyone should hold the market portfolio.

Now let us go back to the risk of individual stocks:

4. Do not look at the risk of a stock in isolation but at its contribution to portfolio risk. This contribution depends on the stock's sensitivity to changes in the value of the portfolio.

5. A stock's sensitivity to changes in the value of the *market* portfolio is known as *beta*. Beta, therefore, measures the marginal contribution of a stock to the risk of the market portfolio.

Now if everyone holds the market portfolio, and if beta measures each security's contribution to the risk of the market portfolio, then it is no surprise that the risk premium demanded by investors is proportional to beta. That is the message of the CAPM.

---

[11]Remember that instead of investing in plant and machinery, the firm could return the money to the shareholders. The opportunity cost of investing is the return that shareholders could expect to earn by buying financial assets. This expected return depends on the market risk of the assets.

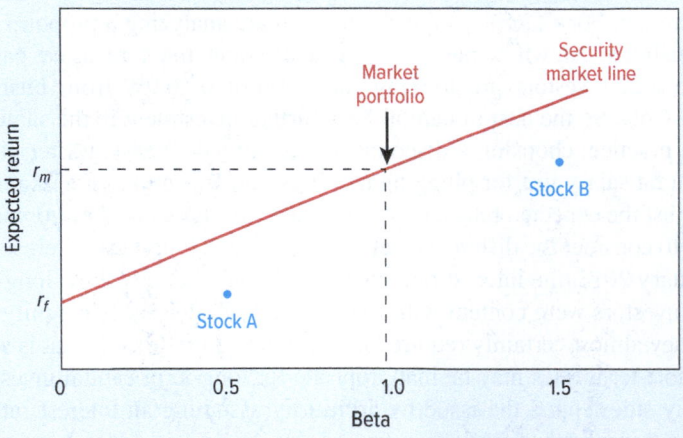

▶ **FIGURE 8.7**

In equilibrium no stock can lie below the security market line. For example, instead of buying stock A, investors would prefer to lend part of their money and put the balance in the market portfolio. And instead of buying stock B, they would prefer to borrow and invest in the market portfolio.

What If a Stock Did Not Lie on the Security Market Line?

Imagine that you encounter stock A in Figure 8.7. Would you buy it? We hope not[12]—if you want an investment with a beta of .5, you could get a higher expected return by investing half your money in Treasury bills and half in the market portfolio. If everybody shares your view of the stock's prospects, the price of A will have to fall until the expected return matches what you could get elsewhere.

What about stock B in Figure 8.7? Would you be tempted by its high return? You wouldn't if you were smart. You could get a higher expected return for the same beta by borrowing 50 cents for every dollar of your own money and investing in the market portfolio. Again, if everybody agrees with your assessment, the price of stock B cannot hold. It will have to fall until the expected return on B is equal to the expected return on the combination of borrowing and investment in the market portfolio.[13]

We have made our point. An investor can always obtain an expected risk premium of $\beta(r_m - r_f)$ by holding a mixture of the market portfolio and a risk-free loan. So in well-functioning markets nobody will hold a stock that offers an expected risk premium of *less* than $\beta(r_m - r_f)$. But what about the other possibility? Are there stocks that offer a higher expected risk premium? In other words, are there any that lie above the security market line in Figure 8.7? If we take all stocks together, we have the market portfolio. Therefore, we know that stocks *on average* lie on the line. Since none lies *below* the line, then there also can't be any that lie *above* the line. Thus each and every stock must lie on the security market line and offer an expected risk premium of

$$r - r_f = \beta(r_m - r_f)$$

8-3   Validity and Role of the Capital Asset Pricing Model

Any economic model is a simplified statement of reality. We need to simplify in order to interpret what is going on around us. But we also need to know how much faith we can place in our model.

---

[12]Unless, of course, we were trying to sell it.
[13]Of course, investing in just A or B only would be stupid; you would hold an undiversified portfolio.

Let us begin with some matters about which there is broad agreement. First, few people quarrel with the idea that investors require some extra return for taking on risk. That is why common stocks have given on average a higher return than U.S. Treasury bills. Who would want to invest in risky common stocks if they offered only the *same* expected return as bills? We would not, and we suspect you would not either.

Second, investors do appear to be concerned principally with those risks that they cannot eliminate by diversification. If this were not so, we should find that stock prices increase whenever two companies merge to spread their risks. And we should find that investment companies which invest in the shares of other firms are more highly valued than the shares they hold. But we do not observe either phenomenon. Mergers undertaken just to spread risk do not increase stock prices, and investment companies are no more highly valued than the stocks they hold.

The capital asset pricing model captures these ideas in a simple way. That is why financial managers find it a convenient tool for coming to grips with the slippery notion of risk and why nearly three-quarters of them use it to estimate the cost of capital.[14] It is also why economists often use the capital asset pricing model to demonstrate important ideas in finance even when there are other ways to prove these ideas. But that does not mean that the capital asset pricing model is ultimate truth. We will see later that it has several unsatisfactory features, and we will look at some alternative theories. Nobody knows whether one of these alternative theories is eventually going to come out on top or whether there are other, better models of risk and return that have not yet seen the light of day.

Tests of the Capital Asset Pricing Model

Imagine that in 1931 ten investors gathered together in a Wall Street bar and agreed to establish investment trust funds for their children. Each investor decided to follow a different strategy. Investor 1 opted to buy the 10% of the New York Stock Exchange stocks with the lowest estimated betas; investor 2 chose the 10% with the next-lowest betas; and so on, up to investor 10, who proposed to buy the stocks with the highest betas. They also planned that at the end of each year they would reestimate the betas of all NYSE stocks and reconstitute their portfolios.[15] And so they parted with much cordiality and good wishes.

In time, the 10 investors all passed away, but their children agreed to meet in early 2018 in the same bar to compare the performance of their portfolios. Figure 8.8 shows how they had fared. Investor 1's portfolio turned out to be much less risky than the market; its beta was only .48. However, investor 1 also realized the lowest return, 8.2% above the risk-free rate of interest. At the other extreme, the beta of investor 10's portfolio was 1.55, about three times that of investor 1's portfolio. But investor 10 was rewarded with the highest return, averaging 15.2% a year above the interest rate. So over this 87-year period, returns did indeed increase with beta.

As you can see from Figure 8.8, the market portfolio over the same 87-year period provided an average return of 12.1% above the interest rate[16] and (of course) had a beta of 1.0. The CAPM predicts that the risk premium should increase in proportion to beta, so that the

BEYOND THE PAGE

Figure 8.8:
Returns and beta

mhhe.com/brealey13e

---

[14]See J. R. Graham and C. R. Harvey, "The Theory and Practice of Corporate Finance: Evidence from the Field," *Journal of Financial Economics* 60 (2001), pp. 187–243. A number of the managers surveyed reported using more than one method to estimate the cost of capital. Seventy-three percent used the capital asset pricing model, while 39% stated they used the average historical stock return and 34% used the capital asset pricing model with some extra risk factors.

[15]Betas were estimated using returns over the previous 60 months.

[16]In Figure 8.8, the stocks in the "market portfolio" are weighted equally. Since the stocks of small firms have provided higher average returns than those of large firms, the risk premium on an equally weighted index is higher than on a value-weighted index. This is one reason for the difference between the 12.1% market risk premium in Figure 8.8 and the 7.7% premium reported in Table 7.1. Also, our 10 investors set up their trust funds in 1931 just before stock prices rebounded from the Great Crash of 1929.

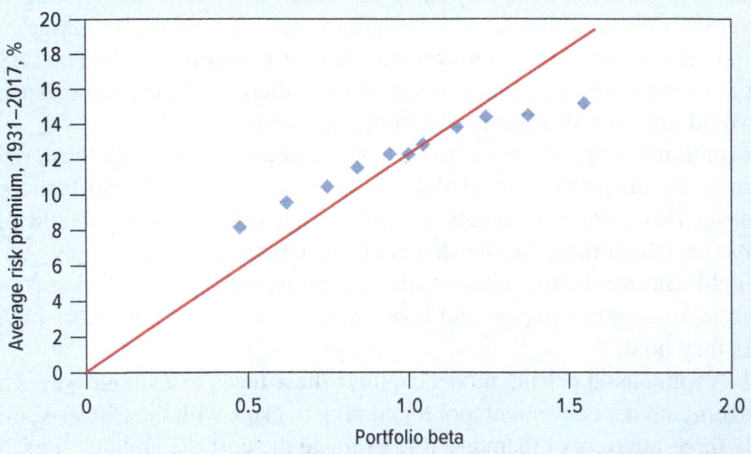

FIGURE 8.8

The capital asset pricing model states that the expected risk premium from any investment should lie on the security market line. The dots show the actual average risk premiums from portfolios with different betas. The high-beta portfolios generated higher average returns, just as predicted by the CAPM. But the high-beta portfolios plotted below the market line, and the low-beta portfolios plotted above. A line fitted to the 10 portfolio returns would be "flatter" than the security market line.

Source: F. Black, "Beta and Return," *Journal of Portfolio Management* 20 (Fall 1993), pp. 8–18. Updates courtesy of Adam Kolasinski.

returns of each portfolio should lie on the upward-sloping security market line in Figure 8.8. Since the market provided a risk premium of 12.1%, investor 1's portfolio, with a beta of .48, should have provided a risk premium of 5.8% and investor 10's portfolio, with a beta of 1.55, should have given a premium of 18.8%. You can see that, while high-beta stocks performed better than low-beta stocks, the difference was not as great as the CAPM predicts.

Although Figure 8.8 provides broad support for the CAPM, critics have pointed out that the slope of the line has been particularly flat in recent years. For example, Figure 8.9 shows how our 10 investors fared between 1966 and 2017. Now it is less clear who is buying the drinks: Returns are pretty much in line with the CAPM with the important exception of the two highest-risk portfolios. Investor 10, who rode the roller coaster of a high-beta portfolio, earned a return that was only marginally above that of the market. Of course, before 1967 the line was correspondingly steeper. This is also shown in Figure 8.9.

What is going on here? It is hard to say. Defenders of the capital asset pricing model emphasize that it is concerned with *expected* returns, whereas we can observe only *actual* returns. Actual stock returns reflect expectations, but they also embody lots of "noise"—the steady flow of surprises that conceal whether on average investors have received the returns they expected. This noise may make it impossible to judge whether the model holds better in one period than another.[17] Perhaps the best that we can do is to focus on the longest period for which there is reasonable data. This would take us back to Figure 8.8, which suggests that expected returns do indeed increase with beta, though less rapidly than the simple version of the CAPM predicts.[18]

The CAPM has also come under fire on a second front: Although return has not risen consistently with beta in recent years, it has been related to other measures. For example, the red line in Figure 8.10 shows the cumulative difference between the returns on small-firm stocks and large-firm stocks. If you had bought the shares with the smallest market capitalizations and sold those with the largest capitalizations, this is how your wealth would have changed. You can see that small-cap stocks did not always do well, but over the long haul, their owners

---

[17]A second problem with testing the model is that the market portfolio should contain all risky investments, including stocks, bonds, commodities, real estate—even human capital. Most market indexes contain only a sample of common stocks.

[18]We say "simple version" because Fischer Black has shown that if there are borrowing restrictions, there should still exist a positive relationship between expected return and beta, but the security market line would be less steep as a result. See F. Black, "Capital Market Equilibrium with Restricted Borrowing," *Journal of Business* 45 (July 1972), pp. 444–455.

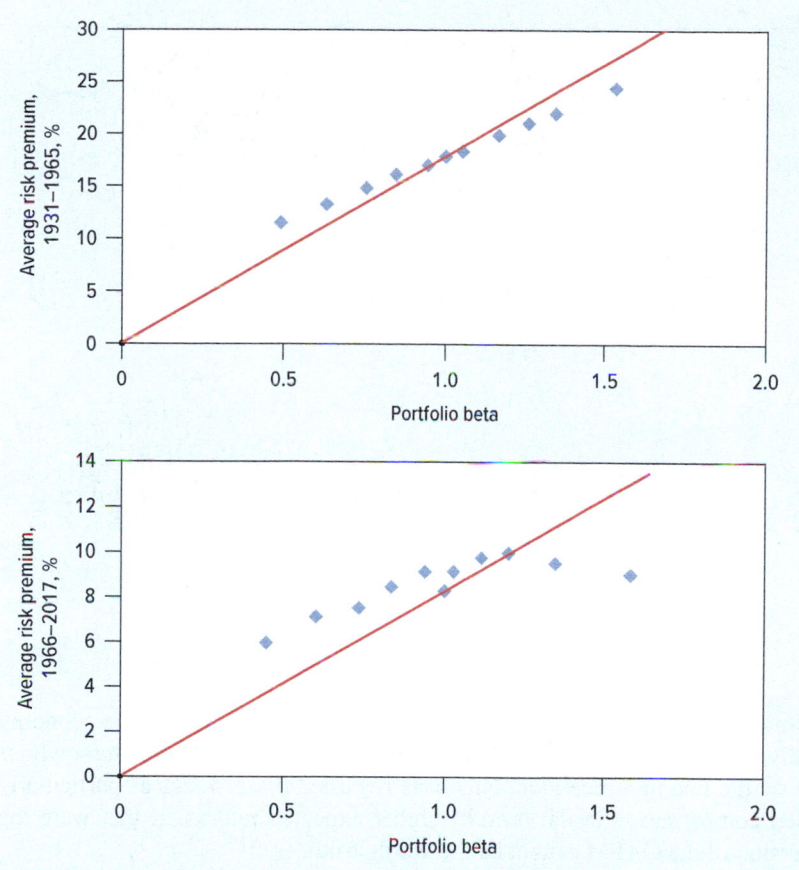

▶ **FIGURE 8.9**

The relationship between beta and actual average return has been weaker since the mid-1960s. Stocks with the highest betas have provided poor returns.

Source: F. Black, "Beta and Return," *Journal of Portfolio Management* 20 (Fall 1993), pp. 8–18. Updates courtesy of Adam Kolasinski.

have made substantially higher returns. Since the end of 1926, the average annual difference between the returns on the two groups of stocks has been 3.2%.

Now look at the green line in Figure 8.10, which shows the cumulative difference between the returns on value stocks and growth stocks. Value stocks here are defined as those with high ratios of book value to market value. Growth stocks are those with low ratios of book to market. Notice that value stocks have provided a higher long-run return than growth stocks.[19] Since 1926, the average annual difference between the returns on value and growth stocks has been 4.9%.

Figure 8.10 does not fit well with the CAPM, which predicts that beta is the *only* reason that expected returns differ. It seems that investors saw risks in "small-cap" stocks and value stocks that were not captured by beta.[20] Take value stocks, for example. Many of these stocks

---

[19]Fama and French calculated the returns on portfolios designed to take advantage of the size effect and the book-to-market effect. See E. F. Fama and K. R. French, "The Cross-Section of Expected Stock Returns," *Journal of Finance* 47 (June 1992), pp. 427–465. When calculating the returns on these portfolios, Fama and French control for differences in firm size when comparing stocks with low and high book-to-market ratios. Similarly, they control for differences in the book-to-market ratio when comparing small- and large-firm stocks. For details of the methodology and updated returns on the size and book-to-market factors see Kenneth French's website (**mba. tuck.dartmouth.edu/pages/faculty/ken.french/data_library.html**).

[20]An investor who bought small-company stocks and sold large-company stocks would have incurred some risk. Her portfolio would have had a beta of .27. This is not nearly large enough to explain the difference in returns. There is no simple relationship between the return on the value- and growth-stock portfolios and beta.

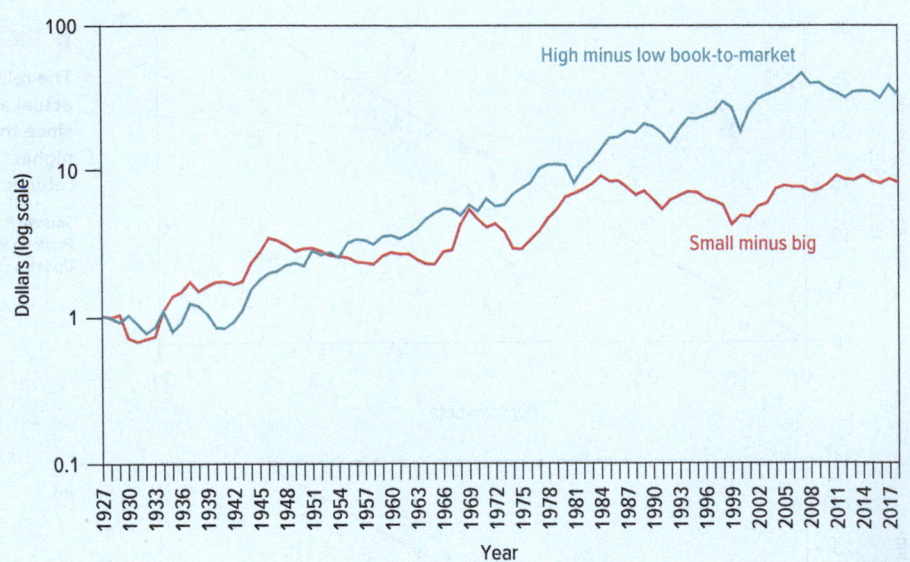

FIGURE 8.10

The red line shows the cumulative difference between the returns on small-firm and large-firm stocks from 1926 to 2017. The green line shows the cumulative difference between the returns on high book-to-market-value stocks (i.e., value stocks) and low book-to-market-value stocks (i.e., growth stocks).

Source: Kenneth French's website, mba.tuck.dartmouth.edu/pages/faculty/ken.french/data_library.html.

may have sold below book value because the firms were in serious trouble; if the economy slowed unexpectedly, the firms might have collapsed altogether. Therefore, investors, whose jobs could also be on the line in a recession, may have regarded these stocks as particularly risky and demanded compensation in the form of higher expected returns. If that were the case, the simple version of the CAPM cannot be the whole truth.

Again, it is hard to judge how seriously the CAPM is damaged by this finding. The relationship among stock returns and firm size and book-to-market ratio has been well documented. However, if you look long and hard at past returns, you are bound to find some strategy that just by chance would have worked in the past. This practice is known as "data mining" or "data snooping." Maybe the size and book-to-market effects are simply chance results that stem from data snooping. If so, they should have vanished once they were discovered. There is some evidence that this is the case. For example, if you look again at Figure 8.10, you will see that since the mid-1980s, small-firm stocks have underperformed just about as often as they have overperformed.

There is no doubt that the evidence on the CAPM is less convincing than scholars once thought. But it will be hard to reject the CAPM beyond all reasonable doubt. Since data and statistics are unlikely to give final answers, the plausibility of the CAPM *theory* will have to be weighed along with the empirical "facts."

BEYOND THE PAGE

The momentum factor

mhhe.com/brealey13e

Assumptions behind the Capital Asset Pricing Model

The capital asset pricing model rests on several assumptions that we did not fully spell out. For example, we assumed that investment in U.S. Treasury bills is risk-free. It is true that there is little chance of default, but bills do not guarantee a *real* return. There is still some uncertainty about inflation. Another assumption was that investors can *borrow* money at the same rate of interest at which they can lend. Generally borrowing rates are higher than lending rates. The model also assumes that all assets are marketable, but some assets, such as your human capital, cannot be bought and sold.

It turns out that many of these assumptions are not crucial, and with a little pushing and pulling, it is possible to modify the capital asset pricing model to handle them. The really important idea is that investors are content to invest their money in a limited number of benchmark portfolios. (In the basic CAPM, these benchmarks are Treasury bills and the market portfolio.)

In these modified CAPMs, expected return still depends on market risk, but the definition of market risk depends on the nature of the benchmark portfolios. In practice, none of these alternative capital asset pricing models is as widely used as the standard version.

8-4 Some Alternative Theories

BEYOND THE PAGE

The consumption CAPM

mhhe.com/brealey13e

The capital asset pricing model pictures investors as solely concerned with the level and uncertainty of their future wealth. But this could be too simplistic. For example, investors may become accustomed to a particular standard of living, so that poverty tomorrow may be particularly difficult to bear if you were wealthy yesterday. Behavioral psychologists have also observed that investors do not focus solely on the *current* value of their holdings, but look back at whether their investments are showing a profit. A gain, however small, may be an additional source of satisfaction. The capital asset pricing model does not allow for the possibility that investors may take account of the price at which they purchased stock and feel elated when their investment is in the black and depressed when it is in the red.[21]

Arbitrage Pricing Theory

The capital asset pricing theory begins with an analysis of how investors construct efficient portfolios. Stephen Ross's **arbitrage pricing theory,** or **APT,** comes from a different family entirely. It does not ask which portfolios are efficient. Instead, it starts by *assuming* that each stock's return depends partly on pervasive macroeconomic influences or "factors" and partly on "noise"—events that are unique to that company. Moreover, the return is assumed to obey the following simple relationship:

$$\text{Return} = a + b_1(r_{\text{factor 1}}) + b_2(r_{\text{factor 2}}) + b_3(r_{\text{factor 3}}) + \cdots + \text{noise}$$

The theory does not say what the factors are: There could be an oil price factor, an interest-rate factor, and so on. The return on the market portfolio *might* serve as one factor, but then again it might not.

Some stocks will be more sensitive to a particular factor than other stocks. ExxonMobil would be more sensitive to an oil price factor than, say, Coca-Cola. If factor 1 picks up unexpected changes in oil prices, b_1 will be higher for ExxonMobil.

For any individual stock, there are two sources of risk. First is the risk that stems from the pervasive macroeconomic factors. This cannot be eliminated by diversification. Second is the risk arising from possible events that are specific to the company. Diversification eliminates specific risk, and diversified investors can therefore ignore it when deciding whether to buy or sell a stock. The expected risk premium on a stock is affected by factor or macroeconomic risk; it is *not* affected by specific risk.

---

[21]We discuss aversion to loss again in Chapter 13. The implications for asset pricing are explored in S. Benartzi and R. Thaler, "Myopic Loss Aversion and the Equity Premium Puzzle," *Quarterly Journal of Economics* 110 (1995), pp. 73–92; and in N. Barberis, M. Huang, and T. Santos, "Prospect Theory and Asset Prices," *Quarterly Journal of Economics* 116 (2001), pp. 1–53.

Arbitrage pricing theory states that the expected risk premium on a stock should depend on the expected risk premium associated with each factor and the stock's sensitivity to each of the factors (b_1, b_2, b_3, etc.). Thus the formula is[22]

$$\text{Expected risk premium} = r - r_f$$

$$= b_1(r_{\text{factor 1}} - r_f) + b_2(r_{\text{factor 2}} - r_f) + \cdots$$

Notice that this formula makes two statements:

1. If you plug in a value of zero for each of the b's in the formula, the expected risk premium is zero. A diversified portfolio that is constructed to have zero sensitivity to each macroeconomic factor is essentially risk-free and therefore must be priced to offer the risk-free rate of interest. If the portfolio offered a higher return, investors could make a risk-free (or "arbitrage") profit by borrowing to buy the portfolio. If it offered a lower return, you could make an arbitrage profit by running the strategy in reverse; in other words, you would *sell* the diversified zero-sensitivity portfolio and *invest* the proceeds in U.S. Treasury bills.

2. A diversified portfolio that is constructed to have exposure to, say, factor 1, will offer a risk premium, which will vary in direct proportion to the portfolio's sensitivity to that factor. For example, imagine that you construct two portfolios, A and B, that are affected only by factor 1. If portfolio A is twice as sensitive as portfolio B to factor 1, portfolio A must offer twice the risk premium. Therefore, if you divided your money equally between U.S. Treasury bills and portfolio A, your combined portfolio would have exactly the same sensitivity to factor 1 as portfolio B and would offer the same risk premium.

   Suppose that the arbitrage pricing formula did *not* hold. For example, suppose that the combination of Treasury bills and portfolio A offered a higher return. In that case investors could make an arbitrage profit by selling portfolio B and investing the proceeds in the mixture of bills and portfolio A.

The arbitrage that we have described applies to well-diversified portfolios, where the specific risk has been diversified away. But if the arbitrage pricing relationship holds for all diversified portfolios, it must generally hold for the individual stocks. Each stock must offer an expected return commensurate with its contribution to portfolio risk. In the APT, this contribution depends on the sensitivity of the stock's return to unexpected changes in the macroeconomic factors.

A Comparison of the Capital Asset Pricing Model and Arbitrage Pricing Theory

Like the capital asset pricing model, arbitrage pricing theory stresses that expected return depends on the risk stemming from economywide influences and is not affected by specific risk. You can think of the factors in arbitrage pricing as representing special portfolios of stocks that tend to be subject to a common influence. If the expected risk premium on each of these portfolios is proportional to the portfolio's market beta, then the arbitrage pricing theory and the capital asset pricing model will give the same answer. In any other case, they will not.

---

[22]There may be some macroeconomic factors that investors are simply not worried about. For example, some macroeconomists believe that money supply doesn't matter and therefore investors are not worried about inflation. Such factors would not command a risk premium. They would drop out of the APT formula for expected return.

How do the two theories stack up? Arbitrage pricing has some attractive features. For example, the market portfolio that plays such a central role in the capital asset pricing model does not feature in arbitrage pricing theory.[23] So we do not have to worry about the problem of measuring the market portfolio, and in principle we can test the arbitrage pricing theory even if we have data on only a sample of risky assets.

Unfortunately, you win some and lose some. Arbitrage pricing theory does not tell us what the underlying factors are—unlike the capital asset pricing model, which collapses *all* macroeconomic risks into a well-defined *single* factor, the return on the market portfolio.

The Three-Factor Model

Look back at the equation for APT. To estimate expected returns, you first need to follow three steps:

Step 1: Identify a reasonably short list of macroeconomic factors that could affect stock returns.

Step 2: Estimate the expected risk premium on each of these factors ($r_{\text{factor 1}} - r_f$, etc.).

Step 3: Measure the sensitivity of each stock to the factors (b_1, b_2, etc.).

One way to shortcut this process is to take advantage of the research by Fama and French, which showed that stocks of small firms and those with a high book-to-market ratio have provided above-average returns. This could simply be a coincidence. But there is also some evidence that these factors are related to company profitability and therefore may be picking up risk factors that are left out of the simple CAPM.[24]

If investors do demand an extra return for taking on exposure to these factors, then we have a measure of the expected return that looks very much like arbitrage pricing theory:

$$r - r_f = b_{\text{market}}(r_{\text{market factor}}) + b_{\text{size}}(r_{\text{size factor}}) + b_{\text{book-to-market}}(r_{\text{book-to-market factor}})$$

This is commonly known as the Fama–French three-factor model. Using it to estimate expected returns is the same as applying the arbitrage pricing theory. Here is an example.[25]

BEYOND THE PAGE

Fama-French 3-factor betas for U.S. stocks.

mhhe.com/brealey13e

Step 1: Identify the Factors Fama and French have already identified the three factors that appear to determine expected returns. The returns on each of these factors are

Factor	Measured by
Market factor	Return on market index *minus* risk-free interest rate
Size factor	Return on small-firm stocks *less* return on large-firm stocks
Book-to-market factor	Return on high book-to-market-ratio stocks *less* return on low book-to-market-ratio stocks

Step 2: Estimate the Risk Premium for Each Factor We will keep to our figure of 7% for the market risk premium. History may provide a guide to the risk premium for the other two factors. As we saw earlier, between 1926 and 2017, the difference between the annual returns on

---

[23]Of course, the market portfolio *may* turn out to be one of the factors, but that is not a necessary implication of arbitrage pricing theory.

[24]E. F. Fama and K. R. French, "Size and Book-to-Market Factors in Earnings and Returns," *Journal of Finance* 50 (1995), pp. 131–155.

[25]The three-factor model was first used to estimate the cost of capital for different industry groups by Fama and French. See E. F. Fama and K. R. French, "Industry Costs of Equity," *Journal of Financial Economics* 43 (1997), pp. 153–193. Fama and French emphasize the imprecision in using either the CAPM or an APT-style model to estimate the returns that investors expect.

small and large capitalization stocks averaged 3.2% a year, while the difference between the returns on stocks with high and low book-to-market ratios averaged 4.9%.

Step 3: Estimate the Factor Sensitivities   Some stocks are more sensitive than others to fluctuations in the returns on the three factors. You can see this from the first three columns of numbers in Table 8.3, which show some estimates of the factor sensitivities of 10 industry groups for the 60 months ending in December 2017. For example, an increase of 1% in the return on the book-to-market factor *reduces* the return on computer stocks by .21% but *increases* the return on oil and gas stocks by 1.10%. In other words, when value stocks (high book-to-market) outperform growth stocks (low book-to-market), computer stocks tend to perform relatively badly and oil and gas stocks do relatively well.

Once you have estimated the factor sensitivities, it is a simple matter to multiply each of them by the expected factor return and add up the results. For example, the expected risk premium on pharmaceutical stocks is $r - r_f = (1.07 \times 7) + (.23 \times 3.2) - (.55 \times 4.9) = 5.5\%$. To calculate the expected return we need to add on the risk-free interest rate, which we assume to be 1.8%. Thus the three-factor model suggests that expected return on pharmaceutical stocks is $1.8 + 5.5 = 7.3\%$.

Compare this figure with the expected return estimate using the capital asset pricing model (the final column of Table 8.3). The three-factor model provides a slightly lower estimate of the expected return for pharmaceutical stocks. Why? Largely because they are growth stocks with a low exposure (−.55) to the book-to-market factor. The three-factor model produces a lower expected return for growth stocks, but it produces a higher figure for value stocks such as those of banks and oil companies that have a high book-to-market ratio.

| | Three-Factor Model | | | | CAPM |
| | Factor Sensitivities | | | | |
	b_{market}	b_{size}	$b_{book\text{-}to\text{-}market}$	Expected Return[a]	Expected Return[b]
Autos	1.20	0.54	0.12	12.5%	11.1%
Banks	1.09	0.23	0.70	13.6	10.0
Chemicals	1.32	0.05	0.18	12.1	11.2
Computers	1.11	−0.17	−0.21	8.0	9.2
Construction	1.24	0.75	−0.07	12.5	11.6
Food	0.73	−0.33	−0.13	5.2	6.4
Oil and gas	1.03	0.17	1.10	14.9	9.6
Pharmaceuticals	1.07	0.23	−0.55	7.3	9.4
Telecoms	0.95	−0.25	0.08	8.1	8.1
Utilities	0.44	−0.22	−0.19	3.3	4.5

❭ **TABLE 8.3**   Estimates of expected equity returns for selected industries using the Fama–French three-factor model and the CAPM

[a]The expected return equals the risk-free interest rate plus the factor sensitivities multiplied by the factor risk premiums, that is, $r_f + (b_{market} \times 7) + (b_{size} \times 3.2) + (b_{book\text{-}to\text{-}market} \times 4.9)$.

[b]Estimated as $r_f + \beta(r_m - r_f)$, that is, $r_f + \beta \times 7$. Note that we used *simple* regression to estimate β in the CAPM formula. This beta may, therefore, be different from b_{market} that we estimated from a *multiple* regression of stock returns on the three factors.

Source: The industry indexes are value-weighted indexes from Kenneth French's website, mba.tuck.dartmouth.edu/pages/faculty/ken.french/data_library.html.

This Fama–French APT model is not widely used in practice to estimate the cost of equity or the WACC. The model requires three betas and three risk premiums, instead of one beta and one market risk premium in the CAPM. Also the three APT betas are not as easy to predict and interpret as the CAPM beta, which is just an exposure to overall market risk. The Fama–French APT is probably less suited to estimating the cost of equity for an individual stock than to providing an alternative way to estimate an industry cost of equity, as in Table 8.3.

The Fama–French model finds its widest use as a way of measuring the performance of mutual funds, pension funds, and other professionally managed portfolios. If a portfolio manager "beats the S&P," it may be because he or she has made a bet on small stocks in a period when small stocks soared—or perhaps he or she had the luck or foresight to avoid growth stocks in a period when growth stocks collapsed. An analyst can evaluate the manager's performance by estimating the portfolio's b_{market}, b_{size}, and $b_{book-to-market}$ and then checking whether the portfolio return is better than the return on a robotically managed portfolio with the same exposures to the Fama–French factors.

SUMMARY

The basic principles of portfolio selection boil down to a commonsense statement that investors try to increase the expected return on their portfolios and to reduce the variability of that return. A portfolio that gives the highest expected return for a given standard deviation, or the lowest standard deviation for a given expected return, is known as an *efficient portfolio*. To work out which portfolios are efficient, an investor must be able to state the expected return and standard deviation of each stock and the degree of correlation between each pair of stocks.

Investors who are restricted to holding common stocks should choose efficient portfolios that suit their attitudes to risk. But investors who can also borrow and lend at the risk-free rate of interest should choose the *best* common stock portfolio *regardless* of their attitudes to risk. Having done that, they can then set the risk of their overall portfolio by deciding what proportion of their money they are willing to invest in stocks. The best efficient portfolio offers the highest ratio of forecasted risk premium to portfolio standard deviation.

For an investor who has only the same opportunities and information as everybody else, the best stock portfolio is the same as the best stock portfolio for other investors. In other words, he or she should invest in a mixture of the market portfolio and a risk-free loan (i.e., borrowing or lending).

A stock's marginal contribution to portfolio risk is measured by its sensitivity to changes in the value of the portfolio. The marginal contribution of a stock to the risk of the *market portfolio* is measured by *beta*. That is the fundamental idea behind the capital asset pricing model (CAPM), which concludes that each security's expected risk premium should increase in proportion to its beta:

$$\text{Expected risk premium} = \text{beta} \times \text{market risk premium}$$

$$r - r_f = \beta(r_m - r_f)$$

The capital asset pricing theory is the best-known model of risk and return. It is plausible and widely used but far from perfect. Actual returns are related to beta over the long run, but the relationship is not as strong as the CAPM predicts, and other factors seem to explain returns better since the mid-1960s. Stocks of small companies, and stocks with high book values relative to market prices, appear to have risks not captured by the CAPM.

The arbitrage pricing theory offers an alternative theory of risk and return. It states that the expected risk premium on a stock should depend on the stock's exposure to several pervasive macroeconomic factors that affect stock returns:

$$\text{Expected risk premium} = b_1(r_{\text{factor } 1} - r_f) + b_2(r_{\text{factor } 2} - r_f) + \cdots$$

Here b's represent the individual security's sensitivities to the factors, and $r_{\text{factor}} - r_f$ is the risk premium demanded by investors who are exposed to this factor.

Arbitrage pricing theory does not say what these factors are. It asks for economists to hunt for unknown game with their statistical toolkits. Fama and French have suggested three factors:

- The return on the market portfolio less the risk-free rate of interest.
- The difference between the return on small- and large-firm stocks.
- The difference between the return on stocks with high book-to-market ratios and stocks with low book-to-market ratios.

In the Fama–French three-factor model, the expected return on each stock depends on its exposure to these three factors.

Each of these different models of risk and return has its fan club. However, all financial economists agree on two basic ideas: (1) Investors require extra expected return for taking on risk, and (2) they appear to be concerned predominantly with the risk that they cannot eliminate by diversification.

Near the end of Chapter 9, we list some Excel Functions that are useful for measuring the risk of stocks and portfolios.

FURTHER READING

A number of textbooks on portfolio selection explain both Markowitz's original theory and some ingenious simplified versions. See, for example,

E. J. Elton, M. J. Gruber, S. J. Brown, and W. N. Goetzmann: *Modern Portfolio Theory and Investment Analysis,* 9th ed. (New York: John Wiley & Sons, 2014).

The literature on the capital asset pricing model is enormous. There are dozens of published tests of the capital asset pricing model. Fischer Black's paper is a very readable example. Discussions of the theory tend to be more uncompromising. Two excellent but advanced examples are Campbell's survey paper and Cochrane's book.

F. Black, "Beta and Return," *Journal of Portfolio Management* 20 (Fall 1993), pp. 8–18.

J. Y. Campbell, "Asset Pricing at the Millennium," *Journal of Finance* 55 (August 2000), pp. 1515–1567.

J. H. Cochrane, *Asset Pricing,* revised ed. (Princeton, NJ: Princeton University Press, 2005).

PROBLEM SETS

 Select problems are available in McGraw-Hill's *Connect.* Please see the preface for more information.

1. **Efficient portfolios** For each of the following pairs of investments, state which would always be preferred by a rational investor (assuming that these are the only investments available to the investor):

   a. Portfolio A, $r = 18\%$ $\sigma = 20\%$; portfolio B, $r = 14\%$ $\sigma = 20\%$.

   b. Portfolio C, $r = 15\%$ $\sigma = 18\%$; portfolio D, $r = 13\%$ $\sigma = 8\%$.

   c. Portfolio E, $r = 14\%$ $\sigma = 16\%$; portfolio F, $r = 14\%$ $\sigma = 10\%$.

2. **Efficient portfolios** Figure 8.11 purports to show the range of attainable combinations of expected return and standard deviation.

    a. Which diagram is incorrectly drawn and why?

    b. Which is the efficient set of portfolios?

    c. If r_f is the rate of interest, mark with an X the optimal stock portfolio.

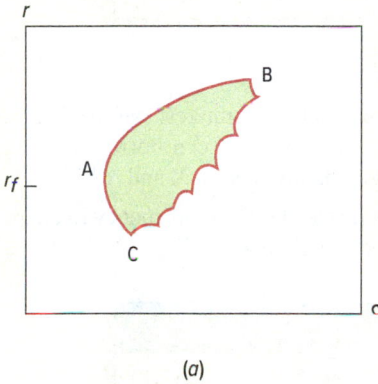

(a)

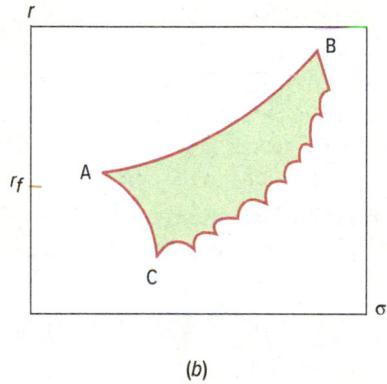

(b)

▶ **FIGURE 8.11**

See Problem 2

3. **Efficient portfolios***

    a. Plot the following risky portfolios on a graph:

	A	B	C	D	E	F	G	H
Expected return (r), (%)	10	12.5	15	16	17	18	18	20
Standard deviation (σ), (%)	23	21	25	29	29	32	35	45

    b. Five of these portfolios are efficient, and three are not. Which are inefficient ones?

    c. Suppose you can also borrow and lend at an interest rate of 12%. Which of the portfolios has the highest Sharpe ratio?

    d. Suppose you are prepared to tolerate a standard deviation of 25%. What is the maximum expected return that you can achieve if you cannot borrow or lend?

    e. What is your optimal strategy if you can borrow or lend at 12% and are prepared to tolerate a standard deviation of 25%? What is the maximum expected return that you can achieve with this risk?

4. **Portfolio risk and return** Look back at the calculation for Southwest Airlines and Amazon in Section 8-1.

    a. Recalculate the expected portfolio return and standard deviation for different values of x_1 and x_2, assuming the correlation coefficient $\rho_{12} = 0$. Plot the range of possible combinations of expected return and standard deviation as in Figure 8.3.

    b. Repeat the problem for $\rho_{12} = +.50$.

5. **Portfolio risk and return** Mark Harrywitz proposes to invest in two shares, X and Y. He expects a return of 12% from X and 8% from Y. The standard deviation of returns is 8% for X and 5% for Y. The correlation coefficient between the returns is .2.

a. Compute the expected return and standard deviation of the following portfolios:

Portfolio	Percentage in X	Percentage in Y
1	50	50
2	25	75
3	75	25

b. Sketch the set of portfolios composed of X and Y.

c. Suppose that Mr. Harrywitz can also borrow or lend at an interest rate of 5%. Show on your sketch how this alters his opportunities. Given that he can borrow or lend, what proportions of the common stock portfolio should be invested in X and Y?

6. **Portfolio risk and return*** Ebenezer Scrooge has invested 60% of his money in share A and the remainder in share B. He assesses their prospects as follows:

	A	B
Expected return (%)	15	20
Standard deviation (%)	20	22
Correlation between returns		0.5

a. What are the expected return and standard deviation of returns on his portfolio?

b. How would your answer change if the correlation coefficient were 0 or −.5?

c. Is Mr. Scrooge's portfolio better or worse than one invested entirely in share A, or is it not possible to say?

7. **Portfolio risk and return*** Here are returns and standard deviations for four investments.

	Return (%)	Standard Deviation (%)
Treasury bills	6	0
Stock P	10	14
Stock Q	14.5	28
Stock R	21	26

Calculate the standard deviations of the following portfolios.

a. 50% in Treasury bills, 50% in stock P.

b. 50% each in Q and R, assuming the shares have
   - Perfect positive correlation.
   - Perfect negative correlation.
   - No correlation.

c. Plot a figure like Figure 8.3 for Q and R, assuming a correlation coefficient of .5.

d. Stock Q has a lower return than R but a higher standard deviation. Does that mean that Q's price is too high or that R's price is too low?

8. **Portfolio risk and return** Percival Hygiene has $10 million invested in long-term corporate bonds. This bond portfolio's expected annual rate of return is 9%, and the annual standard deviation is 10%. Amanda Reckonwith, Percival's financial adviser, recommends that Percival consider investing in an index fund that closely tracks the Standard & Poor's 500 Index. The index has an expected return of 14%, and its standard deviation is 16%.

   a. Suppose Percival puts all his money in a combination of the index fund and Treasury bills. Can he thereby improve his expected rate of return without changing the risk of his portfolio? The Treasury bill yield is 6%.

   b. Could Percival do even better by investing equal amounts in the corporate bond portfolio and the index fund? The correlation between the bond portfolio and the index fund is +.1.

9. **Sharpe ratio*** Use the long-term data on security returns in Sections 7-1 and 7-2 to calculate the historical level of the Sharpe ratio for the market portfolio.

10. **Sharpe ratio** Look back at Problem 9 in Chapter 7. The risk-free interest rate in each of these years was as follows:

	2010	2011	2012	2013	2014
Interest rate (%)	0.12	0.04	0.06	0.02	0.02

   a. Calculate the average return and standard deviation of returns for Ms. Sauros's portfolio and for the market. Use these figures to calculate the Sharpe ratio for the portfolio and the market. On this measure did Ms. Sauros perform better or worse than the market?

   b. Now calculate the average return that you could have earned over this period if you had held a combination of the market and a risk-free loan. Make sure that the combination has the same beta as Ms. Sauros's portfolio. Would your average return on this portfolio have been higher or lower? Explain your results.

11. **Portfolio beta** Refer to Table 7.5.

   a. What is the beta of a portfolio that has 40% invested in ExxonMobil and 60% in Newmont?

   b. Would you invest in this portfolio if you had no superior information about the prospects for these stocks? Devise an alternative portfolio with the same expected return and less risk.

   c. Now repeat parts (a) and (b) with a portfolio that has 40% invested in Travelers and 60% in Amazon.

12. **CAPM*** True or false? Explain or qualify as necessary.

   a. Investors demand higher expected rates of return on stocks with more variable rates of return.

   b. The CAPM predicts that a security with a beta of 0 will offer a zero expected return.

   c. An investor who puts $10,000 in Treasury bills and $20,000 in the market portfolio will have a beta of 2.0.

   d. Investors demand higher expected rates of return from stocks with returns that are highly exposed to macroeconomic risks.

   e. Investors demand higher expected rates of return from stocks with returns that are very sensitive to fluctuations in the stock market.

13. **CAPM** True or false?

   a. The CAPM implies that if you could find an investment with a negative beta, its expected return would be less than the interest rate.

   b. The expected return on an investment with a beta of 2.0 is twice as high as the expected return on the market.

   c. If a stock lies below the security market line, it is undervalued.

14. **CAPM** Suppose that the Treasury bill rate is 6% rather than 2%. Assume that the expected return on the market stays at 9%. Use the betas in Table 8.2.

   a. Calculate the expected return from Johnson & Johnson.

   b. Find the highest expected return that is offered by one of these stocks.

   c. Find the lowest expected return that is offered by one of these stocks.

   d. Would U.S. Steel offer a higher or lower expected return if the interest rate were 6% rather than 2%? Assume that the expected market return stays at 9%.

   e. Would Coca-Cola offer a higher or lower expected return if the interest rate were 8%?

15. **CAPM** The Treasury bill rate is 4%, and the expected return on the market portfolio is 12%. Using the capital asset pricing model:

   a. Draw a graph similar to Figure 8.6 showing how the expected return varies with beta.

   b. What is the risk premium on the market?

   c. What is the required return on an investment with a beta of 1.5?

   d. If an investment with a beta of .8 offers an expected return of 9.8%, does it have a positive NPV?

   e. If the market expects a return of 11.2% from stock X, what is its beta?

16. **Cost of capital*** Epsilon Corp. is evaluating an expansion of its business. The cash-flow forecasts for the project are as follows:

Years	Cash Flow ($ millions)
0	−100
1–10	+15

   The firm's existing assets have a beta of 1.4. The risk-free interest rate is 4% and the expected return on the market portfolio is 12%. What is the project's NPV?

17. **APT** Consider a three-factor APT model. The factors and associated risk premiums are

Factor	Risk Premium (%)
Change in gross national product (GNP)	+5
Change in energy prices	−1
Change in long-term interest rates	+2

   Calculate expected rates of return on the following stocks. The risk-free interest rate is 7%.

   a. A stock whose return is uncorrelated with all three factors.

   b. A stock with average exposure to each factor (i.e., with $b = 1$ for each).

   c. A pure-play energy stock with high exposure to the energy factor ($b = 2$) but zero exposure to the other two factors.

d. An aluminum company stock with average sensitivity to changes in interest rates and GNP, but negative exposure of $b = -1.5$ to the energy factor. (The aluminum company is energy-intensive and suffers when energy prices rise.)

18. **APT** Some true or false questions about the APT:

   a. The APT factors cannot reflect diversifiable risks.

   b. The market rate of return cannot be an APT factor.

   c. There is no theory that specifically identifies the APT factors.

   d. The APT model could be true but not very useful, for example, if the relevant factors change unpredictably.

19. **APT** Consider the following simplified APT model:

Factor	Expected Risk Premium (%)
Market	6.4
Interest rate	−0.6
Yield spread	5.1

Calculate the expected return for the following stocks. Assume $r_f = 5\%$.

	Factor Risk Exposures		
	Market	**Interest Rate**	**Yield Spread**
Stock	(b_1)	(b_2)	(b_3)
P	1.0	−2.0	−0.2
P^2	1.2	0	0.3
P^3	0.3	0.5	1.0

20. **APT** Look again at Problem 19. Consider a portfolio with equal investments in stocks P, P^2, and P^3.

   a. What are the factor risk exposures for the portfolio?

   b. What is the portfolio's expected return?

21. **Three-factor model*** The following table shows the sensitivity of four stocks to the three Fama–French factors. Estimate the expected return on each stock assuming that the interest rate is 2%, the expected risk premium on the market is 7%, the expected risk premium on the size factor is 3.2%, and the expected risk premium on the book-to-market factor is 4.9%.

	Ford	Walmart	Citigroup	Apple
Market	1.24	0.41	1.52	1.25
Size	−0.07	−0.47	−0.01	−0.67
Book-to-market	0.28	−0.25	0.85	−0.72

CHALLENGE

22. **Fund performance** Between 2008 and 2017, the returns on Microfund averaged 10% a year. In his 2017 discussion of performance, the fund president noted that this was 2.5% a year better than the return on the U.S. market, a result that he attributed to the fund's strategy of buying only stocks with outstanding management.

The following table shows the returns on the market, the size and book-to-market factors, and the interest rate during this period:

	Market Risk Premium	Return on Size Factor	Return on Book-to-Market Factor	Interest Rate
2008	−38.34	3.26	0.97	1.60
2009	28.26	9.28	−9.14	0.10
2010	17.37	13.77	−5.17	0.12
2011	0.44	−6.04	−8.41	0.04
2012	16.28	−1.22	9.89	0.06
2013	35.2	7.35	1.54	0.02
2014	11.7	−7.75	−1.65	0.02
2015	0.07	−3.73	−9.48	0.02
2016	13.3	6.66	23.33	0.20
2017	21.5	−4.85	−13.85	0.80

The fund had marketed itself as a way to invest in small and medium-sized stocks, and this was reflected in a beta relative to the size factor of 1.4. It had also traditionally adopted a conservative approach to risk with an estimated market beta of .9. The fund's beta relative to the book-to-market factor was −.4. Evaluate the performance of the fund during this period.

23. **Minimum-risk portfolio** In footnote 4, we noted that the minimum-risk portfolio contained an investment of 53% in Amazon and 47% in Southwest Airlines. Prove it. (*Hint:* You need a little calculus to do so.)

24. **Efficient portfolios** Look again at the set of the three efficient portfolios that we calculated in Section 8-1.

    a. If the interest rate is 5%, which of the three efficient portfolios should you hold?

    b. How would your answer to part (a) change if the interest rate were 2%?

25. **APT** The following question illustrates the APT. Imagine that there are only two pervasive macroeconomic factors. Investments X, Y, and Z have the following sensitivities to these two factors:

Investment	b_1	b_2
X	1.75	0.25
Y	−1.00	2.00
Z	2.00	1.00

We assume that the expected risk premium is 4% on factor 1 and 8% on factor 2. Treasury bills obviously offer zero risk premium.

    a. According to the APT, what is the risk premium on each of the three stocks?

    b. Suppose you buy $200 of X and $50 of Y and sell $150 of Z. What is the sensitivity of your portfolio to each of the two factors? What is the expected risk premium?

    c. Suppose you buy $80 of X and $60 of Y and sell $40 of Z. What is the sensitivity of your portfolio to each of the two factors? What is the expected risk premium?

    d. Finally, suppose you buy $160 of X and $20 of Y and sell $80 of Z. What is your portfolio's sensitivity now to each of the two factors? And what is the expected risk premium?

e. Suggest two possible ways that you could construct a fund that has a sensitivity of .5 to factor 1 only. (*Hint:* One portfolio contains an investment in Treasury bills.) Now compare the risk premiums on each of these two investments.

f. Suppose that the APT did *not* hold and that X offered a risk premium of 8%, Y offered a premium of 14%, and Z offered a premium of 16%. Devise an investment that has zero sensitivity to each factor and that has a positive risk premium.

You can download data for the following questions from **finance.yahoo.com.**

Use the Beyond the Page feature to access an Excel program for calculating the efficient frontier. (We are grateful to Darien Huang for providing us with a copy of this program.) Excel functions SLOPE, STDEV, COVAR, and CORREL are especially useful for answering the following questions.

1. a. Download up to 10 years of monthly returns for 10 different stocks and enter them into the Excel program. Enter some plausible figures for the expected return on each stock and find the set of efficient portfolios. Assume that you cannot borrow or lend.

   b. How does the possibility of short sales improve the choices open to the investor?

2. Find a low-risk stock—Walmart or Kellogg would be a good candidate. Use monthly returns for the most recent three years to confirm that the beta is less than 1.0. Now estimate the annual standard deviation for the stock and the S&P index, and the correlation between the returns on the stock and the index. Forecast the expected return for the stock, assuming the CAPM holds, with a market return of 12% and a risk-free rate of 5%.

   a. Plot a graph like Figure 8.5 showing the combinations of risk and return from a portfolio invested in your low-risk stock and the market. Vary the fraction invested in the stock from 0 to 100%.

   b. Suppose that you can borrow or lend at 5%. Would you invest in some combination of your low-risk stock and the market, or would you simply invest in the market? Explain.

   c. Suppose that you forecasted a return on the stock that is 5 percentage points higher than the CAPM return used in part (b). Redo parts (a) and (b) with the higher forecasted return.

   d. Find a high-risk stock and redo parts (a) and (b).

3. Recalculate the betas for the stocks in Table 8.2 using the latest 60 monthly returns. Recalculate expected rates of return from the CAPM formula, using a current risk-free rate and a market risk premium of 7%. How have the expected returns changed from Table 8.2?

● ● ● ● ●

FINANCE ON THE WEB

BEYOND THE PAGE

Try it! Markowitz portfolio program

mhhe.com/brealey13e

MINI-CASE ● ● ● ● ●

John and Marsha on Portfolio Selection

The scene: John and Marsha hold hands in a cozy French restaurant in downtown Manhattan, several years before the mini-case in Chapter 9. Marsha is a futures-market trader. John manages a $250 million common-stock portfolio for a large pension fund. They have just ordered tournedos financiere for the main course and flan financiere for dessert. John reads the financial pages of *The Wall Street Journal* by candlelight.

John: Wow! Potato futures hit their daily limit. Let's add an order of gratin dauphinoise. Did you manage to hedge the forward interest rate on that euro loan?

Marsha: John, please fold up that paper. (*He does so reluctantly.*) John, I love you. Will you marry me?

John: Oh, Marsha, I love you too, but . . . there's something you must know about me—something I've never told anyone.

Marsha: (*concerned*) John, what is it?

John: I think I'm a closet indexer.

Marsha: What? Why?

John: My portfolio returns always seem to track the S&P 500 market index. Sometimes I do a little better, occasionally a little worse. But the correlation between my returns and the market returns is over 90%.

Marsha: What's wrong with that? Your client wants a diversified portfolio of large-cap stocks. Of course your portfolio will follow the market.

John: Why doesn't my client just buy an index fund? Why is he paying *me*? Am I really adding value by active management? I try, but I guess I'm just an . . . indexer.

Marsha: Oh, John, I know you're adding value. You were a star security analyst.

John: It's not easy to find stocks that are truly over- or undervalued. I have firm opinions about a few, of course.

Marsha: You were explaining why Pioneer Gypsum is a good buy. And you're bullish on Global Mining.

John: Right, Pioneer. (*Pulls handwritten notes from his coat pocket.*) Stock price $87.50. I estimate the expected return as 11% with an annual standard deviation of 32%. That's twice the market standard deviation of 16%.

Marsha: Only 11%? You're forecasting a market return of 12.5%.

John: Yes, I'm using a market risk premium of 7.5% and the risk-free interest rate is about 5%. That gives 12.5%. But Pioneer's beta is only .65. I was going to buy 30,000 shares this morning, but I lost my nerve. I've got to stay diversified.

Marsha: Have you tried modern portfolio theory?

John: MPT? Not practical. Looks great in textbooks, where they show efficient frontiers with 5 or 10 stocks. But I choose from hundreds, maybe thousands, of stocks. Where do I get the inputs for 1,000 stocks? That's a million variances and covariances!

Marsha: Actually only about 500,000, dear. The covariances above the diagonal are the same as the covariances below. But you're right, most of the estimates would be out-of-date or just garbage.

John: To say nothing about the expected returns. Garbage in, garbage out.

Marsha: But John, you don't need to solve for 1,000 portfolio weights. You only need a handful. Here's the trick: Take your benchmark, the S&P 500, as security 1. That's what you would end up with as an indexer. Then consider a few securities you really know something about. Pioneer could be security 2, for example. Global, security 3. And so on. Then you could put your wonderful financial mind to work.

John: I get it: Active management means selling off some of the benchmark portfolio and investing the proceeds in specific stocks like Pioneer. But how do I decide whether Pioneer really improves the portfolio? Even if it does, how much should I buy?

Marsha: Just maximize the Sharpe ratio, dear.

John: I've got it! The answer is yes!

Marsha: What's the question?

John: You asked me to marry you. The answer is yes. Where should we go on our honeymoon?

Marsha: How about Australia? I'd love to visit the Sydney Futures Exchange.

QUESTIONS

1. Table 8.4 reproduces John's notes on Pioneer Gypsum and Global Mining. Calculate the expected return, risk premium, and standard deviation of a portfolio invested partly in the market and partly in Pioneer. (You can calculate the necessary inputs from the betas and standard deviations given in the table. *Hint:* A stock's beta equals its covariance with the market return divided by the variance of the market return.) Does adding Pioneer to the market benchmark improve the Sharpe ratio? How much should John invest in Pioneer and how much in the market?

	Pioneer Gypsum	Global Mining
Expected return	11.0%	12.9%
Standard deviation	32%	24%
Beta	0.65	1.22
Stock price	$87.50	$105.00

❯TABLE 8.4
John's notes on Pioneer Gypsum and Global Mining.

2. Repeat the analysis for Global Mining. What should John do in this case? Assume that Global accounts for .75% of the S&P index.

CHAPTER

9

Risk and the Cost of Capital

Long before the development of modern theories linking risk and return, smart financial managers adjusted for risk in capital budgeting. They knew that risky projects are, other things equal, less valuable than safe ones—that's just common sense. Therefore, they demanded higher rates of return from risky projects, or they based their decisions about risky projects on conservative forecasts of project cash flows.

Today, most companies start with the company cost of capital as a benchmark discount rate for new investments. The company cost of capital is the right discount rate only for investments that have the same risk as the company's overall business. For riskier projects, the opportunity cost of capital is greater than the company cost of capital. For safer projects, it is less.

The company cost of capital is usually estimated as a weighted-average cost of capital—that is, as the average rate of return demanded by investors in the company's debt and equity. The hardest part of estimating the weighted-average cost of capital is figuring out the cost of equity—that is, the expected rate of return to investors in the firm's common stock. Many firms turn to the capital asset pricing model (CAPM) for an answer. The CAPM states that the expected rate of return equals the risk-free interest rate plus a risk premium that depends on beta and the market risk premium.

You can look up betas on financial websites like Yahoo! Finance and Bloomberg, but it's important to remember that these betas are estimates and liable to statistical errors. We will show you how to estimate betas and to check the reliability of these estimates.

Now suppose you're responsible for a specific investment project. How do you know if the project is average risk or above- or below-average risk? We suggest you check whether the project's cash flows are more or less sensitive to the business cycle than the average project. Also check whether the project has higher or lower fixed operating costs (higher or lower operating leverage) and whether it requires large future investments.

Remember that a project's cost of capital depends only on market risk. Diversifiable events can affect project cash flows but they do not increase the cost of capital. Also don't be tempted to add arbitrary fudge factors to discount rates. Fudge factors are too often added to discount rates for projects in unstable parts of the world, for example.

Financial managers usually assume that a project's risk will be the same in every future period, and they use a single risk-adjusted discount rate for all future cash flows. But occasionally managers need to recognize that risk can also vary over time for a given project. For example, some projects are riskier in youth than in old age. We close the chapter by introducing certainty equivalents, which illustrate how risk can change over time.

9-1   Company and Project Costs of Capital

The **company cost of capital** is defined as the expected return on a portfolio of all the company's outstanding debt and equity securities. It is the opportunity cost of capital for an investment in all of the firm's assets, and therefore the appropriate discount rate for the firm's average-risk projects.

If the firm has no debt outstanding, then the company cost of capital is just the expected rate of return on the firm's stock. Many large, successful companies pretty well fit this special case, including Johnson & Johnson (J&J). The estimated beta of Johnson & Johnson's common stock is .81. Suppose that the risk-free interest rate is 2% and the market risk premium is 7%. Then the capital asset pricing model would imply an expected return of 7.7% from J&J's stock:

$$r = r_f + \beta(r_m - r_f) = 2 + .81 \times 7 = 7.7\%$$

If J&J is contemplating an expansion of its existing business, it would make sense to discount the forecasted cash flows at 7.7%.[1]

The company cost of capital is *not* the correct discount rate if the new projects are more or less risky than the firm's existing business. Each project should, in principle, be evaluated at its *own* opportunity cost of capital. This is a clear implication of the value-additivity principle introduced in Chapter 7. For a firm composed of assets A and B, the firm value is

$$\text{Firm value} = \text{PV(AB)} = \text{PV(A)} + \text{PV(B)}$$

$$= \text{sum of separate asset values}$$

Here, PV(A) and PV(B) are valued just as if they were mini-firms in which stockholders could invest directly. Investors would value A by discounting its forecasted cash flows at a rate reflecting the risk of A. They would value B by discounting at a rate reflecting the risk of B. The two discount rates will, in general, be different. If the present value of an asset depended on the identity of the company that bought it, present values would *not* add up, and we know they do add up. (Think of a portfolio of $1 million invested in J&J and $1 million invested in Toyota. Would any reasonable investor say that the portfolio is worth anything more or less than $2 million?)

If the firm considers investing in a third project C, it should also value C as if C were a mini-firm. That is, the firm should discount the cash flows of C at the expected rate of return that investors would demand if they could make a separate investment in C. *The opportunity cost of capital depends on the use to which that capital is put.*

Perhaps we're saying the obvious. Think of J&J: It is a massive health care and consumer products company, with $76 billion in sales in 2017. J&J has well-established consumer products, including Band-Aid® bandages, Tylenol®, and products for skin care and babies. It also invests heavily in much chancier ventures, such as biotech research and development (R&D). Do you think that a new production line for baby lotion has the same cost of capital as an investment in biotech R&D? We don't, though we admit that estimating the cost of capital for biotech R&D could be challenging.

Suppose we measure the risk of each project by its beta. Then J&J should accept any project lying above the upward-sloping security market line that links expected return to risk in Figure 9.1. If the project is high risk, J&J needs a higher prospective return than if the project

---

[1]We have simplified by treating J&J as all-equity-financed. J&J's market-value debt ratio is very low, but not zero. We discuss debt financing and the weighted-average cost of capital later in the chapter.

> ▶ **FIGURE 9.1**
>
> J&J's company cost of capital is about 7.7%. This is the correct discount rate only if the project beta is .81. In general, the correct discount rate increases as project beta increases. J&J should accept projects with rates of return above the security market line relating required return to beta.

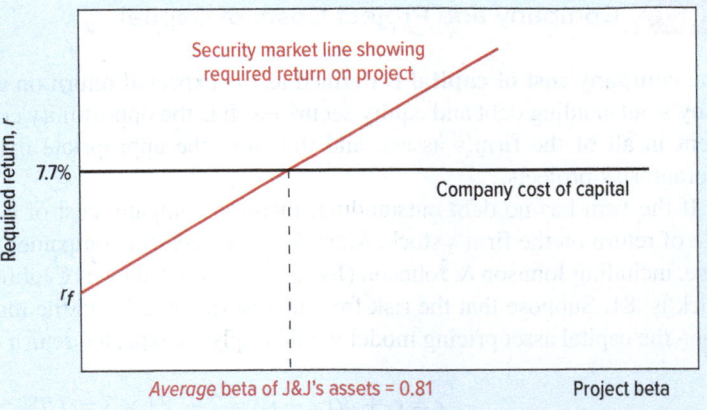

is low risk. That is not the same as accepting any project *regardless of its risk* as long as it offers a higher return than the *company's* cost of capital. In that case, J&J would accept any project above the horizontal cost of capital line in Figure 9.1—that is, any project offering a return of more than 7.7%.

It is clearly silly to suggest that J&J should demand the same rate of return from a very safe project as from a very risky one. If J&J used the company cost of capital rule, it would reject many good low-risk projects and accept many poor high-risk projects. It is also silly to suggest that just because another company has a still lower company cost of capital, it is justified in accepting projects that J&J would reject.

Perfect Pitch and the Cost of Capital

The true cost of capital depends on project risk, not on the company undertaking the project. So why is so much time spent estimating the company cost of capital?

There are two reasons. First, many (maybe most) projects can be treated as average risk—that is, neither more nor less risky than the average of the company's other assets. For these projects the company cost of capital is the right discount rate. Second, the company cost of capital is a useful starting point for setting discount rates for unusually risky or safe projects. It is easier to add to, or subtract from, the company cost of capital than to estimate each project's cost of capital from scratch.

There is a good musical analogy here. Most of us, lacking perfect pitch, need a well-defined reference point, like middle C, before we can sing on key. But anyone who can carry a tune gets *relative* pitches right. Businesspeople have good intuition about *relative* risks, at least in industries they are used to, but not about absolute risk or required rates of return. Therefore, they set a company-wide cost of capital as a benchmark. This is not the right discount rate for everything the company does, but adjustments can be made for more or less risky ventures.

That said, we have to admit that many large companies use the company cost of capital not just as a benchmark, but also as an all-purpose discount rate for every project proposal. Measuring differences in risk is difficult to do objectively, and financial managers shy away from intracorporate squabbles. (You can imagine the bickering: "My projects are safer than yours! I want a lower discount rate!" "No they're not! Your projects are riskier than a naked call option!")[2]

---

[2]A "naked" call option is an option purchased with no offsetting (hedging) position in the underlying stock or in other options. We discuss options in Chapter 20.

When firms force the use of a single company cost of capital, risk adjustment shifts from the discount rate to project cash flows. Top management may demand extra-conservative cash-flow forecasts from extra-risky projects. Or they may refuse to sign off on an extra-risky project unless NPV, computed at the company cost of capital, is well above zero. Such rough-and-ready risk adjustments may be better than none at all.

Debt and the Company Cost of Capital

We defined the company cost of capital as "the expected return on a portfolio of all the company's outstanding debt and equity securities." Thus, the cost of capital is estimated as a blend of the *cost of debt* (the interest rate on the firm's debt) and the *cost of equity* (the expected rate of return demanded by investors in the firm's common stock).

Suppose the company's market-value balance sheet looks like this:

Asset value	100	Debt	$D = 30$ at 7.5%
		Equity	$E = 70$ at 15%
Asset value	100	Firm value	$V = 100$

The values of debt and equity add up to overall firm value ($D + E = V$) and firm value V equals asset value. These figures are all market values, not book (accounting) values. The market value of equity is often much larger than the book value, so the market debt ratio D/V is often much lower than a debt ratio computed from the book balance sheet.

The 7.5% cost of debt is the opportunity cost of capital for the investors who hold the firm's debt. The 15% cost of equity is the opportunity cost of capital for the investors who hold the firm's shares. Neither measures the *company* cost of capital, that is, the opportunity cost of investing in the firm's *assets*. The cost of debt is less than the company cost of capital, because debt is safer than the assets. The cost of equity is greater than the company cost of capital, because the equity of a firm that borrows is riskier than the assets. Equity is not a direct claim on the firm's free cash flow. It is a residual claim that stands behind debt.

The company cost of capital is not equal to the cost of debt or to the cost of equity but is a blend of the two. Suppose you purchased a portfolio consisting of 100% of the firm's debt and 100% of its equity. Then you would own 100% of its assets lock, stock, and barrel. You would not share the firm's free cash flow with anyone; every dollar that the firm pays out would be paid to you.

The expected rate of return on your hypothetical portfolio is the company cost of capital. The expected rate of return is just a weighted average of the cost of debt ($r_D = 7.5\%$) and the cost of equity ($r_E = 15\%$). The weights are the relative market values of the firm's debt and equity, that is, $D/V = 30\%$ and $E/V = 70\%$.[3]

$$\text{Company cost of capital} = r_D D/V + r_E E/V$$

$$= 7.5 \times .30 + 15 \times .70 = 12.75\%$$

This blended measure of the company cost of capital is called the **weighted-average cost of capital** or **WACC** (pronounced "whack"). Calculating WACC is a bit more complicated than our example suggests, however. For example, interest is a tax-deductible expense for

---

[3]Recall that the 30% and 70% weights in your hypothetical portfolio are based on market, not book, values. Now you can see why. If the portfolio were constructed with different book weights—say, 50–50—then the portfolio returns could not equal the asset returns.

corporations, so the after-tax cost of debt is $(1 - T_c)r_D$, where T_c is the marginal corporate tax rate. Suppose $T_c = 21\%$, its rate in the United States in 2018. Then *after-tax WACC* is

$$\text{After-tax WACC} = (1 - T_c)\, r_D\, D/V + r_E\, E/V$$

$$= (1 - .21) \times 7.5 \times .30 + 15 \times .70 = 12.3\%$$

We give another example of the after-tax WACC later in this chapter, and we cover the topic in much more detail in Chapter 19. But now, we turn to the hardest part of calculating WACC, estimating the cost of equity.

9-2   Measuring the Cost of Equity

To calculate the weighted-average cost of capital, you need an estimate of the cost of equity. You decide to use the capital asset pricing model (CAPM). Here you are in good company: As we saw in the last chapter, most large U.S. companies do use the CAPM to estimate the cost of equity, which is the expected rate of return on the firm's common stock.[4] The CAPM says that

$$\text{Expected stock return} = r_f + \beta(r_m - r_f)$$

Now you have to estimate beta. Let us see how that is done in practice.

Estimating Beta

BEYOND THE PAGE

How to estimate beta

mhhe.com/brealey13e

In principle, we are interested in the future beta of the company's stock, but lacking a crystal ball, we turn first to historical evidence. For example, look at the scatter diagram at the top left of Figure 9.2. Each dot represents the return on U.S. Steel stock and the return on the market in a particular month. The plot starts in January 2008 and runs to December 2012, so there are 60 dots in all.

The second diagram on the left shows a similar plot for the returns on Microsoft stock, and the third shows a plot for Consolidated Edison. In each case, we have fitted a line through the points. The slope of this line is an estimate of beta. It tells us how much on average the stock price changed when the market return was 1% higher or lower.

BEYOND THE PAGE

Try It! Comparing beta estimates

mhhe.com/brealey13e

The right-hand diagrams show similar plots for the same three stocks during the subsequent period ending in December 2017. The estimated betas are not constant. For example, the estimate for U.S. Steel is much lower in the first period than in the second. You would have been off target if you had blindly used its beta during the earlier period to predict its beta in the later years. However, you could have been pretty confident that ConEd's beta was much less than U.S. Steel's and that Microsoft's beta was somewhere between the two.[5]

Only a portion of each stock's total risk comes from movements in the market. The rest is firm-specific, diversifiable risk, which shows up in the scatter of points around the fitted lines in Figure 9.2. *R-squared* (R^2) measures the proportion of the total variance in the stock's returns that can be explained by market movements. For example, from 2013 to 2017, the R^2 for Microsoft was .20. In other words, 20% of Microsoft's risk was market risk and 80% was

---

[4] The CAPM is not the last word on risk and return, of course, but the principles and procedures covered in this chapter work just as well with other models such as the Fama–French three-factor model. See Section 8-4.

[5] Remember that to estimate beta, you must regress the *returns* on the stock (the y variable) on the market *returns* (the x variable). You would get a very similar estimate if you simply used the percentage *changes* in the stock price and the market index. But sometimes, people make the mistake of regressing the stock price *level* on the *level* of the index and obtain nonsense results.

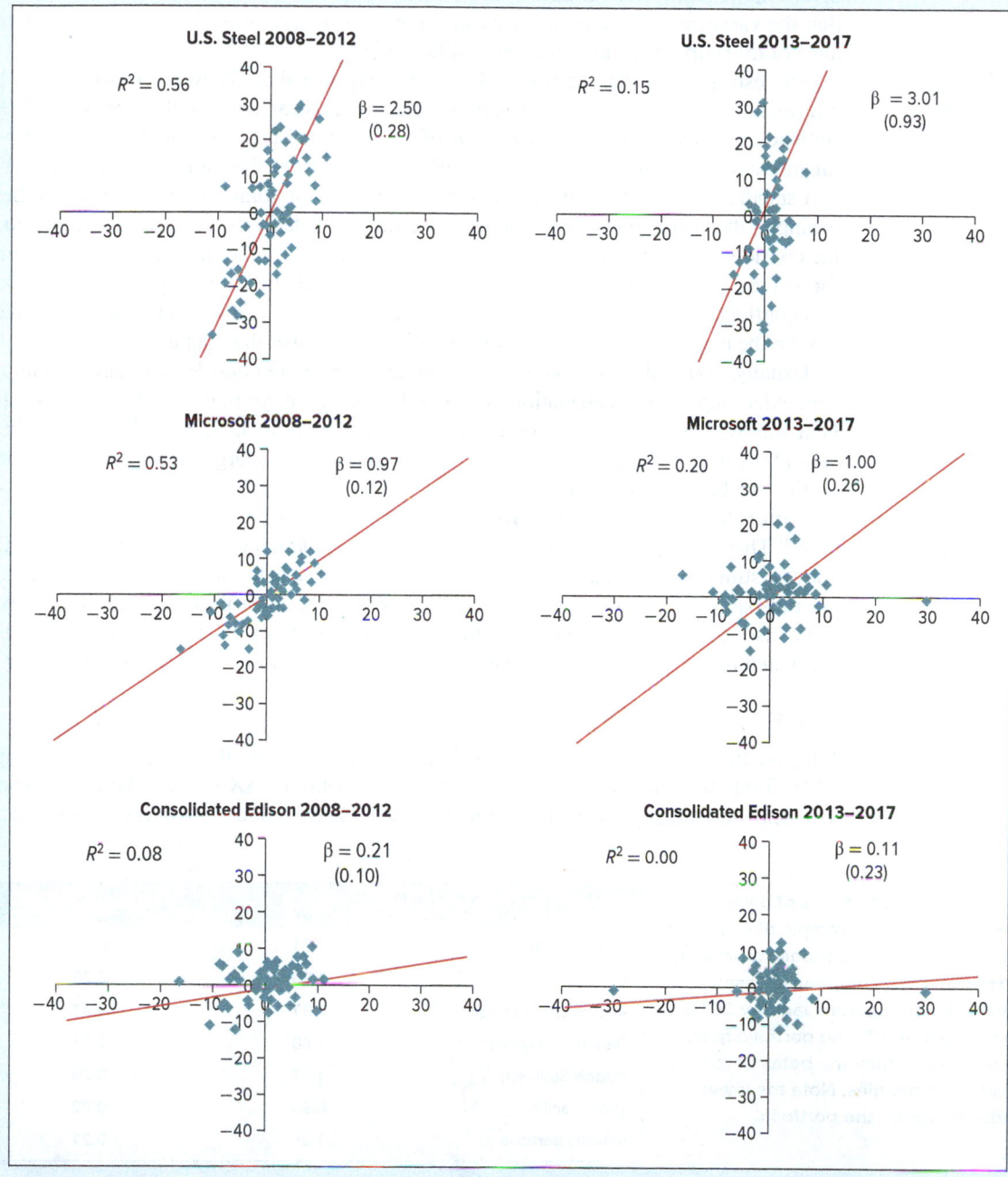

▶ **FIGURE 9.2**

We have used past returns to estimate the betas of three stocks for the periods January 2008 to December 2012 (left-hand diagrams) and January 2013 to December 2017 (right-hand diagrams). Beta is the slope of the fitted line. Notice that in both periods, U.S. Steel had the highest beta and Consolidated Edison the lowest. Standard errors are in parentheses below the betas. The standard error measures the range of possible error in the beta estimate. We also report the proportion of total risk that is due to market movements (R^2).

diversifiable risk.[6] The variance of the returns on Microsoft stock was 439.[7] So we could say that the variance in stock returns that was due to the market was $.2 \times 439 = 88$, and the variance of diversifiable returns was $.80 \times 439 = 351$.

BEYOND THE PAGE

Try It! Beta estimates for U.S. stocks

mhhe.com/brealey13e

The estimates of beta shown in Figure 9.2 are just that. They are based on the stocks' returns in 60 particular months. The noise in the returns can obscure the true beta.[8] Therefore, statisticians calculate the *standard error* of the estimated beta to show the extent of possible mismeasurement. Then they set up a *confidence interval* of the estimated value plus or minus two standard errors. We can be much more confident of some estimates than of others. For example, the standard error on Microsoft's estimated beta in the second period is 0.26. Thus, the confidence interval for the beta is 1.00 plus or minus $2 \times .26$. If you state that the *true* beta for Microsoft is between .48 and 1.52, you have a 95% chance of being right. We can be much less confident of our estimate of U.S. Steel's beta in the 2013–2017 period. Its standard error is .93. So the true beta for U.S. Steel could well be much lower than our estimated figure of 3.01.[9]

Usually, you will have more information (and thus more confidence) than this simple, and somewhat depressing, calculation suggests. For example, you know that ConEd's estimated beta was well below 1 in two successive five-year periods. U.S. Steel's estimated beta was well above 1 in both periods. Nevertheless, there is always a large margin for error when estimating the beta for individual stocks.

Fortunately, the estimation errors tend to cancel out when you estimate betas of *portfolios*.[10] That is why financial managers often turn to *industry betas*. For example, Table 9.1 shows estimates of beta and the standard errors of these estimates for the common stocks of six railroad companies. The standard errors are for the most part close to .3. However, the table also shows the estimated beta for a portfolio of all six railroad stocks. Notice that the estimated industry beta is somewhat more reliable. This shows up in the lower standard error.

The Expected Return on CSX's Common Stock

Suppose that in January 2018 you had been asked to estimate the company cost of capital of CSX. Table 9.1 provides two clues about the true beta of CSX's stock: the direct estimate of 1.35 and the average estimate for the industry of 1.25. We will use the industry estimate of 1.25.

〉TABLE 9.1   Estimates of betas and standard errors for a sample of railroad companies and for an equally weighted portfolio of these companies, based on monthly returns from January 2013 to December 2017. The portfolio beta is more reliable than the betas of the individual companies. Note the lower standard error for the portfolio.

	Beta	Standard Error
Canadian Pacific	1.21	0.27
CSX	1.35	0.29
Kansas City Southern	0.87	0.31
Genesee & Wyoming	1.80	0.31
Norfolk Southern	1.37	0.26
Union Pacific	0.90	0.22
Industry portfolio	1.25	0.21

---

[6]Notice that the first period includes much of the financial crisis, when stocks were more than usually influenced by the market factor. This shows up in the higher R^2s in this period.

[7]This is an annual figure; we annualized the monthly variance by multiplying by 12 (see footnote 19 in Chapter 7). The standard deviation was $\sqrt{439} = 21.0\%$.

[8]Estimates of beta may be distorted if there are extreme returns in one or two months. In such cases, statisticians may prefer to give less weight to the extreme observations or even to omit them entirely.

[9]For this reason, statisticians would generally adjust this estimate of U.S. Steel's beta down toward 1.0. Similarly, they would adjust upward any estimated beta that was below 1.0. For simplicity, in this book we use unadjusted betas, but if you are interested in how to make the adjustment, take a look at the Beyond the Page feature, "How to estimate beta."

[10]If the observations are independent, the standard error of the estimated mean beta declines in proportion to the square root of the number of stocks in the portfolio.

The next issue is what value to use for the risk-free interest rate. In early 2018, the three-month Treasury bill rate was about 1.6%. The one-year interest rate was a little higher, at 2.0%. Yields on longer-maturity U.S. Treasury bonds were higher still, at about 3.0% on 20-year bonds.

The CAPM is a short-term model. It works period by period and calls for a short-term interest rate. But could a 1.6% three-month risk-free rate give the right discount rate for cash flows 10 or 20 years in the future? Well, now that you mention it, probably not.

Financial managers muddle through this problem in one of two ways. The first way simply uses a long-term risk-free rate in the CAPM formula. If this short-cut is used, then the market risk premium must be restated as the average difference between market returns and returns on *long-term* Treasuries.[11]

The second way retains the usual definition of the market risk premium as the difference between market returns and returns on *short-term* Treasury bill rates. But now you have to forecast the expected return from holding Treasury bills over the life of the project. In Chapter 3, we observed that investors require a risk premium for holding long-term bonds rather than bills. Table 7.1 showed that over the past century, this risk premium has averaged about 1.5%. So to get a rough but reasonable estimate of the expected long-term return from investing in Treasury bills, we need to subtract 1.5% from the current yield on long-term bonds. In our example

$$\text{Expected long-term return from bills} = \text{yield on long-term bonds} - 1.5\%$$

$$= 3.0 - 1.5 = 1.5\%$$

This is a plausible estimate of the expected average future return on Treasury bills. We therefore use this rate in our example.

Returning to our CSX example, suppose you decide to use a market risk premium of 7%. Then the resulting estimate for CSX's cost of equity is about 10.3%:

$$\text{Cost of equity} = \text{expected return} = rf + \beta(r_m - r_f)$$

$$= 1.5 + 1.25 \times 7.0 = 10.3\%$$

CSX's After-Tax Weighted-Average Cost of Capital

Now you can calculate CSX's after-tax WACC. The company's cost of debt was about 4.0%. With a 21% corporate tax rate, the after-tax cost of debt was $r_D(1 - T_C) = 4.0 \times (1 - .21) = 3.2\%$. The ratio of debt to overall company value was $D/V = 19.2\%$. Therefore

$$\text{After-tax WACC} = (1 - T_C)r_D D/V + r_E E/V$$

$$= (1 - .21) \times 4.0 \times .192 + 10.3 \times .808 = 8.9\%$$

CSX should set its overall cost of capital to 8.9%, assuming that its CFO agrees with our estimates.

Warning   The cost of debt is always less than the cost of equity. The WACC formula blends the two costs. The formula is dangerous, however, because it suggests that the average cost of capital could be reduced by substituting cheap debt for expensive equity. It doesn't work that

---

[11]This approach gives a security market line with a higher intercept and a lower market risk premium. Using a "flatter" security market line is perhaps a better match to the historical evidence, which shows that the slope of average returns against beta is not as steeply upward-sloping as the CAPM predicts. See Figures 8.8 and 8.9.

way! As the debt ratio D/V increases, the cost of the remaining equity also increases, offsetting the apparent advantage of more cheap debt. We show how and why this offset happens in Chapter 17.

Debt does have a tax advantage, however, because interest is a tax-deductible expense. That is why we use the after-tax cost of debt in the after-tax WACC. We cover debt and taxes in much more detail in Chapters 18 and 19.

CSX's Asset Beta

The after-tax WACC depends on the average risk of the company's assets, but it also depends on taxes and financing. It's easier to think about project risk if you measure it directly. The direct measure is called the **asset beta.**

We calculate the asset beta as a blend of the separate betas of debt (β_D) and equity (β_E). For CSX, we have $\beta_E = 1.25$, and we'll assume $\beta_D = .15$.[12] The weights are the fractions of debt and equity financing, $D/V = .192$ and $E/V = .808$:

$$\text{Asset beta} = \beta_A = \beta_D(D/V) + \beta_E(E/V)$$

$$= .15 \times .192 + 1.25 \times .808 = 1.04$$

Calculating an asset beta is similar to calculating a weighted-average cost of capital. The debt and equity weights D/V and E/V are the same. The logic is also the same: Suppose you purchased a portfolio consisting of 100% of the firm's debt and 100% of its equity. Then you would own 100% of its assets lock, stock, and barrel, and the beta of your portfolio would equal the beta of the assets. The portfolio beta is of course just a weighted average of the betas of debt and equity.

This asset beta is an estimate of the average risk of CSX's railroad business. It is a useful benchmark, but it can take you only so far. Not all railroad investments are average risk. And if you are the first to use railroad-track networks as interplanetary transmission antennas, you will have no asset beta to start with.

How can you make informed judgments about costs of capital for projects or lines of business when you suspect that risk is *not* average? That is our next topic.

9-3   **Analyzing Project Risk**

Suppose that a coal-mining corporation needs to assess the risk of investing in a new company headquarters. The asset beta for coal mining is not helpful. You need to know the beta of real estate. Fortunately, portfolios of commercial real estate are traded. For example, you could estimate asset betas from returns on Real Estate Investment Trusts (REITs) specializing in commercial real estate.[13] The REITs would serve as traded *comparables* for the proposed office building. You could also turn to indexes of real estate prices and returns derived from sales and appraisals of commercial properties.[14]

---

[12]Why is the debt beta positive? Two reasons: First, debt investors worry about the risk of default. Corporate bond prices fall, relative to Treasury-bond prices, when the economy goes from expansion to recession. The risk of default is therefore partly a macroeconomic and market risk. Second, all bonds are exposed to uncertainty about interest rates and inflation. Even Treasury bonds have positive betas when long-term interest rates and inflation are volatile and uncertain.

[13]REITs are investment funds that invest in real estate. You would have to be careful to identify REITs investing in commercial properties similar to the proposed office building. There are also REITs that invest in other types of real estate, including apartment buildings, shopping centers, and timberland.

[14]See Chapter 23 in D. Geltner, N. G. Miller, J. Clayton, and P. Eichholtz, *Commercial Real Estate Analysis and Investments,* 3rd ed. (South-Western College Publishing, 2013).

A company that wants to set a cost of capital for one particular line of business typically looks for *pure plays* in that line of business. Pure-play companies are public firms that specialize in one activity. For example, suppose that J&J wants to set a cost of capital for its pharmaceutical business. It could estimate the average asset beta or cost of capital for pharmaceutical companies that have *not* diversified into consumer products like Band-Aid® bandages or baby powder.

Overall company costs of capital are almost useless for *conglomerates.* Conglomerates diversify into several unrelated industries, so they have to consider industry-specific costs of capital. They therefore look for pure plays in the relevant industries. Take Richard Branson's Virgin Group as an example. The group combines many different companies, including airlines (Virgin Atlantic) and train services (Virgin Rail Group). Fortunately, there are many examples of pure-play airlines and train operators. The trick is picking the comparables with business risks that are most similar to Virgin's companies.

Sometimes good comparables are not available or are not a good match to a particular project. Then the financial manager has to exercise his or her judgment. Here we offer the following advice:

1. *Think about the determinants of asset betas.* Often, the characteristics of high- and low-beta assets can be observed when the beta itself cannot be.

2. *Don't be fooled by diversifiable risk.*

3. *Avoid fudge factors.* Don't give in to the temptation to add fudge factors to the discount rate to offset things that could go wrong with the proposed investment. Adjust cash-flow forecasts instead.

What Determines Asset Betas?

Cyclicality   Many people's intuition associates risk with the variability of earnings or cash flow. But much of this variability reflects diversifiable risk. Lone prospectors searching for gold look forward to extremely uncertain future income, but whether they strike it rich is unlikely to depend on the performance of the market portfolio. Even if they do find gold, they do not bear much market risk. Therefore, an investment in gold prospecting has a high standard deviation but a relatively low beta.

What really counts is the strength of the relationship between the firm's earnings and the aggregate earnings on all real assets. We can measure this either by the *earnings beta* or by the *cash-flow beta.* These are just like a real beta except that changes in earnings or cash flow are used in place of rates of return on securities. Firms with high earnings or cash-flow betas are more likely to have high asset betas.

This means that cyclical firms—firms whose revenues and earnings are strongly dependent on the state of the business cycle—tend to be high-beta firms. Thus, you should demand a higher rate of return from investments whose performance is strongly tied to the performance of the economy. Examples of cyclical businesses include airlines, luxury resorts and restaurants, construction, and steel. (Much of the demand for steel depends on construction and capital investment.) Examples of less-cyclical businesses include food and tobacco products and established consumer brands such as J&J's baby products. MBA programs are another example because spending a year or two at a business school is an easier choice when jobs are scarce. Applications to top MBA programs increase in recessions.

Operating Leverage   A production facility with high fixed costs, relative to variable costs, is said to have high *operating leverage.* High operating leverage means a high asset beta. Let us see how this works.

The cash flows generated by an asset can be broken down into revenue, fixed costs, and variable costs:

$$\text{Cash flow} = \text{revenue} - \text{fixed cost} - \text{variable cost}$$

Costs are variable if they depend on the rate of output. Examples are raw materials, sales commissions, and some labor and maintenance costs. Fixed costs are cash outflows that occur regardless of whether the asset is active or idle, for example, property taxes or the wages of workers under contract.

We can break down the asset's present value in the same way:

$$PV(asset) = PV(revenue) - PV(fixed cost) - PV(variable cost)$$

Or equivalently

$$PV(revenue) = PV(fixed cost) + PV(variable cost) + PV(asset)$$

Those who *receive* the fixed costs are like debtholders in the project; they simply get a fixed payment. Those who receive the net cash flows from the asset are like holders of common stock; they get whatever is left after payment of the fixed costs.

We can now figure out how the asset's beta is related to the betas of the values of revenue and costs. The beta of PV(revenue) is a weighted average of the betas of its component parts:

$$\beta_{revenue} = \beta_{fixed\ cost} \frac{PV(fixed\ cost)}{PV(revenue)}$$

$$+ \beta_{variable\ cost} \frac{PV(variable\ cost)}{PV(revenue)} + \beta_{assets} \frac{PV(asset)}{PV(revenue)}$$

The fixed-cost beta should be close to zero; whoever receives the fixed costs receives a fixed stream of cash flows. The betas of the revenues and variable costs should be approximately the same, because they respond to the same underlying variable, the rate of output. Therefore we can substitute $\beta_{revenue}$ for $\beta_{variable\ cost}$ and solve for the asset beta. Remember, we are assuming $\beta_{fixed\ cost} = 0$. Also, PV(revenue) − PV(variable cost) = PV(asset) + PV(fixed cost).[15]

$$\beta_{assets} = \beta_{revenue} \frac{PV(revenue) - PV(variable\ cost)}{PV(asset)}$$

$$= \beta_{revenue} \left[1 + \frac{PV(fixed\ cost)}{PV(asset)}\right]$$

Thus, given the cyclicality of revenues (reflected in $\beta_{revenue}$), the asset beta is proportional to the ratio of the present value of fixed costs to the present value of the project.

Now you have a rule of thumb for judging the relative risks of alternative designs or technologies for producing the same project. Other things being equal, the alternative with the higher ratio of fixed costs to project value will have the higher project beta. Empirical tests confirm that companies with high operating leverage actually do have high betas.[16]

We have interpreted fixed costs as costs of production, but fixed costs can show up in other forms, for example, as future investment outlays. Suppose that an electric utility commits to build a large electricity-generating plant. The plant will take several years to build, and the costs are fixed obligations. Our operating leverage formula still applies, but with PV(future

---

[15]In Chapter 10, we describe an accounting measure of the degree of operating leverage (DOL), defined as DOL = 1 + fixed costs/profits. DOL measures the percentage change in profits for a 1% change in revenue. We have derived here a version of DOL expressed in PVs and betas.

[16]See B. Lev, "On the Association between Operating Leverage and Risk," *Journal of Financial and Quantitative Analysis* 9 (September 1974), pp. 627–642; and G. N. Mandelker and S. G. Rhee, "The Impact of the Degrees of Operating and Financial Leverage on Systematic Risk of Common Stock," *Journal of Financial and Quantitative Analysis* 19 (March 1984), pp. 45–57.

investment) included in PV(fixed costs). The commitment to invest therefore increases the plant's asset beta. Of course PV(future investment) decreases as the plant is constructed and disappears when the plant is up and running. Therefore the plant's asset beta is only temporarily high during construction.

Other Sources of Risk   So far we have focused on cash flows. Cash-flow risk is not the only risk. A project's value is equal to the expected cash flows discounted at the risk-adjusted discount rate r. If either the risk-free rate or the market risk premium changes, then r will change and so will the project value. A project with very long-term cash flows is more exposed to such shifts in the discount rate than one with short-term cash flows. This project will, therefore, have a high beta even though it may not have high operating leverage or cyclicality.[17]

You cannot hope to estimate the relative risk of assets with any precision, but good managers examine each project from a variety of angles and look for clues as to its riskiness. They know that high market risk is a characteristic of cyclical ventures, of projects with high fixed costs and of projects that are sensitive to marketwide changes in the discount rate. They think about the major uncertainties affecting the economy and consider how their projects are affected by these uncertainties.

Don't Be Fooled by Diversifiable Risk

In this chapter, we have defined risk as the asset beta for a firm, industry, or project. But in everyday usage, "risk" simply means "bad outcome." People think of the risks of a project as a list of things that can go wrong. For example,

- A geologist looking for oil worries about the risk of a dry hole.
- A pharmaceutical-company scientist worries about the risk that a new drug will have unacceptable side effects.
- A plant manager worries that new technology for a production line will fail to work, requiring expensive changes and repairs.
- A telecom CFO worries about the risk that a communications satellite will be damaged by space debris. (This was the fate of an Iridium satellite in 2009, when it collided with Russia's defunct Cosmos 2251. Both were blown to smithereens.)

Notice that these risks are all diversifiable. For example, the Iridium-Cosmos collision was definitely a zero-beta event. These hazards do not affect asset betas and should not affect the discount rate for the projects.

Sometimes, financial managers increase discount rates in an attempt to offset these risks. This makes no sense. Diversifiable risks do not increase the cost of capital.

EXAMPLE 9.1 • Allowing for Possible Bad Outcomes

Project Z will produce just one cash flow, forecasted at $1 million at year 1. It is regarded as average risk, suitable for discounting at a 10% company cost of capital:

$$\text{PV} = \frac{C_1}{1 + r} = \frac{1,000,000}{1.1} = \$909,100$$

---

[17]See J. Y. Campbell and J. Mei, "Where Do Betas Come From? Asset Price Dynamics and the Sources of Systematic Risk," *Review of Financial Studies* 6 (Fall 1993), pp. 567–592. Cornell discusses the effect of duration on project risk in B. Cornell, "Risk, Duration and Capital Budgeting: New Evidence on Some Old Questions," *Journal of Business* 72 (April 1999), pp. 183–200.

But now you discover that the company's engineers are behind schedule in developing the technology required for the project. They are confident it will work, but they admit to a small chance that it will not. You still see the *most likely* outcome as $1 million, but you also see some chance that project Z will generate *zero* cash flow next year.

Now the project's prospects are clouded by your new worry about technology. It must be worth less than the $909,100 you calculated before that worry arose. But how much less? There is *some* discount rate (10% plus a fudge factor) that will give the right value, but we do not know what that adjusted discount rate is.

We suggest you reconsider your original $1 million forecast for project Z's cash flow. Project cash flows are supposed to be *unbiased* forecasts that give due weight to all possible outcomes, favorable and unfavorable. Managers making unbiased forecasts are correct on average. Sometimes, their forecasts will turn out high, other times low, but their errors will average out over many projects.

If you forecast a cash flow of $1 million for projects like Z, you will overestimate the average cash flow, because every now and then you will hit a zero. Those zeros should be "averaged in" to your forecasts.

For many projects, the most likely cash flow is also the unbiased forecast. If there are three possible outcomes with the probabilities shown below, the unbiased forecast is $1 million. (The unbiased forecast is the sum of the probability-weighted cash flows.)

Possible Cash Flow	Probability	Probability-Weighted Cash Flow	Unbiased Forecast
1.2	0.25	0.3	
1.0	0.50	0.5	1.0, or $1 million
0.8	0.25	0.2	

This might describe the initial prospects of project Z. But if technological uncertainty introduces a 10% chance of a zero cash flow, the unbiased forecast could drop to $900,000:

Possible Cash Flow	Probability	Probability-Weighted Cash Flow	Unbiased Forecast
1.2	0.225	0.27	
1.0	0.45	0.45	0.90, or $900,000
0.8	0.225	0.18	
0	0.10	0.0	

The present value is

$$PV = \frac{.90}{1.1} = .818, \text{ or } \$818,000$$

Managers often work out a range of possible outcomes for major projects, sometimes with explicit probabilities attached. We give more elaborate examples and further discussion in Chapter 10. But even when outcomes and probabilities are not explicitly written down, the manager can still consider the good and bad outcomes as well as the most likely one. When the bad outcomes outweigh the good, the cash-flow forecast should be reduced until balance is regained.

Step 1, then, is to do your best to make unbiased forecasts of a project's cash flows. Unbiased forecasts incorporate all possible outcomes, including those that are specific to your project and those that stem from economywide events. Step 2 is to consider whether *diversified* investors would regard the project as more or less risky than the average project. In this step only market risks are relevant.

Avoid Fudge Factors in Discount Rates

Think back to our example of project Z, where we reduced forecasted cash flows from $1 million to $900,000 to account for a possible failure of technology. The project's PV was reduced from $909,100 to $818,000. You could have gotten the right answer by adding a fudge factor to the discount rate and discounting the original forecast of $1 million. But you have to think through the possible cash flows to get the fudge factor, and once you forecast the cash flows correctly, you don't need the fudge factor.

Fudge factors in discount rates are dangerous because they displace clear thinking about future cash flows. Here is an example.

EXAMPLE 9.2 • Correcting for Optimistic Forecasts

The chief financial officer (CFO) of EZ^2 Corp. is disturbed to find that cash-flow forecasts for its investment projects are almost always optimistic. On average they are 10% too high. He therefore decides to compensate by adding 10% to EZ^2's WACC, increasing it from 12% to 22%.[18]

Suppose the CFO is right about the 10% upward bias in cash-flow forecasts. Can he just add 10% to the discount rate?

Project ZZ has level forecasted cash flows of $1,000 per year lasting for 15 years. The first two lines of Table 9.2 show these forecasts and their PVs discounted at 12%. Lines 3 and 4 show the corrected forecasts, each reduced by 10%, and the corrected PVs, which are (no surprise) also reduced by 10% (line 5). Line 6 shows the PVs when the uncorrected forecasts are discounted at 22%. The final line 7 shows the percentage reduction in PVs at the 22% discount rate, compared to the unadjusted PVs in line 2.

Year	1	2	3	4	5	...	10	...	15
1. Original cash-flow forecast	$1,000.00	$1,000.00	$1,000.00	$1,000.00	$1,000.00	...	$1,000.00	...	$1,000.00
2. PV at 12%	$ 892.90	$ 797.20	$ 711.80	$ 635.50	$ 567.40	...	$ 322.00	...	$ 182.70
3. Corrected cash-flow forecast	$ 900.00	$ 900.00	$ 900.00	$ 900.00	$ 900.00	...	$ 900.00	...	$ 900.00
4. PV at 12%	$ 803.60	$ 717.50	$ 640.60	$ 572.00	$ 510.70	...	$ 289.80	...	$ 164.40
5. PV correction	−10.0%	−10.0%	−10.0%	− 10.0%	− 10.0%	...	− 10.0%	...	− 10.0%
6. Original forecast discounted at 22%	$ 819.70	$ 671.90	$ 550.70	$ 451.40	$ 370.00	...	$ 136.90	...	$ 50.70
7. PV "correction" at 22% discount rate	−8.2%	−15.7%	− 22.6%	− 29.0%	− 34.8%	...	− 57.5%	...	− 72.3%

❯TABLE 9.2   The original cash-flow forecasts for the ZZ project (line 1) are too optimistic. The forecasts and PVs should be reduced by 10% (lines 3 and 4). But adding a 10% fudge factor to the discount rate reduces PVs by far more than 10% (line 6). The fudge factor overcorrects for bias and would penalize long-lived projects.

---

[18]The CFO is ignoring Brealey, Myers, and Allen's Second Law, which we cover in Chapter 12.

Line 5 shows the correct adjustment for optimism (10%). Line 7 shows what happens when a 10% fudge factor is added to the discount rate. The effect on the first year's cash flow is a PV "haircut" of about 8%, 2% less than the CFO expected. But later present values are knocked down by much more than 10%, because the fudge factor is compounded in the 22% discount rate. By years 10 and 15, the PV haircuts are 57% and 72%, far more than the 10% bias that the CFO started with.

Did the CFO really think that bias accumulated as shown in line 7 of Table 9.2? We doubt that he ever asked that question. If he was right in the first place, and the true bias is 10%, then adding a 10% fudge factor to the discount rate understates PV dramatically. The fudge factor also makes long-lived projects look much worse than quick-payback projects.[19]

Discount Rates for International Projects

In this chapter we have concentrated on investments in the United States. In Chapter 27, we say more about investments made internationally. Here, we simply warn against adding fudge factors to discount rates for projects in developing economies. Such fudge factors are too often seen in practice.

It's true that markets are more volatile in developing economies, but much of that risk is diversifiable for investors in the United States., Europe, and other developed countries. It's also true that more things can go wrong for projects in developing economies, particularly in countries that are unstable politically. Expropriations happen. Sometimes governments default on their obligations to international investors. Thus it's especially important to think through the downside risks and to give them weight in cash-flow forecasts.

Some international projects are at least partially protected from these downsides. For example, an opportunistic government would gain little or nothing by expropriating the local IBM affiliate, because the affiliate would have little value without the IBM brand name, products, and customer relationships. A privately owned toll road would be a more tempting target, because the toll road would be relatively easy for the local government to maintain and operate.

9-4   Certainty Equivalents—Another Way to Adjust for Risk

BEYOND THE PAGE

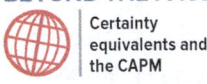

Certainty equivalents and the CAPM

mhhe.com/brealey13e

In practical capital budgeting, a single risk-adjusted rate is used to discount all future cash flows. This assumes that project risk does not change over time, but remains constant year-in and year-out. We know that this cannot be strictly true, for the risks that companies are exposed to are constantly shifting. We are venturing here onto somewhat difficult ground, but there is a way to think about risk that can suggest a route through. It involves converting the expected cash flows to **certainty equivalents.** First we work through an example showing what certainty equivalents are. Then, as a reward for your investment, we use certainty equivalents to uncover what you are really assuming when you discount a series of future cash flows at a single risk-adjusted discount rate. We also value a project where risk changes over time and ordinary discounting fails. Your investment will be rewarded still more when we cover options in Chapters 20 and 21 and forward and futures pricing in Chapter 26. Option-pricing formulas discount certainty equivalents. Forward and futures prices *are* certainty equivalents.

---

[19]The optimistic bias could be worse for distant than near cash flows. If so, the CFO should make the time-pattern of bias explicit and adjust the cash-flow forecasts accordingly.

Valuation by Certainty Equivalents

Think back to the simple real estate investment that we used in Chapter 2 to introduce the concept of present value. You are considering construction of an office building that you plan to sell after one year for $800,000. That cash flow is uncertain with the same risk as the market, so $\beta = 1$. The risk-free interest rate is $r_f = 7\%$, but you discount the $800,000 payoff at a risk-adjusted rate of $r = 12\%$. This gives a present value of $800,000/1.12 = \$714,286$.

Suppose a real estate company now approaches and offers to fix the price at which it will buy the building from you at the end of the year. This guarantee would remove any uncertainty about the payoff on your investment. So you would accept a lower figure than the uncertain payoff of $800,000. But how much less? If the building has a present value of $714,286 and the interest rate is 7%, then

$$PV = \frac{\text{certain cash flow}}{1.07} = \$714,286$$

$$\text{Certain cash flow} = \$764,286,$$

In other words, a certain cash flow of $764,286 has exactly the same present value as an expected but uncertain cash flow of $800,000. The cash flow of $764,286 is therefore known as the *certainty-equivalent cash flow.* To compensate for both the delayed payoff and the uncertainty in real estate prices, you need a return of $800,000 - 714,286 = \$85,714$. One part of this difference compensates for the time value of money. The other part ($800,000 - 764,286 = \$35,714$) is a markdown or haircut to compensate for the risk attached to the forecasted cash flow of $800,000.

Our example illustrates two ways to value a risky cash flow:

Method 1: Discount the risky cash flow at a *risk-adjusted discount rate r* that is greater than r_f.[20] The risk-adjusted discount rate adjusts for both time and risk. This is illustrated by the clockwise route in Figure 9.3.

Method 2: Find the certainty-equivalent cash flow and discount at the risk-free interest rate r_f. When you use this method, you need to ask, What is the smallest *certain* payoff for which I would exchange the risky cash flow? This is called the *certainty equivalent,* denoted by CEQ. Since CEQ is the value equivalent of a safe cash flow, it is discounted at the risk-free rate. The certainty-equivalent method makes *separate* adjustments for risk and time. This is illustrated by the counterclockwise route in Figure 9.3.

We now have two identical expressions for the PV of a cash flow in period 1:[21]

$$PV = \frac{C_1}{1+r} = \frac{CEQ_1}{1+r_f}$$

For cash flows two, three, or t years away,

$$PV = \frac{C_t}{(1+r)^t} = \frac{CEQ_t}{(1+r_f)^t}$$

---

[20]The discount rate r can be less than r_f for assets with negative betas. But actual betas are almost always positive.

[21]CEQ_1 can be calculated directly from the capital asset pricing model. The certainty-equivalent form of the CAPM states that the certainty-equivalent value of the cash flow C_1 is $C_1 - \lambda \, \text{cov}(\tilde{C}_1, \tilde{r}_m)$. $\text{Cov}(\tilde{C}_1, \tilde{r}_m)$ is the covariance between the uncertain cash flow, and the return on the market, $\tilde{r}_m$. Lambda, λ, is a measure of the market price of risk. It is defined as $(r_m - r_f)/\sigma_m^2$. For example, if $r_m - r_f = .08$ and the standard deviation of market returns is $\sigma_m = .20$, then lambda $= .08/.20^2 = 2$.

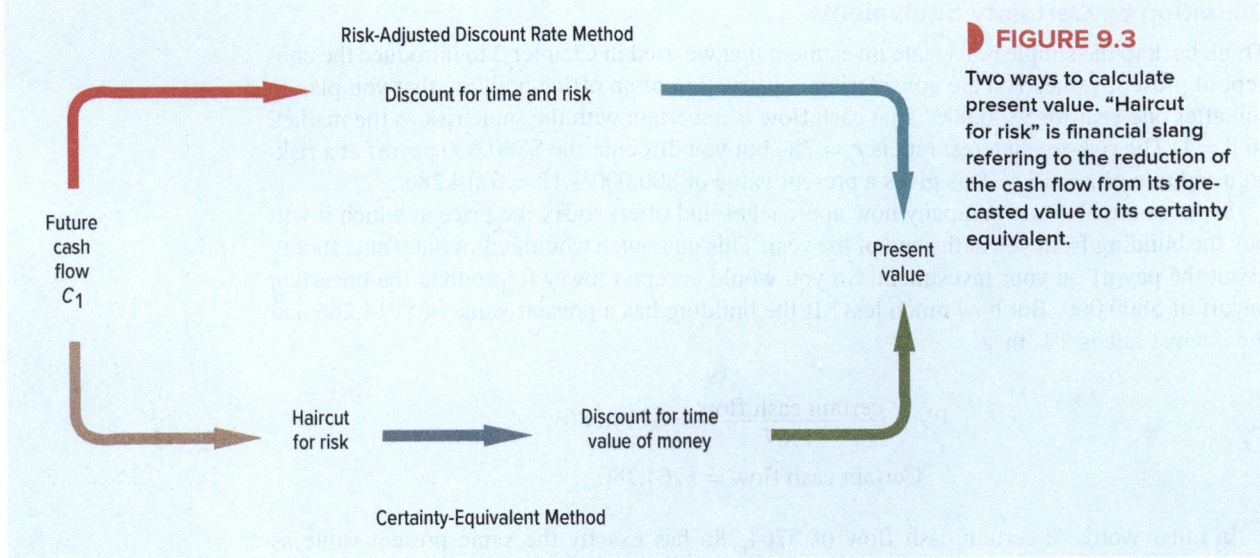

Risk-Adjusted Discount Rate Method

Discount for time and risk

Future
cash
flow
C_1

Haircut
for risk

Discount for time
value of money

Present
value

Certainty-Equivalent Method

FIGURE 9.3

Two ways to calculate present value. "Haircut for risk" is financial slang referring to the reduction of the cash flow from its fore-casted value to its certainty equivalent.

When to Use a Single Risk-Adjusted Discount Rate for Long-Lived Assets

We are now in a position to examine what is implied when a constant risk-adjusted discount rate is used to calculate a present value.

Consider two simple projects. Project A is expected to produce a cash flow of $100 million for each of three years. The risk-free interest rate is 6%, the market risk premium is 8%, and project A's beta is .75. You therefore calculate A's opportunity cost of capital as follows:

$$r = r_f + \beta(r_m - r_f)$$

$$= 6 + .75(8) = 12\%$$

Discounting at 12% gives the following present value for each cash flow:

Project A		
Year	Cash Flow	PV at 12%
1	100	89.3
2	100	79.7
3	100	71.2
		Total PV 240.2

Now compare these figures with the cash flows of project B. Notice that B's cash flows are lower than A's; B's flows are safe, however, and therefore they are discounted at the risk-free interest rate. The *present value* of each year's cash flow is identical for the two projects.

Project B		
Year	Cash Flow	PV at 6%
1	94.6	89.3
2	89.6	79.7
3	84.8	71.2
		Total PV 240.2

In year 1 project A has a risky cash flow of 100. This has the same PV as the safe cash flow of 94.6 from project B. Therefore, 94.6 is the certainty equivalent of 100. Since the two cash flows have the same PV, investors must be willing to give up $100 - 94.6 = 5.4$ in expected year-1 income in order to get rid of the uncertainty.

In year 2, project A has a risky cash flow of 100, and B has a safe cash flow of 89.6. Again both flows have the same PV. Thus, to eliminate the uncertainty in year 2, investors are prepared to give up $100 - 89.6 = 10.4$ of future income. To eliminate uncertainty in year 3, they are willing to give up $100 - 84.8 = 15.2$ of future income.

To value project A, you discounted each cash flow at the same risk-adjusted discount rate of 12%. Now you can see what is implied when you did that. By using a constant rate, you effectively made a larger deduction for risk from the later cash flows:

Year	Forecasted Cash Flow for Project A	Certainty-Equivalent Cash Flow	Deduction for Risk
1	100	94.6	5.4
2	100	89.6	10.4
3	100	84.8	15.2

The second cash flow is riskier than the first because it is exposed to two years of market risk. The third cash flow is riskier still because it is exposed to three years of market risk. This increased risk is reflected in the certainty equivalents that decline by a constant proportion each period.[22]

Therefore, use of a constant risk-adjusted discount rate for a stream of cash flows assumes that risk accumulates at a constant rate as you look farther out into the future. That will be the case if the project's beta remains constant.

A Common Mistake

You sometimes hear people say that because distant cash flows are riskier, they should be discounted at a higher rate than earlier cash flows. That is quite wrong: We have just seen that using the same risk-adjusted discount rate for each year's cash flow implies a larger deduction for risk from the later cash flows. The reason is that the discount rate compensates for the risk borne *per period*. The more distant the cash flows, the greater the number of periods and the larger the *total* risk adjustment.

When You Cannot Use a Single Risk-Adjusted Discount Rate for Long-Lived Assets

Sometimes you will encounter problems where the use of a single risk-adjusted discount rate will get you into trouble. For example, later in the book, we look at how options are valued. Because an option's risk is continually changing, the certainty-equivalent method needs to be used.

Here is a disguised, simplified, and somewhat exaggerated version of an actual project proposal that one of the authors was asked to analyze. The scientists at Vegetron have come up with an electric mop, and the firm is ready to go ahead with pilot production and test marketing. The preliminary phase will take one year and cost $125,000. Management feels that there is only a 50% chance that pilot production and market tests will be successful. If they are, then Vegetron will build a $1 million plant that would generate an expected annual cash

---

[22]Notice how the ratio of the certainty equivalent cash flow (CEQ_t) to the actual cash flow (C_t) declines smoothly. $CEQ_1 = .946 \times C_1$. $CEQ_2 = .946^2 \times C_2 = .896 \times C_2$. And $CEQ_3 = .946^3 \times C_3 = .848 \times C_3$.

flow in perpetuity of $250,000 a year after taxes. If they are not successful, the project will have to be dropped.

The expected cash flows (in thousands of dollars) are

$$C_0 = -125$$
$$C_1 = 50\% \text{ chance of } -1{,}000 \text{ and } 50\% \text{ chance of } 0$$
$$= .5(-1{,}000) + .5(0) = -500$$
$$C_t \text{ for } t = 2, 3, \ldots = 50\% \text{ chance of } 250 \text{ and } 50\% \text{ chance of } 0$$
$$= .5(250) + .5(0) = 125$$

Management has little experience with consumer products and considers this a project of extremely high risk.[23] Therefore management discounts the cash flows at 25%, rather than at Vegetron's normal 10% standard:

$$\text{NPV} = -125 - \frac{500}{1.25} + \sum_{t=2}^{\infty} \frac{125}{(1.25)^t} = -125, \text{ or } -\$125{,}000$$

This seems to show that the project is not worthwhile.

Management's analysis is open to criticism if the first year's experiment resolves a high proportion of the risk. If the test phase is a failure, then there is no risk at all—the project is *certain* to be worthless. If it is a success, there could well be only normal risk from then on. That means there is a 50% chance that in one year Vegetron will have the opportunity to invest in a project of *normal* risk, for which the *normal* discount rate of 10% would be appropriate. Thus the firm has a 50% chance to invest $1 million in a project with a net present value of $1.5 million:

Pilot production and market tests
$$\text{Success} \rightarrow \text{NPV} = -1{,}000 + \frac{250}{.10} = +1{,}500(50\% \text{ Chance})$$
$$\text{Failure} \rightarrow \text{NPV} = 0(50\% \text{ Chance})$$

Thus we could view the project as offering an expected payoff of $.5(1{,}500) + .5(0) = 750$, or $750,000, at $t = 1$ on a $125,000 investment at $t = 0$. Of course, the certainty equivalent of the payoff is less than $750,000, but the difference would have to be very large to justify rejecting the project. For example, if the certainty equivalent is half the forecasted cash flow (an extremely large cash flow haircut) and the risk-free rate is 7%, the project is worth $225,500:

$$\text{NPV} = C_0 + \frac{\text{CEQ}_1}{1 + r}$$
$$= -125 + \frac{.5(750)}{1.07} = 225.5, \text{ or } \$225{,}500$$

This is not bad for a $125,000 investment—and quite a change from the negative-NPV that management got by discounting all future cash flows at 25%.

---

[23] We will assume that they mean high *market risk* and that the difference between 25% and 10% is *not* a fudge factor introduced to offset optimistic cash-flow forecasts.

Estimating Stock and Market Risk

❯Spreadsheets such as Excel have some built-in statistical functions that are useful for calculating risk measures. You can find these functions by clicking *fx* on the Excel toolbar. If you then click on the function that you wish to use, Excel will ask you for the inputs that it needs. At the bottom left of the function box, there is a Help facility with an example of how the function is used.

Here is a list of useful functions for estimating stock and market risk. You can enter the inputs for all these functions as numbers or as the addresses of cells that contain the numbers. Note that different versions of Excel may use slightly different names for these functions.

1. **VAR.P** and **STDEV.P**: Calculate variance and standard deviation of a series of numbers, as shown in Section 7-2.

2. **VAR.S** and **STDEV.S**: Footnote 15 of Chapter 7 noted that when variance is estimated from a sample of observations (the usual case), a correction should be made for the loss of a degree of freedom. VAR.S and STDEV.S provide the corrected measures. For any large sample VAR.S and VAR.P will be similar.

3. **SLOPE**: Useful for calculating the beta of a stock or portfolio.

4. **CORREL**: Useful for calculating the correlation between the returns on any two investments.

5. **COVARIANCE.P** and **COVARIANCE.S**: Portfolio risk depends on the covariance between the returns on each pair of stocks. These functions calculate the covariance.

6. **RSQ**: R-squared is the square of the correlation coefficient and is useful for measuring the proportion of the variance of a stock's returns that can be explained by the market.

7. **AVERAGE**: Calculates the average of any series of numbers.

If, say, you need to know the standard error of your estimate of beta, you can obtain more detailed statistics by going to the *Tools* menu and clicking on *Data Analysis* and then on *Regression*.

Spreadsheet Questions

The following questions provide opportunities to practice each of the Excel functions.

1. (VAR.P and STDEV.P) Choose two well-known stocks and download the latest 61 months of adjusted prices from **finance.yahoo.com.** Calculate the monthly returns for each stock. Now find the variance and standard deviation of the returns for each stock by using VAR.P and STDEV.P. Annualize the variance by multiplying by 12 and the standard deviation by multiplying by the square root of 12.

2. (AVERAGE, VAR.P and STDEV.P) Now calculate the annualized variance and standard deviation for a portfolio that each month has equal holdings in the two stocks. Is the result more or less than the average of the standard deviations of the two stocks? Why?

3. (SLOPE) Download the Standard & Poor's index for the same period (its symbol is ^GSPC). Find the beta of each stock and of the portfolio. (*Note:* You need to enter the stock returns as the Y-values and market returns as the X-values.) Is the beta of the portfolio more or less than the average of the betas of the two stocks?

4. (CORREL) Calculate the correlation between the returns on the two stocks. Use this measure and your earlier estimates of each stock's variance to calculate the variance of a portfolio that is evenly divided between the two stocks. (You may need to reread Section 7-3 to refresh your memory of how

Source: Microsoft Excel

to do this.) Check that you get the same answer as when you calculated the portfolio variance directly.

5. (COVARIANCE.P) Repeat question 4, but now calculate the covariance directly rather than from the correlations and variances.

6. (RSQ) For each of the two stocks calculate the proportion of the variance explained by the market index. Do the results square with your intuition?

7. Use the *Regression* facility under the *Data Analysis* menu to calculate the beta of each stock and of the portfolio (beta here is called the coefficient of the X-variable). Look at the standard error of the estimate in the cell to the right. How confident can you be of your estimates of the betas of each stock? How about your estimate of the portfolio beta?

SUMMARY

In Chapter 8, we set out the basic principles for valuing risky assets. This chapter shows you how to apply those principles when valuing capital investment projects.

Suppose the project has the same market risk as the company's existing assets. In this case, the project cash flows can be discounted at the *company cost of capital*. The company cost of capital is the rate of return that investors require on a portfolio of all of the company's outstanding debt and equity. It is usually calculated as an after-tax *weighted-average cost of capital* (after-tax WACC)— that is, as the weighted average of the after-tax cost of debt and the cost of equity. The weights are the relative market values of debt and equity. The cost of debt is calculated after tax because interest is a tax-deductible expense.

The hardest part of calculating the after-tax WACC is estimation of the cost of equity. Most large, public corporations use the capital asset pricing model (CAPM) to do this. They generally estimate the firm's equity beta from past rates of return for the firm's common stock and for the market, and they check their estimate against the average beta of similar firms.

The after-tax WACC is the correct discount rate for projects that have the same market risk as the company's existing business. Many firms, however, use the after-tax WACC as the discount rate for all projects. This is a dangerous procedure. If the procedure is followed strictly, the firm will accept too many high-risk projects and reject too many low-risk projects. It is *project* risk that counts: The true cost of capital depends on the use to which the capital is put.

Managers, therefore, need to understand why a particular project may have above- or below-average risk. You can often identify the characteristics of a high- or low-beta project even when the beta cannot be estimated directly. For example, you can figure out how much the project's cash flows are affected by the performance of the entire economy. Cyclical projects are generally high-beta projects. You can also look at operating leverage. Fixed production costs increase beta.

Don't be fooled by diversifiable risk. Diversifiable risks do not affect asset betas or the cost of capital, but the possibility of bad outcomes should be incorporated in the cash-flow forecasts. Also be careful not to offset worries about a project's future performance by adding a fudge factor to the discount rate. Fudge factors don't work, and they may seriously undervalue long-lived projects.

There is one more fence to jump. Most projects produce cash flows for several years. Firms generally use the same risk-adjusted rate to discount each of these cash flows. When they do this, they are implicitly assuming that cumulative risk increases at a constant rate as you look further into the future. That assumption is usually reasonable. It is precisely true when the project's future beta will be constant, that is, when risk *per period* is constant.

But exceptions sometimes prove the rule. Be on the alert for projects where risk clearly does not increase steadily. In these cases, you should break the project into segments within which the same discount rate can be reasonably used. Or you should use the certainty-equivalent version of the DCF model, which allows separate risk adjustments to each period's cash flow.

The nearby box provides useful spreadsheet functions for estimating stock and market risk.

● ● ● ● ●

For a useful survey of the issues covered in this chapter, see:

R. Jagannathan, J. Liberti, B. Liu, and I. Meier, "A Firm's Cost of Capital," *Annual Review of Financial Economics* 9 (November 2017), pp. 259–282.

Levi and Welch provide some recommendations for estimating betas in:

Y. Levi and I. Welch, "Best Practice for Cost-of-Capital Estimates," *Journal of Financial and Quantitative Analysis* 52 (April 2017), pp. 427–463.

● ● ● ● ●

 **CONNECT** Select problems are available in McGraw-Hill's *Connect.* Please see the preface for more information.

1. **Definitions** Define the following terms:

   a. Cost of debt.

   b. Cost of equity.

   c. After-tax WACC.

   d. Equity beta.

   e. Asset beta.

   f. Pure-play comparable.

   g. Certainty equivalent.

2. **True/false*** True or false?

   a. The company cost of capital is the correct discount rate for all projects because the high risks of some projects are offset by the low risk of other projects.

   b. Distant cash flows are riskier than near-term cash flows. Therefore, long-term projects require higher risk-adjusted discount rates.

   c. Adding fudge factors to discount rates undervalues long-lived projects compared with quick-payoff projects.

3. **Company cost of capital** Quark Productions ("Give your loved one a quark today.") uses its company cost of capital to evaluate all projects. Will it underestimate or overestimate the value of high-risk projects?

4. **Company cost of capital** The total market value of the common stock of the Okefenokee Real Estate Company is $6 million, and the total value of its debt is $4 million. The treasurer estimates that the beta of the stock is currently 1.5 and that the expected risk premium on the market is 6%. The Treasury bill rate is 4%. Assume for simplicity that Okefenokee debt is risk-free and the company does not pay tax.

   a. What is the required return on Okefenokee stock?

   b. Estimate the company cost of capital.

   c. What is the discount rate for an expansion of the company's present business?

   d. Suppose the company wants to diversify into the manufacture of rose-colored spectacles. The beta of unleveraged optical manufacturers is 1.2. Estimate the required return on Okefenokee's new venture.

5. **Company cost of capital** You are given the following information for Golden Fleece Financial:

Long-term debt outstanding:	$300,000
Current yield to maturity (r_{dept}):	8%
Number of shares of common stock:	10,000
Price per share:	$50
Book value per share:	$25
Expected rate of return on stock (r_{equity}):	15%

Calculate Golden Fleece's company cost of capital. Ignore taxes.

6. **Company cost of capital** Nero Violins has the following capital structure:

Security	Beta	Total Market Value ($ millions)
Debt	0	$100
Preferred stock	0.20	40
Common stock	1.20	299

a. What is the firm's asset beta? (*Hint:* What is the beta of a portfolio of all the firm's securities?)

b. Assume that the CAPM is correct. What discount rate should Nero set for investments that expand the scale of its operations without changing its asset beta? Assume a risk-free interest rate of 5% and a market risk premium of 6%. Ignore taxes.

7. **WACC*** A company is 40% financed by risk-free debt. The interest rate is 10%, the expected market risk premium is 8%, and the beta of the company's common stock is .5. What is the after-tax WACC, assuming that the company pays tax at a 20% rate?

8. **WACC** Binomial Tree Farm's financing includes $5 million of bank loans. Its common equity is shown in Binomial's Annual Report at $6.67 million. It has 500,000 shares of common stock outstanding, which trade on the Wichita Stock Exchange at $18 per share. What debt ratio should Binomial use to calculate its WACC or asset beta? Explain.

9. **Measuring risk** Refer to the top-right panel of Figure 9.2. What proportion of U.S. Steel's returns was explained by market movements? What proportion of risk was diversifiable? How does the diversifiable risk show up in the plot? What is the range of possible errors in the estimated beta?

10. **Measuring risk** Figure 9.4 shows plots of monthly rates of return on three stocks versus those of the market index. The beta and standard deviation of each stock is given beside the plot.

a. Which stock is safest for a diversified investor?

b. Which stock is safest for an undiversified investor who puts all her money in one of these stocks?

c. Consider a portfolio with equal investments in each stock. What would be this portfolio's beta?

d. Consider a well-diversified portfolio composed of stocks with the same beta and standard deviation as Ford. What are the beta and standard deviation of this portfolio's return? The standard deviation of the market portfolio's return is 20%.

e. Use the capital asset pricing model to estimate the expected return on each stock. The risk-free rate is 4%, and the market risk premium is 8%.

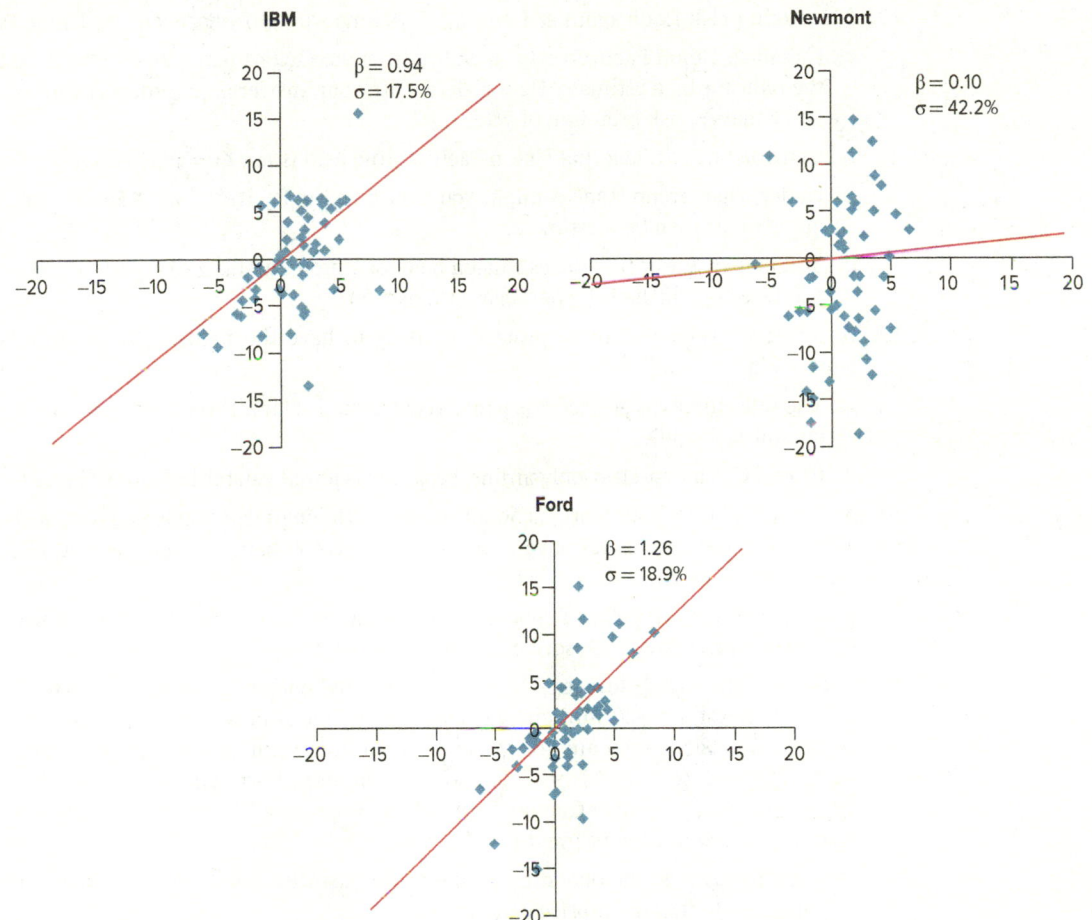

11. **Measuring risk*** The following table shows estimates of the risk of two well-known Canadian stocks:

	Standard Deviation (%)	R^2	Beta	Standard Error of Beta
Sun Life Financial	18.7	0.12	0.86	0.30
Loblaw	19.5	0.06	0.63	0.33

a. What proportion of each stock's risk was market risk, and what proportion was specific risk?

b. What is the variance of the returns for Sun Life Financial stock? What is the specific variance?

c. What is the confidence interval on Loblaw's beta? (See page 234 for a definition of "confidence interval.")

d. If the CAPM is correct, what is the expected return on Sun Life? Assume a risk-free interest rate of 5% and an expected market return of 12%.

e. Suppose that next year, the market provides a 20% return. Knowing this, what return would you expect from Sun Life?

12. **Measuring risk** Look again at Table 9.1. This time we will concentrate on Union Pacific.

    a. Calculate Union Pacific's cost of equity from the CAPM using its own beta estimate and the industry beta estimate. How different are your answers? Assume a risk-free rate of 2% and a market risk premium of 7%.

    b. Can you be confident that Union Pacific's true beta is not the industry average?

    c. Under what circumstances might you advise Union Pacific to calculate its cost of equity based on its own beta estimate?

    d. You now discover that the estimated beta for Union Pacific in the period 2008–2012 was 1.3. Does this influence your answer to part (c)?

13. **Asset betas** Which of these projects is likely to have the higher asset beta, other things equal? Why?

    a. The sales force for project A is paid a fixed annual salary. Project B's sales force is paid by commissions only.

    b. Project C is a first-class-only airline. Project D is a well-established line of breakfast cereals.

14. **Asset betas*** EZCUBE Corp. is 50% financed with long-term bonds and 50% with common equity. The debt securities have a beta of .15. The company's equity beta is 1.25. What is EZCUBE's asset beta?

15. **Asset betas** What types of firms need to estimate industry asset betas? How would such a firm make the estimate? Describe the process step by step.

16. **Betas and operating leverage** You run a perpetual encabulator machine, which generates revenues averaging $20 million per year. Raw material costs are 50% of revenues. These costs are variable—they are always proportional to revenues. There are no other operating costs. The cost of capital is 9%. Your firm's long-term borrowing rate is 6%. Now you are approached by Studebaker Capital Corp., which proposes a fixed-price contract to supply raw materials at $10 million per year for 10 years.

    a. What happens to the operating leverage and business risk of the encabulator machine if you agree to this fixed-price contract?

    b. Calculate the present value of the encabulator machine with and without the fixed-price contract.

17. **Diversifiable risk** Many investment projects are exposed to diversifiable risks. What does "diversifiable" mean in this context? How should diversifiable risks be accounted for in project valuation? Should they be ignored completely?

18. **Fudge factors** John Barleycorn estimates his firm's after-tax WACC at only 8%. Nevertheless, he sets a 15% companywide discount rate to offset the optimistic biases of project sponsors and to impose "discipline" on the capital budgeting process. Suppose Mr. Barleycorn is correct about the project sponsors, who are, in fact, optimistic by 7% on average. Explain why the increase in the discount rate from 8% to 15% will not offset the bias.

19. **Fudge factors** Mom and Pop Groceries has just dispatched a year's supply of groceries to the government of the Central Antarctic Republic. Payment of $250,000 will be made one year hence after the shipment arrives by snow train. Unfortunately, there is a good chance of a coup d'état, in which case the new government will not pay. Mom and Pop's controller therefore decides to discount the payment at 40% rather than at the company's 12% cost of capital.

    a. What's wrong with using a 40% rate to offset political risk?

    b. How much is the $250,000 payment really worth if the odds of a coup d'état are 25%?

20. **Fudge factors*** An oil company is drilling a series of new wells on the perimeter of a producing oil field. About 20% of the new wells will be dry holes. Even if a new well strikes oil, there is still uncertainty about the amount of oil produced: 40% of new wells that strike oil produce only 1,000 barrels a day; 60% produce 5,000 barrels per day.

a. Forecast the annual cash revenues from a new perimeter well. Use a future oil price of $100 per barrel.

b. A geologist proposes to discount the cash flows of the new wells at 30% to offset the risk of dry holes. The oil company's normal cost of capital is 10%. Does this proposal make sense? Briefly explain why or why not.

21. **Certainty equivalents*** A project has a forecasted cash flow of $110 in year 1 and $121 in year 2. The interest rate is 5%, the estimated risk premium on the market is 10%, and the project has a beta of .5. If you use a constant risk-adjusted discount rate, what is

a. The PV of the project?

b. The certainty-equivalent cash flow in year 1 and year 2?

c. The ratio of the certainty-equivalent cash flows to the expected cash flows in years 1 and 2?

22. **Certainty equivalents** A project has the following forecasted cash flows:

Cash Flows ($ thousands)			
C_0	C_1	C_2	C_3
−100	+40	+60	+50

The estimated project beta is 1.5. The market return r_m is 16%, and the risk-free rate r_f is 7%.

a. Estimate the opportunity cost of capital and the project's PV (using the same rate to discount each cash flow).

b. What are the certainty-equivalent cash flows in each year?

c. What is the ratio of the certainty-equivalent cash flow to the expected cash flow in each year?

d. Explain why this ratio declines.

23. **Changing risk** The McGregor Whisky Company is proposing to market diet scotch. The product will first be test-marketed for two years in southern California at an initial cost of $500,000. This test launch is not expected to produce any profits but should reveal consumer preferences. There is a 60% chance that demand will be satisfactory. In this case, McGregor will spend $5 million to launch the scotch nationwide and will receive an expected annual profit of $700,000 in perpetuity. If demand is not satisfactory, diet scotch will be withdrawn. Once consumer preferences are known, the product will be subject to an average degree of risk, and therefore, McGregor requires a return of 12% on its investment. However, the initial test-market phase is viewed as much riskier, and McGregor demands a return of 20% on this initial expenditure. What is the NPV of the diet scotch project?

CHALLENGE

24. **Beta of costs** Suppose that you are valuing a future stream of high-risk (high-beta) cash outflows. High risk means a high discount rate. But the higher the discount rate, the less the present value. This seems to say that the higher the risk of cash outflows, the less you should worry about them! Can that be right? Should the sign of the cash flow affect the appropriate discount rate? Explain.

25. **Fudge factors** An oil company executive is considering investing $10 million in one or both of two wells: Well 1 is expected to produce oil worth $3 million a year for 10 years; well 2 is expected to produce $2 million for 15 years. These are real (inflation-adjusted) cash flows.

The beta for producing wells is .9. The market risk premium is 8%, the nominal risk-free interest rate is 6%, and expected inflation is 4%.

The two wells are intended to develop a previously discovered oil field. Unfortunately there is still a 20% chance of a dry hole in each case. A dry hole means zero cash flows and a complete loss of the $10 million investment.

Ignore taxes and make further assumptions as necessary.

a. What is the correct real discount rate for cash flows from developed wells?

b. The oil company executive proposes to add 20 percentage points to the real discount rate to offset the risk of a dry hole. Calculate the NPV of each well with this adjusted discount rate.

c. What do you say the NPVs of the two wells are?

d. Is there any single fudge factor that could be added to the discount rate for developed wells that would yield the correct NPV for both wells? Explain.

● ● ● ● ●

FINANCE ON THE WEB

You can download data for the following questions from **finance.yahoo.com.**

1. Look at the companies listed in Table 8.2. Calculate monthly rates of return for two successive five-year periods. Calculate betas for each subperiod using the Excel SLOPE function. How stable was each company's beta? Suppose that you had used these betas to estimate expected rates of return from the CAPM. Would your estimates have changed significantly from period to period?

2. Identify a sample of food companies. For example, you could try Campbell Soup (CPB), General Mills (GIS), Kellogg (K), Mondelez International (MDLZ), and Tyson Foods (TSN).

   a. Estimate beta and R^2 for each company, using five years of monthly returns and Excel functions SLOPE and RSQ.

   b. Average the returns for each month to give the return on an equally weighted portfolio of the stocks. Then calculate the industry beta using these portfolio returns. How does the R^2 of this portfolio compare with the average R^2 of the individual stocks?

   c. Use the CAPM to calculate an average cost of equity (r_{equity}) for the food industry. Use current interest rates—take a look at the end of Section 9-2—and a reasonable estimate of the market risk premium.

MINI-CASE ● ● ● ● ●

The Jones Family Incorporated

The Scene: It is early evening in the summer of 2018, in an ordinary family room in Manhattan. Modern furniture, with old copies of *The Wall Street Journal* and the *Financial Times* scattered around. Autographed photos of Jerome Powell and George Soros are prominently displayed. A picture window reveals a distant view of lights on the Hudson River. John Jones sits at a computer terminal, glumly sipping a glass of chardonnay and putting on a carry trade in Japanese yen over the Internet. His wife Marsha enters.

Marsha: Hi, honey. Glad to be home. Lousy day on the trading floor, though. Dullsville. No volume. But I did manage to hedge next year's production from our copper mine. I couldn't get a good quote on the right package of futures contracts, so I arranged a commodity swap.

John doesn't reply.

Marsha: John, what's wrong? Have you been selling yen again? That's been a losing trade for weeks.

John: Well, yes. I shouldn't have gone to Goldman Sachs's foreign exchange brunch. But I've got to get out of the house somehow. I'm cooped up here all day calculating covariances and efficient risk-return trade-offs while you're out trading commodity futures. You get all the glamour and excitement.

Marsha: Don't worry, dear, it will be over soon. We only recalculate our most efficient common stock portfolio once a quarter. Then you can go back to leveraged leases.

John: You trade, and I do all the worrying. Now there's a rumor that our leasing company is going to get a hostile takeover bid. I knew the debt ratio was too low, and you forgot to put on the poison pill. And now you've made a negative-NPV investment!

Marsha: What investment?

John: That wildcat oil well. Another well in that old Sourdough field. It's going to cost $5 million! Is there any oil down there?

Marsha: That Sourdough field has been good to us, John. Where do you think we got the capital for your yen trades? I bet we'll find oil. Our geologists say there's only a 30% chance of a dry hole.

John: Even if we hit oil, I bet we'll only get 75 barrels of crude oil per day.

Marsha: That's 75 barrels day in, day out. There are 365 days in a year, dear.

John and Marsha's teenage son Johnny bursts into the room.

Johnny: Hi, Dad! Hi, Mom! Guess what? I've made the junior varsity derivatives team! That means I can go on the field trip to the Chicago Board Options Exchange. (*Pauses.*) What's wrong?

John: Your mother has made another negative-NPV investment. A wildcat oil well, way up on the North Slope of Alaska.

Johnny: That's OK, Dad. Mom told me about it. I was going to do an NPV calculation yesterday, but I had to finish calculating the junk-bond default probabilities for my corporate finance homework. (*Grabs a financial calculator from his backpack.*) Let's see: 75 barrels a day times 365 days per year times $100 per barrel when delivered in Los Angeles . . . that's $2.7 million per year.

John: That's $2.7 million *next* year, assuming that we find any oil at all. The production will start declining by 5% every year. And we still have to pay $20 per barrel in pipeline and tanker charges to ship the oil from the North Slope to Los Angeles. We've got some serious operating leverage here.

Marsha: On the other hand, our energy consultants project increasing oil prices. If they increase with inflation, price per barrel should increase by roughly 2.5% per year. The wells ought to be able to keep pumping for at least 15 years.

Johnny: I'll calculate NPV after I finish with the default probabilities. The interest rate is 6%. Is it OK if I work with the beta of .8 and our usual figure of 7% for the market risk premium?

Marsha: I guess so, Johnny. But I am concerned about the fixed shipping costs.

John: (*Takes a deep breath and stands up.*) Anyway, how about a nice family dinner? I've reserved our usual table at the Four Seasons.

Everyone exits.

Announcer: Is the wildcat well really negative-NPV? Will John and Marsha have to fight a hostile takeover? Will Johnny's derivatives team use Black–Scholes or the binomial method? Find out in the next episode of The Jones Family Incorporated.

You may not aspire to the Jones family's way of life, but you will learn about all their activities, from futures contracts to binomial option pricing, later in this book. Meanwhile, you may wish to replicate Johnny's NPV analysis.

QUESTIONS

1. Calculate the NPV of the wildcat oil well, taking account of the probability of a dry hole, the shipping costs, the decline in production, and the forecasted increase in oil prices. How long does production have to continue for the well to be a positive-NPV investment? Ignore taxes and other possible complications.

2. Now consider operating leverage. How should the shipping costs be valued, assuming that output is known and the costs are fixed? How would your answer change if the shipping costs were proportional to output? Assume that unexpected fluctuations in output are zero-beta and diversifiable. (*Hint:* The Jones's oil company has an excellent credit rating. Its long-term borrowing rate is only 7%.)

CHAPTER

10

Project Analysis

Having read our earlier chapters on capital budgeting, you may have concluded that the choice of which projects to accept or reject is a simple one. You just need to draw up a set of cash-flow forecasts, choose the right discount rate, and crank out net present value. But finding projects that create value for the shareholders can never be reduced to a mechanical exercise. We therefore devote the next three chapters to ways in which companies can stack the odds in their favor when making investment decisions.

When managers are presented with investment proposals, they do not accept the cash flow forecasts at face value. Instead, they try to understand what makes a project tick and what could go wrong with it. Remember Murphy's law, "if anything can go wrong, it will," and O'Reilly's corollary, "at the worst possible time."

Once you know what makes a project tick, you may be able to reconfigure it to improve its chances of success. And if you understand why a venture may fail, you can decide whether it is worth trying to rule out the possible causes of failure. Maybe further expenditure on market research would clear up those doubts about acceptance by consumers, maybe another drill hole would give you a better idea of the size of the ore body, and maybe some further work on the test bed would confirm the durability of those welds.

If the project really has a negative NPV, the sooner you can identify it, the better. And even if you decide that it is worth going ahead without further analysis, you do not want to be caught by surprise if things go wrong later. You want to know the danger signals and the actions that you might take.

Our first task in this chapter is to show how managers use *sensitivity analysis, break-even analysis,* and *Monte Carlo simulation* to identify the crucial assumptions in investment proposals and to explore what can go wrong. There is no magic in these techniques, just computer-assisted common sense. You do not need a license to use them.

Discounted cash-flow analysis commonly assumes that companies hold assets passively, and it ignores the opportunities to expand the project if it is successful or to bail out if it is not. However, wise managers recognize these opportunities when considering whether to invest. They look for ways to capitalize on success and reduce the costs of failure, and they are prepared to pay up for projects that give them this flexibility. Opportunities to modify projects as the future unfolds are known as *real options.* In the final section of the chapter, we describe several important real options, and we show how to use *decision trees* to set out the possible future choices.

10-1 Sensitivity and Scenario Analysis

Uncertainty means that more things can happen than will happen. Therefore, whenever managers are given a cash-flow forecast, they try to determine what else may happen and the implications of these possible surprise events. This is called *sensitivity analysis.*

Put yourself in the well-heeled shoes of the financial manager of the Otobai Company in Osaka. You are considering the introduction of a high-performance electric scooter for city use. Your staff members have prepared the cash-flow forecasts shown in Table 10.1. Since NPV is positive at the 20% opportunity cost of capital, it appears to be worth going ahead, but before you decide, you want to delve into these forecasts and identify the key variables that determine whether the project succeeds or fails.

The project requires an initial investment of ¥15 billion in plant and machinery, which will have negligible further value when the project comes to an end. As sales build up in the early and middle years of the project, the company will need to make increasing investments in net working capital, which is recovered in later years. After year 6, the company expects sales to

	Cash Flow in Years										
	0	1	2	3	4	5	6	7	8	9	10
1 Cash flow from investment in plant and equipment	−15.00	0.0	0.0	0.0	0.0	0.0	0.0	0.0	0.0	0.0	0.0
2 Cash flow from investment in working capital		−4.10	−1.30	−0.20	−0.30	−0.20	−0.40	1.60	1.90	1.80	1.20
3 Number of units sold		6,800	10,000	16,000	21,500	24,000	25,400	23,400	16,000	10,500	6,000
4 Unit price (¥ millions)		1.50	1.55	1.59	1.64	1.69	1.74	1.80	1.85	1.80	1.75
5 Revenue (3 × 4)		10.20	15.50	25.44	35.26	40.56	44.20	42.12	29.60	18.90	10.50
6 Cost of goods sold (50% of revenue)		5.10	7.75	12.72	17.63	20.28	22.10	21.06	14.80	9.45	5.25
7 Fixed costs	3.00	4.40	4.53	4.67	4.81	4.95	5.10	5.25	5.41	5.57	5.74
8 Depreciation		1.50	1.50	1.50	1.50	1.50	1.50	1.50	1.50	1.50	1.50
9 Pretax profit (5 − 6 − 7 − 8)	−3.00	−0.80	1.72	6.55	11.32	13.83	15.50	14.31	7.89	2.38	−1.99
10 Tax at 40%	−1.20	−0.32	0.69	2.62	4.53	5.53	6.20	5.72	3.16	0.95	−0.80
11 Profit after tax (9 − 10)	−1.80	−0.48	1.03	3.93	6.79	8.30	9.30	8.58	4.73	1.43	−1.19
12 Operating cash flow (8 + 11)	−1.80	1.02	2.53	5.43	8.29	9.80	10.80	10.08	6.23	2.93	0.31
13 Net cash flow (1 + 2 + 12)	−16.80	−3.08	1.23	5.23	7.99	9.60	10.40	11.68	8.13	4.73	1.51
14 Present value (at 20%)	−16.80	−2.57	0.85	3.03	3.85	3.86	3.48	3.26	1.89	0.92	0.24
NPV	2.02										

❭**TABLE 10.1**   Preliminary cash-flow forecasts for Otobai's electric scooter project (figures in ¥ billions unless stated otherwise)

tail off as other companies enter the market, and the company will probably need to reduce the price of the scooter. The cost of goods sold is forecast to be 50% of sales; in addition, there will be fixed costs each year that are unrelated to the level of sales. Taxes at a 40% rate are computed after deducting straight-line depreciation.

These seem to be the important things you need to know, but look out for unidentified variables that could affect these estimates. Perhaps there could be patent problems, or perhaps you will need to invest in service stations that will recharge the scooter batteries. The greatest dangers often lie in these unknown unknowns, or "unk-unks," as scientists call them.

Having found no unk-unks (no doubt you will find them later), you conduct a sensitivity analysis with respect to the required investment in plant and working capital and the forecast unit sales, price, and costs. To do this, the marketing and production staffs are asked to give optimistic and pessimistic estimates for each of the underlying variables. These are set out in the second and third columns of Table 10.2. For example, it is possible that sales of scooters could be 25% below forecast, or you may be obliged to cut the price by 15%. The fourth and fifth columns of the table shows what happens to the project's net present value if the variables are set one at a time to their optimistic and pessimistic values. Your project appears to be by no means a sure thing. The most dangerous variables are cost of goods sold and unit sales. If the cost of goods sold is 70% of sales (and all other variables are as expected), then the project has an NPV of –¥10.7 billion. If unit sales each year turn out to be 25% less than you forecast (and all other variables are as expected), then the project has an NPV of –¥5.9 billion.

Trendy consultants sometimes use a tornado diagram such as Figure 10.1 to illustrate the results of a sensitivity analysis. The bars at the summit of the tornado show the range of NPV outcome due to uncertainty about the level of sales. At the base of the tornado you can see the more modest effect of uncertainty about investment in working capital and the level of fixed costs.[1]

Value of Information

The world is uncertain, and accurate cash-flow forecasts are unattainable. So, if a project has a positive NPV based on your best forecasts, shouldn't you go ahead with it regardless of the fact that there may be later disappointments? Why spend time and effort focusing on the things that could go wrong?

Sensitivity analysis is not a substitute for the NPV rule, but if you know the danger points, you may be able to modify the project or resolve some of the uncertainty before your company undertakes the investment. For example, suppose that the pessimistic value for the cost of goods sold partly reflects the production department's worry that a particular machine will not work

BEYOND THE PAGE

Try It! Scooter project spreadsheets

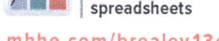

mhhe.com/brealey13e

	Possible Deviations from Forecast, %		NPV (¥billions)	
Variable	Optimistic	Pessimistic	Optimistic	Pessimistic
Capital investment	–30%	+50%	5.77	–4.22
Change in working capital	–40	+40	3.37	0.68
Number of units sold	+30	–25	11.57	–5.94
Unit price	+10	–15	5.20	–2.75
Cost of goods sold (% of sales)	30	70	14.75	–10.71
Fixed costs	–30	+30	6.21	–2.17

❯ **TABLE 10.2**   To undertake a sensitivity analysis of the electric scooter project, we set each variable in turn at its most pessimistic or optimistic value and recalculate the NPV of the project

---

[1]Notice that the term "fixed costs" does not imply that they are certain or cannot change from year to year. It indicates that the costs are not related to the level of sales.

FIGURE 10.1

Tornado diagram for electric scooter project

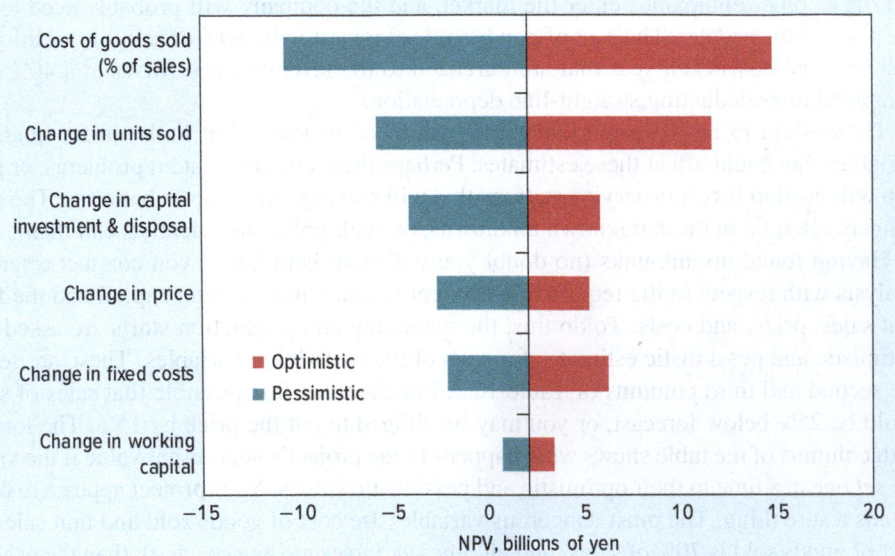

as designed and that the operation will need to be performed by other methods. The chance of this happening is only 1 in 10. But, if it does occur, the extra cost would reduce the NPV of your project by ¥2.5 billion, putting the NPV underwater at $+2.02 - 2.50 = -¥0.48$ billion. Suppose that a ¥100 million pretest of the machine would resolve the uncertainty and allow you to clear up the problem. It clearly pays to invest ¥100 million to avoid a 10% probability of a ¥2.5 billion fall in NPV. You are ahead by $-0.1 + .10 \times 2.5 = ¥0.15$ billion. On the other hand, the value of additional information about working capital is small. Because the project is only marginally unprofitable, even under pessimistic assumptions about working capital, you are unlikely to be in trouble if you have misestimated that variable.

Limits to Sensitivity Analysis

Sensitivity analysis boils down to expressing cash flows in terms of key project variables and then calculating the consequences of misestimating those variables. It forces the manager to identify the crucial determinants of the project's success and indicates where additional information would be most useful or where design changes may be needed.

One drawback to sensitivity analysis is that it always gives somewhat ambiguous results. For example, what exactly does *optimistic* or *pessimistic* mean? The marketing department may be interpreting the terms in a different way from the production department. Ten years from now, after hundreds of projects, hindsight may show that the marketing department's pessimistic limit was exceeded twice as often as that of the production department, but what you may discover 10 years hence is no help now. Of course, you could specify that when you use the terms "pessimistic" and "optimistic," you mean that there is only a 10% chance that the actual value will prove to be worse than the pessimistic figure or better than the optimistic one. However, it is far from easy to extract a forecaster's notion of the true probabilities of possible outcomes.[2]

Another problem with sensitivity analysis is that the underlying variables are likely to be interrelated. For example, if inflation pushes prices to the upper end of your range, it is quite probable that costs will also be inflated. And if sales are unexpectedly high, you may need to invest more in working capital. Sometimes the analyst can get around these problems by

---

[2]If you doubt this, try some simple experiments. Ask the person who repairs your dishwasher to state a numerical probability that it will work for at least one more year. Or construct your own subjective probability distribution of the number of telephone calls you will receive next week. That ought to be easy. Try it. We will also refer in Chapter 11 to evidence that people tend to be overconfident in their forecasts and to understate the possible errors.

defining underlying variables so that they are roughly independent. For example, it made more sense for Otobai to look at cost of goods sold as a proportion of sales rather than as a dollar value. But you cannot push one-at-a-time sensitivity analysis too far. It is impossible to obtain expected, optimistic, and pessimistic values for total project cash flows from the information in Table 10.2.

Sensitivity analysis boils down to expressing cash flows in terms of key project variables and then calculating the consequences of misestimating the variables. It forces the manager to identify the underlying variables, indicates where additional information would be most useful, and helps to expose inappropriate forecasts.

Scenario Analysis

If the variables are interrelated, it may help to consider some alternative plausible scenarios. For example, perhaps the company economist is worried about the possibility of a sharp rise in world oil prices. The direct effect of this would be to encourage the use of electrically powered transportation. The popularity of hybrid cars after a recent oil price increases leads you to estimate that an immediate 20% rise in the price of oil would enable you to increase unit sales by 10% a year. On the other hand, the economist also believes that higher oil prices would stimulate inflation, which would affect selling prices, costs, and working capital. Table 10.3 shows that this scenario of higher oil prices and higher inflation would on balance help your new venture. Its NPV would increase to ¥6.9 billion.

		Cash Flows in Year										
		0	1	2	3	4	5	6	7	8	9	10
1	Cash flow from capital investment	−15.0	0.0	0.0	0.0	0.0	0.0	0.0	0.0	0.0	0.0	0.0
2	Cash flow from change in working capital		−4.3	−1.4	−0.2	−0.3	−0.2	−0.4	−1.7	−2.0	−1.9	−1.3
3	Units sold		7,480	11,000	17,600	23,650	26,400	27,940	25,740	17,600	11,550	6,600
4	Price (¥millions)		1.58	1.62	1.67	1.72	1.77	1.83	1.89	1.94	1.89	1.84
5	Revenue (3 × 4)		11.8	17.8	29.4	40.7	46.8	51.1	48.6	34.1	21.8	12.1
6	Cost of goods sold (50% of sales)		5.9	8.9	14.7	20.3	23.4	25.6	24.3	17.1	10.9	6.1
7	Fixed costs	3.0	4.4	4.5	4.7	4.8	5.0	5.1	5.3	5.4	5.6	5.7
8	Depreciation		1.5	1.5	1.5	1.5	1.5	1.5	1.5	1.5	1.5	1.5
9	Pretax profit (5 − 6 − 7 − 8)	−3.0	0.0	2.9	8.5	14.0	16.9	19.0	17.6	10.2	3.8	−1.2
10	Tax at 40%	−1.2	0.0	1.2	3.4	5.6	6.8	7.6	7.0	4.1	1.5	−0.5
11	Profit after tax (9 − 10)	−1.8	0.0	1.7	5.1	8.4	10.2	11.4	10.5	6.1	2.3	−0.7
12	Operating cash flow (8 + 11)	−1.8	1.5	3.2	6.6	9.9	11.7	12.9	12.0	7.6	3.8	0.8
13	Net cash flow (1 + 2 + 12)	−16.8	−2.6	1.9	6.4	9.6	11.5	12.5	10.3	5.6	1.9	−0.5
14	Present value (at 20%)	−16.8	−2.2	1.3	3.7	4.6	4.6	4.2	2.9	1.3	0.4	−0.1
15	NPV	6.9										

Assumptions:
1. Increase of 10% in unit sales plus 5% in sales price.
2. Increase of 5% in working capital.
3. Cost of goods sold remains at 50% of sales.

❯TABLE 10.3   How the NPV of the electric scooter project would be affected by higher oil prices and increased inflation (figures in ¥billions unless stated otherwise)

Managers often find such **scenario analysis** helpful. It allows them to look at different, but consistent, combinations of variables. Forecasters generally prefer to give an estimate of revenues or costs under a particular scenario than to give some absolute optimistic or pessimistic value.

10-2   Break-Even Analysis and Operating Leverage

Break-Even Analysis

When we undertake a sensitivity analysis of a project or when we look at alternative scenarios, we are asking how serious it would be if sales or costs turn out to be worse than we forecasted. Managers sometimes prefer to rephrase this question and ask how bad things can get before the project NPV turns negative. This exercise is known as *break-even analysis*.

We saw earlier that the profitability of Otobai's project could be severely damaged if unit sales are unexpectedly low. Therefore, management might look at how far unit sales could fall before the project becomes a loser. A 1% annual shortfall in unit sales would turn NPV from ¥2.02 to –¥1.70, a decline of ¥0.32. So NPV would be exactly zero if each year sales fell by $1\% \times (2.02)/(0.32) = 6.3\%$ below forecast.

Table 10.4 shows the break-even points for each of the other variables. You can see, for example, that quite small errors in your forecasts for unit sales, price, and variable costs could cause your project to become a loser. On the other hand, the project would still break even (NPV = 0) if you have underestimated working capital by 60.1%.

Table 10.4 defines break-even as the point at which NPV would be exactly zero. But managers frequently calculate break-even points in terms of accounting profits rather than net present values. For example, look at Table 10.5, which shows the minimum level of sales that Otobai needs each year to avoid a loss on its scooter project. You can see that in year 1, Otobai needs sales of ¥11.80 billion to cover costs and depreciation. In year 2, the break-even sales level rises to ¥12.06 billion.[3]

Should Otobai's manager be relaxed if the project breaks even each year in accounting terms? It is true that its revenues will then be sufficient to cover the operating costs and repay the initial investment. But they will not be sufficient to repay the opportunity cost of capital on that ¥15 billion. A project that breaks even in accounting terms will surely have a negative NPV.

BEYOND THE PAGE

Break-even analysis of Otobai's electric scooter project

mhhe.com/brealey13e

❭**TABLE 10.4**   The percentage change in the estimated value of each variable that produces an NPV of zero for the electric scooter project

	Change in Estimated Value
Capital investment	+16.2%
Working capital	+60.1
Sales	–6.3
Cost of goods sold (% of sales)	+3.2
Fixed costs	+14.5

[3]Notice that because fixed costs change from year to year, so does the break-even level of sales.

		0	1	2	3	4	5	6	7	8	9	10
Cash Flows in Year (figures in ¥billions)												
Revenues		6.00	11.80	12.06	12.34	12.62	12.90	13.20	13.50	13.82	14.14	14.48
Cost of goods sold (50% of sales)		3.00	5.90	6.03	6.17	6.31	6.45	6.60	6.75	6.91	7.07	7.24
Fixed costs		3.00	4.40	4.53	4.67	4.81	4.95	5.10	5.25	5.41	5.57	5.74
Depreciation		0.00	1.50	1.50	1.50	1.50	1.50	1.50	1.50	1.50	1.50	1.50
Pretax profit		0.00	0.00	0.00	0.00	0.00	0.00	0.00	0.00	0.00	0.00	0.00

TABLE 10.5   A project's accounting break-even point is the minimum level of sales required to avoid an accounting loss

Operating Leverage and the Break-Even Point

A project's break-even point depends on the extent to which its costs vary with the level of sales. Suppose that electric scooters fall out of favor. The bad news is that Otobai's sales revenue is less than you had hoped, but you have the consolation that the cost of goods sold is also lower. But, any costs that are fixed do not decline along with sales, and, therefore, any shortfall in sales has a greater impact on profitability. Of course, a high proportion of fixed costs is not all bad. The firm whose costs are fixed fares poorly when demand is low but makes a killing during a boom.

A business with high fixed costs is said to have high operating leverage. Operating leverage is usually defined in terms of accounting profits rather than cash flows[4] and is measured by the percentage change in profits for each 1% change in sales. Thus the **degree of operating leverage (DOL)** is

$$DOL = \frac{\text{percentage change in profits}}{\text{percentage change in sales}}$$

The following simple formula[5] shows how DOL is related to the business's fixed costs (including depreciation) as a proportion of pretax profits:

$$DOL = 1 + \frac{\text{fixed costs including depreciation}}{\text{profits}}$$

For example, in year 2 of the scooter project,

$$DOL = 1 + \frac{(4.5+1.5)}{1.72} = 4.50$$

A 1% increase in the project's year-2 revenues would result in a 4.5% rise in profits.

[4]In Chapter 9, we developed a measure of operating leverage that was expressed in terms of cash flows and their present values. We used this measure to show how beta depends on leverage.

[5]This formula for DOL can be derived as follows. If sales increase by 1%, then variable costs will also increase by 1%, and profits will increase by .01 × (sales − variable costs) = .01 × (pretax profits + fixed costs). Now recall the definition of DOL:

$$DOL = \frac{\text{percentage change in profits}}{\text{percentage change in sales}} = \frac{(\text{change in profits})/(\text{level of profits})}{.01}$$

$$= 100 \times \frac{\text{change in profits}}{\text{level of profits}} = 100 \times \frac{.01 \times (\text{profits} + \text{fixed costs})}{\text{level of profits}}$$

$$= 1 + \frac{\text{fixed costs}}{\text{profits}}$$

10-3   Monte Carlo Simulation

Sensitivity analysis allows you to consider the effect of changing one variable at a time. By looking at the project under alternative scenarios, you can consider the effect of a *limited number* of plausible combinations of variables. **Monte Carlo simulation** is a tool for considering *all* possible combinations. It therefore enables you to inspect the entire distribution of project outcomes.

Imagine that you are a gambler at Monte Carlo. You know nothing about the laws of probability (few casual gamblers do), but a friend has suggested to you a complicated strategy for playing roulette. Your friend has not actually tested the strategy but is confident that it will *on the average* give you a 2.5% return for every 50 spins of the wheel. Your friend's optimistic estimate for any series of 50 spins is a profit of 55%; your friend's pessimistic estimate is a loss of 50%. How can you find out whether these really are the odds? An easy but possibly expensive way is to start playing and record the outcome at the end of each series of 50 spins. After, say, 100 series of 50 spins each, plot a frequency distribution of the outcomes and calculate the average and upper and lower limits. If things look good, you can then get down to some serious gambling.

An alternative is to tell a computer to simulate the roulette wheel and the strategy. In other words, you could instruct the computer to draw numbers out of its digital hat to determine the outcome of each spin of the wheel and then to calculate how much you would make or lose from the particular gambling strategy.

That would be an example of Monte Carlo simulation. In capital budgeting, we replace the gambling strategy with a model of the project and the roulette wheel with a model of the world in which the project operates. Let us see how this might work with our project for an electrically powered scooter.

Simulating the Electric Scooter Project

Step 1: Modeling the Project   The first step in any simulation is to give the computer a precise model of the project. For example, the sensitivity analysis of the scooter project was based on the following implicit model of each year's cash flow:

Cash flow = operating cash flow − investment in working capital

Operating cash flow = (revenue − costs − depreciation) × (1 − tax rate) + depreciation

Revenue = unit sales × unit price

Costs = (revenue × variable cost as a proportion of revenue) + fixed cost

This model of the project was all that you needed for the simpleminded sensitivity analysis that we described above. But if you wish to simulate the whole project, you need to think about how the variables are interrelated. For example, consider the unit sales variable. The marketing department has estimated sales of 6.8 million scooters in the first year of the project's life; of course, you do not know how things will work out. Actual sales will exceed or fall short of expectations by the amount of the department's forecast error:

Sales, year 1 = expected sales, year 1 × (1 + forecast error, year 1)

You expect the forecast error to be zero, but it could turn out to be positive or negative. Suppose, for example, that actual sales turn out to be 7.48 million. That means a forecast error of 10%, or +.1:

Sales, year 1 = 6.8 × (1 + .1) = 7.48 million

You can write sales in the second year in exactly the same way:

Sales, year 2 = expected sales, year 2 × (1 + forecast error, year 2)

At this point, you must consider how the expected sales in year 2 are affected by what happens in year 1. If scooter sales are below expectations in year 1, it is likely that they will continue to be below in subsequent years. Suppose that a shortfall in year 1 leads you to revise down your forecast of sales in year 2 by a like amount. Then:

$$\text{Expected sales, year 2} = \text{actual sales, year 1}$$

Now you can rewrite sales in year 2 in terms of the actual sales in the previous year plus a forecast error:

$$\text{Sales, year 2} = \text{sales, year 1} \times (1 + \text{forecast error, year 2})$$

In the same way, you can describe the expected sales in year 3 in terms of sales in year 2 and so on. This set of equations illustrates how you can describe interdependence between different periods. But you also need to allow for interdependence between different variables. For example, if sales are high, the price of electrically powered scooters is likely to be above forecast. Suppose that this is the only uncertainty and that a 10% addition to sales would lead you to predict a 3% increase in price. Then you could model the first year's price as follows:

$$\text{Price, year 1} = \text{expected price, year 1} \times (1 + .3 \times \text{error in sales forecast, year 1})$$

Then, if variations in sales exert a permanent effect on price, you can define the second year's price as

$$\text{Price, year 2} = \text{expected price, year 2} \times (1 + .3 \times \text{error in sales forecast, year 2}) = \text{actual price, year 1} \times (1 + .3 \times \text{error in sales forecast, year 2})$$

Notice how we have linked each period's selling price to the actual selling prices (including forecast error) in all previous periods. We used the same type of linkage for sales. These linkages mean that forecast errors accumulate; they do not cancel out over time. Thus, uncertainty increases with time: The farther out you look into the future, the more the actual price or sales may depart from your original forecast. The complete model of your project would include a set of equations for each of the variables: sales, price, variable cost, fixed cost, and investment in working capital. Even if you allowed for only a few interdependencies between variables and across time, the result would be quite a complex list of equations. Perhaps that is not a bad thing if it forces you to understand what the project is all about. Model building is like spinach: You may not like the taste, but it is good for you.

Step 2: Specifying Probabilities   Remember the procedure for simulating the gambling strategy? The first step was to specify the strategy, the second was to specify the numbers on the roulette wheel, and the third was to tell the computer to select these numbers at random and calculate the results of the strategy:

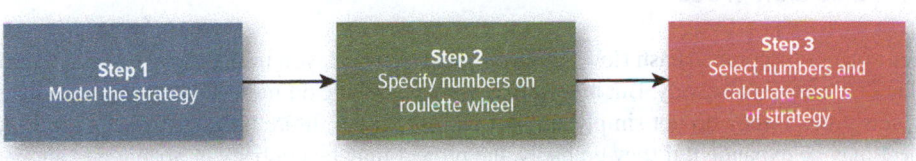

The steps are just the same for your scooter project:

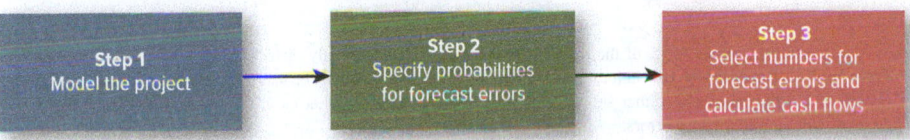

Think about how you might go about specifying your possible errors in forecasting market size. You expect sales in year 1 to be 6.8 million scooters. You obviously don't think you are underestimating or overestimating, so the expected forecast error is zero. On the other hand, the marketing department has given you a range of possible estimates. Sales in year 1 could be as low as 5.7 million scooters or as high as 8.2 million scooters. Thus the forecast error has an expected value of 0 and a range of plus or minus 20%. If the marketing department has, in fact, given you the lowest and highest possible outcomes, actual market size should fall somewhere within this range with near certainty.[6]

That takes care of market size; now you need to draw up similar estimates of the possible forecast errors for each of the other variables that are in your model.

Step 3: Simulate the Cash Flows   The computer now samples from the distribution of the forecast errors, calculates the resulting cash flows for each period, and records them. After many iterations, you begin to get accurate estimates of the probability distributions of the project cash flows—accurate, that is, only to the extent that your model and the probability distributions of the forecast errors are accurate. Remember the GIGO principle: "garbage in, garbage out."

Step 4: Calculate Present Value   The distributions of project cash flows should allow you to calculate the expected cash flows more accurately. In the final step, you need to discount these expected cash flows to find present value.

Simulation, though complicated, has the obvious merit of compelling the forecaster to face up to uncertainty and to interdependencies. Once you have set up your simulation model, it is a simple matter to analyze the principal sources of uncertainty in the cash flows and to see how much you could reduce this uncertainty by improving the forecasts of sales or costs. You may also be able to explore the effect of possible modifications to the project.

Simulation may sound like a panacea for the world's ills, but, as usual, you pay for what you get. Sometimes you pay for more than you get. It is not just a matter of the time spent in building the model. It is extremely difficult to estimate interrelationships between variables and the underlying probability distributions, even when you are trying to be honest. But in capital budgeting, forecasters are seldom completely impartial and the probability distributions on which simulations are based can be highly biased.

In practice, a simulation that attempts to be realistic will also be complex. Therefore, the decision maker may delegate the task of constructing the model to management scientists or consultants. The danger here is that even if the builders understand their creation, the decision maker cannot and therefore does not rely on it. This is a common but ironic experience.

10-4   Real Options and Decision Trees

When you use discounted cash flow (DCF) to value a project, you implicitly assume that the firm will hold the assets passively. But managers are not paid to be dummies. After they have invested in a new project, they do not simply sit back and watch the future unfold. If things go well, the project may be expanded; if they go badly, the project may be cut back or abandoned altogether. Projects that can be modified in these ways are more valuable than those that do not provide such flexibility. The more uncertain the outlook, the more valuable this flexibility becomes.

---

[6]Suppose "near certainty" means "99% of the time." If forecast errors are normally distributed, this degree of certainty requires a range of plus or minus three standard deviations. Other distributions could, of course, be used. For example, the marketing department may view any level of sales of 15% either side of forecast as equally likely. In that case, the simulation would require a uniform (rectangular) distribution of forecast errors.

That sounds obvious, but notice that sensitivity analysis and Monte Carlo simulation do not recognize the opportunity to modify projects.[7] For example, think back to the Otobai electric scooter project. In real life, if things go wrong with the project, Otobai would abandon to cut its losses. If so, the worst outcomes would not be as devastating as our sensitivity analysis and simulation suggested.

Options to modify projects are known as **real options.** Managers may not always use the term "real option" to describe these opportunities; for example, they may refer to "intangible advantages" of easy-to-modify projects. But when they review major investment proposals, these option intangibles are often the key to their decisions.

The Option to Expand

Long-haul airfreight businesses such as UPS need to move a massive amount of goods each day. To handle the growing demand, UPS announced in 2016 that it had agreed to buy 14 Boeing freighter aircraft to add to its existing fleet of more than 500 planes. If business continued to expand, UPS would need more aircraft. But rather than placing additional firm orders, the company secured a place in Boeing's production line by acquiring *options* to buy a further 14 aircraft at a predetermined price. These options did not commit UPS to expand but gave it the flexibility to do so.

Figure 10.2 displays UPS's expansion option as a simple **decision tree.** You can think of it as a game between UPS and fate. Each square represents an action or decision by the company. Each circle represents an outcome revealed by fate. In this case, there is only one outcome— when fate reveals the airfreight demand and UPS's capacity needs. UPS then decides whether to exercise its options and buy the additional aircraft. Here the future decision is easy: Buy the airplanes only if demand is high and the company can operate them profitably. If demand is low, UPS walks away and leaves Boeing with the problem of finding another customer for the planes that were reserved for UPS.

You can probably think of many other investments that take on added value because of the further options they provide. For example,

- When launching a new product, companies often start with a pilot program to iron out possible design problems and to test the market. The company can evaluate the pilot project and then decide whether to expand to full-scale production.

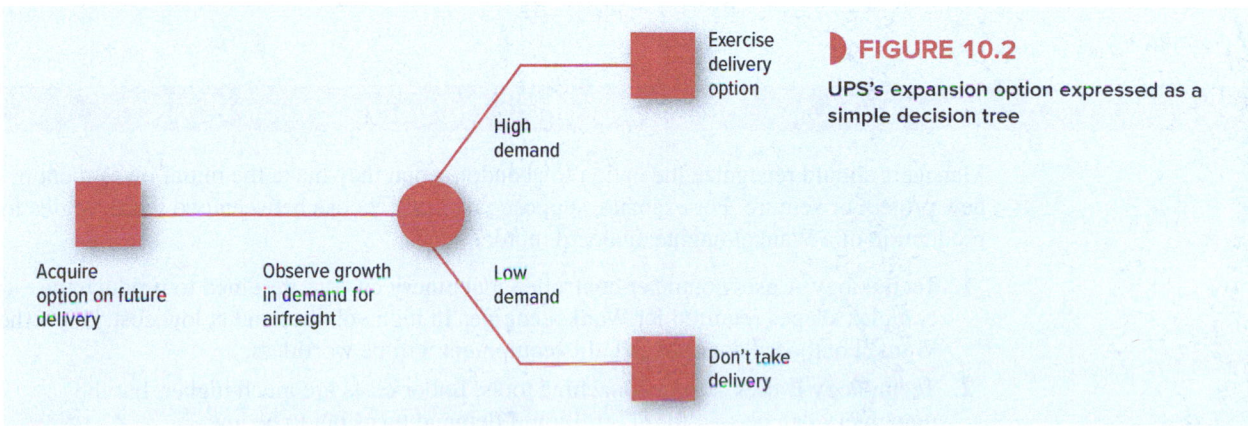

▶ **FIGURE 10.2**

UPS's expansion option expressed as a simple decision tree

---

[7]Some simulation models *do* recognize the possibility of changing policy. For example, when a pharmaceutical company uses simulation to analyze its R&D decisions, it allows for the possibility that the company can abandon the development at each phase.

- When designing a factory, it can make sense to provide extra land or floor space to reduce the future cost of a second production line.

- When building a four-lane highway, it may pay to build six-lane bridges so that the road can be converted later to six lanes if traffic volumes turn out to be higher than expected.

- When building production platforms for offshore oil and gas fields, companies usually allow ample vacant deck space. The vacant space costs more up front but reduces the cost of installing extra equipment later. For example, vacant deck space could provide an option to install water-flooding equipment if oil or gas prices are high enough to justify this investment.

Expansion options do not show up on accounting balance sheets, but managers and investors are well aware of their importance. For example, in Chapter 4 we showed how the present value of growth opportunities (PVGO) contributes to the value of a company's common stock. PVGO equals the forecasted total NPV of future investments. But it is better to think of PVGO as the value of the firm's *options* to invest and expand. The firm is not obliged to grow. It can invest more if the number of positive-NPV projects turns out high, or it can slow down if that number turns out low. The flexibility to adapt investment to future opportunities is one of the factors that makes PVGO so valuable.

The Option to Abandon

If the option to expand has value, what about the decision to bail out? Projects do not just go on until assets expire of old age. The decision to terminate a project is usually taken by management, not by nature. Once the project is no longer profitable, the company will cut its losses and exercise its option to abandon the project.

Some assets are easier to bail out of than others. Tangible assets are usually easier to sell than intangible ones. It helps to have active secondhand markets, which exist mainly for standardized items. Real estate, airplanes, trucks, and certain machine tools are likely to be relatively easy to sell. On the other hand, the knowledge accumulated by a software company's research and development program is a specialized intangible asset and probably would not have significant abandonment value. (Some assets, such as old mattresses, even have *negative* abandonment value; you have to pay to get rid of them. It is costly to decommission nuclear power plants or to reclaim land that has been strip-mined.)

EXAMPLE 10.1 • Bailing Out of the Outboard-Engine Project

Managers should recognize the option to abandon when they make the initial investment in a new project or venture. For example, suppose you must choose between two technologies for production of a Wankel-engine outboard motor.

1. Technology A uses computer-controlled machinery custom-designed to produce the complex shapes required for Wankel engines in high volumes and at low cost. But if the Wankel outboard does not sell, this equipment will be worthless.

2. Technology B uses standard machine tools. Labor costs are much higher, but the machinery can be sold for $17 million if demand turns out to be low.

Just for simplicity, assume that the initial capital outlays are the same for both technologies. If demand in the first year is buoyant, technology A will provide a payoff of $24 million. If demand is sluggish, the payoff from A is $16 million. Think of these payoffs as the project's cash flow in the first year of production plus the value in year 1 of all future cash flows. The corresponding payoffs to technology B are $22.5 million and $15 million:

Payoffs from Producing Outboard ($ millions)		
	Technology A	**Technology B**
Buoyant demand	$24.0	$22.5
Sluggish demand	16.0	15.0[a]

[a] Composed of a cash flow of $1.5 million and a PV in year 1 of 13.5 million.

Technology A looks better in a DCF analysis of the new product because it was designed to have the lowest possible cost at the planned production volume. Yet you can sense the advantage of the flexibility provided by technology B if you are unsure whether the new outboard will sink or swim in the marketplace. If you adopt technology B and the outboard is not a success, you are better off collecting the first year's cash flow of $1.5 million and then selling the plant and equipment for $17 million.

Figure 10.3 summarizes Example 10.1 as a decision tree. The abandonment option occurs at the right-hand boxes for technology B. The decisions are obvious: Continue if demand is buoyant, abandon otherwise. Thus the payoffs to technology B are

Buoyant demand → continue production → payoff of $22.5 million
Sluggish demand → exercise option to sell assets → payoff of 1.5 + 17 = $18.5 million

Technology B provides an insurance policy: If the outboard's sales are disappointing, you can abandon the project and receive $18.5 million. The total value of the project with technology B is its DCF value, assuming that the company does not abandon, *plus* the value of the option to sell the assets for $17 million. When you value this abandonment option, you are placing a value on flexibility.

Production Options

When companies undertake new investments, they generally think about the possibility that they may wish to modify the project at a later stage. After all, today everybody may be demanding round pegs, but, who knows, tomorrow square ones may be all the rage. In that case, you need a plant that provides the flexibility to produce a variety of peg shapes. In just the same way, it may be worth paying up front for the flexibility to vary the inputs. For example, in Chapter 22, we will describe how electric utilities often build in the option to switch between burning oil and burning natural gas. We refer to these opportunities as *production options.*

Timing Options

The fact that a project has a positive NPV does not mean that it is best undertaken now. It might be even more valuable to delay.

Timing decisions are fairly straightforward under conditions of certainty. You need to examine alternative dates for making the investment and calculate its net future value at each of these dates. Then, to find which of the alternatives would add most to the firm's *current* value, you must discount these net future values back to the present:

$$\text{Net present value of investment if undertaken at time } t = \frac{\text{net future value at date } t}{(1+r)^t}$$

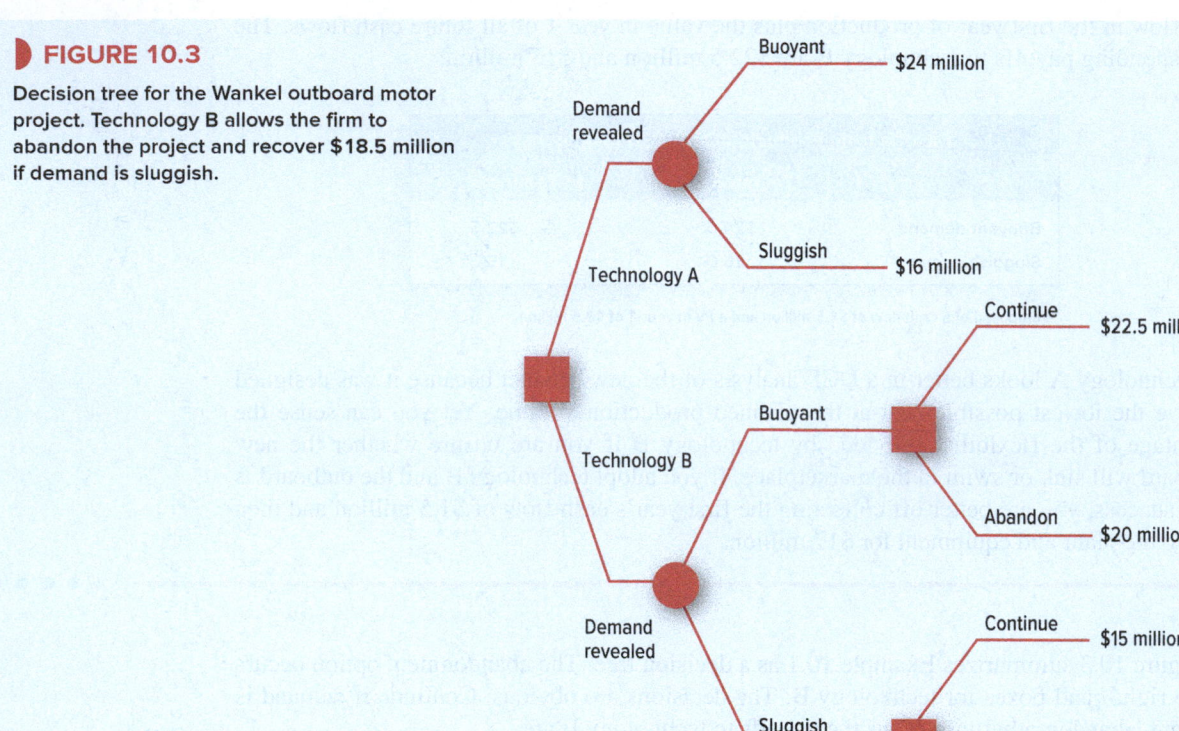

> **FIGURE 10.3**
>
> Decision tree for the Wankel outboard motor project. Technology B allows the firm to abandon the project and recover $18.5 million if demand is sluggish.

Buoyant — $24 million

Demand revealed

Sluggish — $16 million

Technology A

Continue — $22.5 million

Buoyant

Technology B

Abandon — $20 million

Demand revealed

Continue — $15 million

Sluggish

Abandon — $18.5 million

The optimal date to undertake the investment is the one that maximizes its contribution to the value of your firm today. This procedure should already be familiar to you from Chapter 6, where we worked out when it was best to cut a tract of timber.

In the timber-cutting example, we assumed that there was no uncertainty about the cash flows, so that you knew the optimal time to exercise your option. When there is uncertainty, the timing option is much more complicated. An investment opportunity not taken at $t = 0$ might be more or less attractive at $t = 1$; there is rarely any way of knowing for sure. Perhaps it is better to strike while the iron is hot even if there is a chance that it will become hotter. On the other hand, if you wait a bit you might obtain more information and avoid a bad mistake. That is why you often find that managers choose not to invest today in projects where the NPV is only marginally positive and there is much to be learned by delay.

More on Decision Trees

We will return to all these real options in Chapter 22, after we have covered the theory of option valuation in Chapters 20 and 21. But we will end this chapter with a closer look at decision trees.

Decision trees are commonly used to describe the real options imbedded in capital investment projects. But decision trees were used in the analysis of projects years before real options were first explicitly identified. Decision trees can help to illustrate project risk and how future decisions will affect project cash flows. Even if you never learn or use option valuation theory, decision trees belong in your financial toolkit.

The best way to appreciate how decision trees can be used in project analysis is to work through a detailed example.

EXAMPLE 10.2 ● A Decision Tree for Pharmaceutical R&D

Drug development programs may last decades. Usually hundreds of thousands of compounds may be tested to find a few with promise. Then these compounds must survive several stages of investment and testing to gain approval from the Food and Drug Administration (FDA). Only then can the drug be sold commercially. The stages are as follows:

1. *Phase I clinical trials.* After laboratory and clinical tests are concluded, the new drug is tested for safety and dosage in a small sample of humans.

2. *Phase II clinical trials.* The new drug is tested for efficacy (Does it work as predicted?) and for potentially harmful side effects.

3. *Phase III clinical trials.* The new drug is tested on a larger sample of humans to confirm efficacy and to rule out harmful side effects.

4. *Prelaunch.* If FDA approval is gained, there is investment in production facilities and initial marketing. Some clinical trials continue.

5. *Commercial launch.* After making a heavy initial investment in marketing and sales, the company begins to sell the new drug to the public.

Once a drug is launched successfully, sales usually continue for about 10 years, until the drug's patent protection expires and competitors enter with generic versions of the same chemical compound. The drug may continue to be sold off-patent, but sales volume and profits are much lower.

The commercial success of FDA-approved drugs varies enormously. The PV of a "blockbuster" drug at launch can be 5 or 10 times the PV of an average drug. A few blockbusters can generate most of a large pharmaceutical company's profits.[8]

No company hesitates to invest in R&D for a drug that it *knows* will be a blockbuster. But the company will not find out for sure until after launch. Occasionally, a company thinks it has a blockbuster only to discover that a competitor has launched a better drug first.

Sometimes the FDA approves a drug but limits its scope of use. Some drugs, though effective, can only be prescribed for limited classes of patients; other drugs can be prescribed much more widely. Thus the manager of a pharmaceutical R&D program has to assess the odds of clinical success and the odds of commercial success. A new drug may be abandoned if it fails clinical trials—for example, because of dangerous side effects—or if the outlook for profits is discouraging.

Figure 10.4 is a decision tree that illustrates these decisions. We have assumed that a new drug has passed phase I clinical trials with flying colors. Now it requires an investment of $18 million for phase II trials. These trials take two years. The probability of success is 44%.

If the trials are successful, the manager learns the commercial potential of the drug, which depends on how widely it can be used. Suppose that the forecasted PV at launch depends on the scope of use allowed by the FDA. These PVs are shown at the far right of the decision tree: an upside outcome of NPV = $700 million if the drug can be widely used, a most likely case with NPV = $300 million, and a downside case of NPV = $100 million if the drug's scope is greatly restricted.[9] The NPVs are the payoffs at launch after investment in marketing. Launch comes three years after the start of phase III if the drug is approved by the FDA.

---

[8]The website of the Tufts Center for the Study of Drug Development (**http://csdd.tufts.edu**) provides a wealth of information about the costs and risks of pharmaceutical R&D.

[9]The most likely case is not the average outcome because PVs in the pharmaceutical business are skewed to the upside. The average PV is $.25 \times 700 + .5 \times 300 + .25 \times 100 = \$350$ million.

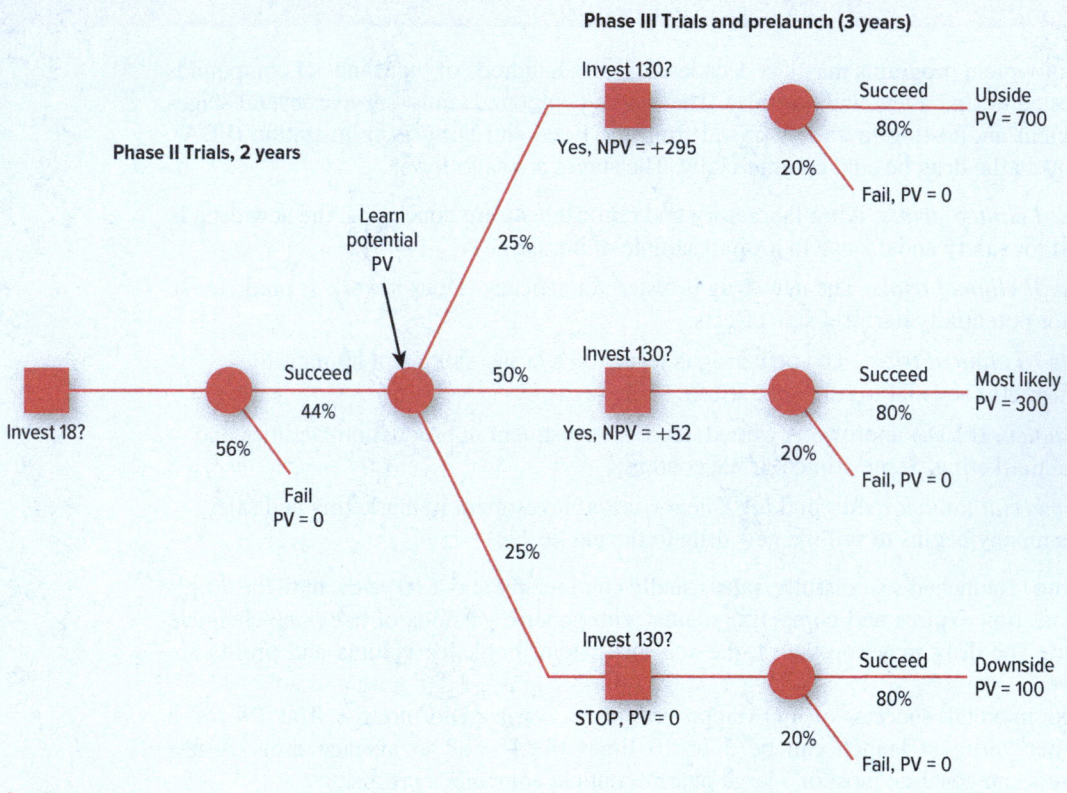

▶ **FIGURE 10.4**

A simplified decision tree for pharmaceutical R&D. A candidate drug requires an $18 million investment for phase II clinical trials. If the trials are successful (44% probability), the company learns the drug's scope of use and updates its forecast of the drug's PV at commercial launch. The investment required for the phase III trials and prelaunch outlays is $130 million. The probability of success in phase III and prelaunch is 80%.

The probabilities of the upside, most likely, and downside outcomes are 25%, 50%, and 25%, respectively.

A further R&D investment of $130 million is required for phase III trials and for the prelaunch period. (We have combined phase III and prelaunch for simplicity.) The probability of FDA approval and launch is 80%.

Now let's value the investments in Figure 10.4. We assume a risk-free rate of 4% and market risk premium of 7%. If FDA-approved pharmaceutical products have asset betas of .8, the opportunity cost of capital is $4 + .8 \times 7 = 9.6\%$.

We work back through the tree from right to left. The NPVs at the start of phase III trials are:

$$\text{NPV(upside)} \quad = -130 + .8 \times \frac{700}{(1.096)^3} = +\$295 \text{ million}$$

$$\text{NPV(most likely)} = -130 + .8 \times \frac{300}{(1.096)^3} = +\$52 \text{ million}$$

$$\text{NPV(downside)} \quad = -130 + .8 \times \frac{100}{(1.096)^3} = -\$69 \text{ million}$$

Since the downside NPV is negative at –$69 million, the $130 million investment at the start of phase III should *not* be made in the downside case. There is no point investing $130 million for an 80% chance of a $100 million payoff three years later. Therefore the value of the R&D program at this point in the decision tree is not –$69 million, but zero.

Now calculate the NPV at the initial investment decision for phase II trials. The payoff two years later depends on whether the drug delivers on the upside, most likely, or downside: a 25% chance of NPV = +$295 million, a 50% chance of NPV = +$52 million, and a 25% chance of cancellation and NPV = 0. These NPVs are achieved only if the phase II trials are successful: There is a 44% chance of success and a 56% chance of failure. The initial investment is $18 million. Therefore, NPV is

$$NPV = -18 + .44 \times \frac{.25 \times 295 + .5 \times 52 + .25 \times 0}{(1.096)^2} = -18 + 37 = +\$19 \text{ million}$$

Thus the phase II R&D is a worthwhile investment, even though the drug has only a 33% chance of making it to launch (.44 × .75 = .33, or 33%).

Notice that we did not increase the 9.6% discount rate to offset the risks of failure in clinical trials or the risk that the drug will fail to generate profits. Concerns about the drug's efficacy, possible side effects, and scope of use are diversifiable risks, which do not increase the risk of the R&D project to the company's diversified stockholders. We were careful to take these concerns into account in the cash-flow forecasts, however. The decision tree in Figure 10.4 keeps track of the probabilities of success or failure and the probabilities of upside and downside outcomes.[10]

Figures 10.3 and 10.4 are both examples of abandonment options. We have not explicitly modeled the investments as options, however, so our NPV calculation is incomplete. We show how to value abandonment options in Chapter 22.

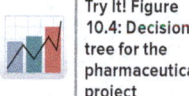

BEYOND THE PAGE

Try It! Figure 10.4: Decision tree for the pharmaceutical project

mhhe.com/brealey13e

Pro and Con Decision Trees

Any cash-flow forecast rests on some assumption about the firm's future investment and operating strategy. Often that assumption is implicit. Decision trees force the underlying strategy into the open. By displaying the links between today's decisions and tomorrow's decisions, they help the financial manager to find the strategy with the highest net present value.

The decision tree in Figure 10.4 is a simplified version of reality. For example, you could expand the tree to include a wider range of NPVs at launch, possibly including some chance of a blockbuster or of intermediate outcomes. You could allow information about the NPVs to arrive gradually, rather than just at the start of phase III. You could introduce the investment decision at phase I trials and separate the phase III and prelaunch stages. You may wish to draw a new decision tree covering these events and decisions. You will see how fast the circles, squares, and branches accumulate.

The trouble with decision trees is that they get so ____ complex so ____ quickly (insert your own expletives). Life is complex, however, and there is very little we can do about it. It is therefore unfair to criticize decision trees because they can become complex. Our criticism is reserved for analysts who let the complexity become overwhelming. The point of decision trees is to allow explicit analysis of possible future events and decisions. They should

---

[10]The market risk attached to the PVs at launch is recognized in the 9.6% discount rate.

be judged not on their comprehensiveness but on whether they show the most important links between today's and tomorrow's decisions. Decision trees used in real life will be more complex than Figure 10.4, but they will nevertheless display only a small fraction of possible future events and decisions. Decision trees are like grapevines: They are productive only if they are vigorously pruned.

● ● ● ● ●

SUMMARY

Good capital budgeting practice tries to identify the major uncertainties in project proposals. An awareness of these uncertainties may suggest ways that the project can be reconfigured to reduce the dangers, or it may point to some additional research that will confirm whether the project is worthwhile.

There are several ways in which companies try to identify and evaluate the threats to a project's success. The first is *sensitivity analysis*. Here the manager considers in turn each forecast or assumption that drives cash flows and recalculates NPV at optimistic and pessimistic values of that variable. The project is "sensitive to" that variable if the resulting range of NPVs is wide, particularly on the pessimistic side.

Sensitivity analysis often moves on to *break-even analysis*, which identifies break-even values of key variables. Suppose the manager is concerned about a possible shortfall in sales. Then it may be helpful to calculate the sales level at which the project just breaks even (NPV = 0) and to consider the odds that sales will fall that far. Break-even analysis is also done in terms of accounting income, although we do not recommend this application. Projects with a high proportion of fixed costs are likely to have higher break-even points. Because a shortfall in sales results in a larger decline in profits when the costs are largely fixed, such projects are said to have high *operating leverage*.

Sensitivity analysis and break-even analysis are easy, and they identify the forecasts and assumptions that really count for the project's success or failure. The important variables do not change one at a time, however. For example, when raw material prices are higher than forecasted, it's a good bet that selling prices will be higher too. The logical response is *scenario analysis*, which examines the effects on NPV of changing several variables at a time.

Scenario analysis looks at a limited number of combinations of variables. If you want to go whole hog and look at all possible combinations, you will have to turn to *Monte Carlo simulation*. In that case, you must build a financial model of the project and specify the probability distribution of each variable that determines cash flow. Then you ask the computer to draw random values for each variable and work out the resulting cash flows. In fact, you ask the computer to do this thousands of times in order to generate complete distributions of future cash flows. With these distributions in hand, you can get a better handle on expected cash flows and project risks. You can also experiment to see how the distributions would be affected by altering project scope or the ranges for any of the variables.

Elementary treatises on capital budgeting sometimes create the impression that once the manager has made an investment decision, there is nothing to do but sit back and watch the cash flows unfold. In practice, companies are constantly modifying their operations. If cash flows are better than anticipated, the project may be expanded; if they are worse, it may be contracted or abandoned altogether. Options to modify projects are known as *real options*. In this chapter, we introduced the main categories of real options: *expansion* options, *abandonment* options, *timing* options, and options providing *flexibility in production*.

Good managers take account of real options when they value a project. One convenient way to summarize real options and their cash-flow consequences is to create a *decision tree*. You identify the things that could happen to the project and the main counteractions that you might take. Then, working back from the future to the present, you can consider which action you *should* take in each case.

Decision trees can help to identify the possible impact of real options on project cash flows, but we largely skirted the issue of how to value real options. We return to this topic in Chapter 22, after we have covered option-valuation methods in the preceding two chapters.

Three not-too-technical references on real options are listed below. Additional references follow Chapter 22.

A. Dixit and R. Pindyck, "The Options Approach to Capital Investment," *Harvard Business Review* 73 (May–June 1995), pp. 105–115.

W. C. Kester, "Today's Options for Tomorrow's Growth," *Harvard Business Review* 62 (March–April 1984), pp. 153–160.

A. Triantis and A. Borison, "Real Options: State of the Practice," *Journal of Applied Corporate Finance* 14 (Summer 2001), pp. 8–24.

FURTHER READING

 **Select problems are available in McGraw-Hill's *Connect*. Please see the preface for more information.**

PROBLEM SETS

1. **Terminology*** Match each of the following terms to one of the definitions or descriptions listed below: sensitivity analysis, scenario analysis, break-even analysis, operating leverage, Monte Carlo simulation, decision tree, real option, tornado diagram.

   a. Recalculation of project NPV by changing several inputs to new but consistent values.

   b. Opportunity to modify a project at a future date.

   c. Analysis of how project NPV changes if different assumptions are made about sales, costs, and other key variables.

   d. The degree to which fixed costs magnify the effect on profits of a shortfall in sales.

   e. A graphical technique for displaying possible future events and decisions taken in response to those events.

   f. A graphical technique that is often used to display the results of a sensitivity analysis.

   g. Determination of the level of future sales at which project profitability or NPV equals zero.

   h. Method for calculating the probability distribution of possible outcomes.

2. **Project analysis** True or false?

   a. Sensitivity analysis is unnecessary for projects with asset betas that are equal to zero.

   b. Sensitivity analysis can be used to identify the variables most crucial to a project's success.

   c. If only one variable is uncertain, sensitivity analysis gives "optimistic" and "pessimistic" values for project cash flow and NPV.

   d. The break-even sales level of a project is higher when break-even is defined in terms of NPV rather than accounting income.

   e. Risk is reduced when most of the costs are fixed.

   f. Monte Carlo simulation can be used to help forecast cash flows.

3. **Sensitivity analysis** Otobai's staff (see Section 10-1) has come up with the following revised estimates for the electric scooter project:

	Optimistic	Pessimistic
% change in capital investment	−20.00	60.00
% change in working capital	−50.00	50.00
% change in units sold	25.00	−20.00
% change in price	20.00	−25.00
Cost of goods sold as % of sales	40.00	75.00
% change in fixed costs	−50.00	70.00

Conduct a sensitivity analysis using the spreadsheets (available in Connect). What are the principal uncertainties in the project?

4. **Sensitivity analysis** The Rustic Welt Company is proposing to replace its old welt-making machinery with more modern equipment. The new equipment costs $9 million (the existing equipment has zero salvage value). The attraction of the new machinery is that it is expected to cut manufacturing costs from their current level of $8 a welt to $4. However, as the following table shows, there is some uncertainty both about future sales and about the performance of the new machinery:

	Pessimistic	Expected	Optimistic
Sales (millions of welts)	0.4	0.5	0.7
Manufacturing cost with new machinery (dollars per welt)	6	4	3
Economic life of new machinery (years)	7	10	13

Conduct a sensitivity analysis of the replacement decision, assuming a discount rate of 12%. Rustic Welt does not pay taxes.

5. **Sensitivity analysis** Use the spreadsheet for the guano project in Chapter 6 to undertake a sensitivity analysis of the project. Make whatever assumptions seem reasonable to you. What are the critical variables? What should the company's response be to your analysis?

6. **Sensitivity analysis** Emperor's Clothes Fashions can invest $5 million in a new plant for producing invisible makeup. The plant has an expected life of five years, and expected sales are 6 million jars of makeup a year. Fixed costs are $2 million a year, and variable costs are $1 per jar. The product will be priced at $2 per jar. The plant will be depreciated straight-line over five years to a salvage value of zero. The opportunity cost of capital is 10%, and the tax rate is 40%.

   a. What is project NPV under these base-case assumptions?

   b. What is NPV if variable costs turn out to be $1.20 per jar?

   c. What is NPV if fixed costs turn out to be $1.5 million per year?

   d. At what price per jar would project NPV equal zero?

7. **Sensitivity analysis*** A project currently generates sales of $10 million, variable costs equal 50% of sales, and fixed costs are $2 million. The firm's tax rate is 21%. What are the effects of the following changes on cash flow?

   a. Sales increase from $10 million to $11 million.

   b. Variable costs increase to 65% of sales.

8. **Scenario analysis**   What is the NPV of the electric scooter project under the following scenario?

Unit sales are 20% below expectations.

Unit price is 10% below expectations.

Unit variable cost remains at 50% of revenue.

Fixed costs increase by 5%.

Investment in plant and equipment and in working capital are unchanged.

9. **Scenario analysis**   You are considering a proposal to produce and market a new sluffing machine. The most likely outcomes for the project are as follows:

Expected sales: 30,000 units per year

Unit price: $50

Variable cost: $30

Fixed cost: $300,000

The project will last for 10 years and requires an initial investment of $1 million, which will be depreciated straight-line over the project life to a final value of zero. The firm's tax rate is 30%, and the required rate of return is 12%.

However, you recognize that some of these estimates are subject to error. Sales could fall 30% below expectations for the life of the project and, if that happens, the unit price would probably be only $40. The good news is that fixed costs could be as low as $200,000, and variable costs would decline in proportion to sales.

a. What is project NPV if all variables are as expected?

b. What is NPV in the worst-case scenario?

10. **Break-even analysis**   Break-even calculations are most often concerned with the effect of a shortfall in sales, but they could equally well focus on any other component of cash flow. Dog Days is considering a proposal to produce and market a caviar-flavored dog food. It will involve an initial investment of $90,000 that can be depreciated for tax straight-line over 10 years. In each of years 1 to 10, the project is forecast to produce sales of $100,000 and to incur variable costs of 50% of sales and fixed costs of $30,000. The corporate tax rate is 30%, and the cost of capital is 10%.

a. Calculate the NPV and accounting break-even levels of fixed costs.

b. Suppose that you are worried that the corporate tax rate will be increased immediately after you commit to the project. Calculate the break-even rate of taxes.

c. How would a rise in the tax rate affect the accounting break-even point?

11. **Break-even analysis**   Dime a Dozen Diamonds makes synthetic diamonds by treating carbon. Each diamond can be sold for $100. The materials cost for a synthetic diamond is $40. The fixed costs incurred each year for factory upkeep and administrative expenses are $200,000. The machinery costs $1 million and is depreciated straight-line over 10 years to a salvage value of zero.

a. What is the accounting break-even level of sales in terms of number of diamonds sold?

b. What is the NPV break-even level of sales assuming a tax rate of 35%, a 10-year project life, and a discount rate of 12%?

12. **Break-even analysis**   Modern Artifacts can produce keepsakes that will be sold for $80 each. Nondepreciation fixed costs are $1,000 per year, and variable costs are $60 per unit. The initial investment of $3,000 will be depreciated straight-line over its useful life of five years to a final value of zero, and the discount rate is 10%.

a. What is the accounting break-even level of sales if the firm pays no taxes?

b. What is the NPV break-even level of sales if the firm pays no taxes?

c. What is the accounting break-even level of sales if the firm's tax rate is 20%?

d. What is the NPV break-even level of sales if the firm's tax rate is 20%?

13. **Break-even analysis**   Define the cash-flow break-even point as the sales volume (in dollars) at which cash flow equals zero.

    a. Is the cash-flow break-even level of sales higher or lower than the zero-profit (accounting) break-even point?

    b. If a project operates at cash-flow break-even [see part (a)] for all future years, is its NPV positive or negative?

14. **Break-even analysis**   A financial analyst has computed both accounting and NPV break-even sales levels for a project using straight-line depreciation over a six-year period. The project manager wants to know what will happen to these estimates if the firm can write off the entire investment in the year that it is made. The firm is in a 21% tax bracket.

    a. Would the accounting break-even level of sales in the first years of the project increase or decrease?

    b. Would the NPV break-even level of sales in the first years of the project increase or decrease?

    c. If you were advising the analyst, would the answer to part (a) or (b) be important to you? Specifically, would you say that the switch to immediate expensing makes the project more or less attractive?

15. **Fixed and variable costs**   In a slow year, Deutsche Burgers will produce 2 million hamburgers at a total cost of $3.5 million. In a good year, it can produce 4 million hamburgers at a total cost of $4.5 million.

    a. What are the fixed costs of hamburger production?

    b. What are the variable costs?

    c. What is the average cost per burger when the firm produces 1 million hamburgers?

    d. What is the average cost when the firm produces 2 million hamburgers?

    e. Why is the average cost lower when more burgers are produced?

16. **Operating leverage**   You estimate that your cattle farm will generate $1 million of profits on sales of $4 million under normal economic conditions and that the degree of operating leverage is 8.

    a. What will profits be if sales turn out to be $3.5 million?

    b. What if they are $4.5 million?

17. **Operating leverage**   Look again at Modern Artifacts in Problem 12.

    a. What is the degree of operating leverage of Modern Artifacts when sales are $7,000?

    b. What is the degree of operating leverage when sales are $12,000?

    c. Why is operating leverage different at these two levels of sales?

18. **Operating leverage**   What is the lowest possible value for the degree of operating leverage for a profitable firm? Show with a numerical example that if Modern Artifacts (see Problem 12) has zero fixed costs and zero depreciation, then DOL = 1 and, in fact, sales and profits are directly proportional, so a 1% change in sales results in a 1% change in profits.

19. **Operating leverage***   A project has fixed costs of $1,000 per year, depreciation charges of $500 a year, annual revenue of $6,000, and variable costs equal to two-thirds of revenues.

    a. If sales increase by 10%, what will be the increase in pretax profits?

    b. What is the degree of operating leverage of this project?

20. **Monte Carlo simulation**   Suppose a manager has already estimated a project's cash flows, calculated its NPV, and done a sensitivity analysis like the one shown in Table 10.2. List the additional steps required to carry out a Monte Carlo simulation of project cash flows.

21. **Real options**   Explain why options to expand or contract production are most valuable when forecasts about future business conditions are most uncertain.

22. **Real options**   Describe the real option in each of the following cases:

    a. Moda di Milano postpones a major investment. The expansion has positive NPV on a discounted cash-flow basis, but top management wants to get a better fix on product demand before proceeding.

    b. Western Telecom commits to production of digital switching equipment specially designed for the European market. The project has a negative NPV, but it is justified on strategic grounds by the need for a strong market position in the rapidly growing, and potentially very profitable, market.

    c. Western Telecom vetoes a fully integrated, automated production line for the new digital switches. It relies on standard, less-expensive equipment. The automated production line is more efficient overall, according to a discounted cash-flow calculation.

    d. Mount Fuji Airways buys a jumbo jet with special equipment that allows the plane to be switched quickly from freight to passenger use or vice versa.

23. **Real options**   True or false?

    a. Decision trees can help identify and describe real options.

    b. The option to expand increases PV.

    c. High abandonment value decreases PV.

    d. If a project has positive NPV, the firm should always invest immediately.

24. **Real options***   A silver mine can yield 10,000 ounces of silver at a variable cost of $32 per ounce. The fixed costs of owning the mine are $40,000 per year regardless of whether the mine is open or closed. In half the years, silver can be sold for $48 per ounce; in the other years, silver can be sold for only $24 per ounce. Ignore taxes.

    a. What is the average cash flow you will receive from the mine if it is always kept in operation and the silver always is sold in the year it is mined?

    b. Now suppose you can costlessly shut down the mine in years of low silver prices. What happens to the average cash flow from the mine?

25. **Real options**   An auto plant that costs $100 million to build can produce a line of flex-fuel cars. The investment will produce cash flows with a present value of $140 million if the line is successful but only $50 million if it is unsuccessful. You believe that the probability of success is only about 50%. You will learn whether the line is successful immediately after building the plant.

    a. Would you build the plant?

    b. Suppose that the plant can be sold for $95 million to another automaker if the auto line is not successful. Now would you build the plant?

    c. Illustrate the option to abandon in part (b) using a decision tree.

26. **Decision trees**   Look back at the Vegetron electric mop project in Section 9-4. Assume that if tests fail and Vegetron continues to go ahead with the project, the $1 million investment would generate only $75,000 a year. Display Vegetron's problem as a decision tree.

27. **Decision trees***   Your midrange guess as to the amount of oil in a prospective field is 10 million barrels, but there is a 50% chance that the amount of oil is 15 million barrels and a 50% chance of 5 million barrels. If the actual amount of oil is 15 million barrels, the present value of the cash flows from drilling will be $8 million. If the amount is only 5 million barrels, the present value will be only $2 million. It costs $3 million to drill the well. Suppose that a seismic test costing $100,000 can immediately verify the amount of oil under the ground. Is it worth paying for the test? Use a decision tree to justify your answer.

28. **Decision trees**   Look again at the decision tree in Figure 10.4. Expand the possible outcomes as follows:

    - Blockbuster: PV = $1.5 billion with 5% probability.
    - Above average: PV = $700 million with 20% probability.
    - Average: PV = $300 million with 40% probability.
    - Below average: PV = $100 million with 25% probability.
    - "Dog": PV = $40 million with 10% probability.

    Redraw the decision tree. Is the $18 million investment in phase II trials still positive NPV?

29. **Decision trees**   Look again at the example in Figure 10.4. The R&D team has put forward a proposal to invest an extra $20 million in expanded phase II trials. The object is to prove that the drug can be administered by a simple inhaler rather than as a liquid. If successful, the scope of use is broadened and the upside PV increases to $1 billion. The probabilities of success are unchanged. Go to the Beyond the Page Excel spreadsheet version of Figure 10.4. Is the extra $20 million investment worthwhile? Would your answer change if the probability of success in the phase III trials falls to 75%?

CHALLENGE

30. **Project analysis**   New Energy is evaluating a new biofuel facility. The plant would cost $4,000 million to build and has the potential to produce up to 40 million barrels of synthetic oil a year. The product is a close substitute for conventional oil and would sell for the same price. The market price of oil currently is fluctuating around $100 per barrel, but there is considerable uncertainty about future prices. Variable costs for the organic inputs to the production process are estimated at $82 per barrel and are expected to be stable. In addition, annual upkeep and maintenance expenses on the facility will be $100 million regardless of the production level. The plant has an expected life of 15 years, and it will be depreciated straight-line over 10 years. Salvage value net of clean-up costs is expected to be negligible. Demand for the product is difficult to forecast. Depending on consumer acceptance, sales might range from 25 million to 35 million barrels annually. The discount rate is 12% and New Energy's tax bracket is 25%.

    a. Find the project NPV for the following combinations of oil price and sales volume. Which source of uncertainty seems most important to the success of the project?

	Oil Price		
Annual Sales (millions of barrels)	**$80/Barrel**	**$100/Barrel**	**$120/Barrel**
25			
30			
35			

    b. At an oil price of $100, what level of annual sales, maintained over the life of the plant, is necessary for NPV break-even? (This will require trial and error unless you are familiar with more advanced features of Excel such as the Goal Seek command.)

    c. At an oil price of $100, what is the accounting break-even level of sales in each year? Why does it change each year? Does this notion of break-even seem reasonable to you?

    d. If each of the scenarios in the table in part (a) is equally likely, what is the NPV of the facility?

    e. Why might the facility be worth building despite your answer to part (d)? (*Hint:* What real option may the firm have to avoid losses in low-oil-price scenarios?)

31. **Monte Carlo simulation**   Look back at the guano project in Section 6-3. Use the Crystal Ball™ software to simulate how uncertainty about inflation could affect the project's cash flows.

32. **Decision trees**   Magna Charter is a new corporation formed by Agnes Magna to provide an executive flying service for the southeastern United States. The founder thinks there will be a ready demand from businesses that cannot justify a full-time company plane but nevertheless need one from time to time. However, the venture is not a sure thing. There is a 40% chance that demand in the first year will be low. If it is low, there is a 60% chance that it will remain low in subsequent years. On the other hand, if the initial demand is high, there is an 80% chance that it will stay high. The immediate problem is to decide what kind of plane to buy. A turboprop costs $550,000. A piston-engine plane costs only $250,000 but has less capacity. Moreover, the piston-engine plane is an old design and likely to depreciate rapidly. Ms. Magna thinks that next year secondhand piston aircraft will be available for only $150,000.

    Table 10.6 shows how the payoffs in years 1 and 2 from both planes depend on the pattern of demand. You can see, for example, that if demand is high in both years 1 and 2, the turbo will provide a payoff of $960,000 in year 2. If demand is high in year 1 but low in year 2, the turbo's payoff in the second year is only $220,000. Think of the payoffs in the second year as the cash flow that year plus the year-2 value of any subsequent cash flows. Also think of these cash flows as certainty equivalents, which can therefore be discounted at the risk-free interest rate of 10%.

    Ms. Magna now has an idea: Why not start out with one piston-engine plane? If demand is low in the first year, Magna Charter can sit tight with this one relatively inexpensive aircraft. On the other hand, if demand is high in the first year she can buy a second piston-engine plane for only $150,000. In this case, if demand continues to be high, the payoff in year 2 from the two piston planes will be $800,000. However, if demand in year 2 were to decline, the payoff would be only $100,000.

    a. Draw a decision tree setting out Magna Charter's choices.

    b. If Magna Charter buys a piston plane, should it expand if demand turns out to be high in the first year?

    c. Given your answer to part (b), would you recommend that Ms. Magna buy the turboprop or the piston-engine plane today?

    d. What would be the NPV of an investment in a piston plane if there were no option to expand? How much extra value is contributed by the option to expand?

Payoffs from the Turboprop						
Year 1 demand		High (0.6)			Low (0.4)	
Year 1 payoff		$150			$30	
Year 2 demand	High (0.8)		Low (0.2)	High (0.4)		Low (0.6)
Year 2 payoff	$960		$220	$930		$140
Payoffs from the Piston Engine						
Year 1 demand		High (0.6)			Low (0.4)	
Year 1 payoff		$100			$50	
Year 2 demand	High (0.8)		Low (0.2)	High (0.4)		Low (0.6)
Year 2 payoff	$410		$180	$220		$100

❯TABLE 10.6
The possible payoffs from Ms. Magna's flying service. (All figures are in thousands. Probabilities are in parentheses.)

MINI-CASE •••••

Waldo County

Waldo County, the well-known real estate developer, worked long hours, and he expected his staff to do the same. So George Chavez was not surprised to receive a call from the boss just as George was about to leave for a long summer's weekend.

Mr. County's success had been built on a remarkable instinct for a good site. He would exclaim "Location! Location! Location!" at some point in every planning meeting. Yet finance was not his strong suit. On this occasion, he wanted George to go over the figures for a new $90 million outlet mall designed to intercept tourists heading downeast toward Maine. "First thing Monday will do just fine," he said as he handed George the file. "I'll be in my house in Bar Harbor if you need me."

George's first task was to draw up a summary of the projected revenues and costs. The results are shown in Table 10.7. Note that the mall's revenues would come from two sources: The company would charge retailers an annual rent for the space they occupied and, in addition, it would receive 5% of each store's gross sales.

Construction of the mall was likely to take three years. The construction costs could be depreciated straight-line over 15 years starting in year 3. As in the case of the company's other developments, the mall would be built to the highest specifications and would not need to be rebuilt until year 17. The land was expected to retain its value, but could not be depreciated for tax purposes.

Construction costs, revenues, operating and maintenance costs, and local real estate taxes were all likely to rise in line with inflation, which was forecasted at 2% a year. Local real estate taxes are deductible for corporate tax. The company's corporate tax rate was 25% and the cost of capital was 9% in nominal terms.

George decided first to check that the project made financial sense. He then proposed to look at some of the things that might go wrong. His boss certainly had a nose for a good retail project, but he was not infallible. The Salome project had been a disaster because store sales had turned out to be 40% below forecast. What if that happened here? George wondered just how far sales could fall short of forecast before the project would be underwater.

Inflation was another source of uncertainty. Some people were talking about a zero long-term inflation rate, but George also wondered what would happen if inflation jumped to, say, 10%.

		Year					
		0	1	2	3	4	5–17
Investment:							
Land		30					
Construction		20	30	10			
Operations:							
Rentals					12	12	12
Share of retail sales					24	24	24
Operating and maintenance costs		2	4	4	10	10	10
Local real estate taxes		2	2	3	4	4	4

❭ **TABLE 10.7**   Projected revenues and costs in real terms for the Downeast Tourist Mall (figures in $ millions)

A third concern was possible construction cost overruns and delays due to required zoning changes and environmental approvals. George had seen cases of 25% construction cost overruns and delays up to 12 months between purchase of the land and the start of construction. He decided that he should examine the effect that this scenario would have on the project's profitability.

"Hey, this might be fun," George exclaimed to Mr. Waldo's secretary, Fifi, who was heading for Old Orchard Beach for the weekend. "I might even try Monte Carlo."

"Waldo went to Monte Carlo once," Fifi replied. "Lost a bundle at the roulette table. I wouldn't remind him. Just show him the bottom line. Will it make money or lose money? That's the bottom line."

"OK, no Monte Carlo," George agreed. But he realized that building a spreadsheet and running scenarios was not enough. He had to figure out how to summarize and present his results to Mr. County.

QUESTIONS

1. What is the project's NPV, given the projections in Table 10.7?

2. Conduct a sensitivity and a scenario analysis of the project. What do these analyses reveal about the project's risks and potential value?

CHAPTER

How to Ensure That Projects Truly Have Positive NPVs

Why is a manager who has learned about discounted cash flow (DCF) like a baby with a hammer? Answer: Because to a baby with a hammer, everything looks like a nail. Our point is that you should not blindly apply DCF without thinking about the reasons that a project may add value. You also need to ensure that the investment process is designed to produce well-researched investment proposals that will add value for shareholders.

We start with the second issue. Investment proposals may emerge from many different parts of the organization. So companies need procedures to ensure that every project is assessed consistently. We review how firms develop budgets for capital investments, how they authorize specific projects, and how they check whether projects perform as promised.

We then ask how managers can distinguish projects that truly have positive NPVs from those that appear worthwhile merely because of forecasting errors? We suggest that they should ask some probing questions about the possible sources of economic gain.

To make good investment decisions, you need to understand your firm's competitive advantages. This is where corporate strategy and finance come together. Good strategy positions the firm to generate the most value from its assets and growth opportunities. The search for good strategy starts with understanding how your firm stacks up versus your competitors and how they will respond to your initiatives. Are your cash-flow forecasts realistic in your competitive environment? What effects will your competitors' actions have on the NPVs of your investments?

The first section in this chapter is concerned with the organization of the investment process. We then review certain common pitfalls in capital budgeting, notably the tendency to apply DCF when market values are already available and no DCF calculations are needed. The third section covers the economic rents that underlie all positive-NPV investments. The final section presents a case study describing how Marvin Enterprises, the gargle blaster company, analyzed the introduction of a radically new product.

11-1 How Firms Organize the Investment Process

The Capital Budget

Senior management needs some forewarning of future investment outlays. So for most large firms, the investment process starts with the preparation of an annual capital budget, which is a list of investment projects planned for the coming year. Smaller investments are not itemized separately in the budget. For example, they may be grouped into the broad category of "machine replacement." Larger investments that significantly affect the company's future will receive greater attention.

Many of the investment proposals that are included in the budget bubble up from the bottom of the organization. But ideas are also likely to come from higher up. For example, the managers of plants A and B cannot be expected to see the potential benefits of closing their plants and consolidating production at a new plant C. We expect divisional managers to propose plant C. Similarly, divisions 1 and 2 may not be eager to give up their own data processing operations to a large central computer. That proposal would come from senior management.

Inconsistent assumptions can creep into these expenditure plans. For example, suppose the manager of your furniture division is bullish on housing starts, but the manager of your appliance division is bearish. The furniture division may push for a major investment in new facilities, while the appliance division may propose a plan for retrenchment. It would be better if both managers could agree on a common estimate of housing starts and base their investment proposals on it. Therefore, many firms begin the capital budgeting process by establishing consensus forecasts of economic indicators, such as inflation and growth in national income, as well as forecasts of particular items that are important to the firm's business, such as housing starts or the prices of raw materials. These forecasts are then used as the basis for the capital budget.

Preparation of the capital budget is not a rigid, bureaucratic exercise. There is plenty of give-and-take and back-and-forth. Divisional managers negotiate with plant managers and fine-tune the division's list of projects. The budget is then reviewed and pruned by senior management and staff that specialize in planning and financial analysis. Usually, there are negotiations between senior management and divisional management, and there may also be special analyses of major outlays or ventures into new areas.

The final capital budget needs to reflect the corporation's strategic plans. These plans take a top-down view of the company. They attempt to identify businesses where the company has a competitive advantage. They also seek to identify businesses that should be sold or allowed to run down. A firm's capital investment choices should reflect both bottom-up and top-down views of the business. Plant and division managers, who do most of the work in bottom-up capital budgeting, may not see the forest for the trees. Strategic planners may have a mistaken view of the forest because they do not look at the trees one by one.

Project Authorizations—and the Problem of Biased Forecasts

Once the budget has been approved, it generally remains the basis for planning over the ensuing year. However, it is not the final sign-off for specific projects. Most companies require appropriation requests for each proposal. Before each investment gets the final go-ahead, it will need to be supported by a more detailed analysis setting out particulars of the project, cash-flow forecasts, and present value calculations.

Many investment projects carry a high price tag and may determine the shape of the firm's business 10 or 20 years in the future. Hence, final approval of appropriation requests tends to be reserved for top management. Companies set ceilings on the size of projects that divisional managers can authorize. Often these ceilings are surprisingly low. For example, a large company, investing $400 million per year, might require top management to approve all projects over $500,000.

The result is that the head office may receive several hundred investment proposals each year. As each proposal travels up the organization, alliances are formed. Thus, once a division has screened its own plants' proposals, the plants in that division unite in competing against outsiders. The final proposal may be silent on the questions and doubts that were raised during the project's travel up the organization.

Project sponsors are liable to be both overconfident and overoptimistic about their pet projects, and these two traits make it particularly difficult for others to judge the merits of a proposal. Most people tend to be overconfident when they forecast. Events they think are almost certain to occur may actually happen only 80% of the time, and events they believe are impossible may happen 20% of the time.[1] Therefore. project risks are understated.

Furthermore, anyone who is keen to get a project accepted is likely to look on the bright side when forecasting the project's cash flows. Such overoptimism seems to be a common feature in financial forecasts. Overoptimism afflicts governments too, probably more than private businesses. How often have you heard of a new dam, highway, or military aircraft that actually cost less than was originally forecasted?

BEYOND THE PAGE

Overoptimism and cost overruns

mhhe.com/brealey13e

Overoptimism is not altogether bad. Psychologists stress that optimism and confidence are likely to increase effort, commitment, and persistence. The problem is that hundreds of appropriation requests may reach senior management each year—all essentially sales documents presented by united fronts and designed to persuade. Alternative schemes have been filtered out at earlier stages. The forecasts have been doctored to ensure that NPV appears positive. One response of senior managers to this problem of biased information is to impose rigid expenditure limits on individual plants or divisions. These limits force the subunits to choose among projects. The firm ends up using capital rationing not because capital is unobtainable, but as a way of decentralizing decisions.

It is probably impossible to eliminate bias completely, but senior managers should take care not to encourage it. For example, if divisional managers believe that success depends on having the largest division rather than the most profitable one, they will propose large expansion projects that they do not truly believe have positive NPVs. Or if new plant managers are pushed to generate increased earnings right away, they will be tempted to propose quick-payback projects even when NPV is sacrificed.

Sometimes senior managers try to offset overoptimism by increasing the hurdle rate for capital expenditure. Suppose the true cost of capital is 10%, but the CFO is frustrated by the large fraction of projects that don't subsequently earn 10%. She therefore directs project sponsors to use a 15% discount rate. In other words, she adds a 5% fudge factor in an attempt to offset forecast bias. But it doesn't work; it never works. Brealey, Myers, and Allen's Second Law[2] explains why. The law states: *The proportion of proposed projects having positive NPVs at the corporate hurdle rate is independent of the hurdle rate.*

The law is not a facetious conjecture. It was tested in a large oil company where staff kept careful statistics on capital investment projects. About 85% of projects had positive NPVs. (The remaining 15% were proposed for other reasons—for example, to meet environmental standards.) One year, after several quarters of disappointing earnings, top management decided that more financial discipline was called for and increased the corporate hurdle rate by several percentage points. But in the following year, the fraction of projects with positive NPVs stayed rock-steady at 85%. If you're worried about bias in forecasted cash flows, the only remedy is careful analysis of the forecasts. Do not add fudge factors to the cost of capital.[3]

---

[1]For example, in a classic test of overconfidence, a large group of students was asked to provide estimates—for example, the number of physicians listed in the Boston yellow pages or the number of automobile imports into the United States. In each case, they were also asked to provide limits within which they were 98% confident that the actual value fell. If these estimated limits were unbiased, the true answer to the questions would fall outside the limits only 2% of the time. But the tests consistently showed that the limits were breached far more often than this (51% of the time in the case of the question about the yellow pages). In other words, the students were much more confident of their estimates than was justified. See M. Alpert and H. Raiffa, "A Progress Report on the Training of Probability Assessors," in D. Kahneman, P. Slovic, L. A. Tversky (eds.), *Judgment under Uncertainty: Heuristics and Biases* (Cambridge, U.K.: Cambridge University Press, 1982), pp. 294–305.

[2]There is no First Law. We think "Second Law" sounds better. There is a Third Law, but that is for another chapter.

[3]Adding a fudge factor to the cost of capital also favors quick-payback projects and penalizes longer-lived projects, which tend to have lower rates of return but higher NPVs. Adding a 5% fudge factor to the discount rate is roughly equivalent to reducing the forecast and present value of the first year's cash flow by 5%. The impact on the present value of a cash flow 10 years in the future is much greater because the fudge factor is compounded in the discount rate. The fudge factor is not too much of a burden for a 2- or 3-year project but is an enormous burden for a 10- or 20-year project.

Postaudits

Most firms keep a check on the progress of large projects by conducting postaudits shortly after the projects have begun to operate. Postaudits identify problems that need fixing, check the accuracy of forecasts, and suggest questions that should have been asked before the project was undertaken. Postaudits pay off mainly by helping managers do a better job when it comes to the next round of investments. After a postaudit, the controller may say, "We should have anticipated the extra training required for production workers." When the next proposal arrives, training will get the attention it deserves.

Postaudits may not be able to measure all of a project's costs and benefits. It is often impossible to split the project away from the rest of the business. Suppose that you have just taken over a trucking firm that operates a delivery service for local stores. You decide to improve service by installing custom software to keep track of packages and to schedule trucks. You also construct a dispatching center and buy five new diesel trucks. A year later, you try a postaudit of the investment in software. You verify that it is working properly and check actual costs of purchase, installation, and operation against projections. But how do you identify the incremental cash inflows? No one has kept records of the extra diesel fuel that would have been used or the extra shipments that would have been lost absent the software. You may be able to verify that service is better, but how much of the improvement comes from the new trucks, how much from the dispatching center, and how much from the software? The only meaningful measures of success are for the delivery business as a whole.

11-2   Look First to Market Values

Let us suppose that you have persuaded all your project sponsors to give honest forecasts. Although those forecasts are unbiased, they are still likely to contain errors, some positive and others negative. The average error will be zero, but that is little consolation because you want to accept only projects with *truly* superior profitability.

Think, for example, of what would happen if you were to jot down your estimates of the cash flows from operating various lines of business. You would probably find that about half *appeared* to have positive NPVs. This may not be because you personally possess any superior skill in operating jumbo jets or running a chain of laundromats but because you have inadvertently introduced large errors into your estimates of the cash flows. The more projects you contemplate, the more likely you are to uncover projects that *appear* to be extremely worthwhile.

What can you do to prevent forecast errors from swamping genuine information? As a senior manager, you can't be expected to check every cash-flow forecast, but you can ask some questions to ensure that each project truly does have a positive NPV. We suggest that you begin by looking at market values.

The BMW and Your Sporting Idol

The following parable should help to illustrate what we mean. Your local BMW dealer is announcing a special offer. For $85,000, you get not only a brand-new BMW 6-Series convertible, but also the chance to enjoy a day's coaching from your favorite sporting hero. You wonder how much you are paying for that day.

There are two possible approaches to the problem. You could evaluate each of the BMW's features, starting with the Turbo V8 engine and ending with the exclusive Nappa leather interior, and conclude that the car is worth $80,000. This would seem to suggest that the day with your sporting hero is costing you $5,000. Alternatively, you might nip round to a couple other BMW dealers and discover that the going market price for the car is $85,000 so that the special offer is costing you nothing. As long as there is a competitive market for BMWs, the latter approach makes more sense.

Security analysts face a similar problem whenever they value a company's stock. They must consider the information that is already known to the market about a company, *and* they must evaluate the information that is known only to them. The information that is known to the market is the BMW; the private information is the day with your sporting idol. Investors have already evaluated the information that is generally known. Security analysts do not need to evaluate this information again. They can *start* with the market price of the stock and concentrate on valuing their private information.

While lesser mortals would instinctively accept the BMW's market value of $85,000, the financial manager is trained to enumerate and value all the costs and benefits from an investment and is therefore tempted to substitute his or her own opinion for the market's. Unfortunately, this approach increases the chance of error. Many capital assets are traded in a competitive market, so it makes sense to *start* with the market price and then ask why you can earn more than your rivals from these assets.

EXAMPLE 11.1 • Investing in a New Department Store

We encountered a department store chain that estimated the present value of the expected cash flows from each proposed store, including the price at which it could eventually sell the store. Although the firm took considerable care with these estimates, it was disturbed to find that its conclusions were heavily influenced by the forecasted selling price of each store. Management disclaimed any particular real estate expertise, but it discovered that its investment decisions were unintentionally dominated by its assumptions about future real estate prices.

Once the financial managers realized this, they always checked the decision to open a new store by asking the following question: "Let us assume that the property is fairly priced. What is the evidence that it is best suited to one of our department stores rather than to some other use?" In other words, *if an asset is worth more to others than it is to you, then beware of bidding for the asset against them.*

Let us take the department store problem a little further. Suppose that the new store costs $100 million.[4] You forecast that it will generate after-tax cash flow of $8 million a year for 10 years. Real estate prices are estimated to grow by 3% a year, so the expected value of the real estate at the end of 10 years is $100 \times (1.03)^{10} = \$134$ million. At a discount rate of 10%, your proposed department store has an NPV of $1 million:

$$\text{NPV} = -100 + \frac{8}{1.10} + \frac{8}{(1.10)^2} + \cdots + \frac{8 + 134}{(1.10)^{10}} = \$1 \text{ million}$$

Notice how sensitive this NPV is to the ending value of the real estate. For example, an ending value of $120 million implies an NPV of –$5 million.

It is helpful to imagine such a business as divided into two parts—a real estate subsidiary that buys the building and a retailing subsidiary that rents and operates it. Then figure out how much rent the real estate subsidiary would have to charge, and ask whether the retailing subsidiary could afford to pay the rent.

---

[4]For simplicity, we assume the $100 million goes entirely to real estate. In real life, there would also be substantial investments in fixtures, information systems, training, and start-up costs.

In some cases, a fair market rental can be estimated from real estate transactions. For example, we might observe that similar retail space recently rented for $10 million a year. In that case, we would conclude that our department store was an unattractive use for the site. Once the site had been acquired, it would be better to rent it out at $10 million than to use it for a store generating only $8 million.

Suppose, on the other hand, that the property could be rented for only $7 million per year. The department store could pay this amount to the real estate subsidiary and still earn a net operating cash flow of 8 − 7 = $1 million. It is therefore the best *current* use for the real estate.[5]

Will it also be the best *future* use? Maybe not, depending on whether retail profits keep pace with any rent increases. Suppose that real estate prices and rents are expected to increase by 3% per year. The real estate subsidiary must charge 7 × 1.03 = $7.21 million in year 2, 7.21 × 1.03 = $7.43 million in year 3, and so on.[6] Figure 11.1 shows that the store's income fails to cover the rental after year 5.

If these forecasts are right, the store has only a five-year economic life; from that point on, the real estate is more valuable in some other use. If you stubbornly believe that the department store is the best long-term use for the site, you must be ignoring potential growth in income from the store.[7]

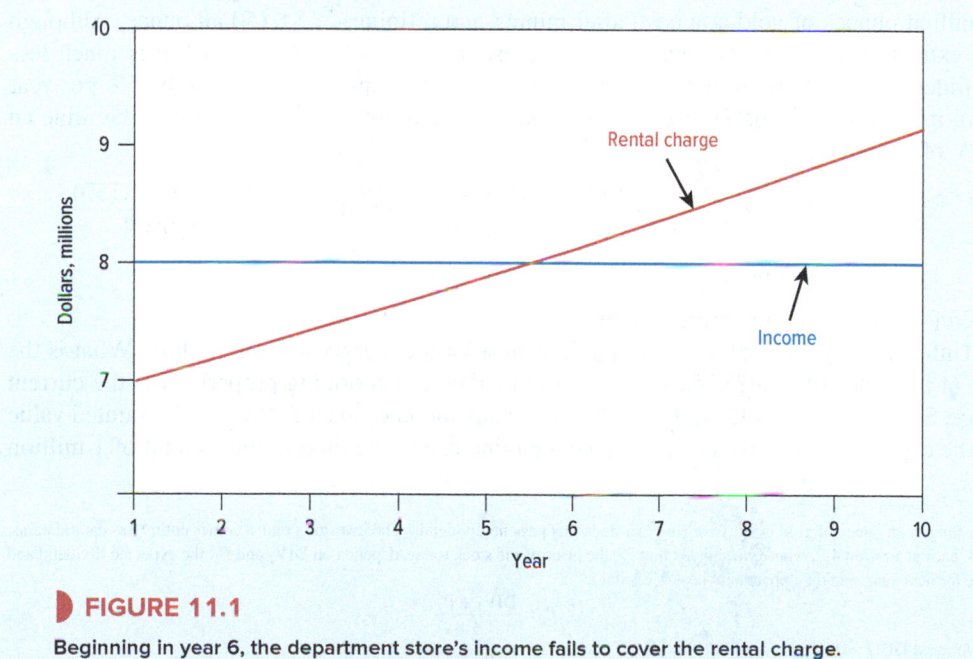

> **FIGURE 11.1**

Beginning in year 6, the department store's income fails to cover the rental charge.

---

[5] The fair market rent equals the profit generated by the real estate's *second*-best use.

[6] This rental stream yields a 10% rate of return to the real estate subsidiary. Each year it gets a 7% "dividend" and 3% capital gain. Growth at 3% would bring the value of the property to $134 million by year 10.

The present value (at $r = .10$) of the growing stream of rents is

$$PV = \frac{7}{r - g} = \frac{7}{.10 - .03} = \$100 \text{ million}$$

This PV is the initial market value of the property.

[7] Another possibility is that real estate rents and values are expected to grow at less than 3% a year. But in that case, the real estate subsidiary would have to charge more than $7 million rent in year 1 to justify its $100 million real estate investment (see footnote 4). That would make the department store even less attractive.

There is a general point here as illustrated in Example 11.1. Whenever you make a capital investment decision, think what bets you are placing. Our department store example involved at least two bets—one on real estate prices and another on the firm's ability to run a successful department store. But that suggests some alternative strategies. For instance, it would be foolish to make a lousy department store investment just because you are optimistic about real estate prices. You would do better to buy real estate and rent it out to the highest bidders. The converse is also true. You shouldn't be deterred from going ahead with a profitable department store because you are pessimistic about real estate prices. You would do better to sell the real estate and *rent* it back for the department store. We suggest that you separate the two bets by first asking, "Should we open a department store on this site, assuming that the real estate is fairly priced?" and then deciding whether you also want to go into the real estate business.

Let us look at another example of how market prices can help you make better decisions.

EXAMPLE 11.2 • Opening a Gold Mine

Kingsley Solomon is considering a proposal to open a new gold mine. He estimates that the mine will cost $500 million to develop and that in each of the next 10 years, it will produce 1 million ounces of gold at a cost, after mining and refining, of $1,150 an ounce. Although the extraction costs can be predicted with reasonable accuracy, Mr. Solomon is much less confident about future gold prices. His best guess is that the price will rise by 5% per year from its current level of $1,500 an ounce. At a discount rate of 10%, this gives the mine an NPV of −$35 million:

$$\text{NPV} = -500 + \frac{.1(1,575 - 1,150)}{1.10} + \frac{.1(1,654 - 1,150)}{(1.10)^2} + \cdots + \frac{.1(2,443 - 1,150)}{(1.10)^{10}}$$

$$= -\$35 \text{ million}$$

Therefore, the gold mine project is rejected.

Unfortunately, Mr. Solomon did not look at what the market was telling him. What is the PV of an ounce of gold? Clearly, if the gold market is functioning properly, it is the current price, $1,500 an ounce. Gold does not produce any income, so $1,500 is the discounted value of the expected future gold price.[8] Since the mine is expected to produce a total of 1 million

---

[8]Investing in an ounce of gold is like investing in a stock that pays no dividends: The investor's return comes entirely as capital gains. Look back at Section 4-2, where we showed that P_0, the price of the stock today, depends on DIV_1 and P_1, the expected dividend and price for next year, and the opportunity cost of capital *r:*

$$P_0 = \frac{\text{DIV}_1 + P_1}{1 + r}$$

But for gold $\text{DIV}_1 = 0$, so

$$P_0 = \frac{P_1}{1 + r}$$

In words, *today's price is the present value of next year's price.* Therefore, we don't have to know either P_1 or r to find the present value. Also since $\text{DIV}_2 = 0$,

$$P_1 = \frac{P_2}{1 + r}$$

and we can express P_0 as

$$P_0 = \frac{P_1}{1 + r} = \frac{1}{1 + r}\left(\frac{P_2}{1 + r}\right) = \frac{P_2}{(1 + r)^2}$$

In general,

$$P_0 = \frac{P_t}{(1 + r)^t}$$

This holds for any asset that pays no dividends, is traded in a competitive market, and costs nothing to store. Storage costs for gold or common stocks are very small compared to asset value.

We also assume that guaranteed future delivery of gold is just as good as having gold in hand today. This is not quite right. As we will see in Chapter 26, gold in hand can generate a small "convenience yield."

ounces (.1 million ounces per year for 10 years), the present value of the revenue stream is $1 \times 1,500 = \$1,500$ million.[9] Suppose that 10% is an appropriate discount rate for the relatively certain extraction costs. Then

$$\text{NPV} = -\text{initial investment} + \text{PV revenues} - \text{PV costs}$$

$$= -500 + 1,500 - \sum_{t=1}^{10} \frac{.1 \times 1,150}{(1.10)^t} = \$293 \text{ million}$$

It looks as if Kingsley Solomon's mine is not such a bad bet after all.[10]

Mr. Solomon's gold, in Example 11.2, was just like anyone else's gold. So there was no point in trying to value it separately. By taking the PV of the gold sales as given, Mr. Solomon was able to focus on the crucial issue: Were the extraction costs sufficiently low to make the venture worthwhile? That brings us to another of those fundamental truths: If others are producing a good or service profitably and (like Mr. Solomon) you can make it more cheaply than them, then you don't need any NPV calculations to know that you are probably onto a good thing.

We confess that our example of Kingsley Solomon's mine is somewhat special. Unlike gold, most commodities are not kept solely for investment purposes, and therefore you cannot automatically assume that today's price is equal to the present value of the future price.[11]

However, here is another way that you may be able to tackle the problem. Suppose that you are considering investment in a new copper mine and that someone offers to buy the mine's future output at a fixed price. If you accept the offer—and the buyer is completely creditworthy—the revenues from the mine are certain and can be discounted at the risk-free interest rate.[12] That takes us back to Chapter 9, where we explained that there are two ways to calculate PV:

- Estimate the expected cash flows and discount at a rate that reflects the risk of those flows.
- Estimate what sure-fire cash flows would have the same values as the risky cash flows. Then discount these *certainty-equivalent* cash flows at the risk-free interest rate.

When you discount the fixed-price revenues at the risk-free rate, you are using the certainty-equivalent method to value the mine's output. By doing so, you gain in two ways: You don't need to estimate future mineral prices, and you don't need to worry about the appropriate discount rate for risky cash flows.

But here's the question: What is the fixed price at which you could agree today to sell your future output? In other words, what is the certainty-equivalent price? Fortunately, for many commodities, there is an active market in which firms fix today the price at which they will buy or sell copper and other commodities in the future. This market is known as the *futures market,* which we will cover in Chapter 26. Futures prices are certainty equivalents, and you can look them up in the daily newspaper. So you don't need to make elaborate forecasts of

---

[9]We assume that the extraction rate does not vary. If it can vary, Mr. Solomon has a valuable operating option to increase output when gold prices are high or to cut back when prices fall. Option pricing techniques are needed to value the mine when operating options are important. See Chapter 22.

[10]As in the case of our department store example, Mr. Solomon is placing two bets: one on his ability to mine gold at a low cost and the other on the price of gold. Suppose that he really does believe that gold is overvalued. That should not deter him from running a low-cost gold mine as long as he can place separate bets on gold prices. For example, he might be able to enter into a long-term contract to sell the mine's output or he could sell gold futures. (We explain *futures* in Chapter 26.)

[11]Abnormal returns are also often calculated using the Fama-French three-factor model that we discussed in Chapter 8. The stock return is adjusted for the market return, the difference between the returns on small- and large-company stocks, and the difference between the returns on high and low book-to-market firms.

[12]We assume that the *volume* of output is certain (or does not have any market risk).

copper prices to work out the PV of the mine's output. The market has already done the work for you; you simply calculate future revenues using the price in the newspaper of copper futures and discount these revenues at the risk-free interest rate.

Of course, things are never as easy as textbooks suggest. Trades in organized futures exchanges are largely confined to deliveries over the next year or so; therefore, your newspaper won't show the price at which you could sell output beyond this period. But financial economists have developed techniques for using the prices in the futures market to estimate the amount that buyers would agree to pay for more-distant deliveries.[13]

Our two examples of gold and copper producers are illustrations of a universal principle of finance: When you have the market value of an asset, *use it*, at least as a starting point in your analysis.

11-3   Economic Rents and Competitive Advantage

Profits that more than cover the cost of capital are known as *economic rents*. Economics 101 teaches us that in the long run, competition eliminates economic rents. That is, in a long-run competitive equilibrium, no company can expand and earn more than the cost of capital on that investment.

Economic rents are earned when an industry has not settled down to equilibrium or when your firm has something valuable that your competitors don't have. For example, suppose that demand takes off unexpectedly and that your firm can expand production capacity more quickly and cheaply than your competitors. This stroke of luck is pretty sure to generate economic rents, at least until other firms manage to catch up.

Some competitive advantages are longer lived. They include patents or proprietary technology; reputation, embodied in respected brand names, for example; economies of scale that customers can't match; protected markets that competitors can't enter; and strategic assets that competitors can't easily duplicate.

Here's an example of strategic assets. Think of the difference between railroads and trucking companies. It's easy to enter the trucking business but nearly impossible to build a brand-new, long-haul railroad.[14] The interstate lines operated by U.S. railroads are strategic assets. With these assets in place, railroads were able to increase revenues and profits rapidly when shipments surged and energy prices increased in the early years of this century. The high cost of diesel fuel was more burdensome for trucks, which are less fuel efficient than railroads. Thus, high energy prices actually handed the railroads a competitive advantage.

Corporate strategy aims to find and exploit sources of competitive advantage. The problem, as always, is how to do it. John Kay advises firms to pick out distinctive capabilities—existing strengths, not just ones that would be nice to have—and then identify the product markets where those capabilities can generate the most value added. The capabilities may come from durable relationships with customers or suppliers, from the skills and experience of employees, from brand names and reputation, and from the ability to innovate.[15]

Michael Porter identifies five aspects of industry structure (or "five forces") that determine which industries are able to provide sustained economic rents.[16] These are the rivalry among

---

[13]After reading Chapter 26, check out E. S. Schwartz, "The Stochastic Behavior of Commodity Prices: Implications for Valuation and Hedging," *Journal of Finance* 52 (July 1997), pp. 923–973; and A. J. Neuberger, "Hedging Long-Term Exposures with Multiple Short-Term Futures Contracts," *Review of Financial Studies* 12 (1999), pp. 429–459.

[14]The Dakota, Minnesota & Eastern Railroad developed plans to build a new line to transport coal from Wyoming to the Midwest. Although the plans were approved by the regulatory authorities, the project was abandoned in 2012 after the railroad was acquired by the Canadian Pacific Railway.

[15]John Kay, *Why Firms Succeed* (New York: Oxford University Press, 1995).

[16]See M. E. Porter, *Competitive Strategy: Techniques for Analyzing Industries and Competitors* (New York: The Free Press, 1980).

existing competitors, the likelihood of new competition, the threat of substitutes, and the bargaining power both of suppliers and customers. With increasing global competition, firms cannot rely so easily on industry structure to provide high returns. Therefore, managers also need to ensure that the firm is positioned *within* its industry so as to secure a competitive advantage. Porter goes on to suggest three ways this can be done—by cost leadership, by product differentiation, and by focus on a particular market niche.[17]

These advantages will protect a firm only if they are durable and can be sustained against competition from other businesses. Warren Buffett stresses that successful businesses require the equivalent of a castle moat to deter marauders:

> I want a business with a moat around it with a very valuable castle in the middle. And then I want the duke who's in charge of that castle to be honest and hard-working and able. . . .
>
> Our managers of the businesses we run, I've got one message to them, which is to widen the moat. And we want to throw crocodiles and sharks and everything else, gators, I guess, into the moat to keep away competitors. And that comes about through service, it comes about through quality of product, it comes about through cost, it comes about sometimes through patents, it comes about through real estate location.[18]

You can see how business strategy and finance reinforce each other. Managers who have a clear understanding of their firm's competitive strengths (and the moats that protect their products and services) are better placed to separate those projects that truly have a positive NPV from those that do not. Therefore, when you are presented with a project that appears to have a positive NPV, do not just accept the calculations at face value. They may reflect simple estimation errors in forecasting cash flows. Probe behind the cash-flow estimates, and *try to identify a source of economic rents*. A positive NPV for a new project is believable only if you believe that your company has some special advantage.

Thinking about competitive advantage can also help ferret out negative-NPV calculations that are negative by mistake. For example, if you are the lowest-cost producer of a profitable product in a growing market, you should invest to expand along with the market. If your calculations show a negative NPV for such an expansion, you have probably made a mistake.

We will work through shortly an extended example that shows how a firm's analysis of its competitive position confirmed that a major investment had a positive NPV. But first we look at an example in which the analysis helped a firm to identify a negative-NPV transaction and avoid a costly mistake.

EXAMPLE 11.3 • How One Company Avoided a $100 Million Mistake

A U.S. chemical producer was about to modify an existing plant to produce a specialty product, polyzone, which was in short supply on world markets.[19] At prevailing raw material and finished-product prices, the expansion would have been strongly profitable. Table 11.1 shows a simplified version of management's analysis. Note the assumed constant spread between selling price and the cost of raw materials. Given this spread, the resulting NPV was about $64 million at the company's 8% real cost of capital—not bad for a $100 million outlay.

Then doubt began to creep in. Notice the outlay for transportation costs. Some of the project's raw materials were commodity chemicals, largely imported from Europe, and much of the polyzone production would be exported back to Europe. Moreover, the U.S. company had no long-run technological edge over potential European competitors. It had a head start perhaps, but was that really enough to generate a positive NPV?

---

[17]See M. E. Porter, *Competitive Advantage: Creating and Sustaining Superior Advantage* (New York: The Free Press, 1985).
[18]Berkshire Hathaway 2000 Annual Report and 2007 talk to students at the University of Florida.
[19]This is a true story, but names and details have been changed to protect the innocent.

	Year 0	Year 1	Year 2	Years 3–10
Investment	100			
Production (millions of pounds per year)[a]	0	0	40	80
Spread ($ per pound)	1.20	1.20	1.20	1.20
Net revenues	0	0	48	96
Production costs[b]	0	0	30	30
Transport[c]	0	0	4	8
Other costs	0	20	20	20
Cash flow	−100	−20	−6	38
NPV (at $r = 8\%$) = $63.56 million				

❯**TABLE 11.1**   NPV calculation for proposed investment in polyzone production by a
U.S. chemical company (figures in $ millions except as noted)

Note: For simplicity, we assume no inflation and no taxes. Plant and equipment have no salvage value after 10 years.
[a] Production capacity is 80 million pounds per year.
[b] Production costs are $.375 per pound after start up ($.75 per pound in year 2, when production is only 40 million pounds).
[c] Transportation costs are $.10 per pound to European ports.

Notice the importance of the price spread between raw materials and finished product. The analysis in Table 11.1 forecasted the spread at a constant $1.20 per pound of polyzone for 10 years. That had to be wrong: European producers, who did not face the U.S. company's transportation costs, would see an even larger NPV and expand capacity. Increased competition would almost surely squeeze the spread. The U.S. company decided to calculate the *competitive* spread—the spread at which a European competitor would see polyzone capacity as zero NPV. Table 11.2 shows management's analysis. The resulting spread of about $.95 per pound was the best *long-run* forecast for the polyzone market, other things constant of course.

	Year 0	Year 1	Year 2	Years 3–10
Investment	100			
Production (millions of pounds per year)	0	0	40	80
Spread ($ per pound)	0.95	0.95	0.95	0.95
Net revenues	0	0	38	76
Production costs	0	0	30	30
Transport	0	0	0	0
Other costs	0	20	20	20
Cash flow	−100	−20	−12	+26
NPV (at $r = 8\%$) = 0				

❯**TABLE 11.2**   What is the competitive spread to a European producer? About $.95 per pound of polyzone. Note that European producers face no transportation costs. Compare Table 11.1 (figures in $ millions except as noted).

How much of a head start did the U.S. producer have? How long before competitors forced the spread down to $.95? Management's best guess was five years. It prepared Table 11.3, which is identical to Table 11.1 except for the forecasted spread, which would shrink to $.95 by the start of year 5. Now the NPV was negative.

	Year 0	Year 1	Year 2	Year 3	Year 4	Years 5–10
Investment	100					
Production (millions of pounds per year)	0	0	40	80	80	80
Spread ($ per pound)		1.20	1.20	1.20	1.20	1.10	0.95
Net revenues	0	0	48	96	88	76
Production costs	0	0	30	30	30	30
Transport	0	0	4	8	8	8
Other costs	0	20	20	20	20	20
Cash flow	−100	−20	−6	38	30	18
NPV (at $r = 8\%$) = −9.8						

❭**TABLE 11.3**   Recalculation of NPV for polyzone investment by U.S. company (figures in $ millions except as noted). If expansion by European producers forces competitive spreads by year 5, the U.S. producer's NPV falls to −$9.8 million. Compare Table 11.1.

The project might have been saved if production could have been started in year 1 rather than 2 or if local markets could have been expanded, thus reducing transportation costs. But these changes were not feasible, so management canceled the project, albeit with a sigh of relief that its analysis had not stopped at Table 11.1.

This is a perfect example of the importance of thinking through sources of economic rents. Positive NPVs are suspect without some long-run competitive advantage. When a company contemplates investing in a new product or expanding production of an existing product, it should specifically identify its advantages or disadvantages over its most dangerous competitors. It should calculate NPV from those competitors' points of view. If competitors' NPVs come out strongly positive, the company had better expect decreasing prices (or spreads) and evaluate the proposed investment accordingly.

11-4 Marvin Enterprises Decides to Exploit a New Technology—an Example

To illustrate some of the problems involved in predicting economic rents, let us leap forward several years and look at the decision by Marvin Enterprises to exploit a new technology.[20]

One of the most unexpected developments of these years was the remarkable growth of a completely new industry. By 2041, annual sales of gargle blasters totaled $1.68 billion, or 240 million units. Although it controlled only 10% of the market, Marvin Enterprises was among the most exciting growth companies of the decade. Marvin had come late into the business, but it had pioneered the use of implanted microcircuits to control the genetic engineering processes used to manufacture gargle blasters. This development had enabled producers to cut the price of gargle blasters from $9 to $7 and had thereby contributed to the dramatic growth in the size of the market. The estimated demand curve in Figure 11.2 shows just how responsive demand is to such price reductions.

---

[20]We thank Stewart Hodges for permission to adapt this example from a case prepared by him, and we thank the BBC for permission to use the term *gargle blasters*.

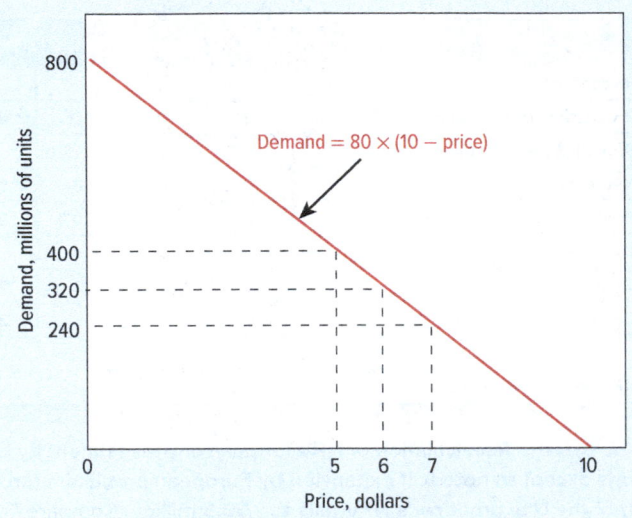

▶ **FIGURE 11.2**

The demand "curve" for gargle blasters shows that for each $1 cut in price there is an increase in demand of 80 million units.

▶ **TABLE 11.4**

Size and cost structure of the gargle blaster industry before Marvin announced its expansion plans

Note: Selling price is $7 per unit. One unit means one gargle blaster.

	Capacity (Millions of Units)				
Technology	Industry	Marvin	Capital Cost per Unit ($)	Manufacturing Cost per Unit ($)	Salvage Value per Unit ($)
First generation (2029)	120	—	17.50	5.50	2.50
Second generation (2037)	120	24	17.50	3.50	2.50

Table 11.4 summarizes the cost structure of the old and new technologies. While companies with the new technology were earning 20% on their initial investment, those with first-generation equipment had been hit by the successive price cuts. Since all Marvin's investment was in the 2037 technology, it had been particularly well placed during this period.

Rumors of new developments at Marvin had been circulating for some time, and the total market value of Marvin's stock had risen to $460 million by January 2042. At that point, Marvin called a press conference to announce another technological breakthrough. Management claimed that its new third-generation process involving mutant neurons enabled the firm to reduce capital costs to $10 and manufacturing costs to $3 per unit. Marvin proposed to capitalize on this invention by embarking on a huge $1 billion expansion program that would add 100 million units to capacity. The company expected to be in full operation within 12 months.

Before deciding to go ahead with this development, Marvin had undertaken extensive calculations on the effect of the new investment. The basic assumptions were as follows:

1. The cost of capital was 20%.

2. The production facilities had an indefinite physical life.

3. The demand curve and the costs of each technology would not change.

4. There was no chance of a fourth-generation technology in the foreseeable future.

5. The corporate income tax, which had been abolished in 2032, was not likely to be reintroduced.

Marvin's competitors greeted the news with varying degrees of concern. There was general agreement that it would be five years before any of them would have access to the new technology. On the other hand, many consoled themselves with the reflection that Marvin's new plant could not compete with an existing plant that had been fully depreciated.

Suppose that you were Marvin's financial manager. Would you have agreed with the decision to expand? Do you think it would have been better to go for a larger or smaller expansion? How do you think Marvin's announcement is likely to affect the price of its stock?

You have a choice. You can go on *immediately* to read *our* solution to these questions. But you will learn much more if you stop and work out your own answer first. Try it.

Forecasting Prices of Gargle Blasters

Up to this point in any capital budgeting problem, we have always given you the set of cash-flow forecasts. In the present case, you have to *derive* those forecasts.

The first problem is to decide what is going to happen to the price of gargle blasters. Marvin's new venture will increase industry capacity to 340 million units. From the demand curve in Figure 11.2, you can see that the industry can sell this number of gargle blasters only if the price declines to $5.75:

$$\text{Demand} = 80 \times (10 - \text{price})$$
$$= 80 \times (10 - 5.75) = 340 \text{ million units}$$

If the price falls to $5.75, what will happen to companies with the 2029 technology? They also have to make an investment decision: Should they stay in business, or should they sell their equipment for its salvage value of $2.50 per unit? With a 20% opportunity cost of capital, the NPV of staying in business is

$$\text{NPV} = -\text{investment} + \text{PV(price} - \text{manufacturing cost)}$$
$$= -2.50 + \frac{5.75 - 5.50}{.20} = -\$1.25 \text{ per unit}$$

Smart companies with 2029 equipment will, therefore, see that it is better to sell off capacity. No matter what their equipment originally cost or how far it is depreciated, it is more profitable to sell the equipment for $2.50 per unit than to operate it and lose $1.25 per unit.

As capacity is sold off, the supply of gargle blasters will decline and the price will rise. An equilibrium is reached when the price gets to $6. At this point 2029 equipment has a zero NPV:

$$\text{NPV} = -2.50 + \frac{6.00 - 5.50}{.20} = \$0 \text{ per unit}$$

How much capacity will have to be sold off before the price reaches $6? You can check that by going back to the demand curve:

$$\text{Demand} = 80 \times (10 - \text{price})$$
$$= 80 \times (10 - 6) = 320 \text{ million units}$$

Therefore Marvin's expansion will cause the price to settle down at $6 a unit and will induce first-generation producers to withdraw 20 million units of capacity.

But after five years, Marvin's competitors will also be in a position to build third-generation plants. As long as these plants have positive NPVs, companies will increase their capacity and force prices down once again. A new equilibrium will be reached when the price reaches $5. At this point, the NPV of new third-generation plants is zero, and there is no incentive for companies to expand further:

$$\text{NPV} = -10 + \frac{5.00 - 3.00}{.20} = \$0 \text{ per unit}$$

Looking back once more at our demand curve, you can see that with a price of $5 the industry can sell a total of 400 million gargle blasters:

$$\text{Demand} = 80 \times (10 - \text{price}) = 80 \times (10 - 5) = 400 \text{ million units}$$

The effect of the third-generation technology is, therefore, to cause industry sales to expand from 240 million units in 2041 to 400 million five years later. But that rapid growth is no protection against failure. By the end of five years, any company that has only first-generation equipment will no longer be able to cover its manufacturing costs and will be *forced* out of business.

The Value of Marvin's New Expansion

We have shown that the introduction of third-generation technology is likely to cause gargle blaster prices to decline to $6 for the next five years and to $5 thereafter. We can now set down the expected cash flows from Marvin's new plant:

	Year 0 (Investment)	Years 1–5 (Revenue – Manufacturing Cost)	Year 6, 7, 8, . . . (Revenue – Manufacturing Cost)
Cash flow per unit ($)	−10	6 − 3 = 3	5 − 3 = 2
Cash flow (100 million units, $ millions)	−1,000	600 − 300 = 300	500 − 300 = 200

Discounting these cash flows at 20% gives us

$$\text{NPV} = -1000 + \sum_{t=1}^{5} \frac{300}{(1.20)^t} + \frac{1}{(1.20)^5}\left(\frac{200}{.20}\right) = \$299 \text{ million}$$

It looks as if Marvin's decision to go ahead was correct. But there is something we have forgotten. When we evaluate an investment, we must consider *all* incremental cash flows. One effect of Marvin's decision to expand is to reduce the value of its existing 2037 plant. If Marvin decided not to go ahead with the new technology, the $7 price of gargle blasters would hold until Marvin's competitors started to cut prices in five years' time. Marvin's decision, therefore, leads to an immediate $1 cut in price. This reduces the present value of its 2037 equipment by

$$24 \text{ million} \times \sum_{t=1}^{5} \frac{1.00}{(1.20)^t} = \$72 \text{ million}$$

Considered in isolation, Marvin's decision has an NPV of $299 million. But it also reduces the value of existing plant by $72 million. The net present value of Marvin's venture is, therefore, 299 − 72 = $227 million.

Alternative Expansion Plans

Marvin's expansion has a positive NPV, but perhaps Marvin would do better to build a larger or smaller plant. You can check that by going through the same calculations as above. First you need to estimate how the additional capacity will affect gargle blaster prices. Then you can calculate the net present value of the new plant and the change in the present value of the existing plant. The total NPV of Marvin's expansion plan is

$$\text{Total NPV} = \text{NPV of new plant} + \text{change in PV of existing plant}$$

We have undertaken these calculations and plotted the results in Figure 11.3. You can see how total NPV would be affected by a smaller or larger expansion.

When the new technology becomes generally available in 2047, firms will construct a total of 280 million units of new capacity.[21] But Figure 11.3 shows that it would be foolish for Marvin to go that far. If Marvin added 280 million units of new capacity in 2042, the discounted value of the cash flows from the new plant would be zero *and* the company would have reduced the value of its old plant by $144 million. To maximize NPV, Marvin should

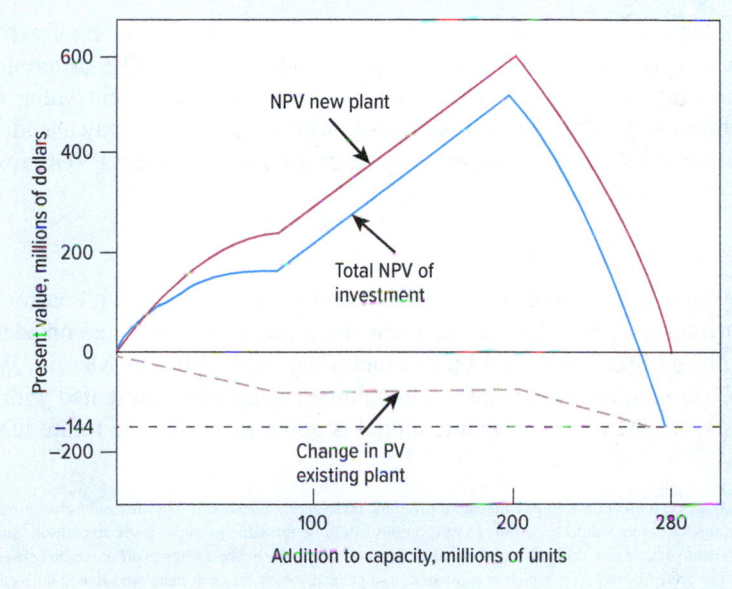

▶ **FIGURE 11.3**

Effect on net present value of alternative expansion plans. Marvin's 100-million-unit expansion has a total NPV of $227 million (total NPV = NPV new plant + change in PV existing plant = 299 − 72 = 227). Total NPV is maximized if Marvin builds 200 million units of new capacity. If Marvin builds 280 million units of new capacity, total NPV is −$144 million.

[21]Total industry capacity in 2047 will be 400 million units. Of this, 120 million units are second-generation capacity, and the remaining 280 million units are third-generation capacity.

construct 200 million units of new capacity and set the price just below $6 to drive out the 2029 manufacturers. Output is, therefore, less and price is higher than either would be under free competition.[22]

The Value of Marvin Stock

Let us think about the effect of Marvin's announcement on the value of its common stock. Marvin has 24 million units of second-generation capacity. In the absence of any third-generation technology, gargle blaster prices would hold at $7 and Marvin's existing plant would be worth

$$PV = 24 \text{ million} \times \frac{7.00 - 3.50}{.20}$$

$$= \$420 \text{ million}$$

Marvin's new technology reduces the price of gargle blasters initially to $6 and after five years to $5. Therefore the value of existing plant declines to

$$PV = 24 \text{ million} \times \left[\sum_{t=1}^{5} \frac{6.00 - 3.50}{(1.20)^t} + \frac{5.00 - 3.50}{.20 \times (1.20)^5} \right]$$

$$= \$252 \text{ million}$$

But the *new* plant makes a net addition to shareholders' wealth of $299 million. So after Marvin's announcement its stock will be worth

$$252 + 299 = \$551 \text{ million}[23]$$

Now here is an illustration of something we talked about in Chapter 4: Before the announcement, Marvin's stock was valued in the market at $460 million. The difference between this figure and the value of the existing plant represented the present value of Marvin's growth opportunities (PVGO). The market valued Marvin's ability to stay ahead of the game at $40 million even before the announcement. After the announcement PVGO rose to $299 million.[24]

The Lessons of Marvin Enterprises

Marvin Enterprises may be just a piece of science fiction, but the problems that it confronts are very real. Whenever Intel considers developing a new microprocessor or Pfizer considers developing a new drug, these firms must face up to exactly the same issues as Marvin. We have tried to illustrate the *kind* of questions that you should be asking when presented with a set of cash-flow forecasts. Of course, no economic model is going to predict the future with

[22]Notice that we are assuming that all customers have to pay the same price for their gargle blasters. If Marvin could charge each customer the maximum price that that customer would be willing to pay, output would be the same as under free competition. Such direct price discrimination is illegal and, in any case, difficult to enforce. But firms do search for indirect ways to differentiate between customers. For example, stores often offer free delivery, which is equivalent to a price discount for customers who live at an inconvenient distance.

[23]To finance the expansion, Marvin is going to have to sell $1,000 million of new stock. Therefore the *total* value of Marvin's stock will rise to $1,551 million. But investors who put up the new money will receive shares worth $1,000 million. The value of Marvin's old shares after the announcement is therefore $551 million.

[24]The market value of Marvin stock will be greater than $551 million if investors expect the company to expand again within the five-year period. In other words, PVGO after the expansion may still be positive. Investors may expect Marvin to stay one step ahead of its competitors or to successfully apply its special technology in other areas.

accuracy. Perhaps Marvin can hold the price above $6. Perhaps competitors will not appreciate the rich pickings to be had in the year 2047. In that case, Marvin's expansion would be even more profitable. But would you want to bet $1 billion on such possibilities? We don't think so.

Investments often turn out to earn far more than the cost of capital because of a favorable surprise. This surprise may in turn create a temporary opportunity for further investments earning more than the cost of capital. But anticipated and more prolonged rents will naturally lead to the entry of rival producers. That is why you should be suspicious of any investment proposal that predicts a stream of economic rents into the indefinite future. Try to estimate *when* competition will drive the NPV down to zero, and think what that implies for the price of your product.

Many companies try to identify the major growth areas in the economy and then concentrate their investment in these areas. But the sad fate of first-generation gargle blaster manufacturers illustrates how rapidly existing plants can be made obsolete by changes in technology. It is fun being in a growth industry when you are at the forefront of the new technology, but a growth industry has no mercy on technological laggards.

Therefore, do not simply follow the herd of investors stampeding into high-growth sectors of the economy. Think of the fate of the dot-com companies in the "new economy" of the late 1990s. Optimists argued that the information revolution was opening up opportunities for companies to grow at unprecedented rates. The pessimists pointed out that competition in e-commerce was likely to be intense and that competition would ensure that the benefits of the information revolution would go largely to consumers. The Finance in Practice box emphasizes that rapid growth is no guarantee of superior profits.

We do not wish to imply that good investment opportunities don't exist. For example, good opportunities frequently arise because the firm has invested money in the past, which gives it the option to expand cheaply in the future. Perhaps the firm can increase its output just by adding an extra production line, whereas its rivals would need to construct an entirely new factory.

Marvin also reminds us to include a project's impact on the rest of the firm when estimating incremental cash flows. By introducing the new technology immediately, Marvin reduced the value of its existing plant by $72 million.

Sometimes the losses on existing plants may completely offset the gains from a new technology. That is why we may see established, technologically advanced companies deliberately slowing down the rate at which they introduce new products. But this can be a dangerous game to play if it opens up opportunities for competitors. For example, for many years Bausch & Lomb was the dominant producer of contact lenses and earned large profits from glass contact lenses that needed to be sterilized every night. Because its existing business generated high returns, the company was slow to introduce disposable lenses. This delay opened up an opportunity for competitors and enabled Johnson & Johnson to introduce disposable lenses.

Marvin's economic rents were equal to the difference between its costs and those of the marginal producer. The costs of the marginal 2029-generation plant consisted of the manufacturing costs plus the opportunity cost of not selling the equipment. Therefore, if the salvage value of the 2029 equipment were higher, Marvin's competitors would incur higher costs and Marvin could earn higher rents. We took the salvage value as given, but it in turn depends on the cost savings from substituting outdated gargle blaster equipment for some other asset. In a well-functioning economy, assets will be used so as to minimize the *total* cost of producing the chosen set of outputs. The economic rents earned by any asset are equal to the total extra costs that would be incurred if that asset were withdrawn.

Cautionary Tales

❯What would be your list of growth industries that have transformed people's lives over the past century? One obvious candidate is the automobile industry. Sales of vehicles in the United States have grown from almost nothing 100 years ago to more than 16.5 million a year today. Many companies foresaw this rapid growth and concluded that it offered a likely source of juicy profits. Wikipedia lists 1,800 U.S. car manufacturers that were established at some point in the United States, with exotic names such as Ben Hur, O-We-Go, and Motor Bob. Almost all these companies blossomed briefly and then withered. Only a handful of U.S. car companies remain today, two of which filed for bankruptcy in 2009 and had to be rescued by the U.S. government.[25]

An equally profitless growth industry has been the aviation sector. Since 1948, the number of passenger miles flown by U.S. airlines has multiplied nearly 300 times. Yet since that date, airlines have, in aggregate, suffered an operating *loss,* and more than 150 airlines have entered into Chapter 11 bankruptcy, in some cases two or three times.[26] While a number of smaller airlines continue to operate, the sector today is dominated by just four companies: American, Delta, United, and Southwest. (Profitability at these companies has recently improved, however, and by early 2017, Warren Buffett's Berkshire Hathaway had acquired large stakes in each company's shares.)

A third and more recent example of a growth industry is the manufacture of computers. With the exception of IBM, the giants of the industry today barely existed in the 1970s. At that time, investors in the industry referred to Snow White and the seven dwarfs. IBM was Snow White and the seven hefty and well-respected dwarfs were the other major mainframe manufacturers— Burroughs, UNIVAC, NCR, Control Data, Honeywell, General Electric, and RCA. In addition to these major producers, there were a number of glamorous dwarflets, such as Amdahl, Wang Laboratories, Data General, and DEC. As the role of the mainframe changed, only Snow White survived as a major force, while the dwarfs and most of their smaller brethren either no longer exist or have exited computer manufacturing.

Do these cautionary stories mean that companies should seek out stagnant or declining industries? Of course not; other things equal, it is better to operate in a growth industry than a declining one. The problem is that the prospect of rapid industry growth attracts competition. And, if the industry is also characterized by rapidly changing technology or consumer taste, then competitive advantage is likely to be less persistent. Think, for example, of Nokia and BlackBerry, whose phones once dominated the smartphone market until they were quickly overtaken by Apple's iPhone and Android phones. The message, in Warren Buffett's words, is that "the key to investing is not assessing how much an industry is going to affect society, or how much it will grow, but rather determining the competitive advantage of any given company and, above all, the durability of that advantage."[27]

When Marvin announced its expansion plans, many owners of first-generation equipment took comfort in the belief that Marvin could not compete with their fully depreciated plant. Their comfort was misplaced. Regardless of past depreciation policy, it paid to scrap first-generation equipment rather than keep it in production. Do not expect that numbers in your balance sheet can protect you from harsh economic reality.

---

[25]Profitless growth in the auto and aviation industries is the subject of a very insightful and entertaining article by Warren Buffett. See C. Loomis, "Mr. Buffett on the Stock Market," *Fortune* (November 22, 1999), pp. 110–115.

[26]Transworld Airlines (TWA) went into bankruptcy three times, prompting jokes about "Chapter 22" and "Chapter 33." TWA is one of nearly 450 U.S. airlines that are no longer operating. See https://en.wikipedia.org/wiki/List_of_defunct_airlines_of_the_United_States.

[27]See C. Loomis, "Mr. Buffett on the Stock Market," op. cit.

All good financial managers want their firms to generate investment ideas with positive NPVs and to weed out the wrong-headed schemes. To do this, they need to establish a well-designed set of procedures for developing and approving investment proposals. For most firms, the investment process starts with approval of the capital budget, which is a list of planned investments over the coming year. The proposed investment projects are evaluated one by one later, based on appropriation requests that provide more detailed information and analysis. They are approved one by one, provided that the requests are convincing.

The appropriation requests that arrive on senior managers' desks will almost always show positive NPVs. But NPVs can be positive for two reasons: (1) The company really can expect to earn superior profits, or (2) there are optimistic biases or errors in cash-flow forecasts. Good managers are wary of these "false positives" and try to keep the odds stacked in their favor by investing in areas where the company has clear competitive advantages. They give careful attention to corporate strategy, which attempts to identify distinct capabilities and deploy them in markets where economic rents can be generated. They avoid expansion where competitive advantages are absent and economic rents are unlikely. They do not project favorable current product prices far into the future without checking whether entry or expansion by competitors will drive future prices down.

Our story of Marvin Enterprises illustrates the origin of rents and how they determine a project's cash flows and net present value.

Any present value calculation, including our calculation for Marvin Enterprises, is subject to error. That's life: There's no other sensible way to value most capital investment projects. But some assets, such as gold, real estate, crude oil, ships, and airplanes, as well as financial assets, such as stocks and bonds, are traded in reasonably competitive markets. When you have the market value of such an asset, use it, at least as a starting point for your analysis.

For a very readable discussion of the problem of overconfidence and other behavioral traits in financial decision making, see:

J. S. Hammond, R. L. Keeney, and H. Raiffa, "The Hidden Traps in Decision Making," *Harvard Business Review* 84 (January 2006), pp. 118–126.

The following papers discuss capital investment and strategy:

P. Barwise, P. Marsh, and R. Wensley, "Must Finance and Strategy Clash?" *Harvard Business Review,* September–October 1989, pp. 85–90.

M. Porter, "What Is Strategy?" *Harvard Business Review,* November–December 1996, pp. 61–78.

S. C. Myers, "Finance Theory and Financial Strategy," *Midland Corporate Finance Journal* 5 (Spring 1987), pp. 6–13. Reprinted from *Interfaces* (January–February 1984).

R. Rumelt, *Good Strategy/ Bad Strategy: The Difference and Why It Matters* (London, U.K.: Profile Books, 2017)

The following book describes how to identify economic rents and positive NPVs:

S. Woolley, *Sources of Value* (Cambridge, U.K.: Cambridge University Press, 2009).

---

connect   **Select problems are available in McGraw-Hill's *Connect.* Please see the preface for more information.**

1. **Capital budgeting process***   True or false?

    a. The approval of a firm's capital budget allows managers to go ahead with any project included in the budget.

    b. Capital budgets and project authorizations are mostly developed "bottom up." Strategic planning is a "top-down" process.

    c. Project sponsors are likely to be overoptimistic.

2. **Capital budgeting process** Explain how each of the following actions or problems can distort or disrupt the capital budgeting process.

   a. Overoptimism by project sponsors.

   b. Inconsistent forecasts of industry and macroeconomic variables.

   c. Capital budgeting organized solely as a bottom-up process.

3. **Capital budgeting process** Draw up an outline or flowchart tracing the capital budgeting process from the initial idea for a new investment project to the completion of the project and the start of operations. Assume the idea for a new obfuscator machine comes from a plant manager in the Deconstruction Division of the Modern Language Corporation.

   Here are some questions your outline or flowchart should consider: Who will prepare the original proposal? What information will the proposal contain? Who will evaluate it? What approvals will be needed, and who will give them? What happens if the machine costs 40% more to purchase and install than originally forecasted? What will happen when the machine is finally up and running?

4. **Biased forecasts** Explain why setting a higher discount rate is not a cure for upward-biased cash-flow forecasts.

5. **Biased forecasts** Look back to the cash flows for projects F and G in Section 5-3. The cost of capital was assumed to be 10%. Assume that the forecasted cash flows for projects of this type are overstated by 8% on average. That is, the forecast for each cash flow from each project should be reduced by 8%. But a lazy financial manager, unwilling to take the time to argue with the projects' sponsors, instructs them to use a discount rate of 18%.

   a. What are the projects' true NPVs?

   b. What are the NPVs at the 18% discount rate?

   c. Are there any circumstances in which the 18% discount rate would give the correct NPVs? (*Hint:* Could upward bias be more severe for more-distant cash flows?)

6. **Market prices** Your brother-in-law wants you to join him in purchasing a building on the outskirts of town. You and he would then develop and run a Taco Palace restaurant. Both of you are extremely optimistic about future real estate prices in this area, and your brother-in-law has prepared a cash-flow forecast that implies a large positive NPV. This calculation assumes sale of the property after 10 years. What further calculations should you do before going ahead?

7. **Market prices** Suppose that you are considering investing in an asset for which there is a reasonably good secondary market. Specifically, your company is Delta Airlines, and the asset is a Boeing 757—a widely used airplane. How does the presence of a secondary market simplify your problem in principle? Do you think these simplifications could be realized in practice? Explain.

8. **Market prices** There is an active, competitive leasing (i.e., rental) market for most standard types of commercial jets. Many of the planes flown by the major domestic and international airlines are not owned by them but leased for periods ranging from a few months to several years. Gamma Airlines, however, owns two long-range DC-11s just withdrawn from Latin American service. Gamma is considering using these planes to develop the potentially lucrative new route from Akron to Yellowknife. A considerable investment in terminal facilities, training, and advertising will be required. Once committed, Gamma will have to operate the route for at least three years. One further complication: The manager of Gamma's international division is opposing commitment of the planes to the Akron–Yellowknife route because of anticipated future growth in traffic through Gamma's new hub in Ulaanbaatar. How would you evaluate the proposed Akron–Yellowknife project? Give a detailed list of the necessary steps in your analysis. Explain how the airplane leasing market would be taken

into account. If the project is attractive, how would you respond to the manager of the international division?

9. **Market prices**   Suppose the current price of gold is $1,200 an ounce. Hotshot Consultants advises you that gold prices will increase at an average rate of 12% for the next two years. After that the growth rate will fall to a long-run trend of 3% per year. What is the present value of 1 million ounces of gold produced in eight years? Assume that gold prices have a beta of 0 and that the risk-free rate is 5.5%.

10. **Market prices***   On the London Metals Exchange, the price for copper to be delivered in one year is $5,500 a ton. (*Note:* Payment is made when the copper is delivered.) The risk-free interest rate is 2% and the expected market return is 8%.

    a. Suppose that you expect to produce and sell 10,000 tons of copper next year. What is the PV of this output? Assume that the sale occurs at the end of the year.

    b. If copper has a beta of 1.2, what is the expected price of copper at the end of the year? What is the certainty-equivalent end-year price?

11. **Market prices**   Photographic laboratories recover and recycle the silver used in photographic film. Stikine River Photo is considering purchase of improved equipment for their laboratory at Telegraph Creek. Here is the information they have:

    - The equipment costs $100,000 and will cost $80,000 per year to run.

    - It has an economic life of 10 years but can be depreciated over 5 years by the straightline method (see Section 6-3).

    - It will recover an additional 5,000 ounces of silver per year.

    - Silver is selling for $40 per ounce. Over the past 10 years, the price of silver has appreciated by 4.5% per year in real terms. Silver is traded in an active, competitive market.

    - Stikine's marginal tax rate is 25%.

    - Stikine's company cost of capital is 8% in real terms. The nominal interest rate is 6%.

    - What is the NPV of the new equipment?

    Make additional assumptions as necessary.

12. **Market prices**   The Cambridge Opera Association has come up with a unique door prize for its December 2019 fund-raising ball: Twenty door prizes will be distributed, each one a ticket entitling the bearer to receive a cash award from the association on December 31, 2020. The cash award is to be determined by calculating the ratio of the level of the Standard and Poor's Composite Index of stock prices on December 31, 2020, to its level on June 30, 2020, and multiplying by $100. Thus, if the index turns out to be 1,000 on June 30, 2020, and 1,200 on December 31, 2020, the payoff will be 100 × (1,200/1,000) = $120.

    After the ball, a black market springs up in which the tickets are traded. What will the tickets sell for on January 1, 2020? On June 30, 2020? Assume the risk-free interest rate is 10% per year. Also assume the Cambridge Opera Association will be solvent at year-end 2020 and will, in fact, pay off on the tickets. Make other assumptions as necessary.

    Would ticket values be different if the tickets' payoffs depended on the Dow Jones Industrial Index rather than the Standard and Poor's Composite?

13. **Market prices**   You are asked to value a large building in northern New Jersey. The valuation is needed for a bankruptcy settlement. Here are the facts:

    - The settlement requires that the building's value equal the PV of the net cash proceeds the railroad would receive if it cleared out the building and sold it for its highest and best nonrailroad use, which is as a warehouse.

    - The building has been appraised at $1 million. This figure is based on actual recent selling prices of a sample of similar New Jersey buildings used as, or available for use as, warehouses.

- If rented today as a warehouse, the building could generate $80,000 per year. This cash flow is calculated after out-of-pocket operating expenses and after real estate taxes of $50,000 per year:

Gross rents	$180,000
Operating expenses	50,000
Real estate taxes	50,000
Net	$80,000

Gross rents, operating expenses, and real estate taxes are uncertain but are expected to grow with inflation.

- However, it would take one year and $200,000 to clear out the railroad equipment and prepare the building for use as a warehouse. The $200,000 would have to be invested immediately.

- The property will be put on the market when ready for use as a warehouse. Your real estate adviser says that properties of this type take, on average, one year to sell after they are put on the market. However, the railroad could rent the building as a warehouse while waiting for it to sell.

- The opportunity cost of capital for investment in real estate is 8% in real terms.

- Your real estate adviser notes that selling prices of comparable buildings in northern New Jersey have declined, in real terms, at an average rate of 2% per year over the last 10 years.

- A 5% sales commission would be paid by the railroad at the time of the sale.

- The railroad pays no income taxes. It would have to pay property taxes.

14. **Market prices**   Sulphur Ridge Mining is considering the development of a new calonium mine at Moose Bend in northern Alberta. The mine would require an upfront investment of $110 million and would produce 100,000 tons of high-grade calonium a year, which is small compared with the current annual worldwide production of 9 million tons. Proved reserves of calonium at the Moose Bend mine are 1.2 million tons. The extraction cost is estimated at $120 a ton and is expected to remain constant in real terms. The market price of calonium is currently $240 a ton, and the consultancy firm, Powder River Associates, is estimating that the real price of calonium will increase by 3% a year in real terms for the foreseeable future. There are several other producers of calonium. Several Canadian mines are believed to be barely breaking even. Others with costs in the $150 to $200 a ton range are making good profits. There are no taxes and the real cost of capital is estimated as 8%. Calonium mining is an environmentally friendly activity, and there are zero costs to shutting down a mine. Should Sulphur Ridge go ahead with the project? Make whatever additional assumptions you think are needed.

15. **Economic rents***   True or false?

    a. A firm that earns the opportunity cost of capital is earning economic rents.

    b. A firm that invests in positive-NPV ventures expects to earn economic rents.

    c. Financial managers should try to identify areas where their firms can earn economic rents, because it is there that positive-NPV projects are likely to be found.

    d. Economic rent is the equivalent annual cost of operating capital equipment.

16. **Economic rents**   We characterized the interstate rail lines owned by major U.S. railroads as "strategic assets" that could generate increased profits. In what conditions would you expect these assets to generate economic rents? Keep in mind that railroads compete with trucking

companies as well as other railroads. Trucking companies have some advantages, including flexibility.

17. **Economic rents**   Thanks to acquisition of a key patent, your company now has exclusive production rights for barkelgassers (BGs) in North America. Production facilities for 200,000 BGs per year will require a $25 million immediate capital expenditure. Production costs are estimated at $65 per BG. The BG marketing manager is confident that all 200,000 units can be sold for $100 per unit (in real terms) until the patent runs out five years hence. After that the marketing manager hasn't a clue about what the selling price will be. What is the NPV of the BG project? Assume the real cost of capital is 9%. To keep things simple, also make the following assumptions:

    • The technology for making BGs will not change. Capital and production costs will stay the same in real terms.

    • Competitors know the technology and can enter as soon as the patent expires, that is, they can construct new plants in year 5 and start selling BGs in year 6.

    • If your company invests immediately, full production begins after 12 months, that is, in year 1.

    • There are no taxes.

    • BG production facilities last 12 years. They have no salvage value at the end of their useful life.

18. **Economic rents**   How would your answer to Problem 17 change if technological improvements reduce the cost of new BG production facilities by 3% per year? Thus a new plant built in year 1 would cost only 25 (1 − .03) = $24.25 million, a plant built in year 2 would cost $23.52 million, and so on. Assume that production costs per unit remain at $65.

19. **Economic rents**   Reevaluate the NPV of the proposed polyzone project (Example 11.3) under each of the following assumptions. What's the right management decision in each case?

    a. Spread in year 4 holds at $1.20 per pound.

    b. The U.S. chemical company can start up polyzone production at 40 million pounds in year 1 rather than year 2.

    c. The U.S. company makes a technological advance that reduces its annual production costs to $25 million. Competitors' production costs do not change.

20. **Equilibrium prices**   Demand for concave utility meters is expanding rapidly, but the industry is highly competitive. A utility meter plant costs $50 million to set up, and it has an annual capacity of 500,000 meters. The production cost is $5 per meter, and this cost is not expected to change. The machines have an indefinite physical life and the cost of capital is 10%. What is the competitive price of a utility meter?

    a. $5

    b. $10

    c. $15

21. **Opportunity costs**   New-model commercial airplanes are much more fuel-efficient than older models. How is it possible for airlines flying older models to make money when its competitors are flying newer planes? Explain briefly.

CHALLENGE PROBLEMS

22. **Economic rents**   The manufacture of polysyllabic acid is a competitive industry. Most plants have an annual output of 100,000 tons. Operating costs are $.90 a ton, and the sales price is $1 a ton. A 100,000-ton plant costs $100,000 and has an indefinite life. Its current scrap value of $60,000 is expected to decline to $57,900 over the next two years,

Phlogiston Inc. proposes to invest $100,000 in a plant that employs a new low-cost process to manufacture polysyllabic acid. The plant has the same capacity as existing units, but operating costs are $.85 a ton. Phlogiston estimates that it has two years' lead over each of its rivals in use of the process but is unable to build any more plants itself before year 2. Also it believes that demand over the next two years is likely to be sluggish and that its new plant will therefore cause temporary overcapacity.

You can assume that there are no taxes and that the cost of capital is 10%.

a. By the end of year 2, the prospective increase in acid demand will require the construction of several new plants using the Phlogiston process. What is the likely NPV of such plants?

b. What does that imply for the price of polysyllabic acid in year 3 and beyond?

c. Would you expect existing plant to be scrapped in year 2? How would your answer differ if scrap value were $40,000 or $80,000?

d. The acid plants of United Alchemists Inc. have been fully depreciated. Can it operate them profitably after year 2?

e. Acidosis Inc. purchased a new plant last year for $100,000 and is writing it down by $10,000 a year. Should it scrap this plant in year 2?

f. What would be the NPV of Phlogiston's venture?

23. **Equilibrium prices** The world airline system is composed of the routes X and Y, each of which requires 10 aircraft. These routes can be serviced by three types of aircraft—A, B, and C. There are 5 type A aircraft available, 10 type B, and 10 type C. These aircraft are identical except for their operating costs, which are as follows:

Annual Operating Cost ($ millions)		
Aircraft Type	**Route X**	**Route Y**
A	1.5	1.5
B	2.5	2.0
C	4.5	3.5

The aircraft have a useful life of five years and a salvage value of $1 million.

The aircraft owners do not operate the aircraft themselves but rent them to the operators. Owners act competitively to maximize their rental income, and operators attempt to minimize their operating costs. Airfares are also competitively determined. Assume the cost of capital is 10%.

a. Which aircraft would be used on which route, and how much would each aircraft be worth?

b. What would happen to usage and prices of each aircraft if the number of type A aircraft increased to 10?

c. What would happen if the number of type A aircraft increased to 15?

d. What would happen if the number of type A aircraft increased to 20?

State any additional assumptions you need to make.

24. **Economic rents** Taxes are a cost, and, therefore, changes in tax rates can affect consumer prices, project lives, and the value of existing firms. The following problem illustrates this. It also illustrates that tax changes that appear to be "good for business" do not always increase

the value of existing firms. Indeed, unless new investment incentives increase consumer demand, they can work only by rendering existing equipment obsolete.

The manufacture of bucolic acid is a competitive business. Demand is steadily expanding, and new plants are constantly being opened. Expected cash flows from an investment in a new plant are as follows:

	0	1	2	3
1. Initial investment	100			
2. Revenues		100	100	100
3. Cash operating costs		50	50	50
4. Tax depreciation		33.33	33.33	33.33
5. Income pretax		16.67	16.67	16.67
6. Tax at 40%		6.67	6.67	6.67
7. Net income		10	10	10
8. After-tax salvage				15
9. Cash flow (7 + 8 + 4 − 1)	− 100	+43.33	+43.33	+58.33
NPV at 20% = 0				

Assumptions:
1. Tax depreciation is straight-line over three years.
2. Pretax salvage value is 25 in year 3 and 50 if the asset is scrapped in year 2.
3. Tax on salvage value is 40% of the difference between salvage value and depreciated investment.
4. The cost of capital is 20%.

a. What is the value of a one-year-old plant? Of a two-year-old plant?

b. Suppose that the government now changes tax depreciation to allow a 100% writeoff in year 1. How does this affect the value of existing one- and two-year-old plants? Existing plants must continue using the original tax depreciation schedule.

c. Would it now make sense to scrap existing plants when they are two rather than three years old?

d. How would your answers change if the corporate income tax were abolished entirely?

MINI-CASE ● ● ● ● ●

Ecsy-Cola[28]

Libby Flannery, the regional manager of Ecsy-Cola, the international soft drinks empire, was reviewing her investment plans for Central Asia. She had contemplated launching Ecsy-Cola in the ex-Soviet republic of Inglistan in 2022. This would involve a capital outlay of $20 million in 2021 to build a bottling plant and set up a distribution system there. Fixed costs (for manufacturing, distribution, and marketing) would then be $3 million per year from 2021 onward. This would be sufficient to make and sell 200 million liters per year—enough for every man, woman, and child in Inglistan to drink four bottles per week! But there would be few savings from building a smaller plant, and import tariffs and transport costs in the region would keep all production within national borders.

---

[28]We thank Anthony Neuberger for suggesting this topic.

The variable costs of production and distribution would be 12 cents per liter. Company policy requires a rate of return of 25% in nominal dollar terms, after local taxes but before deducting any costs of financing. The sales revenue is forecasted to be 35 cents per liter.

Bottling plants last almost forever, and all unit costs and revenues were expected to remain constant in nominal terms. Tax would be payable at a rate of 30%, and under the Inglistan corporate tax code, capital expenditures can be written off on a straight-line basis over four years.

All these inputs were reasonably clear. But Ms. Flannery racked her brain trying to forecast sales. Ecsy-Cola found that the "1–2–4" rule works in most new markets. Sales typically double in the second year, double again in the third year, and after that remain roughly constant. Libby's best guess was that, if she went ahead immediately, initial sales in Inglistan would be 12.5 million liters in 2023, ramping up to 50 million in 2025 and onward.

Ms. Flannery also worried whether it would be better to wait a year. The soft drink market was developing rapidly in neighboring countries, and in a year's time she should have a much better idea whether Ecsy-Cola would be likely to catch on in Inglistan. If it didn't catch on and sales stalled below 20 million liters, a large investment probably would not be justified.

Ms. Flannery had assumed that Ecsy-Cola's keen rival, Sparky-Cola, would not also enter the market. But last week she received a shock when in the lobby of the Kapitaliste Hotel she bumped into her opposite number at Sparky-Cola. Sparky-Cola would face costs similar to Ecsy-Cola. How would Sparky-Cola respond if Ecsy-Cola entered the market? Would it decide to enter also? If so, how would that affect the profitability of Ecsy-Cola's project?

Ms. Flannery thought again about postponing investment for a year. Suppose Sparky-Cola were interested in the Inglistan market. Would that favor delay or immediate action?

Maybe Ecsy-Cola should announce its plans before Sparky-Cola has a chance to develop its own proposals. It seemed that the Inglistan project was becoming more complicated by the day.

QUESTIONS

1. Calculate the NPV of the proposed investment, using the inputs suggested in this case. How sensitive is this NPV to future sales volume?

2. What are the pros and cons of waiting for a year before deciding whether to invest? (*Hint:* What happens if demand turns out high and Sparky-Cola also invests? What if Ecsy-Cola invests right away and gains a one-year head start on Sparky-Cola?)

CHAPTER

12

Agency Problems and Investment

So far we've concentrated on criteria and procedures for identifying capital investments with positive NPVs. If a firm takes all (and only) positive-NPV projects, it maximizes the firm's value. But do the firm's managers want to maximize value?

Managers have no special gene that automatically aligns their personal interests with outside investors' financial objectives. So how do shareholders ensure that top managers do not feather their own nests or grind their own axes? And how do top managers ensure that middle managers and employees try as hard as they can to find and execute positive-NPV projects?

Here we circle back to the principal–agent problems first raised in Chapter 1. Shareholders are the ultimate principals; top managers are the stockholders' agents. But middle managers and employees are, in turn, agents of top management. Thus, senior managers—including the chief financial officer—are simultaneously agents vis-à-vis shareholders and principals vis-à-vis the rest of the firm. The problem is to get everyone working together to maximize value.

This chapter describes how companies grapple with that problem. We first describe the temptations that can divert managers from maximizing shareholder value and then discuss how those temptations are blocked or at least diluted.

Managers' investment decisions are monitored by auditors, lenders, and regulators, as well as by shareholders. In addition, compensation schemes for top management are designed to give managers the right incentives to increase value.

Top managers in the United States usually receive incentive compensation in the form of grants of stock or options. This helps to align the managers' and shareholders' interests, but it may have unpleasant side effects. For example, it can put pressure on managers to worry more about short- rather than long-run returns. We will confront a disturbing fact: It appears that some, maybe most, public corporations seem willing to sacrifice NPV to maintain or increase immediate earnings per share.

Middle managers' compensation depends mostly on accounting measures of profitability. It's not absolute profitability that matters, but profitability relative to the cost of capital. We explain how measures of economic value added (EVA) incorporate the cost of capital and thereby mitigate agency problems in lower layers of the firm. At the end of the chapter, we explore the differences between accounting rates of return and true, economic rates of return. You should be aware of the biases that can hide in accounting measures of profitability.

12-1 What Agency Problems Should You Watch Out For?

The CEO, CFO, and other managers cannot be perfect agents of their shareholders. The managers are human beings who cannot completely set aside their own interests and concerns. It's naïve to think that they will find and invest in all and only positive-NPV investments. Agency costs are incurred when they don't.

Agency costs of investment can't be eliminated, but they can be mitigated. Managers are monitored by shareholders, banks, and other financial institutions, which push back against inefficient investment and waste. Compensation and other incentives can be designed so that managers are rewarded appropriately when they generate value for the firm. Managers are also constrained by law and regulation from taking actions that damage the shareholders. A good combination of monitoring, incentives, and constraints adds up to good corporate governance.

There will be more on monitoring and management compensation later in this chapter and on corporate governance later in the book. We start here by listing several specific agency problems that can interfere with value-maximizing investment.

- *Reduced effort.* Finding and implementing positive-NPV projects can be a high-effort, high-pressure activity. Managers may be drawn to slack off.

- *Perks.* Managers are tempted to spend wastefully on upscale office accommodations, meetings scheduled at luxury resorts, private jets, and so on. Economists refer to these nonpecuniary rewards as private benefits. Ordinary people refer to them as perks.[1]

- *Empire building.* Other things equal, managers prefer to run large businesses rather than small ones. Getting from small to large may not be a positive-NPV undertaking.

- *Entrenching investment.* Suppose manager Q considers two expansion plans. One plan will require a manager with special skills that manager Q just happens to have. The other plan requires only a general-purpose manager. Guess which plan Q will favor? Projects designed to require or reward the skills of existing managers are called *entrenching investments.*[2]

- *Overinvestment.* Entrenching investments and empire building are typical symptoms of overinvestment—that is, investing beyond the point where NPV falls to zero. The temptation to overinvest is highest when the firm has plenty of cash but limited investment opportunities. Michael Jensen called this the *free-cash-flow* problem.[3]

- *Insufficient disinvestment.* There is also a reluctance to *disinvest,* especially when jobs are at stake. Sometimes value is added by selling off a factory or product line or closing down a loss-making business. The reluctance to disinvest amounts to overinvestment on the downside.

Agency Problems Don't Stop at the Top

The CEO, CFO, and other top managers are agents for shareholders as principals. But the top managers must also supervise and set incentives for middle managers. In this case, the top managers are principals and the middle managers agents.

Getting incentives right throughout a large corporation is difficult. So why not bypass these difficulties and let the CFO and his or her immediate staff make the important investment decisions?

The bypass won't work, for at least four reasons. First, top management would have to analyze thousands of projects every year. There's no way to know enough about each one to make intelligent choices. Top management must rely on analysis done at lower levels.

[1]Rajan and Wulf argue that it is wrong to treat all perks as managerial excess. That corporate jet can be an excellent investment if it saves several hours a week that the CEO or CFO would otherwise waste in airports. Also, some large companies require the CEO to fly in the corporate jet for security reasons. See R. Rajan and J. Wulf, "Are Perks Purely Managerial Excess?" *Journal of Financial Economics* 79 (January 2006), pp. 1–33.

[2]A. Shleifer and R. W. Vishny, "Management Entrenchment: The Case of Manager-Specific Investments," *Journal of Financial Economics* 25 (November 1989), pp. 123–140.

[3]M. C. Jensen, "Agency Costs of Free Cash Flow, Corporate Finance and Takeovers," *American Economic Review* 76 (May 1986), pp. 323–329.

Second, the *design* of a capital investment project involves investment decisions that top managers do not see. Think of a proposal to build a new factory. The managers who developed the plan for the factory had to decide its location. Suppose they chose a more expensive site to get closer to a pool of skilled workers. That's an investment decision: additional investment to generate extra cash flow from access to these workers' skills. (Outlays for training could be lower, for example.) Does the additional investment generate additional NPV, compared with building the factory at a cheaper but more remote site? How is the CFO to know? He or she can't afford the time or the technical knowledge to investigate every alternative that was considered but rejected by the project's sponsors.

Third, many capital investments don't appear in the capital budget. These include research and development, worker training, and marketing outlays designed to expand a market or lock in satisfied customers.

Fourth, *small decisions add up*. Operating managers make investment decisions every day. They may carry extra inventories of raw materials so they won't have to worry about being caught short. Managers at the confabulator plant in Quayle City, Kansas, may decide they need one more forklift. They may hold on to an idle machine tool or an empty warehouse that could have been sold. These are not big decisions ($25,000 here, $50,000 there), but thousands of such decisions add up to real money.

Risk Taking

Because managers cannot diversify their risks as readily as the shareholders, one might expect them to be too risk-averse. Indeed, evidence suggests that managers seek a "quiet life" when the pressure to perform is relaxed.[4] But there are plenty of exceptions.

First, the managers who reach the top ranks of a large corporation must have taken some risks along the way. Managers who seek only the quiet life don't get noticed and don't get promoted rapidly.

Second, managers who are compensated with stock options have an incentive to take more risk. As we explain in Chapters 20 and 21, the value of an option increases when the risk of the firm increases.[5]

Third, managers sometimes have nothing to lose by taking on risks. Suppose that a regional office suffers large, unexpected losses. The regional manager's job is on the line, and in response, he or she tries a risky strategy that offers a small probability of a big, quick payoff. If the strategy pays off, the losses are covered and the manager's job may be saved. If it fails, nothing is lost, because the manager would have been fired anyway. This behavior is called *gambling for redemption*.[6]

Fourth, organizations often hesitate to curtail risky activities that are delivering—at least temporarily—rich profits. The financial crisis of 2007–2009 provides sobering examples. Charles Prince, the pre-crisis CEO of Citigroup, was asked why that bank's leveraged lending business was expanding so rapidly. Prince quipped, "When the music stops . . . things will be complicated. But as long as the music is playing, you've got to get up and dance. We're still dancing." Citi later took a $1.5 billion loss on this line of business.

---

[4]S. Mullainathan and M. Bertrand, "Do Managers Prefer a Quiet Life? Corporate Governance and Managerial Preferences," *Journal of Political Economy* 111 (2003), pp. 1043–1075. When corporations are better protected from takeovers, wages increase, fewer new plants are built, and fewer old plants are shut down. Productivity and profitability also decline.

[5]Kelly Shue and Richard Townsend find that increases in CEOs' option awards were followed, on average, by increases in the volatility of their companies' stocks. It appears that the additional volatility was caused by higher financial leverage—that is, increased use of debt vs. equity financing. Chapter 17 explains how financial leverage increases volatility. See K. Shue and R. Townsend, "How Do Quasi-Random Option Grants Affect CEO Risk-Taking?", *Journal of Finance* 72 (December 2017), pp. 2551–2588.

[6]Baring Brothers, a British bank with a 200-year history, was wiped out when one of its traders, Nick Leeson, lost $1.4 billion trading in Japanese stock market indexes from a Barings office in Singapore. Leeson was gambling for redemption. As his losses mounted, he kept doubling and redoubling his trading bets in an attempt to recover his losses.

Example: Agency Costs and Subprime Mortgages "Subprime" refers to mortgage loans made to home buyers with weak credit. Some of these loans were made to naïve buyers who then struggled to keep up with interest and principal payments. Some were made to opportunistic buyers who were willing to bet that real estate prices would keep improving so that they could "flip" their houses at a profit. But prices fell sharply in 2007 and 2008, and many buyers were forced to default.

Why did so many banks and mortgage companies make these loans in the first place? One reason is that they could repackage the loans as mortgage-backed securities and sell them at a profit to other banks and institutional investors. It's clear with hindsight that many buyers of these mortgage-backed securities were, in turn, naïve and paid too much. When housing prices fell and defaults increased, the prices of these securities fell drastically. For example, Merrill Lynch wrote off $50 billion of losses and was sold under duress to Bank of America.

Although there's plenty of blame to pass around for the subprime crisis, some of it must go to the managers who promoted and sold the subprime mortgages. Were they acting in shareholders' interests or their own interests? We doubt that their shareholders would have endorsed the managers' tactics if the shareholders could have seen what was really going on. We think that the managers would have been much more cautious if they had not had the chance for another fat bonus before their game ended. If so, the financial crisis was partly an agency problem, not value maximization run amok.

12.2 Monitoring

Agency costs can be reduced by monitoring a manager's efforts and actions and by intervening when the manager veers off course.

Monitoring can prevent the more obvious agency costs, such as blatant perks. It can confirm that the manager is putting in sufficient time on the job. But monitoring requires time and money. Some monitoring is almost always worthwhile, but a limit is soon reached at which an extra dollar spent on monitoring would not return an extra dollar of value from reduced agency costs. Like all investments, monitoring encounters diminishing returns.

Some agency costs can't be prevented even with the most thorough monitoring. Suppose a shareholder undertakes to monitor capital investment decisions. How could he or she ever know for sure whether a capital budget approved by top management includes (1) *all* the positive-NPV opportunities open to the firm and (2) *no* projects with negative NPVs due to empire-building or entrenching investments? The managers know more about the firm's prospects than outsiders ever can. If the shareholder could identify all projects and their NPVs, then the managers would hardly be needed!

Who actually does the monitoring?

Boards of Directors

In large, public companies, the task of monitoring is delegated to the board of directors, who are elected by shareholders to represent their interests. Boards of directors are sometimes portrayed as passive stooges who always champion the incumbent management. But response to past corporate scandals has tipped the balance toward greater independence. For example, the Sarbanes-Oxley Act (or SOX) requires that public corporations place more independent directors on the board—that is, more directors who are not managers or are not affiliated with management. In large companies, 85% of all directors are now independent.[7]

---

[7] See Spencer Stuart Board Index, www.spencerstuart.com/research-and-insight/spencer-stuart-board-index-2016.

When managers are not up to the job, boards frequently step in. In recent years, the CEOs of Ford, CSX, AIG, and Wells Fargo have all been replaced. Boards outside the United States, which traditionally have been more management friendly, have also become more willing to replace underperforming managers. The list of recent departures includes the heads of Cathay Pacific, LafargeHolcim, Toshiba, Marks and Spencer, and Handelsbanken.

Of course, delegation of monitoring to the board brings its own agency problems. For example, many board members may be long-standing friends of the CEO and may be indebted to the CEO for help or advice. Understandably, they may be reluctant to fire the CEO or enquire too deeply into his or her conduct. Fortunately, the company's directors are not the only people who scrutinize management's actions. Several other groups serve to keep a wary eye on management.

Auditors

The board is required to hire independent accountants to audit the firm's financial statements. If the audit uncovers no problems, the auditors issue an opinion that the financial statements fairly represent the company's financial condition and are consistent with **generally accepted accounting principles (GAAP).**

If problems are found, the auditors will negotiate changes in assumptions or procedures. Managers almost always agree because if acceptable changes are not made, the auditors will issue a *qualified opinion,* which is bad news for the company and its shareholders. A qualified opinion suggests that managers are covering something up and undermines investors' confidence.

A qualified audit opinion may be bad news, but when investors learn of accounting irregularities that have escaped detection, there can be hell to pay. In September 2014, the British supermarket giant Tesco announced that it had discovered material accounting irregularities and had overstated its first half profits by about $420 million. As the scandal unfolded, Tesco's share price fell by some 30%, wiping $8 billion off the market value of the company.

Lenders

Lenders also monitor. When a company takes out a large bank loan, the bank tracks the company's assets, earnings, and cash flow. By monitoring to protect its loan, the bank generally protects shareholders' interests also.[8]

Shareholders

Shareholders also keep an eagle eye on the company's management and board of directors. If they think that a corporation is not pursuing shareholder value with sufficient energy and determination, they can try to force change—for example, by nominating candidates to the board of directors.

There is a breed of *activist investors* who specialize in finding such underperforming companies and trying to convince them to restructure. These include Carl Icahn (Icahn Enterprises), Paul Singer (Elliott Management), Daniel Loeb (Third Point), and Nelson Peltz (Trian Partners). Peltz's fund bought a large stake in DuPont and was able to force DuPont to cut back its operations and research and development (R&D) and to shed 10% of its worldwide workforce. It agreed to merge with Dow Chemical and to split the merged firm into three new, more focused companies. Other recent targets for activist investors include Navistar, Procter & Gamble,

---

[8]The interests of lenders and shareholders are not always aligned—see Chapter 18. But a company's ability to satisfy lenders is normally good news for stockholders, particularly when lenders are well placed to monitor.

and the food giants Mondelez International and Nestlé. A company's shareholders appear to welcome the arrival of an activist investor for the announcement of the acquisition of a 5% holding by an activist prompts a 7 to 8% abnormal return on the stock.[9]

Smaller shareholders can't play the activist investors' game, but they can take the "Wall Street Walk" by selling out and moving on to other investments. The Wall Street Walk can send a powerful message. If enough shareholders bail out, the stock price tumbles. This damages top management's reputation and compensation. A large part of top managers' paychecks comes from stock grants and stock options, which pay off if the stock price rises but are worthless if the price falls below a stated threshold. Thus, a falling stock price has a direct impact on managers' personal wealth. A rising stock price is good for managers as well as stockholders.

Takeovers

A company's management is regularly monitored by other management teams. If the latter believe that the assets are not being used efficiently, then they can try to take over the business and boot out the existing management. We will have more to say in Chapters 31 and 32 about the role of takeovers and the market for corporate control.

12-3   Management Compensation

Monitoring can't be perfect. Therefore, compensation plans must be designed to attract competent managers and to give them the right incentives.

For U.S. public companies, compensation is the responsibility of the *compensation committee* of the board of directors. The Securities and Exchange Commission (SEC) and New York Stock Exchange (NYSE) require that all directors on the compensation committee be independent—that is, not managers or employees and not linked to the company by some other relationship (e.g., a lucrative consulting contract) that would undercut their independence. The committee typically hires outside consultants to advise on compensation trends and on compensation levels in peer companies.

You can see how the information provided by outside consultants may cause compensation to creep up. The problem is that compensation committees don't want to approve below-average compensation. But if every firm wants to be above-average, then the average will ratchet up.[10]

Once the compensation package is approved by the committee, it is described in an annual Compensation Discussion and Analysis (CD&A), which is sent to shareholders along with director nominations and the company's 10-K filing. (The 10-K is the annual report to the SEC.) In January 2011, the SEC gave shareholders a nonbinding say-on-pay vote on the CD&A at least once every three years.[11] The occasional no vote on management compensation is a disagreeable wake-up call for managers and directors. For example, when the shareholders of auto supplier BorgWarner voted "no" in 2015, the company made changes to its compensation program and cut the CEO's incentive award by $2.4 million.

---

[9]A. Brav, W. Jiang, F. Partnoy, and R. Thomas, "Hedge Fund Activism, Corporate Governance, and Firm Performance," *Journal of Finance* 63 (2008), pp. 1729–1775.

[10]Bizjak, Lemmon, and Naveen found that most firms set pay levels at or above the median of the peer group, and some firms go much higher. For example, Coca-Cola and IBM consistently aim for levels in the top quartile of their peers. See J. M. Bizjak, M. L. Lemmon, and L. Naveen, "Has the Use of Peer Groups Contributed to Higher Pay and Less Efficient Compensation?" *Journal of Financial Economics* 90 (November 2008), pp. 152–168.

[11]Other countries that have given shareholders nonbinding votes on compensation include Australia, Sweden, and the U.K. Shareholders in the Netherlands have a binding vote.

To reinforce these safeguards we now have two consulting companies, ISS and Glass Lewis, that review CD&As for thousands of companies, looking especially at pay-for-performance standards. Their clients are mostly institutional investors, who seek advice on how to vote. (A mutual fund or pension fund may own shares in hundreds of companies. The fund may decide to outsource the analysis of CD&As to a company that specializes in governance issues.)

Compensation Facts and Controversies

Studies of executive pay in the United States suggest three general features:

1. As you can see from Figure 12.1, U.S. CEOs tend to be more highly paid than their opposite numbers in other countries. On average, they get double the pay of German CEOs and more than five times the pay of Japanese CEOs.

2. Figure 12.2 shows that average compensation in the United States has risen much more rapidly than inflation. Between 1992 and 2016, total compensation for the CEOs of companies in the Standard & Poor's (S&P) Index has more than tripled in real terms.[12]

3. Figure 12.3 shows that only 12% of compensation for these CEOs comes from salary. The remainder comes from bonuses, stock grants, stock options, and other performance-linked incentives. This proportion of incentive-based compensation has increased sharply and is much higher than in other countries.

We look first at the size of the pay package. Then we turn to its contents.

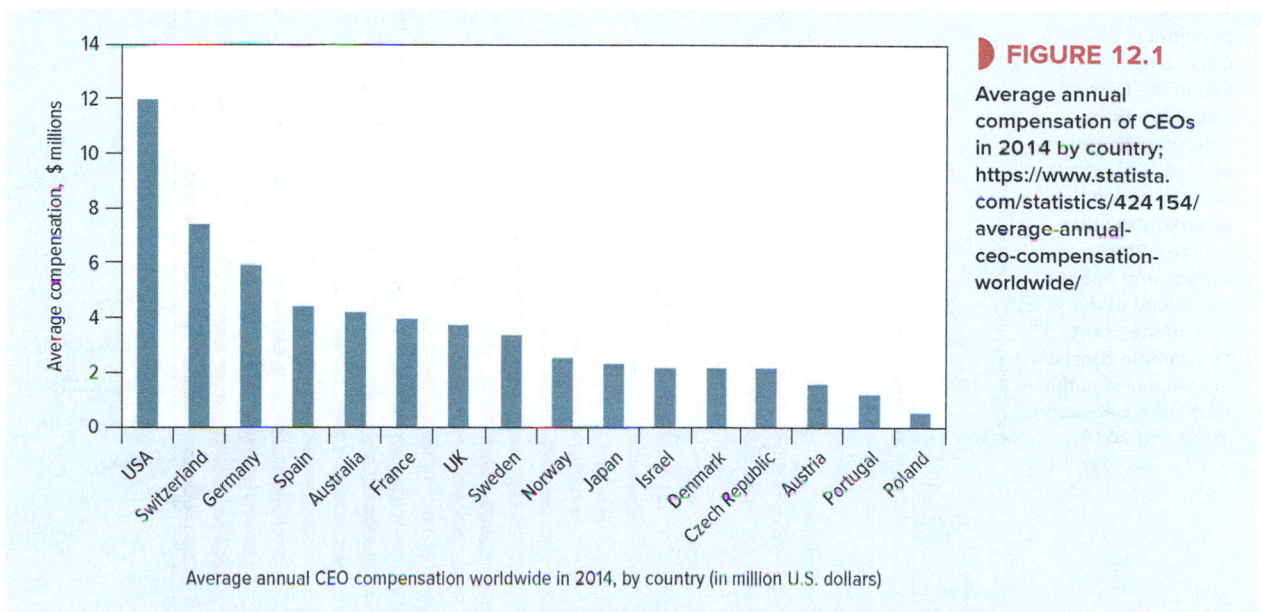

▶ **FIGURE 12.1**

Average annual compensation of CEOs in 2014 by country; https://www.statista.com/statistics/424154/average-annual-ceo-compensation-worldwide/

Average annual CEO compensation worldwide in 2014, by country (in million U.S. dollars)

---

[12]This sharp rise in CEO pay started in the 1970s. For the previous 30 years, pay levels were essentially flat. See C. Frydman and R. Saks, "Executive Compensation: A New View from a Long-Term Perspective, 1936–2005," *Review of Financial Studies* 23 (2010), pp. 2099–2138.

▶ **FIGURE 12.2**

Median total compensation 1992–2016 for CEOs of companies in the S&P Index. Values are shown in inflation-adjusted 2016 dollars.

Source: Execucomp.

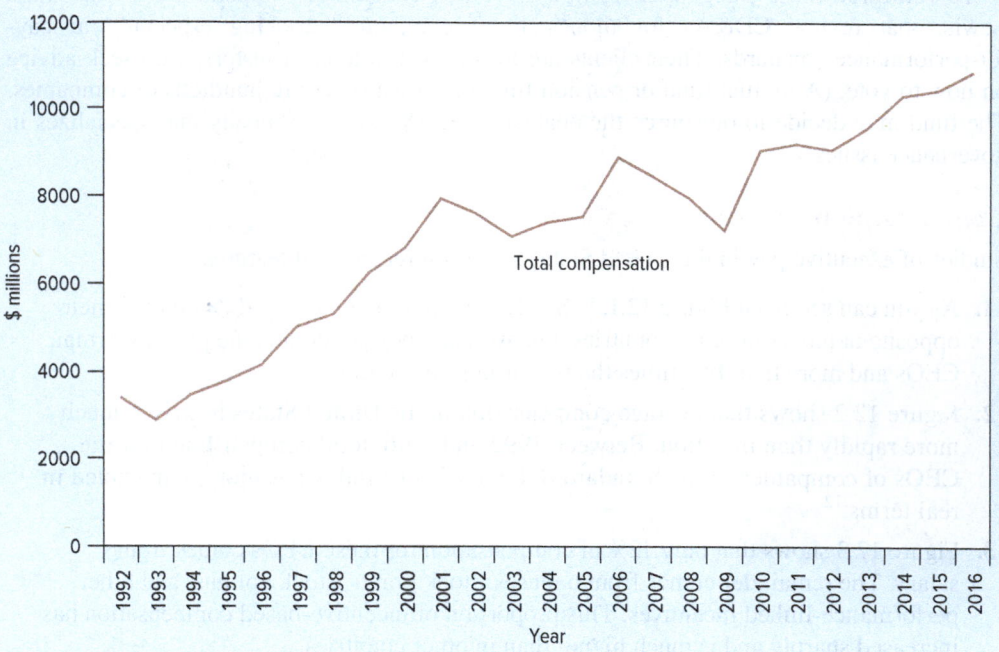

▶ **FIGURE 12.3**

The average percentage of CEO compensation in the form of salaries, bonuses, long-term incentive plans (LTIPs), stock awards, option awards, and other sources. Stock awards and options are valued at the time of the grant. The sample consists of companies in the S&P Index between 1992 and 2016.

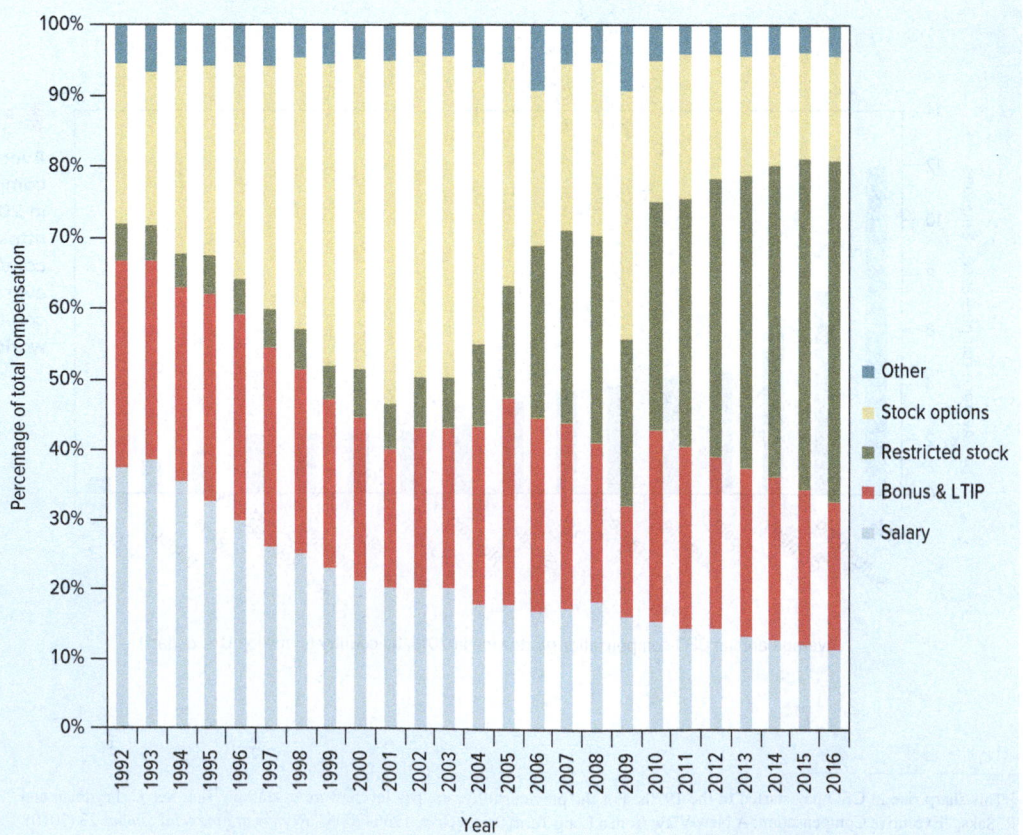

High levels of CEO pay undoubtedly encourage CEOs to work hard and (perhaps more important) offer an attractive carrot to lower-level managers who hope to become CEOs. But there has been widespread concern about "excessive" pay, especially pay for mediocre performance. For example, Robert Nardelli received a $210 million severance package on leaving The Home Depot, and Henry McKinnell received almost $200 million on leaving Pfizer. Both CEOs left behind troubled and underperforming companies. You can imagine the newspaper headlines.

Those headlines were even bigger in 2008 when it was revealed that generous bonuses were to be paid to the senior management of banks that had been bailed out by the government. Merrill Lynch hurried through $3.6 billion in bonuses, including $121 million to just four executives, only days before Bank of America finalized its deal to buy the collapsing firm with the help of taxpayer money. "Bonuses for Boneheads" was the headline in *Forbes* magazine.

It is easy to point to cases where poorly performing managers have received unjustifiably large payouts. But is there a more general problem? Perhaps high levels of pay simply reflect a shortage of talent. After all, CEOs are not alone in earning large sums. The earnings of top professional athletes are equally mouthwatering. The LA Dodgers' Clayton Kershaw was paid $33 million in 2017. The Dodgers must have believed that it was worth paying for a star who would win games and fill up the ballpark.

If star managers are as rare as star baseball players, corporations may need to pay up for CEO talent. Suppose that a superior CEO can add 1% to the value of a large corporation with a market capitalization of $10 billion. One percent on a stock market value of $10 billion is $100 million. If the CEO can really deliver, then a pay package of, say, $20 million per year sounds like a bargain.[13]

There is also a less charitable explanation of managerial pay. This view stresses the close links between the CEO and the other members of the board of directors. If directors are too chummy with the CEO, they may find it difficult to get tough when it comes to setting compensation packages.

So we have two views of the level of managerial pay. One is that it results from arms-length contracting in a tight market for managerial talent. The other is that poor governance and weak boards allow excessive pay. There is evidence for and against both views. For example, CEOs are not the only group to have seen their compensation increase rapidly in recent years. Corporate lawyers, sports stars, and celebrity entertainers have all increased their share of national income, even though their compensation is determined by arms-length negotiation.[14] However, the shortage-of-talent argument cannot account for wide disparities in pay. For example, compare the CEO of Ford (compensation of $22 million in 2016) to the CEO of Toyota (compensation of about $3 million) or to Fed Chairman Jerome Powell ($200,000). It is difficult to argue that Ford's CEO delivered the most value or had the most difficult and important job.

The Economics of Incentive Compensation

The amount of compensation may be less important than how it is structured. The compensation package should encourage managers to maximize shareholder wealth.

Compensation could be based on input (e.g., the manager's effort) or on output (income or value added as a result of the manager's decisions). But input is difficult to measure.

---

[13]Gabaix and Landier argue that high CEO pay is a natural consequence of steadily increasing firm values and the competition for management talent. See X. Gabaix and A. Landier, "Why Has CEO Pay Increased So Much?" *Quarterly Journal of Economics* 123 (February 2008), pp. 49–100.

[14]See S. N. Kaplan and J. D. Rauh, "Wall Street and Main Street: What Contributes to the Rise in the Highest Incomes?" *Review of Financial Studies* 23 (2010), pp. 1004–1050.

How can outside investors observe effort? They can check that the manager clocks in on time, but hours worked does not measure true effort. (Is the manager facing up to difficult and stressful choices, or is he or she just burning time with routine meetings, travel, and paperwork?)

Because effort is not observable, compensation must be based on output—that is, on verifiable results. Trouble is, results depend not just on the manager's contribution, but also on events outside the manager's control. Unless you can separate out the manager's contribution, you face a difficult trade-off. You want to give the manager high-powered incentives, so that he or she does very well when the firm does very well and poorly when the firm underperforms. But suppose the firm is a cyclical business that always struggles in recessions. Then high-powered incentives will force the manager to bear business cycle risk that is not his or her fault.

There are limits to the risks that managers can be asked to bear. So the result is a compromise. Firms do link managers' pay to performance, but fluctuations in firm value are shared by managers and shareholders. Managers bear some of the risks that are beyond their control, and shareholders bear some of the agency costs when managers fail to maximize firm value.

Most major companies around the world now link part of their executive pay to the performance of the companies' stock.[15] Sometimes these incentive schemes constitute the major part of the manager's compensation pay. For example, for the 2017 fiscal year, Larry Ellison, who was CEO of the business software giant Oracle Corporation, received total compensation estimated at $21 million. Only $1 of that amount was salary. The lion's share was in the form of stock and option grants. Moreover, as founder of Oracle, Ellison holds more than 1 *billion* shares in the firm. No one can say for certain how hard Ellison would have worked with a different compensation package. But one thing is clear: He has a huge personal stake in the success of the firm—and in increasing its market value.

Stock options give managers the right (but not the obligation) to buy their company's shares in the future at a fixed exercise price. Usually, the exercise price is set equal to the company's stock price on the day the options are granted. If the company performs well and stock price increases, the manager can buy shares and cash in on the difference between the stock price and the exercise price. If the stock price falls, the manager leaves the options unexercised and hopes for compensation through another channel.

The popularity of stock options was encouraged by U.S. accounting rules, which permitted companies to grant stock options without recognizing any immediate compensation expense. The rules allowed companies to value options at the excess of the stock price over the exercise price on the grant date. But the exercise price was almost always set *equal* to the stock price on that date. Thus, the excess was zero and the stock options were valued at zero. (We show how to calculate the actual value of options in Chapters 20 and 21.) So companies could grant lots of options at no recorded cost and with no reduction in accounting earnings. Naturally, accountants and investors were concerned because earnings were overstated in greater numbers as the volume of option grants increased. After years of controversy, the accounting rules were changed in 2006. U.S. corporations are now required to value executive stock options more realistically and to deduct these values as a compensation expense.

Options also used to have a tax advantage in the United States. Since 1994, compensation of more than $1 million has been considered unreasonable and is not a tax-deductible expense. However, until 2018 there was no restriction on performance-based compensation such as stock options. This exemption was removed by the Tax Cuts and Jobs Act of December 2017.

---

[15]The major exceptions are in China, Japan, India, and South Korea, where such incentive schemes are still used by a minority of large firms.

If you look back at Figure 12.3, you will see that the form of incentive compensation has also undergone significant change. During the 1990s, there was a surge in the use of stock options, and by the year 2000, almost half of a CEO's compensation was typically in the form of options. More recently, companies have increasingly rewarded management with *restricted shares* or, more commonly, with *performance shares.* In the former case, the manager receives a fixed number of shares at the end of a vesting period as long as he or she is still with the company. In the latter case, the number of shares that the manager receives is typically related to his or her performance in the interim.

You can see the advantages of tying compensation to stock price either by the grant of options or stock. When a manager works hard to increase the price, he or she helps shareholders as well as herself. The stock price is a noisy, but objective measure of a firm's financial performance. It is also a forward-looking measure; it incorporates the value of future earnings and future growth opportunities (PVGO). Thus a manager can be rewarded today for ensuring that his or her firm has a good shot at a prosperous future.

But compensation tied to stock price can also have unpleasant side effects. We have already noted how compensation based on stock price forces managers to bear risks that are outside their control. Think of the CEO of an oil company. The company's earnings and stock price depend on worldwide oil prices. When oil prices took off as they did in 1974, 1980 and the early 2000s, did oil-industry CEOs get an extra compensation for being in the right industry at the right time? Bertrand and Mullainathan found that the answer was Yes. Compensation in the oil industry was closely linked to the level of oil prices. But they also found that the link was weaker when shareholders with large blocks of stock sat on the board of directors. It seems that these shareholders resisted large compensation awards that were based just on good luck.[16]

Some companies do attempt to take out the effect of luck by measuring and rewarding performance relative to industry peers. For example, the electric utility Entergy bases part of its incentive compensation on how well Entergy stock performs relative to the Philadelphia Index of 20 of the largest U.S. utilities.

A second problem with performance-related pay is that stock prices depend on investors' expectations of future earnings, and rates of return depend on how well the company performs relative to expectations. Suppose a company announces the appointment of an outstanding new manager. The stock price leaps up in anticipation of improved performance. If the new manager then delivers exactly the good performance that investors expected, the stock will earn only a normal rate of return. In this case, a compensation scheme linked to the stock return after the manager starts would fail to recognize the manager's special contribution.

Stock options can also encourage excessive risk taking. For example, when stock prices fall precipitously, as they did for many firms in the crisis of 2007–2009, existing stock options can be far "underwater" and nearly worthless. Managers holding these options may be tempted to gamble for redemption.

The Specter of Short-Termism

The fourth imperfection may be the most serious. Managers whose pay depends on the stock price are tempted to withhold bad news or manage reported earnings. They are also tempted to postpone or cancel valuable investment projects if the projects would depress earnings in the short run.

CEOs of public companies face constant scrutiny. Much of that scrutiny focuses on earnings. Security analysts forecast earnings per share (EPS), and investors, security analysts, and

---

[16]M. Bertrand and S. Mullainathan, "Are CEOS Rewarded for Luck? The Ones without Principals Are," *Quarterly Journal of Economics* (August 2001), pp. 901–932.

professional portfolio managers wait to see whether the company can meet or beat the forecasts. *Not* meeting the forecasts can be a big disappointment.

Monitoring by security analysts and portfolio managers can help constrain agency problems. But CEOs complain about the "tyranny of EPS" and the apparent short-sightedness of the stock market. (The British call it *short-termism.*) Of course, the stock market is not systematically short-sighted. If it were, growth companies would not sell at the high price–earnings ratios observed in practice.[17] Nevertheless, the pressure on CEOs to generate steady, predictable growth in earnings is real.

CEOs complain about this pressure, but do they do anything about it? Unfortunately the answer appears to be yes, according to Graham, Harvey, and Rajgopal, who surveyed about 400 senior managers.[18] Most of the managers said that accounting earnings were the single most important number reported to investors. Most admitted to adjusting their firms' operations and investments to manage earnings. For example, 80% were willing to decrease discretionary spending in R&D, advertising, or maintenance if necessary to meet earnings targets. Many managers were also prepared to defer or reject investment projects with positive NPVs.

There is a good deal of evidence that firms do indeed manage their earnings. For example, Degeorge, Patel, and Zeckhauser studied a large sample of earnings announcements.[19] With remarkable regularity, earnings per share either met or beat security analysts' forecasts, but only by a few cents. CFOs appeared to report conservatively in good times, building a stockpile of earnings that could be reported later. The rule, it seems, is *Make sure that you report sufficiently good results to keep analysts happy, and, if possible, keep something back for a rainy day.*[20]

How much value was lost because of such adjustments? For a healthy, profitable company, spending a little less on advertising or deferring a project start for a few months may cause no significant damage. But we cannot endorse any sacrifice of fundamental shareholder value done just to manage earnings.

We may condemn earnings management, but in practice it's hard for CEOs and CFOs to break away from the crowd. Graham and his coauthors explain it this way:[21]

> The common belief is that a well-run and stable firm should be able to "produce the numbers". . . even in a year that is somewhat down. Because the market expects firms to be able to hit or slightly exceed earnings targets, and on average firms do just this, problems can arise when a firm does not deliver. . . . The market might assume that not delivering [reveals] potentially serious problems (because the firm is apparently so near the edge that it cannot produce the dollars to hit earnings . . .). As one CFO put it, "if you see one cockroach, you immediately assume that there are hundreds behind the walls."

Thus, we have a cockroach theory explaining why stock prices sometimes fall sharply when a company's earnings fall short, even if the shortfall is only a penny or two.

Of course, private firms do not have to worry about earnings management—which could help explain the increasing number of firms that have been bought out and returned to private

---

[17]Recall from Chapter 4 that the price–earnings ratio equals $1/r_E$, where r_E is the cost of equity, *unless* the firm has valuable growth opportunities (PVGO). The higher the PVGO, the lower the earnings–price ratio and the higher the price–earnings ratio. Thus, the high price–earnings ratios observed for growth companies (much higher than plausible estimates of $1/r_E$) imply that investors forecast large PVGOs. But PVGO depends on investments to be made many years in the future. If investors see significant PVGOs, they cant be systematically short-sighted.

[18]J. R. Graham, C. R. Harvey, and S. Rajgopal, "The Economic Implications of Corporate Financial Reporting," *Journal of Accounting and Economics* 40 (2005), pp. 3–73.

[19]F. Degeorge, J. Patel, and R. Zeckhauser, "Earnings Management to Exceed Thresholds," *The Journal of Business* 72 (January 1999), pp. 1–33.

[20]Sometimes, instead of adjusting their operations, companies meet their target earnings by bending the accounting rules. For example, in August 2009, GE was fined $50 million for creative accounting in earlier years. The SEC said that GE had met or exceeded analysts' profit targets in every quarter from 1995 through 2004, but that its top accountants signed off on improper decisions to make its numbers look better and to avoid missing analysts' earnings expectations.

[21]Graham, Harvey, and Rajgopal, op. cit., p. 29.

ownership. (We discuss "going private" in Chapters 15, 32, and 33.) Firms in some other countries, where quarterly earnings reports are not required and governance is more relaxed, may find it easier to invest for the long run. But such firms will probably accumulate more agency problems. We wish there were simple answers to these trade-offs.

12-4   Measuring and Rewarding Performance: Residual Income and EVA

Almost all top executives of firms with publicly traded shares have compensation packages that depend in part on their firms' stock price performance. But their compensation also includes a bonus that depends on increases in earnings or on other accounting measures of performance. For lower-level managers, compensation packages usually depend more on accounting measures and less on stock returns.

Accounting measures of performance have two advantages:

1. They are based on absolute performance, rather than on performance relative to investors' expectations.

2. They make it possible to measure the performance of junior managers whose responsibility extends to only a single division or plant.

Tying compensation to accounting profits also creates some obvious problems. For example, managers whose pay or promotion depends on short-term profits may cut back on training, advertising, or R&D. This is not a recipe for adding value because these outlays are investments that should pay off in later years. Nevertheless, the outlays are treated as current expenses and deducted from current income. Thus, an ambitious manager is tempted to cut back, thereby increasing current income, leaving longer-run problems to his or her successor.

In addition, accounting earnings and rates of return can be severely biased measures of true profitability. We ignore this problem for now, but return to it in the next section.

Finally, growth in earnings does not necessarily mean that shareholders are better off. Any investment with a positive rate of return (1% or 2% will do) will eventually increase earnings. Therefore, if managers are told to maximize growth in earnings, they will dutifully invest in projects offering 1% or 2% rates of return—projects that destroy value. But shareholders do not want growth in earnings for its own sake, and they are not content with 1% or 2% returns. They want positive-NPV investments, and *only* positive-NPV investments. They want the company to invest only if the expected rate of return exceeds the cost of capital.

Look at Table 12.1, which contains a simplified income statement and balance sheet for your company's Quayle City confabulator plant. There are two methods for judging whether the plant's returns are higher than the cost of capital.

Book return on investment (ROI) is just the ratio of after-tax operating income to the net (depreciated) book value of assets.[22] In Chapter 5, we rejected book ROI as a capital investment criterion, and in fact, few companies now use it for that purpose. However, managers frequently assess the performance of a division or a plant by comparing its ROI with the cost of capital.

Suppose you need to assess the performance of the Quayle City plant. As you can see from Table 12.1, the corporation has $1,000 million invested in the plant, which is generating earnings of $150 million. Therefore, the plant is earning an ROI of 150/1,000 = .15,

---

[22]Notice that investment includes the net working capital (current assets minus current liabilities) required to operate the plant. The investment shown is also called net assets or the net capital invested in the plant. We say "ROI," but you will also hear "return on capital" (ROC). "Return on assets" (ROA) sometimes refers to return on assets defined to include net working capital, as in Table 12.1, but sometimes to return on total assets, where current assets are included but current liabilities are not subtracted. It's prudent to check definitions when reviewing reported ROIs, ROCs, or ROAs. In Chapter 28, we look more carefully at how these measures are calculated.

Income			Assets at Start of Year		
Sales		$550	Net working capital[b]		$ 80
Cost of goods sold[a]		275	Property, plant, and equipment investment		1,170
Selling, general, and administrative expenses		75	*Less* cumulative depreciation		360
		$200	Net investment		$ 810
Taxes at 25%		50	Other assets		110
Net income		$150	Total assets		$1,000

> **TABLE 12.1**   Simplified statements of income and assets for the Quayle City confabulator plant (figures in millions)

[a]Includes depreciation expense.
[b]Current assets less current liabilities.

or 15%.[23] If the cost of capital is (say) 10%, then the plant's activities are adding to shareholder value. The *net* return is 15 − 10 = 5%. If the cost of capital is (say) 20%, then shareholders would have been better off investing $1 billion somewhere else. In this case the net return is negative, at 15 − 20 = −5%.

Residual Income or Economic Value Added (EVA®)[24]

When firms calculate income, they start with revenues and then deduct costs, such as wages, raw material costs, overhead, and taxes. But there is one cost that they do not commonly deduct: the cost of capital. True, they allow for depreciation, but investors are not content with a return of their investment; they also demand a return *on* that investment. As we pointed out in Chapter 10, a business that breaks even in terms of accounting profits is really making a loss; it is failing to cover the cost of capital.

To judge the net contribution to value, we need to deduct the cost of capital contributed to the plant by the parent company and its stockholders. Suppose again that the cost of capital is 10%. Then the dollar cost of capital for the Quayle City plant is .10 × $1,000 = $100 million.

The net gain is therefore $150 − 100 = $50 million. This is the addition to shareholder wealth due to management's hard work (or good luck).

Net income after deducting the dollar return required by investors is called *residual income* or *economic value added (EVA)*. The formula is

$$\text{EVA} = \text{residual income} = \text{income earned} - \text{income required}$$
$$= \text{income earned} - \text{cost of capital} \times \text{investment}$$

For our example, the calculation is

$$\text{EVA} = \text{residual income} = 150 - (.10 \times 1,000) = +\$50 \text{ million}$$

[23]Notice that earnings are calculated after tax but with no deductions for interest paid. The plant is evaluated as if it were all-equity-financed. This is standard practice (see Chapter 6). It helps to separate investment and financing decisions. The tax advantages of debt financing supported by the plant are picked up not in the plant's earnings or cash flows, but in the discount rate. The cost of capital is the after-tax weighted-average cost of capital, or WACC. WACC was briefly introduced in Chapter 9 and will be further explained in Chapters 17 and 19.

[24]The term EVA was coined by the consulting firm Stern Stewart, which popularized and implemented this measure of residual income. Stern Stewart's EVA practice has mostly moved to the follow-on consulting firm EVA Dimensions. EVA is conceptually the same as the residual income measure advocated by some accounting scholars. See R. Anthony, "Accounting for the Cost of Equity," *Harvard Business Review* 51 (1973), pp. 81–102; and "Equity Interest—Its Time Has Come," *Journal of Accountancy* 154 (1982), pp. 76–93.

But if the cost of capital were 20%, EVA would be negative by $50 million.

Net return on investment and EVA are focusing on the same question. When return on investment equals the cost of capital, net return and EVA are both zero. But the net return is a percentage and ignores the scale of the company. EVA recognizes the amount of capital employed and the number of dollars of additional wealth created.

EVA sometimes pops up with different labels. Other consulting firms have their own versions of residual income. McKinsey & Company uses *economic profit (EP),* defined as capital invested multiplied by the spread between return on investment and the cost of capital. This is another way to measure residual income. For the Quayle City plant, with a 10% cost of capital, economic profit is the same as EVA:

$$\text{Economic profit (EP)} = (\text{ROI} - r) \times \text{capital invested}$$
$$= (.15 - .10) \times 1{,}000 = \$50 \text{ million}$$

In Chapter 28, we take a look at EVAs calculated for some well-known companies. But EVA's most valuable contributions happen inside companies. EVA encourages managers and employees to concentrate on increasing value, not just on increasing earnings.

Pros and Cons of EVA

Let us start with the pros. EVA, economic profit, and other residual income measures are clearly better than earnings or earnings growth for measuring performance. A plant that is generating lots of EVA should generate accolades for its managers as well as value for shareholders. EVA may also highlight parts of the business that are not performing up to scratch. If a division is failing to earn a positive EVA, its management is likely to face some pointed questions about whether the division's assets could be better employed elsewhere.

EVA sends a message to managers: Invest if and only if the increase in earnings is enough to cover the cost of capital. This is an easy message to grasp. Therefore, EVA can be used down deep in the organization as an incentive compensation system. It is a substitute for explicit monitoring by top management. Instead of *telling* plant and divisional managers not to waste capital and then trying to figure out whether they are complying, EVA rewards them for careful investment decisions. Of course, if you tie junior managers' compensation to their economic value added, you must also give them power over those decisions that affect EVA. Thus, the use of EVA implies delegated decision making.

EVA makes the cost of capital *visible* to operating managers. A plant manager can improve EVA by (1) increasing earnings or (2) *reducing* capital employed. Therefore, underutilized assets tend to be flushed out and disposed of.

Introduction of residual income measures often leads to surprising reductions in assets employed—not from one or two big capital disinvestment decisions, but from many small ones. Ehrbar quotes a sewing machine operator at Herman Miller Corporation:

> [EVA] lets you realize that even assets have a cost. . . . We used to have these stacks of fabric sitting here on the tables until we needed them. . . . We were going to use the fabric anyway, so who cares that we're buying it and stacking it up there? Now no one has excess fabric. They only have the stuff we're working on today. And it's changed the way we connect with suppliers, and we're having [them] deliver fabric more often.[25]

If you propose to tie a manager's remuneration to her business's profitability, it is clearly better to use EVA than accounting income, which takes no account of the cost of the capital

---

[25]A. Ehrbar, *EVA: The Real Key to Creating Wealth* (New York: John Wiley & Sons, 1998), pp. 130–131.

employed. But what are the limitations of EVA? Here we return to the same question that bedevils stock-based measures of performance. How can you judge whether a low EVA is a consequence of bad management or of factors outside the manager's control? The deeper you go in the organization, the less independence that managers have and therefore the greater the problem in measuring their contribution.

The second limitation with any accounting measure of performance lies in the data on which it is based. We explore this issue in the next section.

12-5   Biases in Accounting Measures of Performance

Anyone using accounting measures of performance had better hope that the accounting numbers are accurate. Unfortunately, they are often not accurate, but biased. Applying EVA or any other accounting measure of performance therefore requires adjustments to the income statements and balance sheets.

For example, think of the difficulties in measuring the profitability of a pharmaceutical research program, where it typically takes 10 to 12 years to bring a new drug from discovery to final regulatory approval and the drug's first revenues. That means 10 to 12 years of guaranteed losses, even if the managers in charge do everything right. Similar problems occur in start-up ventures, where there may be heavy capital outlays but low or negative earnings in the first years of operation. This does not imply negative NPV, so long as operating earnings and cash flows are sufficiently high later on. But EVA and ROI would be negative in the start-up years, even if the project were on track to a strong positive NPV.

The problem in these cases is not with EVA or ROI, but with the accounting data. The pharmaceutical R&D program may be showing accounting losses because generally accepted accounting principles require that outlays for R&D be written off as current expenses. But from an economic point of view, those outlays are an investment, not an expense. If a proposal for a new business predicts accounting losses during a start-up period, but the proposal nevertheless shows a positive NPV, then the start-up losses are really an investment—cash outlays made to generate larger cash inflows when the business hits its stride.

Example: Measuring the Profitability of the Nodhead Supermarket

BEYOND THE PAGE

Try it! Nodhead supermarket

mhhe.com/brealey13e

Supermarket chains invest heavily in building and equipping new stores. The regional manager of a chain is about to propose investing $1 million in a new store in Nodhead. Projected cash flows are

	Year						
	1	2	3	4	5	6	After 6
Cash flow ($ thousands)	100	200	250	298	298	297	0

Of course, real supermarkets last more than six years. But these numbers are realistic in one important sense: It may take two or three years for a new store to build up a substantial, habitual clientele. Thus, cash flow is low for the first few years even in the best locations.

We will assume the opportunity cost of capital is 10%. The Nodhead store's NPV at 10% is zero. It is an acceptable project, but not an unusually good one:

$$NPV = -1,000 + \frac{100}{1.10} + \frac{200}{(1.10)^2} + \frac{250}{(1.10)^3} + \frac{298}{(1.10)^4} + \frac{298}{(1.10)^5} + \frac{297}{(1.10)^6} = 0$$

With NPV = 0, the true (internal) rate of return of this cash-flow stream is also 10%.

	Year					
	1	**2**	**3**	**4**	**5**	**6**
Cash flow	100	200	250	298	298	297
Book value at start of year	1,000	834	667	500	333	167
Book value at end of year	834	667	500	333	167	0
Book depreciation	167	167	167	167	167	167
Book income	−67	33	83	131	131	130
Book ROI	−0.067	0.040	0.125	0.263	0.394	0.782
EVA	−167	−50	17	81	98	114

❭**TABLE 12.2**   Forecasted book income, ROI, and EVA for the proposed Nodhead store. **Book ROI and EVA are underestimated for the first two years and overestimated thereafter.**
Note: There are minor rounding errors in some annual figures.

Table 12.2 shows the store's forecasted *book* profitability, assuming straight-line depreciation over its six-year life. The book ROI is lower than the true return for the first two years and higher afterward.[26] EVA also starts negative for the first two years, then turns positive and grows steadily to year 6. These are typical outcomes, because accounting income is too low when a project or business is young and too high as it matures.

At this point the regional manager steps up on stage for the following soliloquy:

The Nodhead store's a decent investment. But if we go ahead, I won't look very good at next year's performance review. And what if I also go ahead with the new stores in Russet, Gravenstein, and Sheepnose? Their cash-flow patterns are pretty much the same. I could actually appear to lose money next year. The stores I've got won't earn enough to cover the initial losses on four new ones.

Of course, everyone knows new supermarkets lose money at first. The loss would be in the budget. My boss will understand—I think. But what about her boss? What if the board of directors starts asking pointed questions about profitability in my region? I'm under a lot of pressure to generate better earnings. Pamela Quince, the upstate manager, got a bonus for generating a positive EVA. She didn't spend much on expansion.

The regional manager is getting conflicting signals. On the one hand, he is told to find and propose good investment projects. *Good* is defined by discounted cash flow. On the other hand, he is also urged to seek high book income. But the two goals conflict because book income does not measure true income. The greater the pressure for immediate book profits, the more the regional manager is tempted to forgo good investments or to favor quick payback projects over longer-lived projects, even if the latter have higher NPVs.

Measuring Economic Profitability

Let us think for a moment about how profitability should be measured in principle. It is easy enough to compute the true, or economic, rate of return for a common stock that is

---

[26]The errors in book ROI always catch up with you in the end. If the firm chooses a depreciation schedule that overstates a project's return in some years, it must also understate the return in other years. In fact, you can think of a project's IRR as a kind of average of the book returns. It is not a simple average, however. The weights are the project's book values discounted at the IRR. See J. A. Kay, "Accountants, Too, Could Be Happy in a Golden Age: The Accountant's Rate of Profit and the Internal Rate of Return," *Oxford Economic Papers* 28 (1976), pp. 447–460.

continuously traded. We just record cash receipts (dividends) for the year, add the change in price over the year, and divide by the beginning price:

$$\text{Rate of return} = \frac{\text{cash receipts} + \text{change in price}}{\text{beginning price}}$$

$$= \frac{C_1 + (P_1 - P_0)}{P_0}$$

The numerator of the expression for rate of return (cash flow plus change in value) is called **economic income:**

$$\text{Economic income} = \text{cash flow} + \text{change in present value}$$

Any reduction in present value represents **economic depreciation;** any increase in present value represents *negative* economic depreciation. Therefore,

$$\text{Economic income} = \text{cash flow} - \text{economic depreciation}$$

The concept works for any asset. Rate of return equals cash flow plus change in value divided by starting value:

$$\text{Rate of return} = \frac{C_1 + (PV_1 - PV_0)}{PV_0}$$

where PV_0 and PV_1 indicate the present values of the business at the ends of years 0 and 1.

The only hard part in measuring economic income is calculating present value. You can observe market value if the asset is actively traded, but few plants, divisions, or capital projects have shares traded in the stock market. You can observe the present market value of *all* the firm's assets but not of any one of them taken separately.

Accountants rarely even attempt to measure present value. Instead they give us net book value (BV), which is original cost less depreciation computed according to some arbitrary schedule. If book depreciation and economic depreciation are different (they are rarely the same), then book earnings will not measure true earnings. (In fact, it is not clear that accountants should even *try* to measure true profitability. They could not do so without heavy reliance on subjective estimates of value. Perhaps they should stick to supplying objective information and leave the estimation of value to managers and investors.)

It is not hard to *forecast* economic income and rate of return for the Nodhead store. Table 12.3 shows the calculations. From the cash-flow forecasts we can forecast present value at the start of periods 1 to 6. Cash flow minus economic depreciation equals economic income. Rate of return equals economic income divided by start-of-period value.

Of course, these are forecasts. Actual future cash flows and values will be higher or lower. Table 12.3 shows that investors *expect* to earn 10% in each year of the store's six-year life. In other words, investors expect to earn the opportunity cost of capital each year from holding this asset.

Notice that EVA calculated using present value and economic income is zero in each year of the Nodhead project's life. For year 2, for example,

$$\text{EVA} = 100 - (.10 \times 1,000) = 0$$

EVA *should* be zero, because the project's true rate of return is only equal to the cost of capital. EVA will always give the right signal if, and only if, book income equals economic income and asset values are measured accurately.

	Year					
	1	**2**	**3**	**4**	**5**	**6**
Cash flow	100	200	250	298	298	297
PV at start of year	1,000	1,000	900	740	516	270
PV at end of year	1,000	900	740	516	270	0
Economic depreciation	0	100	160	224	246	270
Economic income	100	100	90	74	52	27
Rate of return	0.10	0.10	0.10	0.10	0.10	0.10
EVA	0.00	0.00	0.00	0.00	0.00	0.00

❭**TABLE 12.3**   Forecasted economic income, rate of return, and EVA for the proposed Nodhead store. Economic income equals cash flow minus economic depreciation. Rate of return equals economic income divided by value at start of year. EVA equals income minus cost of capital times value at start of year.

Note: There are minor rounding errors in some annual figures.

Do the Biases Wash Out in the Long Run?

Even if the forecasts for the Nodhead store turn out to be correct, ROI and EVA will be biased if they are based on *book income* and *book value*. That might not be a serious problem if the errors wash out in the long run, when the region settles down to a steady state with an even mix of old and new stores.

It turns out that the errors do not wash out in the steady state. Table 12.4 shows steady-state book ROIs and EVAs for the supermarket chain if it opens one store a year. For simplicity, we assume that the company starts from scratch and that each store's cash flows are carbon copies of the Nodhead store. The true rate of return on each store is, therefore, 10% and the true EVA is zero. But as Table 12.4 demonstrates, steady-state book ROI and estimated EVA *overstate* the true profitability.

Thus, we still have a problem even in the long run. The extent of the error depends on how fast the business grows. We have just considered one steady state with a zero growth rate. Think of another firm with a 5% steady-state growth rate. Such a firm would invest $1,000 the first year, $1,050 the second, $1,102.50 the third, and so on. Clearly, the faster growth means more new projects relative to old ones. The greater weight given to young projects, which have low book ROIs and negative apparent EVAs, the lower the business's apparent profitability.[27]

What Can We Do about Biases in Accounting Profitability Measures?

The dangers in judging profitability by accounting measures are clear from these examples. To be forewarned is to be forearmed. But we can say something beyond just "be careful."

It is natural for firms to set a standard of profitability for plants or divisions. Ideally, that standard should be the opportunity cost of capital for investment in the plant or division. That is the whole point of EVA: to compare actual profits with the cost of capital. But if performance is measured by return on investment or EVA, then these measures need to recognize accounting biases. Ideally, the financial manager should identify and eliminate accounting biases before calculating EVA or net ROI. The managers and consultants that implement these measures work hard to adjust book income closer to economic income. For example,

---

[27]We could repeat the steady-state analysis in Table 12.4 for different growth rates. It turns out that book income will overstate economic income if the growth rate is less than the internal rate of return and understate economic income if the growth rate exceeds the internal rate of return. Biases disappear if the growth rate and internal rate of return are exactly equal.

	Year					
	1	**2**	**3**	**4**	**5**	**6**
Book income for store[a]						
1	−67	33	83	131	131	130
2		−67	33	83	131	131
3			−67	33	83	131
4				−67	33	83
5					−67	33
6						−67
Total book income	−67	−33	50	181	312	443
Book value for store						
1	1,000	834	667	500	333	167
2		1,000	834	667	500	333
3			1,000	834	667	500
4				1,000	834	667
5					1,000	834
6						1,000
Total book value	1,000	1,834	2,501	3,001	3,334	3,501
Book ROI for all stores	−0.067	−0.018	0.020	0.060	0.094	0.126[b]
EVA	−166.73	−216.79	−200.19	−118.91	−20.96	92.66[c]
						▲
						Steady state

〉TABLE 12.4   Book ROI for a group of stores like the Nodhead store. The steady-state book ROI overstates the 10% *economic rate* of return. The steady-state EVA is also biased upward.

Note: There are minor rounding errors in some annual figures.
[a]Book income = cash flow − book depreciation.
[b]Steady-state book ROI.
[c]Steady-state EVA.

they may record R&D as an investment rather than an expense and construct alternative balance sheets showing R&D as an asset.

Accounting biases are notoriously hard to get rid of, however. Thus, many firms end up asking not "Did the widget division earn more than its cost of capital last year?" but "Was the widget division's book ROI typical of a successful firm in the widget industry?" The underlying assumptions are that (1) similar accounting procedures are used by other widget manufacturers and (2) successful widget companies earn their cost of capital.

There are some simple accounting changes that could reduce biases in performance measures. Remember that the biases all stem from *not* using economic depreciation. Therefore, why not switch to economic depreciation? The main reason is that each asset's present value would have to be reestimated every year. Imagine the confusion if this were attempted. You can understand why accountants set up a depreciation schedule when an investment is made and then stick to it. But why restrict the choice of depreciation schedules to the old standbys, such as straight-line? Why not specify a depreciation pattern that at least matches *expected* economic depreciation? For example, the Nodhead store could be depreciated according to the expected economic depreciation schedule shown in Table 12.3. This would avoid any systematic biases. It would break no law or accounting standard. This step seems so simple and effective that we are at a loss to explain why firms have not adopted it.[28]

---

[28]This procedure has been suggested by several authors; see, for example, Zvi Bodie, "Compound Interest Depreciation in Capital Investment," *Harvard Business Review* 60 (May–June 1982), pp. 58–60.

SUMMARY

In an ideal world, managers would make all positive-NPV investments and only positive-NPV investments.[29] But managers are not perfect servants of shareholders. Agency costs are incurred when they do not maximize shareholder value.

Managers may be tempted to slack off or to consume wasteful perks. They may expand in pursuit of prestige and other private benefits. They may favor entrenching investments that reinforce their personal value to the firm. They may overinvest, especially when cash flow is plentiful. They may resist disinvestment even when shrinking adds value.

Of course, managers who are tempted do not automatically give in. They recognize their responsibilities. They want their companies to be efficient and competitive. But they also know they are monitored, not just by shareholders and the board of directors, but also by auditors, regulators, and banks and other lenders. Compensation packages are also designed to align managers' and shareholders' interests.

Compensation for top management typically includes grants of stock, stock options, or bonuses based on stock-price performance. Thus, managers have strong incentives to increase shareholder value. Compensation tied to stock price is not a perfect solution to agency problems, however. It forces managers to bear market or macroeconomic risks that they cannot control. It may also encourage short-termism—that is, an excessive focus on short-term results at the expense of long-term investment. It appears that U.S. CEOs and CFOs are willing to sacrifice long-term value (e.g., by cutting back R&D) in order to make sure that earnings per share look good to investors.

The further you go down a company's organization chart, the more tenuous the link between stock price and a manager's effort and decisions. Therefore, a higher fraction of pay depends on accounting income. But increasing accounting income is not the same thing as increasing value. Accountants do not recognize the cost of capital as an expense. Many companies now tie compensation to economic value added (EVA) or other measures of residual income. These measures start with accounting income but subtract a charge for capital employed. This charge pushes managers and other employees to let go of unneeded assets and to acquire new ones only when the additional earnings exceed the cost of capital.

The usefulness of EVA or other residual income measures depends on accurate measures of income and capital employed. Adjustments to accounting data may be needed to make sure the measures are not misleading.

In principle, companies should use true or economic income instead of accounting income. Economic income equals the cash flow less economic depreciation (i.e., the decline in the present value of the asset). Unfortunately, we can't ask accountants to recalculate each asset's present value each time income is calculated. But it does seem fair to ask why they don't at least try to match book depreciation schedules to typical patterns of economic depreciation.

The more pressing problem is that CEOs and CFOs seem to pay too much attention to earnings, at least in the short run, to maintain smooth growth and to meet earnings targets. They manage earnings, not with improper accounting, but by tweaking operating and investment plans. For example, they may defer a positive-NPV project for a few months to move the project's up-front expenses into the next fiscal year. It's not clear how much value is lost by this kind of behavior, but any value loss is unfortunate.

---

[29]There are, of course, many types of investments that generate no cash flows directly, but are nevertheless required for safety, efficiency, or to meet legal, regulatory, or ethical standards. Examples include investments for safety and pollution control. Companies make these investments even though they may appear to have negative NPVs.

FURTHER READING

Current practices in management remuneration are discussed in:

A. Edmans, X. Gabaix, and D. Jenter, "Executive Compensation: A Survey of Theory and Evidence," European Corporate Governance Institute, June 26, 2017.

R. K. Aggarwal, "Executive Compensation and Incentives," in B. E. Eckbo (ed.), *Handbook of Empirical Corporate Finance* (Amsterdam: Elsevier/North-Holland, 2007), Chapter 7.

R. Rau, "Executive Compensation," *Foundations and Trends in Finance* 10 (2017), pp. 181–362.

The following surveys argue that executive compensation has been excessive, owing partly to weaknesses in corporate governance:

L. Bebchuk and J. Fried, *Pay without Performance: The Unfulfilled Promise of Executive Compensation* (Cambridge, MA: Harvard University Press, 2005).

M. C. Jensen, K. J. Murphy, and E. G. Wruck, "Remuneration: Where We've Been, How We Got to Here, What Are the Problems, and How to Fix Them," 2004, at **www.ssrn.com,** posted July 12, 2004.

The Fall 2005 issue of the Journal of Applied Corporate Finance *focuses on executive pay and corporate governance.*

The following article is worth reading for survey evidence on earnings and corporate reporting:

J. R. Graham, C. R. Harvey, and S. Rajgopal, "The Economic Implications of Corporate Financial Reporting," *Journal of Accounting and Economics* 40 (2005), pp. 3–73.

For easy-to-read descriptions of EVA, see:

G. Bennett Stewart III, *Best Practice EVA: The Definitive Guide to Measuring and Maximizing Shareholder Value* (New York: John Wiley & Sons, 2013).

J. M. Stern and J. S. Shiely, *The EVA Challenge—Implementing Value-Added Change in an Organization* (New York: John Wiley & Sons, 2007).

PROBLEM SETS

 Select problems are available in McGraw-Hill's *Connect.* Please see the preface for more information.

1. **Terminology*** Define the following:
   a. Agency costs in capital investment.
   b. Private benefits.
   c. Empire building.
   d. Entrenching investment.
   e. Delegated monitoring.

2. **Monitoring** Monitoring alone can never completely eliminate agency costs in capital investment. Briefly explain why.

3. **Monitoring** Who monitors the top management of public U.S. corporations? (We have mentioned several types of monitoring in this chapter.)

4. **Management compensation*** True or false?
   a. U.S. CEOs are paid much more than CEOs in other countries.
   b. A large fraction of compensation for U.S. CEOs comes from grants of restricted shares or performance shares.
   c. Stock-option grants give the manager a certain number of shares delivered at annual intervals, usually over five years.
   d. U.S. accounting rules now require recognition of the value of stock-option grants as a compensation expense.

5. **Management compensation** Compare typical compensation and incentive arrangements for (a) top management (e.g., the CEO or CFO) and (b) plant or division managers. What are the chief differences? Can you explain them?

6. **Management compensation** Suppose all plant and division managers were paid only a fixed salary—no other incentives or bonuses.

   a. Describe the agency problems that would appear in capital investment decisions.

   b. How would tying the managers' compensation to EVA alleviate these problems?

7. **Management compensation** We noted that management compensation must, in practice, rely on results rather than on effort. Why? What problems are introduced by not rewarding effort?

8. **Management compensation** Here are a few questions about compensation schemes that tie top management's compensation to the rate of return earned on the company's common stock.

   a. Today's stock price depends on investors' expectations of future performance. What problems does this create?

   b. Stock returns depend on factors outside the managers' control—for example, changes in interest rates or prices of raw materials. Could this be a serious problem? If so, can you suggest a partial solution?

   c. Compensation schemes that depend on stock returns do not depend on accounting data. Is that an advantage? Why or why not?

9. **Management compensation** You chair the compensation committee of the board of directors of Androscoggin Copper. A consultant suggests two stock-option packages for the CEO:

   a. A conventional stock-option plan, with the exercise price fixed at today's stock price.

   b. An alternative plan in which the exercise price depends on the future market value of a portfolio of the stocks of other copper-mining companies. This plan pays off for the CEO only if Androscoggin's stock price performs better than its competitors'. The second plan sets a higher hurdle for the CEO, so the number of shares should be higher than in the conventional plan.

      Assume that the number of shares granted under each plan has been calibrated so that the present values of the two plans are the same. Which plan would you vote for? Explain.

10. **Management compensation** In recent years, several large banks have paid management bonuses partly in bonds and partly in stock. What do you think is the reason for this? Do you think it is a good idea?

11. **Earnings targets** How, in practice, do managers of public firms meet short-run earnings targets? By creative accounting?

12. **Economic income** Fill in the blanks: "A project's economic income for a given year equals the project's _____ less its _____ depreciation. New projects may take several years to reach full profitability. In these cases, book income is _____ than economic income early in the project's life and _____ than economic income later in its life."

13. **Economic income*** Consider the following project:

	Period			
	0	**1**	**2**	**3**
Net cash flow	−100	0	78.55	78.55

The internal rate of return is 20%. The NPV, assuming a 20% opportunity cost of capital, is exactly zero. Calculate the expected economic income and economic depreciation in each year.

BEYOND THE PAGE

Try it! Nodhead supermarket

mhhe.com/brealey13e

14. **Accounting measures of performance** Use the Beyond the Page feature to access the Excel program for measuring the profitability of the Nodhead project. Reconstruct Table 12.4 assuming a steady-state growth rate of 10% per year. Your answer will illustrate a fascinating theorem—namely, that book rate of return equals the economic rate of return when the economic rate of return and the steady-state growth rate are the same.

15. **Accounting measures of performance*** The Modern Language Corporation earned $1.6 million on net assets of $20 million. The cost of capital is 11.5%. Calculate the net ROI and EVA.

16. **Accounting measures of performance** Calculate the year-by-year book and economic profitability for investment in polyzone production, as described in Chapter 11. Use the cash flows and competitive spreads shown in Table 11.2, and assume straight-line depreciation over 10 years. What is the steady-state book rate of return (ROI) for a mature company producing polyzone? Assume no growth and competitive spreads.

17. **Accounting measures of performance** True or false? Explain briefly.

    a. Book profitability measures are biased measures of true profitability for individual assets. However, these biases "wash out" when firms hold a balanced mix of old and new assets.

    b. Systematic biases in book profitability would be avoided if companies used depreciation schedules that matched expected economic depreciation. However, few, if any, firms have done this.

18. **EVA** Here are several questions about economic value added or EVA.

    a. Is EVA expressed as a percentage or a dollar amount?

    b. Write down the formula for calculating EVA.

    c. What is the difference, if any, between EVA and residual income?

    d. What is the point of EVA? Why do firms use it?

    e. Does the effectiveness of EVA depend on accurate measures of accounting income and assets?

19. **EVA*** Herbal Resources is a small but profitable producer of dietary supplements for pets. This is not a high-tech business, but Herbal's earnings have averaged around $1.2 million after tax, largely on the strength of its patented enzyme for making cats nonallergenic. The patent has eight years to run, and Herbal has been offered $4 million for the patent rights. Herbal's assets include $2 million of working capital and $8 million of property, plant, and equipment. The patent is not shown on Herbal's books. Suppose Herbal's cost of capital is 15%. What is its EVA?

20. **EVA** Table 12.5 shows a condensed income statement and balance sheet for Androscoggin Copper's Rumford smelting plant.

    a. Calculate the plant's EVA. Assume the cost of capital is 9%.

    b. As Table 12.5 shows, the plant is carried on Androscoggin's books at $48.32 million. However, it is a modern design, and could be sold to another copper company for $95 million (including net working capital). How should this fact change your calculation of EVA?

❯**TABLE 12.5**
Condensed financial statements for the Rumford smelting plant. See Problem 20 (figures in $ millions).

Income Statement for 2018		Assets, December 31, 2018	
Revenue	$56.66	Net working capital	$ 7.08
Raw materials cost	18.72		
Operating cost	21.09	Investment in plant and equipment	69.33
Depreciation	4.50	Less accumulated depreciation	21.01
Pretax income	$12.35	Net plant and equipment	$48.32
Tax at 21%	2.59		
Net income	$ 9.76	Total assets	$55.40

21. **EVA** Use the Beyond the Page feature to access the Excel program for calculating the profitability of the Nodhead project. Now suppose that the cash flows from Nodhead's new supermarket are as follows:

BEYOND THE PAGE

Try it! Nodhead supermarket

mhhe.com/brealey13e

		Period					
	0	**1**	**2**	**3**	**4**	**5**	**6**
Cash flows ($ thousands)	−1,000	+298	+298	+298	+138	+138	+140

   a. Recalculate economic depreciation. Is it accelerated or decelerated?

   b. Rework Tables 12.2 and 12.3 to show the relationship between (a) the "true" rate of return and book ROI and (b) true EVA and forecasted EVA in each year of the project's life.

22. **EVA** Ohio Building Products (OBP) is considering the launch of a new product that would require an initial investment in equipment of $30,800 (no investment in working capital is required). The forecast profits from the product are as follows:

	Year 1	Year 2
Net revenues	$23,337	$22,152
Depreciation	13,860	16,940
Pretax profit	9,477	5,212
Tax at 21%	3,317	1,824
Net profit	$6,160	$3,388

   No cash flows are forecast after year 2, and the equipment will have no salvage value. The cost of capital is 10%.

   a. What is the project's NPV?

   b. Calculate the expected EVA and the return on investment in each of years 1 and 2.

   c. Why does EVA decline between years 1 and 2, whereas the return on investment is unchanged?

   d. Calculate the present value of the economic value added. How does this figure compare with the project NPV?

   e. What would be the return on investment and EVA if OBP chooses instead to depreciate the investment straight line? Do you think that this would provide a better standard for measuring subsequent performance?

CHALLENGE

23. **Accounting measures of performance** Consider an asset with the following cash flows:

	Year			
	0	**1**	**2**	**3**
Cash flows ($ millions)	−12	+5.20	+4.80	+4.40

   The firm uses straight-line depreciation. Thus, for this project, it writes off $4 million per year in years 1, 2, and 3. The discount rate is 10%.

   a. Show that economic depreciation equals book depreciation.

   b. Show that the book rate of return is the same in each year.

c. Show that the project's book profitability is its true profitability.

d. You've just illustrated another interesting theorem. If the book rate of return is the same in each year of a project's life, the book rate of return equals the IRR.

24. **Accounting measures of performance** In our Nodhead example, true depreciation was decelerated. That is not always the case. For instance, Table 12.6 shows how, on average, the market value of a Boeing 737 has varied with its age[30] and the cash flow needed in each year to provide a 10% return. (For example, if you bought a 737 for $19.69 million at the start of year 1 and sold it a year later, your total profit would be $17.99 + 3.67 - 19.69 = \$1.97$ million, 10% of the purchase cost.)

Many airlines write off their aircraft straight-line over 15 years to a salvage value equal to 20% of the original cost.

a. Calculate economic and book depreciation for each year of the plane's life.

b. Compare the true and book rates of return in each year.

c. Suppose an airline invested in a fixed number of Boeing 737s each year. Would steady-state book return overstate or understate true return?

Start of Year	Market Value	Cash Flow
1	19.69	
2	17.99	$3.67
3	16.79	3.00
4	15.78	2.69
5	14.89	2.47
6	14.09	2.29
7	13.36	2.14
8	12.68	2.02
9	12.05	1.90
10	11.46	1.80
11	10.91	1.70
12	10.39	1.61
13	9.91	1.52
14	9.44	1.46
15	9.01	1.37
16	8.59	1.32

❯ **TABLE 12.6** Estimated market values of a Boeing 737 in January 1987 as a function of age, plus the cash flows needed to provide a 10% true rate of return (figures in $ millions)

[30]We are grateful to Mike Staunton for providing us with these estimates.

Efficient Markets and Behavioral Finance

Up to this point, we have concentrated almost exclusively on the left-hand side of the balance sheet—the firm's capital investment decision. Now we move to the right-hand side and to the problems involved in financing the capital investments. To put it crudely, you've learned how to spend money, now learn how to raise it.

Of course, we haven't totally ignored financing in earlier chapters. We introduced the weighted-average cost of capital, for example. But in most places, we have looked past financing issues and used estimates of the opportunity cost of capital to discount future cash flows. We didn't ask how the cost of capital might be affected by financing.

Now we are turning the problem around. We take the firm's present portfolio of real assets and its future investment strategy as given, and then we determine the best financing strategy. For example,

- Should the firm reinvest most of its earnings in the business, or distribute the cash to shareholders?

- Is it better to distribute cash to stockholders by paying out dividends or by repurchasing stock?

- If the firm needs more money, should it issue more stock or should it borrow?

- Should it borrow short term or long term?

- Should it borrow by issuing a normal long-term bond or a convertible bond (a bond that can be exchanged for stock by the bondholders)?

There are countless other financing trade-offs, as you will see.

The purpose of holding the firm's capital investment decision constant is to separate that decision from the financing decision. Strictly speaking, this assumes that investment and financing decisions are *independent*. In many circumstances, this is a reasonable assumption. The firm is generally free to change its capital structure by repurchasing one security and issuing another. In that case, there is no need to associate a particular investment project with a particular source of cash. The firm can think, first, about which projects to accept and, second, about how they should be financed.

Sometimes decisions about capital structure depend on project choice or vice versa, and in those cases, the investment and financing decisions have to be considered jointly. However, we defer discussion of such interactions of financing and investment decisions until Chapter 19.

We start this chapter by contrasting investment and financing decisions. The objective in each case is the same—to maximize NPV. However, it may be harder to find positive-NPV financing opportunities. The reason it is difficult to add value by clever financing decisions is that capital markets are usually efficient. By this we mean that fierce competition between investors eliminates profit opportunities and causes debt and equity issues to be fairly priced. If you think that sounds like a sweeping statement, you are right. That is why we have devoted this chapter to explaining and evaluating the efficient-market hypothesis.

We define the efficient-market hypothesis more carefully in Section 13-2. The hypothesis comes in three flavors—weak, semistrong, and strong—depending on the types of information available to investors. We review the evidence

for and against each of the flavors. The evidence for efficient markets is mostly convincing, but puzzling anomalies keep cropping up.

Advocates for rational and efficient markets also have a hard time explaining *bubbles.* Every decade seems to find its own bubble: the 1980s real estate and stock market bubble in Japan, the 1990s technology stock bubble, and the real estate bubble that triggered the subprime crisis. Part of the blame for bubbles goes to the incentive and agency problems that can plague even the most rational people, particularly when they are investing other people's money. But bubbles may also reflect patterns of irrational behavior that have been well documented by behavioral psychologists. We describe the main features of *behavioral finance* and the challenge that it poses to the efficient-market hypothesis.

The chapter closes with the five lessons of market efficiency and the implications for the financial manager if markets are not efficient.

• • • • •

13-1   Differences between Investment and Financing Decisions

In some ways, financing decisions are more complex than investment decisions. The number of different securities and financing strategies is well into the hundreds (we have stopped counting). You will have to learn the major families, genera, and species. You will also need to become familiar with the vocabulary of financing. You will learn about *red herrings, greenshoes,* and *bookrunners;* behind each of these terms lies an interesting story.

There are also ways in which financing decisions are much easier than investment decisions. First, financing decisions do not have the same degree of finality as investment decisions. They are easier to reverse. Second, it's harder to make money by smart financing strategies. The reason is that financial markets are more competitive than product markets. This means it is more difficult to find positive-NPV financing strategies than positive-NPV investment strategies.

When the firm looks at capital investment decisions, it does *not* assume that it is facing perfect, competitive markets. It may have only a few competitors that specialize in the same line of business in the same geographical area. And it may own some unique assets that give it an edge over its competitors. Often, these assets are intangible, such as patents, expertise, or reputation. All this opens up the opportunity to make superior profits and find projects with positive NPVs.

In financial markets, your competition is all other corporations seeking funds, to say nothing of the state, local, and federal governments that go to New York, London, Hong Kong, and other financial centers to raise money. The investors who supply financing are comparably numerous, and they are smart. Money attracts brains.

Competition is intense. Competition drives out easy profits for traders and investors who seek mispriced securities. If mispricing is rare, then it is reasonable to assume, at least as a starting point, that prices are right, or as right as human beings can get them.

When we suggest that stock or bond "prices are right," we do not mean that they are stable. A price that is right today will change tomorrow when new information arrives. We only assume that prices incorporate all relevant information available to traders and investors at the time the prices are set. In other words, we assume that prices are set in *efficient financial markets.*

We Always Come Back to NPV

Financial managers separate investment and financing decisions. But the decisions to build a factory or issue a bond both involve valuation of an asset. The fact that you are buying a real asset (the factory) and selling a financial asset (the bond) doesn't matter. In both cases you are concerned with the *value* of what is bought or sold.

For example, consider a new 10-year bond issue by GENX Corporation. The issue will raise $100 million for a new factory. The interest rate is 7%. GENX tried to negotiate a lower rate, but potential investors pointed out that 7% is the prevailing market interest rate on 10-year bonds issued by other companies with the same financial strength and bond rating as GENX. If GENX wants to sell the new bonds for $1,000 each, it will have to pay 7% interest on that $1,000.

Would you purchase the bond at this price? Before doing so, you decide to do a NPV calculation. You write out investment and interest payments.

$$\text{NPV} = -\$1,000 + \text{PV of interest payments at 7\% of } \$1,000 + \text{PV of principal (}\$1,000 \text{ repaid in year 10)}$$

What's the discount rate—that is, what's the opportunity cost of capital? It must be 7%. That's the rate of return you can get on other bonds with the same maturity and risk. Therefore:

$$\text{NPV} = -\$1,000 + \sum_{t=1}^{10} \frac{\$70}{(1.07)^t} + \frac{\$1,000}{(1.07)^{10}} = 0$$

NPV = 0 because buying a GENX bond gives you the prevailing market rate of return.

GENX's CFO now decides to calculate the NPV of the bond issue for GENX. Her calculation is similar to yours, with signs reversed of course. Recall that the bond issue will raise $100 million. NPV of each bond that GENX sells is:

$$\text{NPV} = +\$1,000 - \sum_{t=1}^{10} \frac{\$70}{(1.07)^t} - \frac{\$1,000}{(1.07)^{10}} = 0$$

Again NPV = 0. The CFO is puzzled at first because 7% is less than the 15% rate of return she expects from the new factory. But she realizes that if the bond is fairly priced for investors, it must likewise be fairly priced for her company. She realizes that shareholder value comes from the factory (assuming that 15% exceeds the *factory's* opportunity cost of capital), not from issuing ordinary bonds at the prevailing market interest rate. (Notice how the CFO has separated the investment and financing decisions. She has assigned a separate value to each.)

The bond issue would be positive NPV for GENX only if it could get an interest rate *less* than the prevailing market rate.[1] That opportunity comes occasionally, but it almost always requires some kind of subsidy. Suppose New York State offers to lend at 3% if GENX locates the new factory in New York instead of New Jersey. That offer is positive-NPV:

$$\text{NPV} = +\$1,000 - \sum_{t=1}^{10} \frac{\$30}{(1.07)^t} - \frac{1,000}{(1.07)^{10}} = \$281$$

Each bond that GENX can sell at the subsidized rate of interest has an NPV of $281. Of course, you don't need arithmetic to conclude that borrowing at 3% is a good deal when the market rate is 7%. But the NPV calculation tells you just how much that opportunity is worth.

If, on the other hand, GENX receives no subsidy but issues the bond at the prevailing market interest rate, then the "price is right," and the transaction is zero-NPV for both GENX and the bond investors. In that case, positive NPVs must be sought on the asset side of the balance sheet.

Now we should consider the assumptions embedded in our example. We have ignored transaction costs, which we cover in Chapter 15. We have ignored taxes. We will see in Chapter 18 that interest payments create valuable tax deductions. But our most important

---

[1] NPV would be negative only if GENX were foolish enough to pay more than the market rate or were somehow forced to do so.

assumption was to trust the bond market. We accepted the prevailing interest rate. We did not pause to ask whether that rate was too high or too low. We did not pause to forecast future interest rates. We assumed that the prevailing rate was completely up to date and incorporated all relevant information about all things—past, present and possible future events—that can determine interest rates and bond prices. In other words, we accepted the *efficient market hypothesis* for bonds.

In the next section we begin a review of the evidence for and against this hypothesis. We will focus on the stock market, but the hypothesis also applies to markets for bonds and other securities.

13-2 The Efficient Market Hypothesis

Economists define three levels of market efficiency, depending on the kinds of information incorporated in security prices. In the first level, prices incorporate all information contained in the record of past prices. This is called *weak efficiency*. If weak-form efficiency holds, prices follow random walks. We will explain "random walk" in a moment.

The second level of efficiency requires that prices incorporate all public information, including information from the Internet, the financial press, and other public sources. This is called *semistrong efficiency*. If markets are semistrong efficient, the prices will react immediately to new public information, for example to announcements of earnings per share, a new issue of stock or a merger proposal.

With *strong efficiency,* prices reflect all the information that can be acquired by painstaking analysis of companies and the economy. In such a market we would observe lucky and unlucky investors, but no superior investors who can consistently beat the market.

We will discuss each level of efficiency in its turn.

A Startling Discovery: Price Changes Are Random

As is so often the case with important ideas, the concept of efficient capital markets stemmed from a chance discovery. In 1953, Maurice Kendall, a British statistician, presented a controversial paper to the Royal Statistical Society on the behavior of stock and commodity prices.[2] Kendall had expected to find regular price cycles, but to his surprise they did not seem to exist. Each series appeared to be "a 'wandering' one, almost as if once a week the Demon of Chance drew a random number . . . and added it to the current price to determine the next week's price." In other words, the prices of stocks and commodities seemed to follow a *random walk*.

If you are not sure what we mean by "random walk," you might like to think of the following example: You are given $100 to play a game. At the end of each week a coin is tossed. If it comes up heads, you win 3% of your investment; if it is tails, you lose 2.5%. Therefore, your capital at the end of the first week is either $103.00 or $97.50. At the end of the second week, the coin is tossed again. Now the possible outcomes are:

---

[2]See M. G. Kendall, "The Analysis of Economic Time Series, Part I. Prices," *Journal of the Royal Statistical Society* 96 (1953), pp. 11–25. Kendall's idea was not wholly new. It had been proposed in an almost forgotten thesis written 53 years earlier by a French doctoral student, Louis Bachelier. Bachelier's accompanying development of the mathematical theory of random processes anticipated by five years Einstein's famous work on the random Brownian motion of colliding gas molecules. See L. Bachelier, *Théorie de la Speculation* (Paris: Gauthiers-Villars, 1900). Reprinted in English (A. J. Boness, trans.) in P. H. Cootner (ed.), *The Random Character of Stock Market Prices* (Cambridge, MA: MIT Press, 1964), pp. 17–78.

This process is a random walk with a positive drift of .25% per week.[3] It is a random walk because successive changes in value are independent. That is, the odds each week are the same, regardless of the value at the start of the week or of the pattern of heads and tails in the previous weeks.

When Maurice Kendall suggested that stock prices follow a random walk, he was implying that the price changes are independent of one another just as the gains and losses in our coin-tossing game were independent. Figure 13.1 illustrates this for four stocks from different markets —Microsoft, Marks & Spencer, Philips, and Rio Tinto. Each panel shows the change in price of the stock on successive days. The circled dot in the southeast quadrant of the Microsoft panel refers to a pair of days in which a 2.9% increase was followed by a 2.9% decrease. If there were a systematic tendency for increases to be followed by decreases, there would be many dots in the southeast quadrant and few in the northeast quadrant. It is obvious from a glance that there is very little pattern in these price movements, but we can test this more precisely by calculating the coefficient of correlation between each day's price change and the next. If price movements persisted, the correlation would be positive; if there were no relationship, it would be 0. In our example, the correlation between successive price changes in Microsoft stock was −.037; there was a negligible tendency for price rises to be followed by price falls.[4] For Marks & Spencer, this correlation was also negative at −.020. For Rio Tinto, it was positive at +.010, and for Philips, the correlation was also just positive at +.004.

Figure 13.1 suggests that successive price changes of all four stocks were effectively uncorrelated. Today's price change gave investors almost no clue as to the likely change tomorrow. Does that surprise you? If so, imagine that it were not the case and that changes in Microsoft's stock price were expected to persist for several months. Figure 13.2 provides an example of such a predictable cycle. You can see that an upswing in Microsoft's stock price started last month, when the price was $40, and it is expected to carry the price to $80 next month. What will happen when investors perceive this bonanza? It will self-destruct. Since Microsoft stock is a bargain at $60, investors will rush to buy. They will stop buying only when the stock offers a normal risk-adjusted rate of return. Therefore, as soon as a cycle becomes apparent to investors, they immediately eliminate it by their trading.

You should see now why prices in competitive markets must follow a random walk. If past price changes could be used to predict future price changes, investors could make easy profits. But in competitive markets, there are no such free lunches. As investors try to take advantage of any information in past prices, prices adjust immediately until the superior profits from

BEYOND THE PAGE

Stock prices can appear to have patterns

mhhe.com/brealey13e

---

[3]The drift is equal to the expected outcome: (1/2)(3) + (1/2)(−2.5) = .25%.

[4]The correlation coefficient between successive observations is known as the *autocorrelation coefficient*. An autocorrelation of −.037 implies that, if Microsoft's stock price rose by 1% more than the average yesterday, your best forecast of today's change would be a mere .037% *less* than the average.

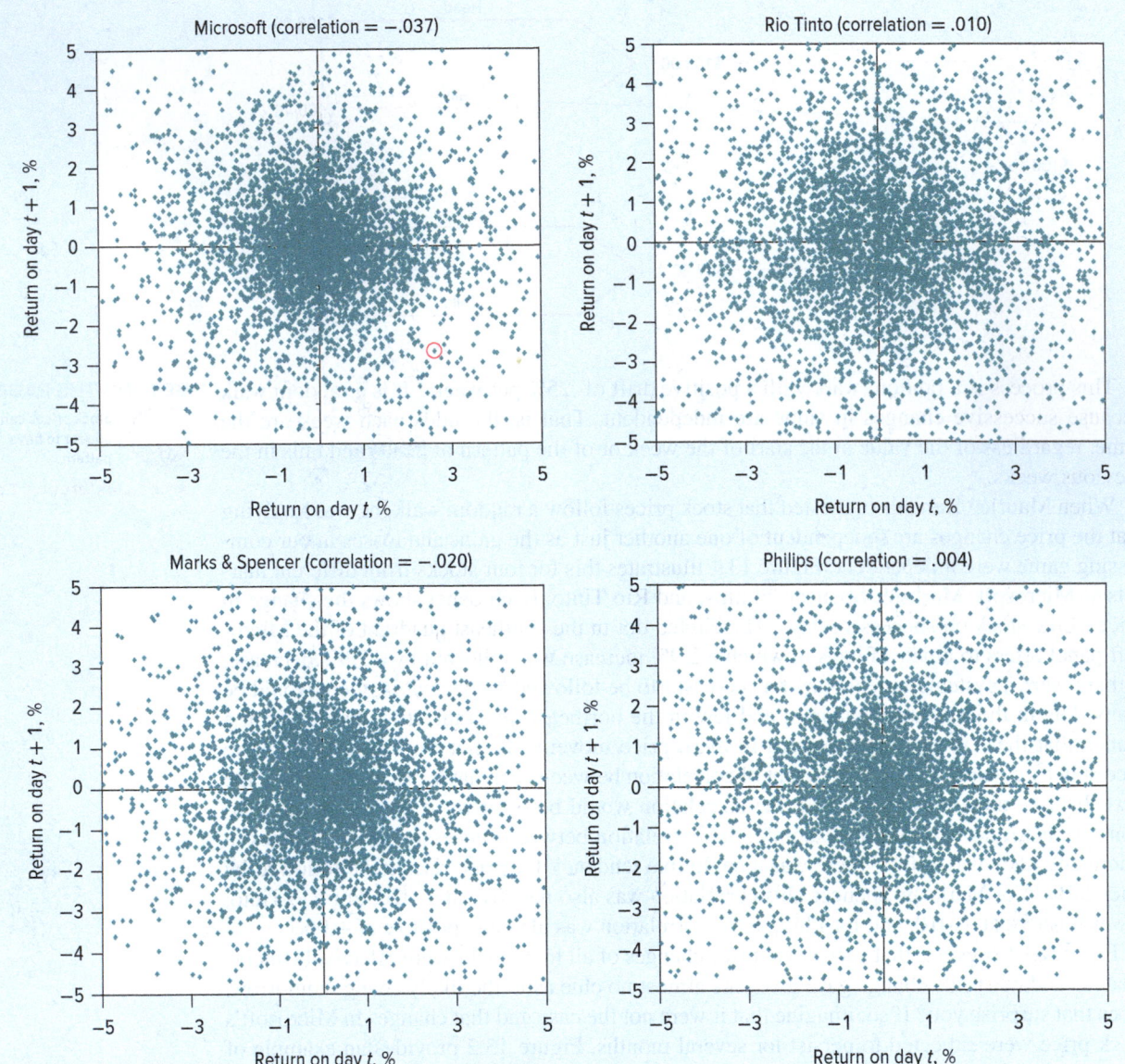

▶ **FIGURE 13.1**   Each dot shows a pair of returns for a stock on two successive days between September 1997 and September 2017. The circled dot for Microsoft records a daily return of +2.9% and then −2.9% on the next day. The scatter diagram shows no significant relationship between returns on successive days.

studying price movements disappear. As a result, all the information in past prices will be reflected in today's stock price, not tomorrow's. Patterns in prices will no longer exist, and price changes in one period will be independent of changes in the next. In other words, the share price will follow a random walk.

Random Walks: The Evidence

Since Maurice Kendall's early discovery, statisticians have undertaken a myriad of tests of the weak form of the efficient market hypothesis. These have confirmed that stock prices throughout the world follow something close to a random walk. We say "close to a random

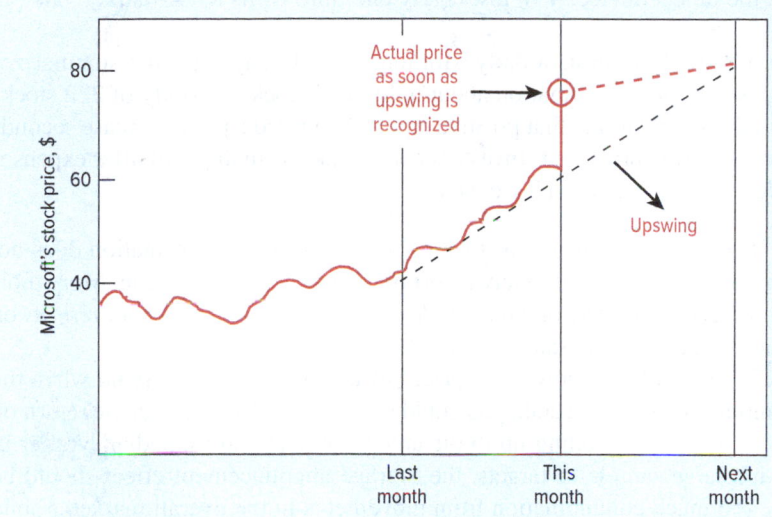

FIGURE 13.2

Cycles self-destruct as soon as they are recognized by investors. The stock price instantaneously jumps to the present value of the expected future price.

In the figure: *Microsoft's stock price, $* (y-axis with values 40, 60, 80). Labels: "Actual price as soon as upswing is recognized", "Upswing". X-axis: Last month, This month, Next month.

walk" because every economic theory has its exceptions and there appear to be some patterns in stock returns.

For example, there is statistical evidence for *momentum:* Stocks that have delivered superior returns over the last few weeks or months tend to deliver superior returns in the future. There is also momentum on the downside: Poorly performing stocks tend to continue to disappoint.[5]

Momentum does not generate easy money for investors. It is a statistical tendency, not a sure thing. Also, pursuit of momentum profits sacrifices diversification and increases risk. Nevertheless, some investment funds specialize in momentum strategies, and a few have done well.

There are also some profit opportunities as prices bounce around in the very short run. But to have any chance of making money from such bounces, you need to be a high-frequency trader with one eye on the computer screen and the other on your annual bonus. You will need super-fast computers with algorithms that trade in high volumes with the aim of capturing a few cents per trade.[6]

Semistrong Market Efficiency: The Evidence

To test for semistrong efficiency, researchers have examined how stock prices respond to public releases of information—for example, news about earnings or dividends, announcements of mergers or takeovers, or macroeconomic developments. Semistrong efficiency means that stock prices respond to relevant news quickly and completely.

There's no doubt that stock prices respond quickly to breaking news. Take Volkswagen's (VW's) diesel emissions scandal as an example. On Friday, September 18, 2015, the U.S. Environmental Protection Agency (EPA) announced that VW had installed "defeat devices" in several models of diesel cars that reduced emissions only when emissions tests were under way. VW's stock price dropped immediately from about $160 to about $130 per share. There was another drop to about $110 per share on Monday, when VW admitted that it had sold 11 million

[5]See N. Jegadeesh and S. Titman, "Returns to Buying Winners and Selling Losers: Implications for Market Efficiency," *Journal of Finance* 48 (March 1993), pp. 65–91. Many practitioners now add a momentum factor to the Fama–French three-factor model, which we discussed in Section 8-3. See M. M. Carhart, "On Persistence in Mutual Fund Performance," *Journal of Finance* 52 (March 1997), pp. 57–82.

[6]High-frequency trading now accounts for roughly half of overall stock market volume. For a readable and critical book on high-frequency trading, see M. Lewis, *Flash Boys: A Wall Street Revolt* (New York: W. W. Norton & Co., 2014).

cars worldwide with the defeat device. VW lost nearly one third of its stock-market value in two days' trading.

Another example: CNBC broadcasts a daily Morning and Midday Call that summarizes security-analyst reports and other information about individual stocks. A study of 322 stocks that were discussed in these calls found that positive reports triggered a price increase seconds after the positive news was first broadcast. Investors could make a small profit after expenses only if they were able to buy in the first 15 seconds.[7]

Abnormal Returns   The quick response of a stock price to new public information does not prove that the new price is right and completely incorporates the new information. More thorough tests of semistrong efficiency rely on *event studies,* which examine *abnormal returns* on samples of stocks that encountered the same type of news release.

Suppose you decide to investigate how stock prices of takeover targets respond when the takeovers are first announced. As a first stab, you could simply calculate the average return on target-company stocks in the days leading up to the announcement and immediately after it. With daily returns on a large sample of targets, the average announcement effect should be clear. There won't be too much contamination from movements in the overall market around the announcement dates because daily market returns average out to a very small number.[8] The potential contamination increases for weekly or monthly returns, however. In these cases you will usually want to adjust for market movements. For example, you can simply subtract out the return on the market:

$$\text{Adjusted stock return} = \text{return on stock} - \text{return on market index}$$

Chapter 8 suggests a refined adjustment based on betas. (Just subtracting the market return assumes that target-firm betas equal 1.0.) This adjustment is called the *market model:*

$$\text{Expected stock return} = \alpha + \beta \times \text{return on market index}$$

Alpha (α) states how much on average the stock price changed when the market index was unchanged. Beta (β) tells us how much *extra* the stock price moved for each 1% change in the market index.[9] Suppose that subsequently the stock price return is $\tilde{r}$ in a month when the market return is $\tilde{r}_m$. In that case, we would conclude that the *abnormal return* for that month is

$$\text{Abnormal stock return} = \text{actual stock return} - \text{expected stock return}$$
$$= \tilde{r} - (\alpha + \beta\tilde{r}_m)$$

This abnormal return should reflect firm-specific news only.[10]

Figure 13.3 illustrates how the release of news affects abnormal returns. It shows the cumulative abnormal return on a sample of U.S. firms that were targets of takeover attempts. Acquiring firms usually have to pay a substantial *takeover premium* to get the deal done, so the target firm's stock price increases as soon as the takeover bid is announced. Figure 13.3 shows the average pattern of the target's stock returns before and after the announcement of a

[7]The price response to negative reports took longer, 15 minutes on average, probably because of the costs and delays of short-selling. See J. A. Busse and T. C. Green, "Market Efficiency in Real Time," *Journal of Financial Economics* 65 (2002), pp. 415–437.

[8]Suppose, for example, that the market return is 12% per year. With 250 trading days in the year, the average daily return is $(1.12)^{1/250} - 1 = .00045$, or .045%.

[9]It is important when estimating α and β that you choose a period in which you believe that the stock behaved normally. If its performance was abnormal, then estimates of α and β cannot be used to measure the returns that investors expected. As a precaution, ask yourself whether your estimates of expected returns look sensible. Methods for estimating abnormal returns are analyzed in A. C. MacKinlay, "Event Studies in Economics and Finance," *Journal of Economic Literature* 35 (1997), pp. 13–39; and also S. P. Kothari and J. B. Warner, "Econometrics of Event Studies," in B. E. Eckbo (ed.), *The Handbook of Empirical Corporate Finance* (Amsterdam: Elsevier/North-Holland, 2007), Chapter 1.

[10]Abnormal returns are also often calculated using the Fama–French three-factor model that we discussed in Chapter 8. The stock return is adjusted for the market return, the difference between the returns on small- and large-company stocks, and the difference between the returns on high and low book-to-market firms.

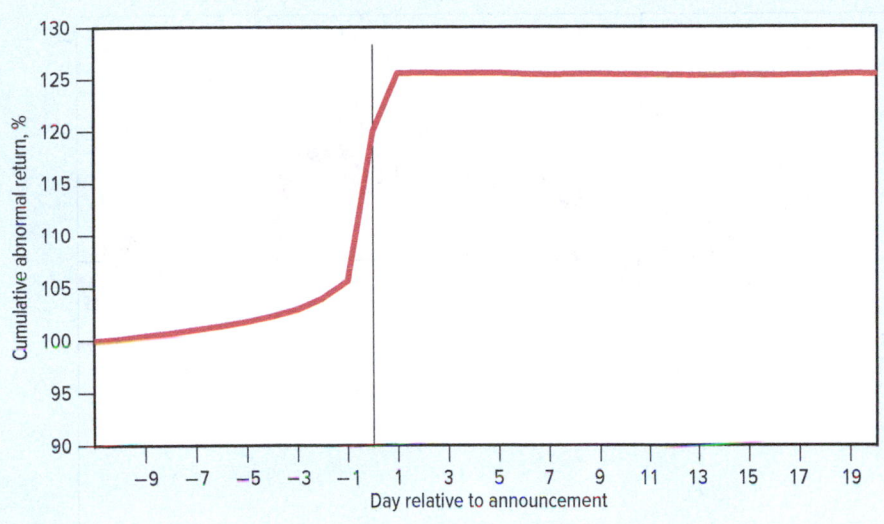

▶ **FIGURE 13.3**

The abnormal performance of the stocks of takeover targets around the announcement date. The prices of target stocks jump up on the day following the announcement, but from then on, there are no unusual price movements. The figure shows the cumulative abnormal returns for 8,668 U.S. targets between 1975 and 2016.

Source: WRDS.

takeover (day 0 in the figure). Stock prices drift up before date zero, as investors gradually realize that a takeover may be coming. On the day of the announcement and the following day, prices jump up by 17.3%.[11] The adjustment to the stock price is immediate and complete. There is no significant further drift in the price, either upward or downward. Thus, within the day, the new stock prices reflect (at least on average) the magnitude of the takeover premium.

Studies of price reactions to takeovers provide good news for semistrong efficiency. But there is also bad news for the hypothesis. One example is the strange case of the "Siamese twins," two securities with claims on the same cash flows, which nevertheless trade separately. Before the two companies merged in July 2005, the Dutch company Royal Dutch Petroleum and the British company Shell Transport & Trading (T&T) were Siamese twins, each with a fixed share in the profits and dividends of the oil giant. Since both companies participated in the same underlying cash flows, you would expect the stock prices to have moved in exact lockstep. But, as you can see from Figure 13.4, the prices of the two shares sometimes diverged substantially.[12]

BEYOND THE PAGE

Long-run IPO returns

mhhe.com/brealey13e

Strong Market Efficiency: The Evidence

Tests of the strong form of the efficient markets hypothesis have examined whether professional portfolio managers can consistently "beat the market." Some researchers have found a slight persistent outperformance, but just as many have concluded that professionally managed funds fail to recoup the costs of management. Look, for example, at Figure 13.4, which compares the returns on diversified equity funds to the Wilshire 5000 Index. You can see that in some years, the mutual funds beat the market, but roughly 60% of the time, it was the other way around.

Figure 13.5 provides a fairly crude comparison because mutual funds have tended to specialize in particular sectors of the market, such as low-beta stocks or large-firm stocks, that may have given below-average returns. To control for such differences, each fund needs to be compared with a benchmark portfolio of similar securities. A number of studies have done this. Most have found that the message was unchanged: The funds earned a lower return than

BEYOND THE PAGE

Mutual fund cumulative returns

mhhe.com/brealey13e

[11]Investors may respond on day 0 if the announcement is made during the hours of trading. Otherwise, they will respond on day 1.
[12]For evidence on the pricing of Siamese twins see K. A. Froot and E. Dabora, "How Are Stock Prices Affected by the Location of Trade?" *Journal of Financial Economics* 53 (August 1999), pp. 189–216; and, for more recent data, A. De Jong, L. Rosenthal, and M. A. Van Dijk, "The Risk and Return of Arbitrage in Dual-Listed Companies," *Review of Finance* 13 (2009), pp. 495–520.

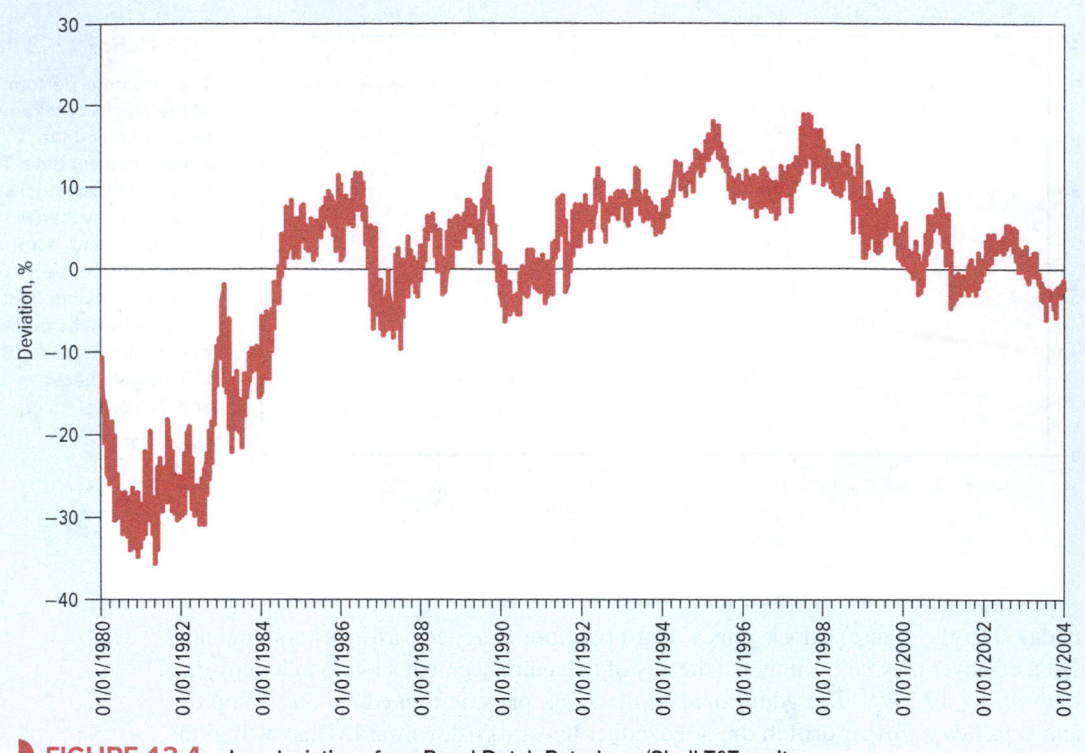

▶ **FIGURE 13.4**   Log deviations from Royal Dutch Petroleum/Shell T&T parity

Source: Mathijs van Dijk, **www.mathijsavandijk.com/dual-listed-companies.**

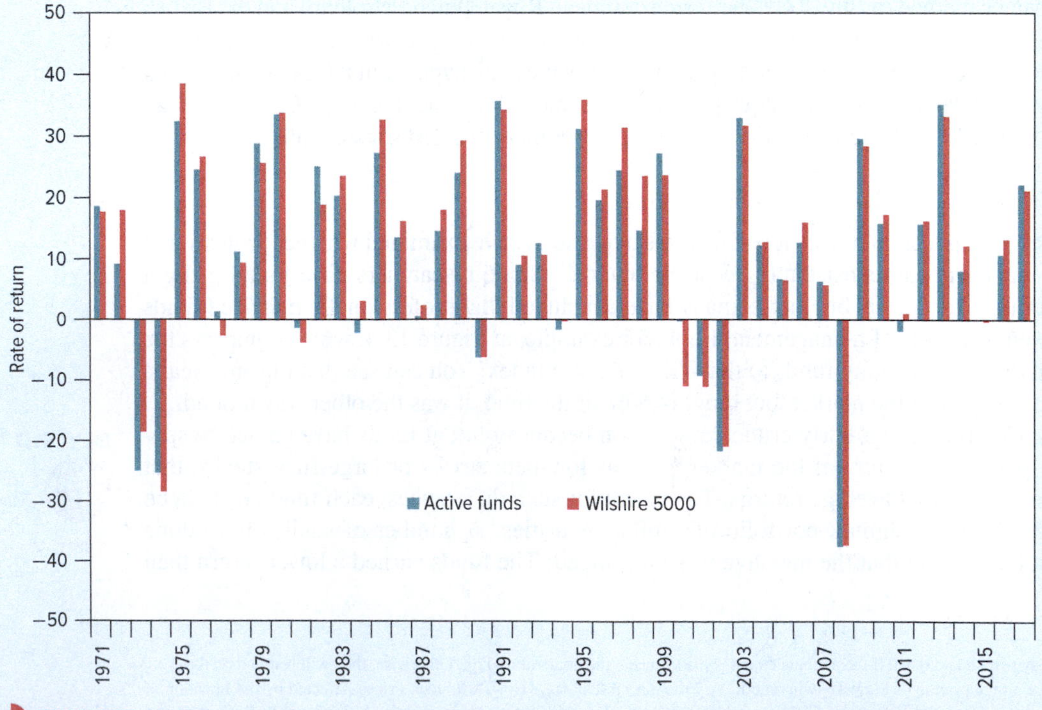

▶ **FIGURE 13.5**   Diversified equity funds versus the Wilshire 5000 Index, 1971–2017. Notice that mutual funds underperform the market in approximately 60% of the years.

the benchmark portfolios *after* expenses and roughly matched the benchmarks *before* expenses.[13]

OK, maybe mutual funds in general don't earn superior returns, but surely some managers are smarter than others and can be relied on to beat their less competent brethren. Unfortunately, it seems difficult to spot the smart ones. For example, a top-quartile fund in one year has no more than an average chance of being in the top quartile the following year.[14] It seems that the top-performing managers in one period have about an average chance of falling on their faces in the next period.

The evidence on efficient markets has convinced many professional and individual investors to give up pursuit of superior performance. They simply "buy the index," which maximizes diversification and cuts costs to the bone. Individual investors can buy *index funds,* which are mutual funds that track stock market indexes. There is no active management, so costs are very low. For example, in mid-2018 management fees for the Vanguard 500 Index Fund, which tracks the S&P 500 Index, were .04% per year for investments over $10,000. The size of this fund was $418 billion.

How far could indexing go? Not to 100%: If all investors hold index funds, then nobody will be collecting information, and prices will not respond to new information when it arrives. An efficient market needs some smart investors who gather information and attempt to profit from it. To provide incentives to gather costly information, prices cannot reflect *all* information.[15] There must be some profits available to allow the costs of information to be recouped. But if the costs are small, relative to the total market value of traded securities, then the financial market can still be close to perfectly efficient.

In some ways, the evidence for strong efficiency is stronger than the evidence for weak or semistrong efficiency. Researchers' statistical tools find patterns, tendencies and anomalies in stock prices. They find examples of lagged responses to public information. Yet it is exceptionally difficult to generate consistent, superior investment performance. Researchers can beat the market in hindsight. Investors with real money have a much harder time of it.

Strong efficiency has important implications for corporate financial managers, who must often decide how to manage investment portfolios. Two examples: Exelon Corporation, which operates the largest fleet of nuclear power plants in the United States, manages a decommissioning trust earmarked to cover future costs of shutting down and decommissioning its nuclear plants. The value of the trust portfolio was $13.3 billion in 2017. Cummins Inc. has a defined-benefit pension plan and sets aside money to invest to cover future pension payments to retired employees in the U.S. and U.K. Its pension assets in 2017 were $5.1 billion.

How should Exelon and Cummins manage these investments? Should they search for portfolio managers that can consistently deliver superior risk-adjusted returns? The evidence for strong-form efficiency indicates that they would be better off minimizing costs by passive indexing of pension fund or other investment portfolios. More and more corporations are doing just that—at least for investments in U.S. stocks and bonds. But they do hire active managers where inefficiencies are more likely—for example, in developing-country stock markets.[16]

BEYOND THE PAGE

Measuring mutual fund performance

mhhe.com/brealey13e

---

[13]See, for example, B. G. Malkiel, "Returns from Investing in Equity Mutual Funds 1971 to 1991," *Journal of Finance* 50 (June 1995), pp. 549–572; and M. M. Carhart, "On Persistence in Mutual Fund Performance," *Journal of Finance* 52 (March 1997), pp. 57–82. Some evidence of slight persistence in performance is provided in E. F. Fama and K. R. French, "Luck versus Skill in the Cross-Section of Mutual Fund Returns," *Journal of Finance* 65 (October 2010), pp. 1915–1947; and in R. Kosowski, A. Timmermann, R. Wermers, and H. White, "Can Mutual Fund 'Stars' Really Pick Stocks? New Evidence from a Bootstrap Analysis," *Journal of Finance* 61 (December 2006), pp. 2551–2595. See also M. J. Gruber, "Another Puzzle: The Growth in Actively Managed Mutual Funds," *Journal of Finance* 51 (July 1996), pp. 783–810; and J. Berk and J. H. Van Binsbergen, "Measuring Skill in the Mutual Fund Industry," *Journal of Financial Economics* 118 (October 2015), pp. 1–20.

[14]See, for example, the Persistence Scorecard, which is published by Standard & Poor's twice a year.

[15]See S. J. Grossman and J. E. Stiglitz, "On the Impossibility of Informationally Efficient Markets," *American Economic Review* 70 (June 1980), pp. 393–408.

[16]A. Dyck, K. V. Lins, and L. Pomorski, "Does Active Management Pay? New International Evidence," *Review of Asset Pricing Studies* 3 (December 2013), pp. 200–228.

Strong-form efficiency has implications for you also. Most readers of this book will be investors. Will you be an active stock-picker? Or will you diversify and minimize management fees by indexing? If you are an active stock-picker, we hope you have fun doing it.

13-3   Bubbles and Market Efficiency

So far, we have asked whether individual stocks are "priced right," given the information that investors can see or acquire. But what about the market as a whole? Are there cases where the overall level of prices cannot be justified by fundamentals? We will look at the evidence in a moment, but first we should note how difficult it is to value common stocks and to determine whether their prices are irrational.

For example, imagine that in mid-2017 you wanted to check whether the stocks forming Standard & Poor's Composite Index were fairly valued. As a first stab, you might use the constant-growth formula that we introduced in Chapter 4. In 2017, the annual dividends paid by the companies in the index were roughly $420 billion. Suppose that these dividends were expected to grow at a steady rate of 4.0% and that investors required a return of 6.0%. Then the constant-growth formula gives a value for the common stocks of

$$\text{PV common stocks} = \frac{\text{DIV}}{r - g} = \frac{420}{.060 - .040} = \$21,000 \text{ billion}$$

which was roughly their value in August 2017. But how confident could you be about these figures? Perhaps the likely dividend growth was only 3.5% per year. In that case, your estimate of the value of the common stocks would decline to

$$\text{PV common stocks} = \frac{\text{DIV}}{r - g} = \frac{420}{.060 - .035} = \$16,800 \text{ billion}$$

In other words, a reduction of just half a percentage point in the expected rate of dividend growth would reduce the value of common stocks by 20%.

The extreme difficulty of valuing common stocks from scratch has two important consequences. First, investors find it easier to price a common stock relative to yesterday's price or relative to today's price of similar securities. In other words, they generally take yesterday's price as correct, adjusting upward or downward on the basis of today's information. If information arrives smoothly, then, as time passes, investors become increasingly confident that today's price level is correct. But when investors lose confidence in the benchmark of yesterday's price, there may be a period of confused trading and volatile prices before a new benchmark is established.

Second, most of the tests of market efficiency are concerned with *relative* prices and focus on whether there are easy profits to be made. It is almost impossible to test whether stocks are *correctly valued* because no one can measure true value with any precision. Take, for example, Pepsi stock, which sold for $116 July 2018. Could we prove that this was its true value? Of course not, but we could be more confident that the price of Pepsi should be somewhat more than double that of Coca-Cola ($45) because Pepsi's earnings and dividends per share were 2.5 times those of Coke and the two companies had similar growth prospects.

It may be impossible to *prove* that market levels are, or are not, consistent with fundamentals. However, every now and again investors seem to be caught up in a speculative frenzy, and asset prices then reach levels that (at least with hindsight) cannot easily be justified by the outlook for profits and dividends. Investors refer to such occasions as *bubbles*. Bubbles can result when prices rise rapidly, and more and more investors join the game on the assumption that prices will *continue* to rise. These bubbles can be self-sustaining for a while. It can be rational to jump on the bandwagon as long as you are sure that there will be greater fools that

BEYOND THE PAGE

Two mysterious crashes

mhhe.com/brealey13e

you can sell out to. But remember that lots of money will be lost, perhaps by you, when the bubble bursts.[17]

The Japanese bubble is a good example. The Nikkei 225 Index increased by about 240% from the start of 1985 to its peak of about 39,000 in January 1990. But stock prices fell sharply after an increase in interest rates. The Nikkei fell to about 23,000 by year-end 1990 and continued an irregular slide downward to about 10,000 in 2010. The index has since recovered, but only to 23,000 in early 2018.

The boom in Japanese stock prices was matched by an even greater explosion in land prices. For example, Ziemba and Schwartz document that the few hundred acres of land under the Emperor's Palace in Tokyo, evaluated at neighborhood land prices, was worth as much as all the land in Canada or California.[18] But then the real estate bubble also burst. By 2005, land prices in the six major Japanese cities had slumped to just 13% of their peak.

Such bubbles are not confined to Japan. Toward the end of the twentieth century, investors in technology stocks saw a remarkable run-up in the value of their holdings. The Nasdaq Composite Index, which has a heavy weighting in high-tech stocks, rose 580% from the start of 1995 to its high in 2000. Then, as rapidly as it began, the boom ended, and by October 2002 the Nasdaq index had fallen 78% from its peak.

Some of the largest gains and losses were experienced by dot-com stocks. For example, Yahoo! shares, which began trading in April 1996, appreciated by 1,400% in four years. In these heady days, some companies found that they could boost their stock price simply by adding ".com" to the company name.[19]

Looking back at the Japanese and dot-com bubbles, it seems difficult to believe that future cash flows could ever have been sufficient to provide investors with a reasonable return.[20] If that is the case, then we must conclude that "bubbles happen." When they do happen, markets cannot be efficient.

13-4 Behavioral Finance

Why might prices depart from fundamental values? Some believe that the answer lies in behavioral psychology. People are not 100% rational 100% of the time. This shows up in investors' attitudes to risk and the way they assess probabilities.

1. *Attitudes toward risk.* Psychologists have observed that, when making risky decisions, people are particularly loath to incur losses. It seems that investors do not focus solely on the current value of their holdings, but look back at whether their investments are showing a profit or a loss. For example, if I sell my holding of IBM stock for $10,000, I may feel on top of the world if the stock only cost me $5,000, but I will be much less happy if it had cost $11,000. This observation is the basis for *prospect theory*.[21] Prospect theory states that (a) the value investors place on a particular outcome is determined by the gains or losses that they have made since the asset was acquired or the holding last reviewed, and (b) investors are particularly averse to the possibility of even a very small loss and need a high return to compensate for it.

---

[17]Bubbles are not necessarily irrational. See M. Brunnermeier, *Asset Pricing under Asymmetric Information: Bubbles, Crashes, Technical Analysis and Herding* (Oxford: Oxford University Press, 2001).

[18]See W. T. Ziemba and S. L. Schwartz, *Invest Japan* (Chicago: Probus Publishing Co., 1992), p. 109.

[19]M. Cooper, O. Dimitrov, and P. R. Rau, "A Rose.com by Any Other Name," *Journal of Finance* 56 (2001), pp. 2371–2388.

[20]For an analysis of Japanese stock prices, see K. French and J. M. Poterba, "Were Japanese Stock Prices Too High?" *Journal of Financial Economics* 29 (October 1991), pp. 337–363. For more on dot-com stock prices, see E. Ofek and M. Richardson, "The Valuation and Market Rationality of Internet Stock Prices," *Oxford Review of Economic Policy* 18 (Autumn 2002), pp. 265–287.

[21]Prospect theory was first set out in D. Kahneman and A. Tversky, "Prospect Theory: An Analysis of Decision under Risk," *Econometrica* 47 (1979), pp. 263–291.

The pain of loss seems also to depend on whether it comes on the heels of earlier losses. Once investors have suffered a loss, they may be even more concerned not to risk a further loss. Conversely, just as gamblers are known to be more willing to make large bets when they are ahead, so investors may be more prepared to run the risk of a stock market dip after they have enjoyed a run of unexpectedly high returns.[22] If they do then suffer a small loss, they at least have the consolation of still being ahead for the year.

When we discussed portfolio theory in Chapters 7 and 8, we pictured investors as forward-looking only. Past gains or losses were not mentioned. All that mattered was the investor's current wealth and the expectation and risk of future wealth. We did not allow for the possibility that Nicholas would be elated because his investment is in the black, while Nicola with an equal amount of wealth would be despondent because hers is in the red.

2. *Beliefs about probabilities.* Most investors do not have a PhD in probability theory and may make systematic errors in assessing the probability of uncertain events. Psychologists have found that, when judging possible future outcomes, individuals tend to look back at what happened in a few similar situations. As a result, they are led to place too much weight on a small number of recent events. For example, an investor might judge that an investment manager is particularly skilled because he has "beaten the market" for three years in a row or that three years of rapidly rising prices are a good indication of future profits from investing in the stock market. The investor may not stop to reflect on how little one can learn about expected returns from three years' experience.

Most individuals are also too *conservative*—that is, too slow to update their beliefs in the face of new evidence. People tend to update their beliefs in the correct direction, but the magnitude of the change is less than rationality would require.

Another systematic bias is *overconfidence*. For example, an American small business has just a 35% chance of surviving for five years. Yet the great majority of entrepreneurs think that they have a better than 70% chance of success.[23] Similarly, most investors think they are better-than-average stock pickers. Two speculators who trade with each other cannot both make money, but nevertheless, they may be prepared to continue trading because each is confident that the other is the patsy.[24] Overconfidence also shows up in the certainty that people express about their judgments. They consistently overestimate the odds that the future will turn out as they say and underestimate the chances of unlikely events.

You can see how these behavioral characteristics may help to explain the Japanese and dot-com bubbles. As prices rose, they generated increased optimism about the future and stimulated additional demand. The more that investors racked up profits, the more confident they became in their views and the more willing they became to bear the risk that next month might not be so good.

BEYOND THE PAGE

Overconfident CFOs

mhhe.com/brealey13e

Sentiment

Behavioral economists stress the importance of investor sentiment in determining stock prices, and they point to evidence of major swings in sentiment. For example, every week the American Association of Individual Investors surveys its members and asks them whether they are bullish, bearish, or neutral on the stock market over the next six months. Anyone who believed that all the good or bad news was already reflected in stock prices would tick the

---

[22]The effect is described in R. H. Thaler and E. J. Johnson, "Gambling with the House Money and Trying to Break Even: The Effects of Prior Outcomes on Risky Choice," *Management Science* 36 (1990), pp. 643–660. The implications of prospect theory for stock returns are explored in N. Barberis, M. Huang, and T. Santos, "Prospect Theory and Asset Prices," *Quarterly Journal of Economics* 116 (February 2001), pp. 1–53.

[23]See D. Kahneman, *Thinking Fast and Slow* (New York: Farrar, Straus, and Giroux, 2011).

[24]For a discussion of the overconfidence bias in financial markets, see K. Daniel and D. Hirshleifer, "Overconfident Investors, Predictable Returns, and Excessive Trading," *Journal of Economic Perspectives* 29 (Fall 2015), pp. 61–88.

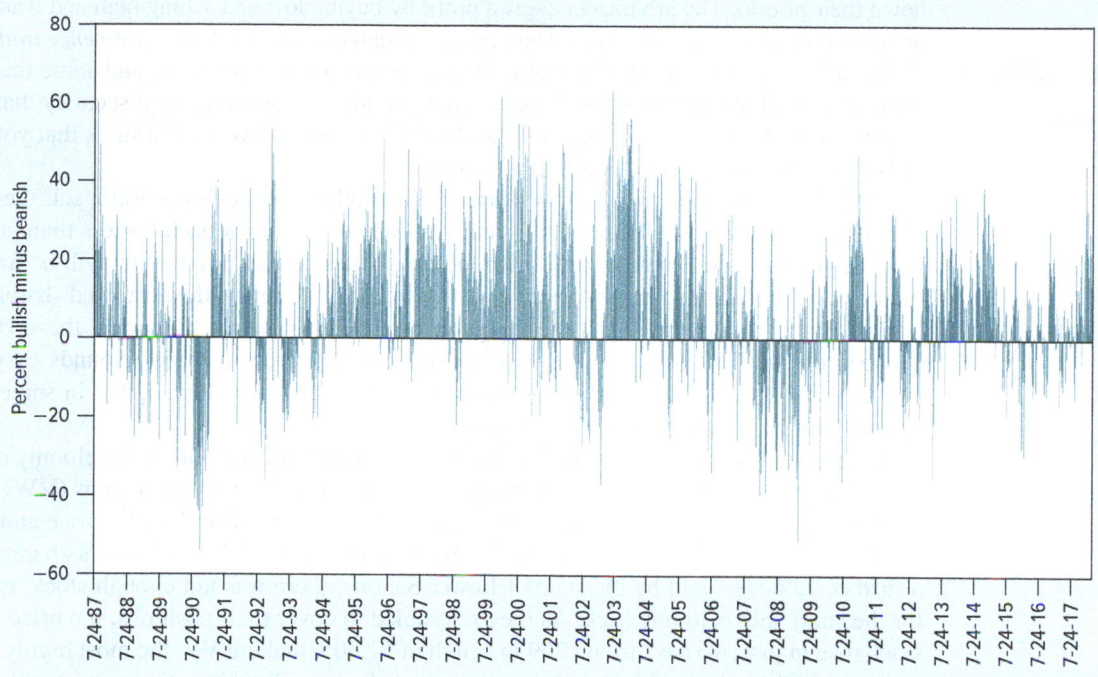

> **FIGURE 13.6**   The spread between the percentage of investors claiming to be bullish and those claiming to be bearish in the weekly sentiment survey of the American Association of Individual Investors

Source: http://www.aaii.com/SentimentSurvey

neutral box. But you can see from Figure 13.6 that private investors swing quite strongly between being bullish or bearish. In January 2000, at the height of the dot-com boom, a massive 75% of investors said they were bullish, 62% more than claimed to be bearish. Perhaps these periods of bullishness and bearishness may explain the short-term momentum effect that we commented on earlier.[25]

Limits to Arbitrage

It is not difficult to believe that amateur investors may sometimes be caught up in a scatty whirl of irrational exuberance.[26] But there are plenty of hard-headed professional investors managing huge sums of money. Why don't these investors bail out of overpriced stocks and force their prices down to fair value? One reason is that there are *limits to arbitrage*—that is, limits on the ability of the rational investors to exploit market inefficiencies.

Strictly speaking, *arbitrage* means an investment strategy that guarantees superior returns without any risk. In practice, arbitrage is defined more casually as a strategy that exploits market inefficiency and generates superior returns if and when prices return to fundamental values. Such strategies can be very rewarding, but they are rarely risk-free.

In an efficient market, if prices get out of line, then arbitrage forces them back. The arbitrageur buys the underpriced securities (pushing up their prices) and sells the overpriced securities (pushing

[25]For evidence on the link between sentiment measures and stock returns, see M. Baker and J. Wurgler, "Investor Sentiment in the Stock Market," *Journal of Economic Perspectives* 21 (2007), pp. 129–151.

[26]The term "irrational exuberance" was coined by Alan Greenspan, former chairman of the Federal Reserve Board, to describe the dot-com boom. It was also the title of a book by Robert Shiller that examined the boom. See R. Shiller, *Irrational Exuberance* (New York: Broadway Books, 2001).

BEYOND THE PAGE

Short sales

mhhe.com/brealey13e

down their prices). The arbitrageur earns a profit by buying low and selling high and waiting for prices to converge to fundamentals. Thus, arbitrage trading is often called *convergence trading*.

But arbitrage is harder than it looks. Trading costs can be significant, and some trades are difficult to execute. For example, suppose that you identify an overpriced security that is *not* in your existing portfolio. You want to "sell high," but how do you sell a stock that you don't own? It can be done, but you have to *sell short*.

To sell a stock short, you borrow shares from another investor's portfolio, sell them, and then wait hopefully until the price falls and you can buy the stock back for less than you sold it for. If you're wrong and the stock price increases, then sooner or later you will be forced to repurchase the stock at a higher price (therefore at a loss) to return the borrowed shares to the lender. But if you're right and the price does fall, you repurchase, pocket the difference between the sale and repurchase prices, and return the borrowed shares. Sounds easy, once you see how short selling works, but there are costs and fees to be paid, and in some cases, you will not be able to find shares to borrow.[27]

The perils of selling short were dramatically illustrated in 2008. Given the gloomy outlook for the automobile industry, several hedge funds decided to sell Volkswagen (VW) shares short in the expectation of buying them back at a lower price. Then in a surprise announcement, Porsche revealed that it had effectively gained control of 74% of VW's shares. Since a further 20% was held by the state of Lower Saxony, there was not enough stock available for the short sellers to buy back. As they scrambled to cover their positions, the price of VW stock rose in just two days from €209 to a high of €1,005, making VW the most highly valued company in the world. Although the stock price drifted rapidly down, those short-sellers who were caught in the *short squeeze* suffered large losses.

The VW example illustrates that the most important limit to arbitrage is the risk that prices will diverge even further before they converge. Thus, an arbitrageur has to have the guts and resources to hold on to a position that may get much worse before it gets better. Take another look at the relative prices of Royal Dutch and Shell T&T in Figure 13.4. Suppose that you were a professional money manager in 1980, when Royal Dutch was about 12% below parity. You decided to buy Royal Dutch, sell Shell T&T short, and wait confidently for prices to converge to parity. It was a long wait. The first time you would have seen any profit on your position was in 1983. In the meantime, the mispricing got worse, not better. Royal Dutch fell to more than 30% below parity in mid-1981. Therefore, you had to report a substantial loss on your "arbitrage" strategy in that year. You were fired and took up a new career as a used-car salesman.

The demise in 1998 of Long Term Capital Management (LTCM) provides another example of the problems with convergence trades. LTCM, one of the largest and most profitable hedge funds of the 1990s, believed that interest rates in the different eurozone countries would converge when the euro replaced the countries' previous currencies. LTCM had taken massive positions to profit from this convergence, as well as massive positions designed to exploit other pricing discrepancies. After the Russian government announced a moratorium on some of its debt payments in August 1998, there was great turbulence in the financial markets, and many of the discrepancies that LTCM was betting on suddenly got much larger.[28] LTCM was losing hundreds of millions of dollars daily. The fund's capital was nearly gone when the Federal Reserve Bank of New York arranged for a group of LTCM's creditor banks to take over LTCM's remaining assets and shut down what was left in an orderly fashion.

---

[27]Investment and brokerage firms identify shares eligible for lending and arrange to make them available to short-sellers. The supply of shares that can be borrowed is limited. You are charged a fee for borrowing the stock, and you are required to put up collateral to protect the lender in case the share price rises and the short-seller is unable to repurchase and return the shares. Putting up collateral is costless if the short-seller gets a market interest rate, but sometimes only lower interest rates are offered.

[28]The Russian debt moratorium was unexpected and unusual because the debt had only recently been issued and was denominated in *roubles*. The government preferred to default rather than to print roubles to service the debt.

LTCM's sudden meltdown has not prevented rapid growth in the hedge fund industry in the 2000s. If hedge funds can push back the limits to arbitrage and avoid the kinds of problems that LTCM ran into, markets will be more efficient going forward. But asking for complete efficiency is probably asking too much. Prices can get out of line and stay out if the risks of an arbitrage strategy outweigh the expected returns.

Incentive Problems and the Financial Crisis of 2008–2009

The limits to arbitrage open the door to individual investors with built-in biases and misconceptions that can push prices away from fundamental values. But there can also be incentive problems that get in the way of a rational focus on fundamentals. We illustrate with a brief look at the financial crisis in 2008 and 2009.

Although U.S. house prices had risen nearly threefold in the decade to 2006, few homeowners foresaw a collapse in the price of their home. After all, the average house price in the U.S. had not fallen since the Great Depression of the 1930s. But in 2006, the bubble burst. By March 2009, U.S. house prices had fallen by nearly a third from their peak.[29]

How could such a boom and crash arise? In part because banks, credit rating agencies, and other financial institutions all had distorted incentives. Purchases of real estate are generally financed with mortgage loans from banks. In most parts of the United States, borrowers can default on their mortgages with relatively small penalties. If property prices fall, they can simply walk away. But if prices rise, they make money. Thus, borrowers may be willing to take large risks, especially if the fraction of the purchase price financed with their own money is small.

Why, then, are banks willing to lend money to people who are bound to default if property prices fall significantly? Since the borrowers benefited most of the time, they were willing to pay attractive up-front fees to banks to get mortgage loans. But the banks could pass on the default risk to somebody else by packaging and reselling the mortgages as mortgage-backed securities (MBSs). Many MBS buyers assumed that they were safe investments because the credit rating agencies said so. As it turned out, the credit ratings were a big mistake. (The rating agencies introduced another agency problem because issuers paid the agencies to rate the MBS issues, and the agencies consulted with issuers over how MBS issues should be structured.)

The "somebody else" was also the government. Many subprime mortgages were sold to FNMA and FHLMC ("Fannie Mae" and "Freddie Mac"). These were private corporations with a special advantage: government credit backup. (The backup was implicit but quickly became explicit when Fannie and Freddie got into trouble in 2008. The U.S. Treasury had to take them over.) Thus, these companies were able to borrow at artificially low rates, channeling money into the mortgage market.

The government was also on the hook because large banks that held subprime MBSs were "too big to fail" in a financial crisis. So the original incentive problem—the temptation of home buyers to take out a large mortgage and hope for higher real estate prices—was never corrected. The government could have cut its exposure by reining in Fannie and Freddie before the crisis but did not do so, perhaps because the government was happy to see more people able to buy their own homes.

Agency and incentive problems are widespread in the financial services industry. In the United States and many other countries, people engage financial institutions such as pension funds and mutual funds to invest their money. These institutions are the investors' agents, but the agents' incentives do not always match the investors' interests. Just as with real estate, these agency relationships can lead to mispricing, and potentially bubbles.[30]

---

[29]Investors who did foresee that the fall in house prices would lead to the subprime debacle were able to earn high profits. For example, John Paulson, the hedge fund manager, earned $3.7 billion in 2007 as a result (*Financial Times*, January 15, 2008, and June 18, 2008).
[30]See F. Allen, "Do Financial Institutions Matter?" *Journal of Finance* 56 (2001), pp. 1165–1175.

The efficient-market hypothesis emphasizes that arbitrage will rapidly eliminate any profit opportunities and drive market prices back to fair value. Behavioral-finance specialists may concede that there are no easy profits, but argue that arbitrage is costly and sometimes slow-working, so that deviations from fair value may persist.

Sorting out the puzzles will take time, but we suggest that financial managers should assume, at least as a starting point, that stock and bond prices are "right" and that there are no free lunches to be had on Wall Street.

The "no free lunch" principle gives us the following five lessons of market efficiency. After reviewing these lessons, we consider what market inefficiency can mean for the financial manager.

Lesson 1: Markets Have No Memory

The weak form of the efficient-market hypothesis states that the sequence of past price changes contains no information about future changes. Economists express the same idea more concisely when they say that the market has no memory. Sometimes financial managers *seem* to act as if this were not the case. For example, after an abnormal market rise, managers prefer to issue equity rather than debt.[31] The idea is to catch the market while it is high. Similarly, they are often reluctant to issue stock after a fall in price. They are inclined to wait for a rebound. But we know that the market has no memory and the cycles that financial managers seem to rely on do not exist.[32]

Sometimes a financial manager will have inside information indicating that the firm's stock is overpriced or underpriced. Suppose, for example, that there is some good news that the market does not know but you do. The stock price will rise sharply when the news is revealed. Therefore, if your company sells shares at the current price, it would offer a bargain to new investors at the expense of present stockholders.

Naturally, managers are reluctant to sell new shares when they have favorable inside information. But such information has nothing to do with the history of the stock price. Your firm's stock could be selling at half its price of a year ago, and yet you could have special information suggesting that it is *still* grossly overvalued. Or it may be undervalued at twice last year's price.

Lesson 2: Trust Market Prices

In an efficient market, you can trust prices because they impound all available information about the value of each security. This means that in an efficient market, there is no way for most investors to achieve consistently superior rates of return. To do so, you not only need to know more than *anyone* else; you need to know more than *everyone* else. This message is important for the financial manager who is responsible for the firm's exchange-rate policy or for its purchases and sales of debt. If you operate on the basis that you are smarter than others at predicting currency changes or interest-rate moves, you will trade a consistent financial policy for an elusive will-o'-the-wisp.

---

[31]See, for example, P. Asquith and D. W. Mullins, Jr., "Equity Issues and Offering Dilution," *Journal of Financial Economics* 15 (January–February 1986), pp. 61–89; and (for the U.K.) P. R. Marsh, "The Choice between Equity and Debt: An Empirical Study," *Journal of Finance* 37 (March 1982), pp. 121–144.

[32]If high stock prices signal expanded investment opportunities and the need to finance these new investments, we would expect to see firms raise more money *in total* when stock prices are historically high. But this does not explain why firms prefer to raise the extra cash at these times by an issue of equity rather than debt.

Procter & Gamble (P&G) supplied a costly example of this point in early 1994, when it lost $102 million in short order. It seems that in 1993, P&G's treasury staff believed that interest rates would be stable and decided to act on this belief to reduce P&G's borrowing costs. They committed P&G to deals with Bankers Trust designed to do just that. Of course, there was no free lunch. In exchange for a reduced interest rate, P&G agreed to compensate Bankers Trust if interest rates rose sharply. Rates did increase dramatically in early 1994, and P&G was on the hook. Then P&G accused Bankers Trust of misrepresenting the transactions—an embarrassing allegation since P&G was hardly investing as a widow or orphan—and sued Bankers Trust.

We take no stand on the merits of this litigation, which was eventually settled. But think of P&G's competition when it traded in the fixed-income markets. Its competition included the trading desks of all the major investment banks, hedge funds, and fixed-income portfolio managers. P&G had no special insights or competitive advantages on the fixed-income playing field. Its decision to place a massive bet on interest rates was about as risky (and painful) as playing leapfrog with a unicorn.

Why was it trading at all? P&G would never invest to enter a new consumer market if it had no competitive advantage in that market. In Chapter 11, we argued that a corporation should not invest unless it can identify a competitive advantage and a source of economic rents. Market inefficiencies may offer economic rents from convergence trades, but few corporations have a competitive edge in pursuing these rents. As a general rule, nonfinancial corporations gain nothing, on average, by speculation in financial markets. They should not try to imitate hedge funds.[33]

The company's assets may also be directly affected by management's faith in its investment skills. For example, one company may purchase another simply because its management thinks that the stock is undervalued. On approximately half the occasions, the stock of the acquired firm will, with hindsight, turn out to be undervalued. But on the other half, it will be overvalued. On average, the value will be correct, so the acquiring company is playing a fair game except for the costs of the acquisition.

Lesson 3: Read the Entrails

If the market is efficient, prices impound all available information. Therefore, if we can only learn to read the entrails, security prices can tell us a lot about the future. For example, in Chapter 23, we show how information in a company's financial statements can help to estimate the probability of bankruptcy. But the market's assessment of the company's securities can also provide important information about the firm's prospects. Thus, if the company's bonds are trading at low prices, you can deduce that the firm is probably in trouble.

Here is another example: Suppose that investors are confident that interest rates are set to rise over the next year. In that case, they will prefer to wait before they make long-term loans, and any firm that wants to borrow long-term money today will have to offer the inducement of a higher rate of interest. In other words, the long-term rate of interest will have to be higher than the one-year rate. Differences between the long-term interest rate and the short-term rate tell you something about what investors expect to happen to short-term rates in the future.

The nearby box shows how market prices reveal opinions about issues as diverse as a presidential election, the weather, or the demand for a new product.

---

[33]There are, of course, some likely exceptions. Hershey and Nestlé are credible traders in cocoa futures markets. The major oil companies probably have special skills and knowledge relevant to energy markets.

Lesson 4: The Do-It-Yourself Alternative

In an efficient market, investors will not pay others for what they can do equally well themselves. As we shall see, many of the controversies in corporate financing center on how well individuals can replicate corporate financial decisions. For example, companies often justify mergers on the grounds that they produce a more diversified and hence more stable firm. But if investors can hold the stocks of both companies, why should they thank the companies for diversifying? It is much easier and cheaper for them to diversify than it is for the firm.

The financial manager needs to ask the same question when considering whether it is better to issue debt or common stock. If the firm issues debt, it will create financial leverage. As a result, the stock will be more risky, and it will offer a higher expected return. But stockholders can obtain financial leverage without the firm's issuing debt; they can borrow on their own accounts. The problem for the financial manager is, therefore, to decide whether there is an advantage to the company issuing debt rather than the individual shareholder.

Lesson 5: Seen One Stock, Seen Them All

The elasticity of demand for any article measures the percentage change in the quantity demanded for each percentage addition to the price. If the article has close substitutes, the elasticity will be strongly negative; if not, it will be near zero. For example, coffee, which is a staple commodity, has a demand elasticity of about $-.2$. This means that a 5% increase in the price of coffee changes sales by $-.2 \times .05 = -.01$; in other words, it reduces demand by only 1%. Consumers are likely to regard different *brands* of coffee as much closer substitutes for each other. Therefore, the demand elasticity for a particular brand could be in the region of, say, -2.0. A 5% increase in the price of Maxwell House relative to that of Folgers would in this case reduce demand by 10%.

Investors don't buy a stock for its unique qualities; they buy it because it offers the prospect of a fair return for its risk. This means that stocks should be like *very* similar brands of coffee, almost perfect substitutes. Therefore, the demand for a company's stock should be highly elastic. If its prospective return is too low relative to its risk, *nobody* will want to hold that stock. If the reverse is true, *everybody* will scramble to buy.

Suppose that you want to sell a large block of stock. Since demand is elastic, you naturally conclude that you need to cut the offering price only very slightly to sell your stock. Unfortunately, that doesn't necessarily follow. When you come to sell your stock, other investors may suspect that you want to get rid of it because you know something they don't. Therefore, they will revise their assessment of the stock's value downward. Demand is still elastic, but the whole demand curve moves down. Elastic demand does not imply that stock prices never change when a large sale or purchase occurs; it *does* imply that you can sell large blocks of stock at close to the market price *as long as you can convince other investors that you have no private information*.

What If Markets Are Not Efficient? Implications for the Financial Manager

Our five lessons depend on efficient markets. What should financial managers do when markets are *not* efficient? The answer depends on the nature of the inefficiency.

What If Your Company's Shares Are Mispriced?   The financial manager may not have special information about future interest rates, but she definitely has special information about the value of her own company's shares. Or investors may have the same information as management, but they may be slow in reacting to that information or may be infected with behavioral biases.

Prediction Markets

❭ Stock markets allow investors to bet on their favorite stocks. Prediction markets allow them to bet on almost anything else. These markets reveal the collective guess of traders on issues as diverse as New York City snowfall, an avian flu outbreak, and the occurrence of a major earthquake.

Prediction markets are conducted on a number of small online exchanges such as the Iowa Electronic Markets and Predictit. Take presidential elections as an example. Prediction markets allowed you to bet that a particular candidate would win. To do so, you could buy a contract that paid $1 if he or she won and nothing otherwise. If you thought that the probability of victory was 55% (say), you would have been prepared to pay up to $.55 for this contract. Someone who was relatively pessimistic about that candidate's chances would have been happy to *sell* you such a contract, for that sale would turn a profit if that candidate were to lose.

With many participants buying and selling, the market price of a contract reveals the collective wisdom of the crowd (or at least of those people who participated in the market). For example, take a look at panel *a* of the accompanying figure. It shows the contract prices through 2012 for a victory by Obama or Romney. For all of this period, those prices pointed to the likelihood of an Obama victory.

Of course, no set of individuals are perfect forecasters, and prediction markets are not unique in performing poorly when the participants have common biases or are focusing on the same information sources. That is what happened in the 2016 presidential election. Panel *b* of the figure shows that at no point during the contest did participants rank Donald Trump's chances as better than evens.

Because prediction markets can pool ideas efficiently, some businesses have also formed internal prediction markets to survey the views of their staff. For example, Google operates an internal market to forecast product launch dates, the number of Gmail users, and other strategic questions.[*]

---

[*]See B. Cowgill and E. Zitzewitz, "Corporate Prediction Markets: Evidence from Google, Ford, and Firm X," *Review of Economic Studies* 82 (October 2015), pp. 1309–1341.

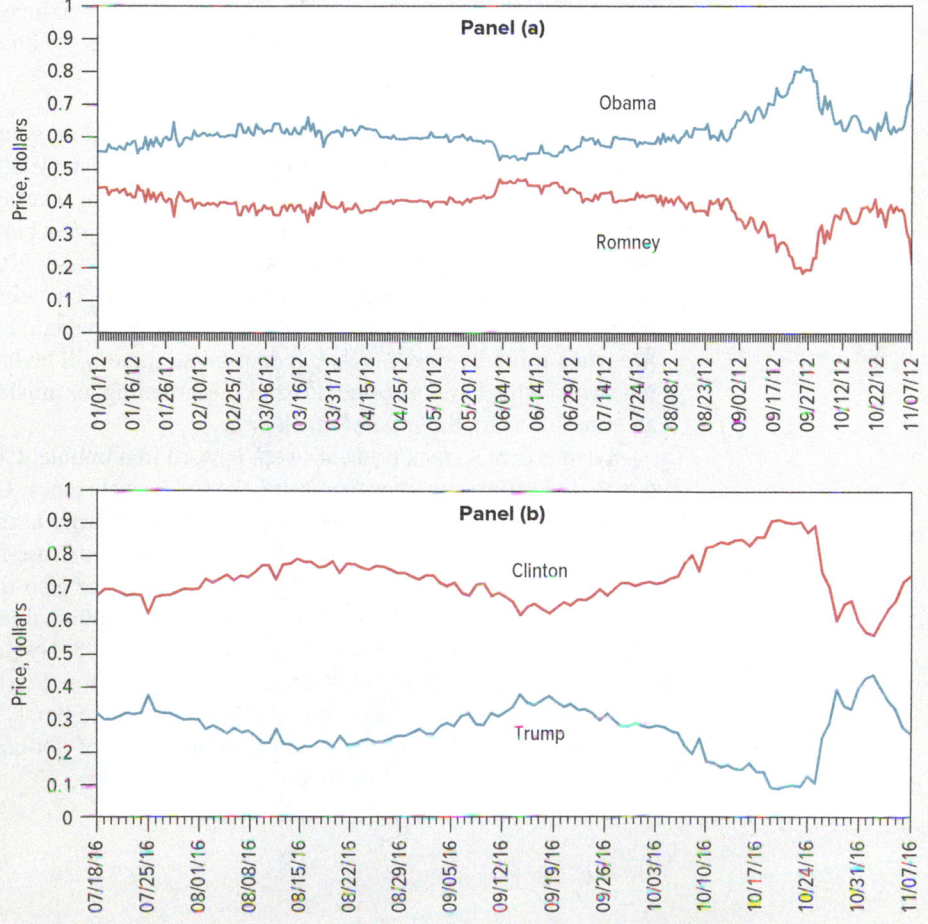

Sometimes you hear managers thinking out loud like this:

Great! Our stock is clearly overpriced. This means we can raise capital cheaply and invest in Project X. Our high stock price gives us a big advantage over our competitors who could not possibly justify investing in Project X.

But that doesn't make sense. If your stock is truly overpriced, you can help your current shareholders by selling additional stock and using the cash to invest in other capital market securities. But you should *never* issue stock to invest in a project that offers a lower rate of return than you could earn elsewhere in the capital market. Such a project would have a negative NPV. You can always do better than investing in a negative-NPV project: Your company can go out and buy common stocks. In an efficient market, such purchases are always *zero* NPV.

What about the reverse? Suppose you know that your stock is *underpriced*. In that case, it certainly would not help your current shareholders to sell additional "cheap" stock to invest in other fairly priced stocks. If your stock is sufficiently underpriced, it may even pay to forgo an opportunity to invest in a positive-NPV project rather than to allow new investors to buy into your firm at a low price. Financial managers who believe that their firm's stock is underpriced may be justifiably reluctant to issue more stock, but they may instead be able to finance their investment program by an issue of debt. In this case the market inefficiency would affect the firm's choice of financing but not its real investment decisions. In Chapter 15, we will have more to say about the financing choice when managers believe their stock is mispriced.

What If Your Firm Is Caught in a Bubble?   On occasion, your company's stock price may be swept up in a bubble like the dot-com boom of the late 1990s. Bubbles can be exhilarating. It's hard not to join in the enthusiasm of the crowds of investors bidding up your firm's stock price.[34] On the other hand, financial management *inside* a bubble poses difficult personal and ethical challenges. Managers don't want to "talk down" a high-flying stock price, especially when bonuses and stock-option payoffs depend on it. The temptation to cover up bad news or manufacture good news can be very strong. But the longer a bubble lasts, the greater the damage when it finally bursts. When it does burst, there will be lawsuits and possibly jail time for managers who have resorted to tricky accounting or misleading public statements in an attempt to sustain the inflated stock price.

When a firm's stock price is swept upward in a bubble, CEOs and financial managers are tempted to acquire another firm using the stock as currency. One extreme example where this arguably happened is AOL's acquisition of Time Warner at the height of the dot-com bubble in 2000. AOL was a classic dot-com company. Its stock rose from $2.34 at the end of 1995 to $75.88 at the end of 1999. Time Warner's stock price also increased during this period, but only from $18.94 to $72.31. AOL's total market capitalization was a small fraction of Time Warner's in 1995, but overtook Time Warner's in 1998. By the end of 1999, AOL's outstanding shares were worth $173 billion, compared with Time Warner's $95 billion. AOL managed to complete the acquisition before the Internet bubble burst. AOL-Time Warner's stock then plummeted, but not by nearly as much as the stocks of dot-com companies that had not managed to find and acquire safer partners.[35]

---

[34]See J. C. Stein, "Rational Capital Budgeting in an Irrational World," *Journal of Business* 69 (October 1996), pp. 429–455.

[35]Pavel Savor and Qi Lu provide evidence that many other firms were able to benefit from stock acquisitions. See "Do Stock Mergers Create Value for Acquirers?" *Journal of Finance* 64 (June 2009), pp. 1061–1097.

The patron saint of the Bolsa (stock exchange) in Barcelona, Spain, is Nuestra Señora de la Esperanza—Our Lady of Hope. She is the perfect patroness, for we all hope for superior returns when we invest. But competition between investors will tend to produce an efficient market. In such a market, prices will rapidly impound any new information, and it will be difficult to make consistently superior returns. We may indeed hope, but all we can rationally *expect* in an efficient market is a return just sufficient to compensate us for the time value of money and for the risks we bear.

The efficient-market hypothesis comes in three different flavors. The weak form of the hypothesis states that prices efficiently reflect all the information in the past series of stock prices. In this case, it is impossible to earn superior returns simply by looking for patterns in stock prices; in other words, prices follow a random walk. The semistrong form of the hypothesis states that prices reflect all published information. That means it is impossible to make consistently superior returns just by reading the newspaper, looking at the company's annual accounts, and so on. The strong form of the hypothesis states that stock prices effectively impound all available information. It tells us that superior information is hard to find because in pursuing it you are in competition with thousands, perhaps millions, of active, intelligent, and greedy investors. The best you can do in this case is to assume that securities are fairly priced and to hope that one day Nuestra Señora will reward your humility.

During the 1960s and 1970s, every article on the topic seemed to provide additional evidence that markets are efficient. But then readers became tired of hearing the same message and wanted to read about possible exceptions. During the 1980s and 1990s, more and more anomalies and puzzles were uncovered. Bubbles, including the dot-com bubble of the 1990s and the real estate bubble of the 2000s, cast doubt on whether markets were always and everywhere efficient.

Limits to arbitrage can explain why asset prices may get out of line with fundamental values. Behavioral finance, which relies on psychological evidence to interpret investor behavior, is also consistent with many of the deviations from market efficiency. Behavioral finance says that investors are averse to even small losses, especially when recent investment returns have been disappointing. Investors may rely too much on a few recent events in predicting the future. They may be overconfident in their predictions and may be sluggish in reacting to new information.

There are plenty of quirks and biases in human behavior, so behavioral finance has plenty of raw material. But if every puzzle or anomaly can be explained by some recipe of quirks, biases, and hindsight, what have we learned? Research in behavioral finance literature is informative and intriguing, but not yet at the stage where a few parsimonious models can account for most of the deviations from market efficiency.

There has been a long-running debate on just how efficient markets are, and there seems no prospect of a universally accepted conclusion any time soon. Perhaps nothing could better illustrate the open nature of this debate than the decision to award the 2013 Nobel Prize in economics jointly to Eugene Fama, who has been dubbed the father of the "efficient market" hypothesis, and to Robert Shiller, whose work has focused on market *inefficiencies*. (The third recipient of the 2013 prize was Lars Hansen for his development of statistical methods that have been widely used to test theories of asset pricing.)[36]

For the corporate treasurer who is concerned with issuing or purchasing securities, the efficient-market theory has obvious implications. In one sense, however, it raises more questions than it answers. The existence of efficient markets does not mean that the financial manager can let financing take care of itself. It provides only a starting point for analysis. It is time to get down to details about securities and issue procedures. We start in Chapter 14.

---

[36]See http://www.nobelprize.org/nobel_prizes/economic-sciences/laureates/2013/ for their Prize Lectures.

FURTHER READING

Malkiel's book is an-easy-to-read book on market efficiency. Fama has written two classic review articles on the topic:

B. G. Malkiel, *A Random Walk Down Wall Street*, 11th ed. (New York: W. W. Norton, 2016).

E. F. Fama, "Efficient Capital Markets: A Review of Theory and Empirical Work," *Journal of Finance* 25 (May 1970), pp. 383–417.

E. F. Fama, "Efficient Capital Markets: II," *Journal of Finance* 46 (December 1991), pp. 1575–1617.

There are several useful surveys of behavioral finance:

N. Barberis and R. H. Thaler, "A Survey of Behavioral Finance," in G. M. Constantinides, M. Harris, and R. M. Stulz (eds.), *Handbook of the Economics of Finance* (Amsterdam: Elsevier Science, 2003).

M. Baker, R. S. Ruback, and J. Wurgler, "Behavioral Corporate Finance: A Survey," in B. E. Eckbo (ed.), *The Handbook of Empirical Corporate Finance* (Amsterdam: Elsevier/North-Holland, 2007), Chapter 4.

R. J. Shiller, "Human Behavior and the Efficiency of the Financial System," in J. B. Taylor and M. Woodford (eds.), *Handbook of Macroeconomics* (Amsterdam: North-Holland, 1999).

A. Shleifer, *Inefficient Markets: An Introduction to Behavioral Finance* (Oxford: Oxford University Press, 2000).

R. H. Thaler (ed.), *Advances in Behavioral Finance* (New York: Russell Sage Foundation, 1993).

D. Hirshleifer, "Behavioral Finance," *Annual Review of Financial Economics* 7 (December 2015), pp. 133–159.

Some conflicting views on market efficiency are provided by:

G. W. Schwert, "Anomalies and Market Efficiency," in G. M. Constantinides, M. Harris, and R. M. Stulz (eds.), *Handbook of the Economics of Finance* (Amsterdam: Elsevier Science, 2003).

M. Rubinstein, "Rational Markets: Yes or No? The Affirmative Case?" *Financial Analysts Journal* 57 (May–June 2001), pp. 15–29.

B. G. Malkiel, "The Efficient Market Hypothesis and Its Critics," *Journal of Economic Perspectives* 17 (Winter 2003), pp. 59–82.

R. J. Shiller, "From Efficient Markets Theory to Behavioral Finance," *Journal of Economic Perspectives* 17 (Winter 2003), pp. 83–104.

E. F. Fama and K. R. French, "Dissecting Anomalies," *Journal of Finance* 63 (August 2008), pp. 1653–1678.

Bubbles are discussed in:

M. Brunnermeier, *Asset Pricing under Asymmetric Information: Bubbles, Crashes, Technical Analysis, and Herding* (Oxford: Oxford University Press, 2001).

A. Scherbina, "Asset Price Bubbles: A Selective Survey," IMF Working Paper 13/45, 2013.

R. J. Shiller, *Irrational Exuberance*, 2nd ed. (Princeton, NJ: Princeton University Press, 2005).

For discussions of the rationality of prices in particular bull markets, see

L. Pastor and P. Veronesi, "Was There a Nasdaq Bubble in the Late 1990s?" *Journal of Financial Economics* 81 (2006), pp. 61–100.

E. Ofek and M. Richardson, "DotCom Mania: The Rise and Fall of Internet Stock Prices," *Journal of Finance* 58 (2003), pp. 1113–1138.

K. French and J. M. Poterba, "Were Japanese Stock Prices Too High?" *Journal of Financial Economics* 29 (October 1991), pp. 337–363.

Select problems are available in McGraw-Hill's *Connect*.
Please see the preface for more information.

PROBLEM SETS

1. **Market efficiency** True or false? The efficient-market hypothesis assumes that

   a. There are no taxes.

   b. There is perfect foresight.

   c. Successive price changes are independent.

   d. Investors are irrational.

   e. There are no transaction costs.

   f. Forecasts are unbiased.

2. **Market efficiency*** True or false?

   a. Financing decisions are less easily reversed than investment decisions.

   b. Tests have shown that there is almost perfect negative correlation between successive price changes.

   c. The semistrong form of the efficient-market hypothesis states that prices reflect all publicly available information.

   d. In efficient markets, the expected return on each stock is the same.

3. **Market efficiency** Which (if any) of these statements are true? Stock prices appear to behave as though successive values

   (a) Are random numbers.

   (b) Follow regular cycles.

   (c) Differ by a random number.

4. **Market efficiency** Supply the missing words: "There are three forms of the efficient-market hypothesis. Tests of randomness in stock returns provide evidence for the _____ form of the hypothesis. Tests of stock price reaction to well-publicized news provide evidence for the _____ form, and tests of the performance of professionally managed funds provide evidence for the _____ form. Market efficiency results from competition between investors. Many investors search for new information about the company's business that would help them to value the stock more accurately. Such research helps to ensure that prices reflect all available information; in other words, it helps to keep the market efficient in the _____ form. Other investors study past stock prices for recurrent patterns that would allow them to make superior profits. Such research helps to ensure that prices reflect all the information contained in past stock prices; in other words, it helps to keep the market efficient in the _____ form."

5. **Market efficiency** How would you respond to the following comments?

   a. "Efficient market, my eye! I know lots of investors who do crazy things."

   b. "Efficient market? Balderdash! I know at least a dozen people who have made a bundle in the stock market."

   c. "The trouble with the efficient-market theory is that it ignores investors' psychology."

   d. "Despite all the limitations, the best guide to a company's value is its written-down book value. It is much more stable than market value, which depends on temporary fashions."

6. **Market efficiency** Respond to the following comments:

   a. "The random-walk theory, with its implication that investing in stocks is like playing roulette, is a powerful indictment of our capital markets."

   b. "If everyone believes you can make money by charting stock prices, then price changes won't be random."

   c. "The random-walk theory implies that events are random, but many events are not random. If it rains today, there's a fair bet that it will rain again tomorrow."

7. **Market efficiency** "If the efficient-market hypothesis is true, the pension fund manager might as well select a portfolio with a pin." Explain why this is not so.

8. **Market efficiency evidence*** Fama and French show that average stock returns on firms with small market capitalizations have been significantly higher than average returns for "large-cap" firms. What are the possible explanations for this result? Does the result disprove market efficiency? Explain briefly.

9. **Market efficiency evidence*** Which of the following observations appear to indicate market inefficiency? Explain whether the observation appears to contradict the weak, semistrong, or strong form of the efficient-market hypothesis.

   a. Tax-exempt municipal bonds offer lower pretax returns than taxable government bonds.

   b. Managers make superior returns on purchases of their company's stock.

   c. There is a positive relationship between the return on the market in one quarter and the change in aggregate profits in the next quarter.

   d. There is some evidence that stocks that have appreciated unusually in the recent past continue to do so in the future.

   e. The stock of an acquired firm tends to appreciate in the period before the merger announcement.

   f. Stocks of companies with unexpectedly high earnings appear to offer high returns for several months after the earnings announcement.

   g. Very risky stocks on average give higher returns than safe stocks.

10. **Market efficiency evidence** Give two or three examples of research results or events that raise doubts about market efficiency. Briefly explain why.

11. **Market efficiency implications** Here again are the five lessons of market efficiency. For each lesson give an example showing the lesson's relevance to financial managers.

    a. Markets have no memory.

    b. Trust market prices.

    c. Read the entrails.

    d. The do-it-yourself alternative.

    e. Seen one stock, seen them all.

12. **Market efficiency implications** Two financial managers, Alpha and Beta, are contemplating a chart showing the actual performance of the Standard and Poor's Composite Index over a five-year period. Each manager's company needs to issue new shares of common stock sometime in the next year.

    Alpha: My company's going to issue right away. The stock market cycle has obviously topped out, and the next move is almost surely down. Better to issue now and get a decent price for the shares.

    Beta: You're too nervous; we're waiting. It's true that the market's been going nowhere for the past year or so, but the figure clearly shows a basic upward trend. The market's on the way up to a new plateau.

    What would you say to Alpha and Beta?

13. **Market efficiency implications** What does the efficient-market hypothesis have to say about these two statements?

    a. "I notice that short-term interest rates are about 1% below long-term rates. We should borrow short-term."

    b. "I notice that interest rates in Japan are lower than rates in the United States. We would do better to borrow Japanese yen rather than U.S. dollars."

14. **Market efficiency implications*** True or false?

    a. If markets are efficient, shareholders should expect to receive only the risk-free interest rate on their investment.

    b. If markets are efficient, investment in the stock market is a mug's game.

    c. If markets are efficient, investors should just invest in firms with good management and an above-average track record.

    d. In an efficient market, investors should expect stocks to sell at a fair price.

15. **Abnormal returns*** Analysis of 60 monthly rates of return on United Futon common stock indicates a beta of 1.45 and an alpha of –.2% per month. A month later, the market is up by 5%, and United Futon is up by 6%. What is Futon's abnormal rate of return?

16. **Abnormal returns** The second column in Table 13.1 shows the monthly return on the British FTSE 100 index from January 2015 through July 2017. The remaining columns show returns on the stocks of two firms—Executive Cheese and Paddington Beer. Both firms announced their earnings in July 2017. Calculate the average abnormal return of the two stocks during the month of the earnings announcement. The earnings of one of these stocks slightly disappointed investors and the earnings of the other were slightly better than expected. Which was which?

❯TABLE 13.1

See Problem 16. Rates of return in percent per month.

Month	Market Return	Executive Cheese Return	Paddington Beer Return
January 2015	2.8	3.6	1.6
February	2.9	7.0	1.5
March	−2.5	−2.2	−0.7
April	2.8	3.1	3.0
May	0.3	0.2	0.1
June	−3.9	−6.5	1.1
July	−0.2	0.1	0.6
August	−6.7	−9.8	−4.6
September	−3.0	−7.2	−5.3
October	4.9	5.8	6.1
November	−0.1	0.2	0.1
December	−1.8	−1.0	−1.2
January 2016	−2.5	−3.1	0.6
February	0.2	0.3	1.7
March	1.3	1.7	2.1
April	1.1	1.1	3.0
May	−0.2	0.1	1.6
June	4.4	7.4	2.8
July	3.4	4.0	0.9
August	0.8	1.2	1.0
September	1.7	5.1	1.3
October	0.8	3.7	−1.6
November	−2.4	−2.7	−1.2
December	5.3	10.7	1.8
January 2017	−0.6	−0.4	−0.7
February	2.3	2.8	2.4
March	0.8	0.7	0.8
April	−1.6	−1.0	−1.2
May	4.4	6.2	−3.7
June	−2.8	−3.2	−1.3
July	2.7	3.0	2.9

17. **Abnormal returns** Here are alphas and betas for Estée Lauder and Caterpillar Tractor for the 60 months ending June 2017. Alpha is expressed as a percent per month.

	Alpha	Beta
Estée Lauder	0.48	0.70
Caterpillar Tractor	−0.41	1.26

Explain how these estimates would be used to calculate an abnormal return.

18. **Behavioral finance** Explain how incentive and agency problems might contribute to mispricing of securities or to bubbles. Give examples.

19. **Behavioral finance** True or false?

a. Most managers tend to be overconfident.

b. Psychologists have found that, once people have suffered a loss, they are more relaxed about the possibility of incurring further losses.

c. Psychologists have observed that people tend to put too much weight on recent events when forecasting.

d. Behavioral biases open up the opportunity for easy arbitrage profits.

20. **Behavioral finance** Many commentators have blamed the subprime crisis on "irrational exuberance." What is your view? Explain briefly.

CHALLENGE

21. **Market efficiency** "The strong form of the efficient-market hypothesis is nonsense. Look at mutual fund X; it has had superior performance for each of the last 10 years." Does the speaker have a point? Suppose that there is a 50% probability that X will obtain superior performance in any year simply by chance.

a. If X is the only fund, calculate the probability that it will have achieved superior performance for each of the past 10 years.

b. Now recognize that there are nearly 10,000 mutual funds in the United States. What is the probability that by chance there is at least 1 out of 10,000 funds that obtained 10 successive years of superior performance?

22. **Bubbles** Some extreme bubbles are obvious with hindsight, *after* they burst. But how would you *define* a bubble? There are many examples of good news and rising stock prices, followed by bad news and falling stock prices. Can you set out rules and procedures to distinguish bubbles from the normal ups and downs of stock prices?

● ● ● ● ●

FINANCE ON THE WEB

Use **finance.yahoo.com** to download daily prices for five U.S. stocks for a recent five-year period. For each stock, construct a scatter diagram of successive returns as in Figure 13.1. Calculate the correlation between the returns on successive days. Do you find any consistent patterns?

An Overview of Corporate Financing

We now begin our analysis of long-term financing decisions—an undertaking we will not complete until Chapter 25. This chapter provides an introduction to corporate financing. It reviews, with a broad brush, several topics that we will explore more carefully later on.

We start the chapter by looking at aggregate data on the sources of financing. Most of the money for new investments comes from profits that companies retain and reinvest. The remainder comes from selling new debt or equity securities. These financing patterns raise several interesting questions. Do companies rely too heavily on internal financing rather than on new issues of debt or equity? Are debt ratios of U.S. corporations dangerously high?

Our second task in the chapter is to review some of the essential features of debt and equity. Lenders and stockholders have different *cash-flow rights* and also different *control rights*. The lenders have first claim on cash flow because they are promised definite cash payments for interest and principal. After the lenders have been paid, whatever cash is left over belongs to the stockholders. Stockholders, on the other hand, have complete control of the firm, providing that they keep their promises to lenders. As owners of the business, they have the ultimate say over what assets the company buys, how the assets are financed, and how they are used. Of course, in large public corporations, the stockholders delegate these decisions to the board of directors, who in turn appoint senior management. In these cases, *effective* control often ends up with the company's management.

The simple division of cash flow among debt and equity glosses over the many different types of debt that companies issue. Therefore, we close our discussion of debt and equity with a brief canter through the main categories of debt. We also pause to describe certain less common forms of equity, particularly preferred stock.

The financial manager is the link between the firm and the financial institutions that provide much of the funds that the companies need, together with help in making payments, managing risk, and so on. We, therefore, introduce you to the major financial institutions and look at the roles that these institutions play in corporate financing and in the economy at large. The financial crisis that started in the summer of 2007 demonstrated the importance of healthy financial markets and institutions. We will review the crisis and its aftermath.

14-1 Patterns of Corporate Financing

Corporations invest in long-term assets, such as property, plant, and equipment, and in current assets, such as inventory and accounts receivable. Figure 14.1 shows where U.S. corporations get the cash to pay for these investments. Most of the cash is generated internally. That is, it comes from cash flow allocated to depreciation and from retained earnings (earnings not paid

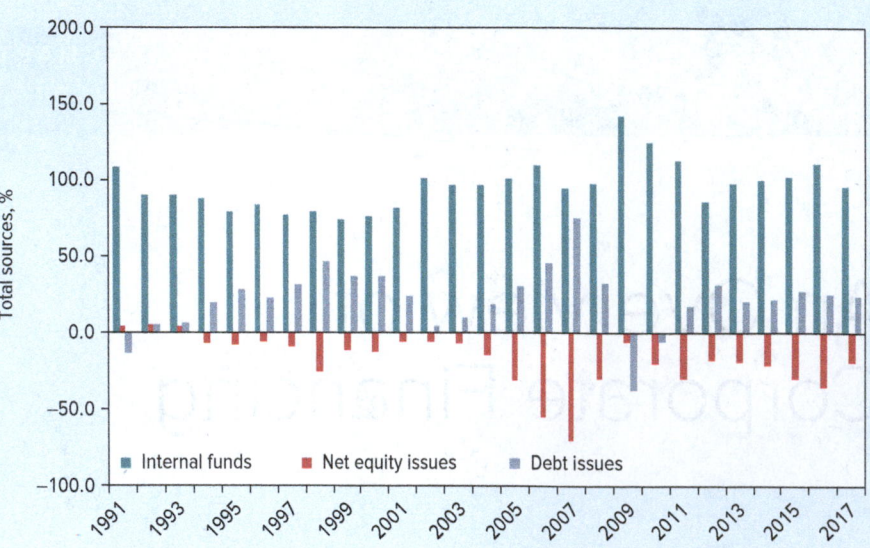

FIGURE 14.1
Sources of funds for U.S. nonfinancial corporations expressed as a fraction of the total

Source: Board of Governors of the Federal Reserve System, Division of Research and Statistics, Flow of Funds Accounts Table F103 at **www.federalreserve.gov/releases/z1/current/default.htm.**

■ Internal funds   ■ Net equity issues   ■ Debt issues

out as cash dividends).[1] U.S. corporations, together with those in other Anglo-Saxon countries, are unusual in their very heavy reliance on internal finance. However, in most industrial countries depreciation and retained earnings remain the largest source of finance. Shareholders are happy for the cash to be plowed back into the firm, provided that it is invested in positive-NPV projects. Every positive-NPV outlay increases shareholder value.

If internal cash flow is not sufficient to pay for the investments, the company faces a financial deficit. To cover the deficit, the company must cut back on dividends in order to increase retained earnings, or it must raise new debt or equity capital from outside investors. So there are two basic financing decisions. First, what fraction of profits should be plowed back into the business rather than paid out to shareholders? Second, what fraction of the financial deficit should be met with debt rather than equity? Thus, the firm needs a payout policy (Chapter 16) and a debt policy (Chapters 17 and 18).

Take a look at U.S. equity issues in Figure 14.1. Net issues were *negative* in almost every year. This means that companies paid out more to shareholders by repurchasing shares than they raised by share issues. (Corporations can buy back their own shares, or they may purchase and retire other firms' shares in the course of mergers and acquisitions.) The choice between cash dividends and repurchases is another aspect of payout policy.

Stock repurchases in the U.S. have typically been larger than new issues of shares. They were especially large in 2006 and 2007, which accounts for the large negative net equity issues in those years. By contrast, debt issues were positive in almost every year.

Do Firms Rely Too Much on Internal Funds?

We have seen that, on average, internal funds (retained earnings plus depreciation) cover most of the cash needed for investment. It seems that internal financing is more convenient than external financing by stock and debt issues. But some observers worry that managers have an irrational or self-serving aversion to external finance. A manager seeking comfortable

---

[1]In Figure 14.1, internally generated cash was calculated by adding depreciation to retained earnings. Depreciation is a noncash expense. Thus, retained earnings understate the cash flow available for reinvestment.

employment could be tempted to forgo a risky but positive-NPV project if it involved launching a new stock issue and facing awkward questions from potential investors. Perhaps managers take the line of least resistance and dodge the "discipline of capital markets."

We do not mean to paint managers as loafers. They sometimes have good reasons for relying on internally generated funds. They may seek to avoid the cost of issuing new securities, for example. Moreover, the announcement of a new equity issue is usually bad news for investors, who worry that the decision signals lower future profits or higher risk.[2] If issues of shares are costly and send a bad-news signal to investors, companies may be justified in looking more carefully at those projects that would require a new stock issue.

How Much Do Firms Borrow?

The mix of debt and equity financing varies widely from industry to industry and from firm to firm. Debt ratios also vary over time for particular firms. These variations are a fact of life: There is no constant, God-given debt ratio, and if there were, it would change. But a few aggregate statistics will do no harm.

Table 14.1 shows the aggregate balance sheet of all U.S. manufacturing corporations. If all these businesses were merged into a single gigantic firm, Table 14.1 would be its balance sheet. Assets and liabilities in the table are entered at book values, that is, accounting values. These do not generally equal market values. The numbers are nevertheless instructive. Notice that firms had long-term debt of $2,779 billion and equity of $4,477 billion. The ratio of long-term debt to long-term debt plus equity was, therefore, $2,779/($2,779 + $4,477) = .38.[3]

Table 14.1 is, of course, only a snapshot. Figure 14.2 provides a longer-term perspective. The debt ratios are lower when computed from market values rather than book values. This is because the market value of equity is generally greater than the book value.

Figure 14.2 shows that book debt ratios are higher today than 50 years ago. Should we be concerned about this? It is true that higher debt ratios mean that more companies will fall into

Assets		$ Billions	Liabilities		$ Billions
Current assets[a]		$ 2,599	Current liabilities[a]		$ 2,088
Fixed assets	$3,696		Long-term debt	$2,779	
Less depreciation	1,990		Other long-term liabilities[b]	1,491	
Net fixed assets		1,705	Total long-term liabilities[b]		4,270
Other long-term assets		6,530	Stockholders' equity		4,477
Total assets		$10,834	Total liabilities and stockholders' equity		$10,834

❭TABLE 14.1   Aggregate balance sheet for manufacturing corporations in the United States, fourth quarter, 2017 (figures in $ billions)

[a]See Table 30.1 for a breakdown of current assets and liabilities.
[b]Includes deferred taxes and several miscellaneous categories.

Source: U.S. Census Bureau, *Quarterly Financial Report Manufacturing, Mining, Trade, and Selected Service Industries*, 2017. Fourth Quarter, issued March 2018 (www.census.gov/econ/qfr).

---

[2]Managers do have insiders' insights and naturally are tempted to issue stock when the price looks good to them, that is, when they are less optimistic than outside investors. The outside investors realize this and will buy a new issue only at a discount from the pre-announcement price. More on stock issues in Chapter 15.
[3]This debt ratio may be understated, because "Other long-term liabilities" probably include some debt-equivalent claims. We will not pause to sort through these other liabilities, however.

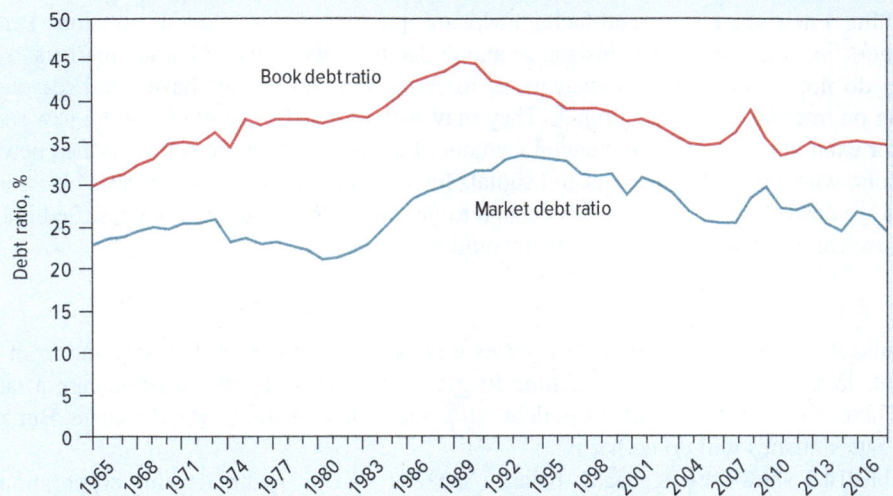

> **FIGURE 14.2**

Ratio of debt to debt plus net worth for nonfinancial corporations, 1965–2017

Source: Board of Governors of the Federal Reserve System, Division of Research and Statistics, Flow of Funds Accounts Table B.103 at www.federalreserve.gov/releases/z1/current/default.htm.

financial distress when a serious recession hits the economy. But all companies live with this risk to some degree, and it does not follow that less risk is better. Finding the optimal debt ratio is like finding the optimal speed limit. We can agree that accidents at 30 miles per hour are generally less dangerous than accidents at 60 miles per hour, but we do not therefore set the speed limit on all roads at 30. Speed has benefits as well as risks. So does debt, as we see in Chapter 18.

It is interesting to compare debt levels of U.S. companies with those of their foreign counterparts. However, in those countries that do not have well-developed bond markets debt means principally short-term bank debt. Therefore, rather than focusing on just long-term debt, it is more instructive to compare the ratio of *total* liabilities to total liabilities plus equity. Figure 14.3 is taken from a study by Claessens, Djankov, and Nenova of 11,000 companies in 46 countries. Korean and Indian companies are among the most highly indebted; those in the United States are relatively conservative in their use of debt.

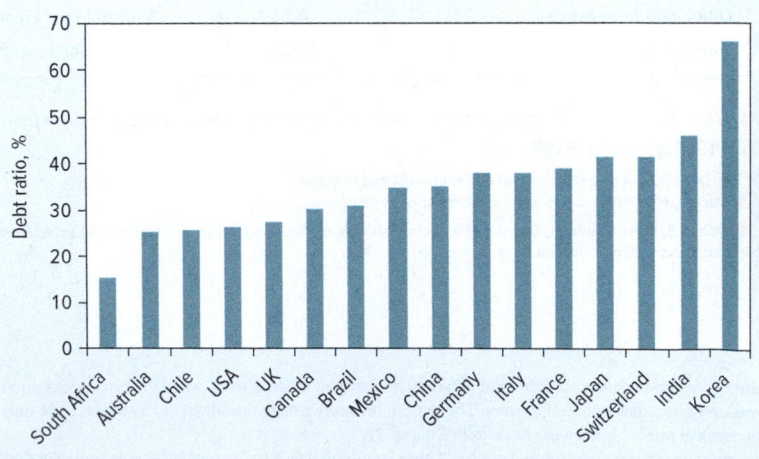

> **FIGURE 14.3**

Median ratios of total liabilities to total liabilities plus equity in different countries, 1995–1996

Source: S. Claessens, S. Djankov, and T. Nenova, "Corporate Risk Around the World," World Bank Policy Research Working Paper 2271, 2000, http://documents.worldbank.org/curated/en/907571468739464629/Corporate-risk-around-the-world.

14-2   Common Stock

Ownership of the Corporation

A corporation is owned by its common stockholders. You can see from Figure 14.4 that in the United States, 39% of this common stock is held directly by individual investors, and a similar proportion belongs to **financial intermediaries** such as mutual funds, pension funds, and insurance companies. Mutual funds and exchange traded funds (ETFs) hold 30% and pension funds a further 12%.[4]

But what do we mean when we say that these stockholders *own* the corporation? The answer is obvious if the company has issued no other securities. Consider the simplest possible case of a corporation financed solely by common stock, all of which is owned by the firm's chief executive officer (CEO). This lucky owner-manager receives all the cash flows and makes all investment and operating decisions. She has complete *cash-flow rights* and also complete *control rights*.

These rights are split up and reallocated as soon as the company borrows money. If it takes out a bank loan, it enters into a contract with the bank promising to pay interest and eventually repay the principal. The bank gets a privileged, but limited, right to cash flows; the residual cash-flow rights are left with the stockholder. Thus common stock is a *residual claim* on the firm's assets and cash flow.

The bank typically protects its claim by imposing restrictions on what the firm can or cannot do. For example, it may require the firm to limit future borrowing, and it may forbid the firm to sell off assets or to pay excessive dividends. The stockholders' control rights are thereby limited. However, the contract with the bank can never restrict or determine all the operating and investment decisions necessary to run the firm efficiently. (No team of lawyers, no matter how long they scribbled, could ever write a contract covering all possible contingencies.[5]) The owner of the common stock retains the residual rights of control over these

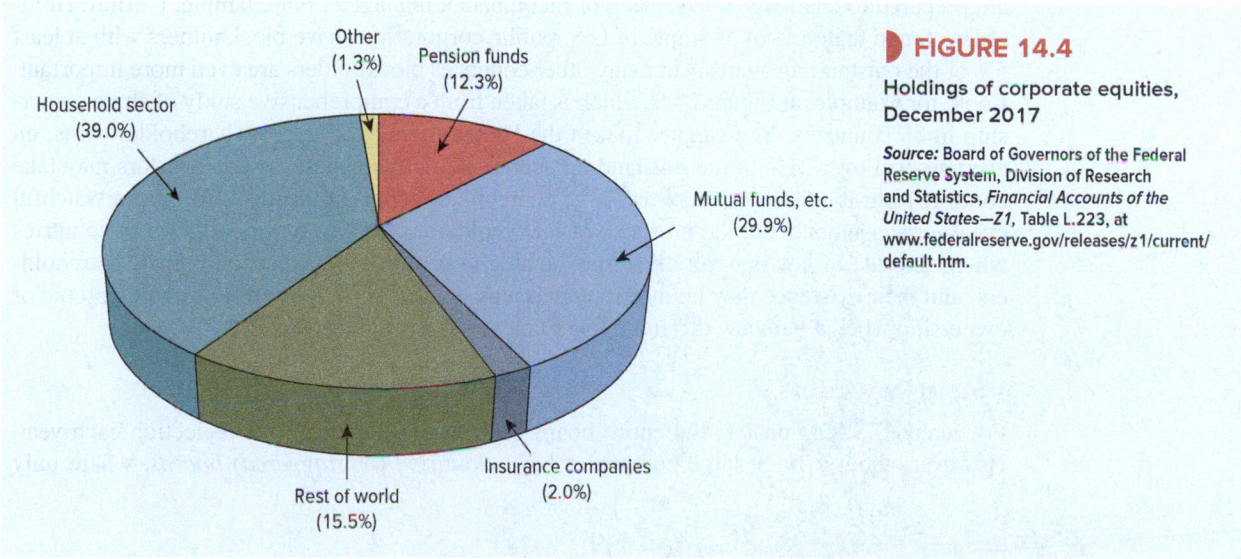

Household sector
(39.0%)

Other
(1.3%)

Pension funds
(12.3%)

Mutual funds, etc.
(29.9%)

Insurance companies
(2.0%)

Rest of world
(15.5%)

▶ **FIGURE 14.4**

Holdings of corporate equities, December 2017

Source: Board of Governors of the Federal Reserve System, Division of Research and Statistics, *Financial Accounts of the United States—Z1*, Table L.223, at www.federalreserve.gov/releases/z1/current/default.htm.

---

[4]Figure 14.4 does not show U.S. holdings of overseas shares. These amount to 20% of the total equity holdings of U.S. investors.
[5]Theoretical economists therefore stress the importance of *incomplete contracts*. Their point is that contracts pertaining to the management of the firm are inevitably incomplete and that someone must exercise residual rights of control. See, for example, O. Hart, *Firms, Contracts, and Financial Structure* (Oxford: Oxford University Press, 1995).

decisions. For example, she may choose to increase the selling price of the firm's products, to hire temporary rather than permanent employees, or to construct a new plant in Miami Beach rather than Hollywood.[6]

Ownership of the firm can of course change. If the firm fails to make the promised payments to the bank, it may be forced into bankruptcy. Once the firm is under the "protection" of a bankruptcy court, shareholders' cash-flow and control rights are tightly restricted and may be extinguished altogether. Unless some rescue or reorganization plan can be implemented, the bank becomes the new owner of the firm and acquires the cash-flow and control rights of ownership. (We discuss bankruptcy in Chapter 32.)

No law of nature says residual cash-flow rights and residual control rights have to go together. For example, one could imagine a situation where the debtholder gets to make all the decisions. But this would be inefficient. Since the benefits of good decisions are felt mainly by the common stockholders, it makes sense to give them control over how the firm's assets are used. Because they have the ultimate right of control and simultaneously have the residual cash flow entitlement, shareholders have an incentive to ensure that management maximizes their wealth.

Public corporations may be owned by tens of thousands of stockholders. The common stockholders in these corporations still have the residual rights over the cash flows and have the ultimate right of control over the company's affairs. In practice, however, their control is limited to an entitlement to vote on appointments to the *board of directors,* and on other crucial matters such as the decision to merge. Many shareholders do not bother to vote. They reason that because they own so few shares, their vote will have little impact on the outcome. The problem is that, if all shareholders think in the same way, they cede effective control and management gets a free hand to look after its own interests.

This free-rider problem was highlighted in a book written in 1932 by Berle and Means.[7] They warned of the emergence of a powerful class of managers that were insulated from outside pressure. Economists today are less convinced that managers enjoy the degree of liberty that Berle and Means envisaged. The majority of corporations have large shareholders who are prepared to challenge self-serving or incompetent managers. For example, Clifford Holderness found that 96% of a sample of U.S. public corporations have blockholders with at least 5% of the outstanding shares.[8] In many other countries blockholders are even more important. Look, for example, at Figure 14.5, which is taken from a comprehensive study of share ownership in 85 countries. You can see that in the United States, the largest shareholder owns, on average, just over 21% of the outstanding shares. In many of these cases, investors may take comfort from the fact that there are large shareholders with an incentive to keep a watchful eye on management. But the presence of blockholders is not always good news. In countries where the rule of law is weak, they may be able to profit at the expense of small shareholders, and their existence may be more a concern than a comfort. We will return to this topic of ownership when we review different governance systems in Chapter 33.

Voting Procedures

For many U.S. companies, the entire board of directors comes up for reelection each year. However, about 1 in 10 large companies have *classified* (or *staggered*) *boards,* where only

BEYOND THE PAGE

Empty voting

mhhe.com/brealey13e

---

[6]Of course, the bank manager may suggest that a particular decision is unwise, or even threaten to cut off future lending, but the bank does not have any *right* to make these decisions.

[7]A. A. Berle and G. C. Means, *The Modern Corporation and Private Property* (New York, The Macmillan Company, 1932).

[8]See C. Holderness, "The Myth of Diffuse Ownership in the United States," *Review of Financial Studies* 22 (April 2009), pp. 1377–1408; and R. La Porta, F. Lopez-de-Silanes, and A. Shleifer, "Corporate Ownership around the World," *Journal of Finance* 54 (1999), pp. 471–517. For a review of the extent and influence of blockholders, see A. Edmans and C. G. Holderness, "Blockholders: A Survey of Theory and Evidence," *The Handbook of the Economics of Corporate Governance,*1 (2017), pp. 541–636.

FIGURE 14.5

Average percentage of equity owned by largest shareholders. (Shareholders from one family are grouped together).

Source: G. Aminadav and E. Papaioannou, "Corporate Control around the World," National Bureau of Economic Research, Working Paper 23010, December 2016 http://www.nber.org/papers/w23010.

a third of the directors are reelected annually. Proponents of such staggered boards argue that they help to insulate management from short-term pressure and allow the company to innovate and take risks. Shareholder activists, on the other hand, complain that staggered elections serve to entrench management since dissident shareholders must wait two years before they can gain majority representation on the board. Consequently, in recent years activists have successfully pressured many companies into declassifying their boards.

On many issues, a simple majority of shareholder votes cast is sufficient to carry the day, but the company charter may specify some decisions that require a *supermajority* of, say, 75% of those eligible to vote. For example, a supermajority vote is sometimes needed to approve a merger or a change to the charter. Such provisions have also attracted shareholder complaints that they help to entrench management and prevent worthwhile takeovers.

The issues on which stockholders are asked to vote are rarely contested, particularly in the case of large, publicly traded firms. Occasionally, there are *proxy contests* in which the firm's existing management and directors compete with outsiders for effective control of the corporation. The odds in a proxy fight are stacked against the outsiders, for the insiders can get the firm to pay all the costs of presenting their case and obtaining votes.[9] But there are a growing number of activist investors who campaign for changes in management policy. If they can gather sufficient shareholder support, the corporation may get the message without incurring a proxy battle. For example, when activist investor Dan Loeb acquired a $3.5 billion stake in Nestlé, the company moved to adopt most of his reforms.

Dual-Class Shares and Private Benefits

Usually, companies have one class of common stock and each share has one vote. Occasionally, however, a firm may have two classes of stock outstanding, which differ in their right to vote. For example, when Facebook made its first issue of common stock, the founders were reluctant to give up control of the company. Therefore, the company created two classes of shares. The A shares, which were sold to the public, had 1 vote each, while the B shares, which were owned by the founders, had 10 votes each. Both classes of shares had the same cash-flow rights, but they had different control rights.

BEYOND THE PAGE

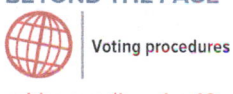   Voting procedures

mhhe.com/brealey13e

BEYOND THE PAGE

Facebook's proposed share issue

mhhe.com/brealey13e

---

[9] In 2010 the SEC proposed Rule 14a-11 that would allow shareholders to add their nominations to the company's proxy material. This was successfully challenged in the courts. However, an SEC rule that allows shareholders to add proposals to change the bylaws was not overturned.

BEYOND THE PAGE

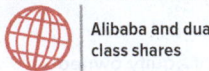

Alibaba and dual-class shares

mhhe.com/brealey13e

When two classes of stock coexist, shareholders with the extra voting power may sometimes use it to toss out bad management or to force management to adopt policies that enhance shareholder value. But as long as both classes of shares have identical cash-flow rights, all shareholders benefit equally from such changes. So here is the question: If everyone gains equally from better management, why do shares with superior voting power typically sell at a premium? The only plausible reason is that there are *private benefits* captured by the owners of these shares. For example, the holder of a block of voting shares might prevent any challenge to his or her management position. The shares might have extra bargaining power in an acquisition. Or they might be held by another company, which could use its voting power and influence to secure a business advantage.

These private benefits of control seem to be much larger in some countries than others. For example, Tatiana Nenova has looked at a number of countries in which firms may have two classes of stock.[10] In the United States, the premium that an investor needed to pay to gain voting control amounted to only 2% of firm value, but in Italy it was over 29% and in Mexico it was 36%. It appears that in these two countries, majority investors are able to secure large private benefits.

BEYOND THE PAGE

The value of voting rights

mhhe.com/brealey13e

Even when only one class of shares exists, minority stockholders may be at a disadvantage; the company's cash flow and potential value may be diverted to management or to one or a few dominant stockholders holding large blocks of shares. In the United States, the law protects minority stockholders from exploitation, but minority stockholders in some countries may not fare so well.[11]

Financial economists sometimes refer to the exploitation of minority shareholders as *tunneling;* the majority shareholder tunnels into the firm and acquires control of the assets for himself. Let us look at tunneling Russian-style.

EXAMPLE 14.1 • Raiding the Minority Shareholders

To grasp how the scam works, you first need to understand *reverse stock splits*. These are often used by companies with a large number of low-priced shares. The company making the reverse split simply combines its existing shares into a smaller, more convenient number of new shares. For example, the shareholders might be given two new shares in place of the three shares that they currently own. As long as all shareholdings are reduced by the same proportion, nobody gains or loses by such a move.

However, the majority shareholder of one Russian company realized that the reverse stock split could be used to loot the company's assets. He therefore proposed that existing shareholders receive 1 new share in place of every 136,000 shares they currently held.[12]

Why did the majority shareholder pick the number "136,000"? Answer: Because the two minority shareholders owned less than 136,000 shares and therefore did not have the right to *any* shares. Instead, they were simply paid off with the par value of their shares, and the majority shareholder was left owning the entire company. The majority shareholders of several other companies were so impressed with this device that they also proposed similar reverse stock splits to squeeze out their minority shareholders.

Such blatant exploitation would not be permitted in the United States or in many other countries.

• • • •

---

[10]T. Nenova, "The Value of Corporate Voting Rights and Control: A Cross-Country Analysis," *Journal of Financial Economics* 68 (June 2003) pp. 325–351.

[11]International differences in the opportunities for dominant shareholders to exploit their position are discussed in S. Johnson et al., "Tunnelling," *American Economic Review* 90 (May 2000), pp. 22–27.

[12]Since a reverse stock split required only the approval of a simple majority of the shareholders, the proposal was voted through.

Equity in Disguise

Common stocks are issued by corporations, but a few equity securities are issued not by corporations but by partnerships or trusts. We will give some brief examples.

Partnerships Plains All American Pipeline LP is a *master limited partnership* that owns crude oil pipelines in the United States and Canada. You can buy "units" in this partnership on the New York Stock Exchange, thus becoming a *limited partner* in Plains All American. The most the limited partners can lose is their investment in the company.[13] In this and most other respects, the partnership units are just like the shares in an ordinary corporation. They share in the profits of the business and receive cash distributions (like dividends) from time to time.

Partnerships avoid corporate income tax; any profits or losses are passed straight through to the partners' tax returns. But various limitations offset this tax advantage. For example, the law regards a partnership merely as a voluntary association of individuals; like its partners, it is expected to have a limited life. A corporation, on the other hand, is an independent legal "person" that can, and often does, outlive all its original shareholders.

Trusts and REITs Would you like to own a part of the oil in the Prudhoe Bay field on the north slope of Alaska? Just call your broker and buy a few units of the BP Prudhoe Bay Royalty Trust. BP set up this trust and gave it a royalty interest in production from BP's share of the Prudhoe Bay revenues. As the oil is produced, each trust unit gets its share of the revenues.

This trust is the passive owner of a single asset: the right to a share of the revenues from BP's Prudhoe Bay production. Operating businesses, which cannot be passive, are rarely organized as trusts, though there are exceptions, notably *real estate investment trusts,* or *REITs* (pronounced "reets").

REITs were created to facilitate public investment in commercial real estate; there are shopping center REITs, office building REITs, apartment REITs, and REITs that specialize in lending to real estate developers. REIT "shares" are traded just like common stocks. The REITs themselves are not taxed, so long as they distribute at least 95% of earnings to the REITs' owners, who must pay whatever taxes are due on the dividends. However, REITs are tightly restricted to real estate investment. You cannot set up a widget factory and avoid corporate taxes by calling it a REIT.

Preferred Stock

Usually, when investors talk about "stock" or "equity," they are referring to common stock. But some companies also issue **preferred stock,** and this too forms part of its equity. Despite its name, preferred stock provides only a small part of most companies' cash needs, and it will occupy less time in later chapters. However, it can be a useful method of financing in mergers and certain other special situations.

Like debt, preferred stock offers a series of fixed payments to the investor. The company can choose *not* to pay a preferred dividend, but in that case it may not pay a dividend to its common stockholders. Most issues of preferred are known as *cumulative preferred stock.* This means that the firm must pay *all* past preferred dividends before common stockholders get a cent. If the company does miss a preferred dividend, the preferred stockholders generally gain some voting rights, so that the common stockholders are obliged to share control of the company with the preferred holders. Directors are also aware that failure to pay the preferred dividend earns the company a black mark with investors, so they do not take such a decision lightly.

---

[13]A partnership can offer limited liability *only* to its limited partners. The partnership must also have one or more general partners, who have unlimited liability. However, general partners can be corporations. This puts the corporation's shield of limited liability between the partnership and the human beings who ultimately own the general partner.

14-3   Debt

When companies borrow money, they promise to make regular interest payments and to repay the principal. However, this liability is limited. Stockholders have the right to default on the debt if they are willing to hand over the corporation's assets to the lenders. Clearly, they will choose to do this only if the value of the assets is less than the amount of the debt.[14]

Debt has first claim on cash flows, but its claim is limited. Therefore, in contrast to equity, it does not have residual cash-flow rights and does not participate in the upsides of the business. Also, unlike equity, debt offers no control rights unless the firm defaults or violates debt covenants. Because lenders are not considered to be owners of the firm, they do not normally have any voting power.

The company's payments of interest are regarded as a cost and are deducted from taxable income. Thus interest is paid from *before-tax* income, whereas dividends on common and preferred stock are paid from *after-tax* income. Therefore, the government provides a tax subsidy for debt that it does not provide for equity (and from time to time complains that companies borrow too much). We discuss debt and taxes in detail in Chapter 18.

We have seen that financial intermediaries own the majority of corporate equity. Figure 14.6 shows that this is also true of the company's bonds. In this case, it is the insurance companies that own the largest stake.[15]

Debt Comes in Many Forms

The financial manager is faced with an almost bewildering choice of debt securities. In Chapter 24, we look in some detail at the different types of corporate debt. For the moment, simply notice that the mixture of debt securities that each company issues reflects the financial manager's response to a number of questions:

1. *Should the company borrow short-term or long-term?* If your company simply needs to finance a temporary increase in inventories ahead of the holiday season, then it may

FIGURE 14.6

Holdings of bonds issued in the United States by U.S. and foreign corporations, December 2017

Source: Board of Governors of the Federal Reserve System, Division of Research and Statistics, *Financial Accounts of the United States—Z1,* Table L.213, at https://www.federalreserve.gov/releases/z1/current/default.htm.

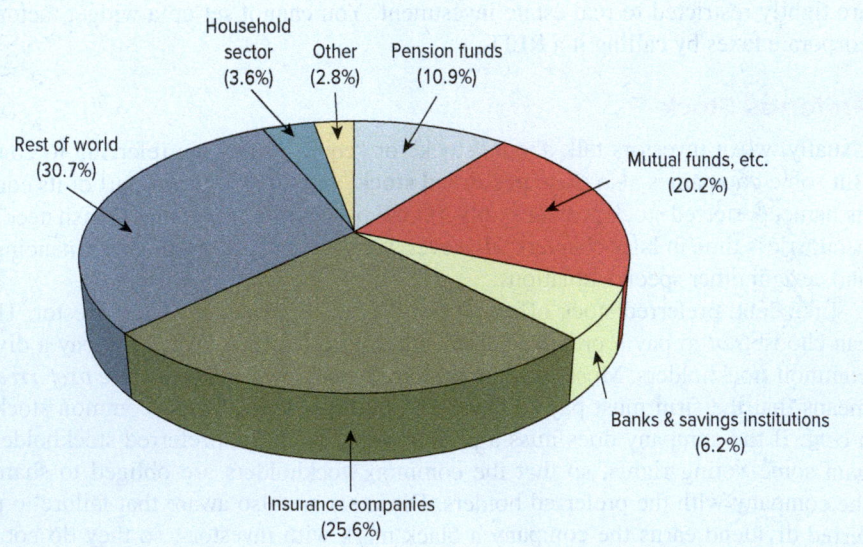

---

[14]In practice, this handover of assets is far from straightforward. Sometimes thousands of lenders have different claims on the firm. Administration of the handover is usually left to the bankruptcy court (see Chapter 32).

[15]Figure 14.6 does not include shorter-term debt such as bank loans. Almost all short-term debt issued by corporations is held by financial intermediaries.

make sense to take out a short-term bank loan. But suppose that the cash is needed to pay for expansion of an oil refinery. Refinery facilities can operate more or less continuously for 15 or 20 years. In that case, it would be more appropriate to issue a long-term bond.[16]

Some loans are repaid in a steady, regular way; in other cases, the entire loan is repaid at maturity. Occasionally the borrower has the option to terminate the loan early.

2. *Should the debt be fixed or floating rate?* The interest payment, or coupon, on long-term bonds is commonly fixed at the time of issue. If a $1,000 bond is issued when long-term interest rates are 10%, the firm continues to pay $100 per year regardless of how interest rates fluctuate.

    Most bank loans and some bonds offer a variable, or *floating,* rate. For example, the interest rate in each period may be set at 1% above LIBOR (London Interbank Offered Rate), which is the interest rate at which major international banks lend dollars to each other. When LIBOR changes, the interest rate on the loan also changes.

3. *Should you borrow dollars or some other currency?* Many firms in the United States borrow abroad. Often they may borrow dollars abroad (foreign investors have large holdings of dollars), but firms with overseas operations may decide to issue debt in a foreign currency. After all, if you need to spend foreign currency, it probably makes sense to borrow foreign currency.

    International bonds have usually been marketed by the London branches of international banks, and have traditionally been known as **eurobonds.** A eurobond may be denominated in dollars, yen, or any other currency. Unfortunately, when the single European currency was established, it was called the *euro.* It is, therefore, easy to confuse a *eurobond* (a bond that is sold internationally) with a bond that is denominated in euros.

4. *What promises should you make to the lender?* Lenders want to make sure that their debt is as safe as possible. Therefore, they may demand that their debt is *senior* to other debt. If default occurs, senior debt is first in line to be repaid. The *junior,* or *subordinated,* debtholders are paid only after all senior debtholders are satisfied (though all debtholders rank ahead of the preferred and common stockholders).

    The firm may also set aside some of its assets specifically for the protection of particular creditors. Such debt is said to be *secured,* and the assets that are set aside are known as *collateral.* Thus, a retailer might offer inventory or accounts receivable as collateral for a bank loan. If the retailer defaults on the loan, the bank can seize the collateral and use it to help pay off the debt.

    Usually, the firm also provides assurances to the lender that it will not take unreasonable risks. For example, a firm that borrows in moderation is less likely to get into difficulties than one that is up to its gunwales in debt. So the borrower may agree to limit the amount of extra debt that it can issue. Lenders are also concerned that, if trouble occurs, others will push ahead of them in the queue. Therefore, the firm may agree not to create new debt that is senior to existing debtholders or to put aside assets for other lenders.

5. *Should you issue straight or convertible bonds?* Companies often issue securities that give the owner an option to convert them into other securities. These options may have

---

[16]A company might choose to finance a long-term project with short-term debt if it wished to signal its confidence in the future. Investors would deduce that, if the company anticipated declining profits, it would not take the risk of being unable to take out a fresh loan when the first one matured. See D. Diamond, "Debt Maturity Structure and Liquidity Risk," *Quarterly Journal of Economics* 106 (1991), pp. 709–737.

a substantial effect on value. The most dramatic example is provided by a **warrant,** which is *nothing but* an option. The owner of a warrant can purchase a set number of the company's shares at a set price before a set date. Warrants and bonds are often sold together as a package.

A **convertible bond** gives its owner the option to exchange the bond for a predetermined number of shares. The convertible bondholder hopes that the issuing company's share price will zoom up so that the bond can be converted at a big profit. But if the shares zoom down, there is no obligation to convert; the bondholder remains a bondholder.

A Debt by Any Other Name

The word *debt* sounds straightforward, but companies make a number of promises that look suspiciously like debt but are treated differently in the accounts. Some of these disguised debts are easily spotted. For example, accounts payable are simply obligations to pay for goods that have already been delivered and are, therefore, like short-term debt.

Other arrangements are less obvious. For example, instead of borrowing to buy new equipment, the company may rent or **lease** it on a long-term basis. In this case, the firm promises to make a series of lease payments to the owner of the equipment. This is just like the obligation to make payments on an outstanding loan. If the firm gets into deep water, it can't choose to miss out on its debt interest, and it can't choose to skip those lease payments.

Here is another example of a disguised debt. When American Airlines filed for bankruptcy in 2011, it had promised its employees pensions valued at $18.5 billion. This obligation was, in effect, a senior debt because American was obligated to make payments to retired employees. Unfortunately, American had set aside only $8.3 billion to meet this obligation.

Pension obligations should be valued by discounting future payments at a debt interest rate. When interest rates change, the present value of pension obligations changes, too. For example, in May 2015, the German airline Lufthansa announced that the present value of its pension obligations increased from €7.2 billion to €10.2 billion in the first quarter of 2015, largely because of a decrease from 2.6% to 1.7% in the interest rate used for discounting.

There is nothing underhanded about lease or pension obligations. They are explained in the notes to a corporation's financial statements when they do not appear explicitly on its balance sheet. Investors recognize the debt-equivalent obligations and the financial risks that they create.[17]

But now and then, a company works hard to ensure that investors do *not* know how much the company has borrowed. For example, Enron was able to borrow $658 million by setting up *special-purpose entities (SPEs),* which raised cash by a mixture of equity and debt and then used these debts to help fund the parent company. None of this debt showed up on Enron's balance sheet, but the debt showed up with a vengeance in Enron's death spiral toward bankruptcy in 2001.

Variety's the Very Spice of Life

We have indicated several dimensions along which corporate securities can be classified. That gives the financial manager plenty of choice in designing securities. As long as you can convince investors of its attractions, you can issue a convertible, subordinated, floating-rate bond denominated in Swedish kronor. Rather than combining features of existing securities, you may create an entirely new one. We can imagine a coal mining company issuing convertible bonds on which the payment fluctuates with coal prices. We know of no such security, but it is perfectly legal to issue it—and who knows?—it might generate considerable interest among investors.

---

[17]For example, see L. Jin, R.C. Merton, and Z. Brodie, "Do a Firm's Equity Returns Reflect the Risk of its Pension Plan?" *Journal of Financial Economics* 81 (2006), pp. 1–26.

That completes our tour of corporate securities. You may feel like the tourist who has just seen 12 cathedrals in five days. But there will be plenty of time in later chapters for reflection and analysis. It is now time to move on and to look at the markets in which the firm's securities are traded and at the financial intermediaries that hold them.

14-4   Financial Markets and Intermediaries

The flow of savings to large public corporations is shown in Figure 14.7. Notice that the savings travel from investors worldwide through financial markets, financial intermediaries, or both. Suppose, for example, that Bank of America raises $300 million by a new issue of shares. An Italian investor buys 6,000 of the new shares for $10 per share. Now Bank of America takes that $60,000, along with money raised by the rest of the issue, and makes a $300 million loan to ExxonMobil. The Italian investor's savings end up flowing through financial markets (the stock market), to a financial intermediary (Bank of America), and finally to Exxon.

Of course, our Italian friend's $60,000 doesn't literally arrive at Exxon in an envelope marked "From L. DaVinci." Investments by the purchasers of the Bank of America's stock issue are pooled, not segregated. Sr. DaVinci would own a share of all of Bank of America's assets, not just one loan to Exxon. Nevertheless, investors' savings are flowing through the financial markets and then the bank to finance Exxon's capital investments.

Suppose that another investor decides to open a checking account with Bank of America. The bank can take the money in this checking account and also lend it on to ExxonMobil. In this case, the savings bypass the financial markets and flow directly to a financial intermediary and from there to Exxon.

We now need to flesh out Figure 14.7 by looking at the main financial markets and intermediaries.

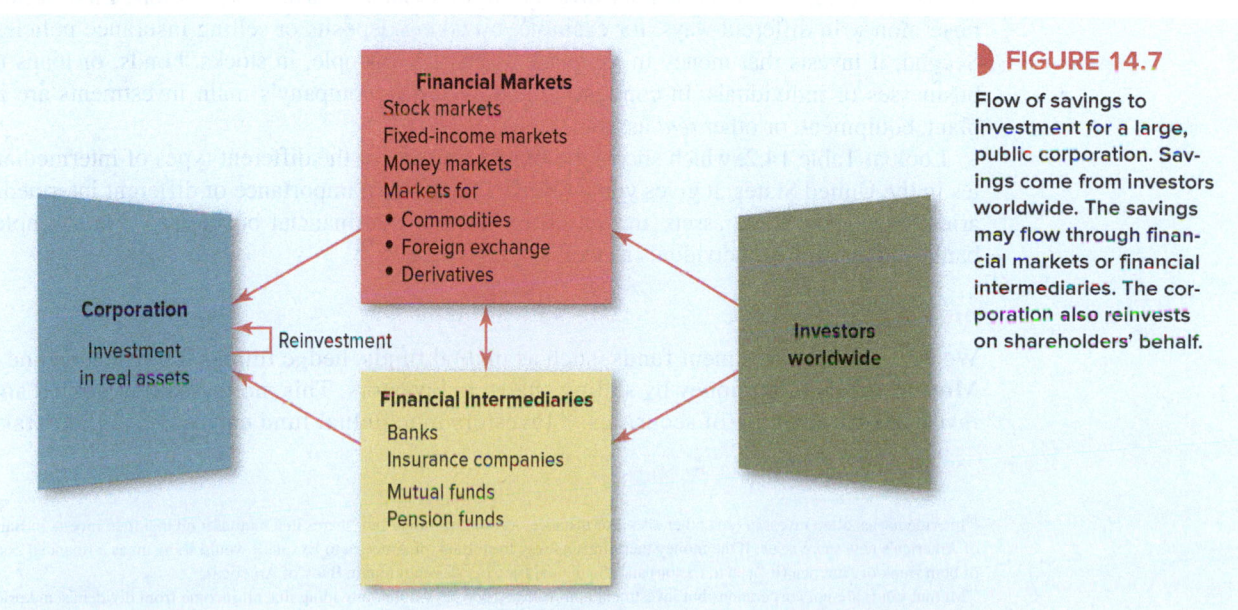

▶ **FIGURE 14.7**

Flow of savings to investment for a large, public corporation. Savings come from investors worldwide. The savings may flow through financial markets or financial intermediaries. The corporation also reinvests on shareholders' behalf.

Financial Markets

A **financial market** is a market where financial assets are issued and traded. In our example, Bank of America used the financial markets to raise money from investors by a new issue of shares. Such issues are known as *primary issues.* But in addition to helping companies to raise cash, financial markets also allow investors to trade stocks or bonds among themselves. For example, Mr. Rosencrantz might decide to raise some cash by selling his Bank of America stock at the same time that Mr. Guildenstern invests his savings in the stock. So they make a trade. The result is simply a transfer of ownership from one person to another, which has no effect on the company's cash, assets, or operations. Such purchases and sales are known as *secondary transactions.*

Some financial assets have less active secondary markets than others. For example, when a bank lends money to a company, it acquires a financial asset (the company's promise to repay the loan with interest). Banks do sometimes sell packages of these loans to other banks, but generally they retain the loan until it is repaid by the borrower. Other financial assets are regularly traded. Some, such as shares of stock, are traded on organized exchanges like the New York, London, or Hong Kong stock exchanges. In other cases, there is no organized exchange, and the assets are traded by a network of dealers. Such markets are known as *over-the-counter (OTC)* markets. For example, in the United States, most government and corporate bonds are traded OTC.

Some financial markets are not used to raise cash but, instead, help firms to manage their risks. In these markets firms can buy or sell derivatives, whose payoffs depend on the prices of other securities or commodities. For example, if a chocolate producer is worried about rising cocoa prices, it can use the derivatives markets to fix the price at which it buys its future cocoa requirements.

BEYOND THE PAGE

Stock exchanges: From clubs to commercial companies

mhhe.com/brealey13e

Financial Intermediaries

A **financial intermediary** is an organization that raises money from investors and provides financing for individuals, companies, and other organizations. Banks, insurance companies, and investment funds are all intermediaries. These intermediaries are important sources of financing for corporations. They are a stop on the road between savings and real investment.

Why is a financial intermediary different from a manufacturing corporation? First, it may raise money in different ways, for example, by taking deposits or selling insurance policies. Second, it invests that money in *financial* assets, for example, in stocks, bonds, or loans to businesses or individuals. In contrast, a manufacturing company's main investments are in plant, equipment, or other *real* assets.

Look at Table 14.2, which shows the financial assets of the different types of intermediaries in the United States. It gives you an idea of the relative importance of different intermediaries. Of course, these assets are not all invested in nonfinancial businesses. For example, banks make loans to individuals as well as to businesses.[18]

Investment Funds

We look first at investment funds, such as mutual funds, hedge funds, and pension funds. **Mutual funds** raise money by selling shares to investors. This money is then pooled and invested in a portfolio of securities.[19] Investors in a mutual fund can increase their stake

---

[18]Intermediaries often invest in each other also. For instance, an investor might buy shares in a mutual fund that then invests in Bank of America's new share issue. If the money then finds its way from Bank of America to Exxon, it would show up as a financial asset of both Bank of America (its loan to Exxon) and the mutual fund (its shareholding in Bank of America).

[19]Mutual funds are not corporations but investment companies. They pay no tax, providing that all income from dividends and price appreciation is passed on to the funds' shareholders. The shareholders pay personal tax on this income.

	$ Billions
Mutual funds	$15,899
Money market funds	2,847
Closed-end funds	275.2
ETFs	3,401
Hedge funds[a]	3,541
Pension funds	19,845
Banks and savings institutions	18,925
Insurance companies	9,340

❭**TABLE 14.2**   **Financial assets of intermediaries in the United States, December 2017**

[a] estimated

Sources: Board of Governors of the Federal Reserve System, Division of Research and Statistics, *Financial Accounts of the United States— Z1,* www.federalreserve.gov; and Preqin, https://www.preqin.com/.

in the fund's portfolio by buying additional shares, or they can sell their shares back to the fund if they wish to cash out. The purchase and sale prices depend on the fund's net asset value (NAV) on the day of purchase or redemption. If there is a net flow of cash into the fund, the manager will use it to buy more stocks or bonds; if there is a net outflow, the fund manager will need to raise the money by selling some of the fund's investments.

There are just over 8,000 equity and bond mutual funds in the United States. In fact, there are more mutual funds than public companies! The funds pursue a wide variety of investment strategies. Some funds specialize in safe stocks with generous dividend payouts. Some specialize in high-tech growth stocks. Some "balanced" funds offer mixtures of stocks and bonds. Some specialize in particular countries or regions. For example, the Fidelity Investments mutual fund group sponsors funds for Canada, Japan, China, Europe, and Latin America.

Mutual funds offer investors low-cost diversification and professional management. For most investors, it's more efficient to buy a mutual fund than to assemble a diversified portfolio of stocks and bonds. Most mutual fund managers also try their best to "beat the market"—that is, to generate superior performance by finding the stocks with better-than-average returns. Whether they can pick winners consistently is another question, which we addressed in Chapter 13. In exchange for their services, the fund's managers take out a management fee. There are also the expenses of running the fund. For mutual funds that invest in stocks, fees and expenses typically add up to nearly 1% per year.

Most mutual funds invest in shares or in a mixture of shares and bonds. However, one particular type of mutual fund, called a money market fund, invests only in short-term safe securities, such as Treasury bills or bank certificates of deposit. Money market funds offer individuals and small- and medium-sized businesses a convenient home in which to park their spare cash. There are nearly 400 money market funds in the United States. Some of these funds are huge. For example, the JPMorgan U.S. Government Money Market Fund had $140 billion in assets in 2017.

Mutual funds are *open-end* funds—they stand ready to issue new shares and to buy back existing shares. In contrast, a **closed-end fund** has a fixed number of shares that are traded on an exchange. If you want to invest in a closed-end fund, you cannot buy new shares from the fund; you must buy existing shares from another stockholder in the fund.

If you simply want low-cost diversification, one option is to buy a mutual fund that invests in all the stocks in a stock market index. For example, the Vanguard Index Fund holds all the stocks in the Standard & Poor's Composite Index. An alternative is to invest in an

BEYOND THE PAGE

Mutual fund assets

mhhe.com/brealey13e

BEYOND THE PAGE

Exchange traded funds

mhhe.com/brealey13e

exchange traded fund, or **ETF,** which is a portfolio of stocks that can be bought or sold in a single trade. These include Standard & Poor's Depository Receipts (SPDRs, or "spiders"), which are portfolios matching Standard & Poor's stock market indexes. You can also buy DIAMONDS, which track the Dow Jones Industrial Average; QUBES or QQQs, which track the Nasdaq 100 index; and Vanguard ETFs that track the U.S. Total Stock Market index, which is a basket of almost all of the stocks traded in the United States. You can also buy ETFs that track foreign stock markets, bonds, or commodities.

ETFs are, in some ways, more efficient than mutual funds. To buy or sell an ETF, you simply make a trade, just as if you bought or sold shares of stock. In this respect, ETFs are like closed-end investment funds. But, with rare exceptions, ETFs do not have managers with the discretion to try to "pick winners." ETF portfolios are tied down to indexes or fixed baskets of securities. ETF issuers make sure that the ETF price tracks the price of the underlying index or basket.

Like mutual funds, **hedge funds** also pool the savings of different investors and invest on their behalf. But they differ from mutual funds in at least three ways. First, because hedge funds usually follow complex investment strategies, access is restricted to knowledgeable investors such as pension funds, endowment funds, and wealthy individuals. Don't try to send a check for $3,000 or $5,000 to a hedge fund; most hedge funds are not in the "retail" investment business. Second, hedge funds are generally established as limited partnerships. The investment manager is the general partner and the investors are the limited partners. Third, hedge funds try to attract the most talented managers by compensating them with potentially lucrative, performance-related fees.[20] In contrast, mutual funds usually charge a fixed percentage of assets under management.

Hedge funds follow many different investment strategies. Some try to make a profit by identifying *overvalued* stocks or markets that they then sell short. Some hedge funds take bets on firms involved in merger negotiations, others look for mispricing of convertible bonds, and some take positions in currencies and interest rates. "Vulture funds" specialize in the securities of distressed corporations. Hedge funds manage less money than mutual funds, but they sometimes take very big positions and have a large impact on the market.

There are other ways to pool and invest savings. Consider a pension plan set up by a corporation or other organization on behalf of its employees. The most common type of plan is the *defined-contribution* plan. In this case, a percentage of the employee's monthly paycheck is contributed to a **pension fund.** (The employer and employee may each contribute 5%, for example.) Contributions from all participating employees are pooled and invested in securities or mutual funds. (Usually, the employees can choose from a menu of funds with different investment strategies.) Each employee's balance in the plan grows over the years as contributions continue and investment income accumulates. The balance in the plan can be used to finance living expenses after retirement. The amount available for retirement depends on the accumulated contributions and on the rate of return earned on the investments.[21]

Pension funds are designed for long-run investment. They provide professional management and diversification. They also have an important tax advantage: Contributions are tax-deductible, and investment returns inside the plan are not taxed until cash is finally withdrawn.[22]

---

[20]Sometimes these fees can be very large indeed. For example, *Forbes* estimated that hedge fund manager James Simons earned $1.6 billion in 2016.

[21]In a *defined-benefit* plan, the employer promises a certain level of retirement benefits (set by a formula), and the *employer* invests in the pension plan. The plan's accumulated investment value has to be large enough to cover the promised benefits. If not, the employer must put in more money. Defined-benefit plans are gradually giving way to defined-contribution plans.

[22]Defined-benefit pension plans share these same advantages, except that the employer invests rather than the employees. In a defined-benefit plan, the advantage of tax deferral on investment income accrues to the employer. This deferral reduces the cost of funding the plan.

All these investment funds provide a stop on the road from savings to corporate investment. For example, suppose your mutual fund purchases part of that new issue of shares by Bank of America. The orange arrows show the flow of savings to investment:

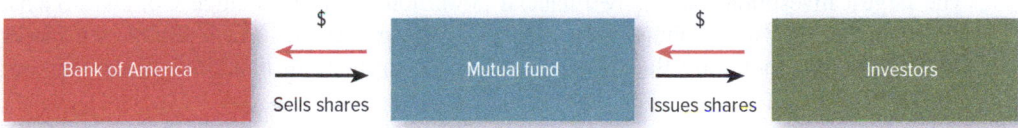

Financial Institutions

Banks and insurance companies are *financial institutions*.[23] A financial institution is an intermediary that does more than just pool and invest savings. Institutions raise financing in special ways, for example, by accepting deposits or selling insurance policies, and they provide additional financial services. Unlike most investment funds, they not only invest in securities but also lend money directly to individuals, businesses, or other organizations.

Commercial Banks   There are just under 5,000 commercial banks in the United States. They vary from giants such as JPMorgan Chase with $2.6 trillion of assets to dwarves like the Emigrant Mercantile Bank with under $4 million.

Commercial banks are major sources of loans for corporations. (In the United States, they are generally not allowed to make equity investments in corporations, although banks in most other countries can do so.) Suppose that a local forest products company negotiates a nine-month bank loan for $2.5 million. The flow of savings is

BEYOND THE PAGE

 World bank rankings

mhhe.com/brealey13e

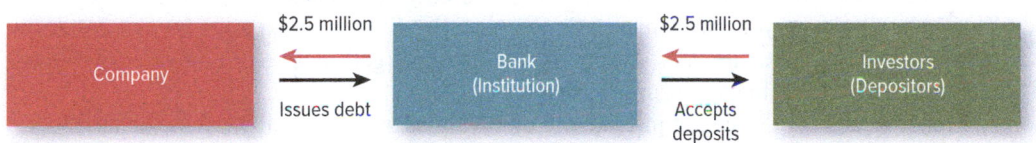

The bank provides debt financing for the company and, at the same time, provides a place for depositors to park their money safely and withdraw it as needed.

We will have plenty more to say about bank loans in Chapter 24.

Investment Banks   We have discussed commercial banks, which raise money from depositors and other investors and then make loans to businesses and individuals. *Investment banks* are different.[24] Investment banks do not take deposits, and they do not usually make loans to companies. Instead, they advise and assist companies in raising financing. For example, investment banks *underwrite* stock offerings by purchasing the new shares from the issuing company at a negotiated price and reselling the shares to investors. Thus, the issuing company gets a fixed price for the new shares, and the investment bank takes responsibility for distributing the shares to thousands of investors. We discuss share issues in more detail in Chapter 15.

Investment banks also advise on takeovers, mergers, and acquisitions. They offer investment advice and manage investment portfolios for individual and institutional investors. They run trading desks for foreign exchange, commodities, bonds, options, and derivatives.

---

[23]We may be drawing too fine a distinction between financial intermediaries and institutions. A mutual fund could be considered a financial institution. But "financial institution" usually suggests a more complicated intermediary, such as a bank.

[24]Banks that accept deposits and provide financing to businesses are called *commercial* banks. *Savings banks* accept deposits and savings accounts and loan the money out mostly to individuals, for example, as mortgage loans to home buyers. Investment banks do not take deposits and do not loan money to businesses or individuals, except as *bridge loans* made as temporary financing for takeovers or other transactions.

Investment banks can invest their own money in start-ups and other ventures. For example, the Australian Macquarie Bank has invested in airports, toll highways, electric transmission and generation, and other infrastructure projects around the world.

The largest investment banks are financial powerhouses. They include Goldman Sachs, Morgan Stanley, Lazard, Nomura (Japan), and Macquarie Bank.[25] In addition, the major commercial banks, including Bank of America and Citigroup, all have investment banking operations.[26]

Insurance Companies   Insurance companies are more important than banks for the *long-term* financing of business. They are massive investors in corporate stocks and bonds, and they often make long-term loans directly to corporations.

Suppose a company needs a loan of $2.5 million for nine years, not nine months. It could issue a bond directly to investors, or it could negotiate a nine-year loan with an insurance company:

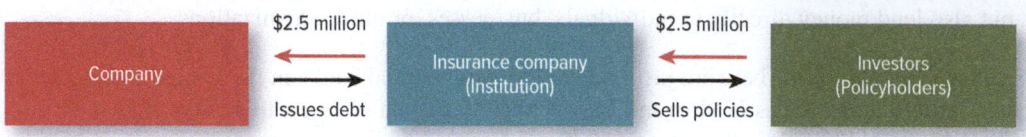

The money to make the loan comes mainly from the sale of insurance policies. Say you buy a fire insurance policy on your home. You pay cash to the insurance company and get a financial asset (the policy) in exchange. You receive no interest payments on this financial asset, but if a fire does strike, the company is obliged to cover the damages up to the policy limit. This is the return on your investment. (Of course, a fire is a sad and dangerous event that you hope to avoid. But if a fire does occur, you are better off getting a return on your investment in insurance than not having insurance at all.)

The company will issue not just one policy but thousands. Normally the incidence of fires "averages out," leaving the company with a predictable obligation to its policyholders as a group. Of course the insurance company must charge enough for its policies to cover selling and administrative costs, pay policyholders' claims, and generate a profit for its stockholders.

14-5   The Role of Financial Markets and Intermediaries

Financial markets and intermediaries provide financing for business. They channel savings to real investment. That much should be loud and clear. But other functions may not be quite so obvious. Financial intermediaries contribute in many ways to our individual well-being and the smooth functioning of the economy. Here are some examples.

The Payment Mechanism

Think how inconvenient life would be if all payments had to be made in cash. Fortunately, checking accounts, credit cards, and electronic transfers allow individuals and firms to send and receive payments quickly and safely over long distances. Banks are the obvious providers of payments services, but they are not alone. For example, if you buy shares in a money

---

[25]Strictly speaking, Goldman Sachs and Morgan Stanley are not investment banks. In 2008, they handed in their investment banking charter in exchange for a banking charter that allows them to accept deposits. However, their principal focus is on investment banking activities.

[26]Bank of America owns Merrill Lynch, one of the largest investment banks. Merrill was rescued by Bank of America in 2008 after making huge losses from mortgage-related investments.

market mutual fund, your money is pooled with that of other investors and is used to buy safe, short-term securities. You can then write checks on this mutual fund investment, just as if you had a bank deposit.

Borrowing and Lending

Financial institutions do not lend only to companies. They also channel savings toward those who can best use them. Thus, if Ms. Jones has more money than she needs now and wishes to save for a rainy day, she can put the money in a bank savings deposit. If Mr. Smith wants to buy a car now and pay for it later, he can borrow money from the bank. In other words, banks provide Jones and Smith with a time machine that allows them to transport their wealth backward and forward over time. Both are happier than if they were forced to spend cash as it arrived.

As we saw in Chapter 1, when individuals have access to borrowing and lending, companies do not have to worry that shareholders may have different time preferences. Companies can simply focus on maximizing firm value and investors can choose separately when they want to spend their wealth.

Notice that banks promise their checking account customers instant access to their money and at the same time make long-term loans to companies and individuals. This mismatch between the liquidity of the bank's liabilities (the deposits) and most of its assets (the loans) is possible only because the number of depositors is sufficiently large that the bank can be fairly sure that they will not all want to withdraw their money simultaneously.

In principle, you don't need financial institutions to provide borrowing and lending. Individuals with cash surpluses, for example, could take out newspaper advertisements to find those with cash shortages. But it can be cheaper and more convenient to use a financial intermediary, such as a bank, to link up the borrower and lender. For example, banks are equipped to check out the would-be borrower's creditworthiness and to monitor the use of cash lent out.[27]

Pooling Risk

Financial markets and institutions allow firms and individuals to pool their risks. For instance, insurance companies make it possible to share the risk of an automobile accident or a household fire. Here is another example. Suppose that you have only a small sum to invest. You could buy the stock of a single company, but then you would be wiped out if that company went belly-up. It is generally better to buy shares in a mutual fund that invests in a diversified portfolio of common stocks or other securities. In this case you are exposed only to the risk that security prices as a whole will fall.

Information Provided by Financial Markets

In well-functioning financial markets, you can *see* what securities and commodities are worth, and you can see—or at least estimate—the rates of return that investors can expect on their savings. The information financial markets provide is often essential to a financial manager's job. Consider these scenarios.

In December, Catalytic Concepts, a manufacturer of catalytic converters, is planning production for the next April. The converters include platinum, which is traded on the New York

---

[27]However, in the past decade a number of *peer-to-peer* lending firms (P2PLs), such as Prosper and Lending Club, have been established. These firms receive applications for loans from individuals or small businesses and then advertise on the Web for interested lenders. Lenders do not know the identity of the borrower, but the peer-to-peer intermediary does provide a credit score and its own credit assessment of the borrower, which is reflected in the interest rate being offered. The P2PL provides a market place that links borrowers and lenders. In addition, it offers credit information, and collects payments from borrowers and forwards them to the lenders. By contrast a bank *owns* its portfolio of loans and offers its depositors instant access to their money.

Mercantile Exchange. How much per ounce should the company budget for purchases of platinum in April? Easy: The company's CFO looks up the market price of platinum on the New York Mercantile Exchange—$1,023 per ounce for delivery in April (this was the price for platinum in August 2017, for delivery the following April). The CFO can lock in that price if she wishes. We explain how in Chapter 26.

Now suppose the CFO of Catalytic Concepts needs to raise $400 million in new financing. She considers an issue of 30-year bonds. If the company's bonds are rated Baa, what interest rate will it have to pay on the new issue? The CFO sees that existing Baa bonds yield 4.40%. The company should be able to sell its new bonds at a similar rate.

Finally, stock prices and company values summarize investors' collective assessment of how well a company is doing, both its current performance and its future prospects. Thus an increase in stock price sends a positive signal from investors to managers.[28] That is why top management's compensation is linked to stock prices. A manager who owns shares in his or her company will be motivated to increase the company's market value. This reduces agency costs by aligning the interests of managers and stockholders. This is one important advantage of going public. A private company can't use its stock price as a measure of performance. It can still compensate managers with shares, but the shares will not be valued in a financial market.

The basic functions of financial markets are the same the world over. So it is not surprising that similar institutions have emerged to perform these functions. In almost every country you will find banks accepting deposits, making loans, and looking after the payments system. You will also encounter insurance companies offering life insurance and protection against accident. If the country is relatively prosperous, other institutions, such as pension funds and mutual funds, will also have been established to help manage people's savings. Of course there are differences in institutional structure. Take banks, for example. In many countries where securities markets are relatively undeveloped, banks play a much more dominant role in financing industry. Often the banks undertake a wider range of activities than they do in the United States. For example, they may take large equity stakes in industrial companies; this would not generally be allowed in the United States.

The Financial Crisis of 2007–2009

BEYOND THE PAGE

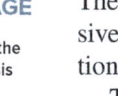

Time line of the financial crisis

mhhe.com/brealey13e

The financial crisis of 2007–2009 raised many questions, but it settled one question conclusively: Financial markets and institutions are important. When financial markets and institutions ceased to operate properly, the world was pushed deeper into a global recession.

The financial crisis had its roots in the easy-money policies that were pursued by the U.S. Federal Reserve and other central banks following the collapse of the Internet and telecom stock bubble in 2000. At the same time, large balance-of-payments surpluses in Asian economies were invested back into U.S. debt securities. This also helped to push down interest rates and contribute to the lax credit.

Banks took advantage of this cheap money to expand the supply of subprime mortgages to low-income borrowers. Many banks tempted would-be homeowners with low initial payments, offset by significantly higher payments later.[29] (Some home buyers were betting on escalating housing prices so that they could resell or refinance before the higher payments

---

[28]We can't claim that investors' assessments of value are always correct. Finance can be a risky and dangerous business—dangerous for your wealth, that is. With hindsight we see horrible mistakes by investors—for example, the gross overvaluation of Internet and telecom companies in 2000. On average, however, it appears that financial markets collect and assess information quickly and accurately.

[29]With a so-called option ARM loan, the minimum mortgage payment was often not even sufficient to cover that month's interest on the loan. The unpaid interest was then added to the amount of the mortgage, so the homeowner was burdened by an ever-increasing mortgage that one day would need to be paid off.

kicked in.) One lender is even said to have advertised what it dubbed its "NINJA" loan—NINJA standing for "No Income, No Job, and No Assets."

Most subprime mortgages were then packaged together into mortgage-backed securities that could be resold. But, instead of selling these securities to investors who could best bear the risk, many banks kept large quantities of the loans on their own books or sold them to other banks.

The widespread availability of mortgage finance fueled a dramatic increase in house prices, which doubled in the five years ending June 2006. At that point, prices started to slide and homeowners began to default on their mortgages. A year later, Bear Stearns, a large investment bank, announced huge losses on the mortgage investments that were held in two of its hedge funds. By the spring of 2008, Bear Stearns was on the verge of bankruptcy, and the U.S. Federal Reserve arranged for it to be acquired by JPMorgan Chase.

The crisis peaked in September 2008, when the U.S. government was obliged to take over the giant federal mortgage agencies Fannie Mae and Freddie Mac, both of which had invested several hundred billion dollars in subprime mortgage-backed securities. Over the next few days, the financial system started to melt down. Both Merrill Lynch and Lehman Brothers were in danger of failing. On September 14, the government arranged for Bank of America to take over Merrill in return for financial guarantees. However, it did nothing to rescue Lehman Brothers, which filed for bankruptcy protection the next day. Two days later, the government reluctantly lent $85 billion to the giant insurance company AIG, which had insured huge volumes of mortgage-backed securities and other bonds against default. The following day, the Treasury unveiled its first proposal to spend $700 billion to purchase "toxic" mortgage-backed securities.

As the crisis unfolded throughout 2007 and 2008, uncertainty about which domino would be next to fall made banks reluctant to lend to one another, and the interest rate that they charged for such loans rose to 4.6% above the rate on U.S. Treasury debt. (Normally, this spread above Treasuries is less than .5%.) The bond market and the market for short-term company borrowing effectively dried up. This had an immediate knock-on effect on the supply of credit to industry, and the economy suffered one of its worst setbacks since the Great Depression.

Few developed economies escaped the crisis. As well as suffering from a collapse in their own housing markets, many foreign banks had made large investments in U.S. subprime mortgages. A roll call of all the banks that had to be bailed out by their governments would fill several pages, but here are just a few members of that unhappy band: the Royal Bank of Scotland in the United Kingdom, UBS in Switzerland, Allied Irish Bank in Ireland, Fortis in Belgium, ING in Holland, Hypo Group in Austria, and WestLb in Germany.

Who was responsible for the financial crisis? In part, the U.S. Federal Reserve for its policy of easy money. The U.S. government also must take some of the blame for encouraging banks to expand credit for low-income housing.[30] The rating agencies were at fault for providing triple-A ratings for many mortgage bonds that shortly afterward went into default. Last but not least, the bankers themselves were guilty of promoting and reselling the subprime mortgages.

The banking crisis and subsequent recession left many governments with huge mountains of debt. By 2010, investors were becoming increasingly concerned about the position of Greece, where for many years government spending had been running well ahead of revenues. Greece's position was complicated by its membership in the single-currency euro club. Although much of the country's borrowing was in euros, the government had no control over

BEYOND THE PAGE

U.S. house prices

mhhe.com/brealey13e

BEYOND THE PAGE

The rise and fall of Lehman Brothers

mhhe.com/brealey13e

---

[30]A rapid expansion of low-income home ownership is generally popular in government circles, and it chimed well with the aspirations set out in President Bush's goals of an "Ownership Society."

its currency and could not simply print more euros to service its debt. Investors began to contemplate the likelihood of a Greek government default and the country's possible exit from the eurozone. The failure of eurozone governments to deal decisively with the Greek problem prompted investors to worry about the prospects for other heavily indebted eurozone countries, such as Ireland, Portugal, Italy, and Spain. After several rescue attempts, Greece finally defaulted in 2011. But it was not the end of the story, and four years later, after failing to get further assistance, Greece defaulted on a loan from the IMF.

At least with hindsight, we can see that the run-up to the financial crisis saw plenty of examples of foolishness and greed. Nearly a decade after the crisis, bankers remain at the bottom of everyone's popularity list. That position has been reinforced by the revelations that several major banks had been rigging the interest rate and foreign exchange markets. But the lesson of the financial crisis and the subsequent scandals is not that we don't need a financial system; it is that we need it to work honestly and well.

Financial markets in the United States and most developed countries work well most of the time, but just like the little girl in the poem, "when they are good, they are very good indeed, but when they are bad, they are horrid." During the financial crisis, markets were very horrid indeed. Think of some of the problems that you would have faced as a financial manager:

BEYOND THE PAGE

The Dodd-Frank Act

mhhe.com/brealey13e

- Many of the world's largest banks teetered on the edge or had to be rescued so that there were few, or no, safe havens for cash.
- Stock and bond prices bounced around like Tigger on stimulants.
- Periodically, markets for some types of security dried up altogether, making it tough to raise cash.
- In the eurozone, investors could not even be confident that governments would be able to service their bonds or retain the euro as their currency.
- From the peak in 2006, manufacturing profits fell away sharply and the number of business bankruptcies tripled.

It must have seemed to financial managers as if they were being assailed from all sides.

We hope that these years were just a very unfortunate blip and that the world has not become permanently more complex and risky.

SUMMARY

Financial managers are faced with two broad financing decisions:

1. How much internally generated cash flow should be plowed back into the business? How much should be paid out to shareholders by cash dividends or share repurchases?
2. To what extent should the firm use debt rather than equity financing?

The answers to these questions depend on the firm's payout policy and debt policy.

Figure 14.1 summarizes how U.S. corporations raise and spend money. Have another look at it and try to get a feel for the numbers. Notice that internally generated cash is the major source of financing for investment. Borrowing is also significant. Net equity issues have been negative, however—that is, share repurchases have been larger than share issues.

Common stock is the simplest form of finance. The common stockholders own the corporation. They get all of the cash flow and assets that are left over after the firm's debts have been paid. Common stock is, therefore, a residual claim that participates in the upsides and downsides of the business. Debt has first claim on cash flows, but its claim is limited. Debt has no control rights unless the firm defaults or violates debt covenants.

Preferred stock is another form of equity financing. Preferreds promise a fixed dividend, but if the board of directors decides to skip the dividend, holders of the preferred have no recourse. The firm must pay the preferred dividends before it pays any dividends on common stock, however.

Debt is the most important source of external financing. Holders of bonds and other corporate debt are promised interest payments and return of principal. If the company cannot make these payments, the debt investors can sue for payment or force bankruptcy. Bankruptcy usually means that the debtholders take over and either sell the company's assets or continue to operate them under new management.

Note that the tax authorities treat interest payments as a cost, and therefore, the company can deduct interest when calculating its taxable income. Interest is paid from pretax income, whereas dividends and retained earnings come from after-tax income. That is one reason preferred stock is a less important source of financing than debt. Preferred dividends are not tax deductible.

The variety of debt instruments is almost endless. The instruments differ by maturity, interest rate (fixed or floating), currency, seniority, security, and whether the debt can be converted into equity.

The majority of the firm's debt and equity is owned by financial intermediaries—notably banks, insurance companies, pension funds, and mutual funds. They finance much of corporate investment, as well as investment in real estate and other assets. They run the payments mechanism, help individuals diversify and manage their portfolios, and help companies manage risk. The crisis of 2007–2009 and its aftermath dramatized the crucial role that these intermediaries play.

FURTHER READING

A useful article for comparing financial structure in the United States and other major industrial countries is:

R. G. Rajan and L. Zingales, "What Do We Know about Capital Structure? Some Evidence from International Data," *Journal of Finance* 50 (December 1995), pp. 1421–1460.

For a discussion of the allocation of control rights and cash-flow rights between stockholders and debtholders, see:

O. Hart, *Firms, Contracts, and Financial Structure* (Oxford: Oxford University Press, 1995).

Robert Merton gives an excellent overview of the functions of financial institutions in:

R. Merton, "A Functional Perspective of Financial Intermediation," *Financial Management* 24 (Summer 1995), pp. 23–41.

The Winter 2009 issue of the Journal of Financial Perspectives *contains several articles on the crisis of 2007–2009. See also:*

V. V. Acharya and M. W. Richardson, eds., *Restoring Financial Stability* (Hoboken, NJ: John Wiley & Sons, 2009).

F. Allen and E. Carletti, "An Overview of the Crisis: Causes, Consequences and Solutions," *International Review of Finance* 10 (March 2010), pp. 1–26.

The following works cover financial crises more generally:

F. Allen and D. Gale, *Understanding Financial Crises* (Oxford: Oxford University Press, 2007).

C. M. Reinhart and K. Rogoff, "The Aftermath of Financial Crises," *American Economic Review* 99 (May 2009), pp. 466–472.

C. M. Reinhart and K. Rogoff, *This Time Is Different: Eight Centuries of Financial Folly* (Princeton: Princeton University Press, 2009).

PROBLEM SETS

McGraw Hill Education **connect** Select problems are available in McGraw-Hill's *Connect*. Please see the preface for more information.

1. **Terminology*** Fill in the blanks, using the following terms: floating rate, common stock, convertible, subordinated, preferred stock, senior, warrant.

   a. If a lender ranks behind the firm's general creditors in the event of default, his or her loan is said to be _____.

   b. Interest on many bank loans is based on a _____ of interest.

   c. A(n) _____ bond can be exchanged for shares of the issuing corporation.

   d. A(n) _____ gives its owner the right to buy shares in the issuing company at a predetermined price.

   e. Dividends on _____ cannot be paid unless the firm has also paid any dividends on its _____.

2. **Company financing** True or false?

   a. In the United States, most common shares are owned by individual investors.

   b. An insurance company is a financial intermediary.

   c. Investments in partnerships cannot be publicly traded.

3. **Sources of funds** True or false?

   a. Net stock issues by U.S. nonfinancial corporations in most years are small but positive.

   b. Most capital investment by U.S. companies is funded by retained earnings and reinvested depreciation.

   c. Debt ratios in the United States are lower than in most other developed economies.

4. **Security holdings*** True or false?

   a. Banks are huge investors in corporate equity.

   b. Insurance companies are huge investors in corporate debt.

   c. Rather than investing directly in corporate equities, most households prefer to pool their risk in a hedge fund.

   d. Many individuals have a current account with an investment bank that then uses the cash to lend to industry.

5. **Company ownership** What do we mean when we say that stockholders have control rights and residual cash flow rights? How in practice do they exercise their control rights?

6. **Classified boards** Saga City has a declassified board with nine directors.

   a. How many directors come up for election each year?

   b. Would Saga be more or less vulnerable to a hostile takeover if it had a classified board?

7. **Voting rights** Suppose that East Corporation has issued voting and nonvoting stock. Investors hope that holders of the voting stock will use their power to vote out the company's incompetent management. Would you expect the voting stock to sell for a higher price? Explain.

8. **Preferred stock*** In 2018, Beta Corporation earned gross profits of $760,000.

   a. Suppose that Beta was financed by a combination of common stock and $1 million of debt. The interest rate on the debt was 10%, and the corporate tax rate in 2018 was 21%. How much profit was available for common stockholders after payment of interest and corporate taxes?

   b. Now suppose that instead of issuing debt, Beta was financed by a combination of common stock and $1 million of preferred stock. The dividend yield on the preferred was 8%, and the corporate tax rate was still 21%. Recalculate the profit available for common stockholders after payment of preferred dividends and corporate taxes.

9. **Corporate debt*** Which of the following features would increase the value of a corporate bond? Which would reduce its value?

   a. The bond is convertible into shares.

   b. The bond is secured by a mortgage on real estate.

   c. The bond is subordinated.

10. **Financial markets and intermediaries.** True or false?

    a. Financing for public corporations must flow through financial markets.

    b. Financing for private corporations must flow through financial intermediaries.

    c. Almost all foreign exchange trading occurs on the floors of the FOREX exchanges in New York and London.

    d. Derivative markets are a major source of finance for many corporations.

11. **Financial markets and intermediaries.** Which of the following are financial markets?

    a. NASDAQ.

    b. Vanguard Explorer Fund.

    c. JPMorgan Chase.

    d. Chicago Mercantile Exchange.

12. **Financial markets and intermediaries*** True or false?

    a. Exchange traded funds are hedge funds that can be bought and sold on the stock exchange.

    b. Hedge funds provide small investors with low-cost diversification.

    c. The sale of insurance policies is a source of financing for insurance companies.

    d. In defined-contribution pension plans, the pension pot depends on the rate of return earned on the contributions by the employer and employee.

13. **Financial markets and intermediaries** Financial markets and intermediaries channel savings from investors to corporate investment. The savings make this journey by many different routes. Give a specific example for each of the following routes:

    a. Investor to financial intermediary, to financial markets, and to the corporation.

    b. Investor to financial markets, to a financial intermediary, and to the corporation.

    c. Investor to financial markets, to a financial intermediary, back to financial markets, and to the corporation.

14. **Financial markets and intermediaries** Explain briefly how each of the following allow individuals or companies to spread their risk:

    a. An exchange traded fund.

    b. Commodity markets.

    c. A life insurance company.

15. **Financial markets and intermediaries** Some individuals are eager to spend income before it arrives; others want to postpone consumption. Give some examples of intermediaries that provide services to these individuals.

16. **The financial crisis** Construct a timeline of the important events in the financial crisis that started in the summer of 2007. When do you think the crisis ended? You will probably want to review some of the entries under Further Reading before you answer.

17. **The financial crisis** We mention several causes of the financial crisis. What other causes can you identify? You will probably want to review some of the entries under Further Reading before you answer.

FINANCE ON THE WEB

1. Use data from **finance.yahoo.com** to work out the financing proportions given in Figure 14.1 for a particular industrial company for some recent year.

2. The website **www.federalreserve.gov/releases/z1/current/default.htm** provides data on sources of funds and an aggregate balance sheet for nonfarm nonfinancial corporations. Look at Table F.102 for the latest year. What proportion of the cash that companies needed was generated internally, and how much had to be raised on the financial markets? Is this the usual pattern? Now look at "new equity issues." Were companies, on average, issuing new equity or buying their shares back?

3. An aggregate balance sheet for U.S. manufacturing corporations can be found on **www.census.gov/econ/qfr**. Find the balance sheet for the latest year. What was the ratio of long-term debt to long-term debt plus equity? What about the ratio of all long-term liabilities to long-term liabilities plus equity?

CHAPTER

15

How Corporations Issue Securities

In Chapter 11, we encountered Marvin Enterprises, one of the most remarkable growth companies of the twenty-first century. It was founded by George and Mildred Marvin, two high-school dropouts, together with their chum Charles P. (Chip) Norton. To get the company off the ground, the three entrepreneurs relied on their own savings together with personal loans from a bank. However, the company's rapid growth meant that they had soon borrowed to the hilt and needed more equity capital. Equity investment in young private companies is generally known as *venture capital*. Such venture capital may be provided by investment institutions or by wealthy individuals who are prepared to back an untried company in return for a piece of the action. In the first part of this chapter, we will explain how companies like Marvin go about raising venture capital.

Venture capital organizations aim to help growing firms over that awkward adolescent period before they are large enough to go public. For a successful firm such as Marvin, there is likely to come a time when it needs to tap a wider source of capital and, therefore, decides to make its first public issue of common stock. The next section of the chapter describes what is involved in such an issue in the United States. We explain the process for registering the offering with the Securities and Exchange Commission, and we introduce you to the underwriters who buy the issue and resell it to the public. We also see that new issues are generally sold below the price at which they subsequently trade. To understand why that is so, we need to make a brief sortie into the field of auction procedures.

A company's first issue of stock is seldom its last. In Chapter 13, we saw that corporations face a persistent financial deficit, which they meet by selling securities. We therefore look at how established corporations go about raising more capital. In the process, we encounter another puzzle: When companies announce a new issue of stock, the stock price generally falls. We suggest that the explanation lies in the information that investors read into the announcement.

If a stock or bond is sold publicly, it can then be traded on the securities markets. But sometimes investors intend to hold on to their securities and are not concerned about whether they can sell them. In these cases, there is little advantage to a public issue, and the firm may prefer to place the securities directly with one or two financial institutions. At the end of this chapter, we explain how companies arrange a private placement.

15-1   Venture Capital

On April 1, 2031, George and Mildred Marvin met with Chip Norton in their research lab (which also doubled as a bicycle shed) to celebrate the incorporation of Marvin Enterprises. The three entrepreneurs had raised $100,000 from savings and personal bank loans and had purchased 1 million shares in the new company. At this *zero-stage* investment, the company's

assets were $90,000 in the bank ($10,000 had been spent for legal and other expenses of setting up the company), plus the *idea* for a new product, the household gargle blaster. George Marvin was the first to see that the gargle blaster, up to that point an expensive curiosity, could be commercially produced using microgenetic refenestrators.

Marvin Enterprises' bank account steadily drained away as design and testing proceeded. Local banks did not see Marvin's idea as adequate collateral, so a transfusion of equity capital was clearly needed. Preparation of a *business plan* was a necessary first step. The plan was a confidential document describing the proposed product, its potential market, the underlying technology, and the resources (time, money, employees, and plant and equipment) needed for success.

Most entrepreneurs are able to spin a plausible yarn about their company. But it is as hard to convince a venture capitalist that your business plan is sound as to get a first novel published.[1] Marvin's managers were able to point to the fact that they were prepared to put their money where their mouths were. Not only had they staked all their savings in the company, but they were mortgaged to the hilt. This *signaled* their faith in the business.

First Meriam Venture Partners was impressed with Marvin's management team and its business plan and agreed to buy 1 million new shares for $1 each. After this *first-stage* financing, the company's market-value balance sheet looked like this:

Marvin Enterprises' First-Stage Balance Sheet (Market Values in $ millions)

Cash from new equity	$1	$1	New equity from venture capital
Other assets, mostly intangible	1	1	Original equity held by entrepreneurs
Value	$2	$2	Value

By agreeing to pay $1 a share for Marvin's stock, First Meriam placed a value of $1 million on the entrepreneurs' original shareholdings. This was First Meriam's estimate of the value of the entrepreneurs' original idea and their commitment to the enterprise. If the estimate was right, the entrepreneurs could congratulate themselves on a $900,000 paper gain over their original $100,000 investment. In exchange, the entrepreneurs gave up half their company and accepted First Meriam's representatives to the board of directors.[2]

The success of a new business depends critically on the effort put in by the managers. Therefore venture capital firms try to structure a deal so that management has a strong incentive to work hard. That takes us back to Chapters 1 and 12, where we showed how the shareholders of a firm (who are the principals) need to provide incentives for the managers (who are their agents) to work to maximize firm value.

If Marvin's management had demanded watertight employment contracts and fat salaries, they would not have found it easy to raise venture capital. Instead, the Marvin team agreed to put up with modest salaries. They could cash in only from appreciation of their stock. If Marvin failed, they would get nothing because First Meriam actually bought *preferred* stock designed to convert automatically into common stock when and if Marvin Enterprises succeeded in an initial public offering or consistently generated more than a target level of earnings. But if Marvin Enterprises had failed, First Meriam would have been first in line to claim any salvageable assets. This raised even further the stakes for the company's management.[3]

---

[1]For evidence on what venture capitalists look for in a potential investment see P. Gompers, W. Gornall, S. N. Kaplan, and I. A. Strebulaev, "How Do Venture Capitalists Make Decisions?" ECGI Finance Working Paper 477/2016 (August 2016), available on http://ssrn.com/abstract_id=2801385.

[2]Venture capital investors do not necessarily demand a majority on the board of directors. Whether they do depends, for example, on how mature the business is and on what fraction they own. A common compromise gives an equal number of seats to the founders and to outside investors; the two parties then agree to one or more additional directors to serve as tie-breakers in case a conflict arises. Regardless of whether they have a majority of directors, venture capital companies are seldom silent partners; their judgment and contacts can often prove useful to a relatively inexperienced management team.

[3]Notice the trade-off here. Marvin's management is being asked to put all its eggs into one basket. That creates pressure for managers to work hard, but it also means that they take on risk that could have been diversified away.

Venture capitalists rarely give a young company up front all the money it will need. At each stage they give enough to reach the next major checkpoint. Thus in spring 2033, having designed and tested a prototype, Marvin Enterprises was back asking for more money for pilot production and test marketing. First Meriam, the original backers, had insisted on pro-rata rights, which gave it the right to participate in subsequent financings. It, therefore, chose to invest $1.5 million in the *second-stage* financing and a further $2.5 million came from two other venture capital partnerships and wealthy individual investors. The balance sheet just after the second stage was as follows:

Marvin Enterprises' First-Stage Balance Sheet (Market Values in $ millions)			
Cash from new equity	$ 4	$ 4	New equity, second stage
Fixed assets	1	5	Equity from first stage
Other assets, mostly intangible	9	5	Original equity held by entrepreneurs
Value	$14	$14	Value

Now the after-the-money valuation was $14 million. First Meriam marked up its original investment to $5 million, and the founders noted an additional $4 million paper gain.

Does this begin to sound like a (paper) money machine? It was so only with hindsight. At stage 1, it wasn't clear whether Marvin would ever get to stage 2; if the prototype hadn't worked, First Meriam could have refused to put up more funds and effectively closed down the business.[4] Or it could have advanced stage 2 money in a smaller amount on less favorable terms. The board of directors could also have fired George, Mildred, and Chip and gotten someone else to try to develop the business.

In Chapter 14, we pointed out that stockholders and lenders differ in their cash-flow rights and control rights. The stockholders are entitled to whatever cash flows remain after paying off the other security holders. They also have control over how the company uses its money, and it is only if the company defaults that the lenders can step in and take control of the company. When a new business raises venture capital, these cash-flow rights and control rights are usually negotiated separately. The venture capital firm will want a say in how that business is run and will demand representation on the board and a significant number of votes. The venture capitalist may agree that it will relinquish some of these rights if the business subsequently performs well. However, if performance turns out to be poor, the venture capitalist may automatically get a greater say in how the business is run and whether the existing management should be replaced.

For Marvin, fortunately, everything went like clockwork. Third-stage *mezzanine financing* was arranged,[5] full-scale production began on schedule, and gargle blasters were acclaimed by music critics worldwide. Marvin Enterprises went public on February 3, 2037. Once its shares were traded, the paper gains earned by First Meriam and the company's founders turned into fungible wealth. Before we go on to this initial public offering, let us look briefly at the venture capital markets today.

The Venture Capital Market

Most new companies rely initially on family funds and bank loans. Some of them continue to grow with the aid of equity investment provided by wealthy individuals known as *angel investors*. However, like Marvin, many adolescent companies raise capital from specialist

BEYOND THE PAGE

U.S. venture
capital investment

mhhe.com/brealey13e

---

[4]If First Meriam had refused to invest at stage 2, it would have been an exceptionally hard sell convincing another investor to step in its place. The other outside investors knew they had less information about Marvin than First Meriam and would have read its refusal as a bad omen for Marvin's prospects.

[5]Mezzanine financing does not necessarily come in the third stage; there may be four or five stages. The point is that mezzanine investors come in late, in contrast to venture capitalists who get in on the ground floor.

venture-capital firms, which pool funds from a variety of investors, seek out fledgling companies to invest in, and then work with these companies as they try to grow. In addition, many large firms act as *corporate venturers* by providing equity capital to new innovative companies. For example, over the past 20 years, Intel has invested in more than 1,300 firms in 56 countries. In a recent development, young start-ups have also used the Web to raise the money from small investors. This development, known as *crowdfunding,* is described in the nearby box.

Figure 15.1 shows the changing level of venture capital investment. During the giddy days of 2000, funds invested nearly $200 billion, but since the end of the dot-com boom, venture capital investment has returned to about $60 billion a year.

Most venture capital funds are organized as limited private partnerships with a fixed life of about 10 years. Pension funds and other investors are the limited partners. The management company, which is the general partner, is responsible for making and overseeing the investments and, in return, receives a fixed fee and a share of the profits, called the *carried interest*.[6] You will find that these venture capital partnerships are often lumped together with similar partnerships that provide funds for companies in distress or that buy out whole companies or divisions of public companies and then take them private. The general term for these activities is *private equity investing*.

Venture capital firms are not passive investors. They tend to specialize in young high-tech firms that are difficult to evaluate and they monitor these firms closely. They also provide ongoing advice to the firms that they invest in and often play a major role in recruiting the senior management team. Their judgment and contacts can be valuable to a business in its early years and can help the firm to bring its products more quickly to market.[7]

Venture capitalists may cash in on their investment in two ways. Once the new business has established a track record, it is frequently sold out to a larger firm. However, many

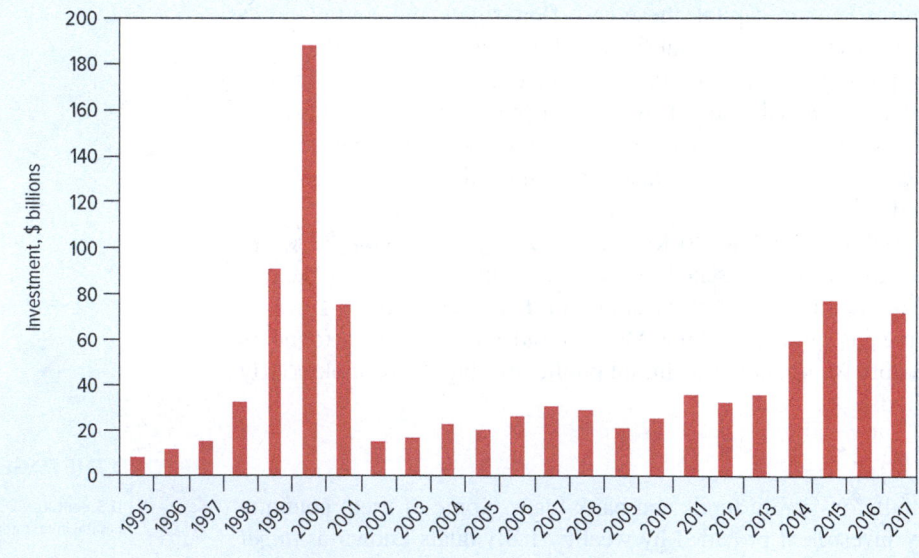

FIGURE 15.1

Venture capital investment in the United States

Source: Thomson Reuters data in MoneyTree Report, Q4, 2017, PricewaterhouseCoopers, National Venture Capital Association.

---

[6]A typical arrangement might be for the management company to receive a fee of 2% *plus* 20% of the profits.
[7]For evidence on the role of venture capitalists in assisting new businesses, see T. Hellman and M. Puri, "The Interaction between Product Market and Financing Strategy: The Role of Venture Capital," *Review of Financial Studies* 13 (2000), pp. 959–984; and S. N. Kaplan and P. Stromberg, "Characteristics, Contracts and Actions: Evidence from Venture Capitalist Analyses," *Journal of Finance* 59 (October 2004), pp. 2177–2210.

entrepreneurs do not fit easily into a corporate bureaucracy and would prefer instead to remain the boss. In this case, the company may decide, like Marvin, to go public and so provide the original backers with an opportunity to "cash out," selling their stock and leaving the original entrepreneurs in control. Approximately 50% of companies going public have been backed by a venture capital company. A thriving venture capital market therefore needs an active stock exchange, such as Nasdaq, that specializes in trading the shares of young, rapidly growing firms.[8]

For every 10 first-stage venture capital investments, only 2 or 3 may survive as successful, self-sufficient businesses. From these statistics come two rules for success in venture capital investment. First, don't shy away from uncertainty; accept a low probability of success. But don't buy into a business unless you can see the chance of a big, public company in a profitable market. There's no sense taking a long shot unless it pays off handsomely if you win. Second, cut your losses; identify losers early, and if you can't fix the problem—by replacing management, for example—throw no good money after bad.

Venture capital firms have had plenty of failures, but they have also provided early financing for many glamorous growth companies such as Intel, Apple, Microsoft, and Google (now renamed Alphabet). Gornall and Strebulaev examined companies that were supported in their early days with venture capital. They estimated that in 2014, these companies accounted for 20% of the market capitalization of U.S. public companies and 44% of spending on R&D.[9]

How successful in general is venture capital investment? Figure 15.2 shows the returns to investors in 775 venture capital funds according to the date that the funds made their initial investment.[10] Overall, the average return on the funds was about 17%, more than 15% higher than that of an equivalent investment in the stock market. However, notice how the returns have depended on the year that the fund was established. Those funds formed before 1998 earned dreamy returns, whereas those that came later to the party for the most part made losses.

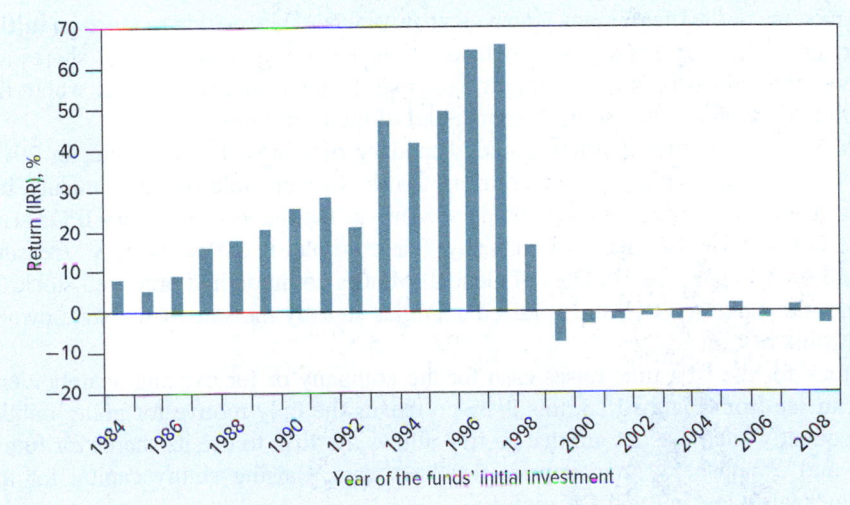

FIGURE 15.2

Average internal rate of return on venture capital funds by year of initial investment

Source: R. S. Harris, T. Jenkinson, and S. N. Kaplan, "Private Equity Performance: What Do We Know," *Journal of Finance* 69 (2014) pp. 1851–1882.

(x-axis: Year of the funds' initial investment; y-axis: Return (IRR), %)

[8]This argument is developed in B. Black and R. Gilson, "Venture Capital and the Structure of Capital Markets: Banks versus Stock Markets," *Journal of Financial Economics* 47 (March 1998), pp. 243–277.

[9]See W. Gornall and I. A. Strebulaev, "The Economic Impact of Venture Capital: Evidence from Public Companies," Stanford University Working Paper (2015).

[10]See R. Harris, T. Jenkinson, and S.Kaplan, "Private Equity Performance: What Do We Know?" *Journal of Finance* 69 (October 2014) pp. 1851–1882. Since you can't look up the value of new start-up businesses in *The Wall Street Journal*, you can never be sure of a firm's success until it is eventually sold, becomes a public company, or goes out of business. For those funds that started up between 1984 and 1998, almost all of the investments fell into these categories. For the later years, the values for many of the investments are based on estimates.

Every Crowd Has a Silver Lining

❭ A new way has emerged for entrepreneurs to finance start-ups. It is known as crowdfunding and uses the Internet to raise money directly from a crowd of individuals.

WobbleWorks is a small toy and robotics firm that was founded in Boston in 2011 by two entrepreneurs. The company needed capital to develop the 3Doodler, a pen that could be used to produce 3-D plastic images. The company's solution was to advertise for backers on Kickstarter, a website for young enterprises that seek to raise capital from a large number of individuals. Possible backers were given about a month to decide whether they wished to support the 3Doodler project and how much they wished to invest. The concept proved enormously popular, and the offer was heavily oversubscribed, with more than 26,000 individuals pledging a total of $2.3 million. Many of these pledges were for less than $25; others were much more substantial. As in the case of many crowdfunded projects, investors in the 3Doodler did not receive shares in the company. Instead, they received early samples of the product.

In 2016, President Obama signed the JOBS Act. This allows companies to raise up to $50 million online in a mini IPO. Thus, for the first time, crowdfunding websites can offer small investors the opportunity to back start-up companies in return for an equity participation in the firm rather than samples of the product. Early evidence suggests that equity crowdfunding is principally used by very small start-ups. Needless to say, such investment is not an activity for the faint-hearted, and the SEC has drawn up a set of rules for these mini IPOs to protect credulous investors.

BEYOND THE PAGE

The Boom in Initial Coin Offerings

mhhe.com/brealey13e

15-2 The Initial Public Offering

There comes a stage in the life of many young companies when they decide to make an **initial public offering** of stock, or **IPO.** This may be a primary offering, in which new shares are sold to raise additional cash for the company. Or it may be a secondary offering, where the existing shareholders decide to cash in by selling part of their holdings.

Many IPOs are a mixture of primary and secondary offerings. For example, in 2014, Alibaba's IPO raised $25 billion. About a third of the shares were sold by the company, but the remainder were sold by existing shareholders. Some of the biggest secondary IPOs arise when a government sells its stake in a company. For example, in 2010, the U.S. Treasury raised $20 billion by selling its holdings of General Motors common and preferred stock. In the same year, the Chinese government raised a similar sum by the sale of the state-owned Agricultural Bank of China.

Selling stock for the first time raises cash for the company or for existing shareholders, but as you can see from Figure 15.3, this is by no means the only motive for going public. The most frequently cited reasons are that an IPO allows the firm to use its shares for future acquisitions and establishes a market price for the shares. Raising equity capital for the company comes fairly low in the list of motives.

The Public-Private Choice

While there are advantages to being a public corporation, there are also drawbacks. In addition to the fact that they may end up selling shares for less than their true worth,[11] there are longer-term costs to operating as a public company. Managers of public companies often

---

[11]We discuss below the evidence that new issues are generally underpriced.

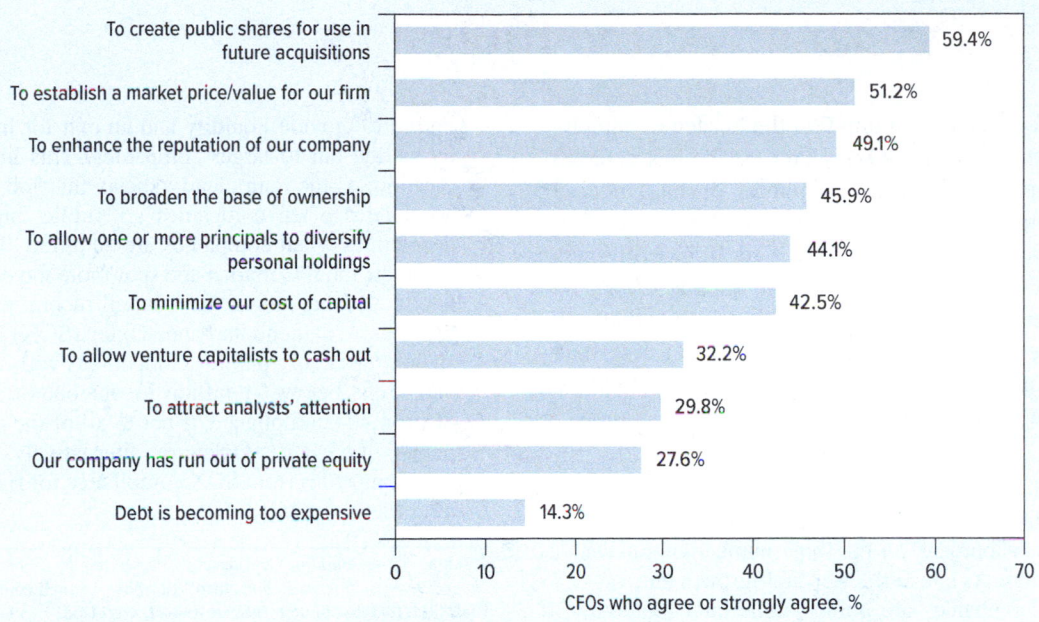

FIGURE 15.3   Survey evidence on the motives for going public.

Source: J. C. Brau and S. E. Fawcett, "Evidence on What CFOs Think about the IPO Process: Practice, Theory and Managerial Implications," *Journal of Applied Corporate Finance* 18 (October 2006), pp. 107–117.

chafe at the constant pressure from shareholders to report increases in profits, and they complain at the red tape involved in running a public company. These complaints about red tape have become more vocal since the passage of the Sarbanes–Oxley Act (SOX), which sought to prevent a repeat of the corporate scandals that brought about the collapse of Enron and WorldCom. As the nearby box suggests, a consequence of SOX has been an increased reporting burden, particularly on small companies and an apparent greater willingness to remain private.[12] Operating as a private company could be tricky if it cut off the company's access to finance, but in recent years, financial institutions have become more willing to provide equity capital to private firms. For example, in 2017, Airbnb raised $1 billion of private equity in a new funding round.

Some large U.S. companies—such as Cargill, Koch Industries, and Mars Inc.—have been private all their corporate lives. Also, you should not think of the issue process in the United States as a one-way street; public firms often go into reverse and return to being privately owned. For example, Dell became a public company in 1988 and then reverted to being private in 2013, when Michael Dell and a private-equity firm bought out the business. For an extreme example of reversal, consider the food service company, Aramark. It began life in 1936 as a private company and went public in 1960. In 1984, a management buyout led to the company going private, and it remained private until 2001 when it had its second public offering. But the experiment did not last long: Five years later, Aramark was once again the object of a buyout that took the company private again. In 2013, Aramark went public for the third time.

---

[12]Companies can alleviate the reporting burden by reducing the number of shareholders to less than 300 and delisting their stock from the exchange. This procedure is known as "going dark." In recent years there has been an increase in the number of companies going dark.

FINANCE IN PRACTICE

Has SOX Damaged the IPO Market?

❯ CEOs frequently complain that the burden of complying with the Sarbanes–Oxley Act (SOX) has deterred U.S. companies from going public or has induced them to list in London rather than New York. In 2011, the President's Council on Jobs and Competitiveness backed this belief. The council noted that 2008 and 2009 experienced fewer venture-backed IPOs than any year since 1985. The number of IPOs of less than $50 million fell from 80% of all IPOs in the 1990s to 20% in the 2000s. The council concluded:

> Well-intentioned regulations aimed at protecting the public from the misrepresentations of a small number of large companies have unintentionally placed significant burdens on the large number of smaller companies. As a result, fewer high-growth entrepreneurial companies are going public, and more are opting to provide liquidity and an exit for investors by selling out to larger companies. This hurts job creation, as the data clearly shows that job growth accelerates when companies go public, but often decelerates when companies are acquired. Thus, to stimulate the IPO market and spur more job creation, nearly all members of the Council recommend that Congress . . . amend Sarbanes-Oxley (SOX) to allow shareholders of public companies with market valuations below $1 billion to opt out of at least Section 404 compliance, if not to all of the requirements, of Sarbanes-Oxley; or, alternatively, exempt new companies from SOX compliance for five years after they go public.*

---

*"Taking Action, Building Confidence," *The President's Council on Jobs and Competitiveness Interim Report*, **http://files.jobs-council.com/jobscouncil/files/2011/10/JobsCouncil_InterimReport_Oct11.pdf**, p. 19.

BEYOND THE PAGE

The largest U.S. private companies

mhhe.com/brealey13e

BEYOND THE PAGE

The JOBS Act

mhhe.com/brealey13e

For some years, fewer U.S. companies have been going public, and many new growth companies that are worth a billion dollars or more have increasingly chosen to remain private. As we write this in 2017, these so-called unicorns include such well-known names as Uber, Dropbox, and Airbnb. While the majority of large businesses in the United States are public corporations, the number of public corporations has fallen by about 50% since its high in 1996. It looks as if the case for remaining private may be stronger than it once was.

In response to such concerns Congress passed the Jumpstart Our Business Startups (JOBS) Act, which eased some of the regulations for small companies that were enacted in SOX. However, not everyone agrees that SOX was responsible for the decline in the number of IPOs. For example, Gao, Ritter, and Zhu point out that the fall in the number of companies going public is concentrated among small venture-backed firms.[13] They argue that it is becoming more difficult for such firms to operate in today's rapidly changing markets, and therefore, rather than going public, it makes more sense for these firms to sell out to larger firms.

In many countries, private companies are more important than in the United States. For example, Germany's medium-sized manufacturers, collectively known as the Mittelstand, account for about 50% of national income and 80% of the workforce. These Mittelstand companies are typically privately held, family-owned businesses that rely heavily on bank borrowing to make good any financial deficit.[14] Increasingly, private equity firms have been stepping in to provide the equity capital that they need.

---

[13]See X. Gao, J. R. Ritter, and Z. Zhu, "Where Have All the IPOs Gone?" *Journal of Financial and Quantitative Analysis* 48 (December 2013), pp. 1663–1692.

[14]Many larger German companies have also chosen to remain private, including the retailers Schwarz Gruppe and Aldi, and the media giant Bertelsmann. For a discussion of the financing of the Mittelstand, see U. Hommel and H. Schneider, "Financing the German Mittelstand," *EIB Papers* 8 (2003), pp. 53–90.

398

Arranging an Initial Public Offering

Let us now look at how Marvin arranged to go public. By 2037, the company had grown to the point at which it needed still more capital to implement its second-generation production technology. At the same time, the company's founders were looking to sell some of their shares.[15] In the previous few months, there had been a spate of IPOs by high-tech companies, and the shares had generally sold like hotcakes. So Marvin's management hoped that investors would be equally keen to buy the company's stock.

Management's first task was to select the *underwriters*. Underwriters act as financial midwives to a new issue. Usually they play a triple role: First they provide the company with procedural and financial advice, then they buy the issue, and finally they resell it to the public.

After some discussion, Marvin settled on Klein Merrick as the managing underwriter and Goldman Stanley as the co-manager. Klein Merrick then formed a syndicate of underwriters who would buy the entire issue and reoffer it to the public.

In choosing Klein Merrick to manage its IPO, Marvin was influenced by Merrick's proposals for making an active market in the stock in the weeks after the issue.[16] Merrick also planned to generate continuing investor interest in the stock by distributing a major research report on Marvin's prospects.[17] Marvin hoped that this report would encourage investors to hold its stock.

Together with Klein Merrick and firms of lawyers and accountants, Marvin prepared a registration statement for the approval of the Securities and Exchange Commission (SEC).[18] This statement is a detailed and somewhat cumbersome document that presents information about the proposed financing and the firm's history, existing business, and plans for the future.

The most important sections of the registration statement are distributed to investors in the form of a prospectus. In the appendix to this chapter, we have reproduced the prospectus for Marvin's first public issue of stock. Real prospectuses would go into much more detail on each topic, but this example should give you some feel for the mixture of valuable information and redundant qualification that characterizes these documents. The Marvin prospectus also illustrates how the SEC insists that investors' eyes are opened to the dangers of purchase (see "Certain Considerations" in the prospectus). Some investors have joked that if they read each prospectus carefully, they would not dare to buy any new issue.

In addition to registering the issue with the SEC, Marvin needed to check that the issue complied with the so-called blue-sky laws of each state that regulate sales of securities within the state.[19] It also arranged for its newly issued shares to be traded on the Nasdaq exchange.

BEYOND THE PAGE

Twitter's IPO prospectus

mhhe.com/brealey13e

---

[15]First Meriam also wanted to cash in on its investment, but venture capital companies usually believe that selling out at the time of the IPO would send a bad signal to investors. Therefore, First Meriam planned to wait until well after the IPO and then either sell its holding or distribute its shares in Marvin to the investors in the First Meriam fund.

[16]On average, the managing underwriter accounts for 40% to 60% of trading volume in the stock during the first 60 days after an IPO. See K. Ellis, R. Michaely, and M. O'Hara, "When the Underwriter Is the Market Maker: An Examination of Trading in the IPO Aftermarket," *Journal of Finance* 55 (June 2000), pp. 1039–1074.

[17]The 40 days after the IPO are designated as a *quiet period*. Merrick is obliged to wait until after this period before commenting on the valuation of the company. Survey evidence suggests that in choosing an underwriter, firms place considerable importance on its ability to provide follow-up research reports. See L. Krigman, W. H. Shaw, and K. L. Womack, "Why Do Firms Switch Underwriters?" *Journal of Financial Economics* 60 (May 2001), pp. 245–284.

[18]The rules governing the sale of securities derive principally from the Securities Act of 1933. The SEC is concerned solely with disclosure and it has no power to prevent an issue as long as there has been proper disclosure. Some public issues are exempt from registration. These include issues by small businesses and loans maturing within nine months.

[19]In 1980, when Apple Computer Inc. went public, the Massachusetts state government decided the offering was too risky and barred the sale of the shares to individual investors in the state. The state relented later after the issue was out and the price had risen. Needless to say, this action was not acclaimed by Massachusetts investors. States do not usually reject security issues by honest firms through established underwriters. We cite the example to illustrate the potential power of state securities laws and to show why underwriters keep careful track of them.

The Sale of Marvin Stock

While Marvin was responding to the SEC's comments on the registration statement, the company and its underwriters began to firm up the issue price. First they looked at the price–earnings ratios of the shares of Marvin's principal competitors. Then they worked through a number of discounted-cash-flow calculations like the ones we described in Chapters 4 and 11. Most of the evidence pointed to a market price in the region of $74 to $76 a share, and the company therefore included this provisional figure in an amended version of the prospectus.[20]

Marvin and Klein Merrick arranged a *road show* to talk to potential investors. Mostly these were institutional investors, such as managers of mutual funds and pension funds. The investors gave their reactions to the issue and indicated to the underwriters how much stock they wished to buy. Some stated the maximum price that they were prepared to pay, but others said that they just wanted to invest so many dollars in Marvin at whatever issue price was chosen. These discussions with fund managers allowed Klein Merrick to build up a book of potential orders.[21] Although the managers were not bound by their responses, they knew that, if they wanted to keep in the underwriters' good books, they should be careful not to go back on their expressions of interest. The underwriters also were not obliged to treat all investors equally. Some investors who were keen to buy Marvin stock were disappointed in the allotment that they subsequently received.

Immediately after it received clearance from the SEC, Marvin and the underwriters met to fix the issue price. Investors had been enthusiastic about the story that the company had to tell and it was clear that they were prepared to pay more than $76 for the stock. Marvin's managers were tempted to go for the highest possible price, but the underwriters were more cautious. Not only would they be left with any unsold stock if they overestimated investor demand, but they also argued that some degree of underpricing was needed to tempt investors to buy the stock. Marvin and the underwriters therefore compromised on an issue price of $80. Potential investors were encouraged by the fact that the offer price was higher than the $74 to $76 proposed in the preliminary prospectus and decided that the underwriters must have encountered considerable enthusiasm for the issue.

Although Marvin's underwriters were committed to buy only 900,000 shares from the company, they chose to sell 1,035,000 shares to investors. This left the underwriters short of 135,000 shares or 15% of the issue. If Marvin's stock had proved unpopular with investors and traded below the issue price, the underwriters could have bought back these shares in the marketplace. This would have helped to stabilize the price and would have given the underwriters a profit on the sale of these extra shares. As it turned out, investors fell over themselves to buy Marvin stock, and by the end of the first day, the stock was trading at $105. The underwriters would have incurred a heavy loss if they had been obliged to buy back the extra shares at $105. However, Marvin had provided underwriters with a *greenshoe* option that allowed them to buy an additional 135,000 shares from the company. This ensured that the underwriters were able to sell the extra shares to investors without fear of loss.

After a mandatory "quiet period" of 40 days following the sale, several of Marvin's underwriters published research reports on the company and recommended buying the stock.

The Underwriters

Marvin's underwriters were prepared to enter into a firm commitment to buy the stock and then offer it to the public. Thus they took the risk that the issue might flop and they would be left with unwanted stock. Occasionally, where the sale of common stock is regarded as

---

[20]The company is allowed to circulate a preliminary version of the prospectus (known as a *red herring*) before the SEC has approved the registration statement.

[21]The managing underwriter is therefore often known as the *bookrunner*.

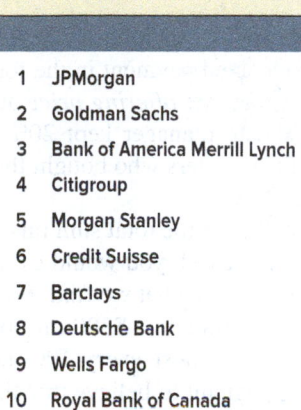

1	JPMorgan
2	Goldman Sachs
3	Bank of America Merrill Lynch
4	Citigroup
5	Morgan Stanley
6	Credit Suisse
7	Barclays
8	Deutsche Bank
9	Wells Fargo
10	Royal Bank of Canada

❯**TABLE 15.1**   The top managing underwriters of equity issues, 2017

Source: Financial Times.

particularly risky, the underwriters may be prepared to handle the sale only on a *best-efforts* basis. In this case the underwriters promise to sell as much of the issue as possible, but they do not guarantee to sell the entire amount.[22]

Successful underwriting requires financial muscle and considerable experience. The names of Marvin's underwriters are, of course, fictitious, but Table 15.1 shows that underwriting is dominated by the major investment banks and large commercial banks. Foreign players are also heavily involved in underwriting securities that are sold internationally.

Underwriting is not always fun. In April 2008, a British bank, HBOS, offered its shareholders two new shares at a price of £2.75 for each five shares that they currently held.[23] The underwriters to the issue, Morgan Stanley and Dresdner Kleinwort, guaranteed that at the end of eight weeks they would buy any new shares that the stockholders did not want. At the time of the offer, HBOS shares were priced at about £5, so the underwriters felt confident that they would not have to honor their pledge. Unfortunately, they reckoned without the turbulent market in bank shares that year. The bank's shareholders worried that the money they were asked to provide would go to bailing out the bondholders and depositors. By the end of the eight weeks, the price of HBOS stock had slumped below the issue price, and the underwriters were left with 932 million unwanted shares worth £3.6 billion.

Companies get to make only one IPO, but underwriters are in the business all the time. Wise underwriters, therefore, realize that their reputation is on the line and will not handle an issue unless they believe the facts have been presented fairly to investors. So, when a new issue goes wrong, the underwriters may be blamed for overhyping the issue and failing in their "due diligence." For example, in December 1999, software company Va Linux went public at $30 a share. The next day, trading opened at $299 a share, but then the price began to sag. Within two years, it had fallen below $2. Disgruntled Va Linux investors sued the underwriters, complaining that the prospectus was "materially false." These underwriters had plenty of company because following the collapse of the dot-com stocks in 2000, investors in many other high-tech IPOs sued the underwriters. As the nearby box explains, there was further embarrassment when it emerged that several well-known underwriters had engaged in "spinning"—that is, allocating stock in popular new issues to managers of their important corporate clients. The underwriter's seal of approval for a new issue no longer seemed as valuable as it once had.

---

[22]The alternative is to enter into an *all-or-none* arrangement. In this case, either the entire issue is sold at the offering price or the deal is called off and the issuing company receives nothing.

[23]This arrangement is known as a *rights issue.* We describe rights issues later in the chapter.

Costs of a New Issue

We have described Marvin's underwriters as filling a triple role—providing advice, buying the new issue, and reselling it to the public. In return, they received payment in the form of a *spread;* that is, they were allowed to buy the shares for less than the *offering price* at which the shares were sold to investors.[24] Klein Merrick as syndicate manager kept 20% of this spread. A further 25% of the spread was used to pay those underwriters who bought the issue. The remaining 55% went to the firms that provided the sales force.

The underwriting spread on the Marvin issue amounted to 7% of the total sum raised from investors. Since many of the costs incurred by underwriters are fixed, you would expect that the percentage spread would decline with issue size. This, in part, is what we find. For example, a $5 million IPO might carry a spread of 10%, while the spread on a $300 million issue might be only 5%. However, Chen and Ritter found that for almost every IPO between $20 and $80 million the spread was exactly 7%.[25] Since it is difficult to believe that there are no scale economies, this clustering at 7% is a puzzle.[26]

In addition to the underwriting fee, Marvin's new issue entailed substantial administrative costs. Preparation of the registration statement and prospectus involved management, legal counsel, and accountants, as well as the underwriters and their advisers. In addition, the firm had to pay fees for registering the new securities, printing and mailing costs, and so on. You can see from the first page of the Marvin prospectus (see this chapter's appendix) that these administrative costs totaled $820,000 or just over 1% of the proceeds.

Underpricing of IPOs

Marvin's issue was costly in yet another way. Since the offering price was less than the true value of the issued securities, investors who bought the issue got a bargain at the expense of the firm's original shareholders.

BEYOND THE PAGE

 Hot IPOs

mhhe.com/brealey13e

These costs of *underpricing* are hidden but nevertheless real. For IPOs, they generally exceed all other issue costs. Whenever any company goes public, it is very difficult to judge how much investors will be prepared to pay for the stock. Sometimes the underwriters misjudge dramatically. For example, when the prospectus for the IPO of eBay was first published, the underwriters indicated that the company would sell 3.5 million shares at a price between $14 and $16 each. However, the enthusiasm for eBay's web-based auction system was such that the underwriters increased the issue price to $18. The next morning, dealers were flooded with orders to buy eBay; more than 4.5 million shares traded, and the stock closed the day at a price of $47.375.

BEYOND THE PAGE

 Chinese IPOs

mhhe.com/brealey13e

We admit that the eBay issue was unusual.[27] But researchers have found that investors who buy at the issue price on average realize very high returns over the following days. For example, one study of more than 13,000 U.S. IPOs from 1960 to 2017 found average underpricing of 16.8%.[28]

---

[24]In the more risky cases, the underwriter usually receives some extra noncash compensation, such as warrants to buy additional common stock in the future.

[25]H. C. Chen and J. R. Ritter, "The Seven Percent Solution," *Journal of Finance* 55 (June 2000), pp. 1105–1131.

[26]Chen and Ritter argue that the fixed spread suggests the underwriting market is not competitive. The U.S. Department of Justice was led to investigate whether the spread constituted evidence of price-fixing. Robert Hansen disagrees that the market is not competitive. Among other things, he provides evidence that the 7% spread is not abnormally profitable and argues that it is part of a competitive and efficient market. See R. Hansen, "Do Investment Banks Compete in IPOs?: The Advent of the "7% Plus Contract"," *Journal of Financial Economics* 59 (2001), pp. 313–346.

[27]It does not, however, hold the record. That honor goes to VA Linux.

[28]Our figure is an equally weighted average of first-day returns and is taken from data on **https://site.warrington.ufl.edu/ritter/ipo-data/.**

How Scandal Hit the Investment Banking Industry

❯ Nineteen ninety-nine looked to be a wonderful year for investment banks. Not only did they underwrite a near-record number of IPOs, but the stocks that they sold leapt by an average of 72% on their first day of trading, earning the underwriters some very grateful clients. Just three years later, the same investment banks were in disgrace. Probing by New York State Attorney General Eliot Spitzer uncovered a chronicle of unethical and shameful behavior during the boom years.

As the dot-com stock market boom developed, investment banking analysts had begun to take on the additional role of promoters of the shares that they analyzed, in the process becoming celebrities with salaries to match. The early run-up in the stock price of dot-com IPOs therefore owed much to hype by the underwriters' analysts, who strongly promoted stocks that they sometimes privately thought were overpriced. One superstar Internet analyst was revealed in internal e-mails to have believed that stocks he was peddling to investors were "junk" and "piece[s] of crap." In many cases, the stocks were indeed junk, and the underwriters who had puffed the IPOs soon found themselves sued by disgruntled investors who had bought at the inflated prices.

The underwriters' troubles deepened when it was disclosed that in a number of cases they had allocated stock in hot new issues to the personal brokerage accounts of the CEOs of major corporate clients. This stock could then be sold, or "spun," for quick profits. Five senior executives of leading telecom companies were disclosed to have received a total of $28 million in profits from their allocation of stocks in IPOs underwritten by one bank. Over the same period, the bank was awarded more than $100 million of business from these five companies. Eliot Spitzer argued that such lucrative perks were really attempts by the banks to buy future business and that the profits therefore belonged to the companies' shareholders rather than the executives. Soon, top executives of several other companies were facing demands from disgruntled shareholders that they return to their companies the profits that they had pocketed from hot initial public offerings.

These scandals that engulfed the investment banking industry resulted in a $1.4 billion payout by the banks and an agreement to separate investment banking and research departments, hire independent consultants, and select independent research providers. But the revelations also raised troubling questions about ethical standards and the pressures that can lead employees to unscrupulous behavior.

Figure 15.4 shows that the United States is not the only country in which IPOs are underpriced. In Saudi Arabia, the gains from buying IPOs have averaged 240%.

You might think that shareholders would prefer not to sell stock in their company for less than its market price, but many investment bankers and institutional investors argue that underpricing is in the interests of the issuing firm. They say that a low offering price on an IPO raises the price when it is subsequently traded in the market and enhances the firm's ability to raise further capital.

There is another possible reason that it may make sense to underprice new issues. Suppose that you successfully bid for a painting at an art auction. Should you be pleased? It is true that you now own the painting, which was presumably what you wanted, but everybody else at the auction apparently thought that the painting was worth less than you did. In other words, your success suggests that you may have overpaid. This problem is known as the *winner's curse*. The highest bidder in an auction is most likely to have overestimated the object's value and, unless bidders recognize this in their bids, the buyer will, on average, overpay. If bidders are aware of the danger, they are likely to adjust their bids down correspondingly.

The same problem arises when you apply for a new issue of securities. For example, suppose that you decide to apply for every new issue of common stock. You will find that you have no difficulty in getting stock in the issues that no one else wants. But, when the issue is

BEYOND THE PAGE

Facebook's IPO

mhhe.com/brealey13e

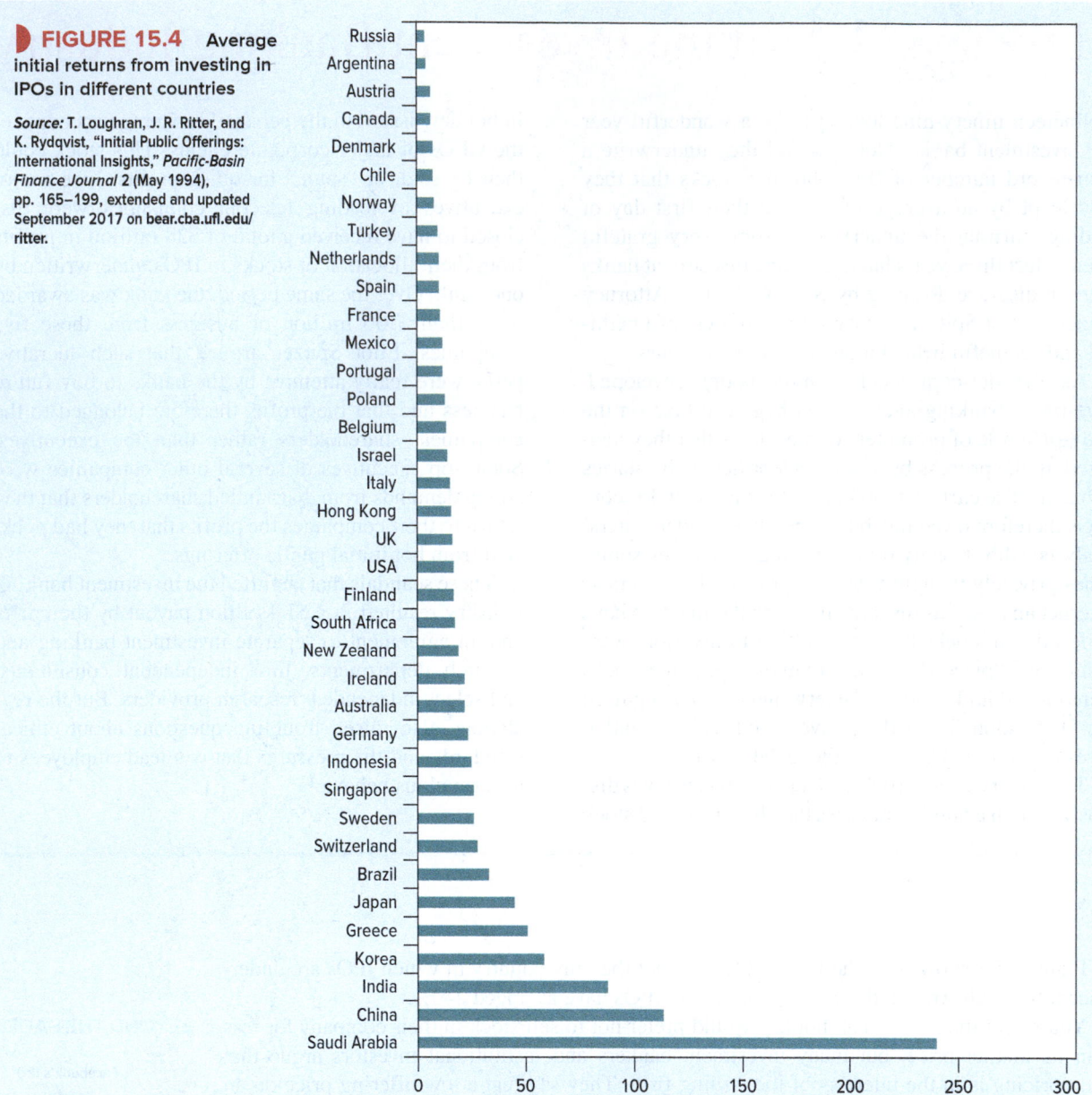

◗ **FIGURE 15.4** **Average initial returns from investing in IPOs in different countries**

Source: T. Loughran, J. R. Ritter, and K. Rydqvist, "Initial Public Offerings: International Insights," *Pacific-Basin Finance Journal* 2 (May 1994), pp. 165–199, extended and updated September 2017 on **bear.cba.ufl.edu/ritter.**

attractive, the underwriters will not have enough stock to go around, and you will receive less stock than you wanted. The result is that your money-making strategy may turn out to be a loser. If you are smart, you will play the game only if there is substantial underpricing on average. Here then we have a possible rationale for the underpricing of new issues. Uninformed investors who cannot distinguish which issues are attractive are exposed to the winner's curse. Companies and their underwriters are aware of this and need to underprice on average to attract the uninformed investors.[29]

---

[29]The winner's curse would disappear if only investors knew what the market price was going to be. One response is to allow trading in a security before it has been issued. This is known as the *gray market,* which in the United States is most common for debt issues. Investors can observe the price in the gray market and can be more confident that they are not overbidding when the actual issue takes place.

These arguments could well justify some degree of underpricing, but it is not clear that they can account for the occasional underpricing of 100% or more. Skeptics point out that such underpricing is largely in the interests of the underwriters, who want to reduce the risk that they will be left with unwanted stock and also to court popularity by allotting stock to favored clients.

If the skeptics are right, you might expect issuing companies to rebel at being asked to sell stock for much less than it is worth. Think back to our example of eBay. If the company had sold 3.5 million shares at the market price of $47.375 rather than $18, it would have netted an additional $103 million. So why weren't eBay's existing shareholders hopping mad? Loughran and Ritter suggest that the explanation lies in behavioral psychology and argue that the cost of underpricing may be outweighed in shareholders' minds by the happy surprise of finding that they are wealthier than they thought. eBay's largest shareholder was Pierre Omidyar, the founder and chairman, who retained his entire holding of 15.2 million shares. The initial jump in the stock price from $18 to $47.375 added $447 million to Mr. Omidyar's wealth. This may well have pushed the cost of underpricing to the back of his mind.[30]

Hot New-Issue Periods

Figure 15.5 shows that the degree of underpricing fluctuates sharply from year to year. In 1999, around the peak of the dot-com boom, new issues raised $65 billion, and the average first-day return on IPOs was 70%. Nearly $37 billion was left on the table that year.[31] But, as the number of new issues slumped, so did the amount of underpricing.

Some observers believe that these hot new-issue periods arise because investors are prone to periods of excessive optimism and would-be issuers time their IPOs to coincide with these periods. Other observers stress the fact that a fall in the cost of capital or an improvement in the economic outlook may mean that a number of new or dormant projects suddenly become

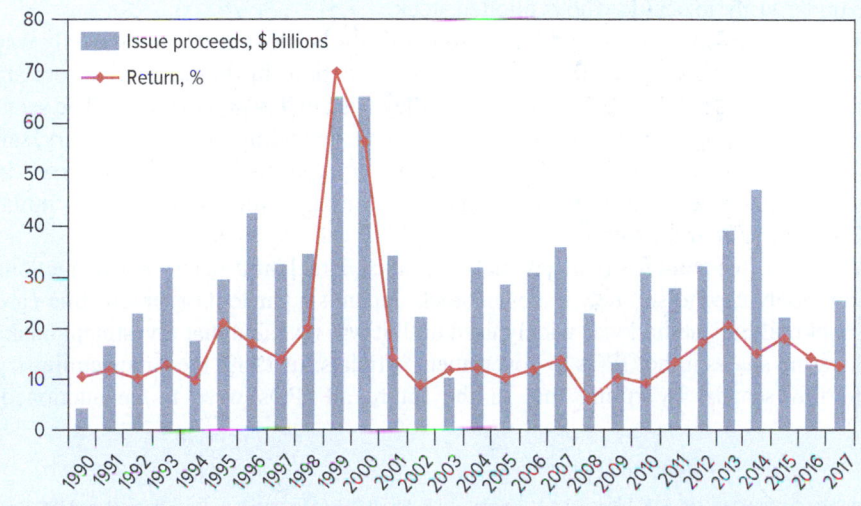

▶ **FIGURE 15.5**

IPO proceeds in the United States and average first-day returns, 1990–2017

Source: J. R. Ritter, "Monthly Number of IPOs and the average first-day return," February, 2018, bear.cba.ufl.edu/ritter.

---

[30]T. Loughran and J. Ritter, "Why Don't Issuers Get Upset about Leaving Money on the Table in IPOs?" *Review of Financial Studies* 15 (2002), pp. 413–444.

[31]The "money left on the table" is the difference between the value placed by investors on the stocks and the amount that investors paid for the stocks.

profitable. At such times, many entrepreneurs rush to raise new cash to invest in these projects.[32]

The Long-Run Performance of IPO Stocks

On average investors who buy IPO stocks at the issue price realize high immediate returns, but how do they fare over the longer run? During the period 1980 to 2015 investors who bought the stock of an IPO at the close of the first day's trading would have lost 18.7% relative to the market over the following three years. This suggests that the initial reaction to the new issues was overenthusiastic. However, much of this poor performance seems to have reflected the fact that IPO stocks were largely those of small growth companies. These companies were generally poor investments during this period. When IPO stocks are compared with those of similar companies, much of the return shortfall disappears.[33]

15-3   Alternative Issue Procedures for IPOs

Table 15.2 summarizes the main steps involved in making an initial public offering of stock in the United States. You can see that Marvin's new issue was a typical IPO in almost every respect. In particular, most IPOs in the United States use the *bookbuilding* method in which the underwriter builds a book of likely orders and uses this information to set the issue price.

The bookbuilding method is, in some ways, like an auction since potential buyers indicate how many shares they are prepared to buy at given prices. However, these indications are not binding and are used only as a guide to fix the price of the issue. The advantage of the bookbuilding method is that it allows underwriters to give preference to those investors whose bids are most helpful in setting the issue price and to offer them a reward in the shape of underpricing.[34] Critics of bookbuilding point to the abuses of the 1990s and emphasize the dangers of allowing the underwriter to decide who is allotted stock.

Bookbuilding has rapidly gained popularity throughout the world, but it is not the only way to sell new stock. One alternative is to conduct an open auction. In this case, investors are invited to submit their bids, stating how many shares they wish to buy and the price. The securities are then sold to the highest bidders. Most governments, including the U.S. Treasury, sell their bonds by auction. In the United States, auctions of common stock are rare. However, in 2004, Google simultaneously raised eyebrows and $1.7 billion in the world's largest initial public offering to be sold by auction.[35]

Fans of auctions often point to countries such as France, Israel, and Japan, where auctions were once commonly used to sell new issues of stock. Japan is a particularly interesting case because the bookbuilding method was widely used until it was revealed that investment banks had been allocating shares in hot IPOs to government officials. In 1989, the finance ministry responded to this scandal by ruling that in the future all IPOs were to be auctioned.

---

[32]For examples of these explanations, see A. P. Ljungqvist, V. Nanda, and R. Singh, "Hot Markets, Investor Sentiment, and IPO Pricing," *Journal of Business* 79 (July 2006), pp. 1667–1702; and L. Pastor and P. Veronesi, "Rational IPO Waves," *Journal of Finance* 60 (2005), pp. 1713–1757.

[33]See, for example, M. Lowry, R. Michaely, and E. Volkova, "Initial Public Offerings: A Synthesis of the Literature and Directions for Future Research," 2017, *Foundations and Trends in Finance,* 11 (February 10, 2017), pp. 154–320.

[34]See L. M. Benveniste and P. A. Spindt, "How Investment Bankers Determine the Offer Price and Allocation of New Issues," *Journal of Financial Economics* 24 (1989), pp. 343–361; and F. Cornelli and D. Goldreich, "Bookbuilding and Strategic Allocation," *Journal of Finance* 56 (December 2001), pp. 2337–2369.

[35]Google's issue was followed in 2005 by a $140 million auction of stock by Morningstar.

TABLE 15.2
The main steps involved in making an initial public offering of stock in the United States

1. About 1 year before the company expects to go public, it appoints the managing underwriter (bookrunner) and co-manager(s). The underwriting syndicate is formed.
2. The arrangement with the underwriters includes agreement on the spread (typically 7% for medium-sized IPOs) and on the greenshoe option (typically allowing the underwriters to increase the number of shares bought by 15%).
3. About 3 months before the issue date, the company files a registration statement with the SEC. A preliminary prospectus (red herring) is issued, and a preliminary price range is proposed.
4. A roadshow is arranged to market the issue to potential investors. The managing underwriter builds a book of potential demand and, if appropriate, sets a new preliminary price range.
5. As soon as the SEC approves the registration statement, the company and underwriters agree on the issue price.
6. The following day, the underwriters allot stock (typically with overallotment), and trading starts.
7. The underwriters cover any short position by buying stock in the market or by exercising their greenshoe option.
8. After the 40-day quiet period, the underwriters are permitted to make forward-looking statements about the company and recommendations to buy the stock.

This resulted in a sharp fall in underpricing. However, in 1997, the restrictions were lifted, bookbuilding returned to favor, and the level of underpricing increased.[36]

Types of Auction: A Digression

Suppose that a government wishes to auction 4 million bonds and three would-be buyers submit bids. Investor A bids $1,020 each for 1 million bonds, B bids $1,000 for 3 million bonds, and C bids $980 for 2 million bonds. The bids of the two highest bidders (A and B) absorb all the bonds on offer and C is left empty-handed. What price do the winning bidders, A and B, pay?

The answer depends on whether the sale is a *discriminatory auction* or a *uniform-price auction*. In a discriminatory auction, every winner is required to pay the price that he or she bid. In this case, A would pay $1,020 and B would pay $1,000. In a uniform-price auction, both would pay $1,000, which is the price of the lowest winning bidder (investor B).

It might seem from our example that the proceeds from a uniform-price auction would be lower than from a discriminatory auction. But this ignores the fact that the uniform-price auction provides better protection against the winner's curse. Wise bidders know that there is little cost to overbidding in a uniform-price auction, but there is potentially a very high cost to doing so in a discriminatory auction.[37] Economists therefore often argue that the uniform-price auction should result in higher proceeds.[38]

Sales of bonds by the U.S. Treasury used to take the form of discriminatory auctions so that successful buyers paid their bid. However, in 1998, the government switched to a uniform-price auction.[39]

---

[36]T. Kaneko and R. Pettway, "Auctions versus Book Building of Japanese IPOs," *Pacific-Basin Journal* 11 (2003), pp. 439–462.

[37]In addition, the price in the uniform-price auction depends not only on the views of B but also on those of A (e.g., if A had bid $990 rather than $1,020, then both A and B would have paid $990 for each bond). Since the uniform-price auction takes advantage of the views of both A and B, it reduces the winner's curse.

[38]Sometimes auctions reduce the winner's curse by allowing uninformed bidders to enter noncompetitive bids, whereby they submit a quantity but not a price. For example, in U.S. Treasury auctions, investors may submit noncompetitive bids and receive their full allocation.

[39]Experience in the United States with uniform-price auctions suggests that they do indeed reduce the winner's curse problem and realize higher prices for the seller. See D. Goldreich, "Underpricing in Discriminatory and Uniform-Price Treasury Auctions," *Journal of Financial and Quantitative Analysis* 42 (June 2007), pp. 443–466.

15-4   Security Sales by Public Companies

A company's first public issue of stock is seldom its last. As the firm grows, it is likely to make further issues of debt and equity. Public companies can issue securities either by offering them to investors at large or by making a rights issue that is limited to existing stockholders. We begin by describing general cash offers, which are now used for almost all debt and equity issues in the United States. We then describe rights issues, which are widely used in other countries for issues of common stock.

General Cash Offers

When a corporation makes a general cash offer of debt or equity in the United States, it goes through much the same procedure as when it first went public. In other words, it registers the issue with the SEC[40] and then sells the securities to an underwriter (or a syndicate of underwriters), who in turn offers the securities to the public. Before the price of the issue is fixed, the underwriter will build up a book of likely demand for the securities, just as in the case of Marvin's IPO.

The SEC's Rule 415 allows large companies to file a single registration statement covering financing plans for up to three years into the future. The actual issues can then be done with scant additional paperwork, whenever the firm needs the cash or thinks it can issue securities at an attractive price. This is called *shelf registration*—the registration statement is "put on the shelf," to be taken down and used as needed.

Think of how you as a financial manager might use shelf registration. Suppose your company is likely to need up to $200 million of new long-term debt over the next year or so. It can file a registration statement for that amount. It then has prior approval to issue up to $200 million of debt, but it isn't obligated to issue a penny. Nor is it required to work through any particular underwriters; the registration statement may name one or more underwriters the firm thinks it may work with, but others can be substituted later.

Now you can sit back and issue debt as needed, in bits and pieces if you like. Suppose Morgan Stanley comes across an insurance company with $10 million ready to invest in corporate bonds. Your phone rings. It's Morgan Stanley offering to buy $10 million of your bonds, priced to yield, say, 8.5%. If you think that's a good price, you say OK and the deal is done, subject only to a little additional paperwork. Morgan Stanley then resells the bonds to the insurance company, it hopes at a higher price than it paid for them, thus earning an intermediary's profit.

Here is another possible deal: Suppose that you perceive a window of opportunity in which interest rates are temporarily low. You invite bids for $100 million of bonds. Some bids may come from large investment banks acting alone; others may come from ad hoc syndicates. But that's not your problem; if the price is right, you just take the best deal offered.

Not all companies eligible for shelf registration actually use it for all their public issues. Sometimes they believe they can get a better deal by making one large issue through traditional channels, especially when the security to be issued has some unusual feature or when the firm believes that it needs the investment banker's counsel or stamp of approval on the issue. Consequently, shelf registration is less often used for issues of common stock or convertible securities than for garden-variety corporate bonds.

International Security Issues

Instead of borrowing in their local market, companies often issue so-called *foreign bonds* in another country's domestic market, in which case the issue will be governed by the rules of that country.

---

[40]In 2005, the SEC created a new category of firm termed "a well-known seasoned issuer" (or WKSI). These firms are exempt from certain filing requirements.

A second alternative is to make an issue of *eurobonds,* which is underwritten by a group of international banks and offered simultaneously to investors in a number of countries. The borrower must provide a prospectus or offering circular that sets out the detailed terms of the issue. The underwriters will then build up a book of potential orders, and finally, the issue will be priced and sold. Very large debt issues may be sold as *global bonds,* with one part sold internationally in the eurobond market and the remainder sold in the company's domestic market.

Equity issues too may be sold overseas. Traditionally, New York has been the natural home for such issues, but in recent years, many companies have preferred to list in London or Hong Kong. This has led many U.S. observers to worry that New York may be losing its competitive edge to other financial centers.

The Costs of a General Cash Offer

Whenever a firm makes a cash offer of securities, it incurs substantial administrative costs, and it needs to compensate the underwriters by selling them securities below the price that they expect to receive from investors.

In addition to these direct costs, the offer price for seasoned stock issues is on average set at about 3% below the previous night's close.[41] While this underpricing is far less than in the case of an IPO, it remains a significant proportion of the cost of an issue of stock.

Table 15.3 lists underwriting spreads for a few recent issues. Notice that the underwriting spreads for debt securities are lower than for common stocks—less than 1% for many issues. Larger issues tend to have lower spreads than smaller issues. This may partly stem

Type	Company	Issue Amount ($ millions)	Underwriting Spread (%)
Common Stock:			
IPO	Alibaba Group	$21,767	1.2%
IPO	Invitation Homes	1,540	4.5
IPO	Mulesoft	221	7.0
IPO	Jounce Therapeutics	102	7.0
IPO	Ichor Holdings	53	7.0
IPO	BeyondSpring	3	7.0
Seasoned	AMC Entertainment Holdings	600	3.5
Seasoned	Keysight Technologies	400	3.5
Seasoned	John Bean Technologies	170	5.5
Seasoned	Intrepid Potash	52	3.9
Seasoned	Akers Biosciences	2	7.0
Debt:			
4.5% notes 2057*	Microsoft	$2,000	0.75%
5.291% notes 2046*	Ford Motor	1,300	0.88
3.75% notes 2046*	United Technologies	1,100	0.88
5.75% convertible senior notes 2021	Ship Finance International	225	2.0

> **TABLE 15.3**
> Gross underwriting spreads of selected issues. Spreads are percentages of gross proceeds.
>
> *Excludes the exercise by the underwriters of greenshoe options.

[41]See O. Altinkilic and R. S. Hansen, "Discounting and Underpricing in Seasoned Equity Offers," *Journal of Financial Economics* 69 (2003), pp. 285–323.

from the fact that there are fixed costs to selling securities, but large issues are generally made by large companies, which are better known and easier for the underwriter to monitor. So do not assume that a small company could make a jumbo issue at a negligible percentage spread.[42]

Figure 15.6 summarizes a study of total issue costs (spreads plus administrative costs) for several thousand issues between 2004 and 2008.

Market Reaction to Stock Issues

Economists who have studied seasoned issues of common stock have generally found that announcement of the issue results in a decline in the stock price of 2% to 4%.[43] While this may not sound overwhelming, the fall in market value is equivalent, on average, to nearly a third of the new money raised by the issue.

What's going on here? One view is that the price of the stock is simply depressed by the prospect of the additional supply. On the other hand, there is little sign that the extent of the price fall increases with the size of the stock issue. There is an alternative explanation that seems to fit the facts better.

Suppose that the CFO of a restaurant chain is strongly optimistic about its prospects. From her point of view, the company's stock price is too low. Yet the company wants to issue shares

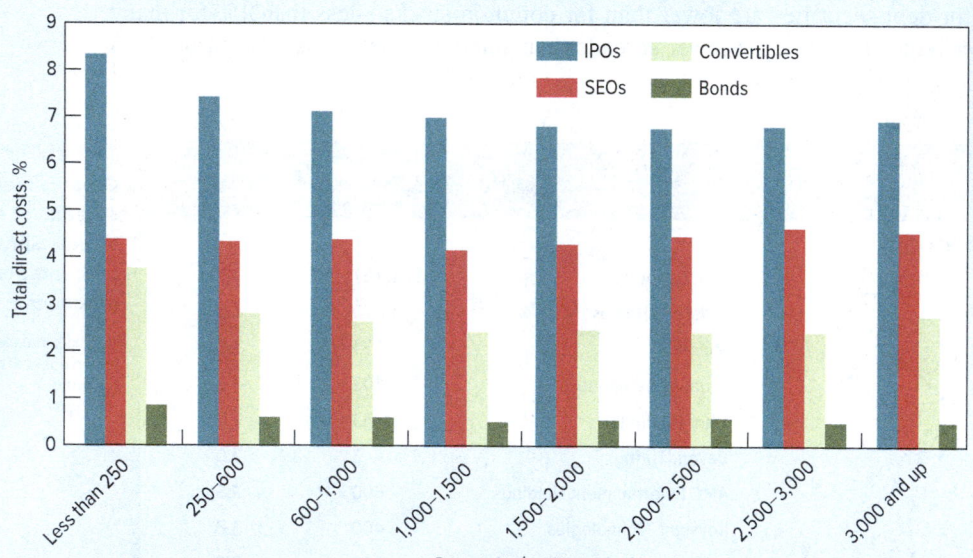

▶ **FIGURE 15.6**   **Total direct costs as a percentage of gross proceeds. The total direct costs for initial public offerings (IPOs), seasoned equity offerings (SEOs), convertible bonds, and straight bonds are composed of underwriter spreads and other direct expenses.**

Source: SDC Platinum.

Notes: There were 5,706 domestic issues between 2004 and 2008. Closed-end funds (SIC 6726), REITS (SIC 6798), ADRs, mortgage-backed, and federal agency (SIC 6011, 6019, 6111 and 999B) issues are excluded.

---

[42]This point is emphasized in O. Altinkiliç and R. S. Hansen, "Are There Economies of Scale in Underwriting Fees? Evidence of Rising External Financing Costs," *Review of Financial Studies* 13 (Spring 2000), pp. 191–218.

[43]See, for example, Altınkılıç and Hansen, "Are There Economies of Scale in Underwriting Fees?"; and K. Jung, Y-C. Kim, and R. Stulz, "Timing, Investment Opportunities, Managerial Discretion, and the Security Issue Decision," *Journal of Financial Economics* 42 (October 1996), pp. 159–185.

to finance expansion into the new state of Northern California.[44] What is she to do? All the choices have drawbacks. If the chain sells common stock, it will favor new investors at the expense of old shareholders. When investors come to share the CFO's optimism, the share price will rise, and the bargain price to the new investors will be evident.

If the CFO could convince investors to accept her rosy view of the future, then new shares could be sold at a fair price. But this is not so easy. CEOs and CFOs always take care to *sound* upbeat, so just announcing "I'm optimistic" has little effect. But supplying detailed information about business plans and profit forecasts is costly and is also of great assistance to competitors.

The CFO could scale back or delay the expansion until the company's stock price recovers. That too is costly, but it may be rational if the stock price is severely undervalued and a stock issue is the only source of financing.

If a CFO knows that the company's stock is *over*valued, the position is reversed. If the firm sells new shares at the high price, it will help existing shareholders at the expense of the new ones. Managers might be prepared to issue stock even if the new cash is just put in the bank.

Of course, investors are not stupid. They can predict that managers are more likely to issue stock when they think it is overvalued and that optimistic managers may cancel or defer issues. Therefore, when an equity issue is announced, they mark down the price of the stock accordingly. Thus the decline in the price of the stock at the time of the new issue may have nothing to do with the increased supply but simply with the information that the issue provides.[45]

Cornett and Tehranian devised a natural experiment that pretty much proves this point.[46] They examined a sample of stock issues by commercial banks. Some of these issues were necessary to meet capital standards set by banking regulators. The rest were ordinary, voluntary stock issues designed to raise money for various corporate purposes. The necessary issues caused a much smaller drop in stock prices than the voluntary ones, which makes perfect sense. If the issue is outside the manager's discretion, announcement of the issue conveys no information about the manager's view of the company's prospects.[47]

Most financial economists now interpret the stock price drop on equity issue announcements as an information effect and not a result of the additional supply.[48] But what about an issue of preferred stock or debt? Are they equally likely to provide information to investors about company prospects? A pessimistic manager might be tempted to get a debt issue out before investors become aware of the bad news, but how much profit can you make for your shareholders by selling overpriced debt? Perhaps 1% or 2%. Investors know that a pessimistic manager has a much greater incentive to issue equity rather than preferred stock or debt. Therefore, when companies announce an issue of preferred or debt, there is a barely perceptible fall in the stock price.[49]

---

[44]Northern California seceded from California and became the fifty-second state in 2027.

[45]This explanation was developed in S. C. Myers and N. S. Majluf, "Corporate Financing and Investment Decisions When Firms Have Information That Investors Do Not Have," *Journal of Financial Economics* 13 (1984), pp. 187–221.

[46]M. M. Cornett and H. Tehranian, "An Examination of Voluntary versus Involuntary Security Issuances by Commercial Banks," *Journal of Financial Economics* 35 (1994), pp. 99–122.

[47]The "involuntary issuers" did make a choice: They could have forgone the stock issue and run the risk of failing to meet the regulatory capital standards. The banks that were more concerned with this risk were more likely to issue. Thus it is no surprise that Cornett and Tehranian found some drop in stock price even for the involuntary issues.

[48]There is another possible information effect. Just as an unexpected increase in the dividend suggests to investors that the company is generating more cash than they thought, the announcement of a new issue may have the reverse implication. However, this effect cannot explain why the announcement of an issue of debt does not result in a similar fall in the stock price.

[49]See L. Shyam-Sunder, "The Stock Price Effect of Risky vs. Safe Debt," *Journal of Financial and Quantitative Analysis* 26 (December 1991), pp. 549–558.

Rights Issues

BEYOND THE PAGE

Rights issues terminology

mhhe.com/brealey13e

Instead of making an issue of stock to investors at large, companies sometimes give their existing shareholders the right of first refusal. Such issues are known as *privileged subscription,* or *rights, issues.* In the United States, rights issues are largely confined to closed-end investment companies. However, in most countries outside the United States, rights issues are the most common method for seasoned equity issues. For example, rights offerings predominate in China, Germany, France, and Brazil.[50]

We have already come across one example of a rights issue—the offer by the British bank HBOS, which ended up in the hands of its underwriters. Let us look more closely at another issue. In 2017, Deutsche Bank needed to raise €8 billion of equity to reduce its debt ratio. It did so by offering its existing shareholders the right to buy one new share for every two that they currently held. The new shares were priced at €11.65, about 35% below the pre-announcement market price of €18.00.

Imagine that just before the rights issue you held two shares of Deutsche Bank valued at 2 × €18 = €36.00. Deutsche's offer would give you the right to buy one new share for an additional outlay of €11.65. If you take up the offer, your holding increases to three shares, and the value increases by the amount of the extra cash to €36.00 + 11.65 = €47.65. Therefore, after the issue the value of each share is no longer €18.00 but a little lower at €47.65/3 = €15.88. This is termed the ex-rights price.

What is the value of the right to buy a new share for €11.65? The answer is €15.88 − €11.65 = €4.23.[51] An investor who could buy a share worth €15.88 for €11.65 would be willing to pay €4.23 for the privilege.[52]

It should be clear on reflection that Deutsche Bank could have raised the same amount of money on a variety of terms. For example, it could have offered shareholders the right to buy one new share at €5.825 for every share that they held. In this case, shareholders would buy twice as many shares at half the price. Our shareholder who initially held two shares would end up with four shares' worth, in total, 2 × €18.00 + 2 × €5.825 = €47.65. The value of each share would be €47.65/4 = €11.91. Under this new arrangement, the ex-rights share price is lower, but you end up with four shares rather than three. The total value of your holding remains the same. Suppose that you wanted to sell your right to buy one new share for €5.825. Investors would be prepared to pay you €6.09 for this right. They would then pay €5.825 to Deutsche Bank and receive a share worth €11.91.

Deutsche's shareholders were given about two weeks to decide whether they wished to take up the offer of new shares. If the stock price in the meantime fell below the issue price, shareholders would have no incentive to buy the new shares. For this reason, companies making a rights issue generally arrange for the underwriters to buy any unwanted stock. Underwriters are not often left holding the baby, but we saw earlier that in the case of the HBOS issue, they were left with a very large (and bouncing) baby.

Our example illustrates that as long as the company successfully sells the new shares, the issue price in a rights offering is irrelevant. That is not the case in a general cash offer. If the

---

[50]See M. Massa, T. Vermaelen, and M. Xu, "Rights Offerings, Trading, and Regulation: A Global Perspective," INSEAD Working Paper 2013/120/FIN, December 13, 2013, available at SSRN: https://ssrn.com/abstract=2340504.

[51]In fact, he should be prepared to pay slightly more because he is not compelled to buy the stock and can choose not to do so. In practice, since the option is usually well in the money and its time to expiration is short, its value is usually negligible.

[52] There is a minor, but potentially confusing, difference between North American and European rights issues. In the Deutsche Bank issue, shareholders needed one right to buy a new share, but they needed to own two shares to receive this right. A similar issue in North America would generally give shareholders one right for each share held. However, they would need more than one right to buy a new share, and each right would be worth correspondingly less. For example, if Deutsche had been a U.S. company, shareholders would have received one right for every share owned, but they would have needed two of these rights to buy one new share. Each right would have been only half as valuable. You may encounter formulas for the value of a right. Remember to check whether the formula is referring to a U.S. or a European issue. Better still, work out the value of a right for yourself.

company sells stock to new shareholders for less than the market will bear, the buyer makes a profit at the expense of existing shareholders. As we noted earlier, general cash offers are typically sold at a small discount of about 3% on the previous day's closing price, so underpricing is not a major worry. But since this cost can be avoided completely by using a rights issue, we are puzzled by the apparent preference of companies for general cash offers.

15-5 Private Placements and Public Issues

Whenever a company makes a public offering, it is obliged to register the issue with the SEC. It could avoid this costly process by selling the securities privately. The rules on what constitutes a *private placement* are complicated. The securities can generally be sold to an unlimited number of financial institutions, but there are restrictions on the number of less wealthy private individuals who can participate.

One of the drawbacks of a private placement is that the investor cannot easily resell the security. However, institutions such as life insurance companies invest huge amounts in corporate debt for the long haul and are less concerned about its marketability. Consequently, an active private placement market has evolved for corporate debt. Often, this debt is negotiated directly between the company and the lender, but if the issue is too large to be absorbed by one institution, the company will generally employ an investment bank to draw up a prospectus and identify possible buyers.

As you would expect, it costs less to arrange a private placement than to make a public issue. This is a particular advantage for companies making smaller issues.

In 1990, the SEC adopted Rule 144A, which relaxed its restrictions on who can buy and trade unregistered securities. The rule allows large financial institutions (known as *qualified institutional buyers*) to trade unregistered securities among themselves. Rule 144A was intended to increase liquidity and reduce interest rates and issue costs for private placements. It was aimed largely at foreign corporations deterred by registration requirements in the United States. The SEC argued that such firms would welcome the opportunity to issue unregistered stocks and bonds that could then be freely traded by large U.S. financial institutions.

Rule 144A issues have proved very popular, particularly with foreign issuers. There has also been an increasing volume of secondary trading in Rule 144A issues.

In this chapter, we have summarized the various procedures for issuing corporate securities. We first looked at how infant companies raise venture capital to carry them through to the point at which they can make their first public issue of stock. We then looked at how companies can make further public issues of securities by a general cash offer. Finally, we reviewed the procedures for a private placement.

SUMMARY

It is always difficult to summarize a summary. Instead, we will remind you of some of the most important implications for the financial manager who must decide how to raise financing.

- *Larger is cheaper.* There are economies of scale in issuing securities. It is cheaper to go to the market once for $100 million than to make two trips for $50 million each. Consequently, firms bunch security issues. That may often mean relying on short-term financing until a large issue is justified. Or it may mean issuing more than is needed at the moment in order to avoid another issue later.

- *Watch out for underpricing.* Underpricing is often a serious hidden cost to the existing shareholders.

- *The winner's curse may be a serious problem with IPOs.* Would-be investors in an initial public offering (IPO) do not know how other investors will value the stock, and they worry that they are likely to receive a larger allocation of the overpriced issues. Careful design of issue procedure may reduce the winner's curse.

- *New stock issues may depress the price.* The extent of this price pressure varies, but for industrial issues in the United States, the fall in the value of the existing stock may amount to a significant proportion of the money raised. This pressure is due to the information that the market reads into the company's decision to issue stock.

- *Shelf registration often makes sense for debt issues by blue-chip firms.* Shelf registration reduces the time taken to arrange a new issue, it increases flexibility, and it may cut underwriting costs. It seems best suited for debt issues by large firms that are happy to switch between investment banks. It seems less suited for issues of unusually risky or complex securities or for issues by small companies that are likely to benefit from a close relationship with an investment bank.

● ● ● ● ●

FURTHER READING

Metrick and Yasuda, Megginson, Gompers, and Gompers and Lerner provide an overview of the venture capital industry, while Sahlman looks at the form of the venture capital contract:

A. Metrick and A. Yasuda, *Venture Capital and the Finance of Innovation,* 2nd ed. (New York: John Wiley & Sons, 2010).

W. L. Megginson, "Toward a Global Model of Venture Capital?" *Journal of Applied Corporate Finance* 16 (Winter 2004), pp. 89–107.

P. Gompers, "Venture Capital," in B. E. Eckbo, ed., *Handbook of Corporate Finance: Empirical Corporate Finance* (Amsterdam: Elsevier/North Holland, 2007).

P. Gompers and J. Lerner, "The Venture Capital Revolution," *Journal of Economic Perspectives* 15 (Spring 2001), pp. 145–168.

W. A. Sahlman, "Aspects of Financial Contracting in Venture Capital," *Journal of Applied Corporate Finance* (Summer 1988), pp. 23–36.

Here are some comprehensive surveys of the literature on new issues:

K. W. Hanley, "The Economics of Primary Markets," Working paper, Lehigh University, July 9, 2017.

M. Lowry, R. Michaely, and E. Volkova "Initial Public Offering: A Synthesis of the Literature and Directions for Future Research," *Foundations and Trends in Finance* 11 (February 10, 2017), pp. 154–320.

B. E. Eckbo, R. W. Masulis, and Ø. Norli, "Security Offerings," in B. E. Eckbo, ed., *Handbook of Corporate Finance: Empirical Corporate Finance* (Amsterdam: Elsevier/North-Holland, 2007).

J. R. Ritter, "Investment Banking and Securities Issuance," in G. M. Constantinides, M. Harris, and R. Stulz, eds., *Handbook of the Economics of Finance* (Amsterdam: Elsevier Science, 2003).

T. Jenkinson and A. P. Ljungqvist, *Going Public: The Theory and Evidence on How Companies Raise Equity Finance,* 2nd ed. (Oxford: Oxford University Press, 1999).

Two useful articles on IPOs are:

R. G. Ibbotson, J. L. Sindelar, and J. R. Ritter, "The Market's Problems with the Pricing of Initial Public Offerings," *Journal of Applied Corporate Finance* 7 (Spring 1994), pp. 66–74.

L. M. Benveniste and W. J. Wilhelm Jr., "Initial Public Offerings: Going by the Book," *Journal of Applied Corporate Finance* 10 (Spring 1997) pp. 98–108.

A useful introduction to the design of auctions is:

P. Milgrom, "Auctions and Bidding: A Primer," *Journal of Economic Perspectives* 3 (1989), pp. 3–22.

PROBLEM SETS

connect   Select problems are available in McGraw-Hill's *Connect*.
Please see the preface for more information.

1. **Vocabulary*** Each of the following terms is associated with one of the events beneath. Can you match them up?

   a. Best efforts

   b. Bookbuilding

   c. Shelf registration

   d. Rule 144A

   Events:

   A. Investors indicate to the underwriter how many shares they would like to buy in a new issue and these indications are used to help set the price.

   B. The underwriter accepts responsibility only to try to sell the issue.

   C. Some issues are not registered but can be traded freely among qualified institutional buyers.

   D. Several tranches of the same security may be sold under the same registration. (A "tranche" is a batch, a fraction of a larger issue.)

2. **Vocabulary** Explain what each of the following terms or phrases means:

   a. Venture capital.

   b. Bookbuilding.

   c. Underwriting spread.

   d. Registration statement.

   e. Winner's curse.

3. **Vocabulary** Here is a further vocabulary quiz. Briefly explain each of the following:

   a. Zero-stage vs. first- or second-stage financing.

   b. Carried interest.

   c. Rights issue.

   d. Road show.

   e. Best-efforts offer.

   f. Qualified institutional buyer.

   g. Blue-sky laws.

   h. Greenshoe option.

4. **Stock issues** True or false?

   a. Venture capitalists typically provide first-stage financing sufficient to cover all development expenses. Second-stage financing is provided by stock issued in an IPO.

   b. Underpricing in an IPO is only a problem when the original investors are selling part of their holdings.

   c. Stock price generally falls when the company announces a new issue of shares. This is attributable to the information released by the decision to issue.

   d. The rights issue will give the shareholder the opportunity to buy one new share for less than the market price.

5. **Venture capital*** Ethelbert.com is a young software company owned by two entrepreneurs. It currently needs to raise $400,000 to support its expansion plans. A venture capitalist is prepared to provide the cash in return for a 40% holding in the company. Under the plans for

the investment, the VC will hold 10,000 shares in the company, and the two entrepreneurs will have combined holdings of 15,000 shares.

a. What is the total after-the-money valuation of the firm?

b. What value is the venture capitalist placing on each share?

6. **Venture capital** Look at Marvin's first attempt to raise financing. (Refer to Section 15.1 and the Marvin Prospectus in the appendix at the end of this chapter.) Suppose that First Meriam decides that Marvin's shares are worth only $0.80 each.

a. How many shares will Marvin need to sell to raise the additional $1 million?

b. What fraction of the firm will Marvin's managers own after the VC investment?

7. **Venture capital** True or false?

a. Venture capital companies know that managers are more likely to work hard if they can be assured of a good steady salary.

b. Venture capital companies generally advance the money in stages.

c. Venture capital companies are generally passive investors and are happy to let the companies in which they are invested get on with the job.

d. Some young companies grow with the aid of equity investment provided by wealthy individuals known as angel investors.

8. **Venture capital** Complete the passage using the following terms: limited partners, venture capital, private, underwriters, general partners, private equity, corporate venturers, partnerships, private, angel investors. (Note: Not all terms will be used)

Equity capital in young businesses is known as ____(a)____, and it is provided by specialist firms; wealthy individuals, known as ____(b)____; and large technology companies that act as ____(c)____. Venture capital funds are organized as ____(d)____. The management companies are the ____(e)____, and pension funds and other investors are the ____(f)____. Venture capital partnerships are often lumped together with similar partnerships that buy whole companies and take them ____(g)____. The general term for these firms is ____(h)____ companies.

9. **Venture capital**

a. "A signal is credible only if it is costly." Explain why management's willingness to invest in Marvin's equity was a credible signal. Was its willingness to accept only part of the venture capital that would eventually be needed also a credible signal?

b. "When managers take their reward in the form of increased leisure or executive jets, the cost is borne by the shareholders." Explain how First Meriam's financing package tackled this problem.

10. **IPOs*** Refer to Section 15.1 and the Marvin Prospectus Appendix at the end of this chapter to answer the following questions.

a. If there is unexpectedly heavy demand for the issue, how many extra shares can the underwriters buy?

b. How many shares are to be sold in the primary offering? How many will be sold in the secondary offering?

c. One day post-IPO, Marvin shares traded at $105. What was the degree of underpricing? How does that compare with the average degree of underpricing for IPOs in the United States?

d. There are three kinds of cost to Marvin's new issue—underwriting expense, administrative costs, and underpricing. What was the total dollar cost of the Marvin issue?

11. **IPOs** Find the prospectus for a recent IPO. How do the issue costs compare with

a. Those of the Marvin issue?

b. Those shown in Table 15.3?

Can you suggest reasons for the differences?

12. **Issue costs** For each of the following pairs of issues, which is likely to involve the lower proportionate underwriting and administrative costs?

   a. A large issue/a small issue.

   b. A bond issue/a common stock issue.

   c. Initial public offering/subsequent issue of stock.

   d. A small private placement of bonds/a small general cash offer of bonds.

13. **Issue costs** In April 2019, Van Dyck Exponents offered 100 shares for sale in an IPO. Half of the shares were sold by the company and the other half by existing shareholders, each of whom sold exactly half of their existing holding. The offering price to the public was $50, and the underwriters received a spread of 7%. The issue was heavily oversubscribed, and on the first day of trading, the stock price rose to $160.

   a. What were the proceeds of the issue to the company? To the shareholders?

   b. How much commission did the underwriters receive?

   c. How much money was left on the table?

   d. What was the cost of the underpricing to the selling shareholders?

14. **Underpricing** In some U.K. IPOs, any investor may be able to apply to buy shares. Mr. Bean has observed that, on average, these stocks are underpriced by about 9% and, for some years, has followed a policy of applying for a constant proportion of each issue. He is therefore disappointed and puzzled to find that this policy has not resulted in a profit. Explain to him why this is so.

15. **Underpricing.** Having heard about IPO underpricing, I put in an order to my broker for 1,000 shares of every IPO he can get for me. After three months, my investment record is as follows:

IPO	Shares Allocated to Me	Price per Share	Initial Return
A	500	$10	7%
B	200	20	12
C	1,000	8	−2
D	0	12	23

   a. What is the average underpricing in dollars of this sample of IPOs?

   b. What is the average initial return on my "portfolio" of shares purchased from the four IPOs that I bid on? When calculating this average initial return, remember to weight by the amount of money invested in each issue.

   c. "You have just encountered the problem of the winners' curse." True or false?

16. **Underpricing.** Fishwick Enterprises has 200,000 shares outstanding, half of which are owned by Jennifer Fishwick and half by her cousin. The two cousins have decided to sell 100,000 shares in an IPO. Half of these shares would be issued by the company to raise new cash, and half would be shares that are currently held by Jennifer Fishwick. Suppose that the shares are sold at an issue price of $50 but rise to $80 by the end of the first day's trading. Suppose also that investors would have been prepared to buy the issue at $80.

   a. What percentage of the company will Jennifer own after the issue?

   b. What will her holding be worth at the end of the first day's trading?

   c. Suppose the issue had been priced at $80. How many shares would the company have needed to sell to raise the same gross proceeds from the IPO?

   d. What in this case would be Jennifer's wealth (cash plus the value of her remaining holding)? Assume Jennifer also needs to sell her shares to raise the same gross proceeds from the IPO.

   e. What is the cost of underpricing to Jennifer in dollars?

17. **Underpricing** Construct a simple example to show the following:

    a. Existing shareholders are made worse off when a company makes a cash offer of new stock below the market price.

    b. Existing shareholders are not made worse off when a company makes a rights issue of new stock below the market price even if the new stockholders do not wish to take up their rights.

18. **Auctions** Spike Equino is the CEO of a private medical equipment company that is proposing to sell 100,000 shares of its stock in an open auction. Suppose the company receives the bids in the following table.

Shares	Price
20,000	$80
10,000	78
15,000	73
25,000	70
10,000	69
8,000	67
14,000	66
15,000	65
30,000	61

    a. What will be the company's total receipts from the sale if the auction is a discriminatory auction?

    b. What if it is a uniform price auction?

    c. In practice, would investors tend to be more cautious in their bidding in a discriminatory or uniform price auction?

19. **Types of seasoned issue*** After each of the following issue methods, we have listed two types of issue. Choose the one more likely to employ that method.

    a. Rights issue (*initial public offer/further sale of an already publicly traded stock*).

    b. Rule 144A issue (*international bond issue/U.S. bond issue by a foreign corporation*).

    c. Private placement (*issue of existing stock/bond issue by an industrial company*).

    d. Shelf registration (*initial public offer/bond issue by a large industrial company*).

20. **Costs of a general cash offer** Why are the costs of debt issues less than those of equity issues? List the possible reasons.

21. **Market reaction to stock issues** There are three reasons that a common stock issue might cause a fall in price:

    a. The price fall is needed to absorb the extra supply.

    b. The issue causes temporary price pressure until it has been digested.

    c. Management has information that stockholders do not have.

    Explain these reasons more fully. Which do you find most plausible? Is there any way that you could seek to test whether you are right?

22. **Rights issues** Associated Breweries is planning to market alcohol-free beer. To finance the venture, it proposes to make a rights issue at $10 of one new share for each two shares held. (The company currently has outstanding 100,000 shares priced at $40 a share.) Assuming that the new money is invested to earn a fair return, give values for the following:

    a. Number of new shares.

    b. Amount of new investment.

    c. Total value of company after issue.

    d. Total number of shares after issue.

    e. Stock price after the issue.

23. **Rights issues** In 2012, the Pandora Box Company made a rights issue at €5 a share of one new share for every four shares held. Before the issue there were 10 million shares outstanding and the share price was €6.

    a. What was the total amount of new money raised?

    b. The rights issue gave the shareholder the opportunity to buy one new share for less than the market price. What was the value of this opportunity?

    c. What was the prospective stock price after the issue?

    d. How far could the total value of the company fall before shareholders would be unwilling to take up their rights?

24. **Rights issues** Problem 23 contains details of a rights offering by Pandora Box. Suppose that the company had decided to issue new stock at €4. How many new shares would it have needed to sell to raise the same sum of money? Recalculate the answers to questions (b) to (d) in Problem 23. Show that the shareholders are just as well off if the company issues the shares at €4 rather than €5.

25. **Rights issues vs. cash offers** Suppose that instead of having a rights issue of new stock at €4 (see Problem 23), Pandora decided to make a general cash offer at €4. Would existing shareholders still be just as well off? Explain.

26. **Private placements** You need to choose between making a public offering and arranging a private placement. In each case, the issue involves $10 million face value of 10-year debt. You have the following data for each:

    - *A public issue:* The interest rate on the debt would be 8.5%, and the debt would be issued at face value. The underwriting spread would be 1.5%, and other expenses would be $80,000.

    - *A private placement:* The interest rate on the private placement would be 9%, but the total issuing expenses would be only $30,000.

    a. What is the difference in the proceeds to the company net of expenses?

    b. Other things being equal, which is the better deal?

    c. What other factors beyond the interest rate and issue costs would you wish to consider before deciding between the two offers?

CHALLENGE PROBLEMS

27. **Venture capital**

    a. Why do venture capital companies prefer to advance money in stages? If you were the management of Marvin Enterprises, would you have been happy with such an arrangement? With the benefit of hindsight did First Meriam gain or lose by advancing money in stages?

    b. The price at which First Meriam would invest more money in Marvin was not fixed in advance. But Marvin could have given First Meriam an *option* to buy more shares at a preset price. Would this have been better?

    c. At the second stage, Marvin could have tried to raise money from another venture capital company in preference to First Meriam. To protect themselves against this, venture capital firms sometimes demand first refusal on new capital issues. Would you recommend this arrangement?

28. **Auctions** Explain the difference between a uniform-price auction and a discriminatory auction. Why might you prefer to sell securities by one method rather than another?

29. **Dilution** Here is recent financial data on Pisa Construction Inc.

Stock price	$40	Market value of firm	$400,000
Number of shares	10,000	Earnings per share	$4
Book net worth	$500,000	Return on investment	8%

Pisa has not performed spectacularly to date. However, it wishes to issue new shares to obtain \$80,000 to finance expansion into a promising market. Pisa's financial advisers think a stock issue is a poor choice because, among other reasons, "sale of stock at a price below book value per share can only depress the stock price and decrease shareholders' wealth." To prove the point they construct the following example: "Suppose 2,000 new shares are issued at \$40 and the proceeds are invested. (Neglect issue costs.) Suppose return on investment does not change. Then

$$\text{Book net worth} = \$580,000$$
$$\text{Total earnings} = .08(580,000) = \$46,400$$
$$\text{Earnings per share} = \frac{46,400}{12,000} = \$3.87$$

Thus, EPS declines, book value per share declines, and share price will decline proportionately to \$38.70."

Evaluate this argument with particular attention to the assumptions implicit in the numerical example.

FINANCE ON THE WEB

Look up a recent IPO on **biz.yahoo.com/ipo** and then use the Edgar database to find the prospectus. (You may find it easiest to look up the company on **finance.yahoo.com** and use the link to SEC filings. In any case, finding the final prospectus can be a matter of trial and error.) Compare the IPO with that of Marvin. For example, who were the existing shareholders? Was the company raising more capital, or were existing shareholders selling? Were existing shareholders prevented by a lock-up agreement from selling more shares? How did the underwriting and other costs compare with those of Marvin? Did the underwriters have a greenshoe option? Did the issue turn out to be underpriced? (The Yahoo! website should help here.) If so, how much money was left on the table?

APPENDIX ● ● ●

Marvin's New-Issue Prospectus[53]

PROSPECTUS

900,000 Shares

Marvin Enterprises Inc.

Common Stock ($.10 par value)

Of the 900,000 shares of Common Stock offered hereby, 500,000 shares are being sold by the Company and 400,000 shares are being sold by the Selling Stockholders. See "Principal and Selling Stockholders." The Company will not receive any of the proceeds from the sale of shares by the Selling Stockholders.

Before this offering there has been no public market for the Common Stock. **These securities involve a high degree of risk. See "Certain Considerations."**

THESE SECURITIES HAVE NOT BEEN APPROVED OR DISAPPROVED BY THE SECURITIES AND EXCHANGE COMMISSION NOR HAS THE COMMISSION PASSED ON THE ACCURACY OR ADEQUACY OF THIS PROSPECTUS. ANY REPRESENTATION TO THE CONTRARY IS A CRIMINAL OFFENSE.

	Price to Public	Underwriting Discount	Proceeds to Company[1]	Proceeds to Selling Stockholders[1]
Per share	$80.00	$5.60	$74.40	$74.40
Total[2]	$72,000,000	$5,040,000	$37,200,000	$29,760,000

[1]Before deducting expenses payable by the Company estimated at $820,000, of which $455,555 will be paid by the Company and $364,445 will be paid by the Selling Stockholders.

[2]The Company and the Selling Stockholders have granted to the Underwriters an option to purchase up to an additional 135,000 shares at the initial public offering price, less the underwriting discount, solely to cover overallotment.

The Common Stock is offered subject to receipt and acceptance by the Underwriters, to prior sale, and to the Underwriters' right to reject any order in whole or in part and to withdraw, cancel, or modify the offer without notice.

Klein Merrick Inc.   February 3, 2037

No person has been authorized to give any information or to make any representations, other than as contained therein, in connection with the offer contained in this Prospectus, and, if given or made, such information or representations must not be relied upon. This Prospectus does not constitute an offer of any securities other than the registered securities to which it relates or an offer to any person in any jurisdiction where such an offer would be unlawful. The delivery of this Prospectus at any time does not imply that information herein is correct as of any time subsequent to its date.

IN CONNECTION WITH THIS OFFERING, THE UNDERWRITERS MAY OVERALLOT OR EFFECT TRANSACTIONS WHICH STABILIZE OR MAINTAIN THE MARKET PRICE OF THE COMMON STOCK OF THE COMPANY AT A LEVEL ABOVE THAT WHICH MIGHT OTHERWISE PREVAIL IN THE OPEN MARKET. SUCH STABILIZING, IF COMMENCED, MAY BE DISCONTINUED AT ANY TIME.

---

[53]Most prospectuses have content similar to that of the Marvin prospectus but go into considerably more detail. Also we have omitted Marvin's financial statements.

Prospectus Summary

The following summary information is qualified in its entirety by the detailed information and financial statements appearing elsewhere in this Prospectus.

The Offering

Common Stock offered by the Company ....500,000 shares

Common Stock offered by the Selling Stockholders..400,000 shares

Common Stock to be outstanding after this offering .... 4,100,000 shares

Use of Proceeds

For the construction of new manufacturing facilities and to provide working capital.

The Company

Marvin Enterprises Inc. designs, manufactures, and markets gargle blasters for domestic use. Its manufacturing facilities employ integrated nanocircuits to control the genetic engineering processes used to manufacture gargle blasters.

The Company was organized in Delaware in 2031.

Proceeds

The net proceeds of this offering are expected to be $36,744,445. Of the net proceeds, approximately $27.0 million will be used to finance expansion of the Company's principal manufacturing facilities. The balance will be used for working capital.

Certain Considerations

Investment in the Common Stock involves a high degree of risk. The following factors should be carefully considered in evaluating the Company:

Substantial Capital Needs The Company will require additional financing to continue its expansion policy. The Company believes that its relations with its lenders are good, but there can be no assurance that additional financing will be available in the future.

Licensing The expanded manufacturing facilities are to be used for the production of a new imploding gargle blaster. An advisory panel to the U.S. Food and Drug Administration (FDA) has recommended approval of this product for the U.S. market but no decision has yet been reached by the full FDA committee.

Dividend Policy

The company has not paid cash dividends on its Common Stock and does not anticipate that dividends will be paid on the Common Stock in the foreseeable future.

Management

The following table sets forth information regarding the Company's directors, executive officers, and key employees.

Name	Age	Position
George Marvin	32	President, Chief Executive Officer, & Director
Mildred Marvin	28	Treasurer & Director
Chip Norton	30	General Manager

George Marvin—George Marvin established the Company in 2031 and has been its Chief Executive Officer since that date. He is a past president of the Institute of Gargle Blasters and has recently been inducted into the Confrérie des Gargarisateurs.

Mildred Marvin—Mildred Marvin has been employed by the Company since 2031.

Chip Norton—Mr. Norton has been General Manager of the Company since 2031. He is a former vice-president of Amalgamated Blasters, Inc.

Executive Compensation

The following table sets forth the cash compensation paid for services rendered for the year 2036 by the executive officers:

Name	Capacity	Cash Compensation
George Marvin	President and Chief Executive Officer	$300,000
Mildred Marvin	Treasurer	220,000
Chip Norton	General Manager	220,000

Certain Transactions

At various times between 2032 and 2035, First Meriam Venture Partners invested a total of $8.5 million in the Company. In connection with this investment, First Meriam Venture Partners was granted certain rights to registration under the Securities Act of 1933, including the right to have their shares of Common Stock registered at the Company's expense with the Securities and Exchange Commission.

Principal and Selling Stockholders

The following table sets forth certain information regarding the beneficial ownership of the Company's voting Common Stock as of the date of this prospectus by (i) each person known by the Company to be the beneficial owner of more than 5 percent of its voting Common Stock, and (ii) each director of the Company who beneficially owns voting Common Stock. Unless otherwise indicated, each owner has sole voting and dispositive power over his or her shares.

	Common Stock					
	Shares Beneficially Owned prior to Offering			Shares Beneficially Owned after Offer[1]		
Name of Beneficial Owner	Number	Percent	Shares to Be Sold	Number	Percent	
George Marvin	375,000	10.4	60,000	315,000	7.7	
Mildred Marvin	375,000	10.4	60,000	315,000	7.7	
Chip Norton	250,000	6.9	80,000	170,000	4.1	
First Meriam Venture Partners	1,700,000	47.2	—	1,700,000	41.5	
TFS Investors	260,000	7.2	—	260,000	6.3	
Centri-Venture Partnership	260,000	7.2	—	260,000	6.3	
Henry Pobble	180,000	5.0	—	180,000	4.4	
Georgina Sloberg	200,000	5.6	200,000	—	—	

[1] Assuming no exercise of the Underwriters' overallotment option.

Lock-up Agreements

The holders of the Common Stock have agreed with the underwriters not to sell, pledge, or otherwise dispose of their shares, other than as specified in this prospectus, for a period of 180 days after the date of the prospectus without the prior consent of Klein Merrick.

Description of Capital Stock

The Company's authorized capital stock consists of 10,000,000 shares of voting Common Stock. As of the date of this Prospectus, there are 10 holders of record of the Common Stock.

Under the terms of one of the Company's loan agreements, the Company may not pay cash dividends on Common Stock except from net profits without the written consent of the lender.

Underwriting

Subject to the terms and conditions set forth in the Underwriting Agreement, the Company has agreed to sell to each of the Underwriters named below, and each of the Underwriters, for whom Klein Merrick Inc. are acting as Representatives, has severally agreed to purchase from the Company, the number of shares set forth opposite its name below.

Underwriters	Number of Shares to Be Purchased
Klein Merrick Inc.	300,000
Goldman Stanley	300,000
Medici Bank	100,000
Canary Wharf Securities	100,000
Bank of New England	100,000

In the Underwriting Agreement, the several Underwriters have agreed, subject to the terms and conditions set forth therein, to purchase all shares offered hereby if any such shares are purchased. In the event of a default by any Underwriter, the Underwriting Agreement provides that, in certain circumstances, purchase commitments of the nondefaulting Underwriters may be increased or the Underwriting Agreement may be terminated.

There is no public market for the Common Stock. The price to the public for the Common Stock was determined by negotiation between the Company and the Underwriters and was based on, among other things, the Company's financial and operating history and condition, its prospects and the prospects for its industry in general, the management of the Company, and the market prices of securities for companies in businesses similar to that of the Company.

Legal Matters

The validity of the shares of Common Stock offered by the Prospectus is being passed on for the Company by Dodson and Fogg and for the Underwriters by Kenge and Carboy.

Experts

The consolidated financial statements of the Company have been so included in reliance on the reports of Hooper Firebrand, independent accountants, given on the authority of that firm as experts in auditing and accounting.

Financial Statements

[Text and tables omitted.]

CHAPTER

16

Payout Policy

Payout policy resolves two questions. First, how much cash should the corporation pay out to its shareholders? Second, should the cash be distributed by paying cash dividends or by repurchasing shares? We will cover these questions in reverse order, "how" before "how much."

Suppose a corporation has surplus cash. Should it distribute that cash by paying a dividend, or should it do so by repurchasing shares? In an ideal, frictionless world, the choice between dividend and repurchase does not matter. In practice, the choice can be important.

First, investors expect a firm that has made regular dividend payments to continue doing so and to increase those payments steadily as earnings increase. Dividends are rarely cut back unless the firm suffers significant, continuing losses, and managers don't increase dividends unless they are confident that the dividend can be maintained. Announcement of a dividend increase is therefore good news for shareholders, who infer that managers are confident about the future. Repurchases, on the other hand, are more flexible and do not convey as much information to investors.

Second, repurchases are tax-advantaged. When shareholders sell, they pay tax at capital gains rates, which have generally been lower than tax rates on dividends.

Repurchases have grown dramatically over the last 30 years, and in the United States, they now rival dividends in importance. Of course, cash dividends are still paid. Large, mature firms distribute huge amounts as dividends. But most of these firms also repurchase shares. Many other firms use repurchases exclusively.

Next we consider "how much." How does a financial manager conclude that cash is really surplus? Before deciding to pay dividends or repurchase shares, the manager asks a series of questions. First, is the business generating positive free cash flow after making all investments with positive NPVs? Is that positive free cash flow likely to continue? Second, is the firm's debt ratio prudent? If the ratio is too high, paying down debt usually takes priority. Third, are the company's holdings of cash a sufficient cushion for unexpected setbacks and a sufficient war chest for unexpected opportunities? If the answer to all three questions is yes, then the cash is truly surplus. If a corporation has surplus cash, it's best to pay the cash back to shareholders. Paying out surplus cash reassures shareholders that the cash will not be wasted on questionable investments or consumed by perks or excessive compensation.

We begin this chapter with a review of how dividends are paid and repurchases carried out. We also consider the *information content* of dividends and repurchases. That is, we consider what investors can learn from managers' payout decisions and how stock prices react to payout announcements. Then we examine the pros and cons of cash dividends versus repurchases. Finally, we discuss how corporations should manage *total* payout—that is, the sum of dividends and repurchases.

BEYOND THE PAGE

The growth in repurchases

mhhe.com/brealey13e

Corporations pay out cash by distributing dividends or by buying back some of their outstanding shares. Repurchases were rare in the early 1980s, but Figure 16.1 shows that the total value of repurchases in the United States is now similar to total dividends.

Figure 16.1 shows that dividends are more stable than repurchases. Notice how repurchases were cut back in the early 2000s and in the crisis of 2007–2009. Dividends also fell in the crisis, but by less than repurchases.

Cash-rich corporations sometimes undertake massive repurchase programs, but they often increase dividends at the same time. Here are four examples:

- Cisco Systems: A $25 billion repurchase program an a 14% increase in dividends.
- Mastercard: A $4 billion repurchase program and an increase in annual dividends from $.88 to $1.00 per share.
- Boeing: An $18 billion repurchase program and a 20% dividend increase to $1.71 per share.
- AbbVie, a pharmaceutical company: $10 billion repurchase program and a dividend increase from $.71 to $.96 per share.

The fraction of public industrial corporations that paid dividends was 57% in 1980. But the fraction decreased steadily in the 1980s and 1990s to about 16% at the turn of the century, then rebounded to about 42% in 2017. Repurchases in 1980 were tiny, but by 2017, about 48% of industrial companies repurchased. The fraction of banks that pay dividends has been much higher than for industrial companies, but the fraction of banks that repurchase has been about the same.[1]

Here is a table of payout practices, by nonfinancial firms, from 2011 to 2017:

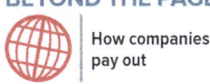

BEYOND THE PAGE

How companies pay out

mhhe.com/brealey13e

		Pay Dividend?	
		Yes	**No**
Repurchase?	**Yes**	23.4%	20.6%
	No	13.9%	42.1%

Source: Compustat.

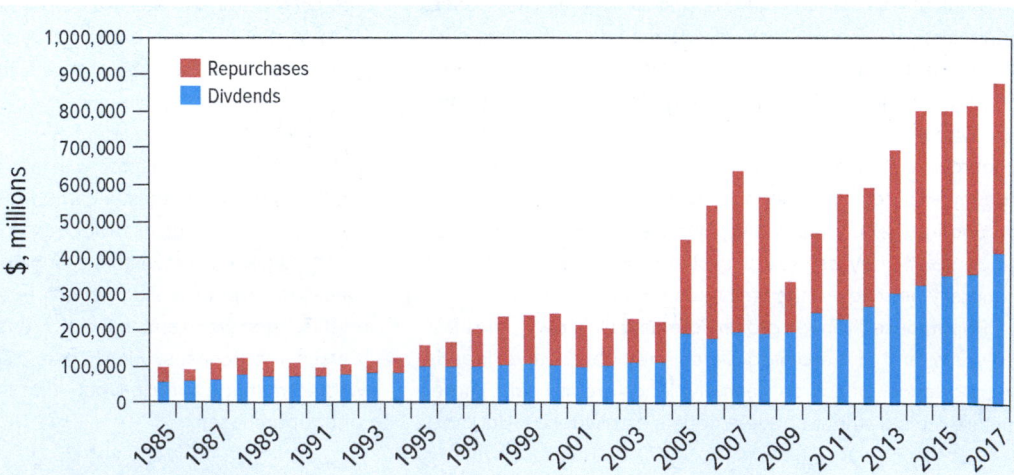

FIGURE 16.1

Dividends and stock repurchases by nonfinancial companies in the United States, 1985–2017 (figures in $ millions)

Source: Standard & Poor's Compustat.

---

[1]E. Floyd, N. Li, and D. J. Skinner, "Payout Policy through the Financial Crisis: The Growth of Repurchases and the Resilience of Dividends," *Journal of Financial Economics* 118 (November 2015), pp. 299–316, Table 1. In Europe, the decline in dividend payers has been especially steep in Germany. See D. J. Denis and I. Osobov, "Why Do Firms Pay Dividends? International Evidence on the Determinants of Dividend Policy," *Journal of Financial Economics* 89 (July 2008), pp. 62–82.

On average in each year, 23.4% of the firms paid a dividend and also repurchased shares. The fraction that paid dividends but did not repurchase was 13.9%. The corresponding fraction for repurchases but no dividends was 20.6%. But 42.1% of firms did not pay dividends or repurchase shares.

Who are the nondividend payers? Some are companies that used to pay dividends, but then fell on hard times and had to cut back. However, most nondividend payers are growth companies that have never paid a dividend and will not pay one in the foreseeable future. The zero-dividend companies also include such household names as Berkshire Hathaway, Alphabet (Google), and Amazon.

How Firms Pay Dividends

On December 18, 2017, Pfizer's board of directors announced a quarterly cash dividend of $.34 per share. Who received this dividend? That may seem an obvious question, but shares trade constantly, and the firm's records of who owns its shares are never fully up to date. So corporations specify a particular day's roster of shareholders who qualify to receive each dividend. For example, Pfizer announced that it would send a dividend check on March 1, 2018 (the payment date), to all shareholders recorded in its books on February 2 (the record date).

One day before the record date, Pfizer stock began to trade ex-dividend. Investors who bought shares on or after that date did not have their purchases registered by the record date and were not entitled to the dividend. Other things equal, a stock is worth less if you miss out on the dividend. So when a stock "goes ex-dividend," its price falls by about the amount of the dividend. Figure 16.2 illustrates the sequence of the key dividend dates. This sequence is the same whenever companies pay a dividend (though of course the actual dates will differ).

Corporations are not free to declare whatever dividend they choose. In some countries, such as Brazil and Chile, companies are obliged by law to pay out a *minimum* proportion of their earnings. Conversely, some restrictions may be imposed by lenders, who are concerned that excessive dividend payments would not leave enough in the kitty to repay their loans. In the United States, state law also helps to protect the firm's creditors against excessive dividend payments. For example, companies are not allowed to pay a dividend out of legal capital, which is generally defined as the par value of outstanding shares.[2]

Most U.S. companies pay a *regular* cash dividend each quarter, but occasionally this is supplemented by a one-off *extra* or *special dividend*. Many companies offer shareholders automatic dividend reinvestment plans (DRIPs). Often, the new shares are issued at a 5% discount from the market price. Sometimes 10% or more of total dividends will be reinvested under such plans.[3]

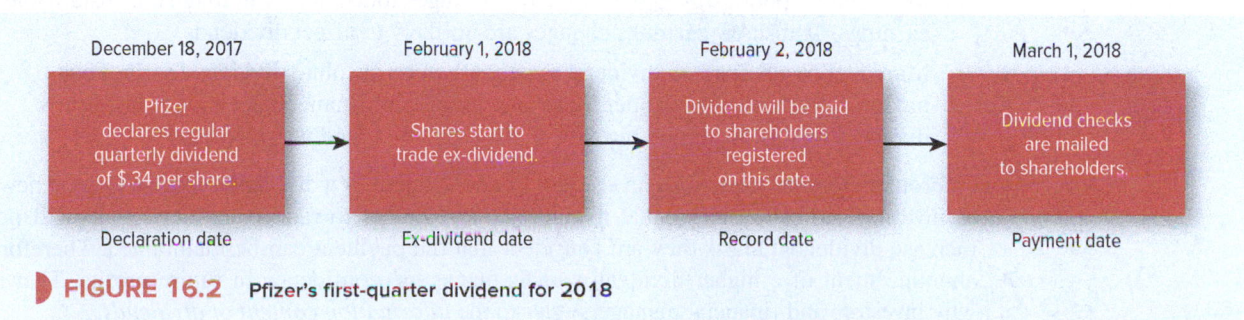

FIGURE 16.2   Pfizer's first-quarter dividend for 2018

---

[2]Where there is no par value, legal capital is defined as part or all of the receipts from the issue of shares. Companies with wasting assets, such as mining companies, are sometimes permitted to pay out legal capital.

[3]Sometimes companies not only allow shareholders to reinvest dividends, but also allow them to buy additional shares at a discount. For an amusing and true rags-to-riches story, see M. S. Scholes and M. A. Wolfson, "Decentralized Investment Banking: The Case of Discount Dividend-Reinvestment and Stock-Purchase Plans," *Journal of Financial Economics* 23 (September 1989), pp. 7–35.

Dividends are not always in the form of cash. Companies also declare *stock dividends*. For example, if the firm pays a stock dividend of 5%, it sends each shareholder 5 extra shares for every 100 shares currently owned. A stock dividend is essentially the same as a stock split. Both increase the number of shares but do not affect the company's assets, profits, or total value. So both reduce value *per share*.[4] In this chapter, we focus on *cash* dividends.

How Firms Repurchase Stock

Instead of paying a dividend to its stockholders, the firm can use the cash to repurchase stock. The reacquired shares are kept in the company's treasury and may be resold if the company needs money. There are four main ways to repurchase stock. By far the most common method is for the firm to announce that it plans to buy its stock in the open market, just like any other investor.[5] However, companies sometimes use a tender offer where they offer to buy back a stated number of shares at a fixed price, which is typically set at about 20% above the current market level. Shareholders can then choose whether to accept this offer. A third procedure is to employ a *Dutch auction*. In this case, the firm states a series of prices at which it is prepared to repurchase stock. Shareholders submit offers declaring how many shares they wish to sell at each price and the company calculates the lowest price at which it can buy the desired number of shares. Finally, repurchase sometimes takes place by direct negotiation with a major shareholder.

In the past, many countries banned or severely restricted the use of stock repurchases. As a result, firms that had amassed large amounts of cash were tempted to invest it at low rates of return rather than hand it back to shareholders, who could have reinvested it in firms that were short of cash. But most of these limitations have now been removed, and many multinational giants now repurchase huge amounts of stock. For example, Royal Dutch Shell, Siemens, Toyota, and Novartis have all spent large sums on buying back their stock.

16-2   The Information Content of Dividends and Repurchases

BEYOND THE PAGE

The Lintner model of payouts

mhhe.com/brealey13e

A survey in 2004 asked senior executives about their companies' dividend policies. Figure 16.3 paraphrases their responses. Three themes stand out:

1. Managers are reluctant to make dividend changes that may have to be reversed. They are particularly worried about having to rescind a dividend increase and, if necessary, would issue shares or borrow to maintain the dividend.

2. Managers "smooth" dividends. Dividend changes follow shifts in long-run, sustainable earnings. Transitory earnings changes are unlikely to affect dividends.

3. Managers focus more on dividend *changes* than on absolute dividend levels. Thus paying a dividend of $2.00 per share is an important financial decision if last year's dividend was $1.50, but no big deal if last year's dividend was also $2.00.

From these responses, you can see why announcement of a dividend increase is good news to investors. Investors know that managers are reluctant to reduce dividends and will not increase dividends unless they are confident that the payment can be maintained. Therefore announcement of a higher dividend signals managers' confidence in future profits. That is why investors and financial managers refer to the *information content of dividends*.

---

[4]The distinction between a stock dividend and a stock split is technical. A stock dividend is shown in the accounts as a transfer from retained earnings to equity capital. A split is shown as a reduction in the par value of each share.

[5]The U.S. Securities and Exchange Commission's rule 10b-18 protects repurchasing firms from accusations of share-price manipulation. Open-market repurchases are subject to several restrictions, however. For example, repurchases cannot exceed a small fraction of daily trading volume.

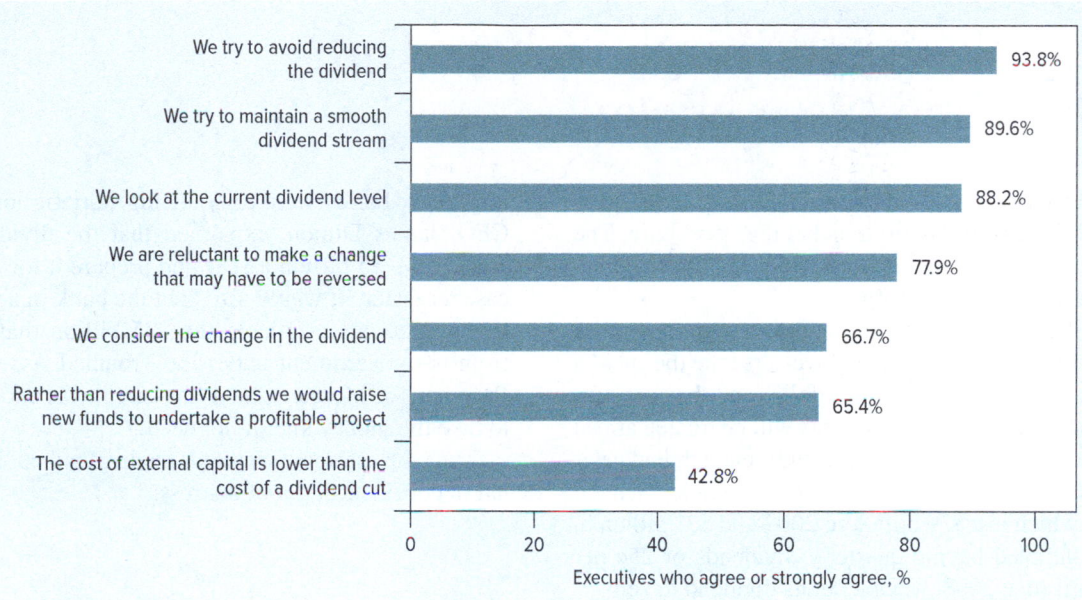

▶ **FIGURE 16.3**   A 2004 survey of financial executives on dividend policy

Source: A. Brav, J. R. Graham, C. R. Harvey, and R. Michaely, "Payout Policy in the 21st Century," *Journal of Financial Economics* 77 (September 2005), pp. 483–527.

The information content of dividends implies that dividend increases predict future profitability. Evidence on this point is somewhat elusive. But Healy and Palepu, who focus on companies that paid a dividend for the first time, find that, on average, earnings jumped 43% in the year a dividend was paid. If managers thought that this was a temporary windfall, they might have been cautious about committing themselves to paying out cash. But it looks as if these managers had good reason to be confident about prospects, for earnings continued to rise in the following years.[6] On the other hand, it appears that dividend increases by companies already paying regular dividends do not predict increases in future earnings. Instead the increases predict *safer* earnings. Managers are more likely to increase dividends when they expect future earnings and cash flow to be less volatile and uncertain than usual. They are less likely to increase dividends, and more likely to cut dividends, when they see unusual risks ahead.[7]

Investors certainly appear to take comfort from an increase in dividends. It is no surprise, therefore, to find that a higher dividend prompts a rise in the stock price, whereas a dividend cut results in a fall in price. For example, in the case of the dividend initiations studied by Healy and Palepu, the dividend announcement resulted in a 4% stock-price increase on average.[8]

Notice that investors do not get excited about the *level* of a company's dividend; they worry about the *change,* which they view as an important indicator of the sustainability of earnings.

Do not assume that all dividend cuts are bad news, however. The nearby box explains how investors endorsed a drastic dividend cut announced in 2009 by JPMorgan Chase.

---

[6]P. Healy and K. Palepu, "Earnings Information Conveyed by Dividend Initiations and Omissions," *Journal of Financial Economics* 21 (1988), pp. 149–175. For an example of a study that finds no information in dividend changes, see G. Grullon, R. Michaely, and B. Swaminathan, "Are Dividend Changes a Sign of Firm Maturity?" *Journal of Business* 75 (July 2002), pp. 387–424.

[7]R. Michaely, S. Rossi and M. Weber, "The Information Content of Dividends: Safer Profits, Not Higher Profits," Chicago Booth Research Paper 17-30, January 2018.

[8]The 4% average return was adjusted for market returns. Healy and Palepu also looked at companies that *stopped* paying a dividend. In this case, the stock price on average declined by 9.5% on the announcement, and earnings fell over the next four quarters.

Good News: JPMorgan Chase Cuts Its Dividend to a Nickel

❯ On February 23, 2009, JPMorgan Chase cut its quarterly dividend from 38¢ to a nickel (5¢) per share. The cut was a surprise to investors, but the bank's share price *increased* by about 5%.

Usually, dividend cuts or omissions are bad news because investors infer trouble. Investors take the cut as a signal of a cash or earnings shortfall—and they are usually right. Managers know that cuts will be treated as bad news, so they usually put off cuts until enough bad news accumulates to force them to act. For example, General Motors, which lost $39 billion in 2007 and $31 billion in 2008, continued paying quarterly dividends of 25¢ per share until June 2008, when it cut its dividend to zero.

JPMorgan Chase, however, acted from a position of relative strength. It remained profitable when other large U.S. banks were announcing horrific losses. Its CEO, James Dimon, explained that the dividend cut would save $5 billion a year and prepare it for a worst-case recession. It would also "put the bank in a position to pay back more quickly the $25 billion that it took from the government under the Troubled Asset Relief Program." JPMorgan Chase has said it was encouraged to take the money and didn't need it.

Thus, investors interpreted the dividend cut as a signal of confidence, not of distress.

Source: R. Sidel and M. Rieker, "J.P. Morgan Makes 87% Cut in its Dividend to a Nickel," *The New York Times,* February 24, 2009, pp. C1, C3.

The Information Content of Share Repurchases

BEYOND THE PAGE

Repurchase motives

mhhe.com/brealey13e

Announcement of a share repurchase is not a commitment to continue repurchases in later years. So the information content of a repurchase announcement is less strongly positive than the announcement of a dividend increase. Nevertheless, a study by Comment and Jarrell, who looked at the announcements of open-market repurchase programs, found that, on average, they resulted in an abnormal price rise of 2%.[9]

Investors may applaud repurchases if they worry that managers would otherwise fritter away the money on perks or unprofitable empire building. Stock repurchases may also be used to signal a manager's confidence in the future. Suppose that you, the manager, believe that your stock is substantially undervalued. You announce that the company is prepared to buy back a fifth of its stock at a price that is 20% above the current market price. But (you say) you are certainly not going to sell any of your own stock at that price. Investors jump to the obvious conclusion—you must believe that the stock is a good value even at 20% above the current price.

When companies offer to repurchase their stock at a premium, senior management and directors usually commit to hold on to their stock.[10] So it is not surprising that researchers have found that announcements of offers to buy back shares above the market price have prompted a larger rise in the stock price, averaging about 11%.[11]

---

[9]R. Comment and G. Jarrell, "The Relative Signalling Power of Dutch-Auction and Fixed Price Self-Tender Offers and Open-Market Share Repurchases," *Journal of Finance* 46 (September 1991), pp. 1243–1271. There is also evidence of continuing superior performance during the years following a repurchase announcement. See D. Ikenberry, J. Lakonishok, and T. Vermaelen, "Market Underreaction to Open Market Share Repurchases," *Journal of Financial Economics* 39 (October 1995), pp. 181–208.

[10]Not only do managers hold on to their stock; on average, they also add to their holdings *before* the announcement of a repurchase. See D. S. Lee, W. Mikkelson, and M. M. Partch, "Managers' Trading around Stock Repurchases," *Journal of Finance* 47 (December 1992), pp. 1947–1961.

[11]See Comment and Jarrell, op. cit.

16-3 Dividends or Repurchases? The Payout Controversy

Announcements of dividends and repurchases can convey information about management's confidence and so affect the stock price. But eventually, the stock price change would happen anyway as information seeps out through other channels. Does payout policy affect value in the long run?

Suppose you are CFO of a successful, profitable public company. The company is maturing. Growth is slowing down, and you plan to distribute free cash flow to stockholders. Does it matter whether you initiate dividends or a repurchase program? Does the choice affect the market value of your firm in any fundamental way?

One of the endearing features of economics is its ability to accommodate not just two, but three opposing points of view. And so it is with the choice between dividends and repurchases. On the right are conservatives who argue that investors pay more for firms with generous, stable dividends. On the left, another group argues that repurchases are better because dividends are taxed at higher effective rates than capital gains. And in the center, a middle-of-the-road party claims that the choice between dividends and repurchases has no effect on value.

Payout Policy Is Irrelevant in Perfect Capital Markets

The middle-of-the-road party was founded in 1961 by Miller and Modigliani (always referred to as "MM"), when they published a proof that dividend policy is value-irrelevant in a world without taxes, transaction costs, and other market imperfections.[12]

MM insisted that one must consider dividend policy only after holding the firm's assets, investments, and borrowing policy fixed. Suppose they were not fixed. For example, suppose that the firm decides to reduce capital investment and to pay out the cash saved as a dividend. In this case, the effect of the dividend on shareholder value is tangled up with the profitability of the foregone investment. Or suppose that the firm decides to borrow more aggressively and to pay out the debt proceeds as dividends. In this case, the effect of the dividend can't be separated from the effect of the additional borrowing.

Think what happens if you want to up the dividend without changing the investment policy or capital structure. The extra cash for the dividend must come from somewhere. If the firm fixes its borrowing, the only way it can finance the extra dividend is to sell more shares. Alternatively, rather than *increasing* dividends and selling new shares, the firm can pay *lower* dividends. With investment policy and borrowing fixed, the cash that is saved can only be used to buy back some of the firm's existing shares. Thus any change in dividend payout must be offset by the sale or repurchase of shares.

Repurchases were rare when MM wrote in 1961, but we can easily apply their reasoning to the choice between dividends and repurchases. A simple example is enough to show MM's irrelevance result in this case. Then we will show that value is also unaffected if the company increases the dividend and finances the increase with an issue of shares.

---

[12]M. H. Miller and F. Modigliani, "Dividend Policy, Growth and the Valuation of Shares," *Journal of Business* 34 (October 1961), pp. 411–433. MM's results were anticipated by J. B. Williams, *The Theory of Investment Value* (Cambridge, MA: Harvard University Press, 1938). Also a proof similar to MM's was developed in J. Lintner, "Dividends, Earnings, Leverage, Stock Prices and the Supply of Capital to Corporations," *Review of Economics and Statistics* 44 (August 1962), pp. 243–269. MM recognized that dividends could convey information, but their proofs focused on value, not information about value. The examples in this section put aside the information content of dividends.

Dividends or Repurchases? An Example

Rational Demiconductor has, at this moment, 1 million shares outstanding and the following market-value balance sheet:

Rational Demiconductor Balance Sheet (Market Values, $ millions)

Surplus cash	$ 1.0	$ 0	Debt
Fixed assets and net working capital	10.0	11.0	Equity market capitalization (1 million shares at $11 per share)
	$11.0	$11.0	

For simplicity we assume it has no debt. All of its fixed assets are paid for. Its working capital includes enough cash to support its operations, so the $1 million cash entered at the top left of its balance sheet is surplus.

Rational's market capitalization is $11 million, so each of its 1 million shares is worth $11. If it now pays out the surplus cash, market capitalization must fall to $10 million:

Rational Demiconductor Balance Sheet (Market Values after Payout, $ millions)

Surplus cash	$ 0	$ 0	Debt
Fixed assets and net working capital	10.0	10.0	Equity market capitalization
	$10.0	$10.0	

But the price *per share* depends on whether the surplus cash is paid out as a dividend or by repurchases. If a dividend of $1 per share is paid, 1 million shares are still outstanding, and stock price is $10. Shareholders' wealth, including the cash dividends, is $10 + 1 = $11 per share.

Suppose Rational pays no cash dividend, but repurchases shares instead. It spends $1 million to repurchase 90,909 shares at $11 each, leaving 909,091 shares outstanding. Stock price remains at $11 ($10 million divided by 909,091 shares). Shareholders' wealth is $11 per share. It doesn't matter whether a particular shareholder decides to sell shares back to the firm. If she sells, she gets $11 per share in cash. If she doesn't want to sell, she retains shares worth $11 each.

Thus, shareholder wealth is the same with dividends as with repurchases. If Rational pays a cash dividend, wealth is $10 + 1 = $11, including the dividend. If Rational repurchases, there is no dividend, but each share is worth $11.

You may hear a claim that share repurchases should increase the stock price. That's not quite right, as our example illustrates. A repurchase does not increase the stock price, but it avoids the fall in stock price that would occur on the ex-dividend day if the amount spent on repurchases were paid out as cash dividends. Repurchases do not guarantee a higher stock price, but only a stock price higher than if a dividend were paid instead. Repurchases also reduce the number of shares outstanding, so future earnings per share are higher than if the same amount were paid out as dividends.

If MM and the middle-of-the-roaders are correct and payout policy does not affect value, then the choice between dividends and repurchases is merely tactical. A company will decide to repurchase if it wants to retain the flexibility to cut back payout if valuable investment opportunities arise. Another company may decide to pay dividends to assure stockholders that it will run a tight ship, paying out free cash flow to limit the temptation for careless spending.

Stock Repurchases and DCF Models of Share Price

Our example looked at a one-time choice between a cash dividend and repurchase program. In practice, a company that pays a dividend today also makes an implicit promise to continue paying dividends in later years, smoothing the dividends and increasing them gradually as earnings grow. Repurchases are not smoothed in the same way as dividends. For example, when oil prices tumbled in 2014, Chevron announced that it was scrapping its stock repurchase program for 2015. The company compared repurchases to a "flywheel" that can store or disperse energy as needed. At the same time that it cut its repurchases, the company stressed that maintaining its current dividend remained "the highest priority."

A repurchase program reduces the number of outstanding shares and increases earnings and dividends per share. Thus we should pause and consider what repurchases imply for the DCF dividend-discount models that we derived and applied in Chapter 4. These models say that stock price equals the PV of future dividends *per share*. How do we apply these models when the number of shares is changing?

There are two valuation approaches for common stocks when repurchases are important:

1. Calculate market capitalization (the aggregate value of *all* shares) by forecasting and discounting all the free cash flow paid out to shareholders. Then calculate price per share by dividing market capitalization by the number of shares currently outstanding. With this approach, you don't have to worry about how payout of free cash flow is split between dividends and repurchases.

2. Calculate the present value of dividends per share, taking account of the increased growth rate of dividends per share caused by the declining number of shares resulting from the repurchases.

The first valuation approach, which focuses on the total free cash flow available for payout to shareholders, is easier and more reliable when future repurchases are erratic or unpredictable.

We illustrate by continuing the Rational Demiconductor example. Suppose that Rational has just paid a cash dividend of $1 per share, reducing ex-dividend market capitalization to $10 million. We now reveal the source of Rational's equity value. Its operations are expected to generate a level, perpetual stream of earnings and free cash flow (FCF) of $1 million per year (no forecasted growth or decline). The cost of capital is $r = .10$, or 10%. Thus, the market capitalization of all of Rational's currently outstanding shares is PV = FCF/r = 1/.10 = $10 million.

BEYOND THE PAGE

Repurchases and the dividend discount model

mhhe.com/brealey13e

Rational Demiconductor Balance Sheet
(Market Values Ex Dividend in Year 0, $ millions)

Surplus cash	$ 0	$ 0	Debt
PV of free cash flow, $1 million per year starting in year 1	10.0	10.0	Equity market capitalization (1 million shares at $10)
	$10.0	$10.0	

The price per share equals market capitalization divided by the shares currently outstanding: $10 million divided by 1 million = $10 per share. This is the first valuation approach.

The second approach requires an assumption about future payout policy. Life is easy if Rational commits to dividends only, no repurchases. In that case, the forecasted dividend stream is level and perpetual at $1 per share. We can use the constant-growth DCF model with a growth rate $g = 0$. Share price is

$$PV = \frac{DIV}{r - g} = \frac{1}{.10 - 0} = \$10$$

But suppose that Rational announces instead that henceforth it will pay out exactly 50% of earnings as dividends and 50% as repurchases. (We assume that stockholders who sell their stock back to the company do not miss out on the dividend.) This means that next year's dividend will be only $.50. On the other hand, Rational will use $500,000 (50% of earnings) to buy back shares. It will repurchase 47,619 shares at the ex-dividend price of $10.50 per share, and shares outstanding will fall to 1,000,000 − 47,619 = 952,381 shares.[13] Thus expected earnings *per share* for year 2 increase to $1 million divided by 952,381 = $1.05 per share. So the $.50 reduction in the dividend for year 1 has been offset by 5% growth in future earnings per share, from $1 to $1.05 in year 2. And if you carry this example forward to year 3 and beyond, you will see that using 50% of earnings for repurchases continues to generate a growth rate in earnings and dividends per share of 5% per year.

So the DCF model comes back to exactly the same value for Rational's shares today, just as MM would predict. The repurchase program decreases next year's dividend from $1.00 to $.50 per share but generates 5% growth in earnings and dividends per share.

$$PV = \frac{DIV_1}{r - g} = \frac{.50}{.10 - .05} = \$10$$

Thus, we can get to Rational's price per share in two ways. The easy first method is to calculate equity market capitalization based on total free cash flow and then divide by the current number of shares outstanding. The second, more difficult method is to forecast and discount dividends per share, taking account of the growth in dividends per share caused by repurchases. We recommend the easy way when repurchases are important. Note also that the second way, which works out nicely in our example, becomes much more difficult to do precisely when repurchases are irregular or unpredictable.

Our example illustrates several general points. First, absent tax effects or other market frictions, today's market capitalization and share price are not affected by how future payout is split between dividends and repurchases. Second, shifting payout to repurchases reduces *current* dividends but produces an offsetting increase in future earnings and dividends per share. Third, when valuing cash flow per share, it is double-counting to include both the forecasted dividends per share and cash received from repurchases. If you sell back your share, you don't get any subsequent dividends.

Dividends and Share Issues

We have considered dividend policy as the choice between cash dividends or repurchases. If we hold total payout constant, smaller dividends mean larger repurchases. But, as we noted earlier, MM derived their dividend-irrelevance theorem when repurchases were rare. So MM asked whether a corporation could increase value by paying *larger* cash dividends. But they still insisted on holding investment and debt-financing policy fixed.

Suppose a company like Rational Demiconductor has paid out any surplus cash. Now it wants to impress investors by paying out an even larger dividend. The extra money must come from somewhere. If the firm fixes its borrowing, the only way it can finance the extra dividend is to print some more shares and sell them. The new stockholders are going to part with their money only if you can offer them shares that are worth as much as they cost. But how can the firm sell more shares when its assets, earnings, investment opportunities, and, therefore, market value are all unchanged? The answer is that there must be a *transfer of value*

---

[13]You can check that next year's ex-dividend price of $10.50 per share is the only price at which repurchase works. Shareholders will not sell their shares for less than $10.50 because then $500,000 would purchase more than 47,619 shares, leaving less than 952,381 shares outstanding and a price above $10.50 when the repurchase is completed. The firm should not offer more than $10.50 because that would repurchase fewer than 47,619 shares and hand a free gift to selling stockholders.

from the old to the new stockholders. The new ones get the newly printed shares, each one worth less than before the extra dividend was announced, and the old ones suffer a capital loss on their shares. The capital loss borne by the old shareholders just offsets the extra cash dividend they receive.

Turn back to the first Rational Demiconductor balance sheet, which shows the company starting with $1 million of surplus cash, $1 per share. Suppose it decides to pay an annual dividend of $2 per share. To do so it will have to issue new shares (sooner or later) to replace the extra $1 million of cash that just went out the door. The ex-dividend stock price is $9, so it will have to issue 111,111 shares to raise $1 million. The issue brings Rational's equity market capitalization back to $1,111,111 \times \$9 = \$10$ million. Thus, Rational's shareholders receive a dividend of $2 versus $1 per share, but the extra cash in their pockets is exactly offset by a lower stock price. They own a smaller fraction of the firm, because Rational had to finance the extra dividend by issuing 111,111 new shares.[14]

Figure 16.4 shows how this transfer of value occurs. Assume that Company Z pays out a third of its total value as a dividend and it raises the money to do so by selling new shares. The capital loss suffered by the old stockholders is represented by the reduction in the size of the red boxes. But that capital loss is exactly offset by the fact that the new money raised (the blue boxes) is paid over to them as dividends. The firm that sells shares to pay higher dividends is simply recycling cash. To suggest that this makes shareholders better off is like advising the cook to cool the kitchen by leaving the refrigerator door open.

Does it make any difference to the old stockholders that they receive an extra dividend payment plus an offsetting capital loss? It might if that were the only way they could get their hands on cash. But as long as there are efficient capital markets, they can raise the cash by selling shares. Thus, the old shareholders can cash in either by persuading the management to pay a higher dividend or by selling some of their shares. In either case there will be a

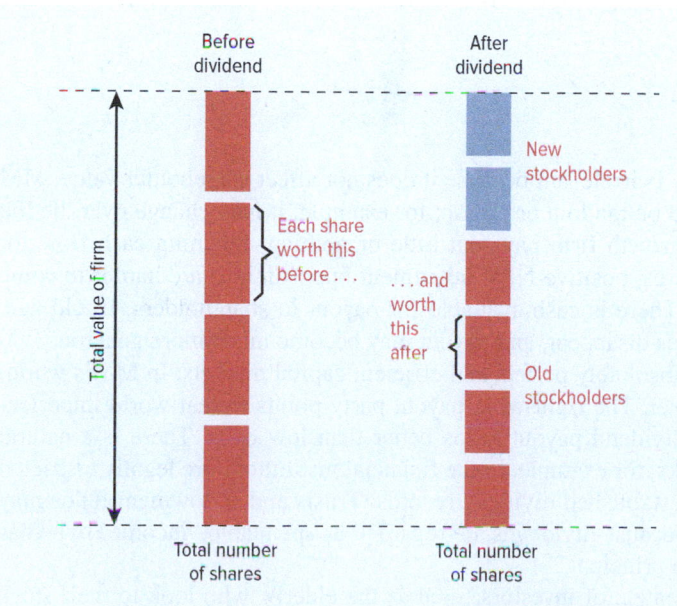

FIGURE 16.4

Company Z pays out a third of its worth as a dividend and raises the money by selling new shares. The transfer of value to the new stockholders is equal to the dividend payment. The total value of the firm is unaffected.

[14]We saw earlier that Rational's repurchase policy caused the dividend to increase by 5% a year ($g = .05$). Now the effect of regular sales of stock is that the dividend per share *declines* by 10% a year ($g = -.10$). Stock price, therefore, equals $2.0/(.10 + .10) = \$10$. Value is unchanged.

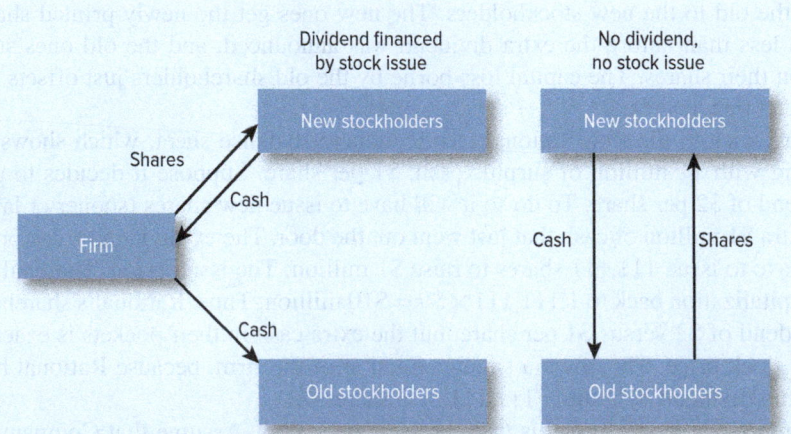

FIGURE 16.5

Two ways of raising cash for the firm's original shareholders. In each case the cash received is offset by a decline in the value of the old stockholders' claim on the firm. If the firm pays a dividend, each share is worth less because more shares have to be issued against the firm's assets. If the old stockholders sell some of their shares, each share is worth the same but the old stockholders have fewer shares.

transfer of value from old to new shareholders. The only difference is that in the former case, this transfer is caused by a dilution in the value of each of the firm's shares, and in the latter case, it is caused by a reduction in the number of shares held by the old shareholders. The two alternatives are compared in Figure 16.5.

Because investors do not need dividends to get their hands on cash, they will not pay higher prices for the shares of firms with high payouts. Therefore, firms should not worry about paying low dividends or no dividends at all.

Of course, this conclusion ignores taxes, issue costs, and a variety of other complications. We turn to these in a moment. The really crucial assumption in our proof is that the new shares are sold at a fair price. The shares that the company sells for $1 million must be worth $1 million. In other words, we have assumed efficient markets.

16-4 The Rightists

MM said that dividend policy is irrelevant because it does not affect shareholder value. MM did not say that payout should be random or erratic; for example, it may change over the life cycle of the firm. A young growth firm pays out little or nothing, retaining cash flow for investment. As the firm matures, positive-NPV investment opportunities are harder to come by and growth slows down. There is cash available for payout to shareholders. In old age, profitable growth opportunities disappear, and payout may become much more generous.

Of course, MM assumed absolutely perfect and efficient capital markets. In MM's world, everyone is a rational optimizer. The right-wing payout party points to real-world imperfections that could make high dividend payout ratios better than low ones. There is a natural clientele for high-payout stocks, for example. Some financial institutions are legally restricted from holding stocks lacking established dividend records. Trusts and endowment funds may prefer high-dividend stocks because dividends are regarded as spendable "income," whereas capital gains are "additions to principal."

There is also a natural clientele of investors, such as the elderly, who look to their stock portfolios for a steady source of cash.[15] In principle, this cash could be easily generated from

BEYOND THE PAGE

Designer funds

mhhe.com/brealey13e

---

[15]See, for example, J. R. Graham and A. Kumar, "Do Dividend Clienteles Exist? Evidence on Dividend Preferences of Retail Investors," *Journal of Finance* 61 (June 2006), pp. 1305–1336; and M. Baker, S. Nagel, and J. Wurgler, "The Effect of Dividends on Consumption," *Brookings Papers on Economic Activity* (2007), pp. 231–291.

stocks paying no dividends at all; the investor could just sell off a small fraction of his or her holdings from time to time. But it is simpler and cheaper for the company to send a quarterly check than for its shareholders to sell, say, one share every three months. Regular dividends relieve many of its shareholders of transaction costs and considerable inconvenience.

Some observers have appealed to behavioral psychology to explain why we may prefer to receive those regular dividends rather than sell small amounts of stock.[16] We are all, they point out, liable to succumb to temptation. Some of us may hanker after fattening foods, while others may be dying for a drink. We could seek to control these cravings by willpower, but that can be a painful struggle. Instead, it may be easier to set simple rules for ourselves ("cut out chocolate," or "wine with meals only"). In just the same way, we may welcome the self-discipline that comes from spending only dividend income, and thereby sidestep the difficult decision of how much we should dip into capital.

Clearly, some clienteles of investors prefer stocks with regular and stable cash dividends. These investors might be willing to pay more for stocks of companies that paid out cash by dividends rather than repurchases. But do they have to pay more? Corporations are free to adjust the supply of dividends to demand. If they could increase their stock prices simply by shifting payout from repurchases to cash dividends, they would presumably have done so already. The investors who prefer cash dividends already have a wide choice of dividend-paying stocks. If the supply of such stocks is sufficient to satisfy those investors, then additional firms have no incentive to switch from repurchases to cash dividends. If this is indeed the outcome, the middle-of-the-road party wins, even if the rightists have correctly identified clienteles that prefer cash dividends.

Payout Policy, Investment Policy, and Management Incentives

Perhaps the most persuasive argument in favor of the rightist position is that paying out funds to shareholders prevents managers from misusing or wasting funds.[17] Suppose a company has plenty of free cash flow but few profitable investment opportunities. Shareholders may not trust the managers to spend retained earnings wisely and may fear that the money will be plowed back into building a larger empire rather than a more profitable one. In such cases, investors may demand higher dividends not because these are valuable in themselves, but because they encourage a more careful, value-oriented investment policy.

Cash-cow corporations may be reluctant to let go of their cash. But their managers know that the stock price is likely to fall if investors sense that the cash will be frittered away. Particularly for top managers holding valuable stock options, this threat of a falling stock price provides an excellent incentive to pay out the surplus cash.

16-5   Taxes and the Radical Left

The left-wing dividend creed is simple: Whenever dividends are taxed more heavily than capital gains, firms should pay the lowest cash dividend they can get away with. Cash available for payout should be used to repurchase shares.

By shifting their distribution policies in this way, corporations can transmute dividends into capital gains. If this financial alchemy results in lower taxes, it should be welcomed by any taxpaying investor. That is the basic point made by the leftist party when it argues for repurchases instead of dividends.

---

[16]See H. Shefrin and M. Statman, "Explaining Investor Preference for Cash Dividends," *Journal of Financial Economics* 13 (June 1984), pp. 253–282.

[17]See F. Easterbrook, "Two Agency Cost Explanations of Dividends," *American Economic Review* 74 (1984), pp. 650–659; and especially M. Jensen, "Agency Costs of Free Cash Flow, Corporate Finance, and Takeovers," *American Economic Review* 76 (May 1986), pp. 323–329.

There is no doubt that high taxes on dividends can make a difference. The leftists quickly run into two problems, however. First, if they are right, why should any firm ever pay a cash dividend? If cash is paid out, repurchases should always be the best channel as long as the firm has taxable shareholders.[18] Second, the difference in the tax rate has now disappeared for both are taxed at rates of 0%, 15%, or a maximum of 20% depending on income.[19] However, capital gains still offer some tax advantage, even at these low rates. Taxes on dividends have to be paid immediately, but taxes on capital gains can be deferred until shares are sold and gains realized. The longer investors wait to sell, the lower the PV of their tax liability.[20]

The distinction between dividends and capital gains is not important for many financial institutions, which operate free of all taxes. For example, pension funds are not taxed. These funds hold $5.7 trillion of common stocks, so their clout in the U.S. stock market is enormous. Only corporations have a tax reason to *prefer* cash dividends. They pay corporate income tax on only 50% of dividends received.[21] So, for each $1 of dividends received, the firm gets to keep $1 − (.50 \times .21) = \$.895$. Thus the effective tax rate is only 10.5%. But corporations have to pay 21% tax on interest income or realized capital gains.

Empirical Evidence on Dividends and Taxes

It is hard to deny that taxes are important to investors. You can see that in the bond market. Interest on municipal bonds is not taxed, and so municipals usually sell at low pretax yields. Interest on federal government bonds is taxed, so these bonds sell at higher pretax yields. It does not seem likely that investors in bonds just forget about taxes when they enter the stock market.

There is some evidence that in the past taxes have affected U.S. investors' choice of stocks.[22] Lightly taxed institutional investors have tended to hold high-yield stocks and retail investors have preferred low-yield stocks. Moreover, this preference for low-yield stocks has been somewhat more marked for high-income individuals. Nevertheless, taxes have not deterred individuals in high-tax brackets from holding substantial amounts of dividend-paying stocks.

If investors are concerned about taxes, we might also expect that when the tax penalty on dividends is high, companies would think twice about increasing dividend payout. Only about a fifth of U.S. financial managers cite investor taxes as an important influence when the firm makes its dividend decision. On the other hand, firms have sometimes responded to major shifts in the way that investors are taxed. For example, when Australia introduced a tax change in 1987 that effectively eliminated the tax penalty on dividends for Australian investors, firms became more willing to increase dividend payout.[23] Or consider the case of the 2011 tax reform in Japan, which raised the top marginal tax rate on dividend income from 10% to

[18]A firm that eliminates dividends and makes regular repurchases may find that the Internal Revenue Service interprets the repurchases as de facto dividends and taxes the payout accordingly. However, in practice this tax risk is a threat only for privately held firms. Nevertheless, public corporations do not usually announce that they are repurchasing shares to save investor taxes on dividends. They may say, "Our stock is a good investment" or "We want to have shares available to finance possible future acquisitions." What do you think of these rationales?

[19]Many investors will also pay a 3.8% Medicare surtax on investment income, bringing the total maximum rate on dividends and capital gains to 23.8%.

[20]When securities are sold, capital gains tax is paid on the difference between the selling price and the purchase price or *basis*. Shares purchased in 2011 for $20 (the basis) and sold in 2017 for $30 would generate a capital gain of $10 per share and a tax of $2.38 at a 23.8% rate.

Suppose sale is deferred one year to 2018. If the interest rate is 5%, the PV of the tax, viewed from 2017, falls to 2.38/1.05 = $2.27. The effective capital gains tax rate is 22.7%. The longer sale is deferred, the lower the effective tax rate.

The effective tax rate falls to zero if the investor dies before selling because under current U.S. estate-tax law, his or her heirs get to "step up" the basis without realizing a taxable gain. Suppose the price is still $30 when the investor dies. The heirs could sell for $30 and pay no tax because they could step up to a $30 basis. The investor's stock holdings may be subject to estate taxes, however.

[21]The taxable fraction of dividends is reduced to 35% if the corporation owns more than 20% of the dividend payer and is eliminated if it owns more than 80%.

[22]See, for example, Y. Grinstein and R. Michaely, "Institutional Holdings and Payout Policy," *Journal of Finance* 60 (June 2005), pp. 1389–1426; and J. R. Graham and A. Kumar, "Do Dividend Clienteles Exist? Evidence on Dividend Preferences of Retail Investors," *Journal of Finance* 61 (June 2006), pp. 1305–1336.

[23]K. Pattenden and G. Twite, "Taxes and Dividend Policy under Alternative Tax Regimes," *Journal of Corporate Finance* 14 (2008), pp. 1–16.

43.6% for individuals who owned between 3% and 5% of the company's stock. More than 50% of these investors sold their stock before the tax hike, and companies that continued to have such large investors rapidly adjusted their payout policies.[24]

If tax considerations are important, we would expect to find a tendency for high-dividend stocks to sell at lower prices and, therefore, to offer higher pretax returns, at least in past decades when tax rates on dividends were much higher than on capital gains. Unfortunately, the evidence for this tendency is ambiguous at best.[25]

Taxes are important, but cannot be the whole story of payout. Many companies paid generous dividends in the 1960s and 1970s, when U.S. tax rates on dividends were much higher than today. The shift from dividends to repurchases accelerated in the 2000s, when tax rates on both dividends and capital gains were much lower than historical levels. Payout has also shifted to repurchases in countries such as Australia which have imputation tax systems that remove the double taxation of dividends.

Nevertheless, it seems safe to say that the tax advantages of repurchases are one reason that they have grown so much in the United States and other developed economies.

Alternative Tax Systems

In the United States, shareholders' returns are taxed twice. They are taxed at the corporate level (corporate tax) and in the hands of the shareholder (income tax or capital gains tax). These two tiers of tax are illustrated in Table 16.1, which shows the after-tax return to the shareholder if the company distributes all its income as dividends. We assume the company earns $100 a share before tax and therefore pays corporate tax of $.21 \times 100 = \$21$. This leaves $79 a share to be paid out as a dividend, which is then subject to a second layer of tax. For example, a shareholder who is taxed at 15% pays tax on this dividend of $.15 \times 79 = \$11.85$. Only a tax-exempt pension fund or charity would retain the full $79.

Of course, dividends are regularly paid by companies that operate under very different tax systems. In some countries, such as Australia and New Zealand, shareholders' returns are not taxed twice. For example, in Australia shareholders are taxed on dividends, but they may deduct from this tax bill their share of the corporate tax that the company has paid. This is known as an *imputation tax system*. Table 16.2 shows how the imputation system works.

Operating income	$100	
Corporate tax at 21%	21	← Corporate tax
After-tax income (paid out as dividends)	$ 79	
Income tax paid by investor at 15%	11.85	← Second tax paid by investor
Net income to shareholder	$ 67.15	

❯ TABLE 16.1 In the United States, returns to shareholders are taxed twice. This example assumes that all income after corporate taxes is paid out as cash dividends to an investor in the top income tax bracket (figures in dollars per share).

---

[24]See K. Onji and M. Orihara, "Taxes, Stock Ownership, and Payout Policy: Evidence from a 2011 Tax Reform in Japan," April 5, 2016, available at SSRN: https://ssrn.com/abstract=2811034.

[25]Two influential early studies found conflicting results. Litzenberger and Ramaswamy estimated that investors priced stocks as if dividend income attracted an extra 14% to 23% of tax. Miller and Scholes used a different methodology and came up with a negligible 4% difference in the tax rate. See R. H. Litzenberger and K. Ramaswamy, "The Effects of Dividends on Common Stock Prices: Tax Effects or Information Effects," *Journal of Finance* 37 (May 1982), pp. 429–443; and M. H. Miller and M. Scholes, "Dividends and Taxes: Some Empirical Evidence," *Journal of Political Economy* 90 (1982), pp. 1118–1141. Subsequent research on dividend taxation and common-stock returns is reviewed in J. Farre-Mensa, R. Michaely, and M. Schmalz, "Payout Policy," in A. Lo and R. C. Merton, eds., *Annual Review of Financial Economics* 6 (December 2014), pp. 75–134.

	Rate of Income Tax Paid by Investor		
	15%	30%	47%
Operating income	$100	$100	$100
Corporate tax ($T_c = 0.30$)	30	30	30
After-tax income	$ 70	$ 70	$ 70
Grossed-up dividend	100	100	100
Income tax	15	30	47
Tax credit for corporate payment	−30	−30	−30
Tax due from shareholder	−$15	$ 0	$ 17
Available to shareholder	85	70	53

> **TABLE 16.2**   Under imputation tax systems, such as that in Australia, shareholders receive a tax credit for the corporate tax that the firm has paid (figures in Australian dollars per share)

Suppose that an Australian company earns pretax profits of A$100 a share. After it pays corporate tax at 30%, the profit is A$70 a share. The company now declares a net dividend of A$70 and sends each shareholder a check for this amount. This dividend is accompanied by a tax credit saying that the company has already paid A$30 of tax on the shareholder's behalf. Thus shareholders are treated as if they received a total, or gross, dividend of 70 + 30 = A$100 and paid tax of A$30. If the shareholder's tax rate is 30%, there is no more tax to pay and the shareholder retains the net dividend of A$70. If the shareholder pays tax at the top personal rate of 47%, then he or she is required to pay an additional $17 of tax; if the tax rate is 15% (the rate at which Australian pension funds are taxed), then the shareholder receives a *refund* of 30 − 15 = A$15.[26]

Under an imputation tax system, millionaires have to cough up the extra personal tax on dividends. If this is more than the tax that they would pay on capital gains, then millionaires would prefer that the company does not distribute earnings. If it is the other way around, they would prefer dividends.[27] Investors with low tax rates have no doubts about the matter. If the company pays a dividend, these investors receive a check from the revenue service for the excess tax that the company has paid; therefore, they prefer high payout rates.

Look once again at Table 16.2 and think what would happen if the corporate tax rate were zero. The shareholder with a 15% tax rate would still end up with A$85, and the shareholder with the 47% rate would still receive A$53. Thus, under an imputation tax system, when a company pays out all its earnings, there is effectively only one layer of tax—the tax on the shareholder. The revenue service collects this tax through the company and then sends a demand to the shareholder for any excess tax or makes a refund for any overpayment.[28]

---

[26]In Australia, shareholders receive a credit for the full amount of corporate tax that has been paid on their behalf. In other countries, the tax credit is less than the corporate tax rate. You can think of the tax system in these countries as lying between the Australian and U.S. systems.

[27]In the case of Australia, the tax rate on capital gains is the same as the tax rate on dividends. However, for securities that are held for more than 12 months, only half of the gain is taxed.

[28]This is only true for earnings that are paid out as dividends. Retained earnings are subject to corporate tax. Shareholders get the benefit of retained earnings in the form of capital gains.

16-6 Payout Policy and the Life Cycle of the Firm

MM said that payout policy does not affect shareholder value. Shareholder value is driven by the firm's investment policy, including its future growth opportunities. Financing policy, including the choice between debt and equity, can also affect value, as we will see in Chapter 18.

In MM's analysis, payout is a residual, a by-product of other financial policies. The firm should make investment and financing decisions, and then can pay out whatever cash is left over. Therefore, decisions about how much to pay out should change over the life cycle of the firm.

MM assumed a perfect and rational world, but many of the complications discussed in this chapter actually reinforce the life cycle of payout. Let's review the life-cycle story.[29]

Young growth firms have plenty of profitable investment opportunities. During this time, it is efficient to retain and reinvest all operating cash flow. Why pay out cash to investors if the firm then has to replace the cash by borrowing or issuing more shares? Retaining cash avoids costs of issuing securities and minimizes shareholders' taxes. Investors are not worried about wasteful overinvestment because investment opportunities are good, and managers' compensation is tied to stock price.

As the firm matures, positive-NPV projects become scarcer relative to cash flow. The firm begins to accumulate cash. Now investors begin to worry about overinvestment or excessive perks. The investors pressure management to start paying out cash. Sooner or later, managers comply—otherwise, stock price stagnates. The payout may come as share repurchases, but initiating a regular cash dividend sends a stronger and more reassuring signal of financial discipline. The commitment to financial discipline can outweigh the tax costs of dividends. (The middle-of-the-road party argues that the tax costs of paying cash dividends may not be that large, particularly in recent years, when U.S. personal tax rates on dividends and capital gains have been low.) Regular dividends may also be attractive to some types of investors, for example, retirees who depend on dividends for living expenses.

As the firm ages, more and more payout is called for. The payout may come as higher dividends or larger repurchases. Sometimes the payout comes as the result of a takeover. Shareholders are bought out, and the firm's new owners generate cash by selling assets and restructuring operations. We discuss takeovers in Chapter 31.

The life cycle of the firm is not always predictable. It's not always obvious when the firm is "mature" and ready to start paying cash back to shareholders. The following three questions can help the financial manager decide:

1. Is the company generating positive free cash flow after making all investments with positive NPVs, and is the positive free cash flow likely to continue?

2. Is the firm's debt ratio prudent?

3. Are the company's holdings of cash a sufficient cushion for unexpected setbacks and a sufficient war chest for unexpected opportunities?

If the answer to all three questions is yes, then the free cash flow is surplus, and payout is called for.

As the nearby box shows, in March 2012, Apple's answer to all three questions was "yes." Yes, it was continuing to accumulate cash at a rate of $30 billion per year. Yes, because it had no debt to speak of. Yes, because no conceivable investment or acquisition could soak up its excess cash flow.

---

[29]Here we are following a life-cycle theory set out in H. DeAngelo, L. DeAngelo, and D. Skinner, "Corporate Payout Policy," *Foundations and Trends in Finance* 3 (2008), pp. 95–287.

Apple Commits to Dividend and Buyback

❯ Figure 16.6 shows how Apple's holdings of cash and marketable securities have grown over the past decade. By the start of 2012, Apple Inc. had accumulated cash and long-term securities of about $100 billion. Steve Jobs, the architect of Apple's explosive growth, had preferred to keep the war chest of cash for investment or possible acquisitions. Jobs's fiscal conservatism may seem quaint when Apple's forecasted income for 2012 was over $40 billion. But Jobs could remember tough times for Apple; the company was near bankruptcy when Jobs took over in 1997. Apple had paid cash dividends in the early 1990s but was forced to stop in 1995 as its cash reserves dwindled.

After Jobs died in October 2011, the pressure from investors for payout steadily increased. "They have a ridiculous amount of cash," said Douglas Skinner, a professor of accounting at the Chicago Booth School of Business. "There is no feasible acquisition that Apple could do that would need that much cash."

On March 19, 2012, Apple announced that it would pay a quarterly dividend of $2.65 per share and spend $10 billion for share buybacks. It forecasted $45 billion in payout over the following three years. Apple's stock price jumped by $15.53 to $601 by the close of trading on the announcement day. Apple's dividend yield went from zero to $(2.65 \times 4)/601 = 1.8\%$.

Was Apple's payout sufficiently generous? Analysts' opinions varied. "A pretty vanilla return-of-cash program" (A. M. Sacconaghi, Bernstein Research). "It's not too piddling, and on the other hand not so large to signal that growth prospects are not what they thought" (David A. Rolfe, Wedgewood Partners). The payout was not so large that it stopped Apple from accumulating cash because, over the following five years, the company more than doubled its holdings of cash and marketable securities.

Postcript: Apple more than kept its payout promise. In the 5 years to 2017, it distributed $224 billion through dividends and repurchases. Nevertheless, by the end of the period, its cash mountain was even higher than at the time of the 2012 announcement. At that point Apple announced a plan to buy back a further $100 billion of stock.

Source: N. Wingfield, "Flush with Cash, Apple Declares a Dividend and Buyback," *The New York Times*, March 20, 2012, pp. B1, B9.

❯ **FIGURE 16.6**

The growth in Apple's holdings of cash and marketable securities, 2002–2017

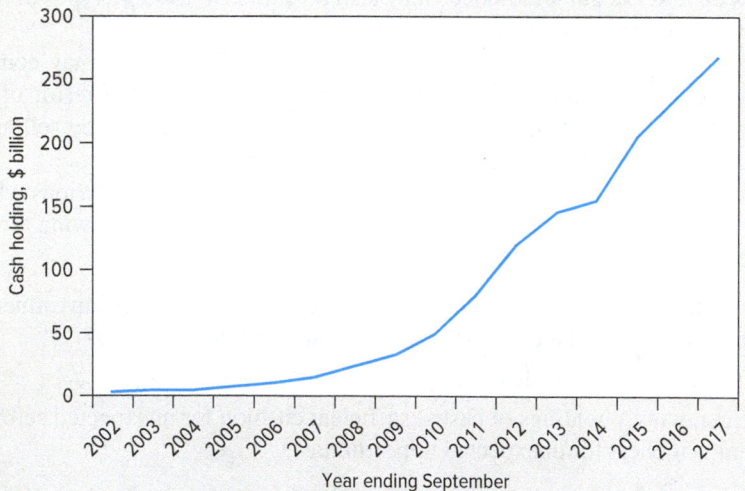

Some critics had argued that Apple should pay out the cash because it was earning interest at less than 1% per year. That was a spurious argument because shareholders had no better opportunities. Safe interest rates were extremely low, and neither Apple nor investors could do anything about it.

Note also two further points. First, Apple did not just initiate a cash dividend. It announced a combination of dividends and repurchases. This two-part payout strategy is now standard for large, mature corporations. Second, Apple did not initiate repurchases because its stock was undervalued but because it had surplus cash. You will hear critics who claim that companies should repurchase shares in bad times, when profits disappoint, and forbear in good times when profits are high. It is true that repurchases are sometimes triggered by management's view that their company's stock is underappreciated by investors. But repurchases are primarily a device for distributing surplus cash to investors. It's no surprise that repurchases increase when profits are high and more surplus cash is available.

Payout and Corporate Governance

Most of this chapter has considered payout policy by public corporations in developed economies with good corporate governance. Payout can play a still more important role in countries where corporations are more opaque and governance less effective.

In some countries, you cannot always trust the financial information that companies provide. A passion for secrecy and a tendency to construct multilayered corporate organizations can produce earnings figures that are doubtful and sometimes meaningless. Thanks to creative accounting, the situation is little better for some companies in the United States, although accounting standards have tightened since passage of the Sarbanes-Oxley legislation in 2002.

How does an investor separate the winners and losers when governance is weak and corporations are opaque? One clue is payout. Investors can't read managers' minds, but they can learn from their actions. They know that a firm that reports good earnings and pays out a significant fraction of the earnings is putting its money where its mouth is. We can understand, therefore, why investors would be skeptical about reported earnings unless they were backed up by consistent payout policy.

Of course, firms can cheat in the short run by overstating earnings and scraping up cash for payout. But it is hard to cheat in the long run because a firm that is not making money will not have cash to pay out. If a firm pays a high dividend or commits to substantial repurchases without generating sufficient cash flow, it will ultimately have to seek additional debt or equity financing. The requirement for new financing would reveal management's game to investors.

The implications for payout in developing countries could go either way. On the one hand, managers who are committed to shareholder value have a stronger motive to pay out cash when corporate governance is weak and corporate financial statements are opaque. Payout makes the firm's reported earnings more credible. On the other hand, weak corporate governance may also weaken managers' commitment to shareholders. In this case they will pay out less, and instead deploy cash more in their own interests. It turns out that dividend payout ratios are on average smaller where governance is weak.[30]

---

[30]See R. LaPorta, F. Lopez de Silanes, A. Shleifer, and R. W. Vishny, "Agency Problems and Dividend Policy around the World," *Journal of Finance* 55 (February 2000), pp. 1–33.

* * * * *

SUMMARY

A corporation's payout policy is the answer to two questions. First, how much cash should the company pay out to its stockholders? Second, should the cash be distributed by paying cash dividends or by repurchasing shares?

The answer to "How much?" is often zero. Younger companies with profitable growth opportunities do not pay out cash and rarely repurchase stock. They finance investment as much as possible with internally generated cash flow. But as they mature, growth opportunities gradually fade away and surplus cash accumulates. Then investors press for payout because they worry that managers will overinvest if too much idle cash is lying around.

Cash is surplus when these three criteria are met:

1. Free cash flow is reliably positive. Recall that free cash flow is the operating cash flow left over after the firm has made all positive-NPV investments.

2. The firm's debt level is prudent and manageable. Otherwise, free cash flow is better used to pay down debt.

3. The firm has a sufficient war chest of cash or unused debt capacity to cover unexpected opportunities or setbacks.

A firm with surplus cash will probably start by repurchasing shares. Repurchases are more flexible than dividends. Once a company announces a regular cash dividend, investors expect the dividend to continue unless the company encounters serious financial trouble. Thus, financial managers do not start or increase a cash dividend unless they are confident that the dividend can be maintained. Announcements of dividend initiations or increases usually cause a stock price increase, because the announcements signal managers' confidence. This is the *information content of dividends*.

Regular cash dividends are paid by mature, profitable firms. But most firms that pay regular cash dividends also repurchase shares. If we lived in an ideally simple and perfect world, the choice between cash dividends and stock repurchase would have no effect on market value. For example, when a company shifts payout from repurchases to cash dividends, then shareholders' extra cash is exactly offset by a lower stock price.

The most obvious and serious market imperfection has been the different tax treatment of dividends and capital gains. U.S. tax rates on dividends have in the past been much higher than on capital gains. By 2018, the tax rate on both dividends and capital gains was equal, although the effective tax rate on capital gains was lower because payment can be deferred until shares are sold. Thus taxes have favored repurchases.

Taxes alone cannot explain payout policy, however. For example, corporations paid out massive sums in cash dividends even in the 1960s, 1970s, and early 1980s, when the top income-tax rate on dividends was 70% or more.

Of course, some investors—widows and orphans, for example—may depend on regular cash dividends. But the supply of dividends should expand to satisfy this clientele, and if the supply of dividends already meets demand, then no single firm can increase its market value simply by paying dividends. (A dividend announcement may be good news for investors, but that news would come out sooner or later through other channels.)

It is difficult to be dogmatic about payout. But remember, if investment and capital-structure decisions are held constant, then arguments about payout policy are largely about shuffling money from one pocket to another. Unless large tax consequences accompany these shuffles, it's unlikely that firm value is much affected by the choice between dividends and repurchases. The short-run choice is tactical. Longer-run payout strategy depends on the life cycle of the firm from youth and growth to profitable maturity.

Investors seem interested in payout mostly because of the information they read into payout decisions. Investors also push mature firms to pay out cash. Committing to a regular cash dividend is a particularly effective signal of financial discipline.

FURTHER READING

For comprehensive reviews of the literature on payout policy, see:

F. Allen and R. Michaely, "Payout Policy," in G. Constantinides, M. Harris, and R. Stulz, eds., *Handbook of the Economics of Finance: Corporate Finance* (Amsterdam: North-Holland, 2003).

H. DeAngelo, L. DeAngelo, and D. Skinner, "Corporate Payout Policy," *Foundations and Trends in Finance* 3 (2008), pp. 95–287.

J. Farre-Mensa, R. Michaely, and M. Schmalz, "Payout Policy," in A. Lo and R. Merton, eds., *Annual Review of Financial Economics* 6 (December 2014), pp. 75–134.

For a survey of managers' attitudes to the payout decision, see:

A. Kalay and M. Lemmon, "Payout Policy," in B. E. Eckbo, ed., *Handbook of Empirical Corporate Finance* (Amsterdam: Elsevier/North-Holland, 2007), Chapter 10.

A. Brav, J. R. Graham, C. R. Harvey, and R. Michaely, "Payout Policy in the 21st Century," *Journal of Financial Economics* 77 (September 2005), pp. 483–527.

 **Select problems are available in McGraw-Hill's *Connect*. Please see the preface for more information.**

PROBLEM SETS

1. **Dividend payments*** In 2017, Entergy paid a regular quarterly dividend of $.89 per share.

   a. Match each of the following dates.

(A1) Friday, October 27	(B1) Record date
(A2) Tuesday, November 7	(B2) Payment date
(A3) Wednesday, November 8	(B3) Ex-dividend date
(A4) Thursday, November 9	(B4) Last with-dividend date
(A5) Friday, December 1	(B5) Declaration date

   b. On one of these dates, the stock price fell by about $.89. Which date? Why?

   c. Entergy's stock price in November 2017 was about $86. What was the dividend yield?

   d. Entergy's forecasted earnings per share for 2017 were about $6.90. What was the payout ratio?

   e. Suppose that Entergy paid a 10% stock dividend. What would happen to the stock price?

2. **Dividend payments** Seashore Salt Co. has surplus cash. Its CFO decides to pay back $4 per share to investors by initiating a regular dividend of $1 per quarter or $4 per year. The stock price jumps to $90 when the payout is announced.

   a. Why does the stock price increase?

   b. What happens to the stock price when the stock goes ex dividend?

3. **Repurchases** Look again at Problem 2. Assume instead that the CFO announces a stock repurchase of $4 per share instead of a cash dividend.

   a. What happens to the stock price when the repurchase is announced? Would you expect the price to increase to $90? Explain briefly.

   b. Suppose the stock is repurchased immediately after the announcement. Would the repurchase result in an additional stock-price increase?

4. **Repurchases** An article on stock repurchase in the *Los Angeles Times* noted: "An increasing number of companies are finding that the best investment they can make these days is in themselves." Discuss this view. How is the desirability of repurchase affected by company prospects and the price of its stock?

5. **Dividends payments and repurchases** Go to the Apple website or to a financial source such as Yahoo! Finance.

   a. Has Apple's dividend increased from the initial quarterly rate of $2.65?

   b. What was the announcement date of the most recent dividend?

   c. When did Apple stock last go ex-dividend?

   d. What happened to the stock price on the ex-dividend date? When was the dividend actually paid?

e. What is Apple's dividend yield?

f. Look up estimates of Apple's EPS for the next year. What is the dividend payout ratio?

g. How much does Apple plan to spend on repurchases in the next year? What is the overall payout ratio (dividends plus repurchases)?

6. **Company dividend policy** Here are several "facts" about typical corporate dividend policies. Which are true and which false?

a. Companies decide each year's dividend by looking at their capital expenditure requirements and then distributing whatever cash is left over.

b. Managers and investors seem more concerned with dividend changes than with dividend levels.

c. Managers often increase dividends temporarily when earnings are unexpectedly high for a year or two.

d. Companies undertaking substantial share repurchases usually finance them with an off-setting reduction in cash dividends.

7. **Company dividend policy** Investors and financial managers focus more on changes in cash dividends than on the level of cash dividends. Why?

8. **Information content of dividends** What is meant by "the information content of dividends"? Explain.

9. **Information content of dividends** Does the good news conveyed by the announcement of a dividend increase mean that a firm can increase its stock price in the long run simply by paying cash dividends? Explain.

10. **Information content of dividends** Generous dividend payouts and high price–earnings multiples are correlated positively. Does this imply that paying out cash as dividends instead of repurchases increases share price? (*Hint:* Could the level of dividends be telling investors something about long-run earnings?)

11. **Payout policy in perfect capital markets** MM insisted that payout policy should be analyzed holding debt and investment policy constant. Why? Explain.

12. **Payout policy in perfect capital markets*** Go back to the first Rational Demiconductor balance sheet. Now assume that Rational wins a lawsuit and is paid $1 million in cash. Its market capitalization rises by that amount. It decides to pay out $2 per share instead of $1 per share. Explain what happens to Rational's stock price over the period of the announcement and over the period of the payment if the payout comes (a) as a cash dividend or (b) as a share repurchase.

13. **Payout policy in perfect capital markets** Go back to the first Rational Demiconductor balance sheet one more time. Assume that Rational does not win the lawsuit (see Problem 12) and is left with only $1 million in surplus cash. Nevertheless Rational decides to pay a cash dividend of $2 per share. What must Rational do to finance the $2 dividend if it holds its debt and investment policies constant? What happens to price per share?

14. **Payout policy in perfect capital markets** Respond to the following comment: "It's all very well saying that I can sell shares to cover cash needs, but that may mean selling at the bottom of the market. If the company pays a regular cash dividend, investors avoid that risk."

15. **Payout policy in perfect capital markets** Here are key financial data for House of Herring Inc.:

Earnings per share for 2025	$5.50
Number of shares outstanding	40 million
Target payout ratio	50%
Planned dividend per share	$2.75
Stock price, year-end 2025	$130

House of Herring plans to pay the entire dividend early in January 2026. All corporate and personal taxes were repealed in 2024.

a. Other things equal, what will be House of Herring's stock price after the planned dividend payout?

b. Suppose the company cancels the dividend and announces that it will use the money saved to repurchase shares. What happens to the stock price on the announcement date? Assume that investors learn nothing about the company's prospects from the announcement. How many shares will the company need to repurchase?

c. Suppose that, instead of canceling the dividend, the company increases dividends to $5.50 per share and then issues new shares to recoup the extra cash paid out as dividends. What happens to the with- and ex-dividend share prices? How many shares will need to be issued? Again, assume investors learn nothing from the announcement about House of Herring's prospects.

16. **Repurchases and the DCF model** Hors d'Age Cheeseworks has been paying a regular cash dividend of $4 per share each year for over a decade. The company is paying out all its earnings as dividends and is not expected to grow. There are 100,000 shares outstanding selling for $80 per share. The company has sufficient cash on hand to pay the next annual dividend.

Suppose that, starting in year 1, Hors d'Age decides to cut its cash dividend to zero and announces that it will repurchase shares instead.

a. What is the immediate stock price reaction? Ignore taxes, and assume that the repurchase program conveys no information about operating profitability or business risk.

b. How many shares will Hors d'Age purchase?

c. Project and compare future stock prices for the old and new policies. Do this for years 1, 2, and 3.

17. **Repurchases and the DCF model*** Surf & Turf Hotels is a mature business, although it pays no cash dividends. Next year's earnings are forecasted at $56 million. There are 10 million outstanding shares. The company has traditionally paid out 50% of earnings by repurchases and reinvested the remaining earnings. With reinvestment, the company has generated steady growth averaging 5% per year. Assume the cost of equity is 12%.

a. Calculate Surf & Turf's current stock price, using the constant-growth DCF model from Chapter 4. (*Hint:* Take the easy route and estimate overall market capitalization.)

b. Now Surf & Turf's CFO announces a switch from repurchases to a regular cash dividend. Next year's dividend will be $2.80 per share. The CFO reassures investors that the company will continue to pay out 50% of earnings and reinvest 50%. All future payouts will come as dividends, however. What would you expect to happen to Surf & Turf's stock price? Why?

18. **Repurchases and the DCF model** House of Haddock has 5,000 shares outstanding and the stock price is $140. The company is expected to pay a dividend of $20 per share next year and thereafter the dividend is expected to grow indefinitely by 5% a year. The president, George Mullet, now makes a surprise announcement: He says that the company will henceforth distribute half the cash in the form of dividends and the remainder will be used to repurchase stock. The repurchased stock will not be entitled to the dividend.

a. What is the total value of the company before and after the announcement? What is the value of one share?

b. What is the expected stream of dividends per share for an investor who plans to retain his shares rather than sell them back to the company? Check your estimate of share value by discounting this stream of dividends per share.

19. **Repurchases and the DCF model** Little Oil has 1 million shares outstanding with a total market value of $20 million. The firm is expected to pay $1 million of dividends next year, and thereafter the amount paid out is expected to grow by 5% a year in perpetuity. Thus, the expected dividend is $1.05 million in year 2, $1.1025 million in year 3, and so on. However, the company has heard that the value of a share depends on the flow of dividends, and therefore, it announces that next year's dividend will be increased to $2 million and that the extra cash will be raised immediately afterward by an issue of shares. After that, the total amount paid out each year will be as previously forecasted—that is, $1.05 million in year 2 and increasing by 5% in each subsequent year.

   a. At what price will the new shares be issued in year 1?

   b. How many shares will the firm need to issue?

   c. What will be the expected dividend payments on these new shares, and what therefore will be paid out to the *old* shareholders after year 1?

   d. Show that the present value of the cash flows to current shareholders remains $20 million.

20. **Repurchases and EPS** Many companies use stock repurchases to increase earnings per share. For example, suppose that a company is in the following position:

Net profit	$10 million
Number of shares before repurchase	1 million
Earnings per share	$10
Price–earnings ratio	20
Share price	$200

   The company now repurchases 200,000 shares at $200 a share. The number of shares declines to 800,000 shares and earnings per share increase to $12.50. Assuming the price–earnings ratio stays at 20, the share price must rise to $250. Discuss.

21. **Dividends and value** We stated in Section 16-3 that MM's proof of dividend irrelevance assumes that new shares are sold at a fair price. Look back at Problem 19. Assume that new shares are issued in year 1 at $10 a share. Show who gains and who loses. Is dividend policy still irrelevant? Why or why not?

22. **Payout and valuation** Look back one last time at Problem 19. How would you value Little Oil if it paid out $500,000 in cash dividends year in and year out, with no expected growth or decline? Remaining free cash flow will be used to repurchase shares. Assume that Little Oil's free cash flow continues to grow at 5% as in Problem 19.

23. **Dividend clienteles** Mr. Milquetoast admires Warren Buffett and believes that Berkshire Hathaway is a good investment. He wants to invest $100,000 in Berkshire Hathaway B shares but hesitates because Berkshire Hathaway has never paid a dividend. He needs to generate $5,000 per year in cash for living expenses. What should Mr. Milquetoast do?

24. **Dividend clienteles** Some types of investors prefer dividend-paying stocks because dividends provide a regular, convenient source of income. Does demand from these investors necessarily lift the prices of dividend-paying stocks relative to stocks of companies that pay no dividends but repurchase shares instead? Explain briefly.

25. **Payout and taxes*** Which of the following U.S. investors have tax reasons to prefer companies that pay out cash by repurchases instead of cash dividends? Which should not care?

   a. A pension fund.

   b. An individual investor in the top income-tax bracket.

   c. A corporation.

   d. An endowment for a charity or university.

26. **Payout policy and taxes** The middle-of-the-road party holds that payout policy doesn't matter because the *supply* of high-, medium-, and low-payout stocks has already adjusted to satisfy investors' demands. Investors who like generous dividends hold stocks that give them all the dividends that they want. Investors who want capital gains see ample low-payout stocks to choose from. Thus, high-payout firms cannot gain by transforming to low-payout firms, or vice versa.

     Suppose the government reduces the tax rate on dividends but not on capital gains. Suppose that before this change the supply of dividends matched investor needs. How would you expect the tax change to affect the total cash dividends paid by U.S. corporations and the proportion of high-versus low-payout companies? Would payout policy still be irrelevant after any dividend supply adjustments are completed? Explain.

27. **Payout policy and the cost of capital** Comment briefly on each of the following statements:

   a. "Unlike American firms, which are always being pressured by their shareholders to increase dividends, Japanese companies pay out a much smaller proportion of earnings and so enjoy a lower cost of capital."

   b. "Unlike new capital, which needs a stream of new dividends to service it, retained earnings have zero cost."

   c. "If a company repurchases stock instead of paying a dividend, the number of shares falls and earnings per share rise. Thus stock repurchase must always be preferred to paying dividends."

28. **Dividends and the firm's life cycle** Halfshell Seafood is still generating good profits, but growth is slowing down. How should its CFO decide when to start up a program of paying out cash to stockholders? What questions should the CFO ask?

CHALLENGE

29. **Dividend policy and the dividend discount model** Consider the following two statements: "Dividend policy is irrelevant," and "Stock price is the present value of expected future dividends." (See Chapter 4.) They *sound* contradictory. This question is designed to show that they are fully consistent.

     The current price of the shares of Charles River Mining Corporation is $50. Next year's earnings and dividends per share are $4 and $2, respectively. Investors expect perpetual growth at 8% per year. The expected rate of return demanded by investors is $r = 12\%$.

     We can use the perpetual-growth model to calculate stock price:

$$P_0 = \frac{\text{DIV}}{r - g} = \frac{2}{.12 - .08} = 50$$

     Suppose that Charles River Mining announces that it will switch to a 100% payout policy, issuing shares as necessary to finance growth. Use the perpetual-growth model to show that current stock price is unchanged.

30. **Dividends and taxes** Suppose that there are just three types of investors with the following tax rates:

	Individual	Corporations	Institutions
Dividends	50%	5%	0%
Capital gains	15	35	0

Individuals invest a total of $80 billion in stock and corporations invest $10 billion. The remaining stock is held by the institutions. All three groups simply seek to maximize their after-tax income.

These investors can choose from three types of stock offering the following pretax payouts per share:

	Low Payout	Medium Payout	High Payout
Dividends	$5	$5	$30
Capital gains	15	5	0

These payoffs are expected to persist in perpetuity. The low-payout stocks have a total market value of $100 billion, the medium-payout stocks have a value of $50 billion, and the high-payout stocks have a value of $120 billion.

a. Who are the marginal investors that determine the prices of the stocks?

b. Suppose that this marginal group of investors requires a 12% after-tax return. What are the prices of the low-, medium-, and high-payout stocks?

c. Calculate the after-tax returns of the three types of stock for each investor group.

d. What are the dollar amounts of the three types of stock held by each investor group?

CHAPTER

17

• • •

Does Debt Policy Matter?

A firm's basic resource is the stream of cash flows produced by its assets. When the firm is financed entirely by common stock, all those cash flows belong to the stockholders. When it issues both debt and equity securities, it splits the cash flows into two streams, a relatively safe stream that goes to the debtholders and a riskier stream that goes to the stockholders.

The firm's mix of debt and equity financing is called its *capital structure*. A firm that finances an investment partly or wholly with debt is said to employ *financial leverage*. Of course, capital structure is not just "debt versus equity." There are many different flavors of debt, at least two flavors of equity (common and preferred), plus hybrids such as convertible bonds. The firm can issue dozens of distinct securities in countless combinations. It attempts to find the particular combination that maximizes the overall market value of the firm.

Are such attempts worthwhile? We must consider the possibility that *no* combination has any greater appeal than any other. Perhaps the really important decisions concern the company's assets, and decisions about capital structure are immaterial.

Modigliani and Miller (MM), who showed that payout policy doesn't matter in perfect capital markets, also showed that financing decisions don't matter in perfect markets. Their famous "proposition 1" states that a firm cannot change its total value just by splitting its cash flows into different streams: The firm's value is determined by its real assets, not by how it is financed. Thus, capital structure is irrelevant as long as the firm's investment decisions are taken as given.

MM's proposition 1 allows complete separation of investment and financing decisions. It implies that any firm could use the capital budgeting procedures presented in Chapters 5 through 12 without worrying about where the money for capital expenditures comes from. In those chapters, we assumed all-equity financing without really thinking about it. If MM are right, that is exactly the right approach. If the firm uses a mix of debt and equity financing, its overall cost of capital will be exactly the same as if it were financed entirely with equity.

Financing decisions do matter in practice, for reasons detailed in Chapters 18 and 19. But we devote this chapter to MM because their proposition is the starting point for all applied capital structure theory. If you don't understand the starting point, you won't understand the destination. For example, the after-tax weighted-average cost of capital (WACC) follows from MM's proposition 1 with one tax adjustment. If you don't understand MM, you won't understand WACC.

MM's proposition amounts to saying, "There is no magic in financial leverage." If you don't understand MM, you may also fall prey to those who claim to see magic in the usually higher rates of return on equity for firms that borrow aggressively. The would-be magicians don't realize that the extra borrowing generates extra financial risk. MM show that the extra financial risk exactly offsets the higher returns.

In Chapter 18, we undertake a detailed analysis of the imperfections that are most likely to make a difference, including taxes, the costs of bankruptcy and financial distress, the costs of writing and enforcing complicated debt contracts, differences created by imperfect information, and the effects of debt on incentives for management. In Chapter 19, we show how such imperfections (especially taxes) affect the weighted-average cost of capital and the value of the firm.

17-1   The Effect of Financial Leverage in a Competitive Tax-Free Economy

Financial managers try to find the combination of securities that has the greatest overall appeal to investors—the combination that maximizes the market value of the firm. Before tackling this problem, we should check whether a policy that maximizes the total value of the firm's securities also maximizes the wealth of the shareholders.

Let D and E denote the market values of the outstanding debt and equity of the Wapshot Mining Company. Wapshot's 1,000 shares sell for $50 apiece. Thus,

$$E = 1,000 \times 50 = \$50,000$$

Wapshot has also borrowed $25,000, and so V, the aggregate market value of all Wapshot's outstanding securities, is

$$V = D + E = \$75,000$$

Wapshot's stock is known as *levered equity.* Its stockholders face the benefits and costs of **financial leverage**, or *gearing.* Suppose that Wapshot "levers up" still further by borrowing an additional $10,000 and paying the proceeds out to shareholders as a special dividend of $10 per share. This substitutes debt for equity capital with no impact on Wapshot's assets.

What will Wapshot's equity be worth after the special dividend is paid? We have two unknowns, E and V:

Old debt	$25,000	$35,000 = D
New debt	$10,000	
Equity		? = E
Firm value		? = V

If V is $75,000 as before, then E must be $V - D = 75,000 - 35,000 = \$40,000$. Stockholders have suffered a capital loss that exactly offsets the $10,000 special dividend. But if V *increases* to, say, $80,000 as a result of the change in capital structure, then $E = \$45,000$ and the stockholders are $5,000 ahead. In general, any increase or decrease in V caused by a shift in capital structure accrues to the firm's stockholders. We conclude that a policy that maximizes the market value of the firm is also best for the firm's stockholders.

This conclusion rests on two important assumptions: first, that Wapshot's shareholders do not gain or lose from payout policy and, second, that after the change in capital structure the old and new debt are together *worth* $35,000.

Payout policy may or may not be relevant, but there is no need to repeat the discussion of Chapter 16. We need only note that shifts in capital structure sometimes force important decisions about payout policy. Perhaps Wapshot's cash dividend has costs or benefits that should be considered in addition to any benefits achieved by its increased financial leverage.

Our second assumption that old plus new debt ends up worth $35,000 seems innocuous. But it could be wrong. Perhaps the new borrowing has increased the risk of the old bonds. If the holders of old bonds cannot demand a higher rate of interest to compensate for the increased risk, the value of their investment is reduced. In this case, Wapshot's stockholders gain at the expense of the holders of old bonds even though the overall value of the firm is unchanged.

But this anticipates issues better left to Chapter 18. In this chapter, we assume that any new issue of debt has no effect on the market value of existing debt.

Enter Modigliani and Miller

Let us accept that the financial manager would like to find the combination of securities that maximizes the value of the firm. How is this done? MM's answer is that the financial manager should stop worrying: In a perfect market any combination of securities is as good as another. The value of the firm is unaffected by its choice of capital structure.[1]

You can see this by imagining two firms that generate the same stream of operating income and differ only in their capital structure. Firm U is unlevered. Therefore the total value of its equity E_U is the same as the total value of the firm V_U. Firm L, on the other hand, is levered. The value of its equity is, therefore, equal to the value of the firm less the value of the debt: $E_L = V_L - D_L$.

Now think which of these firms you would prefer to invest in. If you don't want to take much risk, you can buy common stock in the unlevered firm U. For example, if you buy 1% of firm U's shares, your investment is $0.01V_U$ and you are entitled to 1% of the gross profits:

Dollar Investment	Dollar Return
$0.01V_U$	$0.01 \times$ Profits

Now compare this with an alternative strategy. This is to purchase the same fraction of *both* the debt and the equity of firm L. Your investment and return are then:

	Dollar Investment	Dollar Return
Debt	$0.01D_L$	$0.01 \times$ Interest
Equity	$0.01E_L$	$0.01 \times$ (Profits – interest)
Total	$0.01(D_L + E_L)$	$0.01 \times$ Profits
	$= 0.01V_L$	

Both strategies offer the same payoff: 1% of the firm's profits. The law of one price tells us that in well-functioning markets two investments that offer the same payoff must have the same price. Therefore, $0.01V_U$ must equal $0.01V_L$: The value of the unlevered firm must equal the value of the levered firm.

Suppose that you are willing to run a little more risk. You decide to buy 1% of the outstanding shares in the *levered* firm. Your investment and return are now:

Dollar Investment	Dollar Return
$0.01E_L$	$0.01 \times$ (Profits – interest)
$= 0.01(V_L - D_L)$	

Again, there is an alternative strategy. This is to borrow $.01D_L$ on your own account and purchase 1% of the stock of the unlevered firm.[2] In this case, your strategy gives you 1% of

---

[1]F. Modigliani and M. H. Miller, "The Cost of Capital, Corporation Finance and the Theory of Investment," *American Economic Review* 48 (June 1958), pp. 261–297. MM's basic argument was anticipated in 1938 by J. B. Williams and to some extent by David Durand. See J. B. Williams, *The Theory of Investment Value* (Cambridge, MA: Harvard University Press, 1938); and D. Durand, "Cost of Debt and Equity Funds for Business: Trends and Problems of Measurement," *Conference on Research in Business Finance* (New York: National Bureau of Economic Research, 1952, pp. 215–262).
[2]Rather than borrow on your own account, you might be able to lend $.01$ D_L less than you currently do. The effect is the same.

the profits from V_U, but you have to pay interest on your loan equal to 1% of the interest that is paid by firm L. Your total investment and net return are:

	Dollar Investment	Dollar Return
Borrowing	$-0.01D_L$	$-0.01 \times$ Interest
Equity	$0.01V_U$	$0.01 \times$ Profits
Total	$0.01(V_U - D_L)$	$0.01 \times$ (Profits − interest)

Again, both strategies offer the same payoff: 1% of profits after interest. Therefore, both investments must have the same cost. The investment $0.01(V_U - D_L)$ must equal $0.01(V_L - D_L)$ and V_U must equal V_L.

It does not matter whether the world is full of risk-averse chickens or venturesome lions. All would agree that the value of the unlevered firm U must be equal to the value of the levered firm L. As long as investors can borrow or lend on their own account on the same terms as the firm, they can "undo" the effect of any changes in the firm's capital structure. This is how MM arrived at their famous proposition 1: "The market value of any firm is independent of its capital structure."

The Law of Conservation of Value

MM's argument that debt policy is irrelevant is an application of an astonishingly simple idea. If we have two streams of cash flow, A and B, then the present value of A + B is equal to the present value of A plus the present value of B. That's common sense: If you have a dollar in your left pocket and a dollar in your right, your total wealth is $2. We met this principle of *value additivity* in our discussion of capital budgeting, where we saw that the present value of two assets combined is equal to the sum of their present values considered separately.

In the present context, we are not combining assets but splitting them up. But value additivity works just as well in reverse. We can slice a cash flow into as many parts as we like; the values of the parts will always sum back to the value of the unsliced stream. (Of course, we have to make sure that none of the stream is lost in the slicing. We cannot say, "The value of a pie is independent of how it is sliced," if the slicer is also a nibbler.)

This is really a *law of conservation of value*. The value of an asset is preserved regardless of the nature of the claims against it. Thus proposition 1: Firm value is determined on the *left-hand* side of the balance sheet by real assets—not by the proportions of debt and equity securities issued to buy the assets.

The simplest ideas often have the widest application. For example, we could apply the law of conservation of value to the choice between raising $100 million by issuing preferred stock, common stock, or some combination. The law implies that the choice is irrelevant, assuming perfect capital markets and providing that the choice does not affect the firm's investment and operating policies. If the total value of the equity "pie" (preferred and common combined) is fixed, the firm's owners (its common stockholders) do not care how this equity pie is sliced.

The law also applies to the mix of debt securities issued by the firm. The choices of long-term versus short-term, secured versus unsecured, senior versus subordinated, and convertible versus nonconvertible debt all should have no effect on the overall value of the firm.

Combining assets and splitting them up will not affect values as long as they do not affect investors' choices. When we showed that capital structure does not affect choice, we implicitly assumed that both companies and individuals can borrow and lend at the same risk-free rate of interest. As long as this is so, individuals can undo the effect of any changes in the firm's capital structure.

In practice, corporate debt is not risk-free and firms cannot escape with rates of interest appropriate to a government security. Some people's initial reaction is that this alone invalidates MM's proposition. It is a natural mistake, but capital structure can be irrelevant even when debt is risky.

If a company borrows money, it does not *guarantee* repayment: It repays the debt in full only if its assets are worth more than the debt obligation. The shareholders in the company therefore have limited liability.

Many individuals would like to borrow with limited liability. They might, therefore, be prepared to pay a premium for levered shares *if the supply of levered shares were insufficient to meet their needs.*[3] But there are literally thousands of common stocks of companies that borrow. Therefore, it is unlikely that an issue of debt would induce them to pay a premium for *your* shares.[4]

An Example of Proposition 1

Macbeth Spot Removers is reviewing its capital structure. Table 17.1 shows its current position. The company has no leverage, and all the operating income is paid as dividends to the common stockholders (we assume still that there are no taxes). The expected earnings and dividends per share are $1.50, but this figure is by no means certain—it could turn out to be more or less than $1.50. The price of each share is $10. Because the firm expects to produce a level stream of earnings in perpetuity, the expected return on the share is equal to the earnings–price ratio, 1.50/10.00 = .15, or 15%.

Ms. Macbeth, the firm's president, has concluded that shareholders would be better off if the company had equal proportions of debt and equity. She therefore proposes to issue $5,000 of debt at an interest rate of 10% and use the proceeds to repurchase 500 shares. To support her proposal, Ms. Macbeth has analyzed the situation under different assumptions about operating income. The results of her calculations are shown in Table 17.2.

To illustrate how leverage would affect earnings per share, Ms. Macbeth has also produced Figure 17.1. The brown line shows how earnings per share would vary with operating income

Data				
Number of shares	1,000			
Price per share	$10			
Market value of shares	$10,000			
Outcomes				
Operating income ($)	500	1,000	1,500	2,000
Earnings per share ($)	0.50	1.00	1.50	2.00
Return on shares (%)	5	10	15	20
			Expected outcome	

❯ TABLE 17.1 Macbeth Spot Removers is entirely equity-financed. Although it expects to have an income of $1,500 a year in perpetuity, this income is not certain. This table shows the return to the stockholder under different assumptions about operating income. We assume no taxes.

---

[3] Of course, individuals could *create* limited liability if they chose. In other words, the lender could agree that borrowers need to repay their debt in full only if the assets of company X are worth more than a certain amount. Presumably individuals don't enter into such arrangements because they can obtain limited liability more simply by investing in the stocks of levered companies.

[4] Capital structure is also irrelevant if each investor holds a fully diversified portfolio. In that case he or she owns *all* the risky securities offered by a company (both debt and equity). But anybody who owns *all* the risky securities doesn't care about how the cash flows are divided among different securities.

〉**TABLE 17.2**   Macbeth
Spot Removers is wondering
whether to issue $5,000 of
debt at an interest rate of 10%
and repurchase 500 shares.
This table shows the return to
the shareholder under different
assumptions about operating
income.

Data				
Number of shares	500			
Price per share	$10			
Market value of shares	$5,000			
Market value of debt	$5,000			
Interest at 10%	$500			
Outcomes				
Operating income ($)	500	1,000	**1,500**	2,000
Interest ($)	500	500	**500**	500
Equity earnings ($)	0	500	**1,000**	1,500
Earnings per share ($)	0	1	**2**	3
Return on shares (%)	0	10	**20**	30
			Expected outcome	

▶ **FIGURE 17.1**

Borrowing increases Macbeth's EPS (earnings per
share) when operating income is greater than $1,000
and reduces EPS when operating income is less than
$1,000. Expected EPS rises from $1.50 to $2.

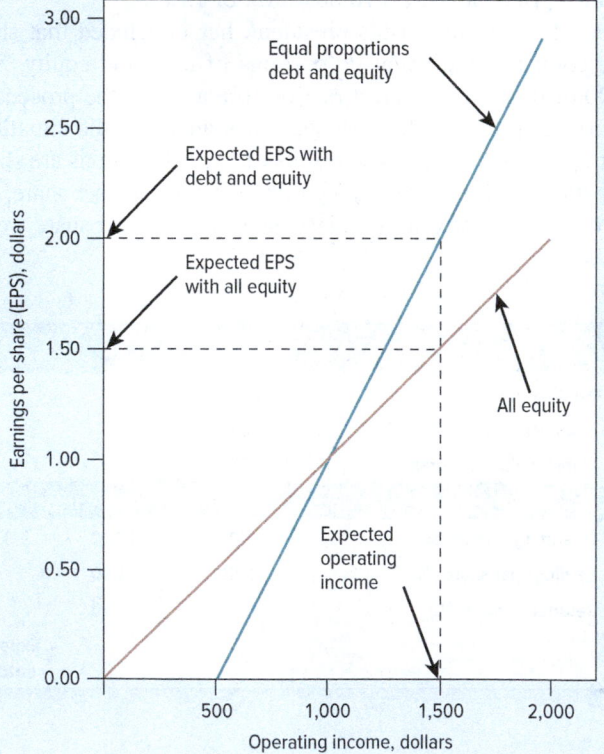

under the firm's current all-equity financing. It is, therefore, simply a plot of the data in Table 17.1.
The green line shows how earnings per share would vary given equal proportions of debt and
equity. It is, therefore, a plot of the data in Table 17.2.

Ms. Macbeth reasons as follows: "It is clear that the effect of leverage depends on the
company's income. If income is greater than $1,000, the return to the equityholder is *increased*

	Operating Income ($)			
	500	**1,000**	**1,500**	**2,000**
Earnings on two shares ($)	1	2	3	4
Less interest at 10% ($)	1	1	1	1
Net earnings on investment ($)	0	1	2	3
Return on $10 investment (%)	0	10	20	30
			Expected outcome	

❭**TABLE 17.3**   Individual investors can replicate Macbeth's leverage

by leverage. If it is less than $1,000, the return is *reduced* by leverage. The return is unaffected when operating income is exactly $1,000. At this point the return on the market value of the assets is 10%, which is exactly equal to the interest rate on the debt. Our capital structure decision, therefore, boils down to what we think about the company's prospects. Since we expect operating income to be above the $1,000 break-even point, I believe we can best help our shareholders by going ahead with the $5,000 debt issue."

As financial manager of Macbeth Spot Removers, you reply as follows: "I agree that leverage will help the shareholder as long as our income is greater than $1,000. But your argument ignores the fact that Macbeth's shareholders have the alternative of borrowing on their own account. For example, suppose that an investor puts up $10 of his or her own money, borrows a further $10, and then invests the total in two unlevered Macbeth shares. The payoff on the investment varies with Macbeth's operating income [as shown in Table 17.3]. This is exactly the same set of payoffs as the investor would get by buying one share in the levered company. [Compare the last two lines of Tables 17.2 and 17.3.] Therefore, a share in the levered company must also sell for $10. If Macbeth goes ahead and borrows, it will not allow investors to do anything that they could not do already, and so it will not increase value."

The argument that you are using is exactly the same as the one MM used to prove proposition 1.

17-2 Financial Risk and Expected Returns

Consider now the implications of MM's proposition 1 for the expected returns on Macbeth stock:

	Current Structure: All Equity	Proposed Structure: Equal Debt and Equity
Expected earnings per share ($)	1.50	2.00
Price per share ($)	10	10
Expected return on share (%)	15	20

Leverage increases the expected stream of earnings per share but *not* the share price. The reason is that the change in the expected earnings stream is exactly offset by a change in the rate at which the earnings are discounted. The expected return on the share (which for a perpetuity is equal to the earnings–price ratio) increases from 15% to 20%. We now show how this comes about.

The expected return on Macbeth's assets r_A is equal to the expected operating income divided by the total market value of the firm's securities:

$$\text{Expected return on assets} = r_A = \frac{\text{expected operating income}}{\text{market value of all securities}}$$

We have seen that in perfect capital markets the company's borrowing decision does not affect *either* the firm's operating income *or* the total market value of its securities. Therefore, the borrowing decision also does not affect the expected return on the firm's assets r_A.

Suppose that an investor holds all of a company's debt and all of its equity. This investor is entitled to all the firm's operating income; therefore, the expected return on the portfolio is just r_A.

The expected return on a portfolio is equal to a weighted average of the expected returns on the individual holdings. Therefore, the expected return on a portfolio consisting of *all* the firm's securities is

Expected return on assets = (proportion in debt × expected return on debt)

+ (proportion in equity × expected return on equity)

$$r_A = \left(\frac{D}{D+E} \times r_D\right) + \left(\frac{E}{D+E} \times r_E\right)$$

This formula is, of course, an old friend from Chapter 9. The overall expected return r_A is called the *company cost of capital* or the *weighted-average cost of capital* (WACC).

We can turn the formula around to solve for r_E, the expected return to equity for a levered firm:

Expected return on equity = expected return on assets

+ (expected return on assets − expected return on debt)

× debt-equity ratio

$$r_E = r_A + (r_A - r_D)\frac{D}{E}$$

Proposition 2

This is MM's proposition 2: The expected rate of return on the common stock of a levered firm increases in proportion to the debt–equity ratio (D/E), expressed in market values; the rate of increase depends on the spread between r_A, the expected rate of return on a portfolio of all the firm's securities, and r_D, the expected return on the debt. Note that $r_E = r_A$ if the firm has no debt.

We can check out this formula for Macbeth Spot Removers. Before the decision to borrow

$$r_E = r_A = \frac{\text{expected operating income}}{\text{market value of all securities}}$$

$$= \frac{1,500}{10,000} = .15, \text{ or } 15\%$$

If the firm goes ahead with its plan to borrow, the expected return on assets r_A is still 15%, but the expected return on equity is

$$r_E = r_A + (r_A - r_D)\frac{D}{E}$$

$$= .15 + (.15 - .10)\frac{5,000}{5,000} = .20, \text{ or } 20\%$$

When the firm was unlevered, equity investors demanded a return of r_A. When the firm is levered, they require a premium of $(r_A - r_D)D/E$ to compensate for the extra risk.

		If operating income falls from	$1,500	to	$500	Change
No debt:	Earnings per share		$1.50		$.50	−$1.00
	Return (r_E)		15%		5%	−10%
50% debt:	Earnings per share		$2.00		0	−$2.00
	Return (r_E)		20%		0	−20%

❭ **TABLE 17.4** Financial leverage increases the risk of Macbeth shares. A $1,000 drop in operating income reduces earnings per share by $1 with all-equity financing, but by $2 with 50% debt.

MM's proposition 1 says that financial leverage has no effect on shareholders' wealth. Proposition 2 says that the rate of return they can expect to receive on their shares increases as the firm's debt–equity ratio increases. How can shareholders be indifferent to increased leverage when it increases expected return? The answer is that any increase in expected return is exactly offset by an increase in financial risk and therefore in shareholders' *required* rate of return.

You can see financial risk at work in our Macbeth example. Compare the risk of earnings per share in Table 17.2 versus Table 17.1. Or look at Table 17.4, which shows how a shortfall in operating income affects the payoff to the shareholders. If the firm is all-equity-financed, a decline of $1,000 in the operating income reduces the return on the shares by 10 percentage points. If the firm issues risk-free debt with a fixed interest payment of $500 a year, then a decline of $1,000 in the operating income reduces the return on the shares by 20 percentage points. In other words, the effect of the proposed leverage is to double the amplitude of the swings in Macbeth's shares. Whatever the beta of the firm's shares before the refinancing, it would be twice as high afterward.

Now you can see why investors require higher returns on levered equity. The required return simply rises to match the increased financial risk.

Leverage and the Cost of Equity

Consider a company with the following market-value balance sheet:

Asset value	$100	Debt (D)	$33.3	at $r_D = 7.25\%$
		Equity (E)	$66.7	at $r_E = 15.5\%$
Asset value	$100	Firm value (V)	$100	

and an overall cost of capital of

$$r_A = r_D\, D/V + r_E\, E/V$$
$$= (7.25 \times 33.3/100) + (15.5 \times 66.7/100) = 12.75\%$$

If the firm is considering a project that has the same risk as the firm's existing business, the appropriate discount rate for the cash flows is 12.75%, the firm's cost of capital.

Suppose the firm changes its capital structure by issuing more debt and using the proceeds to repurchase stock. The implications of MM's Proposition 2 are shown in Figure 17.2. The required return on equity increases with the debt-equity ratio (D/E).[5] Yet, no matter how much

---

[5]Note that the firm's debt ratio (D/V) of .333 corresponds to a debt-equity ratio (D/E) of .333/.667 = .5. Figure 17.2 shows that the required return on equity is 15.5% when the debt-equity ratio = .5.

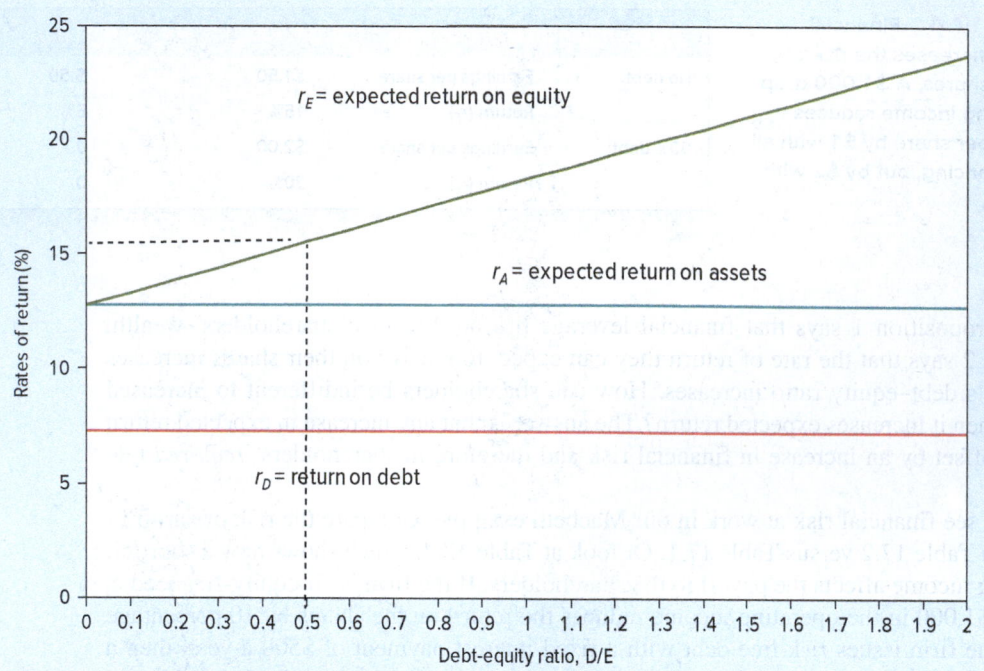

> **FIGURE 17.2**   MM's proposition 2 predicts that if debt is risk-free, the required return on equity r_E increases linearly with the debt-equity ratio, but the return on the package of debt and equity does not change

the firm borrows, the required return on the package of debt and equity, r_A, remains constant at 12.75%. How is it possible for the required return on the package to stay constant when the required return on the individual securities is changing? Answer: Because the proportions of debt and equity in the package are also changing. More debt means that the cost of equity increases but at the same time the *proportion* of equity declines.

In Figure 17.2, we have drawn the rate of interest on the debt as constant no matter how much the firm borrows. This is not wholly realistic. It is true that most large, conservative companies could borrow a little more or less without noticeably affecting the interest rate that they pay. But at higher debt levels, lenders become concerned that they may not get their money back, and they demand higher rates of interest to compensate. Figure 17.3 modifies Figure 17.2 to account for this. You can see that as the firm borrows more, the risk of the debt slowly increases. Proposition 2 continues to predict that the expected return on the package of debt and equity does not change. However, the slope of the r_E line now tapers off as D/E increases. Why? Essentially because holders of risky debt begin to bear part of the firm's operating risk. As the firm borrows more, more of that risk is transferred from stockholders to bondholders.

Let's assume that the firm issues an additional $16.7 of debt and uses the cash to repurchase $16.7 of its equity. The revised market-value balance sheet has debt of $50 rather than $33.3:

Asset value	$100	Debt (*D*)	$50
		Equity (*E*)	$50
Asset value	$100	Firm value (*V*)	$100

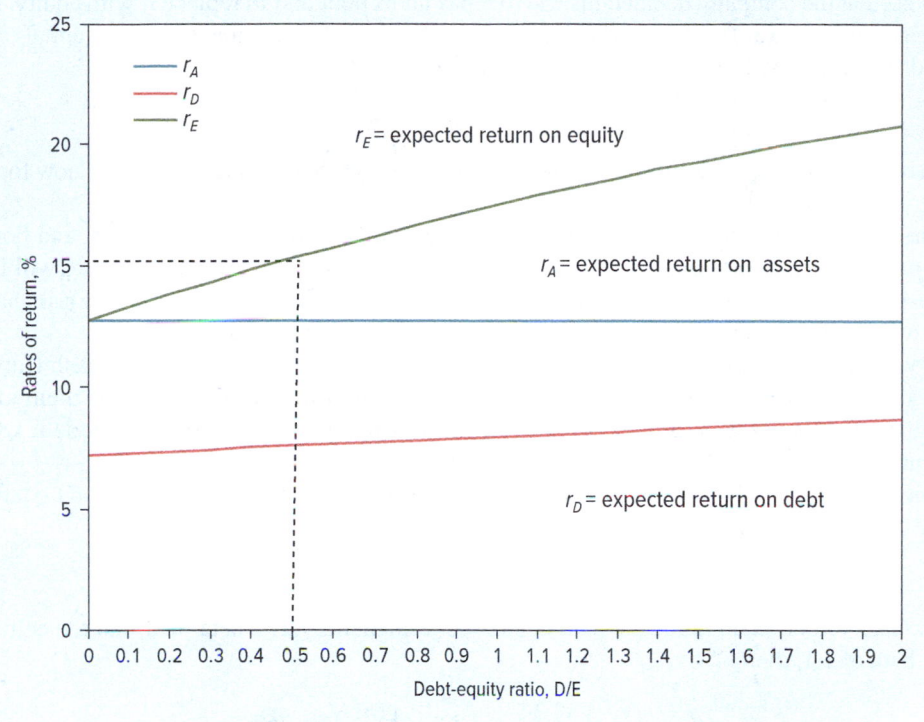

▶ **FIGURE 17.3**
If leverage increases, the risk of the debt increases and debtholders demand a higher interest rate. As lenders take on the extra risk, the expected return on equity increases more slowly. MM's proposition 2 continues to predict that the expected return on the package of debt and equity is unchanged.

The change in financial structure does not affect the amount or risk of the cash flows on the total package of debt and equity. Therefore, if investors required a return of 12.75% on the total package before the refinancing, they must require a 12.75% return on the firm's assets afterward.

Although the required return on the *package* of debt and equity is unaffected, the change in financial structure does affect the required return on the individual securities. Because the company has more debt than before, the debtholders are likely to demand a higher interest rate. Suppose that the expected return on the debt rises to 8%. Now you can write down the basic equation for the return on assets:

$$r_A = r_D \frac{D}{V} + r_E \frac{E}{V}$$

$$= \left(8.0 \times \frac{50}{100}\right) + \left(r_E \times \frac{50}{100}\right) = 12.75\%$$

Solving for the return on equity gives $r_E = 17.5\%$.

Increasing the amount of debt increased debtholder risk and led to a rise in the return that debtholders required (r_D rose from 7.25% to 8.0%). The higher leverage also made the equity riskier and increased the return that shareholders required (r_E rose from 15.5% to 17.5%). However, the weighted-average return on debt and equity was unchanged at 12.75%:

$$r_A = r_D \frac{D}{V} + r_E \frac{E}{V}$$

$$= \left(8.0 \times \frac{50}{100}\right) + \left(17.5 \times \frac{50}{100}\right) = 12.75\%$$

Suppose that the company decided instead to repay all its debt and to replace it with equity. In that case, all the cash flows would go to the equityholders. The company cost of capital, r_A, would stay at 12.75%, and r_E would also be 12.75%.

How Changing Capital Structure Affects Beta

We have looked at how changes in financial structure affect expected return. Let us now look at the effect on beta.

The stockholders and debtholders both receive a share of the firm's cash flows, and both bear part of the risk. For example, if the firm's assets turn out to be worthless, there will be no cash to pay stockholders or debtholders. But debtholders usually bear much less risk than stockholders. Debt betas of large firms are typically in the range of 0 to .2.[6]

If you owned a portfolio of all the firm's securities, you wouldn't share the cash flows with anyone. You wouldn't share the risks with anyone either; you would bear them all. Thus, the firm's asset beta is equal to the beta of a portfolio of all the firm's debt and its equity.

The beta of this hypothetical portfolio is just a weighted average of the debt and equity betas:

$$\beta_A = \beta_{\text{portfolio}} = \beta_D \frac{D}{V} + \beta_E \frac{E}{V}$$

Think back to our example. If the debt before the refinancing has a beta of .1 and the equity has a beta of 1.1, then

$$\beta_A = \left(.1 \times \frac{33.3}{100}\right) + \left(1.1 \times \frac{66.7}{100}\right) = .767$$

What happens after the refinancing? The risk of the total package is unaffected, but both the debt and the equity are now more risky. Suppose that the debt beta stays at .1. We can work out the new equity beta:

$$\beta_A = \beta_{\text{portfolio}} = \beta_D \frac{D}{V} + \beta_E \frac{E}{V}$$

$$.767 = \left(.1 \times \frac{50}{100}\right) + \left(\beta_E \times \frac{50}{100}\right)$$

Solve for the formula for β_E. You will see that it parallels MM's proposition 2 exactly:

$$\beta_E = \beta_A + (\beta_A - \beta_D)D/V = .767 + (.767 - .1)(50/50) = 1.43$$

Our example shows how borrowing creates financial leverage or gearing. Financial leverage does not affect the risk or the expected return on the firm's assets, but it does push up the risk of the common stock. Shareholders demand a correspondingly higher return because of this *financial risk*.

You can use our formulas to *unlever* betas—that is, to go from an observed β_E to β_A. You have the equity beta of 1.43. You also need the debt beta, here .1, and the relative market values of debt (*D/V*) and equity (*E/V*). If debt accounts for 50% of overall value *V*, then the unlevered beta is

$$\beta_A = \left(.1 \times \frac{50}{100}\right) + \left(1.43 \times \frac{50}{100}\right) = .767$$

---

[6]Debt betas are often close to zero but can move into positive territory for two reasons. First, if the risk of default increases, more of the firm's business risk is shifted to lenders. Thus, "junk" debt issues typically have positive betas. Second, changes in interest rates can affect both stock and bond prices, creating a positive correlation between returns on bonds and returns on the stock market. This second reason is most important when long-term interest rates are unusually volatile, as in the United States in the 1970s and early 1980s.

This runs the previous example in reverse. Just remember the basic relationship:

$$\beta_A = \beta_{portfolio} = \beta_D \frac{D}{V} + \beta_E \frac{E}{V}$$

Watch Out for Hidden Leverage

MM did not say that borrowing is a bad thing. But they insisted that financial managers stay on the lookout for the financial risk created by borrowing. That risk can be especially dangerous when the borrowing is not in plain sight. For example, most long-term leases are debt-equivalent obligations, so leases can hide debt. Long-term contracts with suppliers can also be debts in disguise when prices and quantities are fixed. For many firms pension liabilities and liabilities for employees' post-retirement health care are massive off-balance-sheet, debt-equivalent obligations.

EXAMPLE 17.2 • Reeby Sports' Bocce Project

Here is an example of how hidden leverage can fool a company into poor decisions. Reeby Sports is considering launch of a carbon-fiber Bocce shoe. The product will require investment of $500,000 in up-front marketing expenses and $500,000 for new equipment. George Reeby prepares a simple spreadsheet for the new product's expected five-year life and discounts at Reeby Sports' normal 10% cost of capital.[7]

Bocce Shoe Proposal						
	Cash Flow ($1,000s)					
	0	1	2	3	4	5
Marketing	−500	+260	+260	+260	+260	+260
Equipment	−500					
Total	−1,000					
NPV at 10% = −14, or −$14,000						
IRR = 9.4%						

George notes the negative NPV, then calls the equipment salesperson to cancel Reeby Sports' order. The salesperson, anxious to keep her sale, offers to let Reeby Sports buy the equipment now and pay later. She asks whether George will commit to five fixed payments of $122,000 per year. She argues that this will reduce the up-front investment and improve profitability. George revises his spreadsheet:

Bocce Shoe Proposal (Revised)						
	Cash Flow ($1,000s)					
	(Fixed payments of $122,000 per year subtracted)					
	0	1	2	3	4	5
Marketing	−500	+260	+260	+260	+260	+260
Equipment	0	−122	−122	−122	−122	−122
Total	−500	+138	+138	+138	+138	+138
NPV at 10% = +23, or $23,000						
IRR = 11.8%						

---

[7]Reeby Sports has massive tax losses carried forward from the disastrous recession of 2020. Therefore, George's cash-flow projections assume no taxes and ignore depreciation tax shields.

Now George is inclined to go ahead—the NPV and IRR look much better—but Jenny, his investment-banker daughter, points out that the manufacturer is really just lending $500,000 to Reeby Sports at the same 7% interest rate that Reeby Sports would pay to a bank. She explains that the manufacturer would advance $500,000 now in exchange for later fixed payments totaling $5 \times 122,000 = \$610,000$ undiscounted. The payments are obligatory, just like debt service on a bank loan. The effective interest rate is 7%. (You can check that the IRR to the manufacturer from agreeing to payment by installments is 7%.)

Jenny chides her father for mixing up investment and financing decisions. She upbraids him for forgetting about the financial risk created by a debt-financed equipment purchase. She berates him for discounting the cash flows of $138,000 per year (after installment payments) at the 10% cost of capital, which is designed to value *unlevered* cash flows. "Go back to your first spreadsheet, Dad," she instructs.[8] George, fearing chastisement, reproach, and remonstration, agrees.

The hidden leverage in this example is, of course, only thinly disguised. The leverage would be harder to see if, for example, it were wrapped up in a financial lease transaction. See Chapter 25 and the mini-case at the end of this chapter.

• • • •

17-3   No Magic in Financial Leverage

MM's propositions boil down to the simple warning: *There is no magic in financial leverage.* Financial managers who ignore this warning can be sucked into practical mistakes. For example, suppose that someone says, "Shareholders demand—and deserve—higher expected rates of return than bondholders. Therefore, debt is the cheaper source of capital. We can reduce the average cost of capital by borrowing more." Unfortunately, that doesn't follow if the extra borrowing leads stockholders to demand a still higher expected rate of return. According to MM's proposition 2, the cost of equity capital, r_E, increases by just enough to keep the weighted average cost of capital constant. Thus, there are actually two costs of debt. One is the interest rate that lenders require; the other is the higher return that equityholders demand to compensate them for the extra risk resulting from leverage. Mistakes arise when you ignore this second cost.

This is not the only logical short circuit that you are likely to encounter. We have cited two others in Problem 6 at the end of this chapter.

Few financial managers believe that the company cost of capital can be reduced by higher and higher leverage. But is it possible to stake out an intermediate position, in which a moderate degree of leverage increases the expected equity return, r_E, but by less than predicted by MM's proposition 2? In this case, there would be an optimal amount of leverage that minimizes the weighted average cost of capital.

Two arguments could be advanced in support of this position. First, perhaps shareholders do not notice or appreciate the financial risk created by moderate borrowing, although they wake up when debt is "excessive." If so, stockholders in moderately leveraged firms may accept a lower rate of return than they really should.

---

[8]George might try discounting the cash flows in his second spreadsheet at a cost of *equity*. We discuss the "flow to equity" valuation method in Chapter 19. This method mixes investment and financing decisions, however, and is rarely used to value individual projects. George is well-advised to calculate NPV from his first spreadsheet and *then* ask whether the installment sale adds value, compared with other sources of financing.

Does MM Apply to Banks?

❯ Healthy industrial corporations typically operate with debt ratios of around 35%. Most financial managers would not be too concerned if the ratio was a few percentage points higher or lower and would probably find it difficult to put a precise figure on the optimal debt ratio. As we pointed out in Chapter 1, shareholder value is largely created by the company's choice of real assets, not by its financial structure.

This is not so for bankers. Banks operate with very high debt ratios. For example, just before the financial crisis, many major banks had book debt-to-asset ratios of about 97% to 98%. So, it needed only a 2% to 3% fall in the value of their assets to wipe out the total value of the equity. With this sort of leverage, it is not surprising that banks often get into difficulties. This does not mean that banks could, or should, operate with the levels of debt that are typical in industrial companies because a central part of their business is the issue of debt in the form of customer deposits. However, banks could issue substantially more equity than they do without needing to reduce their deposits or increase their assets.

Bank regulators meeting in Basel, Switzerland, have established limits on the amount of leverage that banks should be allowed to have. Following the crisis, these limits were revised downward in the Basel III Accord.

Several countries have imposed even lower limits on the amount of leverage that their banks can undertake.

These moves to make banks issue more equity capital have been vigorously opposed by bankers, who have argued that higher capital ratios would add considerably to their costs. One complaint is that a reduction in leverage would reduce their return on equity. This may be true, but it is beside the point. Increased capital would lower the expected return on equity, but MM would note that it would also reduce the risk of the equity and the return that shareholders require. In a perfect world, these two effects would cancel out so that lower leverage would not increase the cost of capital for banks and would not make shareholders any worse off.

Does bankers' opposition to higher capital requirements simply reflect a failure to understand MM's arguments or are there other more valid reasons for their views? One possibility is tax. As we point out in Section 17-4, debt interest carries with it a tax shield which may be important to a financial institution that operates on relatively fine margins. But that raises a further question: Does it make sense for the government to offer a subsidy that encourages banks to borrow if the effect of that borrowing is to cause periodic banking crises?[9] Would it be better for the government to offer the same tax advantage to banks if they issue extra equity?

That seems naive.[10] The second argument is better. It accepts MM's reasoning as applied to perfect capital markets but holds that actual markets are imperfect. Because of these imperfections, firms that borrow may provide a valuable opportunity for investors. If so, levered shares might trade at premium prices compared with their theoretical values in perfect markets.

Suppose that corporations can borrow more cheaply than individuals. Then investors who want to borrow should do so indirectly by holding the stock of levered firms. They might be willing to live with expected rates of return that do not fully compensate them for the business and financial risk they bear.

---

[9]For a discussion of these issues by four proponents of higher bank capital requirements, see A. R. Admati, P. M. DeMarzo, M. F. Hellwig, and P. Pfleiderer, "Fallacies and Irrelevant Facts in the Debate on Capital Regulation" in C. Goodhart, D. Gabor, J. Vestergaard and I. Erturk, eds., *Central Banks at a Crossroads: Europe and Beyond* (London: Anthem Press, 2014).

[10]This first argument may reflect a confusion between financial risk and the risk of default. Default is not a serious threat when borrowing is moderate; stockholders worry about it only when the firm goes "too far." But as our Macbeth example in Section 17-2 illustrated, stockholders bear financial risk—in the form of increased volatility of rates of return and a higher beta—even when the chance of default is nil.

Is corporate borrowing really cheaper? It's hard to say. Interest rates on home mortgages are not too different from rates on high-grade corporate bonds.[11] Rates on margin debt (borrowing from a stockbroker with the investor's shares tendered as security) are not too different from the rates firms pay banks for short-term loans.

However, suppose that there is a large class of investors for whom corporate borrowing is better than personal borrowing. That clientele would, in principle, be willing to pay a premium for the shares of a levered firm. But maybe it doesn't *have* to pay a premium. Perhaps smart financial managers long ago recognized this clientele and shifted the capital structures of their firms to meet its needs. The shifts would not have been difficult or costly. But if the clientele is now satisfied, it no longer needs to pay a premium for levered shares. Only the financial managers who *first* recognized the clientele extracted any advantage from it.

Maybe the market for corporate leverage is like the market for automobiles. Americans need millions of automobiles and are willing to pay thousands of dollars apiece for them. But that doesn't mean that you could strike it rich by going into the automobile business. You're at least 100 years too late.

Today's Unsatisfied Clienteles Are Probably Interested in Exotic Securities

So far, we have made little progress in identifying cases where firm value might plausibly depend on financing. But our examples illustrate what smart financial managers look for. They look for an *unsatisfied* clientele, investors who want a particular kind of financial instrument but because of market imperfections can't get it or can't get it cheaply.

MM's proposition 1 is violated when the firm, by imaginative design of its capital structure, can offer some *financial service* that meets the needs of such a clientele. Either the service must be new and unique or the firm must find a way to provide some old service more cheaply than other firms or financial intermediaries can.

Now, is there an unsatisfied clientele for garden-variety debt or levered equity? We doubt it. But perhaps you can invent an exotic security and uncover a latent demand for it.

In the next several chapters, we will encounter a number of new securities that have been invented by companies and advisers. These securities take the company's basic cash flows and repackage them in ways that are thought to be more attractive to investors. However, while inventing these new securities is easy, it is more difficult to find investors who will rush to buy them.

Imperfections and Opportunities

BEYOND THE PAGE

Bank regulation and CDOs

mhhe.com/brealey13e

The most serious capital market imperfections are often those created by government. An imperfection that supports a violation of MM's proposition 1 *also* creates a money-making opportunity. Firms and intermediaries will find some way to reach the clientele of investors frustrated by the imperfection.

For many years, the U.S. government imposed a limit on the rate of interest that could be paid on savings accounts. It did so to protect savings institutions by limiting competition for their depositors' money. The fear was that depositors would run off in search of higher yields, causing a cash drain that savings institutions would not be able to meet. Interest-rate regulation provided financial institutions with an opportunity to create value by offering money market funds. These are mutual funds that invest in Treasury bills, commercial paper, and other high-grade, short-term debt instruments. Any saver with a few thousand dollars to invest can gain access to these instruments through a money market fund and can withdraw money

---

[11]One of the authors once obtained a home mortgage at a rate 1/2 percentage point *less* than the contemporaneous yield on long-term AAA bonds.

at any time by writing a check against his or her fund balance. Thus, the fund resembles a checking or savings account that pays close to market interest rates.[12] These money market funds became enormously popular. At the peak of their popularity in 2008, they managed $3.3 trillion of assets.

Long before interest-rate ceilings were finally removed, most of the gains had gone out of issuing money-market funds to individual investors. Once the clientele was finally satisfied, MM's proposition 1 was restored (until the government creates a new imperfection). The moral of the story is this: If you ever find an unsatisfied clientele, do something right away, or capital markets will evolve and steal it from you.

This is actually an encouraging message for the economy as a whole. If MM are right, investors' demands for different types of securities are satisfied at minimal cost. The cost of capital will reflect only business risk. Capital will flow to companies with positive-NPV investments, regardless of the companies' capital structures. This is the efficient outcome.

17-4 A Final Word on the After-Tax Weighted-Average Cost of Capital

MM left us a simple message. When the firm changes its mix of debt and equity securities, the risk and expected returns of these securities change, but the company's overall cost of capital does not change.

Now if you think that message is too neat and simple, you're right. The complications are spelled out in the next two chapters. But we must note one complication here: In the United States and many other countries, interest paid on a firm's borrowing can be deducted from taxable income. Thus, the *after-tax* cost of debt is $r_D(1 - T_c)$, where T_c is the marginal corporate tax rate. So, when companies discount an average-risk project, they do not use the company cost of capital as we have just computed it. Instead they use the after-tax cost of debt to compute the after-tax weighted-average cost of capital or WACC:

$$\text{After-tax WACC} = r_D(1 - T_c)\frac{D}{V} + r_E\frac{E}{V}$$

We briefly introduced this formula in Chapter 9, where we used it to estimate the weighted-average cost of capital for CSX. In 2017, CSX's long-term borrowing rate was $r_D = 4.0\%$, and its estimated cost of equity was $r_E = 10.3\%$. With a 21% corporate tax rate, the after-tax cost of debt was $r_D(1 - T_c) = 4.0(1 - .21) = 3.2\%$. The ratio of debt to overall company value was $D/V = .192$. Therefore,

$$\text{After-tax WACC} = r_D(1 - T_c)\frac{D}{V} + r_E\frac{E}{V}$$

$$= 4.0 \times (1 - .21) \times .192 + 10.3 \times .808 = 8.9\%$$

MM's proposition 2 states that *in the absence of taxes,* the company cost of capital stays the same regardless of the amount of leverage. But if companies receive a tax shield on their interest payments, then the after-tax WACC declines as debt increases. This is illustrated in Figure 17.4, which shows how CSX's WACC changes as the debt–equity ratio changes.

BEYOND THE PAGE

Try It! Figure 17.4: Changing leverage and the cost of capital

mhhe.com/brealey13e

---

[12]Money market funds are not totally safe. In 2008, the Reserve Primary Fund incurred heavy losses on its holdings of Lehman Brothers debt and became only the second money market fund in history to "break the buck" by paying investors only 97 cents on the dollar. Since then, additional regulations have been introduced to prevent a repetition of this failure.

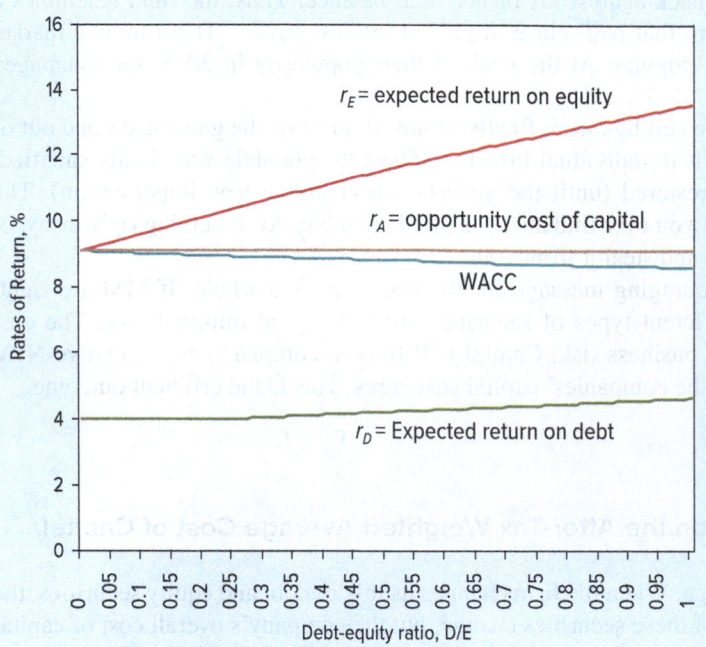

FIGURE 17.4   Estimated after-tax WACC for CSX at different debt–equity ratios. The figure assumes $r_E = 10.3\%$ at a 19.2% debt ratio (equivalent to a 23.76% debt–equity ratio) and a borrowing rate of $r_D = 4.0\%$. We assume that the debt interest rate is effectively constant at lower debt levels but increases at higher debt–equity ratios.

Most large public corporations use an after-tax WACC to discount cash flows from proposed investments. By doing so they are following MM's proposition 1, except for using an after-tax cost of debt.[13]

---

[13]They are also simplifying by using the promised rate of return on debt. Strictly speaking, MM would use the expected rate of return, which is lower than the promised rate of return because of the risk of default. But promised and expected rates of return are usually close for creditworthy companies.

- - - - -

SUMMARY

Think of the financial manager as taking all of the firm's real assets and selling them to investors as a package of securities. Some financial managers choose the simplest package possible: all-equity financing. Some end up issuing dozens of debt and equity securities. The problem is to find the particular combination that maximizes the market value of the firm.

Modigliani and Miller's (MM's) famous proposition 1 states that no combination is better than any other—that the firm's overall market value (the value of all its securities) is independent of capital structure. Firms that borrow do offer investors a more complex menu of securities, but investors yawn in response. The menu is redundant. Any shift in capital structure can be duplicated or "undone" by investors. Why should they pay extra for borrowing indirectly (by holding shares in a levered firm) when they can borrow just as easily and cheaply on their own accounts?

MM agree that borrowing raises the expected rate of return on shareholders' investments. But it also increases the risk of the firm's shares. MM show that the higher risk exactly offsets the increase in expected return, leaving stockholders no better or worse off.

Proposition 1 is an extremely general result. It applies not just to the debt–equity trade-off but to *any* choice of financing instruments. For example, MM would say that the choice between long-term and short-term debt has no effect on firm value.

MM's theory boils down to saying, "There is no magic in financial leverage." Some might object that there is a clientele of investors who are willing to pay a premium for shares of levered firms. But this argument is incomplete. There may be a clientele for levered equity, but that is not enough; this clientele has to be *unsatisfied* and obliged to pay more for levered equity than MM would predict. There are already thousands of levered firms available for investment. Is there still an unsatisfied clientele for garden-variety debt and equity? We doubt it.

Proposition 1 is violated when financial managers find an untapped demand and satisfy it by issuing something new and different. The argument between MM and the traditionalists finally boils down to whether this is difficult or easy. We lean toward MM's view: Finding unsatisfied clienteles and designing exotic securities to meet their needs is a game that's fun to play but hard to win.

If MM are right, the overall cost of capital—the expected rate of return on a portfolio of all the firm's outstanding securities—is the same regardless of the mix of securities issued to finance the firm. The overall cost of capital is usually called the company cost of capital or the weighted-average cost of capital (WACC). MM say that WACC doesn't depend on capital structure. But MM assume away lots of complications. The first complication is taxes. When we recognize that debt interest is tax-deductible, and compute WACC with the after-tax interest rate, WACC declines as the debt ratio increases. There is more—lots more—on taxes and other complications in the next two chapters.

Danger lurks where naïve financial managers try to add value simply by "levering up." MM did not say that borrowing is a bad thing, but they insisted that financial risk offsets the higher average returns from financial leverage. Do not ignore financial risk. Watch out especially for hidden leverage, for example, from financing leases or pension obligations.

FURTHER READING

The fall 1988 issue of the Journal of Economic Perspectives *contains a collection of articles, including one by Modigliani and Miller, that review and assess the MM propositions. The summer 1989 issue of* Financial Management *contains three more articles under the heading "Reflections on the MM Propositions 30 Years Later."*

Two surveys of financial innovation include:

F. Allen and G. Yago, *Financing the Future: Market-Based Innovations for Growth,* Wharton School Publishing-Milken Institute Series on Financial Innovations (Upper Saddle River, NJ: Pearson Education, 2010).

P. Tufano, "Financial Innovation," in G. M. Constantinides, M. Harris, and R. Stulz, eds., *Handbook of the Economics of Finance,* vol. 1A (Amsterdam: Elsevier/North-Holland, 2003), pp. 307–335.

Miller reviews the MM propositions in:

M. H. Miller, "The Modigliani-Miller Propositions after Thirty Years," *Journal of Economic Perspectives,* 2 (Autumn 1988), pp. 99–120.

For a skeptic's view of MM's arguments see:

S. Titman, "The Modigliani and Miller Theorem and the Integration of Financial Markets," *Financial Management* 31 (Spring 2002), pp. 101–115.

PROBLEM SETS

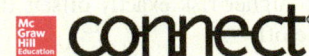 **Select problems are available in McGraw-Hill's *Connect*. Please see the preface for more information.**

1. **Homemade leverage*** Ms. Kraft owns 50,000 shares of the common stock of Copperhead Corporation with a market value of $2 per share, or $100,000 overall. The company is currently financed as follows:

	Market Value
Common stock (8 million shares)	$16 million
Short-term loans	$ 2 million

Copperhead now announces that it is replacing $1 million of short-term debt with an issue of common stock. What action can Ms. Kraft take to ensure that she is entitled to exactly the same proportion of profits as before?

2. **Homemade leverage** Companies A and B differ only in their capital structure. A is financed 30% debt and 70% equity; B is financed 10% debt and 90% equity. The debt of both companies is risk-free.

   a. Rosencrantz owns 1% of the common stock of A. What other investment package would produce identical cash flows for Rosencrantz?

   b. Guildenstern owns 2% of the common stock of B. What other investment package would produce identical cash flows for Guildenstern?

   c. Show that neither Rosencrantz nor Guildenstern would invest in the common stock of B if the total value of company A were less than that of B.

3. **Corporate leverage*** Suppose that Macbeth Spot Removers issues only $2,500 of debt and uses the proceeds to repurchase 250 shares.

   a. Rework Table 17.2 to show how earnings per share and share return now vary with operating income.

   b. If the beta of Macbeth's assets is .8 and its debt is risk-free, what would be the beta of the equity after the debt issue?

4. **Corporate leverage** Reliable Gearing currently is all-equity-financed. It has 10,000 shares of equity outstanding, selling at $100 a share. The firm is considering a capital restructuring. The low-debt plan calls for a debt issue of $200,000 with the proceeds used to buy back stock. The high-debt plan would exchange $400,000 of debt for equity. The debt will pay an interest rate of 10%. The firm pays no taxes.

   a. What will be the debt-to-equity ratio if it borrows $200,000?

   b. If earnings before interest and tax (EBIT) are $110,000, what will be earnings per share (EPS) if Reliable borrows $200,000?

   c. What will EPS be if it borrows $400,000?

5. **MM's propositions** True or false?

   a. MM's propositions assume perfect financial markets, with no distorting taxes or other imperfections.

   b. MM's proposition 1 says that corporate borrowing increases earnings per share but reduces the price–earnings ratio.

   c. MM's proposition 2 says that the cost of equity increases with borrowing and that the increase is proportional to D/V, the ratio of debt to firm value.

d. MM's proposition 2 assumes that increased borrowing does not affect the interest rate on the firm's debt.

e. Borrowing does not increase financial risk and the cost of equity if there is no risk of bankruptcy.

f. Borrowing always increases firm value if there is a clientele of investors with a reason to prefer debt.

6. **MM's propositions** What is wrong with the following arguments?

a. As the firm borrows more and debt becomes risky, both stock- and bondholders demand higher rates of return. Thus, by reducing the debt ratio, we can reduce both the cost of debt and the cost of equity, making everybody better off.

b. Moderate borrowing doesn't significantly affect the probability of financial distress or bankruptcy. Consequently, moderate borrowing won't increase the expected rate of return demanded by stockholders.

c. A capital investment opportunity offering a 10% internal rate of return is an attractive project if it can be 100% debt-financed at an 8% interest rate.

d. The more debt the firm issues, the higher the interest rate it must pay. That is one important reason that firms should operate at conservative debt levels.

7. **MM proposition 1*** Executive Chalk is financed solely by common stock and has outstanding 25 million shares with a market price of $10 a share. It now announces that it intends to issue $160 million of debt and to use the proceeds to buy back common stock.

a. How is the market price of the stock affected by the announcement?

b. How many shares can the company buy back with the $160 million of new debt that it issues?

c. What is the market value of the firm (equity plus debt) after the change in capital structure?

d. What is the debt ratio after the change in structure?

e. Who (if anyone) gains or loses? Now try the next question.

8. **MM proposition 1** Executive Cheese has issued debt with a market value of $100 million and has outstanding 15 million shares with a market price of $10 a share. It now announces that it intends to issue a further $60 million of debt and to use the proceeds to buy back common stock. Debtholders, seeing the extra risk, mark the value of the existing debt down to $70 million.

a. How is the market price of the stock affected by the announcement?

b. How many shares can the company buy back with the $60 million of new debt that it issues?

c. What is the market value of the firm (equity plus debt) after the change in capital structure?

d. What is the debt ratio after the change in structure?

e. Who (if anyone) gains or loses?

9. **MM proposition 1** "MM totally ignore the fact that as you borrow more, you have to pay higher rates of interest." Explain carefully whether this is a valid objection.

10. **MM proposition 1** Here is a limerick:

There once was a man named Carruthers,

Who kept cows with miraculous udders.

He said, "Isn't this neat? They give cream from one teat,

And skim milk from each of the others!"

What is the analogy between Mr. Carruthers's cows and firms' financing decisions? What would MM's proposition 1, suitably adapted, say about the value of Mr. Carruthers's cows? Explain.

11. **MM proposition 2** Spam Corp. is financed entirely by common stock and has a beta of 1.0. The firm is expected to generate a level, perpetual stream of earnings and dividends. The stock has a price–earnings ratio of 8 and a cost of equity of 12.5%. The company's stock is selling for $50. Now the firm decides to repurchase half of its shares and substitute an equal value of debt. The debt is risk-free, with a 5% interest rate. The company is exempt from corporate income taxes. Assuming MM are correct, calculate the following items after the refinancing:

   a. The cost of equity.

   b. The overall cost of capital.

   c. The price–earnings ratio.

   d. The stock price.

   e. The stock's beta.

12. **MM proposition 2.** "Increasing financial leverage increases both the cost of debt (r_{debt}) and the cost of equity (r_{equity}). So the overall cost of capital cannot stay constant." This problem is designed to show that the speaker is confused. Buggins Inc. is financed equally by debt and equity, each with a market value of $1 million. The cost of debt is 5%, and the cost of equity is 10%. The company now makes a further $250,000 issue of debt and uses the proceeds to repurchase equity. This causes the cost of debt to rise to 5.5% and the cost of equity to rise to 10.83%. Assume the firm pays no taxes.

   a. How much debt does the company now have?

   b. How much equity does it now have?

   c. What is the overall cost of capital?

   d. What is the percentage increase in earnings per share after the refinancing?

   e. What is the new price-earnings multiple? (*Hint:* Has anything happened to the stock price?)

13. **MM proposition 2** The common stock and debt of Northern Sludge are valued at $50 million and $30 million, respectively. Investors currently require a 16% return on the common stock and an 8% return on the debt. If Northern Sludge issues an additional $10 million of common stock and uses this money to retire debt, what happens to the expected return on the stock? Assume that the change in capital structure does not affect the risk of the debt and that there are no taxes.

14. **MM proposition 2** Look back to Section 17-1. Suppose that Ms. Macbeth's investment bankers have informed her that since the new issue of debt is risky, debtholders will demand a return of 12.5%, which is 2.5% above the risk-free interest rate.

   a. What are r_A and r_E?

   b. Suppose that the beta of the unlevered stock was .6. What will β_A, β_E, and β_D be after the change to the capital structure?

15. **MM proposition 2** Hubbard's Pet Foods is financed 80% by common stock and 20% by bonds. The expected return on the common stock is 12% and the rate of interest on the bonds is 6%. Assuming that the bonds are default-risk-free, draw a graph that shows the expected return of Hubbard's common stock (r_E) and the expected return on the package of common stock and bonds (r_A) for different debt–equity ratios.

16. **MM proposition 2** Imagine a firm that is expected to produce a level stream of operating profits. As leverage is increased, what happens to

   a. The ratio of the market value of the equity to income after interest?

   b. The ratio of the market value of the firm to income before interest if (i) MM are right and (ii) the traditionalists are right?

17. **MM proposition 2*** Archimedes Levers is financed by a mixture of debt and equity. You have the following information about its cost of capital:

$r_E =$ _____ $r_D = 12\%$ $r_A =$ _____

$\beta_E = 1.5$ $\beta_D =$ _____ $\beta_A =$ _____

$r_f = 10\%$ $r_m = 18\%$ $D/V = 0.5$

Can you fill in the blanks?

18. **MM proposition 2** Look back to Problem 17. Suppose now that Archimedes repurchases debt and issues equity so that $D/V = .3$. The reduced borrowing causes r_D to fall to 11%. How do the other variables change?

19. **Debt clienteles** Can you invent any new kinds of debt that might be attractive to investors? Why do you think they have not been issued?

20. **After-tax WACC*** Gaucho Services starts life with all-equity financing and a cost of equity of 14%. Suppose it refinances to the following market-value capital structure:

Debt (D)	45%	at $r_D = 9.5\%$
Equity (E)	55%	

a. Use MM's proposition 2 to calculate the new cost of equity. Gaucho pays taxes at a marginal rate of $T_c = 40\%$.

b. Calculate Gaucho's after-tax weighted-average cost of capital.

21. **After-tax WACC** Omega Corporation has 10 million shares outstanding, now trading at $55 per share. The firm has estimated the expected rate of return to shareholders at about 12%. It has also issued long-term bonds at an interest rate of 7% and has a debt value of $200 million. It pays tax at a marginal rate of 21%.

a. What is Omega's after-tax WACC?

b. How much higher would WACC be if Omega used no debt at all? (*Hint:* For this problem, you can assume that the firm's overall beta [β_A] is not affected by its capital structure or by the taxes saved because debt interest is tax-deductible.)

22. **After-tax WACC** Gamma Airlines has an asset beta of 1.5. The risk-free interest rate is 6%, and the market risk premium is 8%. Assume the capital asset pricing model is correct. Gamma pays taxes at a marginal rate of 25%. Draw a graph plotting Gamma's cost of equity and after-tax WACC as a function of its debt-to-equity ratio D/E, from no debt to $D/E = 1.0$. Assume that Gamma's debt is risk-free up to $D/E = .25$. Then the interest rate increases to 6.5% at $D/E = .5$, 7% at $D/E = .8$, and 8% at $D/E = 1.0$. As in Problem 21, you can assume that the firm's overall beta (β_A) is not affected by its capital structure or the taxes saved because debt interest is tax-deductible.

CHALLENGE

23. **Investor choice** Consider the following three tickets: Ticket A pays $10 if _____ is elected as president, ticket B pays $10 if _____ is elected, and ticket C pays $10 if neither is elected. (Fill in the blanks yourself.) Could the three tickets sell for less than the present value of $10? Could they sell for more? Try auctioning off the tickets. What are the implications for MM's proposition 1?

24. **Investor choice** People often convey the idea behind MM's proposition 1 by various supermarket analogies, for example, "The value of a pie should not depend on how it is sliced," or, "The cost of a whole chicken should equal the cost of assembling one by buying two drumsticks, two wings, two breasts, and so on."

    Actually proposition 1 doesn't work in the supermarket. You'll pay less for an uncut whole pie than for a pie assembled from pieces purchased separately. Supermarkets charge more for chickens after they are cut up. Why? What costs or imperfections cause proposition 1 to fail in the supermarket? Are these costs or imperfections likely to be important for corporations issuing securities on the U.S. or world capital markets? Explain.

25. **Investor choice** Suppose that new security designs could be patented.[14] The patent holder could restrict use of the new design or charge other firms royalties for using it. What effect would such patents have on MM's capital-structure irrelevance theory?

MINI-CASE ● ● ● ● ●

Claxton Drywall Comes to the Rescue

A law firm (not Dewey, Cheatem, and Howe) is expanding rapidly and must move to new office space. Business is good, and the firm is encouraged to purchase an entire building for $10 million. The building offers first-class office space, is conveniently located near their most important corporate clients, and provides space for future expansion. The firm is considering how to pay for it.

Claxton Drywall, a consultant, encourages the firm not to buy the building but to sign a long-term lease for the building instead. "With lease financing, you'll save $10 million. You won't have to put up any equity investment," Drywall explains.

The senior law partner asks about the terms of the lease. "I've taken the liberty to check," Drywall says. "The lease will provide 100% financing. It will commit you to 20 fixed annual payments of $950,000, with the first payment due immediately."

"The initial payment of $950,000 sounds like a down payment to me," the senior partner observes sourly.

"Good point," Drywall says amiably, "but you'll still save $9,050,000 up front. You can earn a handsome rate of return on that money. For example, I understand you are considering branch offices in London and Brussels. The $9 million would pay the costs of setting up the new offices, and the cash flows from the new offices should more than cover the lease payments. And there's no financial risk—the cash flows from the expansion will cover the lease payments with a safety cushion. There's no reason for you or your partners to worry or to demand a higher-than-normal rate of return."

QUESTIONS

Suppose the present value of the building equals its purchase price of $10 million. Assume that the law firm can finance the offices in London and Brussels from operating cash flow, with cash left over for the lease payments. The firm will not default on the lease payments. For simplicity you can ignore taxes.

1. If the law firm takes the lease, it will invest $950,000 and, in effect, borrow $9,050,000, repaid by 19 installments of $950,000. What is the interest rate on this disguised loan?

2. The law firm could finance 80% of the purchase price with a conventional mortgage at a 7% interest rate. Is the conventional mortgage better than the lease?

3. Construct a simple numerical example to convince Drywall that the lease would expose the law firm to financial risk. [*Hint:* What is the rate of return on the firm's equity investment in the office building if a recession arrives and the market value of the (leased) office building falls to $9 million after one year? What is the rate of return with conventional mortgage financing? With all-equity financing?]

4. Do the investments in London and Brussels have anything to do with the decision to finance the office building? Explain briefly.

---

[14]So far, security designs cannot be patented, but other financial applications have received patent protection. See J. Lerner, "Where Does *State Street* Lead? A First Look at Finance Patents, 1971–2000," *Journal of Finance* 57 (April 2002), pp. 901–930.

How Much Should a Corporation Borrow?

In Chapter 17, we found that debt policy rarely matters in well-functioning capital markets with no frictions or imperfections. Few financial managers would accept that conclusion as a practical guideline. If debt policy doesn't matter, then they shouldn't worry about it—financing decisions could be routine or erratic—it wouldn't matter. Yet financial managers do worry about debt policy. This chapter explains why.

If debt policy were completely irrelevant, then actual debt ratios should vary randomly from firm to firm and industry to industry. Yet in some industries, companies borrow much more heavily than in others. Look, for example, at Table 18.1. You can see that telecoms companies and utilities are large issuers of debt. On the other hand, drug companies and computer software businesses finance largely with equity. Glamorous growth companies rarely use much debt despite rapid expansion and often heavy requirements for capital.

The explanation of these patterns lies partly in the things we left out of the last chapter. We mostly ignored taxes. We assumed bankruptcy was cheap, quick, and painless. It isn't, and there are costs associated with financial distress, even if legal bankruptcy is ultimately avoided. We ignored potential conflicts of interest between the firm's security holders. For example, we did not consider what happens to the firm's "old" creditors when new debt is issued or when a shift in investment strategy takes the firm into riskier territory. We ignored the information problems that favor debt over equity when cash must be raised from new security issues. We ignored the incentive effects of financial leverage on management's investment and payout decisions.

Now we will put all these things back in: taxes first, then the costs of bankruptcy and financial distress. This will lead us to conflicts of interest and to information and incentive problems. In the end, we will have to admit that debt policy does matter.

However, we will not throw away the MM theory we developed so carefully in Chapter 17. We're shooting for a theory *combining* MM's insights plus the effects of taxes, costs of bankruptcy and financial distress, and various other complications. We're not dropping back to a theory based on inefficiencies in the capital market. Instead, we want to see how well-functioning capital markets respond to taxes and the other things covered in this chapter.

Industry	Book Debt Ratio
Pharmaceuticals	.01
Computer software	.06
Semiconductors	.07
Clothing	.17
Machinery	.27
Retail	.28
Autos	.29
Banks	.31
Construction	.35
Oil	.36
Aerospace	.37
Food	.38
Chemicals	.43
Paper	.48
Utilities	.49
Telecoms	.55

❯ **TABLE 18.1**   Median book-value ratios of debt to debt-plus-equity by industry, 2015
Source: WRDS Financial Ratios Suite.

18-1 Corporate Taxes

BEYOND THE PAGE

More industry
debt ratios

mhhe.com/brealey13e

Debt financing has one important advantage under the corporate income tax system in the United States and many other countries. The interest that the company pays is a tax-deductible expense. Thus, the return to bondholders escapes taxation at the corporate level.

There is one restriction on this tax benefit. Since 2018, the net amount of interest that companies can deduct is limited to 30% of taxable earnings before interest, taxes, depreciation, and amortization (EBITDA). From 2022 on, this restriction is tightened to 30% of taxable EBIT. (EBIT is, of course, smaller than EBITDA, so less interest can be deducted.[1])

Most large corporations' interest payments will not hit this constraint, but a few will, with painful results. For example, Dell Technologies carried $52.5 billion of debt at the end of 2017, most as a result of its $67 billion acquisition of EMC in 2016. The company estimated that it would have to pay $200 million per year in extra taxes because of limits on interest deductions. Dell can carry forward unused interest deductions and use them later, if and when the 30% constraint is no longer binding. But the longer the delay, the less the interest tax shields are worth. We predict that Dell will find ways of paying down its debt faster than it would have absent the 30% constraint.

For now, we will assume that the constraint on interest deductions as a percentage of EBITDA or EBIT is not binding. The constraint will merit more thought later in this chapter, however, and also in Chapters 19 and 32.

Table 18.2 shows simple income statements for firm U, which has no debt, and firm L, which has borrowed $1,000 at 8%. L's tax bill is $17 less than U's. This is the *tax shield* provided by the debt of L. In effect the government pays 21% of the interest expense of L. The total income that L can pay out to its bondholders and stockholders increases by that amount.

Tax shields can be valuable assets. Suppose that the debt of L is fixed and permanent. (That is, the company commits to refinance its present debt obligations when they mature and to keep rolling over its debt obligations indefinitely.) Then L can look forward to a permanent stream of cash flows of $17 per year. The risk of these flows is likely to be less than the risk of the operating assets of L. The tax shields depend only on the corporate tax rate[2] and on the ability

	Income Statement of Firm U	Income Statement of Firm L
Earnings before interest and taxes	$1,000	$1,000
Interest paid to bondholders	0	80
Pretax income	$1,000	$ 920
Tax at 21%	210	193
Net income to stockholders	$ 790	$ 727
Total income to both bondholders and stockholders	$0 + 790 = $790	$80 + 727 = $807
Interest tax shield (0.21 × interest)	$0	$17

❭ **TABLE 18.2**   The tax deductibility of interest increases the total income that can be paid out to bondholders and stockholders

---

[1]This restriction is effectively identical to a rule (known as "Zinsschranke") that has been operating in Germany. A similar rule has been proposed by the European Commission as part of a new EU Anti-Tax Avoidance Directive.

[2]Always use the marginal corporate tax rate, not the average rate. Average rates are often much lower than marginal rates because of accelerated depreciation and other tax adjustments. For large corporations, the marginal rate is usually taken as the statutory rate, which was changed to 21% from 2018. However, effective marginal rates can be less than the statutory rate, especially for smaller, riskier companies that cannot be sure that they will earn taxable income in the future.

of L to earn enough to cover interest payments. The corporate tax rate has been pretty stable. And the ability of L to earn its interest payments must be reasonably sure; otherwise it could not have borrowed at 8%. Therefore, we should discount the interest tax shields at a relatively low rate.

But what rate? One common assumption is that the risk of the tax shields is the same as that of the interest payments generating them. Thus, we discount at 8%, the expected rate of return demanded by investors who are holding the firm's debt:

$$PV(\text{tax shield}) = \frac{17}{.08} = \$210$$

In effect, the government assumes 21% of the $1,000 debt obligation of L.

Under these assumptions, the present value of the tax shield is independent of the return on the debt r_D. It equals the corporate tax rate T_c times the amount borrowed D:

$$\text{Interest payment} = \text{return on debt} \times \text{amount borrowed}$$
$$= r_D \times D$$
$$PV(\text{tax shield}) = \frac{\text{coporate tax rate} \times \text{interest payment}}{\text{expected return on debt}}$$
$$= \frac{T_c r_D D}{r_D} = T_c D$$

Of course, PV(tax shield) is less if the firm does not plan to borrow a permanent fixed amount,[3] or if it may not have enough taxable income to use the interest tax shields.[4]

How Do Interest Tax Shields Contribute to the Value of Stockholders' Equity?

MM's proposition 1 amounts to saying that the value of a pie does not depend on how it is sliced. The pie is the firm's assets, and the slices are the debt and equity claims. If we hold the pie constant, then a dollar more of debt means a dollar less of equity value.

But there is really a third slice, the government's. Look at Table 18.3. It shows an expanded balance sheet with *pretax* asset value on the left and the value of the government's tax claim recognized as a liability on the right. MM would still say that the value of the pie—in this case *pretax* asset value— is not changed by slicing. But anything the firm can do to reduce the size of the government's slice obviously makes stockholders better off. One thing it can do is borrow money, which reduces its tax bill and, as we saw in Table 18.2, increases the cash flows to debt and equity investors. The *after-tax* value of the firm (the sum of its debt and equity values as shown in a normal market value balance sheet) goes up by PV(tax shield).

Recasting Johnson & Johnson's Capital Structure

Johnson & Johnson is a large, successful firm that uses relatively little long-term debt. Table 18.4A shows simplified book and market value balance sheets for Johnson & Johnson in December 2017.

---

[3]In this example, we assume that the amount of debt is fixed and stable over time. The natural alternative assumption is a fixed *ratio* of debt to firm value. If the ratio is fixed, then the level of debt and the amount of interest tax shields will fluctuate as firm value fluctuates. In that case, projected interest tax shields can't be discounted at the cost of debt. We cover this point in detail in the next chapter.
[4]If the income of L does not cover interest in some future year, the tax shield is not necessarily lost. The losses can be carried forward and used to shield up to 80% of income in later years.

> **TABLE 18.3**   Normal and expanded market value balance sheets. In a normal balance sheet, assets are valued after tax. In the expanded balance sheet, assets are valued pretax, and the value of the government's tax claim is recognized on the right-hand side. Interest tax shields are valuable because they reduce the government's claim.

Normal Balance Sheet (Market Values)	
Asset value (present value of after-tax cash flows)	Debt
	Equity
Total assets	Total value

Expanded Balance Sheet (Market Values)	
Pretax asset value (present value of pretax cash flows)	Debt
	Government's claim (present value of future taxes)
	Equity
Total pretax assets	Total pretax value

> **TABLE 18.4A**   Simplified balance sheets for Johnson & Johnson, December 2017 (figures in millions)

Notes:
1. Market value is equal to book value for net working capital, long-term debt, and other long-term liabilities. Market value of equity = number of shares times closing price for December 2017. The difference between the market and book values of long-term assets is equal to the difference between the market and book values of equity.
2. PV interest tax shield assumes fixed, perpetual debt, and a 21% tax rate.[5]

Book Values			
Net working capital	$ 12,551	$ 30,675	Long-term debt
Long-term assets	114,215	35,931	Other long-term liabilities
		60,160	Equity
Total net assets	$126,766	$126,766	Total value

Market Values			
Net working capital	$ 12,551	$ 30,675	Long-term debt
PV interest tax shield	6,442	35,931	Other long-term liabilities
Long-term assets	426,257	378,644	Equity
Total net assets	$445,250	$445,250	Total value

Suppose that you were Johnson & Johnson's financial manager with complete responsibility for its capital structure. You decide to borrow an additional $10 billion on a permanent basis and use the proceeds to repurchase shares.

Table 18.4B shows the new balance sheets. The book version simply has $10,000 million more long-term debt and $10,000 million less equity. But we know that Johnson & Johnson's assets must be worth more because its tax bill will be reduced by 21% of the interest on the new debt. In other words, Johnson & Johnson has an increase in PV(interest tax shield), which is worth $T_cD = .21 \times \$10,000$ million $= \$2,100$ million. If the MM theory holds *except* for taxes, firm value must increase by $2,100 million to $447,350 million. Johnson & Johnson's equity ends up worth $370,744 million.

Now you have repurchased $10 billion worth of shares, but Johnson & Johnson's equity value has dropped by only $7.9 billion. Therefore, Johnson & Johnson's stockholders must be $2.1 billion ahead. Not a bad day's work.[6]

---

[5]The 21% corporate tax rate was not enacted until December.
[6]Notice that as long as the bonds are sold at a fair price, all the benefits from the tax shield must go to the shareholders.

Book Values			
Net working capital	$ 12,551	$ 40,675	Long-term debt
Long-term assets	113,829	35,931	Other long-term liabilities
		50,160	Equity
Total net assets	$126,766	$126,766	Total value
Market Values			
Net working capital	$ 12,551	$ 40,675	Long-term debt
PV interest tax shield	8,542	35,931	Other long-term liabilities
Long-term assets	426.257	370,744	Equity
Total net assets	$447,350	$447,350	Total value

❭ **TABLE 18.4B**   Balance sheets for Johnson & Johnson with additional $10 billion of long-term debt substituted for stockholders' equity (figures in millions)

MM and Taxes

We have just developed a version of MM's proposition 1 as corrected by them to reflect corporate income taxes.[7] The new proposition is

$$\text{Value of firm} = \text{value if all-equity-financed} + \text{PV(tax shield)}$$

In the special case of fixed, permanent debt,

$$\text{Value of firm} = \text{value if all-equity-financed} + T_c D$$

Our imaginary financial surgery on Johnson & Johnson provides the perfect illustration of the problems inherent in this "corrected" theory. That $2.1 billion came too easily; it seems to violate the law that there is no such thing as a money machine. And if Johnson & Johnson's stockholders would be richer with $40,675 million of corporate debt, why not $50,675 or $60,675 million? At what debt level should Johnson & Johnson stop borrowing? Our formula implies that firm value and stockholders' wealth continue to go up as D increases. The optimal debt policy appears to be embarrassingly extreme: All firms should be 100% debt-financed.

MM were not that fanatical about it. No one would expect the formula to apply at extreme debt ratios. There are several reasons why our calculations overstate the value of interest tax shields. First, it's wrong to think of debt as fixed and perpetual; a firm's ability to carry debt changes over time as profits and firm value fluctuate. Second, some firms face marginal tax rates less than 21%. Third, you can't use interest tax shields unless there will be future profits to shield—and no firm can be absolutely sure of that. Fourth, the 2017 Tax Cuts and Jobs Act limits the amount of interest that can be deducted to 30% of taxable EBITDA and (after 2021) EBIT. Once a company breaches this limit, additional debt has no further tax advantages over equity.

But none of these qualifications explains why companies like Johnson & Johnson survive and thrive at low debt ratios. It's hard to believe that its financial managers are simply missing the boat.

We seem to have argued ourselves into a blind alley. But there may be two ways out:

1. Perhaps a fuller examination of the U.S. system of corporate *and personal* taxation will uncover a tax disadvantage of corporate borrowing, offsetting the present value of the interest tax shield.

2. Perhaps firms that borrow incur other costs—bankruptcy costs, for example.

We now explore these two escape routes.

---

[7]Interest tax shields are recognized in MM's original article, F. Modigliani and M. H. Miller, "The Cost of Capital, Corporation Finance and the Theory of Investment," *American Economic Review* 48 (June 1958), pp. 261–297. The valuation procedure used in Table 18.4B is presented in their 1963 article, "Corporate Income Taxes and the Cost of Capital: A Correction," *American Economic Review* 53 (June 1963), pp. 433–443.

18-2 Corporate and Personal Taxes

When personal taxes are introduced, the firm's objective is no longer to minimize the *corporate* tax bill; the firm should try to minimize the present value of *all* taxes paid on corporate income. "All taxes" include *personal* taxes paid by bondholders and stockholders.

Figure 18.1 illustrates how corporate and personal taxes are affected by leverage. Depending on the firm's capital structure, a dollar of operating income will accrue to investors either as debt interest or equity income (dividends or capital gains). That is, the dollar can go down either branch of Figure 18.1.

Notice that Figure 18.1 distinguishes between T_p, the personal tax rate on interest, and T_{pE}, the effective personal tax rate on equity income. This rate can be well below T_p, depending on the mix of dividends and capital gains realized by shareholders. The top marginal rate on dividends and capital gains in 2018 is 20% while the top rate on interest income is 37%. Also capital gains taxes can be deferred until shares are sold, so the top *effective* capital gains rate is usually less than 20%.

The firm's objective should be to arrange its capital structure to maximize after-tax income. You can see from Figure 18.1 that corporate borrowing is better if $(1 - T_P)$ is more than $(1 - T_{pE}) \times (1 - T_c)$; otherwise it is worse. The *relative tax* advantage of debt over equity is

$$\text{Relative tax advantage of debt} = \frac{1 - T_p}{(1 - T_{pE})(1 - T_c)}$$

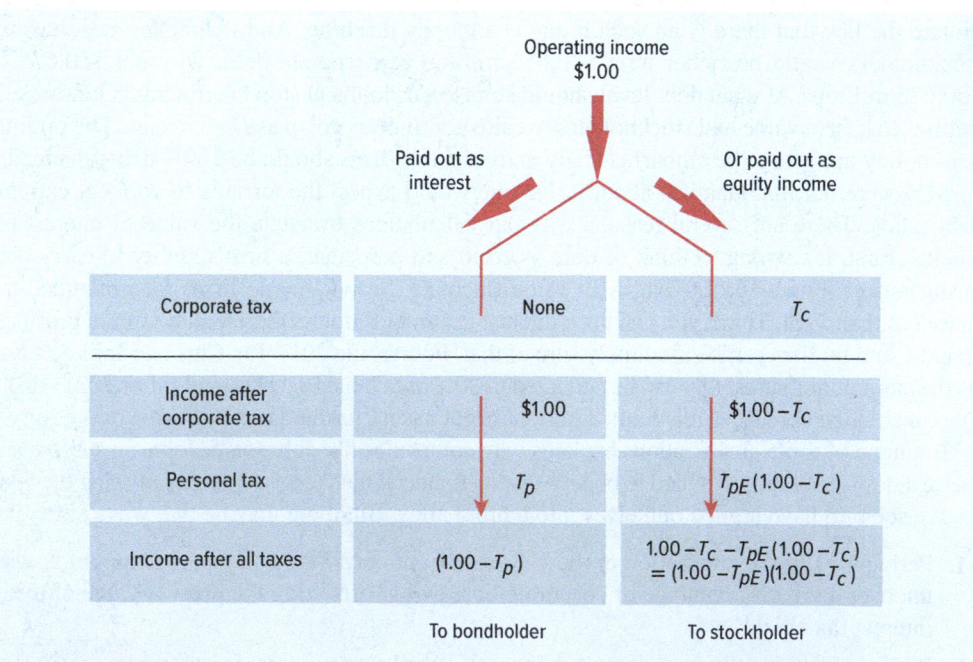

> **FIGURE 18.1**
>
> The firm's capital structure determines whether operating income is paid out as interest or equity income. Interest is taxed only at the personal level. Equity income is taxed at both the corporate and the personal levels. However, T_{pE}, the personal tax rate on equity income, can be less than T_p, the personal tax rate on interest income.

This suggests two special cases. First, suppose that debt and equity income were taxed at the same effective personal rate. With $T_{pE} = T_p$, the relative advantage depends only on the *corporate rate:*

$$\text{Relative advantage} = \frac{1 - T_p}{\left(1 - T_{pE}\right)\left(1 - T_c\right)} = \frac{1}{1 - T_c}$$

In this case, we can forget about personal taxes. The tax advantage of corporate borrowing is exactly as MM calculated it.[8] They do not have to assume away personal taxes. Their theory of debt and taxes requires only that debt and equity income be taxed at the same rate.

The second special case occurs when corporate and personal taxes cancel to make debt policy irrelevant. This requires

$$1 - T_p = (1 - T_{pE})(1 - T_c)$$

This case can happen only if T_c, the corporate rate, is less than the personal rate T_p *and* if T_{pE}, the effective rate on equity income, is small. Merton Miller explored this situation at a time when U.S. tax rates on interest and dividends were much higher than now, but we won't go into the details of his analysis here.[9]

In any event, we seem to have a simple, practical decision rule. Arrange the firm's capital structure to shunt operating income down that branch of Figure 18.1 where the tax is least. Unfortunately that is not as simple as it sounds. What's T_{pE}, for example? The shareholder roster of any large corporation is likely to include tax-exempt investors (such as pension funds or university endowments) as well as millionaires and maybe a billionaire or two. All possible tax brackets will be mixed together. And it's the same with T_p, the personal tax rate on interest. The large corporation's "typical" bondholder might be a tax-exempt pension fund, but many taxpaying investors also hold corporate debt.

Some investors may be much happier to buy your debt than others. For example, you should have no problems inducing pension funds to lend; they don't have to worry about personal tax. But taxpaying investors may be more reluctant to hold debt and will be prepared to do so only if they are compensated by a high rate of interest. Investors paying tax on interest at the top rate of 37% may be particularly reluctant to hold debt. They will prefer to hold common stock or tax-exempt bonds issued by states and municipalities.

To determine the net tax advantage of debt, companies would need to know the tax rates faced by the *marginal* investor—that is, an investor who is equally happy to hold debt or equity. This makes it hard to put a precise figure on the tax benefit, but we can nevertheless provide a back-of-the-envelope calculation. On average, over the past 10 years, large U.S. companies have paid out about half of their earnings. Suppose the marginal investor is in the top tax bracket, paying 37% on interest and 20% on dividends and capital gains.

---

[8]Personal taxes reduce the dollar amount of corporate interest tax shields, but the appropriate discount rate for cash flows after personal tax is also lower. If investors are willing to lend at a prospective return *before* personal taxes of r_D, then they must also be willing to accept a return *after* personal taxes of $r_D(1 - T_p)$, where T_p is the marginal rate of personal tax. Thus we can compute the value after personal taxes of the tax shield on permanent debt:

$$\text{PV(tax shield)} = \frac{T_c \times r_D D \times (1 - T_p)}{r_D \times (1 - T_p)} = T_c D$$

This brings us back to our previous formula for firm value: Value of firm = value if all-equity-financed + $T_c D$

[9]M. H. Miller, "Debt and Taxes," *Journal of Finance* 32 (May 1977), pp. 261–275.

Let's assume that deferred realization of capital gains cuts the effective capital gains rate in half, to $20/2 = 10\%$. Therefore, if the investor invests in the stock of a company with a 50% payout, the tax on each $1.00 of equity income is $T_{pE} = (.5 \times 20) + (.5 \times 10) = 15\%$.

Now we can calculate the effect of shunting a dollar of income down each of the two branches in Figure 18.1:

	Interest	Equity Income
Income before tax	$1.00	$1.00
Less corporate tax at $T_c = .21$	0	0.21
Income after corporate tax	1.00	0.79
Personal tax at $T_p = .37$ and $T_{pE} = .15$	0.37	.119
Income after all taxes	$0.630	$0.671
	Advantage to debt = $0.041	

The advantage to debt financing appears to be about four cents on the dollar.

We should emphasize that our back-of-the-envelope calculation is just that. But it's interesting to see how debt's tax advantage shrinks when we account for the relatively low personal tax rate on equity income.

Most financial managers believe that there is a moderate tax advantage to corporate borrowing, at least for companies that are reasonably sure they can use the corporate tax shields. For companies that cannot benefit from corporate tax shields, there is probably a moderate tax disadvantage.

When we recognize personal taxes, the tax advantage to debt diminishes, but it does not disappear. It still appears that financial managers have passed by some easy tax savings. Perhaps they saw some offsetting disadvantage to increased borrowing. We now explore this second escape route.

BEYOND THE PAGE

Corporate leverage and the Halloween Massacre

mhhe.com/brealey13e

18-3   Costs of Financial Distress

Financial distress occurs when promises to creditors are broken or honored with difficulty. Sometimes financial distress leads to bankruptcy. Sometimes it only means skating on thin ice.

As we will see, financial distress is costly. Investors know that levered firms may fall into financial distress, and they worry about it. That worry is reflected in the current market value of the levered firm's securities. Thus, the value of the firm can be broken down into three parts:

$$\begin{array}{c} \text{Value} \\ \text{of firm} \end{array} = \begin{array}{c} \text{value if} \\ \text{all-equity-financed} \end{array} + \text{PV(tax shield)} - \text{PV}\left(\begin{array}{c} \text{costs of financial} \\ \text{distress} \end{array}\right)$$

The costs of financial distress depend on the probability of distress and the magnitude of costs encountered if distress occurs.

Figure 18.2 shows how the trade-off between the tax benefits and the costs of distress could determine optimal capital structure. PV(tax shield) initially increases as the firm borrows more.

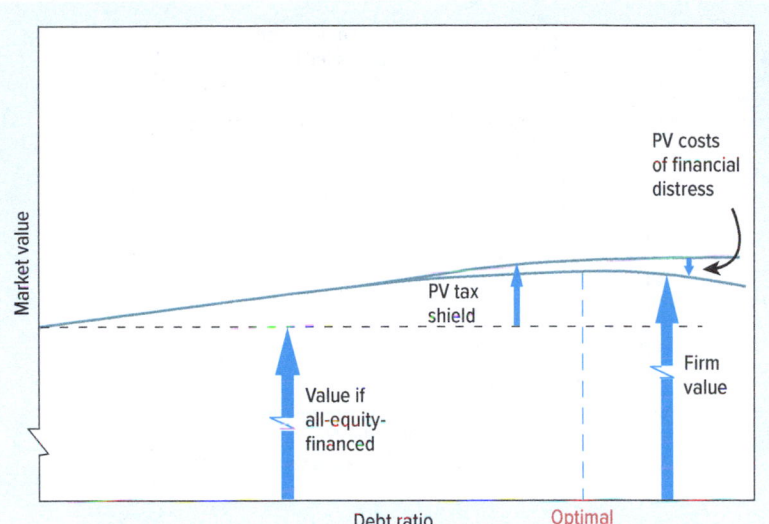

▶ **FIGURE 18.2**

The value of the firm is equal to its value if all-equity-financed plus PV tax shield minus PV costs of financial distress. According to the trade-off theory of capital structure, the manager should choose the debt ratio that maximizes firm value.

At low debt levels, the probability of financial distress should be trivial, and so PV(cost of financial distress) is small and tax advantages dominate. But at some point, the probability of financial distress increases rapidly with additional borrowing; the costs of distress begin to take a substantial bite out of firm value. Also, if the firm can't be sure of profiting from the corporate tax shield, the tax advantage of additional debt is likely to dwindle and eventually disappear. (Once the firm hits the limit on interest deductions at 30% of EBITDA or EBIT, the tax shields from additional borrowing disappear completely.) The theoretical optimum is reached when the present value of tax savings due to further borrowing is just offset by increases in the present value of costs of distress. This is called the *trade-off theory* of capital structure.

Costs of financial distress cover several specific items. Now we identify these costs and try to understand what causes them.

Bankruptcy Costs

You rarely hear anything nice said about corporate bankruptcy. But there is some good in almost everything. Corporate bankruptcies occur when stockholders exercise their *right to default.* That right is valuable; when a firm gets into trouble, limited liability allows stockholders simply to walk away from it, leaving all its troubles to its creditors. The former creditors become the new stockholders, and the old stockholders are left with nothing.

Stockholders in corporations automatically get *limited liability*. But suppose that this were not so. Suppose that there are two firms with identical assets and operations. Each firm has debt outstanding, and each has promised to repay $1,000 (principal and interest) next year. But only one of the firms, Ace Limited, enjoys limited liability. The other firm, Ace Unlimited, does not; its stockholders are personally liable for its debt.[10]

Figure 18.3 compares next year's possible payoffs to the creditors and stockholders of these two firms. The only differences occur when next year's asset value turns out to be less than $1,000. Suppose that next year, the assets of each company are worth only $500. In this

---

[10] Ace Unlimited could be a partnership or sole proprietorship, which does not provide limited liability.

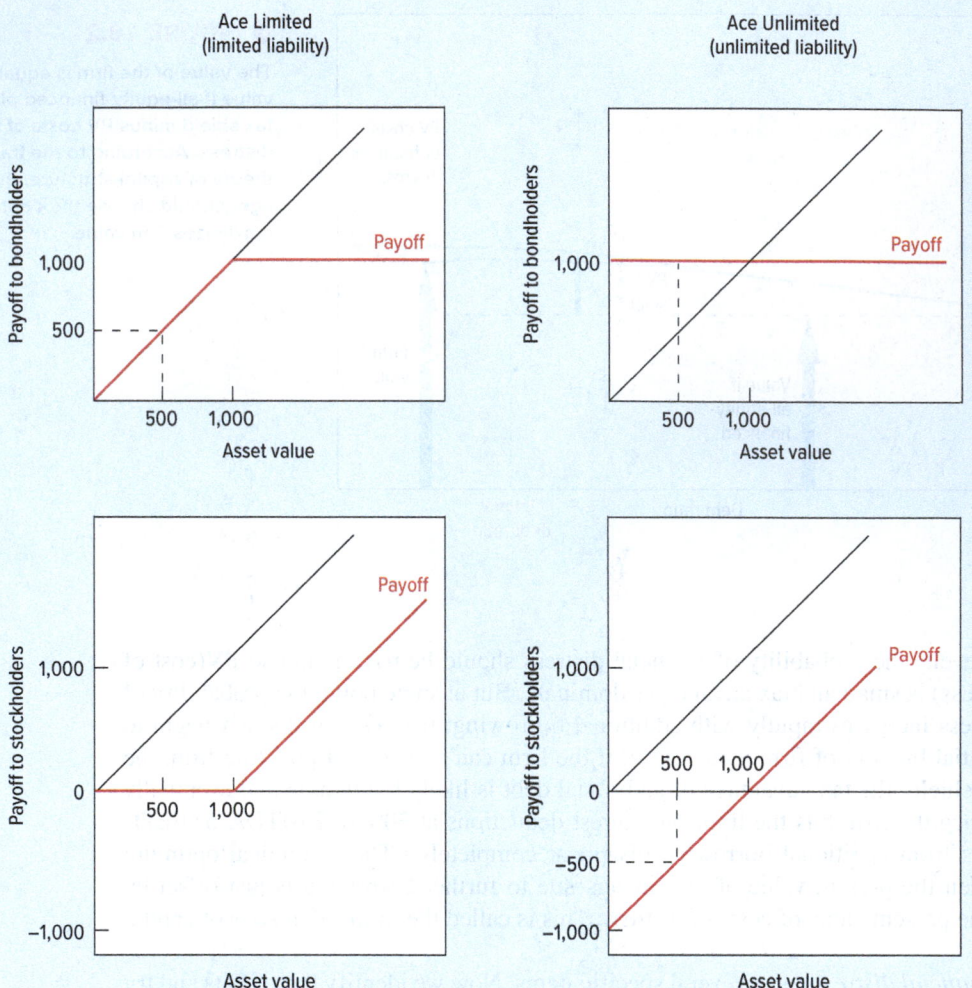

FIGURE 18.3 Comparison of limited and unlimited liability for two otherwise identical firms. If the two firms' asset values are less than $1,000, Ace Limited stockholders default and its bondholders take over the assets. Ace Unlimited stockholders keep the assets, but they must reach into their own pockets to pay off its bondholders. The total payoff to both stockholders and bondholders is the same for the two firms.

case, Ace Limited defaults. Its stockholders walk away; their payoff is zero. Bondholders get the assets worth $500. But Ace Unlimited's stockholders can't walk away. They have to cough up $500, the difference between asset value and the bondholders' claim. The debt is paid whatever happens.

Suppose that Ace Limited does go bankrupt. Of course, its stockholders are disappointed that their firm is worth so little, but that is an operating problem having nothing to do with financing. Given poor operating performance, the right to go bankrupt—the right to default—is a valuable privilege. As Figure 18.3 shows, Ace Limited's stockholders are in better shape than Unlimited's are.

The example illuminates a mistake people often make in thinking about the costs of bankruptcy. Bankruptcies are thought of as corporate funerals. The mourners (creditors and especially shareholders) look at their firm's present sad state. They think of how valuable their securities used to be and how little is left. But they may also think of the lost value as a cost of bankruptcy. That is the mistake. The decline in the value of assets is what the mourning is really about. That has no necessary connection with financing. The bankruptcy is merely a legal mechanism for allowing creditors to take over when the decline in the value of assets triggers a default. Bankruptcy is not the *cause* of the decline in value. It is the result.

Be careful not to get cause and effect reversed. When a person dies, we do not cite the implementation of his or her will as the cause of death.

We said that bankruptcy is a legal mechanism allowing creditors to take over when a firm defaults. *Bankruptcy costs* are the costs of using this mechanism. There are no bankruptcy costs at all shown in Figure 18.3. Note that only Ace Limited can default and go bankrupt. But, regardless of what happens to asset value, the *combined* payoff to the bondholders and stockholders of Ace Limited is always the same as the *combined* payoff to the bondholders and stockholders of Ace Unlimited. Thus, the overall market values of the two firms now (this year) must be identical. Of course, Ace Limited's stock is worth more than Ace Unlimited's stock because of Ace Limited's right to default. Ace Limited's debt is worth correspondingly less.

Our example was not intended to be strictly realistic. Anything involving courts and lawyers cannot be free. Suppose that court and legal fees are $200 if Ace Limited defaults. The fees are paid out of the remaining value of Ace's assets. Thus, if asset value turns out to be $500, creditors end up with only $300. Figure 18.4 shows next year's *total* payoff to bondholders and stockholders net of this bankruptcy cost. Ace Limited, by issuing risky debt, has given lawyers and the court system a claim on the firm if it defaults. The market value of the firm is reduced by the present value of this claim.

It is easy to see how increased leverage affects the present value of the costs of financial distress. If Ace Limited borrows more, it increases the probability of default and the value of the lawyers' claim. It increases PV (costs of financial distress) and reduces Ace's present market value.

The costs of bankruptcy come out of stockholders' pockets. Creditors foresee the costs and foresee that *they* will pay them if default occurs. For this they demand compensation in advance in the form of higher payoffs when the firm does *not* default; that is, they demand a higher promised interest rate. This reduces the possible payoffs to stockholders and reduces the present market value of their shares.

Evidence on Bankruptcy Costs

Bankruptcy costs can add up fast. The failed energy giant Enron paid $757 million in legal, accounting, and other professional fees during the time that it spent in bankruptcy. The costs of sorting out the 65,000 claims on the assets of Lehman Brothers exceed $2 billion.

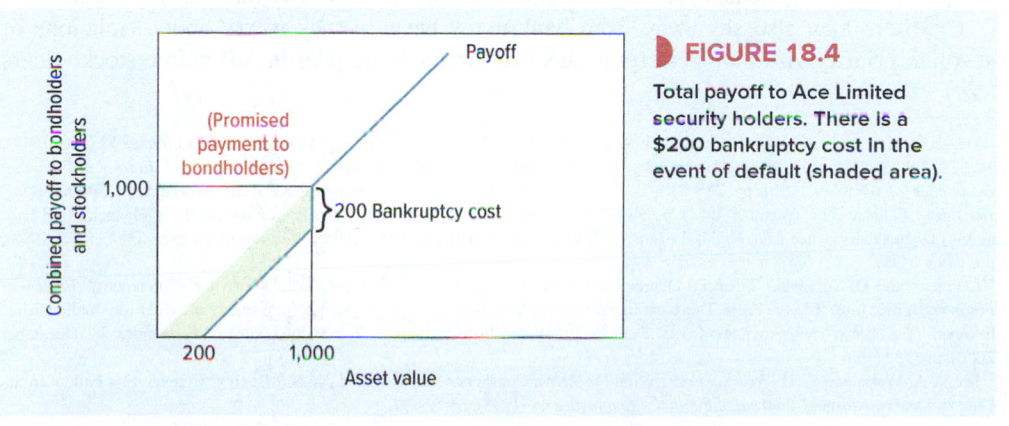

▶ **FIGURE 18.4**

Total payoff to Ace Limited security holders. There is a $200 bankruptcy cost in the event of default (shaded area).

Daunting as such numbers may seem, they are not a large fraction of the companies' asset values. Lawrence Weiss, who studied 31 firms that went bankrupt between 1980 and 1986, found average costs of about 3% of total book assets and 20% of the market value of equity in the year prior to bankruptcy. A study by Andrade and Kaplan of a sample of troubled and highly leveraged firms estimated costs of financial distress amounting to 10% to 20% of predistress market value, although they found it hard to decide whether these costs were caused by financial distress or by the business setbacks that led to distress.[11]

Bankruptcy eats up a larger fraction of asset value for small companies than for large ones. There are significant economies of scale in going bankrupt. For example, a study of smaller U.K. bankruptcies by Franks and Sussman found that fees (legal and accounting) and other costs soaked up roughly 20% to 40% of the proceeds from liquidation of the companies.[12]

Direct versus Indirect Costs of Bankruptcy

So far, we have discussed the *direct* (that is, legal and administrative) costs of bankruptcy. There are indirect costs too, which are nearly impossible to measure. But we have circumstantial evidence indicating their importance.

Managing a bankrupt firm is not easy. Consent of the bankruptcy court is required for many routine business decisions, such as the sale of assets or investment in new equipment. At best, this involves time and effort; at worst, proposals to reform and revive the firm are thwarted by impatient creditors, who stand first in line for cash from asset sales or liquidation of the entire firm.

Sometimes the problem is reversed: The bankruptcy court is so anxious to maintain the firm as a going concern that it allows the firm to engage in negative-NPV activities. When Eastern Airlines entered the "protection" of the bankruptcy court, it still had some valuable, profit-making routes and salable assets such as planes and terminal facilities. The creditors would have been best served by a prompt liquidation, which probably would have generated enough cash to pay off all debt and preferred stockholders. But the bankruptcy judge was keen to keep Eastern's planes flying at all costs, so he allowed the company to sell many of its assets to fund hefty operating losses. When Eastern finally closed down after two years, it was not just bankrupt, but *administratively* insolvent: There was almost nothing for creditors, and the company was running out of cash to pay legal expenses.[13]

We do not know what the sum of direct and indirect costs of bankruptcy amounts to. We suspect it is a significant number, particularly for large firms for which proceedings would be lengthy and complex. Perhaps the best evidence is the reluctance of creditors to force bankruptcy. In principle, they would be better off to end the agony and seize the assets as soon as possible. Instead, creditors often overlook defaults in the hope of nursing the firm over a difficult period. They do this in part to avoid costs of bankruptcy. There is an old financial saying, "Borrow $1,000 and you've got a banker. Borrow $10,000,000 and you've got a partner."

Creditors may also shy away from bankruptcy because they worry about violations of absolute priority. *Absolute priority* means that creditors are paid in full before stockholders

[11]The pioneering study of bankruptcy costs is J. B. Warner, "Bankruptcy Costs: Some Evidence," *Journal of Finance* 32 (May 1977), pp. 337–347. See also L. A. Weiss, "Bankruptcy Resolution: Direct Costs and Violation of Priority of Claims," *Journal of Financial Economics* 27 (October 1990), pp. 285–314; E. I. Altman, "A Further Empirical Investigation of the Bankruptcy Cost Question," *Journal of Finance* 39 (September 1984), pp. 1067–1089; and G. Andrade and S. N. Kaplan, "How Costly Is Financial (not Economic) Distress? Evidence from Highly Leveraged Transactions That Became Distressed," *Journal of Finance* 53 (October 1998), pp. 1443–1493.

[12]J. Franks and O. Sussman, "Financial Distress and Bank Restructuring of Small to Medium Size UK Companies," *Review of Finance* 9 (2005), pp. 65–96. Karin Thorburn found that the Swedish bankruptcy system is reasonably efficient for smaller firms, however. See "Bankruptcy Auctions: Costs, Debt Recovery and Firm Survival," *Journal of Financial Economics* 58 (December 2000), pp. 337–368.

[13]See L. A. Weiss and K. H. Wruck, "Information Problems, Conflicts of Interest, and Asset Stripping: Chapter 11's Failure in the Case of Eastern Airlines," *Journal of Financial Economics* 48 (1998), pp. 55–97.

receive a penny. But sometimes reorganizations provide something for everyone, including consolation prizes for stockholders. Sometimes other claimants move up in the queue. For example, after the Chrysler bankruptcy in 2009, the State of Indiana sued (unsuccessfully) on behalf of local pension funds that had invested in Chrysler bonds. The funds complained bitterly about the terms of sale of the bankrupt company's assets to Fiat, arguing that they would get only $.29 on the dollar, while other, more junior claimants fared better. The Chrysler bankruptcy was a special case, however. One of the key players in the proceedings was the U.S. government, which was anxious to protect tens of thousands of jobs in the middle of a severe recession.

We cover bankruptcy procedures in more detail in Chapter 32.

Financial Distress without Bankruptcy

Not every firm that gets into trouble goes bankrupt. As long as the firm can scrape up enough cash to pay the interest on its debt, it may be able to postpone bankruptcy for many years. Eventually the firm may recover, pay off its debt, and escape bankruptcy altogether.

But the mere threat of financial distress can be costly to the threatened firm. Customers and suppliers are extra cautious about doing business with a firm that may not be around for long. Customers worry about resale value and the availability of service and replacement parts. (This was a serious drag on Chrysler's sales before its bankruptcy in 2009.) Suppliers are disinclined to put effort into servicing the distressed firm's account and may demand cash on the nail for their products. Potential employees are unwilling to sign on and existing staff keep slipping away from their desks for job interviews.

High debt, and thus high financial risk, also appears to reduce firms' appetites for business risk. For example, Luigi Zingales looked at the fortunes of U.S. trucking companies after the trucking industry was deregulated in the late 1970s.[14] The deregulation sparked a wave of competition and restructuring. Survival required new investment and improvements in operating efficiency. Zingales found that conservatively financed trucking companies were more likely to survive in the new competitive environment. High-debt firms were more likely to drop out of the game.

Debt and Incentives

When a firm is in trouble, both bondholders and stockholders want it to recover, but in other respects, their interests may be in conflict. In times of financial distress, the security holders are like many political parties—united on generalities but threatened by squabbling on any specific issue.

Financial distress is costly when these conflicts of interest get in the way of proper operating, investment, and financing decisions. Stockholders are tempted to forsake the usual objective of maximizing the overall market value of the firm and to pursue narrower self-interest instead. They are tempted to play games at the expense of their creditors. We now illustrate how such games can lead to costs of financial distress.

Here is the Circular File Company's book balance sheet:

Circular File Company (Book Values)			
Net working capital	$ 20	$ 50	Bonds outstanding
Fixed assets	80	50	Common stock
Total assets	$100	$100	Total value

---

[14]L. Zingales, "Survival of the Fittest or the Fattest? Exit and Financing in the Trucking Industry," *Journal of Finance* 53 (June 1998), pp. 905–938.

We will assume there is only one share and one bond outstanding. The stockholder is also the manager. The bondholder is somebody else.

Here is its balance sheet in market values—a clear case of financial distress, since the face value of Circular's debt ($50) exceeds the firm's total market value ($30):

Circular File Company (Market Values)

Net working capital	$20	$27	Bonds outstanding
Fixed assets	10	3	Common stock
Total assets	$30	$30	Total value

If the debt matured today, Circular's owner would default, leaving the firm bankrupt. But suppose that the bond actually matures one year hence, that there is enough cash for Circular to limp along for this year, and that the bondholder cannot "call the question" and force bankruptcy before then.

The one-year grace period explains why the Circular share still has value. Its owner is betting on a stroke of luck that will rescue the firm, allowing it to pay off the debt with something left over. The bet is a long shot—the owner wins only if firm value increases from $30 to more than $50.[15] But the owner has a secret weapon: He controls investment and operating strategy.

Risk Shifting: The First Game

Suppose that Circular has $10 cash. The following investment opportunity comes up:

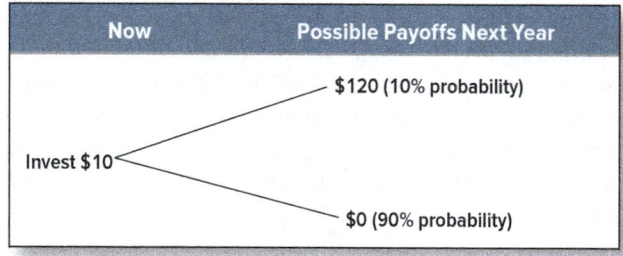

This is a wild gamble and probably a lousy project. But you can see why the owner would be tempted to take it anyway. Why not go for broke? Circular will probably go under anyway, so the owner is essentially betting with the bondholder's money. But the owner gets most of the loot if the project pays off.

Suppose that the project's NPV is −$2 but that it is undertaken anyway, thus depressing firm value by $2. Circular's new balance sheet might look like this:

Circular File Company (Market Values)

Net working capital	$10	$22	Bonds outstanding
Fixed assets	18	6	Common stock
Total assets	$28	$28	Total value

Firm value falls by $2, but the owner is $3 ahead because the bond's value has fallen by $5.[16] The $10 cash that used to stand behind the bond has been replaced by a very risky asset worth only $8.

---

[15]We are not concerned here with how to work out whether $3 is a fair price for stockholders to pay for the bet. We will come to that in Chapter 23 when we discuss risky debt; we will calculate the value of Circular's equity.

[16]We are not calculating this $5 drop. We are simply using it as a plausible assumption. The tools necessary for a calculation come in Chapters 21 and 23.

Thus, a game has been played at the expense of Circular's bondholder. The game illustrates the following general point: Stockholders of levered firms gain when business risk increases. Financial managers who act strictly in their shareholders' interests (and *against* the interests of creditors) will favor risky projects over safe ones. They may even take risky projects with negative NPVs.

This warped strategy for capital budgeting clearly is costly to the firm and to the economy as a whole. Why do we associate the costs with financial distress? Because the temptation to play is strongest when the odds of default are high. A blue-chip company like Exxon Mobil would never invest in our negative-NPV gamble. Its creditors are not vulnerable to one risky project.

Refusing to Contribute Equity Capital: The Second Game

We have seen how stockholders, acting in their immediate, narrow self-interest, may take projects that reduce the overall market value of their firm. These are errors of commission. Conflicts of interest may also lead to errors of omission.

Assume that Circular cannot scrape up any cash and, therefore, cannot take that wild gamble. Instead, a *good* opportunity comes up: a relatively safe asset costing $10 with a present value of $15 and NPV = +$5.

This project will not in itself rescue Circular, but it is a step in the right direction. We might therefore expect Circular to issue $10 of new stock and to go ahead with the investment. Suppose that two new shares are issued to the original owner for $10 cash. The project is taken. The new balance sheet might look like this:

Circular File Company (Market Values)			
Net working capital	$20	$35	Bonds outstanding
Fixed assets	25	10	Common stock
Total assets	$45	$45	Total value

The total value of the firm goes up by $15 ($10 of new capital and $5 NPV). Notice that the Circular bond is no longer worth $25, but $35. The bondholder receives a capital gain of $8 because the firm's assets include a new, safe asset worth $15. The probability of default is less, and the payoff to the bondholder if default occurs is larger.

The stockholder loses what the bondholder gains. Equity value goes up not by $15 but by $15 − $8 = $7. The owner puts in $10 of fresh equity capital but gains only $7 in market value. Going ahead is in the firm's interest but not the owner's.

Again, our example illustrates a general point. If we hold business risk constant, any increase in firm value is shared among bondholders and stockholders. The value of any investment opportunity to the firm's *stockholders* is reduced because project benefits must be shared with bondholders. Thus it may not be in the stockholders' self-interest to contribute fresh equity capital even if that means forgoing positive-NPV investment opportunities.

This problem theoretically affects all levered firms, but it is most serious when firms land in financial distress. The greater the probability of default, the more bondholders have to gain from investments that increase firm value.

And Three More Games, Briefly

As with other games, the temptation to play the next three games is particularly strong in financial distress.

Cash In and Run   Stockholders may be reluctant to put money into a firm in financial distress, but they are happy to take the money out—in the form of a cash dividend, for example. The market value of the firm's stock goes down by less than the amount of the dividend paid, because the decline in *firm* value is shared with creditors. This game is just "refusing to contribute equity capital" run in reverse.[17]

Playing for Time   When the firm is in financial distress, creditors would like to salvage what they can by forcing the firm to settle up. Naturally, stockholders want to delay this as long as they can. There are various devious ways of doing this—for example, through accounting changes designed to conceal the true extent of trouble; by encouraging false hopes of spontaneous recovery; or by cutting corners on maintenance, research and development, and so on—in order to make this year's operating performance look better.

Bait and Switch   This game is not always played in financial distress, but it is a quick way to get *into* distress. You start with a conservative policy, issuing a limited amount of relatively safe debt. Then you suddenly switch and issue a lot more. That makes all your debt risky, imposing a capital loss on the "old" bondholders. Their capital loss is the stockholders' gain.

A dramatic example of bait and switch occurred in October 1988, when the management of RJR Nabisco announced its intention to acquire the company in a *leveraged buyout* (LBO). This put the company "in play" for a transaction in which existing shareholders would be bought out and the company would be "taken private." The cost of the buyout would be almost entirely debt-financed. The new private company would start life with an extremely high debt ratio.

RJR Nabisco had debt outstanding with a market value of about $2.4 billion. The announcement of the coming LBO drove down this market value by $298 million.[18]

What the Games Cost

Why should anyone object to these games so long as they are played by consenting adults? Because playing them means poor decisions about investments and operations. These poor decisions are *agency costs* of borrowing.

The more the firm borrows, the greater is the temptation to play the games (assuming the financial manager acts in the stockholders' interest). The increased odds of poor decisions in the future prompt investors to mark down the present market value of the firm. The fall in value comes out of the shareholders' pockets. Therefore, it is ultimately in their interest to avoid temptation. The easiest way to do this is to limit borrowing to levels at which the firm's debt is safe or close to it.

Banks and other corporate lenders are also not financial innocents. They realize that games may be played at their expense and so protect themselves by rationing the amount that they will lend or by imposing restrictions on the company's actions.

EXAMPLE 18.1 • Ms. Ketchup Faces Credit Rationing

Consider the case of Henrietta Ketchup, a budding entrepreneur with two possible investment projects that offer the following payoffs:

	Now	Investment	Payoff	Probability of Payoff
Project 1		−12	+15	1.0
Project 2		−12	+24	0.5
			0	0.5

---

[17]If stockholders or managers take money out of the firm in anticipation of financial distress or bankruptcy, the bankruptcy court can treat the payout as *fraudulent conveyance* and claw back the money to the firm and its creditors.

[18]We thank Paul Asquith for these figures. RJR Nabisco was finally taken private not by its management but by another LBO partnership. We discuss this LBO in Chapter 32.

Project 1 is surefire and very profitable; project 2 is risky and a rotten project. Ms. Ketchup now approaches her bank and asks to borrow the present value of $10 (she will find the remaining money out of her own purse). The bank calculates that the payoff will be split as follows:

	Expected Payoff to Bank	Expected Payoff to Ms. Ketchup
Project 1	+10	+5
Project 2	$(0.5 \times 10) + (0.5 \times 0) = +5$	$0.5 \times (24 - 10) = +7$

If Ms. Ketchup accepts project 1, the bank's debt is certain to be paid in full; if she accepts project 2, there is only a 50% chance of payment and the expected payoff to the bank is only $5. Unfortunately, Ms. Ketchup will prefer to take project 2, for if things go well, she gets most of the profit, and if they go badly, the bank bears most of the loss. Unless Ms. Ketchup can convince the bank that she will not gamble with its money, the bank will limit the amount that it is prepared to lend.[19]

How can Ms. Ketchup in Example 18.1 reassure the bank of her intentions? The obvious answer is to give it veto power over potentially dangerous decisions. There we have the ultimate economic rationale for all that fine print backing up corporate debt. Debt contracts frequently limit dividends or equivalent transfers of wealth to stockholders; the firm may not be allowed to pay out more than it earns, for example. Additional borrowing is almost always limited. For example, many companies are prevented by existing bond indentures from issuing any additional long-term debt unless their ratio of earnings to interest charges exceeds 2.0.

Sometimes firms are restricted from selling assets or making major investment outlays except with the lenders' consent. The risks of playing for time are reduced by specifying accounting procedures and by giving lenders access to the firm's books and its financial forecasts.

Of course, fine print cannot be a complete solution for firms that insist on issuing risky debt. The fine print has its own costs; you have to spend money to save money. Obviously a complex debt contract costs more to negotiate than a simple one. Afterward it costs the lender more to monitor the firm's performance. Lenders anticipate monitoring costs and demand compensation in the form of higher interest rates; thus the monitoring costs—another agency cost of debt—are ultimately paid by stockholders.

Perhaps the most severe costs of the fine print stem from the constraints it places on operating and investment decisions. For example, an attempt to prevent the risk-shifting game may also prevent the firm from pursuing *good* investment opportunities. At the minimum there are delays in clearing major investments with lenders. In some cases, lenders may veto high-risk investments even if net present value is positive. The lenders are tempted to play a game of their own, forcing the firm to stay in cash or low-risk assets even if good projects are forgone.

---

[19]You might think that if the bank suspects Ms. Ketchup will undertake project 2, it should just raise the interest rate on its loan. In this case, Ms. Ketchup will not want to take on project 2 (they can't both be happy with a lousy project). But Ms. Ketchup also would not want to pay a high rate of interest if she is going to take on project 1 (she would do better to borrow less money at the risk-free rate). So simply raising the interest rate is not the answer.

Debt contracts cannot cover every possible manifestation of the games we have just discussed. Any attempt to do so would be hopelessly expensive and doomed to failure in any event. Human imagination is insufficient to conceive of all the possible things that could go wrong. Therefore, contracts are always *incomplete*. We will always find surprises coming at us on dimensions we never thought to think about.

We hope we have not left the impression that managers and stockholders always succumb to temptation unless restrained. Usually, they refrain voluntarily, not only from a sense of fair play but also on pragmatic grounds: A firm or individual that makes a killing today at the expense of a creditor will be coldly received when the time comes to borrow again. Aggressive game playing is done only by out-and-out crooks and by firms in extreme financial distress. Firms limit borrowing precisely because they don't wish to land in distress and be exposed to the temptation to play.

Costs of Distress Vary with Type of Asset

Suppose your firm's only asset is a large downtown hotel, mortgaged to the hilt. The recession hits, occupancy rates fall, and the mortgage payments cannot be met. The lender takes over and sells the hotel to a new owner and operator. You use your firm's stock certificates for wallpaper.

What is the cost of bankruptcy? In this example, probably very little. The value of the hotel is, of course, much less than you hoped, but that is due to the lack of guests, not to the bankruptcy. Bankruptcy doesn't damage the hotel itself. The direct bankruptcy costs are restricted to items such as legal and court fees, real estate commissions, and the time the lender spends sorting things out.

Suppose we repeat the story of Heartbreak Hotel for Fledgling Electronics. Everything is the same, except for the underlying real assets—not real estate but a high-tech going concern, a growth company whose most valuable assets are technology, investment opportunities, and its employees' human capital.

If Fledgling gets into trouble, the stockholders may be reluctant to put up money to cash in on its growth opportunities. Failure to invest is likely to be much more serious for Fledgling than for the Heartbreak Hotel.

If Fledgling finally defaults on its debt, the lender will find it much more difficult to cash in by selling off the assets. Many of them are intangibles that have value only as a part of a going concern.

Could Fledgling be kept as a going concern through default and reorganization? It may not be as hopeless as putting a wedding cake through a car wash, but there are a number of serious difficulties. First, the odds of defections by key employees are higher than they would be if the firm had never gotten into financial trouble. Special guarantees may have to be given to customers who have doubts about whether the firm will be around to service its products. Aggressive investment in new products and technology will be difficult; each class of creditors will have to be convinced that it is in its interest for the firm to invest new money in risky ventures.

Some assets, like good commercial real estate, can pass through bankruptcy and reorganization largely unscathed;[20] the values of other assets are likely to be considerably diminished. The losses are greatest for the intangible assets that are linked to the health of the firm as a

---

[20]In 1989, the Rockefeller family sold 80% of Rockefeller Center—several acres of extremely valuable Manhattan real estate—to Mitsubishi Estate Company for $1.4 billion. A REIT, Rockefeller Center Properties, held a $1.3 billion mortgage loan (the REIT's only asset) secured by this real estate. But rents and occupancy rates did not meet forecasts, and by 1995, Mitsubishi had incurred losses of about $600 million. Then Mitsubishi quit, and Rockefeller Center was bankrupt. That triggered a complicated series of maneuvers and negotiations. But did this damage the value of the Rockefeller Center properties? Was Radio City Music Hall, one of the properties, any less valuable because of the bankruptcy? We doubt it.

going concern—for example, technology, human capital, and brand image. That may be why debt ratios are low in the pharmaceutical industry, where value depends on continued success in research and development, and in many service industries where value depends on human capital. We can also understand why highly profitable growth companies, such as Microsoft or Google, use mostly equity finance.

The moral of these examples is this: *Do not think only about the probability that borrowing will bring trouble. Think also of the value that may be lost if trouble comes.*

Heartbreak Hotel for Enron? Enron was one of the most glamorous, fast-growing, and (apparently) profitable companies of the 1990s. It played a lead role in the deregulation of electric power markets, both in the United States and internationally. It invested in electric power generation and distribution, gas pipelines, telecommunications networks, and various other ventures. It also built up an active energy trading business. At its peak, the aggregate market value of Enron's common stock exceeded $60 billion. By the end of 2001, Enron was in bankruptcy and its shares were worthless.

With hindsight, we see that Enron was playing many of the games that we described earlier in this section. It was borrowing aggressively and hiding the debt in special-purpose entities (SPEs). The SPEs also allowed it to pump up its reported earnings, playing for time while making more and more risky investments. When the bubble burst, there was hardly any value left.

The collapse of Enron didn't really destroy $60 billion in value because that $60 billion wasn't there in the first place. But there were genuine costs of financial distress. Let's focus on Enron's energy trading business. That business was not as profitable as it appeared, but it was nevertheless a valuable asset. It provided an important service for wholesale energy customers and suppliers who wanted to buy or sell contracts that locked in the future prices and quantities of electricity, natural gas, and other commodities.

What happened to this business when it became clear that Enron was in financial distress and probably headed for bankruptcy? It disappeared. Trading volume went to zero immediately. None of its customers was willing to make a new trade with Enron because it was far from clear that Enron would be around to honor its side of the bargain. With no trading volume, there was no trading business. As it turned out, Enron's trading business more resembled Fledgling Electronics than a tangible asset like Heartbreak Hotel.

The value of Enron's trading business depended on Enron's creditworthiness. The value should have been protected by conservative financing. Most of the lost value can be traced back to Enron's aggressive borrowing. This loss of value was, therefore, a cost of financial distress.

The Trade-Off Theory of Capital Structure

Financial managers often think of the firm's debt–equity decision as a trade-off between interest tax shields and the costs of financial distress. Of course, there is controversy about how valuable interest tax shields are and what kinds of financial trouble are most threatening, but these disagreements are only variations on a theme. Thus, Figure 18.2 illustrates the debt–equity trade-off.

This *trade-off theory* of capital structure recognizes that target debt ratios may vary from firm to firm. Companies with safe, tangible assets and plenty of taxable income to shield ought to have high target ratios. Unprofitable companies with risky, intangible assets ought to rely primarily on equity financing.

If there were no costs of adjusting capital structure, then each firm should always be at its target debt ratio. However, there are costs—and, therefore, delays—in adjusting to the optimum. Firms cannot immediately offset the random events that bump them away from their capital structure targets, so we should see random differences in actual debt ratios among firms having the same target debt ratio.

BEYOND THE PAGE

Do firms have a debt target?

mhhe.com/brealey13e

All in all, this trade-off theory of capital structure choice tells a comforting story. Unlike MM's theory, which seemed to say that firms should take on as much debt as possible, it avoids extreme predictions and rationalizes moderate debt ratios. Also, if you ask financial managers whether their firms have target debt ratios, they will usually say yes—although the target is often specified not as a debt ratio but as a debt rating. For example, the firm might manage its capital structure to maintain a single-A bond rating. Ratio or rating, a target is consistent with the trade-off theory.[21]

But what are the facts? Can the trade-off theory of capital structure explain how companies actually behave?

The answer is "yes and no." On the "yes" side, the trade-off theory successfully explains many industry differences in capital structure. High-tech growth companies, whose assets are risky and mostly intangible, normally use relatively little debt. Airlines can and do borrow heavily because their assets are tangible and relatively safe.[22]

On the "no" side, there are some things the trade-off theory cannot explain. It cannot explain why some of the most successful companies thrive with little debt. Think of Johnson & Johnson, which, as Table 18.4A shows, has little debt. Granted, Johnson & Johnson's most valuable assets are intangible, the fruits of its research and development. We know that intangible assets and conservative capital structures go together. But Johnson & Johnson also has a very large corporate income tax bill (normally about $4 billion) and the highest possible credit rating. It could borrow enough to save tens of millions of dollars without raising a whisker of concern about possible financial distress.

Johnson & Johnson illustrates an odd fact about real-life capital structures: The most profitable companies commonly borrow the least.[23] Here the trade-off theory fails because it predicts exactly the reverse. Under the trade-off theory, high profits should mean more debt-servicing capacity and more taxable income to shield and so should give a *higher* target debt ratio.[24]

It will be interesting to see whether the Tax Cuts and Job Act of 2017 will lead U.S. corporations to rely less on debt. The trade-off theory predicts that the reduction of the tax rate from 35% to 21% will reduce target debt ratios. Corporations with interest payments exceeding 30% of EBITDA or EBIT will have an extra incentive to reduce debt if costs of financial distress are at all important.

On the other hand, it appears that public companies rarely make major shifts in capital structure just because of taxes,[25] and it is hard to detect the present value of interest tax shields in firms' market values.[26] There are large, long-lived differences between average debt ratios of high- versus low-debt companies in the same industry, even after controlling for attributes

---

[21]See J. Graham and C. Harvey, "The Theory and Practice of Corporate Finance: Evidence from the Field," *Journal of Financial Economics* 60 (May 2001), pp. 187–243.

[22]We are not suggesting that all airline companies are safe; many are not. But air*craft* can support debt where air*lines* cannot. If Fly-by-Night Airlines fails, its planes retain their value in another airline's operations. There's a good secondary market in used aircraft, so a loan secured by aircraft can be well protected even if made to an airline flying on thin ice (and in the dark).

[23]For example, in an international comparison, Wald found that profitability was the single largest determinant of firm capital structure. See J. K. Wald, "How Firm Characteristics Affect Capital Structure: An International Comparison," *Journal of Financial Research* 22 (Summer 1999), pp. 161–187.

[24]Here we mean debt as a fraction of the book or replacement value of the company's assets. Profitable companies might not borrow a greater fraction of their market value. Higher profits imply higher market value as well as stronger incentives to borrow.

[25]MacKie-Mason found that taxpaying companies are more likely to issue debt (vs. equity) than nontaxpaying companies. This shows that taxes do affect financing choices. However, it is not necessarily evidence for the trade-off theory. Look back to Section 18-2, and note the special case where corporate and personal taxes cancel to make debt policy irrelevant. In that case, taxpaying firms would see no net tax advantage to debt: Corporate interest tax shields would be offset by the taxes paid by investors in the firm's debt. But the balance would tip in favor of equity for a firm that was losing money and reaping no benefits from interest tax shields. See J. MacKie-Mason, "Do Taxes Affect Corporate Financing Decisions?" *Journal of Finance* 45 (December 1990), pp. 1471–1493.

[26]A study by E. F. Fama and K. R. French, covering over 2,000 firms from 1965 to 1992, failed to find any evidence that interest tax shields contributed to firm value. See "Taxes, Financing Decisions and Firm Value," *Journal of Finance* 53 (June 1998), pp. 819–843.

that the trade-off theory says should be important.[27] But DeAngelo and Roll find the debt ratios of individual companies have fluctuated dramatically when tracked over decades. For example, IBM's book debt ratio peaked at about 40% in the mid-1950s, fell to nearly zero in the mid-1970s, and rose again to about 30% at the turn of the century. International Paper's debt ratio fluctuated between 20% and 40% between 1909 and the end of World War II, then fell to zero until the mid-1960s, when it popped back into the 20% to 40% range. DeAngelo and Roll's case studies suggest that increases in leverage often happened in periods of heavy capital investment and large requirements for external financing.[28]

Graham, Leary, and Roberts find that aggregate leverage for U.S. corporations increased steadily from about 10% in the mid-1940s to about 30% from the early 1970s through 2010. But they were not able to explain the increase by changes in corporate tax rates.[29] Debt ratios in other industrialized countries are equal to or higher than those in the United States. Many of these countries have imputation tax systems, which should eliminate the value of the interest tax shields.[30]

None of this disproves the trade-off theory. As George Stigler emphasized, theories are not rejected by circumstantial evidence; it takes a theory to beat a theory. So we now turn to a completely different theory of financing.

18-4   The Pecking Order of Financing Choices

The pecking-order theory starts with *asymmetric information*—a fancy term indicating that managers know more about their companies' prospects, risks, and values than do outside investors.

Managers obviously know more than investors. We can prove that by observing stock price changes caused by announcements by managers. For example, when a company announces an increased regular dividend, stock price typically rises because investors interpret the increase as a sign of management's confidence in future earnings. In other words, the dividend increase transfers information from managers to investors. This can happen only if managers know more in the first place.

Asymmetric information affects the choice between internal and external financing and between new issues of debt and equity securities. This leads to a *pecking order*, in which investment is financed first with internal funds (reinvested earnings primarily), then by new issues of debt, and finally with new issues of equity. New equity issues are a last resort when the company runs out of debt capacity, that is, when the threat of costs of financial distress brings regular insomnia to existing creditors and to the financial manager.

We will take a closer look at the pecking order in a moment. First, you must appreciate how asymmetric information can force the financial manager to issue debt rather than common stock.

---

[27]M. L. Lemmon, M. R. Roberts, and J. F. Zender, "Back to the Beginning: Persistence and the Cross-Section of Corporate Capital Structure," *Journal of Finance* 63 (August 2008), pp. 1575–1608.

[28]H. DeAngelo and R. Roll, "Capital Structure Instability," *Journal of Applied Corporate Finance* 28 (Fall 2016), pp. 38–52.

[29]J. R. Graham, M. T. Leary, and M. R. Roberts, "The Leveraging of Corporate America: A Long-Run Perspective on Changes in Capital Structure," *Journal of Applied Corporate Finance* 28 (Fall 2016), pp. 29–37.

[30]We described the Australian imputation tax system in Section 16-5. Look again at Table 16.2, supposing that an Australian corporation pays A\$10 of interest. This reduces the corporate tax by A\$3.00; it also reduces the tax credit taken by the shareholders by A\$3.00. The final tax does not depend on whether the corporation or the shareholder borrows. You can check this by redrawing Figure 18.2 for the Australian system. The corporate tax rate T_c will cancel out. Since income after all taxes depends only on investors' tax rates, there is no special advantage to corporate borrowing.

Debt and Equity Issues with Asymmetric Information

To the outside world, Smith & Company and Jones Inc., our two example companies, are identical. Each runs a successful business with good growth opportunities. The two businesses are risky, however, and investors have learned from experience that current expectations are frequently bettered or disappointed. Current expectations price each company's stock at $100 per share, but the true values could be higher or lower:

	Smith & Co.	Jones, Inc.
True value could be higher, say	$120	$120
Best current estimate	100	100
True value could be lower, say	80	80

Now suppose that both companies need to raise new money from investors to fund capital investment. They can do this either by issuing bonds or by issuing new shares of common stock. How would the choice be made? One financial manager—we will not tell you which one—might reason as follows:

> Sell stock for $100 per share? Ridiculous! It's worth at least $120. A stock issue now would hand a free gift to new investors. I just wish those skeptical shareholders would appreciate the true value of this company. Our new factories will make us the world's lowest-cost producer. We've painted a rosy picture for the press and security analysts, but it just doesn't seem to be working. Oh well, the decision is obvious: We'll issue debt, not underpriced equity. A debt issue will save underwriting fees too.

The other financial manager is in a different mood:

> Beefalo burgers were a hit for a while, but it looks like the fad is fading. The fast-food division's gotta find some good new products or it's all downhill from here. Export markets are OK for now, but how are we going to compete with those new Siberian ranches? Fortunately the stock price has held up pretty well—we've had some good short-run news for the press and security analysts. Now's the time to issue stock. We have major investments underway, and why add increased debt service to my other worries?

Of course, outside investors can't read the financial managers' minds. If they could, one stock might trade at $120 and the other at $80.

Why doesn't the optimistic financial manager simply educate investors? Then the company could sell stock on fair terms, and there would be no reason to favor debt over equity or vice versa.

This is not so easy. (Note that both companies are issuing upbeat press releases.) Investors can't be told what to think; they have to be convinced. That takes a detailed layout of the company's plans and prospects, including the inside scoop on new technology, product design, marketing plans, and so on. Getting this across is expensive for the company and also valuable to its competitors. Why go to the trouble? Investors will learn soon enough, as revenues and earnings evolve. In the meantime the optimistic financial manager can finance growth by issuing debt.

Now suppose there are two press releases:

> Jones Inc. will issue $120 million of five-year senior notes.

> Smith & Co. announced plans today to issue 1.2 million new shares of common stock. The company expects to raise $120 million.

As a rational investor, you immediately learn two things. First, Jones's financial manager is optimistic and Smith's is pessimistic. Second, Smith's financial manager is also naive to think that investors would pay $100 per share. The *attempt* to sell stock shows that it must be worth less. Smith might sell stock at $80 per share, but certainly not at $100.[31]

Smart financial managers think this through ahead of time. The end result? Both Smith and Jones end up issuing debt. Jones Inc. issues debt because its financial manager is optimistic and doesn't want to issue undervalued equity. A smart, but pessimistic, financial manager at Smith issues debt because an attempt to issue equity would force the stock price down and eliminate any advantage from doing so. (Issuing equity also reveals the manager's pessimism immediately. Most managers prefer to wait. A debt issue lets bad news come out later through other channels.)

The story of Smith and Jones illustrates how asymmetric information favors debt issues over equity issues. If managers are better informed than investors and both groups are rational, then any company that can borrow will do so rather than issuing fresh equity. In other words, debt issues will be higher in the pecking order.

Taken literally, this reasoning seems to rule out any issue of equity. That's not right because asymmetric information is not always important and there are other forces at work. For example, if Smith had already borrowed heavily, and would risk financial distress by borrowing more, then it would have a good reason to issue common stock. In this case, announcement of a stock issue would not be entirely bad news. The announcement would still depress the stock price—it would highlight managers' concerns about financial distress—but the fall in price would not necessarily make the issue unwise or infeasible.

High-tech, high-growth companies can also be credible issuers of common stock. Such companies' assets are mostly intangible, and bankruptcy or financial distress would be especially costly. This calls for conservative financing. The only way to grow rapidly and keep a conservative debt ratio is to issue equity. If investors see equity issued for these reasons, problems of the sort encountered by Smith's financial manager become much less serious.

With such exceptions noted, asymmetric information can explain the dominance of debt financing over new equity issues, at least for mature public corporations. Debt issues are frequent; equity issues, rare. The bulk of external financing comes from debt, even in the United States, where equity markets are highly information-efficient. Equity issues are even more difficult in countries with less well-developed stock markets.

None of this says that firms ought to strive for high debt ratios—just that it's better to raise equity by plowing back earnings than issuing stock. In fact, a firm with ample internally generated funds doesn't have to sell any kind of security and thus avoids issue costs and information problems completely.

Implications of the Pecking Order

The *pecking-order theory* of corporate financing goes like this.

1. Firms prefer internal finance.
2. They adapt their target dividend payout ratios to their investment opportunities, while trying to avoid sudden changes in dividends.
3. Sticky dividend policies, plus unpredictable fluctuations in profitability and investment opportunities, mean that internally generated cash flow is sometimes more than capital expenditures and other times less. If it is more, the firm pays off debt or invests in

---

[31]A Smith stock issue might not succeed even at $80. Persistence in trying to sell at $80 could convince investors that the stock is worth even less!

marketable securities. If it is less, the firm first draws down its cash balance or sells its holdings of marketable securities.

4. If external finance is required, firms issue the safest security first. That is, they start with debt, then possibly hybrid securities such as convertible bonds, then perhaps equity as a last resort.

In this theory, there is no well-defined target debt–equity mix because there are two kinds of equity, internal and external, one at the top of the pecking order and one at the bottom. Each firm's observed debt ratio reflects its cumulative requirements for external finance.

The pecking order explains why the most profitable firms generally borrow less—not because they have low target debt ratios but because they don't need outside money. Less profitable firms issue debt because they do not have internal funds sufficient for their capital investment programs and because debt financing is first on the pecking order of *external* financing.

In the pecking-order theory, the attraction of interest tax shields is assumed to be second-order. Debt ratios change when there is an imbalance of internal cash flow, net of dividends, and real investment opportunities. Highly profitable firms with limited investment opportunities work down to low debt ratios. Firms whose investment opportunities outrun internally generated funds are driven to borrow more and more.

This theory explains the inverse intraindustry relationship between profitability and financial leverage. Suppose firms generally invest to keep up with the growth of their industries. Then rates of investment will be similar within an industry. Given sticky dividend payouts, the least profitable firms will have less internal funds and will end up borrowing more.

The Trade-Off Theory vs. the Pecking-Order Theory—Some Evidence

In 1995, Rajan and Zingales published a study of debt versus equity choices by large firms in Canada, France, Germany, Italy, Japan, the United Kingdom, and the United States. Rajan and Zingales found that the debt ratios of individual companies seemed to depend on four main factors:[32]

1. *Size.* Large firms tend to have higher debt ratios.

2. *Tangible assets.* Firms with high ratios of fixed assets to total assets have higher debt ratios.

3. *Profitability.* More profitable firms have lower debt ratios.

4. *Market to book.* Firms with higher ratios of market-to-book value have lower debt ratios.

These results convey good news for both the trade-off and pecking-order theories. Trade-off enthusiasts note that large companies with tangible assets are less exposed to costs of financial distress and would be expected to borrow more. They interpret the market-to-book ratio as a measure of growth opportunities and argue that growth companies could face high costs of financial distress and would be expected to borrow less. Pecking-order advocates stress the importance of profitability, arguing that profitable firms use less debt because they can rely on internal financing. They interpret the market-to-book ratio as just another measure of profitability.

---

[32]R. G. Rajan and L. Zingales, "What Do We Know about Capital Structure? Some Evidence from International Data," *Journal of Finance* 50 (December 1995), pp. 1421–1460. The same four factors seem to work in developing economies. See L. Booth, V. Aivazian, A. Demirguc-Kunt, and V. Maksimovic, "Capital Structures in Developing Countries," *Journal of Finance* 56 (February 2001), pp. 87–130.

It seems that we have two competing theories, and they're both right! That's not a comfortable conclusion. So recent research has tried to run horse races between the two theories in order to find the circumstances in which one or the other wins. It seems that the pecking order works best for large, mature firms that have access to public bond markets. These firms rarely issue equity. They prefer internal financing but turn to debt markets if needed to finance investment. Smaller, younger, growth firms are more likely to rely on equity issues when external financing is required.[33]

There is also some evidence that debt ratios incorporate the cumulative effects of *market timing*.[34] Market timing is an example of behavioral corporate finance. Suppose that investors are sometimes irrationally exuberant (as in the late 1990s) and sometimes irrationally despondent. If the financial manager's views are more stable than investors', then he or she can take advantage by issuing shares when the stock price is too high and switching to debt when the price is too low. Thus lucky companies with a history of buoyant stock prices will issue less debt and more shares, ending up with low debt ratios. Unfortunate and unpopular companies will avoid share issues and end up with high debt ratios.

Market timing could explain why companies tend to issue shares after run-ups in stock prices and also why aggregate stock issues are concentrated in bull markets and fall sharply in bear markets.

There are other behavioral explanations for corporate financing policies. For example, Bertrand and Schoar tracked the careers of individual CEOs, CFOs, and other top managers. Their individual "styles" persisted as they moved from firm to firm.[35] For example, older CEOs tended to be more conservative and pushed their firms to lower debt. CEOs with MBA degrees tended to be more aggressive. In general, financial decisions depended not just on the nature of the firm and its economic environment, but also on the personalities of the firm's top management.

The Bright Side and the Dark Side of Financial Slack

Other things equal, it's better to be at the top of the pecking order than at the bottom. Firms that have worked down the pecking order and need external equity may end up living with excessive debt or passing by good investments because shares can't be sold at what managers consider a fair price.

In other words, *financial slack* is valuable. Having financial slack means having cash, marketable securities, readily salable real assets, and ready access to debt markets or to bank financing. Ready access basically requires conservative financing so that potential lenders see the company's debt as a safe investment.

In the long run, a company's value rests more on its capital investment and operating decisions than on financing. Therefore, you want to make sure your firm has sufficient financial slack so that financing is quickly available for good investments. Financial slack is most valuable to firms with plenty of positive-NPV growth opportunities. That is another reason why growth companies usually aspire to conservative capital structures.

---

[33]L. Shyam-Sunder and S. C. Myers found that the pecking-order hypothesis outperformed the trade-off hypothesis for a sample of large companies in the 1980s. See "Testing Static Trade-off against Pecking-Order Models of Capital Structure," *Journal of Financial Economics* 51 (February 1999), pp. 219–244. M. Frank and V. Goyal found that the performance of the pecking-order hypothesis deteriorated in the 1990s, especially for small growth firms. See "Testing the Pecking Order Theory of Capital Structure," *Journal of Financial Economics* 67 (February 2003), pp. 217–248. See also E. Fama and K. French, "Testing Trade-off and Pecking Order Predictions about Dividends and Debt," *Review of Financial Studies* 15 (Spring 2002), pp. 1–33; and M. L. Lemmon and J. F. Zender, "Debt Capacity and Tests of Capital Structure Theories," *Journal of Financial and Quantitative Analysis* 45 (2010), pp. 1161–1187,

[34]M. Baker and J. Wurgler, "Market Timing and Capital Structure," *Journal of Finance* 57 (February 2002), pp. 1–32.

[35]M. Bertrand and A. Schoar, "Managing with Style: The Effect of Managers on Firm Policies," *Quarterly Journal of Economics* 118 (November 2003), pp. 1169–1208.

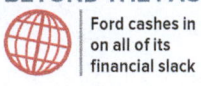

Of course, financial slack is only valuable if you're willing to use it. Take a look at the nearby box, which describes how Ford used up all of its financial slack in one enormous debt issue.

There is also a dark side to financial slack. Too much of it may encourage managers to take it easy, expand their perks, or empire-build with cash that should be paid back to stockholders. In other words, slack can make agency problems worse.

Michael Jensen has stressed the tendency of managers with ample free cash flow (or unnecessary financial slack) to plow too much cash into mature businesses or ill-advised acquisitions. "The problem," Jensen says, "is how to motivate managers to disgorge the cash rather than investing it below the cost of capital or wasting it in organizational inefficiencies."[36]

If that's the problem, then maybe debt is an answer. Scheduled interest and principal payments are contractual obligations of the firm. Debt forces the firm to pay out cash. Perhaps the best debt level would leave just enough cash in the bank, after debt service, to finance all positive-NPV projects, with not a penny left over.

We do not recommend this degree of fine-tuning, but the idea is valid and important. Debt can discipline managers who are tempted to invest too much. It can also provide the pressure to force improvements in operating efficiency. We pick up this theme again in Chapter 32.

Is There a Theory of Optimal Capital Structure?

No. That is, there is no *one* theory that can capture everything that drives thousands of corporations' debt versus equity choices. Instead, there are several theories, each more or less helpful, depending on each particular corporation's assets, operations, and circumstances.

In other words, *relax:* Don't waste time searching for a magic formula for the optimal debt ratio. Remember too that most value comes from the left side of the balance sheet—that is, from the firm's operations, assets, and growth opportunities. Financing is less important. Of course, financing can subtract value rapidly if you screw it up, but you won't do that.

In practice, financing choices depend on the relative importance of the factors discussed in this chapter. In some cases, reducing taxes will be the primary objective. Thus, high debt ratios are found in the lease-financing business (see Chapter 25). Long-term leases are often tax-driven transactions. High debt ratios are also found in developed commercial real estate. For example, modern downtown office buildings can be safe, cash-cow assets if the office space is rented to creditworthy tenants. Bankruptcy costs are small, so it makes sense to lever up and save taxes.

For smaller growth companies, interest tax shields are less important than preserving financial slack. Profitable growth opportunities are valuable only if financing is available when it comes time to invest. Costs of financial distress are high, so it's no surprise that growth companies try to use mostly equity financing.

There's another reason why growth companies borrow less. Their growth opportunities are real options, that is, options to invest in real assets. The options contain lots of hidden financial risk. We will see in Chapters 20 through 22 that an option to buy a real asset is equivalent to a claim on a fraction of the asset's value, minus an implicit debt obligation. The implicit debt obligation is usually larger than the net value of the option itself.

A growth company therefore bears financial risk even if it does not borrow a dime explicitly. It makes sense for such a company to offset the financial risk created by growth options by reducing the amount of debt on its balance sheet. The implicit debt in its growth options ends up displacing explicit debt.

Growth options are less important for mature corporations. Such companies can and usually do borrow more. They often end up following the pecking order. Information problems deter large equity issues, so such firms prefer to finance investment with retained earnings.

[36]M. C. Jensen, "Agency Costs of Free Cash Flow, Corporate Finance and Takeovers," *American Economic Review* 76 (May 1986), pp. 323–329.

They issue more debt when investments outrun retained earnings, and pay down debt when earnings outpace investment.

Sooner or later, a corporation's operations age to the point where growth opportunities evaporate. In that case, the firm may issue large amounts of debt and retire equity, to constrain investment and force payout of cash to investors. The higher debt ratio may come voluntarily or be forced by a takeover.

These examples are not exhaustive, but they give some flavor of how a thoughtful CEO can set financing strategy.

● ● ● ● ●

SUMMARY

Our task in this chapter was to show why capital structure matters. We did not throw away MM's proposition that capital structure is irrelevant; we added to it. However, we did not arrive at any simple, universal theory of optimal capital structure.

The trade-off theory emphasizes interest tax shields and the costs of financial distress. The value of the firm is broken down as

> Value if all-equity-financed + PV(tax shield) − PV(costs of financial distress)

According to this theory, the firm should increase debt until the value from PV(tax shield) is just offset, at the margin, by increases in PV(costs of financial distress).

The costs of financial distress are:

1. Bankruptcy costs
   a. Direct costs such as legal and accounting fees.
   b. Indirect costs reflecting the difficulty of managing a company undergoing liquidation or reorganization.

2. Costs of financial distress short of bankruptcy
   a. Doubts about a firm's creditworthiness can hobble its operations. Customers and suppliers will be reluctant to deal with a firm that may not be around next year. Key employees will be tempted to leave. Highly leveraged firms seem to be less vigorous product-market competitors.
   b. Conflicts of interest between bondholders and stockholders of firms in financial distress may lead to poor operating and investment decisions. Stockholders acting in their narrow self-interest can gain at the expense of creditors by playing "games" that reduce the overall value of the firm.
   c. The fine print in debt contracts is designed to prevent these games. But fine print increases the costs of writing, monitoring, and enforcing the debt contract.

The value of the interest tax shield would be easy to compute if we had only corporate taxes to worry about. In that case, the net tax saving from borrowing would be just the marginal corporate tax rate T_c times $r_D D$, the interest payment. If debt is fixed, the tax shield can be valued by discounting at the borrowing rate r_D. In the special case of fixed, permanent debt

$$PV(\text{tax shield}) = \frac{T_c r_D D}{r_D} = T_c D$$

The U.S. corporate tax rate dropped from 35% to 21% starting in 2018, reducing the tax incentive to borrow. Tax deductions of interest expense were also limited to 30% of EBITDA and (after 2022) to 30% of EBIT. It appears that these limits will affect few public U.S. corporations, but those few will have to think hard about whether additional borrowing is worthwhile.

Also corporate taxes are only part of the story. If investors pay higher taxes on interest income than on equity income (dividends and capital gains), then interest tax shields to the corporation will be partly offset by higher taxes paid by investors. The low (20% maximum) U.S. tax rates on dividends and capital gains have reduced the tax advantage to corporate borrowing.

The trade-off theory balances the tax advantages of borrowing against the costs of financial distress. Corporations are supposed to pick a target capital structure that maximizes firm value. Firms with safe, tangible assets and plenty of taxable income to shield ought to have high targets. Unprofitable companies with risky, intangible assets ought to rely more on equity financing.

This theory of capital structure successfully explains many industry differences in capital structure, but it does not explain why the most profitable firms *within* an industry generally have the most conservative capital structures. Under the trade-off theory, high profitability should mean high debt capacity *and* a strong tax incentive to use that capacity.

There is a competing, pecking-order theory, which states that firms use internal financing when available and choose debt over equity when external financing is required. This explains why the less profitable firms in an industry borrow more—not because they have higher target debt ratios but because they need more external financing and because debt is next on the pecking order when internal funds are exhausted.

The pecking order is a consequence of asymmetric information. Managers know more about their firms than outside investors do, and they are reluctant to issue stock when they believe the price is too low. They try to time issues when shares are fairly priced or overpriced. Investors understand this and interpret a decision to issue shares as bad news. That explains why stock price usually falls when a stock issue is announced.

Debt is better than equity when these information problems are important. Optimistic managers will prefer debt to undervalued equity, and pessimistic managers will be pressed to follow suit. The pecking-order theory says that equity will be issued only when debt capacity is running out and financial distress threatens.

The pecking-order theory stresses the value of financial slack. Without sufficient slack, the firm may be caught at the bottom of the pecking order and be forced to choose between issuing undervalued shares, borrowing and risking financial distress, or passing up positive-NPV investment opportunities.

There is, however, a dark side to financial slack. Surplus cash or credit tempts managers to overinvest or to indulge an easy and glamorous corporate lifestyle. When temptation wins, or threatens to win, a high debt ratio can help: It forces the company to disgorge cash and prods managers and organizations to try harder to be more efficient.

FURTHER READING

The research literature on capital structure is enormous. We cite only a few of the most important and interesting articles. The following review articles give broader surveys:

M. Harris and A. Raviv, "The Theory of Capital Structure," *Journal of Finance* 46 (March 1991), pp. 297–355.

S. C. Myers, "Financing of Corporations," in G. M. Constantinides, M. Harris, and R. Stulz, eds., *Handbook of the Economics of Finance* (Amsterdam: Elsevier North-Holland, 2003).

M. Frank and V. Goyal, "Trade-off and Pecking Order Theories of Debt," in E. Eckbo, ed., *Handbook of Corporate Finance: Empirical Finance,* vol. 2 (Amsterdam: North Holland, 2008).

J. R. Graham and M. T. Leary, "A Review of Empirical Capital Structure Research and Directions for the Future," *Annual Review of Financial Economics* 3 (2011), 309–345.

The Fall 2016 issue of the Journal of Applied Corporate Finance *contains several articles on capital structure decisions in practice.*

The following paper surveys chief financial officers' views about capital structure:

J. Graham and C. Harvey, "How Do CFOs Make Capital Budgeting and Capital Structure Decisions?" *Journal of Applied Corporate Finance* 15 (Spring 2002), pp. 8–23.

 Select problems are available in McGraw-Hill's *Connect.*
Please see the preface for more information.

1. **Tax shields** The present value of interest tax shields is often written as $T_c D$, where D is the amount of debt and T_c is the marginal corporate tax rate. Under what assumptions is this present value calculation correct?

2. **Tax shields*** Compute the present value of interest tax shields generated by these three debt issues. Consider corporate taxes only. Assume that the marginal tax rate is $T_c = .30$.

    a. A $1,000, one-year loan at 8%.

    b. A five-year loan of $1,000 at 8%. Assume no principal is repaid until maturity.

    c. A $1,000 perpetuity at 7%.

3. **Tax shields** Here are book and market value balance sheets of the United Frypan Company (UF):

	Book				Market		
Net working capital	$ 20	$ 40	Debt	Net working capital	$ 20	$ 40	Debt
Long-term assets	80	60	Equity	Long-term assets	140	120	Equity
	$100	$100			$160	$160	

   Assume that MM's theory holds with taxes. There is no growth, and the $40 of debt is expected to be permanent. Assume a 40% corporate tax rate.

    a. How much of the firm's value in dollar terms is accounted for by the debt-generated tax shield?

    b. How much better off will UF's shareholders be if the firm borrows $20 more and uses it to repurchase stock?

4. **Tax shields** Look back at the Johnson & Johnson example in Section 18-1. Suppose Johnson & Johnson increases its long-term debt to $45 billion. It uses the additional debt to repurchase shares. Reconstruct Table 18.4B with the new capital structure. How much additional value is added for Johnson & Johnson shareholders if the table's assumptions are correct?

5. **Tax shields** What is the relative tax advantage of corporate debt if the corporate tax rate is $T_c = .21$, the personal tax rate is $T_p = .37$, but all equity income is received as capital gains and escapes tax entirely ($T_{pE} = 0$)? How does the relative tax advantage change if the company decides to pay out all equity income as cash dividends that are taxed at 20%?

6. **Tax shields*** "The firm can't use interest tax shields unless it has (taxable) income to shield." What does this statement imply for debt policy? Explain briefly.

7. **Tax shields** Suppose that Congress sets the top personal tax rate on interest and dividends at 35% and the top rate on realized capital gains at 15%. The corporate tax rate stays at 21%. Compute the difference between the total corporate plus personal taxes paid on debt and the total taxes on equity income if (a) all capital gains are realized immediately and (b) capital gains are deferred forever. Assume capital gains are half of equity income.

8. **Tax shields** "The trouble with MM's argument is that it ignores the fact that individuals cannot deduct interest for personal income tax." Show why this is not an objection if personal tax rates on interest and equity income are the same.

9. **Bankruptcy costs** On February 29, 2019, when PDQ Computers announced bankruptcy, its share price fell from $3.00 to $.50 per share. There were 10 million shares outstanding. Does that imply bankruptcy costs of 10 × (3.00 − .50) = $25 million? Explain.

10. **Bankruptcy costs** Look at some real companies with different types of assets. What operating problems would each encounter in the event of financial distress? How well would the assets keep their value?

11. **Financial distress** This question tests your understanding of financial distress.

    a. What are the costs of going bankrupt? Define these costs carefully.

    b. "A company can incur costs of financial distress without ever going bankrupt." Explain how this can happen.

    c. Explain how conflicts of interest between bondholders and stockholders can lead to costs of financial distress.

12. **Financial distress*** True or false?

    a. If the probability of default is high, managers and stockholders will be tempted to take on excessively risky projects.

    b. If the probability of default is high, stockholders may refuse to contribute equity even if the firm has safe positive-NPV opportunities.

    c. When a company borrows, the expected costs of bankruptcy come out of the lenders' pockets and do not affect the market value of the shares.

13. **Agency costs** In Section 18-3, we briefly referred to three games: playing for time, cash in and run, and bait and switch.

    For each game, construct a simple numerical example (like the example for the risk-shifting game) showing how shareholders can gain at the expense of creditors. Then explain how the temptation to play these games could lead to costs of financial distress.

14. **Agency costs*** Let us go back to Circular File's market value balance sheet:

Net working capital	$20	$25	Bonds outstanding
Fixed assets	10	5	Common stock
Total assets	$30	$30	Total value

Who gains and who loses from the following maneuvers?

    a. Circular scrapes up $5 in cash and pays a cash dividend.

    b. Circular halts operations, sells its fixed assets, and converts net working capital into $20 cash. Unfortunately the fixed assets fetch only $6 on the secondhand market. The $26 cash is invested in Treasury bills.

    c. Circular encounters an acceptable investment opportunity, NPV = 0, requiring an investment of $10. The firm borrows to finance the project. The new debt has the same security, seniority, etc., as the old.

    d. Suppose that the new project has NPV = +$2 and is financed by an issue of preferred stock.

    e. The lenders agree to extend the maturity of their loan from two years to three in order to give Circular a chance to recover.

15. **Agency costs** The Salad Oil Storage (SOS) Company has financed a large part of its facilities with long-term debt. There is a significant risk of default, but the company is not on the ropes yet. Explain:

    a. Why SOS stockholders could lose by investing in a positive-NPV project financed by an equity issue.

    b. Why SOS stockholders could gain by investing in a negative-NPV project financed by cash.

    c. Why SOS stockholders could gain from paying out a large cash dividend.

16. **Agency costs** The possible payoffs from Ms. Ketchup's projects (see Example 18.1) have not changed but there is now a 40% chance that project 2 will pay off $24 and a 60% chance that it will pay off $0.

    a. Recalculate the expected payoffs to the bank and Ms. Ketchup if the bank lends the present value of $10. Which project would Ms. Ketchup undertake?

    b. What is the maximum amount the bank could lend that would induce Ms. Ketchup to take project 1?

17. **Covenants***

    a. Who benefits from the fine print in bond contracts when the firm gets into financial trouble? Give a one-sentence answer.

    b. Who benefits from the fine print when the bonds are issued? Suppose the firm is offered the choice of issuing (1) a bond with standard restrictions on dividend payout, additional borrowing, etc., and (2) a bond with minimal restrictions but a much higher interest rate? Suppose the interest rates on both (1) and (2) are fair from the viewpoint of lenders. Which bond would you expect the firm to issue? Why?

18. **Trade-off theory** The traditional theory of optimal capital structure states that firms trade off corporate interest tax shields against the possible costs of financial distress due to borrowing. What does this theory predict about the relationship between book profitability and target book debt ratios? Is the theory's prediction consistent with the facts?

19. **Pecking-order theory** "I was amazed to find that the announcement of a stock issue drives down the value of the issuing firm by 30%, on average, of the proceeds of the issue. That issue cost dwarfs the underwriter's spread and the administrative costs of the issue. It makes common stock issues prohibitively expensive."

    a. You are contemplating a $100 million stock issue. On past evidence, you anticipate that announcement of this issue will drive down stock price by 3% and that the market value of your firm will fall by 30% of the amount to be raised. On the other hand, additional equity financing is required to fund an investment project that you believe has a positive NPV of $40 million. Should you proceed with the issue?

    b. Is the fall in market value on announcement of a stock issue an *issue cost* in the same sense as an underwriter's spread? Respond to the quote that begins this question.

    Use your answer to part (a) as a numerical example to explain your response to part (b).

20. **Pecking-order theory** Why does asymmetric information push companies to raise external funds by borrowing rather than by issuing common stock?

21. **Pecking-order theory*** Fill in the blanks: According to the pecking-order theory,

    a. The firm's debt ratio is determined by _____.

    b. Debt ratios depend on past profitability, because _____.

22. **Financial slack** For what kinds of companies is financial slack most valuable? Are there situations in which financial slack should be reduced by borrowing and paying out the proceeds to the stockholders? Explain.

23. **Financial slack*** True or false?

    a. Financial slack means having cash in the bank or ready access to the debt markets.

    b. Financial slack is most valuable to firms with few investment opportunities and poor prospects.

    c. Managers with excessive financial slack may be tempted to spend it on poor investments.

24. **Debt ratios** Rajan and Zingales identified four variables that seemed to explain differences in debt ratios in several countries. What are the four variables?

25. **Leverage targets** Some corporations' debt–equity targets are expressed not as a debt ratio but as a target debt rating on the firm's outstanding bonds. What are the pros and cons of setting a target rating rather than a target ratio?

CHALLENGE

26. **Leverage measures** Most financial managers measure debt ratios from their companies' book balance sheets. Many financial economists emphasize ratios from market-value balance sheets. Which is the right measure in principle? Does the trade-off theory propose to explain book or market leverage? How about the pecking-order theory?

27. **Trade-off theory** The trade-off theory relies on the threat of financial distress. But why should a public corporation ever have to land in financial distress? According to the theory, the firm should operate at the top of the curve in Figure 18.2. Of course market movements or business setbacks could bump it up to a higher debt ratio and put it on the declining, right-hand side of the curve. But in that case, why doesn't the firm just issue equity, retire debt, and move back up to the optimal debt ratio? What are the reasons why companies don't issue stock—or enough stock—quickly enough to avoid financial distress?

FINANCE ON THE WEB

You can download data for the following questions from the Yahoo! Finance website (**www.finance.yahoo.com**).

1. Look up Johnson & Johnson on Yahoo! Finance.

   a. Recalculate book- and market-value balance sheets using the most recent available financial information. Use the same format as for Table 18.4.

   b. Track Johnson & Johnson's long-term debt and debt ratio over the last five years (you will need to go to the company's website to do this). How have they changed? Does it appear that the company has a stable target debt ratio? Do you see any evidence of pecking-order financing?

   c. How much has the company spent to repurchase its own shares? Would the trade-off theory predict share repurchases for a conservatively financed company like Johnson & Johnson?

2. Select three or four companies from the Yahoo! Finance database. Estimate how much more these companies could borrow before they would exhaust taxable profits.

CHAPTER

19

Financing and Valuation

In Chapters 5 and 6, we showed how to value a capital investment project by a four-step procedure:

1. Forecast after-tax cash flows, assuming all-equity financing.
2. Assess the project's risk.
3. Estimate the opportunity cost of capital.
4. Calculate NPV, using the opportunity cost of capital as the discount rate.

There's nothing wrong with this procedure, but now we're going to extend it to include value contributed by financing decisions. There are two ways to do this:

1. *Adjust the discount rate.* To take account of the interest tax shields, companies usually adjust the discount rate downward. They do this by calculating an after-tax weighted average cost of capital (WACC). We introduced the after-tax WACC in Chapters 9 and 17, but here we provide a lot more guidance on how it is calculated and used.
2. *Adjust the present value.* In this case, you start by estimating the base-case value of the firm or project, assuming it is all-equity-financed, and then adjust this base-case value to account for financing.

Adjusted present value (APV)

= base-case value + value of financing side effects

Once you identify and value the financing side effects, calculating APV is no more than addition or subtraction.

This is a how-to-do-it chapter. In the first section, we explain and derive the after-tax WACC and use it to value a project and business. Then in Section 19-2, we work through a more complex and realistic valuation problem. Section 19-3 covers some tricks of the trade: helpful hints on how to estimate inputs and on how to adjust WACC when business risk or capital structure changes. Section 19-4 turns to the APV method. The idea behind APV is simple enough, but tracing through all the financing side effects can be tricky. We conclude the chapter with a question-and-answer section designed to clarify points that managers and students often find confusing. The Appendix covers an important special case—namely, the after-tax valuation of safe cash flows.

This chapter contains several extended numerical examples. To keep things simple, we will follow current U.S. tax law in all of them, using the 21% tax rate and 100% bonus depreciation implemented in 2018. You can explore the effects of different tax rates and depreciation schedules when you tackle the end-of-chapter problems.

19-1 The After-Tax Weighted-Average Cost of Capital

We first addressed problems of valuation and capital budgeting in Chapters 5 and 6. In those early chapters, we said hardly a word about financing decisions. We separated investment from financing decisions. If the investment project was positive-NPV, we assumed that the firm would go ahead, without asking whether financing the project would add or subtract additional value. We were really assuming a Modigliani–Miller (MM) world in which all financing decisions are irrelevant. In a strict MM world, firms can analyze real investments as if they are all-equity-financed; the actual financing plan is a mere detail to be worked out later.

Under MM assumptions, decisions to spend money can be separated from decisions to raise money. Now we reconsider the capital budgeting decision when investment and financing decisions interact and cannot be wholly separated.

One reason financing and investment decisions interact is taxes. Interest is a tax-deductible expense. Think back to Chapters 9 and 17, where we introduced the *after-tax* weighted-average cost of capital:

$$\text{WACC} = r_D(1 - T_c)\frac{D}{V} + r_E\frac{E}{V}$$

Here D and E are the market values of the firm's debt and equity, $V = D + E$ is the total market value of the firm, r_D and r_E are the costs of debt and equity, respectively, and T_c is the marginal corporate tax rate.

Notice that the WACC formula uses the *after-tax* cost of debt $r_D(1 - T_c)$. That is how the after-tax WACC captures the value of interest tax shields. Notice too that all the variables in the WACC formula refer to the firm as a whole. As a result, the formula gives the right discount rate only for projects that are just like the firm undertaking them. The formula works for the "average" project. It is incorrect for projects that are safer or riskier than the average of the firm's existing assets. It is incorrect for projects whose acceptance would lead to an increase or decrease in the firm's target debt ratio.

The WACC is based on the firm's *current* characteristics, but managers use it to discount *future* cash flows. That's fine as long as the firm's business risk and debt ratio are expected to remain constant, but when the business risk and debt ratio are expected to change, discounting cash flows by the WACC is just approximately correct.

Many firms set a single, companywide WACC and update it only if there are major changes in risk and interest rates. The WACC is a common reference point that avoids divisional squabbles about discount rates.[1] But all financial managers need to know how to adjust WACC when business risks and financing assumptions change. We show how to make these adjustments later in this chapter.

EXAMPLE 19.1 • Calculating Sangria's WACC

Sangria is a U.S.-based company whose products aim to promote happy, low-stress lifestyles. Let's calculate Sangria's WACC. Its book and market-value balance sheets are

Sangria Corporation (Book Values, $ millions)			
Asset value	$1,000	$ 500	Debt
		500	Equity
	$1,000	$ 1,000	

---

[1]See Section 9-1 under "Perfect Pitch and the Cost of Capital."

Sangria Corporation (Market Values, $ millions)

Asset value	$1,250	$ 500	Debt
		750	Equity
	$1,250	$1,250	

We calculated the market value of equity on Sangria's balance sheet by multiplying its current stock price ($7.50) by 100 million, the number of its outstanding shares. The company's future prospects are good, so the stock is trading above book value ($7.50 vs. $5.00 per share). However, interest rates have been stable since the firm's debt was issued, so the book and market values of debt are, in this case, equal.

Sangria's cost of debt (the market interest rate on its existing debt and on any new borrowing)[2] is 6%. Its cost of equity (the expected rate of return demanded by investors in Sangria's stock) is 12.5%.

The market-value balance sheet shows assets worth $1,250 million. Of course, we can't observe this value directly because the assets themselves are not traded. But we know what they are worth to debt and equity investors ($500 + 750 = $1,250 million). This value is entered on the left of the market-value balance sheet.

Why did we show the book balance sheet? Only so you could draw a big X through it. Do so now.

Think of the WACC as the expected rate of return on a *portfolio* of the firm's outstanding debt and equity. The portfolio weights depend on market values. The expected rate of return on the market-value portfolio reveals the expected rate of return demanded by investors for committing their hard-earned money to the firm's assets and operations.

When estimating the weighted-average cost of capital, you are not interested in past investments but in current values and expectations for the future. Sangria's true debt ratio is not 50%, the book ratio, but 40% because its assets are worth $1,250 million. The cost of equity, $r_E = .125$, is the expected rate of return from purchase of stock at $7.50 per share, the current market price. It is not the return on book value per share. You can't buy shares in Sangria for $5 anymore.

Sangria is consistently profitable and pays taxes at the marginal rate of 21%.[3] This tax rate is the final input for Sangria's WACC. The inputs are summarized here:

Cost of debt (r_D)	0.06
Cost of equity (r_E)	0.125
Marginal tax rate (T_c)	0.21
Debt ratio (D/V)	500/1,250 = 0.4
Equity ratio (E/V)	750/1,250 = 0.6

The company's after-tax WACC is

$$\text{WACC} = .06 \times (1 - .21) \times .4 + .125 \times .6 = .094, \text{ or } 9.4\%$$

That's how you calculate the weighted-average cost of capital. Now let's see how Sangria would *use* it.

---

[2] Always use an up-to-date interest rate (yield to maturity), not the interest rate when the firm's debt was first issued and not the coupon rate on the debt's book value.
[3] This is the U.S. corporate tax rate starting in 2018. Most U.S. corporations add a few percentage points to the tax rate to cover state income taxes, depending on how their sales, assets, and income are distributed across states.

EXAMPLE 19.2   ●   Using Sangria's WACC to Value a Project

Sangria's enologists have proposed investing $12.5 million in the construction of a perpetual crushing machine, which (conveniently for us) never depreciates and generates a perpetual stream of earnings and cash flow of $1.487 million per year pretax. The project is average risk, so we can use WACC. The after-tax cash flow is:

Pretax cash flow	$1.487 million
Tax at 21%	0.312
After-tax cash flow	$C = $1.175 million

Note: This after-tax cash flow takes no account of interest tax shields on debt supported by the perpetual crusher project. As we explained in Chapter 6, standard capital budgeting practice separates investment from financing decisions and calculates after-tax cash flows as if the project were all-equity-financed. However, the interest tax shields will not be ignored: We are about to discount the project's cash flows by Sangria's WACC, in which the cost of debt is entered after tax. The value of interest tax shields is picked up not as higher after-tax cash flows, but in a lower discount rate.

The crusher generates a perpetual after-tax cash flow of $C = $1.175 million, so NPV is

$$\text{NPV} = -12.5 + \frac{1.175}{.094} = 0$$

NPV = 0 means a barely acceptable investment. The annual cash flow of $1.175 million per year amounts to a 9.4% rate of return on investment (1.175/12.5 = .094), exactly equal to Sangria's WACC.

If project NPV is exactly zero, the return to equity investors must exactly equal the cost of equity, 12.5%. Let's confirm that Sangria shareholders can actually look forward to a 12.5% return on their investment in the perpetual crusher project.

Suppose Sangria sets up this project as a mini-firm. Its market-value balance sheet looks like this:

Perpetual Crusher (Market Values, $ millions)

Asset value	$12.5	$ 5.0	Debt
		7.5	Equity
	$12.5	$12.5	

Calculate the expected dollar return to shareholders:

$$\text{After-tax interest} = r_D(1 - T_c)D = .06 \times (1 - .21) \times 5 = .237$$
$$\text{Expected equity income} = C - r_D(1 - T_c)D = 1.175 - .237 = .938$$

The project's earnings are level and perpetual, so the expected rate of return on equity is equal to the expected equity income divided by the equity value:

$$\text{Expected equity return} = r_E = \frac{\text{expected equity income}}{\text{equity value}}$$

$$= \frac{.938}{7.5} = .125, \text{ or } 12.5\%$$

The expected return on equity equals the cost of equity, so it makes sense that the project's NPV is zero.

● ● ● ● ●

Review of Assumptions

It is appropriate to discount the perpetual crusher's cash flows at Sangria's WACC only if

- The project's business risks are the same as those of Sangria's other assets and remain so for the life of the project.
- Throughout its life, the project supports the same fraction of debt to value as in Sangria's overall capital structure.

You can see the importance of these two assumptions: If the perpetual crusher had greater business risk than Sangria's other assets, or if the acceptance of the project would lead to a permanent, material change in Sangria's debt ratio, then Sangria's shareholders would not be content with a 12.5% expected return on their equity investment in the project.

But users of WACC need not worry about small or temporary fluctuations in debt ratios. Nor should they be misled by the immediate source of financing. Suppose that Sangria decides to borrow $12.5 million to get a quick start on construction of the crusher. This does not necessarily change Sangria's long-term financing targets. The crusher's debt *capacity* is only $5 million. If Sangria decides for convenience to borrow $12.5 million for the crusher, then sooner or later it will have to borrow $12.5 – $5 = $7.5 million *less* for other projects.

We have illustrated the WACC formula only for a project offering perpetual cash flows. But the formula works for any cash-flow pattern as long as the firm adjusts its borrowing to maintain a constant debt ratio over time.[4] When the firm departs from this borrowing policy, WACC is only approximately correct.

Mistakes People Make in Using the Weighted-Average Formula

The weighted-average formula is very useful, but it is also dangerous. It tempts people to make logical errors. For example, manager Q, who is campaigning for a pet project, might look at the formula

$$\text{WACC} = r_D(1 - T_c)\frac{D}{V} + r_E\frac{E}{V}$$

---

[4]We can prove this statement as follows. Denote expected after-tax cash flows (assuming all-equity financing) as $C_1, C_2, \ldots, C_T$. With all-equity financing, these flows would be discounted at the opportunity cost of capital r. But we need to value the cash flows for a firm that is financed partly with debt. Start with value in the next to last period: $V_{T-1} = D_{T-1} + E_{T-1}$. The total cash payoff to debt and equity investors is the cash flow plus the interest tax shield. The expected total return to debt and equity investors is

$$\text{Expected cash payoff in } T = C_T + T_c r_D D_{T-1} \tag{1}$$

$$= V_{T-1}\left(1 + r_D\frac{D_{T-1}}{V_{T-1}} + r_E\frac{E_{T-1}}{V_{T-1}}\right) \tag{2}$$

Assume the debt ratio is constant at $L = D/V$. Equate (1) and (2) and solve for V_{T-1}:

$$V_{T-1} = \frac{C_T}{1 + (1 - T_c)r_D L + r_E(1 - L)} = \frac{C_T}{1 + \text{WACC}}$$

The logic repeats for V_{T-2}. Note that the next period's payoff includes V_{T-1}: Expected cash payoff in $T - 1 = C_{T-1} + T_c r_D D_{T-2} + V_{T-1}$

$$= V_{T-2}\left(1 + r_D\frac{D_{T-2}}{V_{T-2}} + r_E\frac{E_{T-2}}{V_{T-2}}\right)$$

$$V_{T-2} = \frac{C_{T-1} + V_{T-1}}{1 + (1 - T_c)r_D L + r_E(1 - L)} = \frac{C_{T-1} + V_{T-1}}{1 + \text{WACC}} = \frac{C_{T-1}}{1 + \text{WACC}} + \frac{C_T}{(1 + \text{WACC})^2}$$

We can continue all the way back to date 0:

$$V_0 = \sum_{t=1}^{T} \frac{C_t}{(1 + \text{WACC})^t}$$

and think, "Aha! My firm has a good credit rating. It could borrow, say, 90% of the project's cost if it likes. That means $D/V = .9$ and $E/V = .1$. My firm's borrowing rate r_D is 8%, and the required return on equity, r_E, is 15%. The tax rate is now 21%. Therefore,

$$\text{WACC} = .08(1 - .21)(.9) + .15(.1) = .072$$

or 7.2%. When I discount at that rate, my project looks great."

Manager Q is wrong on several counts. First, the weighted-average formula works only for projects that are carbon copies of the firm. The firm isn't 90% debt-financed.

Second, the immediate source of funds for a project has no necessary connection with the hurdle rate for the project. What matters is the project's overall contribution to the firm's borrowing power. A dollar invested in Q's pet project will not increase the firm's debt capacity by $.90. If the firm borrows 90% of the project's cost, it is really borrowing in part against its *existing* assets. Any advantage from financing the new project with more debt than normal should be attributed to the old projects, not to the new one.

Third, even if the firm were willing and able to lever up to 90% debt, its cost of capital would not decline to 7.2%, as Q's naive calculation predicts. You cannot increase the debt ratio without creating financial risk for stockholders and thereby increasing r_E, the expected rate of return they demand from the firm's common stock. Going to 90% debt would certainly increase the borrowing rate, too.

19-2 Valuing Businesses

On most workdays, the financial manager concentrates on valuing projects, arranging financing, and helping to run the firm more effectively. The valuation of the business as a whole is left to investors and financial markets. But on some days, the financial manager has to take a stand on what an entire business is worth. When this happens, a *big* decision is typically in the offing. For example:

- If firm A is about to make a takeover offer for firm B, then A's financial managers have to decide how much the combined business A + B is worth under A's management. This task is particularly difficult if B is a private company with no observable share price.

- If firm C is considering the sale of one of its divisions, it has to decide what the division is worth in order to negotiate with potential buyers.

- When a firm goes public, the investment bank must evaluate how much the firm is worth in order to set the issue price.

- If a mutual fund owns shares in a company that is not traded, then the fund's directors are obliged to estimate a fair value for those shares. If the directors do a sloppy job of coming up with a value, they are liable to find themselves in court.

In addition, thousands of analysts in stockbrokers' offices and investment firms spend every workday burrowing away in the hope of finding undervalued firms. Many of these analysts use the valuation tools we are about to cover.

In Chapter 4, we took a first pass at valuing free cash flows from an entire business. We assumed then that the business was financed solely by equity. Now we will show how WACC can be used to value a company that is financed by a mixture of debt and equity. You just treat the company as if it were one big project. You forecast the company's free cash flows (the hardest part of the exercise) and discount back to present value. But be sure to remember three important points:

1. If you discount at WACC, cash flows have to be projected just as you would for a capital investment project. Do not deduct interest. Calculate taxes as if the company were all-equity-financed. (The value of interest tax shields is not ignored, because the after-tax cost of debt is used in the WACC formula.)

2. Unlike most projects, companies are potentially immortal. But that does not mean that you need to forecast every year's cash flow from now to eternity. Financial managers usually forecast to a medium-term horizon and add a terminal value to the cash flows in the horizon year. The terminal value is the present value at the horizon of all subsequent cash flows. Estimating the terminal value requires careful attention because it often accounts for the majority of the company's value.

3. Discounting at WACC values the assets and operations of the company. If the object is to value the company's equity, that is, its common stock, don't forget to subtract the value of the company's outstanding debt.

Here's an example.

Valuing Rio Corporation

Sangria is tempted to acquire the Rio Corporation, which is also in the business of promoting relaxed, happy lifestyles. Rio has developed a special weight-loss program called the Brazil Diet, based on barbecues, red wine, and sunshine. The firm guarantees that within three months you will have a figure that will allow you to fit right in at Ipanema or Copacabana beach in Rio de Janeiro. But before you head for the beach, you've got the job of working out how much Sangria should pay for Rio.

Rio is a U.S. company. It is privately held, so Sangria has no stock market price to rely on. Rio is in the same line of business as Sangria, so we will assume that it has the same business risk as Sangria, and, like Sangria, its debt capacity is 40% of firm value. Therefore, we can use Sangria's WACC.

Your first task is to forecast Rio's *free cash flow* (FCF). Free cash flow is the amount of cash that the firm can pay out to investors after making all investments necessary for growth. Free cash flow is calculated assuming the firm is all-equity-financed. Discounting the free cash flows at the after-tax WACC gives the total value of Rio (debt *plus* equity). To find the value of its equity, you will need to subtract the 40% of the firm that can be financed with debt.

We will forecast each year's free cash flow out to a *valuation horizon* (H) and predict the business's value at that horizon (PV_H). The cash flows and horizon value are then discounted back to the present:

$$PV = \underbrace{\frac{FCF_1}{1 + WACC} + \frac{FCF_2}{(1 + WACC)^2} + \cdots + \frac{FCF_H}{(1 + WACC)^H}}_{PV \text{ (free cash flow)}} + \underbrace{\frac{PV_H}{(1 + WACC)^H}}_{PV \text{ (horizon value)}}$$

Of course, the business will continue after the horizon, but it's not practical to forecast free cash flow year by year to infinity. PV_H stands in for the value in year H of free cash flow in periods $H + 1$, $H + 2$, etc.

Free cash flow and net income are not the same. They differ in several important ways:

- Income is the return to shareholders, calculated after interest expense. Free cash flow is calculated before interest.

- Income is calculated after various noncash expenses, including depreciation. Therefore, we will add back depreciation when we calculate free cash flow.

- Capital expenditures and investments in working capital do not appear as expenses on the income statement, but they do reduce free cash flow.

Free cash flow can be negative for rapidly growing firms, even if the firms are profitable, because investment exceeds cash flow from operations. Negative free cash flow is normally temporary, fortunately for the firm and its stockholders. Free cash flow turns positive as growth slows down and the payoffs from prior investments start to roll in.

Table 19.1 sets out the information that you need to forecast Rio's free cash flows. We will follow common practice and start with a projection of sales. In the year just ended, Rio had sales of $83.6 million. In recent years, sales have grown between 5% and 8% a year. You forecast that sales will grow about 7% a year for the next three years. Growth will then slow to 4% for years 4 to 6 and to 3% starting in year 7.

The other components of cash flow in Table 19.1 are driven by these sales forecasts. For example, you can see that costs are forecasted at 74% of sales in the first year with a gradual increase to 76.5% of sales in later years, reflecting increased marketing costs as Rio's competitors gradually catch up.

Increasing sales are likely to require further investment in fixed assets and working capital. Rio's net fixed assets are currently about $.79 for each dollar of sales. Unless Rio has surplus capacity or can squeeze more output from its existing plant and equipment, its investment in fixed assets will need to grow along with sales. Therefore, we assume that every dollar of sales growth requires an increase of $.79 in net fixed assets. We also assume that working capital grows in proportion to sales.

Rio's free cash flow is calculated in Table 19.1 as profit after tax, plus depreciation,[5] minus investment. Investment is the change in the stock of (gross) fixed assets and working capital from the previous year. For example, in year 1:

$$\text{Free cash flow} = \text{Profit after tax} + \text{depreciation} - \text{investment in fixed assets}$$
$$- \text{investment in working capital}$$
$$= 10.6 + 9.9 - (109.6 - 95.0) - (11.6 - 11.1) = \$5.3 \text{ million}$$

Estimating Horizon Value

We will forecast cash flows for each of the first six years. After that, Rio's sales are expected to settle down to stable, long-term growth starting in year 7. To find the present value of the cash flows in years 1 to 6, we discount at the 9.4% WACC:

$$\text{PV} = \frac{5.3}{1.094} + \frac{5.2}{1.094^2} + \frac{5.5}{1.094^3} + \frac{8.0}{1.094^4} + \frac{8.3}{1.094^5} + \frac{8.2}{1.094^6} = \$29 \text{ million}$$

Now we need to find the value of the cash flows from year 7 onward. In Chapter 4, we looked at several ways to estimate horizon value. Here we will use the constant-growth DCF formula. This requires a forecast of the free cash flow for year 7, which we have worked out

BEYOND THE PAGE

Try It! Rio's
spreadsheet

mhhe.com/brealey13e

---

[5] For simplicity we have tied depreciation to growth in sales. We have not tracked bonus depreciation on each year's new investments.

		Latest							
	Year				Forecast				
	0	1	2	3	4	5	6	7	
1 Sales	83.6	89.5	95.8	102.5	106.6	110.8	115.2	118.7	
2 Cost of goods sold	63.1	66.2	71.3	76.3	79.9	83.1	87.0	90.8	
3 EBITDA (1 − 2)	20.5	23.3	24.4	26.1	26.6	27.7	28.2	27.9	
4 Depreciation	3.3	9.9	10.6	11.3	11.8	12.3	12.7	13.1	
5 Profit before tax (EBIT) (3 − 4)	17.2	13.4	13.8	14.8	14.9	15.4	15.5	14.8	
6 Tax	3.6	2.8	2.9	3.1	3.1	3.2	3.3	3.1	
7 Profit after tax (5 − 6)	13.6	10.6	10.9	11.7	11.7	12.2	12.2	11.7	
8 Investment in fixed assets (change in gross fixed assets)	11.0	14.6	15.5	16.6	15.0	15.6	16.2	15.9	
9 Investment in working capital	1.0	0.5	0.8	0.9	0.5	0.6	0.6	0.4	
10 Free cash flow (7 + 4 − 8 − 9)	4.9	5.3	5.2	5.5	8.0	8.3	8.2	8.5	
PV free cash flow, years 1–6	29.0								
PV horizon value	77.4			(Horizon value in year 6)			132.7		
PV of company	106.4								
Assumptions:									
Sales growth, %	6.7	7.0	7.0	7.0	4.0	4.0	4.0	3.0	
Costs (percent of sales)	75.5	74.0	74.5	74.5	75.0	75.0	75.5	76.5	
Working capital (percent of sales)	13.3	13.0	13.0	13.0	13.0	13.0	13.0	13.0	
Net fixed assets (percent of sales)	79.2	79.0	79.0	79.0	79.0	79.0	79.0	79.0	
Depreciation (percent of net fixed assets)	5.0	14.0	14.0	14.0	14.0	14.0	14.0	14.0	
Tax rate, %	21.0								
WACC, %	9.4								
Long-term growth forecast, %	3.0								
Fixed assets and working capital									
Gross fixed assets	95.0	109.6	125.1	141.8	156.8	172.4	188.6	204.5	
Less accumulated depreciation	29.0	38.9	49.5	60.8	72.6	84.9	97.6	110.7	
Net fixed assets	66.0	70.7	75.6	80.9	84.2	87.5	91.0	93.8	
Net working capital	11.1	11.6	12.4	13.3	13.9	14.4	15.0	15.4	

❯TABLE 19.1   Free-cash-flow projections and company value for Rio Corporation ($ millions)

Note: Columns may not add exactly because of rounding.

in the final column of Table 19.1, assuming a long-run growth rate of 3% per year.[6] The free cash flow is $8.5 million, so

$$PV_H = \frac{FCF_{H+1}}{WACC - g} = \frac{8.5}{.094 - .03} = \$132.7 \text{ million}$$

$$PV \text{ at year } 0 = \frac{1}{1.094^6} \times 132.7 = \$77.4 \text{ million}$$

---

[6]Notice that expected free cash flow increases by about 4% from year 6 to year 7 because the transition from 4% to 3% sales growth reduces required investment. But sales, investment, and free cash flow will all increase at 3% once the company settles into stable growth. Recall that the first cash flow in the constant-growth DCF formula occurs in the next year, year 7 in this case. Growth progresses at a steady-state 3% from year 7 onward. Therefore, it's OK to use the 3% growth rate in the horizon-value formula.

We now have all we need to value the business:

$$PV(\text{company}) = PV(\text{cash flow years 1 to 6}) + PV(\text{horizon value})$$
$$= \$29.0 + 77.4 = \$106.4 \text{ million}$$

This is the total value of Rio. To find the value of the equity, we simply subtract the 40% of firm value that will be financed with debt:

$$\text{Value of debt} = .40 \times 106.4 = \$42.6 \text{ million}$$

$$\text{Total value of equity} = \$106.4 - 42.6 = \$63.8 \text{ million}$$

If Rio has 1.5 million shares outstanding, its value per share is:

$$\text{Value per share} = 63.8/1.5 = \$42.53$$

Thus, Sangria could afford to pay up to about $42 per share for Rio.

You now have an estimate of the value of Rio Corporation. But how confident can you be in this figure? Notice that only about a quarter of Rio's value comes from cash flows in the first six years. The rest comes from the horizon value. Moreover, this horizon value can change in response to minor changes in assumptions. For example, if the long-run growth rate is 4% rather than 3%, firm value increases from $106.4 million to $110.5 million.

Thus, faster growth increases Rio's horizon value and PV(company). At this point, we must check the two warnings from the concatenator valuation example in Chapter 4. Did we account for the extra investment required to support the faster long-run growth? Yes. Growth at 4% instead of 3% increases year 7's investment in fixed assets from $15.9 to $16.9 million and investment in working capital from $0.4 to $0.6 million. (To confirm this, go to the Rio Spreadsheet Beyond the Page and change the long-run growth rate.) Did we assume that Rio can earn more that its cost of capital in perpetuity? Yes, because the increased investment in year 7 and after added NPV. In other words, the horizon value contains positive PVGO, the present value of growth opportunities.

Will competition eliminate the PVGO? The financial manager will have to think hard about the competitive landscape. Perhaps he or she will decide that the long-run cost forecast at 76.5% of sales is too optimistic.

The financial manager will probably also look at the values that investors place on comparable listed companies. For example, suppose that similar lifestyle companies commonly trade at a ratio of company value to EBITDA of 4.8. Then Sangria's manager might judge that Rio's horizon value is 4.8 × $27.9 million = $133.9 million in year 6 and $78.1 million discounted to year 0. This would suggest that Rio is currently worth $29.0 + 78.1 = $107.1 million, marginally higher than our initial DCF estimate. The manager might also look at the market-to-book ratio for comparable businesses and calculate what Rio would be worth if it sold at a similar ratio.

Financial managers should also check whether a business is worth more dead than alive. Sometimes a company's *liquidation value* exceeds its value as a going concern. Sometimes financial analysts can ferret out idle or underexploited assets that would be worth much more if sold to someone else. Such assets would be valued at their likely sale price and the rest of the business valued without them.

WACC vs. the Flow-to-Equity Method

When valuing Rio, we forecasted the cash flows assuming all-equity financing and we used the WACC to discount these cash flows. The WACC formula picked up the value of the interest tax shields. Then, to find the equity value, we subtracted the value of debt from the total value of the firm.

If our task is to value a firm's equity, there's an obvious alternative to discounting the total cash flows at the firm's WACC: Discount cash flows to equity after interest and after taxes at the cost of equity capital. This is called the *flow-to-equity* method. If the company's debt ratio is constant over time, the flow-to-equity method should give the same answer as discounting total cash flows at the WACC and then subtracting the value of the debt.

Suppose that you are asked to value Rio by the flow-to-equity method, assuming that the company adjusts its debt each year to maintain a constant debt ratio. You are given as a starter an estimate of Rio's horizon value at the end of year 6. Perhaps this value was obtained by discounting subsequent cash flows by Rio's WACC or perhaps it was estimated by looking at how investors value comparable, publicly traded companies. You decide to expand the spreadsheet in Table 19.1 by calculating each year's interest payments and issues or repayments of debt. You recompute taxes, recognizing that the interest payments are a tax-deductible expense. Finally, you discount the free cash flow to equity at the cost of equity, which in our example is $r_E = 12.5\%$.

It sounds straightforward, but in practice, it can be tricky to do it right. The problem arises because each year's interest payment depends on the amount of debt at the start of the year, and this depends in turn on Rio's *value* at the start of the year (remember Rio's debt is a constant proportion of value). So you seem to have a catch-22 situation in which you first need to know Rio's value each year before you can go on to calculate and discount the cash flows to equity. Fortunately, a simple formula allows you to solve simultaneously for the company's value and the cash flow in each year. We won't get into that here, but if you would like to see how the flow-to-equity method can be used to value Rio, click on the nearby Beyond the Page feature to access the worked example.

BEYOND THE PAGE

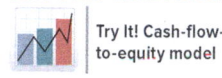

Try It! Cash-flow-to-equity model

mhhe.com/brealey13e

19-3 **Using WACC in Practice**

Some Tricks of the Trade

Sangria had just one asset and two sources of financing. A real company's market-value balance sheet has many more entries, for example:[7]

Current assets, including cash, inventory, and accounts receivable	Current liabilities, including accounts payable and short-term debt
Property, plant, and equipment	Long-term debt (D)
	Preferred stock (P)
Growth opportunities	Equity (E)
Total assets	Total liabilities plus equity

Several questions immediately arise:

---

[7]This balance sheet is for exposition and should not be confused with a real company's books. It includes the value of growth opportunities, which accountants do not recognize, though investors do. It excludes certain accounting entries, for example, deferred taxes.

Deferred taxes arise when a company uses faster depreciation for tax purposes than it uses in reports to investors. That means the company reports more in taxes than it pays. The difference is accumulated as a liability for deferred taxes. In a sense, there is a liability because the Internal Revenue Service "catches up," collecting extra taxes as assets age. But this is irrelevant in capital investment analysis, which focuses on actual after-tax cash flows and uses accelerated tax depreciation.

Deferred taxes should not be regarded as a source of financing or an element of the weighted-average cost of capital formula. The liability for deferred taxes is not a security held by investors. It is a balance sheet entry created for accounting purposes.

Deferred taxes can be important in regulated industries, however. Regulators take deferred taxes into account in calculating allowed rates of return and the time patterns of revenues and consumer prices.

How does the formula change when there are more than two sources of financing?
Easy: There is one cost for each element. The weight for each element is proportional to
its market value. For example, if the capital structure includes both preferred and common
shares,

$$\text{WACC} = r_D(1 - T_c)\frac{D}{V} + r_p\frac{P}{V} + r_E\frac{E}{V}$$

where r_P is investors' expected rate of return on the preferred stock, P is the amount of
preferred stock outstanding, and $V = D + P + E$.

What about short-term debt? Many companies consider only long-term financing when
calculating WACC. They leave out the cost of short-term debt. In principle, this is incorrect. The lenders who hold short-term debt are investors who can claim their share of operating earnings. A company that ignores this claim will misstate the required return on capital
investments.

But "zeroing out" short-term debt is not a serious error if the debt is only temporary,
seasonal, or incidental financing or if it is offset by holdings of cash and marketable securities. Suppose, for example, that one of your foreign subsidiaries takes out a six-month loan
to finance its inventory and accounts receivable. The dollar equivalent of this loan will show
up as a short-term debt. At the same time, headquarters may be lending money by investing
surplus dollars in short-term securities. If this lending and borrowing offset, there is no point
in including the cost of short-term debt in the weighted-average cost of capital, because the
company is not a *net* short-term borrower.

What about other current liabilities? Current liabilities are usually "netted out" by subtracting them from current assets. The difference is entered as net working capital on the
left-hand side of the balance sheet. The sum of long-term financing on the right is called *total
capitalization.*

Net working capital
  = current assets
  − current liabilities
	Long-term debt (*D*)

	Preferred stock (*P*)
Property, plant, and equipment	
Growth opportunities	Equity (*E*)
Total assets	Total capitalization (*V*)

When net working capital is treated as an asset, forecasts of cash flows for capital investment projects must treat increases in net working capital as a cash outflow and decreases as an
inflow. This is standard practice, which we followed in Section 6-2. We also did so when we
estimated the future investments that Rio would need to make in working capital.

Because current liabilities include short-term debt, netting them out against current assets
excludes the cost of short-term debt from the weighted-average cost of capital. We have just
explained why this can be an acceptable approximation. But when short-term debt is an
important, permanent source of financing—as is common for small firms and firms outside
the United States—it should be shown explicitly on the right-hand side of the balance sheet,
not netted out against current assets.[8] The interest cost of short-term debt is then one element
of the weighted-average cost of capital.

How are the costs of financing calculated? You can often use stock market data to get an
estimate of r_E, the expected rate of return demanded by investors in the company's stock. With
that estimate, WACC is not too hard to calculate because the borrowing rate r_D and the debt and

---

[8]Financial practitioners have rules of thumb for deciding whether short-term debt is worth including in WACC. One rule checks
whether short-term debt is at least 10% of total liabilities and net working capital is negative. If so, then short-term debt is almost
surely being used to finance long-term assets and is explicitly included in WACC.

equity ratios D/V and E/V can be directly observed or estimated without too much trouble.[9] Estimating the value and required return for preferred shares is likewise usually not too complicated.

Estimating the required return on other security types can be troublesome. Convertible debt, where the investors' return comes partly from an option to exchange the debt for the company's stock, is one example. We leave convertibles to Chapter 24.

Junk debt, where the risk of default is high, is likewise difficult. The higher the odds of default, the lower the market price of the debt, and the higher is the *promised* rate of interest. But the weighted-average cost of capital is an *expected*—that is, average—rate of return, not a promised one. For example, as we write this in 2018, the three-year bonds issued by Bon-Ton Department Stores are priced at 12.5%% of face value and offer a promised yield of 110%, about 108 percentage points above yields on the highest-quality debt issues maturing at the same time. The price and yield on the Bon-Ton bond demonstrated investors' concern about the company's chronic financial ill-health. But the 110% yield was not an expected return because it did not average in the losses to be incurred if the company were to default. Including 110% as a "cost of debt" in a calculation of WACC would therefore have overstated Bon-Ton's true cost of capital.

This is bad news: There is no easy way of estimating the expected rate of return on most junk debt issues. The good news is that for most debt, the odds of default are small. That means the promised and expected rates of return are close, and the promised rate can be used as an approximation in calculating the weighted-average cost of capital.

Should I use a company or industry WACC? Of course, you want to know what your company's WACC is. Yet industry WACCs are sometimes more useful. Here's an example. Kansas City Southern used to be a portfolio of (1) the Kansas City Southern Railroad, with operations running from the U.S. Midwest south to Texas and Mexico, and (2) Stillwell Financial, an investment-management business that included the Janus mutual funds. It's hard to think of two more dissimilar businesses. Kansas City Southern's overall WACC was not right for either of them. The company would have been well advised to use a railroad industry WACC for its railroad operations and an investment management WACC for Stillwell.[10]

Kansas City Southern spun off Stillwell in 2000 and is now a pure-play railroad. But even now, the company would be wise to check its WACC against a railroad industry WACC. Industry WACCs are less exposed to random noise and estimation errors. Fortunately for Kansas City Southern, there are five large, pure-play railroads (including Canadian Pacific and Canadian National Railway) that the company could use to calculate an industry WACC. Of course, use of an industry WACC for a particular company's investments assumes that the company and industry have approximately the same business risk. Industry WACCs also have to be adjusted (by the three-step procedure given below) if industry-average debt ratios differ from the target debt ratio for the project to be valued.

Don't use industry WACCs blindly. Railroad companies are relatively homogenous, and therefore it may be helpful to look at a railroad WACC. But an industry-average WACC for Miscellaneous Consumer Goods would be almost useless as a guide to the WACC of an individual company.[11]

What tax rate should I use? Taxes are complicated. Corporations can often reduce average tax rates by taking advantage of special provisions (some might say "loopholes") in the

---

[9]Most corporate debt is not actively traded, so its market value cannot be observed directly. But you can usually value a nontraded debt security by looking to securities that *are* traded and that have approximately the same default risk and maturity. See Chapter 23.

For healthy firms the market value of debt is usually not too far from book value, so many managers and analysts use book value for D in the weighted-average cost of capital formula. However, be sure to use *market,* not book, values for E.

[10]We noted the difficulty of estimating expected rates of return on junk debt. This problem largely disappears for industry WACCs, provided that most or all of the companies in the industry sample are not relying on junk-debt financing.

[11]Levi and Welch argue against using industry-average betas to predict betas for individual companies in Y. Levi and I. Welch, "Best Practice for Cost-of-Capital Estimates," *Journal of Financial and Quantitative Analysis* 52 (April 2017), pp. 427–463.

tax code. But the WACC formula calls for the *marginal* tax rate—that is, the cash taxes paid as a percentage of each dollar of additional income generated by a capital-investment project.

The examples in this chapter use 21%, the current U.S. space corporate rate. In practice, U. S. corporations add three or four percentage points to cover state taxation. Thus, a corporation operating nationwide—and paying income taxes in most states—might use a 24% or 25% rate to calculate WACC.

What if the company can't use all its interest tax shields? So far, we have assumed that the company is consistently profitable and will pay taxes at the full statutory rate, which in the United States is now 21%. Thus, the company can still use a new project's depreciation tax shields even if a project endures a period of start-up losses. The project's depreciation expense shields some of the company's overall taxable income. Interest tax shields on debt supported by the new project can be captured in the same way.

Sometimes interest tax shields from new debt cannot be captured immediately because (1) the company is suffering losses overall or (2) its total interest payments exceed 30% of EBITDA.[12] Should the company change its WACC if it finds itself in one or both of these unfortunate states?

Probably not, if the losses or constraint are temporary. Tax losses and nondeductible interest can be carried forward and used to shield future income. (The tax rate in the WACC formula could be reduced to account for delay in using tax shields.) But if the wait to use interest tax shields from additional borrowing is long enough, it may be best to use the APV method, which we explain in the next section.

Adjusting WACC When Debt Ratios and Business Risks Differ

The WACC formula assumes that the project or business to be valued will be financed in the same debt–equity proportions as the company (or industry) as a whole. What if that is not true? For example, what if Sangria's perpetual crusher project supports only 20% debt, versus 40% for Sangria overall?

Moving from 40% to 20% debt may change all the inputs to the WACC formula.[13] Obviously, the financing weights change. But the cost of equity r_E is less because financial risk is reduced. The cost of debt may be lower, too.

Take a look at Figure 19.1, which plots Sangria's WACC and the costs of debt and equity as a function of its debt–equity ratio. The flat line is r, the opportunity cost of capital. Remember, this is the expected rate of return that investors would want from the company if it were all-equity-financed. The opportunity cost of capital depends only on business risk and is the natural reference point.

Suppose Sangria or the perpetual crusher project were all-equity-financed ($D/V = 0$). At that point, WACC and the opportunity cost of capital are identical. Start from that point in Figure 19.1. As the debt ratio increases, the cost of equity increases because of financial risk, but notice that WACC declines. The decline is *not* caused by use of "cheap" debt in place of "expensive" equity. It falls because of the tax shields on debt interest payments. If there were no corporate income taxes, the weighted-average cost of capital would be constant and equal to the opportunity cost of capital at all debt ratios. We showed this in Chapter 17.

Figure 19.1 shows the *shape* of the relationship between financing and WACC, but initially we have numbers only for Sangria's current 40% debt ratio. We want to recalculate WACC at a 20% ratio.

Here is the simplest way to do it. There are three steps.

---

[12]See the summary of the U.S. Tax Cuts and Jobs Act in Chapter 6. The limit on interest deductions changes to 30% of EBIT in 2022.
[13]Even the tax rate could change. For example, Sangria might have enough taxable income to cover interest payments at 20% debt but not at 40% debt. In that case, the effective marginal tax rate would be higher at 20% than 40% debt.

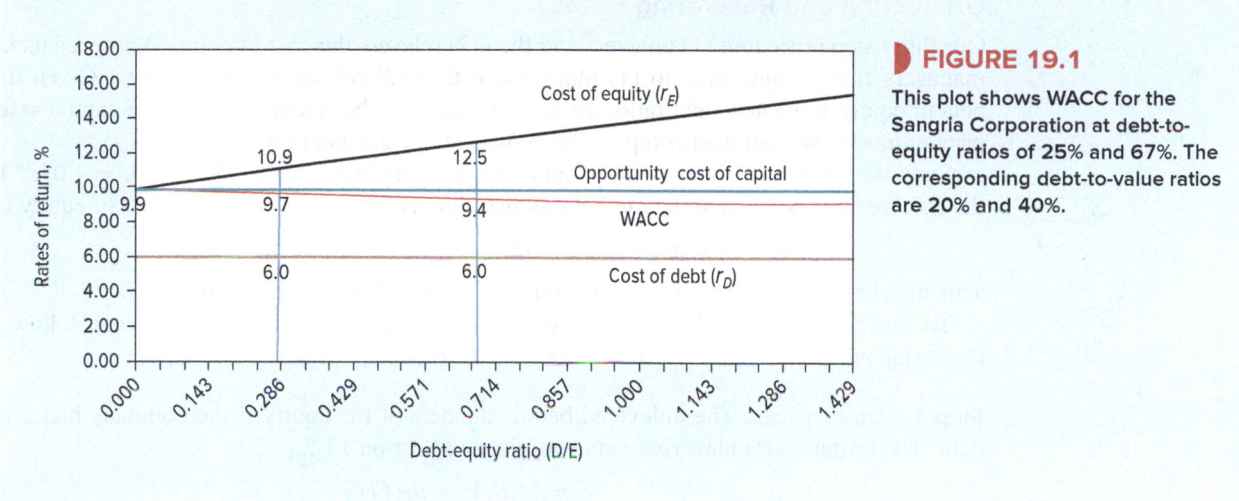

▶ **FIGURE 19.1**

This plot shows WACC for the Sangria Corporation at debt-to-equity ratios of 25% and 67%. The corresponding debt-to-value ratios are 20% and 40%.

Step 1 Calculate the opportunity cost of capital. In other words, calculate WACC and the cost of equity at zero debt. This step is called *unlevering* the WACC. The simplest unlevering formula is

$$\text{Opportunity cost of capital} = r = r_D D/V + r_E E/V$$

This formula comes directly from Modigliani and Miller's proposition 1 (see Section 17-1). If taxes are left out, the weighted-average cost of capital equals the opportunity cost of capital and is independent of leverage.

Step 2 Estimate the cost of debt, r_D, at the new debt ratio, and calculate the new cost of equity.

$$r_E = r + (r - r_D)D/E$$

This formula is Modigliani and Miller's proposition 2 (see Section 17-2). It calls for *D/E*, the ratio of debt to *equity*, not debt to value.

Step 3 Recalculate the weighted-average cost of capital at the new financing weights.

Let's do the numbers for Sangria at *D/V* = .20, or 20%.
Step 1. Sangria's current debt ratio is *D/V* = .4. So the opportunity cost of capital is:

$$r = .06(.4) + .125(.6) = .099, \text{ or } 9.9\%$$

Step 2. We will assume that the debt cost stays at 6% when the debt ratio is 20%. Then

$$r_E = .099 + (.099 - .06)(.25) = .109, \text{ or } 10.9\%$$

Note that the debt–*equity* ratio is .2/.8 = .25.
Step 3. Recalculate WACC.

$$\text{WACC} = .06(1 - .21)(.2) + .109(.8) = .097, \text{ or } 9.7\%$$

Figure 19.1 enters these numbers on the plot of WACC versus the debt–equity ratio.

BEYOND THE PAGE

WACC and changing debt ratios

mhhe.com/brealey13e

Unlevering and Relevering Betas

Our three-step procedure (1) unlevers and then (2) relevers the cost of equity. Some financial managers find it convenient to (1) unlever and then (2) relever the equity beta. Given the beta of equity at the new debt ratio, the cost of equity can be calculated from the capital asset pricing model. We can then compute the WACC at the new debt ratio.

Suppose Sangria's debt and equity betas in our example are $\beta_D = .135$ and $\beta_E = 1.07$.[14] If the risk-free rate is 5%, and the market risk premium is 7.0%, then Sangria's cost of equity is

$$r_E = r_f + (r_m - r_f)\beta_E = .05 + (.07)1.07 = .125, \text{ or } 12.5\%$$

This matches the cost of equity in our example at a 40/60 debt–equity ratio.

To find Sangria's weighted average cost of capital at a 20% debt ratio, we can follow a three-step procedure that pretty much matches the procedure that we used earlier.

Step 1   Unlever beta. The unlevered beta is the beta of the equity if the company had zero debt. The formula for unlevering beta was given in Section 17-2.

$$\beta_A = \beta_D(D/V) + \beta_E(E/V)$$

This equation says that the beta of a firm's assets (β_A) is equal to the beta of a portfolio of all of the firm's outstanding debt and equity securities. An investor who bought such a portfolio would own the assets free and clear and absorb only business risks. For Sangria,

$$\beta_A = \beta_D(D/V) + \beta_E(E/V) = .135(.4) + 1.07(.6) = .696$$

Step 2   Estimate the betas of the debt and equity at the new debt ratio. The formula for relevering beta closely resembles MM's proposition 2, except that betas are substituted for rates of return:

$$\beta_E = \beta_A + (\beta_A - \beta_D)D/E$$

Use this formula to recalculate β_E when D/E changes. If the beta of Sangria's debt stays at .135 when it moves to a debt-equity ratio of $.2/.8 = .25$, then

$$\beta_E = \beta_A + (\beta_A - \beta_D)D/E = .696 + (.696 - .135).25 = .836$$

Step 3   Recalculate the cost of equity and the WACC at the new financing weights:

$$r_E = r_f + (r_m - r_f)\beta_E = .05 + .07(.836) = .109, \text{ or } 10.9\%$$

$$\text{WACC} = .06(1 - .21)(.2) + .8(.109) = .097, \text{ or } 9.7\%$$

This corresponds to the figure that we calculated above and plotted in Figure 19.1.

The Importance of Rebalancing

The formulas for WACC and for unlevering and relevering expected returns are simple, but we must be careful to remember the underlying assumptions. The most important point is *rebalancing*.

Calculating WACC for a company at its existing capital structure requires that the capital structure *won't* change; in other words, the company must rebalance its capital structure to maintain the same market-value debt ratio for the relevant future. Take Sangria Corporation as an example. It starts with a debt-to-value ratio of 40% and a market value of $1,250 million. Suppose that Sangria's products do unexpectedly well in the marketplace and that market value increases to $1,500 million. Rebalancing means that it will then increase debt to $.4 \times 1,500 = \$600$ million, thus regaining a 40% ratio. The proceeds of the additional borrowing could be used to finance other investments or it could be paid out to the stockholders. If market value instead falls, Sangria would have to pay down debt proportionally.

---

[14]Debt betas are generally small, and many managers simplify and assume $\beta_D = 0$. Junk-debt betas can be well above zero, however.

Of course, real companies do not rebalance capital structure in such a mechanical and compulsive way. For practical purposes, it's sufficient to assume gradual but steady adjustment toward a long-run target.[15] But if the firm plans significant changes in capital structure (for example, if it plans to pay off its debt), the WACC formula won't work. In such cases, you should turn to the APV method, which we describe in the next section.

Our three-step procedure for recalculating WACC with a different debt ratio makes a similar rebalancing assumption.[16] Whatever the starting debt ratio, the firm is assumed to rebalance to maintain that ratio in the future.[17]

The Modigliani–Miller Formula, Plus Some Final Advice

What if the firm does not rebalance to keep its debt ratio constant? In this case, the only general approach is adjusted present value, which we cover in the next section. But sometimes financial managers turn to other discount-rate formulas, including one derived by Modigliani and Miller (MM). MM considered a company or project generating a level, perpetual stream of cash flows financed with fixed, perpetual debt. There is then a simple relationship between the after-tax discount rate (r_{MM}) and the opportunity cost of capital (r):[18]

$$r_{MM} = r(1 - T_c D/V)$$

---

[15]Here's another way to interpret the WACC formula's assumption of a constant debt ratio. Assume that the debt *capacity* of a project is a constant fraction of the project's value. ("Capacity" does not mean the maximum amount that could be borrowed against the project, but the amount that managers would optimally choose to borrow.) Discounting at WACC gives the project credit for interest tax shields on the project's debt capacity, even if the firm does not rebalance its capital structure and ends up borrowing more or less than the total capacity of all its projects.

[16]Similar, but not identical. The basic WACC formula is correct whether rebalancing occurs at the end of each period or continuously. The unlevering and relevering formulas used in steps 1 and 2 of our three-step procedure are exact only if rebalancing is continuous so that the debt ratio stays constant day-to-day and week-to-week. However, the errors introduced from annual rebalancing are very small and can be ignored for practical purposes.

[17]Here's why the formulas work with continuous rebalancing. Think of a market-value balance sheet with assets and interest tax shields on the left and debt and equity on the right, with $D + E = PV(\text{assets}) + PV(\text{tax shield})$. The total risk (beta) of the firm's debt and equity equals the blended risk of PV(assets) and PV(tax shield):

$$\beta_D \frac{D}{V} + \beta_E \frac{E}{V} = \alpha \beta_A + (1 - \alpha)\beta_{\text{tax shield}} \qquad (1)$$

where α is the proportion of the total firm value from its assets and $1 - \alpha$ is the proportion from interest tax shields. If the firm readjusts its capital structure to keep D/V constant, then the beta of the tax shield must be the same as the beta of the assets. With rebalancing, an $x\%$ change in firm value V changes debt D by $x\%$. So the interest tax shield $T_c r_D D$ will change by $x\%$ as well. Thus the risk of the tax shield must be the same as the risk of the firm as a whole:

$$\beta_{\text{tax shield}} = \beta_A = \beta_D \frac{D}{V} + \beta_E \frac{E}{V} \qquad (2)$$

This is our unlevering formula expressed in terms of beta. Since expected returns depend on beta:

$$r_A = r_D \frac{D}{V} + r_E \frac{E}{V} \qquad (3)$$

Rearrange formulas (2) and (3) to get the relevering formulas for β_E and r_E. (Notice that the tax rate T_c has dropped out.)

$$\beta_E = \beta_A + (\beta_A - \beta_D)D/E$$
$$r_E = r_A + (r_A - r_D)D/E$$

All this assumes continuous rebalancing. Suppose instead that the firm rebalances once a year, so that the next year's interest tax shield, which depends on this year's debt, is known. Then you can use a formula developed by Miles and Ezzell:

$$r_{\text{Miles-Ezzell}} = r_A - (D/V)r_D T_t \left(\frac{1 + r_A}{1 + r_D}\right)$$

See J. Miles and J. Ezzell, "The Weighted Average Cost of Capital, Perfect Capital Markets, and Project Life: A Clarification," *Journal of Financial and Quantitative Analysis* 15 (September 1980), pp. 719–730.

[18]The formula first appeared in F. Modigliani and M. H. Miller, "Corporate Income Taxes and the Cost of Capital: A Correction," *American Economic Review* 53 (June 1963), pp. 433–443. It is explained more fully in M. H. Miller and F. Modigliani: "Some Estimates of the Cost of Capital to the Electric Utility Industry, 1954–1957," *American Economic Review* 56 (June 1966), pp. 333–391. Given perpetual fixed debt,

$$V = \frac{C}{r} + T_c D$$

$$V = \frac{C}{r(1 - T_c D/V)} = \frac{C}{r_{MM}}$$

Here it's easy to unlever: just set the debt-capacity parameter (D/V) equal to zero.[19]

MM's formula is still used in practice, but it is exact only in the special case where there is a level, perpetual stream of cash flows and fixed, perpetual debt. However, the formula is not a bad approximation for projects that are not perpetual as long as debt is issued in a fixed amount.[20]

So which team do you want to play with, the fixed-debt team or the rebalancers? If you join the fixed-debt team you will be outnumbered. Most financial managers use the plain, after-tax WACC, which assumes constant market-value debt ratios and therefore assumes rebalancing. That makes sense, because the debt *capacity* of a firm or project must depend on its future value, which will fluctuate.

At the same time, we must admit that the typical financial manager doesn't care much if his or her firm's debt ratio drifts up or down within a reasonable range of moderate financial lever-age. The typical financial manager acts as if a plot of WACC against the debt ratio is "flat" (constant) over this range. This too makes sense, if we just remember that interest tax shields are the *only* reason why the after-tax WACC declines in Figures 17.4 and 19.1. The WACC formula doesn't explicitly capture costs of financial distress or any of the other non-tax complications discussed in Chapter 18.[21] All these complications may roughly cancel the value added by inter-est tax shields (within a range of moderate leverage). If so, the financial manager is wise to focus on the firm's operating and investment decisions, rather than on fine-tuning its debt ratio.

19-4 Adjusted Present Value

We now turn to an alternative way to take account of financing decisions. This is to calculate an **adjusted present value** or **APV.** The idea behind APV is to divide and conquer. Instead of capturing the effects of financing by adjusting the discount rate, APV makes a series of present value calculations. The first calculation establishes a base-case value for the project or firm: its value as a separate, all-equity-financed venture. The discount rate for the base-case value is just the opportunity cost of capital. Once the base-case value is set, then each financing side effect is traced out, and the present value of its cost or benefit to the firm is calculated. Finally, all the present values are added together to estimate the project's total contribution to the value of the firm:

$$APV = \text{base-case NPV} + \text{sum of PVs of financing side effects}[22]$$

---

[19]In this case the relevering formula for the cost of equity is

$$r_E = r_A + (1 - T_c)(r_A - r_D)D/E$$

The unlevering and relevering formulas for betas are

$$\beta_A = \frac{\beta_D(1 - T_c)D/E + \beta_E}{1 + (1 - T_c)D/E}$$

and

$$\beta_E = \beta_A + (1 - T_c)(\beta_A - \beta_D)D/E$$

See R. Hamada, "The Effect of a Firm's Capital Structure on the Systematic Risk of Common Stocks," *Journal of Finance* 27 (May 1972), pp. 435–452.

[20]See S. C. Myers, "Interactions of Corporate Financing and Investment Decisions—Implications for Capital Budgeting," *Journal of Finance* 29 (March 1974), pp. 1–25.

[21]Costs of financial distress can show up as rapidly increasing costs of debt and equity, especially at high debt ratios. The costs of financial distress could "flatten out" the WACC curve in Figures 17.4 and 19.1 and finally increase WACC as leverage climbs. Thus some practitioners calculate an industry WACC and take it as constant, at least within the range of debt ratios observed for healthy companies in the industry.

Personal taxes could also generate a flatter curve for after-tax WACC as a function of leverage. See Section 18-2.

[22]The adjusted-present-value rule was developed in S. C. Myers, "Interactions of Corporate Financing and Investment Decisions—Implications for Capital Budgeting," *Journal of Finance* 29 (March 1974), pp. 1–25.

The most important financing side effect is the interest tax shield on the debt supported by the project (a plus). Other possible side effects are the issue costs of securities (a minus) or financing packages subsidized by a supplier or government (a plus).

APV gives the financial manager an explicit view of the factors that are adding or subtracting value. APV can prompt the manager to ask the right follow-up questions. For example, suppose that base-case NPV is positive but less than the costs of issuing shares to finance the project. That should prompt the manager to look around to see if the project can be rescued by an alternative financing plan.

APV for the Perpetual Crusher

APV is easiest to understand in simple numerical examples. Let's apply it to Sangria's perpetual crusher project. We start by showing that APV is equivalent to discounting at WACC if we make the same assumptions about debt policy.

We used Sangria's WACC (9.4%) as the discount rate for the crusher's projected cash flows. The WACC calculation assumed that debt will be maintained at a constant 40% of the future value of the project or firm. In this case, the risk of interest tax shields is the same as the risk of the project.[23] Therefore, we can discount the tax shields at the opportunity cost of capital (r). We calculated the opportunity cost of capital in the last section by unlevering Sangria's WACC to obtain $r = 9.9\%$.

The first step is to calculate base-case NPV. This is the project's NPV with all-equity financing. To find it, we discount after-tax project cash flows of $1.175 million at the opportunity cost of capital of 9.9% and subtract the $12.5 million outlay. The cash flows are perpetual, so

$$\text{Base-case NPV} = -12.5 + \frac{1.175}{.099} = -\$0.63 \text{ million}$$

Thus, the project would not be worthwhile with all-equity financing. But it actually supports debt of $5 million. At a 6% borrowing rate ($r_D = .06$) and a 21% tax rate ($T_c = .21$), annual tax shields are $.21 \times .06 \times 5 = .063$, or $63,000.

What are those tax shields worth? If the firm is constantly rebalancing its debt, we discount at $r = 9.9\%$:

$$\text{PV(interest tax shields, debt rebalanced)} = \frac{63,000}{.099} = \$0.63 \text{ million}$$

APV is the sum of base-case value and PV(interest tax shields):

$$\text{APV} = -0.63 \text{ million} + 0.63 \text{ million} = 0$$

This is exactly the same as we obtained by one-step discounting with WACC. The perpetual crusher is a break-even project by either valuation method.[24]

But with APV, we don't have to hold debt at a constant proportion of value. Suppose Sangria plans to keep project debt fixed at $5 million. In this case, we assume the risk of the tax shields is the same as the risk of the debt and we discount at the 6% rate on debt:

$$\text{PV(tax shields, debt fixed)} = \frac{63,000}{.06} = \$1.05 \text{ million}$$

$$\text{APV} = -0.63 + 1.05 = \$.42 \text{ million}$$

---

[23]That is, $\beta_A = \beta_{\text{tax shields}}$. See footnote 17.
[24]Calculating the present value of the tax shields is straightforward when the project is a perpetuity. When it is not, the expected value of the project changes as time passes and so does the expected tax shield. With a finite project and debt that is a constant proportion of project value, we would need to calculate the expected project value at each future date before calculating the present value of the tax shields. Therefore, whenever the debt ratio is constant, managers use WACC to account for the interest tax shield, and they save APV for times when debt is repaid on a fixed schedule.

Now the project is more attractive. With fixed debt, the interest tax shields are safe and therefore worth more. (Whether the fixed debt is safer for Sangria is another matter. If the perpetual crusher project fails, the $5 million of fixed debt may end up as a burden on Sangria's other assets.)

Other Financing Side Effects

Suppose Sangria has to finance the perpetual crusher by issuing debt and equity. It issues $7.5 million of equity with issue costs of 7% ($.53 million) and $5 million of debt with issue costs of 2% ($.10 million). Assume the debt is fixed once issued, so that interest tax shields are worth $1.05 million. Now we can recalculate APV, taking care to subtract the issue costs:

$$APV = -0.63 + 1.05 - .53 - .10 = -.21 \text{ million, or } -\$210,000$$

The issue costs would result in a negative APV.

Sometimes there are favorable financing side effects that have nothing to do with taxes. For example, suppose that a potential manufacturer of crusher machinery offers to sweeten the deal by leasing it to Sangria on favorable terms. Then to calculate APV you would need to add in the NPV of the lease. Or suppose that a local government offers to lend Sangria $5 million at a very low interest rate if the crusher is built and operated locally. The NPV of the subsidized loan could be added in to APV. (We cover leases in Chapter 25 and subsidized loans in the Appendix to this chapter.)

APV for Entire Businesses

APV can also be used to value entire businesses. Let's take another look at the valuation of Rio. In Table 19.1, we assumed a constant 40% debt ratio and discounted free cash flow at Sangria's WACC. Table 19.2 runs the same analysis, but with a fixed debt schedule.

We'll suppose that Sangria has decided to make an offer for Rio. If successful, it plans to finance the purchase with $62 million of debt. It intends to pay down the debt to $53 million in year 6. Recall Rio's horizon value of $132.7 million, which is calculated in Table 19.1 and shown again in Table 19.2. The debt ratio at the horizon is therefore projected at 53/132.7 = .40, or 40%. Thus, Sangria plans to take Rio back to a normal 40% debt ratio at the horizon.[25] But Rio will be carrying a heavier debt load before the horizon. For example, the $62 million of initial debt is about 56% of company value as calculated in Table 19.1.

Let's see how Rio's APV is affected by this more aggressive borrowing schedule. Table 19.2 shows projections of free cash flows from Table 19.1.[26] Now we need Rio's base-case value. This is its value with all-equity financing, so we discount these flows at the opportunity cost of capital (9.9%), not at WACC. The resulting base-case value for Rio is $28.5 + 75.3 = 103.8 million. Table 19.2 also projects debt levels, interest payments, and interest tax shields. If the debt levels are taken as fixed, then the tax shields should be discounted back at the 6% borrowing rate. The resulting PV of interest tax shields is $3.6 million. Thus,

$$APV = \text{base-case NPV} + PV(\text{interest tax shields})$$
$$= \$103.8 + 3.6 = \$107.5 \text{ million}$$

---

[25]Therefore, we still calculate the horizon value in year 6 by discounting subsequent free cash flows at WACC. The horizon value in year 6 is discounted back to year 0 at the opportunity cost of capital, however.

[26]Many of the assumptions and calculations in Table 19.1 have been hidden in Table 19.2. The hidden rows can be recalled in the Beyond the Page spreadsheets for Tables 19.1 and 19.2.

	Latest Year	Forecast						
	0	**1**	**2**	**3**	**4**	**5**	**6**	**7**
Free cash flow	4.9	5.3	5.2	5.5	8.0	8.3	8.2	8.5
PV free cash flow, years 1–6	28.5							
PV horizon value	75.3			(Horizon value in year 6)			132.7	
Base-case PV of company	103.8							
Debt	62.0	60.0	60.0	58.0	56.0	54.0	53.0	
Interest		3.72	3.60	3.60	3.48	3.36	3.24	
Interest tax shield		0.78	0.76	0.76	0.73	0.71	0.68	
PV interest tax shields	3.6							
APV	107.5							
Tax rate, %	21.0							
Opportunity cost of capital, %	9.9							
WACC, % (to discount horizon value to year 6)	9.4							
Long-term growth forecast, %	3.0							
Interest rate, % (years 1–6)	6.0							
After-tax debt service		4.94	2.84	4.84	4.75	4.65	3.56	

❯**TABLE 19.2**   **APV valuation of Rio Corporation ($ millions)**

an increase of $1.0 million from NPV in Table 19.1. The increase can be traced to the higher early debt levels and to the assumption that the debt levels and interest tax shields are fixed and safe.[27]

Now a difference of $1.0 million is not a big deal, considering all the lurking risks and pitfalls in forecasting Rio's free cash flows. But you can see the advantage of the flexibility that APV provides. The APV spreadsheet allows you to explore the implications of different financing strategies without locking into a fixed debt ratio or having to calculate a new WACC for every scenario.

APV is particularly useful when the debt for a project or business is tied to book value or has to be repaid on a fixed schedule. For example, Kaplan and Ruback used APV to analyze the prices paid for a sample of leveraged buyouts (LBOs). LBOs are takeovers, typically of mature companies, heavily debt-financed. However, the new debt is not intended to be permanent. LBO business plans call for generating extra cash by selling assets, shaving costs, and improving profit margins. The extra cash is used to pay down the LBO debt. Therefore, you can't use WACC as a discount rate to evaluate an LBO because its debt ratio will not be constant.

---

[27]But will Rio really *support* debt at the levels shown in Table 19.2? If not, then the debt must be partly supported by Sangria's other assets, and only part of the $3.6 million in PV(interest tax shields) can be attributed to Rio itself.

APV works fine for LBOs. The company is first evaluated as if it were all-equity-financed. That means that cash flows are projected after tax, but without any interest tax shields generated by the LBO's debt. The tax shields are then valued separately and added to the all-equity value. Any other financing side effects are added also. The result is an APV valuation for the company.[28] Kaplan and Ruback found that APV did a pretty good job explaining prices paid in these hotly contested takeovers, considering that not all the information available to bidders had percolated into the public domain. Kaplan and Ruback were restricted to publicly available data.

APV and Limits on Interest Deductions

The United States now limits the amount of interest that can be deducted for tax to 30% of each year's EBITDA (or 30% of EBIT starting in 2022). Germany has a similar restriction, and the European Commission has proposed an EU-wide limit.

Most companies will not be caught by these rules. But what about the few that are caught? How should a financial manager take limits on interest-expense deductions into account?

Suppose the 30% constraint is and will be binding. Assume the firm is profitable and paying taxes. Then the future interest tax shields generated by a new investment project are proportional to its future EBITDA. The financial manager should forecast EBITDA and the associated tax shields and discount at a rate depending on the risk of EBITDA.[29] The APV formula is the same as before:

$$\text{APV} = \text{base-case NPV} + \text{PV(interest tax shields)}$$

but PV(interest tax shields) now depends on the *project's* forecasted EBITDA.

Those projects that generate plenty of EBITDA will be especially valuable to tax-paying firms that are subject to the 30% constraint. The EBITDA of the project can relax the constraint for the firm as a whole, thus unlocking interest tax shields on the firm's existing debt.

The APV of an entire business or company subject to the 30% constraint should also include the PV of interest tax shields generated by its expected future EBITDA. If the 30% limit on interest deductions is temporary—in one or two low-profit years, for example—then the unused tax shields are not lost but can be carried forward indefinitely and may therefore be merely delayed. The financial manager could assign the tax shields to future years, discount to PV and include them in APV.

APV for International Investments

APV is most useful when financing side effects are numerous and important. This is frequently the case for large international investments, which may have custom-tailored *project financing* and special contracts with suppliers, customers, and governments. Here are a few examples of financing side effects resulting from the financing of a project.

We explain project finance in Chapter 24. It typically means very high debt ratios to start, with most or all of a project's early cash flows committed to debt service. Equity investors have to wait. Since the debt ratio will not be constant, you have to turn to APV.

Project financing may include debt available at favorable interest rates. Most governments subsidize exports by making special financing packages available, and manufacturers of industrial equipment may stand ready to lend money to help close a sale. Suppose, for example, that your project requires construction of an on-site electricity generating plant. You solicit bids from suppliers in various countries. Don't be surprised if the competing suppliers

---

[28]Kaplan and Ruback actually used "compressed" APV, in which all cash flows, including interest tax shields, are discounted at the opportunity cost of capital. S. N. Kaplan and R. S. Ruback, "The Valuation of Cash Flow Forecasts: An Empirical Analysis," *Journal of Finance* 50 (September 1995), pp. 1059–1093.

[29]In most cases the risk of EBITDA will be similar to the risk of the project's overall cash flows. If so the interest tax shields generated by the project's EBITDA can be discounted at the same opportunity cost of capital used to calculate base-case NPV.

sweeten their bids with offers of low interest rate project loans or if they offer to lease the plant on favorable terms. You should then calculate the NPVs of these loans or leases and include them in your project analysis.

Sometimes international projects are supported by contracts with suppliers or customers. Suppose a manufacturer wants to line up a reliable supply of a crucial raw material—powdered magnoosium, say. The manufacturer could subsidize a new magnoosium smelter by agreeing to buy 75% of production and guaranteeing a minimum purchase price. The guarantee is clearly a valuable addition to the smelter's APV: If the world price of powdered magnoosium falls below the minimum, the project doesn't suffer. You would calculate the value of this guarantee (by the methods explained in Chapters 20 to 22) and add it to APV.

Sometimes local governments impose costs or restrictions on investment or disinvestment. For example, Chile, in an attempt to slow down a flood of short-term capital inflows in the 1990s, required investors to "park" part of their incoming money in non-interest-bearing accounts for a period of two years. An investor in Chile during this period could have calculated the cost of this requirement and subtracted it from APV.[30]

19-5   Your Questions Answered

Question: All these cost of capital formulas—which ones do financial managers actually use?

Answer: The after-tax weighted-average cost of capital, most of the time. WACC is estimated for the company, or sometimes for an industry. We recommend industry WACCs when data are available for firms with similar assets, operations, business risks, and growth opportunities.

Of course, conglomerate companies, with divisions operating in two or more unrelated industries, should not use a single company or industry WACC. Such firms should try to estimate a different industry WACC for each operating division.

Question: But WACC is the correct discount rate only for "average" projects. What if the project's financing differs from the company's or industry's?

Answer: Remember, investment projects are usually not separately financed. Even when they are, you should focus on the project's contribution to the firm's overall debt capacity, not on its immediate financing. (Suppose it's convenient to raise all the money for a particular project with a bank loan. That doesn't mean the project itself supports 100% debt financing. The company is borrowing against its existing assets as well as the project.)

But if the project's debt capacity is materially different from the company's existing assets, or if the company's overall debt policy changes, WACC should be adjusted. The adjustment can be done by the three-step procedure explained in Section 19-3.

Question: Could we do one more numerical example?

Answer: Sure. Suppose that WACC has been estimated as follows at a 30% debt ratio:

$$\text{WACC} = r_D(1 - T_c)\frac{D}{V} + r_E\frac{E}{V}$$

$$= .09(1 - .21)(.3) + .15(.7) = .126, \text{ or } 12.6\%$$

What is the correct discount rate at a 50% debt ratio?

Step 1. Calculate the opportunity cost of capital.

$$r = r_D D/V + r_E E/V$$

$$= .09(.3) + .15(.7) = .132, \text{ or } 13.2\%$$

---

[30]Such capital controls have been described as financial roach motels: Money can get in, but it can't get out.

Step 2. Calculate the new costs of debt and equity. The cost of debt will be higher at 50% debt than 30%. Say it is $r_D = .095$. The new cost of equity is

$$r_E = r + (r - r_D)D/E$$
$$= .132 + (.132 - .095)50/50$$
$$= .169, \text{ or } 16.9\%$$

Step 3. Recalculate WACC.

$$\text{WACC} = r_D(1 - T_c)D/V + r_E E/V$$
$$= .095(1 - .21)(.5) + .169(.5) = .122, \text{ or } 12.2\%$$

Question: How do I use the capital asset pricing model to calculate the after-tax weighted-average cost of capital?

Answer: First plug the equity beta into the capital asset pricing formula to calculate r_E, the expected return to equity. Then use this figure, along with the after-tax cost of debt and the debt-to-value and equity-to-value ratios, in the WACC formula.

Of course, the CAPM is not the only way to estimate the cost of equity. For example, you might be able to use the dividend discount model (see Section 4-3).

Question: But suppose I do use the CAPM? What if I have to recalculate the equity beta for a different debt ratio?

Answer: The formula for the equity beta is

$$\beta_E = \beta_A + (\beta_A - \beta_D)D/E$$

where β_E is the equity beta, β_A is the asset beta, and β_D is the beta of the company's debt. The asset beta is a weighted average of the debt and equity betas:

$$\beta_A = \beta_D(D/V) + \beta_E(E/V)$$

Suppose you needed the opportunity cost of capital r. You could calculate β_A and then r from the capital asset pricing model.

Question: I think I understand how to adjust for differences in debt capacity or debt policy. How about differences in business risk?

Answer: If business risk is different, then r, the opportunity cost of capital, is different.

Figuring out the right r for an unusually safe or risky project is never easy. Sometimes the financial manager can use estimates of risk and expected return for companies similar to the project. Suppose, for example, that a traditional pharmaceutical company is considering a major commitment to biotech research. The financial manager could pick a sample of biotech companies, estimate their average beta and cost of capital, and use these estimates as benchmarks for the biotech investment.

But in many cases, it's difficult to find a good sample of matching companies for an unusually safe or risky project. Then the financial manager has to adjust the opportunity cost of capital by judgment. Section 9-3 may be helpful in such cases.

Question: When do I need adjusted present value (APV)?

Answer: The WACC formula picks up only one financing side effect: the value of interest tax shields on debt supported by a project. If there are other side effects—subsidized financing tied to a project, for example—you should use APV.

You can also use APV to break out the value of interest tax shields:

$$\text{APV} = \text{base-case NPV} + \text{PV(tax shield)}$$

Suppose, for example, that you are analyzing a company just after a leveraged buyout. The company has a very high initial debt level but plans to pay down the debt as rapidly as possible. APV could be used to obtain an accurate valuation.

Question: When should personal taxes be incorporated into the analysis?

Answer: Always use T_c, the marginal corporate tax rate, when calculating WACC as a weighted average of the costs of debt and equity. The discount rate is adjusted *only* for corporate taxes.

In principle, APV can be adjusted for personal taxes by replacing the marginal corporate rate T_c with an effective tax rate that combines corporate and personal taxes and reflects the net tax advantage per dollar of interest paid by the firm. We provided back-of-the-envelope calculations of this advantage in Section 18-2. The effective tax rate is almost surely less than T_c, but it is very difficult to pin down the numerical difference. Therefore, in practice T_c is almost always used as an approximation.

Question: Are taxes really that important? Do financial managers really fine-tune the debt ratio to minimize WACC?

Answer: As we saw in Chapter 18, financing decisions reflect many forces beyond taxes, including costs of financial distress, differences in information, and incentives for managers. There may not be a sharply defined optimal capital structure. Therefore most financial managers don't fine-tune their companies' debt ratios, and they don't rebalance financing to keep debt ratios strictly constant. In effect, they assume that a plot of WACC for different debt ratios is "flat" over a reasonable range of moderate leverage.

In this chapter, we considered how financing can be incorporated into the valuation of projects and ongoing businesses. There are two ways to take financing into account. The first is to calculate NPV by discounting at an adjusted discount rate, usually the after-tax weighted-average cost of capital (WACC). The second approach discounts at the opportunity cost of capital and then adds or subtracts the present values of financing side effects. The second approach is called adjusted present value, or APV.

The formula for the after-tax WACC is

$$\text{WACC} = r_D(1 - T_c)\frac{D}{V} + r_E\frac{E}{V}$$

where r_D and r_E are the expected rates of return demanded by investors in the firm's debt and equity securities, D and E are the current *market values* of debt and equity, and V is the total market value of the firm ($V = D + E$). Of course, the WACC formula expands if there are other sources of financing, for example, preferred stock.

Strictly speaking, discounting at WACC works only for projects that are carbon copies of the existing firm—projects with the same business risk that will be financed to maintain the firm's current ratio of debt to market value. But firms can use WACC as a benchmark rate to be adjusted for differences in business risk or financing. We gave a three-step procedure for adjusting WACC for different debt ratios.

Discounting cash flows at the WACC assumes that debt is rebalanced to keep a constant ratio of debt to market value. The amount of debt supported by a project is assumed to rise or fall with the project's after-the-fact success or failure. The WACC formula also assumes that financing matters *only* because of interest tax shields. When this or other assumptions are violated, only APV will give an absolutely correct answer.

APV is, in concept at least, simple. First calculate the base-case NPV of the project or business on the assumption that financing *doesn't* matter. (The discount rate is not WACC, but the opportunity cost of capital.) Then calculate the present values of any relevant financing side effects and add or subtract from base-case value. A capital investment project is worthwhile if

$$\text{APV} = \text{base-case NPV} + \text{PV(financing side effects)}$$

is positive. Common financing side effects include interest tax shields, issue costs, and special financing packages offered by suppliers or governments.

For firms or going-concern businesses, value depends on free cash flow. Free cash flow is the amount of cash that can be paid out to all investors, debt as well as equity, after deducting cash needed for new investment or increases in working capital. Free cash flow does not include the interest tax shields. The WACC formula accounts for interest tax shields by using the after-tax cost of debt. APV adds PV(interest tax shields) to base-case value.

Businesses are usually valued in two steps. First, free cash flow is forecasted out to a valuation horizon assuming all-equity financing and is then discounted back to present value using WACC. Then a horizon value is calculated and also discounted back. Be particularly careful to avoid unrealistically high horizon values. By the time the horizon arrives, competitors will have had several years to catch up. Also, when you are done valuing the business, don't forget to subtract its debt to get the value of the firm's equity.

All of this chapter's examples reflect assumptions about the amount of debt supported by a project or business. Remember not to confuse "supported by" with the immediate source of funds for investment. For example, a firm might, as a matter of convenience, borrow $1 million for a $1 million research program. But the research is unlikely to contribute $1 million in debt capacity; a large part of the $1 million new debt would be supported by the firm's other assets.

Also remember that *debt capacity* is not meant to imply an absolute limit on how much the firm *can* borrow. The phrase refers to how much it *chooses* to borrow against a project or ongoing business.

FURTHER READING

The Harvard Business Review *has published a popular account of APV:*

T. A. Luehrman, "Using APV: A Better Tool for Valuing Operations," *Harvard Business Review* 75 (May–June 1997), pp. 145–154.

There have been dozens of articles on the weighted-average cost of capital and other issues discussed in this chapter. Here are three:

J. Miles and R. Ezzell, "The Weighted Average Cost of Capital, Perfect Capital Markets, and Project Life: A Clarification," *Journal of Financial and Quantitative Analysis* 15 (September 1980), pp. 719–730.

R. A. Taggart Jr., "Consistent Valuation and Cost of Capital Expressions with Corporate and Personal Taxes," *Financial Management* 20 (Autumn 1991), pp. 8–20.

R. S. Ruback, "Capital Cash Flows: A Simple Approach to Valuing Risky Cash Flows," *Financial Management* 31 (Summer 2002), pp. 85–103.

The valuation rule for safe, nominal cash flows is developed in:

R. S. Ruback, "Calculating the Market Value of Riskless Cash Flows," *Journal of Financial Economics* 15 (March 1986), pp. 323–339.

PROBLEM SETS

 **Select problems are available in McGraw-Hill's *Connect*. Please see the preface for more information.**

1. **WACC** True or false? Use of the WACC formula assumes

   a. A project supports a fixed amount of debt over the project's economic life.

   b. The *ratio* of the debt supported by a project to project value is constant over the project's economic life.

   c. The firm rebalances debt each period, keeping the debt-to-value ratio constant.

2. **WACC** The WACC formula seems to imply that debt is "cheaper" than equity—that is, that a firm with more debt could use a lower discount rate. Does this make sense? Explain briefly.

3. **WACC*** Calculate the weighted-average cost of capital (WACC) for Federated Junkyards of America, using the following information:

   - Debt: $75,000,000 book value outstanding. The debt is trading at 90% of book value. The yield to maturity is 9%.

- Equity: 2,500,000 shares selling at $42 per share. Assume the expected rate of return on Federated's stock is 18%.
- Taxes: Federated's marginal tax rate is $T_c = .21$.

4. **WACC*** Suppose Federated Junkyards decides to move to a more conservative debt policy. A year later, its debt ratio is down to 15% ($D/V = .15$). The interest rate has dropped to 8.6%. Recalculate Federated's WACC under these new assumptions. The company's business risk, opportunity cost of capital, and tax rate have not changed. Use the three-step procedure explained in Section 19-3.

5. **WACC** Whispering Pines Inc. is all-equity-financed. The expected rate of return on the company's shares is 12%.
   a. What is the opportunity cost of capital for an average-risk Whispering Pines investment?
   b. Suppose the company issues debt, repurchases shares, and moves to a 30% debt-to-value ratio ($D/V = .30$). What will be the company's weighted-average cost of capital at the new capital structure? The borrowing rate is 7.5% and the tax rate is 21%.

6. **WACC** Table 19.3 shows a *book* balance sheet for the Wishing Well Motel chain. The company's long-term debt is secured by its real estate assets, but it also uses short-term bank loans as a permanent source of financing. It pays 10% interest on the bank debt and 9% interest on the secured debt. Wishing Well has 10 million shares of stock outstanding, trading at $90 per share. The expected return on Wishing Well's common stock is 18%.

   Calculate Wishing Well's WACC. Assume that the book and market values of Wishing Well's debt are the same. The marginal tax rate is 21%.

Cash and marketable securities	100	Bank loan	280
Accounts receivable	200	Accounts payable	120
Inventory	50	Current liabilities	400
Current assets	350		
Real estate	2,100	Long-term debt	1,800
Other assets	150	Equity	400
Total	2,600	Total	2,600

❯**TABLE 19.3**   Book balance sheet for Wishing Well Inc. (figures in $ millions)

7. **WACC** Table 19.4 shows a simplified balance sheet for the Dutch manufacturer Rensselaer Felt. Calculate this company's weighted-average cost of capital. The debt has just been refinanced at an interest rate of 6% (short term) and 8% (long term). The expected rate of return on the company's shares is 15%. There are 7.46 million shares outstanding, and the shares are trading at €46. The tax rate is 25%.

Cash and marketable securities	1,500	Short-term debt	75,600
Accounts receivable	120,000	Accounts payable	62,000
Inventory	125,000	Current liabilities	137,600
Current assets	246,500		
Property, plant, and equipment	212,000	Long-term debt	208,600
Deferred taxes	45,000		
Other assets	89,000	Shareholders' equity	246,300
Total	592,500	Total	592,500

❯**TABLE 19.4**   Simplified book balance sheet for Rensselaer Felt (figures in € thousands)

8. **WACC** See Problem 7. How will Rensselaer's WACC and cost of equity change if it issues €50 million in new equity and uses the proceeds to retire long-term debt? Assume the company's borrowing rates are unchanged. Use the three-step procedure from Section 19-3.

9. **WACC** Nevada Hydro is 40% debt-financed and has a weighted-average cost of capital of 10.2%:

$$\text{WACC} = (1 - Tc)rD\ D/V + rE\ E/V = (1 - .21)(.085)(.40) + .125(.60) = .102$$

Goldensacks Company is advising Nevada Hydro to issue $75 million of preferred stock at a dividend yield of 9%. The proceeds would be used to repurchase and retire common stock. The preferred issue would account for 10% of the pre-issue market value of the firm.

Goldensacks argues that these transactions would reduce Nevada Hydro's WACC to 9.84%:

$$\text{WACC} = (1 - .21)(.085)(.40) + .09(.10) + .125(.50)$$
$$= .0984, \text{ or } 9.84\%$$

Do you agree with this calculation? Explain.

10. **Forecasting cash flow** Suppose Wishing Well (see Problem 6) is evaluating a new motel and resort on a romantic site in Madison County, Wisconsin. Explain how you would forecast the after-tax cash flows for this project. (*Hints:* How would you treat taxes? Interest expense? Changes in working capital?)

11. **Flow-to-equity valuation** What is meant by the flow-to-equity valuation method? What discount rate is used in this method? What assumptions are necessary for this method to give an accurate valuation?

12. **APV** True or false? The APV method

   a. Starts with a base-case value for the project.

   b. Calculates the base-case value by discounting project cash flows, forecasted assuming all-equity financing, at the WACC for the project.

   c. Is especially useful when debt is to be paid down on a fixed schedule.

13. **APV*** A project costs $1 million and has a base-case NPV of exactly zero (NPV = 0). What is the project's APV in the following cases?

   a. If the firm invests, it has to raise $500,000 by a stock issue. Issue costs are 15% of *net* proceeds.

   b. If the firm invests, there are no issue costs, but its debt capacity increases by $500,000. The present value of interest tax shields on this debt is $76,000.

14. **APV** Consider a project lasting one year only. The initial outlay is $1,000, and the expected inflow is $1,200. The opportunity cost of capital is $r = .20$. The borrowing rate is $r_D = .10$, and the tax shield per dollar of interest is $T_c = .21$.

   a. What is the project's base-case NPV?

   b. What is its APV if the firm borrows 30% of the project's required investment?

15. **APV** To finance the Madison County project (see Problem 10), Wishing Well needs to arrange an additional $80 million of long-term debt and make a $20 million equity issue. Underwriting fees, spreads, and other costs of this financing will total $4 million. How would you take this into account in valuing the proposed investment?

16. **APV** Digital Organics (DO) has the opportunity to invest $1 million now ($t = 0$) and expects after-tax returns of $600,000 in $t = 1$ and $700,000 in $t = 2$. The project will last for two years only. The appropriate cost of capital is 12% with all-equity financing, the borrowing rate is 8%, and DO will borrow $300,000 against the project. This debt must be repaid in two equal installments of $150,000 each. Assume debt tax shields have a net value of $.30 per dollar of interest paid. Calculate the project's APV using the procedure followed in Table 19.2.

17. **APV** Consider another perpetual project like the crusher described in Section 19-1. Its initial investment is $1,000,000, and the expected cash inflow is $95,000 a year in perpetuity. The opportunity cost of capital with all-equity financing is 10%, and the project allows the firm to borrow at 7%. The tax rate is 21%.

    Use APV to calculate the project's value.

    a. Assume first that the project will be partly financed with $400,000 of debt and that the debt amount is to be fixed and perpetual.

    b. Then assume that the initial borrowing will be increased or reduced in proportion to changes in the market value of this project.

    Explain the difference between your answers to (a) and (b).

18. **Opportunity cost of capital** Suppose the project described in Problem 17 is to be undertaken by a university. Funds for the project will be withdrawn from the university's endowment, which is invested in a widely diversified portfolio of stocks and bonds. However, the university can also borrow at 7%. The university is tax exempt.

    The university treasurer proposes to finance the project by issuing $400,000 of perpetual bonds at 7% and by selling $600,000 worth of common stocks from the endowment. The expected return on the common stocks is 10%. He therefore proposes to evaluate the project by discounting at a weighted-average cost of capital, calculated as

    $$r = r_D D/V + r_E E/V$$
    $$= .07\,(400,000/1,000,000) + .10\,(600,000/1,000,000)$$
    $$= .088, \text{ or } 8.8$$

    What's right or wrong with the treasurer's approach? Should the university invest? Should it borrow? Would the project's value to the university change if the treasurer financed the project entirely by selling common stocks from the endowment?

19. **APV** Consider a project to produce solar water heaters. It requires a $10 million investment and offers a level after-tax cash flow of $1.75 million per year for 10 years. The opportunity cost of capital is 12%, which reflects the project's business risk.

    a. Suppose the project is financed with $5 million of debt and $5 million of equity. The interest rate is 8% and the marginal tax rate is 21%. An equal amount of the debt will be repaid in each year of the project's life. Calculate APV.

    b. How does APV change if the firm incurs issue costs of $400,000 to raise the $5 million of required equity?

20. **APV and debt capacity** Suppose KCS Corp. buys out Patagonia Trucking, a privately owned business, for $50 million. KCS has only $5 million cash in hand, so it arranges a $45 million bank loan. A normal debt-to-value ratio for a trucking company would be 50% at most, but the bank is satisfied with KCS's credit rating.

    Suppose you were valuing Patagonia by APV in the same format as Table 19.2. How much debt would you include? Explain briefly.

21. **APV and issue costs** The Bunsen Chemical Company is currently at its target debt ratio of 40%. It is contemplating a $1 million expansion of its existing business. This expansion is expected to produce a cash inflow of $130,000 a year in perpetuity.

    The company is uncertain whether to undertake this expansion and how to finance it. The two options are a $1 million issue of common stock or a $1 million issue of 20-year debt. The flotation costs of a stock issue would be around 5% of the amount raised, and the flotation costs of a debt issue would be around 1½%.

    Bunsen's financial manager, Polly Ethylene, estimates that the required return on the company's equity is 14%, but she argues that the flotation costs increase the cost of new equity to 19%. On this basis, the project does not appear viable. On the other hand, she points out that the company can raise new debt on a 7% yield, which would make the cost of new debt 8½%. She therefore recommends that Bunsen should go ahead with the project and finance it with an issue of long-term debt.

Is Ms. Ethylene right? How would you evaluate the project?

22. **APV and limits on interest tax shields** Take another look at the APV calculation for the perpetual crusher project in Section 19-4. This time assume that the corporation investing in the project has hit the 30% constraint on interest deductions as a percentage of EBITDA. How does the constraint change the project's APV?

Notice that the crusher's pretax cash flow of $1.487 million a year is also its EBITDA and EBIT. The project is perpetual, so there is no depreciation or amortization. Assume for simplicity that the constraint is permanently binding, but that the firm will continue to pay tax at the 21% statutory rate.

BEYOND THE PAGE

Try It! Rio's spreadsheet

mhhe.com/brealey13e

23. **WACC and APV** Take another look at the valuations of Rio in Tables 19.1 and 19.2. Now use the live spreadsheets in Connect to show how Rio's value depends on:

   a. The forecasted long-term growth rate.

   b. The required amounts of investment in fixed assets and working capital.

   c. The opportunity cost of capital. (*Note:* You can also vary the opportunity cost of capital in Table 19.1.)

   d. Profitability—that is, cost of goods sold as a percentage of sales.

   e. The assumed amount of debt financing.

24. **Company valuation** Chiara Company's management has made the projections shown in Table 19.5. Use this table as a starting point to value the company as a whole. The WACC for Chiara is 12%, and the forecast long-run growth rate after year 5 is 4%. The company, which is located in South Africa, has ZAR 5 million of debt and 865,000 shares outstanding. What is the value per share?

		Historical				Forecast		
Year	**−2**	**−1**	**0**	**1**	**2**	**3**	**4**	**5**
1. Sales	35,348	39,357	40,123	36,351	30,155	28,345	29,982	30,450
2. Cost of goods sold	17,834	18,564	22,879	21,678	17,560	16,459	15,631	14,987
3. Other costs	6,968	7,645	8,025	6,797	5,078	4,678	4,987	5,134
4. EBITDA (1 − 2 − 3)	10,546	13,148	9,219	7,876	7,517	7,208	9,364	10,329
5. Depreciation	5,671	5,745	5,678	5,890	5,670	5,908	6,107	5,908
6. EBIT (Pretax profit) (4 − 5)	4,875	7,403	3,541	1,986	1,847	1,300	3,257	4,421
7. Tax at 28%	1,365	2,073	991	556	517	364	912	1,238
8. Profit after tax (6 − 7)	3,510	5,330	2,550	1,430	1,330	936	2,345	3,183
9. Change in working capital	325	566	784	−54	−342	−245	127	235
10. Investment (change in gross fixed assets)	5,235	6,467	6,547	7,345	5,398	5,470	6,420	6,598

〉TABLE 19.5   Cash flow projections for Chiara Corp. (ZAR thousands)

CHALLENGE

25. **Miles-Ezzell formula** In footnote 17, we referred to the Miles–Ezzell discount rate formula, which assumes that debt is not rebalanced continuously, but at one-year intervals. Derive this formula. Then use it to unlever Sangria's WACC and calculate Sangria's opportunity cost of capital. Your answer will be slightly different from the opportunity cost that we calculated in Section 19-3. Can you explain why?

26. **Rebalancing** The WACC formula assumes that debt is rebalanced to maintain a constant debt ratio D/V. Rebalancing ties the level of future interest tax shields to the future value of the company. This makes the tax shields risky. Does that mean that fixed debt levels (no rebalancing) are better for stockholders?

27. **Horizon value** Modify Table 19.1 on the assumption that competition eliminates any opportunities to earn more than WACC on new investment after year 7 (PVGO = 0). How does the valuation of Rio change?

Table 19.6 is a simplified book balance sheet for Nike in November 2017. Here is some further information:

FINANCE ON THE WEB

Number of outstanding shares (N)	1.32billion
Price per share (P)	$60
Beta	0.55
Treasury bill rate	0.8%
20-year Treasury bond rate	2.7%
Cost of debt (r_D)	3.8%
Marginal tax rate (from 2018)	21%

a. Calculate Nike's WACC. Use the capital asset pricing model and the additional information given above. Make additional assumptions and approximations as necessary.

b. What is Nike's opportunity cost of capital?

c. Finally, go to **finance.yahoo.com** and update your answers to parts (a) and (b).

Current assets	$16,582	Current liabilities	$ 6,750
Net property, plant, and equipment	4,117	Long-term debt	3,472
Investments and other assets	3,356	Other liabilities	2,075
		Shareholders' equity	11,758
Total	$24,055	Total	$24,055

❱ **TABLE 19.6**   Simplified book balance sheet for Nike, November 2017 (figures in $ millions)

APPENDIX • • •

Discounting Safe, Nominal Cash Flows

Suppose you're considering purchase of a $100,000 machine. The manufacturer sweetens the deal by offering to finance the purchase by lending you $100,000 for five years, with annual interest payments of 5%. You would have to pay 13% to borrow from a bank. Your marginal tax rate is 21% ($T_c = .21$).

How much is this loan worth? If you take it, the cash flows, in thousands of dollars, are

	Period					
	0	**1**	**2**	**3**	**4**	**5**
Cash flow	100	−5	−5	−5	−5	−105
Tax shield		+1.05	+1.05	+1.05	+1.05	+1.05
After-tax cash flow	100	−3.95	−3.95	−3.95	−3.95	−103.95

What is the right discount rate?

Here you are discounting *safe, nominal* cash flows—safe because your company must commit to pay if it takes the loan,[31] and nominal because the payments would be fixed regardless of future inflation. Now, the correct discount rate for safe, nominal cash flows is your company's *after-tax, unsubsidized borrowing rate*,[32] which is $r_D(1 - T_c) = .13(1 - .21) = .1027$. Therefore,

$$NPV = +100 - \frac{3.95}{1.1027} - \frac{3.95}{(1.1027)^2} - \frac{3.95}{(1.1027)^3} - \frac{3.95}{(1.1027)^4} - \frac{103.95}{(1.1027)^5}$$

$$= +23.79, \text{ or } \$23,790$$

The manufacturer has effectively cut the machine's purchase price from $100,000 to $100,000 − $23,790 = $76,210. You can now go back and recalculate the machine's NPV using this fire-sale price, or you can use the NPV of the subsidized loan as one element of the machine's adjusted present value.

A General Rule

Clearly, we owe an explanation of why $r_D(1 - T_c)$ is the right discount rate for safe, nominal cash flows. It's no surprise that the rate depends on r_D, the unsubsidized borrowing rate, for that is investors' opportunity cost of capital, the rate they would demand from your company's debt. But why should r_D be converted to an *after-tax* figure?

Let's simplify by taking a *one-year* subsidized loan of $100,000 at 5%. The cash flows, in thousands of dollars, are

	Period 0	Period 1
Cash flow	100	−105
Tax shield on interest of $5		+1.05
After-tax cash flow	100	−103.95

---

[31] In theory, *safe* means literally "risk-free," like the cash returns on a Treasury bond. In practice, it means that the risk of not paying or receiving a cash flow is small.

[32] In Section 13-1, we calculated the NPV of subsidized financing using the *pretax* borrowing rate. Now you can see that was a mistake. Using the pretax rate implicitly defines the loan in terms of its pretax cash flows, violating a rule promulgated way back in Section 6-1: *Always* estimate cash flows on an after-tax basis.

Now ask, What is the maximum amount X that could be borrowed for one year through regular channels if $103,950 is set aside to service the loan?

"Regular channels" means borrowing at 13% pretax and 10.27% after tax. Therefore, you will need 110.27% of the amount borrowed to pay back principal plus after-tax interest charges. If $1.1027X = 103,950$, then $X = 94,269$. Now if you can borrow $100,000 by a subsidized loan, but only $94,269 through normal channels, the difference ($5,731) is money in the bank. Therefore, it must also be the NPV of this one-period subsidized loan.

When you discount a safe, nominal cash flow at an after-tax borrowing rate, you are implicitly calculating the equivalent loan, the amount you could borrow through normal channels, using the cash flow as debt service. Note that

$$\text{Equivalent loan} = \text{PV(cash flow available for debt service)} = \frac{103,950}{1.1027} = 94,269$$

In some cases, it may be easier to think of taking the lender's side of the equivalent loan rather than the borrower's. For example, you could ask: How much would my company have to invest today to cover next year's debt service on the subsidized loan? The answer is $94,269: If you lend that amount at 13%, you will earn 10.27% after tax, and therefore have 94,269(1.1027) = $103,950. By this transaction, you can in effect cancel, or "zero out," the future obligation. If you can borrow $100,000 and then set aside only $94,269 to cover all the required debt service, you clearly have $5,731 to spend as you please. That amount is the NPV of the subsidized loan.

Therefore, regardless of whether it's easier to think of borrowing or lending, the correct discount rate for safe, nominal cash flows is an after-tax interest rate.[33]

In some ways, this is an obvious result once you think about it. Companies are free to borrow or lend money. If they *lend,* they receive the after-tax interest rate on their investment; if they *borrow* in the capital market, they pay the after-tax interest rate. Thus, the opportunity cost to companies of investing in debt-equivalent cash flows is the after-tax interest rate. This is the adjusted cost of capital for debt-equivalent cash flows.[34]

Some Further Examples

Here are some further examples of debt-equivalent cash flows.

Payout Fixed by Contract

Suppose you sign a maintenance contract with a truck leasing firm, which agrees to keep your leased trucks in good working order for the next two years in exchange for 24 fixed monthly payments. These payments are debt-equivalent flows.

Prejudgment Interest Awards

Court cases involving the award of damages are often complex, and by the time the decision has been reached, many years may have elapsed since the time of the original harm. To compensate for the delay in payment, courts customarily award "prejudgment interest." In other words, they add on an additional award for the return that the claimant could have earned over the period since

---

[33]Borrowing and lending rates should not differ by much if the cash flows are truly safe—that is, if the chance of default is small. Usually your decision will not hinge on the rate used. If it does, ask which offsetting transaction—borrowing or lending—seems most natural and reasonable for the problem at hand. Then use the corresponding interest rate.

[34]All the examples in this section are forward-looking; they call for the value today of a stream of future debt-equivalent cash flows. But similar issues arise in legal and contractual disputes when a *past* cash flow has to be brought forward in time to a present value today. Suppose it's determined that company A should have paid B $1 million 10 years ago. B clearly deserves more than $1 million today because it has lost the time value of money. The time value of money should be expressed as an after-tax borrowing or lending rate or, if no risk enters, as the after-tax risk-free rate. The time value of money is *not* equal to B's overall cost of capital. Allowing B to "earn" its overall cost of capital on the payment allows it to earn a risk premium without bearing risk. For a broader discussion of these issues, see F. Fisher and R. C. Romaine, "Janis Joplin's Yearbook and the Theory of Damages," *Journal of Accounting, Auditing & Finance* 5 (Winter/Spring 1990), pp. 145–157.

the offense. This increment is often larger than the amount of the original damage. For example, when GM was held to have infringed a company's patent, it was ordered to pay $8.8 million in royalties and $11 million in prejudgment interest. A company that has to wait for compensation for damages until long after the damages were incurred has effectively made a debt-equivalent loan to the offender. The award should therefore be increased by the company's *after-tax* interest rate.[35]

Depreciation Tax Shields

Since 2018, U.S. companies have been able to immediately write off most expenditure on capital equipment. In other countries, capital expenditures must generally be written off over their likely life. These deductions generate a depreciation tax shield.

Capital projects are normally valued by discounting the total after-tax cash flows they are expected to generate. Depreciation tax shields contribute to project cash flow, but they are not valued separately; they are just folded into project cash flows along with dozens, or hundreds, of other specific inflows and outflows. The project's opportunity cost of capital reflects the average risk of the resulting aggregate.

However, suppose we ask what depreciation tax shields are worth *by themselves*. For a firm that's sure to pay taxes, depreciation tax shields are a safe, nominal flow. Therefore, they should be discounted at the firm's after-tax borrowing rate.

Perhaps you are CFO of a Polish company that proposes to buy an asset for 500,000 zloty,[36] which can be depreciated straight-line over five years. The corporate tax rate in Poland is 19%. Therefore, the resulting depreciation tax shields are

	Period				
	1	2	3	4	5
Percentage deductions	20	20	20	20	20
Deductions (zloty, thousands)	100	100	100	100	100
Tax shields at $T_c = 0.19$ (zloty, thousands)	19	19	19	19	19

If the pretax borrowing rate is 10%, the after-tax discount rate is $r_D(1 - T_c) = .10(1 - .19) = .081$. The present value of these shields is

$$PV = \frac{19}{1.081} + \frac{19}{(1.081)^2} + \frac{19}{(1.081)^3} + \frac{19}{(1.081)^4} + \frac{19}{(1.081)^5}.$$

$$= +75.7, \text{ or } 75,700 \text{ } zloty$$

A Consistency Check

You may have wondered whether our procedure for valuing debt-equivalent cash flows is consistent with the WACC and APV approaches presented earlier in this chapter. Yes, it is consistent, as we will now illustrate.

Let's look at another very simple numerical example. You are asked to value a $1 million payment to be received from a blue-chip company one year hence. After taxes at 21%, the cash inflow is $790,000. The payment is fixed by contract.

Because the contract generates a debt-equivalent flow, the opportunity cost of capital is the rate investors would demand on a one-year note issued by the blue-chip company, which happens

---

[35]In practice, courts use a variety of methods for calculating prejudgment interest. For a discussion of the issue see Fisher and Romaine, op. cit.
[36]Zloty, the Polish currency, often abbreviated as PLN.

to be 8%. For simplicity, we'll assume this is your company's borrowing rate too. Our valuation rule for debt-equivalent flows is therefore to discount at $r_D(1 - T_c) = .08(1 - .21) = .0632$:

$$PV = \frac{650,000}{1.0632} = \$611,362$$

What is the *debt capacity* of this $650,000 payment? Exactly $611,362. Your company could borrow that amount and pay off the loan completely—principal and after-tax interest—with the $650,000 cash inflow. The debt capacity is 100% of the PV of the debt-equivalent cash flow.

If you think of it that way, our discount rate $r_D(1 - T_c)$ is just a special case of WACC with a 100% debt ratio ($D/V = 1$).

$$WACC = r_D(1 - T_c)D/V + r_E E/V$$
$$= r_D(1 - T_c) \text{ if } D/V = 1 \text{ and } E/V = 0$$

Now let's try an APV calculation. This is a two-part valuation. First, the $650,000 inflow is discounted at the opportunity cost of capital, 8%. Second, we add the present value of interest tax shields on debt supported by the project. Because the firm can borrow 100% of the cash flow's value, the tax shield is $r_D T_c$ APV, and APV is:

$$APV = \frac{650,000}{1.08} + \frac{.08(.21)APV}{1.08}$$

Solving for APV, we get $611,362, the same answer we obtained by discounting at the after-tax borrowing rate. Thus, our valuation rule for debt-equivalent flows is a special case of APV.

QUESTIONS

1. The U.S. government has settled a dispute with your company for $16 million. The government is committed to pay this amount in exactly 12 months. However, your company will have to pay tax on the award at a marginal tax rate of 21%. What is the award worth? The one-year Treasury rate is 5.5%.

2. You are considering a five-year lease of office space for R&D personnel. Once signed, the lease cannot be canceled. It would commit your firm to six annual $100,000 payments, with the first payment due immediately. What is the present value of the lease if your company's borrowing rate is 9% and its tax rate is 21%? The lease payments would be tax-deductible.

Understanding Options

Pop quiz: What do the following events have in common?

- Hershey buys options that put a ceiling on the price that it will pay for its future purchases of cocoa.

- Flatiron offers its president a bonus if the company's stock price exceeds $120.

- Blitzen Computer dips a toe in the water and enters a new market.

- Malted Herring postpones investment in a positive-NPV plant.

- Hewlett-Packard exports partially assembled printers even though it would be cheaper to ship the finished product.

- Dominion installs a dual-fired unit at its Possum Point power station that can use either fuel oil or natural gas.

- in 2017, vTv Therapeutics issues 38,006 warrants. Each warrant entitles its owner to buy an additional Class A share for $5.92.

- Twitter issues $1.8 billion of convertible bonds. Each bond can be exchanged for 12.9 shares.

Answers: (1) Each of these events involves an option, and (2) they illustrate why the financial manager of an industrial company needs to understand options.

Companies regularly use commodity, currency, and interest-rate options to reduce risk. For example, a meat-packing company that wishes to put a ceiling on the cost of beef might take out an option to buy live cattle at a fixed price. A company that wishes to limit its future borrowing costs might take out an option to sell long-term bonds at a fixed price. And so on. In Chapter 26, we explain how firms employ options to limit their risk.

Many capital investments include an embedded option to expand in the future. For instance, the company may invest in a patent that allows it to exploit a new technology, or it may purchase adjoining land that gives it the option in the future to increase capacity. In each case, the company is paying money today for the opportunity to make a further investment. To put it another way, the company is acquiring *growth opportunities.*

Here is another disguised option to invest: You are considering the purchase of a tract of desert land that is known to contain gold deposits. Unfortunately, the cost of extraction is higher than the current price of gold. Does this mean the land is almost worthless? Not at all. You are not obliged to mine the gold, but ownership of the land gives you the option to do so. Of course, if you know that the gold price will remain below the extraction cost, then the option is worthless. But if there is uncertainty about future gold prices, you could be lucky and make a killing.[1]

If the option to expand has value, what about the option to bail out? Projects don't usually go on until the equipment disintegrates. The decision to terminate a project is usually taken by management, not by nature. Once the project is no longer profitable, the company will cut its losses and exercise its option to abandon the project. Some projects have higher abandonment value than others. Those that use standardized

---

[1]In Chapter 11, we valued Kingsley Solomon's gold mine by calculating the value of the gold in the ground and then subtracting the value of the extraction costs. That is correct only if we know that the gold will be mined. Otherwise, the value of the mine is increased by the value of the option to leave the gold in the ground if its price is less than the extraction cost.

equipment may offer a valuable abandonment option. Others may actually cost money to discontinue. For example, it is very costly to decommission an offshore oil platform.

We took a peek at investment options in Chapter 10, and we showed there how to use decision trees to analyze a pharmaceutical company's options to discontinue trials of a new drug. In Chapter 22 we take a more thorough look at these *real* options.

Another important reason why financial managers need to understand options is that they are often tacked on to an issue of corporate securities and so provide the investor or the company with the flexibility to change the terms of the issue. For example, in Chapter 24, we show how warrants or convertibles give their holders an option to buy common stock in exchange for cash or bonds.

In fact, we see in Chapter 23 that whenever a company borrows, it gains an option to walk away from its debts and surrender its assets to the bondholders. If the value of the company's assets at maturity is less than the amount of the debt, the company will choose to default on the payment, and the bondholders will get to keep the company's assets. Thus, when the firm borrows, the lender effectively acquires

the company, and the shareholders obtain the option to buy it back by paying off the debt. This is an extremely important insight. It means that anything that we can learn about traded options applies equally to corporate liabilities.

In this chapter, we use traded stock options to explain how options work, but we hope that our brief survey has convinced you that the interest of financial managers in options goes far beyond traded stock options. That is why we are asking you to invest here to acquire several important ideas for use later.

If you are unfamiliar with the wonderful world of options, it may seem baffling on first encounter. We therefore divide this chapter into three bite-sized pieces. Our first task is to introduce you to call and put options and to show you how the payoff on these options depends on the price of the underlying asset. We then show how financial alchemists can combine options to produce a variety of interesting strategies.

We conclude the chapter by identifying the variables that determine option values. There you encounter some surprising and counterintuitive effects. For example, investors are used to thinking that increased risk reduces present value. But for options it is the other way around.

● ● ● ● ●

20-1 Calls, Puts, and Shares

Investors regularly trade options on common stocks.[2] For example, Table 20.1 reproduces quotes for options on the stock of Amazon.com. You can see that there are two types of options—calls and puts. We explain each in turn.

Call Options and Position Diagrams

A **call option** gives its owner the right to buy stock at a specified *exercise* or *strike price* on or before a specified maturity date. If the option can be exercised only at maturity, it is conventionally known as a *European call;* in other cases (such as the Amazon options shown in Table 20.1), the option can be exercised on or at any time before maturity, and it is then known as an *American call.*

The third column of Table 20.1 sets out the prices in April 2017 of Amazon call options with different exercise prices and exercise dates. Look at the quotes for options maturing in July 2017. The first entry says that for $95.58 you could acquire an option to buy one share[3] of Amazon stock for $820 on or before July 2017. Moving down to the next row, you can see that an option to buy for $40 more ($860 vs. $820) costs nearly $30 less, that is, $66.03. In general, the value of a call option goes down as the exercise price goes up. The more that you need to pay to acquire the stock, the less valuable is the option.

---

[2]The two principal options exchanges in the United States are the International Securities Exchange (ISE) and the Chicago Board Options Exchange (CBOE).

[3]You can't actually buy an option on a single share. Trades are in multiples of 100. The minimum order would be for 100 options on 100 Amazon shares.

)TABLE 20.1

Selected prices of put and call options on Amazon .com stock in April 2017, when the closing stock price was about $900

[a] Long-term options are called "LEAPS."

Source: Yahoo! Finance, finance .yahoo.com.

Maturity Date	Exercise Price	Price of Call Option	Price of Put Option
July 2017	$820	$95.58	$14.40
	860	66.03	24.73
	900	42.80	41.15
	940	25.35	63.63
	980	14.08	92.43
October 2017	$820	$113.30	$28.75
	860	86.65	42.15
	900	**64.30**	**59.55**
	940	45.95	81.18
	980	31.75	110.30
January 2018[a]	$820	$128.23	$40.68
	860	103.08	55.60
	900	81.23	73.15
	940	62.58	94.75
	980	46.83	119.58

Now look at the quotes for options maturing in October 2017 and January 2018. Notice how the option price increases as option maturity is extended. For example, at an exercise price of $900, the July 2017 call option costs $42.80, the October 2017 option costs $64.30, and the January 2018 option costs $81.23. The longer you have to decide whether you want to exercise, the more valuable is the option.

Option analysts often draw a *position diagram* to illustrate the possible payoffs from an option. For example, the position diagram in Figure 20.1*a* shows the possible consequences of investing in Amazon October 2017 call options with an exercise price of $900 (boldfaced in Table 20.1). The outcome from investing in Amazon calls depends on what happens to

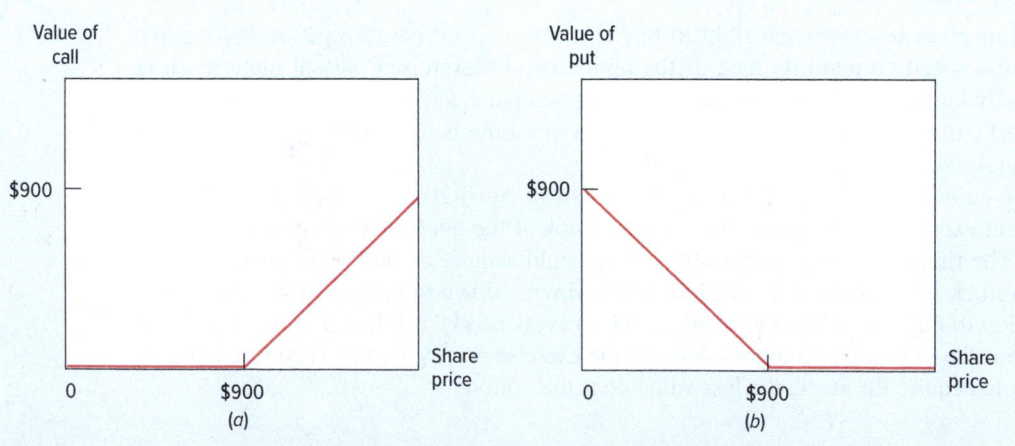

▶ FIGURE 20.1   Position diagrams show how payoffs to owners of Amazon calls and puts (shown by the colored lines) depend on the share price. (*a*) Result of buying Amazon call exercisable at $900. (*b*) Result of buying Amazon put exercisable at $900.

the stock price. If the stock price at the end of this six-month period turns out to be less than the $900 exercise price, it will not make sense to pay the exercise price to obtain the share. Your call will, in that case, be worthless. On the other hand, if the stock price turns out to be greater than $900, it will pay to exercise your option to buy the share. In this case, when the call expires, it will be worth the market price of the share minus the $900 that you must pay to exercise the option. For example, suppose that the price of Amazon stock rises to $980. Your call will then be worth $980 – $900 = $80. That is your payoff, but of course, it is not all profit. Table 20.1 shows that you had to pay $64.30 to buy the call.

Put Options

Now let us look at the Amazon **put options** in the right-hand column of Table 20.1. Whereas a call option gives you the right to *buy* a share for a specified exercise price, a put gives you the right to *sell* the share. For example, the boldfaced entry in the right-hand column of Table 20.1 shows that for $59.55, you could acquire an option to sell Amazon stock for a price of $900 any time before October 2017. The circumstances in which the put turns out to be valuable are just the opposite of those in which the call is profitable. You can see this from the position diagram in Figure 20.1*b*. If Amazon's share price immediately before expiration turns out to be *greater* than $900, you won't want to sell stock at that price. You would do better to sell the share in the market, and your put option will be worthless. Conversely, if the share price turns out to be *less* than $900, it will pay to buy stock at the low price and then take advantage of the option to sell it for $900. In this case, the value of the put option on the exercise date is the difference between the $900 proceeds of the sale and the market price of the share. For example, if the share is worth $800, the put is worth $100:

$$\text{Value of put option at expiration} = \text{exercise price} - \text{market price of the share}$$

$$= \$900 - \$800 = \$100$$

Selling Calls and Puts

Let us now look at the position of an investor who *sells* these investments. If you sell, or "write," a call, you promise to deliver shares if asked to do so by the call buyer. In other words, the buyer's asset is the seller's liability. If the share price is below the exercise price when the option matures, the buyer will not exercise the call and the seller's liability will be zero. If it rises above the exercise price, the buyer will exercise and the seller must give up the shares. The seller loses the difference between the share price and the exercise price received from the buyer. Notice that it is the buyer who always has the option to exercise; option sellers simply do as they are told.

Suppose that the price of Amazon stock turns out to be $980, which is above the option's exercise price of $900. In this case, the buyer will exercise the call. The seller is forced to sell stock worth $980 for only $900 and so has a payoff of – $80.[4] Of course, that $80 loss is the buyer's gain. Figure 20.2*a* shows how the payoffs to the seller of the Amazon call option vary with the stock price. Notice that for every dollar the buyer makes, the seller loses a dollar. Figure 20.2*a* is just Figure 20.1*a* drawn upside down.

In just the same way, we can depict the position of an investor who sells, or writes, a put by standing Figure 20.1*b* on its head. The seller of the put has agreed to pay $900 for the share if the buyer of the put should request it. Clearly the seller will be safe as long as the share price remains above $900 but will lose money if the share price falls below this figure. The worst thing that can happen is that the stock becomes worthless. The seller would then be obliged to pay $900 for a stock worth $0. The payoff to the seller would be –$900.

---

[4]The seller has some consolation, for he or she was paid $64.30 in April for selling the call.

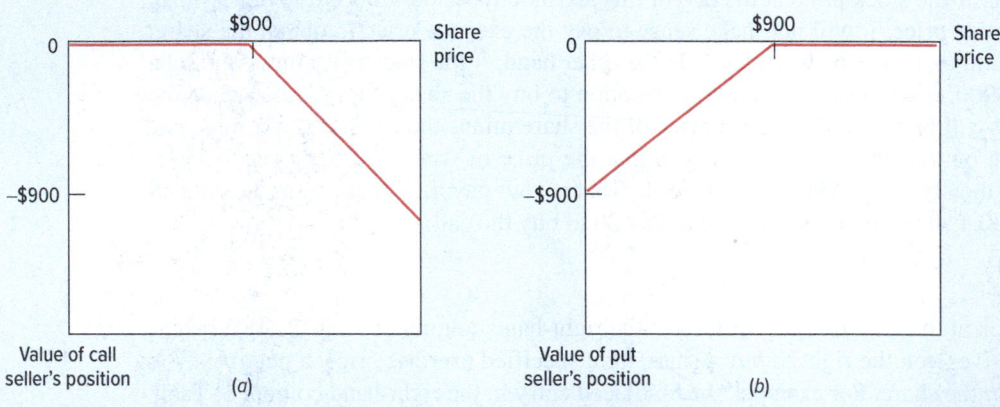

▶ **FIGURE 20.2**   Payoffs to *sellers* of Amazon calls and puts (shown by the colored lines) depend on the share price. (*a*) Result of selling Amazon call exercisable at $900. (*b*) Result of selling Amazon put exercisable at $900.

Position Diagrams Are Not Profit Diagrams

Position diagrams show *only* the payoffs at option exercise; they do not account for the initial cost of buying the option or the initial proceeds from selling it.

This is a common point of confusion. For example, the position diagram in Figure 20.1*a* makes purchase of a call *look* like a sure thing—the payoff is at worst zero, with plenty of upside if Amazon's stock price goes above $900 by October 2017. But compare the *profit diagram* in Figure 20.3*a*, which subtracts the $64.30 *cost* of the call in April 2017 from the payoff at maturity. The call buyer loses money at all share prices less than $900 + 64.30 = $964.30. Take another example: The position diagram in Figure 20.2*b* makes selling a put *look* like a sure loss—the *best* payoff is zero. But the profit diagram in Figure 20.3*b*, which recognizes the $59.55 received by the seller, shows that the seller gains at all prices above $900 – 59.55 = $840.45.[5]

▶ **FIGURE 20.3**

Profit diagrams incorporate the costs of buying an option or the proceeds from selling one. In panel (*a*), we subtract the $64.30 cost of the Amazon call from the payoffs plotted in Figure 20.1*a*. In panel (*b*), we add the $59.55 proceeds from selling the Amazon put to the payoffs in Figure 20.2*b*.

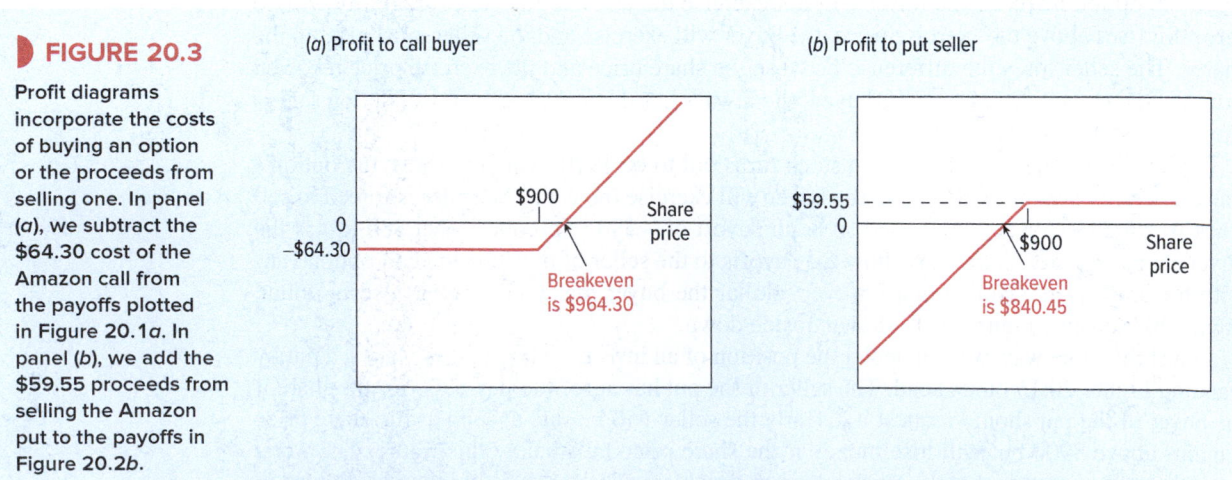

[5]The fact that you have made a profit on your position is not necessarily a cause for rejoicing. The profit needs to compensate you for the risk that you took.

Profit diagrams like those in Figure 20.3 may be helpful to the options beginner, but options experts rarely draw them.[6] Now that you've graduated from the first options class we won't draw them either. We stick to position diagrams, because you have to focus on payoffs at exercise to understand options and to value them properly.

20-2 Financial Alchemy with Options

Look now at Figure 20.4a, which shows the payoff if you buy Amazon stock at $900. You gain dollar-for-dollar if the stock price goes up and you lose dollar-for-dollar if it falls. That's trite; it doesn't take a genius to draw a 45-degree line.

Look now at panel (b), which shows the payoffs from an investment strategy that retains the upside potential of Amazon stock but gives complete downside protection. In this case, your payoff stays at $900 even if the Amazon stock price falls to $800, $500, or zero. Panel (b)'s payoffs are clearly better than panel (a)'s. If a financial alchemist could turn panel (a) into panel (b), you'd be willing to pay for the service.

Now, as you have probably suspected, this financial alchemy is for real. You can do the transmutation shown in Figure 20.4. You do it with options, and we will show you how. Look at row 1 of Figure 20.5. The first diagram again shows the payoff from buying a share of Amazon stock, while the next diagram in row 1 shows the payoffs from buying an Amazon put option with an exercise price of $900. The third diagram shows the effect of combining these two positions. You can see that if Amazon's stock price rises above $900, your put option is valueless, so you simply receive the gains from your investment in the share. However, if the stock price falls below $900, you can exercise your put option and sell your stock for $900. Thus, by adding a put option to your investment in the stock, you have protected yourself against loss.[7] This is the strategy that we depicted in Figure 20.4. Of course, there is no gain without pain. The cost of insuring yourself against loss is the amount that you pay for a put option on Amazon stock with an exercise price of $900. In April 2017, the price of this put was $59.55. This was the going rate for financial alchemists.

We have just seen how put options can be used to provide downside protection. We now show you how call options can be used to get the same result. This is illustrated in row 2 of Figure 20.5. The first diagram shows the payoff from placing the present value of $900 in a

BEYOND THE PAGE

Option payoffs

mhhe.com/brealey13e

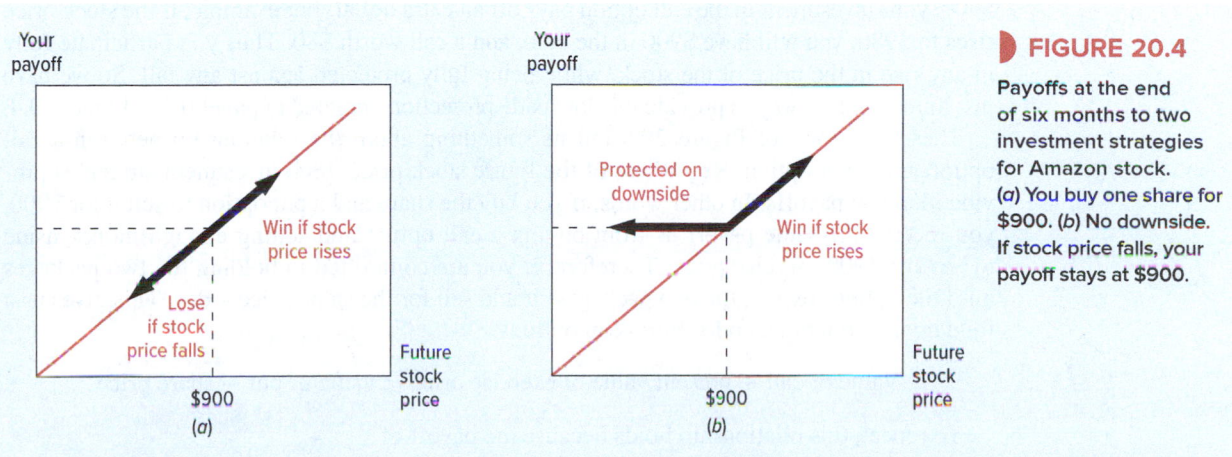

▶ **FIGURE 20.4**

Payoffs at the end of six months to two investment strategies for Amazon stock. (*a*) You buy one share for $900. (*b*) No downside. If stock price falls, your payoff stays at $900.

---

[6]Profit diagrams such as Figure 20.3 deduct the initial cost of the option from the final payoff. They therefore ignore the first lesson of finance—"A dollar today is worth more than a dollar in the future."

[7]This combination of a stock and a put option is known as a *protective put*.

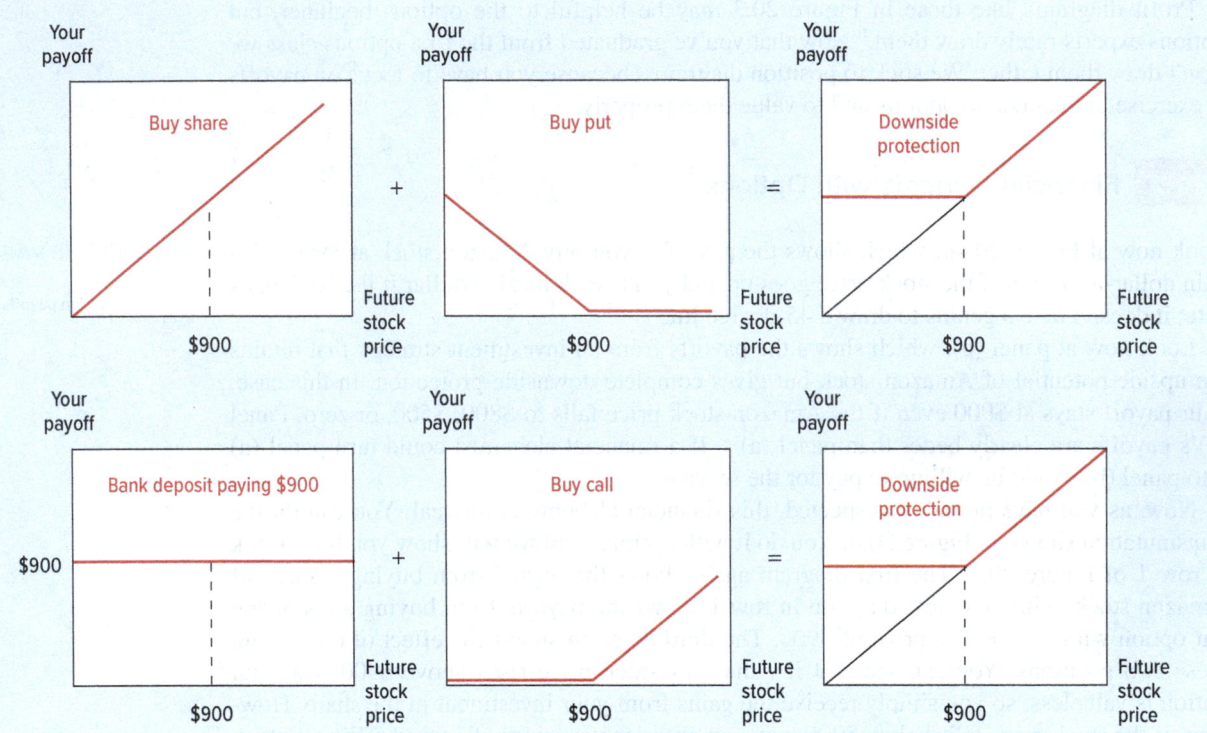

FIGURE 20.5 Each row in the figure shows a different way to create a strategy where you gain if the stock price rises but are protected on the downside (strategy [b] in Figure 20.4)

bank deposit. Regardless of what happens to the price of Amazon stock, your bank deposit will pay off $900. The second diagram in row 2 shows the payoff from a call option on Amazon stock with an exercise price of $900, and the third diagram shows the effect of combining these two positions. Notice that if the price of Amazon stock falls, your call is worthless, but you still have your $900 in the bank. For every dollar that Amazon stock price rises above $900, your investment in the call option pays off an extra dollar. For example, if the stock price rises to $980, you will have $900 in the bank and a call worth $80. Thus you participate fully in any rise in the price of the stock, while being fully protected against any fall. So we have just found another way to provide the downside protection depicted in panel (b) of Figure 20.4.

These two rows of Figure 20.5 tell us something about the relationship between a call option and a put option. Regardless of the future stock price, both investment strategies provide identical payoffs. In other words, if you buy the share and a put option to sell it for $900, you receive the same payoff as from buying a call option and setting enough money aside to pay the $900 exercise price. Therefore, if you are committed to holding the two packages until the options expire, the two packages should sell for the same price today. This gives us a fundamental relationship for European options:

Value of call + present value of exercise price = value of put + share price

To repeat, this relationship holds because the payoff of

buy call, invest present value of exercise price in safe asset[8]

---

[8]The present value is calculated at the *risk-free* rate of interest. It is the amount that you would have to invest today in a bank deposit or Treasury bills to realize the exercise price on the option's expiration date.

is identical to the payoff from

buy put, buy share.

This basic relationship among share price, call and put values, and the present value of the exercise price is called **put–call parity**.[9]

Put–call parity can be expressed in several ways. Each expression implies two investment strategies that give identical results. For example, suppose that you want to solve for the value of a put. You simply need to twist the put–call parity formula around to give

Value of put = value of call + present value of exercise price − share price

From this expression you can deduce that

buy put

is identical to

buy call, invest present value of exercise price in safe asset, sell share.

In other words, if puts are not available, you can get exactly the same payoff by buying calls, putting cash in the bank, and selling shares.

If you find this difficult to believe, look at Figure 20.6, which shows the possible payoffs from each position. The diagram on the left shows the payoffs from a call option on Amazon stock with an exercise price of $900. The second diagram shows the payoffs from placing the present value of $900 in the bank. Regardless of what happens to the share price, this

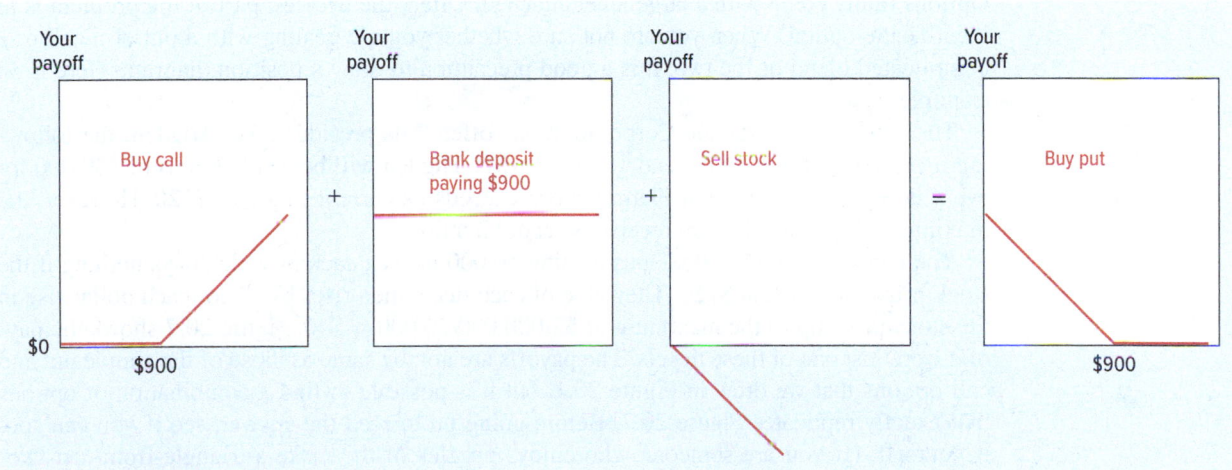

FIGURE 20.6   A strategy of buying a call, depositing the present value of the exercise price in the bank, and selling the stock is equivalent to buying a put

---

[9]Put–call parity holds only if you are committed to holding the options until the final exercise date. It therefore does not hold for American options, which you can exercise *before* the final date. We discuss possible reasons for early exercise in Chapter 21. Also if the stock makes a dividend payment before the final exercise date, you need to recognize that the investor who buys the call misses out on this dividend. In this case the relationship is

Value of call + present value of exercise price = value of put + share price − present value of dividend

investment will pay off $900. The third diagram shows the payoffs from selling Amazon stock. When you sell a share that you don't own, you have a liability—you must sometime buy it back. As they say on Wall Street:

> He who sells what isn't his'n
> Buys it back or goes to pris'n

Therefore, the best that can happen to you is that the share price falls to zero. In that case, it costs you nothing to buy the share back. But for every extra dollar on the future share price, you will need to spend an extra dollar to buy the share. The final diagram in Figure 20.6 shows that the *total* payoff from these three positions is the same as if you had bought a put option. For example, suppose that when the option matures, the stock price is $800. Your call will be worthless, your bank deposit will be worth $900, and it will cost you $800 to repurchase the share. Your total payoff is $0 + 900 - 800 = \$100$, exactly the same as the payoff from the put.

If two investments offer identical payoffs, then they should sell for the same price today. If the law of one price is violated, you have a potential arbitrage opportunity. So let's check whether there are any arbitrage profits to be made from our Amazon calls and puts. In April 2017, the price of a six-month call with a $900 exercise price was $64.30, the interest rate was about .5% for 6 months, and the price of Amazon stock was $900. Therefore the cost of a homemade put was

$$\text{Buy call} + \text{present value of exercise price} - \text{share price} = \text{cost of homemade put}$$

$$64.30 + 900/1.005 - 900 = \$59.82$$

This is almost exactly the same as it would have cost you to buy a put directly.

Spotting the Option

Options rarely come with a large label attached. Often, the trickiest part of the problem is to identify the option. When you are not sure whether you are dealing with a put or a call or a complicated blend of the two, it is a good precaution to draw a position diagram. Here is an example.

The Flatiron and Mangle Corporation has offered its president, Ms. Higden, the following incentive scheme: At the end of the year Ms. Higden will be paid a bonus of $50,000 for every dollar that the price of Flatiron stock exceeds its current figure of $120. However, the maximum bonus that she can receive is set at $2 million.[10]

You can think of Ms. Higden as owning 50,000 tickets, each of which pays nothing if the stock price fails to beat $120. The value of each ticket then rises by $1 for each dollar rise in the stock price up to the maximum of $2,000,000/50,000 = $40. Figure 20.7 shows the payoffs from just one of these tickets. The payoffs are not the same as those of the simple put and call options that we drew in Figure 20.1, but it is possible to find a combination of options that exactly replicates Figure 20.7. Before going on to read the answer, see if you can spot it yourself. (If you are someone who enjoys puzzles of the make-a-triangle-from-just-two-matchsticks type, this one should be a walkover.)

The answer is in Figure 20.8. The solid black line represents the purchase of a call option with an exercise price of $120, and the dotted line shows the sale of another call option with an exercise price of $160. The colored line shows the payoffs from a combination of the purchase and the sale—exactly the same as the payoffs from one of Ms. Higden's tickets.

---

[10]Bonus schemes in many companies follow a pattern similar to Ms. Higden's scheme. See, for example, A. Edmans, X. Gabaix, and D. Jenter, "Executive Compensation: A Survey of Theory and Evidence," European Corporate Governance Institute, June 26, 2017.

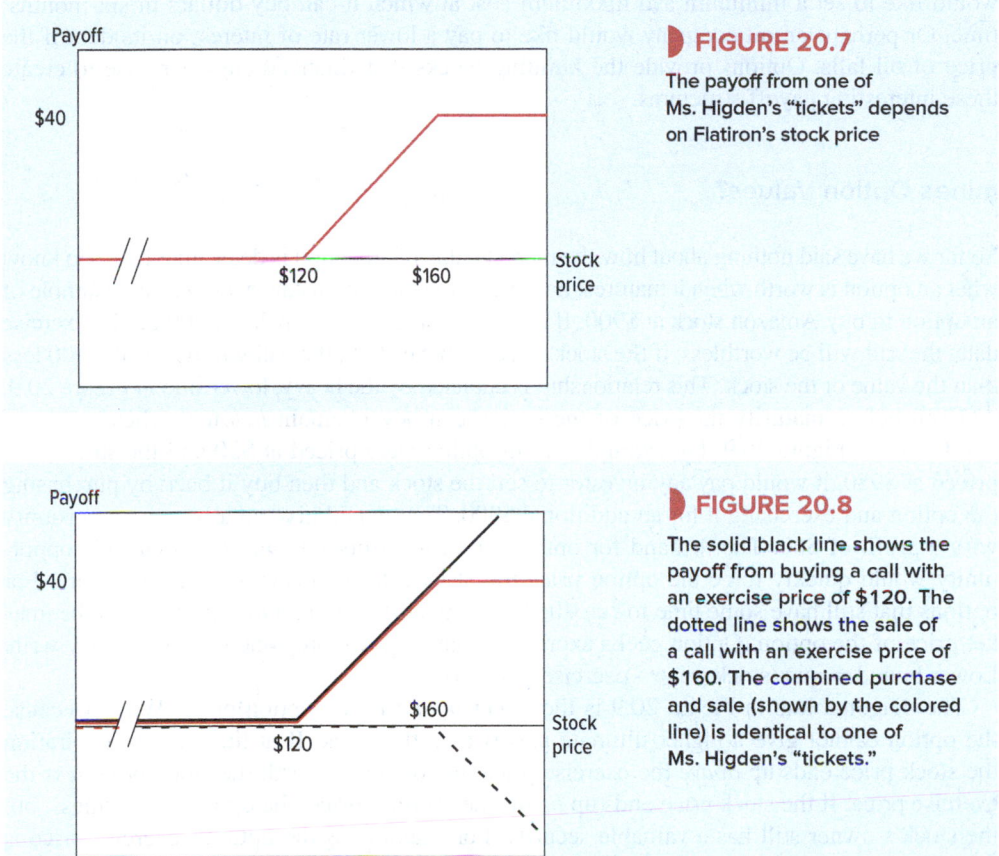

▶ **FIGURE 20.7**

The payoff from one of Ms. Higden's "tickets" depends on Flatiron's stock price

▶ **FIGURE 20.8**

The solid black line shows the payoff from buying a call with an exercise price of $120. The dotted line shows the sale of a call with an exercise price of $160. The combined purchase and sale (shown by the colored line) is identical to one of Ms. Higden's "tickets."

Thus, if we wish to know how much the incentive scheme is costing the company, we need to calculate the difference between the value of 50,000 call options with an exercise price of $120 and the value of 50,000 calls with an exercise price of $160.

We could have made the incentive scheme depend in a much more complicated way on the stock price. For example, the bonus could peak at $2 million and then fall steadily back to zero as the stock price climbs above $160.[11] You could still have represented this scheme as a combination of options. In fact, we can state a general theorem:

> Any set of contingent payoffs—that is, payoffs that depend on the value of some other asset— can be constructed with a mixture of simple options on that asset.

In other words, you can create any position diagram—with as many ups and downs or peaks and valleys as your imagination allows—by buying or selling the right combinations of puts and calls with different exercise prices.[12]

Finance pros often talk about **financial engineering,** which is the practice of packaging different investments to create new tailor-made instruments. Perhaps a German company

---

[11]This is not as nutty a bonus scheme as it may sound. Maybe Ms. Higden's hard work can lift the value of the stock by so much and the only way she can hope to increase it further is by taking on extra risk. You can deter her from doing this by making her bonus start to decline beyond some point. Too bad that before the financial crisis the bonus schemes for some bank CEOs did not contain this feature.

[12]In some cases, you may also have to borrow or lend money to generate a position diagram with your desired pattern. Lending raises the payoff line in position diagrams, as in the bottom row of Figure 20.5. Borrowing lowers the payoff line.

would like to set a minimum and maximum cost at which it can buy dollars in six-months' time. Or perhaps an oil company would like to pay a lower rate of interest on its debt if the price of oil falls. Options provide the building blocks that financial engineers use to create these interesting payoff structures.

20-3   What Determines Option Values?

So far we have said nothing about how the market value of an option is determined. We do know what an option is worth when it matures, however. Consider, for instance, our earlier example of an option to buy Amazon stock at $900. If Amazon's stock price is below $900 on the exercise date, the call will be worthless; if the stock price is above $900, the call will be worth $900 less than the value of the stock. This relationship is depicted by the heavy, lower line in Figure 20.9.

Even before maturity the price of the option can never remain *below* the heavy, lower-bound line in Figure 20.9. For example, if our option were priced at $20 and the stock were priced at $980, it would pay any investor to sell the stock and then buy it back by purchasing the option and exercising it for an additional $900. That would give an arbitrage opportunity with a profit of $60. The demand for options from investors seeking to exploit this opportunity would quickly force the option price up, at least to the heavy line in the figure. For options that still have some time to run, the heavy line is therefore a *lower bound* on the market price of the option. Option geeks express the same idea more concisely when they write Lower bound = max(stock price − exercise price, 0).

The diagonal line in Figure 20.9 is the *upper bound* to the option price. Why? Because the option cannot give a higher ultimate payoff than the stock. If at the option's expiration the stock price ends up *above* the exercise price, the option is worth the stock price *less* the exercise price. If the stock price ends up *below* the exercise price, the option is worthless, but the stock's owner still has a valuable security. For example, if the option's exercise price is $900, then the extra dollar returns realized by stockholders are shown in the following table:

	Stock Payoff	Option Payoff	Extra Payoff from Holding Stock Instead of Option
Option exercised (stock price greater than $900)	Stock price	Stock price − $900	$900
Option expires unexercised (stock price less than or equal to $900)	Stock price	0	Stock price

▶ **FIGURE 20.9**

Value of a call before its expiration date (dashed line). The value depends on the stock price. It is always worth more than its value if exercised now (heavy line). It is never worth more than the stock price itself.

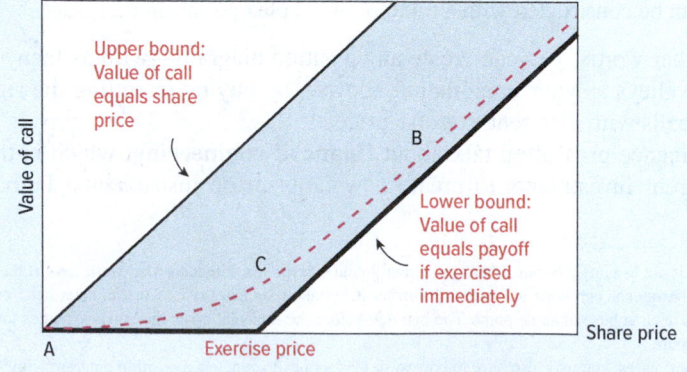

If the stock and the option have the same price, everyone will rush to sell the option and buy the stock. Therefore, the option price must be somewhere in the shaded region of Figure 20.9. In fact, it will lie on a curved, upward-sloping line like the dashed curve shown in the figure. This line begins its travels where the upper and lower bounds meet (at zero). Then it rises, gradually becoming parallel to the upward-sloping part of the lower bound.

But let us look more carefully at the shape and location of the dashed line. Three points, *A, B,* and *C,* are marked on the dashed line. As we explain each point you will see why the option price has to behave as the dashed line predicts.

Point A   *When the stock is worthless, the option is worthless.* A stock price of zero means that there is no possibility the stock will ever have any future value.[13] If so, the option is sure to expire unexercised and worthless, and it is worthless today.

That brings us to our first important point about option value:

The value of an option increases as stock price increases, if the exercise price is held constant.

That should be no surprise. Owners of call options clearly hope for the stock price to rise and are happy when it does.

Point B   *As the stock price increases, the option price approaches the stock price less the present value of the exercise price.* Notice that the dashed line representing the option price in Figure 20.9 eventually becomes parallel to the ascending heavy line representing the lower bound on the option price. The reason is as follows: The higher the stock price, the higher is the probability that the option will eventually be exercised. If the stock price is high enough, exercise becomes a virtual certainty; the probability that the stock price will fall below the exercise price before the option expires becomes trivially small.

If you own an option that you *know* will be exchanged for a share of stock, you effectively own the stock now. The only difference is that you don't have to pay for the stock (by handing over the exercise price) until later, when formal exercise occurs. In these circumstances, buying the call is equivalent to buying the stock but financing part of the purchase by borrowing. The amount implicitly borrowed is the present value of the exercise price. The value of the call is therefore equal to the stock price less the present value of the exercise price.

This brings us to another important point about options. Investors who acquire stock by way of a call option are buying on credit. They pay the purchase price of the option today, but they do not pay the exercise price until they actually take up the option. The delay in payment is particularly valuable if interest rates are high and the option has a long maturity.

Thus, the value of an option increases with both the rate of interest and the time to maturity.

Point C   *The option price always exceeds its minimum value* (except when stock price is zero). We have seen that the dashed and heavy lines in Figure 20.9 coincide when stock price is zero (point *A*), but elsewhere the lines diverge; that is, the option price must exceed the minimum value given by the heavy line. The reason for this can be understood by examining point *C*.

At point *C,* the stock price exactly equals the exercise price. The option is therefore worthless if exercised today. However, suppose that the option will not expire until three months hence. Of course, we do not know what the stock price will be at the expiration date. There is roughly a 50% chance that it will be higher than the exercise price and a 50% chance that it will be lower. The possible payoffs to the option are therefore

---

[13]If a stock *can* be worth something in the future, then investors will pay *something* for it today, although possibly a very small amount.

Outcome	Payoff
Stock price rises (50% probability)	Stock price less exercise price (option is exercised)
Stock price falls (50% probability)	Zero (option expires worthless)

If there is a positive probability of a positive payoff, and if the worst payoff is zero, then the option must be valuable. That means the option price at point *C* exceeds its lower bound, which at point *C* is zero. In general, the option prices will exceed their lower-bound values as long as there is time left before expiration.

One of the most important determinants of the *height* of the dashed curve (i.e., of the difference between actual and lower-bound value) is the likelihood of substantial movements in the stock price. An option on a stock whose price is unlikely to change by more than 1% or 2% is not worth much; an option on a stock whose price may halve or double is very valuable.

As an option holder, you gain from volatility because the payoffs are not symmetric. If the stock price falls *below* the exercise price, your call option will be worthless, regardless of whether the shortfall is a few cents or many dollars. On the other hand, for every dollar that the stock price rises *above* the exercise price, your call will be worth an extra dollar. Therefore, the option holder gains from the increased volatility on the upside, but does not lose on the downside.

A simple example may help to illustrate the point. Consider two stocks, X and Y, each of which is priced at $100. The only difference is that the outlook for Y is much less easy to predict. There is a 50% chance that the price of Y will rise to $150 and a similar chance that it will fall to $70. By contrast, there is a 50–50 chance that the price of X will either rise to $130 or fall to $90.

Suppose that you are offered a call option on each of these stocks with an exercise price of $100. The following table compares the possible payoffs from these options:

	Stock Price Falls	Stock Price Rises
Payoff from option on X	$0	$130 − $100 = $30
Payoff from option on Y	$0	$150 − $100 = $50

In both cases, there is a 50% chance that the stock price will decline and make the option worthless but, if the stock price rises, the option on Y will give the larger payoff. Because the chance of a zero payoff is the same, the option on Y is worth more than the option on X.

Of course, in practice future stock prices may take on a range of different values. We have recognized this in Figure 20.10, where the uncertain outlook for Y's stock price shows up in the wider probability distribution of future prices.[14] The greater spread of outcomes for stock Y again provides more upside potential and, therefore, increases the chance of a large payoff on the option.

Figure 20.11 shows how volatility affects the value of an option. The upper curved line depicts the value of the Amazon call option assuming that Amazon's stock price, like that of stock Y, is highly variable. The lower curved line assumes a lower (and more realistic) degree of volatility.[15]

---

[14] Figure 20.11 continues to assume that the exercise price on both options is equal to the current stock price. This is not a necessary assumption. Also, in drawing Figure 20.11, we have assumed that the distribution of stock prices is symmetric. This also is not a necessary assumption, and we will look more carefully at the distribution of stock prices in the next chapter.

[15] The option values shown in Figure 20.12 were calculated by using the Black-Scholes option-valuation model. We explain this model in Chapter 21 and use it to value the Amazon option.

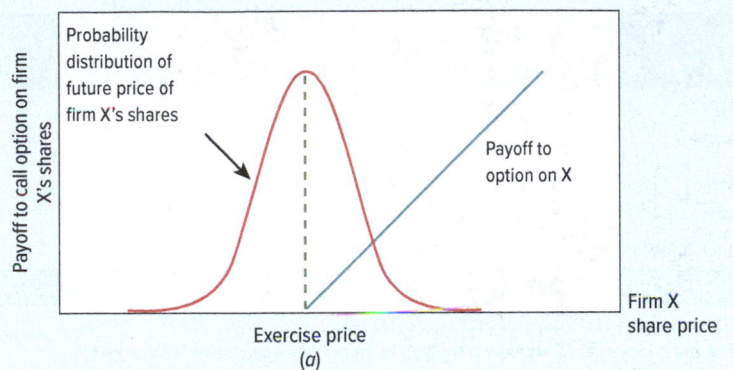

FIGURE 20.10

Call options on the shares of (*a*) firm X and (*b*) firm Y. In each case, the current share price equals the exercise price, so each option has a 50% chance of ending up worthless (if the share price falls) and a 50% chance of ending up "in the money" (if the share price rises). However, the chance of a large payoff is greater for the option on firm Y's shares because Y's stock price is more volatile and therefore has more upside potential.

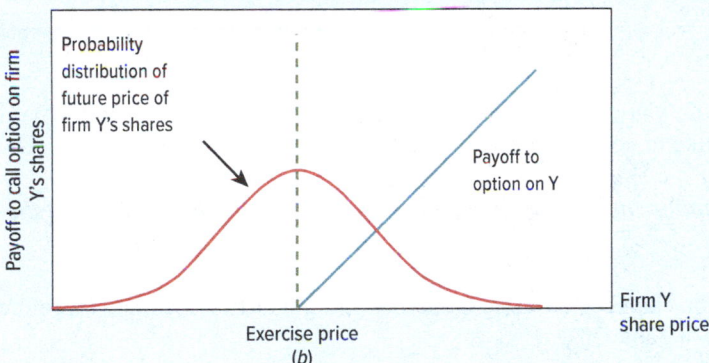

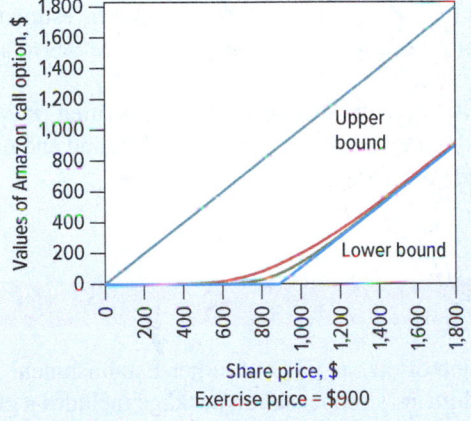

FIGURE 20.11

How the value of the Amazon call option increases with the volatility of the stock price. Each of the curved lines shows the value of the option for different initial stock prices. The only difference is that the upper line assumes a much higher level of uncertainty about Amazon's future stock price.

The probability of large stock price changes during the remaining life of an option depends on two things: (1) the variance (i.e., volatility) of the stock price *per period* and (2) the number of periods until the option expires. If there are t remaining periods, and the variance per period is σ^2, the value of the option should depend on cumulative variability $\sigma^2 t$.[16]

---

[16]Here is an intuitive explanation: If the stock price follows a random walk (Section 13-2), successive price changes are statistically independent. The cumulative price change before expiration is the sum of t random variables. The variance of a sum of independent random variables is the sum of the variances of those variables. Thus, if σ^2 is the variance of the daily price change, and there are t days until expiration, the variance of the cumulative price change is $\sigma^2 t$

> TABLE 20.2

What the price of a call option depends on

*The direct effect of increases in r_f or σ on option price, given the stock price. There may also be indirect effects. For example, an increase in r_f could reduce stock price P. This in turn could affect option price.

1. If There Is an *Increase* in:	The Change in the Call Option Price Is:
Stock price (P)	Positive
Exercise price (EX)	Negative
Interest rate (r_f)	Positive*
Time to expiration (t)	Positive
Volatility of stock price (σ)	Positive*

2. Other Properties of Call Options:

a. *Upper bound.* The option price is always less than the stock price.
b. *Lower bound.* The call price never falls below the payoff to immediate exercise ($P - EX$ or zero, whichever is larger).
c. If the stock is worthless, the call is worthless.
d. As the stock price becomes very large, the call price approaches the stock price less the present value of the exercise price.

Other things equal, you would like to hold an option on a volatile stock (high σ^2). Given volatility, you would like to hold an option with a long life ahead of it (large t).

Thus the value of an option increases with both the volatility of the share price and the time to maturity.

It's a rare person who can keep all these properties straight at first reading. Therefore, we have summed them up in Table 20.2.

Risk and Option Values

In most financial settings, risk is a bad thing; you have to be paid to bear it. Investors in risky (high-beta) stocks demand higher expected rates of return. High-risk capital investment projects have correspondingly high costs of capital and have to beat higher hurdle rates to achieve positive NPV.

For options it's the other way around. As we have just seen, options written on volatile assets are worth *more* than options written on safe assets.[17] If you can understand and remember that one fact about options, you've come a long way.

EXAMPLE 20.1 • Volatility and Executive Stock Options

Suppose you have to choose between two job offers, as CFO of either Establishment Industries or Digital Organics. Establishment Industries' compensation package includes a grant of the stock options described on the left side of Table 20.3. You demand a similar package from Digital Organics, and they comply. In fact, they match the Establishment Industries options in every respect, as you can see on the right side of Table 20.3. (The two companies' current stock prices just happen to be the same.) The only difference is that Digital Organics' stock is 50% more volatile than Establishment Industries' stock (36% annual standard deviation versus 24% for Establishment Industries).

---

[17]This is not as crazy as it may at first sound. *Given the price of the stock,* the option is more valuable when the stock is volatile. However, that same volatility may have reduced the amount that investors are prepared to pay for the stock.

	Establishment Industries	Digital Organics
Number of options	100,000	100,000
Exercise price	$25	$25
Maturity	5 years	5 years
Current stock price	$22	$22
Stock price volatility (standard deviation of return)	24%	36%

❯ **TABLE 20.3**   Which package of executive stock options would you choose? The package offered by Digital Organics is more valuable, because the volatility of that company's stock is higher.

If your job choice hinges on the value of the executive stock options, you should take the Digital Organics offer. The Digital Organics options are written on the more volatile asset and, therefore, are worth more.

We value the two stock-option packages in the next chapter.

SUMMARY

If you have managed to reach this point, you are probably in need of some fresh air and a run round the block. So we will summarize what we have learned so far and take up the subject of options again in the next chapter when you are refreshed.

There are two types of option. An American call is an option to buy an asset at a specified exercise price on or before a specified maturity date. Similarly, an American put is an option to sell the asset at a specified price on or before a specified date. European calls and puts are exactly the same except that they cannot be exercised before the specified maturity date. Calls and puts are the basic building blocks that can be combined to give any pattern of payoffs.

What determines the value of a call option? Common sense tells us that it ought to depend on three things:

1. To exercise an option you have to pay the exercise price. Other things being equal, the less you are obliged to pay, the better. Therefore, the value of a call option increases with the ratio of the asset price to the exercise price.

2. You do not have to pay the exercise price until you decide to exercise the option. Therefore, a call option gives you a free loan. The higher the rate of interest and the longer the time to maturity, the more this free loan is worth. So the value of a call option increases with the interest rate and time to maturity.

3. If the price of the asset falls short of the exercise price, you won't exercise the call option. You will, therefore, lose 100% of your investment in the option no matter how far the asset depreciates below the exercise price. On the other hand, the more the price rises *above* the exercise price, the more profit you will make. Therefore, the option holder does not lose from increased volatility if things go wrong, but gains if they go right. The value of an option increases with the variance per period of the stock return multiplied by the number of periods to maturity.

Always remember that an option written on a risky (high-variance) asset is worth more than an option on a safe asset. It's easy to forget, because in most other financial contexts, increases in risk reduce present value.

**FURTHER
READING**

See Further Readings for Chapter 21.

PROBLEM SETS

 **Select problems are available in McGraw-Hill's *Connect*.
Please see the preface for more information.**

1. **Vocabulary*** Complete the following passage:

   A _____ option gives its owner the opportunity to buy a stock at a specified price that is generally called the _____ price. A _____ option gives its owner the opportunity to sell stock at a specified price. Options that can be exercised only at maturity are called _____ options.

2. **Option payoffs*** Note Figure 20.12 below. Match each diagram, (*a*) and (*b*), with one of the following positions:

   - Call buyer
   - Call seller
   - Put buyer
   - Put seller

3. **Option payoffs** Look again at Figure 20.12. It appears that the investor in panel (*b*) can't lose and the investor in panel (*a*) can't win. Is that correct? Explain. (*Hint:* Draw a profit diagram for each panel.)

4. **Option payoffs** What is a call option worth at maturity if (a) the stock price is zero? (b) the stock price is extremely high relative to the exercise price?

5. **Option payoffs** "The buyer of the call and the seller of the put both hope that the stock price will rise. Therefore the two positions are identical." Is the speaker correct? Illustrate with a position diagram.

6. **Option combinations*** Suppose that you hold a share of stock and a put option on that share. What is the payoff when the option expires if (a) the stock price is below the exercise price? (b) the stock price is above the exercise price?

7. **Option combinations** Dr. Livingstone I. Presume holds £600,000 in East African gold stocks. Bullish as he is on gold mining, he requires absolute assurance that at least £500,000 will be available in six months to fund an expedition. Describe two ways for Dr. Presume to achieve this goal. There is an active market for puts and calls on East African gold stocks, and the rate of interest is 6% per year.

▶ **FIGURE 20.12**

See Problem 2

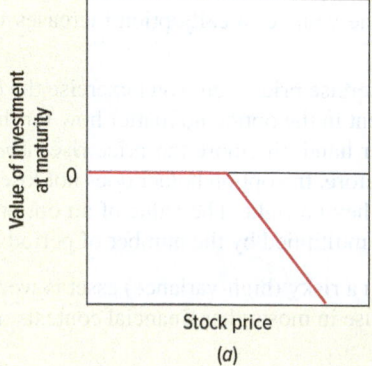
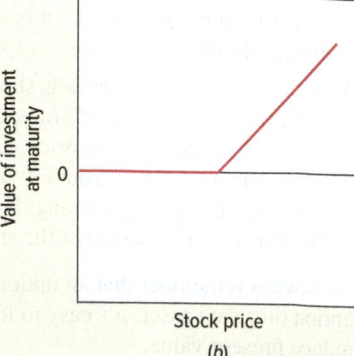

(*a*)   (*b*)

8. **Option combinations*** Suppose you buy a one-year European call option on Wombat stock with an exercise price of $100 and sell a one-year European put option with the same exercise price. The current stock price is $100, and the interest rate is 10%.

   a. Draw a position diagram showing the payoffs from your investments.

   b. How much will the combined position cost you? Explain.

9. **Option combinations** Suppose that Mr. Colleoni borrows the present value of $100, buys a six-month put option on stock Y with an exercise price of $150, and sells a six-month put option on Y with an exercise price of $50.

   a. Draw a position diagram showing the payoffs when the options expire.

   b. Suggest two other combinations of loans, options, and the underlying stock that would give Mr. Colleoni the same payoffs.

10. **Option combinations** Option traders often refer to "straddles" and "butterflies." Here is an example of each:

    - *Straddle:* Buy one call with exercise price of $100 and simultaneously buy one put with exercise price of $100.

    - *Butterfly:* Simultaneously buy one call with exercise price of $100, sell two calls with exercise price of $110, and buy one call with exercise price of $120.

    Draw position diagrams for the straddle and butterfly, showing the payoffs from the investor's net position. Each strategy is a bet on variability. Explain briefly the nature of each bet.

11. **Option combinations** Ms. Higden has been offered yet another incentive scheme (see Section 20-2). She will receive a bonus of $500,000 if the stock price at the end of the year is $120 or more; otherwise she will receive nothing. (Don't ask why anyone should want to offer such an arrangement. Maybe there's some tax angle.)

    a. Draw a position diagram illustrating the payoffs from such a scheme.

    b. What combination of options would provide these payoffs? (*Hint:* You need to buy a large number of options with one exercise price and sell a similar number with a different exercise price.)

12. **Option combinations** Discuss briefly the risks and payoffs of the following positions:

    a. Buy stock and a put option on the stock.

    b. Buy stock.

    c. Buy call.

    d. Buy stock and sell call option on the stock.

    e. Buy bond.

    f. Buy stock, buy put, and sell call.

    g. Sell put.

13. **Put–call parity** Which *one* of the following statements is correct?

    a. Value of put + present value of exercise price = value of call + share price

    b. Value of put + share price = value of call + present value of exercise price

    c. Value of put – share price = present value of exercise price – value of call

    d. Value of put + value of call = share price – present value of exercise price

    The correct statement equates the value of two investment strategies. Plot the payoffs to each strategy as a function of the stock price. Show that the two strategies give identical payoffs.

14. **Put-call parity** A European call and put option have the same maturity. Both are at-the-money, so that the stock price equals the exercise price. The stock does not pay a dividend. Which option should sell for the higher price? Explain.

15. **Put–call parity**

    a. If you can't sell a share short, you can achieve exactly the same final payoff by a combination of options and borrowing or lending. What is this combination?

    b. Now work out the mixture of stock and options that gives the same final payoff as investment in a risk-free loan.

16. **Put–call parity** The common stock of Triangular File Company is selling at $90. A 26-week call option written on Triangular File's stock is selling for $8. The call's exercise price is $100. The risk-free interest rate is 10% per year.

    a. Suppose that puts on Triangular stock are not traded, but you want to buy one. How would you do it?

    b. Suppose that puts *are* traded. What should a 26-week put with an exercise price of $100 sell for?

17. **Put–call parity** What is put–call parity and why does it hold? Could you apply the parity formula to a call and put with different exercise prices?

18. **Put–call parity** There is another strategy involving calls and borrowing or lending that gives the same payoffs as the strategy described in Problem 6. What is the alternative strategy?

19. **Put–call parity** It is possible to buy three-month call options and three-month puts on stock Q. Both options have an exercise price of $60 and both are worth $10. If the interest rate is 5% a year, what is the stock price? (*Hint:* Use put–call parity.)

20. **Put–call parity*** In April 2017, Facebook's stock price was about $145. An eight-month call on the stock, with an exercise price of $145, sold for $10.18. The risk-free interest rate was 1% a year. How much would you be willing to pay for a put on Facebook stock with the same maturity and exercise price? Assume that the Facebook options are European options. (*Note:* Facebook does not pay a dividend.)

21. **Option bounds** Pintail's stock price is currently $200. A one-year *American* call option has an exercise price of $50 and is priced at $75. How would you take advantage of this great opportunity?

22. **Option values*** How does the price of a call option respond to the following changes, other things equal? Does the call price go up or down?

    a. Stock price increases.

    b. Exercise price is increased.

    c. Risk-free rate increases.

    d. Expiration date of the option is extended.

    e. Volatility of the stock price falls.

    f. Time passes, so the option's expiration date comes closer.

23. **Option values** Respond to the following statements.

    a. "I'm a conservative investor. I'd much rather hold a call option on a safe stock like Exxon Mobil than a volatile stock like Amazon."

    b. "I bought an American call option on Fava Farms stock, with an exercise price of $45 per share and three more months to maturity. Fava Farms' stock has skyrocketed from $35 to $55 per share, but I'm afraid it will fall back below $45. I'm going to lock in my gain and exercise my call right now."

24. **Option values** FX Bank has succeeded in hiring ace foreign exchange trader Lucinda Cable. Her remuneration package reportedly includes an annual bonus of 20% of the profits that she generates in excess of $100 million. Does Ms. Cable have an option? Does it provide her with the appropriate incentives?

25. **Option values** Look at actual trading prices of call options on stocks to check whether they behave as the theory presented in this chapter predicts. For example,

    a. Follow several options as they approach maturity. How would you expect their prices to behave? Do they actually behave that way?

    b. Compare two call options written on the same stock with the same maturity but different exercise prices.

    c. Compare two call options written on the same stock with the same exercise price but different maturities.

26. **Option values** Is it more valuable to own an option to buy a portfolio of stocks or to own a portfolio of options to buy each of the individual stocks? Say briefly why.

27. **Option values** You've just completed a month-long study of energy markets and conclude that energy prices will be *much* more volatile in the next year than historically. Assuming you're right, what types of option strategies should you undertake? (*Note:* You can buy or sell options on oil-company stocks or on the price of future deliveries of crude oil, natural gas, fuel oil, etc.)

28. **Option values*** Table 20.4 lists some prices of options on common stocks (prices are quoted to the nearest dollar). The interest rate is 10% a year. Can you spot any mispricing? What would you do to take advantage of it?

CHALLENGE

29. **Option bounds** Problem 21 considered an arbitrage opportunity involving an American option. Suppose that this option was a European call. Show that there is a similar possible arbitrage profit.

30. **Option payoffs** Figure 20.13 shows some complicated position diagrams. Work out the combination of stocks, bonds, and options that produces each of these positions.

31. **Option payoffs** Some years ago the Australian firm Bond Corporation sold a share in some land that it owned near Rome for A$110 million and as a result boosted its annual earnings by A$74 million. A television program subsequently revealed that the buyer was given a put option to sell its share in the land back to Bond for A$110 million and that Bond had paid A$20 million for a call option to repurchase the share in the land for the same price.

    a. What happens if the land is worth more than A$110 million when the options expire? What if it is worth less than A$110 million?

    b. Use position diagrams to show the net effect of the land sale and the option transactions.

    c. Assume a one-year maturity on the options. Can you deduce the interest rate?

    d. The television program argued that it was misleading to record a profit on the sale of land. What do you think?

Stock	Time to Exercise (months)	Exercise Price	Stock Price	Put Price	Call Price
Drongo Corp.	6	$ 50	$80	$20	$52
Ragwort, Inc.	6	100	80	10	15
Wombat Corp.	3	40	50	7	18
Wombat Corp.	6	40	50	5	17
Wombat Corp.	6	50	50	8	10

❯ **TABLE 20.4**
Prices of options on common stocks (in dollars). See Problem 28.

▶ **FIGURE 20.13**

Some complicated position diagrams. See Problem 30.

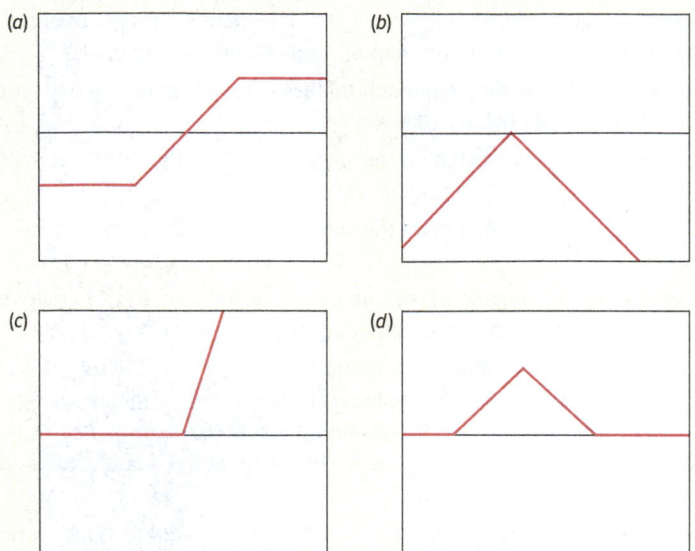

32. **Option values** Three six-month call options are traded on Hogswill stock:

Exercise Price	Call Option Price
$ 90	$ 5
100	11
110	15

How would you make money by trading in Hogswill options? (*Hint:* Draw a graph with the option price on the vertical axis and the ratio of stock price to exercise price on the horizontal axis. Plot the three Hogswill options on your graph. Does this fit with what you know about how option prices should vary with the ratio of stock price to exercise price?) Now look in the newspaper at options with the same maturity but different exercise prices. Can you find any money-making opportunities?

● ● ● ● ●

FINANCE ON THE WEB

Go to **finance.yahoo.com.** Check out the delayed quotes for Amazon options for different exercise prices and maturities. Take the mean of the bid and ask prices.

a. Confirm that higher exercise prices mean lower call prices and higher put prices.

b. Confirm that longer maturity means higher prices for both puts and calls.

c. Choose an Amazon put and call with the same exercise price and maturity. Confirm that put–call parity holds (approximately). (*Note:* You will have to use an up-to-date risk-free interest rate.)

CHAPTER

21

Valuing Options

In Chapter 20, we introduced you to call and put options. Call options give the owner the right to buy an asset at a specified exercise price; put options give the right to sell. We also took the first step toward understanding how options are valued. The value of a call option depends on five variables:

1. The higher the price of the asset, the more valuable an option to buy it.

2. The lower the price that you must pay to exercise the call, the more valuable the option.

3. You do not need to pay the exercise price until the option expires. This delay is most valuable when the interest rate is high.

4. If the stock price is below the exercise price at maturity, the call is valueless regardless of whether the price is $1 below or $100 below. However, for every dollar that the stock price rises above the exercise price, the option holder gains an additional dollar. Thus, the value of the call option increases with the volatility of the stock price.

5. Finally, a long-term option is more valuable than a short-term option. A distant maturity delays the point at which the holder needs to pay the exercise price and increases the chance of a large jump in the stock price before the option matures.

In this chapter, we show how these variables can be combined into an exact option-valuation model—a formula we can plug numbers into to get a definite answer. We first describe a simple way to value options, known as the binomial model. We then introduce the Black–Scholes formula for valuing options. Finally, we provide a checklist showing how these two methods can be used to solve a number of practical option problems.

The most efficient way to value most options is to use a computer. But in this chapter, we will work through some simple examples by hand. We do so because unless you understand the basic principles behind option valuation, you are likely to make mistakes in setting up an option problem, and you won't know how to interpret the computer's answer and explain it to others.

In Chapter 20, we looked at the put and call options on Amazon stock. In this chapter, we stick with that example and show you how to value the Amazon options. But remember *why* you need to understand option valuation. It is not to make a quick buck trading on an options exchange. It is because many capital budgeting and financing decisions have options embedded in them. We discuss a variety of these options in subsequent chapters.

21-1   A Simple Option-Valuation Model

Why Discounted Cash Flow Won't Work for Options

For many years, economists searched for a practical formula to value options until Fischer Black and Myron Scholes finally hit upon the solution. Later we will show you what they found, but first we should explain why the search was so difficult.

Our standard procedure for valuing an asset is to (1) figure out expected cash flows and (2) discount them at the opportunity cost of capital. Unfortunately, this is not practical for options. The first step is messy but feasible, but finding *the* opportunity cost of capital is impossible because the risk of an option changes every time the stock price moves.

When you buy a call, you are taking a position in the stock but putting up less of your own money than if you had bought the stock directly. Thus, an option is always riskier than the underlying stock. It has a higher beta and a higher standard deviation of returns.

How much riskier the option is depends on the stock price relative to the exercise price. A call option that is in the money (stock price greater than exercise price) is safer than one that is out of the money (stock price less than exercise price). Thus a stock price increase raises the option's expected payoff *and* reduces its risk. When the stock price falls, the option's payoff falls *and* its risk increases. That is why the expected rate of return investors demand from an option changes day by day, or hour by hour, every time the stock price moves.

We repeat the general rule: The higher the stock price is relative to the exercise price, the safer is the call option, although the option is always riskier than the stock. The option's risk changes every time the stock price changes.

Constructing Option Equivalents from Common Stocks and Borrowing

If you've digested what we've said so far, you can appreciate why options are hard to value by standard discounted-cash-flow formulas and why a rigorous option-valuation technique eluded economists for many years. The breakthrough came when Black and Scholes exclaimed, "Eureka! We have found it![1] The trick is to set up an *option equivalent* by combining common stock investment and borrowing. The net cost of buying the option equivalent must equal the value of the option."

We'll show you how this works with a simple numerical example. We'll travel back to April 2017 and consider a six-month call option on Amazon stock with an exercise price of $900. We'll pick a day when Amazon stock was also trading at $900, so that this option is *at the money*. The short-term, risk-free interest rate was $r = 0.5\%$ for 6 months, or about 1% a year.

To keep the example as simple as possible, we assume that Amazon stock can do only two things over the option's six-month life. The price could rise by 20% to $900 \times 1.2 = \$1,080$. Alternatively, it could fall by the same proportion to $900 \div 1.2 = \$750$, which is equivalent to a decline of $(900 - 750)/900 = 16.667\%$. The upward move is sometimes written as $u = 1.2$, and the downward move as $d = 1/u = 1/1.2$.

Warning: We will round some of our calculations slightly. So, if you are following along with your calculator, don't worry if your answers differ in the last decimal place.

If Amazon's stock price falls to $750, the call option will be worthless, but if the price rises to $1,080, the option will be worth $1,080 - 900 = \$180$. The possible payoffs to the option are therefore as follows:

	Stock Price = $750	Stock Price = $1,080
1 call option	$0	$180

---

[1] We do not know whether Black and Scholes, like Archimedes, were sitting in bathtubs at the time.

Now compare these payoffs with what you would get if you bought .54545 Amazon share and borrowed the present value of $409.09 from the bank:[2]

	Stock Price = $750	Stock Price = $1,080
0.54545 share	$409.09	$589.09
Repayment of loan + interest	−409.09	−409.09
Total payoff	$ 0	$180.00

Notice that the payoffs from the levered investment in the stock are identical to the payoffs from the call option. Therefore, the law of one price tells us that both investments must have the same value:

$$\text{Value of call} = \text{value of .54545 shares} - \text{value of bank loan}$$
$$= .54545 \times \$900 - 409.09/1.005 = \$83.85$$

Presto! You've valued a call option.

To value the Amazon option, we borrowed money and bought stock in such a way that we exactly replicated the payoff from a call option. This is called a **replicating portfolio.** The number of shares needed to replicate one call is called the **hedge ratio or option delta.** In our Amazon example, one call is replicated by a levered position in .54545 share. The option delta is, therefore, .54545.

How did we know that Amazon's call option was equivalent to a levered position in .54545 share? We used a simple formula that says:

$$\text{Option delta} = \frac{\text{spread of possible option prices}}{\text{spread of possible share prices}} = \frac{180 - 0}{1,080 - 750} = .54545$$

You have learned not only to value a simple option but also learned that you can replicate an investment in the option by a levered investment in the underlying asset. Thus, if you can't buy or sell a call option on an asset, you can create a homemade option by a replicating strategy—that is, you buy or sell delta shares and borrow or lend the balance.

Risk-Neutral Valuation Notice why the Amazon call option should sell for $83.85. If the option price is higher than $83.85, you could make a certain profit by buying .54545 share of stock, selling a call option, and borrowing the present value of $409.09. Similarly, if the option price is less than $83.85, you could make an equally certain profit by selling .54545 share, buying a call, and lending the balance. In either case, there would be an arbitrage opportunity.[3]

If there's a possible arbitrage profit, everyone scurries to take advantage of it. So when we said that the option price had to be $83.85 or there would be an arbitrage opportunity, we did not need to know anything about investor attitudes to risk. High-rolling speculators and total wimps would all jostle each other in the rush to realize a possible arbitrage profit. Thus, the option price cannot depend on whether investors detest risk or do not care a jot.

---

[2]The exact number of shares to buy is 180/330 = .54545. . . as explained below.
[3]Of course, you don't get seriously rich by dealing in .54545 share. But if you multiply each of our transactions by a million, it begins to look like real money.

This suggests an alternative way to value the option. We can *pretend* that all investors are *indifferent* about risk, work out the expected future value of the option in such a world, and discount it back at the risk-free interest rate to give the current value. Let us check that this method gives the same answer.

If investors are indifferent to risk, the expected return on the stock must be equal to the risk-free rate of interest:

$$\text{Expected return on Amazon stock} = 0.5\% \text{ per six months}$$

We know that Amazon stock can either rise by 20% to $1,080 or fall by 16.667% to $750. We can, therefore, calculate the probability of a price rise in our hypothetical risk-neutral world:

$$\text{Expected return} = [\text{probability of rise} \times 20\%]$$
$$+ [(1 - \text{probability of rise}) \times (-6.667\%)]$$
$$= 0.5\%$$

Therefore,

$$\text{Probability of rise} = .46815 \text{ or } 46.815\%$$

Notice that this is *not* the *true* probability that Amazon stock will rise. Since investors dislike risk, they will almost surely require a higher expected return than the risk-free interest rate from Amazon stock. Therefore, the true probability is greater than .46815.

The general formula for calculating the risk-neutral probability of a rise in value is

$$p = \frac{\text{interest rate} - \text{downside change}}{\text{upside change} - \text{downside change}} = \frac{r - d}{u - d}$$

In the case of Amazon:

$$p = \frac{.005 - (-.16667)}{.20 - (-.16667)} = .46815$$

We know that if the stock price rises, the call option will be worth $180; if it falls, the call will be worth nothing. Therefore, if investors are risk-neutral, the expected value of the call option is

$$[\text{Probability of rise} \times 180] + [(1 - \text{probability of rise}) \times 0]$$
$$= (.46815 \times 180) + (.53185 \times 0)$$
$$= \$84.27$$

And the *current* value of the call is

$$\frac{\text{Expected future value}}{1 + \text{interest rate}} = \frac{84.27}{1.005} = \$83.85$$

Exactly the same answer that we got earlier!

We now have two ways to calculate the value of an option:

1. Find the combination of stock and loan that replicates an investment in the option. Since the two strategies give identical payoffs in the future, they must sell for the same price today.

2. Pretend that investors do not care about risk so that the expected return on the stock is equal to the interest rate. Calculate the expected future value of the option in this

BEYOND THE PAGE

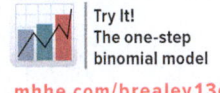 Try It!
The one-step
binomial model

mhhe.com/brealey13e

hypothetical *risk-neutral* world, and discount it at the risk-free interest rate. This idea may seem familiar to you. In Chapter 9, we showed how you can value an investment either by discounting the expected cash flows at a risk-adjusted discount rate or by adjusting the expected cash flows for risk and then discounting these *certainty-equivalent* flows at the risk-free interest rate. We have just used this second method to value the Amazon option. The certainty-equivalent cash flows on the stock and option are the cash flows that would be expected in a risk-neutral world.

Valuing the Amazon Put Option

Valuing the Amazon call option may well have seemed like pulling a rabbit out of a hat. To give you a second chance to watch how it is done, we will use the same method to value another option—this time, the six-month Amazon put option with a $900 exercise price.[4] We continue to assume that the stock price will either rise to $1,080 or fall to $750.

If Amazon's stock price rises to $1,080, the option to sell for $900 will be worthless. If the price falls to $750, the put option will be worth $900 − 750 = $150. Thus, the payoffs to the put are

	Stock Price = $750	Stock Price = $1,080
1 put option	$150	$0

We start by calculating the option delta using the formula that we presented previously:[5]

$$\text{Option delta} = \frac{\text{spread of possible option prices}}{\text{spread of possible stock prices}} = \frac{0 - 150}{1,080 - 750}$$

$$= -.45455$$

Notice that the delta of a put option is always negative; that is, you need to *sell* delta shares of stock to replicate the put. In the case of the Amazon put you can replicate the option payoffs by *selling* .45455 Amazon share and *lending* the present value of $490.91. Since you have sold the share short, you will need to lay out money at the end of six months to buy it back, but you will have money coming in from the loan. Your net payoffs are exactly the same as the payoffs you would get if you bought the put option:

	Stock Price = $750	Stock Price = $1,080
Sale of 0.45455 share	−$340.91	−$490.91
Repayment of loan + interest	+ 490.91	+ 490.91
Total payoff	$150.00	$ 0

Since the two investments have the same payoffs, they must have the same value:

$$\text{Value of put} = -(.45455)\text{ shares} + \text{value of bank loan}$$

$$= -(.45455) \times 900 + 490.91/1.005 = \$79.37$$

---

[4]When valuing *American* put options, you need to recognize the possibility that it will pay to exercise early. We discuss this complication later in the chapter, but it is unimportant for valuing the Amazon put and we ignore it here.

[5]The delta of a put option is always equal to the delta of a call option with the same exercise price minus one. In our example, delta of put = .54545 − 1 = −.45455

Valuing the Put Option by the Risk-Neutral Method   Valuing the Amazon put option with the risk-neutral method is a cinch. We already know that the probability of a rise in the stock price is .46815. Therefore, the expected value of the put option in a risk-neutral world is

$$[\text{Probability of rise} \times 0] + [(1 - \text{probability of rise}) \times 150]$$
$$= (.46815 \times 0) + (.53185 \times \$150)$$
$$= \$79.78$$

And therefore the *current* value of the put is

$$\frac{\text{Expected future value}}{1 + \text{interest rate}} = \frac{79.78}{1.005} = \$79.38$$

Apart from a minor rounding error, the two methods give the same answer.

The Relationship between Call and Put Prices   We pointed out earlier that for European options there is a simple relationship between the values of the call and the put.[6]

Value of put = value of call + present value of exercise price − share price

Since we had already calculated the value of the Amazon call, we could also have used this relationship to find the value of the put:

$$\text{Value of put} = 83.85 + \frac{900}{1.005} - 900 = \$79.37$$

Everything checks.

21-2   **The Binomial Method for Valuing Options**

The essential trick in pricing any option is to set up a package of investments in the stock and the loan that will exactly replicate the payoffs from the option. If we can price the stock and the loan, then we can also price the option. Equivalently, we can pretend that investors are risk-neutral, calculate the expected payoff on the option in this fictitious risk-neutral world, and discount by the rate of interest to find the option's present value.

These concepts are completely general, but the example in the last section used a simplified version of what is known as the **binomial method.** The method starts by reducing the possible changes in the next period's stock price to two, an "up" move and a "down" move. This assumption that there are just two possible prices for Amazon stock at the end of six months is clearly fanciful.

We could make the Amazon problem a trifle more realistic by assuming that there are two possible price changes in each three-month period. This would give a wider variety of six-month prices. And there is no reason to stop at three-month periods. We could go on to take shorter and shorter intervals, with each interval showing two possible changes in Amazon's stock price and giving an even wider selection of six-month prices.

We illustrate this in Figure 21.1. The top diagram shows our starting assumption: just two possible prices at the end of six months. Moving down, you can see what happens when there are two possible price changes every three months. This gives three possible stock prices when the option matures. In Figure 21.1c, we have gone on to divide the six-month period into 26 weekly periods, in each of which the price can make one of two small moves. The distribution of prices at the end of six months is now looking much more realistic.

---

[6]*Reminder:* This formula applies only when the two options have the same exercise price and exercise date.

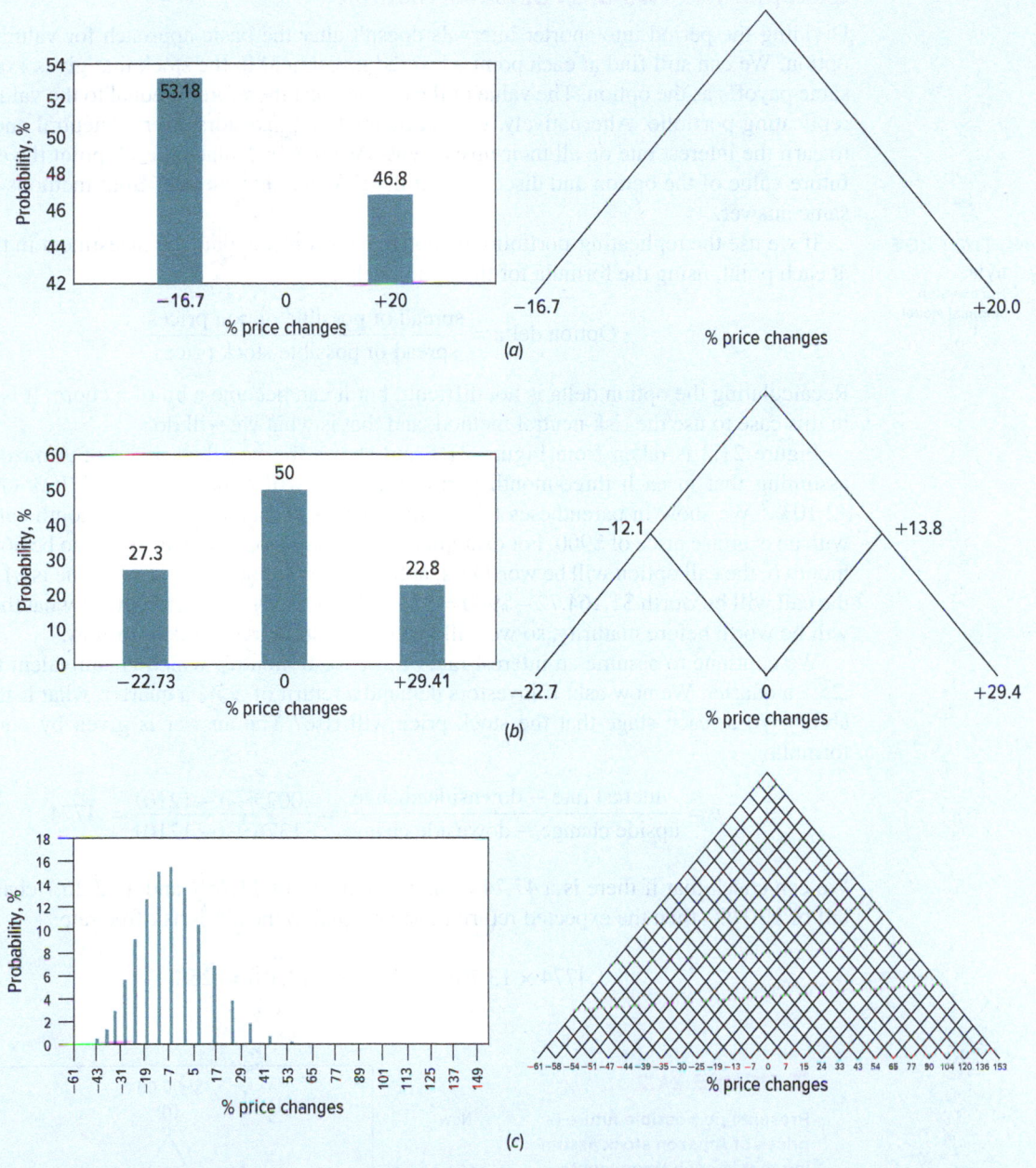

FIGURE 21.1   This figure shows the possible six-month price changes for Amazon stock assuming that the stock makes a single up or down move each six months (Fig. 21.1a); 2 moves, one every three months (Fig. 21.1b); or 26 moves, one every week (Fig. 21.1c). Beside each tree we show a histogram of the possible six-month price changes, assuming investors are risk-neutral.

We could continue in this way to chop the period into shorter and shorter intervals, until eventually we would reach a situation in which the stock price is changing continuously and there is a continuum of possible future stock prices. We demonstrate first with our simple two-step case in Figure 21.1b. Then we work up to the situation where the stock price is changing continuously. Don't panic; that won't be as bad as it sounds.

Example: The Two-Step Binomial Method

Dividing the period into shorter intervals doesn't alter the basic approach for valuing a call option. We can still find at each point a levered investment in the stock that gives exactly the same payoffs as the option. The value of the option must therefore be equal to the value of this replicating portfolio. Alternatively, we can pretend that investors are risk-neutral and expect to earn the interest rate on all their investments. We then calculate at each point the expected future value of the option and discount it at the risk-free interest rate. Both methods give the same answer.

If we use the replicating-portfolio method, we must recalculate the investment in the stock at each point, using the formula for the option delta:

$$\text{Option delta} = \frac{\text{spread of possible option prices}}{\text{spread of possible stock prices}}$$

BEYOND THE PAGE

Try It!
The two-step
binomial model

mhhe.com/brealey13e

Recalculating the option delta is not difficult, but it can become a bit of a chore. It is simpler in this case to use the risk-neutral method, and that is what we will do.

Figure 21.2 is taken from Figure 21.1 and shows the possible prices of Amazon stock, assuming that in each three-month period the price will either rise by 13.76% or fall by 12.10%.[7] We show in parentheses the possible values at maturity of a six-month call option with an exercise price of $900. For example, if Amazon's stock price turns out to be $695.45 in month 6, the call option will be worthless; at the other extreme, if the stock value is $1,164.72, the call will be worth $1,164.72 − $900 = $264.72. We haven't worked out yet what the option will be worth before maturity, so we will just put question marks there for now.

We continue to assume an interest rate of .5% for 6 months, which is equivalent to about .25% a quarter. We now ask: If investors demand a return of .25% a quarter, what is the probability (p) at each stage that the stock price will rise? The answer is given by our simple formula:

$$p = \frac{\text{interest rate} - \text{downside change}}{\text{upside change} - \text{downside change}} = \frac{.0025 - (-.1210)}{.1376 - (-.1210)} = .4774$$

We can check that if there is a 47.74% chance of a rise of 13.76% and a 52.26% chance of a fall of 12.10%, then the expected return must be equal to the .25% risk-free rate:

$$(.4774 \times 13.76) + (.5226 \times -12.10) = .25\%$$

▶ **FIGURE 21.2**

Present and possible future prices of Amazon stock assuming that in each three-month period the price will either rise by 13.76% or fall by 12.10%. Figures in parentheses show the corresponding values of a six-month call option with an exercise price of $900. The interest rate is .25% a quarter.

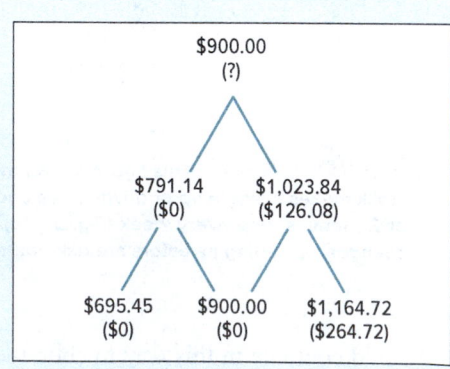

Option Value in Month 3   Now we can find the possible option values in month 3. Suppose that by the end of three months, the stock price has risen to $1,023.84. In that case, investors know that when the option finally matures in month 6, the option value will be either $0 or $264.72. We can therefore use our risk-neutral probabilities to calculate the expected option value at month 6:

$$\text{Expected value of call in month 6} = (\text{probability of rise} \times 264.72) + (\text{probability of fall} \times 0)$$
$$= (.4774 \times 264.72) + (.5226 \times 0) = \$126.39$$

And the value in month 3 is 126.39/1.0025 = $126.08.

What if the stock price falls to $791.14 by month 3? In that case the option is bound to be worthless at maturity. Its expected value is zero, and its value at month 3 is also zero.

Option Value Today   We can now get rid of two of the question marks in Figure 21.2. Figure 21.3 shows that if the stock price in month 3 is $1,023.84, the option value is $126.08, and if the stock price is $791.14, the option value is zero. It only remains to work back to the option value today.

There is a 47.74% chance that the option will be worth $126.08 and a 52.26% chance that it will be valueless. So the expected value in month 3 is

$$(.4774 \times 126.08) + (.5626 \times 0) = \$60.19$$

And the value today is 60.19/1.0025 = $60.05.

The General Binomial Method

Moving to two steps when valuing the Amazon call probably added extra realism. But there is no reason to stop there. We could go on, as in Figure 21.1, to chop the period into smaller and smaller intervals. We could still use the binomial method to work back from the final date to the present. Of course, it would be tedious to do the calculations by hand but simple to do so with a computer.

Since a stock can usually take on an almost limitless number of future values, the binomial method gives a more realistic and accurate measure of the option's value if we work with a large number of subperiods. But that raises an important question. How do we pick sensible figures for the up and down changes in value? For example, why did we pick figures of +13.76% and −12.1% when we revalued Amazon's option with two subperiods? Fortunately,

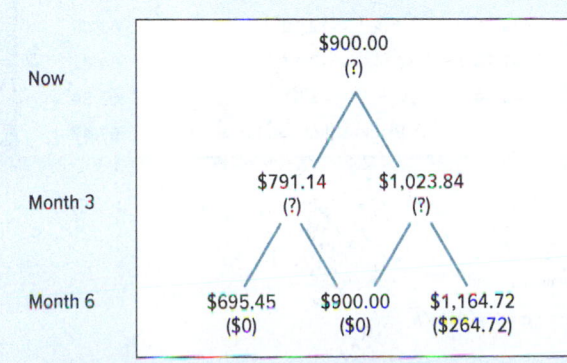

Now	$900.00 (?)		
Month 3	$791.14 (?)	$1,023.84 (?)	
Month 6	$695.45 ($0)	$900.00 ($0)	$1,164.72 ($264.72)

▶ **FIGURE 21.3**

Present and possible future prices of Amazon stock. Figures in parentheses show the corresponding values of a six-month call option with an exercise price of $900.

there is a neat little formula that relates the up and down changes to the standard deviation of stock returns:

$$1 + \text{upside change} = u = e^{\sigma\sqrt{h}}$$
$$1 + \text{downside change} = d = 1/u$$

where

e = base for natural logarithms = 2.718
σ = standard deviation of (continuously compounded) stock returns
h = interval as fraction of a year

When we said that Amazon's stock price could either rise by 20% or fall by 16.667% over six months ($h = .5$), our figures were consistent with a figure of 25.784% for the standard deviation of annual returns:[8]

$$1 + \text{upside change(6-month interval)} = u = e^{.25784\sqrt{.5}} = 1.2$$
$$1 + \text{downside change} = d = 1/u = 1/1.2 = .833$$

To work out the equivalent upside and downside changes when we divide the period into two three-month intervals ($h = .25$), we use the same formula:

$$1 + \text{upside change(3-month interval)} = u = e^{.25784\sqrt{.25}} = 1.1376$$
$$1 + \text{downside change} = d = 1/u = 1/1.1376 = .879$$

BEYOND THE PAGE

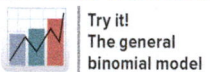

Try it!
The general
binomial model

mhhe.com/brealey13e

The center columns in Table 21.1 show the equivalent up and down moves in the value of the firm if we chop the period into six monthly or 26 weekly periods, and the final column shows the effect on the estimated option value. (We explain the Black–Scholes value shortly.)

The Binomial Method and Decision Trees

Calculating option values by the binomial method is basically a process of solving decision trees. You start at some future date and work back through the tree to the present. Eventually, the possible cash flows generated by future events and actions are folded back to a present value.

❯ **TABLE 21.1** As the number of steps is increased, you must adjust the range of possible changes in the value of the asset to keep the same standard deviation. But you will get increasingly close to the Black–Scholes value of the Amazon call option.

Note: The standard deviation is $\sigma = .25784$.

Number of Steps	Change per Interval (%)		Estimated Option Value
	Upside	Downside	
1	+20.00	−16.67	$83.85
2	+13.76	−12.10	60.05
6	+7.73	−7.17	64.82
26	+3.64	−3.51	66.84
		Black–Scholes value =	67.47

[8]To find the standard deviation given u, we turn the formula around:

$$\sigma = \log(u)/\sqrt{h}$$

where log = natural logarithm. In our example,

$$\sigma = \text{Log}(1.20)/\sqrt{(0.5)} = 0.1823/\sqrt{(0.5)} = 0.25784.$$

Is the binomial method *merely* another application of decision trees, a tool of analysis that you learned about in Chapter 10? The answer is no, for at least two reasons. First, option pricing theory is absolutely essential for discounting within decision trees. Discounting expected cash flows doesn't work within decision trees for the same reason that it doesn't work for puts and calls. As we pointed out in Section 21-1, there is no single, constant discount rate for options because the risk of the option changes as time and the price of the underlying asset change. There is no single discount rate inside a decision tree because, if the tree contains meaningful future decisions, it also contains options. The market value of the future cash flows described by the decision tree has to be calculated by option pricing methods.

Second, option theory gives a simple, powerful framework for describing complex decision trees. For example, suppose that you have the option to abandon an investment. The complete decision tree would overflow the largest classroom whiteboard. But now that you know about options, the opportunity to abandon can be summarized as "an American put." Of course, not all real problems have such easy option analogies, but we can often approximate complex decision trees by some simple package of assets and options. A custom decision tree may get closer to reality, but the time and expense may not be worth it. Most men buy their suits off the rack even though a custom-made Armani suit would fit better and look nicer.

21-3   The Black–Scholes Formula

Look back at Figure 21.1, which showed what happens to the distribution of possible Amazon stock price changes as we divide the option's life into a larger and larger number of increasingly small subperiods. You can see that the distribution of price changes becomes increasingly smooth.

If we continued to chop up the option's life in this way, we would eventually reach the situation shown in Figure 21.4, where there is a continuum of possible stock price changes at maturity. Figure 21.4 is an example of a lognormal distribution. The lognormal distribution is often used to summarize the probability of different stock price changes.[9] It has a number of good commonsense features. For example, it recognizes the fact that the stock price can

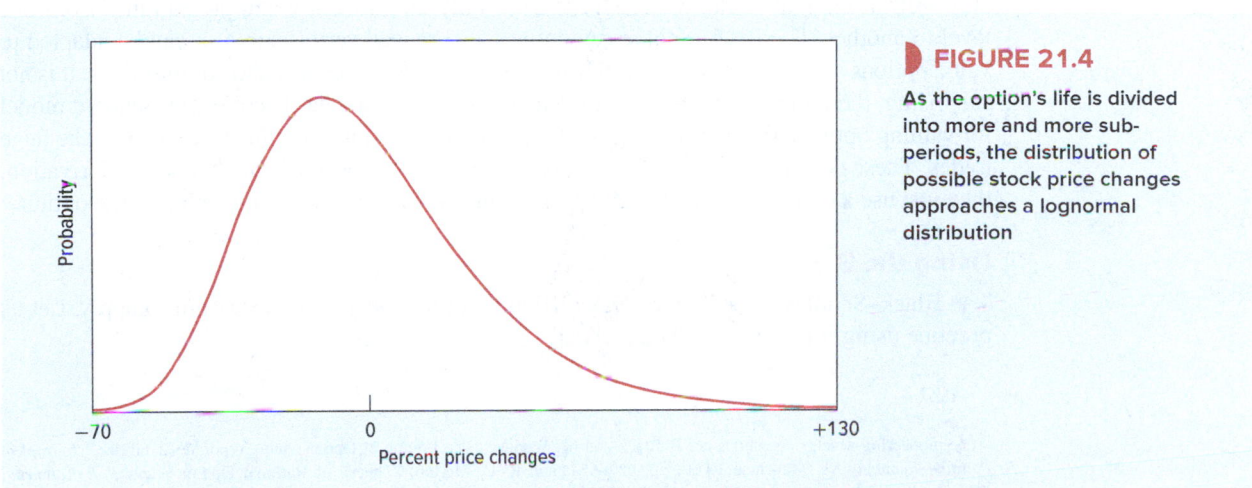

▶ **FIGURE 21.4**

As the option's life is divided into more and more subperiods, the distribution of possible stock price changes approaches a lognormal distribution

[9]When we first looked at the distribution of stock price changes in Chapter 8, we depicted these changes as normally distributed. We pointed out at the time that this is an acceptable approximation for very short intervals, but the distribution of changes over longer intervals is better approximated by the lognormal.

never fall by more than 100% but that there is some, perhaps small, chance that it could rise by much more than 100%.

Subdividing the option life into indefinitely small slices does not affect the principle of option valuation. We could still replicate the call option by a levered investment in the stock, but we would need to adjust the degree of leverage continuously as time went by. Calculating option value when there is an infinite number of subperiods may sound a hopeless task. Fortunately, Black and Scholes derived a formula that does the trick.[10] It is an unpleasant-looking formula, but on closer acquaintance you will find it exceptionally elegant and useful. The formula is

$$\text{Value of call option} = [\text{delta} \times \text{share price}] - [\text{bank loan}]$$
$$\uparrow \qquad\qquad \uparrow \qquad\qquad \uparrow$$
$$[N(d_1) \times P] - [N(d_2) \times \text{PV(EX)}]$$

where

$$d_1 = \frac{\log[P/\text{PV(EX)}]}{\sigma\sqrt{t}} + \frac{\sigma\sqrt{t}}{2}$$

$$d_2 = d_1 - \sigma\sqrt{t}$$

$N(d)$ = cumulative normal probability density function[11]

EX = exercise price of option; PV(EX) is calculated by discounting at the risk-free interest rate r_f

t = number of periods to exercise date

P = price of stock now

σ = standard deviation per period of (continuously compounded) rate of return on stock

Notice that the value of the call in the Black–Scholes formula has the same properties that we identified earlier. It increases with the level of the stock price P and decreases with the present value of the exercise price PV(EX), which in turn depends on the interest rate and time to maturity. It also increases with the time to maturity and the stock's variability ($\sigma\sqrt{t}$).

To derive their formula, Black and Scholes assumed that there is a continuum of stock prices, and therefore to replicate an option, investors must continuously adjust their holding in the stock.[12] Of course, this is not literally possible, but even so, the formula performs remarkably well in the real world, where stocks trade only intermittently and prices jump from one level to another. The Black–Scholes model has also proved very flexible; it can be adapted to value options on a variety of assets such as foreign currencies, bonds, and commodities. It is not surprising, therefore, that it has been extremely influential and has become the standard model for valuing options. Every day, dealers on the options exchanges use this formula to make huge trades. These dealers are not for the most part trained in the formula's mathematical derivation; they just use a computer or a specially programmed calculator to find the value of the option.

Using the Black–Scholes Formula

The Black–Scholes formula may look difficult, but it is very straightforward to apply. Let us practice using it to value the Amazon call.

---

[10] The pioneering articles on options are F. Black and M. Scholes, "The Pricing of Options and Corporate Liabilities," *Journal of Political Economy* 81 (May–June 1973), pp. 637–654; and R. C. Merton, "Theory of Rational Option Pricing," *Bell Journal of Economics and Management Science* 4 (Spring 1973), pp. 141–183.

[11] That is, $N(d)$ is the probability that a normally distributed random variable $\tilde{x}$ will be less than or equal to d. $N(d_1)$ in the Black–Scholes formula is the option delta. Thus the formula tells us that the value of a call is equal to an investment of $N(d_1)$ in the common stock less borrowing of $N(d_2) \times$ PV(EX).

[12] The important assumptions of the Black–Scholes formula are that (1) the price of the underlying asset follows a lognormal random walk, (2) investors can adjust their hedge continuously and costlessly, (3) the risk-free rate is known, and (4) the underlying asset does not pay dividends.

Here are the data that you need:

- Price of stock now $= P = 900$
- Exercise price $=$ EX $= 900$
- Standard deviation of continuously compounded annual returns $= \sigma = .25784$
- Years to maturity $= t = .5$
- Interest rate per annum $= r_f = .5\%$ for 6 months or about 1% per annum[13]

Remember that the Black–Scholes formula for the value of a call is

$$[N(d_1) \times P] - [N(d_2) \times \text{PV(EX)}]$$

where

$$d_1 = \log[P/\text{PV(EX)}]/\sigma\sqrt{t} + \sigma\sqrt{t}/2$$
$$d_2 = d_1 - \sigma\sqrt{t}$$
$$N(d) = \text{cumulative normal probability function}$$

There are three steps to using the formula to value the Amazon call:

Step 1   Calculate d_1 and d_2. This is just a matter of plugging numbers into the formula (noting that "log" means *natural* log):

$$d_1 = \log[P/\text{PV(EX)}]/\sigma\sqrt{t} + \sigma\sqrt{t}/2$$
$$= \log[900/(900/1.005)]/(.25784 \times \sqrt{.5}) + .25784 \times \sqrt{.5}/2$$
$$= .1184$$
$$d_2 = d_1 - \sigma\sqrt{t} = .1184 - .25784 \times \sqrt{.5} = -.0639$$

Step 2   Find $N(d_1)$ and $N(d_2)$. $N(d_1)$ is the probability that a normally distributed variable will be less than d_1 standard deviations above the mean. If d_1 is large, $N(d_1)$ is close to 1.0 (i.e., you can be almost certain that the variable will be less than d_1 standard deviations above the mean). If d_1 is zero, $N(d_1)$ is .5 (i.e., there is a 50% chance that a normally distributed variable will be below the average).

The simplest way to find $N(d_1)$ is to use the Excel function NORMSDIST. For example, if you enter NORMSDIST(.1184) into an Excel spreadsheet, you will see that there is a .5471 probability that a normally distributed variable will be less than .1184 standard deviations above the mean.

Again you can use the Excel function to find $N(d_2)$. If you enter NORMSDIST (−.0639) into an Excel spreadsheet, you should get the answer .4745. In other words, there is a probability of .4745 that a normally distributed variable will be less than .0639 standard deviations *below* the mean.

---

[13]When valuing options, it is more common to use continuously compounded rates to calculate PV(EX) (see Section 2-4). As long as the two rates are equivalent, both methods give the same answer, so why do we bother to mention the subject here? It is simply because most computer programs for valuing options call for a continuously compounded rate. If you enter an annually compounded rate by mistake, the error will usually be small, but you can waste a lot of time trying to trace it.

BEYOND THE PAGE

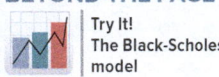

Try It!
The Black-Scholes
model

mhhe.com/brealey13e

Step 3   Plug these numbers into the Black–Scholes formula. You can now calculate the value of the Amazon call:

$$[\text{Delta} \times \text{price}] - [\text{bank loan}]$$
$$= [N(d_1) \times P] - [N(d_2) \times \text{PV(EX)}]$$
$$= [.5471 \times 900] - [.4745 \times (900/1.005)] = 492.43 - 424.96 = \$67.47$$

In other words, you can replicate the Amazon call option by investing $492.43 in the company's stock and borrowing $424.96. Subsequently, as time passes and the stock price changes, you may need to borrow a little more to invest in the stock or you may need to sell some of your stock to reduce your borrowing.

Some More Practice   Suppose you repeat the calculations for the Amazon call for a wide range of stock prices. The result is shown in Figure 21.5. You can see that the option values lie along an upward-sloping curve that starts its travels in the bottom left-hand corner of the diagram. As the stock price increases, the option value rises and gradually becomes parallel to the lower bound for the option value. This is exactly the shape we deduced in Chapter 20 (see Figure 20.9).

The height of this curve of course depends on risk and time to maturity. For example, if the risk of Amazon stock had suddenly increased, the curve shown in Figure 21.5 would rise at every possible stock price. For example, Figure 20.11 shows what would happen to the curve if the risk of Amazon stock doubled.

The Risk of an Option

How risky is the Amazon call option? We have seen that you can exactly replicate a call by a combination of risk-free borrowing and an investment in the stock. So the risk of the option must be the same as the risk of this replicating portfolio. We know that the beta of any portfolio is simply a weighted average of the betas of the separate holdings. So the risk of the option is just a weighted average of the betas of the investments in the loan and the stock.

On past evidence, the beta of Amazon stock is $\beta_{\text{stock}} = 1.5$; the beta of a risk-free loan is $\beta_{\text{loan}} = 0$. You are investing $492.43 in the stock and –$424.96 in the loan. (Notice that the investment in the loan is negative—you are *borrowing* money.) Therefore the beta of the option is $\beta_{\text{option}} = (-424.96 \times 0 + 492.43 \times 1.5)/(-424.96 + 492.43) = 10.95$. Notice that because a call option is equivalent to a levered position in the stock, it is always riskier than the stock itself. In Amazon's case, the option is about 7 times as risky as the stock and 11 times as risky as the market. As time passes and the price of Amazon stock changes, the risk of the option will also change.

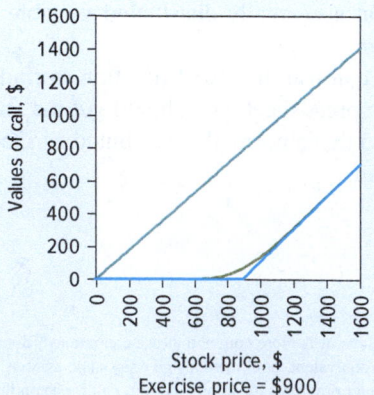

▶ **FIGURE 21.5**

The curved line shows how the value of the Amazon call option changes as the price of Amazon stock changes

The Black–Scholes Formula and the Binomial Method

Look back at Table 21.1, where we used the binomial method to calculate the value of the Amazon call. Notice that, as the number of intervals is increased, the values that you obtain from the binomial method begin to snuggle up to the Black–Scholes value of $67.47.

The Black–Scholes formula recognizes a continuum of possible outcomes. This is usually more realistic than the limited number of outcomes assumed in the binomial method. The formula is also more accurate and quicker to use than the binomial method. So why use the binomial method at all? The answer is that there are many circumstances in which you cannot use the Black–Scholes formula, but the binomial method will still give you a good measure of the option's value. We will look at several such cases in Section 21-5.

21-4   Black–Scholes in Action

To illustrate the principles of option valuation, we focused on the example of Amazon's options. But financial managers turn to the Black–Scholes model to estimate the value of a variety of different options. Here are four examples.

Executive Stock Options

In fiscal year 2017, Larry Ellison, the CEO of Oracle Corporation, received a salary of $1, but he also pocketed $21 million in the form of options and other stock-related awards.

Executive stock options are often an important part of compensation. For many years, companies were able to avoid reporting the cost of these options in their annual statements. However, they must now treat options as an expense just like salaries and wages, so they need to estimate the value of all new options that they have granted. For example, Oracle's financial statements show that in fiscal 2017, the company issued a total of 18 million options with an average life of 4.8 years. Oracle calculated that the average value of these options was $8.18. How did it come up with this figure? It just used the Black–Scholes model assuming a standard deviation of 23%.[14]

Some companies have disguised how much their management is paid by backdating the grant of an option. Suppose, for example, that a firm's stock price has risen from $20 to $40. At that point, the firm awards its CEO options exercisable at $20. That is generous but not illegal. However, if the firm pretends that the options were *actually* awarded when the stock price was $20 and values them on that basis, it will substantially understate the CEO's compensation.[15] The Beyond the Page app discusses the backdating scandal.

Speaking of executive stock options, we can now use the Black–Scholes formula to value the option packages you were offered in Section 20-3 (see Table 20.3). Table 21.2 calculates the value of the options from the safe-and-stodgy Establishment Industries at $5.26 each. The options from risky-and-glamorous Digital Organics are worth $7.40 each. Congratulations.

BEYOND THE PAGE

The Perfect
Payday

mhhe.com/brealey13e

Warrants

When Owens Corning emerged from bankruptcy in 2006, the debtholders became the sole owners of the company. But the old stockholders were not left entirely empty-handed. They

---

[14]Many of the recipients of these options may not have agreed with Oracle's valuation. First, the options were less valuable to their owners if they created substantial undiversifiable risk. Second, if the holders planned to quit the company in the next few years, they were liable to forfeit the options. For a discussion of these issues see J. I. Bulow and J. B. Shoven, "Accounting for Stock Options," *Journal of Economic Perspectives* 19 (Fall 2005), pp. 115–135.

[15]Until 2005, companies were obliged to record as an expense any difference between the stock price when the options were granted and the exercise price. Thus, as long as the options were granted at-the-money (exercise price equals stock price), the company was not obliged to show any expense.

> **TABLE 21.2**   Using the Black–Scholes formula to value the executive stock options for Establishment Industries and Digital Organics (see Table 20.3)

	Establishment Industries	Digital Organics
Stock price (P)	$22	$22
Exercise price (EX)	$25	$25
Interest rate (r_f)	0.04	0.04
Maturity in years (t)	5	5
Standard deviation (σ)	0.24	0.36
$d_1 = \log[P/PV(EX)]/\sigma\sqrt{t} + \sigma\sqrt{t}/2$	0.3955	0.4873
$d_2 = d_1 - \sigma\sqrt{t}$	−0.1411	−0.3177
Call value = $[N(d_1) \times P] - [N(d_2) \times PV(EX)]$	$5.26	$7.40

were given warrants to buy the new common stock at any point in the next seven years for $45.25 a share. Because the stock in the restructured firm was worth about $30 a share, the stock needed to appreciate by 50% before the warrants would be worth exercising. However, this option to buy Owens Corning stock was clearly valuable, and shortly after the warrants started trading, they were selling for $6 each. You can be sure that before shareholders were handed this bone, all the parties calculated the value of the warrants under different assumptions about the stock's volatility. The Black–Scholes model is tailor-made for this purpose.[16]

Portfolio Insurance

Your company's pension fund owns an $800 million diversified portfolio of common stocks that moves closely in line with the market index. The pension fund is currently fully funded, but you are concerned that if it falls by more than 20%, it will start to be underfunded. Suppose that your bank offers to insure you for one year against this possibility. What would you be prepared to pay for this insurance? Think back to Section 20-2 (Figure 20.5), where we showed that you can shield against a fall in asset prices by buying a protective put option. In the present case, the bank would be selling you a one-year put option on U.S. stock prices with an exercise price 20% below their current level. You can get the value of that option in two steps. First use the Black–Scholes formula to value a call with the same exercise price and maturity. Then back out the put value from put–call parity. (You may have to adjust for dividends, but we'll leave that to the next section.)

Calculating Implied Volatilities

So far, we have used our option pricing model to calculate the value of an option given the standard deviation of the asset's returns. Sometimes it is useful to turn the problem around and ask what the option price is telling us about the asset's volatility. For example, the

---

[16]Postscript: Unfortunately, Owens Corning's stock price never reached $45 and the warrants expired worthless.

Chicago Board Options Exchange trades options on several market indexes. As we write this, the Standard and Poor's 500 Index is about 2375, while a seven-month at-the-money call on the index is priced at 89. If the Black–Scholes formula is correct, then an option value of 89 makes sense only if investors believe that the standard deviation of index returns is about 11.4% a year.[17]

The Chicago Board Options Exchange regularly publishes the implied volatility on the Standard and Poor's index, which it terms the VIX (see the nearby box on the "fear index"). There is an active market in the VIX. For example, suppose you feel that the implied volatility is implausibly low. Then you can "buy" the VIX at the current low price and hope to "sell" it at a profit when implied volatility has increased.

You may be interested to compare the current implied volatility that we calculated earlier with Figure 21.6, which shows past measures of implied volatility for the Standard and Poor's index and for the Nasdaq index (VXN). Notice the sharp increase in investor uncertainty at the height of the credit crunch in 2008. This uncertainty showed up in the price that investors were prepared to pay for options.

BEYOND THE PAGE

The option smile

mhhe.com/brealey13e

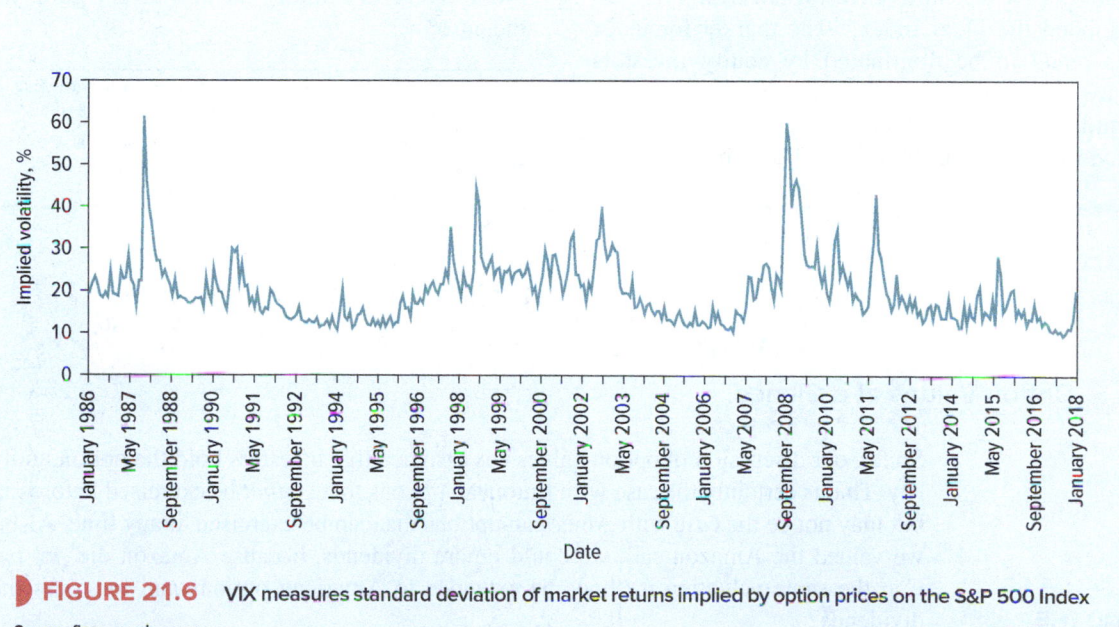

▶ **FIGURE 21.6**   VIX measures standard deviation of market returns implied by option prices on the S&P 500 Index

Source: finance.yahoo.com.

---

[17]In calculating the implied volatility we need to allow for the dividends paid on the shares. We explain how to take these into account in the next section.

The Fear Index*

❯ The Market Volatility Index, or VIX, measures the volatility that is implied by near-term Standard & Poor's 500 Index options and is therefore an estimate of expected *future* market volatility over the next 30 calendar days. Implied market volatilities have been calculated by the Chicago Board Options Exchange (CBOE) since January 1986, though in its current form, the VIX dates back only to 2003.

Investors regularly trade volatility. They do so by buying or selling VIX futures and options contracts. Since these were introduced by the Chicago Board Options Exchange (CBOE), combined trading activity in the two contracts has grown to more than 100,000 contracts per day, making them two of the most successful innovations ever introduced by the exchange.

Because VIX measures investor uncertainty, it has been dubbed the "fear index." The market for index options tends to be dominated by equity investors who buy index puts when they are concerned about a potential drop in the stock market. Any subsequent decline in the value of their portfolio is then offset by the increase in the value of the put option. The more that investors demand such insurance, the higher the price of index put options. Thus VIX is an indicator that reflects the cost of portfolio insurance.

Between January 1986 and February 2018, the VIX has averaged 20.0%, almost identical to the long-term level of market volatility that we cited in Chapter 7. The high point for the index was in October 1987 when the VIX closed the month at 61%,[**] but there have been several other short-lived spikes, for example, at the time of Iraq's invasion of Kuwait and the subsequent response by UN forces.

Although the VIX is the most widely quoted measure of volatility, volatility measures are also available for several other U.S. and overseas stock market indexes (such as the FTSE 100 Index in the U.K. and the CAC 40 in France), as well as for gold, oil, and the euro.

---

[*]For a review of the VIX index, see R. E. Whaley, "Understanding the VIX," *Journal of Portfolio Management 35* (Spring 2009), pp. 98–105.

[**]On October 19, 1987 (Black Monday), the VIX closed at 150. Fortunately, the market volatility returned fairly rapidly to less exciting levels.

21-5 Option Values at a Glance

So far, our discussion of option values has assumed that investors hold the option until maturity. That is certainly the case with European options that *cannot* be exercised before maturity but may not be the case with American options that can be exercised at any time. Also, when we valued the Amazon call, we could ignore dividends, because Amazon did not pay any. Can the same valuation methods be extended to American options and to stocks that pay dividends?

BEYOND THE PAGE

Dilution

mhhe.com/brealey13e

Another question concerns dilution. When investors buy and then exercise traded options, there is no effect on the number of shares issued by the company. But sometimes the company itself may give options to key employees or sell them to investors. When these options are exercised, the number of outstanding shares *does* increase, and therefore the stake of existing stockholders is diluted. Option valuation models need to be able to cope with the effect of dilution. The Beyond the Page feature shows how to do this.

In this section, we look at how the possibility of early exercise and dividends affect option value.

American Calls—No Dividends   Unlike European options, American options can be exercised any time. However, we know that in the absence of dividends, the value of a call option increases with time to maturity. So, if you exercised an American call option early, you would needlessly reduce its value. Because an American call should not be exercised before maturity, its value is the same as that of a European call, and the Black–Scholes model applies to both options.

European Puts—No Dividends   If we wish to value a European put, we can use the put–call parity formula from Chapter 20:

$$\text{Value of put} = \text{value of call} - \text{value of stock} + \text{PV(exercise price)}$$

American Puts—No Dividends   It can sometimes pay to exercise an American put before maturity in order to reinvest the exercise price. For example, suppose that immediately after you buy an American put, the stock price falls to zero. In this case, there is no advantage to holding onto the option because it *cannot* become more valuable. It is better to exercise the put and invest the exercise money. Thus, an American put is always more valuable than a European put. In our extreme example, the difference is equal to the present value of the interest that you could earn on the exercise price. In all other cases, the difference is less.

Because the Black–Scholes formula does not allow for early exercise, it cannot be used to value an American put exactly. But you can use the step-by-step binomial method as long as you check at each point whether the option is worth more dead than alive and then use the higher of the two values.

European Calls and Puts on Dividend-Paying Stocks   Part of the share value comprises the present value of dividends. The option holder is not entitled to dividends. Therefore, when using the Black–Scholes model to value a European option on a dividend-paying stock, you should reduce the price of the stock by the present value of the dividends to be paid before the option's maturity.

Dividends don't always come with a big label attached, so look out for instances where the asset holder gets a benefit and the option holder does not. For example, when you buy foreign currency, you can invest it to earn interest; but if you own an option to buy foreign currency, you miss out on this income. Therefore, when valuing an option to buy foreign currency, you need to deduct the present value of this foreign interest from the current price of the currency.[18]

American Calls on Dividend-Paying Stocks   We have seen that when the stock does not pay dividends, an American call option is *always* worth more alive than dead. By holding on to the option, you not only keep your option open, but also earn interest on the exercise money. Even when there are dividends, you should never exercise early if the dividend you gain is less than the interest you lose by having to pay the exercise price early. However, if the dividend

---

[18]For example, just suppose that it costs $2 to buy £1 and that this pound can be invested to earn interest of 5%. The option holder misses out on interest of .05 × $2 = $.10. So, before using the Black–Scholes formula to value an option to buy sterling, you must adjust the current price of sterling: Adjusted price of sterling = current price − PV(interest) = $2 − .10/1.05 = $1.905

is sufficiently large, you might want to capture it by exercising the option just before the ex-dividend date.

The only general method for valuing an American call on a dividend-paying stock is to use the step-by-step binomial method. In this case, you must check at each stage to see whether the option is more valuable if exercised just before the ex-dividend date than if held for at least one more period.

21-6 The Option Menagerie

Our focus in the past two chapters has been on plain-vanilla puts and calls or combinations of them. An understanding of these options and how they are valued will allow you to handle most of the option problems that you are likely to encounter in corporate finance. However, you may occasionally encounter some more unusual options. We are not going to be looking at them in this book, but just for fun and to help you hold your own in conversations with your investment banker friends, here is a crib sheet that summarizes a few of these exotic options:

Asian (or average) option	The exercise price is equal to the *average* of the asset's price during the life of the option.
Barrier option	Option where the payoff depends on whether the asset price reaches a specified level. A knock-in option (up-and-in call or down-and-in put) comes into existence only when the underlying asset reaches the barrier. Knock-out options (down-and-out call or up-and-out put) *cease* to exist if the asset price reaches the barrier.
Bermuda option	The option is exercisable on discrete dates before maturity.
Caput option	Call option on a put option.
Chooser (as-you-like-it) option	The holder must decide before maturity whether the option is a call or a put.
Compound option	An option on an option.
Digital (binary or cash-or-nothing) option	The option payoff is zero if the asset price is the wrong side of the exercise price and otherwise is a fixed sum.
Lookback option	The option holder chooses as the exercise price any of the asset prices that occurred before the final date.
Rainbow option	Call (put) option on the best (worst) of a basket of assets.

SUMMARY

In this chapter, we introduced the basic principles of option valuation by considering a call option on a stock that could take on one of two possible values at the option's maturity. We showed that it is possible to construct a package of the stock and a loan that would provide exactly the same payoff as the option *regardless* of whether the stock price rises or falls. Therefore, the value of the option must be the same as the value of this replicating portfolio.

We arrived at the same answer by pretending that investors are risk-neutral, so that the expected return on every asset is equal to the interest rate. We calculated the expected future value of the option in this imaginary risk-neutral world and then discounted this figure at the interest rate to find the option's present value.

The general binomial method adds realism by dividing the option's life into a number of subperiods in each of which the stock price can make one of two possible moves. Chopping the period into these shorter intervals doesn't alter the basic method for valuing a call option. We can still replicate the call by a package of the stock and a loan, but the package changes at each stage.

Finally, we introduced the Black–Scholes formula. This calculates the option's value when the stock price is constantly changing and takes on a continuum of possible future values.

An option can be replicated by a package of the underlying asset and a risk-free loan. Therefore, we can measure the risk of any option by calculating the risk of this portfolio. Naked options are often substantially more risky than the asset itself.

When valuing options in practical situations there are a number of features to look out for. For example, you may need to recognize that the option value is reduced by the fact that the holder is not entitled to any dividends.

● ● ● ● ●

FURTHER READING

Three readable articles about the Black–Scholes model are:

F. Black, "How We Came up with the Option Formula," *Journal of Portfolio Management* 15 (1989), pp. 4–8.

F. Black, "The Holes in Black–Scholes," *RISK Magazine* 1 (1988), pp. 27–29.

F. Black, "How to Use the Holes in Black–Scholes," *Journal of Applied Corporate Finance* 1 (Winter 1989), pp. 67–73.

There are a number of good books on option valuation. They include:

J. Hull, *Options, Futures and Other Derivatives,* 10th ed. (Cambridge, UK: Pearson, 2017).

R. L. McDonald, *Derivatives Markets,* 3rd ed. (Cambridge, UK: Pearson, 2012).

P. Wilmott, *Paul Wilmott on Quantitative Finance,* 2nd ed. (New York: John Wiley & Sons, 2006).

● ● ● ● ●

PROBLEM SETS

Select problems are available in McGraw-Hill's *Connect*. Please see the preface for more information.

1. **Binomial model*** Over the coming year, Ragwort's stock price will halve to $50 from its current level of $100 or it will rise to $200. The one-year interest rate is 10%.

   a. What is the delta of a one-year call option on Ragwort stock with an exercise price of $100?

   b. Use the replicating-portfolio method to value this call.

   c. In a risk-neutral world, what is the probability that Ragwort stock will rise in price?

   d. Use the risk-neutral method to check your valuation of the Ragwort option.

   e. If someone told you that in reality there is a 60% chance that Ragwort's stock price will rise to $200, would you change your view about the value of the option? Explain.

2. **Binomial model** Imagine that Amazon's stock price will either rise by 33.3% or fall by 25% over the next six months (see Section 21-1). Recalculate the value of the call option (exercise price = $900) using (a) the replicating portfolio method and (b) the risk-neutral method. Explain intuitively why the option value rises from the value computed in Section 21-1.

3. **Binomial model** The stock price of Heavy Metal (HM) changes only once a month: Either it goes up by 20% or it falls by 16.7%. Its price now is $40. The interest rate is 1% per month.

   a. What is the value of a one-month call option with an exercise price of $40?

   b. What is the option delta?

   c. Show how the payoffs of this call option can be replicated by buying HM's stock and borrowing.

   d. What is the value of a two-month call option with an exercise price of $40?

   e. What is the option delta of the two-month call over the first one-month period?

4. **Binomial model** Suppose a stock price can go up by 15% or down by 13% over the next year. You own a one-year put on the stock. The interest rate is 10%, and the current stock price is $60.

   a. What exercise price leaves you indifferent between holding the put or exercising it now?

   b. How does this break-even exercise price change if the interest rate is increased?

5. **Two-step binomial model*** Take another look at our two-step binomial trees for Amazon in Figure 21.2. Use the risk-neutral method to value six-month call and put options with an exercise price of $750. Assume the Amazon stock price is $900.

6. **Two-step binomial model** Buffelhead's stock price is $220 and could halve or double in each six-month period (equivalent to a standard deviation of 98%). A one-year call option on Buffelhead has an exercise price of $165. The interest rate is 21% a year.

   a. What is the value of the Buffelhead call?

   b. Now calculate the option delta for the second six months if (1) the stock price rises to $440 and (2) the stock price falls to $110.

   c. How does the call option delta vary with the level of the stock price? Explain intuitively why.

   d. Suppose that in month 6, the Buffelhead stock price is $110. How, at that point, could you replicate an investment in the stock by a combination of call options and risk-free lending? Show that your strategy does indeed produce the same returns as those from an investment in the stock.

7. **Two-step binomial model** Suppose that you have an option that allows you to sell Buffelhead stock (see Problem 6) in month 6 for $165 *or* to buy it in month 12 for $165. What is the value of this unusual option?

8. **Two-step binomial model** Johnny Jones's high school derivatives homework asks for a binomial valuation of a 12-month call option on the common stock of the Overland Railroad. The stock is now selling for $45 per share and has an annual standard deviation of 24%. Johnny first constructs a binomial tree like Figure 21.2, in which stock price moves up or down every six months. Then he constructs a more realistic tree, assuming that the stock price moves up or down once every three months, or four times per year.

   a. Construct these two binomial trees.

   b. How would these trees change if Overland's standard deviation were 30%? (*Hint:* Make sure to specify the right up and down percentage changes.)

9. **Option delta***

   a. Can the delta of a call option be greater than 1.0? Explain.

   b. Can it be less than zero?

 c. How does the delta of a call change if the stock price rises?

 d. How does it change if the risk of the stock increases?

10. **Option delta** Suppose you construct an option hedge by buying a levered position in delta shares of stock and selling one call option. As the share price changes, the option delta changes, and you will need to adjust your hedge. You can minimize the cost of adjustments if changes in the stock price have only a small effect on the option delta. Construct an example to show whether the option delta is likely to vary more if you hedge with an in-the-money option, an at-the-money option, or an out-of-the-money option.

11. **Black–Scholes model***

 a. Use the Black-Scholes formula to find the value of the following call option.

  i. Time to expiration 1 year.

  ii. Standard deviation 40% per year.

  iii. Exercise price $50.

  iv. Stock price $50.

  v. Interest rate 4% (effective annual yield).

 b. Now recalculate the value of this call option, but use the following parameter values. Each change should be considered independently.

  i. Time to expiration 2 years.

  ii. Standard deviation 50% per year.

  iii. Exercise price $60.

  iv. Stock price $60.

  v. Interest rate 6%.

 c. In which case did increasing the value of the input *not* increase your calculation of option value?

12. **Black–Scholes model** Use the Black–Scholes formula to value the following options:

 a. A call option written on a stock selling for $60 per share with a $60 exercise price. The stock's standard deviation is 6% per month. The option matures in three months. The risk-free interest rate is 1% per month.

 b. A put option written on the same stock at the same time, with the same exercise price and expiration date.

 Now for each of these options, find the combination of stock and risk-free asset that would replicate the option.

13. **Binomial and Black–Scholes models** The current price of United Carbon (UC) stock is $200. The standard deviation is 22.3% a year, and the interest rate is 21% a year. A one-year call option on UC has an exercise price of $180.

 a. Use the Black–Scholes model to value the call option on UC. You may find it helpful to use the spreadsheet version of Table 21.2, accessible through the Beyond the Page feature.

 b. Use the formula given in Section 21-2 to calculate the up-and-down moves that you would use if you valued the UC option with the one-period binomial method. Now value the option by using that method.

 c. Recalculate the up-and-down moves and revalue the option by using the two-period binomial method.

 d. Use your answer to part (c) to calculate the option delta (1) today, (2) next period if the stock price rises, and (3) next period if the stock price falls. Show at each point how you would replicate a call option with a levered investment in the company's stock.

BEYOND THE PAGE

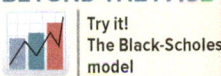

Try it!
The Black-Scholes model

mhhe.com/brealey13e

14. **Option risk** "A call option is always riskier than the stock it is written on." True or false? How does the risk of an option change when the stock price changes?

15. **Option risk***

    a. In Section 21-3, we calculated the risk (beta) of a six-month call option on Amazon stock with an exercise price of $900. Now repeat the exercise for a similar option with an exercise price of $750. Does the risk rise or fall as the exercise price is reduced?

    b. Now calculate the risk of a one-year call on Amazon stock with an exercise price of $750. Does the risk rise or fall as the maturity of the option lengthens?

16. **Warrants** Use the Black–Scholes program from the Beyond the Page feature to value the Owens Corning warrants described in Section 21-4. The standard deviation of Owens Corning stock was 41% a year and the interest rate when the warrants were issued was 5%. Owens Corning did not pay a dividend. Ignore the problem of dilution.

17. **Pension fund insurance** Use the Black–Scholes program to estimate how much you should be prepared to pay to insure the value of your pension fund portfolio for the coming year. Make reasonable assumptions about the volatility of the market and use current interest rates. Remember to subtract the present value of likely dividend payments from the current level of the market index.

18. **American options** For which of the following options *might* it be rational to exercise before maturity? Explain briefly why or why not.

    a. American put on a non-dividend-paying stock.

    b. American call—the dividend payment is $5 per annum, the exercise price is $100, and the interest rate is 10%.

    c. American call—the interest rate is 10%, and the dividend payment is 5% of future stock price. (*Hint:* The dividend depends on the stock price, which could either rise or fall.)

19. **American options** The price of Moria Mining stock is $100. During each of the next two six-month periods the price may either rise by 25% or fall by 20% (equivalent to a standard deviation of 31.5% a year). At month 6, the company will pay a dividend of $20. The interest rate is 10% per six-month period. What is the value of a one-year American call option with an exercise price of $80? Now recalculate the option value, assuming that the dividend is equal to 20% of the with-dividend stock price.

20. **American options** Suppose that you own an American put option on Buffelhead stock (see Problem 6) with an exercise price of $220.

    a. Would you ever want to exercise the put early?

    b. Calculate the value of the put.

    c. Now compare the value with that of an equivalent European put option.

21. **American options** Recalculate the value of the Buffelhead call option (see Problem 6), assuming that the option is American and that at the end of the first six months the company pays a dividend of $25. (Thus, the price at the end of the year is either double or half the *ex*-dividend price in month 6.) How would your answer change if the option were European?

22. **American options** The current price of the stock of Mont Tremblant Air is C$100. During each six-month period it will either rise by 11.1% or fall by 10% (equivalent to an annual standard deviation of 14.9%). The interest rate is 5% per six-month period.

    a. Calculate the value of a one-year European put option on Mont Tremblant's stock with an exercise price of C$102.

    b. Recalculate the value of the Mont Tremblant put option, assuming that it is an American option.

23. **American options** Other things equal, which of these American options are you most likely to want to exercise early?

    a. A put option on a stock with a large dividend or a call on the same stock.

    b. A put option on a stock that is selling below exercise price or a call on the same stock.

    c. A put option when the interest rate is high or the same put option when the interest rate is low.

       Illustrate your answer with examples.

24. **Option exercise** Is it better to exercise a call option on the with-dividend date or on the ex-dividend date? How about a put option? Explain.

CHALLENGE

25. **Option delta** Use the put-call parity formula (see Section 20-2) and the one-period binomial model to show that the option delta for a put option is equal to the option delta for a call option minus 1.

26. **Option delta** Show how the option delta changes as the stock price rises relative to the exercise price. Explain intuitively why this is the case. (What happens to the option delta if the exercise price of an option is zero? What happens if the exercise price becomes indefinitely large?)

27. **Dividends** Your company has just awarded you a generous stock option scheme. You suspect that the board will either decide to increase the dividend or announce a stock repurchase program. Which do you secretly hope they will decide? Explain. (You may find it helpful to refer back to Chapter 16.)

28. **Option risk** Calculate and compare the risk (betas) of the following investments: (a) a share of Amazon stock; (b) a one-year call option on Amazon; (c) a one-year put option; (d) a portfolio consisting of a share of Amazon stock and a one-year put option; (e) a portfolio consisting of a share of Amazon stock, a one-year put option, and the sale of a one-year call. In each case, assume that the exercise price of the option is $900, which is also the current price of Amazon stock.

29. **Option risk** In Section 21-1, we used a simple one-step model to value two Amazon options each with an exercise price of $900. We showed that the call option could be replicated by borrowing $407.06 and investing $490.91 in .54545 share of Amazon stock. The put option could be replicated by selling short $409.10 of Amazon stock and lending $488.46.

    a. If the beta of Amazon stock is 1.5, what is the beta of the call according to the one-step model?

    b. What is the beta of the put?

    c. Suppose that you were to buy one call and invest the present value of the exercise price in a bank loan. What would be the beta of your portfolio?

    d. Suppose instead that you were to buy one share and one put option of Amazon. What would be the beta of your portfolio now?

    e. Your answers to parts (c) and (d) should be the same. Explain.

30. **Option maturity** Some corporations have issued *perpetual* warrants. Warrants are call options issued by a firm, allowing the warrant holder to buy the firm's stock.

    a. What does the Black–Scholes formula predict for the value of an infinite-lived call option on a non-dividend-paying stock? Explain the value you obtain. (*Hint:* What happens to the present value of the exercise price of a long-maturity option?)

    b. Do you think this prediction is realistic? If not, explain carefully why. (*Hints:* What about dividends? What about bankruptcy?)

Look at the stocks listed in Table 7.3. Pick at least three stocks, and find call option prices for each of them on **finance.yahoo.com.** Now find monthly adjusted prices and calculate the standard deviation from the monthly returns using the Excel function STDEV.P. Convert the standard deviation from monthly to annual units by multiplying by the square root of 12.

a. For each stock, pick a traded option with a maturity of about six months and an exercise price equal to the current stock price. Use the Black–Scholes formula and your estimate of standard deviation to value each option. If the stock pays dividends, remember to subtract from the stock price the present value of any dividends that the option holder will miss out on. How close is your calculated value to the traded price of the option?

b. Your answer to part (a) will not exactly match the traded price. Experiment with different values for the standard deviation until your calculated values match the prices of the traded options as closely as possible. What are these implied volatilities? What do the implied volatilities say about investors' forecasts of future volatility?

MINI-CASE ● ● ● ●

Bruce Honiball's Invention

It was another disappointing year for Bruce Honiball, the manager of retail services at the Gibb River Bank. Sure, the retail side of Gibb River was making money, but it didn't grow at all in 2017. Gibb River had plenty of loyal depositors but few new ones. Bruce had to figure out some new product or financial service—something that would generate some excitement and attention.

Bruce had been musing on one idea for some time. How about making it easy *and safe* for Gibb River's customers to put money in the stock market? How about giving them the upside of investing in equities—at least *some* of the upside—but none of the downside?

Bruce could see the advertisements now:

> How would you like to invest in Australian stocks completely risk-free? You can with the new Gibb River Bank *Equity-Linked Deposit.* You share in the good years; we take care of the bad ones.
>
> Here's how it works. Deposit A$100 with us for one year. At the end of that period, you get back your A$100 *plus* A$5 for every 10% rise in the value of the Australian All Ordinaries stock index. But, if the market index falls during this period, the Bank will still refund your A$100 deposit in full.
>
> There's no risk of loss. Gibb River Bank is your safety net.

Bruce had floated the idea before and encountered immediate skepticism, even derision: "Heads they win, tails we lose—is that what you're proposing, Mr. Honiball?" Bruce had no ready answer. Could the bank really afford to make such an attractive offer? How should it invest the money that would come in from customers? The bank had no appetite for major new risks.

Bruce has puzzled over these questions for the past two weeks but has been unable to come up with a satisfactory answer. He believes that the Australian equity market is currently fully valued, but he realizes that some of his colleagues are more bullish than he is about equity prices.

Fortunately, the bank had just recruited a smart new MBA graduate, Sheila Liu. Sheila was sure that she could find the answers to Bruce Honiball's questions. First she collected data on the Australian market to get a preliminary idea of whether equity-linked deposits could work. These data are shown in Table 21.3. She was just about to undertake some quick calculations when she received the following further memo from Bruce:

Sheila, I've got another idea. A lot of our customers probably share my view that the market is overvalued. Why don't we also give them a chance to make some money by offering a "bear market deposit"? If the market goes up, they would just get back their A$100 deposit. If it goes down, they get their A$100 back plus $5 for each 10% that the market falls. Can you figure out whether we could do something like this? Bruce.

QUESTION

1. What kinds of options is Bruce proposing? How much would the options be worth? Would the equity-linked and bear-market deposits generate positive NPV for Gibb River Bank?

Year	Interest Rate	Market Return	Dividend Yield	Year	Interest Rate	Market Return	Dividend Yield
1995	8.0%	20.2%	4.0	2007	6.6	18.0	4.3
1996	7.4	14.6	4.1	2008	7.3	−40.4	6.8
1997	5.5	12.2	3.7	2009	3.2	39.6	5.3
1998	5.0	11.6	3.6	2010	4.3	3.3	4.2
1999	4.9	19.3	3.3	2011	4.8	−11.4	4.4
2000	5.9	5.0	3.3	2012	3.7	18.8	5.1
2001	5.2	10.1	3.3	2013	2.8	19.7	4.5
2002	4.6	−8.1	3.5	2014	2.5	5.0	4.5
2003	4.8	15.9	4.2	2015	2.1	3.8	4.7
2004	5.4	27.6	3.7	2016	1.8	11.6	4.8
2005	5.6	21.1	3.8	2017	1.5	12.5	4.4
2006	5.9	25.0	3.8				

❭ **TABLE 21.3**
Australian interest rates and equity returns, 1995–2017

CHAPTER

Real Options

When you use discounted cash flow (DCF) to value a project, you implicitly assume that your firm will hold the project passively. In other words, you are ignoring the *real options* attached to the project—options that sophisticated managers can take advantage of. You could say that DCF does not reflect the value of management. Managers who hold real options do not have to be passive; they can make decisions to capitalize on good fortune or to mitigate loss. The opportunity to make such decisions clearly adds value whenever project outcomes are uncertain.

Chapter 10 introduced the four main types of real options:

- The option to expand if the immediate investment project succeeds.

- The option to wait (and learn) before investing.

- The option to shrink or abandon a project.

- The option to vary the mix of output or the firm's production methods.

Chapter 10 gave several simple examples of real options. We also showed you how to use decision trees to set out possible future outcomes and decisions. But we did not show you how to value real options. That is our task in this chapter. We apply the concepts and valuation principles you learned in Chapter 21.

For the most part, we work with simple numerical examples. The art and science of valuing real options are illustrated just as well with simple calculations as complex ones. But we also describe several more realistic examples, including

- A strategic investment in the computer business.

- The option to develop commercial real estate.

- The decision to operate or mothball an oil tanker.

- Purchase options on aircraft.

- Investment in pharmaceutical R&D.

These examples show how financial managers can value real options in real life. We also show how managers can create real options, adding value by adding flexibility to the firm's investments and operations.

We should start with a warning. Setting out the possible future choices that the firm may encounter usually calls for a strong dose of judgment. Therefore, do not expect precision when valuing real options. Often, managers do not even try to put a figure on the value of the option but simply draw on their experience to decide whether it is worth paying for additional flexibility. Thus, they might say, "We just don't know whether gargle blasters will catch on, but it probably makes sense to spend an extra $200,000 now to allow for an extra production line in the future."

22-1   The Value of Follow-On Investment Opportunities

It is 1982 and the first personal computer has recently been launched. You are assistant to the chief financial officer (CFO) of Blitzen Computers, an established computer manufacturer casting a profit-hungry eye on the PC market. You are helping the CFO evaluate the proposed introduction of the Blitzen Mark I Micro.

)TABLE 22.1
Summary of cash flows and financial analysis of the Mark I microcomputer ($ millions)

	Year					
	1982	1983	1984	1985	1986	1987
After-tax operating cash flow (1)		+110	+159	+295	+185	0
Capital investment (2)	450	0	0	0	0	0
Increase in working capital (3)	0	50	100	100	−125	−125
Net cash flow (1) − (2) − (3)	−450	+60	+59	+195	+310	+125
NPV at 20% = −$46.45, or about −$46 million						

The Mark I's forecasted cash flows and NPV are shown in Table 22.1. Unfortunately, the Mark I can't meet Blitzen's customary 20% hurdle rate and has a $46 million negative NPV, contrary to top management's strong gut feeling that Blitzen ought to be in the personal computer market.

The CFO has called you in to discuss the project:

"The Mark I just can't make it on financial grounds," the CFO says. "But we've got to do it for strategic reasons. I'm recommending we go ahead."

"But you're missing the all-important financial advantage, Chief," you reply.

"Don't call me 'Chief.' What financial advantage?"

"If we don't launch the Mark I, it will probably be too expensive to enter the micro market later, when Apple, IBM, and others are firmly established. If we go ahead, we have the opportunity to make follow-on investments that could be extremely profitable. The Mark I gives not only its own cash flows, but also a call option to go on with a Mark II micro. That call option is the real source of strategic value."

"So it's strategic value by another name. That doesn't tell me what the Mark II investment's worth. The Mark II could be a great investment or a lousy one—we haven't got a clue."

"That's exactly when a call option is worth the most," you point out perceptively. "The call lets us invest in the Mark II if it's great and walk away from it if it's lousy."

"So what's it worth?"

"Hard to say precisely, but I've done a back-of-the-envelope calculation, which suggests that the value of the option to invest in the Mark II could more than offset the Mark I's $46 million negative NPV. [The calculations are shown in Table 22.2.] If the option to invest is worth $55 million, the total value of the Mark I is its own NPV, −$46 million, plus the $55 million option attached to it, or +$9 million."

"You're just overestimating the Mark II," the CFO says gruffly. "It's easy to be optimistic when an investment is three years away."

"No, no," you reply patiently. "The Mark II is expected to be no more profitable than the Mark I—just twice as big and therefore twice as bad in terms of discounted cash flow. I'm forecasting it to have a negative NPV of about $100 million. But there's a chance the Mark II could be extremely valuable. The call option allows Blitzen to cash in on those upside outcomes. The chance to cash in could be worth $55 million.

"Of course, the $55 million is only a trial calculation, but it illustrates how valuable follow-on investment opportunities can be, especially when uncertainty is high and the product market is growing rapidly. Moreover, the Mark II will give us a call on the Mark III, the Mark III on the Mark IV, and so on. My calculations don't take subsequent calls into account."

"I think I'm beginning to understand a little bit of corporate strategy," mumbles the CFO.

Questions and Answers about Blitzen's Mark II

Question: I know how to use the Black–Scholes formula to value traded call options, but this case seems harder. What number do I use for the stock price? I don't see any traded shares.

〉TABLE 22.2
Valuing the option to invest in the Mark II microcomputer

Assumptions
1. The decision to invest in the Mark II must be made after three years, in 1985.
2. The Mark II investment is double the scale of the Mark I (note the expected rapid growth of the industry). Investment required is $900 million (the exercise price), which is taken as fixed.
3. Forecasted cash inflows of the Mark II are also double those of the Mark I, with present value of $807 million in 1985 and $807/(1.2)^3 = $467 million in 1982.
4. The future value of the Mark II cash flows is highly uncertain. This value evolves as a stock price does with a standard deviation of 35% per year. (Many high-technology stocks have standard deviations higher than 35%.)
5. The annual interest rate is 10%.

Interpretation

The opportunity to invest in the Mark II is a three-year call option on an asset worth $467 million with a $900 million exercise price.

Valuation

$$\text{PV(exercise price)} = \frac{900}{(1.1)^3} = 676$$

$$\text{Call value} = [N(d_1) \times P] - [N(d_2) \times \text{PV(EX)}]$$

$$d_1 = \log[P/\text{PV(EX)}]/\sigma\sqrt{t} + \sigma\sqrt{t}/2$$
$$= \log[.691]/.606 + .606/2 = -.3072$$
$$d_2 = d_1 - \sigma\sqrt{t} = -.3072 - .606 = -.9134$$

$$N(d_1) = .3793, N(d_2) = .1805$$

$$\text{Call value} = [.3793 \times 467] - [.1805 \times 676] = \$55.1 \text{ million}$$

BEYOND THE PAGE

Blitzen

mhhe.com/brealey13e

Answer: With traded call options, you can see the value of the *underlying asset* that the call is written on. Here the option is to buy a nontraded real asset, the Mark II. We can't observe the Mark II's value; we have to compute it.

The Mark II's forecasted cash flows are set out in Table 22.3. The project involves an initial outlay of $900 million in 1985. The cash inflows start in the following year and have a present value of $807 million in 1985, equivalent to $467 million in 1982 as shown in Table 22.3. So the real option to invest in the Mark II amounts to a three-year call on an underlying asset worth $467 million, with a $900 million exercise price.

Notice that real options analysis does *not* replace DCF. You typically need DCF to value the underlying asset.

Question: Table 22.2 uses a standard deviation of 35% per year. Where does that number come from?

〉TABLE 22.3
Cash flows of the Mark II microcomputer, as forecasted from 1982 ($ millions)

	1982		1985	1986	1987	1988	1989	1990
After-tax operating cash flow				+220	+318	+590	+370	0
Increase in working capital				100	200	200	−250	−250
Net cash flow				+120	+118	+390	+620	+250
Present value at 20%	+467	←	+807					
Investment, PV at 10%	676	←	900					
	(PV in 1982)							
Forecasted NPV in 1985			−93					

Answer: We recommend you look for *comparables*—that is, traded stocks with business risks similar to the investment opportunity.[1] For the Mark II, the ideal comparables would be growth stocks in the personal computer business or perhaps a broader sample of high-tech growth stocks. Use the average standard deviation of the comparable companies' returns as the benchmark for judging the risk of the investment opportunity.[2]

Question: Table 22.3 discounts the Mark II's cash flows at 20%. I understand the high discount rate because the Mark II is risky. But why is the $900 million investment discounted at the risk-free interest rate of 10%? Table 22.3 shows the present value of the investment in 1982 of $676 million.

Answer: Black and Scholes assumed that the exercise price is a fixed, certain amount. We wanted to stick with their basic formula. If the exercise price is uncertain, you can switch to a slightly more complicated valuation formula.[3]

Question: Nevertheless, if I had to decide in 1982, once and for all, whether to invest in the Mark II, I wouldn't do it. Right?

Answer: Right. The NPV of a commitment to invest in the Mark II is negative:

$$\text{NPV(1982)} = \text{PV(cash inflows)} - \text{PV(investment)} = \$467 - 676 = -\$209 \text{ million}$$

The option to invest in the Mark II is "out of the money" because the Mark II's value is far less than the required investment. Nevertheless, the option is worth +$55 million. It is especially valuable because the Mark II is a risky project with lots of upside potential. Figure 22.1 shows the probability distribution of the possible present values of the Mark II in 1985. The expected (mean or average) outcome is our forecast of $807,[4] but the actual value could exceed $2 billion.

Question: Could it also be far below $807 million—$500 million or less?

Answer: The downside is irrelevant because Blitzen won't invest unless the Mark II's actual value turns out higher than $900 million. The net option payoffs for all values less than $900 million are zero.

In a DCF analysis, you discount the expected outcome ($807 million), which averages the downside against the upside, the bad outcomes against the good. The value of a call option depends only on the upside. You can see the danger of trying to value a future investment option with DCF.

Question: What's the decision rule?

Answer: Adjusted present value. The best-case NPV of the Mark I project is −$46 million, but accepting it creates the expansion option for the Mark II. The expansion option is worth $55 million, so

$$\text{APV} = -46 + 55 = +\$9 \text{ million}$$

---

[1] You could also use scenario analysis, which we described in Chapter 10. Work out "best" and "worst" scenarios to establish a range of possible future values. Then find the annual standard deviation that would generate this range over the life of the option. For the Mark II, a range from $300 million to $2 billion would cover about 90% of the possible outcomes. This range, shown in Figure 22.1, is consistent with an annual standard deviation of 35%.

[2] Be sure to "unlever" the standard deviations, thereby eliminating volatility created by debt financing. Chapters 17 and 19 covered unlevering procedures for beta. The same principles apply for standard deviation: You want the standard deviation of a portfolio of all the debt and equity securities issued by the comparable firm.

[3] If the required investment is uncertain, you have, in effect, an option to exchange one risky asset (the future value of the exercise price) for another (the future value of the Mark II's cash inflows). See W. Margrabe, "The Value of an Option to Exchange One Asset for Another," *Journal of Finance* 33 (March 1978), pp. 177–186.

[4] We have drawn the future values of the Mark II as a lognormal distribution, consistent with the assumptions of the Black–Scholes formula. Lognormal distributions are skewed to the right, so the average outcome is greater than the most likely outcome. The most likely outcome is the highest point on the probability distribution.

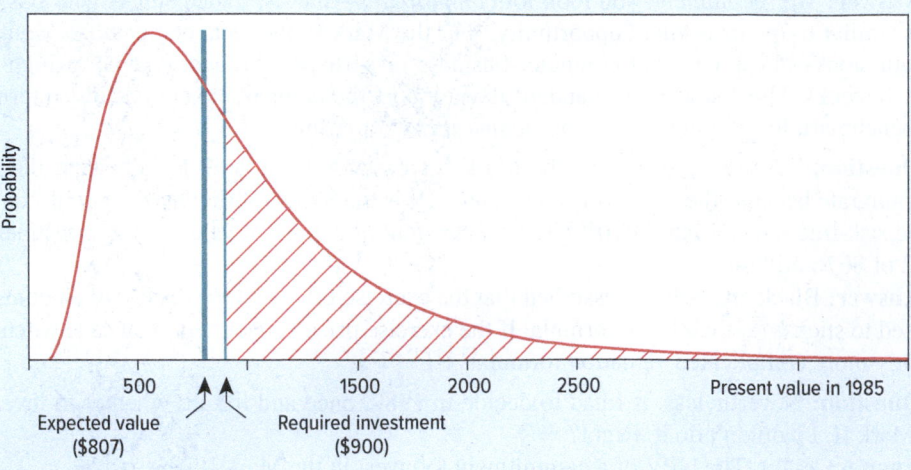

▶ **FIGURE 22.1**

This distribution shows the range of possible present values for the Mark II project in 1985. The expected value is about $800 million, less than the required investment of $900 million. The option to invest pays off in the shaded area above $900 million.

Of course, we haven't counted other follow-on opportunities. If the Mark I and Mark II are successes, there will be an option to invest in the Mark III, possibly the Mark IV, and so on.

Other Expansion Options

You can probably think of many other cases where companies spend money today to create opportunities to expand in the future. A mining company may acquire rights to an ore body that is not worth developing today but could be very profitable if ore prices increase. A real estate developer may invest in worn-out farmland that could be turned into a shopping mall if a new highway is built. A pharmaceutical company may acquire a patent that gives the right but not the obligation to market a new drug. In each case, the company is acquiring a real option to expand.

22-2   The Timing Option

The fact that a project has a positive NPV does not mean that you should go ahead today. It may be better to wait and see how the market develops.

Suppose that you are contemplating a now-or-never opportunity to build a malted herring factory. In this case, you have an about-to-expire call option on the present value of the factory's future cash flows. If the present value exceeds the cost of the factory, the call option's payoff is the project's NPV. But if NPV is negative, the call option's payoff is zero because, in that case, the firm will not make the investment.

Now suppose that you can delay construction of the plant. You still have the call option, but you face a trade-off. If the outlook is highly uncertain, it is tempting to wait and see whether the malted herring market takes off or decays. On the other hand, if the project is truly profitable, the sooner you can capture the project's cash flows, the better. If the cash flows are high enough, you will want to exercise your option right away.

The cash flows from an investment project play the same role as dividend payments on a stock. When a stock pays no dividends, an American call is always worth more alive than dead and should never be exercised early. But payment of a dividend before the option matures reduces the ex-dividend price and the possible payoffs to the call option at maturity. Think of the extreme case: If a company pays out all its assets in one bumper dividend, the stock price must be zero and the call worthless. Therefore, any in-the-money call would be exercised just before this liquidating dividend.

Dividends do not always prompt early exercise, but if they are sufficiently large, call option holders capture them by exercising just before the ex-dividend date. We see managers acting in the same way: When a project's forecasted cash flows are sufficiently large, managers capture the cash flows by investing right away. But when forecasted cash flows are small, managers are inclined to hold on to their call rather than to invest, even when project NPV is positive.[5] This explains why managers are sometimes reluctant to commit to positive-NPV projects. This caution is rational as long as the option to wait is open and sufficiently valuable.

Valuing the Malted Herring Option

Figure 22.2 shows the possible cash flows and end-of-year values for the malted herring project. If you commit and invest $180 million, you have a project worth $200 million. If demand turns out to be low in year 1, the cash flow is only $16 million and the value of the project falls to $160 million. But if demand is high in year 1, the cash flow is $25 million and value rises to $250 million. Although the project lasts indefinitely, we assume that investment cannot be postponed beyond the end of the first year, and therefore we show only the cash flows for the first year and the possible values at the end of the year. Notice that if you undertake the investment right away, you capture the first year's cash flow ($16 million or $25 million); if you delay, you miss out on this cash flow, but you will have more information on how the project is likely to work out.

We can use the binomial method to value this option. The first step is to pretend that investors are risk neutral and to calculate the probabilities of high and low demand in this risk-neutral world. If demand is high in the first year, the malted herring plant has a cash flow of $25 million and a year-end value of $250 million. The total return is $(25 + 250)/200 - 1 = .375$, or 37.5%. If demand is low, the plant has a cash flow of $16 million and a year-end value of $160 million. Total return is $(16 + 160)/200 - 1 = -.12$, or −12%. In a *risk-neutral* world, the expected return would be equal to the interest rate, which we assume is 5%:

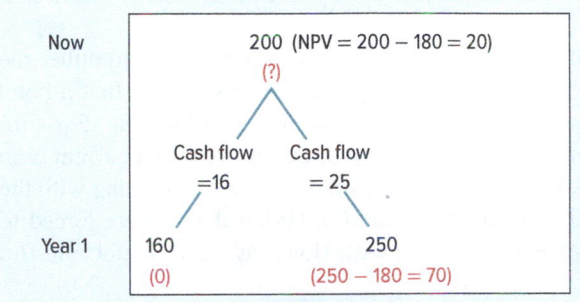

Now	200 (NPV = 200 − 180 = 20)
	(?)
	Cash flow Cash flow
	=16 = 25
Year 1	160 250
	(0) (250 − 180 = 70)

▶ **FIGURE 22.2**

Possible cash flows and end-of-period values for the malted herring project are shown in black. The project costs $180 million, either now or later. The red figures in parentheses show payoffs from the option to wait and to invest later if the project is positive NPV at year 1. Waiting means loss of the first year's cash flows. The problem is to figure out the current value of the option.

---

[5]We have been a bit vague about forecasted project cash flows. If competitors can enter and take away cash that you could have earned, the meaning is clear. But what about the decision to, say, develop an oil well? Here delay doesn't waste barrels of oil in the ground; it simply postpones production and the associated cash flow. The cost of waiting is the decline in today's *present value* of revenues from production. Present value declines if the cash flow from production increases more slowly than the cost of capital.

$$\text{Expected} \atop \text{return} = \left(\text{probability of} \atop \text{high demand}\right) \times 37.5 + \left(1 - \text{probability of} \atop \text{high demand}\right) \times (-12) = 5\%$$

Therefore, the risk-neutral probability of high demand is 34.3%. This is the probability that would generate the risk-free return of 5%.

We want to value a call option on the malted herring project with an exercise price of $180 million. We begin as usual at the end and work backward. The bottom row of Figure 22.2 shows the possible values of this option at the end of the year. If project value is $160 million, the option to invest is worthless. At the other extreme, if project value is $250 million, option value is $250 − 180 − $70 million.

To calculate the value of the option today, we work out the expected payoffs in a risk-neutral world and discount at the interest rate of 5%. Thus, the value of your option to invest in the malted herring plant is

$$\frac{(.343 \times 70) + (.657 \times 0)}{1.05} = \$22.9 \text{ million}$$

But here is where we need to recognize the opportunity to exercise the option immediately. The option is worth $22.9 million if you keep it open, and it is worth the project's immediate NPV (200 − 180 = $20 million) if exercised now. Therefore, we decide to wait and then to invest next year only if demand turns out high.

We have, of course, simplified the malted herring calculations. You won't find many actual investment-timing problems that fit into a one-step binomial tree. But the example delivers an important practical point: A positive NPV is not a sufficient reason for investing. It may be better to wait and see.

Optimal Timing for Real Estate Development

Sometimes it pays to wait for a long time, even for projects with large positive NPVs. Suppose you own a plot of vacant land in the suburbs.[6] The land can be used for a hotel or an office building, but not for both. A hotel could be later converted to an office building, or an office building to a hotel, but only at significant cost. You are therefore reluctant to invest, even if both investments have positive NPVs.

In this case, you have two options to invest, but only one can be exercised. You therefore learn two things by waiting. First, you learn about the general *level* of cash flows from development—for example, by observing changes in the value of developed properties near your land. Second, you can update your estimates of the *relative* size of the hotel's future cash flows versus the office building's.

Figure 22.3 shows the conditions in which you would finally commit to build either the hotel or the office building. The horizontal axis shows the current cash flows that a hotel would generate. The vertical axis shows current cash flows for an office building. For simplicity, we assume that each investment would have an NPV of exactly zero at a current cash flow of 100. Thus, if you were forced to invest today, you would choose the building with the higher cash flow, assuming the cash flow is greater than 100. (What if you were forced to decide today and each building could generate the same cash flow, say, 150? You would flip a coin.)

If the two buildings' cash flows plot in the colored area at the lower right of Figure 22.3, you build the hotel. To fall in this area, the hotel's cash flows have to beat two hurdles. First, they must exceed a minimum level of about 240. Second, they must exceed the office building's cash flows by a sufficient amount. If the situation is reversed, with office building

---

[6]The following example is based on P. D. Childs, T. J. Riddiough, and A. J. Triantis, "Mixed Uses and the Redevelopment Option," *Real Estate Economics* 24 (Fall 1996), pp. 317–339.

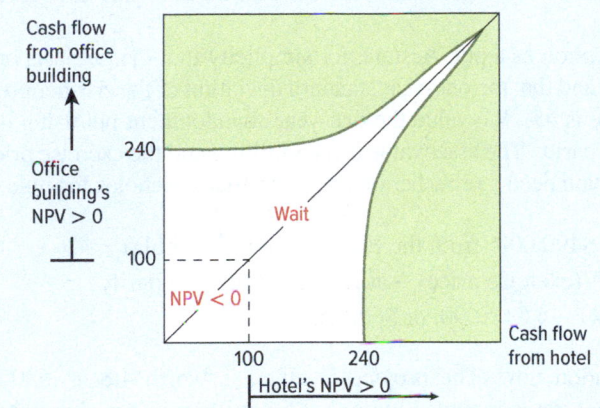

FIGURE 22.3 Development option for vacant land, assuming two mutually exclusive uses, either hotel or office building. The developer should "wait and see" unless the hotel's or office building's cash flows end up in one of the shaded areas.

Source: Adapted from Figure 1 in P. D. Childs, T. J. Riddiough, and A. J. Triantis, "Mixed Uses and the Redevelopment Option," *Real Estate Economics* 24 (Fall 1996), pp. 317–339.

cash flows above the minimum level of 240, and also sufficiently above the hotel's, then you build the office building. In this case, the cash flows plot in the colored area at the top left of the figure.

Notice how the "wait and see" region extends upward along the 45-degree line in Figure 22.3. When the cash flows from the hotel and office building are nearly the same, you become *very* cautious before choosing one over the other.

You may be surprised at how high cash flows have to be in Figure 22.3 to justify investment. There are three reasons. First, building the office building means not building the hotel, and vice versa. Second, the calculations underlying Figure 22.3 assumed cash flows that were small, but growing; therefore, the costs of waiting to invest were small. Third, the calculations did not consider the threat that someone might build a competing hotel or office building right next door. In that case, the "relax and wait" area of Figure 22.3 would shrink dramatically.

22-3 The Abandonment Option

Expansion value is important. When investments turn out well, the quicker and easier the business can be expanded, the better. But suppose bad news arrives, and cash flows are far below expectations. In that case, it is useful to have the option to bail out and recover the value of the project's plant, equipment, or other assets. The option to abandon is equivalent to a put option. You exercise that abandonment option if the value recovered from the project's assets is greater than the present value of continuing the project for at least one more period.

Bad News for the Perpetual Crusher

We introduced the perpetual crusher project in Chapter 19 to illustrate the use of the weighted-average cost of capital (WACC). The project cost $12.5 million and generated expected perpetual cash flows of $1.175 million per year. With WACC = .094, the project was worth PV = 1.175/.094 = $12.5 million. Subtracting the investment of $12.5 million gave NPV = 0.

Several years later, the crusher has not panned out. Cash flows are still expected to be perpetual but are now running at only $450,000 a year. The crusher is therefore worth only $450,000/.094 = $4.8 million. Is this bad news terminal?

Suppose the crusher project can be abandoned, with recovery of $5.2 million from the sale of machinery and real estate. Does abandonment make sense? The immediate gain from abandonment is of course $5.2 − 4.8 = $.4 million. But what if you can wait and reconsider abandonment later? In this case, you have an abandonment option that does not have to be exercised immediately.

We can value the abandonment option as a put. Assume for simplicity that the put lasts one year only (abandon now or at year 1) and that the one-year standard deviation of the crusher project is 30%. The risk-free interest rate is 4%. We value the one-year abandonment put using the Black–Scholes formula and put–call parity. The asset value is $4.8 million and the exercise price is $5.2 million. (See Section 21-3 if you need a refresher on using the Black–Scholes formula.)

$$\text{Call value} = .49 \text{ million or } \$490{,}000 \text{ (from the Black–Scholes formula)}$$
$$\text{Put value} = \text{call value} + \text{PV(exercise price)} - \text{asset value (put–call parity)}$$
$$= .49 + (5.2/1.04) - 4.8 = .690, \text{ or } \$690{,}000$$

Therefore, you decide not to abandon now. The project, if alive, is worth $4.8 + .690 = \$5.49$ million when the abandonment put is included but only $5.2 million if it is abandoned immediately.

You are keeping the project alive not out of stubbornness or loyalty to the crusher, but because there is a chance that cash flows will recover. The abandonment put still protects on the downside if the crusher project deals up further disappointments.

Of course, we have made simplifying assumptions. For example, the recovery value of the crusher is likely to decline as you wait to abandon. So perhaps we are using too high an exercise price. On the other hand, we have considered only a one-year European put. In fact, you have an American put with a potentially long maturity. A long-lived American put is worth more than a one-year European put because you can abandon in year 2, 3, or later if you wish.

Abandonment Value and Project Life

A project's economic life can be just as hard to predict as its cash flows. Yet NPVs for capital-investment projects usually assume fixed economic lives. For example, in Chapter 6 we assumed that the guano project would operate for exactly seven years. Real-option techniques allow us to relax such fixed-life assumptions. Here is the procedure:[7]

1. Forecast cash flows well beyond the project's expected economic life. For example, you might forecast guano production and sales out to year 15.

2. Value the project, including the value of your abandonment put, which allows, but does not require, abandonment before year 15. The actual timing of abandonment will depend on project performance. In the best upside scenarios, project life will be 15 years—it will make sense to continue in the guano business as long as possible. In the worst downside scenarios, project life will be much shorter than 7 years. In intermediate scenarios where actual cash flows match original expectations, abandonment will occur around year 7.

This procedure links project life to the performance of the project. It does not impose an arbitrary ending date, except in the far distant future.

Temporary Abandonment

Companies are often faced with complex options that allow them to abandon a project *temporarily*—that is, to mothball it until conditions improve. Suppose you own an oil tanker operating in the short-term spot market. (In other words, you charter the tanker voyage by

---

[7]See S. C. Myers and S. Majd, "Abandonment Value and Project Life," in *Advances in Futures and Options Research*, F. J. Fabozzi, ed. (Greenwich, CT: JAI Press, 1990).

voyage, at whatever short-term charter rates prevail at the start of the voyage.) The tanker costs $50 million a year to operate, and at current tanker rates, it produces charter revenues of $52.5 million per year. The tanker is therefore profitable but scarcely cause for celebration. Now tanker rates dip by 10%, forcing revenues down to $47.5 million. Do you immediately lay off the crew and mothball the tanker until prices recover? The answer is clearly yes if the tanker operation can be turned on and off like a faucet. But that is unrealistic. There is a fixed cost to mothballing the tanker. You don't want to incur this cost only to regret your decision next month if rates rebound to their earlier level. The higher the costs of mothballing and the more variable the level of charter rates, the greater the loss that you will be prepared to bear before you call it quits and lay up the boat.

Suppose that eventually you do decide to take the boat off the market. You lay up the tanker temporarily.[8] Two years later, your faith is rewarded; charter rates rise, and the revenues from operating the tanker creep above the operating cost of $50 million. Do you reactivate immediately? Not if there are costs to doing so. It makes more sense to wait until the project is well in the black and you can be fairly confident that you will not regret the cost of bringing the tanker back into operation.

These choices are illustrated in Figure 22.4. The teal line shows how the value of an operating tanker varies with the level of charter rates. The black line shows the value of the tanker when mothballed.[9] The level of rates at which it pays to mothball is given by M and the level at which it pays to reactivate is given by R. The higher the costs of mothballing and reactivating and the greater the variability in tanker rates, the farther apart these points will be. You can see that it will pay for you to mothball as soon as the value of a mothballed tanker reaches the value of an operating tanker plus the costs of mothballing. It will pay to reactivate as soon as the value of a tanker that is operating in the spot market reaches the value of a mothballed tanker plus the costs of reactivating. If the level of rates falls below M, the value of the tanker is given by the black line; if the level is greater than R, value is given by the teal line. If rates lie between M and R, the tanker's value depends on whether it happens to be mothballed or operating.

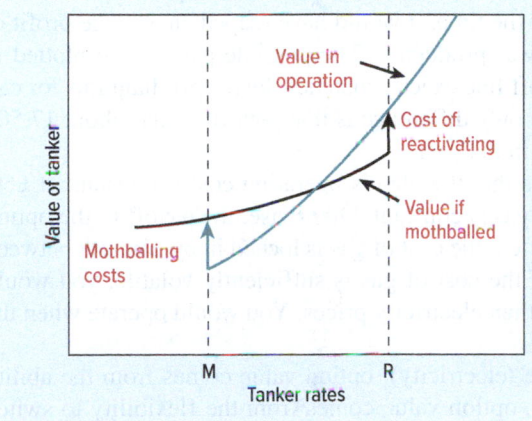

> **FIGURE 22.4**   An oil tanker should be mothballed when tanker rates fall to M, where the tanker's value if mothballed is enough above its value in operation to cover mothballing costs. The tanker is reactivated when rates recover to R.

---

[8]We assume it makes sense to keep the tanker in mothballs. If rates fall sufficiently, it will pay to scrap the tanker.

[9]Dixit and Pindyck estimate these thresholds for a medium-sized tanker and show how they depend on costs and the volatility of freight rates. See A. K. Dixit and R. S. Pindyck, *Investment under Uncertainty* (Princeton, NJ: Princeton University Press, 1994), Chapter 7. Brennan and Schwartz provide an analysis of a mining investment that also includes an option to shut down temporarily. See M. Brennan and E. Schwartz, "Evaluating Natural Resource Investments," *Journal of Business* 58 (April 1985), pp. 135–157.

22-4   Flexible Production and Procurement

Flexible production means the ability to vary production inputs or outputs in response to fluctuating demand or prices. Take the case of CT (combustion-turbine) generating plants, which are designed to deliver short bursts of peak-load electrical power. CTs can't match the thermal efficiency of coal or nuclear power plants, but CTs can be turned on or off on short notice. The coal plants and "nukes" are efficient only if operated on "base load" for long periods.

The profits from operating a CT depend on the *spark spread*—that is, on the difference between the price of electricity and the cost of the natural gas used as fuel. CTs are money-losers at average spark spreads, but the spreads are volatile and can spike to very high levels when demand is high and generating capacity tight. Thus, a CT delivers a series of call options that can be exercised day by day (even hour by hour) when spark spreads are sufficiently high. The call options are normally out-of-the-money (CTs typically operate only about 5% of the time), but the money made at peak prices makes investment in the CTs worthwhile.[10]

The volatility of spark spreads depends on the correlation between the price of electricity and the price of natural gas used as fuel. If the correlation were 1.0, so that electricity and natural gas prices moved together dollar for dollar, the spark spread would barely move from its average value, and the options to operate the gas turbine would be worthless. But, in fact, the correlation is less than 1.0, so the options are valuable. In addition, some CTs are set up to give a further option because they can be run on oil as well as natural gas.[11]

The top panel of Figure 22.5 shows a histogram of electricity prices for the U.K. between March 2001 and August 2017. Prices are set every half hour, so there are nearly 300,000 prices plotted. Prices are quoted as pounds per megawatt-hour (£/MWH). Notice how strongly the histogram is skewed to the right. Although the average price was only £45 per MWH, prices above £100/MWH crop up regularly when electricity demand peaks. The highest price was £5,003/MWH. The occasional high prices are hardly visible in the top panel of Figure 22.5. The bottom panel plots only the prices above £60/MWH.

Suppose you have a CT generating plant in the U.K. that is profitable only at prices above £60/MWH. If the plant was in continuous operation, the profit per MWH would be negative at £45.33 – 60 = –£14.67. But it would be better to leave the plant idle when prices are low and to exercise your option to operate only when prices are above £60. Although the plant would have been idle for nearly three-quarters of the time, it would have reaped an average profit of 95.41 – 60 = £35.41 per MWH when it was producing. The possible payoffs are plotted in the bottom panel of Figure 22.5. The payoff line exactly matches the payoff diagrams for call options with an exercise price of £60. The only difference is that your plant has about 17,500 options every year, one for each half hour in the year.

The payoff line in Figure 22.5 assumes that the plant's operating cost is constant at £60. This is accurate only if the cost of natural gas is constant. Otherwise, the payoff to the option to operate depends on the spark spread. Often, the cost of gas is locked in by contract between the generator and the gas supplier. But if the cost of gas is sufficiently volatile, you would replot Figure 22.5 in spark spreads rather than electricity prices. You would operate when the spark spread is positive.

In this example, the output is the same (electricity); option value comes from the ability to vary the level of output. In other cases, option value comes from the flexibility to switch

---

[10]Here we refer to simple CTs, which are just large gas turbines connected to generators. Combined-cycle CTs add a steam generator to capture exhaust heat from the turbine. The steam is used to generate additional electricity. Combined-cycle units are much more efficient than simple CTs.

[11]Industrial steam and heating systems can also be designed to switch between fuels, depending on relative fuel costs. See N. Kulatilaka, "The Value of Flexibility: The Case of a Dual-Fuel Industrial Steam Boiler," *Financial Management* 22 (Autumn 1993), pp. 271–280.

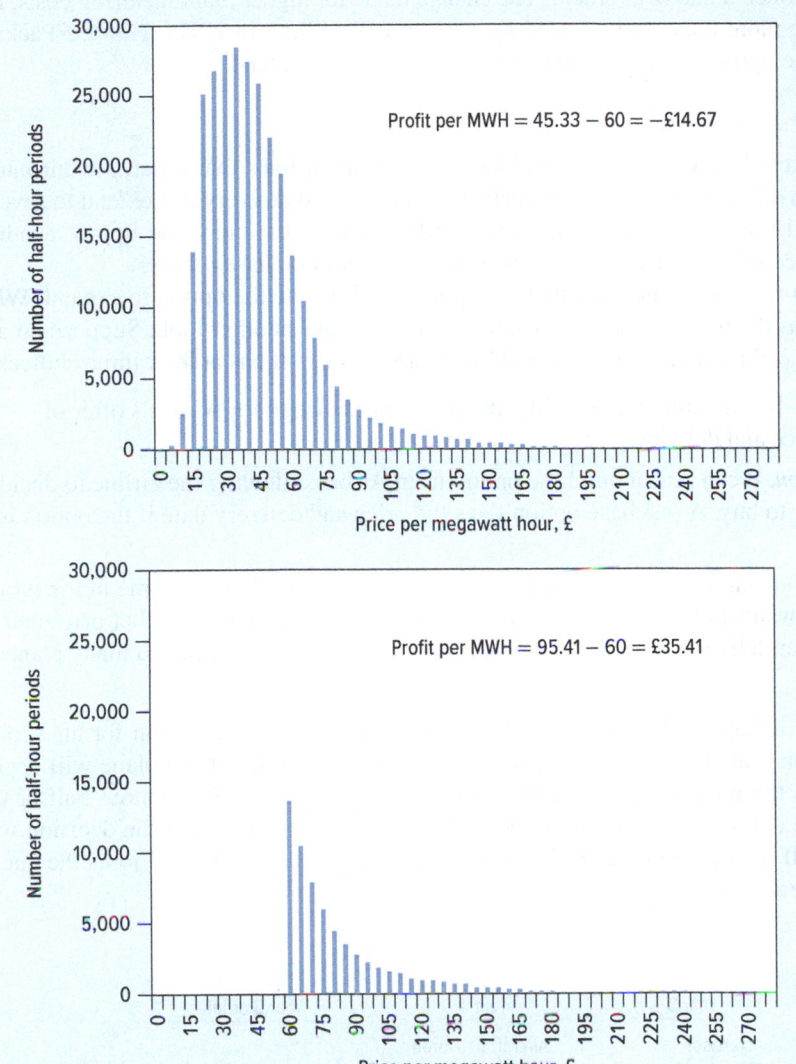

▶ **FIGURE 22.5**

In the U.K., electricity prices are set every half hour. The top panel is a histogram of prices (£/MWH) for March 2001 through August 2017. Note how the histogram is skewed to the right. Many prices exceeded £100/MWH and a few (not visible in the plot) exceeded £500/MWH. The bottom panel shows the payoff to a plant that costs £60/MWH to run. The plant operator has an option to produce with an exercise price of £60.

(Top panel) Profit per MWH = 45.33 − 60 = −£14.67

(Bottom panel) Profit per MWH = 95.41 − 60 = £35.41

from product to product using the same production facilities. For example, textile firms have invested heavily in computer-controlled knitting machines, which allow production to shift from product to product, or from design to design, as demand and fashion dictate.

Flexibility in *procurement* can also have option value. For example, a computer manufacturer planning next year's production must also plan to buy components, such as disk drives and microprocessors, in large quantities. Should it strike a deal today with the component manufacturer? This locks in the quantity, price, and delivery dates. But it also gives up flexibility—for example, the ability to switch suppliers next year or buy at a "spot" price if next year's prices are lower.

For example, Hewlett-Packard used to customize printers for foreign markets and then ship the finished printers. If it did not correctly forecast demand, it was liable to end up with too many printers designed for the German market (say) and too few for the French market. The company's solution was to ship printers that were only partially assembled and then to customize them once it had firm orders. The change made for higher manufacturing costs, but these costs were more than compensated by the extra flexibility. In effect, Hewlett-Packard gained a valuable option to delay the cost of configuring the printers.[12]

Aircraft Purchase Options

For our final example, we turn to the problem confronting airlines that order new airplanes for future use. In this industry, lead times between an order and delivery can extend to several years. Long lead times mean that airlines that order planes today may end up not needing them. You can see why an airline might negotiate an aircraft purchase *option*.

In Section 10-4, we used aircraft purchase options to illustrate the option to expand. What we said there was the truth, but not the whole truth. Let's take another look. Suppose an airline forecasts a need for a new Airbus A320 four years hence.[13] It has at least three choices.

- *Commit now.* It can commit now to buy the plane, in exchange for Airbus's offer of locked-in price and delivery date.
- *Acquire option.* It can seek a purchase option from Airbus, allowing the airline to decide later whether to buy. A purchase option fixes the price and delivery date if the option is exercised.
- *Wait and decide later.* Airbus will be happy to sell another A320 at any time in the future if the airline wants to buy one. However, the airline may have to pay a higher price and wait longer for delivery, especially if the airline industry is flying high and many planes are on order.

The top half of Figure 22.6 shows the terms of a typical purchase option for an Airbus A320. The option must be exercised at year 3, when final assembly of the plane will begin. The option fixes the purchase price and the delivery date in year 4. The bottom half of the figure shows the consequences of "wait and decide later." We assume that the decision will come at year 3. If the decision is "buy," the airline pays the year-3 price and joins the queue for delivery in year 5 or later.

	Year 0	Year 3	Year 4	Year 5 or later
Buy option	Airline and manufacturer set price and delivery date	Exercise? (Yes or no)	Aircraft delivered if option exercised	
Wait	Wait and decide later	Buy now? If yes, negotiate price and wait for delivery.		Aircraft delivered if purchased at year 3

▶ **FIGURE 22.6**   This aircraft purchase option, if exercised at year 3, guarantees delivery at year 4 at a fixed price. Without the option, the airline can still order the plane at year 3, but the price is uncertain and the wait for delivery longer.

Source: Adapted from Figure 17–17 in J. Stonier, "What Is an Aircraft Purchase Option Worth? Quantifying Asset Flexibility Created through Manufacturer Lead-Time Reductions and Product Commonality," *Handbook of Airline Finance*, G. F. Butler and M. R. Keller, eds.

---

[12]Hewlett-Packard's decision is described in P. Coy, "Exploiting Uncertainty," *BusinessWeek,* June 7, 1999, pp. 118–122.
[13]The following example is based on J. E. Stonier, "What Is an Aircraft Purchase Option Worth? Quantifying Asset Flexibility Created through Manufacturer Lead-Time Reductions and Product Commonality," in *Handbook of Airline Finance*, G. F. Butler and M. R. Keller, eds. © 1999 Aviation Week Books.

The payoffs from "wait and decide later" can never be better than the payoffs from an aircraft purchase option since the airline can discard the option and negotiate afresh with Airbus if it wishes. In most cases, however, the airline will be better off in the future with the option than without it; the airline is at least guaranteed a place in the production line, and it may have locked in a favorable purchase price. But how much are these advantages worth today, compared to the wait-and-see strategy?

Figure 22.7 illustrates Airbus's answers to this problem. It assumes a three-year purchase option with an exercise price equal to an A320 price of $45 million. The present value of the purchase option depends on both the NPV of purchasing an A320 at that price and on the forecasted wait for delivery if the airline does *not* have a purchase option but nevertheless decides to place an order in year 3. The longer the wait in year 3, the more valuable it is to have the purchase option today. (Remember that the purchase option holds a place in the A320 production line and guarantees delivery in year 4.)

If the NPV of buying an A320 today is very high (the right-hand side of Figure 22.7), future NPV will probably be high as well, and the airline will want to buy regardless of whether it has a purchase option. In this case, the value of the purchase option comes mostly from the value of guaranteed delivery in year 4.[14] If the NPV is very low, then the option has low value because the airline is unlikely to exercise it. (Low NPV today probably means low NPV in year 3.) The purchase option is worth the most, compared to the wait-and-decide-later strategy, when NPV is around zero. In this case, the airline can exercise the option, getting a good price and early delivery, if future NPV is higher than expected; alternatively, it can walk away from the option if NPV disappoints. Of course, if it walks away, it may still wish to negotiate with Airbus for delivery at a price lower than the option's exercise price.

We have cruised by many of the technical details of Airbus's valuation model for purchase options. But the example does illustrate how real-options models are being built and used. By the way, Airbus offers more than just plain-vanilla purchase options. Airlines can negotiate

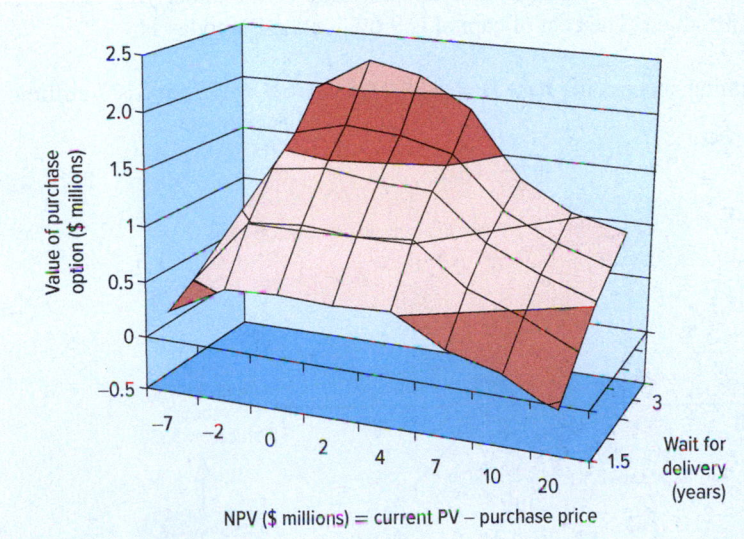

▶ FIGURE 22.7

Value of aircraft purchase option—the extra value of the option versus waiting and possibly negotiating a purchase later. (See Figure 22.6.) The purchase option is worth most when NPV of purchase now is about zero and the forecasted wait for delivery is long.

Source: Adapted from Figure 17–20 in J. Stonier, "What Is an Aircraft Purchase Option Worth? Quantifying Asset Flexibility Created Through Manufacturer Lead-Time Reductions and Product Commonality," in *Handbook of Aviation Finance*, G. F. Butler and M. R. Keller, eds.

---

[14]The Airbus real-options model assumes that future A320 prices will be increased when demand is high, but only to an upper bound. Thus the airline that waits and decides later may still have a positive-NPV investment opportunity if future demand and NPV are high. Figure 22.7 plots the *difference* between the value of the purchase option and this wait-and-see opportunity. This difference can shrink when NPV is high, especially if forecasted waiting times are short.

"rolling options," which lock in price but do not guarantee a place on the production line. (Exercise of the rolling option means that the airline joins the end of the queue.) Airbus also offers a purchase option that includes the right to switch from delivery of an A320 to an A319, a somewhat smaller plane.

22-5 Investment in Pharmaceutical R&D

An investment in research and development (R&D) is really an investment in real options. When your research engineers invent a better mousetrap, they hand you an *option* to manufacture and sell it. New and improved mousetraps can be engineering triumphs but commercial failures. You will make the investment to manufacture and launch the better mousetrap only if the PV of expected cash inflows is greater than the required investment.

The pharmaceutical industry spends massive amounts for R&D to develop options to produce and sell new drugs. We described pharmaceutical R&D in Example 10.2 and in Figure 10.4, which is a simplified decision tree. After you have reviewed that example and figure, take a look at Figure 22.8, which recasts the decision tree as a real option.

The drug candidate in Figure 22.8 requires an immediate investment of $18 million. That investment buys a real option to invest $130 million at year 2 to pay for phase III trials and costs incurred during the prelaunch period. Of course the real option exists only if phase II trials are successful. There is a 56% probability of failure. So after we value the real option, we will have to multiply its value by the 44% probability of success.

The exercise price of the real option is $130 million. The underlying asset is the PV of the drug, assuming that it passes phase III successfully. Figure 10.4 forecasts the expected PV of the drug at launch at $350 million in year 5. We multiply this value by .8 because the decision whether to exercise the option must be taken in year 2, *before* the company knows whether the drug will succeed or fail in phase III and prelaunch. Then we must discount this value back to year 0, because the Black–Scholes formula calls for the value of the underlying asset on the date when the option is valued. The cost of capital is 9.6%, so the PV today is

$$\text{PV at year 0, assuming success in phase II} = .8 \times 350/(1.096)^5 = 177, \text{ or } \$177 \text{ million}$$

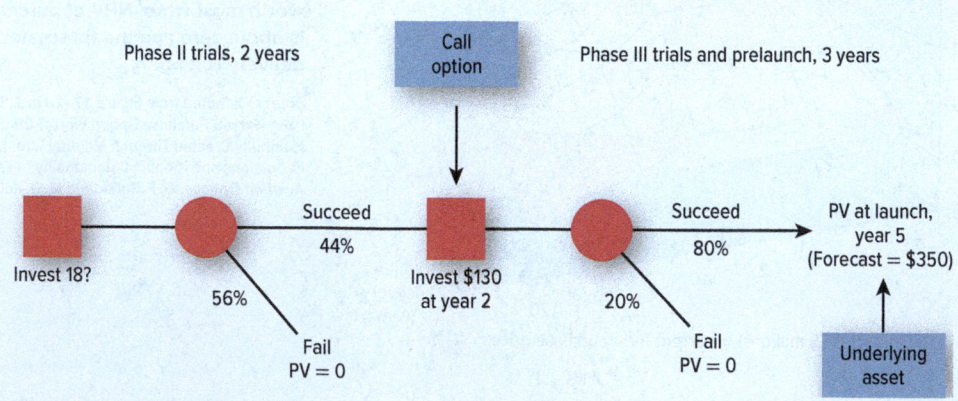

> **FIGURE 22.8**   The decision tree from Figure 10.4 recast as a real option. If phase II trials are successful, the company has a real call option to invest $130 million. If the option is exercised, the company gets an 80% chance of launching an approved drug. The PV of the drug, which is forecasted at $350 million in year 5, is the underlying asset for the call option.

To value the real option, we need a risk-free rate (assume 4%) and a volatility of the value of the drug once launched (assume 20%). With these inputs, the Black–Scholes value of a two-year call on an asset worth $177 million with an exercise price of $130 million is $58.4 million. (Refer to Section 21.3 if you need a refresher on how to use the Black–Scholes formula.)

But there's only a 44% chance that the drug will pass phase II trials. So the company must compare an initial investment of $18 million with a 44% chance of receiving an option worth $58.4 million. The NPV of the drug at year 0 is

$$\text{NPV} = -18 + (.44 \times 58.4) = \$7.7 \text{ million}$$

This NPV is less than the $19 million NPV computed from Figure 10.4.[15] Nevertheless, the R&D project is still a "go."

Of course Figure 22.8 assumes only one decision point, and only one real option, between the start of phase II and the product launch. In practice, there would be other decision points, including a Go/No Go decision after phase III trials but before prelaunch investment. In this case, the payoff to the first option at the end of phase II is the value at that date of the second option. This is an example of a *compound call.*

With two sequential options, you could look up the formula for a compound call in an option pricing manual, or you could build a binomial tree for the R&D project. Suppose you take the binomial route. Once you set up the tree, using risk-neutral probabilities for changes in the value of the underlying asset, you solve the tree as you would solve any decision tree. You work back from the end of the tree, always choosing the decision that gives the highest value at each decision point. NPV is positive if the PV at the start of the tree is higher than the $18 million initial investment.

Despite its simplifying assumptions, our example explains why investors demand higher expected returns from R&D investments than from the products that the R&D may generate. R&D invests in real call options.[16] A call option is always riskier (higher beta) than the underlying asset that is acquired when the option is exercised. Thus, the opportunity cost of capital for R&D is higher than for a new product after the product is launched successfully.[17]

R&D is also risky because it may fail. But the risk of failure is not usually a market or macroeconomic risk. The drug's beta or cost of capital does not depend on the probabilities that a drug will fail in phase II or III. If the drug fails, it will be because of medical or clinical problems, not because the stock market is down. We take account of medical or clinical risks by multiplying future outcomes by the probability of success, not by adding a fudge factor to the discount rate.

---

[15]Note that the Black–Scholes formula treats the exercise price of $130 million as a fixed amount and calculates its PV at a risk-free rate. In Chapter 10, we assumed this investment was just as risky as the drug's postlaunch cash flows. We discounted the investment at the 9.6% overall cost of capital, reducing its PV and thus increasing NPV overall. This is one reason the Black–Scholes formula gives a lower NPV than we calculated in Chapter 10. Of course, the $130 million is only an estimate, so discounting at the risk-free rate may not be correct. You could move from Black–Scholes to the valuation formula for an exchange option, which allows for uncertain exercise prices (see footnote 3). On the other hand, the R&D investment is probably close to a fixed cost because it is not exposed to the risks of the drug's operating cash flows postlaunch. There is a good case for discounting R&D investment at a low rate, even in a decision tree analysis.

[16]You could also value the R&D example as (1) the PV of making all future investments, given success in clinical trials, plus (2) the value of an abandonment put, which will be exercised if clinical trials are successful but the PV of postlaunch cash flows is sufficiently low. NPV is identical because of put–call parity.

[17]The higher cost of capital for R&D is not revealed by the Black–Scholes formula, which discounts certainty-equivalent payoffs at the risk-free interest rate.

Valuing Real Options

In this chapter, we have presented several examples of important real options. In each case, we used the option-pricing methods developed in Chapter 21, as if the real options were traded calls or puts. Was it right to value the real options as if they were traded? Also we said next to nothing about taxes. Shouldn't the risk-free rate be after-tax? What about the practical problems that managers face when they try to value real options in real life? We now address these questions.

A Conceptual Problem?

When we introduced option pricing models in Chapter 21, we showed that the trick is to construct a package of the underlying asset and a loan that would give exactly the same payoffs as the option. If the two investments do not sell for the same price, then there are arbitrage possibilities. But most real assets are not freely traded. This means that we can no longer rely on arbitrage arguments to justify the use of Black–Scholes or binomial option valuation methods.

The risk-neutral method still makes practical sense for real options, however. It's really just an application of the *certainty-equivalent* method introduced in Chapter 9.[18] The key assumption—implicit until now—is that the company's *shareholders* have access to assets with the same risk characteristics (e.g., the same beta) as the capital investments being evaluated by the firm.

Think of each real investment opportunity as having a "double," a security or portfolio with identical risk. Then the expected rate of return offered by the double is also the cost of capital for the real investment and the discount rate for a DCF valuation of the investment project. Now what would investors pay for a real *option* based on the project? The same as for an identical traded option written on the double. This traded option does not have to exist; it is enough to know how it would be valued by investors, who could employ either the arbitrage or the risk-neutral method. The two methods give the same answer, of course.

When we value a real option by the risk-neutral method, we are calculating the option's value if it could be traded. This exactly parallels standard capital budgeting. Shareholders would vote unanimously to accept any capital investment whose market value *if traded* exceeds its cost, as long as they can buy traded securities with the same risk characteristics as the project. This key assumption supports the use of both DCF and real-option valuation methods.

What about Taxes?

So far, this chapter has mostly ignored taxes, but just for simplicity. Taxes have to be accounted for when valuing real options. Take the Mark II microcomputer in Table 22.2 as an example. The Mark II's forecasted PV of $807 million should be calculated from after-tax cash flows generated by the product. The required investment of $900 million should likewise be calculated after-tax.[19]

What about the risk-free discount rate used in the risk-neutral method? It should also be after-tax. Look back to the Chapter 19 Appendix, which demonstrates that the proper discount rate for safe cash flows is the after-tax interest rate. The same logic applies here because projected cash flows in the risk-neutral method are valued as if they were safe.

---

[18]Use of risk-neutral probabilities converts future cash flows to certainty equivalents, which are then discounted to present value at a risk-free rate.

[19]If the capital investment cannot be deducted immediately for tax, you should subtract the PV of any depreciation tax shields from the pre-tax capital investment, thus converting the investment to a net after-tax outlay.

Recall that the value of a real call option can be expressed as a position in the underlying asset minus a loan. Thus, the call behaves like a claim on the underlying asset partly financed with borrowed money. The borrowing does not show up on the corporation's balance sheet, but it is nevertheless really there. The implicit borrowing is a debt-equivalent obligation that must be valued using an after-tax interest rate.[20]

The implicit borrowing creates off-balance-sheet financial leverage. The resulting financial risk is the reason why the real call option's value is more volatile than the value of the underlying asset. (The real option would have a higher beta than the underlying asset if both were traded in financial markets.)

In Chapter 18, we pointed out that highly profitable growth companies like Alphabet and Amazon use mostly equity finance. These companies' real growth options are one explanation. The options contain implicit debt. If the CFOs of these growth firms recognize the implicit debt, or at least the extra financial risk attached to the options, they should reduce ordinary borrowing to compensate. Option leverage therefore displaces ordinary financial leverage. The displacement means that if you forget to count both the debt that is on and off the balance sheet, a growth firm will appear to be less leveraged than it actually is.

Practical Challenges

The challenges in applying real-options analysis are not conceptual but practical. It isn't always easy. We can tick off some of the reasons why.

First, real options can be complex, and valuing them can absorb a lot of analytical and computational horsepower. Whether you want to invest in that horsepower is a matter for business judgment. Sometimes an approximate answer now is more useful than a "perfect" answer later, particularly if the perfect answer comes from a complicated model that other managers will regard as a black box. One advantage of real-options analysis, if you keep it simple, is that it's relatively easy to explain. Complex decision trees can often be described as the payoffs to one or two simple call or put options.

The second problem is lack of *structure*. To quantify the value of a real option, you have to specify its possible payoffs, which depend on the range of possible values of the underlying asset, exercise prices, timing of exercise, etc. In this chapter, we have taken well-structured examples where it is easy to see the road map of possible outcomes. For example, investments in pharmaceutical R&D are well-structured because all new drugs have to go through the same series of clinical trials to get approved by the U.S. Food and Drug Administration. Outcomes are uncertain, but the road map is clear. In other cases, you may not have a road map. For example, reading this book can enhance your personal call option to work in financial management, yet we suspect that you would find it hard to write down how that option would change the binomial tree of your entire future career.

A third problem can arise when your *competitors* have real options. This is not a problem in industries where products are standardized and no single competitor can shift demand and prices. But when you face just a few key competitors, all with real options, then the options can interact. If so, you can't value your options without thinking of your competitors' moves. Your competitors will be thinking in the same fashion.

An analysis of competitive interactions would take us into other branches of economics, including game theory. But you can see the danger of assuming passive competitors. Think of the timing option. A simple real-options analysis will often tell you to wait and learn before investing in a new market. Be careful that you don't wait and learn that a competitor has moved first.[21]

---

[20]The interest on the option debt is also implicit and therefore not tax-deductible. The proof that the discount rate for real options should be after-tax is in S. C. Myers and J. A. Read, Jr., "Real Options, Taxes and Leverage," *Critical Finance Review,* forthcoming.

[21]Being the first mover into a new market is not always the best strategy, of course. Sometimes later movers win. For a survey of real options and product-market competition, see H. Smit and L. Trigeorgis, *Strategic Investment, Real Options and Games* (Princeton, NJ: Princeton University Press, 2004).

Given these hurdles, you can understand why systematic, quantitative valuation of real options is restricted mostly to well-structured problems like the examples in this chapter. The qualitative implications of real options are widely appreciated, however. Real options give the financial manager a conceptual framework for strategic planning and thinking about capital investments. If you can identify and understand real options, you will be a more sophisticated consumer of DCF analysis and better equipped to invest your company's money wisely.

Understanding real options also pays off when you can *create* real options, adding value by adding flexibility to the company's investments and operations. For example, it may be better to design and build a series of modular production plants, each with capacity of 50,000 tons per year of magnoosium alloy, than to commit to one large plant with capacity of 150,000 tons per year. The larger plant will probably be more efficient because of economies of scale. But with the smaller plants, you retain the flexibility to expand in step with demand and to defer investment when demand growth is disappointing.

Sometimes valuable options can be created simply by "overbuilding" in the initial round of investment. For example, oil-production platforms are typically built with vacant deck space to reduce the cost of adding equipment later. Undersea oil pipelines from the platforms to shore are often built with larger diameters and capacity than production from the platform will require. The additional capacity is then available at low cost if additional oil is found nearby. The extra cost of a larger-diameter pipeline is much less than the cost of building a second pipeline later.

SUMMARY

In Chapter 21, you learned the basics of option valuation. In this chapter, we described four important real options:

1. *The option to make follow-on investments.* Companies often cite "strategic" value when taking on negative-NPV projects. A close look at the projects' payoffs reveals call options on follow-on projects in addition to the immediate projects' cash flows. Today's investments can generate tomorrow's opportunities.

2. *The option to wait (and learn) before investing.* This is equivalent to owning a call option on the investment project. The call is exercised when the firm commits to the project. But rather than exercising the call immediately, it's often better to defer a positive-NPV project in order to keep the call alive. Deferral is most attractive when uncertainty is great and immediate project cash flows—which are lost or postponed by waiting—are small.

3. *The option to abandon.* The option to abandon a project provides partial insurance against failure. This is a put option; the put's exercise price is the value of the project's assets if sold or shifted to a more valuable use.

4. *The option to vary the firm's output or its production methods.* Firms often build flexibility into their production facilities so that they can use the cheapest raw materials or produce the most valuable set of outputs. In this case they effectively acquire the option to exchange one asset for another.

We should offer here a healthy warning: The real options encountered in practice are often complex. Each real option brings its own issues and trade-offs. Nevertheless, the tools that you have learned in this and previous chapters can be used in practice. The Black–Scholes formula often suffices to value one-time expansion and abandonment options. For more complex options, it's sometimes easier to switch to binomial trees.

Binomial trees are cousins of decision trees. You work back through binomial trees from future payoffs to present value. Whenever a future decision needs to be made, you figure out the value-maximizing choice, using the principles of option pricing theory, and record the resulting value at the appropriate node of the tree.

Don't jump to the conclusion that real-option valuation methods can replace discounted cash flow (DCF). First, DCF works fine for safe cash flows. It also works for "cash cow" assets—that is, for assets or businesses whose value depends primarily on forecasted cash flows, not on real options. Second, the starting point in most real-option analyses is the present value of an underlying asset. To value the underlying asset, you typically have to use DCF.

Real options are rarely traded assets. When we value a real option, we are estimating its value if it could be traded. This is the standard approach in corporate finance, the same approach taken in DCF valuations. The key assumption is that shareholders can buy traded securities or portfolios with the same risk characteristics as the real investments being evaluated by the firm. If so, they would vote unanimously for any real investment whose market value if traded would exceed the investment required. This key assumption supports the use of both DCF and real-option valuation methods.

Taxes are not tracked specifically in the several real-options examples presented in this chapter. But remember that all cash flows from real options should be projected after corporate tax. The discount rate in the risk-neutral method should also be after-tax.

FURTHER READING

The Further Reading for Chapter 10 lists several introductory articles on real options. The Spring 2005 and 2007 issues of the Journal of Applied Corporate Finance *contain additional articles.*

The Spring 2006 issue contains two further articles:

R. L. McDonald, "The Role of Real Options in Capital Budgeting: Theory and Practice," *Journal of Applied Corporate Finance* 18 (Spring 2006), pp. 28–39.

M. Amram, F. Li, and C. A. Perkins, "How Kimberly-Clark Uses Real Options," *Journal of Applied Corporate Finance* 18 (Spring 2006), pp. 40–47.

The standard texts on real options include:

M. Amram and N. Kulatilaka, *Real Options: Managing Strategic Investments in an Uncertain World* (Boston: Harvard Business School Press, 1999).

T. Copeland and V. Antikarov, *Real Options: A Practitioner's Guide* (New York: Texere, 2003).

A. K. Dixit and R. S. Pindyck, *Investment under Uncertainty* (Princeton, NJ: Princeton University Press, 1994).

H. Smit and L. Trigeorgis, *Strategic Investment, Real Options and Games* (Princeton, NJ: Princeton University Press, 2004).

L. Trigeorgis, *Real Options* (Cambridge, MA: MIT Press, 1996).

Mason and Merton review a range of option applications to corporate finance:

S. P. Mason and R. C. Merton, "The Role of Contingent Claims Analysis in Corporate Finance," in E. I. Altman and M. G. Subrahmanyam, eds., *Recent Advances in Corporate Finance* (Homewood, IL: Richard D. Irwin, Inc., 1985).

Brennan and Schwartz have worked out an interesting application to natural resource investments:

M. J. Brennan and E. S. Schwartz, "Evaluating Natural Resource Investments," *Journal of Business* 58 (April 1985), pp. 135–157.

PROBLEM SETS

 Select problems are available in McGraw-Hill's *Connect*. Please see the preface for more information.

1. **Real options** Respond to the following comments.

    a. "You don't need option pricing theories to value flexibility. Just use a decision tree. Discount the cash flows in the tree at the company cost of capital."

b. "These option pricing methods are just plain nutty. They say that real options on risky assets are worth more than options on safe assets."

c. "Real-options methods eliminate the need for DCF valuation of investment projects."

2. **Real options** Why is quantitative valuation of real options often difficult in practice? List the reasons briefly.

3. **Real options** True or false?

a. Real-options analysis sometimes tells firms to make negative-NPV investments to secure future growth opportunities.

b. Using the Black–Scholes formula to value options to invest is dangerous when the underlying investment project would generate significant immediate cash flows.

c. Binomial trees can be used to evaluate options to acquire or abandon an asset. It's OK to use risk-neutral probabilities in the trees even when the asset beta is 1.0 or higher.

d. It's OK to use the Black–Scholes formula or binomial trees to value real options, even though the options are not traded.

e. A real-options valuation will sometimes reveal that it's better to invest in a series of smaller plants rather than a single large plant.

4. **Real options** Alert financial managers can *create* real options. Give three or four possible examples.

5. **Real options** Describe each of the following situations in the language of options:

a. Drilling rights to undeveloped heavy crude oil in Northern Alberta. Development and production of the oil is a negative-NPV endeavor. (Assume a break-even oil price is C$90 per barrel, versus a spot price of C$80.) However, the decision to develop can be put off for up to five years. Development costs are expected to increase by 5% per year.

b. A restaurant is producing net cash flows, after all out-of-pocket expenses, of $700,000 per year. There is no upward or downward trend in the cash flows, but they fluctuate as a random walk, with an annual standard deviation of 15%. The real estate occupied by the restaurant is owned, not leased, and could be sold for $5 million. Ignore taxes.

c. A variation on part (b): Assume the restaurant faces known fixed costs of $300,000 per year, incurred as long as the restaurant is operating. Thus,

$$\text{Net cash flow = revenue less variable costs − fixed costs}$$
$$\$700,000 = 1,000,000 − 300,000$$

The annual standard deviation of the forecast error of revenue less variable costs is 10.5%. The interest rate is 10%. Ignore taxes.

d. A paper mill can be shut down in periods of low demand and restarted if demand improves sufficiently. The costs of closing and reopening the mill are fixed.

e. A real estate developer uses a parcel of urban land as a parking lot, although construction of either a hotel or an apartment building on the land would be a positive-NPV investment.

f. Air France negotiates a purchase option for 10 Boeing 787s. Air France must confirm the order by 2021. Otherwise Boeing will be free to sell the aircraft to other airlines.

6. **Expansion options*** Look again at the valuation in Table 22.2 of the option to invest in the Mark II project. Consider a change in each of the following inputs. Would the change increase or decrease the value of the expansion option?

a. Increased uncertainty (higher standard deviation).

b. More optimistic forecast (higher expected value) of the Mark II in 1985.

c. Increase in the required investment in 1985.

7. **Expansion options** Look again at Table 22.2. How does the value in 1982 of the option to invest in the Mark II change if

    a. The investment required for the Mark II is $800 million (vs. $900 million)?

    b. The present value of the Mark II in 1982 is $500 million (vs. $467 million)?

    c. The standard deviation of the Mark II's present value is only 20% (vs. 35%)?

8. **Timing options*** You own a parcel of vacant land. You can develop it now, or wait.

    a. What is the advantage of waiting?

    b. Why might you decide to develop the property immediately?

9. **Timing options** Look back at the Malted Herring option in Section 22-2. How did the company's analysts estimate the present value of the project? It turns out that they assumed that the probability of low demand was about 45%. They then estimated the expected payoff as $(.45 \times 176) + (.55 \times 275) = 230$. Discounting at the company's 15% cost of capital gave a present value for the project of $230/1.15 = 200$.

    a. How would this present value change if the probability of low demand was 55%? How would it change if the *project's* cost of capital was higher than the company cost of capital at, say, 20%?

    b. Now estimate how these changes in assumptions would affect the value of the option to delay.

10. **Abandonment options** A start-up company is moving into its first offices and needs desks, chairs, filing cabinets, and other furniture. It can buy the furniture for $25,000 or rent it for $1,500 per month. The founders are of course confident in their new venture, but nevertheless they rent. Why? What's the option?

11. **Abandonment options** Flip back to Tables 6.2 and 6.3, where we assumed an economic life of seven years for IM&C's guano plant. What's wrong with that assumption? How would you undertake a more complete analysis?

12. **Abandonment options** In Section 10-4, we considered two production technologies for a new Wankel-engined outboard motor. Technology A was the most efficient but had no salvage value if the new outboards failed to sell. Technology B was less efficient but offered a salvage value of $17 million.

    Figure 10.3 shows the present value of the project as either $24 or $16 million in year 1 if Technology A is used. Assume that the present value of these payoffs is $18 million at year 0.

    a. With Technology B, the payoffs at year 1 are $22.5 or $15 million. What is the present value of these payoffs in year 0 if Technology B is used? (*Hint:* The payoffs with Technology B are 93.75% of the payoffs from Technology A.)

    b. Technology B allows abandonment in year 1 for $17 million salvage value. You also get cash flow of $1.5 million, for a total of $18.5 million. Calculate abandonment value, assuming a risk-free rate of 7%.

13. **Abandonment options** Take another look at the perpetual crusher example in Section 22-3. Construct a sensitivity analysis showing how the value of the abandonment put changes depending on the standard deviation of the project and the exercise price.

14. **Flexible production and procurement*** Gas turbines are among the least efficient ways to produce electricity, much less thermally efficient than coal or nuclear plants. Why do gas-turbine generating stations exist? What's the option?

15. **R&D** Construct a sensitivity analysis of the value of the pharmaceutical R&D project described in Figure 22.8. What input assumptions are most critical for the NPV of the project? Be sure to check the inputs to valuing the real option to invest at year 2.

BEYOND THE PAGE

Try it! The Black-
Scholes model

mhhe.com/brealey13e

16. **Real option valuation*** You own a one-year call option to buy one acre of Los Angeles real estate. The exercise price is $2 million, and the current, appraised market value of the land is $1.7 million. The land is currently used as a parking lot, generating just enough money to cover real estate taxes. The annual standard deviation is 15% and the interest rate 12%. How much is your call worth? Use the Black–Scholes formula. You may find it helpful to go to the spreadsheet for Chapter 21, which calculates Black–Scholes values (see the Beyond the Page feature).

17. **Real option valuation** A variation on Problem 16: Suppose the land is occupied by a warehouse generating rents of $150,000 after real estate taxes and all other out-of-pocket costs. The present value of the land plus warehouse is again $1.7 million. Other facts are as in Problem 16. You have a European call option. What is it worth?

18. **Real option valuation** You have an option to purchase all of the assets of the Overland Railroad for $2.5 billion. The option expires in nine months. You estimate Overland's current (month 0) present value (PV) as $2.7 billion. Overland generates after-tax free cash flow (FCF) of $50 million at the end of each quarter (i.e., at the end of each three-month period). If you exercise your option at the start of the quarter, that quarter's cash flow is paid out to you. If you do not exercise, the cash flow goes to Overland's current owners.

    In each quarter, Overland's PV either increases by 10% or decreases by 9.09%. This PV includes the quarterly FCF of $50 million. After the $50 million is paid out, PV drops by $50 million. Thus, the binomial tree for the first quarter is (figures in millions):

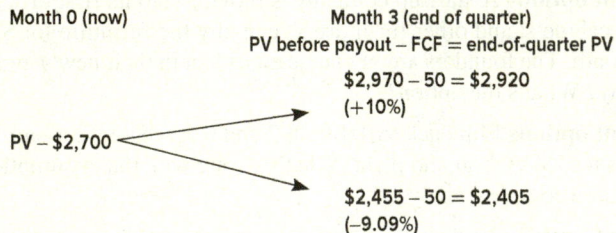

The risk-free interest rate is 2% per quarter.

   a. Build a binomial tree for Overland, with one up or down change for each three-month period (three steps to cover your nine-month option).

   b. Suppose you can only exercise your option now, or after nine months (not at month 3 or 6). Would you exercise now?

   c. Suppose you can exercise now, or at month 3, 6, or 9. What is your option worth today? Should you exercise today, or wait?

19. **Real option valuation** Josh Kidding, who has only read part of Chapter 10, decides to value a real option by (1) setting out a decision tree, with cash flows and probabilities forecasted for each future outcome; (2) deciding what to do at each decision point in the tree; and (3) discounting the resulting expected cash flows at the company cost of capital. Will this procedure give the right answer? Why or why not?

20. **Real option valuation** In binomial trees, risk-neutral probabilities are set to generate an expected rate of return equal to the risk-free interest rate in each branch of the tree. What do you think of the following statement: "The value of an option to acquire an asset increases with the difference between the risk-free rate of interest and the weighted-average cost of capital for the asset"?

21. **Real options and put-call parity** Redo the example in Figure 22.8, assuming that the real option is a put option allowing the company to abandon the R&D program if commercial prospects are sufficiently poor at year 2. Use put-call parity. The NPV of the drug at date 0 should again be +$7.7 million.

CHALLENGE

22. **Complex real options** Suppose you expect to need a new plant that will be ready to produce turbo-encabulators in 36 months. If design A is chosen, construction must begin immediately. Design B is more expensive, but you can wait 12 months before breaking ground. Figure 22.9 shows the cumulative present value of construction costs for the two designs up to the 36-month deadline. Assume that the designs, once built, will be equally efficient and have equal production capacity.

    A standard DCF analysis ranks design A ahead of design B. But suppose the demand for turbo-encabulators falls and the new factory is not needed; then, as Figure 22.9 shows, the firm is better off with design B, provided the project is abandoned before month 24.

    Describe this situation as the choice between two (complex) call options. Then describe the same situation in terms of (complex) abandonment options. The two descriptions should imply identical payoffs, given optimal exercise strategies.

23. **Options and growth** In Chapter 4, we expressed the value of a share of stock as

$$P_0 = \frac{EPS_1}{r} + PVGO$$

    where EPS_1 is earnings per share from existing assets, r is the expected rate of return required by investors, and PVGO is the present value of growth opportunities. PVGO really consists of a portfolio of expansion options.[22]

    a. What is the effect of an increase in PVGO on the standard deviation or beta of the stock's rate of return?

    b. Suppose the CAPM is used to calculate the cost of capital for a growth (high-PVGO) firm. Assume all-equity financing. Will this cost of capital be the correct hurdle rate for investments to expand the firm's plant and equipment, or to introduce new products?

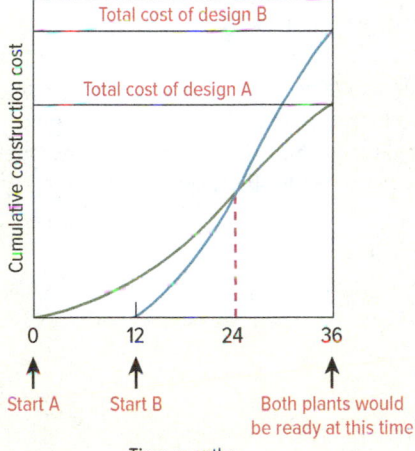

▶ **FIGURE 22.9**

Cumulative construction cost of the two plant designs. Plant A takes 36 months to build; plant B, only 24. But plant B costs more.

---

[22]If this challenge problem intrigues you, check out two articles by Eduardo Schwartz and Mark Moon, who attempt to use real-options theory to value Internet companies: "Rational Valuation of Internet Companies," *Financial Analysts Journal* 56 (May/June 2000), pp. 62–65; and "Rational Pricing of Internet Companies Revisited," *The Financial Review* 36 (November 2001), pp. 7–25.

23

CHAPTER

Credit Risk and the Value of Corporate Debt

We first looked at how to value bonds way back in Chapter 3. We explained in that chapter what bond dealers mean when they refer to spot rates of interest and yields to maturity. We discussed why long-term and short-term bonds may offer different rates of interest and why prices of long-term bonds are affected more by a change in rates. We looked at the difference between nominal and real (inflation-adjusted) interest rates, and we saw how interest rates respond to changes in the prospects for inflation.

All the lessons of Chapter 3 hold good for both government and corporate bonds, but there is also a fundamental distinction between government and corporate issues. When a government borrows money, you can usually be confident that the debt will be repaid in full and on time. This is not true of corporate borrowing. Look, for example, at Figure 23.1. You can see that in 2009, following the financial crisis, companies defaulted on a record $330 billion of debt. Bondholders are aware of the danger that they will not get their money back and so demand a higher yield.

We begin our review of corporate bonds by looking at how yields vary with the likelihood of default. Then in Section 23-2, we look more carefully at the company's decision to default. We show that default is an *option;* if the going becomes too tough, the company has the option to stop payments on its bonds and hand over the business to the debtholders. We know what determines the value of options; therefore, we know the basic variables that must enter into the valuation of corporate bonds.

Our next step is to look at bond ratings and some of the techniques that are used by banks and bond investors to estimate the probability that the borrower will not be able to repay its debts. We will look at statistical models that seek to identify common features of defaulting companies. And we will look at structural models that estimate the probability that a firm's value will fall to the point at which it will choose to default.

23-1 Yields on Corporate Debt

BEYOND THE PAGE

U.S. bond default rate, 1980–2017

mhhe.com/brealey13e

The year 2017 was not a happy one for telecom operator, Frontier Communications. Its share price fell by 85% over the year, and its 11% bonds maturing in 2025 were trading at 79% of face value, where they offered a yield to maturity of 15.8%. A naïve investor who compared this figure with the 2% yield on Treasury bonds might have concluded that Frontier's bonds were a wonderful investment. But the owner would earn a 15.8% return only if the company repaid the debt in full. By 2017, that was looking increasingly doubtful. The company had

614

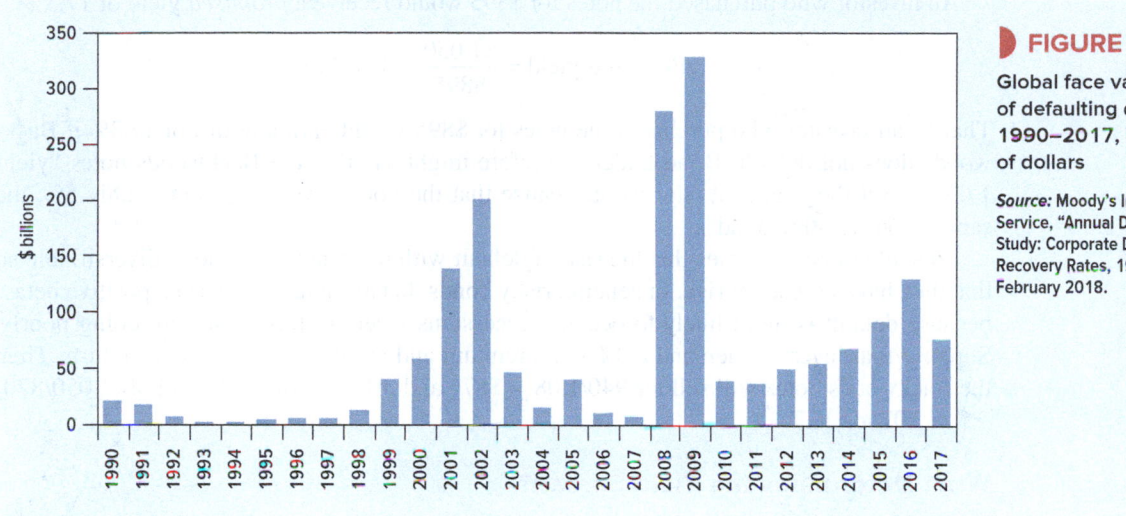

▶ **FIGURE 23.1**

Global face value
of defaulting debt,
1990–2017, in billions
of dollars

Source: Moody's Investor
Service, "Annual Default
Study: Corporate Default and
Recovery Rates, 1920–2017,"
February 2018.

recorded some hefty losses and was on life support. It had nearly $18 billion of debt in issue and just over $3 billion of book equity. Because there was a significant risk that the company would default on its bonds, the *expected* yield was much less than 15.8%.

Corporate bonds, such as the Frontier Communications bond, offer a higher *promised* yield than government bonds, but do they necessarily offer a higher *expected* yield? We can answer this question with a simple numerical example. Suppose that the interest rate on one-year *risk-free* bonds is 5%. Backwoods Chemical Company has issued 5% notes with a face value of $1,000, maturing in one year. What will the Backwoods notes sell for?

If the notes are risk-free, the answer is easy—just discount principal ($1,000) and interest ($50) at 5%:

$$\text{PV of notes} = \frac{\$1,000 + 50}{1.05} = \$1,000$$

Suppose, however, that there is a 20% chance that Backwoods will default and that, if default does occur, holders of its notes receive half the face value of the notes, or $500. In this case, the possible payoffs to the noteholders are

	Payoff	Probability
No default	$1,050	0.8
Default	500	0.2

The expected payment is .8($1,050) + .2($500) = $940.

We can value the Backwoods notes like any other risky asset, by discounting their expected payoff ($940) at the appropriate opportunity cost of capital. We might discount at the risk-free interest rate (5%) if Backwoods's possible default is totally unrelated to other events in the economy. In this case, default risk is wholly diversifiable, and the beta of the notes is zero. The notes would sell for

$$\text{PV of notes} = \frac{\$940}{1.05} = \$895$$

An investor who purchased the notes for $895 would receive a *promised* yield of 17.3%:

$$\text{Promised yield} = \frac{\$1,050}{\$895} - 1 = .173$$

That is, an investor who purchased the notes for $895 would earn a return of 17.3% if Backwoods does not default. Bond traders therefore might say that the Backwoods notes "yield 17.3%." But the smart investor would realize that the notes' *expected* yield is only 5%, the same as on risk-free bonds.

This, of course, assumes that the risk of default with these notes is wholly diversifiable so that they have no market risk. In general, risky bonds do have market risk (i.e., positive betas) because default is more likely to occur in recessions when all businesses are doing poorly. Suppose that investors demand a 3% risk premium and an 8% expected rate of return. Then the Backwoods notes will sell for 940/1.08 = $870 and offer a promised yield of (1,050/870) − 1 = .207, or 20.7%.

What Determines the Yield Spread?

Figure 23.2 shows how the yield spread on U.S. corporate bonds varies with the bond's risk. Bonds rated Aaa by Moody's are the highest-grade bonds and are issued only by a few blue-chip companies. The promised yield on these bonds has on average been about 1% higher than the yield on Treasuries. Baa bonds are rated three notches lower; the yield spread on these bonds has averaged about 2%. At the bottom of the heap are high-yield or "junk" bonds. There is considerable variation in the yield spreads on junk bonds; a typical spread might be about 6% over Treasuries, but spreads can rocket skyward as companies fall into distress.

Remember these are promised yields and companies don't always keep their promises. Many high-yielding bonds have defaulted, while some of the more successful issuers have called and paid off their debt, thus depriving their holders of the prospect of a continuing stream of high coupon payments.

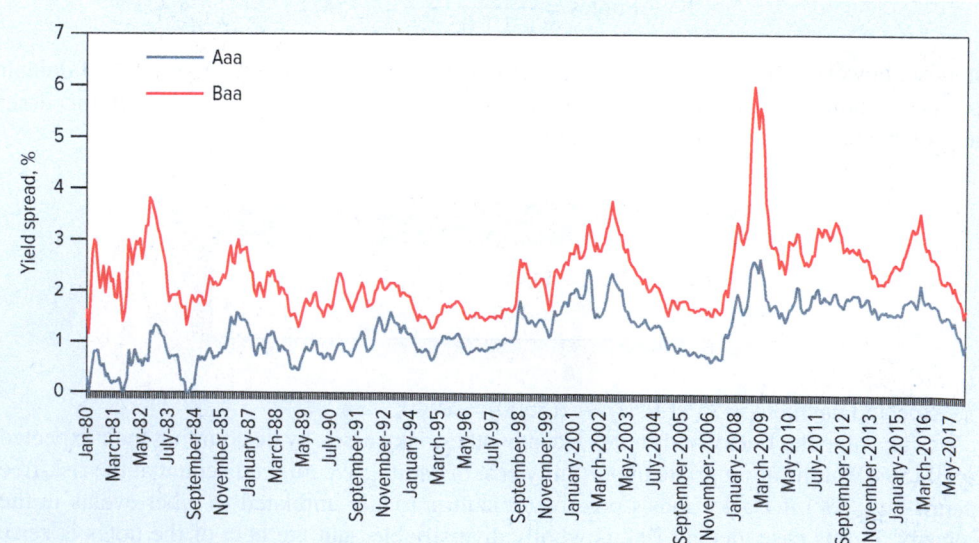

▶ **FIGURE 23.2**

Monthly yield spreads between corporate and 10-year Treasury bonds, 1980–2018

Source: The Federal Reserve Bank of St. Louis, https://fred.stlouisfed.org/

Figure 23.2 also shows that yield spreads can vary quite sharply from one year to the next, particularly for low-rated bonds. For example, they were unusually high in 2000–2002, and 2008–2009. Why is this? The main reason is that, as Figure 23.1 shows, these were periods when defaults were more likely. However, the fluctuations in spreads appear to be too large to be due simply to changing probabilities of default. It seems that there are occasions when investors are particularly reluctant to bear the risk of low-grade bonds and so scurry to the safe haven of government debt.[1]

To understand more precisely what the yield spread measures, compare these two strategies:

Strategy 1: Invest $1,000 in a floating-rate default-free bond yielding 9%.[2]

Strategy 2: Invest $1,000 in a comparable floating-rate corporate bond yielding 10%. At the same time, take out an insurance policy to protect yourself against the possibility of default. You pay an insurance premium of 1% a year, but in the event of default, you are compensated for any loss in the bond's value.

Both strategies provide exactly the same payoff. In the case of strategy 2, you gain a 1% higher yield, but this is exactly offset by the 1% annual premium on the insurance policy. Why does the insurance premium have to be equal to the spread? Because, if it weren't, one strategy would dominate the other and there would be an arbitrage opportunity. The law of one price tells us that two equivalent risk-free investments must cost the same.

Our example tells us how to interpret the spread on corporate bonds. It is equal to the annual premium that would be needed to insure the bond against default.[3]

By the way, you *can* insure corporate bonds; you do so with an arrangement called a *credit default swap* (CDS). If you buy a default swap, you commit to pay a regular insurance premium (or *spread*).[4] In return, if the company subsequently defaults on its debt, the seller of the swap pays you the difference between the face value of the debt and its market value. For example, when American Airlines defaulted in 2011, its unsecured bonds were auctioned for 23.5% of face value. Thus, sellers of default swaps had to pay out 76.5 cents on each dollar of American Airlines's debt that they had insured.

Credit default swaps proved very popular, particularly with banks that need to reduce the risk of their loan books. From almost nothing in 2000, the notional value of default swaps and related products had mushroomed to $62 trillion by the start of the financial crisis.[5] Many of these default swaps were sold by *monoline insurers,* which specialize in providing services to the capital markets. The monolines had traditionally concentrated on insuring relatively safe

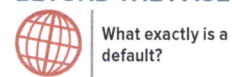

BEYOND THE PAGE

What exactly is a default?

mhhe.com/brealey13e

BEYOND THE PAGE

A most controversial trade

mhhe.com/brealey13e

---

[1]For evidence on the effect of changing risk aversion on bond spreads, see A. Berndt, R. Douglas, D. Duffie, and M. Ferguson, "Corporate Credit Risk Premia," *Review of Finance,* 22 (March 2018), pp. 419–454.

[2]The interest payment on floating-rate bonds goes up and down as the general level of interest rates changes. Thus a floating-rate default-free bond will sell at close to face value on each coupon date. Many governments issue "floaters." The U.S. Treasury does not do so, though some U.S. government agencies do.

[3]For illustration, we have used the example of a floating-rate bond to demonstrate the equivalence between the yield spread and the cost of default insurance. But the spread on a fixed-rate corporate bond should be effectively identical to that on a floater.

[4]In the case of low-grade bonds, when the regular spread does not sufficiently protect the seller against the possibility of an early default, the buyer of the default swap may also be asked to pay an up-front fee.

[5]*Notional value* refers to the total face value of bonds covered by CDS contacts. The *present value* of a CDS contract at its creation is usually zero. That is, the buyer of credit protection usually pays no money up front. Then the present value fluctuates, increasing as and if credit risk increases, but is always smaller than the notional value unless the bond turns out to be totally worthless. Data on credit derivatives are published by the International Swap Dealers Association (ISDA) at **www.isda.org.**

municipal debt but had been increasingly prepared to underwrite corporate debt, as well as many securities that were backed by subprime mortgages. By 2008, insurance companies had sold protection on $2.4 trillion of bonds. As the outlook for many of these bonds deteriorated, investors began to question whether the insurance companies had sufficient capital to make good on their guarantees.

One of the largest providers of credit protection was AIG Financial Products, part of the giant insurance group, AIG, with a portfolio of more than $440 billion of credit guarantees. AIG's clients never dreamed that the company would be unable to pay up: Not only was AIG triple-A rated, but it had promised to post generous collateral if the value of the insured securities dropped or if its own credit rating fell. So confident was AIG of its strategy that the head of its financial products group claimed that it was hard "to even see a scenario within any kind of realm of reason that would see us losing one dollar in any of these transactions." But in September 2008, this unthinkable scenario occurred when the credit rating agencies downgraded AIG's debt, and the company found itself obliged to provide $32 billion of additional collateral within the next 15 days. Had AIG defaulted, everyone who had bought a CDS contract from the company would have suffered large losses on these contracts. To save AIG from imminent collapse, the Federal Reserve stepped in with an $85 billion rescue package.

23-2 Valuing the Option to Default

The difference between a corporate bond and a comparable Treasury bond is that the company has the option to default whereas the government supposedly doesn't.[6] That default option is valuable. If you don't believe us, think about whether (other things equal) you would prefer to be a shareholder in a company with limited liability or in a company with unlimited liability. Of course, you would prefer to have the option to walk away from your company's debts. Unfortunately, every silver lining has its cloud, and the drawback to having a default option is that corporate bondholders expect to be compensated for giving it to you. That is why corporate bonds sell at lower prices and offer higher yields than government bonds.

We can illustrate the nature of the default option by returning to the plight of Circular File Company, which we discussed in Chapter 18. Circular File borrowed $50 per share, but then fell on hard times, and the market value of its assets fell to $30. Circular's bond and stock prices fell to $27 and $3, respectively. Thus Circular's *market-value* balance sheet is:

	Circular File Company	
Asset value	$30	$27	Bond
		3	Stock
	$30	$30	Firm value

---

[6]But governments cannot print the currencies of other countries. Therefore, they may be forced into default on their foreign currency debt. For example, we saw in Chapter 3 how Argentina defaulted on $95 billion of foreign currency debt and, how Greece defaulted in 2012. Very occasionally, governments have even defaulted on their own currency's debt. For example, in 1998, the Russian government defaulted on $36 billion of ruble debt.

If Circular's debt were due and payable now, the firm could not repay the $50 it originally borrowed. It would default, leaving bondholders with assets worth $30 and shareholders with nothing. The reason that Circular stock has a market value of $3 is that the debt is *not* due immediately, but one year from now. A stroke of good fortune could increase firm value enough to pay off the bondholders in full, with something left over for the stockholders.

Circular File is not compelled to repay the debt at maturity. If the value of its assets is less than the $50 that it owes, it will choose to default on the debt and the bondholders will get to keep the assets. Circular's bondholders have, in effect, bought a safe bond but, at the same time, given the shareholders a put option to sell the firm's assets to the bondholders for the amount of the debt. The exercise price of the put is $50, the face value of the bond. If the value of the company's assets when the bond matures is greater than $50, Circular will not exercise its option to default. If the assets' value is less than $50, it will pay Circular to exercise its option and to hand over the assets to settle the debt.

Now you can see why bond traders, investors, and financial managers refer to *default puts*. When a firm defaults, its stockholders are, in effect, exercising their default put. The put's value is the value of limited liability—the value of the stockholders' right to walk away from their firm's debts in exchange for handing over the firm's assets to its creditors. In the case of Circular File, this option to default is extremely valuable because default is likely to occur. At the other extreme, the value of IBM's option to default is trivial compared with the value of IBM's assets. Default on IBM bonds is possible but extremely unlikely. Option traders would say that for Circular File, the put option is "deep in the money" because today's asset value ($30) is well below the exercise price ($50). For IBM, the put option is far "out of the money" because the value of IBM's assets greatly exceeds the amount of IBM's debt.

Valuing corporate bonds should be a two-step process:

$$\text{Bond value} = \text{bond value assuming no chance of default}$$
$$-\text{value of put option on assets}$$

The first step is easy: Calculate the bond's value assuming no default risk. (Discount promised interest and principal payments at the rate offered by Treasuries.) The second step requires you to calculate the value of a put written on the firm's assets, where the maturity of the put equals the maturity of the bond and the exercise price of the put equals the promised payment.

In Chapter 18, we assumed that the value of Circular's bond was $27. Now we can see where that figure could have come from. Suppose that the standard deviation of the returns on Circular's assets is 60% a year and that the risk-free interest rate is 10%. The current value of Circular's assets is $30, and the exercise price of the default option is $50. If you enter these data into the Black–Scholes model, you find that the value of Circular's default put is $18.6. You can now value its bond:

$$\text{Value of Circular's bond} = \text{value of default-free bonds} - \text{value of default put}$$
$$= 50/1.1 \qquad\qquad - 18.6$$
$$= \$26.9 \text{ (about } \$27)$$

BEYOND THE PAGE

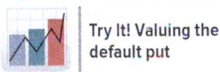 Try It! Valuing the default put

mhhe.com/brealey13e

The value of Circular's equity is equal to the value of its assets less the value of its debt. So the equity is worth about $3 (30 − 26.9 = $3.1).

Before you get too gung-ho about valuing the default option, we should warn you that, in practice, you would encounter complications that make the valuation of corporate bonds considerably more difficult than it sounds. For example, we assumed that Circular File is committed to making a single payment of $50 at the end of the year. But suppose, instead, that it has issued a 10-year bond that pays interest annually. In this case, there are 10 payments rather than just one. When each payment comes due, Circular has the option to make the coupon payment or to default. If it makes the payment, Circular obtains a second option to default when the second interest payment becomes due. The reward to making this payment is that the stockholders get a third put option, and so on. (This is an example of a *compound put option*.)

Of course, if the firm does not make any of these payments when due, bondholders take over, and stockholders are left with nothing. In other words, if Circular decides to exercise its default option, it gives up all subsequent default options.

Valuing the 10-year bond when it is issued is equivalent to valuing the first of the 10 options. But you cannot value the first option without valuing the nine that follow. Even this example understates the practical difficulties because large firms may have dozens of outstanding debt issues with different interest rates and maturities, and before the current debt matures, they may make further issues. Consequently, when bond traders evaluate a corporate bond, they do not immediately reach for their option calculator. They are more likely to start by identifying bonds with similar maturity and risk of default and look at the yield spreads offered by these bonds.

Valuing the default put may be challenging, but, now we know that limited liability is an option, we also know what the value of that option depends on. The following table shows how the value of the option to default depends on the underlying variables:[7]

If there is an increase in:	Value of default put:
Value of company's assets	Declines
Standard deviation of asset value	Rises
Amount of outstanding debt	Rises
Debt maturity	Rises
Default-free interest rate	Declines
Dividend payments	Rises

We have seen that corporate bonds sell for lower promised yields than comparable Treasury bonds. Can we explain the size of these yield spreads in terms of the default put that attaches to corporate bonds? Feldhütter and Schaefer believe that the answer is yes in the case of investment-grade bonds. For these bonds, they find that default risk can do a fairly good job of explaining the typical yield spread.[8] However, yields on junk bonds appear to be higher than their default experience would justify. It seems that investors in junk bonds demand additional yield to compensate for their relative lack of liquidity.

---

[7] Notice that the effect of an interest rate rise on the value of a put option is the opposite of its effect on the value of a call. Circular's option to extinguish the debt is more valuable when interest rates are high. The effect of changes in the interest rate is generally modest.

[8] P. Feldhütter and S. Schaefer, "The Myth of the Credit Spread Puzzle," *Review of Financial Studies* 31 (August 2018), pp. 2897–2942.

The Value of Corporate Equity

We saw in Chapter 20 that the value of a put option is identical to the value of a call option with the same exercise price, plus the present value of the exercise price, and less the value of the underlying asset. Think what this means for the value of Circular File's default put:

Value of option to default = value of call option on Circular's assets

+ present value of Circular's debt at the risk-free interest rate

− value of Circular's assets

If you twist this formula around, you get:

$$\begin{aligned}
\text{Value of call option on Circular's assets} &= \text{value of Circular's assets} - \left(\begin{array}{c}\text{present value of}\\\text{Circular's debt at the}\\\text{risk-free interest rate}\end{array}\right) - \left(\begin{array}{c}\text{value of put}\\\text{option to default}\end{array}\right)\\
&= \text{value of Circular's assets} - \text{value of Circular's debt}
\end{aligned}$$

The expression on the right-hand side is simply the value of Circular's equity. This tells us that you can think of Circular's bondholders as effectively owning the company now, but the shareholders have the option to buy it back from them at the end of the year by paying off the debt. Thus, the balance sheet of Circular File can be expressed as follows:

BEYOND THE PAGE

Try It! Leverage and debt betas

mhhe.com/brealey13e

Circular File Company (Market Values)

Asset value	$30	$26.9	Bond value = asset value − value of call
		3.1	Stock value = value of call
	$30	$ 30	Firm value = asset value

A Digression: Valuing Government Financial Guarantees

When American Airlines declared bankruptcy in 2011, its pension plan had liabilities of $18.5 billion and assets of just $8.3 billion. But the 130,000 workers and retirees did not face a destitute old age. Their pensions were largely guaranteed by the Pension Benefit Guaranty Corporation (PBGC).[9]

Pension promises don't always appear on the company's balance sheet, but they are a long-term liability just like the promises to bondholders. The guarantee by the PBGC changes the pension promises from a risky liability to a safe one. If the company goes belly-up and there are insufficient assets to cover the pensions, the PBGC makes up most of the difference.

The government recognizes that the guarantee provided by the PBGC is costly. Thus, shortly after assuming the liability for the American Airlines plan, the PBGC calculated that the discounted value of payments on defaulted plans and those close to default amounted to $98 billion.

Unfortunately, these calculations ignore the risk that other firms in the future may fail and hand over their pension liability to the PBGC. To calculate the cost of the guarantee, we need to think about what the value of company pension promises would be without any guarantee:

Value of guarantee = value of guaranteed pensions

− value of pension promises without a guarantee

---

[9] There are limits to pension payments made by the PBGC to retired employees. Employees with large pensions are not made whole.

With the guarantee, the pensions are as safe as a promise by the U.S. government;[10] *without* the guarantee, the pensions are like an ordinary debt obligation of the firm. We already know what the difference is between the value of safe government debt and risky corporate debt. It is the value of the firm's right to hand over the assets of the firm and to walk away from its obligations. Thus, the value of the pension guarantee is the value of this put option.

In a paper prepared for the Congressional Budget Office, Wendy Kiska, Deborah Lucas, and Marvin Phaup show how option pricing models can help to give a better measure of the cost to the PBGC of pension guarantees.[11] Their estimates suggest that the value of the PBGC's guarantees was substantially higher than its published estimate.

The PBGC is not the only government body to provide financial guarantees. For example, the Federal Deposit Insurance Corporation (FDIC) guarantees bank deposit accounts, the Federal Family Education Loan (FFEL) program guarantees loans to students, the Small Business Administration (SBA) provides partial guarantees for loans to small businesses, and so on. The government's liability under these programs is enormous. Fortunately, option pricing is leading to a better way to calculate their cost.

23-3   Bond Ratings and the Probability of Default

Banks and other financial institutions not only want to know the value of the loans that they have made, but they also need to know the risk that they are incurring. Some rely on the judgments of specialized bond rating services. Others have developed their own models for measuring the probability that the borrower will default. We describe bond ratings first and then discuss two classes of model for predicting default.

The relative quality of most traded bonds can be judged by bond ratings. There are three principal rating services—Moody's, Standard & Poor's, and Fitch.[12] Table 23.1 summarizes these ratings. For example, the highest-quality bonds are rated triple-A (Aaa) by Moody's, then come double-A (Aa) bonds, and so on. Bonds rated Baa or above are known as *investment-grade* bonds.[13] Commercial banks, many pension funds, and other financial institutions are not allowed to invest in bonds unless they are investment-grade.[14]

Bonds rated below Baa are termed **high-yield** or **junk bonds.** Most junk bonds used to be *fallen angels*—that is, bonds of companies that had fallen on hard times. But during the 1980s, new issues of junk bonds multiplied 10-fold, as more and more companies issued large quantities of low-grade debt to finance takeovers. The result was that for the first time, corporate midgets were able to take control of corporate giants.

Issuers of these junk bonds often had debt ratios of 90% to 95%. Many worried that this threatened the health of corporate America and, as default rates on corporate debt rose to 10% in the early 1990s, the market for new issues of junk bonds dried up. Since then, the market for junk debt has had its ups and downs, but as interest rates on Treasuries dwindled in the years following the financial crisis, investors sought higher yields, and new issues of junk bonds boomed.

---

[10]The pension guarantee is not ironclad. If the PBGC cannot meet its obligations, the government is not committed to providing the extra cash. But few doubt that it would do so.

[11]Congressional Budget Office, "The Risk Exposure of the Pension Benefit Guaranty Corporation," Washington, DC, September 2005.

[12]The SEC has been concerned about the power wielded by the three bond-rating agencies. It has therefore approved seven new nationally recognized statistical rating organizations (NRSOs): DBRS, A.M. Best, Egan-Jones Ratings, Morningstar Credit Ratings (previously known as Realpoint), Kroll Bond Rating, HR Ratings de Mexico, and Japan Credit Rating.

[13]Rating services also provide a finer breakdown. Thus, a bond might be rated A-1, A-2, or A-3 (the lowest A rating). In addition, the rating service may announce that it has put an issue on its watch list for a possible upgrade or downgrade.

[14]Investment-grade bonds can usually be entered at face value on the books of banks and life insurance companies.

Moody's	Standard & Poor's and Fitch
Investment-Grade Bonds:	
Aaa	AAA
Aa	AA
A	A
Baa	BBB
Junk Bonds:	
Ba	BB
B	B
Caa	CCC
Ca	CC
C	C

❭**TABLE 23.1** Key to bond ratings. The highest-quality bonds are rated triple-A. Investment-grade bonds have to be the equivalent of Baa or higher. Bonds that don't make this cut are called "high-yield" or "junk" bonds.

Bond ratings are judgments about firms' financial and business prospects. There is no fixed formula by which ratings are calculated. Nevertheless, investment bankers, bond portfolio managers, and others who follow the bond market closely can get a fairly good idea of how a bond will be rated by looking at a few key numbers, such as the firm's debt ratio, the ratio of earnings to interest, the operating margin, and the return on assets. Table 23.2 shows how these ratios vary with the firm's bond rating.

Figure 23.3 shows that bond ratings do reflect the probability of default. Since 1970, no U.S. bonds that were initially rated triple-A by Moody's have defaulted in the year after issue and only 1 in 700 have defaulted within 10 years of issue. (The Aaa default rate is not plotted in Figure 23.3. It would be invisible.) At the other extreme, about half of Caa to C bonds have defaulted by year 10. Of course, bonds do not usually fall suddenly from grace. As time passes and the company becomes progressively more shaky, the agencies revise downward the bond's rating to reflect the increasing probability of default.

Rating agencies don't always get it right. When Enron went belly-up in 2001, investors protested that only two months earlier the company's debt had an investment-grade rating. Rating agencies also did not win many friends during the financial crisis of 2007–2009, when many of the mortgage-backed debts that had been given triple-A ratings defaulted. And when agencies *do* downgrade a company's debt, they are often accused of precipitate action that increases the cost of borrowing.

Ratio	Aaa	Aa	A	Baa	Ba	B	C
Operating margin (%)	22.0	17.1	17.6	14.1	11.2	8.9	4.1
Pretax return on assets (%)	20.9	15.6	13.8	10.9	9.1	7.1	4.0
Debt ratio	19.3	50.2	38.6	46.2	51.7	72.0	98.0
Cash coverage ratio	28.9	15.1	9.7	5.9	3.5	1.7	0.6

❭**TABLE 23.2** How financial ratios differ according to a firm's bond rating. Median ratios for U.S. nonfinancial firms by bond rating.

Source: Moody's Financial Metrics:, "Key Ratios by Rating and Industry for North American Non-Financial Corporations," December 2013.

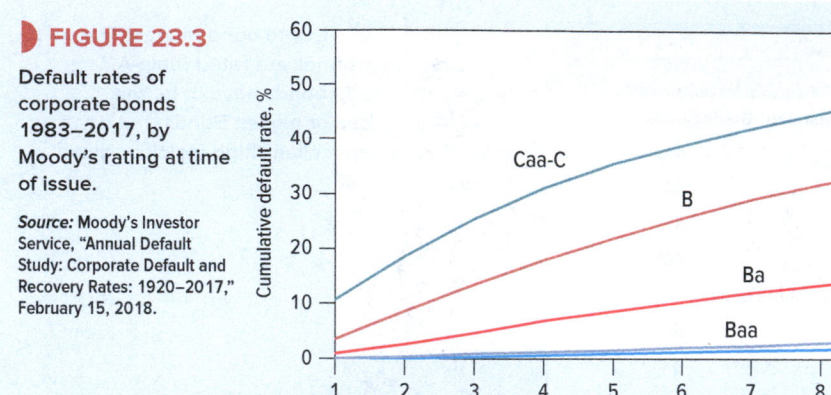

▶ **FIGURE 23.3**

Default rates of corporate bonds 1983–2017, by Moody's rating at time of issue.

Source: Moody's Investor Service, "Annual Default Study: Corporate Default and Recovery Rates: 1920–2017," February 15, 2018.

23-4   Predicting the Probability of Default

Statistical Models of Default

If you apply for a credit card or a bank loan, you will probably be asked to complete a questionnaire that provides details about your job, home, and financial health. This information is then used to calculate an overall credit score.[15] If you do not make the grade on the score, you are likely to be refused credit or subjected to a more detailed analysis. In a similar way, mechanical credit scoring systems are used by banks to assess the risk of their corporate loans and by firms when they extend credit to customers.

Suppose that you are given the task of developing a system that will help to decide which businesses are poor credits. You start by comparing the financial statements of companies that went bankrupt over a 40-year period with those of surviving firms. Figure 23.4 shows what you find. Panel (*a*) illustrates that, as early as four years before they went bankrupt, failing firms were earning a much lower return on assets (ROA) than firms that survived. Panel (*b*) shows that, on average, they also had a high ratio of liabilities to assets, and Panel (*c*) shows that EBITDA (earnings before interest, taxes, and depreciation) was low relative to the firms' total liabilities. In each case, these indicators of the firms' financial health steadily deteriorated as bankruptcy approached.

Rather than focusing on individual ratios, it makes sense to combine the ratios into a single score that can separate the creditworthy sheep from the impecunious goats. That means estimating an equation that relates the risk of bankruptcy to a set of financial variables. Most statistical bankruptcy models focus on a relatively small set of accounting ratios. There is general agreement that the probability of bankruptcy is higher for firms that have low and declining profitability, high debt ratios and low interest coverage, and decreasing cash reserves and working capital.[16]

---

[15]The most commonly used consumer credit score is the FICO score, which is used by the three main credit agencies—Experian, TransUnion, and Equifax. The agencies also use their own proprietary scoring system, VantageScore.

[16]An early example of these models is the Z-score model proposed by Edward Altman in E. I. Altman, "Financial Ratios, Discriminant Analysis and the Prediction of Corporate Bankruptcy," *Journal of Finance,* 23 (September 1968), pp. 589–609. For two more recent examples that make use of both accounting and market data, see T. Shumway, "Forecasting Bankruptcy More Accurately: A Simple Hazard Model," *Journal of Business* 74 (2001), pp. 101–124; and J. Y. Campbell, J. Hilscher, and J. Szilagyi, "In Search of Distress Risk," *Journal of Finance* 63 (December 2008), pp. 2899–2939.

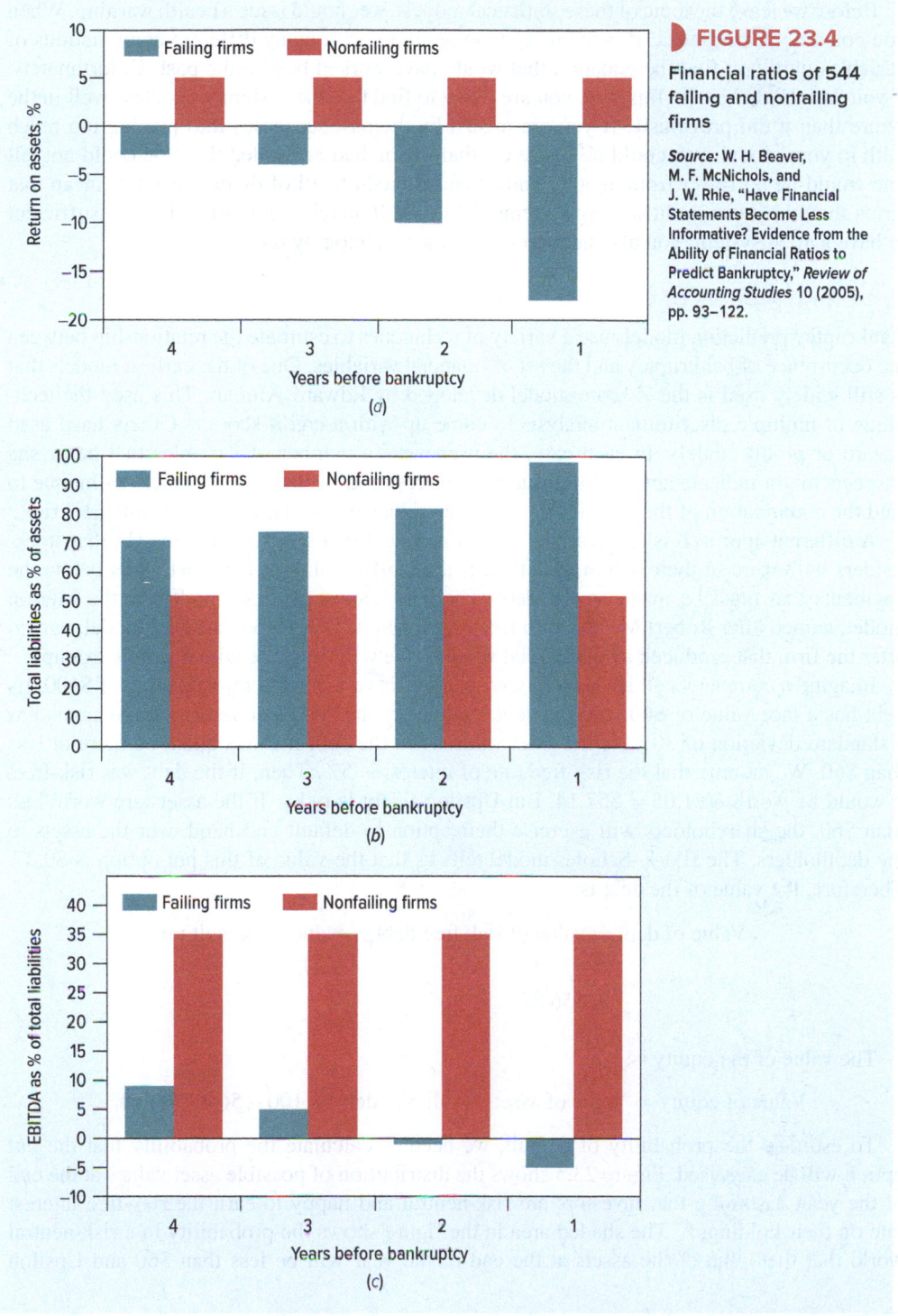

> **FIGURE 23.4**

Financial ratios of 544 failing and nonfailing firms

Source: W. H. Beaver, M. F. McNichols, and J. W. Rhie, "Have Financial Statements Become Less Informative? Evidence from the Ability of Financial Ratios to Predict Bankruptcy," *Review of Accounting Studies* 10 (2005), pp. 93–122.

For small businesses, there may be little alternative to the use of accounting data, but for large, publicly traded firms, it is also possible to take advantage of the information in security prices. Low and volatile stock returns, a low market-to-book ratio, and a low stock price all seem to provide additional information on impending bankruptcy.

Before we leave the topic of these statistical models, we should issue a health warning. When you construct a risk index, it is tempting to experiment with many different combinations of variables until you find the equation that would have worked best in the past. Unfortunately, if you "mine" the data in this way, you are likely to find that the system works less well in the future than it did previously. If you are misled by the past successes into placing too much faith in your model, you could be worse off than if you had pretended that you could not tell one would-be borrower from another and extended credit to all of them. Does this mean that firms should not use credit scoring systems? Not a bit. It merely implies that it is not sufficient to have a good system; you also need to know how much to rely on it.

Structural Models of Default

Bankruptcy prediction models use a variety of techniques to estimate the relationship between the occurrence of bankruptcy and the set of financial variables. One of the earliest models that is still widely used is the Z-score model developed by Edward Altman. This used the technique of multiple discriminant analysis to come up with a credit score.[17] Others have used hazard or probit models. In each case, the user picks a number of variables that he or she suspects might indicate approaching financial distress and then uses a statistical technique to find the combination of these variables that best predicts which firms will become bankrupt.

A different approach is to develop a structural model that builds on the insight that stockholders will exercise their option to default if the market value of the assets falls below the payments that must be made on the debt. The best known of these models is the Merton model, named after Robert Merton who first developed it,[18] or Moody's KMV model, named after the firm that produced a commercial version. We will illustrate with a simple example.

Imagine a company, call it Upsilon, whose assets have a current market value of $100. Its debt has a face value of $60, and the debt matures in one year. The return on the assets has a standard deviation of 30%, so the asset value when the debt matures could be more or less than $60. We assume that the risk-free rate of interest is 5%. Then, if the debt was risk-free, it would be worth 60/1.05 = $57.14. But Upsilon's debt is risky: If the assets are worth less than $60, the shareholders will exercise their option to default and hand over the assets to the debtholders. The Black–Scholes model tells us that the value of this put option is $0.27. Therefore, the value of the debt is:

$$\text{Value of debt} = \text{value of risk-free debt} - \text{value of default put}$$
$$= 57.14 \qquad\qquad - 0.27$$
$$= \$56.87$$

The value of the equity is:

$$\text{Value of equity} = \text{Value of assets} - \text{value of debt} - 100 - 56.87 = 43.13$$

To estimate the probability of default, we need to calculate the probability that the put option will be exercised. Figure 23.5 shows the distribution of possible asset values at the end of the year, assuming that investors are risk-neutral and happy to earn the risk-free interest rate on their holdings.[19] The shaded area in the figure shows the probability in a risk-neutral world that the value of the assets at the end of the year will be less than $60 and Upsilon

---

[17] Altman's Z-score model is described in E. I. Altman and E. Hotchkiss, *Corporate Financial Distress and Bankruptcy*, 3rd ed. (New York: John Wiley, 2006).

[18] See R.C. Merton, "On the Pricing of Corporate Debt: The Risk Structure of Interest Rates," *Journal of Finance* 29 (1974), pp. 449–470.

[19] If you wish to estimate the actual, rather than risk-neutral, probability that Upsilon will default, you need to use the expected return on the assets rather than the risk-free interest rate.

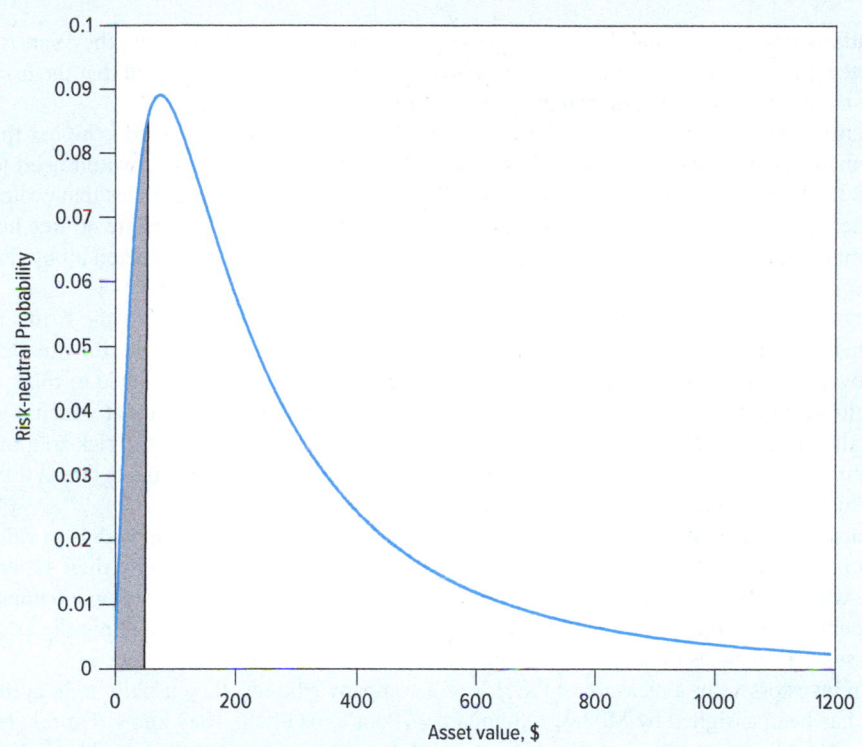

> **FIGURE 23.5**   Upsilon has issued one-year debt with a face value of $60. The shaded area shows that there is a 4.3% risk-neutral probability that the value of the company's assets at the end of the year will be less than $60, in which case, the company will choose to default.

will default. If you look back at the Black–Scholes formula in Section 21-4, you will see the expression $N(d_2)$. The probability that the option will be exercised is equal to $1 - N(d_2)$. In the case of Upsilon,

$$\text{Risk-neutral probability of default} = 1 - N(d_2) = .043, \text{ or } 4.3\%$$

There is a 4.3% chance that Upsilon will default.

The Merton model of default has obvious attractions. It has a theoretical base. So the relevant variables are pretty well known, and you do not need to go prospecting among past data to find variables that may be indications of impending default. But when you apply the model in practice, you inevitably encounter complications. For example, unless you can observe the value of the company's debts, you can't observe the value of its assets or measure their volatility.[20] Also, companies may have several debt issues, each with a different maturity. You could use an average time to maturity, but, if you are concerned with the probability of default in the short run, you may wish to place more weight on debt that will shortly need to be repaid.

---

[20]Merton proposed an ingenious way to back out asset value and volatility from the value and volatility of the equity.

SUMMARY

Corporations have limited liability. If companies are unable to pay their debts, they can file for bankruptcy. Lenders are aware that they may receive less than they are owed and that the *expected* yield on a corporate bond is less than the *promised yield.*

Because of the possibility of default, the promised yield on a corporate bond is higher than on a government bond. You can think of this extra yield as the amount that you would need to pay to insure the bond against default. There is an active market for insurance policies that protect the debtholder against default. These policies are called credit default swaps. There are no free lunches in financial markets. So the extra yield you get for buying a corporate bond is eaten up by the cost of insuring against default.

The company's option to default is equivalent to a put option. If the value of the firm's assets is less than the amount of the debt, it will pay for the company to default and to allow the lenders to take over the assets in settlement of the debt. This insight tells us what we need to think about when valuing corporate debt—the current value of the firm relative to the point at which it would default, the volatility of the assets, the maturity of the debt payments, and the risk-free interest rate. Unfortunately, most companies have several loans outstanding with payments due at different times. This considerably complicates the task of valuing the put option.

Because of these complications, bond investors do not regularly use option models to value the default option that is attached to a corporate bond. More commonly, they rely on their experience to judge whether the spread between the yield on a corporate bond and the yield on a comparable government issue compensates for the possibility of default. Spreads can change rapidly as investors reassess the chances of default or become more or less risk-averse.

When investors want a measure of the risk of a company's bonds, they usually look at the rating that has been assigned by Moody's, Standard & Poor's, or Fitch. They know that bonds with investment-grade ratings (at least triple-B) are much less likely to default than bonds with a junk rating.

Banks, rating services, and consulting firms have also developed a number of models for estimating the likelihood of default. Statistical models take accounting ratios or other indicators of corporate health, and weight them to produce a single measure of default. Structural models, such as the Merton model, take a different tack and seek to measure the probability that the market value of the firm's assets will fall to the point at which the firm will choose to default rather than try to keep up with its debt payments.

FURTHER READING

The websites of the main credit rating agencies contain a variety of useful reports on credit risk. (See in particular **www.moodys.com, www.standardandpoors.com,** and **www.fitch.com.**)

Altman and Hotchkiss provide a review of credit scoring models in:

E. I. Altman and E. Hotchkiss, *Corporate Financial Distress and Bankruptcy,* 3rd ed. (New York: John Wiley, 2006).

Books that discuss corporate bonds and credit risk include:

A. Saunders and L. Allen, *Credit Risk Measurement,* 3rd ed. (New York: John Wiley, 2010).

J. B. Caouette, E. I. Altman, P. Narayanan, and R. Nimmo, *Managing Credit Risk,* 2nd ed. (New York: John Wiley, 2008).

D. Duffie, *Measuring Corporate Default Risk* (Oxford, U.K.: Oxford University Press, 2011).

D. Duffie and K. J. Singleton, *Credit Risk: Pricing, Measurement and Management* (Princeton, NJ: Princeton University Press, 2003).

connect   Select problems are available in McGraw-Hill's *Connect*. Please see the preface for more information.

1. **Expected yield** You own a 5% bond maturing in two years and priced at 87%. Suppose that there is a 10% chance that at maturity the bond will default and you will receive only 40% of the promised payment. What is the bond's promised yield to maturity? What is its expected yield (i.e., the possible yields weighted by their probabilities)?

2. **Bond ratings*** In February 2018, Aaa bonds yielded 3.38%, Baa bonds yielded 4.51%, and comparable Treasuries yielded 2.86%.

   a. What was the credit spread on Aaa bonds?

   b. What was the spread on Baa bonds?

   c. What do you think would be the difference in price (as a percent of face value) between a typical 5% 10-year Baa bond and a similar Treasury bond?

3. **Bond ratings** It is 2030 and the yields on corporate bonds are as follows:

Aaa	A	Ba
8%	10%	12%

   Tau Corp wishes to raise $10 million by an issue of 9% 10-year bonds. What will be the likely issue price (as a percent of face value) if Tau is rated (a) Aaa, (b) A, or (c) Ba?

4. **Default option** The difference between the value of a government bond and a similar corporate bond is equal to the value of an option. What is this option, and what is its exercise price?

5. **Default option*** Other things equal, would you expect the difference between the price of a Treasury bond and a corporate bond to increase or decrease with

   a. The company's business risk?

   b. The degree of leverage?

   c. The time to maturity?

6. **Default option** Company A has issued a single zero-coupon bond maturing in 10 years. Company B has issued a coupon bond maturing in 10 years. Explain why it is more complicated to value B's debt than A's.

7. **Default option** How much would it cost you to insure the bonds of Backwoods Chemical against default? (See Section 23-1.)

8. **Default option** Digital Organics has 10 million outstanding shares trading at $25 per share. It also has a large amount of debt outstanding, all coming due in one year. The debt pays interest at 8%. It has a face value of $350 million but is trading at a market value of only $280 million. The one-year risk-free interest rate is 6%.

   a. Write out the put–call parity formula for Digital Organics's stock, debt, and assets.

   b. What is the value of the company's option to default on its debt?

9. **Default option** Square File's assets are worth $100. It has $80 of zero-coupon debt outstanding that is due to be repaid at the end of two years. The risk-free interest rate is 5%, and the standard deviation of the returns on Square File's assets is 40% per year. Calculate the present value of the company's debt and equity.

10. **Predicting default probability*** A friend has mentioned that she has read somewhere that the following variables can be used to predict bankruptcy: (a) the company debt ratio; (b) the interest coverage; (c) the amount of cash relative to sales or assets; (d) the return on assets;

BEYOND THE PAGE

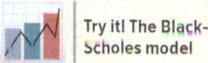 Try it! The Black–Scholes model

mhhe.com/brealey13e

(e) the market-to-book ratio; (f) the recent return on the stock; (g) the volatility of the stock returns. The problem is that she can't remember whether a high value of each variable implies a high or a low probability of bankruptcy. Can you help her out?

11. **Predicting default probability*** What variables are required to use the Merton model to calculate the risk-neutral probability that a company will default on its debt?

12. **Predicting default probability** Company X has borrowed $150 maturing this year and $50 maturing in 10 years. Company Y has borrowed $200 maturing in five years. In both cases, asset value is $140. Sketch a scenario in which X does not default but Y does.

13. **Predicting default probability** Discuss the problems with developing a numerical credit scoring system for evaluating personal loans. You can only test your system using data for applicants who have in the past been granted credit. Is this a potential problem?

BEYOND THE PAGE

Try it! The Black–Scholes model

mhhe.com/brealey13e

14. **Predicting default probability** Look back at Section 23-4. Suppose that the standard deviation of the return on Upsilon's assets is 50%. Recalculate the probability that the company will default.

CHALLENGE

15. **Default option** Look back at the first Backwoods Chemical example at the start of Section 23-1. Suppose that the firm's book balance sheet is

Backwoods Chemical Company (Book Values)			
Net working capital	$ 400	$1,000	Debt
Net fixed assets	1,600	1,000	Equity (net worth)
Total assets	$2,000	$2,000	Total value

BEYOND THE PAGE

Try it! The Black–Scholes model

mhhe.com/brealey13e

The debt has a one-year maturity and a promised interest payment of 9%. Thus, the promised payment to Backwoods's creditors is $1,090. The market value of the assets is $1,200, and the standard deviation of asset value is 45% per year. The risk-free interest rate is 9%. Calculate the value of Backwoods's debt and equity.

FINANCE ON THE WEB

1. Go to **finance.yahoo.com** and select three industrial companies that have been experiencing difficult times.

   a. Are the companies' troubles reflected in their financial ratios? (You may find it helpful to refer to Figure 23.4.)

   b. Now look at the company's bond rating. Do the two measures provide consistent messages?

CHAPTER

24

...

The Many Different Kinds of Debt

In Chapters 17 and 18, we discussed how much a company should borrow. But companies also need to think about what *type* of debt to issue. They can choose to issue short- or long-term debt, straight or convertible bonds; they can issue in the United States or in the international debt market; and they can either sell the debt publicly or place it privately with a few large investors.

As a financial manager, you need to choose the type of debt that makes sense for your company. For example, if a firm has only a temporary need for funds, it will generally issue short-term debt. Firms with a substantial overseas business may prefer to issue foreign currency debt. Sometimes competition between lenders opens a window of opportunity in a particular sector of the debt market. The effect may be only a few basis points reduction in yield, but on a large issue, that can translate into savings of several million dollars. Remember the saying, "A million dollars here and a million there—pretty soon it begins to add up to real money."[1]

Figure 24.1 provides a road map through this chapter. Our initial focus is on the long-term bond market. We start with the more standard bonds. We examine the differences between senior and junior bonds and between secured and unsecured bonds, including a special kind of secured bond called an *asset-backed bond*. We describe how bonds may be repaid by means of a sinking fund and how the borrower or the lender may have an option for early repayment. As we review these different features of corporate debt, we try to explain why sinking funds, repayment options, and the like exist. They are not simply matters of custom or neutral mutations; there are generally good reasons for their use.

Our next task is to look at some less common bonds, starting with convertible bonds and their close relative, the package of bonds and warrants. We also illustrate the enormous variety of bond designs by looking at a few unusual bonds and at some of the motives for innovation in the bond market.

The rest of the chapter is concerned with shorter-term debt, much of which is supplied by banks. Often, companies arrange a *revolving line of credit* with a bank that allows them to borrow up to an agreed amount whenever they need financing. This is often intended to tide the firm over when it has a temporary shortage of cash and is therefore repaid in only a few months. However, banks also make *term loans* that sometimes extend for five years or more. Some loans are too large to be made by a single bank. We describe how such loans are syndicated among a group of banks. We also look at how banks protect their loans by imposing restrictions on the borrower and by requiring security.

Rather than borrowing from a bank, large blue-chip companies sometimes bypass the banking system and regularly issue their own short-term debt to investors. This is called *commercial paper*. Somewhat longer-term loans that are marketed on a regular basis are known as *medium-term notes*. We discuss both in turn.

In the Appendix to the chapter, we look at another form of private placement known as project finance. This is the glamorous part of the debt market. The words *project finance* conjure up images of multibillion-dollar loans to finance huge ventures in exotic parts of the world. You'll find there's something to the popular image, but it's not the whole story.

---

[1] The remark was made by the late Senator Everett Dirksen. However, he was talking billions.

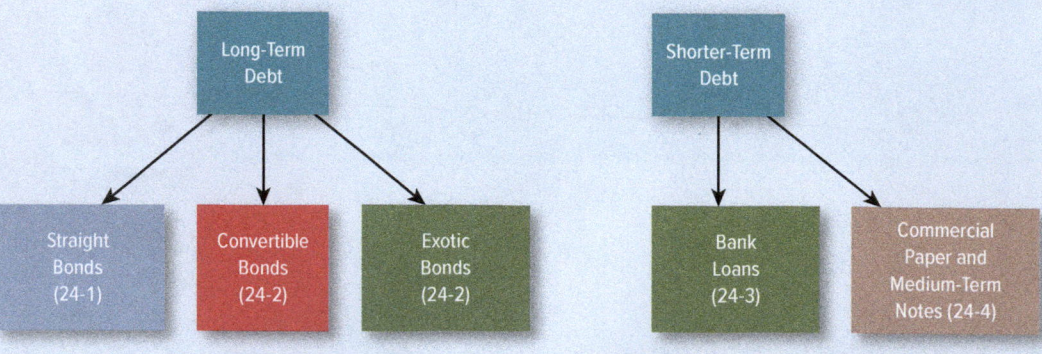

▶ **FIGURE 24.1**   **The principal species of corporate debt and the sections of this chapter in which they are discussed**

We should point out that many debts are not shown on the company's balance sheet. For example, companies have occasionally disguised the debt by establishing *special-purpose entities (SPEs),* which raise cash by a mixture of equity and debt and then use that cash to help fund the parent company. By making use of SPEs, Enron kept a large amount of its debt off-balance-sheet, but that did not stop the company from going bankrupt. Since the Enron scandal, accountants have moved to tighten up the rules on disclosing SPE debt.

Companies have other important long-term liabilities that we do *not* discuss in this chapter. For instance, long-term leases are very similar to debt. The user of the equipment agrees to make a series of lease payments and, if it defaults, it may be forced into bankruptcy. We discuss leases in Chapter 25.

Postretirement health benefits and pension promises can also be huge liabilities. For example, in 2003 General Motors had a pension deficit of $19 billion. To reduce this deficit, GM made a large issue of bonds and invested the majority of the proceeds in its pension fund. You could say that the effect was to increase the company's debt, but the economic reality was that it substituted one long-term obligation (the new debt) for another (its pension obligation). Management of pension plans is outside the scope of this book, but financial managers spend a good deal of time worrying about the pension "debt."

24-1   Long-Term Bonds

Bond Terms

Applied Materials (AMAT) supplies equipment and software for the manufacture of semi-conductors. In 2011, AMAT issued 30-year bonds to help finance an acquisition. The bond was a plain-vanilla issue; in other words, it was pretty well standard in every way. To give you some feel for the bond contract (and for some of the language in which it is couched), we have summarized in Table 24.1 the terms of the issue. We will look in turn at its principal features.

The AMAT bond was issued in 2011 and is due to mature 30 years later in 2041. It was issued in denominations of $1,000. So, at maturity, the company will repay the principal amount of $1,000 to the holder of each bond.

The annual interest or *coupon* payment on the bond is 5.85% of $1,000, or $58.50. This interest is payable semiannually, so every six months the bondholder receives interest of 58.50/2 = $29.25. Most U.S. bonds pay interest semiannually, but in many other countries it is common to pay interest annually.[2]

---

[2]If a bond pays interest semiannually, investors usually calculate a *semiannually* compounded yield to maturity on the bond. In other words, the yield is quoted as twice the six-month yield. When bonds pay interest annually, it is conventional to quote their yields to maturity on an *annually* compounded basis. For more on this, see Section 3-1.

❯TABLE 24.1
Summary of terms
of bond issue by
Applied Materials
(AMAT)

Issue date	June 8, 2011
Amount issued	$600 million
Maturity	June 15, 2041
Denomination, face value, or principal	$1,000
Interest	5.85% per annum payable June 15 and December 15. First payment due December 2011.
Offered	Issued at a price of 99.592% plus accrued interest (proceeds to company 98.717%)
Joint book-running managers	Citi, JPMorgan
Registered	Issued in fully registered form only
Trustee	U.S. Bank National Association
Security	Not secured. Company will not permit to have any lien on its property or assets without equally and ratably securing the debt securities.
Seniority	Senior notes ranking pari passu with other unsecured unsubordinated debt.
Change of control event	If a change of control occurs and the notes are simultaneously downrated to below investment grade the company will offer to repurchase the notes.
Sinking fund	None.
Callable	At whole or in part at the option of the Company with at least 30 days, but not more than 60 days, notice at the greater of (*i*) 100% of the principal amount or (*ii*) the sum of the scheduled remaining payments discounted at 30 basis points above the Treasury rate.
Moody's rating at issue date	A3

The regular interest payment on a bond is a hurdle that the company must keep jumping. If AMAT ever fails to make the payment, lenders can demand their money back instead of waiting until matters deteriorate further.[3] Thus, regular interest payments provide added protection for lenders.

Sometimes bonds are sold with a lower coupon payment but at a significant discount on their face value, so investors receive much of their return in the form of capital appreciation.[4] The ultimate is the zero-coupon bond, which pays no interest at all; in this case, the entire return consists of capital appreciation.[5]

The AMAT interest payment is fixed for the life of the bond, but in some issues the payment varies with the general level of interest rates. For example, the payment may be set at 1% over the U.S. Treasury bill rate or (more commonly) over the **London interbank offered rate (LIBOR),** which is the rate at which international banks borrow from one another. Sometimes these *floating-rate notes* specify a minimum (or floor) interest rate, or they may specify a maximum (or cap) on the rate.[6] You may also come across "collars," which stipulate both a maximum and a minimum payment.

---

[3]There is one type of bond on which the borrower is obliged to pay interest only if it is covered by the year's earnings. These so-called income bonds are rare and have largely been issued as part of railroad reorganizations.

[4]Any bond that is issued at a discount is known as an *original issue discount bond*. A zero-coupon bond is often called a "pure discount bond." The capital appreciation on a discount bond is not taxed as income as long as it amounts to less than .25% a year (IRS Code Section 1272).

[5]The ultimate of ultimates was an issue of a perpetual zero-coupon bond on behalf of a charity.

[6]Instead of issuing a capped floating-rate loan, a company sometimes issues an uncapped loan and at the same time buys a cap from a bank. The bank pays the interest in excess of the specified level.

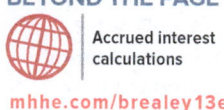
The AMAT bonds have a face value of $1,000 and were sold to investors at 99.592% of face value. In addition, buyers had to pay any *accrued interest*. This is the amount of any future interest that has accumulated by the time of the purchase. For example, investors who bought bonds for delivery on (say) October 15, would have only two months to wait before receiving their first interest payment. Therefore, the four months of accrued interest would be $(120/360) \times 5.85 = 1.95\%$, and the investor would need to pay the purchase price of the bond plus 1.95%.[7]

Although the AMAT bonds were offered to the public at a price of 99.592%, the company received only 98.717%. The difference represents the underwriters' spread. Of the $597.6 million raised, $592.3 million went to the company and $5.3 million (or about .9%) went to the underwriters.

Moving down Table 24.1, you see that the AMAT's bonds are *registered*. This means that the company's registrar records the ownership of each bond and the company pays the interest and final principal amount directly to each owner. Almost all bonds in the United States are issued in registered form, but in many countries, companies may issue *bearer* bonds. In this case, the bond certificate constitutes the primary evidence of ownership, so the bondholder must return the certificate to the company to claim the final repayment of principal.

The AMAT bonds were sold publicly to investors. Before it could sell the bonds, it needed to file a registration statement for approval of the SEC and to prepare a prospectus. The bond was issued under an **indenture,** or **trust deed,** between the company and a trustee. U.S. Bank National Association, which is the trust company for the issue, represents the bondholders. It must see that the terms of the indenture are observed and look after the bondholders in the event of default. The bond indenture is a turgid legal document that is bedtime reading only for insomniacs.[8] However, the main provisions are described in the prospectus to the issue.

Security and Seniority

Sometimes a company sets aside particular assets for the protection of the bondholder. For example, utility company bonds are often secured. In this case, if the company defaults on its debt, the trustee or lender may take possession of the relevant assets. If these are insufficient to satisfy the claim, the remaining debt will have a general claim, alongside any unsecured debt, on the other assets of the firm.

Unsecured bonds maturing in 10 years or fewer are usually called **notes,** while longer-term issues may be called bonds (as in the case of the AMAT bond) or **debentures.**[9] Like most bond issues by industrial and financial companies, the AMAT bonds are unsecured. In that case, it is common for the issue to include a so-called negative pledge clause that promises that the company will not issue any secured bonds without offering the same security to its unsecured bonds.

The majority of secured bonds are **mortgage bonds.** These sometimes provide a claim against a specific building, but they are more often secured on all of the firm's property.[10]

---

[7]In the U.S. corporate bond market, accrued interest is calculated on the assumption that a year is composed of twelve 30-day months; in some other markets (such as the U.S. Treasury bond market) calculations recognize the actual number of days in each calendar month.

[8]For example, the indenture for the AMAT bond states, "Unless and until it is exchanged in whole or in part for securities in definitive form, this security may not be transferred except as a whole by the depositary to a nominee of the depositary or by a nominee of the depositary to the depositary or to another nominee of the depositary or by the depositary or any such nominee to a successor depositary or a nominee of such successor depositary. Unless this global security is presented by an authorized representative of the depositary to the company or its agent for registration of transfer, exchange or payment, and any security issued is registered in the name of any entity as may be requested by an authorized representative of the depositary (and any payment is made to such entity as may be requested by an authorized representative of the depositary), any transfer, pledge or other use hereof for value or otherwise by or to any person is wrongful inasmuch as the registered owner hereof has an interest herein." Try saying that three times very fast.

[9]In some countries, such as the U.K. and Australia, "debenture" means a secured bond.

[10]If a mortgage is *closed,* no more bonds may be issued against the mortgage. However, usually there is no specific limit to the amount of bonds that may be secured (in which case the mortgage is said to be *open*). Many mortgages are secured not only by existing property but also by "after-acquired" property. However, if the company buys only property that is already mortgaged, the bondholder would have only a junior claim on the new property. Therefore, mortgage bonds with after-acquired property clauses also limit the extent to which the company can purchase additional mortgaged property.

Of course, the value of any mortgage depends on the extent to which the property has alternative uses. A custom-built machine for producing buggy whips will not be worth much when the market for buggy whips dries up.

Companies that own securities may use them as collateral for a loan. For example, holding companies are firms whose main assets consist of common stock in a number of subsidiaries. So, when holding companies wish to borrow, they generally use these investments as collateral. In such cases, the problem for the lender is that the stock is junior to all other claims on the assets of the subsidiaries, and so these *collateral trust bonds* usually include detailed restrictions on the freedom of the subsidiaries to issue debt or preferred stock.

A third form of secured debt is the **equipment trust certificate.** This is most frequently used to finance new railroad rolling stock but may also be used to finance trucks, aircraft, and ships. Under this arrangement, a trustee obtains formal ownership of the equipment. The company makes a down payment on the cost of the equipment, and the balance is provided by a package of equipment trust certificates with different maturities that might typically run from 1 to 15 years. Only when all these debts have finally been paid off does the company become the formal owner of the equipment. Bond rating agencies such as Moody's or Standard & Poor's usually rate equipment trust certificates one grade higher than the company's regular debt.

Bonds may be senior claims or they may be subordinated to the senior bonds or to *all* other creditors.[11] If the firm defaults, the senior bonds come first in the pecking order. The subordinated lender gets in line behind the general creditors but ahead of the preferred stockholders and the common stockholders.

As you can see from Figure 24.2, if default does occur, it pays to hold senior secured bonds. On average, investors in these bonds can expect to recover over 50% of the amount of the loan. At the other extreme, recovery rates for junior unsecured bondholders are only 14% of the face value of the debt.

Asset-Backed Securities

Instead of borrowing money directly, companies sometimes bundle up a group of assets and then sell the cash flows from these assets. This issue is known as an *asset-backed security,* or *ABS.* The debt is secured, or backed, by the underlying assets.

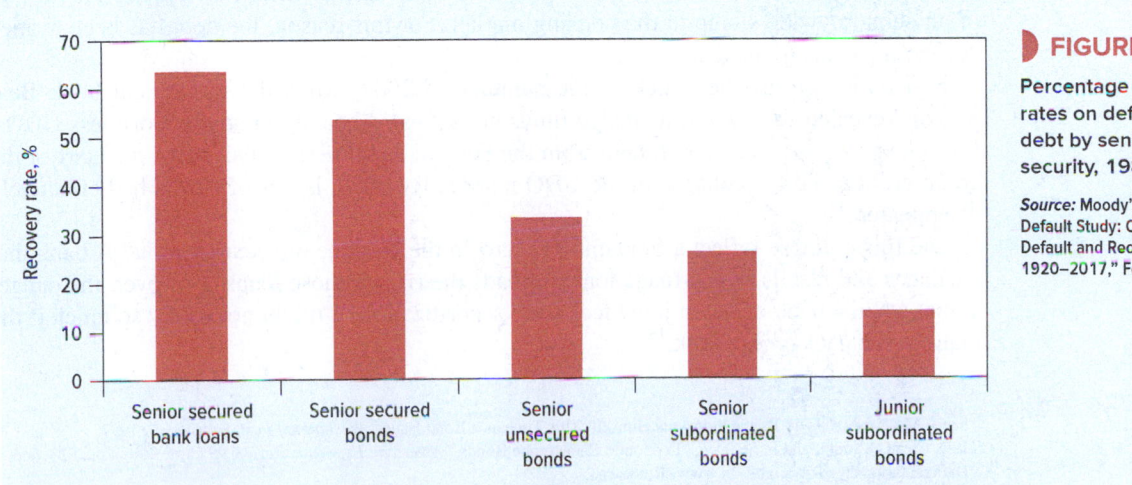

▶ **FIGURE 24.2**

Percentage recovery rates on defaulting debt by seniority and security, 1983–2017

Source: Moody's "Annual Default Study: Corporate Default and Recovery Rates, 1920–2017," February 2018.

---

[11]If a bond does not specifically state that it is junior, you can assume that it is senior.

Suppose your company has made a large number of mortgage loans to buyers of homes or commercial real estate. However, you don't want to wait until the loans are paid off; you would like to get your hands on the money now. Here is what you do. You establish a separate, special-purpose company that buys a package of the mortgage loans. To finance this purchase, the company sells *mortgage-backed securities.* The holders of these bonds simply receive a share of the mortgage payments. For example, if interest rates fall and the mortgages are repaid early, holders of the bonds are also repaid early. That is not generally popular with these holders because they get their money back just when they don't want it—when interest rates are low.

Instead of issuing one class of bonds, a pool of mortgages can be bundled and then split into different slices (or *tranches*), known as *collateralized debt obligations,* or *CDOs.* For example, mortgage payments might be used first to pay off one class of security holders and only then will other classes start to be repaid. The senior tranches have first claim on the cash flows and therefore may be attractive to conservative investors such as insurance companies or pension funds. The riskiest (or *equity*) tranche can then be sold to hedge funds or mutual funds that specialize in low-quality debt.

Real estate lenders are not unique in wanting to turn future cash receipts into up-front cash. Automobile loans, student loans, and credit card receivables are also often bundled and remarketed as an asset-backed security. Indeed, investment bankers seem able to repackage any set of cash flows into a loan. In 1997, David Bowie, the British rock star, established a company that then purchased the royalties from his current albums. The company financed the purchase by selling $55 million of 10-year notes. The royalty receipts were used to make the principal and interest payments on the notes. When asked about the singer's reaction to the idea, his manager replied, "He kind of looked at me cross-eyed and said 'What?'"[12]

The process of bundling a number of future cash flows into a single security is called *securitization.* You can see the arguments for securitization. As long as the risks of the individual loans are not perfectly correlated, the risk of the package is less than that of any of the parts. In addition, securitization distributes the risk of the loans widely and, because the package can be traded, investors are not obliged to hold it to maturity.

In the years leading up to the financial crisis, the proportion of new mortgages that were securitized expanded sharply, while the quality of the mortgages declined. By 2007, more than half of the new issues of CDOs involved exposure to subprime mortgages. Because the mortgages were packaged together, investors in these CDOs were protected against the risk of default on an individual mortgage. However, even the senior tranches were exposed to the risk of an economywide slump in the housing market. For this reason, the debt has been termed "economic catastrophe debt."[13]

Economic catastrophe struck in the summer of 2007, when the investment bank Bear Stearns revealed that two of its hedge funds had invested heavily in nearly worthless CDOs. Bear Stearns was rescued with help from the Federal Reserve, but it signaled the start of the credit crunch and the collapse of the CDO market. By 2009, issues of CDOs had effectively disappeared.[14]

Did this collapse reflect a fundamental flaw in the practice of securitization? A bank that packages and resells its mortgage loans spreads the risk of those loans. However, the danger is that when a bank can earn juicy fees from securitization, it might not worry so much if the loans in the package are junk.[15]

---

[12] See J. Matthews, "David Bowie Reinvents Himself, This Time as a Bond Issue," *Washington Post,* February 7, 1997.

[13] J. D. Coval, J. Jurek, and E. Stafford, "Economic Catastrophe Bonds," *American Economic Review* 99 (June 2009), pp. 628–666.

[14] Data on issuance are available on **www.sifma.org.**

[15] CDO fees for the originating bank were in the region of 1.5% to 1.75%, more than three times the amount that the bank could earn from underwriting an investment-grade bond. However, many banks during the crisis seem to have persuaded themselves that the underlying mortgages were *not* junk and kept a large portion of the loans on their own books. See, for example, V. Acharya and M. Richardson (eds.), *Restoring Financial Stability* (Hoboken, NJ: Wiley, 2009).

Call Provisions

Back to our AMAT bond. The bond includes a call option that allows the company to repay the debt early. This can be a valuable option if AMAT wishes to reduce its leverage or tidy up its outstanding debt. The price at which companies could call their bonds used to be set at a fixed number. In this case, issuers had an incentive to call the bonds whenever they were worth more than the call price. This was not popular with investors. These days, it is more common to link the call price to an estimate of the bond's value. Thus, if interest rates fall and the bond increases in value, AMAT must pay more than face value to buy back its bonds. The formula for determining this price seeks to ensure that AMAT can never buy back the bond for less than it is worth.

Very occasionally you come across bonds that give *investors* the repayment option. Extendible bonds give them the option to extend the bond's life, while retractable (or *puttable*) bonds give investors the right to demand early repayment. Puttable bonds exist largely because bond indentures cannot anticipate every action the company may take that could harm the bondholder. If the value of the bonds is reduced, the put option allows the bondholders to demand repayment.

Puttable loans can sometimes get their issuers into BIG trouble. During the 1990s, many loans to Asian companies gave their lenders a repayment option. Consequently, when the Asian crisis struck in 1997, these companies were faced by a flood of lenders demanding their money back.

Sinking Funds

The AMAT bond must be repaid in its entirety in 2041. But in many cases, a bond issue is repaid on a regular basis before maturity. To do this, the company makes a series of payments into a *sinking fund*. If the payment is in the form of cash, the trustee selects bonds by lottery and uses the cash to redeem them at their face value.[16] Alternatively, the company can choose to buy bonds in the marketplace and pay these into the fund. This is a valuable option for the company. If the bond price is low, the firm will buy the bonds in the market and hand them to the sinking fund; if the price is high, it will call the bonds by lottery.

Generally, there is a mandatory fund that *must* be satisfied and an optional fund that can be satisfied if the borrower chooses. We saw earlier that interest payments provide a regular test of solvency. A sinking fund provides an additional hurdle that the firm must keep jumping. If it cannot pay the cash into the sinking fund, the lenders can demand their money back. That is why long-dated, lower-quality issues involve larger sinking funds. Higher-quality bonds generally have a lighter sinking fund requirement if they have one at all.

Unfortunately, a sinking fund is a weak test of solvency if the firm is allowed to repurchase bonds in the market. Since the *market* value of the debt declines as the firm approaches financial distress, the sinking fund becomes a hurdle that gets progressively lower as the hurdler gets weaker.

Bond Covenants

Investors in corporate bonds know that there is a risk of default. But they still want to make sure that the company plays fair. They don't want it to gamble with their money. Therefore, the loan agreement usually includes a number of *debt covenants* that prevent the company from purposely increasing the value of its default option.[17] These covenants may be relatively light for blue-chip companies but more restrictive for smaller, riskier borrowers.

Lenders worry that after they have made the loan, the company may pile up more debt and so increase the chance of default. They protect themselves against this risk by prohibiting the company from making further debt issues unless the ratio of debt to equity is below a specified limit.

---

[16]Every investor dreams of buying up the entire supply of a sinking-fund bond that is selling way below face value and then forcing the company to buy the bonds back at face value. Cornering the market in this way is fun to dream about but difficult to do.

[17]We described in Section 18-3 some of the games that managers can play at the expense of bondholders.

Not all debts are created equal. If the firm defaults, the senior debt comes first in the pecking order and must be paid off in full before the junior debtholders get a cent. Therefore, when a company issues senior debt, the lenders will place limits on further issues of senior debt. But they won't restrict the amount of *junior* debt that the company can issue. Because the senior lenders are at the front of the queue, they view the junior debt in the same way that they view equity: They would be happy to see an issue of either. Of course, the converse is not true. Holders of the junior debt *do* care both about the total amount of debt and the proportion that is senior to their claim. As a result, an issue of junior debt generally includes a restriction on both total debt and senior debt.

All bondholders worry that the company may issue more secured debt. An issue of mortgage bonds often imposes a limit on the amount of secured debt. This is not necessary when you are issuing unsecured debentures. As long as the debenture holders are given an equal claim, they don't care how much you mortgage your assets. Therefore, unsecured bonds usually include a so-called negative-pledge clause, in which the unsecured holders simply say, "Me too."[18] We saw earlier that the AMAT bonds include a negative pledge clause.

Instead of borrowing money to buy an asset, companies may enter into a long-term agreement to rent or lease it. For the debtholder, this is very similar to secured borrowing. Therefore, debt agreements also include limitations on leasing.

We have talked about how an unscrupulous borrower can try to increase the value of the default option by issuing more debt. But this is not the only way that such a company can exploit its existing bondholders. For example, the value of the default option is increased when the company pays out some of its assets to stockholders. In the extreme case a company could sell all its assets and distribute the proceeds to shareholders as a bumper dividend. That would leave nothing for the lenders. To guard against such dangers, debt issues may restrict the amount that the company may pay out in the form of dividends or repurchases of stock.[19]

Take a look at Table 24.2, which summarizes the principal covenants in a large sample of senior bond issues. These covenants prevent the company from taking certain actions that

Type of Covenant	Percentage of Bonds with Covenants	
	Investment-Grade Bonds	Other Bonds
Merger restrictions	92%	93%
Dividends or other payment restrictions	6	44
Borrowing covenants	74	67
Default-related events[a]	52	71
Change in control	24	74

❭**TABLE 24.2**   Percentage of a sample of bonds with covenant restrictions. Sample consists of 4,478 senior bonds issued between 1993 and 2007.

[a]For example, default on other loans, rating changes, or declining net worth.

Source: S. Chava, P. Kumar, and A. Warga, "Managerial Agency and Bond Covenants," *Review of Financial Studies* 23 (2010), pp. 1120–1148.

---

[18]"Me too" is not acceptable legal jargon. Instead the bond agreement may state that the company "will not consent to any lien on its assets without securing the existing bonds equally and ratably."

[19]A dividend restriction might typically prohibit the company from paying dividends if their cumulative amount would exceed the sum of (1) cumulative net income, (2) the proceeds from the sale of stock or conversion of debt, and (3) a dollar amount equal to one year's dividend.

would reduce the value of their bonds. Notice that investment-grade bonds tend to have fewer restrictions than high-yield bonds. For example, restrictions on the amount of any dividends or repurchases are less common in the case of investment-grade bonds.

These debt covenants *do* matter. Asquith and Wizman, who studied the effect of leveraged buyouts on the value of the company's debt, found that when there were no restrictions on further debt issues, dividend payments, or mergers, the buyout led to a 5.2% fall in the value of existing bonds.[20] Those bonds that were protected by strong covenants against excessive borrowing increased in price by 2.6%.

Unfortunately, it is not easy to cover all loopholes, as the bondholders of Marriott Corporation discovered in 1992. They hit the roof when the company announced plans to divide its operations into two separate businesses. One business, Marriott International, would manage Marriott's hotel chain and receive most of the revenues, while the other, Host Marriott, would own all the company's real estate and be responsible for servicing essentially all of the old company's $3 billion of debt. As a result, the price of Marriott's bonds plunged nearly 30%, and investors began to think about how they could protect themselves against such *event risks*. It is now more common for bondholders to insist on clauses that oblige the borrower to repay the debt if there is a change of control and the bonds are downrated. You can see that the AMAT bond included such a clause.

Privately Placed Bonds

The AMAT notes were registered with the SEC and sold publicly. However, bonds may also be placed privately with a few financial institutions, though the market for privately placed bonds is much smaller than the public market.[21]

As we saw in Section 15-5, it costs less to arrange a private placement than to make a public debt issue. But there are other differences between a privately placed bond and its public counterpart.

First, if you place an issue privately with one or two financial institutions, it may be necessary to sign only a simple promissory note. This is just an IOU that lays down certain conditions that the borrower must observe. However, when you make a public issue of debt, you must worry about who is supposed to represent the bondholders in any subsequent negotiations and what procedures are needed for paying interest and principal. Therefore, the contract has to be more complicated.

The second characteristic of publicly issued bonds is that they are somewhat standardized products. They *have* to be—investors are constantly buying and selling without checking the fine print in the agreement. This is not so necessary in private placements, so the debt can be custom-tailored for firms with special problems or opportunities. The relationship between borrower and lender is much more intimate. Imagine a $200 million debt issue placed privately with an insurance company, and compare it with an equivalent public issue held by 200 anonymous investors. The insurance company can justify a more thorough investigation of the company's prospects and, therefore, may be more willing to accept unusual terms or conditions.[22]

These features of private placements give them a particular niche in the corporate debt market—namely, relatively low-grade loans to small- and medium-sized firms.[23] These are

---

[20]P. Asquith and T. Wizman, "Event Risk, Covenants, and Bondholder Returns in Leveraged Buyouts," *Journal of Financial Economics* 27 (September 1990), pp. 195–213. Leveraged buyouts (LBOs) are company acquisitions that are financed by large issues of (usually unsecured) debt. We describe LBOs in Chapter 32.

[21]D. J. Denis and V. T. Mihov estimated that the value of privately placed bond issues is less than 20% that of total bond issues. See D. J. Denis and V. T. Mihov, "The Choice among Bank Debt, Non-Bank Private Debt and Public Debt: Evidence from New Corporate Borrowings," *Journal of Financial Economics* 70 (2003), pp. 3–28.

[22]Of course, debt with the same terms could be offered publicly, but then 200 separate investigations would be required—a much more expensive proposition.

[23]See D. J. Denis and V. T. Mihov, "The Choice among Bank Debt, Non-Bank Private Debt, and Public Debt: Evidence from New Corporate Borrowings," op.cit.

the firms that face the highest costs in public issues, that require the most detailed investigation, and that may require specialized, flexible loan arrangements.

Of course, the advantages of private placements are not free, for the lenders demand a higher rate of interest to compensate them for holding an illiquid asset. It is difficult to generalize about the difference in interest rates between private placements and public issues, but a typical differential is 50 basis points, or .50 percentage point.

Foreign Bonds and Eurobonds

AMAT's bonds were registered with the SEC, denominated in dollars, and were marketed to investors in the United States and overseas. If the company had needed the cash for a project in another country, it might have preferred to issue debt in that country's currency. For example, it could have sold sterling bonds in the U.K. or Swiss franc bonds in Switzerland. Foreign currency bonds that are sold to local investors in another country are known as *foreign bonds*. Many foreign companies issue their bonds in the United States, making it by far the largest market for foreign bonds. Japan and Switzerland are also substantial markets. Foreign bonds have a variety of nicknames. For example, a bond sold by a foreign company in the United States is known as a *yankee bond,* a bond sold by a foreign firm in Japan is a *samurai,* and one sold in Switzerland is an *alpine.*

Of course, any firm that raises money from local investors in a foreign country is subject to the rules of that country and oversight by its financial regulator. For example, when a foreign company issues publicly traded bonds in the United States, it must first register the issue with the SEC. However, as long as the bonds are not publicly traded, foreign firms borrowing in the United States can avoid registration by complying with the SEC's Rule 144A. Rule 144A bonds can be bought and sold only by large financial institutions.[24]

Instead of issuing a bond in a particular country's market, a company may market a bond issue internationally. Issues that are denominated in one country's currency but marketed internationally outside that country are known as *eurobonds* and are usually made in one of the major currencies, such as the U.S. dollar, the euro, or the yen. For example, AMAT could have issued a dollar bond just to overseas investors. As long as the issue is not marketed to U.S. investors, it does not need to be registered with the SEC.[25] Eurobond issues are marketed by international syndicates of underwriters, such as the London branches of large U.S., European, and Japanese banks and security dealers. Be careful not to confuse a eurobond (which is outside the oversight of any domestic regulator and may be in any currency) with a bond that is marketed in a European country and denominated in euros.[26]

The eurobond market arose during the 1960s because the U.S. government imposed a tax on the purchase of foreign securities and discouraged American corporations from exporting capital. Consequently, both European and American multinationals were forced to tap an international market for capital. The tax was removed in 1974. Since firms can now choose whether to borrow in New York or London, the interest rates in the two markets are usually similar. However, the eurobond market is not directly subject to regulation by the U.S. authorities, and therefore, the financial manager needs to be alert to small differences in the cost of borrowing in one market rather than another.

---

[24]We described Rule 144A in Section 15-5.

[25]You should not, however, get the impression that the eurobond market is some lawless wilderness. Eurobond contracts typically state that the issue is subject to either British or New York law.

[26]To make matters more confusing, the term "eurobond" has also been used to refer to bonds that in the future might be issued jointly by eurozone governments.

24-2 **Convertible Securities and Some Unusual Bonds**

Unlike the common or garden bond, a convertible security can change its spots. It starts life as a bond (or preferred stock) but subsequently may turn into common stock. For example, in March 2017, Tesla issued $850 million of 2.375% convertible senior notes due in 2022. Each bond can be converted at any time into 3.0534 shares of common stock. Thus the owner has a five-year option to return the bond to the company and receive 3.0534 shares of common stock in exchange. The number of shares into which each bond can be converted is called the bond's **conversion ratio.** The conversion ratio of the Tesla bond is 3.0534.

To receive these shares, the owner of the convertible must surrender bonds with a face value of $1,000. This means that to receive *one* share, the owner needs to surrender a face amount of $1,000/3.0534 = $327.75. This is the bond's **conversion price.** Anybody who bought the bond at $1,000 to convert it into stock paid the equivalent of $327.75 a share, 25% above the stock price at the time of the convertible issue.

You can think of a convertible bond as equivalent to a straight bond plus an option to acquire common stock. When convertible bondholders exercise this option, they do not pay cash; instead they give up their bonds in exchange for shares. If Tesla's bonds had not been convertible, they would probably have been worth about $870 at the time of issue. The difference between the price of a convertible bond and the price of an equivalent straight bond represents the value that investors place on the conversion option. For example, an investor who paid $1,000 in 2017 for the Tesla convertible would have paid about $1,000 − $870 = $130 for the five-year option to acquire 3.0534 shares.

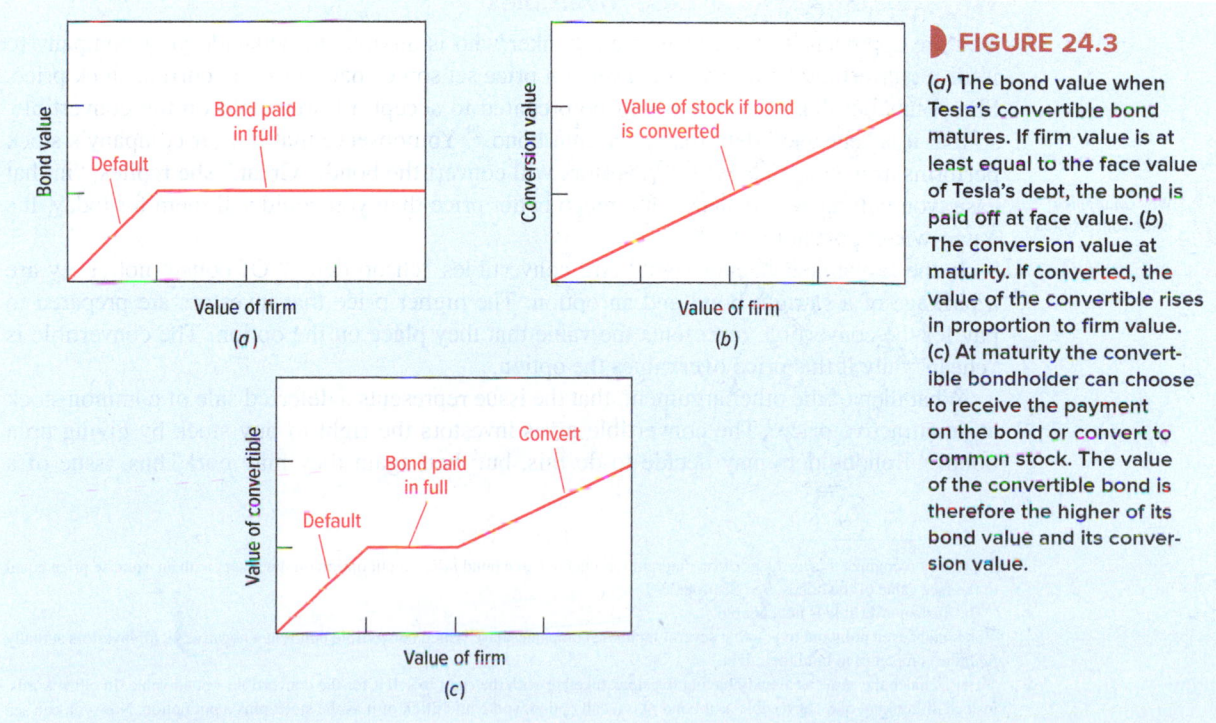

FIGURE 24.3

(*a*) The bond value when Tesla's convertible bond matures. If firm value is at least equal to the face value of Tesla's debt, the bond is paid off at face value. (*b*) The conversion value at maturity. If converted, the value of the convertible rises in proportion to firm value. (*c*) At maturity the convertible bondholder can choose to receive the payment on the bond or convert to common stock. The value of the convertible bond is therefore the higher of its bond value and its conversion value.

The Value of a Convertible at Maturity

By the time that the Tesla convertible matures, investors need to choose whether to stay with the bond or convert to common stock. Figure 24.3*a* shows the possible bond values at maturity.[27] Notice that the bond value is simply the face value as long as Tesla does not default. However, if the value of the company's assets is sufficiently low, the bondholders will receive *less* than the face value and, in the extreme case that the assets are worthless, they will receive nothing. You can think of the bond value as a lower bound, or "floor," to the price of the convertible. But that floor has a nasty slope and, when the company falls on hard times, the bond may not be worth much.

Figure 24.3*b* shows the value of the shares that investors receive if they choose to convert. If Tesla's assets at that point are worthless, the shares into which the convertible can be exchanged are also worthless. But, as the value of the assets rises, so does the conversion value.

Tesla's convertible cannot sell for less than its conversion value. If it did, investors would buy the convertible, exchange it rapidly for stock, and sell the stock. Their profit would be equal to the difference between the conversion value and the price of the convertible. Therefore, there are two lower bounds to the price of the convertible: its bond value and its conversion value. Investors will not convert if the convertible is worth more as a bond; they *will* do so if the conversion value at maturity exceeds the bond value. In other words, the price of the convertible at maturity is represented by the higher of the two lines in Figures 24.3*a* and *b*. This is shown in Figure 24.3*c*.

Forcing Conversion

Many issuers of convertible bonds have an option to buy (or *call*) the bonds back at their face value whenever its stock price is 30% or so above the bond's conversion price.[28] If the company does announce that it will call the bonds, it makes sense for investors to convert immediately. Thus, a call can *force* conversion.

Why Do Companies Issue Convertibles?

You are approached by an investment banker who is anxious to persuade your company to issue a convertible bond with a conversion price set somewhat above the current stock price. She points out that investors would be prepared to accept a lower yield on the convertible, so that it is "cheaper" debt than a straight bond.[29] You observe that if your company's stock performs as well as you expect, investors will convert the bond. "Great," she replies, "in that case, you will have sold shares at a much better price than you could sell them for today. It's a win-win opportunity."

Is the investment banker right? Are convertibles "cheap debt"? Of course not. They are a package of a straight bond and an option. The higher price that investors are prepared to pay for the convertible represents the value that they place on the option. The convertible is "cheap" only if this price overvalues the option.

What then of the other argument, that the issue represents a deferred sale of common stock at an attractive price? The convertible gives investors the right to buy stock by giving up a bond.[30] Bondholders may decide to do this, but then again they may not. Thus, issue of a

---

[27]You may recognize this as the position diagram for a default-free bond *minus* a put option on the assets with an exercise price equal to the face value of the bonds. See Section 23-2.

[28]The Tesla convertible is not callable.

[29]She might even point out to you that several Japanese companies have issued convertible bonds at a negative yield. Investors actually *paid* the companies to hold their debt.

[30]That is much the same as already having the stock together with the right to sell it for the convertible's bond value. In other words, instead of thinking of a convertible as a bond plus a call option, you could think of it as the stock plus a put option. Now you can see why it is wrong to think of a convertible as equivalent to the sale of stock; it is equivalent to the sale of both stock and a put option. If there is any possibility that investors will want to hold on to their bond, this put option has value.

convertible bond *may* amount to a deferred stock issue. But if the firm needs equity capital, a convertible issue is an unreliable way of getting it.

John Graham and Campbell Harvey surveyed companies that had seriously considered issuing convertibles. In 58% of the cases, management considered convertibles an inexpensive way to issue "delayed" common stock. Forty-two percent of the firms viewed convertibles as less expensive than straight debt.[31] Taken at their face value, these arguments don't make sense. But we suspect that these phrases encapsulate some more complex and rational motives.

Notice that convertibles tend to be issued by smaller and more speculative firms. These issues are almost invariably unsecured and generally subordinated. Now put yourself in the position of a potential investor. You are approached by a firm with an untried product line that wants to issue some junior unsecured debt. You know that if things go well, you will get your money back, but if they do not, you could easily be left with nothing. Since the firm is in a new line of business, it is difficult to assess the chances of trouble. Therefore, you don't know what the fair rate of interest is. Also, you may be worried that once you have made the loan, management will be tempted to run extra risks. It may take on additional senior debt, or it may decide to expand its operations and go for broke on your money. In fact, if you charge a very high rate of interest, you could be encouraging this to happen.

What can management do to protect you against a wrong estimate of the risk and to assure you that its intentions are honorable? In crude terms, it can give you a piece of the action. You don't mind the company running unanticipated risks as long as you share in the gains as well as the losses.[32] Convertible securities make sense whenever it is unusually costly to assess the risk of debt or whenever investors are worried that management may not act in the bondholders' interest.[33]

The relatively low coupon rate on convertible bonds may also be a convenience for rapidly growing firms facing heavy capital expenditures.[34] They may be willing to provide the conversion option to reduce immediate cash requirements for debt service. Without that option, lenders might demand extremely high (promised) interest rates to compensate for the probability of default. This would not only force the firm to raise still more capital for debt service but also increase the risk of financial distress. Paradoxically, lenders' attempts to protect themselves against default may actually increase the probability of financial distress by increasing the burden of debt service on the firm.

Valuing Convertible Bonds

We have seen that a convertible bond is equivalent to a package of a bond and an option to buy stock. This means that the option-valuation models that we described in Chapter 21 can also be used to value the option to convert. We don't want to repeat that material here, but we should note three wrinkles that you need to look out for when valuing a convertible:

1. *Dividends.* If you hold the common stock, you may receive dividends. The investor who holds an option to convert into common stock misses out on these dividends. In fact, the convertible holder loses out every time a cash dividend is paid because the dividend

[31]See J. R. Graham and C. R. Harvey, "The Theory and Practice of Finance: Evidence from the Field," *Journal of Financial Economics* 60 (2001), pp. 187–243.

[32]In the survey referred to above, a further 44% of the respondents reported that an important factor in their decision was the fact that convertibles were attractive to investors who were unsure about the riskiness of the company.

[33]Changes in risk are more likely when the firm is small and its debt is low-grade. Therefore, we should find that convertible bonds of such firms offer their holders a larger potential ownership share. This is indeed the case. See C. M. Lewis, R. J. Rogalski, and J. K. Seward, "Understanding the Design of Convertible Debt," *Journal of Applied Corporate Finance* 11 (Spring 1998), pp. 45–53.

[34]Of course, the firm could also make an equity issue rather than an issue of straight debt or convertibles. However, a convertible issue sends a better signal to investors than an issue of common stock. As we explained in Chapter 15, announcement of a stock issue prompts worries of overvaluation and usually depresses the stock price. Convertibles are hybrids of debt and equity and send a less negative signal. If the company is likely to need equity, its willingness to issue a convertible and take the chance that the stock price will rise enough to lead to conversion also signals management's confidence in the future. See J. Stein, "Convertible Bonds as, 'Back-door', Equity Financing," *Journal of Financial Economics* 32 (1992), pp. 3–21.

reduces the stock price and thus reduces the value of the conversion option. If the dividends are high enough, it may even pay to convert before maturity to capture the extra income. We showed how dividend payments affect option value in Section 21-5.

2. *Dilution.* The second complication arises because conversion increases the number of outstanding shares. Therefore, exercise means that each shareholder is entitled to a smaller proportion of the firm's assets and profits.[35] This problem of *dilution* never arises with traded options. If you buy an option through an option exchange and subsequently exercise it, you have no effect on the number of shares outstanding.

3. *Changing bond value.* When investors convert to shares, they give up their bond. The exercise price of the option is therefore the value of the bond that they are relinquishing. But this bond value is not constant. If the bond value at issue is less than the face value (and it usually is less), it is likely to change as maturity approaches. Also, the bond value varies as interest rates change and as the company's credit standing changes. If there is some possibility of default, investors cannot even be certain of what the bond will be worth *at maturity*. In Chapter 21, we did not get into the complication of uncertain exercise prices.

A Variation on Convertible Bonds: The Bond–Warrant Package

Instead of issuing a convertible bond, companies sometimes sell a package of straight bonds and warrants. Warrants are simply long-term call options that give the investor the right to buy the firm's common stock. For example, in 2017 the German chemical giant, BASF, placed a $600 million package of bonds and warrants maturing in 2023. The exercise price of the warrants was set at 112.45 euros, 25% above the price of the stock at the time of issue.

Convertible bonds consist of a package of a straight bond and an option. An issue of bonds and warrants also contains a straight bond and an option. But there are some differences:

1. *Warrants are usually issued privately.* Packages of bonds with warrants tend to be more common in private placements. By contrast, most convertible bonds are issued publicly.

2. *Warrants can be detached.* When you buy a convertible, the bond and the option are bundled together. You cannot sell them separately. This may be inconvenient. If your tax position or attitude to risk inclines you to bonds, you may not want to hold options as well. Warrants are sometimes also "nondetachable," but usually you can keep the bond and sell the warrant.

3. *Warrants are exercised for cash.* When you convert a bond, you simply exchange your bond for common stock. When you exercise warrants, you generally put up extra cash, though occasionally you have to surrender the bond or can choose to do so. This means that the bond–warrant package and the convertible bond have different effects on the company's cash flow and on its capital structure.

4. *A package of bonds and warrants may be taxed differently.* There are some tax differences between warrants and convertibles. Suppose that you are wondering whether to issue a convertible bond at 100. You can think of this convertible as a package of a straight bond worth, say, 90 and an option worth 10. If you issue the bond and option separately, the IRS will note that the bond is issued at a discount and that its price will rise by 10 points over its life. The IRS will allow you, the issuer, to spread this prospective price appreciation over the life of the bond and deduct it from your taxable profits. The IRS will also allocate the prospective price appreciation to the taxable income of the bondholder. Thus, by issuing a package of bonds and warrants rather than a convertible, you may reduce the tax paid by the issuing company and increase the tax paid by the investor.

---

[35]In their financial statements, companies recognize the possibility of dilution by showing how earnings would be affected by the issue of the extra shares.

5. *Warrants may be issued on their own.* Warrants do not have to be issued in conjunction with other securities. Often they are used to compensate investment bankers for underwriting services. Many companies also give their executives long-term options to buy stock. These executive stock options are not usually called warrants, but that is exactly what they are. Companies can also sell warrants on their own directly to investors, though they rarely do so.

Innovation in the Bond Market

Domestic bonds and eurobonds, fixed- and floating-rate bonds, coupon bonds and zeros, callable and puttable bonds, straight bonds and convertible bonds—you might think that this would give you as much choice as you need. Yet almost every day some new type of bond seems to be issued. Table 24.3 lists some of the more interesting bonds that have been invented in recent years.[36] Earlier in the chapter, we described asset-backed securities, and in Chapter 26, we discuss catastrophe bonds whose payoffs are linked to the occurrence of natural disasters.

Some financial innovations appear to serve little or no economic purpose; they may flower briefly but then wither. For example, toward the end of the 1990s in the United States, there was a bout of new issues of **floating-price convertibles,** or, as they were more commonly called, **death-spiral,** or toxic, convertibles. When death-spiral convertibles are issued, the conversion price is set below the current stock price. Moreover, each bond is convertible not into a fixed *number* of shares but into shares with a fixed *value*. Therefore, the more the share price falls, the more shares that the convertible bondholder is entitled to. With a normal convertible, the value of the conversion option falls whenever the value of the firm's assets falls; so the convertible holder shares some of the pain with the stockholders. With a death-spiral convertible, the holder is entitled to shares with a fixed value, so the entire effect of the decrease in the asset price falls on the common stockholders. Death-spiral convertibles were issued largely by companies that were already in desperate straits, and, when the issuers failed to recover, the toxic chicken came home to roost. After the initial flurry of issues in the United States, death-spiral convertibles seem now to have been consigned to the garbage heap of unsuccessful innovations.

Asset-backed securities	Many small loans are packaged together and resold as a bond.
Catastrophe (CAT) bonds	Payments are reduced in the event of a specified natural disaster.
Contingent convertibles (cocos)	Bonds that convert automatically into equity as the value of the company falls.
Equity-linked bonds	Payments are linked to the performance of a stock market index.
Liquid yield option notes (LYONs)	Puttable, callable, convertible, zero-coupon debt.
Longevity bonds	Bonds whose payments are reduced or eliminated if there is a fall in mortality rates.
Mortality bonds	Bonds whose payments are reduced or eliminated if there is a jump in mortality rates.
Pay-in-kind bonds (PIKs)	Issuer can choose to make interest payments either in cash or in more bonds with an equivalent face value.
Credit-linked bonds	Coupon rate changes as company's credit rating changes.
Reverse floaters (yield-curve notes)	Floating-rate bonds that pay a higher rate of interest when other interest rates fall and a lower rate when other rates rise.
Step-up bonds	Bonds whose coupon payments are increased over time.

❭ **TABLE 24.3**   **Some examples of innovation in bond design**

---

[36]For a more comprehensive list of innovations, see K. A. Carow, G.R. Erwin, and J. J. McConnell, "A Survey of U.S Corporate Financing Innovations: 1970–1997," *Journal of Applied Corporate Finance* 12 (Spring 1999), pp. 55–69.

Many other innovations seem to have a more obvious purpose. Here are some important motives for creating new securities:

1. *Investor choice.* Sometimes new financial instruments are created to widen investor choice. Economists refer to such securities as helping to "complete the market." This was the idea behind the 2013 issue of nearly $180 million of *mortality,* or *death bonds* by the French insurance company SCOR. One of the big risks for a life insurance company is a pandemic or other disaster that results in a sharp increase in the death rate. SCOR's bond, therefore, offers investors a higher interest rate for taking on some of that risk. Holders of the bonds will lose their entire investment if U.S. death rates for two consecutive years are unusually high. Mortality bonds widen investor choice. They allow insurance companies to protect themselves against adverse changes in mortality and they spread the risk widely around the market.

BEYOND THE PAGE

Longevity swaps

mhhe.com/brealey13e

2. *Government regulation and tax.* Merton Miller has described new government regulations and taxes as the sand in the oyster that stimulates the design of new types of security. For example, we have already seen how the eurobond market was a response to the U.S. government's imposition of a tax on purchases of foreign securities.

   Asset-backed securities provide another instance of a market that was encouraged by regulation. To reduce the likelihood of failure, banks are obliged to finance part of their loan portfolio with equity capital. Many banks were able to reduce the amount of capital that they needed to hold by packaging up their loans or credit card receivables and selling them off as bonds. Bank regulators have worried about this. They think that banks may be tempted to sell off their riskiest loans and to keep their safest ones. They have therefore introduced new regulations that will link the capital requirement to the riskiness of the loans.

3. *Reducing agency costs.* We have already seen how convertible bonds may reduce agency cost. Here is another example. At the turn of the century, investors were worried by the huge spending plans of telecom companies. So when Deutsche Telecom, the German telecom giant, decided to sell $15 billion of bonds in 2000, it agreed to increase the coupon rate on the bonds by 50 basis points if ever its bonds were downgraded to below investment grade by Moody's or Standard & Poor's. Deutsche Telecom's credit-linked bonds protected investors against possible future attempts by the company to exploit existing bondholders by loading on more debt.

BEYOND THE PAGE

Contingent convertibles

mhhe.com/brealey13e

   Here is yet another example where bond design can help to solve agency problems. Bankers love to borrow rather than issue equity. The problem is that when banks encounter heavy weather, the shareholders may refuse to come to the rescue with more capital. One suggested remedy is for the banks to issue *contingent convertible bonds* (or *cocos*). These are bonds that convert automatically into equity if the bank hits trouble. For example, in 2016 the Spanish bank, BBVA, issued €500 million of perpetual cocos. If BBVA's capital falls below a specified level, the cocos reduce the bank's leverage by changing into equity.

   Dreaming up these new financial instruments is only half the battle. The other problem is to produce them efficiently. Think, for example, of the problems of packaging together several hundred million dollars' worth of credit card receivables and allocating the cash flows to a diverse group of investors. That requires good computer systems. The deal also needs to be structured so that, if the issuer goes bankrupt, the receivables will not be part of the bankruptcy estate. That depends on the development of legal structures that will stand up in the event of a dispute.

24-3   Bank Loans

Bonds are generally long-term loans and more often than not are issued publicly by the borrowing company. It is now time to look at shorter-term debt. This is not usually issued publicly and is largely supplied by banks. Whereas the typical bond issue has a maturity of 10 years, the bank loan is generally repaid in about 3 years.[37] Of course, there is plenty of variation around these figures.

In the United States, bank loans are a less important source of finance than the bond market, but for many smaller firms, they are the *only* source of borrowing. Bank loans come in a variety of flavors. Here are a few of the ways that they differ.

Commitment

Companies sometimes wait until they need the money before they apply for a bank loan, but about 90% of commercial loans by U.S. banks are made under commitment. In this case, the company establishes a line of credit that allows it to borrow up to an established limit from the bank. This line of credit may be an **evergreen credit** with no fixed maturity, but more commonly, it is a **revolving credit** (*revolver*) with a fixed maturity. One other common arrangement is a 364-day facility that allows the company, over the next year, to borrow, repay, and re-borrow as its need for cash varies.[38]

Credit lines are relatively expensive; in addition to paying interest on any borrowings, the company must pay a commitment fee on the unused amount. In exchange for this extra cost, the firm receives a valuable option: It has guaranteed access to the bank's money at a fixed spread over the general level of interest rates.

The growth in the use of credit lines has changed the role of banks. They are no longer simply lenders; they are also in the business of providing companies with liquidity insurance.

Maturity

Many bank loans are for only a few months. For example, a company may need a short-term **bridge loan** to finance the purchase of new equipment or the acquisition of another firm. In this case, the loan serves as interim financing until the purchase is completed and long-term financing arranged. Often, a short-term loan is needed to finance a temporary increase in inventory. Such a loan is described as **self-liquidating;** in other words, the sale of goods provides the cash to repay the loan.

Banks also provide longer-maturity loans, known as **term loans.** A term loan typically has a maturity of four to five years. Usually it is repaid in level amounts over this period, though there is sometimes a large final *balloon* payment or just a single *bullet* payment at maturity. Banks can accommodate the precise repayment pattern to the anticipated cash flows of the borrower. For example, the first repayment might be delayed a year until the new factory is completed. Term loans are often renegotiated before maturity. Banks are willing to do this if the borrower is an established customer, remains creditworthy, and has a sound business reason for making the change.[39]

---

[37] See D. J. Denis and V. T. Mihov, "The Choice among Bank Debt, Non-Bank Private Debt, and Public Debt: Evidence from New Corporate Borrowings," *Journal of Financial Economics* 70 (2003), pp. 3–28.

[38] Banks originally promoted 364-day facilities because they did not need to set aside capital for commitments of less than a year.

[39] One study of private debt agreements found that over 90% are renegotiated before maturity. In most cases, this is not because of financial distress. See M. R. Roberts and A. Sufi, "Renegotiation of Financial Contracts: Evidence from Private Credit Agreements," *Journal of Financial Economics* 93 (2009), pp. 159–184.

FINANCE IN PRACTICE

〉 LIBOR

Each day at around 11 a.m. in London, a panel of major banks provide estimates of the interest rate at which they could borrow funds from another bank in reasonable market size. They produce these estimates for seven maturities that range from overnight to one year. In each case, the top and bottom quarter of the estimates are dropped, and the remainder are averaged to provide the set of rates known as LIBOR. The rates most commonly quoted as LIBOR are for borrowing U.S. dollars, but similar sets of LIBOR are also produced for four other currencies—the euro, the Japanese yen, the pound sterling, and the Swiss Franc. LIBOR rates are published by the ICE Benchmark Administration (ICE).*

Figure 24.4 plots the difference between the interest rate on three-month Treasury bills and LIBOR. This spread is known as the TED spread. For many years the TED spread was typically less than 50 basis points (.5%), but in 2008, it widened dramatically, at one point reaching 360 basis points (3.6%). Suddenly, the choice of benchmark for bank loans began to be very important.

> **FIGURE 24.4**

Month-end values for the spread between the interest rate on three-month Treasury bills and LIBOR (the TED spread), August 2004 to February 2018

Source: Federal Reserve Bank of St. Louis.

*In the case of euro deposits, the European Banking Federation calculates an alternative measure, known as Euribor. You can find historical values for LIBOR at http://research.stlouisfed.org/fred2/series/TEDRATE and for Euribor at www.euribor.org.

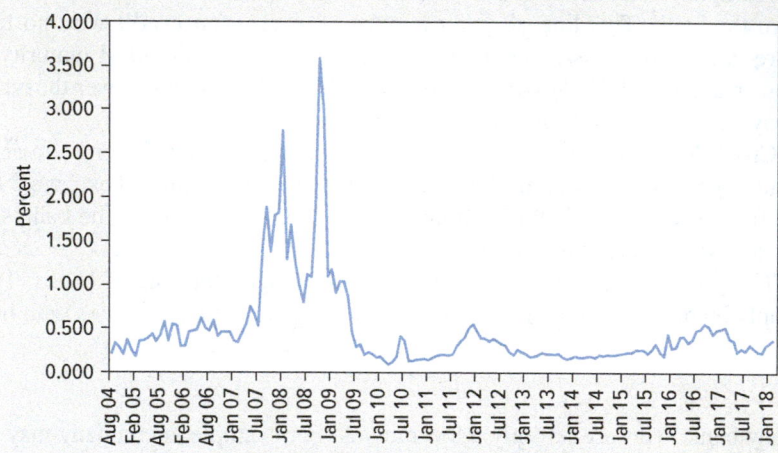

Rate of Interest

Most short-term bank loans are made at a fixed rate of interest, which is often quoted as a discount. For example, if the interest rate on a one-year loan is stated as a discount of 5%, the borrower receives $100 − $5 = $95 and undertakes to pay $100 at the end of the year. The return on such a loan is not 5%, but 5/95 = .0526, or 5.26%.

For longer-term bank loans the interest rate is usually linked to the general level of interest rates. The most common benchmarks are LIBOR, the federal funds rate,[40] or the bank's prime rate. Thus, if the rate is set at "1% over LIBOR," the borrower may pay 5% in the first three months when LIBOR is 4%, 6% in the next three months when LIBOR is 5%, and so on. The nearby box describes how LIBOR is set and its relationship to the Treasury bill rate.

BEYOND THE PAGE

The LIBOR scandal

mhhe.com/brealey13e

Syndicated Loans

Some bank loans and credit lines are too large for a single lender. In these cases, the borrower may pay an arrangement fee to one or more lead banks, which then parcel out the loan or credit

---

[40]The federal funds rate is the rate at which banks lend excess reserves to each other.

line among a syndicate of banks.[41] For example, in 2017 JPMorgan, Citigroup, Mizuho Bank, and Goldman Sachs arranged a syndicated loan facility for Sprint Communications. The package consisted of a $4.0 billion term loan and a $2.0 billion revolving credit facility. The term loan had a seven-year maturity and was priced at 2.5% over LIBOR. The interest rate on the revolving credit facility was 1.75% to 2.75% over LIBOR.[42] In addition, Sprint was required to pay a commitment fee of .25% to .45% on any unused portion of the revolving credit.

The syndicate arrangers serve as underwriters to the loan. They price the loan, market it to other banks, and may also guarantee to take on any unsold portion. The arrangers', first step is to prepare an *information memo* that provides potential lenders with information on the loan. The syndicate desk will then try to sound out the level of interest in the deal before the loan is finally priced and marketed to interested buyers. If the borrower has good credit or if the arranging bank has a particularly good reputation, the majority of the loan is likely to be syndicated. In other cases the arranging bank may need to demonstrate its faith in the deal by keeping a high proportion of the loan on its own books.[43]

Bank loans used to be illiquid; once the bank had made a loan, it was stuck with it. This is no longer the case so that banks with an excess demand for loans may solve the problem by selling a portion of their existing loans to other institutions. For example, about 20% of syndicated loans are subsequently resold, and these sales are reported weekly in *The Wall Street Journal*.[44]

Security

If a bank is concerned about a firm's credit risk, it will ask the firm to provide security for the loan. This is most common for longer-term bank loans, more than half of which are secured.[45] Sometimes the bank will take a *floating lien*. This gives it a general claim if the firm defaults. However, it does not specify the assets in detail, and it sets few restrictions on what the company can do with the assets.

More commonly, banks require specific collateral. For example, suppose that there is a significant delay between the time that you ship your goods and when your customers pay you. If you need the money up front, you can borrow by using these receivables as collateral. First, you must send the bank a copy of each invoice and provide it with a claim against the money that you receive from your customers. The bank may then lend up to 80% of the value of the receivables. Each day, as you make more sales, your collateral increases and you can borrow more money. Each day, some customers also pay their bills. This money is placed in a special collateral account under the bank's control and is periodically used to reduce the amount of the loan. Therefore, as the firm's business fluctuates, so does the amount of the collateral and the size of the loan.

You can also use inventories as security for a loan. For example, if your goods are stored in a warehouse, you need to arrange for an independent warehouse company to provide the bank with a receipt showing that the goods are held on the bank's behalf. The bank will generally

---

[41]For a standard loan to a blue-chip company, the fee for arranging a syndicated loan may be as low as 10 basis points, while a complex deal with a highly leveraged firm may carry a fee of up to 250 basis points. For good reviews of the syndicated loan market, see S. C. Miller, "A Guide to the Loan Market," Standard & Poor's, September 2011 (**www.standardandpoors.com**); and B. Gadanecz, "The Syndicated Loan Market: Structure, Development and Implications," *BIS Quarterly Review,* December 2004, pp. 75–89 (**www.bis.org**).

[42]In the case of both facilities, Sprint had the option to link the interest rate to an alternative measure of the short-term interest rate.

[43]See A. Sufi, "Information Asymmetry and Financing Arrangements: Evidence from Syndicated Loans," *Journal of Finance* 62 (April 2007), pp. 629–668.

[44]Loan sales generally take one of two forms: *assignments* or *participations*. In the former case, a portion of the loan is transferred with the agreement of the borrower. In the second case, the lead bank maintains its relationship with the borrower but agrees to pay over to the buyer a portion of the cash flows that it receives.

[45]The results of a survey of the terms of business lending by banks in the United States are published quarterly in the *Federal Reserve Bulletin* (see **www.federalreserve.gov/releases/E2**).

be prepared to lend up to 50% of the value of the inventories. When the loan is repaid, the bank returns the warehouse receipt, and you are free to remove the goods.[46]

Banks are naturally choosey about the security that they will accept. They want to make sure that they can identify and sell the collateral if you default. They may be happy to lend against a warehouse full of a standard nonperishable commodity, but they would turn up their nose at a warehouse of ripe Camembert.

Banks also need to ensure that the collateral is safe and that the borrower doesn't sell the assets and run off with the money. This is what happened in the great salad oil swindle. Fifty-one banks and companies made loans of nearly $200 million to the Allied Crude Vegetable Oil Refining Corporation. In return, the company agreed to provide security in the form of storage tanks full of valuable salad oil. Unfortunately, cursory inspections failed to notice that the tanks contained seawater and sludge. When the fraud was discovered, the president of Allied went to jail and the 51 lenders were left out in the cold, looking for their $200 million.

BEYOND THE PAGE

Hazards of secured bank lending

mhhe.com/brealey13e

Loan Covenants

We saw earlier that bond issues may contain covenants, which restrict companies from taking actions that would increase the risk of their debt. For publicly issued bonds, these restrictions are often mild and are generally *incurrence covenants.* In other words, they might say that the company may not issue more debt unless the interest cover is greater than five times. In the case of privately placed debt, such as the Sprint syndicated loan, the covenants are generally more severe, and include *maintenance covenants.* For example, these may say that the company is in violation if interest cover falls below five times regardless of whether that is a result of taking on more debt or is simply caused by declining earnings.

Since privately placed debt keeps the borrower on a fairly short leash, it is quite common for a covenant to be breached. This is not as calamitous as it may sound. As long as the borrower is in good financial health, the lender may simply adjust the terms of the covenant. Only if covenants continue to be violated will the lender choose to take more drastic action.

Covenants on bank loans and privately placed bonds are principally of three kinds.[47] The first and most common covenant sets a maximum fraction of net income that can be paid out as dividends. A second set of covenants, called *sweeps,* state that all or part of the loan must be repaid if the borrower makes a large sale of assets or a substantial issue of debt. The third group places conditions on key financial ratios, such as the borrower's debt ratio, and interest coverage ratio, or current ratio. For example, the Sprint loan requires the company to maintain a specified debt ratio and interest cover.

24-4   Commercial Paper and Medium-Term Notes

Commercial Paper

Banks borrow money from one group of firms or individuals and relend the money to another group. They make their profit by charging the borrowers a higher rate of interest than they offer the lender.

Sometimes it is convenient to have a bank in the middle. It saves the lenders the trouble of looking for borrowers and assessing their creditworthiness, and it saves the borrowers the

---

[46]It is not always practicable to keep inventory in a warehouse. For example, automobile dealers need to display their cars in a show-room. One solution is to enter into a floor-planning arrangement in which the finance company or bank holds title to the cars until they are sold. When the cars are sold, the proceeds are used to repay the loan. The interest or "flooring charge" depends on how long the cars have been in the showroom.

[47]For an analysis of loan covenants in privately placed debt see M. Bradley and M. R. Roberts, "The Structure and Pricing of Corporate Debt Covenants," *Quarterly Journal of Finance* 5 (June 2015), pp. 1–37.

trouble of looking for lenders. Depositors do not care about the identity of the borrowers: They need only satisfy themselves that the bank as a whole is safe.

There are also occasions on which it is *not* worth paying an intermediary to perform these functions. Large well-known companies can bypass the banking system by issuing their own short-term unsecured notes. These notes are known as **commercial paper (CP).** Both foreign and domestic financial institutions, such as bank holding companies and finance companies,[48] also issue commercial paper, sometimes in very large quantities. The major issuers of commercial paper have set up their own marketing departments and sell their paper directly to investors, often using the web to do so. Smaller companies sell through dealers who receive a fee for marketing the issue.

Commercial paper in the United States has a maximum maturity of nine months, though most paper is for less than 60 days. Buyers generally hold it to maturity, but the company or dealer that sells the paper is usually prepared to repurchase it earlier.

Commercial paper is not risk-free. When California was mired in the energy crisis of 2001, Southern California Edison and Pacific Gas and Electric defaulted on $1.4 billion of commercial paper. And in 2008, Lehman Brothers filed for bankruptcy with $3 billion of paper outstanding. But such defaults are rare. The majority of commercial paper is issued by high-grade, nationally known companies,[49] and the issuers generally support their borrowing by arranging a backup line of credit with a bank, which guarantees that they can find the money to repay the paper.[50]

Because investors are reluctant to buy commercial paper that does not have the highest credit rating, companies cannot rely on the commercial paper market to always provide them with the short-term capital that they need. For example, when the rating services downgraded the commercial paper of Ford and General Motors, both companies were forced to sharply reduce their sales of paper.

When Lehman Brothers filed for bankruptcy in September 2008, the commercial paper market nosedived. The spread between the interest rates on commercial paper and Treasury bills doubled, while the market closed entirely for low-grade issuers. Many firms that found themselves shut out of the commercial paper market rushed to borrow on their bank lines of credit. Firms that had no such alternative source of borrowing were forced to cut back on their investment plans.[51] Only after the Fed announced plans to buy large quantities of high-grade paper did the market begin to return to normal.

In addition to unsecured commercial paper, there is also a market for *asset-backed commercial paper*. In this case, the company sells its assets to a special-purpose vehicle that then issues the paper. For example, as the auto companies reduced their sales of unsecured commercial paper, they increasingly relied on asset-backed paper secured by the firm's receivables. As the customers paid their bills, the cash was passed through to the holders of this paper.

By 2007, asset-backed paper accounted for almost half the commercial paper market, but weaknesses surfaced after a number of banks set up structured investment vehicles (SIVs) that invested in mortgage-backed securities financed by asset-backed paper. Because the buyers of the commercial paper bore the credit risk, the banks had less incentive to worry about the quality of the underlying mortgages. Once it became clear to investors that this quality was very low, many of the SIVs found it impossible to refinance the maturing paper and went into default.

BEYOND THE PAGE

Commercial paper and the financial crisis

mhhe.com/brealey13e

---

[48]A *bank holding company* is a firm that owns both a bank and nonbanking subsidiaries.

[49]Moody's, Standard & Poor's, and Fitch publish quality ratings for commercial paper. For example, Moody's provides three ratings, from P-1 (i.e., Prime 1, the highest-grade paper) to P-3. Most investors are reluctant to buy low-rated paper. For example, money-market funds are largely limited to holding P-1 paper.

[50]For top-tier issuers, the credit line is generally 75% of the amount of paper; for lower-grade issuers, it is 100%. The company may not be able to draw on this line of credit if it does not satisfy bank covenants. Therefore, lower-rated companies may need to back their paper with an irrevocable line of credit.

[51]For an analysis of firm reaction to the collapse of the commercial paper market, see P. Gao and H. Yun, "Commercial Paper, Lines of Credit, and the Real Effects of the Financial Crisis of 2008: Firm-Level Evidence from the Manufacturing Industry," working paper, University of Notre Dame, 2010.

Medium-Term Notes

New issues of securities do not need to be registered with the SEC as long as they mature within 270 days. So by limiting the maturity of commercial paper issues, companies can avoid the delays and expense of registration. However, large blue-chip companies also make regular issues of unsecured **medium-term notes (MTNs).**

You can think of MTNs as a hybrid between corporate bonds and commercial paper. Like bonds, they are relatively long-term instruments; their maturity is never less than 270 days, though it is typically less than 10 years.[52] On the other hand, like commercial paper, MTNs are not underwritten but are sold on a regular basis either through dealers or, occasionally, directly to investors. Dealers support a secondary market in these MTNs and are prepared to buy the notes back before maturity.[53]

Borrowers such as finance companies, which always need cash, welcome the flexibility of MTNs. For example, a company may tell its dealers the amount of money that it needs to raise that week, the range of maturities that it can offer, and the maximum interest that it is prepared to pay. It is then up to the dealers to find the buyers. Investors may also suggest their own terms to one of the dealers, and, if these terms are acceptable, the deal is done.

---

[52]Occasionally, an MTN registration may be used to issue much longer term bonds. For example, Disney has even used its MTN program to issue a 100-year bond.

[53]In Chapter 15, we encountered SEC Rule 415, which allows companies to file a single registration statement covering financing plans for up to three years in the future (*shelf registration*). Since the interest rates on MTN issues are adjusted frequently, an active MTN market was feasible only after the passage of Rule 415 in 2005.

SUMMARY

You should now have a fair idea of what you are letting yourself in for when you make an issue of bonds. The detailed bond agreement is set out in the indenture between your company and a trustee, but the main provisions are summarized in the prospectus to the issue. The indenture states whether the bonds are senior or subordinated, and whether they are secured or unsecured. Most bonds are unsecured debentures or notes. This means that they are general claims on the corporation. The principal exceptions are utility mortgage bonds, collateral trust bonds, and equipment trust certificates. In the event of default, the trustee to these issues can repossess the company's assets to pay off the debt. Sometimes firms raise money using asset-backed securities, which involve bundling assets together and selling the cash flows from them.

Some long-term bond issues have a sinking fund. This means that the company must set aside enough money each year to retire a specified number of bonds. A sinking fund reduces the average life of the bond, and it provides a yearly test of the company's ability to service its debt. It therefore helps to protect the bondholders against the risk of default.

Long-dated bonds may be callable before maturity. This option to call the bond may be valuable to a company that wishes to reduce its leverage or tidy up its outstanding debt.

Lenders usually seek to prevent the borrower from taking actions that would damage the value of their loans. Here are some examples of debt covenants:

1. The loan agreement may limit the amount of additional borrowing by the company.

2. Unsecured loans may incorporate a negative pledge clause, which prohibits the company from securing additional debt without giving equal treatment to the existing unsecured bonds.

3. Lenders may place a limit on the company's dividend payments or repurchases of stock.

Bonds can be issued in the public markets in the United States, in which case they must be registered with the SEC. Alternatively, if they are issued to a limited number of buyers, they can be privately placed. They can also be issued in a foreign bond market or in the Eurobond market.

Eurobonds are marketed simultaneously in a number of foreign countries by the London branches of international banks and security dealers.

Most bonds start and finish their lives as bonds, but convertible bonds give their owner the option to exchange the bond for common stock. The *conversion ratio* measures the number of shares into which each bond can be exchanged. You can think of a convertible bond as equivalent to a straight bond plus a call option on the stock. Sometimes, instead of issuing a convertible, companies may decide to issue a package of bonds and options (or *warrants*) to buy the stock. If the stock price rises above the exercise price, the investor may then keep the bond and exercise the warrants for cash.

There is an enormous variety of bond issues and new forms of bonds are spawned almost daily. By a process of natural selection, some of these new instruments become popular and may even replace existing species. Others are ephemeral curiosities. Some innovations succeed because they widen investor choice or reduce agency costs. Others owe their origin to tax rules and government regulation.

Many corporations, particularly smaller ones, obtain finance from banks. Bank loans usually have shorter maturities than bonds. Most result from commitments. Firms pay a commitment fee to keep a credit line open that they can draw upon when they need the cash.

Many bank loans are short term at a fixed rate of interest. The interest rate on longer-term bank loans is usually linked to LIBOR or some other index of interest rates. Often bank loans are provided by a syndicate of banks if the amount needed is too large to be provided by a single bank. Loans are frequently secured by collateral such as receivables, inventories, or securities. Covenants are usually more restrictive than with bonds.

Commercial paper and medium-term notes are a cheaper alternative to bank loans for many large firms. They can be sold directly to lenders or through dealers. Commercial paper can be unsecured or asset-backed. Medium-term notes are a hybrid between bonds and commercial paper. They are longer term than commercial paper but are sold in a similar way.

● ● ● ● ●

FURTHER READING

A useful general work on debt securities is:

F. J. Fabozzi (ed.), *The Handbook of Fixed Income Securities,* 8th ed. (New York: McGraw-Hill, 2011).

For an excellent guide to syndicated lending see:

Standard & Poor's, *A Guide to the Loan Market,* September 2011.

For nontechnical discussions of the pricing of convertible bonds and the reasons for their use, see:

M. J. Brennan and E. S. Schwartz, "The Case for Convertibles," *Journal of Applied Corporate Finance* 1 (Summer 1988), pp. 55–64.

C. M. Lewis, R. J. Rogalski, and J. K. Seward, "Understanding the Design of Convertible Debt," *Journal of Applied Corporate Finance* 11 (Spring 1998), pp. 45–53.

For a useful description of the commercial paper market and its difficulties in the crash of 2007–2009, see:

M. Kacperczyk and P. Schnabl, "When Safe Proved Risky: Commercial Paper during the Financial Crisis of 2007–2009," *Journal of Economic Perspectives* 24 (Winter 2010), pp. 29–50.

The readings listed at the end of Chapter 17 include several articles on financial innovation.

● ● ● ● ●

PROBLEM SETS

connect   Select problems are available in McGraw-Hill's *Connect.* Please see the preface for more information.

1. **Bond terms** Use Table 24.1 (but not the text) to answer the following questions:

   a. Who are the principal underwriters for the AMAT bond issue?

   b. What is the percentage underwriting spread?

   c. How many dollars does the company receive for each bond after deduction of the underwriters' spread?

   d. Is the bond "bearer" or "registered"?

   e. Who is the trustee for the issue?

2. **Bond terms** Look at Table 24.1:

   a. The AMAT bond was issued on June 8, 2011, at 99.592%. How much would you have to pay to buy one bond delivered on June 15? Don't forget to include accrued interest.

   b. When is the first interest payment on the bond, and what is the total dollar amount of the payment?

   c. On what date do the bonds finally mature, and what is the amount to be paid on each bond at maturity?

3. **Bond terms** Find the terms and conditions of a recent bond issue and compare them with those of the AMAT issue.

4. **Bond terms*** Select the most appropriate term from within the parentheses:

   a. (High-grade bonds/Low-grade bonds) generally have only light sinking-fund requirements.

   b. Equipment trust certificates are usually issued by (railroads/bank holding companies).

   c. Mortgage pass-through certificates are an example of (an asset-backed security/a convertible bond).

5. **Bond terms** Suppose that the AMAT bond was issued at face value and that investors continue to demand a yield of 5.85%. Sketch what you think would happen to the bond price as the first interest payment date approaches and then passes. What about the price of the bond plus accrued interest (sometimes known as the *dirty price*)?

6. **Bond terms** Bond prices can fall either because of a change in the general level of interest rates or because of an increased risk of default. To what extent do floating-rate bonds protect the investor against each of these risks?

7. **Security and seniority**

   a. As a senior bondholder, would you like the company to issue more junior debt to finance its investment program, would you prefer it not to do so, or would you not care?

   b. You hold debt secured on the company's existing property. Would you like the company to issue more unsecured debt to finance its investments, would you prefer it not to do so, or would you not care?

8. **Security and seniority*** Proctor Power has fixed assets worth $200 million and net working capital worth $100 million. It is financed partly by equity and partly by three issues of debt. These consist of $250 million of First Mortgage Bonds secured only on the company's fixed assets, $100 million of senior debentures, and $120 million of subordinated debentures. If the debt were due today, how much would each debtholder be entitled to receive?

9. **Security and seniority** Elixir Corporation has just filed for bankruptcy. Elixir is a holding company whose assets consist of real estate worth $80 million and 100% of the equity of its two operating subsidiaries. It is financed partly by equity and partly by an issue of $400 million of senior collateral trust bonds that are just about to mature. Subsidiary A has issued directly $320 million of debentures and $15 million of preferred stock. Subsidiary B has issued $180 million of senior debentures and $60 million of subordinated debentures. A's assets have a market value of $500 million, and B's have a value of $220 million. How much will each security holder receive if the assets are sold and distributed strictly according to precedence?

10. **Security and seniority**

    a. Residential mortgages may stipulate either a fixed rate or a variable rate. As a *borrower*, what considerations might cause you to prefer one rather than the other?

    b. Why might holders of mortgage pass-through certificates wish the mortgages to have a floating rate?

11. **Sinking funds** For each of the following sinking funds, state whether the fund increases or decreases the value of the bond at the time of issue (or whether it is impossible to say):

    a. An optional sinking fund operating by drawings at par.

    b. A mandatory sinking fund operating by drawings at par *or* by purchases in the market.

    c. A mandatory sinking fund operating by drawings at par.

12. **Call provisions**

    a. Look at Table 24.1. Suppose that AMAT decides to call the bond one year before it is due to expire. The interest rate on one-year Treasury bonds is 2%. What price must AMAT pay to call the bonds?

    b. Now suppose that the interest rate on Treasury bonds is 10%. What price must AMAT pay to call its bonds?

13. **Covenants** Alpha Corp. is prohibited from issuing more senior debt unless net tangible assets exceed 200% of senior debt. Currently, the company has outstanding $100 million of senior debt and has net tangible assets of $250 million. How much more senior debt can Alpha Corp. issue?

14. **Covenants** Explain carefully why bond indentures may place limitations on the following actions:

    a. Sale of the company's assets.

    b. Payment of dividends to shareholders.

    c. Issue of additional senior debt.

15. **Private placements** Explain the three principal ways in which the terms of private placement bonds commonly differ from those of public issues.

16. **Convertible bonds** True or false?

    a. Convertible bonds are usually senior claims on the firm.

    b. The higher the conversion ratio, the more valuable the convertible.

    c. The higher the conversion price, the more valuable the convertible.

    d. Convertible bonds do not share fully in the price of the common stock, but they provide some protection against a decline.

17. **Convertible bonds*** Maple Aircraft has issued a 4¾% convertible subordinated debenture due 2023. The conversion price is $47.00 and the debenture is callable at 102.75% of face value. The market price of the convertible is 91% of face value, and the price of the common is $41.50. Assume that the value of the bond in the absence of a conversion feature is about 65% of face value.

    a. What is the conversion ratio of the debenture?

    b. If the conversion ratio were 50, what would be the conversion price?

    c. What is the conversion value?

    d. At what stock price is the conversion value equal to the bond value?

    e. Can the market price be less than the conversion value?

    f. How much is the convertible holder paying for the option to buy one share of common stock?

    g. By how much does the common have to rise by 2023 to justify conversion?

18. **Convertible bonds** The Surplus Value Company had $10 million (face value) of convertible bonds outstanding in 2015. Each bond has the following features.

Face value	$1,000
Conversion price	$25
Current call price	105 (percent of face value)
Current trading price	130 (percent of face value)
Maturity	2022
Current stock price	$30 (per share)
Interest rate	10% (coupon as percent of face value)

   a. What is the bond's conversion value?

   b. Can you explain why the bond is selling above conversion value?

   c. Should Surplus call? What will happen if it does so?

19. **Convertible bonds** Sweeney Pies has issued a zero-coupon 10-year bond that can be converted into 10 Sweeney shares. Comparable straight bonds are yielding 8%. Sweeney stock is priced at $50 a share.

   a. Suppose that you had to make a now-or-never decision on whether to convert or to stay with the bond. Which would you do?

   b. If the convertible bond is priced at $550, how much are investors paying for the option to buy Sweeney shares?

   c. If, after one year, the value of the conversion option is unchanged, what is the value of the convertible bond?

20. **Convertible bonds** Iota Microsystems' 10% convertible is about to mature. The conversion ratio is 27.

   a. What is the conversion price?

   b. The stock price is $47. What is the conversion value?

   c. Should you convert?

21. **Convertible bonds** Zenco Inc. is financed by 3 million shares of common stock and by $5 million face value of 8% convertible debt maturing in 2029. Each bond has a face value of $1,000 and a conversion ratio of 200. What is the value of each convertible bond at maturity if Zenco's net assets are worth:

   a. $30 million?

   b. $4 million?

   c. $20 million?

   d. $5 million?

   Draw a figure similar to Figure 24.4c showing how the value of each convertible bond at maturity varies with the value of Zenco's net assets.

22. **Bank loans*** Match each of the following terms with one of the definitions below

   A. Revolving credit

   B. Bridge loan

   C. Term loan

   D. Syndicated loan

   E. Commitment fee

   F. Maintenance covenant

       a. Requirement that borrower keeps in the future to a certain condition—for example, a minimum debt ratio.

b. Rather like a corporate credit card, it allows the company to choose to borrow up to a certain limit and to repay.

c. Loan that is parceled out among a group of banks.

d. Longer term bank loan with a fixed maturity.

e. Fee paid on unused portion of a revolving credit.

f. Short-term bank loan taken out until more permanent funding can be arranged.

23. **Bank loans** Suppose that you are a banker responsible for approving corporate loans. Nine firms are seeking secured loans. They offer the following assets as collateral:

a. Firm A, a heating oil distributor, offers a tanker load of fuel oil in transit from the Middle East.

b. Firm B, a wine wholesaler, offers 1,000 cases of Beaujolais Nouveau located in a field warehouse.

c. Firm C, a stationer, offers an account receivable for office supplies sold to the City of New York.

d. Firm D, a bookstore, offers its entire inventory of 15,000 used books.

e. Firm E, a wholesale grocer, offers a boxcar full of bananas.

f. Firm F offers 100 ounces of gold.

g. Firm G, a government securities dealer, offers its portfolio of Treasury bills.

h. Firm H, a boat builder, offers a half-completed luxury yacht. The yacht will take four more months to complete.

Which of these assets are most likely to be good collateral? Which are likely to be poor collateral? Explain.

24. **Bank loans, commercial paper, and medium-term notes*** Complete the passage below by selecting the most appropriate terms from the following list:

floating lien, revolving credit, medium-term note, warehouse receipt, unsecured, commitment fee, commercial paper.

Companies with fluctuating needs for cash often arrange a _____ with their bank that allows them to borrow up to a specified amount. In addition to paying interest on any borrowings, the company must pay a _____ on any unused amount.

Secured short-term loans are sometimes covered by a _____, which gives it a general claim on the firm's assets. Generally, however, the borrower pledges specific assets. For example, a loan may be secured by inventory. In this case, an independent warehouse company provides the bank with a _____, showing that the goods are held on the bank's behalf and releases those goods only on instructions.

Banks are not the only source of short-term debt. Many large companies issue their own _____ debt directly to investors, often on a regular basis. If the maturity is less than 270 days, the debt does not need to be registered with the SEC and is known as _____. A company may also have a program to sell longer-maturity debt to investors on a continuing basis. This is called a _____ program.

25. **Bank loans, commercial paper, and medium-term notes** Term loans usually require firms to pay a fluctuating interest rate. For example, the interest rate may be set at 1% over LIBOR. LIBOR can sometimes vary by several percentage points within a single year. Suppose that your firm has decided to borrow $40 million for five years and that it has three alternatives:

a. Borrow from a bank at 1.5% over LIBOR, currently 6.5%. The proposed loan agreement requires no principal payments until the loan matures in year 5.

b. Issue 26-week commercial paper, currently yielding 7%. Since funds are required for five years, the commercial paper will need to be rolled over semiannually; that is, financing the $40 million will require 10 successive commercial paper sales.

c. Issue a five-year medium-term note at a fixed rate of 7.5%. As in the case of the bank loan, no principal has to be repaid until the end of year 5.

What factors would you consider in analyzing these alternatives? In what circumstances would you prefer each of these possible loans?

CHALLENGE

26. **Tax benefits** Dorlcote Milling has outstanding a $1 million 3% mortgage bond maturing in 10 years. The coupon on any new debt issued by the company is 10%. The finance director, Mr. Tulliver, cannot decide whether there is a tax benefit to repurchasing the existing bonds in the marketplace and replacing them with new 10% bonds. What do you think? Does it matter whether bond investors are taxed?

27. **Convertible bonds** This question illustrates that when there is scope for the firm to vary its risk, lenders may be more prepared to lend if they are offered a piece of the action through the issue of a convertible bond. Ms. Blavatsky is proposing to form a new start-up firm with initial assets of $10 million. She can invest this money in one of two projects. Each has the same expected payoff, but one has more risk than the other. The relatively safe project offers a 40% chance of a $12.5 million payoff and a 60% chance of an $8 million payoff. The risky project offers a 40% chance of a $20 million payoff and a 60% chance of a $5 million payoff.

    Ms. Blavatsky initially proposes to finance the firm by an issue of straight debt with a promised payoff of $7 million. Ms. Blavatsky will receive any remaining payoff. Show the possible payoffs to the lender and to Ms. Blavatsky if (a) she chooses the safe project and (b) she chooses the risky project. Which project is Ms. Blavatsky likely to choose? Which will the lender want her to choose?

    Suppose now that Ms. Blavatsky offers to make the debt convertible into 50% of the value of the firm. Show that in this case the lender receives the same expected payoff from the two projects.

28. **Convertible bonds** Occasionally, it is said that issuing convertible bonds is better than issuing stock when the firm's shares are undervalued. Suppose that the financial manager of the Butternut Furniture Company does have inside information indicating that the Butternut stock price is too low. Butternut's future earnings will in fact be higher than investors expect. Suppose further that the inside information cannot be released without giving away a valuable competitive secret. Clearly, selling shares at the present low price would harm Butternut's existing shareholders. Will they also lose if convertible bonds are issued? If they do lose in this case, is the loss more or less than it would be if common stock were issued?

    Now suppose that investors forecast earnings accurately but still undervalue the stock because they overestimate Butternut's actual business risk. Does this change your answers to the questions posed in the preceding paragraph? Explain.

MINI-CASE ● ● ● ●

The Shocking Demise of Mr. Thorndike

It was one of Morse's most puzzling cases. That morning, Rupert Thorndike, the autocratic CEO of Thorndike Oil, was found dead in a pool of blood on his bedroom floor. He had been shot through the head, but the door and windows were bolted on the inside, and there was no sign of the murder weapon.

Morse looked in vain for clues in Thorndike's bedroom and office. He had to take another tack. He decided to investigate the financial circumstances surrounding Thorndike's demise. The company's capital structure was as follows:

- 5% debentures: $250 million face value. The bonds mature in 10 years and offer a yield of 12%.

- Stock: 30 million shares, which closed at $9 a share the day before the murder.

- 10% subordinated convertible notes: The notes mature in one year and are convertible at any time at a conversion ratio of 110. The day before the murder these notes were priced at 5% more than their conversion value.

Yesterday, Thorndike had flatly rejected an offer by T. Spoone Dickens to buy all of the common stock for $10 a share. With Thorndike out of the way, it appeared that Dickens's offer would be accepted, much to the profit of Thorndike Oil's other shareholders.[54]

Thorndike's two nieces, Doris and Patsy, and his nephew, John, all had substantial investments in Thorndike Oil and had bitterly disagreed with Thorndike's dismissal of Dickens's offer. Their stakes are shown in the following table:

	5% Debentures (Face Value)	Shares of Stock	10% Convertible Notes (Face Value)
Doris	$4 million	1.2 million	$0 million
John	0	0.5	5
Patsy	0	1.5	3

All debt issued by Thorndike Oil would be paid off at face value if Dickens's offer went through. Holders of the convertible notes could choose to convert and tender their shares to Dickens.

Morse kept coming back to the problem of motive. Which niece or nephew, he wondered, stood to gain most by eliminating Thorndike and allowing Dickens's offer to succeed?

QUESTION

1. Help Morse solve the case. Which of Thorndike's relatives stood to gain most from his death?

---

[54]Rupert Thorndike's shares would go to a charitable foundation formed to advance the study of financial engineering and its crucial role in world peace and progress. The managers of the foundation's endowment were not expected to oppose the takeover.

APPENDIX • • •

Project Finance

Project finance loans are loans that are tied as closely as possible to the fortunes of a particular project and that minimize the exposure of the parent. These loans are usually referred to simply as **project finance** and are a specialty of large international banks.

Project finance means debt supported by the project, not by the project's sponsoring companies. Debt ratios are nevertheless very high for most project financings. They can be high because the debt is protected not just by the project's assets, but also by a variety of contracts and guarantees provided by customers, suppliers, and local governments as well as by the project's owners.

Some Common Features

No two project financings are alike, but they have some common features. Typically, the parent will set up a special-purpose company to own and manage the project. This company will then enter into a package of contracts that ensures the project will generate the cash flows needed to service the debt. Three components of this package are particularly important.

First, the lenders need to be confident that the project will be built on time and to specifications. This is the role of the engineering, procurement, and construction (EPC) contract between the project company and the plant's constructors.

Second, the lenders need to know that the project will be able to generate sufficient revenues to enable it to service the loans. Therefore, the project company will generally enter into a long-term, off-take contract with the business that is buying the product (the *offtaker*).

A third set of contracts involve the government of the host country. The lenders require assurance that the government will not impose new taxes or limit its ability to access the currency markets. If possible, it can be helpful to have the involvement of the World Bank or an international development bank to ensure that the government plays fair.

The effect of this web of contracts is to shift much of the project's risk away from the special-purpose company. As a result, the project company commonly has very little equity, and about 70% of the capital for the project is typically provided in the form of bank debt or other privately placed borrowing. This debt is supported by the project cash flows; if these flows are insufficient, the lenders do not have any recourse against the parent companies.

BEYOND THE PAGE

Revenue guarantees for project finance

mhhe.com/brealey13e

The Role of Project Finance

Project finance is widely used in developing countries to fund power, telecommunications, mining, and transportation projects, but it is also used in the major industrialized countries. In the United States, project finance has been most commonly used to fund power plants. For example, an electric utility company may get together with an industrial company to construct a cogeneration plant that provides electricity to the utility and waste heat to a nearby industrial plant. The utility stands behind the cogeneration project and guarantees its revenue stream. Banks are happy to lend a high proportion of the cost of the project because they know that once the project is up and running, the cash flow is insulated from most of the risks facing normal businesses.[55]

Project financing is costly to arrange,[56] and the project debt usually carries a relatively high interest rate. So why don't companies simply finance the projects by borrowing against

---

[55]There are some interesting regulatory implications to this arrangement. When a utility builds a power plant, it is entitled to a fair return on its investment: Regulators are supposed to set customer charges that will allow the utility to earn its cost of capital. Unfortunately, the cost of capital is not easily measured and is a natural focus for argument in regulatory hearings. But when a utility buys electric power, the cost of capital is rolled into the contract price and treated as an operating cost. In this case, the pass-through to the customer may be less controversial.

[56]Total transaction costs for infrastructure projects average 3% to 5% of the amount invested. See M. Klein, J. So, and B. Shin, "Transaction Costs in Private Infrastructure Projects—Are They Too High?" The World Bank Group, October 1996.

their existing assets? Notice that most of the projects have limited lives and employ established technologies. They generate substantial free cash flow, and there are few options to make profitable follow-on investments. If such investments are funded with project finance, management has little discretion over how the cash flows are used. Instead, the debt-service requirements ensure that the cash must be returned to investors rather than frittered away on unprofitable future ventures.[57]

EXAMPLE 24A.1 • Project Finance for a Power Station

In 2005, the Indonesian government designated a new ultra-supercritical coal-fired power plant in Central Java as a top priority. The $4.2 billion investment was planned to be the first public-private partnership infrastructure project in Indonesia, and a model for future projects.

Electricity generation and distribution in Indonesia is the responsibility of the government-owned company, PLN. To get the Central Java project off the ground, PLN engaged International Finance Corporation (IFC), which is the project-finance arm of the World Bank, to provide advice on structuring the development. IFC worked with key stakeholders, including the PLN, the Ministry of Finance, the newly established Indonesia Infrastructure Guarantee Fund (IIGF), and potential investors to structure a bankable transaction. IFC recommended that the project be set up as a public-private partnership and that a private-sector investor should be appointed to build, own, and operate the plant for its first 25 years. At the end of that period, the operator would transfer the plant to PLN, which would then run it for the remainder of its useful life (a minimum of 40 years).

The first step was to appoint a private-sector investor that was both technically competent and prepared to sell the output of the plant to PLN at a competitive price. Four consortia from Japan and China submitted bids to build and run the project. In 2011, the project was awarded to a special-purpose company, BPI, which was owned in roughly equal proportions by J-Power (a Japanese electric utility company), Itochu Corporation (a Japanese conglomerate with major coal interests), and Adaro Power (part of an Indonesian energy group). Before going ahead with the project, BPI needed to enter into a series of contracts that would protect it against risks that were beyond its control. Foremost among these was a long-term Power Purchase Agreement with PLN. If PLN was unable to meet its obligations, any losses to BPI would be made good by the Indonesia Infrastructure Guarantee Fund, which was backed by the World Bank. These guarantees were buttressed by force majeure clauses that protected BPI from political or natural risks.

BPI needed to hire a consortium of companies to be the engineering, procurement, and construction contractors for the project, and it needed to arrange financing. The security provided by the power purchase agreement and guarantees meant that BPI's equity in the project could be highly levered. Eighty percent of the $3.4 billion cost of the project was in the form of bank loans. Most of this was provided by the Japan Bank for International Cooperation (JBIC), and the remainder came from seven Japanese and two Singaporean banks. JBIC provided a political risk guarantee for the portion financed by these private institutions.

The original plan called for all the agreements to be signed in 2013 and for the plant to be in operation by 2016, but large project financings are rarely plain sailing. The project encountered opposition from landowners and environmental groups. It was not until June 2016 that the project was finally signed off and construction could begin.

---

[57]Because the project is an independent company, it cannot drag down the parent company if something does go badly wrong with the project.

QUESTIONS

1. Explain when it makes sense to use project finance rather than a direct debt issue by the parent company.

2. Look back at the Central Java project. There were many other ways that the project could have been financed. For example, PLN could have invested in the power plant and hired a consortium to run it. Alternatively, the consortium could have owned the power plant directly and funded its cost by a mixture of new borrowing and the sale of shares. What do you think were the advantages of setting up a separately financed company to undertake the project?

**APPENDIX
FURTHER
READING**

Discussions of project finance include:

B. C. Esty, *Modern Project Finance: A Casebook* (New York: John Wiley, 2003).

B. C. Esty, "Returns on Project-Financed Investments: Evolution and Managerial Implications," *Journal of Applied Corporate Finance* 15 (Spring 2002), pp. 71–86.

R. A. Brealey, I. A. Cooper, and M. Habib, "Using Project Finance to Fund Infrastructure Investments," *Journal of Applied Corporate Finance* 9 (Fall 1996), pp. 25–38.

Leasing

Most of us occasionally rent a car, bicycle, or boat. Usually, such personal rentals are short-lived; we may rent a car for a day or week. But in corporate finance, longer-term rentals are common. A rental agreement that extends for a year or more and involves a series of fixed payments is called a lease.

Firms lease as an alternative to buying capital equipment. Trucks and farm machinery are often leased; so are railroad cars, aircraft, and ships. Just about every kind of asset can be leased. For example, two pandas in Washington's National Zoo are leased from the Chinese government at a cost of $500,000 each per year.

Every lease involves two parties. The *user* of the asset is called the *lessee.* The lessee makes periodic payments to the *owner* of the asset, who is called the *lessor.* For example, if you sign an agreement to rent an apartment for a year, you are the lessee and the owner is the lessor.

You often see references to the *leasing industry.* This refers to lessors. (Almost all firms are lessees to at least a minor extent.) Who are the lessors?

Some of the largest lessors are equipment manufacturers. For example, IBM is a large lessor of computers, and Deere is a large lessor of agricultural and construction equipment.

The other two major groups of lessors are banks and independent leasing companies. Leasing companies play an enormous role in the airline business. For example, in 2017 GE Capital Aviation Services, a subsidiary of GE Capital, owned and leased out 1,950 commercial aircraft. The world's airlines rely largely on leasing to finance their fleets.

Leasing companies offer a variety of services. Some act as lease brokers (arranging lease deals) as well as being lessors. Others specialize in leasing automobiles, trucks, and standardized industrial equipment; they succeed because they can buy equipment in quantity; service it efficiently; and if necessary, resell it at a good price.

We begin this chapter by cataloging the different kinds of leases and some of the reasons for their use. Then we show how short-term, or cancelable, lease payments can be interpreted as equivalent annual costs. The remainder of the chapter analyzes long-term leases used as alternatives to debt financing.

25-1 What Is a Lease?

Leases come in many forms, but in all cases the **lessee** (user) promises to make a series of payments to the **lessor** (owner). The lease contract specifies the monthly or semiannual payments, with the first payment usually due as soon as the contract is signed. The payments are generally level, but their time pattern can be tailored to the user's needs. For example, suppose that a manufacturer leases a machine to produce a complex new product. There will be a year's "shakedown" period before volume production starts. In this case, it might be possible to arrange for lower payments during the first year of the lease.

When a lease is terminated, the leased equipment reverts to the lessor. However, the lease agreement often gives the user the option to purchase the equipment or take out a new lease.

Some leases are short-term or can be canceled by the lessee before the end of the contract period. These are generally known as **operating leases.** Others extend over most of the estimated economic life of the asset and cannot be canceled or can be canceled only if the lessor is reimbursed for any losses. These are called **financial, capital,** or **full-payout leases.**

Financial leases are a *source of financing*. Signing a financial lease contract is like borrowing money. There is an immediate cash inflow because the lessee is relieved of having to pay for the asset. But the lessee also assumes a binding obligation to make the payments specified in the lease contract. The user could have borrowed the full purchase price of the asset by accepting a binding obligation to make interest and principal payments to the lender. Thus the cash-flow consequences of leasing and borrowing are similar. In either case, the firm raises cash now and pays it back later. Later in this chapter, we compare leasing and borrowing as financing alternatives.

Leases also differ in the services provided by the lessor. Under a **full-service,** or **rental, lease,** the lessor promises to maintain and insure the equipment and to pay any property taxes due on it. In a **net lease,** the lessee agrees to maintain the asset, insure it, and pay any property taxes. Financial leases are usually net leases.

Most financial leases are arranged for brand new assets. The lessee identifies the equipment, arranges for the leasing company to buy it from the manufacturer, and signs a contract with the leasing company. This is called a **direct lease.** In other cases, the firm sells an asset it already owns and leases it back from the buyer. These **sale and lease-back** arrangements are common in real estate. For example, firm X may wish to raise cash by selling an office or factory but still retain use of the building. It could do this by selling the building for cash to a leasing company and simultaneously signing a long-term lease contract. For example, in 2009 HSBC sold its head office building in London for £772.5 million, or about $1.3 billion. HSBC then leased the building back.[1] Thus legal ownership of the building passed to the new owner, but the right to use it remained with HSBC.

You may also encounter **leveraged leases.** These are financial leases in which the lessor borrows part of the purchase price of the leased asset, using the lease contract as security for the loan. This does not change the lessee's obligations, but it can complicate the lessor's analysis considerably.

25-2 Why Lease?

You hear many suggestions about why companies should lease equipment rather than buy it. Let us look at some sensible reasons and then at four more dubious ones.

Sensible Reasons for Leasing

Short-Term Leases Are Convenient   Suppose you want the use of a car for a week. You could buy one and sell it seven days later, but that would be silly. Quite apart from the fact that registering ownership is a nuisance, you would spend some time selecting a car, negotiating purchase, and arranging insurance. Then at the end of the week you would negotiate resale and cancel the registration and insurance. You might also have a hard time explaining to suspicious would-be buyers why you are selling the car so soon. When you need a car only for a short time, it clearly makes sense to rent it. You save the trouble of registering ownership,

---

[1]This was not the first time that HSBC had leased its head office. In 2007 it sold the building for £1.09 billion and leased it back. It repurchased the building one year later for £838 million.

and you know the effective cost. In the same way, it pays a company to lease equipment that it needs for only a year or two. Of course, this kind of lease is always an operating lease.[2]

Sometimes the cost of short-term rentals may seem prohibitively high, or you may find it difficult to rent at any price. This can happen for equipment that is easily damaged by careless use. The owner knows that short-term users are unlikely to take the same care they would with their own equipment. When the danger of abuse becomes too high, short-term rental markets do not survive. Thus, it is easy enough to buy a Lamborghini Gallardo, provided your pockets are deep enough, but it is much harder to rent one.

Cancellation Options Are Valuable   Some leases that *appear* expensive really are fairly priced once the option to cancel is recognized. We return to this point in the next section.

Maintenance Is Provided   Under a full-service lease, the user receives maintenance and other services. Many lessors are well equipped to provide efficient maintenance. However, bear in mind that these benefits will be reflected in higher lease payments.

Standardization Leads to Low Administrative and Transaction Costs   Suppose that you operate a leasing company that specializes in financial leases for trucks. You are effectively lending money to a large number of firms (the lessees) that may differ considerably in size and risk. But, because the underlying asset is in each case the same salable item (a truck), you can safely "lend" the money (lease the truck) without conducting a detailed analysis of each firm's business. You can also use a simple, standard lease contract. This standardization makes it possible to "lend" small sums of money without incurring large investigative, administrative, or legal costs.

For these reasons leasing is often a relatively cheap source of cash for the small company with few tangible assets to support a debt issue.[3] It offers secure financing on a flexible, piecemeal basis, with lower transaction costs than in a bond or stock issue.

Tax Shields Can Be Used   The lessor owns the leased asset and deducts its depreciation from taxable income. If the depreciation tax shields are more valuable to the lessor than to the asset's user, it may make sense for the lessor to own the equipment and pass on some of the tax benefits to the lessee in the form of low lease payments.

Lessors May Fare Better Than Lenders in Bankruptcy   Lessors in financial leases are in many ways similar to secured lenders, but lessors may fare better in bankruptcy. If a lessee defaults on a lease payment, you might think that the lessor could pick up the leased asset and take it home. But if the bankruptcy court decides that the asset is "essential" to the lessee's business, it *affirms* the lease. Then the bankrupt firm can continue to use the asset. It must still make the lease payments, however. This can be good news for the lessor, who is paid while other creditors cool their heels. Even secured creditors are not paid until the bankruptcy process works itself out.

If the lease is not affirmed but *rejected,* the lessor can recover the leased asset. If it is worth less than the present value of the remaining lease payments, the lessor can try to recoup this loss. But in this case the lessor must get in line with unsecured creditors.

---

[2]The market for used cars suffers from a "lemons" problem since the seller typically knows more about the quality of the car than the would-be buyer. Because off-lease used cars are generally of above-average quality, leasing can help to alleviate this problem. Igal Hendel and Alessandro Lizzeri argue that this may help to explain the prevalence of car leasing. See I. Hendel and A. Lizzeri, "The Role of Leasing under Adverse Selection," *Journal of Political Economy* 110 (February 2002), pp. 113–143. Thomas Gilligan uses a similar argument to analyze the market for aircraft leasing. See T. W. Gilligan, "Lemons and Leases in the Used Business Aircraft Market," *Journal of Political Economy* 112 (2004), pp. 1157–1180.

[3]For evidence that leasing is relatively more common in such firms, see J. R. Graham and M. T. Leary, "A Review of Empirical Capital Structure Research and Directions for the Future," *Annual Review of Financial Economics* 3 (2011), pp. 309–345.

Unfortunately for lessors, there is a third possibility. A lessee in financial distress may be able to renegotiate the lease, forcing the lessor to accept lower lease payments. For example, in 2001 American Airlines (AA) acquired most of the assets of Trans World Airlines (TWA). TWA was bankrupt, and AA's purchase contract was structured so that AA could decide whether to affirm or reject TWA's aircraft leases. AA contacted the lessors and threatened to reject. The lessors realized that rejection would put about 100 leased aircraft back in their laps to sell or re-lease, probably at fire-sale prices. (The market for used aircraft was not strong at the time.) The lessors ended up accepting renegotiated lease rates that were about half what TWA had been paying.[4]

Lessees May Sidestep the Limitation on Debt Interest   The 2017 Tax Cuts and Jobs Act limited the tax deductibility of interest payments to 30% of earnings before interest and depreciation. Companies that are up against this limit may find it convenient to lease new equipment rather than to borrow in order to buy it. The rental payments on the lease are fixed obligations like debt interest, but there is no restriction on the company's ability to deduct them when calculating its tax liability.

Some Dubious Reasons for Leasing

Leasing Avoids Capital Expenditure Controls   In many companies, lease proposals are scrutinized as carefully as capital expenditure proposals, but in others, leasing may enable an operating manager to avoid the approval procedures needed to buy an asset. Although this is a questionable reason for leasing, it may be influential, particularly in the public sector. For example, city hospitals have sometimes found it politically more convenient to lease their medical equipment than to ask the city government to provide funds for purchase.

Leasing Preserves Capital   Leasing companies provide "100% financing"; they advance the full cost of the leased asset. Consequently, they often claim that leasing preserves capital, allowing the firm to save its cash for other things.

But the firm can also "preserve capital" by borrowing money. If Greymare Bus Lines leases a $100,000 bus rather than buying it, it does conserve $100,000 cash. It could also (1) buy the bus for cash and (2) borrow $100,000, using the bus as security. Its bank balance ends up the same whether it leases or buys and borrows. It has the bus in either case, and it incurs a $100,000 liability in either case. What's so special about leasing?

Leases May Be Off-Balance-Sheet Financing   In the United States, the Financial Accounting Standards Board (FASB) distinguishes between financial leases and operating leases. It defines financial leases as leases that meet any one of the following requirements:

1. The lease agreement transfers ownership to the lessee by the time that the lease expires.
2. The lessee can purchase the asset for a bargain price when the lease expires.
3. The lease lasts for at least 75% of the asset's estimated economic life.
4. The present value of the lease payments is at least 90% of the asset's value.

For many years, only financial leases needed to be shown on the balance sheet. Therefore, if a firm could structure a lease so that it was classified as an operating lease, it could understate the true degree of financial leverage. As a result, more than a trillion dollars in lease obligations were not recorded on company balance sheets. In 2016, the FASB moved to plug this gap by introducing new rules that require all leases with terms of more than a year to be shown on

---

[4]If the leases had been rejected, the lessors would have had a claim only on TWA's assets and cash flows, not AA's. The renegotiation of the TWA leases is described in E. Benmelech and N. K. Bergman, "Liquidation Values and the Credibility of Financial Contract Renegotiation: Evidence from U.S. Airlines," *Quarterly Journal of Economics* 123 (2008), pp. 1635–1677.

the balance sheet. From 2019, when the new rules start to come into effect, the opportunities for companies to use leasing as a way to hide their leverage will largely disappear.[5]

25-3 Operating Leases

Remember our discussion of *equivalent annual* costs in Chapter 6? We defined the equivalent annual cost of, say, a machine as the annual rental payment sufficient to cover the present value of all the costs of owning and operating it.

In Chapter 6's examples, the rental payments were hypothetical—just a way of converting a present value to an annual cost. But in the leasing business the payments are real. Suppose you decide to lease a machine tool for one year. What will the rental payment be in a competitive leasing industry? The lessor's equivalent annual cost, of course.

Example of an Operating Lease

The boyfriend of the daughter of the CEO of Establishment Industries takes her to the senior prom in a pearly white stretch limo. The CEO is impressed. He decides Establishment Industries ought to have one for VIP transportation. Establishment's CFO prudently suggests a one-year operating lease instead and approaches Acme Limolease for a quote.

Table 25.1 shows Acme's analysis. Suppose it buys a new limo for $75,000 that it plans to lease out for seven years (years 0 through 6). The table gives Acme's forecasts of operating, maintenance, and administrative costs, the latter including the costs of negotiating the lease, keeping track of payments and paperwork, and finding a replacement lessee when Establishment's year is up. For simplicity, we assume zero inflation and use a 7% real cost of capital.

	Year						
	0	**1**	**2**	**3**	**4**	**5**	**6**
Initial cost	−75	0	0	0	0	0	0
Maintenance costs etc.	−12	−12	−12	−12	−12	−12	−12
Tax shield on costs	+2.52	+2.52	+2.52	+2.52	+2.52	+2.52	+2.52
Depreciation tax shield[a]	+15.75	0	0	0	0	0	0
Total	−68.73	−9.48	−9.48	−9.48	−9.48	−9.48	−9.48
PV at 7% = −113.92[b]							
Break-even rent (level)	−25.01	−25.01	−25.01	−25.01	−25.01	−25.01	−25.01
Tax	+5.25	+5.25	+5.25	+5.25	+5.25	+5.25	+5.25
Break-even rent after tax	−19.75	−19.75	−19.75	−19.75	−19.75	−19.75	−19.75
PV at 7% = −113.92[b]							

❭ **TABLE 25.1**   Calculating the zero-NPV rental rate (or equivalent annual cost) for Establishment Industries' pearly white stretch limo (figures in $ thousands). The break-even rent is set so that the PV of after-tax lease payments equals 113.92, the PV of the after-tax cost of buying and operating the limo.

Note: We assume no inflation and a 7% real cost of capital. The tax rate is 21%.
[a]The depreciation tax shield is calculated assuming that EI can write-off the full amount of the investment immediately. We ignore the special depreciation rules for luxury automobiles.
[b]Note that the first payment of these annuities comes immediately. The standard annuity factor must be multiplied by $1 + r = 1.07$.

---

[5]However, financial and operating leases will continue to be treated differently in the income and cash-flow statements.

We also assume that the limo will have zero salvage value at the end of year 6. The present value of all costs, partially offset by the value of depreciation tax shields,[6] is $113,920. Now, how much does Acme have to charge to break even?

Acme can afford to buy and lease out the limo only if the rental payments forecasted over six years have a present value of at least $113,920. We follow common leasing practice and assume rental payments in advance.[7] The problem, then, is to calculate a six-year annuity due with a present value of $113,920.

As Table 25.1 shows, the required annuity is $19,750.[8] This annuity's present value (after taxes) exactly equals the present value of the after-tax costs of owning and operating the limo. The annuity provides Acme with a competitive expected rate of return (7%) on its investment. Acme could try to charge Establishment Industries more than $19,750, but if the CFO is smart enough to ask for bids from Acme's competitors, the winning lessor will end up receiving this amount.

Remember that Establishment Industries is not compelled to use the limo for more than one year. Acme may have to find several new lessees over the limo's economic life. Even if Establishment continues, it can renegotiate a new lease at whatever rates prevail in the future. Thus Acme does not know what it can charge in year 1 or afterward. If pearly white falls out of favor with teenagers and CEOs, Acme is probably out of luck.

In real life, Acme would have several further things to worry about. For example, how long will the limo stand idle when it is returned at year 1? If idle time is likely before a new lessee is found, then lease rates have to be higher to compensate.[9]

In an operating lease, the *lessor* absorbs these risks, not the lessee. The discount rate used by the lessor must include a premium sufficient to compensate its shareholders for the risks of buying and holding the leased asset. In other words, Acme's 7% real discount rate must cover the risks of investing in stretch limos. (As we see in the next section, risk bearing in *financial* leases is fundamentally different.)

BEYOND THE PAGE

Try It! Leasing
spreadsheets

mhhe.com/brealey13e

Lease or Buy?

If you need a car or limo for only a day or a week you will surely rent it; if you need one for five years you will probably buy it. In between, there is a gray region in which the choice of lease or buy is not obvious. The decision rule should be clear in concept, however: If you need an asset for your business, *buy it if the equivalent annual cost of ownership and operation is less than the best lease rate you can get from an outsider.* In other words, buy if you can rent to yourself cheaper than you can rent from others. (Again we stress that this rule applies to *operating* leases.)

If you plan to use the asset for an extended period, your equivalent annual cost of owning the asset will usually be less than the operating lease rate. The lessor has to mark up the lease rate to cover the costs of negotiating and administering the lease, the foregone revenues when the asset is off-lease and idle, and so on. These costs are avoided when the company buys and rents to itself.

There are two cases in which operating leases may make sense even when the company plans to use an asset for an extended period. First, the lessor may be able to buy and manage

---

[6]The depreciation tax shields are safe cash flows if the tax rate does not change and Acme is sure to pay taxes. If 7% is the right discount rate for the other flows in Table 25.1, the depreciation tax shields deserve a lower rate. A more refined analysis would discount safe depreciation tax shields at an after-tax borrowing or lending rate. See the Appendix to Chapter 19 or the next section of this chapter.

[7]In Section 6–3, the hypothetical rentals were paid *in arrears*.

[8]This is a level annuity because we are assuming that (1) there is no inflation and (2) the services of a six-year-old limo are no different from a brand-new limo's. If users of aging limos see them as obsolete or unfashionable, or if purchase costs of new limos are declining, then lease rates have to decline as limos age. This means that rents follow a *declining* annuity. Early users have to pay more to make up for declining rents later.

[9]If, say, limos were off-lease and idle 20% of the time, lease rates would have to be 25% above those shown in Table 25.1.

the asset at less expense than the lessee. For example, the major truck leasing companies buy thousands of new vehicles every year. That puts them in an excellent bargaining position with truck manufacturers. These companies also run very efficient service operations, and they know how to extract the most salvage value when trucks wear out and it is time to sell them. A small business, or a small division of a larger one, cannot achieve these economies and often finds it cheaper to lease trucks than to buy them.

Second, operating leases often contain useful options. Suppose Acme offers Establishment Industries the following two leases:

1. A one-year lease for $26,000.
2. A six-year lease for $28,000, *with the option to cancel the lease* at any time from year 1 on.[10]

The second lease has obvious attractions. Suppose Establishment's CEO becomes fond of the limo and wants to use it for a second year. If rates increase, lease 2 allows Establishment to continue at the old rate. If rates decrease, Establishment can cancel lease 2 and negotiate a lower rate with Acme or one of its competitors.

Of course, lease 2 is a more costly proposition for Acme: In effect it gives Establishment an insurance policy protecting it from increases in future lease rates. The difference between the costs of leases 1 and 2 is the annual insurance premium. But lessees may happily pay for insurance if they have no special knowledge of future asset values or lease rates. A leasing company acquires such knowledge in the course of its business and can generally sell such insurance at a profit.

Airlines face fluctuating demand for their services and the mix of planes that they need is constantly changing. Most airlines, therefore, lease a proportion of their fleet on a short-term, cancelable basis and are willing to pay a premium to lessors for bearing the cancelation risk. Specialist aircraft lessors are prepared to bear this risk because they are well-placed to find new customers for any aircraft that are returned to them. Aircraft owned by specialist lessors spend less time parked and more time flying than aircraft owned by airlines.[11]

Be sure to check out the options before you sign (or reject) an operating lease.[12]

25-4   Valuing Financial Leases

For operating leases, the decision centers on "lease versus buy." For *financial* leases, the decision amounts to "lease versus borrow." Financial leases extend over most of the economic life of the leased equipment. They are *not* cancelable. The lease payments are fixed obligations equivalent to debt service.

Financial leases make sense when the company is prepared to take on the business risks of owning and operating the leased asset. If Establishment Industries signs a *financial* lease for the stretch limo, it is stuck with that asset. The financial lease is just another way of borrowing money to pay for the limo.

Financial leases do offer special advantages to some firms in some circumstances. However, there is no point in further discussion of these advantages until you know how to value financial lease contracts.

---

[10]Acme might also offer a one-year lease for $28,000 but give the lessee an option to *extend* the lease on the same terms for up to five additional years. This is, of course, identical to lease 2. It doesn't matter whether the lessee has the (put) option to cancel or the (call) option to continue.

[11]A. Gavazza, "Asset Liquidity and Financial Contracts: Evidence from Aircraft Leases," *Journal of Financial Economics* 95 (January 2010), pp. 62–84.

[12]McConnell and Schallheim calculate the value of options in operating leases under various assumptions about asset risk, depreciation rates, etc. See J. J. McConnell and J. S. Schallheim, "Valuation of Asset Leasing Contracts," *Journal of Financial Economics* 12 (August 1983), pp. 237–261.

Example of a Financial Lease

Imagine yourself in the position of Thomas Pierce III, president of Greymare Bus Lines. Your firm was established by your grandfather, who was quick to capitalize on the growing demand for transportation between Widdicombe and nearby townships. The company has owned all its vehicles from the time the company was formed; you are now reconsidering that policy. Your operating manager wants to buy a new bus costing $100,000. The bus will last only eight years before going to the scrap yard. You are convinced that investment in the additional equipment is worthwhile. However, the representative of the bus manufacturer has pointed out that her firm would also be willing to lease the bus to you for eight annual payments of $16,200 each. Greymare would remain responsible for all maintenance, insurance, and operating expenses.

Table 25.2 shows the direct cash-flow consequences of signing the lease contract. (An important indirect effect is considered later.) The consequences are as follows:

1. Greymare does not have to pay for the bus. This is equivalent to a cash inflow of $100,000.

2. Greymare no longer owns the bus and so cannot depreciate it. Therefore it gives up a valuable depreciation tax shield. In Table 25.2, we have assumed that the bus could be written-off immediately for tax.

3. Greymare must pay $16,200 per year for eight years to the lessor. The first payment is due immediately and the last at the end of year 7.

4. However, these lease payments are fully tax-deductible. At a 21% marginal tax rate, the lease payments generate tax shields of $3,400 per year. You could say that the after-tax cost of the lease payment is $16,200 − $3,400 = $12,800.

BEYOND THE PAGE

Try It! Leasing
spreadsheets

mhhe.com/brealey13e

We must emphasize that Table 25.2 assumes that Greymare will pay taxes at the full 21% marginal rate. If the firm were sure to lose money, and therefore pay no taxes, lines 2 and 4 would be left blank. The depreciation tax shields are worth nothing to a firm that pays no taxes, for example.

Table 25.2 also assumes the bus will be worthless when it goes to the scrap yard at the end of year 7. Otherwise there would be an entry for salvage value lost.

Warning: Notice also that we assume for simplicity that all the cash flows occur on just one day each year. So today, Greymare saves the cost of buying the bus, makes the up-front lease payment, and settles up any tax consequences. Exactly 365 days later, it makes a further lease payment and pays $3,400 less in taxes. Elsewhere in the book, we have made similar simplifying assumptions, but leasing is a business with narrow margins; when you need to calculate the value of a lease, it pays to be precise about the exact timing of each cash flow.

	Year							
	0	**1**	**2**	**3**	**4**	**5**	**6**	**7**
Cost of new bus	+100							
Lost depreciation tax shield	−21	0	0	0	0	0	0	0
Lease payment	−16.2	−16.2	−16.2	−16.2	−16.2	−16.2	−16.2	−16.2
Tax shield of lease payment	+3.4	+3.4	+3.4	+3.4	+3.4	+3.4	+3.4	+3.4
Cash flow of lease	+66.2	−12.8	−12.8	−12.8	−12.8	−12.8	−12.8	−12.8

❭**TABLE 25.2**   Cash-flow consequences of the lease contract offered to Greymare Bus Lines (figures in $ thousands)

Who Really Owns the Leased Asset?

To a lawyer or a tax accountant, that would be a silly question: The lessor is clearly the *legal* owner of the leased asset. That is why the lessor is allowed to deduct depreciation from taxable income.

From an *economic* point of view, you might say that the *user* is the real owner because, in a *financial* lease, the user faces the risks and receives the rewards of ownership. Greymare cannot cancel a financial lease. If the new bus turns out to be hopelessly costly and unsuited for Greymare's routes, that is Greymare's problem, not the lessor's. If it turns out to be a great success, the profit goes to Greymare, not the lessor. The success or failure of the firm's business operations does not depend on whether the buses are financed by leasing or some other financial instrument.

In many respects, a financial lease is equivalent to a secured loan. The lessee must make a series of fixed payments; if the lessee fails to do so, the lessor can repossess the asset. Thus, we can think of a balance sheet like this:

Greymare Bus Lines (Figures in $ thousands)			
Bus	100	100	Loan secured by bus
All other assets	1,000	450	Other loans
		550	Equity
Total assets	1,100	1,100	Total liabilities

as being economically equivalent to a balance sheet like this:

Greymare Bus Lines (Figures in $ thousands)			
Bus	100	100	Financial lease
All other assets	1,000	450	Other loans
		550	Equity
Total assets	1,100	1,100	Total liabilities

Having said this, we must immediately qualify. Legal ownership can make a big difference when a financial lease expires because the lessor gets the asset. Once a secured loan is paid off, the user owns the asset free and clear.

Leasing and the Internal Revenue Service

We have already noted that the lessee loses the tax depreciation of the leased asset but can deduct the lease payment in full. The *lessor,* as legal owner, uses the depreciation tax shield but must report the lease payments as taxable rental income.

However, the Internal Revenue Service is suspicious by nature and will not allow the lessee to deduct the entire lease payment unless it is satisfied that the arrangement is a genuine lease and not a disguised installment purchase or secured loan agreement.[13]

Some leases are designed *not* to qualify as a true lease for tax purposes. Suppose a manufacturer finds it convenient to lease a new computer but wants to keep the depreciation tax shields. This is easily accomplished by giving the manufacturer the option to purchase the computer for $1 at the end of the lease.[14] Then the Internal Revenue Service treats the lease as

BEYOND THE PAGE

Leases and the IRS

mhhe.com/brealey13e

---

[13]For example, the IRS will disallow the lease if the lessee has an option to acquire the asset for a nominal sum. The lessee will almost certainly exercise such a bargain-purchase option, leaving the lessor with no chance of future ownership. Special-purpose assets that can only be used by the lessee will also be disqualified because the lessee will end up owning them.

[14]Such leases are known as *$1 out leases.*

an installment sale, and the manufacturer can deduct depreciation and the interest component of the lease payment for tax purposes. But the lease is still a lease for all other purposes.

A First Pass at Valuing a Lease Contract

When we left Thomas Pierce III, president of Greymare Bus Lines, he had just set down in Table 25.2 the cash flows of the financial lease proposed by the bus manufacturer.

These cash flows are typically assumed to be about as safe as the interest and principal payments on a secured loan issued by the lessee. This assumption is reasonable for the lease payments because the lessor is effectively lending money to the lessee. But the various tax shields might carry enough risk to deserve a higher discount rate. For example, Greymare might be confident that it could make the lease payments but not confident that it could earn enough taxable income to use these tax shields. In that case, the cash flows generated by the tax shields would probably deserve a higher discount rate than the borrowing rate used for the lease payments.

A lessee might, in principle, end up using a separate discount rate for each line of Table 25.2, each rate chosen to fit the risk of that line's cash flow. But established, profitable firms usually find it reasonable to simplify by discounting the types of flows shown in Table 25.2 at a single rate based on the rate of interest the firm would pay if it borrowed rather than leased. We assume Greymare's borrowing rate is 10%.

At this point, we must go back to our discussion in the Appendix to Chapter 19 of debt-equivalent flows. When a company lends money, it pays tax on the interest it receives. Its net return is the after-tax interest rate. When a company borrows money, it can deduct interest payments from its taxable income. The net cost of borrowing is the after-tax interest rate. Thus the after-tax interest rate is the effective rate at which a company can transfer debt-equivalent flows from one time period to another. Therefore, to value the incremental cash flows stemming from the lease, we need to discount them at the after-tax interest rate.

Since Greymare can borrow at 10%, we should discount the lease cash flows at $r_D(1 - T_c) = .10(1 - .21) = .079$, or 7.9%. This gives

$$\text{NPV lease} = +66.2 - \frac{12.80}{1.079} - \frac{12.80}{(1.079)^2} - \frac{12.80}{(1.079)^3} - \frac{12.80}{(1.079)^4}$$
$$- \frac{2.80}{(1.079)^5} - \frac{12.80}{(1.079)^6} - \frac{12.80}{(1.079)^7}$$
$$= -.66, \text{ or } - \$660$$

Since the lease has a negative NPV, Greymare is better off buying the bus.

A positive or negative NPV is not an abstract concept; in this case Greymare's shareholders really are $660 poorer if the company leases. Let us now check how this situation comes about.

Look once more at Table 25.2. The lease cash flows are

	Year							
	0	1	2	3	4	5	6	7
Lease cash flows, thousands	+66.20	−12.80	−12.80	−12.80	−12.80	−12.80	−12.80	−12.80

The lease payments are contractual obligations like the principal and interest payments on secured debt. Thus, you can think of the incremental lease cash flows in years 1 through 7 as the "debt service" of the lease. Table 25.3 shows a loan with *exactly* the same debt service as

	Year							
	0	**1**	**2**	**3**	**4**	**5**	**6**	**7**
Amount borrowed	66.86	59.34	51.23	42.48	33.04	22.85	11.86	0
Interest paid at 10%		−6.69	−5.93	−5.12	−4.25	−3.30	−2.29	−1.19
Interest tax shield at 21%		+1.40	+1.25	+1.08	+0.89	+0.69	+0.48	+0.25
Interest paid after tax		−5.28	−4.69	−4.05	−3.36	−2.61	−1.81	−0.94
Principal repaid		−7.52	−8.11	−8.75	−9.44	−10.19	−10.99	−11.86
Net cash flow of equivalent loan	66.86	−12.80	−12.80	−12.80	−12.80	−12.80	−12.80	−12.80

❭**TABLE 25.3**   Details of the equivalent loan to the lease offered to Greymare Bus Lines (figures in $ thousands; cash outflows shown with negative sign)

the lease. The initial amount of the loan is $66.86 thousand. If Greymare borrowed this sum, it would need to pay interest in the first year of .10 × 66.86 = 6.69 and would *receive* a tax shield on this interest of .21 × 6.69 = 1.40. Greymare could then repay 7.52 of the loan, leaving a net cash outflow of 12.80 (exactly the same as for the lease) in year 1 and an outstanding debt at the start of year 2 of 59.34.

As you walk through the calculations in Table 25.3, you see that it costs exactly the same to service a loan that brings an immediate inflow of 66.86 as it does to service the lease, which brings in only 66.20. That is why we say that the lease has a net present value of 66.86 − 66.20 = −.66, or −$660. If Greymare leases the bus rather than raising an *equivalent loan,* there will be $660 less in Greymare's bank account.

Our example illustrates two general points about leases and equivalent loans. First, if you can devise a borrowing plan that gives the same cash flow as the lease in every future period but a higher immediate cash flow, then you should not lease. If, however, the equivalent loan provides the same future cash outflows as the lease but a lower immediate inflow, then leasing is the better choice.

Second, our example suggests two ways to value a lease:

1. *Hard way.* Construct a table like Table 25.3 showing the equivalent loan.

2. *Easy way.* Discount the lease cash flows at the *after-tax* interest rate that the firm would pay on an equivalent loan. Both methods give the same answer—in our case an NPV of −$660.[15]

The Story So Far

We concluded that the lease contract offered to Greymare Bus Lines was *not* attractive because the lease provided $660 less financing than the equivalent loan. The underlying principle is as follows: A financial lease is superior to buying and borrowing if the financing provided by the lease exceeds the financing generated by the equivalent loan.

The principle implies this formula:

$$\text{Net value of lease} = \text{initial financing provided} - \sum_{t=1}^{N} \frac{\text{lease cash flow}}{[1 + r_D (1 - T_c)]^t}$$

---

[15]Sometimes the easy way is not possible. For example, the company's tax rate may vary over the period of the lease. In that case, you will need to fall back on the hard way. Later in the section, we will encounter another case where you will need to construct the equivalent loan.

where N is the length of the lease. Initial financing provided equals the cost of the leased asset minus any immediate lease payment or other cash outflow attributable to the lease.[16]

Notice that the value of the lease is its incremental value relative to borrowing via an equivalent loan. A positive lease value means that *if* you acquire the asset, lease financing is advantageous. It does not prove you should acquire the asset.

However, sometimes favorable lease terms rescue a capital investment project. Suppose that Greymare had decided *against* buying a new bus because the NPV of the $100,000 investment was −$5,000 assuming normal financing. The bus manufacturer could rescue the deal by offering a lease with a value of, say, +$8,000. By offering such a lease, the manufacturer would in effect cut the price of the bus to $92,000, giving the bus-lease package a positive value to Greymare. We could express this more formally by treating the lease's NPV as a favorable financing side effect that adds to project adjusted present value (APV):[17]

$$APV = NPV \text{ of project} + NPV \text{ of lease}$$
$$= -5,000 + 8,000 = +\$3,000$$

Notice also that our formula applies to net financial leases. Any insurance, maintenance, and other operating costs picked up by the lessor have to be evaluated separately and added to the value of the lease. If the asset has salvage value at the end of the lease, that value should be taken into account also.

Suppose, for example, that the bus manufacturer offers to provide routine maintenance that would otherwise cost $2,000 per year after tax. However, Mr. Pierce reconsiders and decides that the bus will probably be worth $10,000 after eight years. (Previously he assumed the bus would be worthless at the end of the lease.) Then the value of the lease increases by the present value of the maintenance savings and decreases by the present value of the lost salvage value.

Maintenance and salvage value are harder to predict than the cash flows shown in Table 25.2, and normally deserve a higher discount rate. Suppose that Mr. Pierce uses 12%. Then the maintenance savings are worth

$$\sum_{t=0}^{7} \frac{2000}{(1.12)^t} = \$11,100$$

The lost salvage value is worth $10,000/(1.12)^8 = \$4,000$.[18] Remember that we previously calculated the value of the lease as −$660. The revised value is, therefore, −660 + 11,100 − 4,000 = $6,550. Now the lease looks like a good deal.

Financial Leases When There Is No Interest Tax Shield

In Table 25.3, we devised a loan that Greymare could take out that had exactly the same cash flows as the lease. In that table, we assumed that Greymare could deduct the interest on this loan when it calculated its taxable income. But the 2017 Tax Cuts and Jobs Act limited the amount of interest that companies can deduct to 30% of earnings before interest and depreciation. Suppose that Greymare has borrowed heavily and cannot deduct additional interest payments for tax. This restriction applies to interest expense on borrowing by Greymare but not to lease payments, even though they are equivalent to debt service. Therefore, leasing the bus allows Greymare to sidestep the restriction on interest deductibility.

---

[16]The principles behind lease valuation were originally set out in S. C. Myers, D. A. Dill, and A. J. Bautista, "Valuation of Financial Lease Contracts," *Journal of Finance* 31 (June 1976), pp. 799–819; and J. R. Franks and S. D. Hodges, "Valuation of Financial Lease Contracts: A Note," *Journal of Finance* 33 (May 1978), pp. 657–669.

[17]See Chapter 19 for the general definition and description of APV.

[18]For simplicity, we have assumed that maintenance expenses are paid at the start of the year and that salvage value is measured at the *end* of year 8.

If Greymare borrows to finance the bus, it will not enjoy any interest tax shields until its earnings recover. So the cost of debt during this period is no longer equal to the after-tax interest rate, and it no longer makes sense to value the lease cash flows by discounting them at this rate. Since the easy way to value the lease doesn't work, you need to turn to the hard way and calculate how much Greymare could borrow if it set aside the future lease cash flows to service the loan. If the amount that Greymare could borrow is less than the immediate cash inflow on the lease, then leasing is the better option.[19]

25-5   When Do Financial Leases Pay?

We have examined the value of a lease from the viewpoint of the lessee. The lessor's criterion is simply the reverse. As long as lessor and lessee are in the same tax bracket, every cash outflow to the lessee is an inflow to the lessor, and vice versa. In our numerical example, the bus manufacturer would project cash flows in a table like Table 25.2, but with the signs reversed. The value of the lease to the bus manufacturer would be

$$\text{Value of lease to lessor} = -66.20 + \frac{12.80}{1.079} + \frac{12.80}{(1.079)^2} + \frac{12.80}{(1.079)^3} + \frac{12.80}{(1.079)^4}$$

$$+ \frac{12.80}{(1.079)^5} + \frac{12.80}{(1.079)^6} + \frac{12.80}{(1.079)^7}$$

$$= +.66 \text{ or } \$660$$

In this case, the values to lessee and lessor exactly offset ($-\$660 + \$660 = 0$). The lessor can win only at the lessee's expense.

But both lessee and lessor can win if their tax rates differ. Suppose that Greymare paid no tax ($T_c = 0$). Then the only cash flows of the bus lease would be

	Year							
	0	1	2	3	4	5	6	7
Cost of new bus	+100							
Lease payment	−16.2	−16.2	−16.2	−16.2	−16.2	−16.2	−16.2	−16.2

These flows would be discounted at 10% because $r_D(1 - T_c) = r_D$ when $T_c = 0$. The value of the lease is

$$\text{Value of lease} = +100 - \sum_{t=0}^{7} \frac{16.2}{(1.10)^t}$$

$$= +100 - 95.07 = +4.93, \text{ or } \$4,930$$

In this case, there is a net gain of $660 to the lessor (who has the 21% tax rate) *and* a net gain of $4,930 to the lessee (who pays zero tax). This mutual gain is at the expense of the government. On the one hand, the government gains from the lease contract because it can tax the lease payments. On the other hand, the contract allows the lessor to take advantage of depreciation and interest tax shields that are of no use to the lessee. However, because the

[19]The trick in doing this is to work back from the final year, when the loan will be fully paid off. The amount of the loan at the *start* of that year plus the final interest payment, less any tax shield, can then be set equal to the final lease payment. If you are still not sure how to calculate the equivalent loan, take a look at the Beyond the Page Spreadsheet.

depreciation is accelerated and the interest rate is positive, the government suffers a net loss in the present value of its tax receipts as a result of the lease.

Now you should begin to understand the circumstances in which the government incurs a loss on the lease and the other two parties gain. Other things being equal, the combined gains to lessor and lessee are highest when

- The lessor's tax rate is substantially higher than the lessee's.
- The depreciation tax shield is received early in the lease period.
- The lease period is long and the lease payments are concentrated toward the end of the period.
- The interest rate r_D is high—if it were zero, there would be no advantage in present value terms to postponing tax.

Leasing around the World

In most developed economies, leasing is widely used to finance investment in plant and equipment.[20] But there are important differences in the treatment of long-term financial leases for tax and accounting purposes. For example, some countries allow the lessor to use depreciation tax shields, just as in the United States. In other countries, the lessee claims depreciation deductions. Accounting usually follows suit.

A number of *big-ticket* leases are cross-border deals. Cross-border leasing can be attractive when the lessor is located in a country that offers generous depreciation allowances. The ultimate cross-border transaction occurs when *both* the lessor *and* the lessee can claim depreciation deductions. Ingenious leasing companies look for such opportunities to *double-dip*. Tax authorities look for ways to stop them.[21]

25-6   Leveraged Leases

Big-ticket leases are usually *leveraged leases.* The structure of a leveraged lease is summarized in Figure 25.1. In this example, the leasing company (or a syndicate of several leasing companies) sets up a special-purpose entity (SPE) to buy and lease a commercial aircraft. The SPE raises up to 80% of the cost of the aircraft by borrowing, usually from insurance companies or other financial institutions. The leasing company puts up the remaining 20% as the equity investment in the lease.

Once the lease is up and running, lease payments begin, and depreciation and interest tax shields are generated. All (or almost all) of the lease payments go to debt service. The leasing company gets no cash inflows until the debt is paid off, but does get all depreciation and interest deductions, which generate tax losses that can be used to shield other income.

By the end of the lease, the debt is paid off and the tax shields exhausted. At this point, the lessee has the option to purchase the aircraft. The leasing company gets the purchase price if the lessee's purchase option is exercised and takes back the aircraft otherwise. (In some cases, the lessee also has an early buyout option partway through the term of the lease.)

The debt in a leveraged lease is *nonrecourse.* The lenders have first claim on the lease payments and on the aircraft if the lessee can't make scheduled payments but no claim on the leasing company. Thus, the lenders must depend solely on the airline lessee's credit and on the airplane as collateral.

---

[20]For example, in 2016 leasing in Europe accounted for 26% of new investment in vehicles and equipment (**www.leaseurope.org**).
[21]Currently in the United States, the tax authorities seem to be winning. The American Jobs Creation Act (JOBS) of 2004 eliminated much of the profit from cross-border leases.

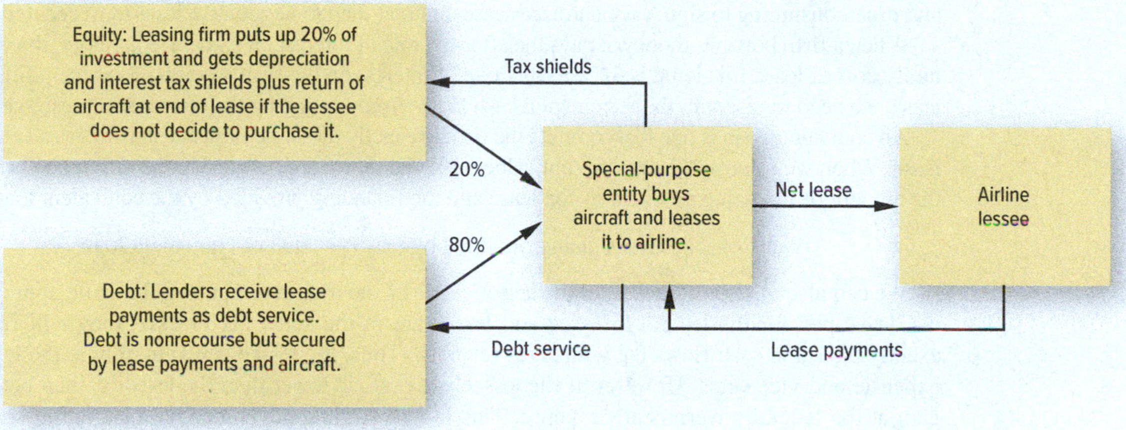

> **FIGURE 25.1**   Structure of a leveraged lease for commercial aircraft

So the leasing company puts up only 20% of the money, gets 100% of the tax shields, but is not on the hook if the lease transaction falls apart. Does this sound like a great deal? Don't jump to that conclusion, because the lenders will demand a higher interest rate in exchange for giving up recourse. In efficient debt markets, paying extra interest to avoid recourse should be a zero-NPV transaction—otherwise, one side of the deal would get a free ride at the expense of the other. Nevertheless, nonrecourse debt, as part of the overall structure shown in Figure 25.1, is a customary and convenient financing method.[22]

---

[22]Leveraged leases have special tax and accounting requirements, which we won't go into here. Also, the equity investment in leveraged leases can be tricky to value because the stream of after-tax cash flows changes sign more than once. That is no problem if you use the NPV rule, but it causes difficulties if you wish to calculate the internal rate of return (IRR). This requires use of modified internal rates of return, if you insist on using IRRs. We discussed multiple IRRs and modified IRRs in Section 5-3. Also take a look at Problem 24 at the end of this chapter.

A lease is just an extended rental agreement. The owner of the equipment (the *lessor*) allows the user (the *lessee*) to operate the equipment in exchange for regular lease payments.

SUMMARY

There is a wide variety of possible arrangements. Short-term, cancelable leases are known as *operating leases*. In these leases, the lessor bears the risks of ownership. Long-term, noncancelable leases are called *financial, capital,* or *full-payout* leases. In these leases the lessee bears the risks. Financial leases are *sources of financing* for assets the firm wishes to acquire and use for an extended period.

The key to understanding operating leases is equivalent annual cost. In a competitive leasing market, the annual operating lease payment will be forced down to the lessor's equivalent annual cost. Operating leases are attractive to equipment users if the lease payment is less than the *user's* equivalent annual cost of buying the equipment. Operating leases make sense when the user needs the equipment only for a short time, when the lessor is better able to bear the risks of obsolescence, or when the lessor can offer a good deal on maintenance. Remember too that operating leases often have valuable options attached.

A financial lease extends over most of the economic life of the leased asset and cannot be canceled by the lessee. Signing a financial lease is like signing a secured loan to finance purchase of the leased asset. With financial leases, the choice is not "lease versus buy" but "lease versus borrow."

Many companies have sound reasons for financing via leases. For example, companies that are not paying taxes can usually strike a favorable deal with a tax-paying lessor. Also, it may be less costly and time-consuming to sign a standardized lease contract than to negotiate a long-term secured loan.

When a firm borrows money, it pays the after-tax rate of interest on its debt. Therefore, the opportunity cost of lease financing is the after-tax rate of interest on the firm's bonds. To value a financial lease, we need to discount the incremental cash flows from leasing by the after-tax interest rate.

An equivalent loan is one that commits the firm to exactly the same future cash flows as a financial lease. When we calculate the net present value of the lease, we are measuring the difference between the amount of financing provided by the lease and the financing provided by the equivalent loan:

$$\text{Value of lease} = \text{financing provided by lease} - \text{value of equivalent loan}$$

We can also analyze leases from the lessor's side of the transaction, using the same approaches we developed for the lessee. If lessee and lessor are in the same tax bracket, they will receive exactly the same cash flows but with signs reversed. Thus, the lessee can gain only at the lessor's expense, and vice versa. However, if the lessee's tax rate is lower than the lessor's, then both can gain at the federal government's expense. This is a tax-timing advantage because the lessor gets interest and depreciation tax shields early in the lease.

Leveraged leases are three-way transactions that include lenders as well as the lessor and lessee. Lenders advance up to 80% of the cost of the leased equipment and lessors put in the rest as an equity investment. The lenders get first claim on the lease payments and on the asset but have no recourse to the equity lessors if the lessee can't pay. The lessor's return comes mostly from interest and depreciation tax shields early in the lease and the value of the leased asset at the end of the lease. Leveraged leases are common in big-ticket, cross-border lease-financing transactions.

FURTHER READING

A useful general reference on leasing is:

P. K. Nevitt and F. J. Fabozzi, *Equipment Leasing,* 4th ed. (Hoboken, NJ: John Wiley & Sons, 2008).

Smith and Wakeman discuss the economic motives for leasing:

C. W. Smith Jr. and L. M. Wakeman, "Determinants of Corporate Leasing Policy," *Journal of Finance* 40 (July 1985), pp. 895–908.

The options embedded in many operating leases are discussed in:

J. J. McConnell and J. S. Schallheim, "Valuation of Asset Leasing Contracts," *Journal of Financial Economics* 12 (August 1983), pp. 237–261.

S. R. Grenadier, "Valuing Lease Contracts: A Real Options Approach," *Journal of Financial Economics* 38 (July 1995), pp. 297–331.

S. R. Grenadier, "An Equilibrium Analysis of Real Estate Leases," *Journal of Business* 78 (2005), pp. 1173–1214.

PROBLEM SETS

 **Select problems are available in McGraw-Hill's *Connect*. Please see the preface for more information.**

1. **Types of lease*** The following terms are often used to describe leases:
   a. Direct
   b. Full-service
   c. Operating
   d. Financial
   e. Net

    f. Leveraged

    g. Sale and lease-back

Match one or more of these terms with each of the following statements:

    A. The initial lease period is shorter than the economic life of the asset.

    B. The initial lease period is long enough for the lessor to recover the cost of the asset.

    C. The lessor provides maintenance and insurance.

    D. The lessee provides maintenance and insurance.

    E. The lessor buys the equipment from the manufacturer.

    F. The lessor buys the equipment from the prospective lessee.

    G. The lessor finances the lease contract by issuing debt and equity claims against it.

2. **Reasons for leasing** Some of the following reasons for leasing are rational. Others are irrational or assume imperfect or inefficient capital markets. Which of the following reasons are the rational ones?

    a. The lessee's need for the leased asset is only temporary.

    b. Specialized lessors are better able to bear the risk of obsolescence.

    c Leasing provides 100% financing and thus preserves capital.

    d. Leasing allows firms with low marginal tax rates to "sell" depreciation tax shields.

    e. Leasing increases earnings per share.

    f. Leasing reduces the transaction cost of obtaining external financing.

    g. Leasing avoids restrictions on capital expenditures.

    h. Leasing is attractive when interest payments exceed 30% of EBITDA and there are no interest tax shields from additional borrowing.

3. **Lease treatment in bankruptcy** What happens if a bankrupt lessee affirms the lease? What happens if the lease is rejected?

4. **Lease treatment in bankruptcy** How does the position of an equipment lessor differ from the position of a secured lender when a firm falls into bankruptcy? Assume that the secured loan would have the leased equipment as collateral. Which is better protected, the lease or the loan? Does your answer depend on the value of the leased equipment if it were sold or re-leased?

5. **Lease characteristics*** True or false?

    a. Lease payments are usually made at the start of each period. Thus, the first payment is usually made as soon as the lease contract is signed.

    b. A sensible motive for financial leases is that they provide off-balance-sheet financing.

    c. The cost of capital for a financial lease is the pretax interest rate the company would pay on a bank loan.

    d. An equivalent loan's principal plus after-tax interest payments exactly match the after-tax cash flows of the lease.

    e. A financial lease should not be undertaken unless it provides more financing than the equivalent loan.

    f. It makes sense for firms that pay no taxes to lease from firms that do.

    g. Other things equal, the net tax advantage of leasing increases as nominal interest rates increase.

6. **Operating leases** Explain why the following statements are true:

    a. In a competitive leasing market, the annual operating lease payment equals the lessor's equivalent annual cost.

    b. Operating leases are attractive to equipment users if the lease payment is less than the user's equivalent annual cost.

7. **Operating leases*** Acme has branched out to rentals of office furniture to start-up companies. Consider a $3,000 desk. Desks last for six years and can be depreciated immediately. What is the break-even operating lease rate for a new desk? Assume that lease rates for old and new desks are the same and that Acme's pretax administrative costs are $400 per desk in each of years 1 to 6. The cost of capital is 9% and the tax rate is 21%. Lease payments are made in advance, that is, at the start of each year. The inflation rate is zero.

8. **Inflation and operating leases** In Problem 7, we assumed identical lease rates for old and new desks.

   a. How does the initial break-even lease rate change if the expected inflation rate is 5% per year? Assume that the real cost of capital does not change. (*Hint:* Look at the discussion of equivalent annual costs in Chapter 6.)

   b. How does your answer to part (a) change if wear and tear force Acme to cut lease rates by 10% in real terms for every year of a desk's age?

9. **Technological change and operating leases** Look at Table 25.1. How would the initial break-even operating lease rate change if rapid technological change in limo manufacturing reduces the costs of new limos by 5% per year? (*Hint:* We discussed technological change and equivalent annual costs in Chapter 6.)

10. **Valuing financial leases** Look again at Problem 7. Suppose a blue-chip company requests a six-year financial lease for a $3,000 desk. The company has just issued five-year notes at an interest rate of 6% per year. What is the break-even rate in this case? Assume administrative costs drop to $200 per year. Explain why your answers to Problem 7 and this question differ.

11. **Valuing financial leases*** Suppose that National Waferonics has before it a proposal for a four-year financial lease of a Waferooney machine. The firm constructs a table like Table 25.2. The bottom line of its table shows the lease cash flows:

	Year 0	Year 1	Year 2	Year 3
Lease cash flow	+62,000	−26,800	−22,200	−17,600

   These flows reflect the cost of the machine, depreciation tax shields, and the after-tax lease payments. Ignore salvage value. Assume the firm could borrow at 10% and faces a 21% marginal tax rate.

   a. What is the value of the equivalent loan?

   b. What is the value of the lease?

   c. Suppose the machine's NPV under normal financing is −$5,000. Should National Waferonics invest? Should it sign the lease?

12. **Valuing Financial Leases** Look again at the National Waferonics lease in Problem 11. Suppose that National Waferonics is highly levered and is unable to deduct further interest payments for tax.

   a. Does this make a lease more or less attractive?

   b. Recalculate the NPV of the lease by constructing an equivalent loan. (*Hint:* Start with the final year. The final repayment of the loan with interest should be set equal to the cash flow on the lease.)

Questions 14 to 17 all refer to Greymare's bus lease. To answer them you may find it helpful to use the Beyond the Page live Excel spreadsheets in Connect.

13. **Valuing financial leases** Look again at the bus lease described in Table 25.2.

   a. What is the value of the lease if Greymare's marginal tax rate is $T_c = .30$?

   b. What would the lease value be if the tax rate is 21%, but for tax purposes, the initial investment had to be written off in equal amounts over years 1 through 5?

BEYOND THE PAGE

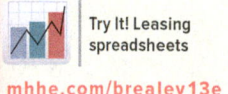

Try It! Leasing
spreadsheets

mhhe.com/brealey13e

14. **Valuing financial leases** In Section 25-5, we showed that the lease offered to Greymare Bus Lines had a positive NPV of $660 if Greymare paid no tax and a +$4,930 NPV to a lessor paying 21% tax. What is the minimum lease payment the lessor could accept under these assumptions? What is the maximum amount that Greymare could pay?

15. **Valuing financial leases** In Section 25-5, we listed four circumstances in which there are potential gains from leasing. Check them out by conducting a sensitivity analysis on the Greymare Bus Lines lease, assuming that Greymare does not pay tax. Try, in turn, (a) a lessor tax rate of 50% (rather than 21%), (b) straight-line depreciation in years 1 to 6 (rather than immediate expensing), (c) a four-year lease with four annual rentals (rather than an eight-year lease), and (d) an interest rate of 20% (rather than 10%). In each case, find the minimum rental that would satisfy the lessor and calculate the NPV to the lessee.

16. **Valuing financial leases** In Section 25-5 we stated that if the interest rate were zero, there would be no advantage in postponing tax and therefore no advantage in leasing. Value the Greymare Bus Lines lease with an interest rate of zero. Assume that Greymare does not pay tax. Can you devise any lease terms that would make both a lessee and a lessor happy? (If you can, we would like to hear from you.)

17. **Valuing financial leases** A lease with a varying rental schedule is known as a structured lease. Try structuring the Greymare Bus Lines lease to increase value to the lessee while preserving the value to the lessor. Assume that Greymare does not pay tax. (*Note:* In practice, the tax authorities will allow some structuring of rental payments but might be unhappy with some of the schemes you devise.)

18. **Valuing financial leases** Nodhead College needs a new computer. It can either buy it for $250,000 or lease it from Compulease. The lease terms require Nodhead to make six annual payments (prepaid) of $62,000. Nodhead pays no tax. Compulease pays tax at 30%. Compulease can depreciate the computer for tax purposes straight-line over five years. The computer will have no residual value at the end of year 5. The interest rate is 8%.

    a. What is the NPV of the lease for Nodhead College?

    b. What is the NPV for Compulease?

    c. What is the overall gain from leasing?

19. **Valuing financial leases** The Safety Razor Company has a large tax-loss carry-forward and does not expect to pay taxes for another 10 years. The company is therefore proposing to lease $100,000 of new machinery. The lease terms consist of eight equal lease payments prepaid annually. The lessor can write the machinery off over seven years using straight-line depreciation. There is no salvage value at the end of the machinery's economic life. The tax rate is 30%, and the rate of interest is 10%. Wilbur Occam, the president of Safety Razor, wants to know the maximum lease payment that his company should be willing to make and the minimum payment that the lessor is likely to accept. Can you help him?

20. **Nonrecourse debt** Lenders to leveraged leases hold nonrecourse debt. What does "nonrecourse" mean? What are the benefits and costs of nonrecourse debt to the equity investors in the lease?

21. **Leveraged leases** How does a leveraged lease differ from an ordinary, long-term financial lease? List the key differences.

22. **Leveraged leases** How would the lessee in Figure 25.1 evaluate the NPV of the lease? Sketch the correct valuation procedure. Then suppose that the equity lessor wants to evaluate the lease. Again sketch the correct procedure. (*Hint:* APV. How would you calculate the combined value of the lease to lessee and lessor?)

CHALLENGE

23. **Valuing leases** Magna Charter has been asked to operate a Beaver bush plane for a mining company exploring north and west of Fort Liard. Magna will have a firm one-year contract with the mining company and expects that the contract will be renewed for the five-year

duration of the exploration program. If the mining company renews at year 1, it will commit to use the plane for four more years.

Magna Charter has the following choices:

- Buy the plane for $500,000.

- Take a one-year operating lease for the plane. The lease rate is $118,000, paid in advance.

- Arrange a five-year, noncancelable financial lease at a rate of $75,000 per year, paid in advance.

These are net leases; all operating costs are absorbed by Magna Charter.

How would you advise Agnes Magna, the charter company's CEO? For simplicity assume five-year, straight-line depreciation for tax purposes. The company's tax rate is 30%. The weighted-average cost of capital for the bush-plane business is 14%, but Magna can borrow at 9%. The expected inflation rate is 4%.

Ms. Magna thinks the plane will be worth $300,000 after five years. But if the contract with the mining company is not renewed (there is a 20% probability of this outcome at year 1), the plane will have to be sold on short notice for $400,000.

If Magna Charter takes the five-year financial lease and the mining company cancels at year 1, Magna can sublet the plane, that is, rent it out to another user.

Make additional assumptions as necessary.

24. **Leasing and IRRs** Reconstruct Table 25.2 as a leveraged lease, assuming that the lessor borrows $80,000, 80% of the cost of the bus, nonrecourse at an interest rate of 11%. All lease payments are devoted to debt service (interest and principal) until the loan is paid off. Assume that the bus is worth $10,000 at the end of the lease. Calculate after-tax cash flows on the lessor's equity investment of $20,000. What is the IRR of the equity cash flows? Is there more than one IRR? How would you value the lessor's equity investment?

25. **Valuing leases** Suppose that the Greymare lease gives the company the option to purchase the bus at the end of the lease period for $1. How would this affect the tax treatment of the lease? Recalculate its value to Greymare and the manufacturer. Could the lease payments be adjusted to provide a positive NPV to both parties?

CHAPTER

26

Managing Risk

Life is punctuated by unforeseen and unforeseeable shocks. Wars, banking and currency crises, political upheavals, pandemics, and natural catastrophes such as earthquakes and floods can all cause severe economic disruption. For example, if you want to make your hair stand on end, look at Table 26.1, which lists some of the greatest macroeconomic disasters in the past 100 years.[1]

Major catastrophes such as those in Table 26.1 are, fortunately, rare. However, most companies are hit from time to time by potentially ruinous shocks. Good managers try to ensure that their companies are not overwhelmed by them. They check that their company has reserve borrowing power to tide them over difficult periods, they maintain sufficient liquid assets to protect the firm from a possible banking or currency crisis, and they ensure that the firm is not overly dependent on a single source of materials or a single outlet for its products.

Most of the time we take risk as God-given. A company's cash flow is exposed to changes in demand, raw material costs, technology, and a seemingly endless list of other uncertainties. There's nothing the manager can do about it other than to ensure that the business is not overwhelmed.

That's not wholly true. The manager can avoid some risks. We have already come across one way to do so: Firms can use real options to provide flexibility. For example, a petrochemical plant that is designed to use either oil or natural gas as a feedstock reduces the risk of an unfavorable shift in the price of raw materials. As another example, think of a company that employs standard machine tools rather than custom machinery and thereby lowers the cost of bailing out if its products do not sell. In other words, the standard machinery provides the firm with a valuable abandonment option.

We covered real options in Chapter 22. This chapter explains how companies also use financial contracts to protect against various hazards. We discuss the pros and cons of corporate insurance policies that protect against specific risks, such as fire, floods, or environmental damage. We then describe forward and futures contracts, which can be used to lock in the future price of commodities such as oil, copper, or soybeans. Financial forward and futures contracts allow the firm to lock in the prices of financial assets such as interest rates or foreign exchange rates. We also describe swaps, which are packages of forward contracts.

Most of this chapter describes how financial contracts may be used to reduce business risks. But why bother? Why should shareholders care whether the company's future profits are linked to future changes in interest rates, exchange rates, or commodity prices? We start the chapter with that question.

---

[1] R. Barro and J. F. Ursua, "Rare Macroeconomic Disasters," *Annual Review of Economics* 4 (2012), pp. 83–109.

Country	Event	Trough Year	Decline in Real GDP per Head (%)
Argentina	Currency crisis	2002	−22
Chile	Pinochet revolution	1975	−24
Germany	Aftermath of WWII	1946	−74
Greece	WWII	1942	−66
Indonesia	Asian currency crisis	1999	−16
Japan	WWII	1944	−50
Russia	Revolution	1921	−62
Spain	Civil war	1938	−31
United States	Great depression	1933	−29
Venezuela	Maduro government	2018	−62Est

❭**TABLE 26.1**   **Major economic disasters**

26-1   Why Manage Risk?

Financial transactions undertaken *solely* to reduce risk do not add value in perfect and efficient markets. Why not? There are two basic reasons.

- *Reason 1: Hedging is a zero-sum game.* A corporation that insures or hedges a risk does not eliminate it. It simply passes the risk to someone else. For example, suppose that a heating-oil distributor contracts with a refiner to buy all of next winter's heating-oil deliveries at a fixed price. This contract is a *zero-sum game* because the refiner loses what the distributor gains, and vice versa.[2] If next winter's price of heating oil turns out to be unusually high, the distributor wins from having locked in a below-market price, but the refiner is forced to sell below the market. Conversely, if the price of heating oil is unusually *low,* the refiner wins because the distributor is forced to buy at the high fixed price. Of course, neither party knows next winter's price at the time that the deal is struck, but they consider the range of possible prices, and in an efficient market they negotiate terms that are fair (zero-NPV) on both sides of the bargain.

- *Reason 2: Investors' do-it-yourself alternative.* Corporations cannot increase the value of their shares by undertaking transactions that investors can easily do on their own. When the shareholders in the heating-oil distributor made their investment, they were presumably aware of the risks of the business. If they did not want to be exposed to the ups and downs of energy prices, they could have protected themselves in several ways. Perhaps they bought shares in both the distributor and refiner, and do not care whether one wins next winter at the other's expense.

Of course, shareholders can adjust their exposure only when companies keep investors fully informed of the transactions that they have made. For example, when a group of European central banks announced in 1999 that they would limit their sales of gold, the gold price immediately shot up. Investors in gold-mining shares rubbed their hands at the prospect of rising profits. But when they discovered that some mining companies had protected

---

[2]In game theory, "zero-sum" means that the payoffs to all players add up to zero, so that one player can win only at the others' expense.

themselves against price fluctuations and would *not* benefit from the price rise, the hand-rubbing by investors turned to hand-wringing.[3]

Some stockholders of these gold-mining companies wanted to make a bet on rising gold prices; others didn't. But all of them gave the same message to management. The first group said, "Don't hedge! I'm happy to bear the risk of fluctuating gold prices, because I think gold prices will increase." The second group said, "Don't hedge! I'd rather do it myself." We have seen this do-it-yourself principle before. Think of other ways that the firm could reduce risk. It could do so by diversifying, for example, by acquiring another firm in an unrelated industry. But we know that investors can diversify on their own, and so diversification by corporations is redundant.[4]

Corporations can also lessen risk by borrowing less. But we showed in Chapter 17 that just reducing financial leverage does not make shareholders any better or worse off, because they can instead reduce financial risk by borrowing less (or lending more) in their personal accounts. Modigliani and Miller (MM) proved that a corporation's debt policy is irrelevant in perfect financial markets. We could extend their proof to say that risk management is also irrelevant in perfect financial markets.

Of course, in Chapter 18, we decided that debt policy *is* relevant, not because MM were wrong, but because of other things, such as taxes, agency problems, and costs of financial distress. The same line of argument applies here. If risk management affects the value of the firm, it must be because of "other things," not because risk shifting is inherently valuable.

Let's review the reasons that risk-reducing transactions can make sense in practice.[5]

Reducing the Risk of Cash Shortfalls or Financial Distress

Transactions that reduce risk make financial planning simpler and reduce the odds of an embarrassing cash shortfall. This shortfall might mean only an unexpected trip to the bank, but a financial manager's worst nightmare is landing in a financial pickle and having to pass up a valuable investment opportunity for lack of funds. In extreme cases an unhedged setback could trigger financial distress or even bankruptcy.

Banks and bondholders recognize these dangers. They try to keep track of the firm's risks, and before lending, they may require the firm to carry insurance or to implement hedging programs. Risk management and conservative financing are therefore substitutes, not complements. Thus, a firm might hedge part of its risk in order to operate safely at a higher debt ratio.

Smart financial managers make sure that cash (or ready financing) will be available if investment opportunities expand. That happy match of cash and investment opportunities does not necessarily require hedging, however. Let's contrast two examples.

Cirrus Oil produces from several oil fields and also invests to find and develop new fields. Should it lock in future revenues from its existing fields by hedging oil prices? Probably not, because its investment opportunities expand when oil prices rise and contract when they fall. Locking in oil prices could leave it with too much cash when oil prices fall and too little, relative to its investment opportunities, when prices rise.

Cumulus Pharmaceuticals sells worldwide and half of its revenues are received in foreign currencies. Most of its R&D is done in the United States. Should it hedge at least some of its

---

[3]The news was worst for the shareholders of Ashanti Goldfields, the huge Ghanaian mining company. Ashanti had gone to the opposite extreme and placed a bet that gold prices would fall. The 1999 price rise nearly drove Ashanti into bankruptcy.

[4]See Section 7-5 and also our discussion of diversifying mergers in Chapter 31. Note that diversification reduces overall risk, but not market risk.

[5]There may be other, special reasons not covered here. For example, governments are quick to tax profits but may be slow to rebate taxes when there are losses. In the United States, losses cannot be set against earlier tax payments but can only be carried forward and used to shield future profits. Thus a firm with volatile income and more frequent losses has a higher effective tax rate. A firm can reduce the fluctuations in its income by hedging. For most firms, this motive for risk reduction is not a big deal. See J. R. Graham and C. W. Smith, Jr., "Tax Incentives to Hedge," *Journal of Finance* 54 (December 1999), pp. 2241–2262.

foreign exchange exposure? Probably yes, because pharmaceutical R&D programs are very expensive, long-term investments. Cumulus can't turn its R&D program on or off depending on a particular year's earnings, so it may wish to stabilize cash flows by hedging against fluctuations in exchange rates.

Agency Costs May Be Mitigated by Risk Management

In some cases, hedging can make it easier to monitor and motivate managers. Suppose your confectionery division delivers a 60% profit increase in a year when cocoa prices fall by 12%. Does the division manager deserve a stern lecture or a pat on the back? How much of the profit increase is due to good management and how much to lower cocoa prices? If the cocoa prices were hedged, it's probably good management. If they were not hedged, you will have to sort things out with hindsight, probably by asking, "What would profits have been if cocoa prices had been hedged?"

The fluctuations in cocoa prices are outside the manager's control. But she will surely worry about cocoa prices if her bottom line and bonus depend on them. Hedging prices ties her bonus more closely to risks that she can control and allows her to spend worrying time on these risks.

Hedging external risks that would affect individual managers does not necessarily mean that the *firm* ends up hedging. Some large firms allow their operating divisions to hedge away risks in an internal "market." The internal market operates with real (external) market prices, transferring risks from the division to the central treasurer's office. The treasurer then decides whether to hedge the firm's aggregate exposure.

This sort of internal market makes sense for two reasons. First, divisional risks may cancel out. For example, your refining division may benefit from an increase in heating-oil prices at the same time that your distribution division suffers. Second, because operating managers do not trade actual financial contracts, there is no danger that the managers will cause the firm to take speculative positions. For example, suppose that profits are down late in the year, and hope for end-year bonuses is fading. Could you be tempted to make up the shortfall with a quick score in the cocoa futures market? Well . . . not you, of course, but you can probably think of some acquaintances who would try just one speculative fling.

The dangers of permitting operating managers to make real speculative trades should be obvious. The manager of your confectionery division is an amateur in the cocoa futures market. If she were a skilled professional trader, she would probably not be running chocolate factories.[6]

Risk management requires some degree of centralization. These days many companies appoint a chief risk officer to develop a risk strategy for the company as a whole. The risk manager needs to come up with answers to the following questions:

1. *What are the major risks that the company is facing and what are the possible consequences?* Some risks are scarcely worth a thought, but there are others that might cause a serious setback or even bankrupt the company.

2. *Is the company being paid for taking these risks?* Managers are not paid to avoid all risks, but if they can reduce their exposure to risks for which there are no corresponding rewards, they can afford to place larger bets when the odds are stacked in their favor.

3. *How should risks be controlled?* Should the company reduce risk by building extra flexibility into its operations? Should it change its operating or financial leverage? Or should it insure or hedge against particular hazards?

---

[6]Amateur speculation is doubly dangerous when the manager's initial trades are losers. At that point, the manager is already in deep trouble and has nothing more to lose by going for broke. "Going for broke" is often called "gambling for redemption."

The Evidence on Risk Management

Which firms use financial contracts to manage risk? Almost all do to some extent. For example, they may have contracts that fix prices of raw materials or output, at least for the near future. Most take out insurance policies against fire, accidents, and theft. In addition, as we shall see, managers employ a variety of specialized tools for hedging risk. These are known collectively as *derivatives*. A survey of the world's 500 largest companies found that most of them use derivatives to manage their risk.[7] Eighty-three percent of the companies employ derivatives to control interest rate risk. Eighty-eight percent use them to manage currency risk, and 49% to manage commodity price risk.

Risk policies differ. For example, some natural resource companies work hard to hedge their exposure to price fluctuations; others shrug their shoulders and let prices wander as they may. Explaining why some hedge and others don't is not easy. Peter Tufano's study of the gold-mining industry suggests that managers' personal risk aversion may have something to do with it. Hedging of gold prices appears to be more common when top management has large personal shareholdings in the company. It is less common when top management holds lots of stock options. (Remember that the value of an option falls when the risk of the underlying security is reduced.) David Haushalter's study of oil and gas producers found the firms that hedged the most had high debt ratios, no debt ratings, and low dividend payouts. It seems that for these firms hedging programs were designed to improve the firms' access to debt finance and to reduce the likelihood of financial distress.[8]

BEYOND THE PAGE

Derivatives usage

mhhe.com/brealey13e

26-2   Insurance

Most businesses buy insurance against a variety of hazards—the risk that their plants will be damaged by fire; that their ships, planes, or vehicles will be involved in accidents; that the firm will be held liable for environmental damage; and so on.

When a firm takes out insurance, it is simply transferring the risk to the insurance company. Insurance companies have some advantages in bearing risk. First, they may have considerable experience in insuring similar risks, so they are well placed to estimate the probability of loss and price the risk accurately. Second, they may be skilled at providing advice on measures that the firm can take to reduce the risk, and they may offer lower premiums to firms that take this advice. Third, an insurance company can *pool* risks by holding a large, diversified portfolio of policies. The claims on any individual policy can be highly uncertain, yet the claims on a portfolio of policies may be very stable. Of course, insurance companies cannot diversify away market or macroeconomic risks; firms generally use insurance policies to reduce their diversifiable risk and they find other ways to avoid macro risks.

Insurance companies also suffer some *disadvantages* in bearing risk, and these are reflected in the prices they charge. Suppose your firm owns a $1 billion offshore oil platform. A meteorologist has advised you that there is a 1-in-10,000 chance that in any year the platform will be destroyed in a storm. Thus, the *expected* loss from storm damage is $1 billion/10,000 = $100,000.

The risk of storm damage is almost certainly not a macroeconomic risk and can potentially be diversified away. So you might expect that an insurance company would be prepared

---

[7]International Swap Dealers Association (ISDA), "2009 Derivatives Usage Survey," **www.isda.org**.
[8]See P. Tufano, "The Determinants of Stock Price Exposure: Financial Engineering and the Gold Mining Industry," *Journal of Finance* 53 (June 1998), pp. 1015–1052; and G. D. Haushalter, "Financing Policy, Basis Risk and Corporate Hedging : Evidence from Oil and Gas Producers," *Journal of Finance* 55 (February 2000), pp. 107–152.

to insure the platform against such destruction as long as the premium was sufficient to cover the expected loss. In other words, a fair premium for insuring the platform should be $100,000 a year.[9] Such a premium would make insurance a zero-NPV deal for your company. Unfortunately, no insurance company would offer a policy for only $100,000. Why not?

- *Reason 1: Administrative costs.* An insurance company, like any other business, incurs a variety of costs in arranging the insurance and handling any claims. For example, disputes about the liability for environmental damage can eat up millions of dollars in legal fees. Insurance companies need to recognize these costs when they set their premiums.

- *Reason 2: Adverse selection.* Suppose that an insurer offers life insurance policies with "no medical exam needed, no questions asked." There are no prizes for guessing who will be most tempted to buy this insurance. Our example is an extreme case of the problem of *adverse selection.* Unless the insurance company can distinguish between good and bad risks, the latter will always be most eager to take out insurance. Insurers increase premiums to compensate or require the owners to share any losses.

- *Reason 3: Moral hazard.* Two farmers met on the road to town. "George," said one, "I was sorry to hear about your barn burning down." "Shh," replied the other, "that's tomorrow night." The story is an example of another problem for insurers, known as *moral hazard.* Once a risk has been insured, the owner may be less careful to take proper precautions against damage. Insurance companies are aware of this and factor it into their pricing.

The extreme forms of adverse selection and moral hazard (like the fire in the farmer's barn) are rarely encountered in professional corporate finance. But these problems arise in more subtle ways. That oil platform may not be a "bad risk," but the oil company knows more about the platform's weaknesses than the insurance company does. The oil company will not purposely scuttle the platform, but once insured it could be tempted to save on maintenance or structural reinforcements. Thus, the insurance company may end up paying for engineering studies or for a program to monitor maintenance. All these costs are rolled into the insurance premium.

When the costs of administration, adverse selection, and moral hazard are small, insurance may be close to a zero-NPV transaction. When they are large, insurance is a costly way to protect against risk.

Many insurance risks are *jump risks;* one day there is not a cloud on the horizon and the next day the hurricane hits. The risks can also be huge. For example, the attack on the World Trade Center on September 11, 2001, cost insurance companies about $36 billion; the Japanese tsunami involved payments of $35–$40 billion; Hurricanes Katrina, Harvey, and Irma are each estimated to cost companies in excess of $40 billion.

If the losses from such disasters can be spread more widely, the cost of insuring them should decline. Therefore, insurance companies have been looking for ways to share catastrophic risks with investors. One solution is for the companies to issue *catastrophe bonds* (or *Cat bonds*). If a catastrophe occurs, the payment on a Cat bond is reduced or eliminated.[10] For example, in 2017, the insurance company, Swiss Re, issued $925 million worth of Cat bonds. The bonds cover the company for three years against any losses from earthquakes in California.

---

[9]If the premium is paid at the beginning of the year and the claim is not settled until the end, then the zero-NPV premium equals the discounted value of the expected claim or $100,000/(1 + r)$.

[10]For a discussion of Cat bonds and other techniques to spread insurance risk, see N. A. Doherty, "Financial Innovation in the Management of Catastrophe Risk," *Journal of Applied Corporate Finance* 10 (April 2005), pp. 84–95; K. Froot, "The Market for Catastrophe Risk: A Clinical Examination," *Journal of Financial Economics* 60 (2001), pp. 529–571; and J. D. Cummins, "CAT Bonds and Other Risk-Linked Securities: State of the Market and Recent Developments," *Risk Management and Insurance Review* 11 (Spring 2008), pp. 23–47.

26-3 Reducing Risk with Options

Managers regularly buy options on currencies, interest rates, and commodities to limit downside risk. Consider, for example, the problem faced by the Mexican government. A hefty portion of its revenue comes from Pemex, the state-owned oil company. So, when oil prices fall, the government may be compelled to reduce its planned spending.

The government's solution has been to arrange an annual hedge against a possible fall in the oil price. Although the details of its hedging program are a closely guarded secret, it is reported that in 2017 the Mexican government bought put options that gave it the right to sell about 250 million barrels of oil over the coming year at an exercise price of $46 per barrel. If oil prices rose above this figure, Mexico would reap the benefit. But if oil prices fell below $46, the payoff to the put options would exactly offset the revenue shortfall. In effect, the options put a floor of $46 a barrel on the value of its oil. Of course, the hedge did not come free. The Mexican government was said to have spent $1.25 billion to buy the contracts from a group of international banks.

Figure 26.1 illustrates the nature of Mexico's insurance strategy. Panel *a* shows the revenue derived from selling 250 million barrels of oil. As the price of oil rises or falls, so do the government's revenues. Panel *b* shows the payoffs to the government's options to sell 250 million barrels at $46 a barrel. The payoff on these options rises as oil prices fall below $46 a barrel. This payoff exactly offsets any decline in oil revenues. Panel *c* shows the government's total revenues after buying the put options. For prices below $46 per barrel, revenues are fixed at $250 \times \$46 = \$11,500$ million. But for every dollar that oil prices rise above $46, revenues increase by $250 million. The profile in panel *c* should be familiar to you. It represents the payoffs to the protective put strategy that we first encountered in Section 20-2.[11]

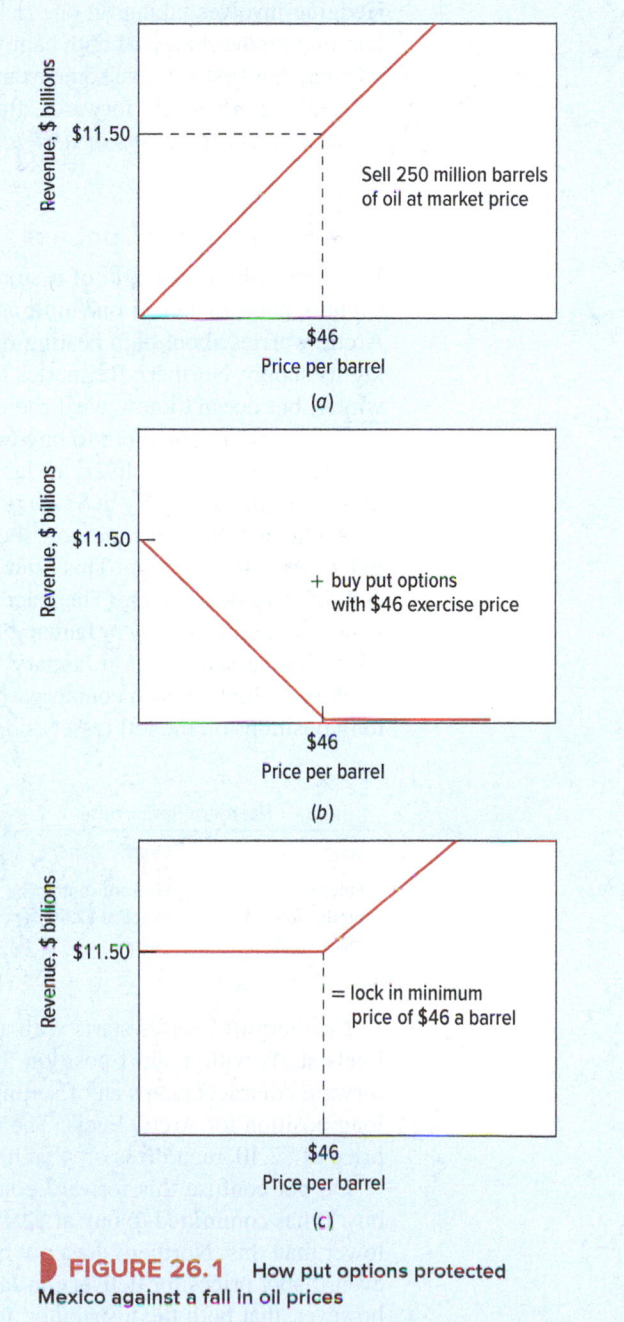

FIGURE 26.1 How put options protected Mexico against a fall in oil prices

---

[11]The Mexican government option position was slightly more complicated than our description. On some of the production, it agreed to take a hit if prices fell below some minimum price.

Hedging involves taking on one risk to offset another. It potentially removes all uncertainty, eliminating the chance of both happy and unhappy surprises. We explain shortly how to set up a hedge, but first we give some examples and describe some tools that are specially designed for hedging. These are forwards, futures, and swaps. Together with options, they are known as *derivative instruments* or *derivatives* because their value depends on the value of another asset.

A Simple Forward Contract

We start with an example of a simple **forward contract.** Arctic Fuels, the heating-oil distributor, plans to deliver one million gallons of heating oil to its retail customers next January. Arctic worries about high heating-oil prices next winter and wants to lock in the cost of buying its supply. Northern Refineries is in the opposite position. It will produce heating oil next winter, but doesn't know what the oil can be sold for. So the two firms strike a deal: Arctic Fuels agrees in September to buy one million gallons from Northern Refineries at $2.40 per gallon, to be paid on delivery in January. Northern agrees to sell and deliver one million gallons to Arctic in January at $2.40 per gallon.

Arctic and Northern are now the two *counterparties* in a forward contract. The **forward price** is $2.40 per gallon. This price is fixed today, in September in our example, but payment and delivery occur later. (The price for immediate delivery is called the **spot price.**) Arctic, which has agreed to *buy* in January, has the *long* position in the contract. Northern Refineries, which has agreed to *sell* in January, has the *short* position.

We can think of each counterparty's long and short positions in balance-sheet format, with long positions on the left (asset) side and short positions on the right (liability) side.

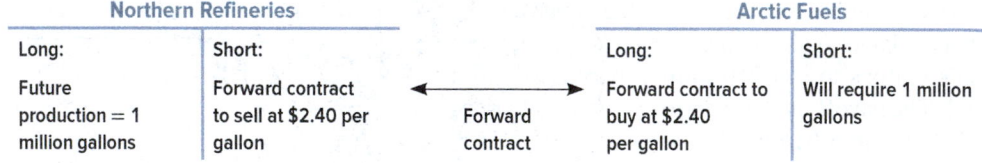

Northern Refineries				**Arctic Fuels**	
Long:	Short:			Long:	Short:
Future production = 1 million gallons	Forward contract to sell at $2.40 per gallon	← Forward contract →		Forward contract to buy at $2.40 per gallon	Will require 1 million gallons

Northern Refineries starts with a long position because it will produce heating oil. Arctic Fuels starts with a short position, because it will have to buy to supply its customers. The forward contract creates an offsetting short position for Northern Refineries and an offsetting long position for Arctic Fuels. The offsets mean that each counterparty ends up locking in a price of $2.40, regardless of what happens to future spot prices.

Do not confuse this forward contract with an option. Arctic does not have the option to buy. It has committed to buy at $2.40 per gallon, even if spot prices in January turn out much lower than this. Northern does not have the option to sell. It cannot back away from the deal, even if spot prices for delivery in January turn out much higher than $2.40 per gallon. Note, however, that both the distributor and refiner have to worry about *counterparty risk,* that is, the risk that the other party will not perform as promised.

We confess that our heating oil example glossed over several complications. For example, we assumed that the risk of both companies is reduced by locking in the price of heating oil. But suppose that the retail price of heating oil moves up and down with the wholesale price. In that case the heating-oil distributor is naturally hedged because costs and revenues move together. Locking in costs with a futures contract could actually make the distributor's profits *more* volatile.

BEYOND THE PAGE

The pros and cons of hedging airline fuel costs

mhhe.com/brealey13e

Futures Exchanges

Our heating-oil distributor and refiner do not have to negotiate a one-off, bilateral contract. Each can go to an exchange where standardized forward contracts on heating oil are traded. The distributor would buy contracts and the refiner would sell.

Here we encounter some tricky vocabulary. When a standardized forward contract is traded on an exchange, it is called a **futures contract**—same contract, but a different label. The exchange is called a **futures exchange.** The distinction between "futures" and "forward" does not apply to the contract, but to how the contract is traded. We describe futures trading in a moment.

Table 26.2 lists a few of the most important commodity futures contracts and the exchanges on which they are traded.[12] Our refiner and distributor can trade heating-oil futures

Future	Exchange	Future	Exchange
Corn	CBOT, DCE	Aluminum	LME, SHFE
Wheat	CBOT	Copper	COMEX, LME, MCX, SHFE
		Gold	COMEX, MCX
Palm oil	CME, DCE	Lead	LME, MCX
Soybeans	CBOT, TGE	Nickel	LME, MCX
Soybean meal	CBOT, DCE	Silver	COMEX, MCX, TOCOM
Soybean oil	CBOT, DCE	Tin	LME
		Zinc	LME, MCX, SHFE
Live cattle	CME		
Lean hogs	CME	Crude oil	ICE, MCX, NYMEX, TOCOM
		Gas oil	ICE, NFX
Cocoa	ICE, NYMEX	Heating oil	ICE, NYMEX
Coffee	ICE	Natural gas	ICE, NYMEX
Cotton	ICE	Unleaded gasoline	ICE, NYMEX, TOCOM
Lumber	CME		
Orange juice	ICE	Electricity	NYMEX
Rubber	SHFE, TOCOM		
Sugar	ICE, NYMEX, ZCE		

▶ TABLE 26.2   **Some important commodity futures and some of the exchanges on which they are traded**

Key to abbreviations:

CBOT	Chicago Board of Trade (part of CME Group)	MCX	Multi Commodity Exchange (India)
CME	Chicago Mercantile Exchange	NYMEX	New York Mercantile Exchange (part of CME Group)
COMEX	Commodity Exchange Division (part of CME Group)	SHFE	Shanghai Futures Exchange
DCE	Dalian Commodity Exchange (China)	TGE	Tokyo Grain Exchange
ICE	Intercontinental Exchange	TOCOM	Tokyo Commodity Exchange
LME	London Metal ExchangeTGE	ZCE	Zhengzhou Commodity Exchange (China)
NFX	Nasdaq FuturesTOCOM		

---

[12]By the time you read this, the list of futures contracts will almost certainly be out of date because thinly traded contracts are terminated and new contracts are introduced. The list of futures exchanges may also be out of date. There have been plenty of mergers in recent years. In July 2007, the CME and CBOT merged to form the CME Group, and the following year, the group acquired NYMEX Holdings, which operated the NYMEX and COMEX exchanges. Also in 2007, the Intercontinental Exchange (ICE) acquired the New York Board of Trade and NYSE merged with Euronext, which owned the futures exchange, LIFFE. Six years later, NYSE Euronext was itself acquired by the ICE, which kept Euronext's futures business but split off its stock exchange operation.

on the New York Mercantile Exchange (NYMEX). A forest products company and a home-builder can trade lumber futures on the Chicago Mercantile Exchange (CME). A wheat farmer and a miller can trade wheat futures on the Chicago Board of Trade (CBOT) or on a smaller regional exchange.

For many firms, the wide fluctuations in interest rates and exchange rates have become at least as important a source of risk as changes in commodity prices. Financial futures are similar to commodity futures, but instead of placing an order to buy or sell a commodity at a future date, you place an order to buy or sell a financial asset at a future date. Table 26.3 lists some important financial futures. Like Table 26.2 it is far from complete. For example, you can also trade futures on the Thai stock market index, the Chilean peso, Spanish government bonds, and many other financial assets.

Almost every day, some new futures contract seems to be invented. At first, there may be just a few private deals between a bank and its customers, but if the idea proves popular, one of the futures exchanges will try to muscle in on the business. For example, in 2017 the Chicago Mercantile Exchange and the CBOE Futures Exchange began to offer futures contracts on the bitcoin.

The Mechanics of Futures Trading

When you buy or sell a futures contract, the price is fixed today but payment is not made until later. You will, however, be asked to put up **margin** in the form of either cash or Treasury bills to demonstrate that you have the money to honor your side of the bargain. As long as you earn interest on the margined securities, there is no cost to you.

In addition, futures contracts are **marked to market.** This means that each day any profits or losses on the contract are calculated; you pay the exchange any losses and receive any profits. For example, suppose that in September Arctic Fuels buys 1 million gallons of

Future	Exchange	Future	Exchange
U.S. Treasury bonds	CBOT	U.S. house prices	CME
U.S. Treasury notes	CBOT		
German government bonds (bunds)	Eurex, ICE	S&P 500 Index	CME
Japanese government bonds (JGBs)	CME, JPX, SGX	French equity index (CAC)	Euronext
British government bonds (gilts)	ICE	German equity index (DAX)	Eurex
U.S. Treasury bills	CME	Japanese equity index (Nikkei)	CME, JPX, SGX
		U.K. equity index (FTSE)	ICE
LIBOR	CME	Euro	CME, Eurex
Euribor	CME, ICE	Japanese yen	CME
Eurodollar deposits	CME, ICE		
Euroyen deposits	CME, SGX, TFX	Bitcoins	CBOE, CME

❯TABLE 26.3   Some important financial futures and some of the exchanges on which they are traded

Key to abbreviations:

CBOE	CBOE Global Markets		ICE	Intercontinental Exchange
CBOT	Chicago Board of Trade (part of CME Group)		JPX	Japan Exchange Group
CME	Chicago Mercantile Exchange		SGX	Singapore Exchange
Eurex	Eurex Exchange		TFX	Tokyo Financial Futures Exchange

January heating-oil futures contracts at a futures price of $2.40 per gallon. The next day the price of the January contract increases to $2.44 per gallon. Arctic now has a profit of $.04 × 1,000,000 = $40,000. The exchange's clearinghouse therefore pays $40,000 into Arctic's margin account. If the price then drops back to $2.42, Arctic's margin account pays $20,000 back to the clearing house.

Of course, Northern Refineries is in the opposite position. Suppose it sells 1 million gallons of January heating-oil futures contracts at a futures price of $2.40 per gallon. If the price increases to $2.44 cents per gallon, it loses $.04 × 1,000,000 = $40,000 and must pay this amount into the clearinghouse. Notice that neither the distributor nor the refiner has to worry about whether the other party will honor the other side of the bargain. The futures exchange guarantees the contracts and protects itself by settling up profits or losses each day. Futures trading eliminates counterparty risk.

Now consider what happens over the life of the futures contract. We're assuming that Arctic and Northern take offsetting long and short positions in the January contract (not directly with each other, but with the exchange). Suppose that a severe cold snap pushes the spot price of heating oil in January up to $2.60 per gallon. Then the futures price at the end of the contract will also be $2.60 per gallon.[13] So Arctic gets a cumulative profit of (2.60 − 2.40) × 1,000,000 = $200,000. It can take delivery of 1 million gallons, paying $2.60 per gallon, or $2,600,000. Its *net* cost, counting the profits on the futures contract, is $2,600,000 − 200,000 = $2,400,000, or $2.40 per gallon. Thus it has locked in the $2.40 per gallon price quoted in September when it first bought the futures contract. You can easily check that Arctic's net cost always ends up at $2.40 per gallon, regardless of the spot price and ending futures price in January.

Northern Refineries suffers a cumulative loss on the futures contract of $200,000 if the January price is $2.60. That's the bad news; the good news is that it can sell and deliver heating oil for $2.60 per gallon. Its net revenues are $2,600,000 − 200,000 = $2,400,000, or $2.40 per gallon, the futures price in September. Again, you can easily check that Northern's net selling price always ends up at $2.40 per gallon.

Taking delivery directly from an exchange can be costly and inconvenient. For example, the NYMEX heating-oil contract calls for delivery in New York Harbor. Arctic Fuels will be better off taking delivery from a local source such as Northern Refineries. Northern Refineries will likewise be better off delivering heating oil locally than shipping it to New York. Therefore, both parties will probably close out their futures positions just before the end of the contract, and take their profits or losses.[14] Nevertheless the NYMEX futures contract has allowed them to hedge their risks.

The effectiveness of this hedge depends on the correlation between changes in heating-oil prices locally and in New York Harbor. Prices in both locations will be positively correlated because of a common dependence on world energy prices. But the correlation is not perfect. What if a local cold snap hits Arctic Fuels's customers but not New York? A long position in NYMEX futures won't hedge Arctic Fuels against the resulting increase in the local spot price. This is an example of **basis risk.** We return to the problems created by basis risk later in this chapter.

Trading and Pricing Financial Futures Contracts

Financial futures trade in the same way as commodity futures. Suppose your firm's pension fund manager thinks that the French stock market will outperform other European markets over the next six months. She forecasts a 10% six-month return. How can she place a bet? She can buy French stocks, of course. But she could also buy futures contracts on the CAC index

---

[13]Recall that the spot price is the price for immediate delivery. The futures contract also calls for immediate delivery when the contract ends in January. Therefore, the ending price of a futures or forward contract must converge to the spot price at the end of the contract.
[14]Some financial futures contracts *prohibit* delivery. All positions are closed out at the spot price at contract maturity.

of French stocks, which are traded on the Euronext exchange. Suppose she buys 15 six-month futures contracts at 5,000. Each contract pays off 10 times the level of the index, so she has a long position of $15 \times 10 \times 5{,}000 = €750{,}000$. This position is marked to market daily. If the CAC goes up, the exchange puts the profits into your fund's margin account; if the CAC falls, the margin account falls too. If your pension manager is right about the French market, and the CAC ends up at 5,500 after six months, then your fund's cumulative profit on the futures position is $15 \times (5{,}500 - 5{,}000) \times 10 = €75{,}000$.

If you want to buy a security, you have a choice. You can buy for immediate delivery at the spot price, or you can "buy forward" by placing an order for future delivery at the futures price. You end up with the same security either way, but there are two differences. First, if you buy forward, you don't pay up front, and so you can earn interest on the purchase price.[15] Second, you miss out on any interest or dividend that is paid in the meantime. This tells us the relationship between spot and futures prices:

$$F_t = S_0(1 + r_f - y)^t$$

where F_t is the futures price for a contract lasting t periods, S_0 is today's spot price, r_f is the risk-free interest rate, and y is the dividend yield or interest rate.[16] The following example shows how and why this formula works.

EXAMPLE 26.1 • Valuing Index Futures

Suppose that the six-month CAC futures contract trades at 5,000 when the current (spot) CAC index is 5,045.41. The interest rate is 1% per year (about .5% over six months) and the dividend yield on the index is 2.8 (about 1.4% over six months). These numbers fit the formula perfectly because

$$F_t = 5{,}045.41 \times (1 + .005 - .014) = 5{,}000$$

But why are the numbers consistent?

Suppose you just buy the CAC index for 5,045.41 today. Then in six months, you will own the index and also have dividends of $.014 \times 5{,}045.41 = 70.64$. But you decide to buy a futures contract for 5,000 instead, and you put €5,045.41 in the bank. After six months, the bank account has earned interest at .5%, so you have $5{,}045.41 \times 1.005 = 5{,}070.64$, enough to buy the index for 5,000 with €70.64 left over—just enough to cover the dividend you missed by buying futures rather than spot. You get what you pay for.[17]

• • • •

---

[15]In the Appendix to Chapter 19, we pointed out that companies effectively earn the after-tax interest rate when they lend and they pay the after-tax interest rate when they borrow. Therefore, when we value the leverage provided by a forward contract, we should also use the after-tax rather than the pretax rate. You will generally see the formula for the value of a forward contract written without a tax term. For convenience we have followed that convention here, but when valuing a forward contract, remember to use the after-tax rate. See S. C. Myers and J. A. Read, Jr., "Real Options, Taxes and Leverage," *Critical Finance Review,* forthcoming.

[16]This formula is strictly true only for forward contracts that are not marked to market. Otherwise, the value of the future depends on the path of interest rates over the life of the contract. In practice, this qualification is usually not important, and the formula works for futures as well as forward contracts.

[17]We can derive our formula as follows. Let S_6 be the value of the index after six months. Today S_6 is unknown. You can invest S_0 in the index today and get $S_6 + yS_0$ after six months. You can also buy the futures contract, put S_0 in the bank, and use your bank balance to pay the futures price F_6 in six months. In the latter strategy you get $S_6 - F_6 + S_0 (1 + r_f)$ after six months. Since the investment is the same, and you get S_6 with either strategy, the payoffs must be the same:

$$S_6 + yS_0 = S_6 - F_6 + S_0 (1 + rf)$$
$$F_6 = S_0 (1 + r_f - y)$$

Here we assume that r_f and y are six-month rates. If they are monthly rates, the general formula is $F_t = S_0 (1 + r_f - y)^t$, where t is the number of months. If they are annual rates, the formula is $F_t = S_0 (1 + r_f - y)^{t/12}$.

Spot and Futures Prices—Commodities

The difference between buying *commodities* today and buying commodity futures is more complicated. First, because payment is again delayed, the buyer of the future earns interest on her money. Second, she does not need to store the commodities and, therefore, saves warehouse costs, wastage, and so on. On the other hand, the futures contract gives no *convenience yield*, which is the value of being able to get your hands on the real thing. The manager of a supermarket can't burn heating-oil futures if there's a sudden cold snap, and he can't stock the shelves with orange juice futures if he runs out of inventory at 1 p.m. on a Saturday.

Let's express storage costs and convenience yield as fractions of the spot price. For commodities, the futures price for t periods ahead is[18]

$$F_t = S_0(1 \times r_f + \text{storage costs} - \text{convenience yield})^t$$

It's interesting to compare this formula with the formula for a financial future. Convenience yield plays the same role as dividends or interest foregone (y) on securities. But financial assets cost nothing to store, and storage costs do not appear in the formula for financial futures.

Usually, you can't observe storage cost or convenience yield, but you can infer the difference between them by comparing spot and futures prices. This difference—that is, convenience yield less storage cost—is called *net convenience yield* (net convenience yield = convenience yield − storage costs).

EXAMPLE 26.2 • Calculating Net Convenience Yield

In December 2017, the spot price of crude oil was $57.57 a barrel and the six-month futures price was $56.91 per barrel. The interest rate was about 1.2% for six months. Thus

$$F_t = S_0(1 + r_f + \text{storage costs} - \text{convenience yield})$$
$$\$56.91 = 57.57(1.012 - \text{net convenience yield})$$

So net convenience yield was positive, that is, net convenience yield = convenience yield − storage costs = .0235 or 2.35% over six months, equivalent to an annual net convenience yield of 4.8%. Evidently the convenience yield from having crude oil in the storage tanks was slightly greater than the storage cost of those inventories.

• • • • •

Figure 26.2 plots the annualized net convenience yield for crude oil since 1983. Notice how much the spread between the spot and futures price can bounce around. When there are shortages or fears of an interruption of supply, traders may be prepared to pay a hefty premium for the convenience of having inventories of crude oil rather than the promise of future delivery. The reverse is true when storage tanks are full to the brim as in 2016.

There is one further complication that we should note. There are some commodities that cannot be stored at all. You cannot easily store electricity, for example. As a result, electricity supplied in, say, six-months' time is a different commodity from electricity available now, and there is no simple link between today's price and that of a futures contract to buy or sell at the end of six months. Of course, generators and electricity users will have their own views

---

[18]This formula could overstate the futures price if no one is willing to hold the commodity, that is, if inventories fall to zero or some absolute minimum.

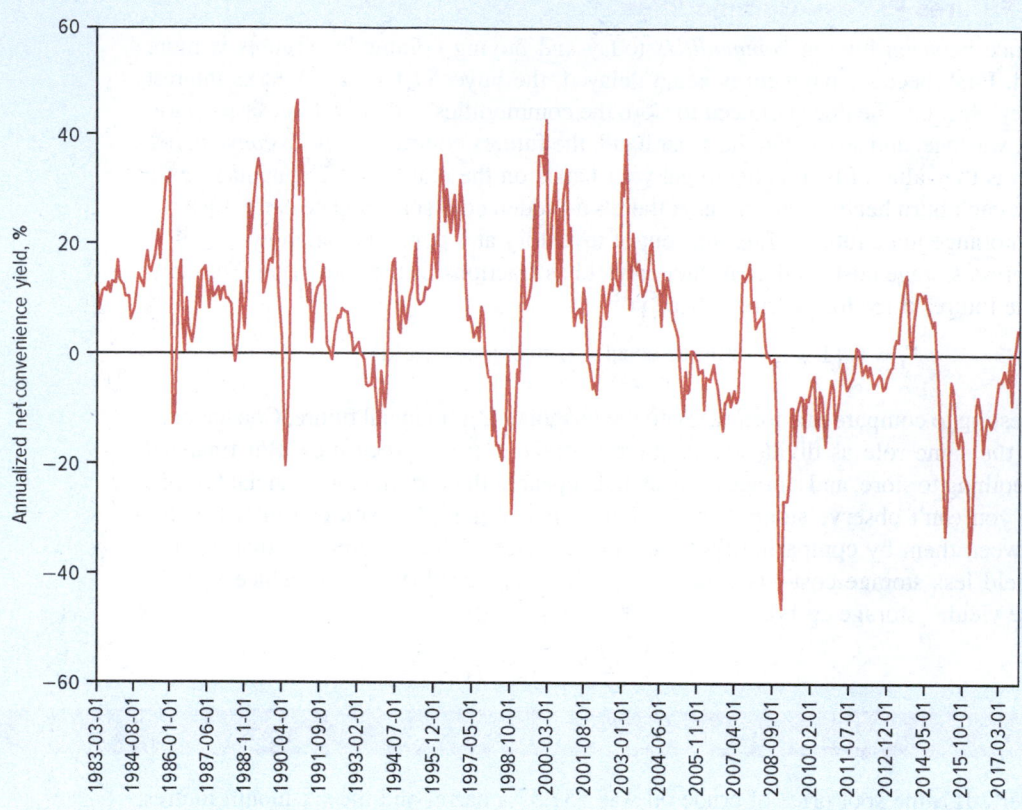

> **FIGURE 26.2**

Annualized percentage net convenience yield (convenience yield less storage costs) for crude oil

Source: www.quandl.com.

of what the spot price is likely to be, and the futures price will reveal these views to some extent.[19]

More about Forward Contracts

Each day, billions of dollars of futures contracts are bought and sold. This liquidity is possible only because futures contracts are standardized and mature on a limited number of dates each year.

Fortunately, there is usually more than one way to skin a financial cat. If the terms of futures contracts do not suit your particular needs, you may be able to buy or sell a tailor-made forward contract. The main forward market is in foreign currency. We discuss this market in Chapter 27.

---

[19]Critics and proponents of futures markets sometimes argue about whether the markets provide "price discovery." That is, they argue about whether futures prices reveal traders' forecasts of spot prices when the futures contract matures. If one of these fractious personalities comes your way, we suggest that you respond with a different question: Do futures prices reveal information about spot prices that is not already in *today's* spot price? Our formulas reveal the answer to this question. There is useful information in futures prices, but it is information about convenience yields and storage costs, or about dividend or interest payments in the case of financial futures. Futures prices reveal information about spot prices only when a commodity is not stored or cannot be stored. Then the link between spot and futures prices is broken, and futures prices can assist with price discovery.

It is also possible to enter into a forward interest rate contract. For example, suppose you know that at the end of three months you are going to need a six-month loan. If you are worried that interest rates will rise over the three-month period, you can lock in the interest rate on the loan by buying a *forward rate agreement (FRA)* from a bank.[20] For example, the bank might sell you a 3-against-9 month (or 3 × 9) FRA at 7%. If, at the end of three months, the six-month interest rate is higher than 7%, then the bank will make up the difference;[21] if it is lower, then you must pay the bank the difference.[22]

Homemade Forward Rate Contracts

Suppose that you borrow $90.91 for one year at 10% and lend $90.91 for two years at 12%. These interest rates are for loans made today; therefore, they are spot interest rates.

The cash flows on your transactions are as follows:

	Year 0	Year 1	Year 2
Borrow for 1 year at 10%	+90.91	−100	
Lend for 2 years at 12%	−90.91	____	+114.04
Net cash flow	0	−100	+114.04

Notice that you do not have any net cash outflow today but you have contracted to pay out money in year 1. The interest rate on this forward commitment is 14.04%. To calculate this forward interest rate, we simply worked out the extra return for lending for two years rather than one:

$$\text{Forward interest rate} = \frac{(1 + 2\text{-year spot rate})^2}{1 + 1\text{-year spot rate}} - 1$$

$$= \frac{(1.12)^2}{1.10} - 1 = .1404, \text{ or } 14.04\%$$

In our example, you manufactured a forward loan by borrowing short term and lending long. But you can also run the process in reverse. If you wish to fix today the rate at which you borrow next year, you borrow long and lend the money until you need it next year.

26-5 Swaps

Some company cash flows are fixed. Others vary with the level of interest rates, rates of exchange, prices of commodities, and so on. These characteristics may not always result in the desired risk profile. For example, a company that pays a fixed rate of interest on its debt might prefer to pay a floating rate, while another company that receives cash flows in euros might prefer to receive them in yen. Swaps allow them to change their risk in these ways.

The market for swaps is huge. In 2017, the total notional amount of interest rate and currency swaps outstanding was more than $300 trillion. By far, the major part of this figure

---

[20]Note that the party that profits from a rise in rates is described as the "buyer." In our example, you would be said to "buy three against nine months" money, meaning that the forward rate agreement is for a six-month loan in three months' time.
[21]The interest rate is usually measured by LIBOR. LIBOR (London interbank offered rate) is the interest rate at which major international banks in London borrow dollars (or euros, yen, etc.) from each other.
[22]These payments would be made when the loan matures nine months from now.

	Year					
	0	**1**	**2**	**3**	**4**	**5**
Homemade swap:						
1. Borrow \$66.67 at 6% fixed rate	+66.67	−4	−4	−4	−4	−(4 + 66.67)
2. Lend \$66.67 at LIBOR floating rate	−66.67	+0.05 × 66.67	+ $LIBOR_1$ × 66.67	+ $LIBOR_2$ × 66.67	+ $LIBOR_3$ × 66.67	+ $LIBOR_4$ × 66.67 + 66.67
Net cash flow	0	−4 +0.05 × 66.67	−4 + $LIBOR_1$ × 66.67	−4 + $LIBOR_2$ × 66.67	−4 + $LIBOR_3$ × 66.67	−4 + $LIBOR_4$ × 66.67
Standard fixed-to-floating swap:						
Net cash flow	0	−4 +0.05 × 66.67	−4 + $LIBOR_1$ × 66.67	−4 + $LIBOR_2$ × 66.67	−4 + $LIBOR_3$ × 66.67	−4 + $LIBOR_4$ × 66.67

❯ **TABLE 26.4**   The top panel shows the cash flows in millions of dollars to a homemade fixed-to-floating interest rate swap. The bottom panel shows the cash flows to a standard swap transaction.

consisted of interest rate swaps.[23] We therefore show first how interest rate swaps work and then describe a currency swap. We conclude with a brief look at some other types of swap.

Interest Rate Swaps

Friendly Bancorp has made a five-year, \$50 million loan to fund part of the construction cost of a large cogeneration project. The loan carries a fixed interest rate of 8%. Annual interest payments are therefore \$4 million. Interest payments are made annually, and all the principal will be repaid at year 5.

Suppose that instead of receiving fixed interest payments of \$4 million a year, the bank would prefer to receive floating-rate payments. It can do so by swapping the \$4 million, five-year annuity (the fixed interest payments) into a five-year floating-rate annuity. We show first how Friendly Bancorp can make its own homemade swap. Then we describe a simpler procedure.

The bank (we assume) can borrow at a 6% fixed rate for five years.[24] Therefore, the \$4 million interest it receives can support a fixed-rate loan of 4/.06 = \$66.67 million. The bank can now construct the homemade swap as follows: It borrows \$66.67 million at a fixed interest rate of 6% for five years and simultaneously lends the same amount at LIBOR. We assume that LIBOR is initially 5%.[25] LIBOR is a short-term interest rate, so future interest receipts will fluctuate as the bank's investment is rolled over.

The net cash flows to this strategy are shown in the top portion of Table 26.4. Notice that there is no net cash flow in year 0 and that in year 5 the principal amount of the short-term investment is used to pay off the \$66.67 million loan. What's left? A cash flow equal to the

---

[23]Data on swaps are provided by the International Swaps and Derivatives Association (**www.isda.org**) and the Bank for International Settlements (**www.bis.org**).

[24] The spread between the bank's 6% borrowing rate and the 8% lending rate is the bank's profit on the project financing.

[25]Maybe the short-term interest rate is below the five-year interest rate because investors expect interest rates to rise.

difference between the interest earned (LIBOR × 66.67) and the $4 million outlay on the fixed loan. The bank also has $4 million per year coming in from the project financing, so it has transformed that fixed payment into a floating payment keyed to LIBOR.

Of course, there's an easier way to do this, shown in the bottom portion of Table 26.3. The bank can just enter into a five-year swap.[26] Naturally, Friendly Bancorp takes this easier route. Let's see what happens.

Friendly Bancorp calls a swap dealer, which is typically a large commercial or investment bank, and agrees to *swap* the payments on a $66.67 million fixed-rate loan for the payments on an equivalent floating-rate loan. The swap is known as a fixed-to-floating interest rate swap and the $66.67 million is termed the *notional principal* amount of the swap. Friendly Bancorp and the dealer are the counterparties to the swap.

The dealer is quoting a rate for five-year swaps of 6% against LIBOR.[27] This figure is sometimes quoted as a spread over the yield on U.S. Treasuries. For example, if the yield on five-year Treasury notes is 5.25%, the swap spread is .75%.

The first payment on the swap occurs at the end of year 1 and is based on the starting LIBOR rate of 5%.[28] The dealer (who pays floating) owes the bank 5% of $66.67 million, while the bank (which pays fixed) owes the dealer $4 million (6% of $66.67 million). The bank, therefore, makes a net payment to the dealer of 4 − (.05 × 66.67) = $.67 million:

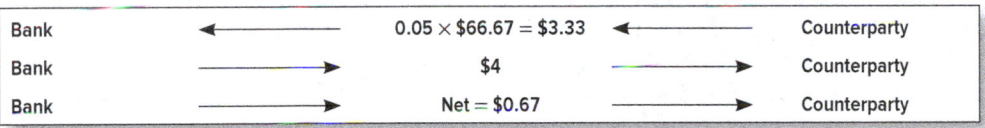

The second payment is based on LIBOR at year 1. Suppose it increases to 6%. Then the net payment is zero:

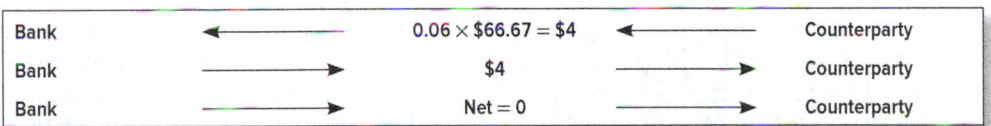

The third payment depends on LIBOR at year 2, and so on.

The *notional value* of this swap is $66.67 million. The fixed and floating interest rates are multiplied by the notional amount to calculate dollar amounts of fixed and floating interest. But the notional value vastly overstates the economic value of the swap. At creation, the economic value of the swap is zero because the NPV of the cash flows to each counterparty is zero. The NPV drifts away from zero as time passes and interest rates change. But the economic value will always be far less than notional value. Careless references to notional values give the impression that swap markets are impossibly gigantic; in fact, they are merely very large.

The economic value of a swap depends on the path of long-term interest rates. For example, suppose that after two years, interest rates are unchanged, so a 6% note issued by the bank would continue to trade at its face value. In this case, the swap still has zero value. (You can

---

[26]Both strategies are equivalent to a series of forward contracts on LIBOR. The forward prices are $4 million each for LIBOR$_1$ × $66.67, LIBOR$_2$ × $66.67, and so on. Separately negotiated forward prices would not be $4 million for any one year, but the PVs of the "annuities" of forward prices would be identical.

[27]Notice that the swap rate always refers to the interest rate on the fixed leg of the swap. Rates are generally quoted against LIBOR, though dealers will also be prepared to quote rates against other short-term debt.

[28]More commonly, interest rate swaps are based on three-month LIBOR and involve quarterly cash payments.

confirm this by checking that the NPV of a new three-year homemade swap is zero.) But if long rates increase over the two years to 7% (say), the value of a three-year note falls to

$$PV = \frac{4}{1.07} + \frac{4}{(1.07)^2} + \frac{4 + 66.67}{(1.07)^3} = \$64.92 \text{ million}$$

Now the fixed payments that the bank has agreed to make are less valuable and the swap is worth $66.67 - 64.92 = \$1.75$ million.

How do we know the swap is worth $1.75 million? Consider the following strategy:

1. The bank can enter a new three-year swap deal in which it agrees to *pay* LIBOR on the same notional principal of $66.67 million.

2. In return it receives fixed payments at the new 7% interest rate, that is, $.07 \times 66.67 = \$4.67$ per year.

The new swap cancels the cash flows of the old one, but it generates an extra $.67 million for three years. This extra cash flow is worth

$$PV = \sum_{t=1}^{3} \frac{.67}{(1.07)^t} = \$1.75 \text{ million}$$

Remember, ordinary interest rate swaps have no initial cost or value (NPV = 0), but their value drifts away from zero as time passes and long-term interest rates change. One counterparty wins as the other loses.

In our example, the swap dealer loses from the rise in interest rates. Dealers will try to hedge the risk of interest rate movements by engaging in a series of futures or forward contracts or by entering into an offsetting swap with a third party. As long as Friendly Bancorp and the other counterparty honor their promises, the dealer is fully protected against risk. The recurring nightmare for swap managers is that one party will default, leaving the dealer with a large unmatched position. This is another example of counterparty risk.

The market for interest rate swaps is large and liquid. Consequently, financial analysts often look at swap rates when they want to know how interest rates vary with maturity. For example, Figure 26.3 shows swap rates in December 2017 for the U.S. dollar, the euro, and the British pound. You can see that in each country, long-term interest rates are much higher than short-term rates, though the level of swap rates varies from one country to another.

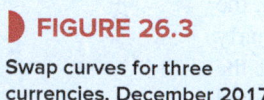

> **FIGURE 26.3**

Swap curves for three currencies, December 2017

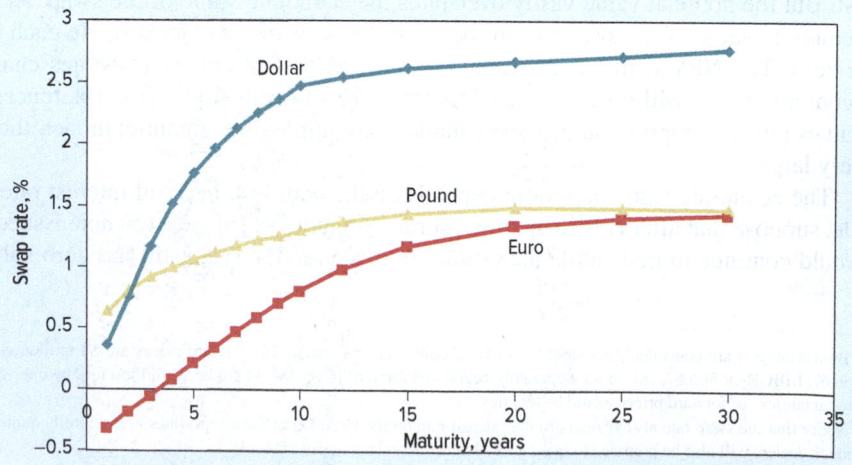

Currency Swaps

We now look briefly at an example of a currency swap.

Suppose that the Possum Company needs 11 million euros to help finance its European operations. We assume that the euro interest rate is about 5%, whereas the dollar rate is about 6%. Since Possum is better known in the United States, the financial manager decides not to borrow euros directly. Instead, the company issues $10 million of five-year 6% notes in the United States. Then it arranges with a counterparty to swap this dollar loan into euros. Under this arrangement the counterparty agrees to pay Possum sufficient dollars to service its dollar loan, and in exchange Possum agrees to make a series of annual payments in euros to the counterparty.

Here are Possum's cash flows (in millions):

	Year 0		Year 1–4		Year 5	
Stock	**Dollars**	**Euros**	**Dollars**	**Euros**	**Dollars**	**Euros**
1. Issue dollar loan	+10		−0.6		−10.6	
2. Swap dollars for euros	−10	+8	+0.6	−0.4	+10.6	−8.4
3. Net cash flow	0	+8	0	−0.4	0	−8.4

Look first at the cash flows in year 0. Possum receives $10 million from its issue of dollar notes, which it then pays over to the swap counterparty. In return the counterparty sends Possum a check for €8 million. (We assume that at current rates of exchange $10 million is worth €8 million.)

Now move to years 1 through 4. Possum needs to pay interest of 6% on its debt issue, which works out at .06 × 10 = $.6 million. The swap counterparty agrees to provide Possum each year with sufficient cash to pay this interest and in return Possum makes an annual payment to the counterparty of 5% of €8 million, or €.4 million. Finally, in year 5 the swap counterparty pays Possum enough to make the final payment of interest and principal on its dollar notes ($10.6 million), while Possum pays the counterparty €8.4 million.

The combined effect of Possum's two steps (line 3) is to convert a 6% dollar loan into a 5% euro loan. You can think of the cash flows for the swap (line 2) as a series of contracts to buy euros in years 1 through 5. In each of years 1 through 4 Possum agrees to purchase $.6 million at a cost of .4 million euros; in year 5 it agrees to buy $10.6 million at a cost of 8.4 million euros.[29]

Some Other Swaps

While interest rate and currency swaps are the most popular type of contract, there is a wide variety of other possible swaps or related contracts. For example, in Chapter 23 we encountered credit default swaps that allow investors to insure themselves against the default on a corporate bond.

Inflation swaps allow a company to protect against inflation risk. One party in the swap receives a fixed payment while the other receives a payment that is linked to the rate of inflation. In effect, the swap creates a made-to-measure inflation-linked bond, which can be of any maturity.[30]

---

[29]Usually in a currency swap the two parties make an initial payment to each other (i.e., Possum pays the bank $10 million and receives €8 million). However, this is not necessary, and Possum might prefer to buy the €8 million from another bank.

[30]If the inflation swap involves only a single payment, it is known as a *zero-coupon swap*. If it provides a sequence of payments, each linked to the rate of inflation, it is called a *year-on-year swap*.

You can also enter into a *total return swap* where one party (party A) makes a series of agreed payments and the other (party B) pays the total return on a particular asset. This asset might be a common stock, a loan, a commodity, or a market index. For example, suppose that B owns $10 million of IBM stock. It now enters into a two-year swap agreement to pay A each quarter the total return on this stock. In exchange A agrees to pay B interest of LIBOR + 1%. B is known as the *total return payer* and A is the *total return receiver.* Suppose LIBOR is 5%. Then A owes B 6% of $10 million, or about 1.5% a quarter. If IBM stock returns more than this, there will be a net payment from B to A; if the return is less than 1.5%, A must make a net payment to B. Although ownership of the IBM stock does not change hands, the effect of this total return swap is the same as if B had sold the asset to A and bought it back at an agreed future date.

26-6   How to Set Up a Hedge

There can be many ways to hedge a risk exposure. Some hedges are zero maintenance: Once established, the financial manager can walk away and worry about other matters. Other hedges are dynamic: They work only if adjusted at frequent intervals.

The forward contract between Northern Refineries and Arctic Fuels, which we described in Section 26-4, was zero maintenance because each counterparty locked in the price of heating oil at $2.40 per gallon, regardless of the future path of heating-oil prices. Now we look at an example where the financial manager will probably implement a *dynamic hedge.*

Hedging Interest Rate Risk

Potterton Leasing has acquired a warehouse and leased it to a manufacturer for fixed payments of $2 million per year for 20 years. The lease cannot be canceled by the manufacturer, so Potterton has a safe, debt-equivalent asset. The interest rate is 10%, and we ignore taxes for simplicity. The PV of Potterton's rental income is $17 million:

$$PV = \frac{2}{1.1} + \frac{2}{(1.1)^2} + \cdots + \frac{2}{(1.1)^{20}} = 17.0 \text{ million}$$

The lease exposes Potterton to interest rate risk. If interest rates increase, the PV of the lease payments falls. If interest rates decrease, the PV rises. Potterton's CFO therefore decides to issue an offsetting debt liability:

PV (lease)	PV (debt)
= $17 million	= $17 million

Thus, Potterton is long $17 million and also short $17 million. But it may not be hedged. Simply borrowing $17 million at some arbitrary maturity does *not* eliminate interest rate risk. Suppose the CFO took out a *one-year,* $17 million bank loan, with a plan to refinance the loan annually. Then she would be borrowing short and lending long (via the 20-year lease), which amounts to a $17 million bet that interest rates will fall. If instead they rise, her company will end up paying more interest in years 2 to 20, with no compensating increase in the lease cash flows.

To hedge interest rate risk, the CFO needs to design the debt issue so that any change in interest rates has the same (and thus offsetting) impact on both the PV of the lease payments and the PV of the debt. There are two ways to accomplish this:

1. *Zero-maintenance hedge.* Issue debt requiring interest and principal payments of exactly $2 million per year for 20 years. This debt would be similar to a real estate mortgage with level payments. In this case, lease payments would exactly cover debt

service in each year. The PVs of the lease payments and the offsetting debt would always be identical, regardless of the level of future interest rates.

2. *Duration hedge.* Issue debt with the same *duration* as the lease payments. Here, debt service does not have to match the lease payments in each (or any) year. If durations are matched, then small changes in interest rates—say, from 10% down to 9.5% or up to 10.5%—will have the same impact on the PVs of the lease payments and the debt.

The duration-matching strategy is usually more convenient, but it is not zero maintenance because durations will drift out of line as interest rates change and time passes. Thus, the CFO will have to revisit and reset the hedge. She will have to execute a dynamic strategy to make duration matching work.

Potterton's CFO first calculates the duration of the lease payments:[31]

$$\text{Duration} = \frac{1}{\text{PV}}\big\{[\text{PV}(C_1) \times 1] + [\text{PV}(C_2) \times 2] + [\text{PV}(C_3) \times 3] + \cdots\big\}$$

$$= \frac{1}{17.0}\left\{\left[\frac{2}{1.10} \times 1\right] + \left[\frac{2}{1.10^2} \times 2\right] + \cdots + \left[\frac{2}{1.10^{20}} \times 20\right]\right\}$$

$$= 7.5 \text{ years}$$

Therefore, to hedge its interest rate risk, Potterton needs to issue a package of bonds with a duration of 7.5 years. The simplest solution is to issue a 12-year bond with a 10% coupon, which has a 7.5-year duration. But this is not the only possible strategy. For example, the company could issue $7.9 million of 10% 20-year bonds and $9.1 million of 10% 8-year bonds. The duration of this package would also be 7.5 years.[32]

Figure 26.4 plots the PVs of the lease payments and the 12-year bond as a function of the interest rate. Both the PV curves are downward-sloping but convex; note how each curve comes down steeply at low interest rates but flattens out at higher interest rates.

Now compare the slope of the PV curve for the lease payments with the slope of the 12-year bond. The slopes are identical at the current 10% interest rate because the duration is identical at this rate. Therefore, so long as the interest rate does not stray too far from the current level of 10%, the PV of the lease cash flows change by almost the same amount as the PV of the bond. In this case, Potterton is hedged. But you can see from Figure 26.4 that if interest rates change by, say, 5%, the value of the lease payments changes by a little bit more than the value of the bond. In this case, Potterton's CFO will have to reset the hedge.

She will also need to reset the hedge at some point even if interest rates do not change because the duration of the 12-year bond will decrease faster than that of the 20-year lease. For example, think forward 12 years: The bond will mature, while the lease will still have 8 years to run.

Duration is not a complete measure of interest rate risk. It measures only exposure to the level of interest rates, not to changes in the shape of the term structure. Duration in effect assumes that the term structure is "flat." It is widely used, however, because it is a good first approximation to interest rate risk exposure. The mini-case at the end of this chapter offers another opportunity to use this concept.

Hedge Ratios and Basis Risk

In our example of Potterton Leasing, the CFO matched lease cash flows worth $17 million against debt worth $17 million. In other words, the hedge ratio for Potterton was exactly 1.

---

[31] Look back at Section 3-2 if you need a revision session on calculating duration.
[32] The duration of the 20-year bonds is 9.37 years and that of the 8-year bonds is 5.87 years. The duration of the package is $(7.9 \times 9.37 + 9.1 \times 5.87)/17 = 7.5$ years.

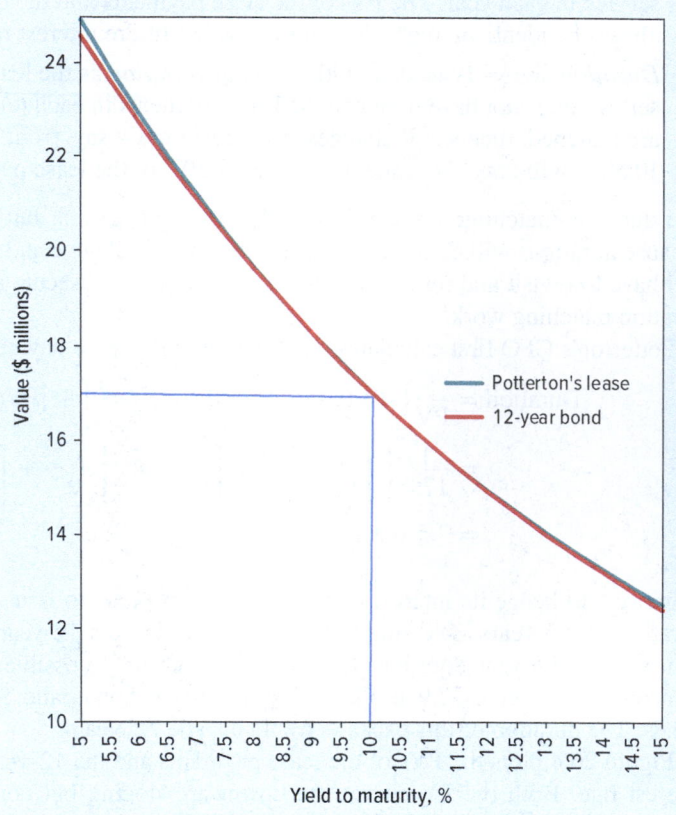

▶ **FIGURE 26.4**

Hedging Potterton's interest rate risk by matching duration. The PV of the lease cash inflows is shown by the blue curve; the PV of a 10% 12-year bond is shown by the red curve. Both have a duration of 7.5 years, so the slopes of the PV curves are identical at the current 10% interest rate. Therefore, Potterton's net exposure to small changes in interest rates is zero.

Hedge ratios can be much higher or lower than 1. For example, suppose a farmer owns 100,000 bushels of wheat and wishes to hedge by selling wheat futures. In practice, the wheat that the farmer owns and the wheat that he sells in the futures markets are unlikely to be identical. If he sells wheat futures on the Kansas City exchange, he agrees to deliver hard, red winter wheat in Kansas City in September. But perhaps he is growing northern spring wheat many miles from Kansas City; in this case, the prices of the two wheats will not move exactly together.

Figure 26.5 shows how changes in the prices of the two types of wheat may have been related in the past. The slope of the fitted line shows that a 1% change in the price of Kansas wheat was, on average, associated with an .8% change in the price of the farmer's wheat. Because the price of the farmer's wheat is relatively insensitive to changes in Kansas prices, he needs to sell .8 × 100,000 bushels of wheat futures to minimize risk.

Let us generalize. Suppose that you already own an asset, A (e.g., wheat), and you wish to hedge against changes in the value of A by making an offsetting sale of another asset, B (e.g., wheat futures). Suppose also that percentage changes in the value of A are related in the following way to percentage changes in the value of B:

$$\text{Expected change in value of A} = \alpha + \delta(\text{change in value of B})$$

Delta (δ) measures the sensitivity of A to changes in the value of B. It is also equal to the hedge ratio—that is, the number of units of B that should be sold to hedge the purchase of A. You minimize risk if you offset your position in A by the sale of delta units of B.

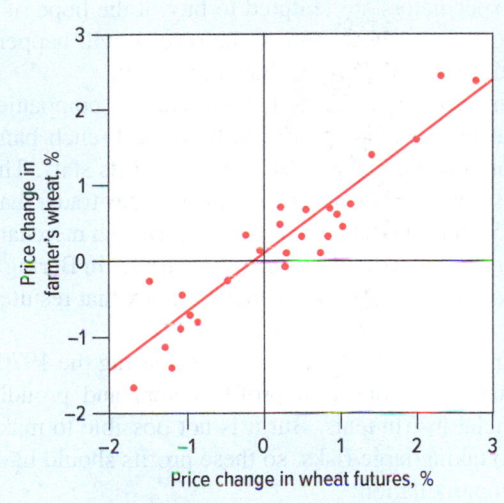

FIGURE 26.5

Hypothetical plot of past changes in the price of the farmer's wheat against changes in the price of Kansas City wheat futures. A 1% change in the futures price implies, on average, a .8% change in the price of the farmer's wheat.

The trick in setting up a hedge is to estimate the delta or hedge ratio. Our farmer could use past experience to do so, but often a strong dose of judgment is called for. For example, suppose that Antarctic Air would like to protect itself against a hike in oil prices. As the financial manager, you need to decide how much a rise in oil price would affect firm value.

Suppose the company spent $200 million on fuel last year. Other things equal, a 10% increase in the price of oil will cost the company an extra $.1 \times 200 = \$20$ million. But perhaps you can partially offset the higher costs by charging higher ticket prices, in which case earnings will fall by less than $20 million. Or perhaps an oil price rise will lead to a slowdown in business activity and therefore lower passenger numbers. In that case earnings will decline by more than $20 million. Working out the likely effect on firm value is even trickier because it depends on whether the rise is likely to be permanent. Perhaps the price rise will induce an increase in production or encourage consumers to economize on energy usage.

Whenever the two sides of the hedge do not move exactly together, there will be some basis risk. That is not a problem for the CFO of Potterton. As long as interest rates do not change sharply, any changes in the value of Potterton's lease should be almost exactly offset by changes in the value of the debt. In this case there is no basis risk, and Potterton is perfectly hedged.

Our wheat farmer is less fortunate. The scatter of points in Figure 26.5 shows that it is not possible for the farmer to construct a perfect hedge using wheat futures. Since the underlying commodity (the farmer's wheat) and the hedging instrument (Kansas City wheat futures) are imperfectly correlated, some basis risk remains.

BEYOND THE PAGE

WTI and Brent oil futures

mhhe.com/brealey13e

26-7   Is "Derivative" a Four-Letter Word?

Our wheat farmer sold wheat futures to reduce business risk. But if you were to copy the farmer and sell futures without an offsetting holding of wheat, you would increase risk, not reduce it. You would be *speculating*.

Speculators in search of large profits (and prepared to tolerate large losses) are attracted by the leverage that derivatives provide. By this we mean that it is not necessary to lay out much money up front and the profits or losses may be many times the initial outlay. "Speculation" has an ugly ring, but a successful derivatives market needs speculators who are prepared to take on risk and provide more cautious people such as farmers or millers with the protection they need. For example, if there is an excess of farmers wishing to sell wheat futures, the price

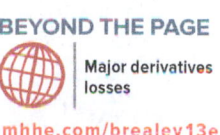

BEYOND THE PAGE

Major derivatives losses

mhhe.com/brealey13e

BEYOND THE PAGE

LTCM

mhhe.com/brealey13e

BEYOND THE PAGE

Metallgesellschaft

mhhe.com/brealey13e

BEYOND THE PAGE

The World's
Poorest Man

mhhe.com/brealey13e

of futures will be forced down until enough speculators are tempted to buy in the hope of a profit. If there is a surplus of millers wishing to buy wheat futures, the reverse will happen. The price of wheat futures will be forced *up* until speculators are drawn in to sell.

Speculation may be necessary to a thriving derivatives market, but it can get companies into serious trouble. The nearby Beyond the Page feature describes how the French bank Société Générale took a €4.9 billion bath from unauthorized trading by one of its staff. The bank has plenty of company. In 2011, Swiss bank UBS reported that a rogue trader had notched up losses of $2.3 billion. And in 1995, Baring Brothers, a blue-chip British merchant bank with a 200-year history, became insolvent. The reason: Nick Leeson, a trader in Baring's Singapore office, had placed very large bets on the Japanese stock market index that resulted in losses of $1.4 billion.

These tales of woe have some cautionary messages for all corporations. During the 1970s and 1980s, many firms turned their treasury operations into profit centers and proudly announced their profits from trading in financial instruments. But it is not possible to make large profits in financial markets without also taking large risks, so these profits should have served as a warning rather than a matter for congratulation.

An Airbus 380 weighs 400 tons, flies at nearly 600 miles per hour, and is inherently very dangerous. But we don't ground A380s; we just take precautions to ensure that they are flown with care. Similarly, it is foolish to suggest that firms should ban the use of derivatives, but it makes obvious sense to take precautions against their misuse. Here are two bits of horse sense:

- *Precaution 1: Don't be taken by surprise.* By this we mean that senior management needs to monitor regularly the value of the firm's derivatives positions and to know what bets the firm has placed. At its simplest, this might involve asking what would happen if interest rates or exchange rates were to change by 1%. But large banks and consultants have also developed sophisticated models for measuring the risk of derivatives positions.

- *Precaution 2: Place bets only when you have some comparative advantage that ensures the odds are in your favor.* If a bank were to announce that it was drilling for oil or launching a new soap powder, you would rightly be suspicious about whether it had what it takes to succeed. You should be equally suspicious if an oil producer or consumer products company announced that it was placing a bet on interest rates or currencies.

Imprudent speculation in derivatives is undoubtedly an issue of concern for the company's shareholders, but is it a matter for more general concern? Some people believe, like Warren Buffett, that derivatives are "financial weapons of mass destruction." They point to the huge volume of trading in derivatives and argue that speculative losses could lead to major defaults that might threaten the whole financial system. These worries have led to increased regulation of derivatives markets.

Now, this is not the place for a discussion of regulation, but we should warn you about careless measures of the size of the derivatives markets and the possible losses. In June 2017, the notional value of outstanding derivative contracts was $628 trillion.[33] This is a very large sum, but it tells you nothing about the money that was being put at risk. For example, suppose that a bank enters into a $10 million interest rate swap and the other party goes bankrupt the next day. How much has the bank lost? Nothing. It hasn't paid anything up front; the two parties simply promised to pay sums to each other in the future. Now the deal is off.

Suppose that the other party does not go bankrupt until a year after the bank entered into the swap. In the meantime interest rates have moved in the bank's favor, so it should be receiving more money from the swap than it is paying out. When the other side defaults on the deal,

---

[33]Bank for International Settlements, *Derivatives Statistics* (**www.bis.org/statistics/derstats.htm**).

the bank loses the difference between the interest that it is due to receive and the interest that it should pay. But it doesn't lose $10 million.[34]

The only meaningful measure of the potential loss from default is the amount that it would cost firms showing a profit to replace their positions.

---

[34]This does not mean that firms don't worry about the possibility of default, and there are a variety of ways that they try to protect themselves. In the case of swaps, firms are reluctant to deal with banks that do not have the highest credit rating.

As a manager, you are paid to take risks, but you are not paid to take just any risks. Some risks are simply bad bets, and others could jeopardize the value of the firm. Hedging risks, when it is practical to do so, can make sense if it reduces the chance of cash shortfalls or financial distress. In some cases, hedging can also make it easier to monitor and motivate operating managers. Relieving managers of risk outside their control helps them concentrate on what can be controlled.

Most businesses insure against possible losses. Insurance companies specialize in assessing risks and can pool risks by holding a diversified portfolio of policies. Insurance works less well when policies are taken up by companies that are most at risk (*adverse selection*) or when the insured company is tempted to skip on maintenance or safety procedures (*moral hazard*).

Firms can also hedge with options and with forward and futures contracts. A forward contract is an advance order to buy or sell an asset. The forward price is fixed today, but payment is not made until the delivery date at the end of the contract. Forward contracts that are traded on organized futures exchanges are called futures contracts. Futures contracts are standardized and traded in huge volumes. The futures markets allow firms to lock in future prices for dozens of different commodities, securities, and currencies.

Instead of buying or selling a standardized futures contract, you may be able to arrange a tailor-made forward contract with a bank. Firms can protect against changes in foreign exchange rates by buying or selling forward currency contracts. Forward rate agreements (FRAs) provide protection against changes in interest rates. You can construct homemade forward contracts. For example, if you borrow for two years and at the same time lend for one year, you have effectively taken out a forward loan.

Firms also hedge with swap contracts. For example, a firm can make a deal to pay interest to a bank at a fixed long-term rate and receive interest from the bank at a floating short-term rate. The firm swaps a fixed for a floating rate. Such a swap could make sense if the firm has relatively easy access to short-term borrowing but dislikes the exposure to fluctuating short-term interest rates.

The theory of hedging is straightforward. You find two closely related assets. You then buy one and sell the other in proportions that minimize the risk of your net position. If the assets are *perfectly* correlated, you can make the net position risk-free. If they are less than perfectly correlated, you will have to absorb some basis risk.

The trick is to find the hedge ratio or delta—that is, the number of units of one asset that is needed to offset changes in the value of the other asset. Sometimes the best solution is to look at how the prices of the two assets have moved together in the past. For example, suppose you observe that a 1% change in the value of B has been accompanied on average by a 2% change in the value of A. Then delta equals 2.0; to hedge each dollar invested in A, you need to sell two dollars of B.

On other occasions theory can help to set up the hedge. For example, the effect of a change in interest rates on an asset's value depends on the asset's duration. If two assets have the same duration, they will be equally affected by fluctuations in interest rates.

Many of the hedges described in this chapter are static. Once you have set up the hedge, you can take a long vacation, confident that the firm is well protected. However, some hedges, such as those that match durations, are dynamic. As time passes and prices change, you need to rebalance your position to maintain the hedge.

Hedging and risk reduction sound as wholesome as mom's apple pie. But remember that hedging solely to reduce risk cannot add value. It is a zero-sum game: Risks aren't eliminated, just shifted to some counterparty. And remember that your shareholders can also hedge by adjusting the composition of their portfolios or by trading in futures or other derivatives. Investors won't reward the firm for doing something that they can do perfectly well for themselves.

Some companies have decided that speculation is much more fun than hedging. This view can lead to serious trouble. We do not believe that speculation makes sense for an industrial company, but we caution against assuming that derivatives are a threat to the financial system.

FURTHER READING

Three general articles on corporate risk management are:

K. A. Froot, D. S. Scharfstein, and J. C. Stein, "A Framework for Risk Management," *Harvard Business Review* 72 (November–December 1994), pp. 59–71.

B. W. Nocco and R. M. Stulz, "Enterprise Risk Management: Theory and Practice," *Journal of Applied Corporate Finance* 18 (Fall 2006), pp. 8–20.

C. H. Smithson and B. Simkins, "Does Risk Management Add Value? A Survey of the Evidence," *Journal of Applied Corporate Finance* 17 (Summer 2005), pp. 8–17.

The Summer 2005 and Fall 2006 issues of the Journal of Applied Corporate Finance *are devoted to risk management, and current news and developments are discussed in* Risk *magazine. You may also wish to refer to the following texts:*

J. C. Hull, *Options, Futures, and Other Derivatives,* 10th ed. (Cambridge, England: Pearson, 2017).

C. H. Smithson, *Managing Financial Risk,* 3rd ed. (New York: McGraw-Hill, 1998).

R. M. Stulz, *Risk Management and Derivatives* (Cincinnati, OH: Thomson-Southwestern Publishing, 2003).

Schaefer's paper is a useful review of how duration measures are used to immunize fixed liabilities:

S. M. Schaefer, "Immunisation and Duration: A Review of Theory, Performance and Applications," *Midland Corporate Finance Journal* 2 (Autumn 1984), pp. 41–59.

PROBLEM SETS

   **Select problems are available in McGraw-Hill's** *Connect.* **Please see the preface for more information.**

1. **Vocabulary check*** Define the following terms:
   a. Spot price
   b. Forward vs. futures contract
   c. Long vs. short position
   d. Basis risk
   e. Mark to market
   f. Net convenience yield

2. **Insurance** Large businesses spend millions of dollars annually on insurance. Why? Should they insure against all risks or does insurance make more sense for some risks than others?

3. **Catastrophe bonds** On some catastrophe bonds, payments are reduced if the claims against the issuer exceed a specified sum. In other cases, payments are reduced only if claims against the entire industry exceed some sum. What are the advantages and disadvantages of the two structures? Which involves more basis risk? Which may create a problem of moral hazard?

4. **Futures and options** A gold-mining firm is concerned about short-term volatility in its revenues. Gold currently sells for $1,300 an ounce, but the price is extremely volatile and could fall as low as $1,220 or rise as high as $1,380 in the next month. The company will bring 1,000 ounces to the market next month.

   a. What will be total revenues if the firm remains unhedged for gold prices of $1,220, $1,300, and $1,380 an ounce?

   b. The futures price of gold for delivery one month ahead is $1,310. What will be the firm's total revenues at each gold price if the firm enters into a one-month futures contract to deliver 1,000 ounces of gold?

   c. What will total revenues be if the firm buys a one-month put option to sell gold for $1,300 an ounce? The put option costs $110 per ounce.

5. **Futures and options** Petrochemical Parfum (PP) is concerned about a possible increase in the price of heavy fuel oil, which is one of its major inputs. Show how PP can use either options or futures contracts to protect itself against a rise in the price of crude oil. Show how the payoffs in each case would vary if the oil price were $70, $80, or $90 a barrel. What are the advantages and disadvantages for PP of using futures rather than options to reduce risk? Assume the current price of oil is $70 per barrel, the futures price is $80, and the option exercise price is $80.

6. **Futures contracts*** True or false?

   a. Hedging transactions in an active futures market have zero or slightly negative NPVs.

   b. When you buy a futures contract, you pay now for delivery at a future date.

   c. The holder of a financial futures contract misses out on any dividend or interest payments made on the underlying security.

   d. The holder of a commodities futures contract does not have to pay for storage costs, but foregoes convenience yield.

7. **Futures contracts** List some of the commodity futures contracts that are traded on exchanges. Who do you think could usefully reduce risk by buying each of these contracts? Who do you think might wish to sell each contract?

8. **Marking to market*** Yesterday, you sold six-month futures on the German DAX stock market index at a price of 13,200. Today, the DAX closed at 13,150 and DAX futures closed at 13,250. You get a call from your broker, who reminds you that your futures position is marked to market each day. Is she asking you to pay money, or is she about to offer to pay you?

9. **Futures prices** Calculate the value of a six-month futures contract on a Treasury bond. You have the following information:

   • Six-month interest rate: 10% per year, or 4.9% for six months.

   • Spot price of bond: 95.

   • The bond pays an 8% coupon, 4% every six months.

10. **Futures prices*** In December 2017, six-month futures on the Australian S&P/ASX 200 Index traded at 5,947. Spot was 6,001. The interest rate was 1.8% a year, and the dividend yield was about 4.4% a year. Were the futures fairly priced?

11. **Futures prices** If you buy a nine-month T-bill future, you undertake to buy a $1 million three-month bill in nine months' time. Suppose that Treasury bills and notes currently offer the following yields

Months to Maturity	Annual Yield
3	6%
6	6.5
9	7
12	8

What is the dollar value of a nine-month bill future?

Commodity	Spot Price	Futures Price	Comments
Magnoosium	$2,550 per ton	$2,728.50 per ton	Monthly storage cost = monthly convenience yield.
Frozen quiche	$0.50 per pound	$0.514 per pound	Six months' storage costs = $.10 per pound; six months' convenience yield = $.05 per pound.
Nevada Hydro 8s of 2002	77	78.39	4% semiannual coupon payment is due just before futures contract expires.
Costaguanan pulgas (currency)	9,300 pulgas = $1	6,900 pulgas = $1	Costaguanan interest rate is 95% per year.
Establishment Industries common stock	$95	$97.54	Establishment pays dividends of $2 per quarter. Next dividend is paid two months from now.
Cheap white wine	$12,500 per 10,000-gal tank	$14,200 per 10,000-gal tank	Six months' convenience yield = $250 per tank. Your company has surplus storage and can store 50,000 gallons at no cost.

❱ **TABLE 26.5**   Spot and six-month futures prices for selected commodities and securities. See Problem 12.

12. **Futures prices** Table 26.5 contains spot and six-month futures prices for several commodities and financial instruments. There may be some money-making opportunities. See if you can find them, and explain how you would trade to take advantage of them. The interest rate is 14.5%, or 7% over the six-month life of the contracts.

13. **Futures prices** The following table shows 2014 gold futures prices for varying contract lengths. Gold is predominantly an investment good, not an industrial commodity. Investors hold gold because it diversifies their portfolios and because they hope its price will rise. They do not hold it for its convenience yield.

	Contract Length (months)		
	3	6	9
Futures price	$1,188.5	$1,189.5	$1,190.0

Calculate the interest rate faced by traders in gold futures, assuming a zero net convenience yield, for each of the contract lengths shown above. The spot price is $1,188.2 per ounce.

14. **Futures prices** Consider the commodities and financial assets listed in Table 26.6. The risk-free interest rate is 6% a year, and the term structure is flat.

   a. Calculate the six-month futures price for each case.

   b. Explain how a magnoosium producer would use a futures market to lock in the selling price of a planned shipment of 1,000 tons of magnoosium six months from now.

   c. Suppose the producer takes the actions recommended in your answer to part (b), but after one month magnoosium prices have fallen to $2,200. What happens? Will the producer have to undertake additional futures market trades to restore its hedged position?

   d. Does the biotech index futures price provide useful information about the expected future performance of biotech stocks?

   e. Suppose Allen Wrench stock falls suddenly by $10 per share. Investors are confident that the cash dividend will not be reduced. What happens to the futures price?

Asset	Spot Price	Comments
Magnoosium	$2,800 per ton	Net convenience yield = 4% per year
Oat bran	$0.44 per bushel	Net convenience yield = 0.5% per month
Biotech stock index	$140.2	Dividend = 0
Allen Wrench Co. common stock	$58.00	Cash dividend = $2.40 per year
5-year Treasury note	$108.93	8% coupon
Westonian ruple	3.1 ruples = $1	12% interest rate in ruples

❯ **TABLE 26.6**   Spot prices for selected commodities and financial assets. See Problem 14.

    f. Suppose interest rates suddenly fall to 4%. The term structure remains flat. What happens to the six-month futures price on the five-year Treasury note? What happens to a trader who shorted 100 notes at the futures price calculated in part (a)?

    g. An importer must make a payment of one million ruples three months from now. Explain *two* strategies the importer could use to hedge against unfavorable shifts in the ruple–dollar exchange rate.

15. **Convenience yield** Calculate convenience yield for magnoosium scrap from the following information:

- Spot price: $2,550 per ton.
- Futures price: $2,408 for a one-year contract.
- Interest rate: 12%.
- Storage costs: $100 per year.

16. **Convenience yield** Residents of the northeastern United States suffered record-setting low temperatures throughout November and December 2024. Spot prices of heating oil rose 25%, to over $7 a gallon.

    a. What effect did this have on the net convenience yield and on the relationship between futures and spot prices?

    b. In late 2025 refiners and distributors were surprised by record-setting *high* temperatures. What was the effect on net convenience yield and spot and futures prices for heating oil?

17. **Convenience yield** After a record harvest, grain silos are full to the brim. Are storage costs likely to be high or low? What does this imply for the *net* convenience yield?

18. **Convenience yield** In March 2018, six-month bitcoin futures were priced at $7,925. The spot price was $7,946. The six-month interest rate was 1.92%.

    a. What was the convenience yield?

    b. Is your answer to part (a) consistent with what you would expect? Explain.

19. **Interest rate swaps** A year ago, a bank entered into a $50 million five-year interest rate swap. It agreed to pay company A each year a fixed rate of 6% and to receive in return LIBOR. When the bank entered into this swap, LIBOR was 5%, but now interest rates have risen, so on a four-year interest rate swap the bank could expect to pay 6.5% and receive LIBOR.

    a. Is the swap showing a profit or loss to the bank?

    b. Suppose that at this point company A approaches the bank and asks to terminate the swap. If there are four annual payments still remaining, how much should the bank charge A to terminate?

20. **Interest rate swaps** In September 2020, swap dealers were quoting a rate for five-year euro interest-rate swaps of 4.5% against Euribor (the short-term interest rate for euro loans).

Euribor at the time was 4.1%. Suppose that A arranges with a dealer to swap a €10 million five-year fixed-rate loan for an equivalent floating-rate loan in euros.

a. Assume the swap is fairly priced. What is the value of this swap at the time that it is entered into?

b. Suppose that immediately after A has entered into the swap, the long-term interest rate rises by 1%. Who gains and who loses?

c. What is now the value of the swap for each €1,000 of notional value?

21. **Total return swaps** Is a total return swap on a bond the same as a credit default swap (see Section 23-1)? Why or why not?

22. **Hedging** "Speculators want futures contracts to be incorrectly priced; hedgers want them to be correctly priced." Why?

23. **Hedging** "Northern Refineries does not avoid risk by selling oil futures. If prices stay above $2.40 a gallon, then it will actually have lost by selling oil futures at that price." Is this a fair comment?

24. **Hedging** What is meant by "delta" (δ) in the context of hedging? Give examples of how delta can be estimated or calculated.

25. **Hedging*** You own a $1 million portfolio of aerospace stocks with a beta of 1.2. You are very enthusiastic about aerospace but uncertain about the prospects for the overall stock market. Explain how you could hedge out your market exposure by selling the market short. How much would you sell? How in practice would you go about "selling the market"?

26. **Hedging**

a. Marshall Arts has just invested $1 million in long-term Treasury bonds. Marshall is concerned about increasing volatility in interest rates. He decides to hedge using bond futures contracts. Should he buy or sell such contracts?

b. The treasurer of Zeta Corporation plans to issue bonds in three months. She is also concerned about interest rate volatility and wants to lock in the price at which her company could sell 5% coupon bonds. How would she use bond futures contracts to hedge?

27. **Hedging** Phoenix Motors wants to lock in the cost of 10,000 ounces of platinum to be used in next quarter's production of catalytic converters. It buys three-month futures contracts for 10,000 ounces at a price of $1,300 per ounce.

a. Suppose the spot price of platinum falls to $1,200 in three months' time. Does Phoenix have a profit or loss on the futures contract? Has it locked in the cost of purchasing the platinum it needs?

b. How do your answers change if the spot price of platinum increases to $1,400 after three months?

28. **Hedging** Legs Diamond owns shares in a Vanguard Index 500 mutual fund worth $1 million on July 15. (This is an index fund that tracks the Standard and Poor's 500 Index.) He wants to cash in now, but his accountant advises him to wait six months so as to defer a large capital gains tax. Explain to Legs how he can use stock index futures to hedge out his exposure to market movements over the next six months. Could Legs "cash in" without actually selling his shares?

29. **Hedging** Price changes of two gold-mining stocks have shown strong positive correlation. Their historical relationship is

Average percentage change in A = .001 + .75 (percentage change in B)

Changes in B explain 60% of the variation of the changes in A ($R^2 = .6$).

a. Suppose you own $100,000 of A. How much of B should you sell to minimize the risk of your net position?

b. What is the hedge ratio?

c. Here is the historical relationship between stock A and gold prices:

Average percentage change in A = −.002 + 1.2 (percentage change in gold price)

If $R^2 = .5$, can you lower the risk of your net position by hedging with gold (or gold futures) rather than with stock B? Explain.

30. **Hedging** Your investment bank has an investment of $100 million in the stock of the Swiss Roll Corporation and a short position in the stock of the Frankfurter Sausage Company. Here is the recent price history of the two stocks:

Month	Percentage Price Change	
	Frankfurter Sausage	**Swiss Roll**
January	−10	−10
February	−10	−5
March	−10	0
April	+10	0
May	+10	+5
June	+10	+10

On the evidence of these six months, how large would your short position in Frankfurter Sausage need to be to hedge as far as possible against movements in the price of Swiss Roll?

31. **Duration hedging*** Securities A, B, and C have the following cash flows:

	Year 1	Year 2	Year 3
A	$ 40	$40	$ 40
B	120	—	—
C	10	10	110

a. Calculate their durations if the interest rate is 8%.

b. Suppose that you have an investment of $10 million in A. What combination of B and C would hedge this investment against interest rate changes?

c. Now suppose that you have a $10 million investment in B. How would you hedge?

32. **Basis risk*** What is basis risk? In which of the following cases would you expect basis risk to be serious?

a. A broker owning a large block of Disney common stock hedges by selling index futures.

b. An Iowa corn farmer hedges the selling price of her crop by selling Chicago corn futures.

c. An importer must pay 900 million euros in six months. He hedges by buying euros forward.

CHALLENGE

33. **Interest rate swaps** Phillip's Screwdriver Company has borrowed $20 million from a bank at a floating interest rate of 2 percentage points above three-month Treasury bills, which now yield 5%. Assume that interest payments are made quarterly and that the entire principal of the loan is repaid after five years.

Phillip's wants to convert the bank loan to fixed-rate debt. It could have issued a fixed-rate five-year note at a yield to maturity of 9%. Such a note would now trade at par. The five-year Treasury note's yield to maturity is 7%.

a. Is Phillip's stupid to want long-term debt at an interest rate of 9%? It is borrowing from the bank at 7%.

b. Explain how the conversion could be carried out by an interest rate swap. What will be the initial terms of the swap? (Ignore transaction costs and the swap dealer's profit.)

One year from now short and medium-term Treasury yields *decrease* to 6%, so the term structure then is flat. (The changes actually occur in month 5.) Phillip's credit standing is unchanged; it can still borrow at 2 percentage points over Treasury rates.

c. What net swap payment will Phillip's make or receive?

d. Suppose that Phillip's now wants to cancel the swap. How much would it need to pay the swap dealer? Or would the dealer pay Phillip's? Explain.

FINANCE ON THE WEB

1. The websites of the major commodities exchanges provide futures prices. Calculate the *annualized* net convenience yield for a commodity of your choice. (*Note:* You may need to use the futures price of a contract that is about to mature as your estimate of the current spot price.)

2. You can find swap rates for the U.S. dollar and the euro on **www.ft.com**. Plot the current swap curves as in Figure 26.3.

3. You can find spot and futures prices for a variety of equity indexes on **www.wsj.com**. Pick one and check whether it is fairly priced. You will need to do some detective work to find the dividend yield on the index and the interest rate.

MINI-CASE •••••

Rensselaer Advisers

You are a vice president of Rensselaer Advisers (RA), which manages portfolios for institutional investors (primarily corporate pension plans) and wealthy individuals. In mid-2018, RA had about $1.1 billion under management, invested in a wide range of common-stock and fixed-income portfolios. Its management fees average 55 basis points (.55%), so RA's total revenue for 2018 is about .0055 × $1.1 billion = $6.05 million.

You are attempting to land a new client, Madison Mills, a conservative, long-established manufacturer of papermaking felt. Madison has established a defined-benefit pension plan for its employees. RA would manage the pension assets that Madison has set aside to cover defined-benefit obligations for retired employees.

Defined benefit means that an employer is committed to pay retirement income according to a formula. For example, annual retirement income could equal 40% of the employee's average salary in the five years prior to retirement. In a defined-benefit plan, retirement income does not depend on the performance of the pension assets. If the assets in the fund are not sufficient to cover pension benefits, the company is required to contribute enough additional cash to cover the shortfall. Thus, the PV of promised retirement benefits is a debt-equivalent obligation of the company.[35]

Table 26.7 shows Madison's obligations to its already retired employees from 2019 to 2040. Each of these employees receives a fixed dollar amount each month. Total dollar payments decline as the employees die off. The PV of the obligations in Table 26.7 is about $89 million at the current (2018) 5% long-term interest rate. Table 26.7 also calculates the duration of the obligations at 7.87 years.

Madison has set aside $90 million in pension assets to cover the obligations in Table 26.7, so this part of its pension plan is fully funded.[36] The pension assets are now invested in a diversified portfolio of common stocks, corporate bonds, and notes.

Year	Date (t)	Payment	PV at 5%	PV × t
2019	1	10,020,000	9,542,857	9,542,857
2020	2	9,009,500	8,171,882	16,343,764
2021	3	8,522,000	7,361,624	22,084,872
2022	4	8,434,500	6,939,084	27,756,336
2023	5	7,858,500	6,157,340	30,786,702
2024	6	7,794,000	5,816,003	34,896,017
2025	7	7,729,500	5,493,211	38,452,479
2026	8	7,639,500	5,170,714	41,365,714
2027	9	6,440,500	4,151,604	37,364,434
2028	10	6,330,000	3,886,071	38,860,709
2029	11	6,242,500	3,649,860	40,148,465
2030	12	6,205,000	3,455,176	41,462,114
2031	13	5,775,500	3,062,871	39,817,322
2032	14	5,600,700	2,828,734	39,602,277
2033	15	5,432,000	2,612,885	39,193,273
2034	16	5,140,000	23,54,693	3,76,75,092
2035	17	4,234,900	1,847,673	31,410,438
2036	18	4,123,000	1,713,192	30,837,450
2037	19	3,890,000	1,539,405	29,248,697
2038	20	3,500,600	1,319,339	26,386,786
2039	21	3,400,500	1,220,584	25,632,254
2040	22	3,340,600	1,141,984	25,123,641
			SUM =	703,991,694
			PV =	89,436,787
			DURATION =	7.87

> **〉TABLE 26.7**
> **Madison Mills Pension Fund, projected benefits for retired employees**

---

[35]In *defined contribution* plans, the corporation contributes to the pension fund on behalf of its employees. Each employee has a claim on part of the fund, just as if the employee held shares in a mutual fund. Employees' retirement benefits depend on their balances in the fund at retirement. If the benefits fall short of an employee's plans or expectations, he or she has no recourse to the company.
[36]Madison must also set pension assets aside for current employees. For this mini-case, we concentrate only on retired employees' benefits.

After reviewing Madison's existing portfolio, you schedule a meeting with Hendrik van Wie, Madison's CFO. Mr. van Wie stresses Madison's conservative management philosophy and warns against "speculation." He complains about the performance of the previous manager of the pension assets. He suggests that you propose a plan of investing in safe assets in a way that minimizes exposure to equity markets and changing interest rates. You promise to prepare an illustration of how this goal could be achieved.

Later, you discover that RA has competition for Madison's investment management business. SPX Associates is proposing a strategy of investing 70% of the portfolio ($63 million) in index funds tracking the U.S. stock market and 30% of the portfolio ($27 million) in U.S. Treasury securities. SPX argues that their strategy is "safe in the long run" because the U.S. stock market has delivered an average risk premium of about 7% per year. In addition, SPX argues that the growth in its stock market portfolio will far outstrip Madison's pension obligations. SPX also claims that the $27 million invested in Treasuries will provide ample protection against short-term stock market volatility. Finally, SPX proposes to charge an investment management fee of only 20 basis points (.20%). RA had planned to charge 30 basis points (.30%).

QUESTIONS

1. Prepare a memo for Mr. van Wie explaining how RA would invest to minimize both risk and exposure to changing interest rates. Give an example of a portfolio that would accomplish this objective. Explain how the portfolio would be managed as time passes and interest rates change. Also explain why SPX's proposal is not advisable for a conservative company like Madison.

   RA manages several fixed-income portfolios. For simplicity, you decide to propose a mix of the following three portfolios:

   - A portfolio of long-term Treasury bonds with an average duration of 14 years.
   - A portfolio of Treasury notes with an average duration of 7 years.
   - A portfolio of short-term Treasury bills and notes with an average duration of 1 year.

   The term structure is flat, and the yield on all three portfolios is 5%.

2. Sorry, you lost. SPX won and implemented its proposed strategy. Now the recession of 2019 has knocked down U.S. stock prices by 20%. The value of the Madison portfolio, after paying benefits for 2019, has fallen from $90 million to $78 million. At the same time interest rates have dropped from 5% to 4% as the Federal Reserve relaxes monetary policy to combat the recession.

   Mr. van Wie calls again, chastened by the SPX experience, and he invites a new proposal to invest the pension assets in a way that minimizes exposure to the stock market and changing interest rates. Update your memo with a new example of how to accomplish Mr. van Wie's objectives. You can use the same portfolios and portfolio durations as in Question 1. You will have to recalculate the PV and duration of the pension benefits from 2019 onward. Assume a flat term structure with all interest rates at 4%. (*Hint:* Madison's pension obligations are now *under*funded. Nevertheless, you can hedge interest rate risk if you increase the duration of the pension assets.)

CHAPTER

27

Managing International Risks

The last chapter grappled with risks from changing interest rates and volatile commodity prices. Corporations that operate internationally face still more hazards from currency fluctuations and political risks.

To understand currency risk, you first have to understand how the foreign exchange market works and how currency exchange rates are determined. We cover those topics first, with special emphasis on the linkages between exchange rates and cross-country differences in interest rates and inflation. Then we describe how corporations assess and hedge their currency exposures.

We also review international capital investment decisions. Cash flows for an investment project in Germany, say, must be forecasted in euros, with attention to German inflation rates and taxes. But euro cash flows require a euro discount rate. How should that rate be estimated? Should it depend on whether the investing company is located in the United States, Germany, or another country? Should the discount rate be adjusted for the risk that the euro may fall relative to other currencies? (The answer to the last question is no. The answers to the preceding questions are not so clear-cut.)

We conclude the chapter with a discussion of political risk. Political risk means possible adverse acts by a hostile foreign government, for example, discriminatory taxes or limits on the profits that can be taken out of the country. Sometimes governments expropriate businesses with minimal compensation. We explain how companies structure their operations and financing to reduce their exposure to political risks.

27-1 The Foreign Exchange Market

An American company that imports goods from France may need to buy euros to pay for the purchase. An American company exporting to France may receive euros, which it sells in exchange for dollars. Both firms make use of the foreign exchange market.

The foreign exchange market has no central marketplace. Business is conducted electronically. The principal dealers are the larger commercial banks and investment banks. A corporation that wants to buy or sell currency usually does so through a commercial bank. Turnover in the foreign exchange market is huge. In London in April 2016, $2,406 billion of currency changed hands each day. That is equivalent to an annual turnover of about $878 trillion ($878,000,000,000,000). New York, Singapore, Hong Kong, and Tokyo together accounted for a further $2,625 billion of turnover per day.[1]

---

[1]The results of the triennial survey of foreign exchange business are published on **www.bis.org/forum/research.htm**.

			Forward Rates		
	Abbreviation	Spot Rate	3 Months	6 Months	1 Year
Europe:					
Euro	EUR or €	1.1758	1.1800	1.1845	1.1916
Czech Republic (koruna)	CZK	21.853	21.605	21.549	21.388
Hungary (forint)	HUF	267.28	265.703	264.438	261.520
Poland (zloty)	PLN	3.5773	3.5691	3.5668	3.5618
Russia (ruble)	RUB	58.879	59.453	60.205	61.501
Sweden (krona)	SEK	8.4976	8.4388	8.3886	8.2836
Switzerland (franc)	CHF	.99059	.98222	.97504	.96089
United Kingdom (pound)	GBP or £	1.3321	1.3383	1.3428	1.3520
Americas:					
Brazil (real)	BRL	3.3124	3.3333	3.3664	3.4364
Canada (dollar)	CAD	1.2881	1.2854	1.2841	1.2820
Chile (peso)	CLP	635.93	635.77	636.62	639.14
Mexico	MXN	19.131	19.417	19.728	20.371
Pacific/Middle East/Africa:					
Australia (dollar)	AUD	1.3077	1.3082	1.3084	1.3084
China (yuan)	CNY	6.6076	6.6542	6.6947	6.7668
India (rupee)	INR	64.148	64.358	65.407	66.676
Israel (shekel)	ILS	3.5144	3.5010	3.4854	3.4511
Japan (yen)	JPY or ¥	112.61	111.94	111.34	109.99
New Zealand (dollar)	NZD	1.4294	1.4312	1.4323	1.4339
South Africa (rand)	ZAR	13.180	13.365	13.555	13.942
South Korea (won)	KRW	1,089.2	1,087.3	1,085.7	1,082.1
Turkey (lira)	TRY	3.8676	3.9739	4.0899	4.3306

❭ **TABLE 27.1   Spot and forward exchange rates, December 2017**

Source: CME Group.

[a]Rates show the number of units of foreign currency per U.S. dollar, except for the euro and the U.K. pound, which show the number of U.S. dollars per unit of foreign currency.

Table 27.1 shows a sample of exchange rates in December 2017. Exchange rates are generally expressed in terms of the number of units of the foreign currency needed to buy one U.S. dollar (USD). This is termed an *indirect quote*. In the first column of Table 27.1, the indirect quote for the Brazilian real shows that you could buy 3.3124 reals for $1. This is often written as BRL3.3124/USD1.

A *direct* exchange rate quote states how many dollars you can buy for one unit of foreign currency. The euro and the British pound sterling are usually shown as direct quotes.[2] For example, Table 27.1 shows that GBP1 is equivalent to USD1.3321 or, more concisely,

[2]The euro is the common currency of the European Monetary Union. The 19 members of the Union are Austria, Belgium, Cyprus, Estonia, Finland, France, Germany, Greece, Ireland, Italy, Latvia, Lithuania, Luxembourg, Malta, Netherlands, Portugal, Slovenia, Slovakia, and Spain.

USD1.3321/GBP1. If £1 buys $1.3321, then $1 must buy 1/1.3321 = GBP.7507. Thus, the indirect quote for the pound is GBP.7507/USD1.[3]

The exchange rates in the second column of Table 27.1 are the prices of currency for immediate delivery. These are known as **spot rates of exchange.** The spot rate for the real is BRL3.3124/USD1, and the spot rate for the pound is USD1.3321/GBP1.

In addition to the spot exchange market, there is a *forward market*. In the forward market you buy and sell currency for future delivery. If you know that you are going to pay out or receive foreign currency at some future date, you can insure yourself against loss by buying or selling forward. Thus, if you need one million reals in three months, you can enter into a three-month *forward contract*. The **forward exchange rate** on this contract is the price you agree to pay in three months when the one million reals are delivered. If you look again at Table 27.1, you will see that the three-month forward rate for the real is quoted at BRL3.3333/USD1. If you buy reals for three months' delivery, you get more reals for your dollar than if you buy them spot. In this case, the real is said to trade at a forward *discount* relative to the dollar because forward reals are cheaper than spot ones. Expressed as an annual rate, the forward discount is[4]

$$4 \times \left(\frac{3.3124}{3.3333} - 1 \right) = -.0251, \text{ or } -2.51\%$$

You could also say that the *dollar* was selling at a *forward premium*.

A forward purchase or sale is a made-to-measure transaction between you and the bank. It can be for any currency, any amount, and any delivery day. You could buy, say, 99,999 Vietnamese dong or Haitian gourdes for a year and a day forward as long as you can find a bank ready to deal. Most forward transactions are for six months or less, but the long-term currency swaps that we described in Chapter 26 are equivalent to a bundle of forward transactions. When firms want to enter into long-term forward contracts, they usually do so through a currency swap.[5]

There is also an organized market for currency for future delivery known as the currency *futures* market. Futures contracts are highly standardized; they are for specified amounts and for a limited choice of delivery dates.[6]

When you buy a forward or futures contract, you are committed to taking delivery of the currency. As an alternative, you can take out an *option* to buy or sell currency in the future at a price that is fixed today. Made-to-measure currency options can be bought from the major banks, and standardized options are traded on the options exchanges.

27-2 Some Basic Relationships

You can't develop a consistent international financial policy until you understand the reasons for the differences in exchange rates and interest rates. We consider the following four problems:

- *Problem 1.* Why is the dollar rate of interest different from, say, the rate on Ruritanian pesos (RUPs)?

- *Problem 2.* Why is the forward rate of exchange for the peso different from the spot rate?

---

[3]Foreign exchange dealers usually refer to the exchange rate between pounds and dollars as *cable*. In Table 27.1, cable is 1.3321.
[4]Here is an occasional point of confusion. Since the quote for the real is indirect, we calculate the premium by taking the ratio of the spot rate to the forward rate. If we use *direct* quotes, then we need to calculate the ratio of the forward rate to the spot rate. In the case of the real, the forward discount with direct quotes is 4 × [(1/3.3333)/(1/3.3124) − 1] = −.0251, or −2.51%.
[5]Notice that spot and short-term forward trades are sometimes undertaken together. For example, a company might need the use of Brazilian reals for one month. In this case, it would buy reals spot and simultaneously sell them forward.
[6]See Chapter 26 for a further discussion of the difference between forward and futures contracts.

- *Problem 3.* What determines next year's expected spot rate of exchange between dollars and pesos?
- *Problem 4.* What is the relationship between the inflation rate in the United States and the inflation rate in Ruritania?

Suppose that individuals were not worried about risk and that there were no barriers or costs to international trade on capital flows. In that case, the spot exchange rates, forward exchange rates, interest rates, and inflation rates would stand in the following simple relationship to one another:

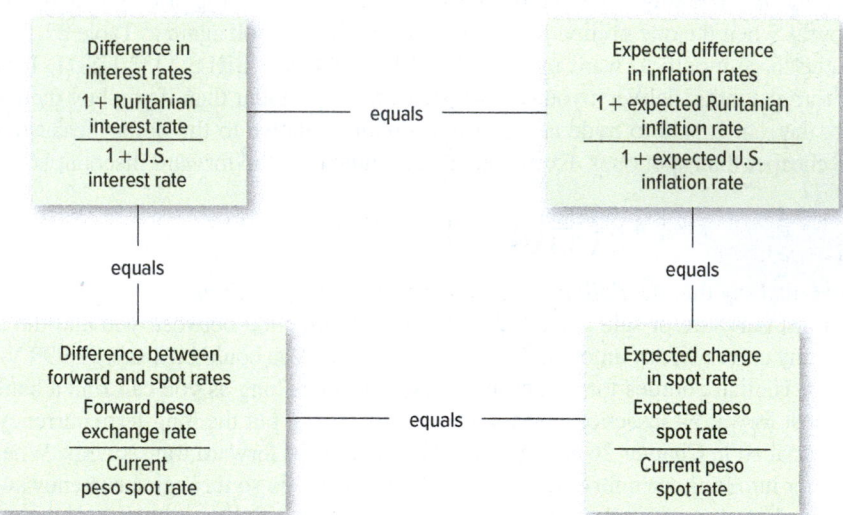

Why should this be so?

Interest Rates and Exchange Rates

Suppose that you have $1,000 to invest for one year. U.S. dollar deposits are offering an interest rate of 5%; Ruritanian peso deposits are offering (an attractive?) 15.5%. Where should you put your money? Does the answer sound obvious? Let's check:

- *Dollar loan.* The rate of interest on one-year dollar deposits is 5%. Therefore, at the end of the year you get $1,000 \times 1.05 = \text{USD}1,050$.
- *Peso loan.* The current exchange rate is RUP50/USD1. Therefore, for $1,000, you can buy $1,000 \times 50 = \text{RUP}50,000$. The rate of interest on a one-year peso deposit is 15.5%. Therefore, at the end of the year you get $50,000 \times 1.155 = \text{RUP}57,750$. Of course, you don't know what the exchange rate is going to be in one year's time. But that doesn't matter. You can fix today the price at which you sell your pesos. The one-year forward rate is RUP55/USD1. Therefore, by selling forward, you can make sure that you will receive $57,750/55 = \$1,050$ at the end of the year.

Thus, the two investments offer the same rate of return. They have to—they are both risk-free. If the domestic interest rate were different from the *covered* foreign interest rate, you would have a money machine.

When you make the peso loan, you receive a higher interest rate. But you get an offsetting loss because you sell pesos forward at a lower price than you pay for them today. The interest rate differential is

$$\frac{1 + \text{Ruritanian interest rate}}{1 + \text{U.S. interest rate}}$$

And the differential between the forward and spot exchange rates is

$$\frac{\text{Forward peso exchange rate}}{\text{Current peso spot rate}}$$

Interest rate parity theory says that the difference in interest rates must equal the difference between the forward and spot exchange rates:

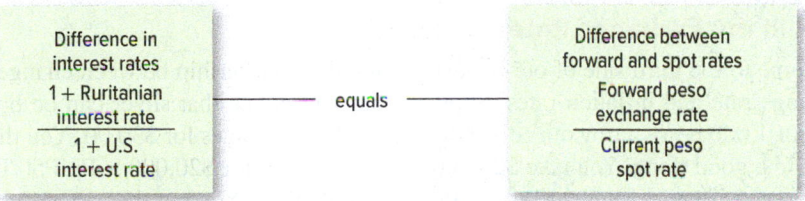

In our example,

$$\frac{1.155}{1.05} = \frac{55}{50}$$

The Forward Premium and Changes in Spot Rates

Now let's consider how the forward premium is related to changes in spot rates of exchange. If people didn't care about risk, the forward rate of exchange would depend solely on what people expected the spot rate to be. For example, if the one-year forward rate on pesos is RUP55/USD1, that could only be because traders expect the spot rate in one year's time to be RUP55/USD1. If they expected it to be, say, RUP60/USD1, nobody would be willing to buy pesos forward. They could get more pesos for their dollar by waiting and buying spot.

Therefore the *expectations theory* of exchange rates tells us that the percentage difference between the forward exchange rate and today's spot rate is equal to the expected change in the spot rate:

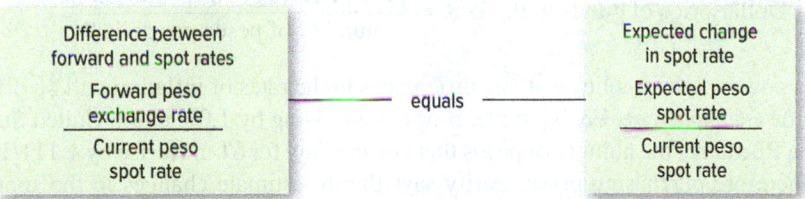

Of course, this assumes that traders don't care about risk. If they do care, the forward rate can be either higher or lower than the expected spot rate. For example, suppose that you have contracted to receive one million pesos in three months. You can wait until you receive the money before you change it into dollars, but this leaves you open to the risk that the price of the peso may fall over the next three months. Your alternative is to sell the peso forward. In this case, you are fixing today the price at which you will sell your pesos. Since you avoid risk by selling forward, you may be willing to do so even if the forward price of pesos is a little *lower* than the expected spot price.

Other companies may be in the opposite position. They may have contracted to pay out pesos in three months. They can wait until the end of the three months and then buy pesos, but this leaves them open to the risk that the price of the peso may rise. It is safer for these companies to fix the price today by *buying* pesos forward. These companies may, therefore, be willing to buy forward even if the forward price of the peso is a little *higher* than the expected spot price.

Thus, some companies find it safer to *sell* the peso forward, while others find it safer to *buy* the peso forward. When the first group predominates, the forward price of pesos is likely to be less than the expected spot price. When the second group predominates, the forward price is likely to be greater than the expected spot price. On average you would expect the forward price to underestimate the expected spot price just about as often as it overestimates it.

Changes in the Exchange Rate and Inflation Rates

Now we come to the third side of our quadrilateral—the relationship between changes in the spot exchange rate and inflation rates. Suppose that you notice that silver can be bought in Ruritania for 1,000 pesos a troy ounce and sold in the United States for $30.00. You think you may be on to a good thing. You take $20,000 and exchange it for $20,000 × RUP50/USD1 = 1,000,000 pesos. That's enough to buy 1,000 ounces of silver. You put this silver on the first plane to the United States, where you sell it for $30,000. You have made a gross profit of $10,000. Of course, you have to pay transportation and insurance costs out of this, but there should still be something left over for you.

Money machines don't exist—not for long, anyway. As others notice the disparity between the price of silver in Ruritania and the price in the United States, the price will be forced up in Ruritania and down in the United States until the profit opportunity disappears. Arbitrage ensures that the dollar price of silver is about the same in the two countries. Of course, silver is a standard and easily transportable commodity, but the same forces should act to equalize the domestic and foreign prices of other goods. Those goods that can be bought more cheaply abroad will be imported, and that will force down the price of domestic products. Similarly, those goods that can be bought more cheaply in the United States will be exported, and that will force down the price of the foreign products.

This is often called *purchasing power parity*.[7] Just as the price of goods in Walmart stores must be roughly the same as the price of goods in Target, so the price of goods in Ruritania when converted into dollars must be roughly the same as the price in the United States:

$$\text{Dollar price of goods in the U.S.} = \frac{\text{peso price of goods in Ruritania}}{\text{number of pesos per dollar}}$$

Purchasing power parity implies that any differences in the rates of inflation will be offset by a change in the exchange rate. For example, if prices are rising by 1.0% in the United States and by 11.1% in Ruritania, the number of pesos that you can buy for $1 must rise by 1.111/1.01 − 1, or 10%. Therefore purchasing power parity says that to estimate changes in the spot rate of exchange, you need to estimate differences in inflation rates:[8]

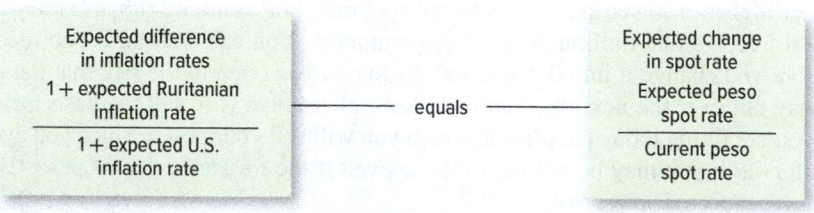

---

[7]Economists use the term *purchasing power parity* to refer to the notion that the level of prices of goods in general must be the same in the two countries. They tend to use the phrase *law of one price* when they are talking about the price of a single good.

[8]In other words, the *expected* difference in inflation rates equals the *expected* change in the exchange rate. Strictly interpreted, purchasing power parity also implies that the *actual* difference in the inflation rates always equals the *actual* change in the exchange rate.

In our example,

$$\text{Current spot rate} \times \text{expected difference in inflation rates} = \text{expected spot rate}$$

$$50 \times \frac{1.111}{1.010} = 55$$

Interest Rates and Inflation Rates

Now for the fourth leg! Just as water always flows downhill, so capital tends to flow where returns are greatest. But investors are not interested in *nominal* returns; they care about what their money will buy. So, if investors notice that real interest rates are higher in Ruritania than in the United States, they will shift their savings into Ruritania until the expected real returns are the same in the two countries. If the expected real interest rates are equal, then the difference in nominal interest rates must be equal to the difference in the expected inflation rates:[9]

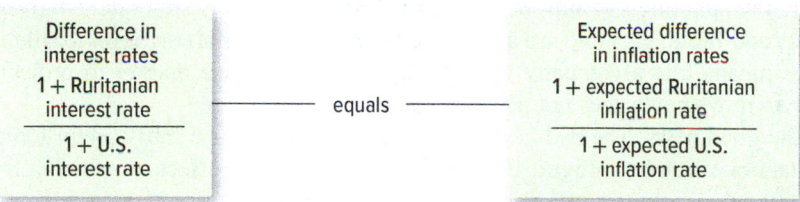

In Ruritania the real one-year interest rate is 4%:

$$\text{Ruritanian expected real interest rate} = \frac{1 + \text{Ruritanian nominal interest rate}}{1 + \text{Ruritanian expected inflation rate}} - 1$$

$$= \frac{1.155}{1.111} - 1 = .040$$

In the United States it is also 4%:

$$\text{U.S. expected real interest rate} = \frac{1 + \text{U.S. nominal interest rate}}{1 + \text{U.S. expected inflation rate}} - 1$$

$$= \frac{1.050}{1.010} - 1 = .040$$

Is Life Really That Simple?

We have described four theories that link interest rates, forward rates, spot exchange rates, and inflation rates. Of course, such simple economic theories are not going to provide an exact description of reality. We need to know how well they predict actual behavior. Let's check.

1. Interest Rate Parity Theory   Interest rate parity theory says that the peso rate of interest covered for exchange risk should be the same as the dollar rate. Before the financial crisis of 2007–2009, interest rate parity almost always held, provided money could be moved easily between deposits in the different currencies. In fact, dealers would *set* the forward price of pesos by looking at the difference between the interest rates on deposits of dollars and pesos. However, during the financial crisis this relationship broke down. Du, Tepper and Verdahlan provide evidence that the relationship was persistently violated for some time following 2009 among

---

[9]In Section 3-5, we discussed Irving Fisher's theory that money interest rates change to reflect changes in anticipated inflation. Here we argue that international differences in money interest rates also reflect differences in anticipated inflation. This theory is sometimes known as the *international Fisher effect*.

the major currencies. They argue that this persistence was partly due to new leverage restrictions on banks, which increased arbitrage costs and caused them to shy away from such activity.[10]

2. The Expectations Theory of Forward Rates   How well does the expectations theory explain the level of forward rates? Scholars who have studied exchange rates have found that forward rates typically exaggerate the likely change in the spot rate. When the forward rate appears to predict a sharp rise in the spot rate (a forward premium), the forward rate tends to overestimate the rise in the spot rate. Conversely, when the forward rate appears to predict a fall in the currency (a forward discount), it tends to overestimate this fall.[11]

This finding is *not* consistent with the expectations theory. Instead it looks as if sometimes companies are prepared to give up return to *buy* forward currency and other times they are prepared to give up return to *sell* forward currency. In other words, forward rates seem to contain a risk premium, but the sign of this premium swings backward and forward.[12] You can see this from Figure 27.1. Almost half the time the forward rate for the U.K. pound *overstates* the likely future spot rate and half the time it *understates* the likely spot rate. *On average,* the forward rate and future spot rate are almost identical. This is important news for the financial manager; it means that a company that always uses the forward market to protect against exchange rate movements does not pay any extra for this insurance.

That's the good news. The bad news is that the forward rate is a fairly awful forecaster of the spot rate. For example, in Figure 27.1 the large error in 1985 reflects the total failure of the forward rate to anticipate the 34% rise in the value of sterling.

3. Purchasing Power Parity Theory   What about the third side of our quadrilateral—purchasing power parity theory? No one who has compared prices in foreign stores with

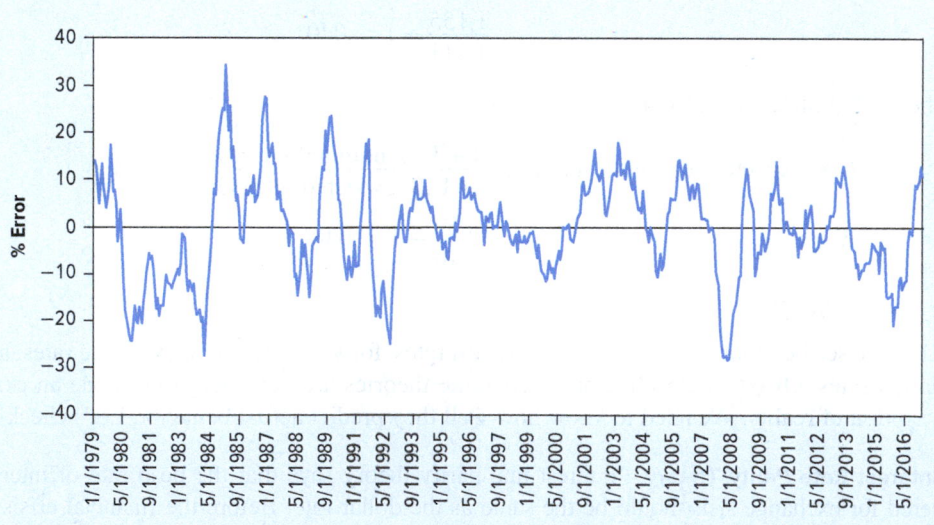

► **FIGURE 27.1**

Percentage error from using the one-year forward rate for U.K. pounds to forecast next year's spot rate. Note that the forward rate overestimates and underestimates the spot rate with about equal frequency.

Source: Bank of England.

---

[10]See W. Du, A. Tepper, and A. Verdelhan, "Deviations from Covered Interest Rate Parity," *Journal of Finance,* 73 (February 2018), pp.915–957. However, for evidence that deviations from interest rate parity theory are fading away, see H. Mance, "Cross-Currency Basis, RIP?" FT Alphaville, October 11, 2017, **https://ftalphaville.ft.com/2017/10/11/2194672/cross-currency-basis-rip/**

[11]Many researchers have even found that, when the forward rate predicts a rise, the spot rate is more likely to fall, and vice versa. For a readable discussion of this puzzling finding, see K. A. Froot and R. H. Thaler, "Anomalies: Foreign Exchange," *Journal of Economic Perspectives* 4 (1990), pp. 179–192.

[12]For evidence that forward exchange rates contain risk premiums that are sometimes positive and sometimes negative, see, for example, E. F. Fama, "Forward and Spot Exchange Rates," *Journal of Monetary Economics* 14 (1984), pp. 319–338.

Country	Local Price Converted to U.S. Dollars ($)
Brazil	5.11
Canada	5.26
China	3.17
Egypt	1.93
Euro area	4.84
India	2.82
Japan	3.43
Norway	6.24
Russia	2.29
South Africa	2.45
Switzerland	6.76
Turkey	2.83
United Kingdom	4.41
United States	5.28

❭**TABLE 27.2**   Price of Big Mac hamburgers in different countries

Source: "The Mac Strikes Back," *The Economist,* January 20, 2018, http://www.economist.com/content/big-mac-index.

prices at home really believes that prices are the same throughout the world. Look, for example, at Table 27.2, which shows the price of a Big Mac in different countries. Notice that at current rates of exchange a Big Mac costs $6.76 in Switzerland but only $5.28 in the United States. To equalize prices in the two countries, the number of Swiss francs that you could buy for your dollar would need to increase by 6.76/5.28 − 1 = .28, or 28%.

This suggests a possible way to make a quick buck. Why don't you buy a hamburger to-go in (say) Egypt for the equivalent of $1.93 and take it for resale in Switzerland, where the price in dollars is $6.76? The answer, of course, is that the gain would not cover the costs. The same good can be sold for different prices in different countries because transportation is costly and inconvenient.[13]

On the other hand, there is clearly some relationship between inflation and changes in exchange rates. For example, between 2012 and 2017 prices in Malawi rose by 270% relative to prices in the United States. Or, to put it another way, you could say that the relative purchasing power of money in Malawi declined by almost two-thirds. If exchange rates had not adjusted, exporters in Malawi would have found it impossible to sell their goods. But, of course, exchange rates did adjust. In fact, the value of the Malawian kwacha fell by 78% relative to the U.S. dollar.

In Figure 27.2, we have plotted the relative change in purchasing power for a sample of countries against the change in the exchange rate. Malawi is tucked in the bottom left-hand corner. You can see that although the relationship is far from exact, large differences in inflation rates are generally accompanied by an offsetting change in the exchange rate.[14]

Strictly speaking, purchasing power parity theory implies that the differential inflation rate is always identical to the change in the spot rate. But we don't need to go as far as that. We

---

[13]Of course, even within a currency area there may be considerable price variations. The price of a Big Mac, for example, differs substantially from one part of the United States to another.

[14]Note that some of the countries represented in Figure 27.2 have highly controlled economies, so that their exchange rates are not those that would exist in an unrestricted market. The interest rates shown in Figure 27.4 are subject to a similar caveat.

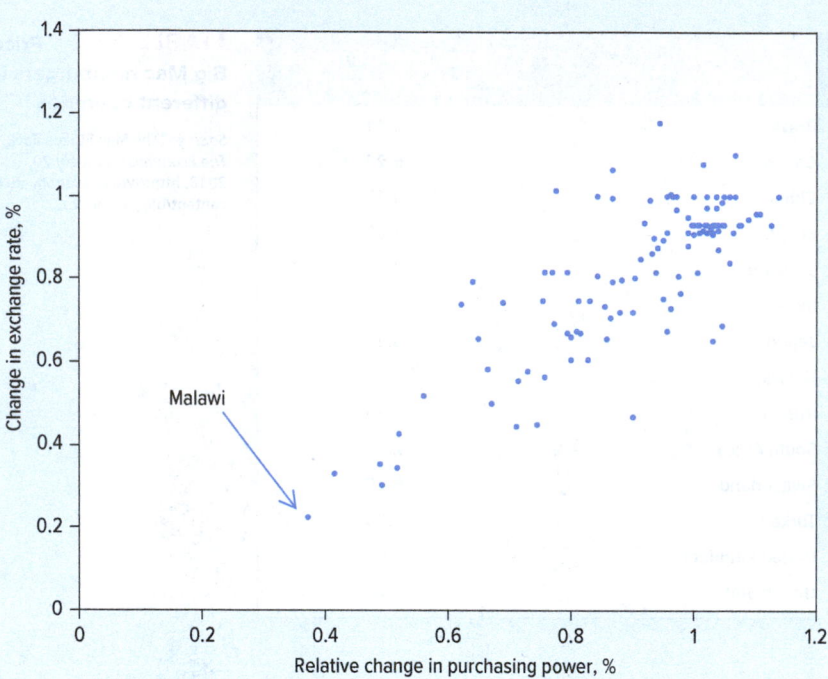

FIGURE 27.2

A decline in the exchange rate and a decline in a currency's purchasing power tend to go hand in hand. In this diagram each of the 120 points represents the experience of a different country in the period 2012–2017. The vertical axis shows the change in the value of the foreign currency relative to the dollar. The horizontal axis shows the change in the purchasing power relative to that of the USA. The point in the lower left is Malawi.

Source: IMF, International Financial Statistics.

should be content if the *expected* difference in the inflation rates equals the *expected* change in the spot rate. That's all we wrote on the third side of our quadrilateral. Look, for example, at Figure 27.3. The blue line in the first plot shows that in 2014 £1 sterling bought only 32% of the dollars that it did at the start of the twentieth century. But this decline in the value of sterling was largely matched by the higher inflation rate in the U.K. The red line shows that the inflation-adjusted, or *real,* exchange rate ended the century at roughly the same level as it began.[15] The second and third plots show the experiences of France and Italy, respectively. The fall in nominal exchange rates for both countries is much greater. Adjusting for changes in currency units, the equivalent of one French franc in 2014 bought about 1% of the dollars that it did at the start of 1900. The equivalent of one Italian lira bought about .4% of the number of dollars. In both cases the real exchange rates in 2014 are not much different from those at the beginning of the twentieth century. Of course, real exchange rates do change, sometimes quite sharply. For example, the real value of sterling fell by 13% in two weeks following the Brexit vote in 2017. However, if you were a financial manager called on to make a long-term forecast of the exchange rate, you could not have done much better than to assume that changes in the value of the currency would offset the difference in inflation rates.

4. Equal Real Interest Rates   Finally we come to the relationship between interest rates in different countries. Do we have a single world capital market with the same *real* rate of interest in all countries? Does the difference in money interest rates equal the difference in the expected inflation rates?

---

[15]The real exchange rate is equal to the nominal exchange rate multiplied by the inflation differential. For example, suppose that the value of sterling falls from $1.65 = £1 to $1.50 = £1 at the same time that the price of goods rises 10% faster in the United Kingdom than in the United States. The inflation-adjusted, or real, exchange rate is unchanged at

$$\text{Nominal exchange rate} \times (1 + i_£)/(1 + i_\$) = 1.50 \times 1.1 = \$1.65/£$$

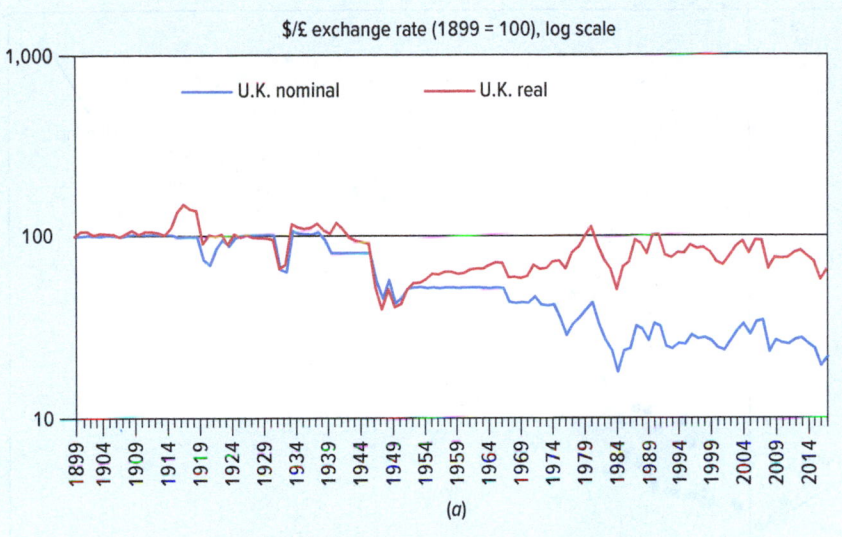

$/£ exchange rate (1899 = 100), log scale

— U.K. nominal   — U.K. real

(a)

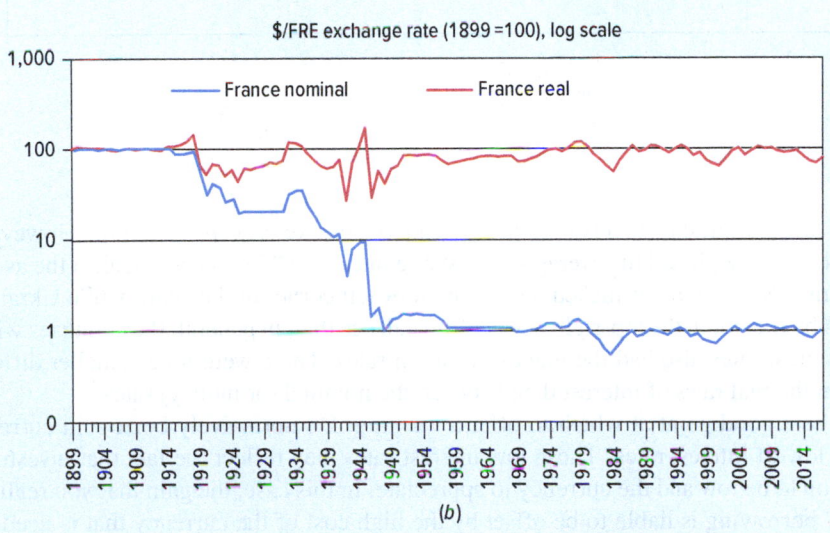

$/FRE exchange rate (1899 =100), log scale

— France nominal   — France real

(b)

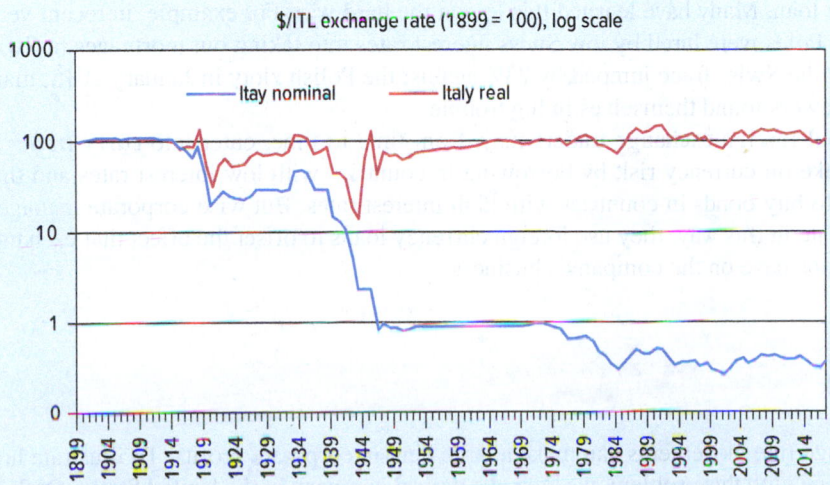

$/ITL exchange rate (1899 = 100), log scale

— Itay nominal   — Italy real

(c)

> **FIGURE 27.3**
>
> Nominal versus real exchange rates in the U.K., France, and Italy. December 1899 = 100. (Values are shown on log scale.)
>
> *Source:* E. Dimson, P. R. Marsh, and M. Staunton, *Triumph of the Optimist: 101 Years of Global Investment Returns* (Princeton, NJ: Princeton University Press, 2002), with updates provided by the authors.

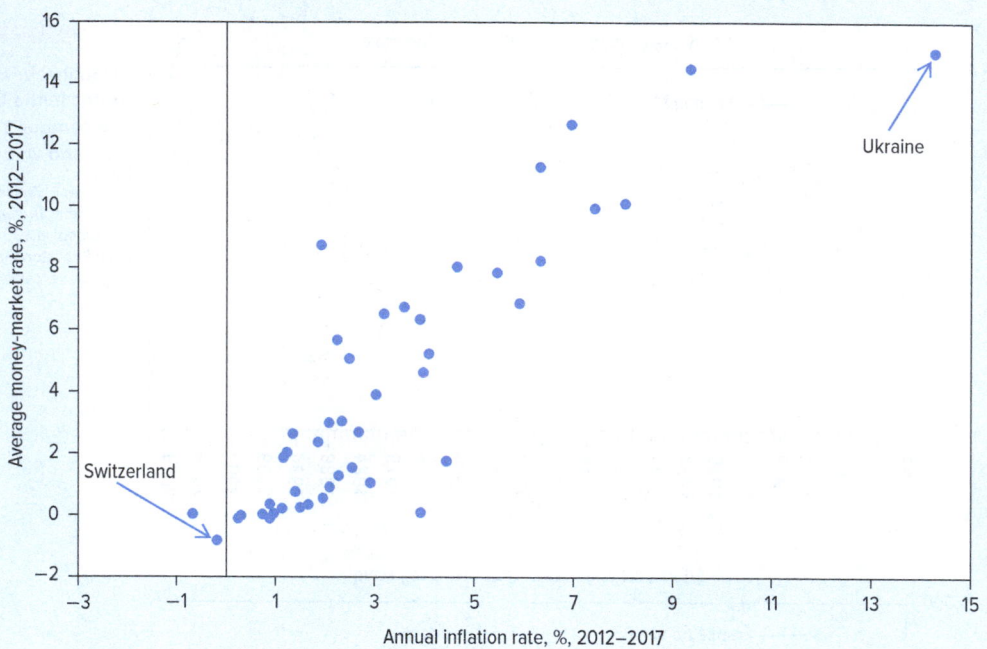

FIGURE 27.4

Countries with the highest interest rates generally have the highest inflation. In this diagram each of the 45 points represents the experience of a different country.

Source: IMF, International Financial Statistics.

This is not an easy question to answer since we cannot observe *expected* inflation. However, in Figure 27.4, we have plotted the average interest rate in each of 45 countries against the average inflation rate. Switzerland is tucked into the bottom-left corner of the chart, while Ukraine is represented by the dot in the top-right corner. You can see that, in general, the countries with the highest interest rates also had the highest inflation rates. There were much smaller differences between the real rates of interest than between the nominal (or money) rates.

This may be a good point at which to offer a warning: Do not naively borrow in currencies with the lowest interest rates. Those low interest rates may reflect the fact that investors expect inflation to be low and the currency to appreciate. In this case, the gain that you realize from "cheap" borrowing is liable to be offset by the high cost of the currency that is needed to service the loan. Many have learned this lesson the hard way. For example, in recent years over 500,000 Poles were lured by low Swiss interest rates into taking out mortgages in Swiss francs. When the Swiss franc jumped by 23% against the Polish zloty in January 2015, many of those borrowers found themselves in big trouble.

Professional foreign exchange traders may, from time to time, enter into *carry trades* in which they take on currency risk by borrowing in countries with low interest rates and then use the cash to buy bonds in countries with high interest rates. But wise corporate managers do not speculate in this way; they use foreign currency loans to offset the effect that exchange rate fluctuations have on the company's business.

27-3 Hedging Currency Risk

Sharp exchange rate movements can make a large dent in corporate profits. To illustrate how companies cope with this problem, we look at a typical company in the United States, Outland Steel, and walk through its foreign exchange operations.

EXAMPLE 27.1 • Outland Steel

Outland Steel has a small but profitable export business. Contracts involve substantial delays in payment, but since the company has a policy of always invoicing in dollars, it is fully protected against changes in exchange rates. Recently, the export department has become unhappy with this practice and believes that it is causing the company to lose valuable export orders to firms that are willing to quote in the customer's own currency.

You sympathize with these arguments, but you are worried about how the firm should price long-term export contracts when payment is to be made in foreign currency. If the value of that currency declines before payment is made, the company may suffer a large loss. You want to take the currency risk into account, but you also want to give the sales force as much freedom of action as possible.

Notice that Outland can insure against its currency risk by selling the foreign currency forward. This means that it can separate the problem of negotiating sales contracts from that of managing the company's foreign exchange exposure. The sales force can allow for currency risk by pricing on the basis of the forward exchange rate. And you, as financial manager, can decide whether the company *ought* to hedge.

What is the cost of hedging? You sometimes hear managers say that it is equal to the difference between the forward rate and *today's* spot rate. That is wrong. If Outland does not hedge, it will receive the spot rate at the time that the customer pays for the steel. Therefore, the cost of insurance is the difference between the forward rate and the expected spot rate when payment is received.

Insure or speculate? We generally vote for insurance. First, it makes life simpler for the firm and allows it to concentrate on its main business. Second, it does not cost much. (In fact, the cost is zero on average if the forward rate equals the expected spot rate, as the expectations theory of forward rates implies.) Third, the foreign currency market seems reasonably efficient, at least for the major currencies. Speculation should be a zero-NPV game, unless financial managers have information that is not available to the pros who make the market.

Is there any other way that Outland can protect itself against exchange loss? Of course. It can borrow foreign currency against its foreign receivables, sell the currency spot, and invest the proceeds in the United States. Interest rate parity theory tells us that in free markets the difference between selling forward and selling spot should be equal to the difference between the interest that you have to pay overseas and the interest that you can earn at home.

Our discussion of Outland's export business illustrates four practical implications of our simple theories about forward exchange rates. First, you can use forward rates to adjust for exchange risk in contract pricing. Second, the expectations theory suggests that protection against exchange risk is usually worth having. Third, interest rate parity theory reminds us that you can hedge either by selling forward or by borrowing foreign currency and selling spot. Fourth, the cost of forward cover is not the difference between the forward rate and *today's* spot rate; it is the difference between the forward rate and the expected spot rate when the forward contract matures.

Perhaps we should add a fifth implication. You don't make money simply by buying currencies that go up in value and selling those that go down. For example, suppose that you buy Narnian leos and sell them after a year for 2% more than you paid for them. Should you give yourself a pat on the back? That depends on the interest that you have earned on your leos. If the interest rate on leos is 2 percentage points less than the interest rate on dollars, the profit on the currency is exactly canceled out by the reduction in interest income. Thus you make money from currency speculation only if you can predict whether the exchange rate will change by more or less than the interest rate differential. In other words, you must be able to predict whether the exchange rate will change by more or less than the forward premium or discount.

BEYOND THE PAGE

Operational hedging by auto producers

mhhe.com/brealey13e

Transaction Exposure and Economic Exposure

The exchange risk from Outland Steel's export business is due to delays in foreign currency payments and is therefore referred to as *transaction exposure*. Transaction exposure can be easily identified and hedged. Consider, for example, its exports to Europe. Since a 1% fall in the value of the euro results in a 1% fall in Outland's dollar receipts, for every euro that Outland is owed by its customers, it needs to sell forward one euro.[16]

However, Outland may still be affected by currency fluctuations even if its customers do not owe it a cent. For example, Outland may be in competition with Swedish steel producers. If the value of the Swedish krona falls, Outland will need to cut its prices in order to compete.[17] Outland can protect itself against such an eventuality by selling the krona forward. In this case the loss on Outland's steel business will be offset by the profit on its forward sale.

Notice that Outland's exposure to the krona is not limited to specific transactions that have already been entered into. Financial managers often refer to this broader type of exposure as *economic exposure*.[18] Economic exposure is less easy to measure than transaction exposure. For example, it is clear that the value of Outland Steel is positively related to the value of the krona, so to hedge its position it needs to sell kronor forward. But, in practice, it may be hard to say exactly how many kronor Outland needs to sell.

BEYOND THE PAGE

Operational hedging and the Swiss franc

mhhe.com/brealey13e

Large Swiss companies, such as Nestlé or the Swatch Group, sell their products around the world. Therefore, like Outland Steel, they need to manage their economic exposure. One solution is to undertake operational hedging by balancing production closely with sales. Look, for example, at Table 27.3, which summarizes the overseas sales and costs for a sample of well-known Swiss companies. Notice that in the case of Nestlé and Swiss Re, sales and costs are almost perfectly matched. These companies are, therefore, relatively immune to fluctuations in the exchange rate. By contrast, in the case of Swatch and Richemont, a substantial

Company	Activity	Swiss Franc		Euro		U.S. Dollar		Other	
		Sales	Costs	Sales	Costs	Sales	Costs	Sales	Costs
Adecco	Employment agency	2	2	48	45	20	19	30	34
Holcim	Cement	4	6	10	10	21	25	65	59
Lindt & Sprüngli	Chocolate	5	12	43	35	40	25	12	28
Nestlé	Food producer	2	5	30	30	30	30	38	35
Novartis	Pharmaceuticals	2	15	26	25	36	40	36	20
Richemont	Luxury goods	5	20	30	20	50	40	15	20
Swatch Group	Luxury goods	10	30	30	20	50	25	10	25
Swiss Re	Insurance	3	5	20	20	40	40	37	35

❯**TABLE 27.3**   **The proportion of sales and costs for major Swiss companies that derive from particular currency areas**

Source: UBS.

---

[16]To put it another way, the hedge ratio is 1.0.

[17]Of course, if purchasing power parity always held, the fall in the value of the krona would be matched by higher inflation in Sweden. The risk for Outland is that the *real* value of the krona may decline so that when measured in dollars, Swedish costs are lower than previously. Unfortunately, it is much easier to hedge against a change in the *nominal* exchange rate than against a change in the *real* rate.

[18]Financial managers also refer to *translation exposure,* which measures the effect of an exchange rate change on the company's financial statements.

proportion of production costs arise in Switzerland, and therefore both companies are exposed to an appreciation of the Swiss franc.

In addition to operational hedging, companies can also control exchange rate risk by using financial hedges. They do this by borrowing in foreign currencies, selling currency forward, or using foreign currency derivatives such as swaps and options. For example, in 2014 Swatch used forwards primarily to reduce its exposure to the euro and dollar. At the end of the year, these forward contracts totaled nearly 1.5 billion Swiss francs.

27-4 Exchange Risk and International Investment Decisions

Suppose that the Swiss pharmaceutical company, Roche, is evaluating a proposal to build a new plant in the United States. To calculate the project's net present value, Roche forecasts the following dollar cash flows from the project:

Cash Flows ($ millions)					
C_0	C_1	C_2	C_3	C_4	C_5
−1,300	400	450	510	575	650

These cash flows are stated in dollars. So to calculate their net present value Roche discounts them at the dollar cost of capital. (Remember dollars need to be discounted at a *dollar* rate, not the Swiss franc rate.) Suppose this cost of capital is 12%. Then

$$\text{NPV} = -1,300 + \frac{400}{1.12} + \frac{450}{1.12^2} + \frac{510}{1.12^3} + \frac{575}{1.12^4} + \frac{650}{1.12^5} = \$513 \text{ million}$$

To convert this net present value to Swiss francs, the manager can simply multiply the dollar NPV by the spot rate of exchange. For example, if the spot rate is CHF1.2/$, then the NPV in Swiss francs is

$$\text{NPV in francs} = \text{NPV in dollars} \times \text{CHF/\$} = 513 \times 1.2 = 616 \text{ million francs}$$

Notice one very important feature of this calculation. Roche does not need to forecast whether the dollar is likely to strengthen or weaken against the Swiss franc. No currency forecast is needed because the company can hedge its foreign exchange exposure. In that case, the decision to accept or reject the pharmaceutical project in the United States is totally separate from the decision to bet on the outlook for the dollar. For example, it would be foolish for Roche to accept a poor project in the United States just because management is optimistic about the outlook for the dollar; if Roche wishes to speculate in this way it can simply buy dollars forward. Equally, it would be foolish for Roche to reject a good project just because management is pessimistic about the dollar. The company would do much better to go ahead with the project and sell dollars forward. In that way, it would get the best of both worlds.[19]

When Roche ignores currency risk and discounts the dollar cash flows at a dollar cost of capital, it is implicitly assuming that the currency risk is hedged. Let us check this by calculating the number of Swiss francs that Roche would receive if it hedged the currency risk by selling forward each future dollar cash flow.

---

[19]There is a general point here that is not confined to currency hedging. Whenever you face an investment that appears to have a positive NPV, decide what it is that you are betting on and then think whether there is a more direct way to place the bet. For example, if a copper mine looks profitable only because you are unusually optimistic about the price of copper, then maybe you would do better to buy copper futures or the shares of other copper producers rather than opening a copper mine.

We need first to calculate the forward rate of exchange between dollars and francs. This depends on the interest rates in the United States and Switzerland. For example, suppose that the dollar interest rate is 6% and the Swiss franc interest rate is 4%. Then interest rate parity theory tells us that the one-year forward exchange rate is

$$s_{CHF/\$} \times (1 + r_{CHF})/(1 + r_\$) = \frac{1.2 \times 1.04}{1.06} = 1.177$$

Similarly, the two-year forward rate is

$$s_{CHF/\$} \times (1 + r_{CHF})^2/(1 + r_\$)^2 = \frac{1.2 \times 1.04^2}{1.06^2} = 1.155$$

So, if Roche hedges its cash flows against exchange rate risk, the number of Swiss francs it will receive in each year is equal to the dollar cash flow times the forward rate of exchange:

Cash Flows (millions of Swiss francs)					
C_0	C_1	C_2	C_3	C_4	C_5
$-1,300 \times 1.2$	400×1.177	450×1.155	510×1.133	575×1.112	650×1.091
$= -1,560$	$= 471$	$= 520$	$= 578$	$= 639$	$= 709$

These cash flows are in Swiss francs and therefore they need to be discounted at the risk-adjusted Swiss franc discount rate. Since the Swiss rate of interest is lower than the dollar rate, the risk-adjusted discount rate must also be correspondingly lower. The formula for converting from the required dollar return to the required Swiss franc return is[20]

$$(1 + \text{Swiss franc return}) = (1 + \text{dollar return}) \times \frac{(1 + \text{Swiss franc interest rate})}{(1 + \text{dollar interest rate})}$$

In our example,

$$(1 + \text{Swiss franc return}) = 1.12 \times \frac{1.04}{1.06} = 1.099$$

Thus the risk-adjusted discount rate in dollars is 12%, but the discount rate in Swiss francs is only 9.9%.

All that remains is to discount the Swiss franc cash flows at the 9.9% risk-adjusted discount rate:

$$NPV = -1,560 + \frac{471}{1.099} + \frac{520}{1.099^2} + \frac{578}{1.099^3} + \frac{639}{1.099^4} + \frac{709}{1.099^5}$$

$$= 616 \text{ million francs}$$

Everything checks. We obtain exactly the same net present value by (1) ignoring currency risk and discounting Roche's dollar cash flows at the dollar cost of capital and (2) calculating the cash flows in francs on the assumption that Roche hedges the currency risk and then discounting these Swiss franc cash flows at the franc cost of capital.

---

[20]The following example should give you a feel for the idea behind this formula. Suppose the spot rate for Swiss francs is CHF 1.2 = $1. Interest rate parity tells us that the forward rate must be $1.2 \times 1.04/1.06 = $ CHF 1.177/$. Now suppose that a share costs $100 and will pay an expected $112 at the end of the year. The cost to Swiss investors of buying the share is $100 \times 1.2 = $ CHF 120. If the Swiss investors sell forward the expected payoff, they will receive an expected $112 \times 1.177 = $ CHF 131.9. The expected return in Swiss francs is $131.9/120 - 1 = .099$, or 9.9%. More simply, the Swiss franc return is $1.12 \times 1.04/1.06 - 1 = .099$.

To repeat: When deciding whether to invest overseas, separate out the investment decision from the decision to take on currency risk. This means that your views about future exchange rates should NOT enter into the investment decision. The simplest way to calculate the NPV of an overseas investment is to forecast the cash flows in the foreign currency and discount them at the foreign currency cost of capital. The alternative is to calculate the cash flows that you would receive if you hedged the foreign currency risk. In this case, you need to translate the foreign currency cash flows into your own currency *using the forward exchange rate* and then discount these domestic currency cash flows at the domestic cost of capital. If the two methods don't give the same answer, you have made a mistake.

When Roche analyzes the proposal to build a plant in the United States, it is able to ignore the outlook for the dollar *only because it is free to hedge the currency risk.* Because investment in a pharmaceutical plant does not come packaged with an investment in the dollar, the opportunity for firms to hedge allows for better investment decisions.

The Cost of Capital for International Investments

Roche should discount dollar cash flows at a dollar cost of capital. But how should a Swiss company like Roche calculate a cost of capital in dollars for an investment in the United States? There is no simple, consensus procedure for answering this question, but we suggest the following procedure as a start.

First you need to decide on the risk of a U.S. pharmaceutical investment to a Swiss investor. You could look at the betas of a sample of U.S. pharmaceutical companies *relative to the Swiss market index.*

Why measure betas relative to the Swiss index, while a U.S. counterpart such as Merck would measure betas relative to the U.S. index? The answer lies in Section 7-4, where we explained that risk cannot be considered in isolation; it depends on the other securities in the investor's portfolio. Beta measures risk *relative to the investor's portfolio.* If U.S. investors already hold the U.S. market, an additional dollar invested at home is just more of the same. But if Swiss investors hold the Swiss market, an investment in the United States can reduce their risk because the Swiss and U.S. markets are not perfectly correlated. That explains why an investment in the United States can be lower risk for Roche's shareholders than for Merck's shareholders. It also explains why Roche's shareholders may be willing to accept a relatively low expected return from a U.S. investment.[21]

Suppose that you decide that the investment's beta relative to the Swiss market is .8 and that the market risk premium in Switzerland is 7.4%. Then the required return on the project can be estimated as

$$\text{Required return} = \text{Swiss interest rate} + (\text{beta} \times \text{Swiss market risk premium})$$

$$= 4 + (.8 \times 7.4) = 9.9$$

This is the project's cost of capital measured in Swiss francs. We used it to discount the expected *Swiss franc* cash flows if Roche hedged the project against currency risk. We cannot use it to discount the *dollar* cash flows from the project.

To discount the expected *dollar* cash flows, we need to convert the Swiss franc cost of capital to a dollar cost of capital. This means running our earlier calculation in reverse:

$$(1 + \text{dollar return}) = (1 + \text{Swiss franc return}) \times \frac{(1 + \text{dollar interest rate})}{(1 + \text{Swiss franc interest rate})}$$

---

[21]When an investor holds an efficient portfolio, the expected reward for risk on each stock in the portfolio is proportional to its beta *relative to the portfolio.* So if the Swiss market index is an efficient portfolio for Swiss investors, then these investors will want Roche to invest in the United States if the expected rate of return more than compensates for the investment's beta relative to the Swiss index.

In our example,

$$(1 + \text{dollar return}) = 1.099 \times \frac{1.06}{1.04} = 1.12$$

We used this 12% dollar cost of capital to discount the forecasted dollar cash flows from the project.

When a company measures risk relative to its domestic market as in our example, its managers are implicitly assuming that shareholders hold simply domestic stocks. That is not a bad approximation, particularly in the United States. Although U.S. investors can reduce their risk by holding an internationally diversified portfolio of shares, they generally invest only a small proportion of their money overseas. Why they are so shy is a puzzle. It looks as if they are worried about the costs of investing overseas, such as the extra costs involved in identifying which stocks to buy, or the possibility of unfair treatment by foreign companies or governments.

The world is getting smaller and "flatter," however, and investors everywhere are increasing their holdings of foreign securities. Pension funds and other institutional investors have diversified internationally, and dozens of mutual funds have been set up for people who want to invest abroad. If investors throughout the world held the world portfolio, then costs of capital would converge. The cost of capital would still depend on the risk of the investment, but not on the domicile of the investing company. There is some evidence that for large U.S. firms it does not make much difference whether a U.S. or global beta is used. For firms in smaller countries, the evidence is not so clear-cut and sometimes a global beta may be more appropriate.[22]

27-5 Political Risk

So far, we have focused on the management of exchange rate risk, but managers also worry about political risk. By this they mean the threat that a government will change the rules of the game—that is, break a promise or understanding—*after* the investment is made. Of course political risks are not confined to overseas investments. Businesses in every country are exposed to the risk of unanticipated actions by governments or the courts. But in some parts of the world foreign companies are particularly vulnerable.

A number of consultancy services offer analyses of political and economic risks and draw up country rankings.[23] For example, Table 27.4 is an extract from the 2016 political risk rankings provided by the PRS Group. Each country is scored on 15 separate dimensions. You can see that Norway comes top of the class overall, while Syria languishes at the bottom.

Some managers dismiss political risk as an act of God, like a hurricane or earthquake. But the most successful multinational companies structure their business to reduce political risk. Foreign governments are not likely to expropriate a local business if it cannot operate without the support of its parent. For example, the foreign subsidiaries of American computer manufacturers or pharmaceutical companies would have relatively little value if they were cut off from the know-how of their parents. Such operations are much less likely to be expropriated than, say, a mining operation that can be operated as a stand-alone venture.

We are not recommending that you turn your silver mine into a pharmaceutical company, but you may be able to plan your overseas manufacturing operations to improve your

---

[22]See R. M. Stulz, "The Cost of Capital in Internationally Integrated Markets: The Case of Nestlé," *European Financial Management* 1, no. 1 (1995), pp. 11–22; R. S. Harris, F. C. Marston, D. R. Mishra, and T. J. O'Brien, "Ex Ante Cost of Equity Estimates of S&P 500 Firms: The Choice between Global and Domestic CAPM," *Financial Management* 32 (Autumn 2003), pp. 51–66; and Standard & Poor's, "Domestic vs. Global CAPM," *Global Cost of Capital Report,* 4th Quarter 2003.

[23]For a discussion of these services see C. Erb, C. R. Harvey, and T. Viskanta, "Political Risk, Economic Risk, and Financial," *Financial Analysts Journal* 52 (1996), pp. 29–46. Also, Campbell Harvey's webpage (**http://people.duke.edu/~charvey/**) is a useful source of information on political risk.

Maximum Score 100		
Country	Total Score	Rank
Norway	88.3	1
Switzerland	88.0	2
Singapore	87.3	3
Sweden	85.8	5
Germany	84.3	6
Japan	82.5	9
Canada	81.0	15=
Korea, Republic	81.0	15=
United Kingdom	79.8	18
United States	79.3	19
Australia	78.0	23=
Italy	75.3	34
France	73.5	43=
China	71.3	55=
India	69.8	63=
Greece	68.5	70=
Argentina	64.5	85
Brazil	63.3	97=
Russia	62.5	103
Turkey	62.3	107=
Venezuela	48.3	137=
Syria	37.0	140

Note: = denotes a tie

❭**TABLE 27.4**   **Political risk scores for a sample of countries, 2016**

Source: International Country Risk Guide, a publication of The PRS Group, Inc. (www.prsgroup.com), 2016.

bargaining position with foreign governments. For example, Ford has integrated its overseas operations so that the manufacture of components, subassemblies, and complete automobiles is spread across plants in a number of countries. None of these plants would have much value on its own, and Ford can switch production between plants if the political climate in one country deteriorates.

Multinational corporations have also devised financing arrangements to help keep foreign governments honest. For example, suppose your firm is contemplating an investment of $500 million to reopen the San Tomé silver mine in Costaguana with modern machinery, smelting equipment, and shipping facilities.[24] The Costaguanan government agrees to invest in roads and other infrastructure and to take 20% of the silver produced by the mine in lieu of taxes. The agreement is to run for 25 years.

The project's NPV on these assumptions is quite attractive. But what happens if a new government comes into power five years from now and imposes a 50% tax on "any precious metals exported from the Republic of Costaguana"? Or changes the government's share of output from 20% to 50%? Or simply takes over the mine "with fair compensation to be determined in due course by the Minister of Natural Resources of the Republic of Costaguana"?

---

[24]The early history of the San Tomé mine is described in Joseph Conrad's *Nostromo.*

No contract can absolutely restrain sovereign power. But you can arrange project financing to make these acts as painful as possible for the foreign government. For example, you might set up the mine as a subsidiary corporation, which then borrows a large fraction of the required investment from a consortium of major international banks. If your firm guarantees the loan, make sure the guarantee stands only if the Costaguanan government honors its contract. The government will be reluctant to break the contract if that causes a default on the loans and undercuts the country's credit standing with the international banking system.

If possible, you should arrange for the World Bank (or one of its affiliates) to finance part of the project or to guarantee your loans against political risk.[25] Few governments have the guts to take on the World Bank. Here is another variation on the same theme. Arrange to borrow, say, $450 million through the Costaguanan Development Agency. In other words, the development agency borrows in international capital markets and relends to the San Tomé mine. Your firm agrees to stand behind the loan as long as the government keeps its promises. If it does keep them, the loan is your liability. If not, the loan is *its* liability.

Political risk is not confined to the risk of expropriation. Multinational companies are always exposed to the criticism that they siphon funds out of countries in which they do business, and, therefore, governments are tempted to limit their freedom to repatriate profits. This is most likely to happen when there is considerable uncertainty about the rate of exchange, which is usually when you would most like to get your money out. Here, again, a little forethought can help. For example, there are often more onerous restrictions on the payment of dividends to the parent than on the payment of interest or principal on debt. Royalty payments and management fees are less sensitive than dividends, particularly if they are levied equally on all foreign operations.

Calculating NPVs for investment projects becomes exceptionally difficult when political risks are significant. You have to estimate cash flows and project life with extra caution. You may want to take a peek at the discounted payback period (see Chapter 5), on the theory that quick-payback projects are less exposed to political risks. But do not try to compensate for political risks by adding casual fudge factors to discount rates. Fudge factors spawn bias and confusion, as we explained in Chapter 9.

---

[25]In the appendix to Chapter 24, we described how the backing of the World Bank helped to arrange financing for the Central Java power project.

• • • • •

SUMMARY

The international financial manager has to cope with different currencies, interest rates, and inflation rates. To produce order out of chaos, the manager needs some model of how they are related. We described four very simple but useful theories.

Interest rate parity theory states that the interest differential between two countries must be equal to the difference between the forward and spot exchange rates. In the international markets, arbitrage ensures that parity generally holds. There are two ways to hedge against exchange risk: One is to take out forward cover; the other is to borrow or lend abroad. Interest rate parity tells us that the costs of the two methods should be the same.

The expectations theory of exchange rates tells us that the forward rate equals the expected spot rate. In practice, forward rates seem to incorporate a risk premium, but this premium is about equally likely to be negative as positive.

In its strict form, purchasing power parity states that $1 must have the same purchasing power in every country. That doesn't square well with the facts because differences in inflation rates are not perfectly related to changes in exchange rates. This means that there may be some genuine exchange risks in doing business overseas. On the other hand, a financial manager, who needs to make a long-term forecast of the exchange rate, cannot do much better than to assume that the real exchange rate will not change.

Finally, we saw that in an integrated world capital market real rates of interest would have to be the same. In practice, government regulation and taxes can cause differences in real interest rates. But do not simply borrow where interest rates are lowest. Those countries are also likely to have the lowest inflation rates and the strongest currencies.

With these precepts in mind, we showed how you can use forward markets or the loan markets to hedge transactions exposure, which arises from delays in foreign currency payments and receipts. But the company's financing choices also need to reflect the impact of a change in the exchange rate on the value of the entire business. This is known as economic exposure. Companies protect themselves against economic exposure either by hedging in the financial markets or by building plants overseas.

Because companies can hedge their currency risk, the decision to invest overseas does not involve currency forecasts. There are two ways for a company to calculate the NPV of an overseas project. The first is to forecast the foreign currency cash flows and to discount them at the foreign currency cost of capital. The second is to translate the foreign currency cash flows into domestic currency assuming that they are hedged against exchange rate risk. These domestic currency flows can then be discounted at the domestic cost of capital. The answers should be identical.

In addition to currency risk, overseas operations may be exposed to extra political risk. However, firms may be able to structure the financing to reduce the chances that government will change the rules of the game.

FURTHER READING

There are a number of useful textbooks in international finance. Here is a small selection:

P. Sercu, *International Finance: Theory into Practice* (Princeton, NJ: Princeton University Press, 2009).

D. K. Eiteman, A. I. Stonehill, and M. H. Moffett, *Multinational Business Finance,* 13th ed. (Cambridge, England: Pearson, 2012).

A. C. Shapiro, *Multinational Financial Management,* 10th ed. (New York: John Wiley & Sons, 2013).

Here are some general discussions of international investment decisions and associated exchange risks:

G. Allayannis, J. Ihrig, and J. P. Weston, "Exchange-Rate Hedging: Financial versus Operational Strategies," *American Economic Review* 91 (May 2001), pp. 391–395.

D. R. Lessard, "Global Competition and Corporate Finance in the 1990s," *Journal of Applied Corporate Finance* 3 (Winter 1991), pp. 59–72.

M. D. Levi and P. Sercu, "Erroneous and Valid Reasons for Hedging Foreign Exchange Rate Exposure," *Journal of Multinational Finance Management* 1 (1991), pp. 25–37.

Listed below are a few of the articles on the relationship between interest rates, exchange rates, and inflation:

Forward and spot exchange rates

M. D. Evans and K. K. Lewis, "Do Long-Term Swings in the Dollar Affect Estimates of the Risk Premia?" *Review of Financial Studies* 8 (1995), pp. 709–742.

Interest rate parity

K. Clinton, "Transactions Costs and Covered Interest Arbitrage: Theory and Evidence," *Journal of Political Economy* 96 (April 1988), pp. 358–370.

Purchasing power parity

K. Froot and K. Rogoff, "Perspectives on PPP and Long-run Real Exchange Rates," in G. Grossman and K. Rogoff (eds.), *Handbook of International Economics* (Amsterdam: North-Holland Publishing Company, 1995).

K. Rogoff, "The Purchasing Power Parity Puzzle," *Journal of Economic Literature* 34 (June 1996), pp. 647–668.

A. M. Taylor and M. P. Taylor, "The Purchasing Power Parity Debate," *Journal of Economic Perspectives* 18 (Autumn 2004), pp. 135–158.

PROBLEM SETS

 **Select problems are available in McGraw-Hill's *Connect*. Please see the preface for more information.**

1. **Exchange rates*** Look at Table 27.1.

   a. How many Japanese yen do you get for your dollar?

   b. What is the three-month forward rate for yen?

   c. Is the yen at a forward discount or premium on the dollar?

   d. Use the one-year forward rate to calculate the annual percentage discount or premium on yen.

   e. If the one-year interest rate on dollars is 2.5% annually compounded, what do you think is the one-year interest rate on yen?

   f. According to the expectations theory, what is the expected spot rate for yen in three months' time?

   g. According to purchasing power parity theory, what then is the expected difference in the three-month rate of price inflation in the United States and Japan?

2. **Exchange rates** Table 27.1 shows the 3-month forward rate on the South African rand.

   a. Is the dollar at a forward discount or premium on the rand?

   b. What is the annual *percentage* discount or premium?

   c. If you have no other information about the two currencies, what is your best guess about the spot rate on the rand three months hence?

   d. Suppose that you expect to receive 100,000 rand in three months. How many dollars is this likely to be worth?

3. **Some basic relationships** Define each of the following theories in a sentence or simple equation:

   a. Interest rate parity.

   b. Expectations theory of forward rates.

   c. Purchasing power parity.

   d. International capital market equilibrium (relationship of real and nominal interest rates in different countries).

4. **Interest rate parity** Look again at Table 27.1. Which countries would you expect to have a lower 1-year interest rate than the United States?

5. **Interest rate parity** The following table shows interest rates and exchange rates for the U.S. dollar and the Lilliputian nano. The spot exchange rate is 15 nanos = $1. Complete the missing entries:

	1 Month	3 Months	1 Year
Dollar interest rate (annually compounded)	4.0	4.5	?
Nano interest rate (annually compounded)	8.2	?	9.8
Forward nanos per dollar	?	?	15.6
Forward discount on nano (% per year)	?	4.8	?

TABLE 27.5
Interest rates and exchange rates
[a]Number of units of foreign currency that can be exchanged for $1.

	Interest Rate (%)	Spot Exchange Rate[a]	1-Year Forward Exchange Rate[a]
United States (dollar)	3	—	—
Costaguana (pulga)	23	10,000	11,942
Westonia (ruple)	5	2.6	2.65
Gloccamorra (pint)	8	17.1	18.2
Anglosaxophonia (wasp)	4.1	2.3	2.28

6. **Interest rate parity** Look at Table 27.1. If the three-month interest rate on dollars is 0.2%, what do you think is the three-month interest rate on the Brazilian real? Explain what would happen if the rate were substantially above your figure.

7. **Interest rate parity** Table 27.5 shows the annual interest rate (annually compounded) and exchange rates against the dollar for different currencies. Are there any arbitrage opportunities? If so, how would you secure a positive cash flow today, while zeroing out all future cash flows?

8. **Purchasing power parity** In March 2017, the exchange rate for the Narnian leo was L2,419 = $1. Inflation in the year to March 2018 was about 30% in Narnia and 2% in the United States.

   a. If purchasing power parity held, what should have been the nominal exchange rate in March 2018?

   b. The actual exchange rate in March 2018 in the midst of a currency crisis was L8,325 = $1. What was the change in the *real* exchange rate?

9. **Interest rates and exchange rates** Penny Farthing, the treasurer of International Bicycles Inc. has noticed that the interest rate in Japan is below the rates in most other countries. Therefore, she is suggesting that the company should make an issue of Japanese yen bonds. Does this make sense?

10. **Currency risk** Suppose that in 2023 one- and two-year interest rates are 5.2% in the United States and 1.0% in Japan. The spot exchange rate is ¥120.22/$. Suppose that one year later interest rates are 3% in both countries, while the value of the yen has appreciated to ¥115.00/$.

    a. Benjamin Pinkerton from New York invested in a U.S. two-year zero-coupon bond at the start of the period and sold it after one year. What was his return?

    b. Madame Butterfly from Osaka bought some dollars. She also invested in the two-year U.S. zero-coupon bond and sold it after one year. What was her return in yen?

    c. Suppose that Ms. Butterfly had correctly forecasted the price at which she sold her bond and that she hedged her investment against currency risk. How could she have hedged? What would have been her return in yen?

11. **Currency risk** Companies may be affected by changes in the nominal exchange rate or in the real exchange rate. Explain how this can occur. Which changes are easiest to hedge against?

12. **Currency risk** You have bid for a possible export order that would provide a cash inflow of €1 million in six months. The spot exchange rate is $1.3549 = €1 and the six-month forward rate is $1.3620 = €1. There are two sources of uncertainty: (1) the euro could appreciate or depreciate and (2) you may or may not receive the export order. Illustrate in each case the final payoffs if (a) you sell 1 million euros forward, and (b) you buy a six-month option to sell euros with an exercise price of $1.3620/€.

13. **Currency risk*** In December 2017, an American investor buys 1,000 shares in a Mexican company at a price of 500 pesos each. The share does not pay any dividend. A year later she sells the shares for 550 pesos each. The exchange rates when she buys the stock are shown in Table 27.1. Suppose that the exchange rate at the time of sale is 20 pesos = $1.

a. How many dollars does she invest?

b. What is her total return in pesos? In dollars?

c. Do you think that she has made an exchange rate profit or loss? Explain.

14. **Currency hedging*** An importer in the United States is due to take delivery of clothing from Mexico in six months. The price is fixed in Mexican pesos. Which of the following transactions could eliminate the importer's exchange risk?

a. Sell six-month call options on pesos.

b. Buy pesos forward.

c. Sell pesos forward.

d. Sell pesos in the currency futures market.

e. Borrow pesos; buy dollars at the spot exchange rate.

f. Sell pesos at the spot exchange rate; lend dollars.

15. **Currency hedging** A U.S. company has committed to pay 10 million kronor to a Swedish company in one year. What is the cost (in present value) of covering this liability by buying kronor forward? The Swedish interest rate is .6%, and exchange rates are shown in Table 27.1. Briefly explain.

16. **Currency hedging** A firm in the United States is due to receive payment of €1 million in eight years' time. It would like to protect itself against a decline in the value of the euro, but finds it difficult to get forward cover for such a long period. Is there any other way in which it can protect itself?

17. **Currency hedging** Suppose you are the treasurer of Lufthansa, the German international airline. How is company value likely to be affected by exchange rate changes? What policies would you adopt to reduce exchange rate risk?

18. **Currency hedging** A Ford dealer in the United States may be exposed to a devaluation of the yen if this leads to a cut in the price of Japanese cars. Suppose that the dealer estimates that a 1% decline in the value of the yen would result in a permanent decline of 5% in the dealer's profits. How should she hedge against this risk, and how should she calculate the size of the hedge position? (*Hint:* You may find it helpful to refer to Section 26-6.)

19. **Currency hedging** "Last year we had a substantial income in sterling, which we hedged by selling sterling forward. In the event sterling appreciated. So our decision to sell forward cost us a lot of money. I think that in the future we should either stop hedging our currency exposure or just hedge when we think sterling is overvalued." As financial manager, how would you respond to your chief executive's comment?

20. **Investment decisions** Carpet Baggers Inc. is proposing to construct a new bagging plant in a country in Europe. The two prime candidates are Germany and Switzerland. The forecasted cash flows from the proposed plants are as follows:

	C_0	C_1	C_2	C_3	C_4	C_5	C_6	IRR (%)
Germany (millions of euros)	−60	+10	+15	+15	+20	+20	+20	15.0
Switzerland (millions of Swiss francs)	−120	+20	+30	+30	+35	+35	+35	12.8

The spot exchange rate for euros is \$1.3/€, while the rate for Swiss francs is CHF 1.5/\$. The interest rate is 5% in the United States, 4% in Switzerland, and 6% in the euro countries. The financial manager has suggested that, if the cash flows were stated in dollars, a return in excess of 10% would be acceptable.

Should the company go ahead with either project? If it must choose between them, which should it take?

21. **Investment decisions*** It is the year 2021 and Pork Barrels Inc. is considering construction of a new barrel plant in Spain. The forecasted cash flows in millions of euros are as follows:

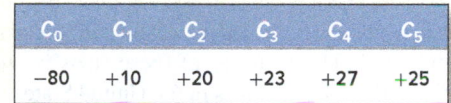

C_0	C_1	C_2	C_3	C_4	C_5
−80	+10	+20	+23	+27	+25

The spot exchange rate is \$1.2 = €1. The interest rate in the United States is 8%, and the euro interest rate is 6%. You can assume that pork barrel production is effectively risk-free.

a. Calculate the NPV of the euro cash flows from the project. What is the NPV in dollars?

b. What are the dollar cash flows from the project if the company hedges against exchange rate changes? What is the NPV of these flows?

c. Suppose that the company expects the euro to depreciate by 5% a year. How does this affect the value of the project?

CHALLENGE

22. **Currency hedging** Alpha and Omega are U.S. corporations. Alpha has a plant in Hamburg that imports components from the United States, assembles them, and then sells the finished product in Germany. Omega is at the opposite extreme. It also has a plant in Hamburg, but it buys its raw material in Germany and exports its output back to the United States. How is each firm likely to be affected by a fall in the value of the euro? How could each firm hedge itself against exchange risk?

Find the foreign exchange rate tables in the online version of *The Wall Street Journal* (**www.wsj .com**) or the *Financial Times* (**www.ft.com**).

FINANCE ON THE WEB

1. a. How many U.S. dollars are worth one Canadian dollar today?

   b. How many Canadian dollars are worth one U.S. dollar today?

   c. Suppose that you arrange today to buy Canadian dollars in 90 days. How many Canadian dollars could you buy for each U.S. dollar?

   d. If forward rates simply reflect market expectations, what is the likely spot exchange rate for the Canadian dollar in 90 days' time?

   e. Look at the table of money rates in the same issue. What is the three-month interest rate on dollars?

   f. Can you deduce the likely three-month interest rate for the Canadian dollar?

   g. You can also buy currency for future delivery in the financial futures market. Look at the table of futures prices. What is the rate of exchange for Canadian dollars to be delivered in approximately six months' time?

2. a. How many Swiss francs can you buy for \$1?

   b. How many Hong Kong dollars can you buy?

   c. What rate do you think a Swiss bank would quote for buying or selling Hong Kong dollars? Explain what would happen if it quoted a cross-rate that was substantially above your figure.

MINI-CASE ·····

Exacta, s.a.

Exacta, s.a., is a major French producer, based in Lyons, of precision machine tools. About two-thirds of its output is exported. The majority of these sales is within the European Union. However, the company also has a thriving business in the United States, despite strong competition from several U.S. firms. Exacta usually receives payment for exported goods within two months of the invoice date, so that at any point in time, only about one-sixth of annual exports to the United States is exposed to currency risk.

The company believes that its North American business is now large enough to justify a local manufacturing operation, and it has recently decided to establish a plant in South Carolina. Most of the output from this plant will be sold in the United States, but the company believes that there should also be opportunities for future sales in Canada and Mexico.

The South Carolina plant will involve a total investment of $380 million and is expected to be in operation by the year 2021. Annual revenues from the plant are expected to be about $420 million, and the company forecasts net profits of $52 million a year. Once the plant is up and running, it should be able to operate for several years without substantial additional investment.

Although there is widespread enthusiasm for the project, several members of the management team have expressed anxiety about possible currency risk. M. Pangloss, the finance director, reassured them that the company was not a stranger to currency risk; after all, the company was already exporting about $320 million of machine tools each year to the United States and has managed to exchange its dollar revenue for euros without any major losses. But not everybody was convinced by this argument. For example, the CEO, Mme. B. Bardot, pointed out that the $380 million to be invested would substantially increase the amount of money at risk if the dollar fell relative to the euro. Mme. Bardot was notoriously risk-averse on financial matters and would push for complete hedging if practical.

M. Pangloss attempted to reassure the CEO. At the same time, he secretly shared some of the anxieties about exchange rate risk. Nearly all the revenues from the South Carolina plant would be in U.S. dollars, and the bulk of the $380 million investment would likewise be incurred in the United States. About two-thirds of the operating costs would be in dollars, but the remaining one-third would represent payment for components brought in from Lyons plus the charge by the head office for management services and use of patents. The company has yet to decide whether to invoice its U.S. operation in dollars or euros for these purchases from the parent company.

M. Pangloss is optimistic that the company can hedge itself against currency risk. His favored solution is for Exacta to finance the plant by a $380 million issue of dollar bonds. That way the dollar investment would be offset by a matching dollar liability. An alternative is for the company to sell forward at the beginning of each year the expected revenues from the U.S. plant. But he realizes from experience that these simple solutions might carry hidden dangers. He decides to slow down and think more systematically about the additional exchange risk from the U.S. operation.

QUESTIONS

1. What would Exacta's true exposure be from its new U.S. operations, and how would it change from the company's current exposure?

2. Given that exposure, what would be the most effective and inexpensive approach to hedging?

CHAPTER

28

Financial Analysis

Good financial managers plan for the future. They check that they will have enough cash to pay the upcoming tax bill or dividend payment. They think about how much investment the firm will need to make and about how they might finance that investment. They reflect on whether they are well placed to ride out an unexpected downturn in demand or an increase in the cost of materials.

In Chapter 29, we will describe how financial managers develop both short- and long-term financial plans. But knowing where you stand today is a necessary prelude to contemplating where you might be in the future. Therefore, in this chapter we show how the firm's financial statements help you

to understand the firm's overall performance and how some key financial ratios may alert senior management to potential problem areas.

You have probably heard stories of whizzes who can take a company's accounts apart in minutes, calculate some financial ratios, and divine the company's future. Such people are like abominable snowmen: often spoken of but never truly seen. Financial ratios are no substitute for a crystal ball. They are just a convenient way to summarize large quantities of financial data and to compare firms' performance. The ratios help you to ask the right questions; they seldom answer them.

28-1 Financial Ratios

Financial ratios are usually easy to calculate. That's the good news. The bad news is that there are so many of them. To make it worse, the ratios are often presented in long lists that seem to require memorization rather than understanding.

We can mitigate the bad news by taking a moment to preview what the ratios are measuring and how they connect to the ultimate objective of value added for shareholders.

Shareholder value depends on good investment decisions. The financial manager evaluates investment decisions by asking several questions, including these: How profitable are the investments relative to the cost of capital? How should profitability be measured? What does profitability depend on? (We will see that it depends on efficient use of assets and on the profits on each dollar of sales.)

Shareholder value also depends on good financing decisions. Again, there are obvious questions: Is the available financing sufficient? The firm cannot grow unless financing is available. Is the financing strategy prudent? The financial manager should not put the firm's assets and operations at risk by operating at a dangerously high debt ratio. Does the firm have

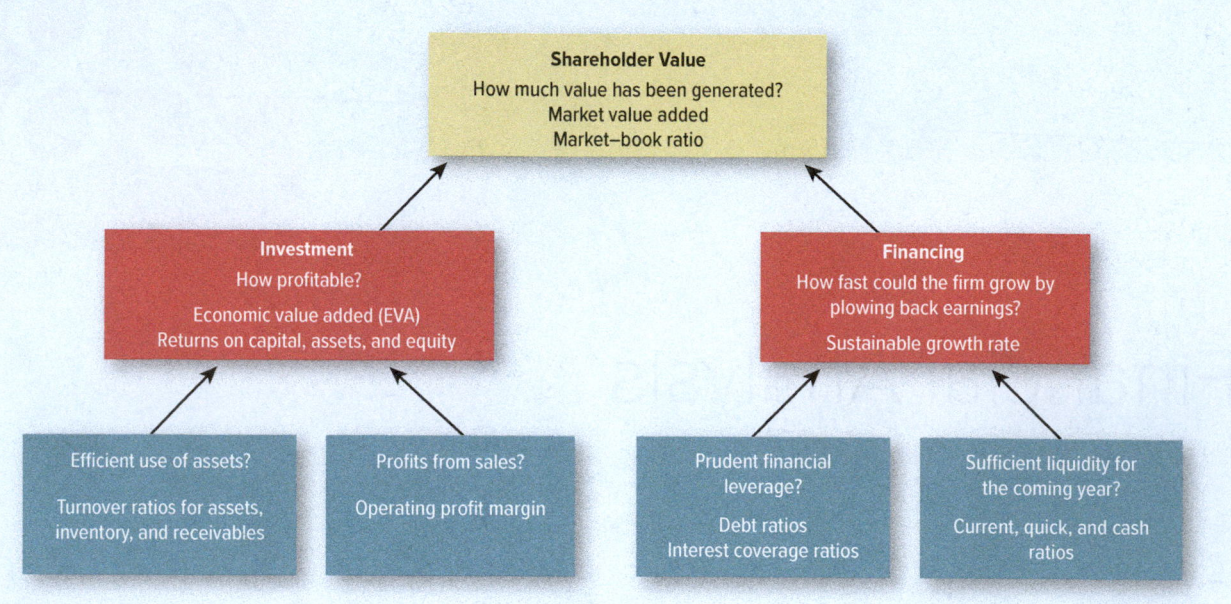

▶ **FIGURE 28.1**   **An organization chart for financial ratios, showing how common financial ratios and other measures relate to shareholder value.**

sufficient liquidity (a cushion of cash or assets that can be readily sold for cash)? The firm has to be able to pay its bills and respond to unexpected setbacks.

Figure 28.1 summarizes these questions in more detail. The boxes on the left are for investment, those on the right for financing. In each box, we have posed a question and given examples of financial ratios or other measures that can help to answer it. For example, the bottom box on the far left asks about efficient use of assets. Three ratios that measure asset efficiency are turnover ratios for assets, inventory, and accounts receivable. The two bottom boxes on the right ask whether financial leverage is prudent and whether the firm has sufficient liquidity for the coming year. The ratios for tracking financial leverage include various debt ratios; the ratios for liquidity are the current, quick, and cash ratios.

Figure 28.1 serves as a road map for this chapter. We will show how to calculate these and other common financial ratios and explain how they relate to the objective of shareholder value.

28-2 Financial Statements

Public companies have a variety of stakeholders, such as shareholders, bondholders, bankers, suppliers, employees, and management. All these stakeholders need to monitor the firm and to ensure that their interests are being served. They rely on the company's financial statements to provide the necessary information. Public companies in the United States report to their shareholders quarterly and annually. The annual financial statements are filed with the SEC on form 10-K and the quarterly statements are filed on form 10-Q. Therefore you often hear financial analysts refer loosely to the company's "10-K" or its "10-Q."

When reviewing a company's financial statements, it is important to remember that accountants still have a fair degree of leeway in reporting earnings and book values. For example, they have discretion in the choice of depreciation method and the speed at which the firm's assets are written off.

The Rise and Stall of Convergence in Accounting Standards

❯ The International Financial Reporting Standards (IFRS), which are set by the London-based International Accounting Standards Board (IASB), aim to harmonize financial reporting around the world. They are the basis for reporting by listed firms throughout the European Union. In addition, some 100 other countries, such as Australia, Canada, Brazil, and India have adopted them or plan to do so, while China has modified its accounting standards to be largely in line with IFRS.

For some years, the SEC has worked to bring U.S. accounting standards more in line with international rules. For example, until 2007, foreign companies that traded on U.S. stock exchanges were required to show how their accounts differed from U.S. GAAP. This was a very expensive exercise that cost some companies millions of dollars annually and caused many to delist their stocks. These companies can now simply report results using international accounting standards. Subsequently, in August 2008, the SEC released its plans to allow some large U.S. multinationals, representing approximately $2.5 trillion in market capitalization, to eventually use IFRS for financial statements.

This shift from GAAP to IFRS would involve a major change in the way that accountants in the United States approach their task. IFRS tend to be "principles based," which means that there are no hard-and-fast codes to follow. Instead, companies must be ready to defend their accounting practices in light of the general principles laid out in the IFRS. By contrast, in the United States, GAAP are accompanied by thousands of pages of prescriptive regulatory guidance and interpretations from auditors and accounting groups. For example, more than 160 pieces of authoritative literature relate to how and when companies record revenue. This leaves less room for judgment, but detailed rules rapidly become out of date, and unscrupulous companies have been able to structure transactions so that they keep to the letter but not the spirit of the rules.

By 2014, it had become clear that the SEC's plan to move to IFRS was effectively dead and that, while the SEC and IASB would continue to collaborate on accounting rules, there was little prospect of any agreement over a single global standard that included the United States.

Although accountants around the world are working toward common practices, there are still considerable variations in the accounting rules of different countries. For investors and multinational companies these variations in accounting rules can be irksome. Accounting bodies have therefore been getting together to see whether they can iron out some of the differences. It is not a simple task, as the nearby box illustrates.

28-3 Home Depot's Financial Statements

Your task is to assess the financial standing of Home Depot, the home improvement company. Perhaps you are a mutual fund manager trying to decide whether to allocate $25 million of new money to Home Depot stock. You could be an investment banker seeking business from the company or a bondholder concerned with its credit standing. You could be the financial manager of Home Depot or of one of its competitors.

In each case, your first step is to assess the company's current condition. You have before you the latest balance sheet and income statement.

The Balance Sheet

Table 28.1 sets out a simplified balance sheet for Home Depot for fiscal years 2017 and 2016. It provides a snapshot of the company's assets at the end of the year and the sources of the money that was used to buy those assets.

745

Assets	End of Fiscal 2017#	End of Fiscal 2016*	Liabilities and Shareholders' Equity	End of Fiscal 2017#	End of Fiscal 2016*
Current assets			**Current liabilities**		
Cash and marketable securities	$ 3,595	$ 2,538	Debt due for repayment	$ 2,761	$ 1,252
Receivables	1,952	2,029	Accounts payable	7,244	7,000
Inventories	12,748	12,549	Other current liabilities	6,189	5,881
Other current assets	638	608	Total current liabilities	$16,194	$14,133
Total current assets	$18,933	$17,724	Long-term debt	$24,267	$22,349
Fixed assets			Other long-term liabilities	2,614	2,151
Tangible fixed assets			Total liabilities	$43,075	$38,633
Property, plant, and equipment	$41,414	$40,426	Shareholders' equity:		
Less accumulated depreciation	19,339	18,512	Common stock and other paid-in capital	10,281	$ 9,008
Net tangible fixed assets	$22,075	$21,914	Retained earnings	39,935	35,519
Intangible asset (goodwill)	$ 2,275	$ 2,093	Treasury stock	−48,762	−40,194
Other assets	1,246	1,235	Total shareholders' equity	1,454	$ 4,333
			Total liabilities and shareholders' equity	$44,529	$42,966
Total assets	$44,529	$42,966			

> **TABLE 28.1** Balance sheet of Home Depot, fiscal 2017 and 2016 (figures in $ millions)

#Year ending January 28, 2018
*Year ending January 29, 2017

The assets are listed in declining order of liquidity. For example, the accountant lists first those assets that are most likely to be turned into cash in the near future. They include cash itself, marketable securities and receivables (that is, bills to be paid by the firm's customers), and inventories of raw materials, work in process, and finished goods. These assets are all known as *current assets*.

The remaining assets on the balance sheet consist of long-term, usually illiquid, assets such as warehouses, stores, fixtures, and vehicles. The balance sheet does not show up-to-date market values of these long-term assets. Instead, the accountant records the amount that each asset originally cost and deducts a fixed annual amount for depreciation of buildings, plant, and equipment. The balance sheet does not include all the company's assets. Some of the most valuable ones are intangible, such as reputation, skilled management, and a well-trained labor force. Accountants are generally reluctant to record these assets in the balance sheet unless they can be readily identified and reasonably valued.[1]

Now look at the right-hand portion of Home Depot's balance sheet, which shows where the money to buy the assets came from. The accountant starts by looking at the liabilities, that is, the money owed by the company. First come those liabilities that need to be paid off in the near future. These *current liabilities* include debts that are due to be repaid within the next year and payables (that is, amounts owed by the company to its suppliers).

---

[1]Home Depot's balance sheet does include an entry for "goodwill." This reflects the difference between the price paid to acquire a company and that company's book value.

The difference between the current assets and current liabilities is known as the *net current assets* or *net working capital*. It roughly measures the company's potential reservoir of cash. For Home Depot in 2017,

$$\text{Net working capital} = \text{current assets} - \text{current liabilities}$$
$$= 18,933 - 16,194 = \$2,739$$

The bottom portion of the balance sheet shows the sources of the cash that was used to acquire the net working capital and fixed assets. Some of the cash has come from the issue of bonds and leases that will not be repaid for many years. After all these long-term liabilities have been paid off, the remaining assets belong to the common stockholders. The company's equity is simply the total value of the net working capital and fixed assets less the long-term liabilities. Part of this equity has come from the sale of shares to investors, and the remainder has come from earnings that the company has retained and invested on behalf of the shareholders.

The Income Statement

If Home Depot's balance sheet resembles a snapshot of the firm at a particular point in time, its income statement is like a video. It shows how profitable the firm has been over the past year.

Look at the summary income statement in Table 28.2. You can see that during 2017, Home Depot sold goods worth $100,978 million.[2] The total cost of purchasing and selling these goods was $66,548 + $17,864 = $84,412 million. In addition to these out-of-pocket expenses, Home Depot also deducted depreciation of $1,811 million for the value of the fixed assets used up in producing the goods. Thus Home Depot's earnings before interest and taxes (EBIT) were

$$\text{EBIT} = \text{total revenues} - \text{costs} - \text{depreciation}$$
$$= 100,978 - 84,412 - 1,811$$
$$= \$14,755 \text{ million}$$

Of this sum, $1,057 million went to pay the interest on the short- and long-term debt (remember debt interest is paid out of pretax income) and a further $5,068 million went to the government in the form of taxes. The $8,630 million that was left over belonged to the shareholders. Home Depot paid out $4,212 million as dividends and reinvested the remainder in the business.

❯TABLE 28.2 Income Statement of Home Depot, fiscal 2017 (figures in $ millions)

	$ millions
Net sales	$100,978
Cost of goods sold	66,548
Selling, general, and administrative expenses	17,864
Depreciation	1,811
Earnings before interest and income taxes (EBIT)	$ 14,755
Interest expense	1,057
Taxable income	$ 13,698
Taxes	5,068
Net income	$ 8,630
Allocation of net income	
Dividends	4,212
Addition to retained earnings	4,418

[2]For simplicity, we have added $74 million of investment income to net sales

28-4 Measuring Home Depot's Performance

You want to use Home Depot's financial statements to assess its financial performance and current standing. Where do you start?

At the close of fiscal 2017, Home Depot's common stock was priced at $204.92 per share. There were 1,170 million shares outstanding, so total **market capitalization** was 1,170 × $204.92 = $239,756 million. This is a big number, of course, but Home Depot is a sizable company. Its shareholders have, over the years, invested billions in the company. Therefore, you decide to compare Home Depot's market capitalization with the book value of its equity. The book value measures shareholders' cumulative investment in the company.

At the end of fiscal 2017, the book value of Home Depot's equity was $1,454 million. Therefore, the **market value added,** the difference between the market value of the firm's shares and the amount of money that shareholders have invested in the firm, was $239,756 − $1,454 = $238,302 million.[3] In other words, Home Depot's shareholders have contributed just over $1 billion and ended up with shares worth about $240 billion. They have accumulated nearly $239 billion in market value added.

The consultancy firm, EVA Dimensions, calculates market value added for a large sample of U.S. companies. Table 28.3 shows a few of the firms from EVA Dimensions' list. Apple is top of the class. It has created nearly $800 billion of wealth for its shareholders. Bank of America languishes near the bottom; the market value of its shares is $66 billion *less* than the amount that shareholders have invested in the firm.

These two firms are large. Their managers have lots of assets to work with. A small firm could not hope to create so much extra value as firms like Johnson & Johnson or Walmart or to lose as much as Bank of America. Therefore, financial managers and analysts also like to calculate how much value has been added for each dollar that shareholders have invested. To do this, they compute the ratio of market value to book value. For example, Home Depot's **market-to-book ratio** is[4]

$$\text{Market-to-book ratio} = \frac{\text{market value of equity}}{\text{book value of equity}}$$

$$= \frac{239,756}{1,454} = 164.9$$

Stock	Market Value Added	Market-to-Book Ratio	Stock	Market Value Added	Market-to-Book Ratio
Apple	782,164	7.15	Freeport-McMoran	−5,781	0.85
Microsoft	461,134	5.84	CBS	−16,858	0.65
Johnson & Johnson	277,722	3.38	AIG	−30,134	0.64
Walmart	209,010	3.41	Conoco	−53,141	0.47
Coca-Cola	202,102	8.59	Bank of America	−65,878	0.80

〉TABLE 28.3   Stock market measures of company performance, September 2017 (dollar values in millions). Companies are ranked by market value added.
Source: EVA Dimensions.

---

[3]Market value added is usually *defined* as the difference between the market value of the firm's capital (debt plus equity) and the book value of the capital. In practice, since the market and book value of debt are generally not too different, market value added is usually *measured* as the difference in the market and book values of the equity.

[4]The market-to-book ratio can also be calculated by dividing stock price by book value per share.

In other words, Home Depot has multiplied the value of its shareholders' investment 164.9 times. This is a very large number, but Home Depot has been buying back its stock and, as a result, the book value of the equity has been reduced by the cost of the repurchases. A very active repurchase program can reduce the book equity to zero.[5] This makes it very difficult to interpret ratios that include book equity in the denominator.

Table 28.3 also shows market-to-book ratios for our sample of U.S. companies. Notice that Coca-Cola has a much higher market-to-book ratio than Johnson & Johnson. But Johnson & Johnson's market value added is higher because of its larger scale.

The market value performance measures in Table 28.3 have three drawbacks. First, the market value of the company's shares reflects investors' expectations about *future* performance. Investors pay attention to current profits and investment, of course, but market-value measures can, nevertheless, be noisy measures of current performance.

Second, measures of market performance are only a first step toward understanding the reasons for the performance. Are the measures an indication of the manager's competence? Are they a reflection of events that are outside the manager's control, or do they just suggest fluctuations in investor sentiment?

Third, you can't look up the market value of privately owned companies whose shares are not traded. Nor can you observe the market value of divisions or plants that are parts of larger companies. You may use market values to satisfy yourself that Home Depot as a whole has performed well, but you can't use them to drill down to look at the performance of, say, its overseas stores or particular U.S. stores. To do this, you need accounting measures of profitability. We start with economic value added (EVA).

Economic Value Added

When accountants draw up an income statement, they start with revenues and then deduct operating and other costs. But one important cost is *not* included: the cost of the capital that the company has raised from investors. Therefore, to see whether the firm has truly created value, we need to measure whether it has earned a profit after deducting *all* costs, including its cost of capital.

The cost of capital is the minimum acceptable rate of return on capital investment. It is an *opportunity* cost of capital, because it equals the expected rate of return on investment opportunities open to investors in financial markets. The firm creates value for investors only if it can earn more than its cost of capital, that is, more than its investors can earn by investing on their own.

The profit after deducting all costs, *including the cost of capital,* is called the company's **economic value added** or **EVA.** We encountered EVA in Chapter 12, where we looked at how firms often link executive compensation to accounting measures of performance. Let's calculate EVA for Home Depot.

Total long-term capital, sometimes called *total capitalization,* is the sum of long-term debt and shareholders' equity. Home Depot entered fiscal 2017 with a total capitalization of $26,682 million, which was made up of $22,349 million of long-term debt and $4,333 million of shareholders' equity. This was the cumulative amount that had been invested in the past by the debt- and equityholders. Home Depot's weighted-average cost of capital was about 8.2%. Therefore, investors who provided the $26,682 million required the company to earn at least .082 × 26,682 = $2,188 million for its debt- and equityholders.

In 2017, Home Depot's after-tax interest and net income totaled (1 − .35) × 1,057 + 8,630 = $9,317 million (the tax rate in 2017 was 35%). If you deduct the total cost of the company's capital

[5]It can even result in a negative ratio. For example, stock repurchases by McDonald's have led to negative book equity.

from this figure, you can see that it earned $9,317 − 2,188 = $7,129 million *more* than investors required. This was Home Depot's residual income, or EVA:

$$\text{EVA} = (\text{after-tax interest} + \text{net income}) - (\text{cost of capital} \times \text{capital})$$
$$= 9,317 - 2,188 = \$7,129 \text{ million}$$

Sometimes it is helpful to re-express EVA as follows:

$$\text{EVA} = \left(\frac{\text{after-tax interest} + \text{net income}}{\text{total capital}} - \text{cost of capital} \right) \times \text{total capital}$$
$$= (\text{return on capital} - \text{cost of capital}) \times \text{total capital}$$

The **return on capital** or **ROC** is equal to the total profits that the company has earned for its debt- and equityholders, divided by the amount of money that they have contributed. If the company earns a higher return on its capital than investors require, EVA is positive.

In the case of Home Depot, with a 35% tax rate the return on capital was

$$\frac{\text{After-tax interest} + \text{net income}}{\text{total capital}} = \frac{(1 - .35) \times 1,057 + 8,630}{26,682} = .349, \text{ or } 34.9\%$$

Home Depot's cost of capital was about 8.2%. So,

$$\text{EVA} = (\text{return on capital} - \text{cost of capital}) \times \text{total capital}$$
$$= (.349 - .082) \times 26,682 = \$7,129$$

The first four columns of Table 28.4 show measures of EVA for our sample of large companies. Apple again heads the list. It earned $37.6 billion more than was needed to satisfy investors. By contrast, Bank of America was a laggard. Although it earned an accounting profit of $18.4 billion, this figure was calculated before deducting the cost of the capital that was employed. After deducting the cost of the capital, Bank of America made an EVA *loss* of $2.4 billion.

	1. After - Tax Interest + Net Income	2. Cost of Capital (WACC, %)	3. Total Long-Term Capital	4. EVA = 1 − (2 × 3)	5. Return on Capital (ROC, %) (1 ÷ 3)
Apple	$52,051	7.1	$203,569	$37,638	25.6
Microsoft	20,626	7.1	61,619	16,269	33.5
Johnson & Johnson	17,599	5.7	112,367	11,160	15.7
Walmart	14,891	2.8	206,206	9,076	7.2
Coca-Cola	8,713	5.8	44,678	6,144	19.5
CBS	1,863	6.1	55,820	−1,559	3.3
Freeport-McMoran	1,710	7.1	52,991	−2,068	3.2
Bank of America	18,370	6.7	310,587	−2,439	5.9
AIG	457	6.4	90,107	−5,300	0.5
Conoco	−1,494	6.7	102,820	−8,373	−1.5

❭**TABLE 28.4**   Accounting measures of company performance, September 2017 (dollar values in millions). Companies are ranked by economic value added (EVA).

Note: EVAs do not compute exactly because of rounding in column 2.

Source: EVA Dimensions.

Accounting Rates of Return

EVA measures how many dollars a business is earning after deducting the cost of capital. Other things equal, the more assets the manager has to work with, the greater the opportunity to generate a large EVA. The manager of a small division may be highly competent, but if that division has few assets, she is unlikely to rank high in the EVA stakes. Therefore, when comparing managers, it can also be helpful to measure the firm's return *per dollar of investment*.

Three common return measures are the return on capital (ROC), the return on equity (ROE), and the return on assets (ROA). All are based on accounting information and are therefore known as *book rates of return*.

Return on Capital[6] We have already calculated Home Depot's return on capital in 2017:

$$\text{ROC} = \frac{\text{after-tax interest} + \text{net income}}{\text{total capital}} = \frac{(1 - .35) \times 1,057 + 8,630}{26,682} = .349, \text{or } 34.9\%$$

The company's cost of capital (WACC) was about 8.2%. So we can say that the company earned nearly 27% more than shareholders demanded.

Notice that, when we calculated Home Depot's return on capital, we summed the company's *after-tax* interest and net income.[7] The reason that we subtracted the tax shield on debt interest was that we wished to calculate the income that the company would have earned with all-equity financing. The tax advantages of debt financing are picked up when we compare the company's return on capital with its weighted-average cost of capital (WACC).[8] WACC already includes an adjustment for the interest tax shield.[9] More often than not, financial analysts ignore this refinement and use the gross interest payment to calculate ROC. It is only approximately correct to compare this measure with the weighted-average cost of capital.

The last column in Table 28.4 shows the return on capital for our sample of well-known companies. Notice that Microsoft's return on capital was 33.5%, more than 26 percentage points higher than its cost of capital. Although Microsoft had a higher return than Apple, it had a slightly lower EVA. This was because it had far fewer dollars invested than Apple.

Return on Equity We measure the **return on equity (ROE)** as the income to shareholders per dollar invested. Home Depot had net income of $8,630 million in 2017 and stockholders' equity of $4,333 million at the start of the year. So its return on equity was

$$\text{ROE} = \frac{\text{net income}}{\text{equity}} = \frac{8,630}{4,333} = 1.992, \text{ or } 199.2\%$$

Has the company provided an adequate return for shareholders? To answer that question, we need to compare it with the company's cost of equity. Home Depot's cost of equity capital in 2017 was about 9.0%, so its return on equity was dramatically higher than its cost of equity, but remember once again our earlier warning about the effect of repurchases on the book value of Home Depot's equity.

---

[6]The expression, *return on capital*, is commonly used when calculating the profitability of an entire firm. When measuring the profitability of an individual plant, the equivalent measure is generally called *return on investment* (or *ROI*).

[7]This figure is called the company's net operating profit after tax, or NOPAT:

$$\text{NOPAT} = \text{after-tax interest} + \text{net income}$$

In the case of Home Depot:

$$\text{NOPAT} = (1-.35) \times 1,057 + 8,630 = \$9,317$$

[8]For the same reason, we used the after-tax interest payment when we calculated Home Depot's EVA.

[9]Remember WACC is a weighted average of the *after-tax* rate of interest and the cost of equity.

Return on Assets   **Return on assets (ROA)** measures the income available to debt and equity investors per dollar of the firm's *total* assets. Total assets (which equal total liabilities plus shareholders' equity) are greater than total capital because total capital does not include current liabilities.[10] With a 35% tax rate the return on Home Depot's assets was

$$ROA = \frac{(\text{after-tax interest} + \text{net income})}{\text{total assets}} = \frac{(1 - .35) \times 1,057 + 8,630}{42,966} = .217, \text{ or } 21.7\%$$

When we subtract the tax shield on Home Depot's interest payments, we are asking how much the company would have earned if all-equity-financed. This adjustment is helpful when comparing the profitability of firms with very different capital structures. Again, this refinement is ignored more often than not, and ROA is calculated using the gross interest payment. Sometimes analysts take no account of interest payments and measure ROA as the income for equityholders divided by total assets. This measure ignores entirely the income that the assets have generated for debtholders.

We will see shortly how Home Depot's return on assets is determined by the sales that these assets generate and the profit margin that the company earns on its sales.

Problems with EVA and Accounting Rates of Return

Rate of return and economic value added have some obvious attractions as measures of performance. Unlike market-value-based measures, they show current performance and are not affected by the expectations about future events that are reflected in today's stock market prices. Rate of return and economic value added can also be calculated for an entire company or for a particular plant or division. However, remember that both measures are based on book (balance sheet) values for assets. Debt and equity are also book values. Accountants do not show every asset on the balance sheet, yet our calculations take accounting data at face value. For example, we ignored the fact that Home Depot has invested large sums in marketing to establish its brand name. This brand name is an important asset, but its value is not shown on the balance sheet. If it were shown, the book values of assets, capital, and equity would increase, and Home Depot would not appear to earn such high returns.

EVA Dimensions, which produced the data in Tables 28.3 and 28.4, does make a number of adjustments to the accounting data. However, it is impossible to include the value of all assets or to judge how rapidly they depreciate. For example, did Microsoft really earn a return of 33% and add $16 billion of economic value? It's difficult to say, because its investment over the years in Windows and other software is not shown on the balance sheet and cannot be measured exactly.

Remember also that the balance sheet does not show the current market values of the firm's assets. The assets in a company's books are valued at their original cost less any depreciation. Older assets may be grossly undervalued in today's market conditions and prices. So a high return on assets indicates that the business has performed well by making profitable investments in the past, but it does not necessarily mean that you could buy the same assets today at their reported book values. Conversely, a low return suggests some poor decisions in the past, but it does not always mean that today the assets could be employed better elsewhere.

28-5   Measuring Efficiency

We began our analysis of Home Depot by calculating how much value the company has added for its shareholders and how much profit it is earning after deducting the cost of the capital that it employs. We examined the company's rates of return on capital, equity, and total assets

---

[10]Although it is sometimes done, it is not correct to compare return on assets with WACC. Current liabilities are ignored when calculating WACC.

and found that its return has been higher than the cost of capital. Our next task is to probe a little deeper to understand the reasons for the company's success. What factors contribute to a firm's overall profitability? One factor clearly must be the efficiency with which it uses its various assets.

Asset Turnover Ratio   The asset turnover, or sales-to-assets, ratio shows how much sales volume is generated by each dollar of total assets, and therefore it measures how hard the firm's assets are working. For Home Depot, each dollar of assets produced $2.35 of sales:

$$\text{Asset turnover} = \frac{\text{sales}}{\text{total assets at start of year}} = \frac{100{,}978}{42{,}966} = 2.35$$

BEYOND THE PAGE

Is it better to use average or start-of-year assets?

mhhe.com/brealey13e

Technical note: Like a number of other financial ratios, the sales-to-assets ratio compares a flow measure (sales over the entire year) with a snapshot measure (assets at a point in time). But which point in time should you use? We calculated the ratio of Home Depot's sales to assets at the start of the year, but frequently analysts use the *average* of the firm's assets at the start and end of the year. The idea is that this better measures the assets that the firm had to work with assets *during* the year.[11] In the case of Home Depot, the two ratios are effectively identical:

$$\text{Asset turnover} = \frac{\text{sales}}{\text{average total assets}} = \frac{100{,}978}{(44{,}529 + 42{,}966)/2} = 2.31$$

There is no obvious *best* measure. If assets are turned over very slowly, it may be better to use the value at the start of the year; if they are turned over fast, as is often the case, it may be preferable to use the average measure. However, it's probably not worth getting too steamed up over the matter. After all, both measures rest on the doubtful assumption that the asset levels at the close of each financial year are typical of the rest of the year. But, like many retailers, Home Depot ends its financial year in January/February just after the busy holiday season, when inventories and receivables are unusually low.

The asset turnover ratio measures how efficiently the business is using its entire asset base. But you also might be interested in how hard *particular types* of assets are being put to use. Here are a couple of examples.

Inventory Turnover   Efficient firms don't tie up more capital than they need in raw materials and finished goods. They hold only a relatively small level of inventories, and they turn over those inventories rapidly. The balance sheet shows the cost of inventories rather than the amount that the finished goods will eventually sell for. So it is usual to compare the level of inventories with the cost of goods sold rather than with sales. In Home Depot's case,

$$\text{Inventory turnover} = \frac{\text{cost of goods sold}}{\text{inventory at start of year}} = \frac{66{,}548}{12{,}549} = 5.3$$

Another way to express this measure is to look at how many days of output are represented by inventories. This is equal to the level of inventories divided by the daily cost of goods sold:

$$\text{Inventory period} = \frac{\text{inventory at start of year}}{\text{daily cost of goods sold}} = \frac{12{,}549}{66{,}548/365} = 69 \text{ days}$$

Receivables Turnover   Receivables are sales for which the company has not yet been paid. The receivables turnover ratio measures the firm's sales as a proportion of its receivables. For Home Depot,

$$\text{Receivables turnover} = \frac{\text{sales}}{\text{receivables at start of year}} = \frac{100{,}978}{2{,}029} = 49.8$$

---

[11]Sometimes it is convenient to use a snapshot figure at the end of the year, although this is not strictly appropriate.

If customers are quick to pay, unpaid bills will be a relatively small proportion of sales and the receivables turnover will be high. Therefore, a comparatively high ratio often indicates an efficient credit department that is quick to follow up on late payers. Sometimes, however, a high ratio indicates that the firm has an unduly restrictive credit policy and offers credit only to customers who can be relied on to pay promptly.[12]

Another way to measure the efficiency of the credit operation is by calculating the average length of time for customers to pay their bills. The faster the firm turns over its receivables, the shorter the collection period. Home Depot's customers pay their bills in about 7.3 days:

$$\text{Accounts receivable period} = \frac{\text{receivables at start of year}}{\text{average daily sales}} = \frac{2{,}029}{100{,}978/365} = 7.3 \text{ days}$$

The receivables turnover ratio and the inventory turnover ratio may help to highlight particular areas of inefficiency, but they are not the only possible indicators. For example, Home Depot might compare its sales per square foot with those of its competitors,[13] a steel producer might calculate the cost per ton of steel produced, an airline might look at revenues per passenger-mile, and a law firm might look at revenues per partner. A little thought and common sense should suggest which measures are likely to produce the most helpful insights into your company's efficiency.

28-6   Analyzing the Return on Assets: The Du Pont System

We have seen that every dollar of Home Depot's assets generates $2.35 of sales. But a company's success depends not only on the volume of its sales but also on how profitable those sales are. This is measured by the profit margin.

Profit Margin   The profit margin measures the proportion of sales that finds its way into profits. It is sometimes defined as

$$\text{Profit margin} = \frac{\text{net income}}{\text{sales}} = \frac{8{,}630}{100{,}978} = .0855, \text{ or } 8.55\%$$

This definition can be misleading. When companies are partly financed by debt, a portion of the profits from the sales must be paid as interest to the firm's lenders. We would not want to say that a firm is less profitable than its rivals simply because it employs debt finance and pays out part of its profits as interest. Therefore, when we are calculating the profit margin, it is useful to add back the after-tax debt interest to net income. This gives an alternative measure of profit margin, which is called the operating profit margin:

$$\text{Operating profit margin} = \frac{\text{after-tax interest} + \text{net income}}{\text{sales}}$$

$$= \frac{(1 - .35) \times 1{,}057 + 8{,}630}{100{,}978}$$

$$= .0923, \text{ or } 9.23\%$$

The Du Pont System

We calculated earlier that Home Depot has earned a return of 21.7% on its assets. The following equation shows that this return depends on two factors—the sales that the company generates from its assets (asset turnover) and the profit that it earns on each dollar of sales (operating profit margin):

---

[12]Where possible, it makes sense to look only at *credit* sales. Otherwise, a high ratio might simply indicate that a small proportion of sales is made on credit.
[13]For example, Home Depot reports its sales per square foot as part of its financial statements.

$$\text{Return on assets} = \frac{\text{after-tax interest} + \text{net income}}{\text{assets}} = \frac{\text{sales}}{\text{assets}} \times \frac{\text{after-tax interest} + \text{net income}}{\text{sales}}$$

$$\uparrow \qquad\qquad\qquad \uparrow$$
$$\text{asset turnover} \qquad \text{operating profit margin}$$

This breakdown of ROA into the product of asset turnover and margin is often called the **Du Pont formula,** after the chemical company that popularized the formula. In Home Depot's case, the formula gives the following breakdown of ROA:

$$\text{ROA} = \text{asset turnover} \times \text{operating profit margin} = 2.35 \times .0923 = .217$$

All firms would like to earn a higher return on their assets, but their ability to do so is limited by competition. The Du Pont formula helps to identify the constraints that firms face. Fast-food chains, which have high asset turnover, tend to operate on low margins. Classy hotels have relatively low turnover ratios but tend to compensate with higher margins.

Firms often seek to improve their profit margins by acquiring a supplier. The idea is to capture the supplier's profit as well as their own. Unfortunately, unless they have some special skill in running the new business, any gain in profit margin is offset by a decline in asset turnover. Other things equal, vertical integration brings higher profit margins and lower asset turnover.

A few numbers may help to illustrate this point. Table 28.5 shows the sales, profits, and assets of Admiral Motors and its components supplier, Diana Corporation. Both earn a 10% return on assets, though Admiral has a lower operating profit margin (20% versus Diana's 25%). Since all of Diana's output goes to Admiral, Admiral's management reasons that it would be better to merge the two companies. That way, the merged company would capture the profit margin on both the auto components and the assembled car.

The bottom row of Table 28.5 shows the effect of the merger. The merged firm does indeed earn the combined profits. Total sales remain at $20 million, however, because all the components produced by Diana are used within the company. With higher profits and unchanged sales, the profit margin increases. Unfortunately, the asset turnover is *reduced* by the merger since the merged firm has more assets. This exactly offsets the benefit of the higher profit margin. The return on assets is unchanged.

Figure 28.2 shows evidence of the trade-off between asset turnover and operating profit margin. You can see that industries with high average turnover ratios tend to have lower average profit margins. Conversely, high margins are typically associated with low turnover. The two curved lines in the figure trace out the combinations of profit margin and turnover that result in an ROA of either 3% or 10%. Despite the enormous dispersion across industries in both margin and turnover, that variation tends to be offsetting, so for most industries, the return on assets lies between 3% and 10%. The notable exception is mining, which was suffering badly in 2017 from low commodity prices.

	Sales	Profits	Assets	Asset Turnover	Profit Margin	ROA
Admiral Motors	$20	$4	$40	0.50	20%	10%
Diana Corporation	8	2	20	0.40	25	10
Diana Motors (the merged firm)	20	6	60	0.33	30	10

》TABLE 28.5 Merging with suppliers or customers generally increases the profit margin, but this increase is offset by a reduction in asset turnover

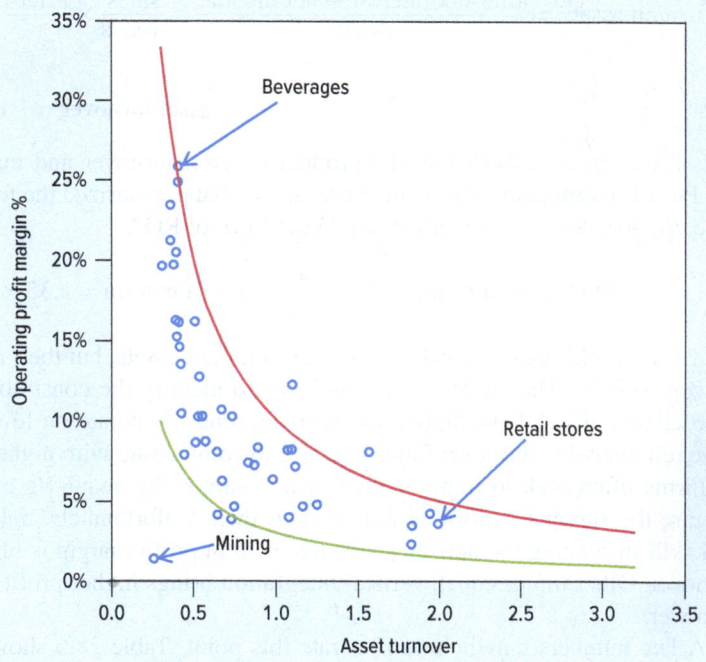

▶ **FIGURE 28.2**

Asset turnover and operating profit margin for 45 U.S. industries in the year ending September 2017. High asset turnover tends to be associated with low profit margins.

Source: U.S. Census Bureau, *Quarterly Financial Report Manufacturing, Mining, Trade, and Selected Service Industries*, Third Quarter 2017.

28-7 Measuring Leverage

When a firm borrows money, it promises to make a series of interest payments and then to repay the amount that it has borrowed. If profits rise, the debtholders continue to receive only the fixed interest payment, so all the gains go to the shareholders. Of course, the reverse happens if profits fall. In this case, shareholders bear the greater part of the pain. If times are sufficiently hard, a firm that has borrowed heavily may not be able to pay its debts. The firm is then bankrupt, and shareholders lose most or all of their investment.

Because debt increases the returns to shareholders in good times and reduces them in bad times, it is said to create *financial leverage*. Leverage ratios measure how much financial leverage the firm has taken on. CFOs keep an eye on leverage ratios to ensure that lenders are happy to continue to take on the firm's debt.

Debt Ratio Financial leverage is usually measured by the ratio of long-term debt to total long-term capital. (Here "long-term debt" should include not just bonds or other borrowing but also financing from long-term leases.)[14] For Home Depot,

$$\text{Long-term debt ratio} = \frac{\text{long-term debt}}{\text{long-term debt} + \text{equity}} = \frac{24{,}267}{24{,}267 + 1{,}454} = .94, \text{ or } 94\%$$

This means that 94 cents of every dollar of long-term capital is in the form of debt.

Leverage is also measured by the debt–equity ratio. For Home Depot,

$$\text{Long-term debt–equity ratio} = \frac{\text{long-term debt}}{\text{equity}} = \frac{24{,}267}{1{,}454} = 16.69, \text{ or } 16.69\%$$

---

[14]A finance lease is a long-term rental agreement that commits the firm to make regular payments. This commitment is just like the obligation to make payments on an outstanding loan. See Chapter 25.

Home Depot's long-term debt ratio is very high for U.S. nonfinancial companies, but the CFO could fairly point out that the book value of the equity substantially understates its market value. Home Depot's long-term debt is less than 2% of Home Depot's market capitalization.

Some companies deliberately operate at very high debt levels. For example, in Chapter 32, we look at leveraged buyouts (LBOs). Firms that are acquired in a leveraged buyout usually issue large amounts of debt. When LBOs first became popular in the 1990s, these companies had average debt ratios of about 90%. Many of them flourished and paid back their debtholders in full; others were not so fortunate.

Notice that our measure of leverage ignores short-term debt. That probably makes sense if the short-term debt is temporary or is matched by similar holdings of cash, but if the company is a regular short-term borrower, it may be preferable to widen the definition of debt to include all liabilities. In this case,

$$\text{Total debt ratio} = \frac{\text{total liabilities}}{\text{total assets}} = \frac{43{,}075}{44{,}529} = .97 \text{ or } 97\%$$

Therefore, Home Depot is financed 97% with long- and short-term liabilities and 3% with equity.[15] We could also say that its ratio of total debt to equity is 43,075/1,454 = 29.6.

Managers sometimes refer loosely to a company's leverage, but we have just seen that leverage may be measured in different ways. This is not the first time we have come across several ways to define a financial ratio. There is no law stating how a ratio should be defined. So be warned: Do not use a ratio without understanding how it has been calculated.

Times-Interest-Earned Ratio   Another measure of financial leverage is the extent to which interest obligations are covered by earnings. Banks prefer to lend to firms whose earnings cover interest payments with room to spare. *Interest coverage* is measured by the ratio of earnings before interest and taxes (EBIT) to interest payments. For Home Depot,[16]

$$\text{Times-interest-earned} = \frac{\text{EBIT}}{\text{interest payments}} = \frac{14{,}755}{1{,}057} = 14.0$$

The company enjoys a comfortable interest coverage or *times-interest-earned* ratio. Sometimes lenders are content with coverage ratios as low as 2 or 3.

The regular interest payment is a hurdle that companies must keep jumping if they are to avoid default. Times-interest-earned measures how much clear air there is between hurdle and hurdler. The ratio is only part of the story, however. For example, it doesn't tell us whether Home Depot is generating enough cash to repay its debt as it comes due.

Cash Coverage Ratio   In Chapter 26, we pointed out that depreciation is deducted when calculating the firm's earnings, even though no cash goes out the door. Suppose we add back depreciation to EBIT to calculate operating cash flow.[17] We can then calculate a *cash* coverage ratio. For Home Depot,

$$\text{Cash coverage} = \frac{\text{EBIT} + \text{depreciation}}{\text{interest payments}} = \frac{14{,}755 + 1{,}811}{1{,}057} = 15.7$$

---

[15]In this case, the debt consists of all liabilities, including current liabilities.

[16]The numerator of times-interest-earned can be defined in several ways. Sometimes depreciation is excluded. Sometimes it is just earnings plus interest'—that is, earnings before interest but *after* tax. This last definition seems nutty to us because the point of times-interest-earned is to assess the risk that the firm won't have enough money to pay interest. If EBIT falls below interest obligations, the firm won't have to worry about taxes. Interest is paid before the firm pays taxes.

[17]Earnings before interest, taxes, depreciation, and amortization are often termed EBITDA.

Leverage and the Return on Equity

When the firm raises cash by borrowing, it must make interest payments to its lenders. This reduces net profits. On the other hand, if a firm borrows instead of issuing equity, it has fewer equityholders to share the remaining profits. Which effect dominates? An extended version of the Du Pont formula helps us answer this question. It breaks down the return on equity (ROE) into four parts:

$$\text{ROE} = \frac{\text{net income}}{\text{equity}}$$

$$= \underbrace{\frac{\text{assets}}{\text{equity}}}_{\substack{\text{leverage}\\\text{ratio}}} \times \underbrace{\frac{\text{sales}}{\text{assets}}}_{\substack{\text{asset}\\\text{turnover}}} \times \underbrace{\frac{\text{after-tax interest} + \text{net income}}{\text{sales}}}_{\substack{\text{operating}\\\text{profit margin}}} \times \underbrace{\frac{\text{net income}}{\text{after-tax interest} + \text{net income}}}_{\text{“debt burden”}}$$

Notice that the product of the two middle terms is the return on assets. It depends on the firm's production and marketing skills and is unaffected by the firm's financing mix. However, the first and fourth terms do depend on the debt–equity mix. The first term, assets/equity, which we call the *leverage ratio,* can be expressed as (equity + liabilities)/equity, which equals 1 + total-debt-to-equity ratio. The last term, which we call the "debt burden," measures the proportion by which interest expense reduces net income.

Suppose that the firm is financed entirely by equity. In this case, both the leverage ratio and the debt burden are equal to 1, and the return on equity is identical to the return on assets. If the firm borrows, however, the leverage ratio is greater than 1 (assets are greater than equity) and the debt burden is less than 1 (part of the profits is absorbed by interest). Thus, leverage can either increase or reduce return on equity. You will usually find, however, that leverage increases ROE when the firm is performing well and ROA exceeds the interest rate.

28-8 Measuring Liquidity

If you are extending credit to a customer or making a short-term bank loan, you are interested in more than the company's leverage. You want to know whether the company can lay its hands on the cash to repay you. That is why credit analysts and bankers look at several measures of **liquidity.** Liquid assets can be converted into cash quickly and cheaply.

Think, for example, what you would do to meet a large unexpected bill. You might have some money in the bank or some investments that are easily sold, but you would not find it so easy to turn your old sweaters into cash. Companies, likewise, own assets with different degrees of liquidity. For example, accounts receivable and inventories of finished goods are generally quite liquid. As inventories are sold off and customers pay their bills, money flows into the firm. At the other extreme, real estate may be very *illiquid.* It can be hard to find a buyer, negotiate a fair price, and close a deal on short notice.

Managers have another reason to focus on liquid assets: Their book (balance sheet) values are usually reliable. The book value of a catalytic cracker may be a poor guide to its true value, but at least you know what cash in the bank is worth. Liquidity ratios also have some *less* desirable characteristics. Because short-term assets and liabilities are easily changed, measures of liquidity can rapidly become outdated. You might not know what the catalytic cracker is worth, but you can be fairly sure that it won't disappear overnight. Cash in the bank can disappear in seconds.

Also, assets that seem liquid sometimes have a nasty habit of becoming illiquid. This happened during the subprime mortgage crisis in 2007. Some financial institutions had set up funds known as *structured investment vehicles (SIVs)* that issued short-term debt backed by residential mortgages. As mortgage default rates began to climb, the market in this debt dried up and dealers became very reluctant to quote a price. Investors who were forced to sell found that the prices that they received were less than half the debt's estimated value.

Bankers and other short-term lenders applaud firms that have plenty of liquid assets. They know that when they are due to be repaid, the firm will be able to get its hands on the cash. But more liquidity is not always a good thing. For example, efficient firms do not leave excess cash in their bank accounts. They don't allow customers to postpone paying their bills, and they don't leave stocks of raw materials and finished goods littering the warehouse floor. In other words, high levels of liquidity may indicate sloppy use of capital. Here, EVA can help because it penalizes managers who keep more liquid assets than they really need.

Net-Working-Capital-to-Total-Assets Ratio   Current assets include cash, marketable securities, inventories, and accounts receivable. Current assets are mostly liquid. The difference between current assets and current liabilities is known as *net working capital*. Since current assets usually exceed current liabilities, net working capital is generally positive. For Home Depot,

$$\text{Net working capital} = 18{,}933 - 16{,}194 = \$2{,}739 \text{ million}$$

Net working capital was 6.2% of total assets:

$$\frac{\text{Net working capital}}{\text{total assets}} = \frac{2{,}739}{44{,}529} = .062, \text{ or } 6.2\%$$

Current Ratio   The current ratio is just the ratio of current assets to current liabilities:

$$\text{Current ratio} = \frac{\text{current assets}}{\text{current liabilities}} = \frac{18{,}933}{16{,}194} = 1.17$$

Home Depot has $1.17 in current assets for every dollar in current liabilities.

Changes in the current ratio can be misleading. For example, suppose that a company borrows a large sum from the bank and invests it in marketable securities. Current liabilities rise and so do current assets. If nothing else changes, net working capital is unaffected but the current ratio changes. For this reason, it is sometimes preferable to net short-term investments against short-term debt when calculating the current ratio.

Quick (Acid-Test) Ratio   Some current assets are closer to cash than others. If trouble comes, inventory may not sell at anything above fire-sale prices. (Trouble typically comes *because* the firm can't sell its inventory of finished products for more than production cost.) Thus, managers often exclude inventories and other less liquid components of current assets when comparing current assets to current liabilities. They focus instead on cash, marketable securities, and bills that customers have not yet paid. This results in the quick ratio:

$$\text{Quick ratio} = \frac{\text{cash} + \text{marketable securities} + \text{receivables}}{\text{current liabilities}} = \frac{3{,}595 + 1{,}952}{16{,}194} = .343$$

Cash Ratio   A company's most liquid assets are its holdings of cash and marketable securities. That is why analysts also look at the cash ratio:

$$\text{Cash ratio} = \frac{\text{cash} + \text{marketable securities}}{\text{current liabilities}} = \frac{3{,}595}{16{,}194} = .222$$

A low cash ratio may not matter if the firm can borrow on short notice. Who cares whether the firm has actually borrowed from the bank or whether it has a guaranteed line of credit so it can borrow whenever it chooses? None of the standard measures of liquidity takes the firm's "reserve borrowing power" into account.

Interpreting Financial Ratios

We have shown how to calculate some common summary measures of Home Depot's performance and financial condition. Now you need some way to judge whether they are high or low. In some cases, there may be a natural benchmark. For example, if a firm has negative economic value added or a return on capital less than the cost of that capital, it has not created wealth for its shareholders.

But what about some of our other measures? There is no right level for, say, the asset turnover or profit margin, and if there were, it would almost certainly vary from year to year and industry to industry. Therefore, when assessing company performance, managers usually look first at how the financial ratios have changed over time, and then they look at how their measures stack up in comparison with companies in the same line of business.

We will first compare Home Depot's position in 2017 with its performance in earlier years. For example, Figure 28.3 plots Home Depot's return on assets since 1996. We know that ROA = asset turnover × operating profit margin. Figure 28.3 shows that beginning in 1999, there was a steady decline in the company's ability to generate sales from its assets, though for a while this effect was largely offset by a rise in the profit margin. When the downturn in the housing market in 2008 also led to a sharp decline in the profit margin, Home Depot's ROA fell dramatically. The turnaround came under new management in 2009, and in each of the following years, the company was able to increase both the rate of asset turnover and the profit margin.

Managers also need to ask themselves how the company's performance compares with that of its principal competitors. Table 28.6 sets out some key performance measures for Home Depot and Lowe's.[18] Home Depot has the higher asset turnover ratio and operating profit margin and these combine to produce a higher return on assets. Home Depot has higher book debt ratios, but, thanks to its greater profitability, it has the higher interest cover. Its assets also appear to be more liquid.

Home Depot and Lowe's are fairly close competitors, and it makes sense to compare their financial ratios. However, all financial ratios must be interpreted in the context of industry norms. For example, you would not expect a soft-drink manufacturer to have the same

BEYOND THE PAGE

Try It! Financial ratios for U.S. companies

mhhe.com/brealey13e

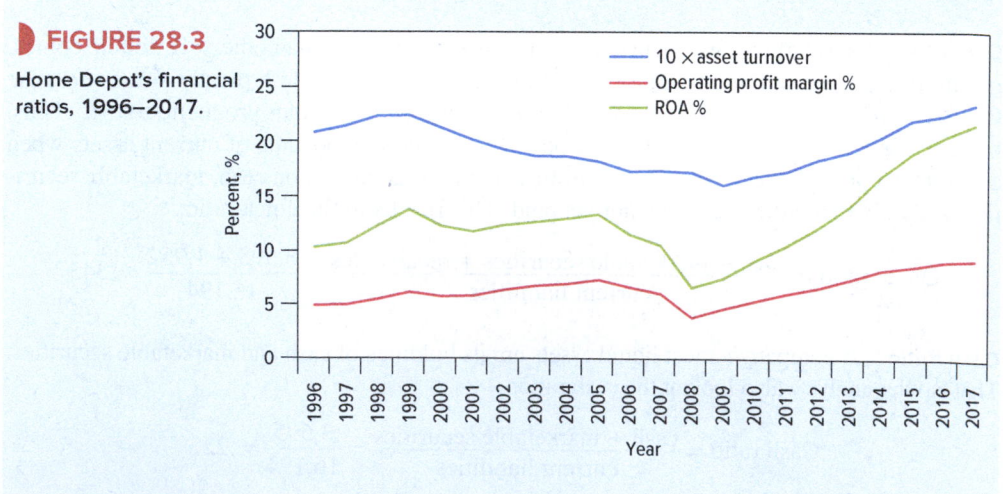

▶ **FIGURE 28.3**

Home Depot's financial ratios, 1996–2017.

---

[18]We do not report a measure of receivables turnover for Lowe's, since the company sells most of its receivables to a third party.

			Fiscal 2017	
			Home Depot	Lowe's Companies
Performance Measures:				
Market value added ($ millions)	Market value of equity – book value of equity		$238,302	$80,467
Market-to-book ratio	Market value of equity/book value of equity		164.9	13.5
EVA ($ millions)	(After-tax interest + net income) – (cost of capital × capital)		$6,366	$2,150
Return on capital (ROC, %)	(After-tax interest + net income)/total capital		34.9	18.5
Return on equity (ROE, %)	Net income/equity		199.2	53.6
Return on assets (ROA, %)	(After-tax interest + net income)/total assets		21.7	11.2
Efficiency Measures:				
Asset turnover	Sales/total assets at start of year		2.35	1.99
Inventory turnover	Cost of goods sold/inventory at start of year		5.3	4.3
Days in inventory	Inventory at start of year/daily cost of goods sold		68.8	84.4
Receivables turnover[a]	Sales/receivables at start of year		49.8	n.a.
Average collection period (days)[a]	Receivables at start of year/daily sales		7.3	n.a.
Profit margin (%)	Net income/sales		8.55	5.03
Operating profit margin (%)	(After-tax interest + net income)/sales		9.23	5.63
Leverage Measures:				
Long-term debt ratio	Long-term debt/(long-term debt + equity)		0.94	0.73
Total debt ratio	Total liabilities/total assets		0.97	0.83
Times-interest-earned	EBIT/interest payments		14.0	9.7
Cash coverage ratio	(EBIT + depreciation)/interest payments		15.7	12.0
Liquidity Measures:				
Net-working-capital-to-total-assets ratio	Net working capital/total assets		0.06	0.02
Current ratio	Current assets/current liabilities		1.17	1.06
Quick ratio	(Cash + marketable securities + receivables)/current liabilities		0.34	0.05
Cash ratio	(Cash + marketable securities)/current liabilities		0.22	0.05

❭TABLE 28.6   Selected financial ratios for Home Depot and Lowe's, 2017

[a]Lowe's sells most of its receivables to a third party.

profit margin as a jeweler or the same leverage as a finance company. You can see this from Table 28.7, which presents some financial ratios for a sample of industry groups.

Notice the large variation across industries. Some of these differences, particularly in profitability measures, may arise from chance; for example, in 2017 the sun shone less kindly on the oil industry. But other differences may reflect more fundamental factors. For example, telecoms and utility companies tend to have high debt ratios, which persist in good years and bad. In comparison, business equipment companies tend to borrow far less. We pointed out earlier that some businesses are able to generate a high level of sales from relatively few assets. You can see that this is the case for retail companies. On the other hand, these companies earn a relatively low profit margin on these sales. By contrast, utilities turn over their assets more slowly but earn a much higher margin of profit on their sales.

	Market-to-Book Ratio	Return on Equity (%)	Asset Turnover	Inventory Turnover	Receivables Turnover	Profit Margin (%)	Long-Term Debt Ratio	Total Debt Ratio	Times-Interest-Earned	Current Ratio	Quick Ratio	Cash Ratio
Autos	2.19	14.1	1.26	6.97	6.45	3.8	.29	.46	5.99	2.05	1.38	.39
Beer and liquor	3.55	12.2	0.82	3.99	9.07	9.5	.22	.42	6.52	2.31	.98	.19
Business equipment	2.09	3.2	0.82	4.14	6.14	2.3	.09	.24	5.72	2.80	2.13	1.18
Chemicals	2.04	9.1	0.80	4.48	6.28	5.2	.43	.53	5.23	2.36	1.48	.59
Clothing	2.19	15.1	1.37	3.10	8.99	5.9	.17	.29	20.60	2.73	1.77	.61
Construction	1.70	7.7	1.06	5.83	7.01	3.2	.35	.44	3.80	2.12	1.49	.32
Electrical equipment	1.82	3.7	0.88	3.79	5.85	2.3	.14	.31	5.32	2.64	1.67	.70
Food	2.77	10.0	0.98	5.84	11.41	6.3	.38	.47	7.89	1.97	1.12	.29
Oil	0.84	−15.8	0.26	18.85	5.72	−35.1	.36	.47	−3.12	1.32	1.15	.37
Paper	2.65	14.7	1.04	5.81	8.07	4.4	.48	.60	7.32	1.58	1.07	.21
Retail	1.99	11.4	1.96	4.64	52.34	2.3	.28	.49	8.54	1.64	.69	.31
Steel	1.17	1.2	1.04	5.35	7.08	−0.6	.34	.43	3.13	2.93	1.47	.33
Telecom	1.84	3.4	0.47	16.76	7.12	3.4	.55	.58	1.92	1.71	1.55	.58
Utilities	1.17	6.2	0.28	11.91	9.22	8.6	.49	.54	3.46	.86	.71	.07

❭TABLE 28.7 Median financial ratios for publicly traded North American companies, December 2015

Source: WRDS Financial Ratios Suite.

SUMMARY

Managers use financial statements to monitor their own company's performance, to help understand the policies of a competitor, and to check on the financial health of customers. But there is a danger of being overwhelmed by the sheer volume of data in a company's Annual Report.[19] That is why managers use a few salient ratios to summarize the firm's market valuation, profitability, efficiency, capital structure, and liquidity. We have described some of the more popular financial ratios.

We offer the following general advice to users of these ratios:

1. Financial ratios seldom provide answers, but they do help you to ask the right questions.

2. There is no international standard for financial ratios. A little thought and common sense are worth far more than blind application of formulas.

3. You need a benchmark for assessing a company's financial position. It is generally useful to compare the company's current financial ratios with the equivalent ratios in the past and with the ratios of other firms in the same business.

SUMMARY

There are some good general texts on financial statement analysis. See, for example:

K. G. Palepu and P. M. Healy, *Business Analysis and Valuation,* 5th ed. (Cincinnati, OH: South-Western Publishing, 2013).

L. Revsine, D. Collins, B. Johnson, F. Mittelstaedt, and L. Soffer, *Financial Reporting and Analysis,* 7th ed. (New York: McGraw-Hill/Irwin, 2017).

S. Penman, *Financial Statement Analysis and Security Valuation,* 5th ed. (New York: McGraw-Hill/Irwin, 2012).

FURTHER READING

 **Select problems are available in McGraw-Hill's *Connect*. Please see the preface for more information.**

PROBLEM SETS

1. **Financial Statements** Construct a balance sheet for Galactic Enterprises given the following data:

Cash balances	$25,000
Inventories	$30,000
Net plant and equipment	$140,000
Accounts receivable	$35,000
Accounts payable	$24,000
Long-term debt	$130,000

What is shareholders' equity?

2. **Performance measures** Keller Cosmetics maintains an operating profit margin of 8% and a sales-to-assets ratio of 3. It has assets of $500,000 and equity of $300,000. Assume that interest payments are $30,000 and the tax rate is 25%.

a. What is the return on assets?

b. What is the return on equity?

---

[19]HSBC's 2007 *Annual Report* totaled 454 pages. The *Financial Times* reported that Britain's postal service was obliged to limit the number that its postmen carried in order to prevent back injuries.

3. **Performance measures*** Table 28.8 gives abbreviated balance sheets and income statements for Walmart. At the end of fiscal 2017, Walmart had 2,960 million shares outstanding with a share price of $106. The company's weighted-average cost of capital was about 5%. Assume the marginal corporate tax rate was 35%. Calculate:

a. Market value added.

b. Market-to-book ratio.

c. Economic value added.

d. Return on start-of-the-year capital.

	Fiscal 2017	Fiscal 2016
Balance Sheet		
Assets		
Current assets:		
Cash and marketable securities	6,756	$ 6,867
Accounts receivable	5,614	5,835
Inventories	43,783	43,046
Other current assets	3,511	1,941
Total current assets	$ 59,664	$ 57,689
Fixed assets:		
Net fixed assets	$114,818	$114,178
Other long-term assets	30,040	26,958
Total assets	$204,522	$198,825
Liabilities and Shareholders' Equity		
Current liabilities:		
Accounts payable	$ 46,092	$ 41,433
Other current liabilities	32,429	25,495
Total current liabilities	$ 78,521	$ 66,928
Long-term debt	36,825	42,018
Other long-term liabilities	11,307	12,081
Total liabilities	$126,653	$121,027
Total shareholders' equity	77,869	77,798
Total liabilities and shareholders' equity	$204,522	$198,825
Income Statement		
Net sales	$500,343	$485,873
Cost of goods sold	373,396	361,256
Selling, general, and administrative expenses	95,981	91,773
Depreciation	10,529	10,080
Earnings before interest and tax (EBIT)	$ 20,437	$ 22,764
Interest expense	2,178	2,267
Taxable income	$ 18,259	$ 20,497
Tax	4,600	6,204
Net income	$ 13,659	$ 14,293

❯ **TABLE 28.8**   Balance sheets and income statement for Walmart, fiscal 2017 and 2016 (figures in $ millions)

4. **Performance measures** Describe some alternative measures of a firm's overall performance. What are their advantages and disadvantages? In each case, discuss what benchmarks you might use to judge whether performance is satisfactory.

5. **Financial ratios*** Look again at Table 28.8, which gives abbreviated balance sheets and income statements for Walmart. Assume Walmart had a 35% marginal corporate tax rate in 2017. Calculate the following using balance-sheet figures from the start of the year:

   a. Return on assets.

   b. Operating profit margin.

   c. Sales-to-assets ratio.

   d. Inventory turnover.

   e. Debt–equity ratio.

   f. Current ratio.

   g. Quick ratio.

6. **Financial ratios** There are no universally accepted definitions of financial ratios, but five of the following ratios are clearly incorrect. Substitute the correct definitions.

   a. Debt–equity ratio = (long-term debt + value of leases)/(long-term debt + value of leases + equity)

   b. Return on equity = (EBIT − tax)/average equity

   c. Profit margin = net income/sales

   d. Days in inventory = sales/(inventory/365)

   e. Current ratio = current liabilities/current assets

   f. Sales-to-net-working-capital = average sales/average net working capital

   g. Quick ratio = (current assets − inventories)/current liabilities

   h. Times-interest-earned = interest earned × long-term debt

7. **Financial ratios** True or false?

   a. A company's debt–equity ratio is always less than 1.

   b. The quick ratio is always less than the current ratio.

   c. The return on equity is always less than the return on assets.

8. **Financial ratios** Sara Togas sells all its output to Federal Stores. The following table shows selected 2017 financial data, in millions, for the two firms:

	Sales	Interest Payment	Net Income	Assets at Start of Year
Federal Stores	$100	$4	$10	$50
Sara Togas	20	1	4	20

   The company's tax rate is 35%. Calculate the sales-to-assets ratio, the operating profit margin, and the return on assets for the two firms. Now assume that the two companies merge. If Federal continues to sell goods worth $100 million, how will the three ratios change?

9. **Financial ratios*** As you can see, someone has spilled ink over some of the entries in the balance sheet and income statement of Transylvania Railroad (Table 28.9). Can you use the following information to work out the missing entries? (*Note:* For this problem, use the following definitions: inventory turnover = COGS/average inventory; receivables collection period = average receivables/[sales/365].)

   - Long-term debt ratio: .4.
   - Times-interest-earned: 8.0.

〉**TABLE 28.9** Balance sheet and income statement of Transylvania Railroad (figures in $ millions)

	December 2018	December 2017
Balance Sheet		
Cash	🔲🔲🔲	20
Accounts receivable	🔲🔲🔲	34
Inventory	🔲🔲🔲	26
Total current assets	🔲🔲🔲	80
Fixed assets (net)	🔲🔲🔲	25
Total	🔲🔲🔲	105
Notes payable	25	20
Accounts payable	30	35
Total current liabilities	🔲🔲🔲	55
Long-term debt	🔲🔲🔲	20
Equity	🔲🔲🔲	30
Total	115	105
Income Statement		
Sales	🔲🔲🔲	
Cost of goods sold	🔲🔲🔲	
Selling, general, and administrative expenses	10	
Depreciation	20	
EBIT	🔲🔲🔲	
Interest	🔲🔲🔲	
Earnings before tax	🔲🔲🔲	
Tax	🔲🔲🔲	
Earnings available for common stock	🔲🔲🔲	

- Current ratio: 1.4.
- Quick ratio: 1.0.
- Cash ratio: .2.
- Inventory turnover: 5.0.
- Receivables collection period: 73 days.
- Tax rate = .4.

10. **Efficiency ratios**

    a. If a firm's assets of $10,000 represent 200 days' sales, what is its annual sales?

    b. What is its asset turnover ratio?

11. **Efficiency ratios** If Microcharge's customers take on average 60 days to pay their bills, what is its receivables turnover?

12. **Efficiency ratios** Magic Flutes has total receivables of $3,000, which represent 20 days' sales. Total assets are $75,000. The firm's operating profit margin is 5%. Find the firm's sales-to-assets ratio and return on assets

13. **Leverage ratios** A firm has a long-term debt–equity ratio of .4. Shareholders' equity is $1 million. Current assets are $200,000, and total assets are $1.5 million. If the current ratio is 2.0, what is the ratio of debt to total long-term capital?

14. **Leverage ratios** Consider this simplified balance sheet for Geomorph Trading:

Current assets	$100	$60	Current liabilities
Long-term assets	500	280	Long-term debt
		70	Other liabilities
		190	Equity
	$600	$600	

   a. Calculate the ratio of debt to equity.

   b. What are Geomorph's net working capital and total long-term capital? Calculate the ratio of debt to total long-term capital.

15. **Leverage ratios** Discuss alternative measures of financial leverage. Should the market value of equity be used or the book value? Is it better to use the market value of debt or the book value? How should you treat off-balance-sheet obligations such as pension liabilities? How would you treat preferred stock?

16. **Leverage ratios** Suppose that a firm has both fixed-rate and floating-rate debt outstanding. What effect will a decline in interest rates have on the firm's times-interest-earned ratio? What about the ratio of the market value of debt to that of equity? Would you judge that leverage has increased or decreased?

17. **Leverage and liquidity ratios** Look again at the balance sheet for Geomorph in Problem 14 . Suppose that at year-end Geomorph had $30 in cash and marketable securities. Immediately after the year-end it used a line of credit to borrow $20 for one year, which it invested in additional marketable securities. Would the company appear to be (a) more or less liquid, (b) more or less highly leveraged? Make any additional assumptions that you need.

18. **Liquidity ratios** Airlux Antarctica has current assets of $300 million, current liabilities of $200 million and a crash—sorry—*cash* ratio of .05. How much cash and marketable securities does it hold?

19. **Liquidity ratios** How would the following actions affect a firm's current ratio?

   a. Inventory is sold.

   b. The firm takes out a bank loan to pay its suppliers.

   c. The firm arranges a line of credit with a bank that allows it to borrow at any time to pay its suppliers.

   d. A customer pays its overdue bills.

   e. The firm uses cash to purchase additional inventories.

20. **Interpreting financial ratios** This question reviews some of the difficulties encountered in interpreting accounting numbers.

   a. Give four examples of important assets, liabilities, or transactions that may not be shown on the company's books.

   b. How does investment in intangible assets, such as research and development, distort accounting ratios? Give at least two examples.

21. **Interpreting financial ratios** Here are some data for five companies in the same industry:

	Company Code				
	A	**B**	**C**	**D**	**E**
EBIT	10	30	100	−3	80
Interest expense	5	15	50	2	1

You have been asked to calculate a measure of times-interest-earned for the industry. Discuss the possible ways that you might calculate such a measure. Does changing the method of calculation make a significant difference to the end result?

22. **Interpreting financial ratios** How would rapid inflation affect the accuracy and relevance of a manufacturing company's balance sheet and income statement? Does your answer depend on how much debt the firm has issued?

23. **Interpreting financial ratios** Suppose that you wish to use financial ratios to estimate the risk of a company's stock. Which of those that we have described in this chapter are likely to be helpful? Can you think of other accounting measures of risk?

24. **Interpreting financial ratios** Look up some firms that have been in trouble. Plot the changes over the preceding years in the principal financial ratios. Are there any patterns?

CHALLENGE

25. **Calculating EVA** We noted that, when calculating EVA, you should calculate income as the sum of the after-tax interest payment and net income. Why do you need to deduct the tax shield? Would an alternative be to use a different measure of the cost of capital? Or would you get the same result if you simply deducted the cost of equity from net income (as is often done)?

26. **Return on capital** Sometimes analysts use the average of capital at the start and end of the year to calculate return on capital. Provide some examples to illustrate when this does and does not make sense. (*Hint:* Start by assuming that capital increases solely as a result of retained earnings.)

27. **Leverage ratios** Take another look at Geomorph Trading's balance sheet in Problem 14 and consider the following additional information:

Current Assets		Current Liabilities		Other Liabilities	
Cash	$15	Payables	$35	Deferred tax	$32
Inventories	35	Taxes due	10	Unfunded pensions	22
Receivables	50	Bank loan	15	R&R reserve	16
	$100		$60		$70

The "R&R reserve" covers the future costs of removal of an oil pipeline and environmental restoration of the pipeline route.

There are many ways to calculate a debt ratio for Geomorph. Suppose you are evaluating the safety of Geomorph's debt and want a debt ratio for comparison with the ratios of other companies in the same industry. Would you calculate the ratio in terms of total liabilities or total capitalization? What would you include in debt—the bank loan, the deferred tax account, the R&R reserve, the unfunded pension liability? Explain the pros and cons of these choices.

Use data from Yahoo! Finance (**finance.yahoo.com**) to answer the following questions.

1. Select two companies that are in a similar line of business and find their simplified balance sheets and income statements. Then draw up common-size statements for each company and compute the principal financial ratios. Compare and contrast the companies based on these data.

2. Look up the latest financial statements for a company of your choice and calculate the following ratios for the latest year:

   a. Return on capital.

   b. Return on equity.

   c. Operating profit margin.

   d. Days in inventory.

   e. Debt ratio.

   f. Times-interest-earned.

   g. Current ratio.

   h. Quick ratio.

3. Select five companies and, using their financial statements, compare the days in inventory and average collection period for receivables. Can you explain the differences between the companies?

CHAPTER

Financial Planning

This chapter is concerned with financial planning. We look first at short-term planning where the focus is on ensuring that the firm does not run out of cash. Short-term planning is, therefore, often termed *cash budgeting.* In the second half of the chapter we look at how firms also use financial planning models to develop a coherent *long-term* strategy.

The principal short-term assets are inventory, accounts receivable, cash, and marketable securities. Decisions on these assets cannot be made in isolation. For example, suppose that the marketing manager wishes to give customers more time to pay for their purchases. This reduces the firm's future cash balances. Or perhaps the production manager adopts a just-in-time system for ordering from suppliers. That allows the firm to get by on smaller inventories and frees up cash.

Managers concerned with short-term financial decisions can avoid many of the difficult conceptual issues encountered elsewhere in this book. In that respect short-term decisions are easier than long-term decisions, but they are not less important. A firm can identify extremely valuable capital investment opportunities, find the precise optimal debt ratio, follow the perfect dividend policy, and yet founder because no one bothers to raise the cash to pay this year's bills. Hence the need for short-term planning.

Short-term planning rarely looks further ahead than the next 12 months. It seeks to ensure that the firm has enough cash to pay its bills and makes sensible short-term borrowing and lending decisions. But the financial manager also needs to think about the investments that will be needed to meet the firm's *long-term* goals and the financing that must be arranged. Long-term financial planning focuses on the implications of alternative financial strategies. It allows managers to avoid some surprises and consider how they should react to surprises that *cannot* be avoided. And it helps to establish goals for the firm and to provide standards for measuring performance.

29-1 Links between Short-Term and Long-Term Financing Decisions

Short-term financial decisions differ in two ways from long-term decisions such as the purchase of plant and equipment or the choice of capital structure. First, they generally involve short-lived assets and liabilities, and, second, they are usually easily reversed. Compare, for example, a 60-day bank loan with an issue of 20-year bonds. The bank loan is clearly a short-term decision. The firm can repay it two months later and be right back where it started. A firm might conceivably issue a 20-year bond in January and retire it in March, but it would be extremely inconvenient and expensive to do so. In practice, the bond issue is a long-term decision, not only because of the bond's 20-year maturity but also because the decision to issue it cannot be reversed on short notice.

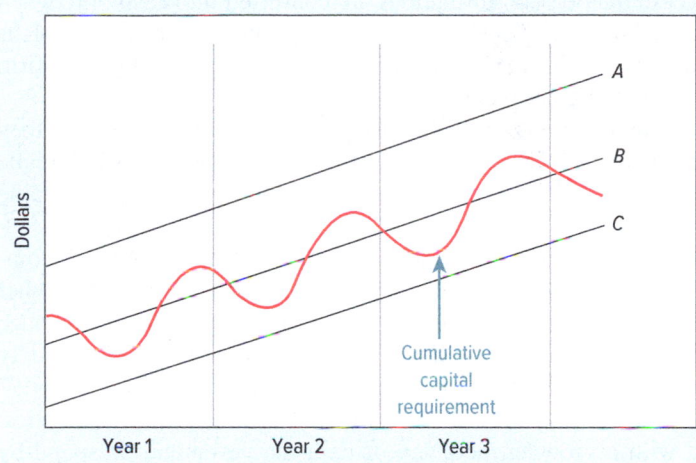

FIGURE 29.1

The firm's cumulative capital requirement (red line) is the cumulative investment in all the assets needed for the business. This figure shows that the requirement grows year by year, but there is some seasonal fluctuation within each year. The requirement for short-term financing is the difference between long-term financing (lines A, B, and C) and the cumulative capital requirement. If long-term financing follows line C, the firm always needs short-term financing. At line B, the need is seasonal. At line A, the firm never needs short-term financing. There is always extra cash to invest.

All businesses require capital—that is, money invested in plant, machinery, inventories, accounts receivable, and all the other assets it takes to run a business. These assets can be financed by either long-term or short-term sources of capital. Let us call the total investment the firm's *cumulative capital requirement.* For most firms the cumulative capital requirement grows irregularly, like the wavy line in Figure 29.1. This line shows a clear upward trend as the firm's business grows. But the figure also shows seasonal variation around the trend, with the capital requirement peaking late in each year. In addition, there would be unpredictable week-to-week and month-to-month fluctuations, but we have not attempted to show these in Figure 29.1.

When long-term financing does not cover the cumulative capital requirement, the firm must raise short-term capital to make up the difference. When long-term financing *more* than covers the cumulative capital requirement, the firm has surplus cash available. Thus the amount of long-term financing raised, given the capital requirement, determines whether the firm is a short-term borrower or lender.

Lines A, B, and C in Figure 29.1 illustrate this. Each depicts a different long-term financing strategy. Strategy A implies a permanent cash surplus, which can be invested in short-term securities. Strategy C implies a permanent need for short-term borrowing. Under B, which is probably the most common strategy, the firm is a short-term lender during part of the year and a borrower during the rest.

What is the *best* level of long-term financing relative to the cumulative capital requirement? It is hard to say. There is no convincing theoretical analysis of this question. We can make practical observations, however. First, most financial managers attempt to "match maturities" of assets and liabilities.[1] That is, they largely finance long-lived assets like plant and machinery with long-term borrowing and equity. Second, most firms make a permanent investment in net working capital (current assets less current liabilities). This investment is financed from long-term sources.

Current assets can be converted into cash more easily than long-term assets. So firms with large holdings of current assets enjoy greater liquidity. Of course, some of these assets are

---

[1] A survey by Graham and Harvey found that managers considered that the desire to match the maturity of the debt with that of the assets was the single most important factor in their choice between short- and long-term debt. See J. R. Graham and C. R. Harvey, "The Theory and Practice of Corporate Finance: Evidence from the Field," *Journal of Financial Economics* 60 (May 2001), pp. 187–243. Stohs and Mauer confirm that firms with a preponderance of short-term assets do indeed tend to issue short-term debt. See M. H. Stohs and D. C. Mauer, "The Determinants of Corporate Debt Maturity Structure," *Journal of Business* 69 (July 1996), pp. 279–312.

more rapidly converted into cash than others. Inventories are converted into cash only when the goods are produced, sold, and paid for. Receivables are more liquid; they become cash as customers pay their outstanding bills. Short-term securities can generally be sold if the firm needs cash on short notice and are therefore more liquid still.

Whatever the motives for maintaining liquidity, they seem more powerful today than they used to be. You can see from Figure 29.2 that, particularly in the easy-money years before the financial crisis, firms in the United States increased their holdings of cash and marketable securities.

Some firms choose to hold more liquidity than others. For example, many high-tech companies, such as Intel and Cisco, hold huge amounts of short-term securities. On the other hand, firms in old-line manufacturing industries—such as chemicals, paper, or steel—manage with a far smaller reserve of liquidity. Why is this? One reason is that companies with rapidly growing profits may generate cash faster than they can redeploy it in new positive-NPV investments. This produces a surplus of cash that can be invested in short-term securities. Of course, companies faced with a growing mountain of cash may eventually respond by adjusting their payout policies. In Chapter 16, we saw how Apple sought to reduce its cash mountain by paying a special dividend and repurchasing its stock.

There are some advantages to holding a large reservoir of cash, particularly for smaller firms that face relatively high costs of raising funds on short notice. For example, biotech firms require large amounts of cash to develop new drugs. Therefore, these firms generally have substantial cash holdings to fund their R&D programs. If these precautionary reasons for holding liquid assets are important, we should find that small companies in relatively high-risk industries are more likely to hold large cash surpluses. A study by Tim Opler and others confirms that this is, in fact, the case.[2]

Financial managers of firms with a surplus of long-term financing and with cash in the bank don't have to worry about finding the money to pay next month's bills. The cash can help to protect the firm against a rainy day and give it the breathing space to make changes to operations. However, there are also drawbacks to surplus cash. Holdings of marketable

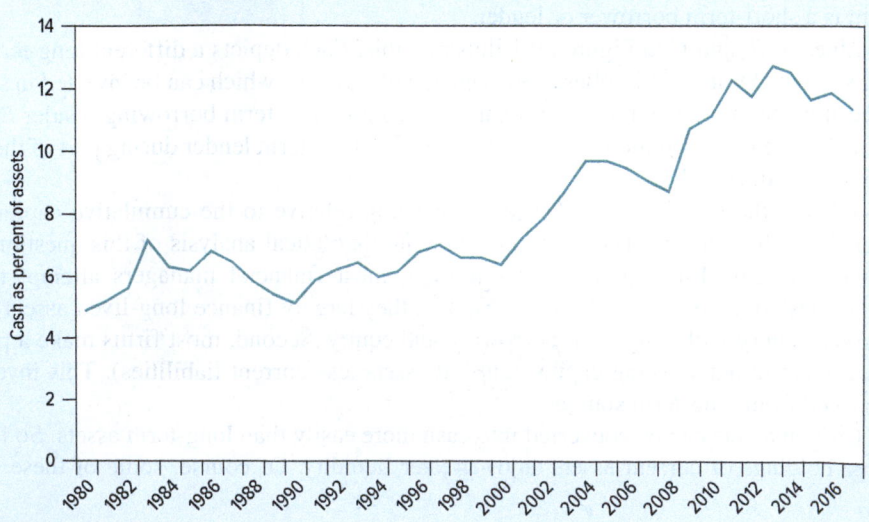

▶ **FIGURE 29.2**

Median ratio of cash to assets for U.S. nonfinancial firms, 1980–2017

Source: Compustat.

[2]T. Opler, L. Pinkowitz, R. Stulz, and R. Williamson, "The Determinants and Implications of Corporate Cash Holdings," *Journal of Financial Economics* 52 (April 1999), pp. 3–46.

securities are at best a zero-NPV investment for a taxpaying firm.[3] Also, managers of firms with large cash surpluses may be tempted to run a less tight ship and may simply allow the cash to seep away in a succession of operating losses. For example, at the end of 2007, General Motors held $27 billion in cash and short-term investments. But shareholders valued GM stock at less than $14 billion. It seemed that shareholders realized (correctly) that the cash would be used to support ongoing losses and to service GM's huge debts.

Pinkowitz and Williamson looked at the value that investors place on a firm's cash and found that on average shareholders valued a dollar of cash at $1.20.[4] They placed a particularly high value on liquidity in the case of firms with plenty of growth opportunities. At the other extreme, they found that when a firm was likely to face financial distress, a dollar of cash within the firm was often worth less than a dollar to the shareholders.[5]

29-2 Tracing Changes in Cash

Table 29.1 shows the 2018 income statement for Dynamic Mattress Company, and Table 29.2 compares the firm's 2017 and 2018 year-end balance sheets. You can see that Dynamic's cash balance increased from $20 million to $30.4 million in 2018.

What caused this increase? Did the extra cash come from Dynamic's issue of long-term debt, from reinvested earnings, from cash released by reducing inventory, or from extra credit extended by Dynamic's suppliers? (Note the increase in accounts payable.) The answer is provided in the company's cash flow statement shown in Table 29.3. A positive sign in the table shows that the activity increased the company's cash balance; a negative sign shows that it reduced the cash balance.

Cash flow statements classify cash flows into those from operating activities, investing activities, and financing activities. Sources of cash are shown as positive numbers; uses of

BEYOND THE PAGE

Try It! Dynamic Mattress's short-term plan

mhhe.com/brealey13e

TABLE 29.1 Income statement for Dynamic Mattress Company, 2018 (figures in $ millions)

		2018
1	Sales	2,200.0
2	Costs	2,024.0
3	Depreciation	23.5
4	EBIT (1 − 2 − 3)	152.5
5	Interest	6.0
6	Pretax income (4 − 5)	146.5
7	Tax at 50%	73.3
8	Net income (6 − 7)	73.3
	Dividend	46.8
	Reinvested earnings	26.5

[3]If, as most people believe, there is a tax advantage to borrowing there must be a corresponding tax disadvantage to lending, since the firm must pay tax at the corporate rate on the interest that it receives from Treasury bills. In this case investment in Treasury bills has a negative NPV. See Section 18-1.
[4]L. Pinkowitz and R. Williamson. "What is the Market Value of a Dollar of Corporate Cash," *Journal of Applied Corporate Finance* 19 (2007), pp. 74–81.
[5]The apparent implication is that the firm should distribute the cash to shareholders. However, debtholders may place restrictions on dividend payments to the shareholders.

>TABLE 29.2
Year-end balance sheets for 2018 and 2017 for Dynamic Mattress Company (figures in $ millions)

	2018	2017	
Assets			
Current assets:			
Cash	30.4	20.0	+10.4
Marketable securities	25.0	0.0	+25.0
Accounts receivable	150.0	124.0	+26.0
Inventory	171.6	183.0	−11.4
Total current assets	377.0	327.0	+50.0
Fixed assets:			
Property, plant, and equipment	375.0	345.0	+30.0
Less accumulated depreciation	100.0	76.5	+23.5
Net fixed assets	275.0	268.5	+6.5
Total assets	652.0	595.5	+56.5
Liabilities and Shareholders' Equity			
Current liabilities:			
Bank loans	0.0	25.0	−25.0
Accounts payable	135.0	110.0	+25.0
Total current liabilities	135.0	135.0	0.0
Long-term debt	90.0	60.0	+30.0
Shareholders' equity	427.0	400.5	+26.5
Total liabilities and shareholders' equity	652.0	595.5	+56.5

>TABLE 29.3 Statement of cash flows for Dynamic Mattress Company, 2018 (figures in $ millions)

Cash flows from operating activities:	
Net income	+73.3
Depreciation	+23.5
Decrease (increase) in accounts receivable	−26.0
Decrease (increase) in inventories	+11.4
Increase (decrease) in accounts payable	+25.0
Net cash flow from operating activities	+107.2
Cash flows from investing activities:	
Investment in fixed assets	−30.0
Cash flows from financing activities:	
Dividends	−46.8
Sale (purchase) of marketable securities	−25.0
Increase (decrease) in long-term debt	+30.0
Increase (decrease) in short-term debt	−25.0
Repurchase of common stock	0.0
Net cash flow from financing activities	−66.8
Increase (decrease) in cash balance	+10.4

cash are shown as negative numbers. Dynamic's cash flow statement shows that Dynamic *generated* cash from the following sources:

1. It earned $73.3 million of net income (*operating activity*).

2. It set aside $23.5 million as depreciation. Remember that depreciation is *not* a cash out-lay. Thus, it must be added back to obtain Dynamic's cash flow (*operating activity*).

3. It reduced inventory, releasing $11.4 million (*operating activity*).

4. It increased its accounts payable, in effect borrowing an additional $25 million from its suppliers (*operating activity*).

5. It issued $30 million of long-term debt (*financing activity*).

Dynamic's cash flow statement shows that it *used* cash for the following purposes:

1. It allowed accounts receivable to expand by $26 million (*operating activity*). In effect, it lent this additional amount to its customers.

2. It invested $30 million (*investing activity*). This shows up as the increase in gross fixed assets in Table 29.2.

3. It paid a $46.8 million dividend (*financing activity*). (*Note:* The $26.5 million increase in Dynamic's equity in Table 29.2 is due to reinvested earnings: $73.3 million of equity income, less the $46.8 million dividend.)

4. It purchased $25 million of marketable securities (*financing activity*).

5. It repaid $25 million of short-term bank debt (*financing activity*).[6]

Look again at Table 29.3. Notice that to calculate cash flows from operating activities, we start with net income and then make two adjustments. First, since depreciation is *not* a cash outlay, we must add it back to net income.[7] Second, we need to recognize the fact that the income statement shows sales and expenditures when they are made, rather than when cash changes hands. For example, think of what happens when Dynamic sells goods on credit. The company records a profit at the time of sale, but there is no cash inflow until the bills are paid. Because there is no cash inflow, there is no change in the company's cash balance, although there is an increase in working capital in the form of an increase in accounts receivable. No net addition to cash would be shown in a cash flow statement like Table 29.3. The increase in cash from operations would be offset by an increase in accounts receivable. Later, when the bills are paid, there is an increase in the cash balance. However, there is no further profit at this point and no increase in working capital. The increase in the cash balance is exactly matched by a decrease in accounts receivable.

Table 29.3 adjusts the cash flow from operating activities *downward* by $26 million to reflect the additional credit that Dynamic has extended to its customers. On the other hand, in 2018 Dynamic reduced its inventories and increased the amount that is owed to its suppliers. The cash flow from operating activities is adjusted *upward* to reflect these changes.

If you draw up a balance sheet at the beginning of the process, you see cash. If you delay a little, you find the cash replaced by inventories of raw materials and, still later, by inventories

---

[6]This is principal repayment, not interest. Sometimes interest payments are explicitly recognized as a use of funds. If so, cash flow from operations would be defined *before* interest'—that is, as net income plus interest plus depreciation.

[7]There is a potential complication here because the depreciation figure shown in the company's report to shareholders is rarely the same as the depreciation figure used to calculate tax. The reason is that firms can minimize their current tax payments by using *accelerated* depreciation when computing their taxable income. As a result, the shareholder books (which generally use straight-line depreciation) overstate the firm's current tax liability. Accelerated depreciation does not eliminate taxes; it only delays them. Since the ultimate liability has to be recognized, the additional taxes that will need to be paid are shown on the balance sheet as a deferred tax liability. In the statement of cash flows, any increase in deferred taxes is treated as a source of funds. In the Dynamic Mattress example, we ignore deferred taxes.

of finished goods. When the goods are sold, the inventories give way to accounts receivable, and, finally, when the customers pay their bills, the firm draws out its profit and replenishes the cash balance.

There is only one constant in this process—namely, working capital. That is one reason (net) working capital is a useful summary measure of current assets and liabilities. The strength of the working capital measure is that it is unaffected by seasonal or other temporary movements between different current assets or liabilities. But the strength is also its weakness, for the working capital figure hides a lot of interesting information. In our example, cash was transformed into inventory, then into receivables, and back into cash again. But these assets have different degrees of risk and liquidity. You can't pay bills with inventory or with receivables. You must pay with cash.

The Cash Cycle

Think about the regular financing that Dynamic needs in order to maintain regular operations. The company conducts a very simple business. It buys raw materials for cash, processes them into finished goods, and then sells these goods on credit. The whole cycle of operations looks like this:

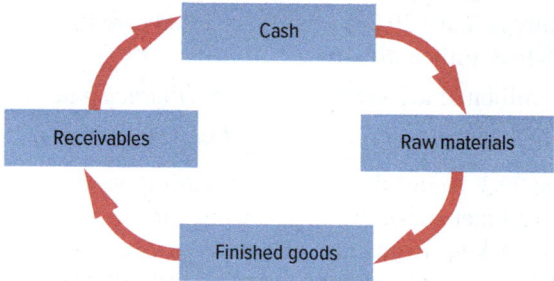

The delay between Dynamic's initial investment in inventories and the final sale date is called the *inventory period* (a measure that should be familiar to you from Chapter 28). The delay between the time that the goods are sold and when the customers finally pay their bills is the *accounts receivable period* (another measure that should be familiar). The total length of time from the purchase of raw materials until the final payment by the customer is termed the *operating cycle:*

$$\text{Operating cycle} = \text{inventory period} + \text{accounts receivable period}$$

Dynamic is not out of cash, however, for this entire cycle of operations. Although the company starts by purchasing raw materials, it does not pay for them immediately. The longer that it defers payment, the shorter the time that the firm is out of cash. The interval between the firm's payment for its raw materials and the collection of payment from the customer is known as the cash cycle or cash conversion period:

$$\text{Cash cycle} = \text{operating cycle} - \text{accounts payable period}$$
$$= (\text{inventory period} + \text{accounts receivable period}) - \text{accounts payable period}$$

This is illustrated in Figure 29.3.

We can calculate the cash cycle for Dynamic Mattress. Suppose that it purchases materials on day 0 but does not pay for them until day 24 (payable period = 24 days). By day 29, Dynamic has converted the raw materials into finished mattresses, which are then sold (inventory period = 29). Twenty-one days later, on day 50, Dynamic's customers pay for their

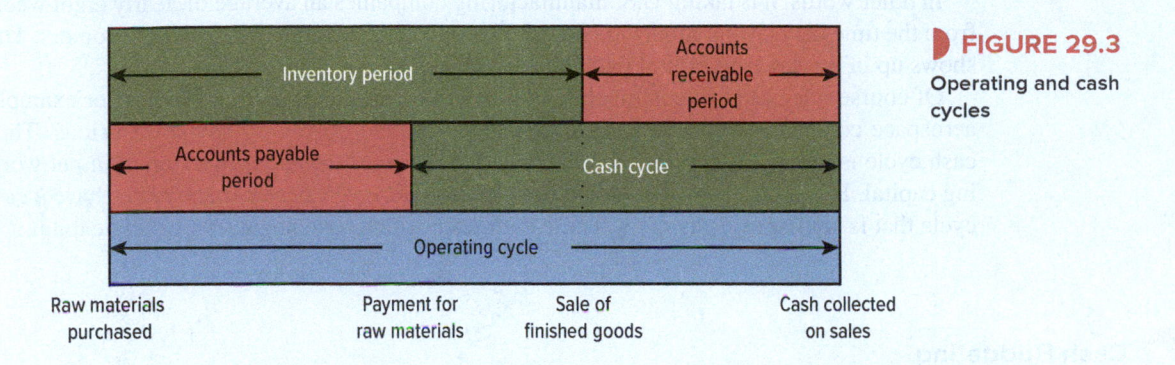

purchases (receivables period = 21). Thus, cash went out of the door on day 24 and did not come back in again until day 50. For Dynamic:

Cash cycle (days) = inventory period + accounts receivable period − accounts payable period

$$26 \quad = \quad 29 \quad + \quad 21 \quad - \quad 24$$

It is interesting to compare Dynamic's cash cycle with that of other U.S. corporations. Table 29.4 provides the information necessary to estimate the average cycle for manufacturing firms:[8]

Average inventory period = inventory at start of year/daily cost of goods sold
= 786/(5,820/365) = 49.3 days

Average receivables period = receivables at start of year/daily sales
= 700/(6,552/365) = 39.0 days

Average payment period = payables at start of year/daily cost of goods sold
= 579/(5,820/365) = 36.3 days

The cash cycle is therefore

Inventory period + receivables period − payables period = 49.3 + 39.0 − 36.3 = 52.0 days

Income Statement	
Sales	$6,552
Cost of goods sold	5,820
Balance Sheet, Start of Year	
Inventory	$786
Accounts receivable	700
Accounts payable	579

❭ **TABLE 29.4** Data used to calculate the cash cycle for U.S. manufacturing firms in 2017 (figures in billions)

Note: Cost of goods sold includes selling, general, and administrative expenses.

Source: U.S. Department of Commerce, *Quarterly Financial Report for Manufacturing, Mining, and Trade Corporations 2017 Quarter 4,* December 2017, Tables 1.0 and 1.1.

---

[8]Because inventories are valued at cost, we divide inventory levels by cost of goods sold rather than sales revenue to obtain the inventory period. This way, both numerator and denominator are measured by cost. The same reasoning applies to the accounts payable period. On the other hand, because accounts receivable are valued at product price, we divide average receivables by daily sales revenue to find the receivables period.

In other words, it is taking U.S. manufacturing companies an average of nearly eight weeks from the time they lay out money on inventories to collect payment from their customers. This shows up in the working capital that companies need to maintain.

Of course, the cash cycle is much longer in some businesses than in others. For example, aerospace companies typically hold large inventories and offer long payment periods. Their cash cycle is nearly six months, and they need to make a substantial investment in net working capital. By contrast, retail companies with their low investment in receivables have a cash cycle that is similar to Dynamic's. These companies often have negative working capital.

29-3 Cash Budgeting

Table 29.3 showed why Dynamic's cash balance rose in 2018. But its financial manager also needs to forecast the company's cash needs in 2019 and ensure that the company will be able to pay its upcoming bills. These forecasts are set out in the firm's cash budget and are then used to draw up a plan for investing any cash surpluses or financing any deficit.

There are three steps to preparing a cash budget:

Step 1   Forecast the sources of cash. The largest inflow of cash usually comes from payments by the firm's customers.

Step 2   Forecast the uses of cash.

Step 3   Calculate whether the firm is facing a cash shortage or surplus. The company then uses these forecasts to draw up a plan for raising or investing cash.

We will illustrate these steps by continuing with the example of Dynamic Mattress.

Step 1. Forecast the Sources of Cash   Most of Dynamic's cash inflow comes from the sales of mattresses. Therefore, we start with a sales forecast by quarter for 2019:[9]

	First Quarter	Second Quarter	Third Quarter	Fourth Quarter
Sales ($ millions)	560	502	742	836

But unless customers pay cash on delivery, these sales will become accounts receivable before they become cash. Cash flow comes from collections on accounts receivable.

Most firms keep track of the average time it takes customers to pay their bills. From this, they can forecast what proportion of a quarter's sales is likely to be converted into cash in that quarter and what proportion is likely to be carried over to the next quarter as accounts receivable.

Suppose that 70% of Dynamic's sales are paid for in the immediate quarter and the remaining 30% in the next. Table 29.5 shows forecast collections under this assumption. For example, you can see that in the first quarter, collections from current sales are 70% of $560, or $392 million. But the firm also collects 30% of the previous quarter's sales, or .3 × $396.7 = $119.0 million. Therefore, total collections are $392 + $119.0 = $511.0 million.

Dynamic started the first quarter with $150.0 million of accounts receivable. The quarter's sales of $560 million were added to accounts receivable, but $511.0 million of collections

---

[9]Most firms would forecast by month instead of by quarter. Sometimes weekly or even daily forecasts are made. But presenting a monthly forecast would triple the number of entries in Table 29.5 and subsequent tables. We wanted to keep the examples as simple as possible.

		First Quarter	Second Quarter	Third Quarter	Fourth Quarter
1	Receivables at start of period	150	199	181.6	253.6
2	Sales	560	502	742	836
	Collections				
	Sales in current period (70%)	392	351.4	519.4	585.2
	Sales in last period (30%)	119[a]	168	150.6	222.6
3	Total collections	511	519.4	670	807.8
4	Receivables at end of period 1 + 2 − 3	199	181.6	253.6	281.8

〉**TABLE 29.5**   To forecast Dynamic Mattress's collections on accounts receivable, you have to forecast sales and collection rates in 2019 (figures in $ millions)

[a]We assume that sales in the last quarter of the previous year were $396.7 million.

were subtracted. Therefore, as Table 29.5 shows, Dynamic ended the quarter with accounts receivable of 150 + 560 − 511 = $199 million. The general formula is

Ending accounts receivable = beginning accounts receivable + sales − collections

Step 2: Forecast the Uses of Cash   So much for the incoming cash. Now for the outgoing. There always seem to be many more uses for cash than there are sources. The second section of Table 29.6 shows how Dynamic expects to use cash. For simplicity, we have condensed the uses into five categories:

1. *Payments of accounts payable.* Dynamic has to pay its bills for raw materials, parts, electricity, and so on. The cash-flow forecast assumes all these bills are paid on time, although Dynamic could probably delay payment to some extent. Delayed payment is sometimes called stretching payables. Stretching is one source of short-term financing, but for most firms, it is an expensive source because, by stretching, they lose discounts given to firms that pay promptly. (This is discussed in more detail in Chapter 30.)

2. *Increase in inventories.* The expected increase in sales in 2019 requires additional investment in inventories.

3. *Labor, administrative, and other expenses.* This category includes all other regular business expenses.

4. *Capital expenditures.* Note that Dynamic Mattress plans a major outlay of cash in the first quarter to pay for a long-lived asset.

5. *Taxes, interest, and dividend payments.* This includes dividend payments to stockholders and interest on currently outstanding long-term debt. It does not include interest on any additional borrowing to meet cash requirements in 2019. At this stage in the analysis, Dynamic does not know how much it will have to borrow, or whether it will have to borrow at all.

Step 3: Calculate the Cash Balance   The forecasted net inflow of cash (sources minus uses) is shown by the shaded line in Table 29.6. Note the large negative figure for the first quarter: a $141.0 million forecast outflow. There is a smaller forecast outflow in the second quarter and then substantial cash inflows in the second half of the year.

BEYOND THE PAGE

Try It! Dynamic Mattress's short-term plan

mhhe.com/brealey13e

	First Quarter	Second Quarter	Third Quarter	Fourth Quarter
Sources of cash:				
Collections on accounts receivable	511.0	519.4	670.0	807.8
Other	0	0	77.0	0
Total sources	511.0	519.4	747.0	807.8
Uses of cash:				
Payments on accounts payable	250.0	250.0	267.0	261.0
Increase in inventory	150.0	150.0	170.0	180.0
Labor and other expenses	136.0	136.0	136.0	136.0
Capital expenditures	70.0	10.0	8.0	14.5
Taxes, interest, and dividends	46.0	46.0	46.0	46.0
Total uses	652.0	592.0	627.0	637.5
Sources minus uses	−141.0	−72.6	120.0	170.3
Calculation of short-term borrowing requirement:				
Cash at start of period	30.4	−110.6	−183.2	−63.2
Change in cash balance	−141.0	−72.6	120.0	170.3
Cash at end of period	−110.6	−183.2	−63.2	107.1
Minimum operating balance	25.0	25.0	25.0	25.0
Cumulative financing required	135.6	208.2	88.2	−82.1

❱**TABLE 29.6** Dynamic Mattress's cash budget for 2019 (figures in $ millions)

The bottom part of Table 29.6 calculates how much financing Dynamic will have to raise if its cash-flow forecasts are right. It starts the year with $30.4 million in cash. There is a $141.0 million cash outflow in the first quarter, so Dynamic will have to obtain at least $141.0 − 30.4 = $110.6 million of additional financing. This would leave the firm with a forecasted cash balance of exactly zero at the start of the second quarter.

Most financial managers regard a planned cash balance of zero as driving too close to the edge of the cliff. They establish a minimum operating cash balance to absorb unexpected cash inflows and outflows. We assume that Dynamic's minimum operating cash balance is $25 million. This means it will have to raise $110.6 + $25 = $135.6 million in the first quarter and $72.6 million more in the second quarter. Thus, its *cumulative* financing requirement is $208.2 million by the second quarter. Fortunately, this is the peak: The cumulative requirement declines in the third quarter by $120 million to $88.2 million. In the final quarter, Dynamic is out of the woods: Its cash balance is $107.1 million, well above its minimum operating balance.

29-4 Dynamic's Short-Term Financial Plan

Our next task is to develop a short-term financial plan that covers the forecasted requirements in the most economical way. We move on to that topic after two general observations:

1. The large cash outflows in the first two quarters do not necessarily spell trouble for Dynamic Mattress. In part, they reflect the capital investment made in the first quarter: Dynamic is spending $70 million, but it should be acquiring an asset worth that much

or more. The cash outflows also reflect low sales in the first half of the year; sales recover in the second half.[10] If this is a predictable seasonal pattern, the firm should have no trouble borrowing to help it get through the slow months.

2. Table 29.6 is only a best guess about future cash flows. It is a good idea to think about the uncertainty in your estimates. For example, you could undertake a sensitivity analysis, in which you inspect how Dynamic's cash requirement would be affected by a shortfall in sales or by a delay in collections.

Dynamic's cash budget defines its problem. Its financial manager must find short-term financing to cover the firm's forecast cash requirements. There are dozens of sources of short-term financing, but, for simplicity, we will assume that Dynamic has just two options:

1. *Bank loan.* Dynamic has an existing arrangement with its bank, allowing it to borrow up to $100 million at an interest rate of 10% per year, or 2.5% per quarter. It can borrow and repay the loan whenever it chooses, but the company may not exceed its credit limit.

2. *Stretching payables.* Dynamic can also raise capital by putting off payment of its bills. The financial manager believes that Dynamic can defer up to $100 million in each quarter. Thus, $100 million can be saved in the first quarter by not paying bills in that quarter. (Note that the cash-flow forecasts in Table 29.6 assumed that these bills will be paid in the first quarter.) If deferred, these payments must be made in the second quarter, but up to $100 million of the second quarter bills can be deferred to the third quarter, and so on.

Stretching payables is often costly, even if no ill will is incurred.[11] The reason is that suppliers may offer discounts for prompt payment. Dynamic loses this discount if it pays late. In this example, we assume the lost discount is 5% of the amount deferred. In other words, if a $100 payment is delayed, the firm must pay $105 in the next quarter. This is similar to borrowing at a quarterly interest rate of 5%, or equivalently at an annualized rate over 20% (more precisely, $1.05^4 - 1 = .216$, or 21.6%).

Dynamic Mattress's Financing Plan

With these two options, the short-term financing strategy is obvious. Use the bank loan first, if necessary up to the $100 million limit. If there is still a shortage of cash, stretch payables.

Table 29.7 shows the resulting plan. In the first quarter of 2019, the plan calls for borrowing the full amount from the bank ($100 million) and stretching $10.6 million of payables (see lines 1 and 2 of Panel B). In addition, the company sells the $25 million of marketable securities it held at the end of 2018. Thus, it raises $100 + $10.6 + $25 = $135.6 million of cash in the first quarter (see the last line of Panel B).

In the second quarter, Dynamic needs to raise an additional $72.6 million to support its operations. It also owes interest of $2.5 million on its bank loan. It must retire the payables that it stretched last quarter. With the 5% interest on that implicit loan from its suppliers, this adds $10.6 + $.5 million to the funds it must raise in the second quarter. Finally, to compensate for the interest it had been earning on the securities it sold in the first quarter, it will require another $.5 million. In total, therefore, it must come up with $86.7 million in the second quarter.

---

[10]Maybe people buy more mattresses late in the year when the nights are longer.
[11]In fact, ill will is likely to be incurred. Firms that stretch payments risk being labeled as credit risks. Since stretching is so expensive, suppliers reason that customers will resort to it only when they cannot obtain credit at reasonable rates elsewhere. Suppliers naturally are reluctant to act as the lender of last resort.

	First Quarter	Second Quarter	Third Quarter	Fourth Quarter
A. Cash requirements:				
Cash required for operations[a]	135.6	72.6	−120.0	−170.3
Interest on bank loan[b]	0	2.5	2.5	1.9
Interest on stretched payables[c]	0	0.5	4.3	0
Repayment of last quarter's stretched payables	0	10.6	86.7	0
Lost interest on securities sold[d]	0	0.5	0.5	0.5
Total cash required	135.6	86.7	−25.9	−167.9
B. Cash raised in quarter from:				
Bank loan	100.0	0	0	0
Stretched payables	10.6	86.7	0	0
Securities sold	25.0	0	0	0
Total cash raised	135.6	86.7	0	0
C. Repayments:				
Repayment of bank loan	0	0	25.9	74.1
D. Addition to cash balances and security holdings:				
Addition	0	0	0	93.9
E. Bank loan outstanding:				
Beginning of quarter	0	100.0	100.0	74.1
End of quarter	100.0	100.0	74.1	0

❯**TABLE 29.7**   Dynamic Mattress's financial plan for 2019 (figures in $ millions)

[a]Cash required for operations in each quarter equals the change in cumulative financing required from the last line of Table 29.6. A negative cash requirement implies a positive cash flow from operations.
[b]The interest rate on the bank loan is 2.5% per quarter, applied to the bank loan outstanding at the start of the quarter. Thus, the interest due in the second quarter is .025 × $100 million = $2.5 million.
[c]The "interest" cost of the stretched payables is 5% of the payment deferred. For example, in the second quarter, 5% of the $10.5 million of deferred payments is about $0.53 million.
[d]The interest loss on securities sold is 2% per quarter. Thus, in the second quarter, Dynamic needs to find an additional .02 × $25 million = $.5 million.

In the third quarter, the firm generates a $120 million cash-flow surplus from operations. Part of that surplus, $86.7 million, is used to pay off the stretched payables from the second quarter, as it is required to do. A small portion is used to pay interest on its outstanding loans. It uses the remaining cash-flow surplus, $25.9 million (last line of Panel A), to pay down its bank loan. In the fourth quarter, the firm has a surplus from operations of $170.3 million. It pays off the interest and remaining principal on the bank loan and is able to invest $93.9 million in cash and marketable securities.

Evaluating the Plan

Does the plan shown in Table 29.7 solve Dynamic's short-term financing problem? No—the plan is feasible, but Dynamic can probably do better. The most glaring weakness is its reliance on stretching payables, an extremely expensive financing device. Remember that it costs Dynamic 5% per quarter to delay paying bills—an effective interest rate of greater than 20% per year.

The first plan would merely stimulate the financial manager to search for cheaper sources of short-term borrowing. The financial manager would ask several other questions as well. For example:

1. Does Dynamic need a larger reserve of cash or marketable securities to guard against, say, its customers stretching their payables (thus slowing down collections on accounts receivable)?

2. Does the plan yield satisfactory current and quick ratios?[12] Its bankers may be worried if these ratios deteriorate.

3. Are there intangible costs to stretching payables? Will suppliers begin to doubt Dynamic's creditworthiness?

4. Does the plan for 2019 leave Dynamic in good financial shape for 2020? (Here the answer is yes because Dynamic will have paid off all short-term borrowing by the end of the year.)

5. Should Dynamic try to arrange long-term financing for the major capital expenditure in the first quarter? This seems sensible, following the rule of thumb that long-term assets deserve long-term financing. It would also dramatically reduce the need for short-term borrowing. A counterargument is that Dynamic is financing the capital investment only temporarily by short-term borrowing. By year-end, the investment is paid for by cash from operations. Thus, Dynamic's initial decision not to seek immediate long-term financing may reflect a preference for ultimately financing the investment with retained earnings.

6. Perhaps the firm's operating and investment plans can be adjusted to make the short-term financing problem easier. Is there any easy way of deferring the first quarter's large cash outflow? For example, suppose that the large capital investment in the first quarter is for new mattress-stuffing machines to be delivered and installed in the first half of the year. The new machines are not scheduled to be ready for full-scale use until August. Perhaps the machine manufacturer could be persuaded to accept 60% of the purchase price on delivery and 40% when the machines are installed and operating satisfactorily.

7. Should Dynamic release cash by reducing the level of other current assets? For example, it could reduce receivables by getting tough with customers who are late paying their bills. (The cost is that, in the future, these customers may take their business elsewhere.) Or it may be able to get by with lower inventories of mattresses. (The cost here is that it may lose business if there is a rush of orders that it cannot supply.)

Short-term financing plans must be developed by trial and error. You lay out one plan, think about it, and then try again with different assumptions on financing and investment alternatives. You continue until you can think of no further improvements. Trial and error is important because it helps you understand the real nature of the problem the firm faces. Here we can draw a useful analogy between the process of planning and Chapter 10's discussion of project analysis. In Chapter 10, we described sensitivity analysis and other tools used by firms to find out what makes capital investment projects tick and what can go wrong with them. Dynamic's financial manager faces the same kind of task here: not just to choose a plan but to understand what can go wrong and what will be done if conditions change unexpectedly.[13]

---

[12]These ratios are discussed in Chapter 28.
[13]This point is even more important in *long-term* financial planning.

A Note on Short-Term Financial Planning Models

Working out a consistent short-term plan requires burdensome calculations. Fortunately, much of the arithmetic can be delegated to a computer. Many large firms have built short-term financial planning models to do this. Smaller companies do not face so much detail and complexity and often find it easier to work with a spreadsheet program on a personal computer. In either case, the financial manager specifies forecasted cash requirements or surpluses, interest rates, credit limits, etc., and the model grinds out a plan like the one shown in Table 29.7.

The computer also produces balance sheets, income statements, and any special reports the financial manager may require. Smaller firms that do not want custom-built models can rent general-purpose models offered by banks, accounting firms, management consultants, or specialized computer software firms.

Most of these models simply work out the consequences of the assumptions specified by the financial manager. *Optimization models* for short-term financial planning are also available. These models are usually linear-programming models. They search for the best plan from a range of alternative policies. These models help when the firm faces complex problems where trial and error might never identify the best combination of alternatives.

Of course, the best plan for one set of assumptions may prove disastrous if the assumptions are wrong. Thus the financial manager always needs to explore the implications of alternative assumptions about future cash flows, interest rates, and so on.

29-5 Long-Term Financial Planning

It's been said that a camel looks like a horse designed by a committee. If a firm made every decision piecemeal, it would end up with a financial camel. That is why smart financial managers also need to plan for the long term and to consider the financial actions that will be needed to support the company's long-term growth. Here is where finance and strategy come together. A coherent long-term plan demands an understanding of how the firm can generate superior returns by its choice of industry and by the way that it positions itself within that industry.

Long-term planning involves capital budgeting on a grand scale. It focuses on the investment by each line of business and avoids getting bogged down in details. Of course, some individual projects may be large enough to have significant individual impact. For example, the telecom giant Verizon has spent billions of dollars to deploy fiber-optic-based broadband technology to its residential customers. You can bet that this project was explicitly analyzed as part of its long-range financial plan. Normally, however, planners do not work on a project-by-project basis. Instead, they are content with rules of thumb that relate average levels of fixed and short-term assets to annual sales, and do not worry so much about seasonal variations in these relationships. In such cases, the likelihood that accounts receivable may rise as sales peak in the holiday season would be a needless detail that would distract from more important strategic decisions.

Why Build Financial Plans?

Firms spend considerable time and resources in long-term planning. What do they get for this investment?

Contingency Planning   Planning is not just forecasting. Forecasting concentrates on the most likely outcomes, but planners worry about unlikely events as well as likely ones. If you think ahead about what could go wrong, then you are less likely to ignore the danger signals and you can respond faster to trouble.

Companies have developed a number of ways of asking "what if" questions about both individual projects and the overall firm. For example, managers often work through the consequences of their decisions under different scenarios. One scenario might envisage high interest rates contributing to a slowdown in world economic growth and lower commodity prices. A second scenario might involve a buoyant domestic economy, high inflation, and a weak currency. The idea is to formulate responses to inevitable surprises. What will you do, for example, if sales in the first year turn out to be 10% below forecast? A good financial plan should help you adapt as events unfold.

Considering Options   Planners need to think whether there are opportunities for the company to exploit its existing strengths by moving into a wholly new area. Often they may recommend entering a market for "strategic" reasons—that is, not because the immediate investment has a positive net present value but because it establishes the firm in a new market and creates options for possibly valuable follow-on investments.

For example, Verizon's costly fiber-optic initiative gives the company the *real option* to offer additional services that may be highly valuable in the future, such as the rapid delivery of an array of home entertainment services. The justification for the huge investment lies in these potential growth options.

Forcing Consistency   Financial plans draw out the connections between the firm's plans for growth and the financing requirements. For example, a forecast of 25% growth might require the firm to issue securities to pay for necessary capital expenditures, while a 5% growth rate might enable the firm to finance these expenditures by using only reinvested profits.

Financial plans should help to ensure that the firm's goals are mutually consistent. For example, the chief executive might say that she is shooting for a profit margin of 10% and sales growth of 20%, but financial planners need to think about whether the higher sales growth may require price cuts that will reduce the profit margin.

Moreover, a goal that is stated in terms of accounting ratios is not operational unless it is translated back into what that means for business decisions. For example, a higher profit margin can result from higher prices, lower costs, or a move into new, high-margin products. Why then do managers define objectives in this way? In part, such goals may be a code to communicate real concerns. For example, a target profit margin may be a way of saying that in pursuing sales growth, the firm has allowed costs to get out of control. The danger is that everyone may forget the code and the accounting targets may be seen as goals in themselves. No one should be surprised when lower-level managers focus on the goals for which they are rewarded. For example, when Volkswagen set a goal of a 6.5% profit margin, some VW groups responded by developing and promoting expensive, high-margin cars. Less attention was paid to marketing cheaper models, which had lower profit margins but higher sales volume. As soon as this became apparent, Volkswagen announced that it would de-emphasize its profit margin goal and would instead focus on return on investment. It hoped that this would encourage managers to get the most profit out of every dollar of invested capital.

A Long-Term Financial Planning Model for Dynamic Mattress

Financial planners often use a financial planning model to help them explore the consequences of alternative strategies. We will drop in again on the financial manager of Dynamic Mattress to see how she uses a simple spreadsheet program to draw up the firm's long-term plan.

Long-term planning is concerned with the big picture. Therefore, when constructing long-term planning models it is generally acceptable to collapse all current assets and liabilities into a single figure for net working capital. Table 29.8 replaces Dynamic's latest balance sheets with condensed versions that report only net working capital rather than individual current assets or liabilities.

	2018	2017
Net working capital	242.0	192.0
Fixed assets:		
Gross investment	375.0	345.0
Less depreciation	100.0	76.5
Net fixed assets	275.0	268.5
Total net assets	517.0	460.5
Long-term debt	90.0	60.0
Shareholders' equity	427.0	400.5
Long-term liabilities and net worth[a]	517.0	460.5

❭**TABLE 29.8**   Condensed year-end balance sheets for 2018 and 2017 for Dynamic Mattress Company (figures in $ millions)

[a]When only net working capital appears on a firm's balance sheet, this figure (the sum of long-term liabilities and net worth) is often referred to as total capitalization.

Suppose that Dynamic's analysis of the industry leads it to forecast a 20% annual growth in the company's sales and profits over the next five years. Can the company realistically expect to finance this out of retained earnings and borrowing, or should it plan for an issue of equity? Spreadsheet programs are tailor-made for such questions. Let's investigate.

The basic sources and uses relationship tells us that the sources of funds must be sufficient to cover the uses. If the company's operations do not provide sufficient cash to pay for the uses, then it will need to raise additional capital from external sources. Dynamic's external capital requirement equals the difference between the cash that the firm will need for its investments and dividend payments and the funds that it will generate from its business operations.

External capital required = (investment in net working capital + investment in fixed assets
+ dividends) − cash flow from operations

Thus, there are three steps to finding how much extra capital Dynamic will need and the implications for its debt ratio.

Step 1   Project next year's net income plus depreciation, assuming the planned 20% increase in revenues. These projections are shown in Panel A of Table 29.9.The first column shows net income for Dynamic in the latest year (2018) and is taken from Table 29.1. The remaining columns show the forecasted values for the following five years.

BEYOND THE PAGE

Try it! Dynamic Mattress's long-term plan

mhhe.com/brealey13e

Step 2   Project what additional investment in net working capital and fixed assets will be needed to support this increased activity and how much of the net income will be paid out as dividends. The sum of these expenditures gives you the total *uses* of capital. If the total uses of capital exceed the cash flow generated by operations, Dynamic will need to raise additional long-term capital. Panel B of Table 29.9 shows these capital requirements. The first column shows that in 2018 Dynamic needed to raise $30 million of new capital. The remaining columns forecast its capital needs for the following five years. For example, you can see that Dynamic will need to issue $67.9 million of debt in 2019 if it is to expand at the planned rate and not sell more shares.

Step 3   Finally, construct a forecast, or pro forma, balance sheet that incorporates the additional assets and the new levels of debt and equity. For example, the first column of Panel C of Table 29.9 shows the latest condensed balance sheet for Dynamic Mattress. The remaining columns show that the company's equity grows by the additional retained earnings (net income less dividends), while long-term debt increases steadily to $607.8 million.

		2018	2019	2020	2021	2022	2023
	PANEL A						
	Income statement						
1	Revenues	2,200.0	2,640.0	3,168.0	3,801.6	4,561.9	5,474.3
2	Costs (92% of revenues)	2,024.0	2,428.8	2,914.6	3,497.5	4,197.0	5,036.4
3	Depreciation (9% of net fixed assets at start of year)	23.5	24.8	29.7	35.6	42.8	51.3
4	EBIT (1 − 2 − 3)	152.5	186.5	223.7	268.5	322.2	386.6
5	Interest (10% of long-term debt at start of year)	6.0	9.0	15.8	24.0	34.0	46.1
6	Income before tax (4 − 5)	146.5	177.5	207.9	244.4	288.1	340.5
7	Tax at 50%	73.3	88.7	104.0	122.2	144.1	170.2
8	Net income (6 − 7)	73.3	88.7	104.0	122.2	144.1	170.2
9	Dividends (60% of net income)	46.8	53.2	62.4	73.3	86.4	102.1
10	Reinvested earnings (8 − 9)	26.5	35.5	41.6	48.9	57.6	68.1
	PANEL B						
	Sources of capital						
11	Net Income plus depreciation (8 + 3)	96.8	113.5	133.7	157.9	186.8	221.6
	Uses of capital						
12	Investment in net working capital	50.0	48.4	58.1	69.7	83.6	100.4
13	Investment in fixed assets	30.0	79.8	95.7	114.8	137.8	165.4
14	Dividends (9)	46.8	53.2	62.4	73.3	86.4	102.1
15	Total uses of capital	126.8	181.4	216.2	257.9	307.9	367.9
16	External capital required (15 − 11)	30.1	67.9	82.5	100.0	121.0	146.3
	PANEL C						
	Balance sheet (year-end)						
	Assets:						
17	Net working capital	242.0	290.4	348.5	418.2	501.8	602.2
18	Net fixed assets	275.0	330.0	396.0	475.2	570.2	684.3
19	Total assets (17 + 18)	517.0	620.4	744.5	893.4	1,072.1	1,286.5
	Liabilities and equity:						
20	Long-term debt (note a)	90.0	157.9	240.4	340.4	461.5	607.8
21	Shareholders' equity (note b)	427.0	462.5	504.1	553.0	610.6	678.7
22	Total liabilities and shareholders' equity (20 + 21)	517.0	620.4	744.5	893.4	1,072.1	1,286.5
	Financial ratios						
23	Debt ratio	0.17	0.25	0.32	0.38	0.43	0.47
24	Interest cover	25.4	20.7	14.2	11.2	9.5	8.4

Columns may not add because of rounding.

Note a: Long-term debt, the balancing item increases by external financing.

Note b: Shareholders' equity equals previous year's value plus reinvested earnings.

❭TABLE 29.9   Actual (2018) and forecasted operating cash flows for Dynamic Mattress Company (figures in $ millions)

Over the five-year period, Dynamic Mattress is forecasted to borrow an additional $517.8 million, and by year 2023, its debt ratio will have risen from 17% to 47%. The interest payments would still be comfortably covered by earnings, and most financial managers could live with this amount of debt. However, the company could not continue to borrow at that rate beyond five years, and the debt ratio might be close to the limit set by the company's banks and bondholders.

An obvious alternative is for Dynamic to issue a mix of debt and equity, but there are other possibilities that the financial manager may want to explore. One option may be to hold back dividends during this period of rapid growth. An alternative may be to investigate whether the company could cut back on net working capital. For example, it may be able to economize on inventories or speed up the collection of receivables. The model makes it easy to examine these alternatives.

We stated earlier that financial planning is not just about exploring how to cope with the most likely outcomes. It also needs to ensure that the firm is prepared for unlikely or unexpected ones. For example, management would certainly wish to check that Dynamic Mattress could cope with a cyclical decline in sales and profit margins. Sensitivity analysis or scenario analysis can help to do this.

Pitfalls in Model Design

The Dynamic Mattress model that we have developed is too simple for practical application. You probably have already thought of several ways to improve it—by keeping track of the outstanding shares, for example, and printing out earnings and dividends per share. Or you might want to distinguish between short-term lending and borrowing opportunities, now buried in working capital.

The model that we developed for Dynamic Mattress is known as a *percentage of sales model*. Almost all the forecasts for the company are proportional to the forecasted level of sales. However, in reality many variables will *not* be proportional to sales. For example, important components of working capital such as inventory and cash balances will generally rise less rapidly than sales. In addition, fixed assets such as plant and equipment are not usually added in small increments as sales increase. The Dynamic Mattress plant may well be operating at less than full capacity, so that the company can initially increase output without *any* additions to capacity. Eventually, however, if sales continue to increase, the firm may need to make a large new investment in plant and equipment.

But beware of adding too much complexity: There is always the temptation to make a model bigger and more detailed. You may end up with an exhaustive model that is too cumbersome for routine use. The fascination of detail, if you give in to it, distracts attention from crucial decisions like stock issues and payout policy.

Choosing a Plan

Financial planning models help the manager to develop consistent forecasts of crucial financial variables. For example, if you wish to value Dynamic Mattress, you need forecasts of future free cash flows. These are easily derived up to the end of the planning period from our financial planning model.[14] However, a planning model does not tell you whether the plan is optimal. It does not even tell you which alternatives are worth examining. For example, we saw that Dynamic Mattress is planning for a rapid growth in sales and earnings per share. But is that good news for the shareholders? Well, not necessarily; it depends on the opportunity cost of the capital that Dynamic Mattress needs to invest. If the new investment earns more

---

[14]Look back at Table 19.1, where we set out the free cash flows for Rio Corporation. A financial planning model would be a natural tool for deriving these figures.

than the cost of capital, it will have a positive NPV and add to shareholder wealth. If the investment earns less than the cost of capital, shareholders will be worse off, even though the company expects steady growth in earnings.

The capital that Dynamic Mattress needs to raise depends on its decision to pay out 60% of its earnings as a dividend. But the financial planning model does not tell us whether this dividend payment makes sense or what mixture of equity or debt the company should issue. In the end the management has to decide. We would like to tell you exactly how to make the choice, but we can't. There is no model that encompasses all the complexities encountered in financial planning and decision making.

As a matter of fact, there never will be one. This bold statement is based on Brealey, Myers, and Allen's Third Law:[15]

> *Axiom:* The number of unsolved problems is infinite.
>
> *Axiom:* The number of unsolved problems that humans can hold in their minds is at any time limited to 10.
>
> *Law:* Therefore in any field there will always be 10 problems that can be addressed but that have no formal solution.

BMA's Third Law implies that no model can find the best of all financial strategies.[16]

29-6 Growth and External Financing

We started this chapter by noting that financial plans force managers to be consistent in their goals for growth, investment, and financing. Before leaving the topic of financial planning, we should look at some general relationships between a firm's growth objectives and its financing needs.

We saw in Table 29.9 that with a 20% growth rate, the firm needs to raise $67.9 million of new capital in 2019. The faster the planned growth rate the greater the need for external financing. Table 29.10 shows how required external financing responds to a changing growth rate. Notice that at a 5.9% growth rate required external financing is zero. At higher growth rates, the firm requires additional capital. At lower growth rates, reinvested earnings exceed

Growth Rate (%)	Required External Financing ($ millions)
0	−28.5
5.9	0
10	19.7
20	67.9
30	116.1

❯ **TABLE 29.10** **Required external financing for Dynamic Mattress in 2019. Higher growth rates require more external capital.**

---

[15]The Second Law is presented in Section 11-1.

[16]It is possible to build linear programming models that help search for the best strategy subject to specified assumptions and conditions. These models can be more effective in screening alternative financial strategies.

the addition to assets and there is a surplus of funds from internal sources; this shows up as negative required external financing.

We can generalize the relationship between a firm's growth objectives and its financing needs. If net assets are proportional to sales, then the additional assets required to support any growth in sales is

$$\text{Additional net assets required} = \text{growth rate} \times \text{initial net assets} \qquad \textbf{(29.1)}$$

and

$$\text{Required external financing} = (\text{growth rate} \times \text{initial net assets}) - \text{reinvested earnings} \qquad \textbf{(29.2)}$$

The maximum growth rate that a firm can achieve without raising external funds is called the internal growth rate. If we set external financing to zero in Equation 29.2, then we can solve for the internal growth rate

$$\text{Internal growth rate} = \frac{\text{reinvested earnings}}{\text{net assets}} \qquad \textbf{(29.3)}$$

We can gain more insight into what determines this growth rate by multiplying the top and bottom of the expression for internal growth rate by *net income* and *equity* as follows:

$$\text{Internal growth rate} = \frac{\text{reinvested earnings}}{\text{net income}} \times \frac{\text{net income}}{\text{equity}} \times \frac{\text{equity}}{\text{net assets}} \qquad \textbf{(29.4)}$$
$$= \text{plowback ratio} \times \text{return on equity} \times \text{equity/net assets}$$

A firm can achieve a higher growth rate without raising external capital if (1) it plows back a high proportion of its earnings, (2) it has a high return on equity (ROE), and (3) it has a low debt-to-asset ratio.[17]

Instead of focusing on how rapidly the company can grow without any external financing, Dynamic Mattress's financial manager may be interested in the growth rate that can be sustained without additional equity issues. Of course, if the firm is able to raise enough debt, virtually any growth rate can be financed. It makes more sense to assume that the firm has settled on an optimal capital structure that it will maintain. Thus, the firm issues only enough debt to keep the debt–equity ratio constant. The sustainable growth rate is the highest growth rate the firm can maintain without increasing its financial leverage. It turns out that the sustainable growth rate depends only on the plowback rate and the return on equity:

$$\text{Sustainable growth rate} = \text{plowback ratio} \times \text{return on equity} \qquad \textbf{(29.5)}$$

For Dynamic Mattress,

$$\text{Sustainable growth rate} = .40 \times .1815 = .0726, \text{ or } 7.26\%$$

We first encountered this formula in Chapter 4, where we used it to value common stocks.[18]

These simple formulas remind us that firms may grow rapidly in the short term by relying on debt finance, but such growth can rarely be maintained without incurring excessive debt levels.

---

[17]In practice, calculating the internal growth rate can be a bit tricky since the return on equity *depends* on the growth rate.

[18]Calculating sustainable growth is also more tricky than it sounds. Because the return on equity depends on the growth rate, it is necessary to solve simultaneously for the return on equity and the growth rate that leaves leverage unchanged. The solution is easily found using the Excel solver tool.

Short-term financial planning is concerned with the management of the firm's short-term, or current, assets and liabilities. The most important current assets are cash, marketable securities, accounts receivable, and inventory. The most important current liabilities are short-term loans and accounts payable. The difference between current assets and current liabilities is called net working capital.

The nature of the firm's short-term financial planning problem is determined by the amount of long-term capital it raises. A firm that issues large amounts of long-term debt or common stock, or that retains a large part of its earnings, may find it has permanent excess cash. In such cases, there is never any problem paying bills, and short-term financial planning consists of managing the firm's portfolio of marketable securities. A firm holding a reserve of cash is able to buy itself time to react to a short-term crisis. This may be important for growth firms that find it difficult to raise cash on short notice. However, large cash holdings can lead to complacency. We suggest that firms with permanent cash surpluses ought to consider returning the excess cash to their stockholders.

Other firms raise relatively little long-term capital and end up as permanent short-term debtors. Most firms attempt to find a golden mean by financing all fixed assets and part of current assets with equity and long-term debt. Such firms may invest cash surpluses during part of the year and borrow during the rest of the year.

The starting point for short-term financial planning is an understanding of sources and uses of cash. Firms forecast their net cash requirements by estimating collections on accounts receivable, adding other cash inflows, and subtracting all cash outlays. If the forecasted cash balance is insufficient to cover day-to-day operations and to provide a buffer against contingencies, the company will need to find additional finance. The search for the best short-term financial plan inevitably proceeds by trial and error. The financial manager must explore the consequences of different assumptions about cash requirements, interest rates, sources of finance, and so on. Firms use computerized financial models to help in this process. These models range from simple spreadsheet programs that merely help with the arithmetic to linear programming models that search for the best financial plan.

Short-term financial planning focuses on the firm's cash flow over the coming year. But the financial manager also needs to consider what financial actions will be needed to support the firm's plans for growth over the next 5 or 10 years. Most firms, therefore, prepare a long-term financial plan that describes the firm's strategy and projects its financial consequences. The plan establishes financial goals and is a benchmark for evaluating subsequent performance.

The process that produces this plan is valuable in its own right. First, planning forces the financial manager to consider the combined effects of all the firm's investment and financing decisions. This is important because these decisions interact and should not be made independently. Second, planning requires the manager to consider events that could upset the firm's progress and to devise strategies to be held in reserve for counterattack when unhappy surprises occur.

There is no theory or model that leads straight to *the* optimal financial strategy. As in the case of short-term planning, many different strategies may be projected under a range of assumptions about the future. The dozens of separate projections that may need to be made generate a heavy load of arithmetic. We showed how you can use a simple spreadsheet model to analyze Dynamic Mattress's long-term strategy.

The following text is concerned with liquidity management and short-term planning:

K. Parkinson and J. G. Kallberg, *Corporate Liquidity: A Guide to Managing Working Capital* (Burr Ridge, IL: Irwin/McGraw-Hill, 1993).

Long-term financial models are discussed in:

J. R. Morris and J. P. Daley, *Introduction to Financial Models for Management and Planning,* 2nd ed. (Boca Raton, FL: Chapman & Hall/CRC Finance Series, 2017).

PROBLEM SETS

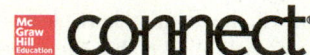 **CONNECT** Select problems are available in McGraw-Hill's *Connect*. Please see the preface for more information.

1. **Sources and uses of cash** State whether each of the following events is a source or use of cash, or neither.

   a. An automobile manufacturer increases production in response to a forecasted increase in demand. Unfortunately, the demand does not increase.

   b. Competition forces the firm to give customers more time to pay for their purchases.

   c. Rising commodity prices increase the value of raw material inventories by 20%.

   d. The firm sells a parcel of land for $100,000. The land was purchased five years earlier for $200,000.

   e. The firm repurchases its own common stock.

   f. The firm doubles its quarterly dividend.

   g. The firm issues $1 million of long-term debt and uses the proceeds to repay a short-term bank loan.

2. **Sources and uses of cash** Table 29.11 shows Dynamic Mattress's year-end 2016 balance sheet, and Table 29.12 shows its income statement for 2017. Work out the statement of cash flows for 2017. Group these items into sources of cash and uses of cash.

Balance Sheet (year-end)	2016	2017
Assets:		
Cash	29.0	20.0
Marketable Securities	10.0	0.0
Accounts Receivable	110.0	124.0
Inventory	100.0	183.0
Total Current Assets	249.0	327.0
Fixed Assets:		
Property, Plant and Equipment	330.0	345.0
Less: Accumulated Depreciation	70.0	76.5
Net Fixed Assets:	260.0	268.5
Total Assets:	509.0	595.5
Liabilities and Equity:		
Bank Loans	20.0	25.0
Accounts Payable	75.0	110.0
Total Current Liabilites	95.0	135.0
Long Term Debt	25.0	60.0
Shareholder's Equity	389.0	400.5
Total Liability and Shareholder's Equity:	509.0	595.5

〉**TABLE 29.11** Year-end balance sheet for Dynamic Mattress for 2016 and 2017 (figures in $ millions). See Problem 2.

Sales	$1,500
Operating costs	1,405
	$ 95
Depreciation	6.5
	$ 88.5
Interest	5
Pretax income	$ 83.5
Tax at 50%	41.8
Net income	$ 41.8

》TABLE 29.12   Income statement for Dynamic Mattress for 2017 (figures in $ millions). See Problem 2.

Notes: Dividend = $30.
Retained earnings = $11.8.

2. **Sources and uses of cash** What will be the effect of each of the following transactions on cash, net working capital, and the current ratio? Assume that the current ratio is above 1.0.

   a. The firm borrows $1,000 in a short-term loan from its bank and pays $500 in accounts payable.

   b. The firm issues $1,000 in long-term bonds and uses the proceeds to pay $800 in payables and purchase $200 in marketable securities.

3. **Sources and uses of cash and working capital*** Listed below are six transactions that Dynamic Mattress might make. Indicate how each transaction would affect (1) cash and (2) working capital. The transactions are

   a. Pay out an extra $10 million cash dividend.

   b. Receive $2,500 from a customer who pays a bill resulting from a previous sale.

   c. Pay $50,000 previously owed to one of its suppliers.

   d. Borrow $10 million long term and invest the proceeds in inventory.

   e. Borrow $10 million short term and invest the proceeds in inventory.

   f. Sell $5 million of marketable securities for cash.

4. **Cash cycle** In fiscal 2017 and 2016, Estée Lauder's financial statements included the following items. What was its cash cycle?

	$ millions	
	2017	**2016**
Inventory	$1,479	$1,264
Receivables	1,395	1,258
Payables	2,634	2,349
Sales	11,824	11,262
Cost of goods sold	2,437	2,181

5. **Cash cycle*** What effect will each of the following have on the cash cycle?

   a. The inventory turnover falls from 80 to 60 days.

   b. Customers are given a larger discount for cash transactions.

   c. The firm adopts a policy of reducing accounts payable.

   d. The firm starts producing more goods in response to customers' advance orders instead of producing ahead of demand.

   e. A temporary glut in the commodity market induces the firm to stock up on raw materials while prices are low.

6. **Cash cycle** A firm is considering several policy changes to increase sales. It plans to increase the variety of goods it keeps in inventory, but this will increase inventory by $100,000. It will offer more liberal sales terms, but this will result in receivables increasing by $650,000. These actions are forecasted to increase sales by $8 million a year. Cost of goods sold will remain at 80% of sales. Because of the firm's increased purchases for its own production needs, payables will increase by $350,000. What effect will these changes have on the firm's cash cycle?

7. **Collections on receivables*** Here is a forecast of sales by National Bromide for the first four months of 2019 (figures in $ thousands):

	Month 1	Month 2	Month 3	Month 4
Cash sales	15	24	18	14
Sales on credit	100	120	90	70

On the average 50% of credit sales are paid for in the current month, 30% are paid in the next month, and the remainder are paid in the month after that. What is the expected cash inflow from operations in months 3 and 4?

8. **Collections on receivables** If a firm pays its bills with a 30-day delay, what fraction of its purchases will be paid in the current quarter? In the following quarter? What if the delay is 60 days?

9. **Forecasts of payables** Dynamic Futon forecasts the following purchases from suppliers:

	Jan.	Feb.	Mar.	Apr.	May	June
Value of goods ($ millions)	32	28	25	22	20	20

a. Forty percent of goods are supplied cash-on-delivery. The remainder are paid with an average delay of one month. If Dynamic Futon starts the year with payables of $22 million, what is the forecasted level of payables for each month?

b. Suppose that from the start of the year the company stretches payables by paying 40% after one month and 20% after two months. (The remainder continue to be paid cash on delivery.) Recalculate payables for each month assuming that there are no cash penalties for late payment.

10. **Cash budget** Table 29.13 lists data from the budget of Ritewell Publishers. Half the company's sales are for cash on the nail; the other half are paid for with a one-month delay.

	February	March	April
Total sales	$200	$220	$180
Purchases of materials:			
For cash	70	80	60
For credit	40	30	40
Other expenses	30	30	30
Taxes, interest, and dividends	10	10	10
Capital investment	100	0	0

❭**TABLE 29.13**   Selected budget data for Ritewell Publishers. See Problem 11.

	February	March	April
Sources of cash:			
Collections on cash sales			
Collections on accounts receivables			
Total sources of cash			
Uses of cash:			
Payments of accounts payable			
Cash purchases of materials			
Other expenses			
Capital expenditures			
Taxes, interest, and dividends			
Total uses of cash			
Net cash inflow			
Cash at start of period	100		
+ Net cash inflow			
= Cash at end of period			
+ Net cash inflow			
+ Minimum operating cash balance	100	100	100
= Cumulative short-term financing required			

❯**TABLE 29.14**   Cash budget for Ritewell Publishers. See Problem 11.

The company pays all its credit purchases with a one-month delay. Credit purchases in January were $30, and total sales in January were $180. Complete the cash budget in Table 29.14.

11. **Short-term financial plans**

    a. Paymore places orders for goods equal to 75% of its sales forecast for the next quarter. What will orders be in each quarter of the coming year if the sales in the current quarter are expected to be $320 and the sales forecasts for the next five quarters are as follows?

	Quarter in Coming Year				Following Year
	First	Second	Third	Fourth	First Quarter
Sales forecast, $	372	360	336	334	384

    b. Paymore pays for two-thirds of the purchases immediately and pays for the remaining purchases in the next quarter. Calculate Paymore's cash payments in the coming year.

    c. Paymore's customers pay their bills with a two-month delay. What are the expected cash receipts from sales in the coming year?

    d. Now suppose that Paymore's other expenses are $105 a quarter. Calculate the expected net cash flow for each quarter in the coming year.

    e. Suppose that Paymore's starting cash balance is $40 and its minimum acceptable balance is $30. Work out the short-term financing requirements for the coming year.

12. **Short-term financial plans** Which items in Table 29.7 would be affected by the following events?

    a. Interest rates rise.

    b. Suppliers demand interest for late payment.

    c. Dynamic receives an unexpected bill in the third quarter from the Internal Revenue Service for underpayment of taxes in previous years.

13. **Short-term financial plans** Each of the following events affects one or more tables in Sections 29-2 and 29-3. Show the effects of each event by adjusting the tables listed in parentheses:

    a. Dynamic repays only $10 million of short-term debt in 2018 (Tables 29.2 and 29.3).

    b. Dynamic issues an additional $40 million of long-term debt in 2018 and invests $25 million in a new warehouse (Tables 29.1, 29.2, and 29.3).

    c. In 2018, Dynamic reduces the quantity of stuffing in each mattress. Customers don't notice, but operating costs fall by 10% (Tables 29.1, 29.2, and 29.3).

    d. Starting in the third quarter of 2019, Dynamic employs new staff members who prove very effective in persuading customers to pay more promptly. As a result, 90% of sales are paid for immediately and 10% are paid in the following quarter (Tables 29.5 and 29.6).

    e. Starting in the first quarter of 2019, Dynamic cuts wages by $20 million a quarter (Table 29.6).

    f. In the second quarter of 2019, a disused warehouse catches fire mysteriously. Dynamic receives a $50 million check from the insurance company (Table 29.6).

    g. Dynamic's treasurer decides he can scrape by on a $10 million operating cash balance (Table 29.6).

BEYOND THE PAGE

Try It! Dynamic Mattress's spreadsheet

mhhe.com/brealey13e

14. **Short-term financial plans** Work out a short-term financing plan for Dynamic Mattress Company, assuming the limit on the line of credit is raised from $100 to $120 million. Otherwise keep to the assumptions used in developing Table 29.7.

BEYOND THE PAGE

Try It! Dynamic Mattress's spreadsheet

mhhe.com/brealey13e

15. **Short-term financial plans** Dynamic Mattress decides to lease its new mattress-stuffing machines rather than buy them. As a result, capital expenditure in the first quarter is reduced by $50 million, but the company must make lease payments of $2.5 million for each of the four quarters. Assume that the lease has no effect on tax payments until after the fourth quarter. Construct two tables like Tables 29.6 and 29.7 showing Dynamic's cumulative financing requirement and a new financing plan. Check your answer using Dynamic's spreadsheet.

BEYOND THE PAGE

Try It! Dynamic Mattress's spreadsheet

mhhe.com/brealey13e

16. **Long-term financial plans** True or false?

    a. Financial planning should attempt to minimize risk.

    b. The primary aim of financial planning is to obtain better forecasts of future cash flows and earnings.

    c. Financial planning is necessary because financing and investment decisions interact and should not be made independently.

    d. Firms' planning horizons rarely exceed three years.

    e. Financial planning requires accurate forecasting.

    f. Financial planning models should include as much detail as possible.

17. **Long-term financial plans** Corporate financial plans are often used as a basis for judging subsequent performance. What do you think can be learned from such comparisons? What problems are likely to arise, and how might you cope with these problems?

18. **Long-term financial plans** Our long-term planning model of Dynamic Mattress is an example of a top-down planning model. Some firms use a bottom-up financial planning model,

which incorporates forecasts of revenues and costs for particular products, advertising plans, major investment projects, and so on. What sort of firms would you expect to use each type, and what would they use them for?

19. **Long-term financial plans** The balancing item in the Dynamic long-term planning model is borrowing. What is meant by balancing item? How would the model change if dividends were made the balancing item instead? In that case how would you suggest that planned borrowing be determined?

20. **Long-term financial plans** Construct a new model for Dynamic Mattress based on your answer to Problem 19. Does your model generate a feasible financial plan for 2019? (*Hint:* If it doesn't, you may have to allow the firm to issue stock.)

21. **Long-term financial plans**

    a. Use the Dynamic Mattress model in Table 29.9 and the spreadsheets to produce pro forma income statements, balance sheets, and statements of cash flows for 2019–2023. Assume business as usual, except that sales and costs are now planned to expand by 30% per year, as are fixed assets and net working capital. The interest rate is forecasted to remain at 10% and stock issues are ruled out. Dynamic also sticks to its 60% dividend payout ratio.

    b. What are the firm's debt ratio and interest coverage under this plan?

    c. Can the company continue to finance expansion by borrowing?

22. **Long-term financial plans*** Table 29.15 summarizes the 2019 income statement and end-year balance sheet of Drake's Bowling Alleys. Drake's financial manager forecasts a 10% increase in sales and costs in 2020. The ratio of sales to average assets is expected to remain at .40. Interest is forecasted at 5% of debt at the start of the year.

    a. What is the implied level of assets at the end of 2020?

    b. If the company pays out 50% of net income as dividends, how much cash will Drake need to raise in the capital markets in 2020?

    c. If Drake is unwilling to make an equity issue, what will be the debt ratio at the end of 2020?

23. **Long-term financial plans** Abbreviated financial statements for Archimedes Levers are shown in Table 29.16. If sales increase by 10% in 2018 and all other items, including debt, increase correspondingly, what must be the balancing item? What will be its value?

BEYOND THE PAGE

Try It! Dynamic
Mattress's
spreadsheet

mhhe.com/brealey13e

BEYOND THE PAGE

Try It! Dynamic
Mattress's
spreadsheet

mhhe.com/brealey13e

Income Statement		
Sales	$1,000	(40% of average assets)[a]
Costs	750	(75% of sales)
Interest	25	(5% of debt at start of year)[b]
Pretax profit	225	
Tax	90	(40% of pretax profit)
Net income	$135	
Balance Sheet		
Net assets	$2,600	Debt	$500
		Equity	2,100
Total	$2,600	Total	$2,600

❯ **TABLE 29.15** Financial statements for Drake's Bowling Alleys, 2019 (figures in thousands). See Problem 23.

[a]Assets at the end of 2018 were $2,400,000.

[b]Debt at the end of 2018 was $500,000.

Income Statement	
Sales	$4,000
Costs, including interest	3,500
Net income	$500

Balance Sheet, Year-End					
	2018	2017		2018	2017
Net assets	$3,200	$2,700	Debt	$1,200	$1,033
			Equity	2,000	1,667
Total	$3,200	$2,700	Total	$3,200	$2,700

❯TABLE 29.16   Financial statements for Archimedes
Levers, 2018. See Problem 24.

24. **Long-term financial plans** The financial statements of Eagle Sport Supply are shown in Table 29.17. For simplicity, "Costs" include interest. Assume that Eagle's assets are proportional to its sales.

   a. Find Eagle's required external funds if it maintains a dividend payout ratio of 50% and plans a growth rate of 15% in 2020.

   b. If Eagle chooses not to issue new shares of stock, what variable must be the balancing item? What will its value be?

   c. Now suppose that the firm plans instead to increase long-term debt only to $1,100 and does not wish to issue any new shares of stock. Why must the dividend payment now be the balancing item? What will its value be?

25. **Forecast growth rate** What is the maximum possible growth rate for Archimedes (see Problem 24) if it maintains its return on equity, the payout ratio is set at 50% and

   a. No external debt or equity is to be issued?

   b. The firm maintains a fixed debt ratio but issues no equity?

26. **Forecast growth rate**

   a. What is the internal growth rate of Eagle Sport (see Problem 25) if the dividend payout ratio is fixed at 50% and the equity-to-asset ratio is fixed at two-thirds?

   b. What is the sustainable growth rate?

Income Statement	
Sales	$950
Costs	250
Pretax income	700
Taxes (at 28.6%)	200
Net income	$500

Balance Sheet, Year-End					
	2019	2018		2019	2018
Net assets	$3,000	$2,700	Debt	$1,000	$900
			Equity	2,000	1,800
Total	$3,000	$2,700	Total	$3,000	$2,700

❯TABLE 29.17   Financial statements for Eagle Sport
Supply, 2019. See Problem 25.

27. **Forecast growth rate** Bio-Plasma Corp. is growing at 30% per year. It is all-equity-financed and has total assets of $1 million. Its return on equity is 20%. Its plowback ratio is 40%.

    a. What is the internal growth rate?

    b. What is the firm's need for external financing this year?

    c. By how much would the firm increase its internal growth rate if it reduced its payout rate to zero?

    d. By how much would such a move reduce the need for external financing? What do you conclude about the relationship between dividend policy and requirements for external financing?

CHALLENGE

29. **Long-term plans** Table 29.18 shows the 2019 financial statements for the Executive Cheese Company. Annual depreciation is 10% of fixed assets at the beginning of the year, plus 10%

Income Statement	
Revenue	$1,785
Fixed costs	53
Variable costs (80% of revenue)	1,428
Depreciation	80
Interest (at 11.8%)	24
Taxes (at 40%)	80
Net income	$120

Balance Sheet, Year-End		
	2019	2018
Assets:		
Net working capital	$400	$340
Fixed assets	800	680
Total assets	$1,200	$1,020
Liabilities:		
Debt	$ 240	$ 204
Book equity	960	816
Total liabilities	$1,200	$1,020

Sources and Uses	
Sources:	
Net income	$120
Depreciation	80
Borrowing	36
Stock issues	104
Total sources	$340
Uses:	
Increase in net working capital	$60
Investment	200
Dividends	80
Total uses	$340

❯TABLE 29.18   **Financial statements for Executive Cheese Company, 2019 (figures in thousands)**

of new investment. The company plans to invest a further $200,000 per year in fixed assets for the next five years and net working capital is expected to remain a constant proportion of fixed assets. The company forecasts that the ratio of revenues to total assets at the start of each year will remain at 1.75. Fixed costs are expected to remain at $53, and variable costs at 80% of revenue. The company's policy is to pay out two-thirds of net income as dividends and to maintain a book debt ratio of 20%.

a. Construct a model for Executive Cheese like the one in Table 29.9.

b. Use your model to produce a set of financial statements for 2020.

FINANCE ON THE WEB

Look up the financial statements for any company on **finance.yahoo.com.** Make some plausible forecasts for future growth and the asset base needed to support that growth. Then use a spreadsheet program to develop a five-year financial plan. What financing is needed to support the planned growth? How vulnerable is the company to an error in your forecasts?

30

Working Capital Management

Most of this book is devoted to long-term financial decisions, including capital budgeting and debt policy. It is now time to look at the financial management of current assets and liabilities. "Current" or "short-term" mean that the asset or liability will mature or be replaced in 12 months or less.

Current assets and liabilities are collectively labeled **working capital.** Table 30.1 shows the composition of working capital of all U.S. manufacturing companies in 2017. The asset side of this working-capital balance sheet includes cash and short-term investments, inventories and accounts receivable (payments due from customers). The liability side includes accounts payable (payments the firm must make to suppliers), short-term borrowing, income taxes due, and the current part of long-term debt, that is, principal payments that come due in the next 12 months. There is also a large entry collecting various other current liabilities. Current assets are larger than current liabilities, so **net working capital** (current assets minus current liabilities) was positive.

The percentages in Table 30.1 show that working capital is not small change. For example, accounts receivable and inventories each accounted for 7% or more of total book assets. The sum of all current assets was 24% of total book assets.

But don't be too quick to take these average percentages as normal. There is wide variation across companies and industries, as we will see in a moment. The composition of your firm's working capital will depend on the nature of its business and its relationships with customers and suppliers. It may also depend on your firm's cumulative free cash flow. A company that generates more cash than it invests will often build up large holdings of cash and short-term investments. We will note the "cash mountains" accumulated by Apple, Facebook, and a few other highly profitable companies.

Current Assets					Current Liabilities
Cash	$389	3.6%	$263	2.4%	Short-term loans
Other short-term financial Investments	210	1.9	644	5.9	Accounts payable
Accounts receivable	755	7.0	26	0.2	Accrued income taxes
Inventories	827	7.6	207	1.9	Current payments due on long-term debt
Other current assets	417	3.8	941	8.7	Other current liabilities
Total	$2,599	24.0%	$2,088	19.3%	Total
Net working capital	$511				

❭**TABLE 30.1**
Current assets and liabilities for U.S. manufacturing corporations, 4th quarter 2017 ($ billions). Percentages show the size of each short-term asset or liability relative to total book assets.

Source: U.S. Census Bureau, Quarterly Financial Report for U.S. Manufacturing, Mining, and Trade Corporations, Table 1, www.census.gov/econ/qfr/index.html.

The components of working capital all have to be managed. We will focus mostly on inventories, accounts receivable, and cash. The management of inventories boils down to a trade-off, of the costs of holding inventories against the benefit of having buffer stocks to meet unexpected needs. The management of accounts receivable requires a credit policy for customers. The management of cash requires having cash on hand for day-to-day transactions, while at the same time sweeping up excess cash that would otherwise sit idle.

Excess cash is usually invested in short-term financial instruments, including Treasury bills, commercial paper, and repos (repurchase agreements). At the end of the chapter, we describe these money market securities and show how to compare their yields.

● ● ● ● ●

30-1 The Composition of Working Capital

The financial manager cannot freely choose the amount of investment in inventories or accounts receivable or the size of accounts payable; the amounts will depend in large part on the nature of the firm's operations and the industry it is in.

Figure 30.1 shows the relative importance of working capital in different industries. For example, current assets account for nearly 75% of total book assets of pharmaceutical companies but less than 10% of total book assets of railroads. For some industries, current assets means principally inventory; for others, it means accounts receivable or cash and securities. Retail firms hold large inventories. Receivables are relatively more important for auto producers. Cash and securities make up the bulk of current assets of computer and pharmaceutical companies.

Table 30.2 presents working-capital balance sheets for four U.S. corporations: Cummins, a manufacturer, mostly of diesel engines; Macy's department stores; electric utility Entergy; and trucking company J. B. Hunt.

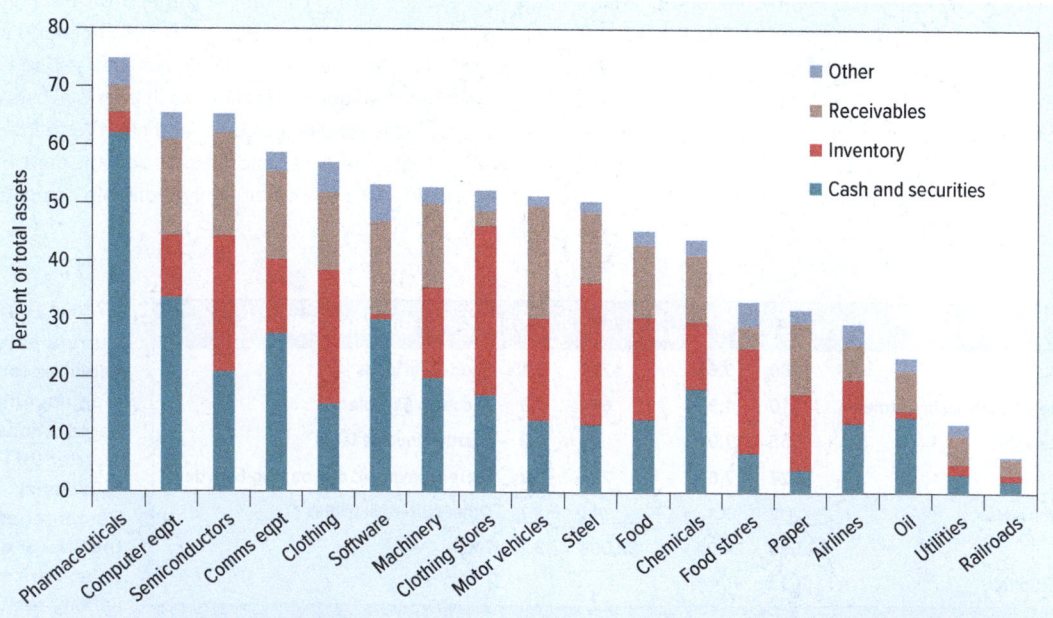

▶ **FIGURE 30.1**   **Current assets as a percentage of total assets in different industries in fourth quarter 2017**

Source: U.S. Census Bureau, Quarterly Financial Report for U.S. Manufacturing, Mining, and Trade Corporations, www.census.gov/econ/qfr/index.html.

Cummins Inc. (Manufacturing)

Current Assets			Current Liabilities		
Cash and short-term investments	$1,444	8.0%	Accounts payable	$4,128	22.9%
Accounts receivable	3,532	19.6%	Short-term debt	640	3.6%
Inventories	3,146	17.5%			
Other current assets	934	5.2%	Other current liabilities	990	5.5%
Current assets	$9,056	50.3%	Current liabilities	$5,758	32.0%
Net working capital	$3,298	18.3%			
Total assets	$17,992				

Macy's (department stores)

Current Assets			Current Liabilities		
Cash and short-term investments	$534	2.6%	Accounts payable	$5,338	26.4%
Accounts receivable	219	1.1%	Short-term debt	309	1.5%
Inventories	7,065	34.9%			
Other current assets	432	2.1%	Other current liabilities	0	0.0%
Current assets	$8,250	40.8%	Current liabilities	$5,647	27.9%
Net working capital	$2,603	12.9%			
Total assets	$20,215				

Entergy (electric utility)

Current Assets			Current Liabilities		
Cash and short-term investments	$546	1.2%	Accounts payable	$1,599	3.4%
Accounts receivable	1,313	2.8%	Short-term debt	2,224	4.8%
Inventories	879	1.9%			
Other current assets	733	1.6%	Other current liabilities	638	1.4%
Current assets	$3,471	7.5%	Current liabilities	$4,461	9.6%
Net working capital	−$990	−2.1%			
Total assets	$46,398				

J. B. Hunt (trucking)

Current Assets			Current Liabilities		
Cash and short-term investments	$8	0.2%	Accounts payable	$682	16.8%
Accounts receivable	859	21.2%	Short-term debt	0	0.0%
Inventories	0	0.0%			
Other current assets	140	3.5%	Other current liabilities	0	0.0%
Current assets	$1,007	24.8%	Current liabilities	$682	16.8%
Net working capital	$325	8.0%			
Total assets	$4,054				

❯ **TABLE 30.2** Components of working capital for four U.S. corporations, third quarter 2017 ($ millions). Short-term debt includes principal amounts of long-term debt due within one year. Net working capital equals current assets minus current liabilities. Percentages show the size of each short-term asset or liability relative to total book assets.

The composition of Cummins's working capital was not too different from the manufacturing aggregate in Table 30.1, although its net working capital was a larger fraction of net book assets. Cummins keeps extensive inventories of raw materials, work in progress, and finished goods awaiting sale. Its inventory of $3,146 million was 17.5% of total book assets. It carried about $3.5 billion in accounts receivable, but accounts payable were even larger at about $4.1 billion. Cummins was, in effect, financing its current assets partly with accounts payable because $4.1 billion due to its suppliers remained to be paid.

Macy's current assets were dominated by inventory. Its shelves and warehouses were stocked with goods awaiting sale to retail customers. Other current assets were much less important. The most important current liability was accounts payable at about $5.3 billion. Like Cummins, Macy's got short-term financing by deferring payments to suppliers.

Entergy's current assets and liabilities were much smaller fractions of its total assets than for Cummins and Macy's. Entergy's inventories were small, which makes sense when you realize that its main product, electricity, cannot be stored and has to be produced at the instant it is consumed. Note also that Entergy's current liabilities included about $2.2 billion of debt maturing in the coming year. Its current liabilities were larger than its current assets, so its net working capital was negative at slightly less than $1 billion. (There is nothing necessarily odd or dangerous about negative working capital. It happens frequently.)

J. B. Hunt, a much smaller company than the other three in Table 30.2, carried no inventories at all. It transports goods; it does not buy and hold them in inventory for resale. Hunt's working capital was dominated by large positions in receivables (21.2% of total assets) and payables (16.8% of total assets). It used no short-term debt financing.

We provide Table 30.2 just to alert you to the diversity that can be found in firms' working-capital accounts and to illustrate some industry patterns. We now turn to the management of working capital, starting with inventory.

30-2 Inventories

Most firms keep inventories of raw materials, work in process, or finished goods awaiting sale and shipment. But they are not obliged to do so. For example, they could buy materials day by day, as needed. But then they would pay higher prices for ordering in small lots, and they would risk production delays if the materials were not delivered on time. They can avoid that risk by ordering more than the firm's immediate needs. Similarly, firms could do away with inventories of finished goods by producing only what they expect to sell tomorrow. But this too could be a dangerous strategy. A small inventory of finished goods may mean shorter and more costly production runs, and it may not be sufficient to meet an unexpected increase in demand.

There are also costs to holding inventories that must be set against these benefits. Money tied up in inventories does not earn interest, storage and insurance must be paid for, and there may be risk of spoilage or obsolescence. Firms need to strike a sensible balance between the benefits of holding inventory and the costs.

EXAMPLE 30.1 ● The Inventory Trade-Off

Akron Wire Products uses 255,000 tons a year of wire rod. Suppose that it orders Q tons at a time from the manufacturer. Just before delivery, Akron has effectively no inventories. Just *after* delivery it has an inventory of Q tons. Thus Akron's inventory of wire rod roughly follows the sawtooth pattern in Figure 30.2.

There are two costs to this inventory. First, each order that Akron places involves a handling and delivery cost. Second, there are carrying costs, such as the cost of storage and the opportunity cost of the capital that is invested in inventory. Akron can reduce the order costs by placing fewer and larger orders. On the other hand, a larger order size increases the average quantity held in inventory, so that the carrying costs rise. Good inventory management requires a trade-off between these two types of cost.

This is illustrated in Figure 30.3. We assume here that each order that Akron places involves a fixed order cost of $450, while the annual carrying cost of the inventory works out at about $55 a ton. You can see how a larger order size results in lower order costs but higher carrying costs. The sum of the two costs is minimized when the size of each order is $Q = 2,043$ tons. The optimal order size (2,043 tons in our example) is termed the *economic order quantity, or EOQ.*[1]

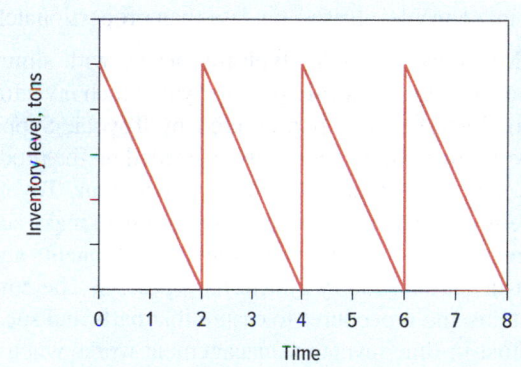

▶ **FIGURE 30.2**

A simple inventory rule. The company waits until inventories of materials are about to be exhausted and then reorders a constant quantity.

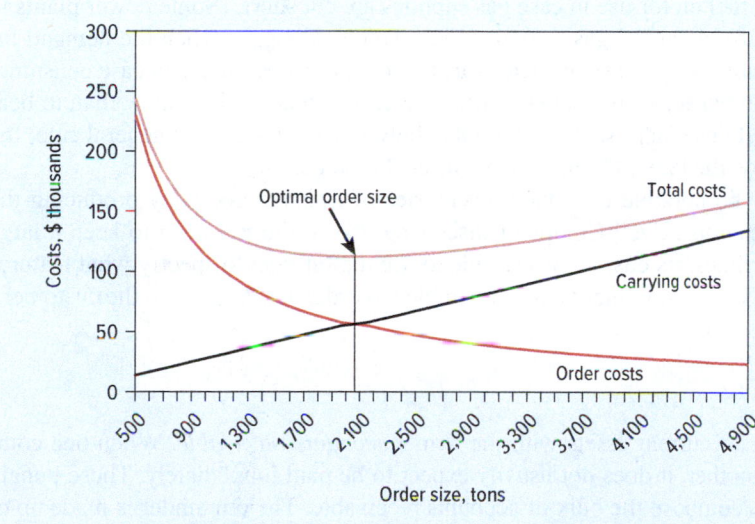

▶ **FIGURE 30.3**

As the inventory order size is increased, order costs fall and inventory carrying costs rise. Total costs are minimized when the saving in order costs is equal to the increase in carrying costs.

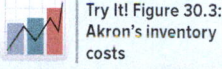
Our example was not wholly realistic. For instance, most firms do not use up their inventory of raw material at a constant rate, and they would not wait until stocks had completely run

---

[1]Where the firm uses up materials at a constant rate, as in our example, there is a simple formula for calculating the economic order quantity (or EOQ). Its optimal size = $Q = \sqrt{(2 \times \text{sales} \times \text{cost per order/carrying cost})}$. In our example $Q = \sqrt{(2 \times 255{,}000 \times 450/55)}$ = 2,043 tons.

out before they were replenished. But this simple model does capture some essential features of inventory management:

- Optimal inventory levels involve a trade-off between carrying costs and order costs.
- Carrying costs include the cost of storing goods as well as the cost of capital tied up in inventory.
- A firm can manage its inventories by waiting until they reach some minimum level and then replenish them by ordering a predetermined quantity.[2]
- When carrying costs are high and order costs are low, it makes sense to place more frequent orders and maintain lower levels of inventory.
- Inventory levels do not rise in direct proportion to sales. As sales increase, the optimal inventory level rises, but less than proportionately.

Manufacturers today typically get by with slimmer inventories than they used to. Some have adopted a *just-in-time* strategy in which inventories of parts and subassemblies are nearly zero. Just-in-time was pioneered by Toyota. Suppliers deliver parts and subassemblies to Toyota's assembly plants only as needed on the production line. Deliveries are made throughout the day at intervals as short as one hour. Toyota can operate successfully with minimal inventories only because it and its suppliers make sure that traffic snarl-ups, strikes, and other hazards do not interrupt the flow of components and bring production to a standstill. Thus a just-in-time inventory system has its costs. The company and its suppliers have to maintain systems and procedures to ensure that parts and subassemblies really do arrive just in time.

Just-in-time inventory management works when the flow of production is steady and predictable, so that no significant buffer is needed for unexpected changes or requirements. But in most circumstances inventory buffers are needed. For example, a gas-fired power plant may hold a supply of fuel oil for use in case gas supplies are cut short. (Some power plants in New England switch from natural gas to fuel oil in severe cold snaps, when the demand for gas for residential heating soars.) Department stores hold extra merchandise in case consumer demand is higher than expected. It's better to bear the cost of holding inventory than to bear the risk of disgruntled customers staring at empty shelves. As a rough and general rule, the greater the uncertainty, the larger the inventory buffer should be.

Sometimes it may be possible to reduce inventories of finished goods by producing the goods to order. For example, Dell Computer discovered that it did not need to keep a large stock of finished machines. Its customers are able to use the Internet to specify what features they want on their PCs. The computer is then assembled to order and shipped to the customer.[3]

30-3   Credit Management

We continue our tour of current assets with the firm's *accounts receivable*. When one company sells goods to another, it does not usually expect to be paid immediately. These unpaid bills, or **trade credit,** compose the bulk of accounts receivable. The remainder is made up of **consumer credit,** that is, bills that are awaiting payment by the final customer.

Management of trade credit requires answers to five sets of questions:

1. How long are you going to give customers to pay their bills? Are you prepared to offer a cash discount for prompt payment?

2. Do you require some formal IOU from the buyer or do you just ask him or her to sign a receipt?

---

[2]This is known as a *reorder point* (or *two-bin*) *system*. Some firms use instead a *periodic review system*, where the firm reviews inventory levels periodically and tops the inventory up to the desired amount.

[3]These examples of just-in-time and build-to-order production are taken from T. Murphy, "JIT When ASAP Isn't Good Enough," *Ward's Auto World*, May 1999, pp. 67–73; R. Schreffler, "Alive and Well," *Ward's Auto World*, May 1999, pp. 73–77; and "A Long March: Mass Customization," *The Economist*, June 12, 2001, pp. 63–65.

3. How do you determine which customers are likely to pay their bills?

4. How much credit are you prepared to extend to each customer? Do you play it safe by turning down any doubtful prospects? Or do you accept the risk of a few bad debts as part of the cost of building a large regular clientele?

5. How do you collect the money when it becomes due? What do you do about reluctant payers or deadbeats?

We discuss each of these topics in turn.

Terms of Sale

Not all sales involve credit. For example, if you are supplying goods to a wide variety of irregular customers, you may demand cash on delivery (COD). And, if your product is custom-designed, it may be sensible to ask for cash before delivery (CBD) or to ask for *progress payments* as the work is carried out.

When we look at transactions that do involve credit, we find that each industry seems to have its own particular practices.[4] These norms have a rough logic. For example, firms selling consumer durables may allow the buyer a month to pay, while those selling perishable goods, such as cheese or fresh fruit, typically demand payment in a week. Similarly, a seller may allow more extended payment if its customers are in a low-risk business, if their accounts are large, if they need time to check the quality of the goods, or if the goods are not quickly resold.

To encourage customers to pay before the final date, it is common to offer a cash discount for prompt settlement. For example, pharmaceutical companies commonly require payment within 30 days but may offer a 2% discount to customers who pay within 10 days. These terms are referred to as "2/10, net 30."

If goods are bought on a recurrent basis, it may be inconvenient to require separate payment for each delivery. A common solution is to pretend that all sales during the month in fact occur at the end of the month (EOM). Thus goods may be sold on terms of 8/10 EOM, net 60. This arrangement allows the customer a cash discount of 8% if the bill is paid within 10 days of the end of the month; otherwise the full payment is due within 60 days of the invoice date.

Cash discounts are often very large. For example, a customer who buys on terms of 2/10, net 30 may decide to forgo the cash discount and pay on the thirtieth day. This means that the customer obtains an extra 20 days' credit but pays about 2% more for the goods. This is equivalent to borrowing money at a rate of 44.6% per annum.[5] Of course, any firm that delays payment beyond the due date gains a cheaper loan but damages its reputation.

The Promise to Pay

Repetitive sales to domestic customers are almost always made on *open account*. The only evidence of the customer's debt is the record in the seller's books and a receipt signed by the buyer.

If you want a clear commitment from the buyer before you deliver the goods, you can arrange a **commercial draft**.[6] This works as follows: You draw a draft ordering payment by the customer and send this to the customer's bank together with the shipping documents. If immediate payment is required, the draft is termed a *sight draft;* otherwise it is known as a *time draft*. Depending on whether it is a sight draft or a time draft, the customer either pays up or acknowledges the debt by signing it and adding the word *accepted*. The bank then hands

---

[4] Standard credit terms in different industries are reported in C. K. Ng, J. K. Smith, and R. L. Smith, "Evidence on the Determinants of Credit Terms Used in Interfirm Trade," *Journal of Finance* 54 (June 1999), pp. 1109–1129.

[5] The cash discount allows you to pay $98 rather than $100. If you do not take the discount, you get a 20-day loan, but you pay 2/98 = 2.04% more for your goods. The number of 20-day periods in a year is 365/20 = 18.25. A dollar invested for 18.25 periods at 2.04% per period grows to $(1.0204)^{18.25} = \$1.446$, a 44.6% return on the original investment. If a customer is happy to borrow at this rate, it's a good bet that he or she is desperate for cash (or can't work out compound interest). For a discussion of this issue, see J. K. Smith, "Trade Credit and Informational Asymmetry," *Journal of Finance* 42 (September 1987), pp. 863–872.

[6] Commercial drafts are sometimes known by the general term *bills of exchange*.

the shipping documents to the customer and forwards the money or **trade acceptance** to you, the seller.

If your customer's credit is shaky, you can ask the customer to arrange for a bank to *accept* the time draft and thereby guarantee the customer's debt. These **bankers' acceptances** are often used in overseas trade. The bank guarantee makes the debt easily marketable. If you don't want to wait for your money, you can sell the acceptance to a bank or to another firm that has surplus cash to invest.

Credit Analysis

There are a number of ways to find out whether customers are likely to pay their debts. For existing customers an obvious indication is whether they have paid promptly in the past. For new customers you can use the firm's financial statements to make your own assessment, or you may be able to look at how highly investors value the firm.[7] However, the simplest way to assess a customer's credit standing is to seek the views of a specialist in credit assessment. For example, in Chapter 23, we described how bond rating agencies, such as Moody's and Standard and Poor's, provide a useful guide to the riskiness of the firm's bonds.

Bond ratings are usually available only for relatively large firms. However, you can obtain information on many smaller companies from a credit agency. Dun and Bradstreet is by far the largest of these agencies and its database contains credit information on millions of businesses worldwide. Credit bureaus are another source of data on a customer's credit standing. In addition to providing data on small businesses, they can also provide an overall credit score for individuals.[8]

Finally, firms can also ask their bank to undertake a credit check. It will contact the customer's bank and ask for information on the customer's average balance, access to bank credit, and general reputation.

Of course you don't want to subject each order to the same credit analysis. It makes sense to concentrate your attention on the large and doubtful orders.

The Credit Decision

Let us suppose that you have taken the first three steps toward an effective credit operation. In other words, you have fixed your terms of sale; you have decided on the contract that customers must sign; and you have established a procedure for estimating the probability that they will pay up. Your next step is to work out which of your customers should be offered credit.

If there is no possibility of repeat orders, the decision is relatively simple. Figure 30.4 summarizes your choice. On one hand, you can refuse credit. In this case, you make neither profit nor loss. The alternative is to offer credit. Suppose that the probability that the customer will pay up is p. If the customer does pay, you receive additional revenues (REV) and you incur additional costs; your net gain is the present value of REV − COST. Unfortunately, you can't be certain that the customer will pay; there is a probability $(1 - p)$ of default. Default means that you receive nothing and incur the additional costs. The *expected* profit from each course of action is therefore as follows:

	Expected Gain
Refuse credit	0
Grant credit	pPV(REV − COST) − $(1 - p)$PV(COST)

---

[7] We discussed how you can use these sources of information in Section 23-4.
[8] We discussed credit scoring models in Section 23-4. Credit bureau scores are often called "FICO scores" because most credit bureaus use a credit scoring model developed by Fair Isaac and Company. FICO scores are provided by the three major credit bureaus'— Equifax, Experian, and TransUnion.

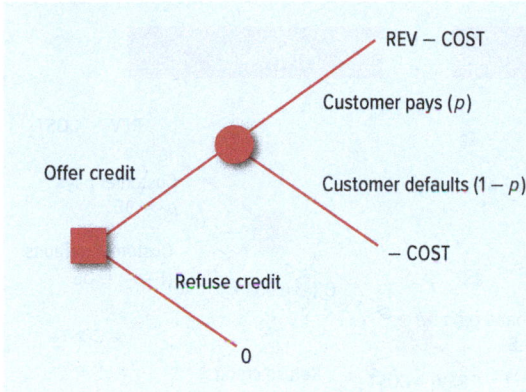

FIGURE 30.4

If you refuse credit, you make neither profit nor loss. If you offer credit, there is a probability *p* that the customer will pay and you will make **REV − COST**; there is a probability (1 − *p*) that the customer will default and you will lose **COST**.

You should grant credit if the expected gain from doing so is positive.

Consider, for example, the case of the Cast Iron Company. On each nondelinquent sale Cast Iron receives revenues with a present value of $1,200 and incurs costs with a value of $1,000. Therefore the company's expected profit if it offers credit is

$$p\text{PV}(\text{REV} - \text{COST}) - (1 - p)\text{PV}(\text{COST}) = p \times 200 - (1 - p) \times 1,000$$

If the probability of collection is 5/6, Cast Iron can expect to break even:

$$\text{Expected profit} = \frac{5}{6} \times 200 - \left(1 - \frac{5}{6}\right) \times 1,000 = 0$$

Therefore Cast Iron's policy should be to grant credit whenever the chances of collection are better than 5 out of 6.

So far, we have ignored the possibility of repeat orders. But one of the reasons for offering credit today is that it may help to get yourself a good, regular customer. Figure 30.5 illustrates the problem. Cast Iron has been asked to extend credit to a new customer. You can find little information on the firm, and you believe that the probability of payment is no better than .8. If you grant credit, the expected profit on this customer's order is

$$\text{Expected profit on initial order} = p_1 \text{PV}(\text{REV} - \text{COST}) - (1 - p_1)\text{PV}(\text{COST})$$
$$= (.8 \times 200) - (.2 \times 1,000) = -\$40$$

You decide to refuse credit.

This is the correct decision if there is no chance of a repeat order. But look again at the decision tree in Figure 30.5. If the customer does pay up, there will be a repeat order next year. Because the customer has paid once, you can be 95% sure that he or she will pay again. For this reason any repeat order is very profitable:

$$\text{Next year's expected profit on repeat order} = p_2 \text{PV}(\text{REV} - \text{COST}) - (1 - p_2)\text{PV}(\text{COST})$$
$$= (.95 \times 200) - (.05 \times 1,000) = \$140$$

Now you can reexamine today's credit decision. If you grant credit today, you receive the expected profit on the initial order *plus* the possible opportunity to extend credit next year:

$$\text{Total expected profit} = \text{expected profit on initial order}$$
$$+ \text{ probability of payment and repeat order}$$
$$\times \text{PV(next year's expected profit on repeat order)}$$
$$= -40 + .80 \times \text{PV}(140)$$

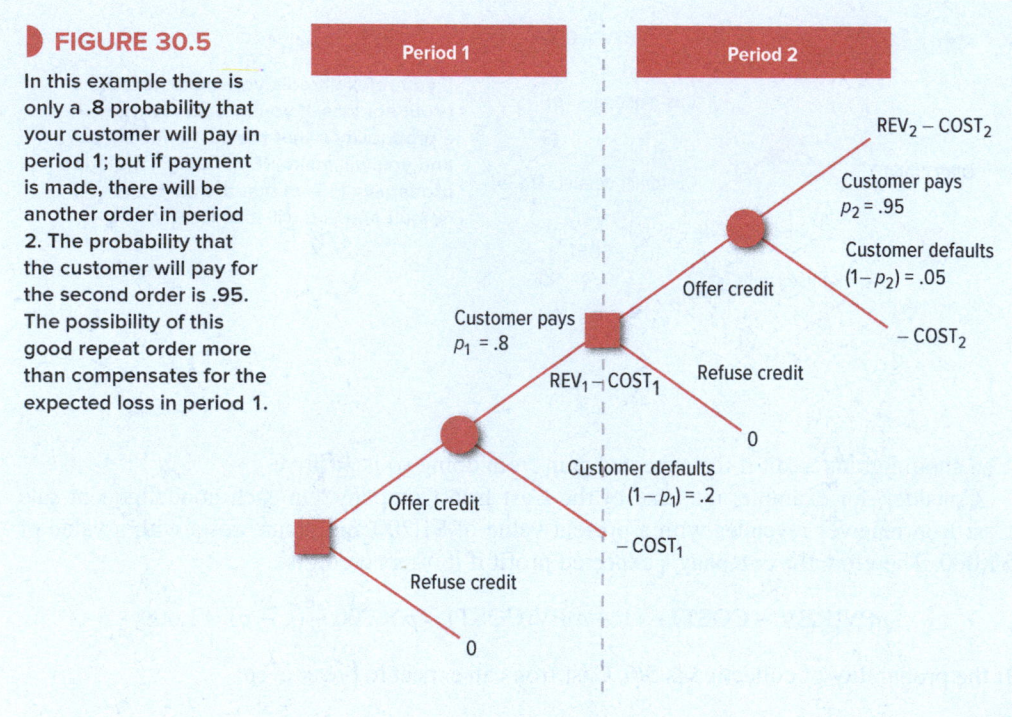

FIGURE 30.5

In this example there is only a .8 probability that your customer will pay in period 1; but if payment is made, there will be another order in period 2. The probability that the customer will pay for the second order is .95. The possibility of this good repeat order more than compensates for the expected loss in period 1.

At any reasonable discount rate, you ought to extend credit. Notice that you should do so even though you expect to take a loss on the initial order. The expected loss is more than outweighed by the possibility that you will secure a reliable and regular customer. Cast Iron is not committed to making further sales to the customer, but by extending credit today, it gains a valuable *option* to do so. It will exercise this option only if the customer demonstrates its creditworthiness by paying promptly.

Of course real-life situations are generally far more complex than our simple Cast Iron examples. Customers are not all good or all bad. Many of them pay consistently late; you get your money, but it costs more to collect and you lose a few months' interest. Then there is the uncertainty about repeat sales. There may be a good chance that the customer will give you further business, but you can't be sure of that and you don't know for how long she will continue to buy.

Like almost all financial decisions, credit allocation involves a strong dose of judgment. Our examples are intended as reminders of the issues involved rather than as cookbook formulas. Here are the basic things to remember.

1. *Maximize profit.* As credit manager, you should not focus on minimizing the number of bad accounts; your job is to maximize expected profit. You must face up to the following facts: The best that can happen is that the customer pays promptly; the worst is default. In the best case, the firm receives the full additional revenues from the sale less the additional costs; in the worst, it receives nothing and loses the costs. You must weigh the chances of these alternative outcomes. If the margin of profit is high, you are justified in a more liberal credit policy; if it is low, you cannot afford many bad debts.[9]

---

[9]Look back at our first Cast Iron example, where we concluded that the company is justified in granting credit if the probability of collection is greater than 5/6. If the customer pays, Cast Iron will earn a profit margin of 200/1200 = 1/6. In other words, the company is justified in granting credit if the probability of payment exceeds 1 − profit margin.

2. *Concentrate on the dangerous accounts.* You should not expend the same effort on analyzing all credit applications. If an application is small or clear-cut, your decision should be largely routine; if it is large or doubtful, you may do better to move straight to a detailed credit appraisal. Most credit managers don't make decisions on an order-by-order basis. Instead, they set a credit limit for each customer. The sales representative is required to refer the order for approval only if the customer exceeds this limit.

3. *Look beyond the immediate order.* The credit decision is a dynamic problem. You cannot look only at the present. Sometimes it may be worth accepting a relatively poor risk as long as there is a good chance that the customer will become a regular and reliable buyer. New businesses must, therefore, be prepared to incur more bad debts than established businesses. This is part of the cost of building a good customer list.

Collection Policy

The final step in credit management is to collect payment. When a customer is in arrears, the usual procedure is to send a statement of account and to follow this at intervals with increasingly insistent letters or telephone calls. If none of these has any effect, most companies turn the debt over to a collection agent or an attorney.

Large firms can reap economies of scale in record keeping, billing, and so on, but the small firm may not be able to support a fully fledged credit operation. However, the small firm may be able to obtain some scale economies by farming out part of the job to a **factor.**

Factoring typically works as follows. The factor and the client agree on a credit limit for each customer. The client then notifies the customer that the factor has purchased the debt. Thereafter, whenever the client makes a sale to an approved customer, it sends a copy of the invoice to the factor, and the customer makes payment directly to the factor. Most commonly the factor does not have any recourse to the client if the customer fails to pay, but sometimes the client assumes the risk of bad debts. There are, of course, costs to factoring, and the factor typically charges a fee of 1% or 2% for administration and a roughly similar sum for assuming the risk of nonpayment. In addition to taking over the task of debt collection, most factoring agreements also provide financing for receivables. In these cases, the factor pays the client 70% to 80% of the value of the invoice in advance at an agreed interest rate. Of course, factoring is not the only way to finance receivables; firms can also raise money by borrowing against their receivables.

Factoring is common in Europe, but in the United States it accounts for only a small proportion of debt collection. It is most common in industries such as clothing and toys. These industries are characterized by many small producers and retailers that do not have long-term relationships. Because a factor may be employed by a number of manufacturers, it sees a larger proportion of the transactions than any single firm, and therefore is better placed to judge the creditworthiness of each customer.[10]

There is always a potential conflict of interest between the collection operation and the sales department. Sales representatives commonly complain that they no sooner win new customers than the collection department frightens them off with threatening letters. The collection manager, on the other hand, bemoans the fact that the sales force is concerned only with winning orders and does not care whether the goods are subsequently paid for.

---

[10]If you don't want help with collection but do want protection against bad debts, you can obtain credit insurance. For example, most governments have established agencies to insure export business. In the United States, this insurance is provided by the Export-Import Bank in association with a group of insurance companies known as the Foreign Credit Insurance Association (FCIA). Banks are much more willing to lend when exports have been insured. (The Export Import Bank's congressional authorization was suspended for part of 2015. As of early 2018, its authorization extends to September 2019.)

There are also many instances of cooperation between the sales force and the collection department. For example, the specialty chemical division of a major pharmaceutical company actually made a business loan to an important customer that had been suddenly cut off by its bank. The pharmaceutical company bet that it knew its customer better than the customer's bank did. The bet paid off. The customer arranged alternative bank financing, paid back the pharmaceutical company, and became an even more loyal customer. It was a nice example of financial management supporting sales.

It is not common for suppliers to make business loans in this way, but they lend money indirectly whenever they allow a delay in payment. Trade credit can be an important source of funds for indigent customers that cannot obtain a bank loan. But that raises an important question: If the bank is unwilling to lend, does it make sense for you, the supplier, to continue to extend trade credit? Here are two possible reasons why it may make sense: First, as in the case of our pharmaceutical company, you may have more information than the bank about the customer's business. Second, you need to look beyond the immediate transaction and recognize that your firm may stand to lose some profitable future sales if the customer goes out of business.[11]

30-4 Cash

In June 2018, Amazon held $16.7 billion in cash and $8.3 billion in short-term securities. Short-term securities pay interest; cash doesn't. So why do firms such as Amazon hold such large amounts of cash? Why don't they arrange for the bank to "sweep" the cash at the end of the day into an interest-bearing investment, such as a money-market mutual fund?

There are at least two reasons. First, cash may be left in non-interest-bearing accounts to compensate banks for the services they provide. Second, large corporations may have literally hundreds of accounts with dozens of different banks. It is often better to leave idle cash in these accounts than to monitor every account every day in order to make daily transfers between them.

One major reason for this proliferation of bank accounts is decentralized management. You cannot give a subsidiary operating autonomy without giving its managers the right to spend and receive cash. Good cash management nevertheless implies some degree of centralization. It is impossible to maintain your desired cash inventory if all the subsidiaries in the group are responsible for their own private pools of cash. And you certainly want to avoid situations in which one subsidiary is investing its spare cash at 5% while another is borrowing at 8%. It is not surprising, therefore, that even in highly decentralized companies there is generally central control over cash balances and bank relations.

How Purchases Are Paid For

Many small, face-to-face purchases are made with paper currency. But you probably would not want to use cash to buy a new car, and you can't use cash to make a purchase over the Internet. There are a variety of ways that you can pay for larger purchases or send payments to another location. Some of the more important ways are set out in Table 30.3.

Look now at Figure 30.6. You can see that there are large differences in the ways that people around the world pay for their purchases. For example, checks are almost unknown in Germany, the Netherlands, and Sweden.[12] Most payments in these countries are by debit card or credit transfer. By contrast, Americans love to write checks. Each year individuals and firms in the United States write about 12 billion checks.

---

[11]For some evidence on the determinants of the supply and demand for trade credit, see M. A. Petersen and R. G. Rajan, "Trade Credit: Theories and Evidence," *Review of Financial Studies* 10 (July 1997), pp. 661–691.

[12]For a discussion of the changing pattern of payment methods, see "Innovations in Retail Payments," Committee on Payment and Settlement Systems, Bank for International Settlements, Basel, Switzerland, May 2012.

❯TABLE 30.3

Check When you write a check, you are instructing your bank to pay a specified sum on demand to the particular firm or person named on the check.
Credit card A credit card, such as a Visa card or MasterCard, gives you a line of credit that allows you to make purchases up to a specified limit. At the end of each month, either you pay the credit card company in full for these purchases or you make a specified minimum payment and are charged interest on the outstanding balance.
Charge card A charge card may look like a credit card and you can spend money with it as with a credit card. But with a charge card, the day of reckoning comes at the end of each month, when you must pay for all purchases that you have made. In other words, you must pay off the entire balance each month.
Debit card A debit card allows you to have your purchases from a store charged directly to your bank account. The deduction is usually made electronically and is immediate. Debit cards may be used to make withdrawals from a cash machine (ATM).
Credit transfer With a credit transfer you ask your bank to set up a standing order to make a regular set payment to a supplier. For example, standing orders are often used to make regular fixed mortgage payments.
Direct payment A direct payment (or debit) is an instruction to your bank to allow a company to collect varying amounts from your account, as long as you have been given advance notice of the amount and date. For example, an electric utility company may ask you to arrange an automatic payment of your electricity bills from your bank account.

Small, face-to-face purchases are commonly paid for with paper currency, but here are some of the other ways to pay your bills

But throughout the world the use of checks is on the decline. For one-off purchases they are being replaced by credit or debit cards. In addition, mobile phone technology and the Internet are encouraging the development of new infant payment systems. For example,

- Electronic bill presentment and payment (or EBPP) allows companies to bill customers and receive payments via the Internet. EBPP is forecasted to grow rapidly.

- Stored-value cards (or e-money) let you transfer cash value to a card that can be used to buy a variety of goods and services. For example, Hong Kong's Octopus card system, which was developed to pay for travel fares, has become a widely used electronic cash system throughout the territory.

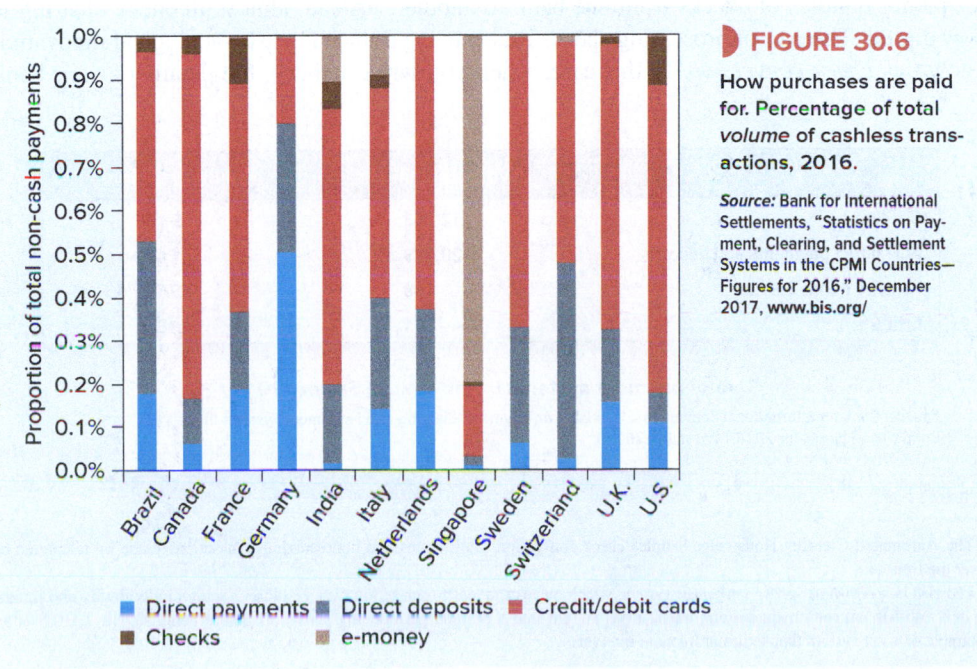

❯ FIGURE 30.6

How purchases are paid for. Percentage of total *volume* of cashless transactions, 2016.

Source: Bank for International Settlements, "Statistics on Payment, Clearing, and Settlement Systems in the CPMI Countries—Figures for 2016," December 2017, www.bis.org/

There are three main ways that firms send and receive money electronically. These are direct payments, direct deposits, and wire transfers.

Recurring expenditures, such as utility bills, mortgage payments, and insurance premiums, are increasingly settled by *direct payment* (also called *automatic debit* or *direct debit*). In this case, the firm's customers simply authorize it to debit their bank account for the amount due. The company provides its bank with a file showing details of each customer, the amount to be debited, and the date. The payment then travels electronically through the **Automated Clearing House (ACH)** system. The firm knows exactly when the cash is coming in and avoids the labor-intensive process of handling thousands of checks.

The ACH system also allows money to flow in the reverse direction. Thus while a *direct payment* transaction provides an automatic debit, a *direct deposit* constitutes an automatic credit. Direct deposits are used to make bulk payments such as wages or dividends. Again the company provides its bank with a file of instructions. The bank then debits the company's account and transfers the cash via the ACH to the bank accounts of the firm's employees or shareholders.

The volume of direct payments and deposits has increased rapidly. You can see from Table 30.4 that the total value of these transactions is over double that of checks.[13]

Large-value payments *between* companies are usually made electronically through Fedwire or CHIPS. Fedwire is operated by the Federal Reserve system and connects more than 6,000 financial institutions to the Fed and, thereby, to each other.[14] CHIPS is a bank-owned system. It mainly handles eurodollar payments and foreign exchange transactions and is used for more than 95% of cross-border payments in dollars. Table 30.4 shows that the *number* of payments by Fedwire and CHIPS is relatively small, but the sums involved are huge.

Speeding Up Check Collections

Although checks are rarely used for large-value payments, they continue to be widely used for smaller nonrecurring transactions. Check handling is a cumbersome and labor-intensive task. However, changes to legislation in the United States at the beginning of the century have helped to reduce costs and speed up collections. The Check Clearing for the 21st Century Act, usually known as Check 21, allows banks to send digital images of checks to one another rather than sending the checks themselves. Thus, cargo planes no longer crisscross the country taking bundles of checks from one bank to another. Instead, almost all check clearing is now digital. The cost of processing checks is also being reduced by a technological innovation known as *check conversion*. In this case, when you write a check, the details of your bank

	Volume (millions)	Value ($ trillions)
Checks	12,263	$ 19
ACH direct payments and deposits	20,329	43
Fedwire Funds Service	148	767
CHIPS	111	364

❯**TABLE 30.4**   Use of payment systems in the United States, 2016

Source: Bank for International Settlements, "Statistics on Payment, Clearing and Settlement Systems in the CPSS Countries—Figures for 2016," December 2017.

---

[13]The Automated Clearing House also handles check conversion transactions and nonrecurring transactions made by telephone or over the Internet.

[14]Fedwire is a *real-time, gross settlement system,* which means that each transaction over Fedwire is settled individually and immediately. With a net settlement system, transactions are put into a pot and periodically netted off before being settled. CHIPS is an example of a net system that settles at frequent intervals.

account and the amount of the payment are automatically captured at the point of sale, your check is handed back to you, and your bank account is immediately debited.

Firms that receive a large volume of checks have devised a number of ways to ensure that the cash becomes available as quickly as possible. For example, a retail chain may arrange for each branch to deposit receipts in a collection account at a local bank. Surplus funds are then periodically transferred electronically to a **concentration account** at one of the company's principal banks. There are two reasons that concentration banking allows the company to gain quicker use of its funds. First, because the store is nearer to the bank, transfer times are reduced. Second, because the customer's check is likely to be drawn on a local bank, the time taken to clear the check is also reduced.

Concentration banking is often combined with a **lockbox system.** In this case, the firm's customers are instructed to send their payments to a regional post-office box. The local bank then takes on the administrative chore of emptying the box and depositing the checks in the company's local deposit account.

International Cash Management

Cash management in domestic firms is child's play compared with cash management in large multinational corporations operating in dozens of countries, each with its own currency, banking system, and legal structure.

A single centralized cash management system is an unattainable ideal for these companies, although they are edging toward it. For example, suppose that you are treasurer of a large multinational company with operations throughout Europe. You could allow the separate businesses to manage their own cash, but that would be costly and would almost certainly result in each one accumulating little hoards of cash. The solution is to set up a regional system. In this case the company establishes a local concentration account with a bank in each country. Any surplus cash is swept daily into a central multicurrency account in London or another European banking center. This cash is then invested in marketable securities or used to finance any plants or subsidiaries that have a cash shortage.

Payments can also be made out of the regional center. For example, to pay wages in each European country, the company just needs to send its principal bank a computer file of the payments to be made. The bank then finds the least costly way to transfer the cash from the company's central accounts and arranges for the cash to be credited on the correct day to the employees in each country.

Rather than actually moving cash between local bank accounts and a regional concentration account, the company may employ a multinational bank with branches in each country and then arrange for the bank to *pool* all the cash surpluses and shortages. In this case no money is transferred between accounts. Instead, the bank just adds together the credit and debit balances, and pays the firm interest on any surplus.

When a company's international branches trade with each other, the number of cross-border transactions can multiply rapidly. Rather than having payments flowing in all directions, the company can set up a netting system. Each branch can then calculate its net position and undertake a single transaction with the netting center. Several industries have set up netting systems for their members. For example, more than 200 airlines have come together to establish a netting system for the foreign currency payments that they must make to each other.

Paying for Bank Services

Much of the work of cash management—processing checks, transferring funds, running lockboxes, helping keep track of the company's accounts—is done by banks. And banks provide many other services not so directly linked to cash management, such as handling payments and receipts in foreign currency, or acting as custodian for securities.

All these services need to be paid for. Usually payment is in the form of a monthly fee, but banks may agree to waive the fee as long as the firm maintains a minimum average balance in an interest-free deposit. Banks are prepared to do this because, after setting aside a portion of the money in a reserve account with the Fed, they can relend the money to earn interest. Demand deposits earmarked to pay for bank services are termed *compensating balances*. They used to be a very common way to pay for bank services, but since banks have been permitted to pay interest on demand deposits, there has been a steady trend away from using compensating balances and toward direct fees.

30-5 Marketable Securities

In December 2017, Apple was sitting on a $285 billion mountain of cash and fixed-income investments, amounting to about 70% of the company's total assets. Of this sum, $9.5 billion was kept as cash and the remainder was invested as follows:

Fixed-Income Investments	Value at Cost ($ billions)
Money market and mutual funds	$ 9.278
U.S. Treasury and agency securities	65.193
Non–U.S. government securities	8.797
Certificates of deposit and time deposits	6.307
Commercial paper	5.384
Corporate securities	156.868
Municipal securities	0.963
Mortgage- and asset-backed securities	22.778
Total	$275.568

Apple's massive investments in securities came from the torrent of free cash flow produced year after year by its operations. But its investments were interesting for at least two further reasons. First, Apple did not limit its investments to short-term securities. For example, it held $129.3 billion in long-term corporate bonds, included under "Corporate securities." Second, U.S. tax law has pushed it to leave most of its investments on the books of its overseas subsidiaries. The 35% U.S. tax rate, which was higher than in most other countries, penalized U.S. corporations that repatriated foreign income. That is no longer the case, as we will soon see.

Tax Strategies

Most countries have *territorial* corporate income taxes: They tax income earned in their own countries but not outside their borders. The United States, on the other hand, has taxed its corporations' *worldwide* income. (The U.S. switched to a territorial tax in 2018—more on that later.) Here is how the U.S. tax system used to work. Suppose that Apple's Irish subsidiary earned profits worth $100,000 in 2017. The subsidiary paid $12,500 at Ireland's 12.5% corporate tax rate. The U.S. rate in 2017 was 35%, one of the highest corporate tax rates in the world, but the Irish tax could be taken as a credit against U.S. tax. So Apple would have to pay an additional U.S. tax of $.35 \times 100,000 - 12,500 = \$22,500$ as soon as its Irish subsidiary sent the profits home. But why pay the extra tax? Why not just leave the money in Ireland? The U.S. tax on foreign income was paid only when income was repatriated.

That is exactly what Apple and other U.S. companies with profits abroad did. [The list of companies with the largest accumulations of overseas profits also includes Microsoft,

Alphabet (Google), Cisco Systems, Pfizer, Abbott Labs, and Johnson & Johnson.] They paid other countries' taxes, almost always at lower rates than 35%, but declined to bring the profits home. The amount of profits left abroad was estimated at more than $2 trillion in 2017.

Starting in 2018, the United States moved to a territorial system with a corporate tax rate reduced to 21%. U.S. corporations are no longer taxed on foreign income and no longer have an incentive to leave profits abroad in low-tax countries. But there is a one-time repatriation tax on profits accumulated abroad through the end of 2017. The tax rate is 15.5% on profits invested in cash and securities and 8% on profits invested in illiquid assets such as plant and equipment. The tax is payable in installments over the eight-year period 2018–2025. So Apple will have to pay tax on its accumulated overseas profits, although at a lower rate than if it had brought the profits home in 2017 or earlier.

In January 2018, Apple responded to the change in the tax law by announcing that it would pay U.S. tax of $38 billion to repatriate $252 billion of profits.

Investment Choices

Most companies do not have the luxury of such huge cash surpluses, but they also park any cash that is not immediately needed in short-term investments. The market for these investments is known as the **money market.** The money market has no physical marketplace. It consists of a loose collection of banks and dealers linked together by telephones or through the Web. But a huge volume of securities is regularly traded on the money market, and competition is vigorous.

Most large corporations manage their own money market investments, but small companies sometimes find it more convenient to hire a professional investment management firm or to put their cash into a money market fund. This is a mutual fund that invests only in low-risk, short-term securities.

The relative safety of money market funds has made them particularly popular at times of financial stress. During the credit crunch of 2008, fund assets mushroomed as investors fled from plunging stock markets. Then it was revealed that one fund, the Reserve Primary Fund, had incurred heavy losses on its holdings of Lehman Brothers' commercial paper. The fund became only the second money market fund in history to "break the buck" by offering just 97 cents on the dollar to investors who cashed in their holdings. That week, investors pulled nearly $200 billion out of money market funds, prompting the government to offer emergency insurance to investors.

Calculating the Yield on Money Market Investments

Many money market investments are pure discount securities. This means that they don't pay interest. The return consists of the difference between the amount you pay and the amount you receive at maturity. Unfortunately, it is no good trying to persuade the Internal Revenue Service that this difference represents capital gain. The IRS is wise to that one and will tax your return as ordinary income.

Interest rates on money market investments are often quoted on a discount basis. For example, suppose that three-month bills are issued at a discount of 5%. This is a rather complicated way of saying that the price of a three-month bill is $100 - (3/12) \times 5 = 98.75$. Therefore, for every $98.75 that you invest today, you receive $100 at the end of three months. The return over three months is $100/98.75 - 1 = .0127$, or 1.27%. This is equivalent to an annual yield of 5.16%. Note that the return is always higher than the discount. When you read that an investment is selling at a discount of 5%, it is very easy to slip into the mistake of thinking that this is its return.[15]

---

[15] To confuse things even more, dealers in the money market often quote rates as if there were only 360 days in a year. So a discount of 5% on a bill maturing in 91 days translates into a price of $100 - 5 \times (91/360) = 98.74\%$.

Returns on Money Market Investments

When we value long-term debt, it is important to take account of default risk. Almost anything may happen in 30 years, and even today's most respectable company may get into trouble eventually. Therefore, corporate bonds offer higher yields than Treasury bonds.

Short-term debt is not risk-free, but generally the danger of default is less for money market securities issued by corporations than for corporate bonds. There are two reasons for this. First, the range of possible outcomes is smaller for short-term investments. Even though the distant future may be clouded, you can usually be confident that a particular company will survive for at least the next month. Second, for the most part, only well-established companies can borrow in the money market. If you are going to lend money for just a few days, you can't afford to spend too much time in evaluating the loan. Thus, you will consider only blue-chip borrowers.

Despite the high quality of money market investments, there are often significant differences in yield between corporate and U.S. government securities. Why is this? One answer is the risk of default. Another is that the investments have different degrees of liquidity or "moneyness." Investors like Treasury bills because they are easily turned into cash on short notice. Securities that cannot be converted so quickly and cheaply into cash need to offer relatively high yields. During times of market turmoil investors may place a particularly high value on having ready access to cash. On these occasions the yield on illiquid securities can increase dramatically.

The International Money Market

In Chapter 24, we pointed out that there are two main markets for dollar bonds. There is the domestic market in the United States, and there is the eurobond market centered in London. There is also an international market for short-term dollar investments, which is known as the *eurodollar* market. Eurodollars have nothing to do with the euro, the currency of the European Monetary Union (EMU). They are simply dollars deposited in a bank in Europe.

Just as there is both a domestic U.S. money market and a eurodollar market, so there is both a domestic Japanese money market and a market in London for euroyen. So, if a U.S. corporation wishes to make a short-term investment in yen, it can deposit the yen with a bank in Tokyo or it can make a euroyen deposit in London. Similarly, there is both a domestic money market in the euro area as well as a money market for euros in London.[16] And so on.

Major international banks in London lend dollars to one another at the *London interbank offered rate* (LIBOR). Similarly, they lend yen to each other at the yen LIBOR interest rate, and they lend euros at the *euro interbank offered rate,* or *Euribor.* These interest rates are used as a benchmark for pricing many types of short-term loans in the United States and in other countries. For example, a corporation in the United States may issue a floating-rate note with interest payments tied to dollar LIBOR.

If we lived in a world without regulation and taxes, the interest rate on a eurodollar loan would have to be the same as the rate on an equivalent domestic dollar loan. However, the international debt markets thrive because governments attempt to regulate domestic bank lending. When the U.S. government limited the rate of interest that banks in the United States could pay on domestic deposits, companies could earn a higher rate of interest by keeping their dollars on deposit in Europe. As these restrictions have been removed, differences in interest rates have largely disappeared.

In the late 1970s, the U.S. government was concerned that its regulations were driving business overseas to foreign banks and the overseas branches of American banks. To attract some of this business back to the States, the government in 1981 allowed U.S. and foreign

---

[16]Occasionally (but only occasionally) referred to as "euroeuros."

banks to establish *international banking facilities (IBFs).* An IBF is the financial equivalent of a free-trade zone; it is physically located in the United States, but it is not required to maintain reserves with the Federal Reserve and depositors are not subject to any U.S. tax.[17] However, there are tight restrictions on what business an IBF can conduct. In particular, it cannot accept deposits from domestic U.S. corporations or make loans to them.

Money Market Instruments

The principal money market instruments are summarized in Table 30.5. We describe each in turn.

U.S. Treasury Bills   The first item in Table 30.5 is U.S. Treasury bills. These are usually issued weekly and mature in four weeks, three months, six months, or one year.[18] Sales are by a uniform-price auction. This means that all successful bidders are allotted bills at the same price.[19] You don't have to participate in the auction to invest in Treasury bills. There is also an excellent secondary market in which billions of dollars of bills are bought and sold every day.

Federal Agency Securities   "Agency securities" is a general term used to describe issues by government agencies and government-sponsored enterprises (GSEs). Although most of this debt is not guaranteed by the U.S. government,[20] investors have generally assumed that the government would step in to prevent a default. That view was reinforced in 2008, when the two giant mortgage companies, the Federal National Mortgage Association (Fannie Mae) and the Federal Home Loan Mortgage Corporation (Freddie Mac) ran into trouble and were taken into government ownership.

Agencies and GSEs borrow both short and long term. The short-term debt consists of discount notes, which are similar to Treasury bills. They are actively traded and often held by corporations. These notes have traditionally offered somewhat higher yields than U.S. Treasuries. One reason is that agency debt is not quite as marketable as Treasury issues. In addition, unless the debt has an explicit government guarantee, investors have demanded an extra return to compensate for the (small?) possibility that the government would allow the agency to default.

Short-Term Tax-Exempts   Short-term notes are also issued by states, municipalities, and agencies such as state universities and school districts.[21] These have one particular attraction—the interest is not subject to federal tax.[22] Of course, this tax advantage of municipal debt is usually recognized in its price. For many years, triple-A municipal debt yielded 10% to 30% less than equivalent Treasury debt.

Most tax-exempt debt is relatively low risk, and is often backed by an insurance policy, which promises to pay out if the municipality is about to default.[23] However, in the turbulent

----

[17]For these reasons, dollars held on deposit in an IBF are classed as eurodollars.

[18]Three-month bills actually mature 91 days after issue, six-month bills mature in 182 days, and one-year bills mature in 364 days. For information on bill auctions, see **www.publicdebt.treas.gov**.

[19]A small proportion of bills is sold to *noncompetitive* bidders. Noncompetitive bids are filled at the same price as the successful competitive bids.

[20]Exceptions are the Government National Mortgage Association (Ginnie Mae), the Small Business Administration, the General Services Administration (GSA), the Farm Credit Financial Assistance Corporation, the Agency for International Development, the Department of Veterans' Affairs (VINNIE MAE), and the Private Export Funding Corporation (PEFCO). Their debts are backed by the "full faith and credit" of the U.S. government.

[21]Some of these notes are *general obligations* of the issuer; others are *revenue securities*, and in these cases, payments are made from rent receipts or other user charges.

[22]This advantage is partly offset by the fact that Treasury securities are free of state and local taxes.

[23]Defaults on tax-exempts have been rare and, for the most part, have involved not-for-profit hospitals. However, there have been a number of major defaults of tax-exempt debt. In 1983, Washington Public Power Supply System (unfortunately known as WPPSS or "WOOPS") defaulted on $2.25 billion of bonds. In 1994, Orange County in California also defaulted after losing $1.7 billion on its investment portfolio. In 2011, Jefferson Country, Alabama, declared bankruptcy with $4.2 billion in municipal debt. The record for municipal bankruptcies is held by Detroit, which filed for bankruptcy in 2013 with $18 to $20 billion of debt.

Investment	Borrower	Maturities When Issued	Marketability	Basis for Calculating Interest	Comments
Treasury bills	U.S. government	4 weeks, 3 months, 6 months, or 1 year	Excellent secondary market	Discount	Auctioned weekly
Government agency and GSE benchmark bills and discount notes	Ginnie Mae, Fannie Mae, Freddie Mac, etc.	Overnight to 360 days	Very good secondary market	Discount	Benchmark bills by regular auction; discount notes sold through dealers
Tax-exempt municipal notes	Municipalities, states, school districts, etc.	3 months to 1 year	Good secondary market	Usually interest-bearing with interest at maturity	Tax-anticipation notes (TANs), revenue anticipation notes (RANs), bond anticipation notes (BANs), etc.
Tax-exempt variable-rate demand notes (VRDNs)	Municipalities, states, state universities, etc.	10 to 40 years	Good secondary market	Variable interest rate	Long-term bonds with put options to demand repayment
Nonnegotiable time deposits and negotiable certificates of deposit (CDs)	Commercial banks, savings and loans	Usually 1 to 3 months; also longer-maturity variable-rate CDs	Fair secondary market for negotiable CDs	Interest-bearing with interest at maturity	Receipt for time deposit
Commercial paper (CP)	Industrial firms, finance companies, and bank holding companies; also municipalities	Maximum 270 days; usually 60 days or less	Dealers or issuer will repurchase paper	Usually discount	Unsecured promissory note; may be placed through dealer or directly with investor
Medium-term notes (MTNs)	Largely finance companies and banks; also industrial firms	Minimum 270 days; usually less than 10 years	Dealers will repurchase notes	Interest-bearing; usually fixed rate	Unsecured promissory note placed through dealer
Bankers' acceptances (BAs)	Major commercial banks	1 to 6 months	Fair secondary market	Discount	Demand to pay that has been accepted by a bank
Repurchase agreements (repos)	Dealers in U.S. government securities	Overnight to about 3 months; also open repos (continuing contracts)	No secondary market	Repurchase price set higher than selling price; difference quoted as repo interest rate	Sales of government securities by dealer with simultaneous agreement to repurchase

❭TABLE 30.5   Money market investments in the United States

markets of 2008 even the backing of an insurance company did little to reassure investors, who worried that the insurers themselves could be in trouble. The tax advantage of "munis" no longer seemed quite so important.

Variable-Rate Demand Notes   There is no law preventing firms from making short-term investments in long-term securities. If a firm has $1 million set aside for an income tax payment, it could buy a long-term bond on January 1 and sell it on April 15, when the taxes must be paid. However, the danger with this strategy is obvious. What happens if bond prices fall by 10% between January and April? There you are with a $1 million liability to the Internal Revenue Service, bonds worth only $900,000, and a very red face. Of course, bond prices could also go up, but why take the chance? Corporate treasurers entrusted with excess funds for short-term investments are naturally averse to the price volatility of long-term bonds.

One solution is to buy municipal variable-rate demand notes (VRDNs). These are long-term securities, whose interest payments are linked to the level of short-term interest rates. Whenever the interest rate is reset, investors have the right to sell the notes back to the issuer for their face value.[24] This ensures that on these reset dates the price of the notes cannot be less than their face value. Therefore, although VRDNs are long-term loans, their prices are very stable. In addition, the interest on municipal debt has the advantage of being tax-exempt. So a municipal variable-rate demand note offers a relatively safe, tax-free, short-term haven for your $1 million of cash.

Bank Time Deposits and Certificates of Deposit   If you make a time deposit with a bank, you are lending money to the bank for a fixed period. If you need the money before maturity, the bank usually allows you to withdraw it but exacts a penalty in the form of a reduced rate of interest.

In the 1960s, banks introduced the **negotiable certificate of deposit (CD)** for time deposits of $1 million or more. In this case, when a bank borrows, it issues a certificate of deposit, which is simply evidence of a time deposit with that bank. If a lender needs the money before maturity, it can sell the CD to another investor. When the loan matures, the new owner of the CD presents it to the bank and receives payment.[25]

Commercial Paper and Medium-Term Notes   As discussed in detail in Chapter 24, these consist of unsecured, short- and medium-term debt issued by companies on a regular basis.

Bankers' Acceptances   We saw earlier in the chapter how bankers' acceptances (BAs) may be used to finance exports or imports. An acceptance begins life as a written demand for the bank to pay a given sum at a future date. Once the bank accepts this demand, it becomes a negotiable security that can be bought or sold through money-market dealers. Acceptances by the large U.S. banks generally mature in one to six months and involve very low credit risk.

Repurchase agreements,   or *repos,* are effectively secured loans that are typically made to a government security dealer. They work as follows: The investor buys part of the dealer's holding of Treasury securities and simultaneously arranges to sell them back again at a later date at a specified higher price.[26] The borrower (the dealer) is said to have entered into a *repo;* the lender (who buys the securities) is said to have a *reverse repo.*

Repos sometimes run for several months, but more frequently, they are just overnight (24-hour) agreements. No other domestic money-market investment offers such liquidity. Corporations can treat overnight repos almost as if they were interest-bearing demand deposits.

Suppose that you decide to invest cash in repos for several days or weeks. You don't want to keep renegotiating agreements every day. One solution is to enter into an *open repo* with a security dealer. In this case, there is no fixed maturity to the agreement; either side is free to withdraw at one day's notice. Alternatively, you may arrange with your bank to transfer any excess cash automatically into repos.

Auction-Rate Preferred Stock   Common stock and preferred stock have an interesting tax advantage for corporations since firms pay tax on only 50% of the dividends that they receive. So, for each $1 of dividends received, the firm gets to keep $1 - (.50 \times .21) = \$.895$. Thus

---

[24]Issuers generally support their borrowing by arranging a backup line of credit with a bank, which ensures that they can find the money to repay the notes.

[25]Some CDs are not negotiable and are simply identical to time deposits. For example, banks may sell low-value nonnegotiable CDs to individuals.

[26]To reduce the risk of repos, it is common to lend less than the market value of the security. This difference is known as a *haircut.*

the effective tax rate is only 10.5%. This is higher than the zero tax rate on the interest from municipal debt but much lower than the 21% rate that the company pays on other debt interest.

Suppose that you consider investing your firm's spare cash in some other corporation's preferred stock. The 10.5% tax rate is very tempting. On the other hand, you worry that the price of the preferred shares may change if long-term interest rates change. You can reduce that worry by investing in preferred shares whose dividend payments are linked to the general level of interest rates.[27]

Varying the dividend payment doesn't quite do the trick because the price of the preferred stock could still fall if the risk increases. So, a number of companies added another wrinkle to floating-rate preferred. Instead of being tied rigidly to interest rates, the dividend can be reset periodically by means of an auction that is open to all investors. Investors can state the yield at which they are prepared to buy the stock. Existing shareholders who require a higher yield simply sell their stock to the new investors at its face value.

Auction-rate preferred stock is similar to a variable-rate demand note except that the issuer is not obliged to buy the stock back. If no new investors turn up at the auction, the existing shareholders are left holding the baby. That is what happened in 2008. Angry shareholders, who were unable to sell their stock, complained that banks had fraudulently marketed the issues as equivalent to cash, and many of the banks that originally handled the issues agreed to buy them back. Auction-rate preferred stock no longer seemed such a safe haven for cash.

---

[27]The company *issuing* preferred stock must pay dividends out of after-tax income. So most tax-paying firms would prefer to issue debt rather than floating-rate preferred. However, there are plenty of firms that are not paying taxes and cannot make use of the interest tax shield. Moreover, they have been able to issue floating-rate preferred at yields *lower* than they would have to pay on a debt issue. The corporations buying the preferreds are happy with these lower yields because 50% of the dividends they receive escape tax.

SUMMARY

This chapter examines the current assets and liabilities on the firm's book balance sheet. The most important current assets are inventories, accounts receivable, cash, and short-term investments. The most important current liabilities are accounts payable and short-term debt, which includes both short-term loans and principal payments on long-term debt coming due in the next 12 months.

Current assets and liabilities constitute the firm's working capital. The difference between current assets and liabilities is its net working capital.

The composition of working capital varies widely across industries. For example, supermarket chains and other retail businesses must keep large inventories on their shelves and at local warehouses. Railroads and trucking companies, on the other hand, transport other companies' inventories but hold little or none of their own.

Some companies rely on short-term debt to help finance inventories and accounts receivable. Most companies also get short-term financing from accounts payable. Accounts payable can be low-cost financing if suppliers do not demand cash on delivery (COD) and the firm pays its bills quickly enough to pocket discounts for prompt payment.

Inventories consist of raw materials, work in process, and finished goods. There are benefits to holding inventories. For example, a stock of raw materials reduces the risk that the firm will be forced to shut down production because of an unexpected shortage. But inventories also tie up capital and are expensive to store. The task of the production manager is to strike a sensible balance between these benefits and costs. In recent years, many companies have decided that they can get by on lower inventories than before. For example, some have adopted *just-in-time* systems that allow the firm to keep inventories to a minimum by receiving a regular flow of components and raw materials throughout the day.

Credit management (the management of receivables) involves five steps:

1. Establish the length of the payment period and the size of any cash discounts for customers who pay promptly.

2. Decide the form of the contract with your customer. For example, if your customer's credit is shaky, you can ask the customer to arrange a banker's acceptance. In this case payment is guaranteed by the customer's bank.

3. Assess your customer's creditworthiness. You can either do your own homework or rely on a credit agency or credit bureau that specializes in gathering information about the credit standing of firms or individuals.

4. Establish sensible credit limits. Remember your aim is not to minimize the number of bad debts, but to maximize profits. Remember also not to be too shortsighted in reckoning the expected profit. It may be worth accepting marginal applicants if there is a chance that they may become regular and reliable customers.

5. Collect. You need to be resolute with the truly delinquent customers, but you do not want to offend the good ones by writing demanding letters just because their check has been delayed in the mail.

Firms need cash on hand to pay suppliers, meet payrolls, buy equipment, pay debt service, and for all the other transactions required to keep a business humming along smoothly. But idle cash earns no interest. Firms therefore establish systems and procedures to transfer excess cash into central accounts at concentration banks. The transfers are almost always made electronically. The central accounts can then provide cash to plants or subsidiaries that will need it. Remaining cash is invested in the money market, perhaps overnight in repurchase transactions or perhaps in securities with maturities of weeks or months. Companies with permanent cash surpluses sometimes also invest in long-term securities. We noted Apple's extensive holdings of long-term corporate debt.

FURTHER READING

Here are some general textbooks on working capital management:

J. S. Sagner, *Working Capital Management: Applications and Case Studies* (New York: John Wiley & Sons, 2014).

J. Zietlow, M. Hill, and T. Maness, *Short-Term Financial Management,* rev. 5th ed., (San Diego, CA: Cognella Publishing, 2016).

A standard text on the practice and institutional background of credit management is:

R. H. Cole and L. Mishler, *Consumer and Business Credit Management,* 11th ed. (New York: McGraw-Hill, 1998).

For a more analytical discussion of credit policy, see:

S. Mian and C. W. Smith, "Extending Trade Credit and Financing Receivables," *Journal of Applied Corporate Finance* 7 (Spring 1994), pp. 75–84.

M. A. Petersen and R. G. Rajan, "Trade Credit: Theories and Evidence," *Review of Financial Studies* 10 (Fall 1997), pp. 661–691.

A useful book on cash management is:

M. Allman-Ward and J. Sagner, *Essentials of Managing Corporate Cash* (New York: Wiley, 2003).

Two readable discussions of why some companies maintain more liquidity than others are:

A. Dittmar, "Corporate Cash Policy and How to Manage It with Stock Repurchases," *Journal of Applied Corporate Finance* 20 (Summer 2008), pp. 22–34.

L. Pinkowitz and R. Williamson, "What Is the Market Value of a Dollar of Corporate Cash?" *Journal of Applied Corporate Finance* 19 (Summer 2007), pp. 75–84.

For descriptions of the money-market and short-term lending opportunities, see:

F. J. Fabozzi, *The Handbook of Fixed Income Securities,* 8th ed. (New York: McGraw-Hill, 2012).

F. J. Fabozzi, S. V. Mann, and M. Choudhry, *The Global Money Markets* (New York: John Wiley, 2002).

Chapter 4 of *U.S. Monetary Policy and Financial Markets,* available on the New York Federal Reserve website, **www.ny.frb.org.**

PROBLEM SETS

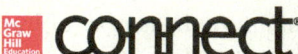

Select problems are available in McGraw-Hill's *Connect*. Please see the preface for more information.

1. **Components of working capital** Take a look at Figure 30.1. Why do food stores hold large inventories? Why do railroads hold small inventories? Why do you think that pharmaceutical companies hold so much cash and securities? Answer briefly.

2. **Components of working capital*** True or false?

   a. Companies with negative net working capital are usually in financial trouble.

   b. Principal payments on long-term debt are shown as current liabilities if due within the next 12 months.

   c. Accounts payable are usually a small fraction of the firm's total liabilities.

   d. Accounts receivable are usually the largest category of current assets.

   e. Less profitable companies typically hold larger cash balances as a precautionary measure.

   f. Well-managed companies invest the majority of their excess cash in short-term securities. They avoid the risks of investing in long-term bonds.

3. **Inventory*** True or false?

   a. Just-in-time inventory systems reduce the cost of managing inventory to zero.

   b. Companies hold larger inventories of finished goods when customer demand fluctuates unpredictably.

   c. Other things equal, higher real interest rates should lead to lower inventories.

   d. Other things equal, lower costs of storage should lead to lower inventories.

4. **Inventory** What are the trade-offs involved in the decision of how much inventory the firm should carry?

5. **Inventory** Central banks pushed short-term interest rates down to extremely low levels in the financial crisis that started in 2008. Some Treasury bill rates in Europe were negative. Other things equal, how would you expect corporations' inventory levels to respond to such a large reduction in interest rates?

6. **Inventory** Take another look at Example 30.1. Suppose a rise in interest rates increases carrying cost per ton from $55 to $75. What is the effect on economic order quantity?

7. **Inventory** Polar Express Railroad keeps a $5 million inventory of spare parts on hand for repairing unexpected breakdowns and equipment failures. The inventory is held in one centralized warehouse at a storage cost of $330,000 per year. The inventory has been financed by a short-term bank loan at 6.5% interest.

   The operations manager has proposed moving the parts from the centralized warehouse to ten storage locations at the hubs of the Polar Express network. The required total inventory would increase to $7 million because some parts would have to be held in inventory at all 10 locations. Storage costs would increase to $600,000 per year. But having the parts at the hubs would save $400,000 per year in the labor cost of repairs. Also repairs would be completed quicker, improving customer service.

Evaluate the operations manager's proposal. Assume the opportunity cost of capital is the interest rate on the bank loan.

8. **Credit terms*** Listed below are some common terms of sale. Can you explain what each means?

   a. 2/30, net 60.

   b. 2/5, EOM, net 30.

   c. COD.

9. **Credit terms** Some of the items in Problem 8 involve a cash discount. For each of these, calculate the rate of interest paid by customers who pay on the due date instead of taking the cash discount.

10. **Credit terms** Phoenix Lambert currently sells its goods cash on delivery. However, the financial manager believes that by offering credit terms of 2/10 net 30 the company can increase sales by 4%, without significant additional costs. If the interest rate is 6% and the profit margin is 5%, would you recommend offering credit? Assume first that all customers take the cash discount. Then assume that they all pay on day 30.

11. **Credit terms** Until recently, Augean Cleaning Products sold its products on terms of net 60, with an average collection period of 75 days. In an attempt to induce customers to pay more promptly, it has changed its terms to 2/10, EOM, net 60. The initial effect of the changed terms is as follows:

	Average Collection Periods (Days)	
Percent of Sales with Cash Discount	**Cash Discount**	**Net**
60	30[a]	80

[a] Some customers deduct the cash discount even though they pay after the specified date.

Calculate the effect of the changed terms. Assume

- Sales volume is unchanged.
- The interest rate is 12%.
- There are no defaults.
- Cost of goods sold is 80% of sales.

12. **Credit terms** Company X sells on a 1/30, net 60 basis. Customer Y buys goods invoiced at $1,000.

   a. How much can Y deduct from the bill if Y pays on day 30?

   b. What is the effective annual rate of interest if Y pays on the due date rather than on day 30?

   c. How would you expect payment terms to change under the following conditions?

      i. The goods are perishable.

      ii. The goods are not rapidly resold.

      iii. The goods are sold to high-risk firms.

13. **Credit policy*** The Branding Iron Company sells its irons for $50 apiece wholesale. Production cost is $40 per iron. There is a 25% chance that wholesaler Q will go bankrupt within the next six months. Q orders 1,000 irons and asks for six months' credit. Should you accept the order? Assume that the discount rate is 10% per year, there is no chance of a repeat order, and Q will pay either in full or not at all.

14. **Credit policy** Look back at Section 30-3. Cast Iron's costs have increased from $1,000 to $1,050. Assuming there is no possibility of repeat orders, answer the following:

    a. When should Cast Iron grant or refuse credit?

    b. If it costs $12 to determine whether a customer has been a prompt or slow payer in the past, when should Cast Iron undertake such a check?

15. **Credit policy** Look back at the discussion in Section 30-3 of credit decisions with repeat orders. If $p_1 = .8$, what is the minimum level of p_2 at which Cast Iron is justified in extending credit?

16. **Credit policy** How should your willingness to grant credit be affected by differences in (a) the profit margin, (b) the interest rate, (c) the probability of repeat orders? In each case, illustrate your answer with a simple example.

17. **Credit policy** As treasurer of the Universal Bed Corporation, Aristotle Procrustes is worried about his bad debt ratio, which is currently running at 6%. He believes that imposing a more stringent credit policy might reduce sales by 5% and reduce the bad debt ratio to 4%. If the cost of goods sold is 80% of the selling price, should Mr. Procrustes adopt the more stringent policy?

18. **Credit policy** Jim Khana, the credit manager of Velcro Saddles, is reappraising the company's credit policy. Velcro sells on terms of net 30. Cost of goods sold is 85% of sales, and fixed costs are a further 5% of sales. Velcro classifies customers on a scale of 1 to 4. During the past five years, the collection experience was as follows:

Classification	Defaults as Percent of Sales	Average Collection Period in Days for Nondefaulting Accounts
1	0	45
2	2.0	42
3	10.0	40
4	20.0	80

    The average interest rate was 15%.

    What conclusions (if any) can you draw about Velcro's credit policy? What other factors should be taken into account before changing this policy?

19. **Credit policy** Look again at the last problem. Suppose (a) that it costs $95 to classify each new credit applicant and (b) that an almost equal proportion of new applicants falls into each of the four categories. In what circumstances should Mr. Khana not bother to undertake a credit check?

20. **Credit management** True or false?

    a. Exporters who require greater certainty of payment arrange for the customers to sign a bill of lading in exchange for a sight draft.

    b. It makes sense to monitor the credit manager's performance by looking at the proportion of bad debts.

    c. If a customer refuses to pay despite repeated reminders, the company usually turns the debt over to a factor or an attorney.

21. **Cash management** Complete the passage that follows by choosing the appropriate terms from the following list: *lockbox banking, Fedwire, CHIPS, concentration banking.*

    Firms can increase their cash resources by speeding up collections. One way to do this is to arrange for payments to be made to regional offices that pay the checks into local banks.

This is known as _____. Surplus funds are then transferred from the local bank to one of the company's main banks. Transfers can be made electronically by the _____ or _____ systems. Another technique is to arrange for a local bank to collect the checks directly from a post office box. This is known as _____.

22. **Cash management*** True or false?

    a. "Money market" refers to the system of electronic cash transfers between corporations and within the banking industry.

    b. The eurodollar market is a market for exchanging dollars for euros or vice versa.

    c. Most large corporations maintain many bank accounts.

    d. Yields quoted on a discount basis are always lower than the true interest rate.

    e. The cost of holding excess cash is lower when interest rates are lower.

23. **Cash management** Knob Inc. is a nationwide distributor of furniture hardware. The company now uses a central billing system for credit sales of $180 million annually. First National, Knob's principal bank, offers to establish a new concentration banking system for a flat fee of $100,000 per year. The bank estimates that mailing and collection time can be reduced by three days. By how much will Knob's cash balances be increased under the new system? How much extra interest income will the new system generate if the extra funds are used to reduce borrowing under Knob's line of credit with First National? Assume that the borrowing rate is 12%. Finally, should Knob accept First National's offer if collection costs under the old system are $40,000 per year?

24. **Lockboxes** Anne Teak, the financial manager of a furniture manufacturer, is considering operating a lockbox system. She forecasts that 300 payments a day will be made to lockboxes with an average payment size of $1,500. The bank's charge for operating the lockboxes is $.40 a check. What reduction in the time to collect and process each check is needed to justify the lockbox system?

25. **Lockboxes** The financial manager of JAC Cosmetics is considering opening a lockbox in Pittsburgh. Checks cleared through the lockbox will amount to $10,000 per day. The lockbox will make cash available to the company three days earlier than is currently the case.

    a. Suppose that the bank offers to run the lockbox for a $20,000 compensating balance. Is the lockbox worthwhile?

    b. Suppose that the bank offers to run the lockbox for a fee of $.10 per check cleared instead of a compensating balance. What must the average check size be for the fee alternative to be less costly? Assume an interest rate of 6% per year.

    c. Why did you need to know the interest rate to answer part (b) but not to answer part (a)?

26. **Payment systems** A parent company settles the collection account balances of its subsidiaries once a week. (That is, each week it transfers any balances in the accounts to a central account.) The cost of a wire transfer is $10. A check costs $.80. Cash transferred by wire is available the same day, but the parent must wait three days for checks to clear. Cash can be invested at 12% per year. How much money must be in a collection account before it pays to use a wire transfer?

27. **Money-market yields** In October 2008, six-month (182-day) Treasury bills were issued at a discount of 1.4%. What was the annual yield?

28. **Money-market yields*** A three-month Treasury bill and a six-month bill both sell at a discount of 10%. Which offers the higher annual yield?

29. **Money-market yields** In Section 30-5, we described a three-month bill that was issued on an annually compounded yield of 5%. Suppose that one month has passed and the investment still offers the same annually compounded return. What is the percentage discount? What was your return over the month?

30. **Money-market yields** Look again at Problem 29. Suppose another month has passed, so the bill has only one month left to run. It is now selling at a discount of 3%. What is the yield? What was your realized return over the two months?

31. **Money-market securities** For each item below, choose the investment that best fits the accompanying description:

    a. Maturity often overnight (repurchase agreements/bankers' acceptances).

    b. Maturity never more than 270 days (tax-exempts/commercial paper).

    c. Issued by the U.S. Treasury (tax-exempts/three-month bills).

    d. Quoted on a discount basis (certificates of deposit/Treasury bills).

    e. Sold by auction (tax-exempts/Treasury bills).

32. **Money-market securities** Consider three securities:

    a. A floating-rate bond.

    b. A preferred share paying a fixed dividend.

    c. A floating-rate preferred.

    If you were responsible for short-term investment of your firm's excess cash, which security would you probably prefer to hold? Could your answer depend on your firm's tax rate? Explain briefly.

33. **Money-market securities** Look up current interest rates offered by short-term investment alternatives. Suppose that your firm has $1 million excess cash to invest for the next two months. How would you invest this cash? How would your answer change if the excess cash were $5,000, $20,000, $100,000, or $100 million?

34. **Tax-exempts** In 2006, agency bonds sold at a yield of 5.32%, while high-grade tax-exempts of comparable maturity offered 3.7% annually. If an investor receives the same *after-tax* return from corporates and tax-exempts, what is that investor's marginal rate of tax? What other factors might affect an investor's choice between the two types of securities?

35. **Taxation**. What is a *territorial* corporate income tax system? How does it differ from the U.S. tax system that was in place before 2018? Explain why the U.S. system in 2017 and earlier forced U.S companies to leave and invest profits abroad.

36. **Tax-exempts** The IRS prohibits companies from borrowing money to buy tax-exempts and deducting the interest payments on the borrowing from taxable income. Should the IRS prohibit such activity? If it didn't, would you advise the company to borrow to buy tax-exempts?

37. **After-tax yields** Suppose you are a wealthy individual paying 37% tax on interest income, 20% on dividends, and zero tax on municipal notes. What is the expected after-tax yield on each of the following investments?

    a. A municipal note yielding 6.5% pretax.

    b. A Treasury bill yielding 8% pretax.

    c. A floating-rate preferred stock yielding 7.5% pretax.

    How would your answer change if the investor is a corporation paying tax at 21%? What other factors would you need to take into account when deciding where to invest the corporation's spare cash?

CHALLENGE

38. **Credit policy** Galenic Inc. is a wholesaler for a range of pharmaceutical products. Before deducting any losses from bad debts, Galenic operates on a profit margin of 5%. For a long time, the firm has employed a numerical credit scoring system based on a small number of key ratios. This has resulted in a bad debt ratio of 1%.

    Galenic recently commissioned a detailed statistical study of the payment record of its customers over the past eight years and, after considerable experimentation, identified five variables that could form the basis of a new credit scoring system. On the evidence of the past eight years, Galenic calculates that for every 10,000 accounts, it would have experienced the following default rates:

	Number of Accounts		
Credit Score under Proposed System	**Defaulting**	**Paying**	**Total**
Greater than 80	60	9,100	9,160
Less than 80	40	800	840
Total	100	9,900	10,000

By refusing credit to firms with a low credit score (less than 80), Galenic calculates that it would reduce its bad debt ratio to 60/9,160, or just under .7%. While this may not seem like a big deal, Galenic's credit manager reasons that this is equivalent to a decrease of one-third in the bad debt ratio and would result in a significant improvement in the profit margin.

a. What is Galenic's current profit margin, allowing for bad debts?

b. Assuming that the firm's estimates of default rates are right, how would the new credit scoring system affect profits?

c. Why might you suspect that Galenic's estimates of default rates will not be realized in practice? What are the likely consequences of overestimating the accuracy of such a credit scoring scheme?

d. Suppose that one of the variables in the proposed scoring system is whether the customer has an existing account with Galenic (new customers are more likely to default). How would this affect your assessment of the proposal?

39. **The cost of capital for current assets** Look again at Problem 7, which asked you to assume that the 6.5% interest rate was the opportunity cost of capital. Was that a reasonable assumption? What should the opportunity cost of capital for inventory depend on? Would it ever make sense to use the firm's overall weighted average cost of capital? What if the inventory was not spare parts for a railroad, but a risky commodity, for example crude oil stocks held as raw material for a petrochemical plant? Discuss and explain.

FINANCE ON THE WEB

1. The three main credit bureaus maintain useful websites with examples of their business and consumer reports. Log on to **www.equifax.com** and look at the sample report on a small business. What information do you think would be most useful if you were considering granting credit to the firm?

2. Log on to the Federal Reserve site at **www.federalreserve.gov** and look up current money market interest rates. Suppose your business has $7 million set aside for an expenditure in three months. How would you choose to invest it in the meantime? Would your decision be different if there were some chance that you might need the money earlier?

31

Mergers

The scale and pace of merger activity in the United States have been remarkable. Table 31.1 lists just a few recent mergers. Notice the high proportion of cross-border mergers between firms in different countries. Look also at Figure 31.1, which shows the number of mergers involving U.S. companies for each year from 1985 to 2017. In 2017, a record year for merger activity, companies were involved in 15,000 deals totaling $1.7 trillion. During such periods of intense merger activity, management spends significant amounts of time either searching for firms to acquire or worrying about whether some other firm will acquire them.

A merger adds value only if the two companies are worth more together than apart. This chapter covers why two companies could be worth more together and how to get the merger deal done if they are. Many marriages between companies are amicable, but sometimes one party is dragged unwillingly to the altar. So we also look at what is involved in hostile takeovers.

Industry	Acquiring Company	Selling Company	Payment ($ billions)
Telecom	AT&T	TimeWarner	$85
Chemicals	Dow Chemical	DuPont	79
Pharmacy/health insurance	CVS Health	Aetna	69
Agrichemicals	Bayer (Germany)	Monsanto	66
Eyewear	Essilor (France)	Luxottica (Italy)	54
Media	Disney	21st Century Fox	52
Tobacco	British American Tobacco (UK)	Reynolds American	49
Agrichemicals	China National Chemical (China)	Syngenta (Switzerland)	43
Semiconductors	Qualcomm	NXP Semiconductors (Holland)	38
Telecom	Comcast	Sky (UK)	31
Pharmaceuticals	Johnson & Johnson	Actelion (Switzerland)	30
Aerospace	United Technologies	Rockwell Collins	30
Food	Keurig Green Mountain	Dr Pepper Snapple	19
Railway transportation equipment	Siemens Mobility Division (Germany)	Alstom (France)	16
Food retailing	Amazon	Whole Foods	14

❯**TABLE 31.1** Some important merger announcements in 2017

Note: Several of these mergers were pending and subject to regulatory approval. In other cases, there may be rival acquirers.

We proceed as follows:

- *Motives.* Sources of value added.

- *Dubious motives.* Don't be tempted.

- *Benefits and costs.* It's important to estimate them consistently.

- *Mechanics.* Legal, tax, and accounting issues.

- *Takeover battles and tactics.* We look at merger tactics and show some of the economic forces driving merger activity.

- *Mergers and the economy.* How can we explain merger waves? Who gains and who loses as a result of mergers?

Mergers are partly about economies from combining two firms, but they are also about who gets to run the company. Pick a merger, and you'll almost always find that one firm is the protagonist and the other is the target. The top management of the target firm usually departs after the merger.

Financial economists now view mergers as part of a broader *market for corporate control*. The activity in this market goes far beyond ordinary mergers. It includes leveraged buyouts (LBOs), spin-offs, and divestitures, as well as nationalizations and privatizations where the government acquires or sells a business. These are the subject of the next chapter.

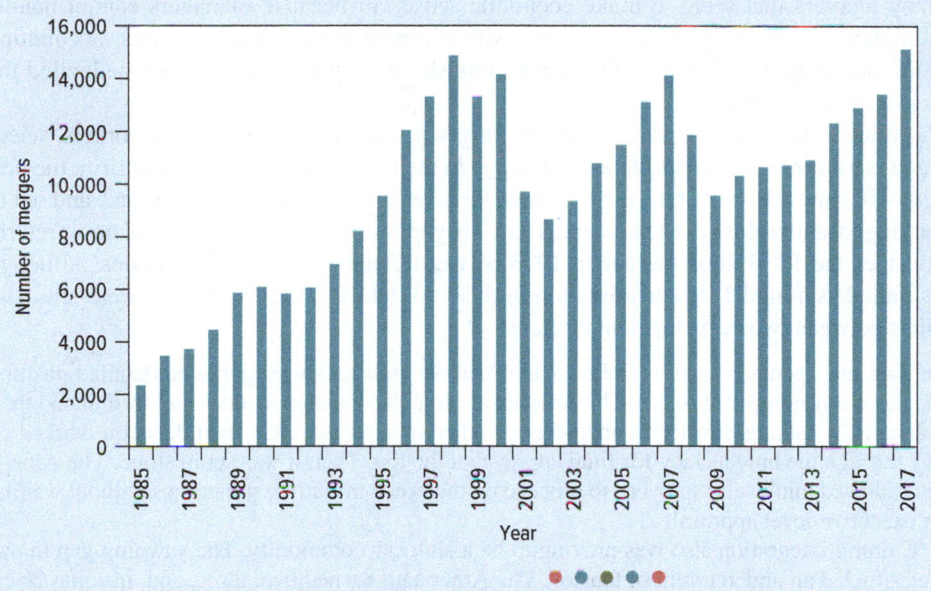

▶ **FIGURE 31.1**

The number of mergers involving U.S. companies, 1985–2017

Source: Institute for Mergers, Acquisitions, and Alliances, https://imaa-institute.org

---

31-1 **Sensible Motives for Mergers**

Mergers can be *horizontal, vertical,* or *conglomerate.* A **horizontal merger** is one that takes place between two firms in the same line of business. Most of the mergers listed in Table 31.1 are horizontal.

A **vertical merger** involves companies at different stages of production. The buyer expands back toward the source of raw materials or forward in the direction of the ultimate consumer. AT&T's acquisition of Time Warner is an example. It has been described as a combination of a "pipe" and a "content" company; it gives AT&T control over the entertainment content that it had previously passed through to its customers.

A **conglomerate merger** involves companies in unrelated lines of businesses. For example, the Indian Tata Group is a huge, widely diversified company. Its acquisitions have been as diverse as Eight O'Clock Coffee, Corus Steel, Jaguar Land Rover, the Ritz Carlton (Boston), and British Salt. No U.S. company is as diversified as Tata, but in the 1960s and 1970s, it was common in the United States for unrelated businesses to merge. Much of the action in the 1980s and 1990s came from breaking up the conglomerates that had been formed 10 to 20 years earlier.

With these distinctions in mind, we are about to consider motives for mergers—that is, reasons two firms may be worth more together than apart. We proceed with some trepidation. The motives, though they often lead the way to real benefits, are sometimes just mirages that tempt unwary or overconfident managers into takeover disasters. This was the case for AOL, which in 2000 spent a record-breaking $156 billion to acquire Time Warner. The aim was to create a company that could offer consumers a comprehensive package of media and information products. It didn't work.

Even more embarrassing was Bank of America's 2008 acquisition of mortgage lender Countrywide for $4 billion. The bank's chief executive hailed the acquisition as a rare chance to become No. 1 in home loans. But after the housing bubble burst, the soured loans made by Countryside ended up costing Bank of America an estimated $40 billion in operating losses, fines, and compensation payments.

Many mergers that seem to make economic sense fail because managers cannot handle the complex task of integrating two firms with different production processes, accounting methods, and corporate cultures. The nearby box shows how these difficulties bedeviled the merger of three Japanese banks.

The value of most businesses depends on *human* assets—managers, skilled workers, scientists, and engineers. If these people are not happy in their new roles in the merged firm, the best of them will leave. Beware of paying too much for assets that go down in the elevator and out to the parking lot at the close of each business day. They may drive into the sunset and never return.

Consider the $38 billion merger in 1998 between Daimler-Benz and Chrysler. Although it was hailed as a model for consolidation in the auto industry, the early years were rife with conflicts between two very different cultures:

> German management-board members had executive assistants who prepared detailed position papers on any number of issues. The Americans didn't have assigned aides and formulated their decisions by talking directly to engineers or other specialists. A German decision worked its way through the bureaucracy for final approval at the top. Then it was set in stone. The Americans allowed midlevel employees to proceed on their own initiative, sometimes without waiting for executive-level approval. . . .
>
> Cultural integration also was proving to be a slippery commodity. The yawning gap in pay scales fueled an undercurrent of tension. The Americans earned two, three, and, in some cases, four times as much as their German counterparts. But the expenses of U.S. workers were tightly controlled compared with the German system. Daimler-side employees thought nothing of flying to Paris or New York for a half-day meeting, then capping the visit with a fancy dinner and a night in an expensive hotel. The Americans blanched at the extravagance.[1]

Nine years after acquiring Chrysler, Daimler threw in the towel and announced that it was offloading an 80% stake in Chrysler to a leveraged-buyout firm, Cerberus Capital Management. Daimler actually paid Cerberus $677 million to take Chrysler off its hands. Cerberus in return assumed about $18 billion in pension and employee health care liabilities and agreed to invest $6 billion in Chrysler and its finance subsidiary.

There are also occasions when the merger does achieve gains but the buyer nevertheless loses because it pays too much. For example, the buyer may overestimate the value of stale inventory or underestimate the costs of renovating old plant and equipment, or it may overlook the warranties on a defective product. Buyers need to be particularly careful about environmental liabilities. If there is pollution from the seller's operations or toxic waste on its property, the costs of cleaning up will probably fall on the buyer.

Now we turn to the possible sources of merger *synergies*—that is, the possible sources of added value.

---

[1] Bill Vlasic, and Bradley A Stertz., "Taken for a Ride," *BusinessWeek*, June 5, 2000. Used with permission of Bloomberg L.P. ©2017. All rights reserved.

Those Elusive Synergies

When three of Japan's largest banks combined to form Mizuho Bank, the result was a bank with assets of $1.5 trillion, more than twice those of the world leader, Deutsche Bank. The name "Mizuho" means "rich rice harvest," and the bank's management forecasted that the merger would yield a rich harvest of synergies. In a message to shareholders, the bank president claimed that the merger would create "a comprehensive financial services group that will surge forward in the 21st century." He predicted that the bank would "lead the new era through cutting-edge comprehensive financial services . . . by exploiting to the fullest extent the Group's enormous strengths, which are backed by a powerful customer base and state-of-the-art financial and information technologies." The cost of putting the banks together was forecasted at ¥130 billion, but management predicted future benefits of ¥466 billion a year.

Within a few months of the announcement, reports began to emerge of squabbles among the three partners. One problem area was IT. Each of the three merging banks had a different supplier for its computer system. At first, it was proposed to use just one of these three systems, but then the banks decided to connect the three different systems together using "relay" computers.

Three years after the initial announcement, the new company opened for business on April 1, 2002. Five days later, computer glitches resulted in a spectacular foul-up. Some 7,000 of the bank's cash machines did not work, 60,000 accounts were debited twice for the same transaction, and millions of bills went unpaid. *The Economist* reported that two weeks later, Tokyo Gas, the biggest gas company, was still missing ¥2.2 billion in payments, and the top telephone company, NTT, which was looking for ¥12.7 billion, was forced to send its customers receipts marked with asterisks in place of figures because it did not know which of about 760,000 bills had been paid.

One of the objectives behind the formation of Mizuho was to exploit economies in its IT systems. The launch fiasco illustrated dramatically that it is easier to predict such merger synergies than to realize them.

Sources: The creation of Mizuho Bank and its launch problems are described in "Undispensable: A Fine Merger Yields One Fine Mess," *The Economist*, April 27, 2002, p. 72; "Big, Bold, but . . .", *Euromoney*, December 2000, pp. 30–35; and "Godzilla Bank," *Forbes*, March 20, 2000, pp. 132–133.

Economies of Scale

Many mergers are intended to reduce costs and achieve economies of scale. For example, when Heinz and Kraft Foods announced plans to merge in 2015, they forecast annual cost savings of $1.5 billion by the end of 2017. These savings would mostly come from economies of scale in the North American market, where there would be opportunities to shut down less efficient manufacturing facilities and reduce labor costs. Also, the larger combined sales would help the company to drive better bargains with retailers and restaurants.[2]

Achieving these *economies of scale* is the natural goal of horizontal mergers. But such economies have been claimed in conglomerate mergers, too. The architects of these mergers have pointed to the economies that come from sharing central services such as office management and accounting, financial control, executive development, and top-level management.[3]

Economies of Vertical Integration

Vertical mergers seek to gain control over the production process by expanding back toward the output of the raw material or forward to the ultimate consumer. One way to achieve this is to merge with a supplier or a customer.

---

[2] See "Analysis of the Kraft-Heinz Merger," *Forbes*, March 30, 2015.

[3] Economies of scale are enjoyed when the average unit cost of production goes down as production increases. One way to achieve economies of scale is to spread fixed costs over a larger volume of production.

Vertical integration facilitates coordination and administration. We illustrate via an extreme example. Think of an airline that does not own any planes. If it schedules a flight from Boston to San Francisco, it sells tickets and then rents a plane for that flight from a separate company. This strategy might work on a small scale, but it would be an administrative nightmare for a major carrier, which would have to coordinate hundreds of rental agreements daily. In view of these difficulties, it is not surprising that all major airlines have integrated backward, away from the consumer, by buying and flying airplanes rather than simply patronizing rent-a-plane companies.

When trying to explain differences in integration, economists often stress the problems that may arise when two business activities are inextricably linked. For example, production of components may require a large investment in highly specialized equipment. Or a smelter may need to be located next to the mine to reduce the costs of transporting the ore. It may be possible in such cases to organize the activities as separate firms operating under a long-term contract. But such a contract can never allow for every conceivable change in the way that the activities may need to interact. Therefore, when two parts of an operation are highly dependent on each other, it often makes sense to combine them within the same vertically integrated firm, which then has control over how the assets should be used.[4]

Nowadays the tide of vertical integration seems to be flowing out. Companies are finding it more efficient to *outsource* the provision of many services and various types of production. For example, back in the 1950s and 1960s, General Motors was deemed to have a cost advantage over its main competitors, Ford and Chrysler, because a greater fraction of the parts used in GM's automobiles were produced in-house. By the 1990s, Ford and Chrysler had the advantage: They could buy the parts cheaper from outside suppliers. This was partly because the outside suppliers tended to use nonunion labor at lower wages. But it also appears that manufacturers have more bargaining power versus independent suppliers than versus a production facility that's part of the corporate family. In 1998 GM decided to spin off Delphi, its automotive parts division, as a separate company. After the spin-off, GM continued to buy parts from Delphi in large volumes, but it negotiated the purchases at arm's length.

Complementary Resources

Many small firms are acquired by large ones that can provide the missing ingredients necessary for the small firms' success. The small firm may have a unique product but lack the engineering and sales organization required to produce and market it on a large scale. The firm could develop engineering and sales talent from scratch, but it may be quicker and cheaper to merge with a firm that already has ample talent. The two firms have *complementary resources*—each has what the other needs—and so it may make sense for them to merge. Also, the merger may open up opportunities that neither firm would pursue otherwise.

In recent years, many of the major pharmaceutical firms have faced the loss of patent protection on their more profitable products and have not had an offsetting pipeline of promising new compounds. This has prompted an increasing number of acquisitions of biotech firms. For example, in 2017 Bristol Myers acquired IFM Therapeutics, a start-up company with two pre-clinical immunotherapy programs. Bristol Myers calculated that IFM's drugs would fit well with its own range of immunotherapy treatments. At the same time, IFM obtained the resources that it needed to bring its products to market.

Surplus Funds

Here's another argument for mergers: Suppose that your firm is in a mature industry. It is generating a substantial amount of cash, but it has few profitable investment opportunities.

---

[4]For example, in 2006 the European Commission challenged Philips's proposed acquisition of Intermagnetics. However, Philips successfully argued that for some years, it had taken over 99% of Intermagnetics output and that the combination of the two companies would facilitate the development of new MRI systems.

Ideally, such a firm should distribute the surplus cash to shareholders by increasing its dividend payment or repurchasing stock. Unfortunately, energetic managers are often reluctant to adopt a policy of shrinking their firm in this way. If the firm is not willing to purchase its own shares, it can instead purchase another company's shares. Firms with a surplus of cash and a shortage of good investment opportunities often turn to mergers *financed by cash* as a way of redeploying their capital.

Some firms have excess cash and do not pay it out to stockholders or redeploy it by wise acquisitions. Such firms often find themselves targeted for takeover by other firms that propose to redeploy the cash for them. During the oil price slump of the early 1980s, many cash-rich oil companies found themselves threatened by takeover. This was not because their cash was a unique asset. The acquirers wanted to capture the companies' cash flow to make sure it was not frittered away on negative-NPV oil exploration projects. We return to this *free-cash-flow* motive for takeovers later in this chapter.

Eliminating Inefficiencies

Cash is not the only asset that can be wasted by poor management. There are always firms with unexploited opportunities to cut costs and increase sales and earnings. Such firms are natural candidates for acquisition by other firms with better management. In some instances, "better management" may simply mean the determination to force painful cuts or realign the company's operations. Notice that the motive for such acquisitions has nothing to do with benefits from combining two firms. Acquisition is simply the mechanism by which a new management team replaces the old one.

A merger is not the only way to improve management, but sometimes it is the only simple and practical way. Managers are naturally reluctant to fire or demote themselves, and stockholders of large public firms do not usually have much *direct* influence on how the firm is run or who runs it.[5]

If this motive for merger is important, one would expect to observe that acquisitions often precede a change in the management of the target firm. This seems to be the case. For example, Martin and McConnell found that the chief executive is four times more likely to be replaced in the year after a takeover than during earlier years.[6] The firms they studied had generally been poor performers; in the four years before acquisition their stock prices had lagged behind those of other firms in the same industry by 15%. Apparently many of these firms fell on bad times and were rescued, or reformed, by merger.

Industry Consolidation

The biggest opportunities to improve efficiency seem to come in industries with too many firms and too much capacity. These conditions can trigger a wave of mergers and acquisitions, which then force companies to cut capacity and employment and release capital for reinvestment elsewhere in the economy. For example, when U.S. defense budgets fell after the end of the Cold War, a round of consolidating takeovers followed in the defense industry. The consolidation was inevitable, but the takeovers accelerated it.

The banking industry is another example. During the financial crisis many banking mergers involved rescues of failing banks by larger and stronger rivals. But most earlier bank mergers involved successful banks that sought to achieve economies of scale. The United States entered the 1980s with far too many banks, largely as a result of outdated restrictions on

---

[5]It is difficult to assemble a large-enough block of stockholders to effectively challenge management and the incumbent board of directors. Stockholders can have enormous indirect influence, however. Their displeasure shows up in the firm's stock price. A low stock price may encourage a takeover bid by another firm.

[6]K. J. Martin and J. J. McConnell, "Corporate Performance, Corporate Takeovers, and Management Turnover," *Journal of Finance* 46 (June 1991), pp. 671–687.

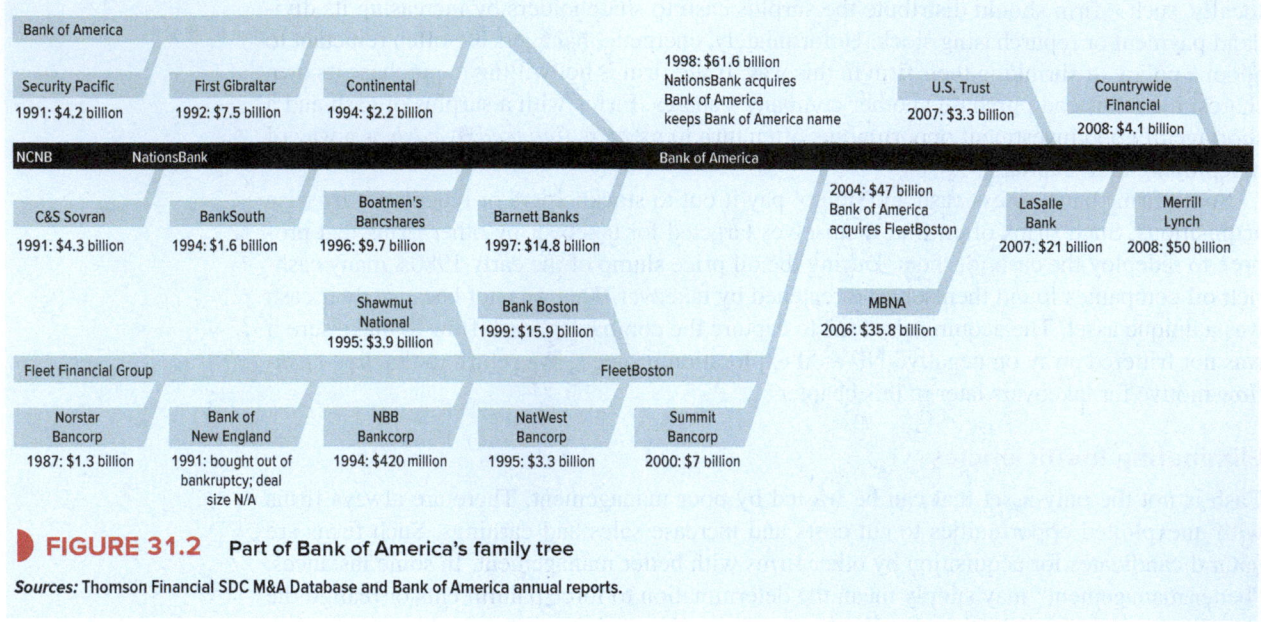

FIGURE 31.2   Part of Bank of America's family tree

Sources: Thomson Financial SDC M&A Database and Bank of America annual reports.

interstate banking. As these restrictions eroded and communications and technology improved, small banks were swept up into regional or "super-regional" banks, and the number of banks declined from over 14,000 to little more than 5,000. For example, look at Figure 31.2, which shows some of the acquisitions by Bank of America and its predecessor companies. The main motive for these mergers was to reduce costs.[7]

Europe also experienced a wave of bank mergers as companies sought to gain the financial muscle to compete in a Europe-wide banking market. These include the mergers of UBS and Swiss Bank Corp (1997), BNP and Banque Paribas (1998), Hypobank and Bayerische Vereinsbank (1998), Banco Santander and Banco Central Hispanico (1999), Unicredit and Capitalia (2007), and Commerzbank and Dresdner Bank (2009).

31-2 Some Dubious Reasons for Mergers

The benefits that we have described so far all make economic sense. Other arguments sometimes given for mergers are dubious. Here are a few of the dubious ones.

Diversification

We have suggested that the managers of a cash-rich company may prefer to see it use that cash for acquisitions rather than distribute it as extra dividends. That is why we often see cash-rich firms in stagnant industries merging their way into fresh woods and pastures new.

What about diversification as an end in itself? It is obvious that diversification reduces risk. Isn't that a gain from merging?

The trouble with this argument is that diversification is easier and cheaper for the stockholder than for the corporation. There is little evidence that investors pay a premium for diversified firms; in fact, as we will explain in Chapter 32, discounts are more common.

---

[7]A study of 41 large bank mergers calculated present values of cost savings averaging 12% of the combined market values of the merging banks. See. J. F. Houston, C. M. James, and M. D. Ryngaert, "Where Do Merger Gains Come From? Bank Mergers from the Perspective of Insiders and Outsiders," *Journal of Financial Economics* 60 (May 2001), pp. 285–331.

The Appendix to this chapter provides a simple proof that corporate diversification does not increase value in perfect markets as long as investors' diversification opportunities are unrestricted. This is the *value-additivity* principle introduced in Chapter 7.

Increasing Earnings per Share: The Bootstrap Game

Some acquisitions that offer no evident economic gains nevertheless produce several years of rising earnings per share. To see how this can happen, let us look at the acquisition of Muck and Slurry by the well-known conglomerate World Enterprises.

The position before the merger is set out in the first two columns of Table 31.2. Because Muck and Slurry has relatively poor growth prospects, its stock's price–earnings ratio is lower than World Enterprises' (line 3). The merger, we assume, produces no economic benefits, and so the firms should be worth exactly the same together as they are apart. The market value of World Enterprises after the merger should be equal to the sum of the separate values of the two firms (line 6).

Since World Enterprises' stock is selling for double the price of Muck and Slurry stock (line 2), World Enterprises can acquire the 100,000 Muck and Slurry shares for 50,000 of its own shares. Thus, World will have 150,000 shares outstanding after the merger.

Total earnings double as a result of the merger (line 5), but the number of shares increases by only 50%. Earnings *per share* rise from $2.00 to $2.67. We call this the *bootstrap effect* because there is no real gain created by the merger and no increase in the two firms' combined value. Since the stock price is unchanged, the price–earnings ratio falls (line 3).

Figure 31.3 illustrates what is going on here. Before the merger $1 invested in World Enterprises bought 5 cents of current earnings and rapid growth prospects. On the other hand, $1 invested in Muck and Slurry bought 10 cents of current earnings but slower growth prospects. If the *total* market value is not altered by the merger, then $1 invested in the merged firm gives 6.7 cents of immediate earnings but slower growth than World Enterprises offered alone. Muck and Slurry shareholders get lower immediate earnings but faster growth. Neither side gains or loses provided everybody understands the deal.

Financial manipulators sometimes try to ensure that the market does *not* understand the deal. Suppose that investors are fooled by the exuberance of the president of World Enterprises and by plans to introduce modern management techniques into its new Earth Sciences Division (formerly known as Muck and Slurry). They could easily mistake the 33% postmerger

	World Enterprises before Merger	Muck and Slurry	World Enterprises after Merger
1. Earnings per share	$2.00	$2.00	$2.67
2. Price per share	$40	$20	$40
3. Price–earnings ratio	20	10	15
4. Number of shares	100,000	100,000	150,000
5. Total earnings	$200,000	$200,000	$400,000
6. Total market value	$4,000,000	$2,000,000	$6,000,000
7. Current earnings per dollar invested in stock (line 1 ÷ line 2)	$0.05	$0.10	$0.067

❯TABLE 31.2   Impact of merger on market value and earnings per share of World Enterprises

Note: When World Enterprises purchases Muck and Slurry, there are no gains. Therefore, total earnings and total market value should be unaffected by the merger. But earnings per share increase. World Enterprises issues only 50,000 of its shares (priced at $40) to acquire the 100,000 Muck and Slurry shares (priced at $20).

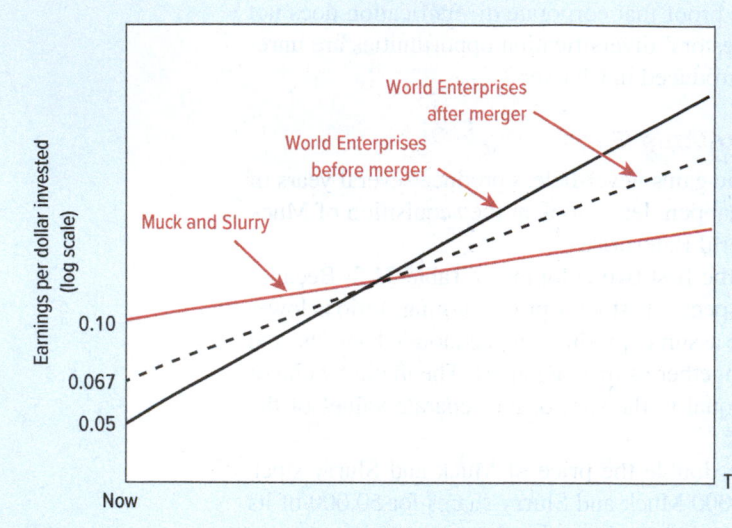

FIGURE 31.3

Effects of merger on earnings growth. By merging with Muck and Slurry, World Enterprises increases current earnings but accepts a slower rate of future growth. Its stockholders should be no better or worse off unless investors are fooled by the bootstrap effect.

Source: S. C. Myers, "A Framework for Evaluating Mergers," in *Modern Developments in Financial Management,* ed. S. C. Myers (New York: Frederick A. Praeger, Inc., 1976), Figure 1, p. 639. Copyright © 1976 Praeger.

increase in earnings per share for real growth. If they do, the price of World Enterprises stock rises and the shareholders of both companies receive something for nothing.

This is a "bootstrap" or "chain letter" game. It generates earnings growth not from capital investment or improved profitability, but from purchase of slowly growing firms with low price–earnings ratios. If this fools investors, the financial manager may be able to puff up stock price artificially. But to keep fooling investors, the firm has to continue to expand by merger *at the same compound rate.* Clearly, this cannot go on forever; one day, expansion must slow down or stop. At this point, earnings growth falls dramatically and the house of cards collapses.

This game is not often played these days, but you may still encounter managers who would rather acquire firms with low price–earnings ratios. Beware of false prophets who suggest that you can appraise mergers just by looking at their immediate impact on earnings per share.

Lower Financing Costs

You often hear it said that a merged firm is able to borrow more cheaply than its separate units could. In part this is true. We have already seen (in Section 15-4) that there are economies of scale in making new issues. Therefore, if firms can make fewer, larger security issues by merging, there are genuine savings.

But when people say that borrowing costs are lower for the merged firm, they usually mean something more than lower issue costs. They mean that when two firms merge, the combined company can borrow at lower interest rates than either firm could separately. This, of course, is exactly what we should expect in a well-functioning bond market. While the two firms are separate, they do not guarantee each other's debt; if one fails, the bondholder cannot ask the other for money. But after the merger, each enterprise effectively does guarantee the other's debt; if one part of the business fails, the bondholders can still take their money out of the other part. Because these mutual guarantees make the debt less risky, lenders demand a lower interest rate.

Does the lower interest rate mean a net gain to the merger? Not necessarily. Compare the following two situations:

- *Separate issues.* Firm A and firm B each make a $50 million bond issue.
- *Single issue.* Firms A and B merge, and the new firm AB makes a single $100 million issue.

Of course AB would pay a lower interest rate, other things being equal. But it does not make sense for A and B to merge just to get that lower rate. Although AB's shareholders do gain from the lower rate, they lose by having to guarantee each other's debt. In other words, they get the lower interest rate only by giving bondholders better protection. There is no *net* gain.

In Section 23-2, we showed that

$$\text{Bond value} = \begin{matrix}\text{Bond value} \\ \text{assuming no} \\ \text{chance of default}\end{matrix} - \begin{matrix}\text{Value of} \\ \text{shareholders's (put)} \\ \text{option to default}\end{matrix}$$

A merger of A and B increases bond value (or reduces the interest payments necessary to support a *given* bond value) only by reducing the value of stockholders' option to default. In other words, the value of the default option for AB's $100 million issue is less than the combined value of the two default options on A's and B's separate $50 million issues.

Now suppose that A and B each borrow $50 million and *then* merge. If the merger is a surprise, it is likely to be a happy one for the bondholders. The bonds they thought were guaranteed by one of the two firms end up guaranteed by both. The stockholders lose in this case because they have given bondholders better protection but have received nothing in exchange.

There is one situation in which mergers can create value by making debt safer. Consider a firm that covets interest tax shields but is reluctant to borrow more because of worries about financial distress. (This is the trade-off theory described in Chapter 18.) Merging decreases the probability of financial distress, other things equal. If it allows increased borrowing, and increased value from the interest tax shields, there can be a net gain to the merger.[8]

31-3   Estimating Merger Gains and Costs

Suppose that you are the financial manager of firm A and you want to analyze the possible purchase of firm B. The first thing to think about is whether there is an *economic gain* from the merger. There is an economic gain *only if the two firms are worth more together than apart*. For example, if you think that the combined firm would be worth PV_{AB} and that the separate firms are worth PV_A and PV_B, then

$$\text{Gain} = PV_{AB} - (PV_A + PV_B) = \Delta PV_{AB}$$

If this gain is positive, there is an economic justification for merger. But you also have to think about the *cost* of acquiring firm B. Take the easy case in which payment is made in cash. Then the cost of acquiring B is equal to the cash payment minus B's value as a separate entity. Thus,

$$\text{Cost} = \text{cash paid} - PV_B$$

The net present value to A of a merger with B is measured by the difference between the gain and the cost. Therefore, you should go ahead with the merger if its net present value, defined as

$$\text{NPV} = \text{gain} - \text{cost}$$
$$= \Delta PV_{AB} - (\text{cash paid} - PV_B)$$

is positive.

---

[8]This merger rationale was first suggested by W. G. Lewellen, "A Pure Financial Rationale for the Conglomerate Merger," *Journal of Finance* 26 (May 1971), pp. 521–537. If you want to see some of the controversy and discussion that this idea led to, look at R. C. Higgins and L. D. Schall, "Corporate Bankruptcy and Conglomerate Merger," *Journal of Finance* 30 (March 1975), pp. 93–113; and D. Galai and R. W. Masulis, "The Option Pricing Model and the Risk Factor of Stock," *Journal of Financial Economics* 3 (January–March 1976), especially pp. 66–69.

We like to write the merger criterion in this way because it focuses attention on two distinct questions. When you estimate the benefit, you concentrate on whether there are any gains to be made from the merger. When you estimate cost, you are concerned with the division of these gains between the two companies.

An example may help make this clear. Firm A has a value of $200 million, and B has a value of $50 million. Merging the two would allow cost savings with a present value of $25 million. This is the gain from the merger. Thus,

$$PV_A = \$200$$
$$PV_B = \$50$$
$$Gain = \Delta PV_{AB} = +\$25$$
$$PV_{AB} = \$275 \text{ million}$$

Suppose that B is bought for cash—say, for $65 million. The cost of the merger is

$$Cost = cash\ paid - PV_B$$
$$= 65 - 50 = \$15 \text{ million}$$

Note that the stockholders of firm B—the people on the other side of the transaction—are ahead by $15 million. *Their* gain is *your* cost. They have captured $15 million of the $25 million merger gain. Thus when we write down the NPV of the merger from A's viewpoint, we are really calculating the part of the gain that A's stockholders get to keep. The NPV to A's stockholders equals the overall gain from the merger less that part of the gain captured by B's stockholders:

$$NPV = 25 - 15 = +\$10 \text{ million}$$

Just as a check, let's confirm that A's stockholders really come out $10 million ahead. They start with a firm worth $PV_A = \$200$ million. They end up with a firm worth $275 million and then have to pay out $65 million to B's stockholders.[9] Thus their net gain is

$$NPV = wealth\ with\ merger - wealth\ without\ merger$$
$$= (PV_{AB} - cash) - PV_A$$
$$= (\$275 - \$65) - \$200 = +\$10 \text{ million}$$

Suppose investors do not anticipate the merger between A and B. The announcement will cause the value of B's stock to rise from $50 million to $65 million, a 30% increase. If investors share management's assessment of the merger gains, the market value of A's stock will increase by $10 million, only a 5% increase.

It makes sense to keep an eye on what investors think the gains from merging are. If A's stock price falls when the deal is announced, then investors are sending the message that the merger benefits are doubtful or that A is paying too much for them.

Right and Wrong Ways to Estimate the Benefits of Mergers

Some companies begin their merger analyses with a forecast of the target firm's future cash flows. Any revenue increases or cost reductions attributable to the merger are included in the forecasts, which are then discounted back to the present and compared with the purchase price:

$$\begin{array}{c} \text{Estimated} \\ \text{net gain} \end{array} = \begin{array}{c} \text{DCF valuation} \\ \text{of target, including} \\ \text{merger benefits} \end{array} - \begin{array}{c} \text{cash required} \\ \text{for acquisition} \end{array}$$

---

[9]We are assuming that PV_A includes enough cash to finance the deal, or that the cash can be borrowed at a market interest rate. Notice that the value to A's stockholders after the deal is done and paid for is $275 − 65 = $210 million—a gain of $10 million.

This is a dangerous procedure. Even the brightest and best-trained analyst can make large errors in valuing a business. The estimated net gain may come up positive not because the merger makes sense but simply because the analyst's cash-flow forecasts are too optimistic. On the other hand, a good merger may not be pursued if the analyst fails to recognize the target's potential as a stand-alone business.

Our procedure *starts* with the target's stand-alone market value (PV_B) and concentrates on the *changes* in cash flow that would result from the merger. *Ask yourself why the two firms should be worth more together than apart.*

The same advice holds when you are contemplating the sale of part of your business. There is no point in saying to yourself, "This is an unprofitable business and should be sold." Unless the buyer can run the business better than you can, the price you receive will reflect the poor prospects.

Sometimes you may come across managers who believe that there are simple rules for identifying good acquisitions. They may say, for example, that they always try to buy into growth industries or that they have a policy of acquiring companies that are selling below book value. But our comments in Chapter 11 about the characteristics of a good investment decision also hold true when you are buying a whole company. *You add value only if you can generate additional economic rents*—some competitive edge that other firms can't match and the target firm's managers can't achieve on their own.

One final piece of horse sense: Often, two companies bid against each other to acquire the same target firm. In effect, the target firm puts itself up for auction. In such cases, ask yourself whether the target is worth more to you than to the other bidder. If the answer is no, you should be cautious about getting into a bidding contest. Winning such a contest may be more expensive than losing it. If you lose, you have simply wasted your time; if you win, you have probably paid too much.

More on Estimating Costs—What If the Target's Stock Price Anticipates the Merger?

The cost of a merger is the premium that the buyer pays over the seller's stand-alone value. How can that value be determined? If the target is a public company, you can start with its market value; just observe price per share and multiply by the number of shares outstanding. But bear in mind that if investors *expect* A to acquire B, or if they expect *somebody* to acquire B, the market value of B may overstate its stand-alone value.

This is one of the few places in this book where we draw an important distinction between market value (MV) and the true, or "intrinsic," value (PV) of the firm as a separate entity. The problem here is not that the market value of B is wrong but that it may not be the value of firm B as a separate entity. Potential investors in B's stock will see two possible outcomes and two possible values:

Outcome	Market Value of B's Stock
1. No merger	PV_B: Value of B as a separate firm
2. Merger occurs	PV_B *plus* some part of the benefits of the merger

If the second outcome is possible, MV_B, the stock market value we observe for B, will overstate PV_B. This is exactly what should happen in a competitive capital market. Unfortunately, it complicates the task of a financial manager who is evaluating a merger.

Here is an example: Suppose that just before A and B's merger announcement we observe the following:

	Firm A	Firm B
Market price per share	$200	$100
Number of shares	1,000,000	500,000
Market value of firm	$200 million	$50 million

Firm A intends to pay $65 million cash for B. If B's market price reflects only its value as a separate entity, then

$$\text{Cost} = (\text{cash paid} - PV_B)$$
$$= (65 - 50) = \$15 \text{ million}$$

However, suppose that B's share price has *already* risen by $12 because of rumors that B might get a favorable merger offer. That means that its intrinsic value is overstated by $12 \times 500,000 = \$6$ million. Its true value, PV_B, is only $44 million. Then

$$\text{Cost} = (65 - 44) = \$21 \text{ million}$$

Since the merger gain is $25 million, this deal still makes A's stockholders better off, but B's stockholders are now capturing the lion's share of the gain.

Notice that if the market made a mistake, and the market value of B was *less* than B's true value as a separate entity, the cost could be negative. In other words, B would be a *bargain* and the merger would be worthwhile from A's point of view, even if the two firms were worth no more together than apart. Of course, A's stockholders' gain would be B's stockholders' loss because B would be sold for less than its true value.

Firms have made acquisitions just because their managers believed they had spotted a company whose intrinsic value was not fully appreciated by the stock market. However, we know from the evidence on market efficiency that "cheap" stocks often turn out to be expensive. It is not easy for outsiders, whether investors or managers, to find firms that are truly undervalued by the market. Moreover, if the shares are really bargain-priced, A doesn't need a merger to profit by its special knowledge. It can just buy up B's shares on the open market and hold them passively, waiting for other investors to wake up to B's true value.

If firm A is wise, it will not go ahead with a merger if the cost exceeds the gain. Firm B will not consent if A's gain is so big that B loses. This gives us a range of possible cash payments that would allow the merger to take place. Whether the payment is at the top or the bottom of this range depends on the relative bargaining power of the two participants.

Estimating Cost When the Merger Is Financed by Stock

Many mergers involve payment wholly or partly in the form of the acquirer's stock. When a merger is financed by stock, cost depends on the value of the shares in the new company received by the shareholders of the selling company. If the sellers receive N shares, each worth P_{AB}, the cost is

$$\text{Cost} = N \times P_{AB} - PV_B$$

Just be sure to use the price per share *after the merger is announced* and its benefits are appreciated by investors.

Suppose that A offers 325,000 (.325 million) shares instead of $65 million in cash. A's share price before the deal is announced is $200. If B is worth $50 million stand-alone,[10] the cost of the merger *appears* to be

$$\text{Apparent cost} = .325 \times 200 - 50 = \$15 \text{ million}$$

However, the apparent cost may not be the true cost. A's stock price is $200 before the merger announcement. At the announcement it ought to go up.

Given the gain and the terms of the deal, we can calculate share prices and market values after the deal. The new firm will have 1.325 million shares outstanding and will be worth $275 million.[11] The new share price is 275/1.325 = $207.55. The true cost is

$$\text{Cost} = .325 \times 207.55 - 50 = \$17.45 \text{ million}$$

This cost can also be calculated by figuring out the gain to B's shareholders. They end up with .325 million shares, or 24.5% of the new firm AB. Their gain is

$$.245(275) - 50 = \$17.45 \text{ million}$$

In general, if B's shareholders are given the fraction x of the combined firms,

$$\text{Cost} = x\,\text{PV}_{AB} - \text{PV}_{B}$$

We can now understand the first key distinction between cash and stock as financing instruments. If cash is offered, the cost of the merger is unaffected by the merger gains. If stock is offered, the cost depends on the gains because the gains show up in the postmerger share price.

Stock financing mitigates the effect of overvaluation or undervaluation of either firm. Suppose, for example, that A overestimates B's value as a separate entity, perhaps because it has overlooked some hidden liability. Thus, A makes too generous an offer. Other things being equal, A's stockholders are better off if it is a stock offer rather than a cash offer. With a stock offer, the inevitable bad news about B's value will fall partly on the shoulders of B's stockholders.

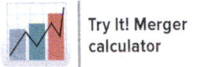

BEYOND THE PAGE

Try It! Merger calculator

mhhe.com/brealey13e

Asymmetric Information

There is a second key difference between cash and stock financing for mergers. A's managers will usually have access to information about A's prospects that is not available to outsiders. Economists call this *asymmetric information*.

Suppose A's managers are more optimistic than outside investors. They may think that A's shares will really be worth $215 after the merger, $7.45 higher than the $207.55 market price we just calculated. If they are right, the true cost of a stock-financed merger with B is

$$\text{Cost} = .325 \times 215 - 50 = \$19.88$$

B's shareholders would get a "free gift" of $7.45 for every A share they receive—an extra gain of $7.45 × .325 = 2.42, that is, $2.42 million.

---

[10]In this case, we assume that B's stock price has *not* risen on merger rumors and accurately reflects B's stand-alone value.
[11]In this case, no cash is leaving the firm to finance the merger. In our example of a cash offer, $65 million would be paid out to B's stockholders, leaving the final value of the firm at 275 − 65 = $210 million. There would only be one million shares outstanding, so share price would be $210. The cash deal is better for A's shareholders in this example.

Of course, if A's managers were really this optimistic, they would strongly prefer to finance the merger with cash. Financing with stock would be favored by *pessimistic* managers who think their company's shares are *over*valued.

Does this sound like "win-win" for A—just issue shares when overvalued, cash otherwise? No, it's not that easy, because B's shareholders, and outside investors generally, understand what's going on. Suppose you are negotiating on behalf of B. You find that A's managers keep suggesting stock rather than cash financing. You quickly infer that A's managers are pessimistic, mark down your own opinion of what the shares are worth, and drive a harder bargain.

This asymmetric-information story explains why the share prices of buying firms generally fall when stock-financed mergers are announced.[12] Andrade, Mitchell, and Stafford found an average market-adjusted fall of 1.5% on the announcement of stock-financed mergers between 1973 and 1998. There was a small *gain* (.4%) for a sample of cash-financed deals.[13]

31-4   The Mechanics of a Merger

Buying a company is a much more complicated affair than buying a piece of machinery. Thus we should look at some of the problems encountered in arranging mergers. In practice, these arrangements are often *extremely* complex, and specialists must be consulted. We are not trying to replace those specialists; we simply want to alert you to the kinds of legal, tax, and accounting issues that they deal with.

Mergers, Antitrust Law, and Popular Opposition

Mergers can get bogged down in the federal antitrust laws. The most important statute here is the Clayton Act of 1914, which forbids an acquisition whenever "in any line of commerce or in any section of the country" the effect "*may be* substantially to lessen competition, or to *tend* to create a monopoly."

Antitrust law can be enforced by the federal government in either of two ways: by a civil suit brought by the Justice Department or by a proceeding initiated by the Federal Trade Commission (FTC).[14] The Hart–Scott–Rodino Antitrust Act of 1976 requires that these agencies be informed of all acquisitions of stock greater than about $75 million. Thus, almost all large mergers are reviewed at an early stage.[15] Both the Justice Department and the FTC then have the right to seek injunctions delaying a merger. An injunction is often enough to scupper the companies' plans. For example, when Halliburton proposed a $28 billion acquisition of Baker Hughes in 2014, the Justice Department filed a lawsuit to block the merger. The companies tried to deal with the Department's objections by selling off various business lines to other players. But by 2016 it had become obvious that they could not assuage concerns that the merger would create too much market power, and the companies scrapped their merger plan.

Companies that do business outside the United States also have to worry about foreign antitrust laws. For example, GE's $46 billion takeover bid for Honeywell was blocked by the European Commission, which argued that the combined company would have too much power in the aircraft industry.

---

[12]The same reasoning applies to stock issues. See Sections 15-4 and 18-4.

[13]See G. Andrade, M. Mitchell, and E. Stafford, "New Evidence and Perspectives on Mergers," *Journal of Economic Perspectives* 15 (Spring 2001), pp. 103–120. This result confirms earlier work, including N. Travlos, "Corporate Takeover Bids, Methods of Payment, and Bidding Firms' Stock Returns," *Journal of Finance* 42 (September 1987), pp. 943–963; and J. R. Franks, R. S. Harris, and S. Titman, "The Postmerger Share-Price Performance of Acquiring Firms," *Journal of Financial Economics* 29 (March 1991), pp. 81–96.

[14]Competitors or third parties who think they will be injured by the merger can also bring antitrust suits.

[15]The target has to be notified also, and it in turn informs investors. Thus the Hart–Scott–Rodino Act effectively forces an acquiring company to "go public" with its bid.

Sometimes trustbusters will object to a merger, but then relent if the companies agree to divest certain assets and operations. For example, when Dow Chemical and DuPont announced plans to merge, the Justice Department required the companies to sell parts of their crop-protection business and two petrochemical plants.

Mergers may also be stymied by political pressures and popular resentment even when no formal antitrust issues arise. In recent years national governments in Europe have become involved in almost all high-profile cross-border mergers and are likely to intervene actively in any hostile bid. For example, the news in 2005 that PepsiCo might bid for Danone aroused considerable hostility in France. The prime minister added his support to opponents of the merger and announced that the French government was drawing up a list of strategic industries that should be protected from foreign ownership. It was unclear whether yogurt production would be one of these strategic industries.

Economic nationalism is not confined to Europe. In 2006, Congress voiced its opposition to the takeover of Britain's P&O by the Dubai company DP World. The acquisition went ahead only after P&O's ports in the United States were excluded from the deal. In 2018, the United States blocked Singapore-based Broadcom's takeover bid for the U.S. chipmaker Qualcomm. The U.S. government cited "national security concerns" about giving a foreign entity access to U.S. technology.

The Form of Acquisition

Suppose you are confident that the purchase of company B will not be challenged on antitrust grounds. Next you will want to consider the form of the acquisition.

One possibility is literally to *merge* the two companies, in which case one company automatically assumes *all* the assets and *all* the liabilities of the other. Such a merger must have the approval of at least 50% of the stockholders of each firm.[16]

An alternative is simply to buy the seller's stock in exchange for cash, shares, or other securities. In this case the buyer can deal individually with the shareholders of the selling company. The seller's managers may not be involved at all. Their approval and cooperation are generally sought, but if they resist, the buyer will attempt to acquire an effective majority of the outstanding shares. If successful, the buyer has control and can complete the merger and, if necessary, toss out the incumbent management.

The third approach is to buy some or all of the seller's assets. In this case, ownership of the assets needs to be transferred, and payment is made to the selling firm rather than directly to its stockholders.

Merger Accounting

When one company buys another, its management worries about how the purchase will show up in its financial statements. Before 2001, the company had a choice of accounting method, but in that year, the Financial Accounting Standards Board (FASB) introduced new rules that required the buyer to use the *purchase method* of merger accounting. This is illustrated in Table 31.3, which shows what happens when A Corporation buys B Corporation, leading to the new AB Corporation. The two firms' initial balance sheets are shown at the top of the table. Below this we show what happens to the balance sheet when the two firms merge. We assume that B Corporation has been purchased for $18 million, 180% of book value.

Why did A Corporation pay an $8 million premium over B's book value? There are two possible reasons. First, the true values of B's *tangible assets*—its working capital, plant, and equipment—may be greater than $10 million. We will assume that this is *not* the reason; that is, we assume that the assets listed on its balance sheet are valued there

---

[16]Corporate charters and state laws sometimes specify a higher percentage.

Balance Sheet of A Corporation			
NWC	20	30	D
FA	80	70	E
	100	100	

Balance Sheet of B Corporation			
NWC	1	0	D
FA	9	10	E
	10	10	

Balance Sheet of AB Corporation			
NWC	21	30	D
FA	89	88	E
Goodwill	8		
	118	118	

❭TABLE 31.3

Accounting for the merger of A Corporation and B Corporation assuming that A Corporation pays $18 million for B Corporation (figures in $ millions)

Key: NWC = net working capital; FA = net book value of fixed assets; D = debt; E = book value of equity.

correctly.[17] Second, A Corporation may be paying for an *intangible asset* that is not listed on B Corporation's balance sheet. For example, the intangible asset may be a promising product or technology. Or it may be no more than B Corporation's share of the expected economic gains from the merger.

A Corporation is buying an asset worth $18 million. The problem is to show that asset on the left-hand side of AB Corporation's balance sheet. B Corporation's tangible assets are worth only $10 million. This leaves $8 million. Under the purchase method, the accountant takes care of this by creating a new asset category called *goodwill* and assigning $8 million to it.[18] As long as the goodwill continues to be worth at least $8 million, it stays on the balance sheet and the company's earnings are unaffected.[19] However, the company is obliged each year to estimate the fair value of the goodwill. If the estimated value ever falls below $8 million, the goodwill is "impaired" and the amount shown on the balance sheet must be adjusted downward and the write-off deducted from that year's earnings. Some companies have found that this can make a nasty dent in profits. For example, when the new accounting rules were introduced, AOL was obliged to write down the value of its assets by $54 billion.

Some Tax Considerations

An acquisition may be either taxable or tax-free. If payment is in the form of cash, the acquisition is regarded as taxable. In this case the selling stockholders are treated as having *sold* their shares, and they must pay tax on any capital gains. If payment is largely in the form of shares, the acquisition is tax-free and the shareholders are viewed as *exchanging* their old shares for similar new ones; no capital gains or losses are recognized.

The tax status of the acquisition also affects the taxes paid by the merged firm afterward. After a tax-free acquisition, the merged firm is taxed as if the two firms had always been together. In a taxable acquisition, the assets of the selling firm are revalued, the resulting write-up or write-down is treated as a taxable gain or loss, and tax depreciation is recalculated on the basis of the restated asset values.

A very simple example will illustrate these distinctions. In 2008, Captain B forms Seacorp, which purchases a fishing boat for $300,000. Assume, for simplicity, that the boat is depreciated for tax purposes over 20 years on a straight-line basis (no salvage value). Thus,

---

[17]If B's tangible assets are worth more than their previous book values, they would be reappraised and their current values entered on AB Corporation's balance sheet.

[18]If part of the $8 million consisted of payment for identifiable intangible assets such as patents, the accountant would place these under a separate category of assets. Identifiable intangible assets that have a finite life need to be written off over their life.

[19]Goodwill is depreciated for tax purposes, however.

	Taxable Merger	Tax-Free Merger
Impact on Captain B	Captain B must recognize a $30,000 capital gain.	Capital gain can be deferred until Captain B sells the Baycorp shares.
Impact on Baycorp	Boat is revalued at $280,000. Tax depreciation increases to $280,000/10 = $28,000 per year (assuming 10 years of remaining life).	Boat's value remains at $150,000, and tax depreciation continues at $15,000 per year.

>**TABLE 31.4**   Possible tax consequences when Baycorp buys Seacorp for $330,000. Captain B's original investment in Seacorp was $300,000. Just before the merger Seacorp's assets were $50,000 of marketable securities and one boat with a book value of $150,000 but a market value of $280,000.

annual depreciation is $300,000/20 = $15,000, and in 2018, the boat has a net book value of $150,000. But Captain B finds that, owing to careful maintenance, inflation, and good times in the local fishing industry, the boat is really worth $280,000. In addition, Seacorp holds $50,000 of marketable securities.

Now suppose that Captain B sells the firm to Baycorp for $330,000. The possible tax consequences of the acquisition are shown in Table 31.4. In this case, Captain B may ask for a tax-free deal to defer capital gains tax. But Baycorp can afford to pay more in a taxable deal because depreciation tax shields are larger.

Cross-Border Mergers and Tax Inversion

In 2013, the U.S pharmaceutical company Actavis took over Warner-Chilcott of Ireland. As part of the deal, the company announced that it would reincorporate in Ireland, where the corporate tax rate is 12.5%–much lower than the combined U.S. federal and state corporate tax rate at that time. One year later, the company acquired Forest Labs, which, as a result, also changed its headquarters to Ireland.

Both deals were examples of *tax inversion*. Before 2018, the United States taxed profits of U.S. corporations even if the profits were earned overseas.[20] Other countries had a territorial system and taxed only profits that were earned domestically. Therefore, when a U.S. corporation relocated abroad because of a merger, it still needed to pay U.S. tax on its U.S. profits, but it no longer paid U.S. tax on profits earned elsewhere. Since the corporate tax rate in the United States was much higher than in most other developed countries, there was a strong incentive for U.S. companies to move their domicile abroad. One way to do this was to arrange to be acquired by a foreign company.

Starting in 2018, the United States switched over to a territorial tax system. As a result, tax is paid on income earned in the United States but not on overseas income. Therefore, the incentive to change the company's domicile by merger has disappeared.[21]

31-5   **Proxy Fights, Takeovers, and the Market for Corporate Control**

The shareholders are the owners of the firm. But most shareholders do not feel like the boss, and with good reason. Try buying one share of IBM stock and marching into the boardroom for a chat with your employee, the CEO. (However, if you own 50 million IBM shares, the CEO will travel to see you.)

---

[20]But the U.S. tax on foreign profits was not paid until the profits were brought home. Therefore, the tax could be postponed by reinvesting outside the United States Many large U.S. companies accumulated "cash mountains" overseas. See Section 30-5.
[21]See Sections 6-2 and 30-5 for descriptions of the main provisions of the 2017 Tax Cuts and Jobs Act.

The *ownership* and *management* of large corporations are separated. Shareholders elect the board of directors but have little direct say in most management decisions. Agency costs arise when managers or directors are tempted to make decisions that are not in the shareholders' interests.

As we pointed out in Chapter 1, there are many forces and constraints working to keep managers' and shareholders' interests in line. But what can be done to ensure that the board has engaged the most talented managers? What happens if managers are inadequate? What if the board is derelict in monitoring the performance of managers? Or what if the firm's managers are fine but the resources of the firm could be used more efficiently by merging with another firm? Can we count on managers to pursue policies that might put them out of a job?

These are all questions about the *market for corporate control,* the mechanisms by which firms are matched up with owners and management teams who can make the most of the firm's resources. You should not take a firm's current ownership and management for granted. If it is possible for the value of the firm to be enhanced by changing management or by reorganizing under new owners, there will be incentives for someone to make the change.

There are three ways to change the management of a firm: (1) a successful proxy contest in which a group of shareholders votes in a new board of directors who then pick a new management team, (2) a takeover of one company by another, and (3) a leveraged buyout of the firm by a private group of investors. We focus here on the first two methods and postpone discussion of buyouts until the next chapter.

Proxy Contests

Shareholders elect the board of directors to keep watch on management and replace unsatisfactory managers. If the board is lax, shareholders are free to elect a different board.

When a group of investors believes that the board and its management should be replaced, they can launch a proxy contest at the next annual meeting. A *proxy* is the right to vote another shareholder's shares. In a proxy contest, the dissident shareholders attempt to obtain enough proxies to elect their own slate to the board of directors. Once the new board is in control, management can be replaced and company policy changed. A proxy fight is therefore a direct contest for control of the corporation. Many proxy fights are initiated by major shareholders who consider the firm poorly managed. In other cases a fight may be a prelude to the merger of two firms. The proponent of the merger may believe that a new board will better appreciate the advantages of combining the two firms.

Proxy contests are expensive and difficult to win. Dissidents who engage in proxy fights must use their own money, but management can use the corporation's funds and lines of communications with shareholders to defend itself. To level the playing field somewhat, the SEC has introduced new rules to make it easier to mount a proxy fight.

Institutional shareholders, such as large hedge funds, have become more aggressive in pressing for managerial accountability and have been able to gain concessions by initiating proxy fights. For example, in 2017, hedge fund manager Nelson Peltz sought to persuade Procter & Gamble to make changes to its corporate structure and its brand policy. After failing to persuade management to offer him a board seat, he launched a proxy battle. The contest cost the two sides a reported $60 million and resulted in a victory for Peltz by a margin of .002%. Peltz believed that as a board member, he would be better placed to secure reforms.

Takeovers

The alternative to a proxy fight is for the would-be acquirer to make a *tender offer* directly to the shareholders. If the offer is successful, the new owner is free to make any management changes. The management of the target firm may advise its shareholders to accept the offer, or it may fight the bid in the hope that the acquirer will either raise its offer or throw in the towel.

In the United States, the rules for tender offers are set largely by the Williams Act of 1968 and by state laws. The Williams Act obliges firms that own 5% or more of another company's shares to tip their hand by reporting their holding to the SEC and to outline their intentions in a Schedule 13(d) filing. This filing is often an invitation for other bidders to enter the fray and to force up the takeover premium. The consolation for the initial bidder is that if its bid is ultimately unsuccessful, it may be able to sell off its holding in the target at a substantial profit.

The courts act as a referee to see that contests are conducted fairly. The problem in setting these rules is that it is unclear who requires protection. Should the management of the target firm be given more weapons to defend itself against unwelcome predators? Or should it simply be encouraged to sit the game out? Or should it be obliged to conduct an auction to obtain the highest price for its shareholders?[22] And what about would-be acquirers? Should they be forced to reveal their intentions at an early stage, or would that allow other firms to piggyback on their good ideas by entering bids of their own? Keep these questions in mind as we review a recent takeover battle.

Valeant Bids for Allergan

Allergan is a U.S. specialty pharmaceutical company, best known as the maker of Botox. In 2014, its independence was threatened by the Canadian firm, Valeant, which, in an unusual move, teamed up with the hedge fund, Pershing Square, to acquire Allergan. Between February and April 2014, Bill Ackman, the manager of Pershing, built up a holding of 9.7% of Allergan's shares. Then on April 21, Valeant announced its offer for Allergan of $47 billion in a mixture of stock and cash, a premium of about 17% over Allergan's previous day's market value.

Allergan's management rejected the offer as undervaluing the company. It accused Valeant of following a strategy of gobbling up acquisitions and starving them of funds. In turn, Valeant accused Allergan's management of spending too freely on research and development and on sales and marketing. It promised that it would cut the combined company's R&D spending by more than two-thirds.

As soon as Allergan became aware of Valeant's offer, the board sought to protect itself by putting in place a poison pill. If any single shareholder acquired a holding of more than 10% of Allergan stock, the poison pill would allow Allergan to offer its other shareholders additional shares at a substantial discount. The immediate effect of Allergan's pill was to stop Pershing from increasing its holding.

In May, Valeant moved to anticipate any antitrust objections to the merger by selling off the rights to some of its skin care products that competed with Allergan's. It then raised its offer to $49.4 billion, and three days later, raised it again to $53 billion. Subsequently, in October, Valeant wrote to Allergan that it was prepared to raise its offer to at least $59 billion, though it stopped short of actually doing so.

As Allergan's board continued to reject Valeant's offers, Pershing proposed to call a special meeting of Allergan's shareholders to replace the board with new members who would be more receptive to Valeant's bid. Such a meeting would require the support of 25% of Allergan's shareholders. Because the poison pill effectively grouped together any shareholders who acted jointly, Pershing needed to be sure that any demand for a special meeting would

---

[22]In 1986, the directors of Revlon were held to be in breach of their duty of loyalty when they did not accept the highest bid for the firm's stock. The Delaware Supreme Court held that when it became inevitable that the company would be sold or broken up, the "directors' role changed from defenders of the corporate bastion to auctioneers charged with getting the best price for the stockholders."

not trigger the poison pill. Whether Pershing would get the necessary support depended heavily on the response of arbitrageurs who owned at least 20% of Allergan's shares.[23]

In the end, Pershing did not need the support of Allergan's shareholders for a special meeting. Allergan settled the pending litigation by agreeing to hold the meeting in December, giving Pershing the chance to attempt its threatened replacement of Allergan's board.

But not everything was going well for Pershing and Valeant. In November 2014, a federal district court ruled that there were serious questions as to whether Pershing's collaboration with Valeant involved insider trading and enjoined Pershing Square from voting its shares at Allergan's special meeting unless it disclosed the facts underlying its exposure to liability for insider trading.

Although the poison pill could not prevent Pershing from calling the special meeting to unseat Allergan's directors, it did give Allergan breathing space. So, while the parties were fighting their battles in the courts, Allergan started looking around for a more congenial partner. At first, it thought it had found one in Salix Pharmaceuticals. A combined company of Allergan and Salix would have been too large a fish for Valeant to swallow. Reports of the negotiations with Salix led Pershing to threaten that if Allergan went ahead with a bid for Salix, Pershing would immediately bring litigation against Allergan's board for breach of fiduciary duty. But by then, Allergan had become disenchanted with the possible Salix merger. Shortly afterward, it found a more attractive partner in Actavis. In November 2014, Allergan agreed to a $66 billion offer from Actavis, and the long, acrimonious battle for Allergan was finally over.

Postscript: Allergan still continued to make the headlines. After the merger, Actavis sold off much of its existing business and changed its name to Allergan. In 2015, Allergan again found itself involved in a merger negotiation as the pharmaceutical giant Pfizer launched, but subsequently withdrew, a friendly $160 billion bid for the company.

Valeant also stayed in the news, but it was not news that its shareholders wanted to hear. Its shares plummeted more than 90% after the company uncovered accounting irregularities, warned of a potential default on its $30 billion of debt, and revealed it was under investigation by the SEC.

Takeover Defenses

What are the lessons from the battle for Allergan? First, the example illustrates some of the strategies of modern merger warfare. Firms such as Allergan that are worried about being taken over usually prepare their defenses in advance. Often they persuade shareholders to agree to *shark-repellent* changes to the corporate charter. For example, the charter may be amended to require that any merger must be approved by a *supermajority* of 80% of the shares rather than the normal 50%. Although shareholders are generally prepared to go along with management's proposals, it is doubtful whether such shark-repellent defenses are truly in their interest. Managers who are protected from takeover appear to enjoy higher remuneration and to generate less wealth for their shareholders.[24]

Many firms follow Allergan's example and deter potential bidders by devising poison pills that make the company unappetizing. For example, the poison pill may give existing shareholders the right to buy the company's shares at half price as soon as a bidder acquires more than 15% of the shares. The bidder is not entitled to the discount. Thus, the bidder resembles Tantalus—as soon as it has acquired 15% of the shares, control is lifted away from its reach. These and other lines of defense are summarized in Table 31.5.

---

[23]Arbitrageurs such as hedge funds speculate on the likely success of takeover bids. They specialize in deciding whether to accept a bid, wait in case someone else produces a better offer, or sell their stock in the market.

[24]A. Agrawal and C. R. Knoeber, "Managerial Compensation and the Threat of Takeover," *Journal of Financial Economics* 47 (February 1998), pp. 219–239; and P. A. Gompers, J. L. Ishii, and A. Metrick, "Corporate Governance and Equity Prices," *Quarterly Journal of Economics* 118 (2003), pp. 107–156.

Pre-Offer Defenses	Description
Shark-repellent charter amendments:	
Staggered (or *classified*) board	The board is classified into three equal groups. Only one group is elected each year. Therefore, the bidder cannot gain control of the target immediately.
Supermajority	A high percentage of shares, typically 80%, is needed to approve a merger.
Fair price	Mergers are restricted unless a fair price (determined by formula or appraisal) is paid.
Restricted voting rights	Shareholders who acquire more than a specified proportion of the target have no voting rights unless approved by the target's board.
Waiting period	Unwelcome acquirers must wait for a specified number of years before they can complete the merger.
Other:	
Poison pill	Existing shareholders are issued rights that, if there is a significant purchase of shares by a bidder, can be used to purchase additional stock in the company at a bargain price.
Poison put	Existing bondholders can demand repayment if there is a change of control as a result of a hostile takeover.
Post-Offer Defenses	
Litigation	Target files suit against bidder for violating antitrust or securities laws.
Asset restructuring	Target buys assets that bidder does not want or that will create an antitrust problem.
Liability restructuring	Target issues shares to a friendly third party, increases the number of shareholders, or repurchases shares from existing shareholders at a premium.

❯**TABLE 31.5**   A summary of takeover defenses

Why did Allergan's management contest the takeover bid? One possible reason was to extract a higher price for the stock, for Valeant was twice led to raise its offer. But on other occasions the target's management may reject a bid because it wishes to protect its position within the firm. Companies sometimes reduce these conflicts of interest by offering their managers *golden parachutes*—that is, generous payoffs if the managers lose their jobs as a result of a takeover. It may seem odd to reward managers for being taken over. However, if a soft landing overcomes their opposition to takeover bids, a few million may be a small price to pay.

Any management team that tries to develop improved weapons of defense must expect challenge in the courts. In the early 1980s, the courts tended to give managers the benefit of the doubt and respect their business judgment about whether a takeover should be resisted. But the courts' attitudes to takeover battles have shifted. For example, in 1993 a court blocked Viacom's agreed takeover of Paramount on the grounds that Paramount directors did not do their homework before turning down a higher offer from QVC. Paramount was forced to give up its poison-pill defense and the stock options that it had offered to Viacom. Such decisions have led managers to become more careful in opposing bids, and they do not throw themselves blindly into the arms of any white knight.

At the same time, companies have acquired some new defensive weapons. In 1987, the Supreme Court upheld state laws that allow companies to deprive an investor of voting rights as soon as the investor's share in the company exceeds a certain level. Since then, state anti-takeover laws have proliferated. Many allow boards of directors to block mergers with hostile bidders for several years and to consider the interests of employees, customers, suppliers, and their communities in deciding whether to try to block a hostile bid.

Anglo-Saxon countries used to have a near-monopoly on hostile takeovers. That is no longer the case. Takeover activity in Europe often exceeds that in the United States, and in recent years, some of the most bitterly contested takeovers have involved European companies.

For example, Mittal's $27 billion takeover of Arcelor resulted from a fierce and highly politicized five-month battle. Arcelor used every defense in the book—including inviting a Russian company to become a leading shareholder.

Mittal is now based in Europe, but it began operations in Indonesia. This illustrates another change in the merger market. Acquirers are also no longer confined to the major industrialized countries. They now include Brazilian, Indian, and Chinese companies. For example, Tetley Tea, Anglo-Dutch steelmaker Corus, and Jaguar and Land Rover have all been acquired by Indian conglomerate Tata Group. In China, Lenovo acquired IBM's personal computer business, Geely bought Volvo from Ford, and China National Chemical bought Syngenta, the Swiss agrichemical busines. In Brazil, Vale purchased Inco, the Canadian nickel producer, and Cutrale-Safra bought the U.S. banana company Chiquita Brands.

Who Gains Most in Mergers?

As our brief history illustrates, in mergers sellers generally do better than buyers. Why do sellers earn higher returns? There are two reasons. First, buying firms are typically larger than selling firms. In many mergers, the buyer is so much larger that even substantial net benefits would not show up clearly in the buyer's share price. Suppose, for example, that company A buys company B, which is only one-tenth A's size. Suppose the dollar value of the net gain from the merger is split equally between A and B.[25] Each company's shareholders receive the same *dollar* profit, but B's receive 10 times A's *percentage* return.

The second, and more important, reason is the competition among potential bidders. Once the first bidder puts the target company "in play," one or more additional suitors often jump in, sometimes as white knights at the invitation of the target firm's management. Every time one suitor tops another's bid, more of the merger gain slides toward the target. At the same time, the target firm's management may mount various legal and financial counterattacks, ensuring that capitulation, if and when it comes, is at the highest attainable price.

Identifying attractive takeover candidates and mounting a bid are high-cost activities. So why should anyone incur these costs if other bidders are likely to jump in later and force up the takeover premium? Mounting a bid may be more worthwhile if a company can first accumulate a holding in the target company. The Williams Act allows a company to acquire a toehold of up to 5% of the target's shares before it is obliged to reveal its holding and outline its plans. So, even if the bid is ultimately unsuccessful, the company may be able to sell off its holding in the target at a substantial profit.

Bidders and targets are not the only possible winners. Other winners include investment bankers, lawyers, accountants, and in some cases arbitrageurs such as hedge funds, which speculate on the likely success of takeover bids.[26] "Speculate" has a negative ring, but it can be a useful social service. A tender offer may present shareholders with a difficult decision. Should they accept, should they wait to see if someone else produces a better offer, or should they sell their stock in the market? This dilemma presents an opportunity for hedge funds, which specialize in answering such questions. In other words, they buy from the target's shareholders and take on the risk that the deal will not go through.

---

[25]In other words, the *cost* of the merger to A is one-half the gain ΔPV_{AB}.

[26]Strictly speaking, an arbitrageur is an investor who takes a fully hedged, that is, riskless, position. But arbitrageurs in merger battles often take very large risks indeed. Their activities are known as "risk arbitrage."

31-6   **Merger Waves and Merger Profitability**

Merger Waves

Look back at Figure 31.1, which shows the number of mergers in the United States for each year since 1985. Notice that mergers come in waves. There was an upsurge in merger activity from 1967 to 1969 and then again in the late 1980s and 1990s. Another merger boom got under way in 2003, petered out with the onset of the credit crisis, and resumed in 2013. These were generally periods of rising stock prices

We don't really understand why merger activity is so volatile and why it seems to be associated with booming stock markets. If mergers are prompted by economic motives, at least one of these motives must be "here today and gone tomorrow," and it must somehow be associated with high stock prices. But none of the economic motives that we review in this chapter has anything to do with the general level of the stock market. None burst on the scene in the 1960s, departed in 1970, and reappeared for most of the 1980s and again in the mid-1990s and early 2000s. Some mergers may result from mistakes in valuation on the part of the stock market. In other words, the buyer may believe that investors have underestimated the value of the seller or may hope that they will overestimate the value of the combined firm. But we see (with hindsight) that mistakes are made in bear markets as well as bull markets. Why don't we see just as many firms hunting for bargain acquisitions when the stock market is low? It is possible that "suckers are born every minute," but it is difficult to believe that they can be harvested only in bull markets.

Merger activity in each wave tends to be concentrated in a relatively small number of industries and is often prompted by deregulation. For example, deregulation of telecoms and banking in the 1990s led to a spate of mergers in both industries.[27] Changes in technology or the pattern of demand can also prompt a spate of mergers. For example, the reduction in defense expenditures following the end of the cold war led to a wave of consolidations among defense companies.

Merger Announcements and the Stock Price

Look back at Figure 13.3, which shows the performance of the stocks of U.S. target firms around the time of the merger announcement. On average, the announcement was associated with an abnormal return of 17.3% for the target shareholders. This is the premium that investors expected the acquirer would need to pay to consummate the merger. Of course, this is an average figure; selling shareholders sometimes obtained much higher returns. When Hewlett-Packard won its takeover battle to buy data-storage company 3Par, it paid a premium of 230% for 3Par's stock.

Selling shareholders clearly do well from mergers. But what about shareholders of the acquiring firm? A similar picture to Figure 13.3 would show that they have roughly broken even in the weeks surrounding the bid. Perhaps the acquirers' shareholders were unduly pessimistic about the merger, but there is no sign that they became more enthusiastic later.

Since the selling shareholders gain and the buyers roughly break-even, it looks as if on average the merging firms are worth more together than apart. For example, Andrade, Mitchell, and Stafford found that between 1973 and 1998, the overall value of merging U.S. firms,

---

[27]See G. Andrade, M. Mitchell, and E. Stafford, "New Evidence and Perspectives on Mergers," *Journal of Economic Perspectives* 15 (Spring 2001), pp. 103–120, and J. Harford, "What Drives Merger Waves?" *Journal of Financial Economics* 77 (September 2005), pp. 529–560.

buyer and seller combined, increased by 1.8%. However, the gains are at best fairly small and accrue to the seller rather than the buyer.[28]

Merger Profitability

Studies of the stock price reaction to merger announcements may show how investors *expect* mergers to work out. But can we say whether mergers do subsequently enhance profitability? The problem here is that we don't know how companies would have fared if they had not merged. Ravenscroft and Scherer, who looked at mergers during the 1960s and early 1970s, argued that productivity declined in the years following a merger.[29] But studies of later merger activity suggest that mergers do seem to improve real productivity. For example, Paul Healy, Krishna Palepu, and Richard Ruback examined 50 large mergers between 1979 and 1983 and found an average increase of 2.4 percentage points in the companies' pretax returns.[30] They argue that this gain came from generating a higher level of sales from the same assets. There was no evidence that the companies were mortgaging their long-term future by cutting back on long-term investments; expenditures on capital equipment and research and development tracked industry averages.[31]

Do Mergers Generate Net Benefits?

There are undoubtedly good acquisitions and bad acquisitions. But if, on average, mergers appear to break even for the buyer, why do we observe so much merger activity? Some believe that the explanation lies in behavioral traits. The managers of acquiring firms may be driven by hubris or overconfidence in their ability to run the target firm better than its existing management, so the acquirers pay too much. There is some evidence to support this view. For example, one study documents large losses to more aggressive acquirers in the merger wave of 1998–2001.[32] Another study of closely fought takeover contests found that winners' stock returns were 24% less than the losers' over the three years post-merger.[33]

Warren Buffet summarizes the situation as follows:

> Many managements apparently were overexposed in impressionable childhood years to the story in which the imprisoned handsome prince is released from a toad's body by a kiss from a beautiful princess. Consequently, they are certain their managerial kiss will do wonders for the profitability of Company T[arget]. . . . We've observed many kisses but very few miracles. Nevertheless, many managerial princesses remain serenely confident about the future potency of their kisses—even after their corporate backyards are knee-deep in unresponsive toads.[34]

---

[28]See G. Andrade, M. Mitchell, and E. Stafford, op. cit.

[29]See D. J. Ravenscraft and F. M. Scherer, "Mergers and Managerial Performance," in J. C. Coffee Jr., L. Lowenstein, and S. Rose-Ackerman, eds., *Knights, Raiders, and Targets: The Impact of the Hostile Takeover* (New York: Oxford University Press, 1988).

[30]See P. Healy, K. Palepu, and R. Ruback, "Does Corporate Performance Improve after Mergers?" *Journal of Financial Economics* 31 (April 1992), pp. 135–175. The study examined the pretax returns of the merged companies relative to industry averages. A study by Lichtenberg and Siegel came to similar conclusions. Before merger, acquired companies had lower levels of productivity than did other firms in their industries, but by seven years after the control change, two-thirds of the productivity gap had been eliminated. See F. Lichtenberg and D. Siegel, "The Effect of Control Changes on the Productivity of U.S. Manufacturing Plants," *Journal of Applied Corporate Finance* 2 (Summer 1989), pp. 60–67.

[31]Maintained levels of capital spending and R&D are also observed by Lichtenberg and Siegel, op. cit.; and B. H. Hall, "The Effect of Takeover Activity on Corporate Research and Development," in A. J. Auerbach, ed., *Corporate Takeovers: Causes and Consequences* (Chicago: University of Chicago Press, 1988).

[32]See S. B. Moeller, F. P. Schlingemann, and R. M. Stulz, "Wealth Destruction on a Massive Scale? A Study of Acquiring Firm Returns in the Recent Merger Wave," *Journal of Finance* 60 (March 2005), pp. 757–782.

[33]See U. Malmendier, E. Moretti, and F. Peters, "Winning by Losing: Evidence on the Long-Run Effects of Mergers," *The Review of Financial Studies*, 31 (August 2018), pp. 3212–3264.

[34]Warren Buffett, Berkshire Hathaway Annual Report, 1981.

Why do so many firms make acquisitions that appear to destroy value? We have suggested that overconfidence may be an explanation, but we should also not dismiss more charitable explanations. For example, McCardle and Viswanathan have pointed out that firms can enter or expand in a product market either by building a new plant or by buying an existing business. If the market is shrinking, it makes more sense for the firm to expand by acquisition. Hence, when it announces the acquisition, firm value may drop simply because investors conclude that the product market is no longer growing. The acquisition in this case does not destroy value; it just signals the stagnant state of the market.[35]

We have discussed the impact of mergers on the companies directly involved, but the most important effects may be felt by the managers of other companies. Since poorly performing firms are more likely to be targets, the threat of takeover may spur the whole of corporate America to try harder. Unfortunately, we don't know whether, on balance, the threat of merger makes for active days or sleepless nights.

---

[35]K. F. McCardle and S. Viswanathan, "The Direct Entry versus Takeover Decision and Stock Price Performance around Takeovers," *Journal of Business* 67 (January 1994), pp. 1–43.

SUMMARY

A merger generates synergies—that is, added value—if the two firms are worth more together than apart. Suppose that firms A and B merge to form a new entity, AB. Then the gain from the merger is

$$\text{Gain} = PV_{AB} - (PV_A + PV_B) = \Delta PV_{AB}$$

Gains from mergers may reflect economies of scale, economies of vertical integration, improved efficiency, the combination of complementary resources, or redeployment of surplus funds. In some cases the object is to install a more efficient management team or to force shrinkage and consolidation in an industry with excess capacity or too many small, inefficient companies. There are also dubious reasons for mergers. There is no value added by merging just to diversify risks, to reduce borrowing costs, or to pump up earnings per share.

You should go ahead with the acquisition if the gain exceeds the cost. Cost is the premium that the buyer pays for the selling firm over its value as a separate entity. It is easy to estimate when the merger is financed by cash. In that case,

$$\text{Cost} = \text{cash paid} - PV_B$$

When payment is in the form of shares, the cost naturally depends on what those shares are worth after the merger is complete. If the merger is a success, B's stockholders will share the merger gains.

The mechanics of buying a firm are much more complex than those of buying a machine. First, you have to make sure that the purchase does not fall afoul of the antitrust laws or other governmental constraints. Second, you have a choice of procedures: You can merge all the assets and liabilities of the seller into those of your own company; you can buy the stock of the seller rather than the company itself; or you can buy the individual assets of the seller. Third, you have to worry about the tax status of the merger.

Mergers are often amicably negotiated between the management and directors of the two companies; but if the seller is reluctant, the would-be buyer can decide to make a tender offer. We sketched some of the offensive and defensive tactics used in takeover battles. We also observed that when the target firm loses, its shareholders typically win: Selling shareholders earn large abnormal returns, while the bidding firm's shareholders roughly break even. The typical merger appears to generate positive net benefits for investors, but competition among bidders, plus active defense by target management, pushes most or all of the gains toward the selling shareholders.

Mergers come and go in waves. Merger activity thrives in periods of economic expansion and buoyant stock prices. Mergers are most frequent in industries that are coping with change, for example, changes in technology or regulation. The wave of mergers in banking and telecoms, for instance, can be traced to deregulation of these industries in the 1990s.

· · · · ·

FURTHER READING

Here are three general works on mergers:

R. Bruner, *Applied Mergers and Acquisitions* (Hoboken, NJ: John Wiley & Sons, 2004).

J. F. Weston, M. L. Mitchell, and J. H. Mulherin, *Takeovers, Restructuring and Corporate Governance,* 4th ed. (Upper Saddle River, NJ: Prentice-Hall, 2013).

S. Betton, B. E. Eckbo, and K. S. Thorburn, "Corporate Takeovers," in B. E. Eckbo (ed.), *Handbook of Empirical Corporate Finance* (Amsterdam: Elsevier/North-Holland, 2007), Chapter 15.

Historical information about mergers is reviewed in:

G. Andrade, M. Mitchell, and E. Stafford, "New Evidence and Perspectives on Mergers," *Journal of Economic Perspectives* 15 (Spring 2001), pp. 103–120.

S. J. Everett, "The Cross-Border Mergers and Acquisitions Wave of the Late 1990s," in R. E. Baldwin and L. A. Winters (eds.), *Challenges to Globalization* (Chicago: University of Chicago Press, 2004).

J. Harford, "What Drives Merger Waves?" *Journal of Financial Economics* 77 (September 2005), pp. 529–560.

B. Holmstrom and S. N. Kaplan, "Corporate Governance and Merger Activity in the U.S.: Making Sense of the 1980s and 1990s," *Journal of Economic Perspectives* 15 (Spring 2001), pp. 121–144.

Finally, here are some informative case studies:

S. N. Kaplan (ed.), *Mergers and Productivity* (Chicago: University of Chicago Press, 2000). This is a collection of case studies.

R. Bruner, "An Analysis of Value Destruction and Recovery in the Alliance and Proposed Merger of Volvo and Renault," *Journal of Financial Economics* 51 (1999), pp. 125–166.

· · · · ·

PROBLEM SETS

 **Select problems are available in McGraw-Hill's *Connect*. Please see the preface for more information.**

1. **Mergers*** True or false?

   a. Sellers almost always gain in mergers.

   b. Buyers usually gain more than sellers.

   c. Firms that do unusually well tend to be acquisition targets.

   d. Merger activity in the United States varies dramatically from year to year.

   e. On the average, mergers produce large economic gains.

   f. Tender offers require the approval of the selling firm's management.

   g. The cost of a merger to the buyer equals the gain realized by the seller.

2. **Mergers** True or false?

   a. Under purchase accounting any difference between the amount paid for the target's assets and their book value is shown as goodwill in the merged company's balance sheet.

   b. In a tax-free merger, the acquirer can write up the value of the target's assets and deduct a higher depreciation charge.

   c. If a company receives payment from the Internal Revenue Service, it is known as "tax inversion."

d. Both the Justice Department and the FTC can seek injunctions to delay a merger where there may be anti-trust issues.

e. Stock financing for mergers mitigates the effect of over- or under-valuation of the target.

3. **Merger types*** Are the following hypothetical mergers horizontal, vertical, or conglomerate?

a. IBM acquires Dell Computer.

b. Dell Computer acquires Walmart.

c. Walmart acquires Tyson Foods.

d. Tyson Foods acquires IBM.

4. **Merger motives** Which of the following motives for mergers make economic sense?

a. Merging to achieve economies of scale.

b. Merging to reduce risk by diversification.

c. Merging to redeploy cash generated by a firm with ample profits but limited growth opportunities.

d. Merging to combine complementary resources.

e. Merging just to increase earnings per share.

5. **Merger motives** Examine several recent mergers and suggest the principal motives for merging in each case.

6. **Merger motives** Suppose you obtain special information—information unavailable to investors—indicating that Backwoods Chemical's stock price is 40% undervalued. Is that a reason to launch a takeover bid for Backwoods? Explain carefully.

7. **Merger motives** Respond to the following comments.

a. "Our cost of debt is too darn high, but our banks won't reduce interest rates as long as we're stuck in this volatile widget-trading business. We've got to acquire other companies with safer income streams."

b. "Merge with Fledgling Electronics? No way! Their P/E's too high. That deal would knock 20% off our earnings per share."

c. "Our stock's at an all-time high. It's time to make our offer for Digital Organics. Sure, we'll have to offer a hefty premium to Digital stockholders, but we don't have to pay in cash. We'll give them new shares of our stock."

8. **Merger motives*** The Muck and Slurry merger has fallen through (see Section 31-2). But World Enterprises is determined to report earnings per share of $2.67. It therefore acquires the Wheelrim and Axle Company. You are given the following facts:

	World Enterprises	Wheelrim and Axle	Merged Firm
Earnings per share	$2.00	$2.50	$2.67
Price per share	$40	$25	?
Price–earnings ratio	20	10	?
Number of shares	100,000	200,000	?
Total earnings	$200,000	$500,000	?
Total market value	$4,000,000	$5,000,000	?

Once again, there are no gains from merging. In exchange for Wheelrim and Axle shares, World Enterprises issues just enough of its own shares to ensure its $2.67 earnings per share objective.

a. Complete the table for the merged firm.

b. How many shares of World Enterprises are exchanged for each share of Wheelrim and Axle?

c. What is the cost of the merger to World Enterprises?

d. What is the change in the total market value of the World Enterprises shares that were outstanding before the merger?

9. **Merger gains and costs** Velcro Saddles is contemplating the acquisition of Skiers' Airbags Inc. The values of the two companies as separate entities are $20 million and $10 million, respectively. Velcro Saddles estimates that by combining the two companies, it will reduce marketing and administrative costs by $500,000 per year in perpetuity. Velcro Saddles can either pay $14 million cash for Skiers' or offer Skiers' a 50% holding in Velcro Saddles. The opportunity cost of capital is 10%.

a. What is the gain from merger?

b. What is the cost of the cash offer?

c. What is the cost of the stock alternative?

d. What is the NPV of the acquisition under the cash offer?

e. What is its NPV under the stock offer?

10. **Merger gains and costs** As financial manager of Corton Inc., you are investigating a possible acquisition of Denham. You have the basic data given in the following table. You estimate that investors expect a steady growth of about 6% in Denham's earnings and dividends. Under new management, this growth rate would be increased to 8% per year without the need for additional capital.

	Corton	Denham
Forecast earnings per share	$5.00	$1.50
Forecast dividend per share	$3.00	$0.80
Number of shares	1,000,000	600,000
Stock price	$90	$20

a. What is the gain from the acquisition?

b. What is the cost of the acquisition if Corton pays $25 in cash for each share of Denham?

c. What is the cost of the acquisition if Corton offers one share of Corton for every three shares of Denham?

d. How would the cost of the cash offer change if the expected growth rate of Corton was not changed by the merger?

e. How would the cost of the share offer change if the expected growth rate was not changed by the merger?

11. **Merger gains and costs*** Gobi Desserts is bidding to take over Universal Puddings. Gobi has 3,000 shares outstanding, selling at $50 per share. Universal has 2,000 shares outstanding, selling at $17.50 a share. Gobi estimates the economic gain from the merger to be $15,000.

a. If Universal can be acquired for $20 a share, what is the NPV of the merger to Gobi?

b. What will Gobi sell for when the market learns that it plans to acquire Universal for $20 a share?

c. What will Universal sell for?

d. What are the percentage gains to the shareholders of each firm?

e. Now suppose that the merger takes place through an exchange of stock. On the basis of the premerger prices of the firms, Gobi sells for $50, so instead of paying $20 cash, Gobi issues .40 of its shares for every Universal share acquired. What will be the stock price of the merged firm?

f. What is the NPV of the merger to Gobi when it uses an exchange of stock? Why does your answer differ from part (a)?

12. **Merger gains and costs** Winterbourne is considering a takeover of Monkton Inc. Winterbourne has 10 million shares outstanding, which sell for $40 each. Monkton has 5 million shares outstanding, which sell for $20 each. If the merger gains are estimated at $25 million, what is the highest price per share that Winterbourne should be willing to pay to Monkton shareholders?

13. **Merger gains and costs** If Winterbourne from Problem 12 has a price-earnings ratio of 12 and Monkton has a P/E ratio of 8, what should be the P/E ratio of the merged firm? Assume in this case that the merger is financed by an issue of new Winterbourne shares. Monkton will get one Winterbourne share for every two Monkton shares held. In the short run the merger has no effect on the earnings outlook for the two businesses.

14. **Merger gains and costs** Sometimes the stock price of a possible target company rises in anticipation of a merger bid. Explain how this complicates the bidder's evaluation of the target company.

15. **Merger gains and costs** Examine a recent merger in which at least part of the payment made to the seller was in the form of stock. Use stock market prices to obtain an estimate of the gain from the merger and the cost of the merger.

16. **Merger accounting** Look again at Table 31.3. Suppose that B Corporation's fixed assets are reexamined and found to be worth $12 million instead of $9 million. How would this affect the AB Corporation's balance sheet under purchase accounting? How would the value of AB Corporation change? Would your answer depend on whether the merger is taxable?

17. **Taxation** Explain the distinction between a tax-free and a taxable merger. Are there circumstances in which you would expect buyer and seller to agree to a taxable merger?

18. **Taxation** Which of the following transactions are not likely to be classed as tax-free?

    a. An acquisition of assets.

    b. A merger in which payment is entirely in the form of voting stock.

19. **Merger tactics*** Connect each term to its correct definition or description.

    a. poison pill

    b. tender offer

    c. shark repellent

    d. merger

    e. tax inversion

    f. proxy contest

        A. Changes in the corporate charter that are designed to deter an unwelcome takeover

        B. Measure in which shareholders are issued rights to buy shares if the bidder acquires a large stake in the firm

        C. Relocation of company domicile to low-tax country often by way of merger

        D. Offer to buy shares directly from stockholders

        E. One company assumes all the assets and all the liabilities of another

        F. Attempt to gain control of a firm by winning the votes of its stockholders

20. **Merger tactics** In Section 31-5, we described how Valeant and its ally, Pershing Square, lost the battle to acquire Allergan. Sometimes, the losers in a takeover battle can also win if they

own a toehold stake in the target's stock. Between April and June 2014, Pershing acquired a 9.7% stake in Allergan at an estimated average price of $128 a share. In November, Actavis offered $219 per share for each of Allergan's 299 million shares. What was Pershing's profit on its holding?

CHALLENGE

21. **Takeover tactics** Examine a hostile acquisition and discuss the tactics employed by both the predator and the target companies. Do you think that the management of the target firm was trying to defeat the bid or to secure the highest price for its stockholders? How did each announcement by the protagonists affect their stock prices?

22. **Merger regulation** How do you think mergers should be regulated? For example, what defenses should target companies be allowed to employ? Should managers of target firms be compelled to seek out the highest bids? Should they simply be passive and watch from the sidelines?

APPENDIX

Conglomerate Mergers and Value Additivity

A pure conglomerate merger is one that has no effect on the operations or profitability of either firm. If corporate diversification is in stockholders' interests, a conglomerate merger would give a clear demonstration of its benefits. But if present values add up, the conglomerate merger would not make stockholders better or worse off.

In this appendix, we examine more carefully our assertion that present values add. It turns out that values *do* add as long as capital markets are perfect and investors' diversification opportunities are unrestricted.

Call the merging firms A and B. Value additivity implies

$$PV_{AB} = PV_A + PV_B$$

where

PV_{AB} = market value of combined firms just after merger

PV_A, PV_B = separate market values of A and B just before merger

For example, we might have

$$PV_A = \$100 \text{ million } (\$200 \text{ per share} \times 500{,}000 \text{ shares outstanding})$$

and

$$PV_B = \$200 \text{ million } (\$200 \text{ per share} \times 1{,}000{,}000 \text{ shares outstanding})$$

Suppose A and B are merged into a new firm, AB, with one share in AB exchanged for each share of A or B. Thus, there are 1,500,000 AB shares issued. *If* value additivity holds, then PV_{AB} must equal the sum of the separate values of A and B just before the merger—that is, $300 million. That would imply a price of $200 per share of AB stock.

But note that the AB shares represent a portfolio of the assets of A and B. Before the merger, investors could have bought one share of A and two of B for $600. Afterward, they can obtain a claim on *exactly* the same real assets by buying three shares of AB.

Suppose that the opening price of AB shares just after the merger is $200, so that $PV_{AB} = PV_A + PV_B$. Our problem is to determine if this is an equilibrium price—that is, whether we can rule out excess demand or supply at this price.

For there to be excess demand, there must be some investors who are willing to increase their holdings of A and B as a consequence of the merger. Who could they be? The only thing new created by the merger is diversification, but those investors who want to hold assets of A *and* B will have purchased A's and B's stock before the merger. The diversification is redundant and consequently won't attract new investment demand.

Is there a possibility of excess supply? The answer is yes. For example, there will be some shareholders in A who did not invest in B. After the merger they cannot invest solely in A, but only in a fixed combination of A and B. Their AB shares will be less attractive to them than the pure A shares, so they will sell part of or all their AB stock. In fact, the only AB shareholders who will *not* wish to sell are those who happened to hold A and B in exactly a 1:2 ratio in their premerger portfolios!

Since there is no possibility of excess demand but a definite possibility of excess supply, we seem to have

$$PV_{AB} \leq PV_A + PV_B$$

That is, corporate diversification can't help, but it may hurt investors by restricting the types of portfolios they can hold. This is not the whole story, however, since investment demand for AB shares might be attracted from other sources if PV_{AB} drops below $PV_A + PV_B$. To illustrate, suppose there are two other firms, A* and B*, which are judged by investors to have the same risk characteristics as A and B, respectively. Then before the merger,

$$r_A = r_{A*} \quad \text{and} \quad r_B = r_{B*}$$

where r is the rate of return expected by investors. We'll assume $r_A = r_{A*} = .08$ and $r_B = r_{B*} = .20$.

Consider a portfolio invested one-third in A* and two-thirds in B*. This portfolio offers an expected return of 16%:

$$r = x_{A*} r_{A*} + x_{B*} r_{B*}$$
$$= \tfrac{1}{3}(.08) + \tfrac{2}{3}(.20) = .16$$

A similar portfolio of A and B before their merger also offered a 16% return.

As we have noted, a new firm AB is really a portfolio of firms A and B, with portfolio weights of ⅓ and ⅔. It is therefore equivalent in risk to the portfolio of A* and B*. Thus, the price of AB shares must adjust so that it likewise offers a 16% return.

What if AB shares drop below $200, so that PV_{AB} is less than $PV_A + PV_B$? Since the assets and earnings of firms A and B are the same, the price drop means that the expected rate of return on AB shares has risen above the return offered by the A*B* portfolio. That is, if r_{AB} exceeds ⅓r_A + ⅔r_B, then r_{AB} must also exceed ⅓r_{A*} + ⅔r_{B*}. But this is untenable: Investors A* and B* could sell part of their holdings (in a 1:2 ratio), buy AB, and obtain a higher expected rate of return with no increase in risk.

On the other hand, if PV_{AB} rises above $PV_A + PV_B$, the AB shares will offer an expected return less than that offered by the A*B* portfolio. Investors will unload the AB shares, forcing their price down.

A stable result occurs only if AB shares stick at $200. Thus, value additivity will hold exactly in a perfect-market equilibrium if there are ample substitutes for the A and B assets. If A and B have unique risk characteristics, however, then PV_{AB} can fall below $PV_A + PV_B$. The reason is that the merger curtails investors' opportunity to tailor their portfolios to their own needs and preferences. This makes investors worse off, reducing the attractiveness of holding the shares of firm AB.

In general, the condition for value additivity is that investors' opportunity set—that is, the range of risk characteristics attainable by investors through their portfolio choices—is independent of the particular portfolio of real assets held by the firm. Diversification per se can never expand the opportunity set given perfect security markets. Corporate diversification may reduce the investors' opportunity set, but only if the real assets the corporations hold lack substitutes among traded securities or portfolios.

In rare cases, the firm may be able to expand the opportunity set. It can do so if it finds an investment opportunity that is unique—a real asset with risk characteristics shared by few or no other financial assets. In this lucky event, the firm should not diversify, however. It should set up the unique asset as a separate firm so as to expand investors' opportunity set to the maximum extent. If Gallo by chance discovered that a small portion of its vineyards produced wine comparable to Chateau Margaux, it would not throw that wine into the Hearty Burgundy vat.

Corporate Restructuring

In the last chapter, we described how mergers and acquisitions change a company's ownership and management team and often force major shifts in corporate strategy. But this is not the only way that company structure can be altered. In this chapter, we look at a variety of other mechanisms for changing ownership and control, including leveraged buyouts (LBOs), spin-offs, and carve-outs.

The first section starts with a famous takeover battle, the leveraged buyout of RJR Nabisco. The rest of the section offers a general review of LBOs and leveraged restructurings. The main point of these transactions is not just to change control, although existing management is often booted out, but also to change incentives for managers and improve financial performance.

RJR Nabisco was an early example of a **private-equity** deal. Section 32-2 takes a closer look at how private-equity investment funds are structured and how the private-equity

business has developed since the 1980s. Private-equity funds usually end up holding a portfolio of companies in different industries. In this respect, they resemble the conglomerates that dominated takeover activity in the 1960s. These conglomerates are mostly gone—it seems that private equity is a superior financial technology for doing the tasks that conglomerates used to do. Our review of conglomerates' weaknesses helps us to understand the strengths of private equity.

Section 32-3 considers other ways that companies may change their structure. These include spin-offs, asset sales, and privatizations.

Some companies choose to restructure, but others have it thrust upon them. None more so than those that fall on hard times and can no longer service their debts. The chapter therefore concludes by looking at how distressed companies either work out a solution with their debtors or go through a formal bankruptcy process.

32-1 Leveraged Buyouts

Leveraged buyouts (LBOs) differ from ordinary acquisitions in two immediately obvious ways. First, the target company goes private, and its shares no longer trade on the open market. Second, the acquirer finances a large fraction of the purchase price by bank loans and bonds, which are secured by the assets and cash flows of the target company. Some, if not all, of the bonds are junk—that is, below investment-grade. Equity financing for LBOs comes from private-equity investment partnerships, which we describe shortly. In the case of the earlier LBOs, debt ratios of 90% were not uncommon, though in recent years, LBOs have been financed with nearly equal amounts of debt and equity.

When a buyout is led by existing management, the transaction is called a **management buyout** or **MBO.** In the 1970s and 1980s, many MBOs were arranged for unwanted divisions

of large diversified companies. Smaller divisions outside the companies' main lines of business sometimes failed to attract top management's interest and commitment, and divisional management chafed under corporate bureaucracy. Many such divisions flowered when spun off as MBOs. Their managers, pushed by the need to generate cash for debt service and encouraged by a substantial personal stake in the business, found ways to cut costs and compete more effectively.

LBO activity shifted to buyouts of entire businesses, including large, mature, public corporations. The years 2006 and 2007 witnessed an exceptional volume of such deals. They included the acquisition of TXU, a Texas utility, in a record $45 billion cash-and-debt buyout. The company was acquired by a group led by private-equity firms Kohlberg Kravis Roberts and TPG Capital. The underlying bet was that increasing natural gas prices would provide the company's coal-based generating plants with an edge. It did not happen. Natural gas prices declined as production by fracking took off, and in 2014, TXU (now renamed Energy Future Holdings) became one of the country's largest nonfinancial bankruptcies.

One of the most interesting deals of 2007 was DaimlerChrysler's decision to sell an 80% stake in Chrysler to Cerberus Capital Management. Chrysler, one of Detroit's original Big Three automakers, merged into DaimlerChrysler in 1998, but the expected synergies between the Chrysler and Mercedes-Benz product lines were hard to grasp. The Chrysler division had some profitable years, but lost $1.5 billion in 2006. Prospects looked grim. DaimlerChrysler (now Daimler AG) *paid* Cerberus $677 million to take Chrysler off its hands. Cerberus assumed about $18 billion in pension and employee health-care liabilities, however, and agreed to invest $6 billion in Chrysler and its finance subsidiary.[1] Two years later, Chrysler filed for bankruptcy, wiping out Cerberus's investment. Subsequently, Chrysler was acquired by Fiat.

With the onset of the credit crisis, the LBO boom of 2006–2007 withered rapidly. Although buyout firms entered 2008 with large amounts of capital to invest, banks and investment institutions became much more wary of lending to LBOs. By 2009, the value of buyout deals had fallen by 90% from its 2007 high. Since then, the market has slowly recovered, but the targets have generally been tiddlers compared with those of the boom years. Table 32.1 lists some recent transactions.

Industry	Lead Partnership	Target	Year	Value ($ billions)
Coffee	JAB	Keurig Green Mountain	2016	$13.9
Retailing	BC Partners	PetSmart	2015	8.7
Software	Carlyle Group	Veritas	2015	8.0
Health care	Hellman & Friedman	Multiplan	2016	7.5
Security systems	Apollo Management	ADT	2016	7.0
Software	Vista Equity Partners	Solera	2015	6.4
Health care	Blackstone	Team Health Holdings	2016	6.1
Electric power	Energy Capital	Calpine	2017	5.6
Software	Permira	Informatica	2015	5.3

❭TABLE 32.1   Some recent leveraged buyouts (values in $ billions)

The RJR Nabisco LBO

The largest, most dramatic, and best documented LBO of the 1980s was the $25 billion takeover of RJR Nabisco by the private-equity partnership, Kohlberg Kravis Roberts (KKR). The players, tactics, and controversies of LBOs are writ large in this case.

---

[1]Cerberus had previously purchased a controlling stake in GMAC, General Motors' finance subsidiary.

The battle for RJR began in October 1988 when the board of directors of RJR Nabisco revealed that Ross Johnson, the company's chief executive officer, had formed a group of investors that proposed to buy all of RJR's stock for $75 per share in cash and take the firm private. RJR's share price immediately moved to about $75, handing shareholders a 36% gain over the previous day's price of $56. At the same time, RJR's bonds fell because it was clear that existing bondholders would soon have a lot more company.[2]

Johnson's offer lifted RJR onto the auction block. Once the company was in play, its board of directors was obliged to consider other offers, which were not long in coming. Four days later, KKR bid $90 per share, $79 in cash plus PIK preferred stock valued at $11. (PIK means "pay in kind." The company could choose to pay preferred dividends with more preferred shares rather than cash.)

The resulting bidding contest had as many turns and surprises as a Dickens novel. In the end it was Johnson's group against KKR. KKR bid $109 per share, after adding $1 per share (roughly $230 million) in the last hour.[3] The KKR bid was $81 in cash, convertible subordinated bonds valued at about $10, and PIK preferred shares valued at about $18. Johnson's group bid $112 in cash and securities.

But the RJR board chose KKR. Although Johnson's group had offered $3 a share more, its security valuations were viewed as "softer" and perhaps overstated. The Johnson group's proposal also contained a management compensation package that seemed extremely generous and had generated an avalanche of bad press.

But where did the merger benefits come from? What could justify offering $109 per share, about $25 billion in all, for a company that only 33 days previously was selling for $56 per share? KKR and other bidders were betting on two things. First, they expected to generate billions in additional cash from interest tax shields, reduced capital expenditures, and sales of assets that were not strictly necessary to RJR's core businesses. Asset sales alone were projected to generate $5 billion. Second, they expected to make the core businesses significantly more profitable, mainly by cutting back on expenses and bureaucracy. Apparently, there was plenty to cut, including the RJR "Air Force," which at one point included 10 corporate jets.

In the year after KKR took over, a new management team set out to sell assets and cut back operating expenses and capital spending. There were also layoffs. As expected, high interest charges meant a net loss of nearly a billion dollars in the first year, but pretax operating income actually increased, despite extensive asset sales.

Inside the firm, things were going well. But outside there was confusion, and prices in the junk bond market were declining rapidly, implying much higher future interest charges for RJR and stricter terms on any refinancing. In 1990, KKR made an additional equity investment in the firm and the company retired some of its junk bonds. RJR's chief financial officer described the move as "one further step in the deleveraging of the company."[4] For RJR, the world's largest LBO, it seemed that high debt was a temporary, not a permanent, virtue.

RJR, like many other firms that were taken private through LBOs, enjoyed only a short period as a private company. It went public again in 1991 with the sale of $1.1 billion of stock. KKR progressively sold off its investment, and its last remaining stake in the company was sold in 1995 at roughly the original purchase price.

Barbarians at the Gate?

The RJR Nabisco LBO crystallized views on LBOs, the junk bond market, and the takeover business. For many it exemplified all that was wrong with finance in the late 1980s, especially

---

[2] N. Mohan and C. R. Chen track the abnormal returns of RJR securities in "A Review of the RJR Nabisco Buyout," *Journal of Applied Corporate Finance* 3 (Summer 1990), pp. 102–108.

[3] The whole story is reconstructed by B. Burrough and J. Helyar in *Barbarians at the Gate: The Fall of RJR Nabisco* (New York: Harper & Row 1990)—see especially Chapter 18—and in a movie with the same title.

[4] C. Anders, "RJR Swallows Hard, Offers $5-a-Share Stock," *The Wall Street Journal*, December 18, 1990, pp. C1–C2.

the willingness of "raiders" to carve up established companies, leaving them with enormous debt burdens, basically in order to get rich quick.[5]

There was plenty of confusion, stupidity, and greed in the LBO business. Not all the people involved were nice. On the other hand, LBOs generated large increases in market value, and most of the gains went to the selling shareholders, not to the raiders. For example, the biggest winners in the RJR Nabisco LBO were the company's stockholders.

The most important sources of added value came from making RJR Nabisco leaner and meaner. The company's new management was obliged to pay out massive amounts of cash to service the LBO debt. It also had an equity stake in the business and, therefore, strong incentives to sell off nonessential assets, cut costs, and improve operating profits.

LBOs are almost by definition *diet deals.* But there were other motives. Here are some of them.

The Junk Bond Markets   LBOs and debt-financed takeovers may have been driven by artificially cheap funding from the junk bond markets. With hindsight, it seems that investors underestimated the risks of default in junk bonds. Default rates climbed painfully, reaching 10.3% in 1991.[6] The market also became temporarily much less liquid after the demise in 1990 of Drexel Burnham, the investment banking firm that was the chief market maker in junk bonds.

Leverage and Taxes   Borrowing money saves taxes, as we explained in Chapter 18. But taxes were not the main driving force behind LBOs. The value of interest tax shields was simply not big enough to explain the observed gains in market value.[7] For example, Richard Ruback estimated the present value of additional interest tax shields generated by the RJR LBO at $1.8 billion.[8] But the gain in market value to RJR stockholders was about $8 billion.

High levels of leverage remain an essential characteristic of LBOs. But the interest tax shields that LBOs can use are now limited. Starting in 2018, the amount of interest payments that can be deducted for tax purposes is limited to 30% of EBITDA. Most public companies will not be affected by this restriction, but it could have serious consequences for LBOs.

Of course, if interest tax shields were the main motive for LBOs' high debt, then LBO managers would not be so concerned to pay down debt. We saw that this was one of the first tasks facing RJR Nabisco's new management.

Other Stakeholders   We should look at the total gain to all investors in an LBO, not just to the selling stockholders. It's possible that the latter's gain is just someone else's loss and that no value is generated overall.

Bondholders are the obvious losers. The debt that they thought was secure can turn into junk when the borrower goes through an LBO. We noted how market prices of RJR debt fell sharply when Ross Johnson's first LBO offer was announced. But again, the losses suffered by bondholders in LBOs are not nearly large enough to explain stockholder gains. For example, Mohan and Chen's estimate of losses to RJR bondholders was at most $575 million[9]—painful to the bondholders, but far below the stockholders' gain.

[5]This view has persisted in some quarters: In April 2005, Franz Müntefering, chairman of the German Social Democratic Party, branded private-equity investors as a plague of "locusts" bent on devouring German industry. Try an Internet search on "private equity" with "locusts."

[6]See E. I. Altman and G. Fanjul, "Defaults and Returns in the High Yield Bond Market: The Year 2003 in Review and Market Outlook," Monograph, Salomon Center, Leonard N. Stern School of Business, New York University, 2004.

[7]There are some tax *costs* to LBOs. For example, selling shareholders realize capital gains and pay taxes that otherwise would be deferred. See M. C. Jensen, S. N. Kaplan, and L. Stiglin, "Effects of LBOs on Tax Revenues of the U.S. Treasury," *Tax Notes* 42 (February 6, 1989), pp. 727–733.

[8]R. J. Ruback, "RJR Nabisco," case study, Harvard Business School, Cambridge, MA, 1989.

[9]N. Mohan and C. R. Chen, op. cit.

Leverage and Incentives   Managers and employees of LBOs work harder and often smarter. They have to generate cash for debt service. Moreover, managers' personal fortunes are riding on the LBOs' success. They become owners rather than organization men and women.

It's hard to measure the payoff from better incentives, but there is some evidence of improved operating efficiency in LBOs. Kaplan, who studied 48 MBOs during the 1980s, found average increases in operating income of 24% three years after the buyouts. Ratios of operating income and net cash flow to assets and sales increased dramatically. He observed cutbacks in capital expenditures but not in employment. Kaplan concludes that these "operating changes are due to improved incentives rather than layoffs."[10]

We have reviewed several motives for LBOs. We do not say that all LBOs are good. On the contrary, there have been many cases of poor judgment, as the bankruptcies of TXU and Chrysler illustrated. Yet, we do quarrel with those who portray LBOs solely as undertaken by Wall Street barbarians breaking up the traditional strengths of corporate America.

Leveraged Restructurings

The essence of a leveraged buyout is of course leverage. So why not take on the leverage and dispense with the buyout? Here is one well-documented success story of a *leveraged restructuring.*[11]

In 1989, Sealed Air was a very profitable company. The problem was that its profits were coming too easily because its main products were protected by patents. When the patents expired, strong competition was inevitable, and the company was not ready for it. The years of relatively easy profits had resulted in too much slack:

> We didn't need to manufacture efficiently; we didn't need to worry about cash. At Sealed Air, capital tended to have limited value attached to it—cash was perceived as being free and abundant.[12]

The company's solution was to borrow the money to pay a $328 million special cash dividend. In one stroke the company's debt increased 10 times. Its book equity went from $162 million to *minus* $161 million. Debt went from 13% of total book assets to 136%. The company hoped that this leveraged restructuring would "disrupt the status quo, promote internal change," and simulate "the pressures of Sealed Air's more competitive future." The shakeup was reinforced by new performance measures and incentives, including increases in stock ownership by employees.

It worked. Sales and operating profits increased steadily without major new capital investments, and net working capital *fell* by half, releasing cash to help service the company's debt. The stock price quadrupled in the five years following the restructuring.

Sealed Air's restructuring was not typical. It is an exemplar chosen with hindsight. It was also undertaken by a successful firm under no outside pressure. But it clearly shows the motive for most leveraged restructurings. They are designed to force mature, successful, but overweight companies to disgorge cash, reduce operating costs, and use assets more efficiently.

---

[10]S. Kaplan, "The Effects of Management Buyouts on Operating Performance and Value," *Journal of Financial Economics* 24 (October 1989), pp. 217–254. For more recent evidence on changes in employment, see S. J. Davis, J. Haltiwanger, R. S. Jarmin, J. Lerner, and J. Miranda, "Private Equity and Employment," U.S. Census Bureau Center for Economic Studies Paper No. CES-WP-08-07, January 2009.

[11]K. H. Wruck, "Financial Policy as a Catalyst for Organizational Change: Sealed Air's Leveraged Special Dividend," *Journal of Applied Corporate Finance* 7 (Winter 1995), pp. 20–35.

[12]K. H. Wruck, op.cit

LBOs and Leveraged Restructurings

The financial characteristics of LBOs and leveraged restructurings are similar. The three main characteristics of LBOs are:

1. *High debt.* The debt is not intended to be permanent. It is designed to be paid down. The requirement to generate cash for debt service is intended to curb wasteful investment and force improvements in operating efficiency. Of course, this solution only makes sense for companies that are generating lots of cash and have few investment opportunities.

2. *Incentives.* Managers are given a greater stake in the business via stock options or direct ownership of shares.

3. *Private ownership.* The LBO goes private. It is owned by a partnership of private investors who monitor performance and can act right away if something goes awry. But private ownership is not intended to be permanent. The most successful LBOs go public again as soon as debt has been paid down sufficiently and improvements in operating performance have been demonstrated.

Leveraged restructurings share the first two characteristics but continue as public companies.

32-2   The Private-Equity Market

Private-Equity Partnerships

Figure 32.1 shows how a private-equity investment fund is organized. The fund is a partnership, not a corporation. The *general partner* sets up and manages the partnership. The *limited partners* put up almost all of the money. Limited partners are generally institutional investors, such as pension funds, endowments, and insurance companies. Wealthy individuals may also

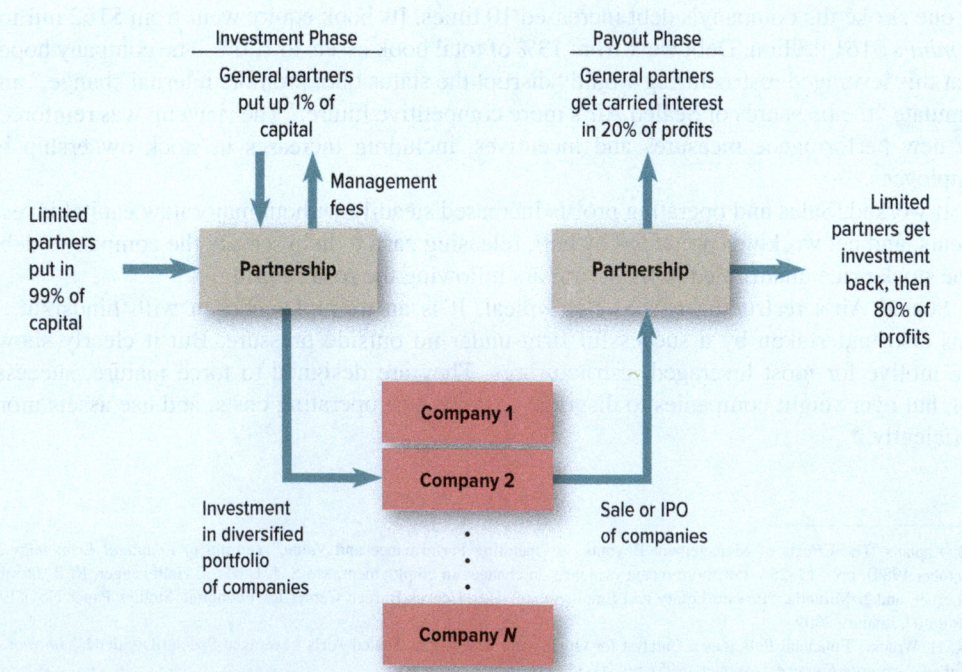

▶ **FIGURE 32.1**

Organization of a typical private-equity partnership. The limited partners, having put up almost all of the money, get first crack at the proceeds from sale or IPO of the portfolio companies. Once their investment is returned, they get 80% of any profits. The general partners, who organize and manage the partnership, get a 20% carried interest in profits.

participate. The limited partners have limited liability, like shareholders in a corporation, but do not participate in management.

Once the partnership is formed, the general partners seek out companies to invest in. For example, we saw in Chapter 15 how venture capital partnerships look for high-tech start-ups or adolescent companies that need capital to grow. LBO funds, on the other hand, look for mature businesses with ample free cash flow that need restructuring. Some funds specialize in particular industries, for example, biotech, real estate, or energy. However, buyout funds like KKR's and Cerberus's look for opportunities almost anywhere.

The partnership agreement has a limited term, which is typically 10 years. The portfolio companies must then be sold and the proceeds distributed. So the general partners cannot reinvest the limited partners' money. Of course, once a fund is proved successful, the general partners can usually go back to the limited partners, or to other institutional investors, and form another fund.

For example, Blackstone, one of the largest private-equity partnerships, formed six private-equity funds between 1987 and 2010. Then in 2015, it announced the formation of a new fund, Blackstone Capital Partners VII, with more than 250 limited partners. These investors committed to provide up to $18 billion.

The general partners of a private-equity fund get a management fee, usually 1% or 2% of capital committed.[13] plus a *carried interest* in 20% of any profits earned by the partnership. In other words, the limited partners get paid off first, but then get only 80% of any further returns. The general partners therefore have a call option on 20% of the partnership's total future payoff, with an exercise price set by the limited partners' investment.[14]

You can see some of the advantages of private-equity partnerships:

- Carried interest gives the general partners plenty of upside. They are strongly motivated to earn back the limited partners' investment and deliver a profit.

- Carried interest, because it is a call option, gives the general partners incentives to take risks. Venture capital funds take the risks inherent in start-up companies. Buyout funds amplify business risks with financial leverage.

- There is no separation of ownership and control. The general partners can intervene in the fund's portfolio companies any time performance lags or strategy needs changing.

- There is no free-cash-flow problem: Limited partners don't have to worry that cash from a first round of investments will be dribbled away in later rounds. Cash from the first round *must* be distributed to investors.

The foregoing are good reasons why private equity grew. But some contrarians say that rapid growth also came from irrational exuberance and speculative excess. These contrarian investors stayed on the sidelines and waited glumly (but hopefully) for the crash.

The popularity of private equity has also been linked to the costs and distractions of public ownership, including the costs of dealing with Sarbanes-Oxley and other legal and regulatory requirements. Many CEOs and CFOs feel pressured to meet short-term earnings targets. Perhaps they spend too much time worrying about these targets and about day-to-day changes in stock price. Perhaps going private avoids public investors' "short-termism" and makes it easier to invest for the long run. But recall that for private equity, the long run is the life of the partnership, 8 or 10 years at most. General partners *must* find a way to cash out of the companies in the partnership's portfolio. There are only two ways to cash out: an IPO or a *trade sale* to another company. Many of today's private-equity deals will be future IPOs.

---

[13]LBO and buyout funds also extract fees for arranging financing for their takeover transactions.

[14]The structure and compensation of private-equity partnerships are described in A. Metrick and A. Yasuda, "The Economics of Private Equity Funds," *Review of Financial Studies* 23 (2010), pp. 2303–2341.

Company	Business	Company	Business
Clear Channel	Outdoor advertising	Nanthealth	Health care
Eastman Kodak	Cameras	Pacific Biosciences	Biotechnology
Gogo	In-flight wi-fi	Transportadora de gas (Argentina)	Natural gas production
Hilton Worldwide	Hotels	Vivint Solar	Security and home automation
Michaels Companies	Arts and crafts stores	Warrior Met Coal	Coal producer

❭**TABLE 32.2**   The Blackstone Group invests in many different industries. Here are a few of its portfolio holdings in December 2017.

Source: Nasdaq.

Thus, private-equity investors need public markets. The firms that seek divorce from public shareholders may well have to remarry them later.

Are Private-Equity Funds Today's Conglomerates?

A conglomerate is a firm that diversifies across a number of unrelated businesses. Is Blackstone a conglomerate? Table 32.2, which lists some of Blackstone's holdings, suggests that it is. Blackstone funds have invested in dozens of industries.

Does this mean that private equity today performs the tasks that public conglomerates used to do? Before answering that question, let's take a brief look at the history of U.S. conglomerates.

Conglomerates were fashionable in the 1960s when a merger boom created more than a dozen sprawling conglomerates. Table 32.3 shows that by the 1970s, some of these conglomerates had achieved amazing spans of activity. The largest conglomerate, ITT, was operating in 38 different industries and ranked eighth in sales among U.S. corporations.

Most of these conglomerates were broken up in the 1980s and 1990s. In 1995 ITT, which had already sold or spun off several businesses, split what was left into three separate firms. One acquired ITT's interests in hotels and gambling; the second took over ITT's automotive parts, defense, and electronics businesses; and the third specialized in insurance and financial services.

What advantages were claimed for the conglomerates of the 1960s and 1970s? First, diversification across industries was supposed to stabilize earnings and reduce risk. That's hardly compelling because shareholders can diversify much more efficiently on their own.

Second, a widely diversified firm can operate an internal capital market. Free cash flow generated by divisions in mature industries (cash cows) can be funneled within the company to those divisions (stars) with plenty of profitable growth opportunities. Consequently, there is no need for fast-growing divisions to raise finance from outside investors.

Sales Rank	Company	Number of Industries
8	International Telephone & Telegraph (ITT)	38
15	Tenneco	28
42	Gulf & Western Industries	4
51	Litton Industries	19
66	LTV	18

❭**TABLE 32.3**

The largest conglomerates of 1979, ranked by sales compared with U.S. industrial corporations. Most of these companies have been broken up.

Source: A. Chandler and R. S. Tetlow (eds.), *The Coming of Managerial Capitalism*, p. 772. The McGraw-Hill Companies, Inc, 1985. See also J. Baskin and P. J. Miranti, Jr., *A History of Corporate Finance* (Cambridge, UK: Cambridge University Press, 1997), ch. 7.

There are some good arguments for internal capital markets. The company's managers probably know more about its investment opportunities than outside investors do, and transaction costs of issuing securities are avoided. Nevertheless, it appears that attempts by conglomerates to allocate capital investment across many unrelated industries were more likely to subtract value than add it. Trouble is, internal capital markets are not really markets but combinations of central planning (by the conglomerate's top management and financial staff) and intracompany bargaining. Divisional capital budgets depend on politics as well as pure economics. Large, profitable divisions with plenty of free cash flow may have the most bargaining power; they may get generous capital budgets while smaller divisions with good growth opportunities are reined in.

Internal Capital Markets in the Oil Business Misallocation in internal capital markets is not restricted to pure conglomerates. For example, Lamont found that when oil prices fell by half in 1986, diversified oil companies cut back capital investment in their non-oil divisions. The non-oil divisions were forced to "share the pain," even though the drop in oil prices did not diminish their investment opportunities. *The Wall Street Journal* reported one example:[15]

> Chevron Corp. cut its planned 1986 capital and exploratory budget by about 30% because of the plunge in oil prices . . . . A Chevron spokesman said that the spending cuts would be across the board and that no particular operations will bear the brunt.
>
> About 65% of the $3.5 billion budget will be spent on oil and gas exploration and production—about the same proportion as before the budget revision.
>
> Chevron also will cut spending for refining and marketing, oil and natural gas pipelines, minerals, chemicals, and shipping operations.

Why cut back on capital outlays for minerals, say, or chemicals? Low oil prices are generally good news, not bad, for chemical manufacturing, because oil distillates are an important raw material.

By the way, most of the oil companies in Lamont's sample were large, blue-chip companies. They could have raised additional capital from investors to maintain spending in their non-oil divisions. They chose not to. We do not understand why.

All large companies must allocate capital among divisions or lines of business. Therefore, they all have internal capital markets and must worry about mistakes and misallocations. But the danger probably increases as the company moves from a focus on one, or a few related industries, to unrelated conglomerate diversification. Look again at Table 32.3: How could top management of ITT keep accurate track of investment opportunities in 38 different industries?

Conglomerates face further problems. Their divisions' market values can't be observed independently, and it is difficult to set incentives for divisional managers. This is particularly serious when managers are asked to commit to risky ventures. For example, how would a biotech start-up fare as a division of a traditional conglomerate? Would the conglomerate be as patient and risk-tolerant as investors in the stock market? How are the scientists and clinicians doing the biotech R&D rewarded if they succeed? We don't mean to say that high-tech innovation and risk-taking are impossible in public conglomerates, but the difficulties are evident.

The third argument for traditional conglomerates came from the idea that good managers were fungible; in other words, it was argued that modern management would work as well in the manufacture of auto parts as in running a hotel chain. Thus conglomerates were supposed to add value by removing old-fashioned managers and replacing them with ones trained in the new management science.

---

[15]O. Lamont, "Cash Flow and Investment: Evidence from Internal Capital Markets," *Journal of Finance* 52 (March 1997), pp. 83–109. *The Wall Street Journal* quotation appears on pp. 89–90. © 1997 Dow Jones & Company, Inc. A more recent example was the decision in January 2015 by Royal Dutch Shell and Qatar Petroleum to abandon plans to build a $6.5 billion petrochemical plant because it was "commercially infeasible" in the current energy market. There may have been good reasons for the decision, but it was not because oil had become much cheaper in 2015. Lower oil prices would presumably lead to lower production costs for petrochemicals, increased demand, and hence higher profitability for the plant.

Private-Equity Fund	Public Conglomerate
Widely diversified, investment in unrelated industries	Widely diversified, investment in unrelated industries
Limited-life partnership forces sale of portfolio companies	Public corporations designed to operate divisions for the long run
No financial links or transfers between portfolio companies	Internal capital market
General partners "do the deal," then monitor; lenders also monitor	Hierarchy of corporate staff evaluates divisions' plans and performance
Managers' compensation depends on exit value of company	Divisional managers' compensation depends mostly on earnings—"smaller upside, softer downside"

❭**TABLE 32.4**   Private-equity fund vs. public conglomerate. Both diversify, investing in a portfolio of unrelated businesses, but their financial structures are otherwise fundamentally different.

Source: Adapted from G. Baker and C. Montgomery, "Conglomerates and LBO Associations: A Comparison of Organizational Forms," working paper, Harvard Business School, Cambridge, MA, July 1996.

There was some truth in this claim. The best of the conglomerates did add value by targeting companies that needed fixing—companies with slack management, surplus assets, or excess cash that was not being invested in positive-NPV projects. These conglomerates targeted the same types of companies that LBO and private-equity funds would target later. The difference is that conglomerates would buy companies, try to improve them, and then manage them for the long run. The long-run management was the most difficult part of the game. Conglomerates would buy, fix, and hold. Private equity buys, fixes, and sells. By selling (cashing out), private equity avoids the problems of managing the conglomerate firm and running internal capital markets.[16] You could say that private-equity partnerships are temporary conglomerates.

Table 32.4 summarizes a comparison by Baker and Montgomery of the financial structure of a private-equity fund and of a typical public conglomerate. Both are diversified, but the fund's limited partners do not have to worry that free cash flow will be plowed back into unprofitable investments. The fund has no internal capital market. Monitoring and compensation of management also differ. In the fund, each company is run as a separate business. The managers report directly to the owners, the fund's partners. Each company's managers own shares or stock options in that company, not in the fund. Their compensation depends on their firm's market value in a trade sale or IPO.

In a public conglomerate, these businesses would be divisions, not freestanding companies. Ownership of the conglomerate would be dispersed, not concentrated. The divisions would not be valued separately by investors in the stock market, but by the conglomerate's corporate staff, the very people who run the internal capital market. Managers' compensation wouldn't depend on divisions' market values because no shares in the divisions would be traded and the conglomerate would not be committed to selling the divisions or spinning them off.

---

[16]Economists have tried to measure whether corporate diversification adds or subtracts value. Berger and Ofek estimate an average conglomerate discount of 12% to 15%. That is, the estimated market value of the whole is 12% to 15% less than the sum of the values of the parts. The chief cause of the discount seems to be overinvestment and misallocation of investment. See P. Berger and E. Ofek, "Diversification's Effect on Firm Value," *Journal of Financial Economics* 37 (January 1995), pp. 39–65. But not everyone is convinced that the conglomerate discount is real. Other researchers have found smaller discounts or pointed out statistical problems that make the discount hard to measure. See, for example, J. M. Campa and S. Kedia, "Explaining the Diversification Discount," *Journal of Finance* 57 (August 2002), pp. 1731–1762; and B. Villalonga, "Diversification Discount or Premium? New Evidence from the Business Information Tracking Service," *Journal of Finance* 59 (April 2004), pp. 479–506.

You can see the arguments for focus and against corporate diversification. But we must be careful not to push the arguments too far. For example, in Chapter 33, we will find that conglomerates, though rare in the United States, are common, and apparently successful, in many parts of the world. They include such giants as Siemens in Germany, Philips in the Netherlands, Sumitomo in Japan, and Samsung in Korea.

32-3 Fusion and Fission in Corporate Finance

Figure 32.2 shows some of AT&T's acquisitions and divestitures. Before 1984, AT&T controlled most of the local and virtually all of the long-distance telephone service in the United States. (Customers used to speak of the ubiquitous "Ma Bell.") Then in 1984, the company accepted an antitrust settlement requiring local telephone services to be spun off to seven new, independent companies. AT&T was left with its long-distance business plus Bell Laboratories, Western Electric (telecommunications manufacturing), and various other assets. As the communications industry became increasingly competitive, AT&T acquired several other businesses, notably in computers, cellular telephone service, and cable television. Some of these acquisitions are shown as the green incoming arrows in Figure 32.2.

AT&T was an unusually active acquirer. It was a giant company trying to respond to rapidly changing technologies and markets. But AT&T was simultaneously *divesting* dozens of other businesses. For example, its credit card operations (the AT&T Universal Card) were sold to Citicorp. AT&T also created several new companies by spinning off parts of its business. For example, in 1996 it spun off Lucent (incorporating Bell Laboratories and Western Electric) and its computer business (NCR). Only six years earlier, AT&T had paid $7.5 billion to acquire NCR. These and several other important divestitures are shown as the green outgoing arrows in Figure 32.1.

Figure 32.2 is not the end of AT&T's story. In 2004, AT&T was acquired by Cingular Wireless, which retained the AT&T name. In 2005, this company in turn merged with SBC

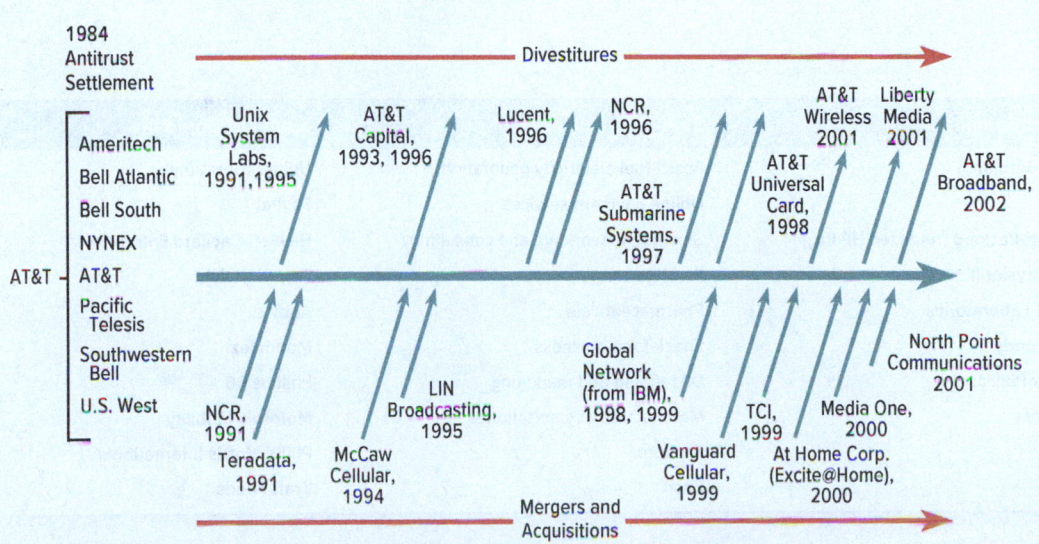

FIGURE 32.2 The effects of AT&T's antitrust settlement in **1984**, and a few of AT&T's acquisitions and divestitures from **1991** to **2003**. Divestitures are shown by the outgoing green arrows. When two years are given, the transaction was completed in two steps.

Communications Inc., a descendant of Southwestern Bell. By that point, there was not much left of the original AT&T, but the name survived. Recent events include AT&T's acquisition of Direct TV for $48.5 billion in 2015 and its 2017 bid of $35 billion for Time Warner. The Time Warner bid was challenged by the U.S. Department of Justice, however. In early 2018, litigation was under way, and it is not clear whether the deal would go through.

In the market for corporate control, *fusion*—that is, mergers and acquisitions—gets most of the attention and publicity. But *fission*—the sale or distribution of assets or operating businesses—can be just as important, as the top half of Figure 32.2 illustrates. In many cases, businesses are sold in LBOs or MBOs. But other transactions are common, including spin-offs, carve-outs, divestitures, asset sales, and privatizations. We start with spin-offs.

Spin-Offs

A **spin-off** (or *split-up*) is a new, independent company created by detaching part of a parent company's assets and operations. Shares in the new company are distributed to the parent company's stockholders.[17] When e-Bay acquired PayPal in 2002, it stated that it was a natural extension of eBay's trading platform. But the two companies proved to have very different cultures and were often in conflict. So in 2015, eBay announced that it intended to spin off PayPal in order "to capitalize on their respective growth opportunities in the rapidly changing global commerce and payments landscape."

eBay was not alone in deciding to spin off. Table 32.5 lists a few other notable spinoffs of recent years.

Spin-offs widen investor choice by allowing them to invest in just one part of the business. More important, they can improve incentives for managers. Companies sometimes refer to divisions or lines of business as "poor fits." By spinning these businesses off, management of the parent company can concentrate on its main activity. If the businesses are independent, it is easier to see the value and performance of each and to reward managers by giving them stock or stock options in their company. Also, spin-offs relieve investors of the worry that funds will be siphoned from one business to support unprofitable capital investments in another. For example, when Dow and DuPont announced their plan to merge and

Parent Company	Spin-Off's Business	Spun-Off Company	Year
E.ON (Germany)	Fossil-fuel electricity generation	Uniper (Germany)	2016
eBay	Online payment services	PayPal	2015
Hewlett-Packard (renamed HP Inc.)	Servers, networking, and consulting	Hewlett-Packard Enterprises	2015
Fiat Chrysler (Italy)	Prestige cars	Ferrari (Italy)	2015
Abbott Laboratories	Pharmaceuticals	AbbVie	2013
Kraft Foods	Snack-food business	Mondelez	2012
ConocoPhillips	Oil refining and marketing	Phillips 66	2012
Motorola	Manufacture of smartphones	Motorola Mobility	2011
Altria	Tobacco	Philip Morris International	2008
Altria	Food	Kraft Foods	2007

❯**TABLE 32.5**   Some notable recent spinoffs

---

[17]The value of the shares that shareholders receive is taxed as a dividend unless they are given at least 80% of the shares in the new company.

then split the proposed merged company into three separate businesses, the accompanying press release commented that these businesses:

> . . . will include a leading global pure-play Agriculture company; a leading global pure-play Material Science company; and a leading technology and innovation-driven Specialty Products company. Each of the businesses will have clear focus, an appropriate capital structure, a distinct and compelling investment thesis, scale advantages, and focused investments in innovation to better deliver superior solutions and choices for customers. (DuPont press release, December 11, 2015)

Investors generally greet the announcement of a spin-off as good news.[18] Their enthusiasm appears to be justified, for spin-offs seem to bring about more efficient capital investment decisions by each company and improved operating performance.[19]

Carve-Outs

Carve-outs are similar to spin-offs, except that shares in the new company are not given to existing shareholders but are sold in a public offering. For example, when the German utility, E.ON decided to exit fossil-fuel electricity generation, it spun off this business into a separate company. Its rival, RWE, went in the opposite direction. It separated its wind and solar business into a new company, Innogy, and sold a 24% stake in the company by means of an IPO. This decision to carve out Innogy brought RWE €4.6 billion of much-needed cash, which it would not have received if it had spun-off the business.

Most carve-outs leave the parent with majority control of the subsidiary, usually about 80% ownership.[20] This may not reassure investors who are worried about a lack of focus or a poor fit, but it does allow the parent to set the manager's compensation based on the performance of the subsidiary's stock price. Sometimes companies carve out a small proportion of the shares to establish a market for the subsidiary's stock and subsequently spin off the remainder of the shares. For example, in 2014 Fiat Chrysler announced plans to sell a 10% stake in Ferrari on the stock market and then to spin off the remaining shares to its stockholders. The nearby box describes how the computer company, Palm, was first carved and then spun.

Perhaps the most enthusiastic carver-outer of the 1980s and 1990s was Thermo Electron, with operations in health care, power generation equipment, instrumentation, environmental protection, and various other areas. By 1997, it had carved out stakes in seven publicly traded subsidiaries, which in turn had carved out 15 further public companies. The 15 were grandchildren of the ultimate parent, Thermo Electron. The company's management reasoned that the carve-outs would give each company's managers responsibility for their own decisions and expose their actions to the scrutiny of the capital markets. For a while, the strategy seemed to work, and Thermo Electron's stock was a star performer. But the complex structure began to lead to inefficiencies, and in 2000, Thermo Electron went into reverse. It reacquired many of the subsidiaries that the company had carved out only a few years earlier, and it spun off several of its progeny, including Viasys Health Care and Kadant Inc., a manufacturer

---

[18]For example, between 1970 and 2015, the announcement of a spin-off was associated with an average abnormal return of 2.5% (authors' calculations). See also P. J. Cusatis, J. A. Miles, and J. R. Woolridge, "Restructuring through Spin-offs: The Stock Market Evidence," *Journal of Financial Economics* 33 (June 1993), pp. 293–311.

[19]See R. Gertner, E. Powers, and D. Scharfstein, "Learning about Internal Capital Markets from Corporate Spin-offs," *Journal of Finance* 57 (December 2002), pp. 2479–2506; L. V. Daley, V. Mehrotra, and R. Sivakumar, "Corporate Focus and Value Creation: Evidence from Spin-offs," *Journal of Financial Economics* 45 (August 1997), pp. 257–281; T. R. Burch and V. Nanda, "Divisional Diversity and the Conglomerate Discount: Evidence from Spin-offs," *Journal of Financial Economics* 70 (October 2003), pp. 69–78; and A. K. Dittmar and A. Shivdasani, "Divestitures and Divisional Investment Policies," *Journal of Finance* 58 (December 2003), pp. 2711–2744. But G. Colak and T. M. Whited argue that apparent increases in value are due to econometric problems rather than actual increases in investment efficiency. See "Spin-offs, Divestitures and Conglomerate Investment," *Review of Financial Studies* 20 (May 2007), pp. 557–595.

[20]The parent must retain an 80% interest to consolidate the subsidiary with the parent's tax accounts. Otherwise, the subsidiary is taxed as a freestanding corporation.

How Palm was Carved and Spun

❯ When 3Com acquired U.S. Robotics in 1997, it also became the owner of Palm, a small start-up business developing handheld computers. It was a lucky purchase, for over the next three years, the Palm Pilot came to dominate the market for handheld computers. But as Palm began to take up an increasing amount of management time, 3Com concluded that it needed to return to its knitting and focus on its basic business of selling computer network systems. In 2000, it announced that it would carve out 5% of its holding of Palm through an initial public offering and then spin off the remaining 95% of Palm shares by giving 3Com shareholders about 1.5 Palm shares for each 3Com share that they owned.

The Palm carve-out occurred at close to the peak of the high-tech boom and got off to a dazzling start. The shares were issued in the IPO at $38 each. On the first day of trading, the stock price touched $165 before closing at $95. Therefore, anyone owning a share of 3Com stock could look forward later in the year to receiving about 1.5 shares of Palm worth $1.5 \times 95 = \$142.50$. But apparently 3Com's shareholders were not fully convinced that their newfound wealth was for real, for on the same day 3Com's stock price closed at $82, or more than $60 a share *less* than the market value of the shares in Palm that they were due to receive.*

Three years after 3Com spun off its holding in Palm, Palm itself entered the spin-off business by giving shareholders stock in PalmSource, a subsidiary that was responsible for developing and licensing the Palm™ operating system. The remaining business, renamed palmOne, would focus on making mobile gadgets. The company gave three reasons for its decision to split into two. First, like 3Com's management, Palm's management believed that the company would benefit from clarity of focus and mission. Second, it argued that shareholder value could "be enhanced if investors could evaluate and choose between both businesses separately, thereby attracting new and different investors." Finally, it seemed that Palm's rivals were reluctant to buy software from a company that competed with them in making handheld hardware.

---

*This difference would seem to present an arbitrage opportunity. An investor who bought 1 share of 3Com and sold short 1.5 shares of Palm would earn a profit of $60 and own 3Com's other assets for free. The difficulty in executing this arbitrage is explored in O. A. Lamont and R. H. Thaler, "Can the Market Add and Subtract? Mispricing in Tech Stock Carve-Outs," *Journal of Political Economy* 111 (April 2003), pp. 227–268.

---

of paper-making and paper-recycling equipment. Then in November 2006, Thermo Electron merged with Fisher Scientific.

Asset Sales

The simplest way to divest an asset is to sell it. An *asset sale* or *divestiture* means sale of a part of one firm to another. This may consist of an odd factory or warehouse, but sometimes whole divisions are sold. Asset sales are another way of getting rid of "poor fits." They may also be required by the FTC or Justice Department as a condition for approving a merger. Such sales are frequent. For example, one study found that more than 30% of assets acquired in a sample of hostile takeovers were subsequently sold.[21]

Maksimovic and Phillips examined a sample of about 50,000 U.S. manufacturing plants each year from 1974 to 1992. About 35,000 plants in the sample changed hands during that period. One-half of the ownership changes were the result of mergers or acquisitions of entire firms, but the other half resulted from asset sales—that is, sale of part or all of a division.[22] Asset sales sometimes raise huge sums of money. For example, in 2017, the Anglo-Australian mining giant, BHP Billiton, announced that it was selling its U.S. shale oil assets for $10 billion. BHP was under pressure from activist investors to reduce its oil exposure.

---

[21]See S. Bhagat, A. Shleifer, and R. Vishny, "Hostile Takeovers in the 1980s: The Return to Corporate Specialization," *Brookings Papers on Economic Activity: Microeconomics,* 1990, pp. 1–84.
[22]V. Maksimovic and G. Phillips, "The Market for Corporate Assets: Who Engages in Mergers and Asset Sales and Are There Efficiency Gains?" *Journal of Finance* 56 (December 2001), pp. 2019–2065, Table 1, p. 2030.

Announcements of asset sales are good news for investors in the selling firm and on average the assets are employed more productively after the sale.[23] It appears that asset sales transfer business units to the companies that can manage them most effectively.

Privatization and Nationalization

A **privatization** is a sale of a government-owned company to private investors. In recent years, almost every government in the world seems to have a privatization program. Here are some examples of recent privatization news:

- Japan sells the West Japan Railway Company (March 2004).
- Germany privatizes Postbank, the country's largest retail bank (June 2004).
- France sells 30% of EDF (Electricité de France; December 2005).
- China sells Industrial and Commercial Bank of China (October 2006).
- Poland sells Tauron Polska Energia (March 2011).
- U.K. sells Royal Mail (October 2013).
- Greece sells 67% stake in port of Piraeus (April 2016).
- Brazil decides to privatize its biggest power utility (August 2017).

Most privatizations are more like carve-outs than spin-offs because shares are sold for cash rather than distributed to the ultimate "shareholders"—that is, the citizens of the selling country. But several former communist countries, including Russia, Poland, and the Czech Republic, privatized by means of vouchers distributed to citizens. The vouchers could be used to bid for shares in the companies that were being privatized. Thus, the companies were not sold for cash, but for vouchers.[24]

Privatizations have raised enormous sums for governments. China raised $22 billion from the privatization of the Industrial and Commercial Bank of China. The Japanese government's successive sales of its holding of NTT (Nippon Telegraph and Telephone) brought in $100 billion.

In many cases, governments have retained a stake in the privatized company or have taken stakes in companies that have hitherto been entirely privately owned. The idea is that the government can represent the wider interests of society and help to safeguard jobs. But you can see the dangers that may arise when the company is subject to political interference.

The motives for privatization seem to boil down to the following three points:

1. *Increased efficiency.* Through privatization, the enterprise is exposed to the discipline of competition and insulated from political influence on investment and operating decisions. Managers and employees can be given stronger incentives to cut costs and add value.

2. *Share ownership.* Privatizations encourage share ownership. Many privatizations give special terms or allotments to employees or small investors.

3. *Revenue for the government.* Last but not least.

There were fears that privatizations would lead to massive layoffs and unemployment, but that does not appear to be the case. While it is true that privatized companies operate more efficiently and thus reduce employment, they also grow faster as privatized companies, which increases employment. In many cases the net effect on employment has been positive.

BEYOND THE PAGE

Voucher privatization in Czechoslovakia

mhhe.com/brealey13e

---

[23]Ibid.

[24]There is extensive research on voucher privatizations. See, for example, M. Boycko, A. Shleifer, and R. Vishny, "Voucher Privatization," *Journal of Financial Economics* 35 (April 1994), pp. 249–266; and R. Aggarwal and J. T. Harper, "Equity Valuation in the Czech Voucher Privatization Auctions," *Financial Management* 29 (Winter 2000), pp. 77–100.

On other dimensions, the impact of privatization is almost always positive. A review of research on the issue concludes that the firms "almost always become more efficient, more profitable, . . . financially healthier and increase their capital investment spending."[25]

The process of privatization is not a one-way street. It can sometimes go into reverse, and publicly owned firms may be taken over by the government. For example, as part of his aim to construct a socialist republic in Venezuela, Hugo Chavez nationalized firms in the banking, oil, power, telecom, steel, and cement sectors.

In some other countries, temporary nationalization has been a pragmatic last resort for governments rather than part of a long-term strategy. For example, in 2008, the U.S. government took control of the giant mortgage companies Fannie Mae and Freddie Mac when they were threatened with bankruptcy.[26] In 2012, the Japanese government agreed to provide 1 trillion yen in return for a majority holding in Tepco, operator of the stricken Fukushima nuclear plant.

32-4 Bankruptcy

BEYOND THE PAGE

U.S. bankruptcy filings

mhhe.com/brealey13e

Some firms are forced to reorganize by the onset of financial distress. At this point they need to agree to a reorganization plan with their creditors or file for bankruptcy. We list the largest nonfinancial U.S. bankruptcies in Table 32.6. The credit crunch also ensured a good dollop of large financial bankruptcies. Lehman Brothers tops the list. It failed in September 2008 with assets of $691.1 billion. Two weeks later, Washington Mutual went the same way with assets of $327.9 billion.

Bankruptcy proceedings in the United States may be initiated by the creditors, but in the case of public corporations it is usually the firm itself that decides to file. It can choose one of two procedures, which are set out in Chapters 7 and 11 of the 1978 Bankruptcy Reform Act. The purpose of Chapter 7 is to oversee the firm's death and dismemberment, while Chapter 11 seeks to nurse the firm back to health.

❭**TABLE 32.6**
The largest nonfinancial bankruptcies

Source: New Generation Research, Inc., www.bankruptcydata.com.

Company	Bankruptcy Date	Total Assets Prebankruptcy ($ billions)
WorldCom	July 2002	$103.9
General Motors	June 2009	91.0
Enron	December 2001	65.5
Conseco	December 2002	61.4
Energy Future Holdings	April 2014	41.0
Chrysler	April 2009	39.3
Pacific Gas and Electric	April 2001	36.2
Texaco	April 1987	34.9
Global Crossing	January 2002	30.2
General Growth Properties	April 2009	29.6
Lyondell Chemical Company	January 2009	27.4
Calpine	December 2005	27.2
UAL	December 2002	25.2

---

[25]W. L. Megginson and J. M. Netter, "From State to Market: A Survey of Empirical Studies on Privatization," *Journal of Economic Literature* 39 (June 2001), p. 381.
[26]The credit crisis prompted a number of company nationalizations throughout the world, such as that of Northern Rock in the U.K., Hypo Real Estate in Germany, Landsbanki in Iceland, and Anglo-Irish Bank in Ireland.

Most small firms make use of Chapter 7. In this case, the bankruptcy judge appoints a trustee, who then closes the firm down and auctions off the assets. The proceeds from the auction are used to pay off the creditors. Secured creditors can recover the value of their collateral. Whatever is left over goes to the unsecured creditors, who take assigned places in a queue. (Secured creditors join as unsecured to the extent that their collateral is not worth enough to repay the secured debt.) The court and the trustee are first in line. Wages come next, followed by federal and state taxes and debts to some government agencies such as the Pension Benefit Guarantee Corporation. The remaining unsecured creditors mop up any remaining crumbs from the table.[27] Frequently, the trustee needs to prevent some creditors from trying to jump the gun and collect on their debts, and sometimes the trustee retrieves property that a creditor has recently seized.

Managers of small firms that are in trouble know that Chapter 7 bankruptcy means the end of the road and, therefore, try to put off filing as long as possible. For this reason, Chapter 7 proceedings are often launched not by the firm, but by its creditors.

When large public companies can't pay their debts, they generally attempt to rehabilitate the business. This is in the shareholders' interests; they have nothing to lose if things deteriorate further and everything to gain if the firm recovers. The procedures for rehabilitation are set out in Chapter 11. Most companies find themselves in Chapter 11 because they can't pay their debts. But sometimes companies have filed for Chapter 11 not because they run out of cash, but to deal with burdensome labor contracts or lawsuits. For example, Delphi, the automotive parts manufacturer, filed for bankruptcy in 2005. Delphi's North American operations were running at a loss, partly because of high-cost labor contracts with the United Auto Workers (UAW) and partly because of the terms of its supply contract with GM, its largest customer. Delphi sought the protection of Chapter 11 to restructure its operations and to negotiate better terms with the UAW and GM.

The aim of Chapter 11 is to keep the firm alive and operating while a plan of reorganization is worked out.[28] During this period, other proceedings against the firm are halted, and the company usually continues to be run by its existing management.[29] The responsibility for developing the plan falls on the debtor firm but, if it cannot devise an acceptable plan, the court may invite anyone to do so—for example, a committee of creditors.

The plan goes into effect if it is accepted by the creditors and confirmed by the court. Each *class* of creditors votes separately on the plan. Acceptance requires approval by at least one-half of votes cast in each class, and those voting "aye" must represent two-thirds of the value of the creditors' aggregate claim against the firm. The plan also needs to be approved by two-thirds of the shareholders. Once the creditors and the shareholders have accepted the plan, the court normally approves it, provided that each class of creditors is in favor and that the creditors will be no worse off under the plan than they would be if the firm's assets were liquidated and the proceeds distributed. Under certain conditions the court may confirm a plan even if one or more classes of creditors votes against it,[30] but the rules for a "cramdown" are complicated, and we will not attempt to cover them here.

The reorganization plan is basically a statement of who gets what; each class of creditors gives up its claim in exchange for new securities or a mixture of new securities and cash. The problem is to design a new capital structure for the firm that will (1) satisfy the

BEYOND THE PAGE

Cramdowns

mhhe.com/brealey13e

---

[27]On average there isn't much left. See M. J. White, "Survey of Evidence on Business Bankruptcy," in *Corporate Bankruptcy,* ed. J. S. Bhandari and L. A. Weiss (Cambridge, UK: Cambridge University Press, 1996).

[28]To keep the firm alive, it may be necessary to continue to use assets that were offered as collateral, but this denies secured creditors access to their collateral. To resolve this problem, the Bankruptcy Reform Act makes it possible for a firm operating under Chapter 11 to keep such assets as long as the creditors who have a claim on them are compensated for any decline in their value. Thus, the firm might make cash payments to the secured creditors to cover economic depreciation of the assets.

[29]Occasionally, the court appoints a trustee to manage the firm.

[30]But at least one class of creditors must vote for the plan; otherwise, the court cannot approve it.

creditors and (2) allow the firm to solve the *business* problems that got the firm into trouble in the first place.[31] Sometimes satisfying these two conditions requires a plan of baroque complexity, involving the creation of a dozen or more new securities.

BEYOND THE PAGE

Chapter 55

mhhe.com/brealey13e

The Securities and Exchange Commission (SEC) plays a role in many reorganizations, particularly for large, public companies. Its interest is to ensure that all relevant and material information is disclosed to the creditors before they vote on the proposed plan of reorganization.

Chapter 11 proceedings are often successful, and the patient emerges fit and healthy. But in other cases, rehabilitation proves impossible, and the assets are liquidated under Chapter 7. Sometimes the firm may emerge from Chapter 11 for a brief period before it is once again submerged by disaster and back in the bankruptcy court. For example, the venerable airline TWA came out of Chapter 11 bankruptcy at the end of 1993, was back again less than two years later, and then for a third time in 2001, prompting jokes about "Chapter 22" and "Chapter 33."[32]

Is Chapter 11 Efficient?

Here is a simple view of the bankruptcy decision: Whenever a payment is due to creditors, management checks the value of the equity. If the value is positive, the firm makes the payment (if necessary, raising the cash by an issue of shares). If the equity is valueless, the firm defaults on its debt and files for bankruptcy. If the assets of the bankrupt firm can be put to better use elsewhere, the firm is liquidated and the proceeds are used to pay off the creditors; otherwise, the creditors become the new owners and the firm continues to operate.[33]

In practice, matters are rarely so simple. For example, we observe that firms often petition for bankruptcy even when the equity has a positive value. And firms often continue to operate even when the assets could be used more efficiently elsewhere. The problems in Chapter 11 usually arise because the goal of paying off the creditors conflicts with the goal of maintaining the business as a going concern. We described in Chapter 18 how the assets of Eastern Airlines seeped away in bankruptcy. When the company filed for Chapter 11, its assets were more than sufficient to repay in full its liabilities of $3.7 billion. But the bankruptcy judge was determined to keep Eastern flying. When it finally became clear that Eastern was a terminal case, the assets were sold off and the creditors received less than $900 million. The creditors would clearly have been better off if Eastern had been liquidated immediately; the unsuccessful attempt at resuscitation cost the creditors $2.8 billion.[34]

Here are some further reasons that Chapter 11 proceedings do not always achieve an efficient solution:

1. Although the reorganized firm is legally a new entity, it is entitled to the tax-loss carry-forwards belonging to the old firm. If the firm is liquidated rather than reorganized, the tax-loss carry-forwards disappear. Thus, there is a tax incentive to continue operating the firm even when its assets could be sold and put to better use elsewhere.

2. If the firm's assets are sold, it is easy to determine what is available to pay creditors. However, when the company is reorganized, it needs to conserve cash. Therefore, claimants are often paid off with a mixture of cash and securities. This makes it less easy to judge whether they receive a fair shake.

---

[31]Although Chapter 11 is designed to keep the firm in business, the reorganization plan often involves the sale or closure of large parts of the business.

[32]One study found that after emerging from Chapter 11, about one in three firms reentered bankruptcy or privately restructured their debt. See E. S. Hotchkiss, "Postbankruptcy Performance and Management Turnover," *Journal of Finance* 50 (March 1995), pp. 3–21.

[33]If there are several classes of creditors in this simplistic model, the junior creditors initially become the owners of the company and are responsible for paying off the senior debt. They now face exactly the same decision as the original owners. If their newly acquired equity is valueless, they will also default and turn over ownership to the next class of creditors.

[34]These estimates of creditor losses are taken from L. A. Weiss and K. H. Wruck, "Information Problems, Conflicts of Interest, and Asset Stripping: Chapter 11's Failure in the Case of Eastern Airlines," *Journal of Financial Economics* 48 (April 1998), pp. 55–97.

3. Senior creditors, who know they are likely to get a raw deal in a reorganization, may press for a liquidation. Shareholders and junior creditors prefer a reorganization. They hope that the court will not interpret the creditors' pecking order too strictly and that they will receive consolation prizes when the firm's remaining value is sliced up.

4. Although shareholders and junior creditors are at the bottom of the pecking order, they have a secret weapon—they can play for time. When they use delaying tactics, the junior creditors are betting on a stroke of luck that will rescue their investment. On the other hand, the senior claimants know that time is working against them, so they may be prepared to settle for a lower payoff as part of the price for getting the plan accepted. Also, prolonged bankruptcy cases are costly, as we pointed out in Chapter 18. Senior claimants may see their money seeping into lawyers' pockets and decide to settle quickly.

But bankruptcy practices do change, and in recent years, Chapter 11 proceedings have become more creditor-friendly.[35] For example, equity investors and junior debtholders used to find that managers were willing allies in dragging out a settlement, but these days, the managers of bankrupt firms often receive a key-employee retention plan, which provides them with a large bonus if the reorganization proceeds quickly and a smaller one if the company lingers on in Chapter 11. For large public bankruptcies, this has contributed to a reduction in the time spent in bankruptcy from about 840 days in 2007 to 430 in 2017.[36]

While a reorganization plan is being drawn up, the company is likely to need additional working capital. It has, therefore, become increasingly common to allow the firm to buy goods on credit and to borrow money (known as *debtor in possession,* or *DIP,* debt). The lenders, who frequently comprise the firm's existing creditors, receive senior claims and can insist on stringent conditions. DIP lenders therefore have considerable influence on the outcome of the bankruptcy proceedings.

As creditors have gained more influence, shareholders of the bankrupt firms have received fewer and fewer crumbs. In recent years, the court has faithfully observed the pecking order in about 90% of Chapter 11 settlements.

In 2009, GM and Chrysler both filed for bankruptcy. They were not only two of the largest bankruptcies ever, but they were also extraordinary legal events. With the help of billions of fresh money from the U.S. Treasury, the companies were in and out of bankruptcy court with blinding speed, compared with the normal placid pace of Chapter 11. The U.S. government was deeply involved in the rescue and the financing of New GM and New Chrysler. The nearby box explains some of the financial issues raised by the Chrysler bankruptcy. The GM bankruptcy raised similar issues.

Workouts

If Chapter 11 reorganizations are not efficient, why don't firms bypass the bankruptcy courts and get together with their creditors to work out a solution? Many firms that are in distress *do* first seek a negotiated settlement, or *workout.* For example, they can seek to delay payment of the debt or negotiate an interest rate holiday. However, shareholders and junior creditors know that senior creditors are anxious to avoid formal bankruptcy proceedings. So they are likely to be tough negotiators, and senior creditors generally need to make concessions to reach agreement.[37] The larger the firm, and the more complicated its capital structure, the less likely it is that everyone will agree to any proposal.

---

[35]For a discussion of these changes see S. T. Bharath, V. Panchapagesan, and I. M. Werner, "The Changing Nature of Chapter 11," working paper, Ohio State University, November 2010. Available at SSRN: **https://ssrn.com/abstract=1102366** or **http://dx.doi .org/10.2139/ssrn.1102366.**

[36]The numbers refer to bankruptcies that were not prepackaged. See **http://lopucki.law.ucla.edu.**

[37]Franks and Torous show that creditors make even greater concessions to junior creditors in informal workouts than in Chapter 11. See J. R. Franks and W. N. Torous, "A Comparison of Financial Recontracting in Distressed Exchanges and Chapter 11 Reorganizations," *Journal of Financial Economics* 35 (May 1994), pp. 349–370.

Sometimes the firm does agree to an informal workout with its creditors and then files under Chapter 11 to obtain the approval of the bankruptcy court. Such *prepackaged* or *prenegotiated bankruptcies* reduce the likelihood of subsequent litigation and allow the firm to gain the special tax advantages of Chapter 11.[38] For example, in 2014 Energy Future Holdings, the electric utility company, arranged a *prepack* after reaching agreement with its creditors. Since 1980, about 30% of U.S. bankruptcies have been prepackaged or prenegotiated.[39]

BEYOND THE PAGE

International bankruptcy procedures

mhhe.com/brealey13e

Alternative Bankruptcy Procedures

The U.S. bankruptcy system is often described as a debtor-friendly system. Its principal focus is on rescuing firms in distress. But this comes at a cost because there are many instances in which the firm's assets would be better deployed in other uses. Michael Jensen, a critic of Chapter 11, has argued that "the U.S. bankruptcy code is fundamentally flawed. It is expensive, it exacerbates conflicts of interest among different classes of creditors, and it often takes years to resolve individual cases." Jensen's proposed solution is to require that any bankrupt company be put immediately on the auction block and the proceeds distributed to claimants in accordance with the priority of their claims.[40]

In some countries, the bankruptcy system is even more friendly to debtors. For example, in France the primary duties of the bankruptcy court are to keep the firm in business and preserve employment. Only once these duties have been performed does the court have a responsibility to creditors. Creditors have minimal control over the process, and it is the court that decides whether the firm should be liquidated or preserved. If the court chooses liquidation, it may select a bidder who offers a lower price but better prospects for employment.

The UK is at the other end of the scale. When a British firm is unable to pay its debts, the control rights pass to the creditors. Most commonly, a designated secured creditor appoints a *receiver,* who assumes direction of the firm, sells sufficient assets to repay the secured creditors, and ensures that any excess funds are used to pay off the other creditors according to the priority of their claims.

Davydenko and Franks, who have examined alternative bankruptcy systems, found that banks responded to these differences in the bankruptcy code by adjusting their lending practices. Nevertheless, as you would expect, lenders recover a smaller proportion of their money in those countries that have a debtor-friendly bankruptcy system. For example, in France the banks recover on average only 47% of the money owed by bankrupt firms, while in the UK, the corresponding figure is 69%.[41]

Of course, the grass is always greener elsewhere. In the United States and France, critics complain about the costs of trying to save businesses that are no longer viable. By contrast, in countries such as the UK, bankruptcy laws are blamed for the demise of healthy businesses and Chapter 11 is held up as a model of an efficient bankruptcy system.

---

[38]In a prepackaged bankruptcy, the debtor gains agreement to the reorganization plan before the filing. In a prenegotiated bankruptcy, the debtor negotiates the terms of the plan only with the principal creditors.

[39]Data from Lynn LoPucki's Bankruptcy Research Database at **http://lopucki.law.ucla.edu.**

[40]M. C. Jensen, "Corporate Control and the Politics of Finance," *Journal of Applied Corporate Finance* 4 (Summer 1991), pp. 13–34. An ingenious alternative set of bankruptcy procedures is proposed in L. Bebchuk, "A New Approach to Corporate Reorganizations," *Harvard Law Review* 101 (1988), pp. 775–804; and P. Aghion, O. Hart, and J. Moore, "The Economics of Bankruptcy Reform," *Journal of Law, Economics and Organization* 8 (1992), pp. 523–546.

[41]S. A. Davydenko and J. R. Franks, "Do Bankruptcy Codes Matter? A Study of Defaults in France, Germany and the U.K.," *Journal of Finance* 63 (2008), pp. 565–608. For descriptions of bankruptcy in Sweden and Finland, see P. Stromberg, "Conflicts of Interest and Market Illiquidity in Bankruptcy Auctions: Theory and Tests," *Journal of Finance* 55 (December 2000), pp. 2641–2692; and S. A. Ravid and S. Sundgren, "The Comparative Efficiency of Small-Firm Bankruptcies: A Study of the U.S. and Finnish Bankruptcy Codes," *Financial Management* 27 (Winter 1998), pp. 28–40.

The Controversial Chrysler Bankruptcy

❯ Chrysler was the weakest of the Big Three U.S. auto manufacturers. We have noted its purchase in 2007 by the private-equity fund Cerberus. By 2009, in the midst of the financial crisis and recession, Chrysler was headed for the dustbin unless it could arrange a rescue from the U.S. government. The rescue came *after* Chrysler's bankruptcy, however. Cerberus's stake was wiped out.

Chrysler filed for bankruptcy on April 30, 2009. It owed $6.9 billion to secured lenders, $5.3 billion to trade creditors (parts suppliers, for example), and $10 billion to a Voluntary Employees' Beneficiary Association (VEBA) trust set up to fund health and other benefits promised to retired employees. It also had unfunded pension liabilities, obligations to dealers, and warranty obligations to customers.

Just six weeks later, on June 11, the bankruptcy was resolved when all of Chrysler's assets and operations were sold to a new corporation for $2 billion. The $2 billion gave secured creditors 29 cents on the dollar. Fiat agreed to take over management of New Chrysler and received a 35% equity stake. New Chrysler received $6 billion in fresh loans from the U.S. Treasury and the Canadian government, in addition to $9.5 billion lent earlier. The Treasury and Canadian government also got 8% and 2% equity stakes, respectively.

The secured bondholders were, of course, unhappy. The court and government did not pause to see if Chrysler was really worth only $2 billion or if a higher value could have been achieved by breaking up the company. But the unsecured creditors must have been unhappier still, right? The sale for $2 billion left nothing to them.

Wrong! The trade creditors got a $5.3 billion debt claim on New Chrysler, 100 cents on the dollar. The unfunded pension liabilities and dealer and warranty obligations were likewise carried over dollar-for-dollar to New Chrysler. The VEBA trust got a $4.6 billion claim and a 55% equity stake.

We noted that junior creditors and stockholders sometimes get small slices of reorganized companies that emerge from bankruptcy. These consolation prizes are referred to as *violations of absolute priority* because absolute priority pays senior creditors in full before junior creditors or stockholders get anything. But the Chrysler bankruptcy was resolved with *reverse priority*: Junior claims were honored and senior claims mostly wiped out.

What this means for U.S. bankruptcy law and practice is not clear. Perhaps Chrysler's 42-day bankruptcy was a one-off deal never to be repeated, except by GM. But now secured investors worry that "junior creditors might leapfrog them if things don't work out."*

---

* George J. Schultze, quoted in M. Roe and D. Skeel, "Assessing the Chrysler Bankruptcy," *Michigan Law Review* 108 (March 2010), pp. 728–772. This article reviews the legal issues created by the reverse priority of creditors in the sale to New Chrysler. See also A. D. Goolsbee, and A. B. Krueger, "A Retrospective Look at Rescuing and Restructuring General Motors and Chrysler," *Journal of Economic Perspectives* 29 (2015), pp. 3–24.

SUMMARY

A corporation's structure is not immutable. Companies frequently reorganize by adding new businesses or disposing of existing ones. They may alter their capital structure, and they may change their ownership and control. In this chapter, we looked at some of the mechanisms by which companies transform themselves.

We started with leveraged buyouts (LBOs). An LBO is a takeover or buyout of a company or division that is financed mostly with debt. The LBO is owned privately, usually by an investment partnership. Debt financing is not the objective of most LBOs; it is a means to an end. Most LBOs are diet deals. The cash requirements for debt service force managers to shed unneeded assets, improve operating efficiency, and forego wasteful expenditure. The managers and employees are given a significant stake in the business, so they have strong incentives to make these improvements.

A leveraged restructuring is in many ways similar to an LBO. In this case, the company puts *itself* on a diet. Large amounts of debt are added and the proceeds are paid out to shareholders. The company is forced to generate cash to service the debt, but there is no change in control and the company stays public.

Most investments in LBOs are made by private-equity partnerships. The limited partners, who put up most of the money, are mostly institutional investors, including pension funds, endowments, and insurance companies. The general partners, who organize and manage the funds, receive a management fee and get a carried interest in the fund's profits. We called these partnerships "temporary conglomerates." They are conglomerates because they create a portfolio of companies in unrelated industries. They are temporary because the partnership has a limited life, usually about 10 years. At the end of this period, the partnership's investments must be sold or taken public again in IPOs. Private-equity funds do not buy and hold; they buy, fix, and sell. Investors in the partnership therefore do not have to worry about wasteful reinvestment of free cash flow.

The private-equity market has prospered. In contrast to these temporary conglomerates, public conglomerates have been declining in the United States. In public companies, unrelated diversification seems to destroy value—the whole is worth less than the sum of its parts. There are two possible reasons for this. First, since the value of the parts can't be observed separately, it is harder to set incentives for divisional managers. Second, conglomerates' internal capital markets are inefficient. It is difficult for management to appreciate investment opportunities in many different industries, and internal capital markets are prone to overinvestment and cross-subsidies.

Of course, companies shed assets as well as acquire them. Assets may be divested by spin-offs, carve-outs, or asset sales. In a spin-off, the parent firm splits off part of its business into a separate public company and gives its shareholders stock in the company. In a carve-out, the parent raises cash by separating off part of its business and selling shares in this business through an IPO. These divestitures are generally good news to investors; it appears that the divisions are moving to better homes, where they can be well managed and more profitable. The same improvements in efficiency and profitability are observed in privatizations, which are spin-offs or carve-outs of businesses owned by governments.

Companies in distress may reorganize by getting together with their creditors to arrange a workout. For example, they may agree to a delay in repayment. If a workout proves impossible, the company needs to file for bankruptcy. Chapter 11 of the Bankruptcy Act, which is used by most large public companies, seeks to reorganize the company and put it back on its feet again. However, the goal of paying off the company's creditors often conflicts with the aim of keeping the business going. As a result, Chapter 11 sometimes allows a firm to continue to operate when its assets could be better used elsewhere and the proceeds used to pay off creditors.

Chapter 11 tends to favor the debtor. But in some other countries, the bankruptcy system is designed almost exclusively to recover as much cash as possible for the lenders. While U.S. critics of Chapter 11 complain about the costs of saving businesses that are not worth saving, commentators elsewhere bemoan the fact that their bankruptcy laws are causing the breakup of potentially healthy businesses.

● ● ● ● ●

FURTHER READING

The following paper provides a general overview of corporate restructuring:

B. E. Eckbo and K. S. Thorburn, "Corporate Restructuring: Breakups and LBOs," in B. E. Eckbo (ed.), *Handbook of Empirical Corporate Finance* (Amsterdam: Elsevier/North-Holland, 2007), Chapter 16.

The papers by Kaplan and Stein and Kaplan and Stromberg provide evidence on the evolution and performance of LBOs. Jensen, the chief proponent of the free-cash-flow theory of takeovers, gives a spirited and controversial defense of LBOs:

S. N. Kaplan and J. C. Stein, "The Evolution of Buyout Pricing and Financial Structure (Or What Went Wrong) in the 1980s," *Journal of Applied Corporate Finance* 6 (Spring 1993), pp. 72–88.

S. N. Kaplan and P. Stromberg, "Leveraged Buyouts and Private Equity," *Journal of Economic Perspectives* 23 (2009), pp. 121–146.

M. C. Jensen, "The Eclipse of the Public Corporation," *Harvard Business Review* 67 (September/October 1989), pp. 61–74.

The Summer 2006, Fall 2011, and Winter 2014 issues of the Journal of Applied Corporate Finance *include several articles on private equity. Privatization is surveyed in:*

W. L. Megginson, *The Financial Economics of Privatization* (Oxford, UK: Oxford University Press, 2005).

The following books and articles survey the bankruptcy process. Bris, Welch, and Zhu give a detailed comparison of bankrupt firms' experience in Chapter 7 versus Chapter 11:

E. I. Altman and E.S. Hotchkiss, *Corporate Financial Distress and Bankruptcy: Predict and Avoid Bankruptcy, Analyze and Invest in Distressed Debt,* 3rd ed. (New York: John Wiley & Sons, 2006).

E. S. Hotchkiss, K. John, R. M. Mooradian, and K. S. Thorburn, "Bankruptcy and the Resolution of Financial Distress," in B. E. Eckbo (ed.), *Handbook of Empirical Corporate Finance* (Amsterdam: Elsevier/North-Holland, 2007), Chapter 14.

L. Senbet and J. Seward, "Financial Distress, Bankruptcy and Reorganization," in R. A. Jarrow, V. Maksimovic, and W. T. Ziemba (eds.), *North-Holland Handbooks of Operations Research and Management Science: Finance,* vol. 9 (New York: Elsevier, 1995), pp. 921–961.

J. S. Bhandari, L. A. Weiss, and B. E. Adler (eds.), *Corporate Bankruptcy: Economic and Legal Perspectives* (Cambridge, UK: Cambridge University Press, 2008).

A. Bris, I. Welch, and N. Zhu, "The Costs of Bankruptcy: Chapter 7 Liquidation versus Chapter 11 Reorganization," *Journal of Finance* 61 (June 2006), pp. 1253–1303.

Here are several good case studies on topics covered in this chapter:

B. Burrough and J. Helyar, *Barbarians at the Gate: The Fall of RJR Nabisco* (New York: Harper & Row, 1990).

G. P. Baker, "Beatrice: A Study in the Creation and Destruction of Value," *Journal of Finance* 47 (July 1992), pp. 1081–1119.

K. H. Wruck, "Financial Policy as a Catalyst for Organizational Change: Sealed Air's Leveraged Special Dividend," *Journal of Applied Corporate Finance* 7 (Winter 1995), pp. 20–35.

J. Allen, "Reinventing the Corporation: The "Satellite" Structure of Thermo Electron," *Journal of Applied Corporate Finance* 11 (Summer 1998), pp. 38–47.

R. Parrino, "Spinoffs and Wealth Transfers: The Marriott Case," *Journal of Financial Economics* 43 (February 1997), pp. 241–274.

C. Eckel, D. Eckel, and V. Singal, "Privatization and Efficiency: Industry Effects of the Sale of British Airways," *Journal of Financial Economics* 43 (February 1997), pp. 275–298.

L. A. Weiss and K. H. Wruck, "Information Problems, Conflicts of Interest, and Asset Stripping: Chapter 11's Failure in the Case of Eastern Airlines," *Journal of Financial Economics* 48 (April 1998), pp. 55–97.

W. Megginson and D. Scannapieco, "The Financial and Economic Lessons of Italy's Privatization Program," *Journal of Applied Corporate Finance* 18 (Summer 2006), pp. 56–65.

PROBLEM SETS

 **Select problems are available in McGraw-Hill's** *Connect.* **Please see the preface for more information.**

1. **Vocabulary** Define the following terms:
   a. LBO
   b. MBO
   c. Spin-off

    d. Carve-out

    e. Asset sale

    f. Privatization

    g. Leveraged restructuring

2. **Leveraged buyouts*** True or false?

    a. One of the first tasks of an LBO's financial manager is to pay down debt.

    b. Once an LBO or MBO goes private, it almost always stays private.

    c. Many early MBOs were arranged for unwanted divisions of large diversified companies.

    d. "Carried interest" refers to the deferral of interest payments on LBO debt.

    e. Private-equity partnerships have limited lives. The main purpose is to force the general partners to seek out quick-payback investments.

    f. Managers of private-equity partnerships have an incentive to make risky investments.

3. **Leveraged buyouts** Read *Barbarians at the Gate* (Further Reading). What agency costs can you identify? (*Hint:* See Chapter 12.) Do you think the LBO was well-designed to reduce these costs?

4. **Leveraged buyouts** For what kinds of firm would an LBO or MBO transaction *not* be productive?

5. **Leveraged buyouts** The Sealed Air leveraged restructuring is described in the Chapter 18 Beyond the Page feature. Outline the similarities and differences between the RJR Nabisco LBO and the Sealed Air restructuring. Were the economic motives the same? Were the results the same? Do you think it was an advantage for Sealed Air to remain a public company?

6. **Private-equity partnerships** Private-equity partnerships have a limited term. What are the advantages of this arrangement?

7. **Private-equity partnerships** Explain the structure of a private-equity partnership. Pay particular attention to incentives and compensation. What types of investment were such partnerships designed to make?

8. **Private-equity partnerships** We described carried interest as an option. What kind of option? How does this option change incentives in a private-equity partnership? Can you think of circumstances where these incentive changes would be perverse—that is, potentially value-destroying? Explain.

9. **Conglomerates** What advantages have been claimed for public conglomerates?

10. **Conglomerates** List the disadvantages of traditional U.S. conglomerates. Can private-equity firms overcome these disadvantages?

11. **Restructuring*** True or false?

    a. Carve-out or spin-off of a division improves incentives for the division's managers.

    b. The announcement of a spin-off is generally followed by a sharp fall in the stock price.

    c. Privatizations are generally followed by massive layoffs.

    d. On average, privatization seems to improve efficiency and add value.

12. **Divestitures** Examine some recent examples of divestitures. What do you think were the underlying reasons for them? How did investors react to the news?

13. **Privatization** "Privatization appears to bring efficiency gains because public companies are better able to reduce agency costs." Why do you think this may (or may not) be true?

14. **Privatization** What are the government's motives in a privatization?

15. **Bankruptcy** What is the difference between Chapter 7 and Chapter 11 bankruptcies?

16. **Bankruptcy*** True or false?

    a. When a company becomes bankrupt, it is usually in the interests of stockholders to seek a liquidation rather than a reorganization.

    b. In Chapter 11, a reorganization plan must be presented for approval by each class of creditor.

    c. In a reorganization, creditors may be paid off with a mixture of cash and securities.

    d. When a company is liquidated, one of the most valuable assets to be sold off is the tax-loss carry-forward.

17. **Bankruptcy** We described several problems with Chapter 11 bankruptcy. Which of these problems could be mitigated by negotiating a prepackaged bankruptcy?

18. **Bankruptcy** Explain why equity can sometimes have a positive value even when companies file for bankruptcy.

33 CHAPTER

Governance and Corporate Control around the World

Much of corporate finance (and much of this book) assumes a particular financial structure—public corporations with actively traded shares and relatively easy access to financial markets. But there are other ways to organize and finance business ventures. The arrangements for ownership, control, and financing vary greatly around the world. In this chapter, we consider some of these differences.

Corporations raise cash from financial markets and also from financial institutions. Markets are relatively more important in the United States, United Kingdom, and other "Anglo-Saxon" economies. Financial institutions, particularly banks, are relatively more important in many other countries, including Germany, Japan, and among emerging economies such as China and India. In bank-based systems, individual investors are less likely to hold corporate debt and equity directly. Instead, ownership passes through banks, insurance companies, and other financial intermediaries.

This chapter starts with an overview of financial markets, financial institutions, and sources of financing. We contrast continental Europe, Japan, and China and India to the United States and United Kingdom. Then Section 33-2 looks more closely at ownership, control, and governance. Here we start with the United States and United Kingdom and then turn to Japan, Germany, and the rest of the world. Section 33-3 asks whether these differences matter. For example, do well-functioning financial markets and institutions contribute to economic development and growth? What are the advantages and disadvantages of market-based versus bank-based systems?

Before starting on this worldwide tour, remember that the principles of financial management apply throughout the journey. The concepts and basic tools of the trade do not vary. For example, all companies in all countries should recognize the opportunity cost of capital (although the cost of capital is even harder to measure where stock markets are small or erratic). Discounted cash flow still makes sense. Real options are encountered everywhere. And even in bank-based financial systems, corporations participate in world financial markets—by trading foreign exchange or hedging risks in futures markets, for instance.

33-1 Financial Markets and Institutions

In most of this book, we have assumed that a large part of debt financing comes from public bond markets. Nothing in principle changes when a firm borrows from a bank instead. But in some countries, bond markets are stunted and bank financing is more important. Figure 33.1 shows the total values of bank loans, private (nongovernment) bonds, and stock markets in

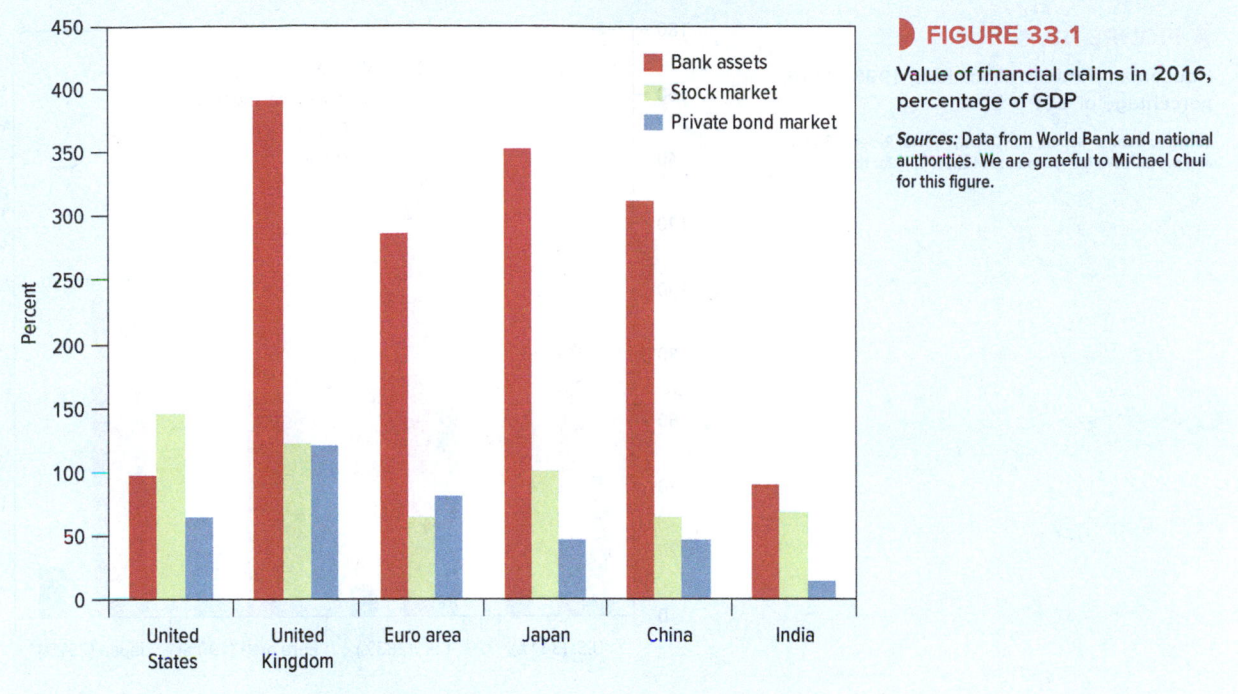

FIGURE 33.1

Value of financial claims in 2016, percentage of GDP

Sources: Data from World Bank and national authorities. We are grateful to Michael Chui for this figure.

different parts of the world in 2016. To measure these financial claims on a comparable basis, the amounts are scaled by gross domestic product (GDP).[1]

Company financing in the United States is different from that in most other countries. The United States not only has a large amount of bank loans outstanding, but there is also a large stock market *and* a large corporate bond market. Thus, the United States is said to have a market-based financial system. Stock market value is also high in the United Kingdom, but bank loans are much more important than the bond market. However, this is because the UK is an international banking center, so the bank loan figure includes eurocurrency loans. The figure does not represent just domestic loans. In Europe, Japan, and China, bank financing again outpaces bond markets, but the stock market is relatively small. In India, the financial system is less developed overall, with banks in particular being relatively small compared to most other countries. Most countries in Europe, including Germany, France, Italy, and Spain, have bank-based financial systems. So do many Asian countries, including Japan, China, and India.

Let's look at these regions from a different perspective. Figure 33.2 shows the financial investments made by households, again scaled by GDP.[2] ("Households" means individual investors.) Household portfolios are divided into four categories: bank deposits, insurance policies and mutual and pension funds, equity securities, and "other." Notice the differences in the total amounts of financial assets in Figure 33.2. Summing the columns for each country and region, the amount of financial assets is 344% of GDP in the United States, 283% in the United Kingdom, 190% in Europe, and 292% in Japan. This does not mean that European investors are poor, just that they hold less wealth in the form of financial assets. Figure 33.2 excludes other important investment categories, such as real estate or privately owned businesses. It also excludes the value of pensions provided by governments.

[1]For more detailed data and discussion of the material in this section, see F. Allen, M. Chui, and A. Maddaloni, "Financial Structure and Corporate Governance in Europe, the USA, and Asia," in *Handbook of European Financial Markets and Institutions*, X. Freixas, P. Hartmann, and C. Mayer, eds. (Oxford, UK: Oxford University Press, 2008), pp. 31–67.

[2]Data for China and India are not available for this and the following figures that summarize portfolio allocations.

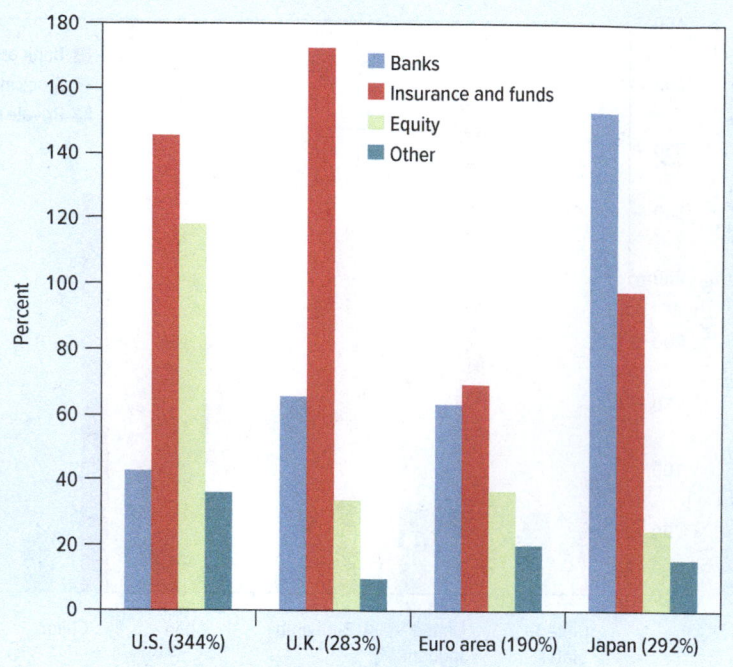

▶ **FIGURE 33.2**

Household portfolio allocations, 1995–2016, percentage of GDP

Sources: Bank of Japan, EUROSTAT, Federal Reserve Board, and the IMF. We are grateful to Michael Chui for this figure.

In the United States, a large fraction of households' portfolios is held directly in equity securities, mostly common stocks. Therefore, individual investors can potentially play an important role in corporate governance. Direct equity holdings are smallest in Japan. Japanese households could not play a significant direct role in corporate governance even if they wanted to. They can't vote shares that they don't own.

Where direct equity investment is small, household investments in bank deposits, insurance policies, and mutual and pension funds are correspondingly large. In the United Kingdom, the insurance and funds category dominates, with bank deposits in second place. In Europe, bank deposits and insurance and funds run a close race for first. In Japan, bank deposits win by a mile, with insurance and funds in second place and equities a distant third.

Figure 33.2 tells us that in many parts of the world, there are relatively few individual stockholders. Most individuals don't invest directly in equity markets, but indirectly, through insurance companies, mutual funds, banks, and other financial intermediaries. Of course, the thread of ownership traces back through these intermediaries to individual investors. All assets are ultimately owned by individuals. There are no Martian or extraterrestrial investors that we know of.[3]

Now let's look at financial institutions. Figure 33.3 shows the financial assets held by financial institutions, including banks, mutual funds, insurance companies, pension funds, and other intermediaries. These investments are smaller in the United States, relative to GDP, than in other countries (as expected in the U.S. market-based system). Financial institutions in the United Kingdom, Europe, and Japan have invested large sums in loans and in deposits. Holdings of equity are highest in the United Kingdom. These holdings are mainly owned by insurance companies and pension funds.

We've covered households and financial institutions. Is there any other source for corporate financing? Yes, financing can come from other corporations. Take a look at Figure 33.4, which shows the financial assets held by nonfinancial corporations. Perhaps the most striking

---

[3]There may be owners not yet present on this planet, however. For example, endowments of educational, charitable, and religious organizations are partly held in trust for future generations.

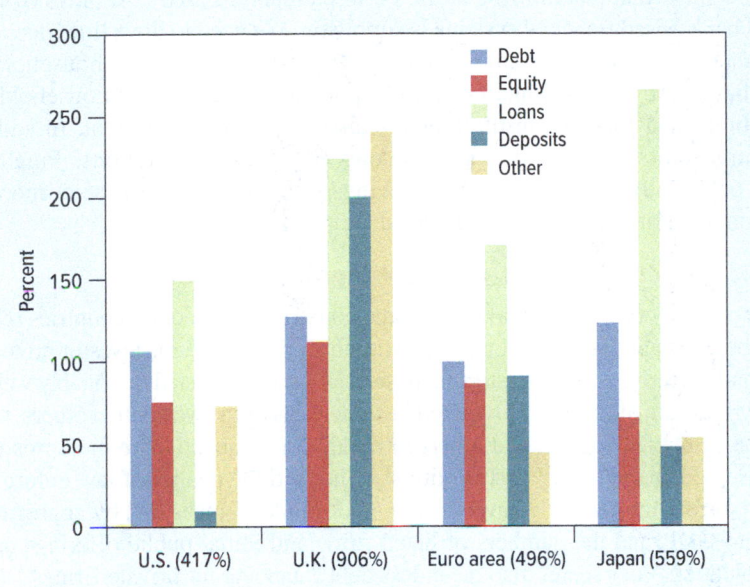

FIGURE 33.3

Financial institutions' portfolio allocations, 1995–2016, percentage of GDP

Sources: Bank of Japan, EUROSTAT, Federal Reserve Board, and the IMF. We are grateful to Michael Chui for this figure.

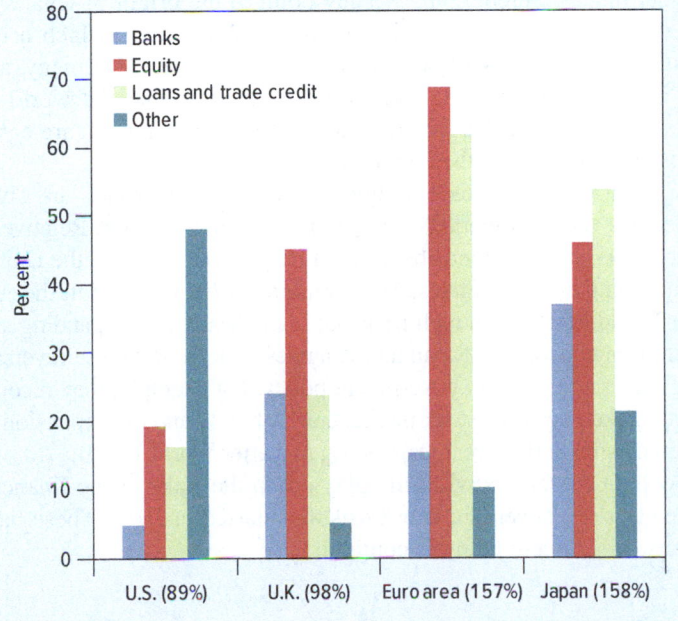

FIGURE 33.4

Nonfinancial corporations' portfolio allocations, 1995–2016, percentage of GDP

Sources: Bank of Japan, EUROSTAT, Federal Reserve Board, and the IMF. We are grateful to Michael Chui for this figure.

feature is the large amount of equity held by firms in Europe. The amount of equity held in Japan and the United Kingdom is also large. In the United States it is relatively small. As we will see, these holdings of shares by other nonfinancial corporations have important implications for corporate ownership and governance.

Another interesting aspect of Figure 33.4 is the large amount of intercompany loans and trade credit in Europe and Japan. Many Japanese firms rely heavily on trade-credit financing— that is, on accounts payable to other firms. Of course, the other firms see the reverse side of trade credit: They are providing financing in the form of accounts receivable.

Figures 33.1 to 33.4 show that just drawing a line between market-based, "Anglo-Saxon" financial systems and bank-based financial systems is simplistic. We need to dig a little deeper when comparing financial systems. For example, more equity is held directly by households in the United States than in the United Kingdom, and the portfolio allocations of households, nonfinancial corporations, and financial institutions are also significantly different. In addition, we noted the large cross-holdings of shares among European corporations. Finally, Japanese households put significantly more of their savings in banks and Japanese corporations use trade credit much more than in other advanced economies.

Investor Protection and the Development of Financial Markets

What explains the importance of financial markets in some countries, while other countries rely less on markets and more on banks and other financial institutions? One answer is investor protection. Stock and bond markets thrive where investors in these markets are protected reasonably well.

Investors' property rights are much better protected in some parts of the world than others. La Porta, Lopez-de-Silanes, Shleifer, Vishny, and others have developed quantitative measures of investor protection based on shareholders' and creditors' rights and the quality of law enforcement. Countries with poor scores generally have smaller stock markets, measured by aggregate market value relative to GDP, and the numbers of listed firms and initial public offerings are smaller relative to population. Poor scores also mean less debt financing for private firms.[4]

BEYOND THE PAGE

Country measures of governance

mhhe.com/brealey13e

It's easy to understand why poor protection of outside investors stunts the growth of financial markets. A more difficult question is why protection is good in some countries and poor in others. La Porta, Lopez-de-Silanes, Shleifer, and Vishny point to the origin of legal systems. They distinguish legal systems derived from the common-law tradition, which originated in England, from systems based on civil law, which evolved in France, Germany, and Scandinavia. The English, French, and German systems have spread around the world by conquest, imperialism, and imitation. Both shareholders and creditors, it is argued, are better protected by the law in countries that adopted the common-law tradition.

But Rajan and Zingales[5] point out that France, Belgium, and Germany, which are civil-law countries, had well-developed financial markets early in the twentieth century. Relative to GDP, these countries' financial markets were then about the same size as markets in the United Kingdom and bigger than those in the United States. These rankings were reversed in the second half of the century after World War II, although financial markets are now expanding and playing a greater role in European economies. Rajan and Zingales believe that these reversals can be attributed to political trends and shifts in government policy. For example, they recount the backlash against financial markets after the stock market crash of 1929 and the expansion of government regulation and ownership in the Great Depression and after World War II.

It remains to be seen how political factors will fully play out in the wake of the financial crisis of 2007–2009 and the eurozone sovereign debt crisis that started in 2010. These have already had significant effects, which seem likely to continue.

33-2   Ownership, Control, and Governance

Who owns the corporation? In the United States and United Kingdom, we just say "the stockholders." There is usually just one class of common stock, and each share has one vote. Some stockholders may have more influence than others, but only because they own more shares. In other countries, ownership is not so simple, as we see later in this section.

---

[4] R. La Porta, F. Lopez-de-Silanes, A. Shleifer, and R. Vishny, "Legal Determinants of External Finance," *Journal of Finance* 52 (July 1997), pp. 1131–1150, and "Law and Finance," *Journal of Political Economy* 106 (December 1998), pp. 1113–1155; and S. Djankov, C. McLiesh, and A. Shleifer, "Private Credit in 129 Countries," *Journal of Financial Economics* 84 (2007), pp. 299–329.
[5] R. Rajan and L. Zingales, *Saving Capitalism from the Capitalists* (New York: Crown Business, 2003).

What is the corporation's financial objective? Normally we just say "to maximize stockholder value." According to U.S. and UK corporation law, managers have a *fiduciary duty* to the shareholders. In other words, they are legally required to act in the interests of shareholders. Consider the classic illustration provided by an early case involving the Ford Motor Company. Henry Ford announced a special dividend, but then reneged, saying that the cash earmarked for the dividend would be spent for the benefit of employees. A shareholder sued on the grounds that corporations existed for the benefit of shareholders and the management did not have the right to improve the lot of workers at shareholders' expense. Ford lost the case.[6]

The idea that the corporation should be run in the interests of the shareholders is thus embedded in the law in the United States and United Kingdom. The board of directors is supposed to represent shareholders' interests. But laws and customs differ in other countries. Now we look at some of these differences. We start with Japan.

Ownership and Control in Japan

Traditionally the most notable feature of Japanese corporate finance has been the **keiretsu.** A keiretsu is a network of companies, usually organized around a major bank. Japan is said to have a *main bank* system, with long-standing relationships between banks and firms. There are also long-standing business relationships between a keiretsu's companies. For example, a manufacturing company might buy most of its raw materials from group suppliers and in turn sell much of its output to other group companies.

The bank and other financial institutions at the keiretsu's center own shares in most of the group companies (though a commercial bank in Japan is limited to 5% ownership of each company). Those companies may, in turn, hold the bank's shares or each other's shares. Because of the cross-holdings, the number of shares available for purchase by outside investors is much lower than the total number outstanding.

The keiretsu is tied together in other ways. Most debt financing comes from the keiretsu's main bank or from affiliated financial institutions. Managers may sit on the boards of directors of other group companies, and a "presidents' council" of the CEOs of the most important group companies meets regularly.

Think of the keiretsu as a system of corporate governance, where power is divided among the main bank, the group's largest companies, and the group as a whole. This confers certain financial advantages. First, firms have access to additional "internal" financing—internal to the group, that is. Thus a company with a capital budget exceeding operating cash flows can turn to the main bank or other keiretsu companies for financing. This avoids the cost or possible bad-news signal of a public sale of securities. Second, when a keiretsu firm falls into financial distress, with insufficient cash to pay its bills or fund necessary capital investments, a workout can usually be arranged. New management can be brought in from elsewhere in the group, and financing can be obtained, again "internally."

Hoshi, Kashyap, and Scharfstein tracked capital expenditure programs of a large sample of Japanese firms—many, but not all, members of keiretsus. The keiretsu companies' investments were more stable and less exposed to the ups and downs of operating cash flows or to episodes of financial distress.[7] It seems that the financial support of the keiretsus enabled members to invest for the long run, regardless of temporary setbacks.

Corporation law in Japan resembles that in the United States, but there are some important differences. For example, in Japan it is easier for shareholders to nominate and elect directors. Also, management remuneration must be approved at general meetings of shareholders.[8] Nevertheless,

---

[6]Subsequently, it appeared that Henry Ford reneged on the dividend so that he could purchase blocks of shares at depressed prices!

[7]T. Hoshi, A. Kashyap, and D. Scharfstein, "Corporate Structure, Liquidity and Investment: Evidence from Japanese Industrial Groups," *Quarterly Journal of Economics* 106 (February 1991), pp. 33–60, and "The Role of Banks in Reducing the Costs of Financial Distress in Japan," *Journal of Financial Economics* 27 (September 1990), pp. 67–88.

[8]These requirements have led to a unique feature of Japanese corporate life, the *sokaiya*, who are racketeers who demand payment in exchange for not disrupting shareholders' meetings.

ordinary shareholders do not, in fact, have much influence. Japanese boards traditionally had 40 or 50 members, with only a handful who are potentially independent of management. However, in recent years, many Japanese companies have changed to U.S.-style boards with fewer members and more independent directors. However, it is still the case that the CEO has tremendous influence. As long as the financial position of a Japanese corporation is sound, the CEO and senior management control the corporation. Outside stockholders have very little influence.

Given this control, plus the cross-holdings within industrial groups, it's no surprise that hostile takeovers are exceedingly rare in Japan. Also, Japanese corporations have been stingy with dividends, which probably reflects the relative lack of influence of outside shareholders. On the other hand, Japanese CEOs do not use their power to generate large sums of personal wealth. They are not well paid, compared to CEOs in most other developed countries. (Look back to Figure 12.1 for average top-management compensation levels for Japan and other countries.)

Cross-holdings reached a peak around 1990 when about 50% of corporations' shares were held by other Japanese companies and financial institutions. Starting in the mid-1990s, a banking crisis began to emerge in Japan. This led firms to sell off bank shares because they viewed them as bad investments. Banks and firms in financial distress, such as Nissan, sold off other companies' shares to raise funds. By 2004, the level of cross-holdings had fallen to 20%. They rose again in the next few years as companies in the steel and other industries began to worry about hostile takeovers, which was the original motivation for acquisition of cross-holdings in the 1950s and 1960s.[9]

One of the most important changes in Japan in recent years has been the introduction of economic reforms by Prime Minister Shinzo Abe. These reforms are commonly known as Abenomics. Changes in corporate governance have been a major component of these. Their purpose is to make managers more responsible to shareholders and make companies more competitive, profitable, and transparent. The Tokyo Stock Exchange (TSE) and the government's Financial Services Agency introduced a new, but legally nonbinding, Corporate Governance Code in 2015. The two most important suggestions are the appointment of two independent outside directors and the disclosure of the company's policy regarding cross-shareholding in the hope that this will help reduce the amount of cross-shareholdings. It remains to be seen how effective the code will be in the long run, but the fact that foreign ownership of TSE-listed firms has been above 30% in recent years should increase companies', willingness to adopt it.[10]

Ownership and Control in Germany

Traditionally, banks in Germany played a significant role in corporate governance. This involved providing loans, owning large amounts of equity directly, and the proxy voting of shares held on behalf of customers. Over time, this role has changed significantly. The relationship between the largest German bank, Deutsche Bank, and one of the largest German companies, Daimler AG, provides a good illustration.

Panel *a* of Figure 33.5 shows the 1990 ownership structure of Daimler, or as it was known then, Daimler-Benz. The immediate owners were Deutsche Bank with 28%, Mercedes Automobil Holding with 25%, and the Kuwait Government with 14%. The remaining 32% of the shares were widely held by about 300,000 individual and institutional investors. But this was only the top layer. Mercedes Automobil's holding was half owned by holding companies "Stella" and "Stern," for short. The rest of its shares were widely held. Stella's shares were in

---

[9]See H. Miyajima and F. Kuroki, "The Unwinding of Cross-Shareholding in Japan: Causes, Effects and Implications," in *Corporate Governance in Japan: Institutional Change and Organizational Diversity,* ed. M. Aoki, G. Jackson, and H. Miyajima (Oxford and New York: Oxford University Press, 2007), pp. 79–124. Also see "Criss-Crossed Capitalism," *The Economist* print edition, November 6, 2008.

[10]See, for example, H. Patrick, "Japan's Abenomics Bumps Along," Center on Japanese Economy and Business Occasional Paper 74, 2016, Columbia University, available at **https://academiccommons.columbia.edu/catalog/ac:194322**.

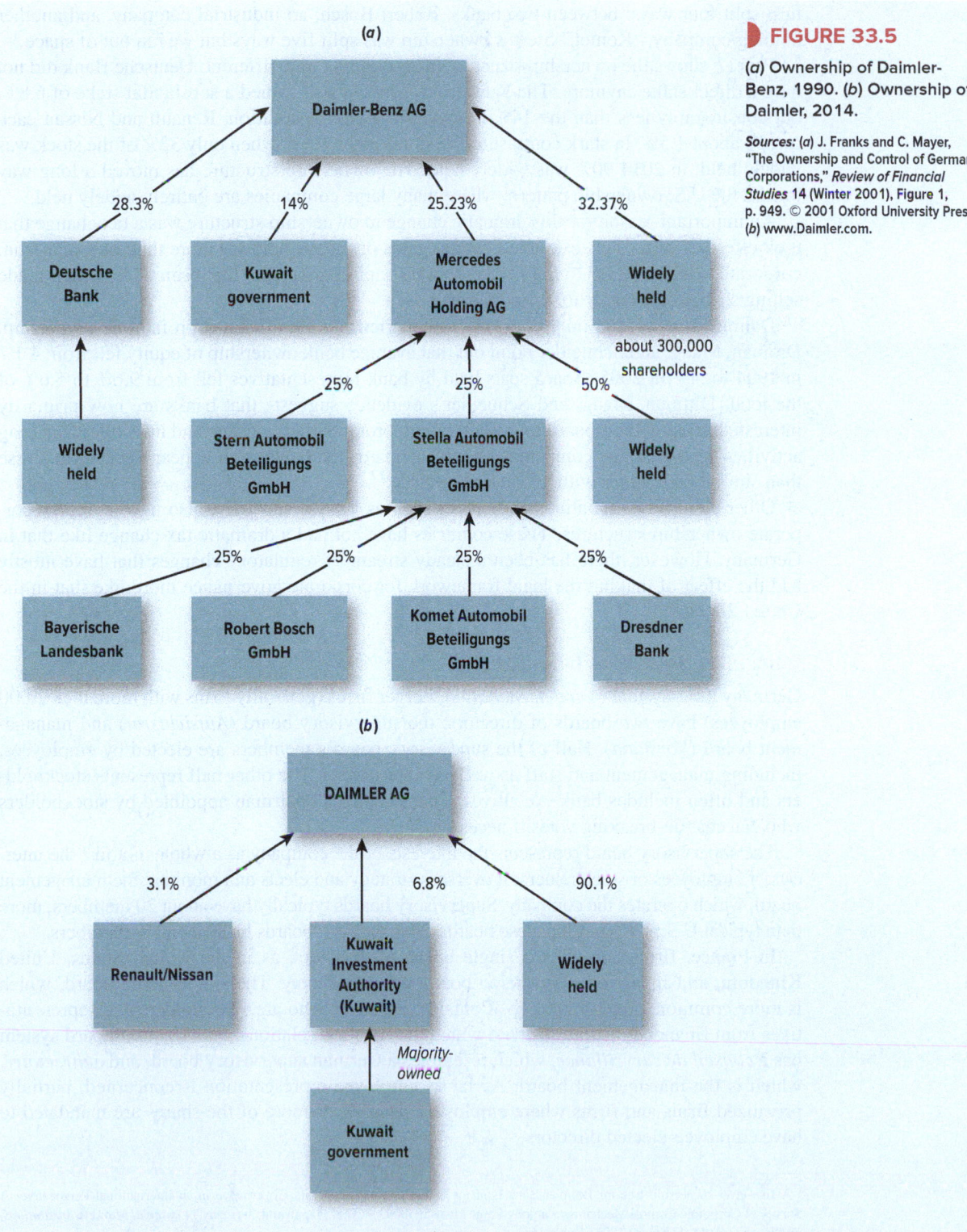

(a)

Daimler-Benz AG

28.3% — **Deutsche Bank**

14% — **Kuwait government**

25.23% — **Mercedes Automobil Holding AG**

32.37% — **Widely held**

about 300,000 shareholders

Widely held

25% — **Stern Automobil Beteiligungs GmbH**

25% — **Stella Automobil Beteiligungs GmbH**

50% — **Widely held**

25% — **Bayerische Landesbank**

25% — **Robert Bosch GmbH**

25% — **Komet Automobil Beteiligungs GmbH**

25% — **Dresdner Bank**

(b)

DAIMLER AG

3.1% — **Renault/Nissan**

6.8% — **Kuwait Investment Authority (Kuwait)**

90.1% — **Widely held**

Majority-owned

Kuwait government

▶ **FIGURE 33.5**

(*a*) Ownership of Daimler-Benz, 1990. (*b*) Ownership of Daimler, 2014.

Sources: (*a*) J. Franks and C. Mayer, "The Ownership and Control of German Corporations," *Review of Financial Studies* 14 (Winter 2001), Figure 1, p. 949. © 2001 Oxford University Press. (*b*) www.Daimler.com.

turn split four ways: between two banks, Robert Bosch, an industrial company, and another holding company, "Komet." Stern's ownership was split five ways but we ran out of space.[11]

Panel *b* shows the ownership structure in 2014. It is quite different. Deutsche Bank did not have a direct stake anymore. The Kuwait government still owned a substantial stake of 6.8%, but considerably less than the 14% it owned in 1990. In addition, Renault and Nissan each owned about 1.5%. In stark contrast to the situation in 1990, when only 32% of the stock was widely held, in 2014 90% was widely held. The ownership structure has moved a long way toward the U.S. ownership pattern, where many large companies are entirely widely held.

An important reason for this dramatic change in ownership structure was a tax change that took effect in 2002. This exempted capital gains on shares held for more than one year from corporate taxation. Prior to that, the corporate capital gains rate had been 52%, which made selling shares very costly for corporations.

Daimler was not the only company to experience a significant drop in bank ownership. Dittman, Maug, and Schneider point out that average bank ownership of equity fell from 4.1% in 1994 to .4% in 2005. Board seats held by bank representatives fell from 9.6% to 5.6% of the total. Dittman, Maug, and Schneider's evidence suggests that banks are now primarily interested in using their board representation to promote their lending and investment banking activities. However, the companies on whose boards the bankers sit appear to perform worse than similar companies without such a presence.[12]

Other countries in continental Europe, such as France and Italy, also have complex corporate ownership structures. These countries have not had a dramatic tax change like that in Germany. However, there has been a steady stream of regulatory changes that have mostly had the effect of making the legal framework for corporate governance more like that in the United States.[13]

European Boards of Directors

Germany has a system of *codetermination.* Larger firms (generally firms with more than 2,000 employees) have *two* boards of directors: the supervisory board (*Aufsichtsrat*) and management board (*Vorstand*). Half of the supervisory board's members are elected by employees, including management and staff as well as labor unions. The other half represents stockholders and often includes bank executives. There is also a chairman appointed by stockholders who can cast tie-breaking votes if necessary.

The supervisory board represents the interests of the company as a whole, not just the interests of employees or stockholders. It oversees strategy and elects and monitors the management board, which operates the company. Supervisory boards typically have about 20 members, more than typical U.S., UK, and Japanese boards. Management boards have about 10 members.

In France, firms can elect a single board of directors, as in the United States, United Kingdom, and Japan, or a two-tiered board, as in Germany. The single-tiered board, which is more common, consists mostly of outside directors, who are shareholders and representatives from financial institutions with which the firm has relationships. The two-board system has a *conseil de surveillance,* which resembles a German supervisory board, and a *directoire,* which is the management board. As far as employee representation is concerned, partially privatized firms and firms where employees own 3% or more of the shares are mandated to have employee-elected directors.

---

[11]A five-layer ownership tree for Daimler-Benz is given in S. Prowse, "Corporate Governance in an International Perspective: A Survey of Corporate Control Mechanisms among Large Firms in the U.S., U.K., Japan and Germany," *Financial Markets, Institutions, and Instruments* 4 (February 1995), Table 16.

[12]See I. Dittmann, E. Maug, and C. Schneider, "Bankers on the Boards of German Firms: What They Do, What They Are Worth, and Why They Are (Still) There," *Review of Finance,* 14 (2010), pp. 35–71.

[13]See L. Enriques and P. Volpin, "Corporate Governance Reforms in Continental Europe," *Journal of Economic Perspectives* 21 (2007), pp. 117–140.

Shareholders versus Stakeholders

It is often suggested that companies should be managed on behalf of all *stakeholders,* not just shareholders. Other stakeholders include employees, customers, suppliers, and the communities where the firm's plants and offices are located.

Different countries take very different views. In the United States, UK, and other "Anglo-Saxon" economies, the idea of maximizing shareholder value is widely accepted as the chief financial goal of the firm.

In other countries, workers' interests are put forward much more strongly. In Germany, for example, as discussed previously, workers in large companies have the right to elect up to half of the directors to the companies' supervisory boards. As a result they have a significant role in the governance of the firm and less attention is paid to the shareholders.[14] In Japan managers usually put the interests of employees and customers on a par with, or even ahead of, the interests of shareholders.

Figure 33.6 summarizes the results of interviews with executives from large companies in five countries. Japanese, German, and French executives think that their firms should be

FIGURE 33.6

(*a*) Whose company is it? The views of 378 managers from five countries. (*b*) Which is more important—job security for employees or shareholder dividends? The views of 399 managers from five countries.

Source: M. Yoshimori, "Whose Company Is It? The Concept of the Corporation in Japan and the West," *Long Range Planning* 28 (August 1995), pp. 2–3, 33–44. Elsevier Science.

---

[14]The following quote from the German banker Carl Fürstenberg (1850–1933) offers an extreme version of how shareholders were once regarded by German managers: "Shareholders are stupid and impertinent—stupid because they give their money to somebody else without any effective control over what this person is doing with it and impertinent because they ask for a dividend as a reward for their stupidity." Quoted by M. Hellwig, "On the Economics and Politics of Corporate Finance and Corporate Control," in *Corporate Governance,* ed. X. Vives (Cambridge, UK: Cambridge University Press, 2000), p. 109.

run for all stakeholders, while U.S. and UK executives say that shareholders must come first. When asked about the trade-off between job security and dividends, most U.S. and UK executives believe dividends should come first. By contrast, almost all Japanese executives and the majority of French and German executives believe that job security should come first.

As capital markets have become more global, companies in all countries face greater pressure to adopt wealth creation for shareholders as a primary goal. Some German companies, including Daimler and Deutsche Bank, have announced their primary goal as wealth creation for shareholders. In Japan, there has also been some movement in this direction as the proportion of foreign ownership of corporations has significantly increased in recent years.

Perhaps we should not make too much of these differences in objectives. Competitive forces alone oblige German and Japanese companies to run a tight ship. Likewise, a focus by U.S. companies on shareholder wealth does not mean that they can afford to rip off their customers or employees. As we pointed out in Chapter 1, corporations add value by establishing a reputation with all their stakeholders for fair dealing and integrity. That message is borne out in a study by Alex Edmans, which found that those U.S. companies with the most satisfied employees have also provided superior returns for their shareholders.[15]

Ownership and Control in Other Countries

Figure 33.7 repeats Figure 14.5, and shows the concentration of ownership in different countries. In the United States, Canada, South Korea, and Japan ownership of listed companies tends to be relatively dispersed, but Figure 33.7 shows that this is not true everywhere. For example, in France and Germany, the largest shareholder owns, on average, nearly half of the outstanding stock. Ownership is even more concentrated in Russia and Argentina.

La Porta, Lopez-de-Silanes, and Shleifer surveyed corporate ownership in 27 developed economies.[16] They found relatively few firms with actively traded shares and dispersed ownership. The pattern of significant ownership by banks and other financial institutions is also uncommon. Instead, firms are typically controlled by wealthy families or the state.

▷ **FIGURE 33.7**

Average percentage of equity owned by largest shareholders. (Shareholders from one family are grouped together).

Source: G. Aminadav and E. Papaioannou, "Corporate Control around the World," National Bureau of Economic Research, Working Paper 23010, December 2016 http://www.nber.org/papers/w23010.

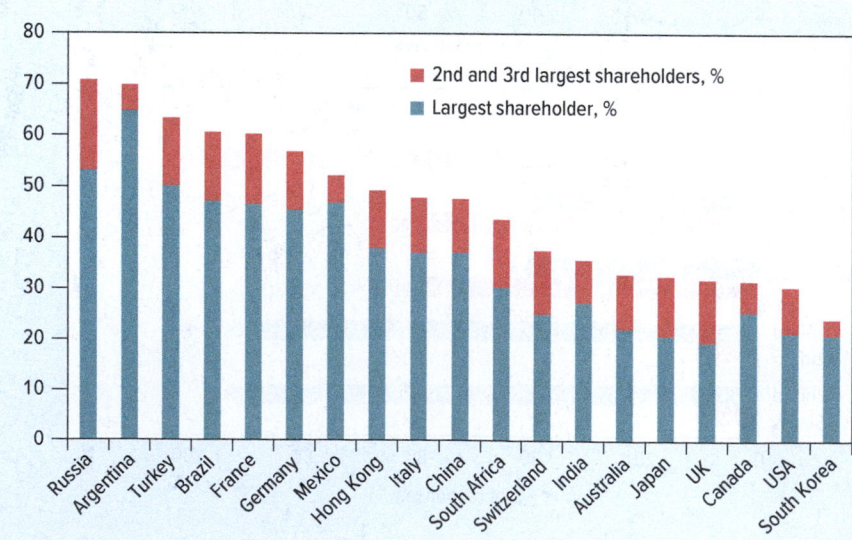

[15]See A. Edmans, "The Link Between Job Satisfaction and Firm Value, With Implications for Corporate Social Responsibility," *Academy of Management Perspectives* 26 (2012), pp. 1–19.
[16]R. La Porta, F. Lopez-de-Silanes, and A. Shleifer, "Corporate Ownership around the World," *Journal of Finance* 54 (1999), pp. 471–517.

The ultimate controlling shareholders typically have secure voting control even when they do not have the majority stake in earnings, dividends, or asset values.

State involvement is particularly important in China, where the central and local government has a controlling interest in almost a quarter of listed firms. In Europe, family control is common in France, Germany, Greece, and Italy. It is also widespread in South America and in Asia, with the principal exception of Japan.

Family control does not usually mean a direct majority stake in the public firm. Control is usually exercised by cross-shareholdings, pyramids, and dual-class shares. We have already discussed cross-holdings. Pyramids and dual-class shares need further explanation.

Pyramids   Pyramids are common in Asian countries as well as several European countries.[17] In a pyramid, control is exercised through a sequence of controlling positions in several layers of companies. The actual operating companies are at the bottom of the pyramid. Above each operating company is a first holding company, then a second one, then perhaps others still higher in the pyramid.[18] Look, for example, at Figure 33.8, which shows the principal shareholders of the French luxury goods company, LVMH. This company is controlled

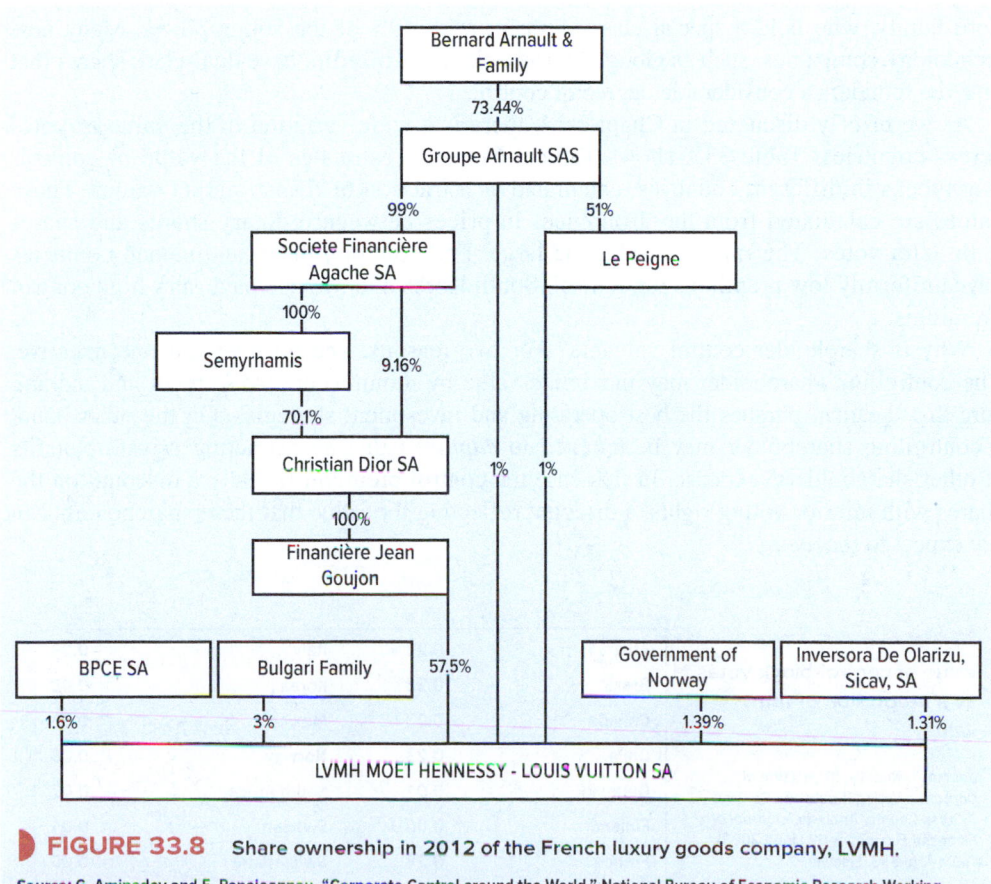

FIGURE 33.8   Share ownership in 2012 of the French luxury goods company, LVMH.

Source: G. Aminadav and E. Papaioannou, "Corporate Control around the World," National Bureau of Economic Research Working Paper, December 2016, http://www.nber.org/papers/w23010.

---

[17]L. A. Bebchuk, R. Kraakman, and G. R. Triantis, "Stock Pyramids, Cross-Ownership, and Dual Class Equity," in *Concentrated Corporate Ownership*, ed. R. Morck (Chicago: University of Chicago Press, 2000), pp. 295–318.
[18]A holding company is a firm whose only assets are controlling blocks of shares in other companies.

by Financière Jean Goujon, whose only business is to hold a 57.5% stake in LVMH. Jean Goujon is wholly owned by Christian Dior, which in turn, is controlled by Semyrhamis, whose main purpose is to hold Christian Dior shares. This company is a wholly owned subsidiary of Financière Agache, which also holds a direct 9.2% stake in Christian Dior. Financière Agache is a 99% controlled subsidiary of the private company Groupe Arnault SAS, which is the holding company of Bernard Arnault and his family. Groupe Arnault SAS also controls 51% of the firm Le Peigne, which holds 1% of the shares of LVMH. In sum, LVMH is controlled by Bernard Arnault and his family, who indirectly hold about a 61.5% stake (57.5% via Financière Jean Goujon, 2% via Financière Agache, 1% via Groupe Arnault SAS, and 1% via Le Peigne).

Dual-Class Equity   Another way to maintain control is to hold stock with extra voting rights. Extra votes can be attached to a special class of shares. For example, a firm's Class A shares could have 10 votes and the Class B shares only 1. *Dual-class equity* occurs frequently in many countries, including Brazil, Canada, Denmark, Finland, Germany, Italy, Mexico, Norway, South Korea, Sweden, and Switzerland. Stocks with different voting rights also occur (but less frequently) in Australia, Chile, France, Hong Kong, South Africa, the United Kingdom, and the United States.[19] For example, the Ford Motor Company is still controlled by the Ford family, who hold a special class of shares with 40% of the voting power. Many new technology companies, such as Google, Facebook, and LinkedIn, have dual-class shares that give the founders a considerable degree of control.

As we briefly discussed in Chapter 14, there is a wide variation in the value of votes across countries. Table 33.1 shows Tatiana Nenova's estimates of the value of controlling blocks in different countries, calculated as a fraction of firms' market values. These values are calculated from the differences in prices between ordinary shares and shares with extra votes. The range of values is large. For example, the Scandinavian countries have uniformly low premiums for control. South Korea and Mexico have very high control premiums.

Why is shareholder control valuable? For two reasons, one positive and one negative. The controlling shareholder may maximize value by monitoring management and making sure that the firm pursues the best operating and investment strategies. On the other hand, a controlling shareholder may be tempted to *capture* value by extracting private benefits at other shareholders' expense. In this case the control premium is really a discount on the shares with inferior voting rights, a discount reflecting the value that these shareholders can *not* expect to receive.

> **TABLE 33.1**   The value of control-block votes as a proportion of firm value
>
> *Source:* T. Nenova, "The Value of Corporate Voting Rights and Control: A Cross-Country Analysis," *Journal of Financial Economics* 68 (June 2003), Table 4, p. 336. Elsevier.

Australia	0.23	Italy	0.29
Brazil	0.23	Korea	0.48
Canada	0.03	Mexico	0.36
Chile	0.23	Norway	0.06
Denmark	0.01	South Africa	0.07
Finland	0.00	Sweden	0.01
France	0.28	Switzerland	0.06
Germany	0.09	United Kingdom	0.10
Hong Kong	−0.03	United States	0.02

---

[19]Dual-class equity is forbidden in Belgium, China, Japan, Singapore, and Spain.

Conglomerates Revisited

Of course, there are also examples of U.S. companies that are controlled by families or by investors holding large blocks of stock. But in these cases, control is exercised for a single firm, not a group of firms. Elsewhere in the world, and particularly in countries without fully developed financial markets, control extends to groups of firms in several different industries. These industrial groups are really conglomerates.

In Korea, for example, the 20 largest conglomerates own about 40% of the country's total corporate assets. These *chaebols* are also strong exporters: Names like Samsung and Hyundai are recognized worldwide. Conglomerates are also common in Latin America. One of the more successful, the Chilean holding company Quinenco, is a dizzying variety of businesses, including hotels and brewing, mobile telephone services, banking, and the manufacture of copper cable. Widely diversified groups are also common in India. The largest, the Tata Group, spans 80 companies in various industries, including steel, electric power, real estate, telecommunications, and financial services. All of these companies are public, but control rests with the group and ultimately with the Tata family.

The United States had a conglomerate merger wave in the 1960s and 1970s, but diversification didn't deliver value in the longer run, and most of the conglomerates of that era have dissolved. But conglomerates survive and grow in developing economies. Why?

Family ownership is part of the answer. A wealthy family can reduce risk while maintaining control and expanding the family business into new industries. Of course, the family could also diversify by buying shares of other companies. But where financial markets are limited and investor protection is poor, internal diversification can beat out financial diversification. Internal diversification means running an internal capital market, but if a country's financial markets and institutions are substandard, an internal capital market may not be so bad after all.

"Substandard" does not just mean lack of scale or trading activity. It may mean government regulations limiting access to bank financing or requiring government approval before bonds or shares are issued.[20] It may mean poor information. If accounting standards are loose and companies are secretive, monitoring by outside investors becomes especially costly and difficult, and agency costs proliferate.

Internal diversification may also be the only practical way to grow. You can't be big *and* focused in a small, closed economy, because the scale of one-industry companies is limited by the local market. Size can be an advantage if larger companies have easier access to international financial markets, which is important if local financial markets are inefficient. Size also means political power, which is especially important in managed economies or in countries where the government economic policy is unpredictable.

Many widely diversified business groups have been efficient and successful, particularly in countries like Korea that have grown rapidly. But there is also a dark side. Sometimes conglomerate business groups *tunnel* resources between the group companies at the expense of outside minority shareholders. Group company X can transfer value to Y by lending it money at a low interest rate, buying some of Y's output at high prices or selling X's assets to Y at low prices. Bertrand, Mehta, and Mullainathan found evidence of widespread tunneling in India.[21] Johnson, Boone, Breach, and Friedman note that the temptation to tunnel is stronger during a recession or financial crisis and argue that tunneling—and poor corporate governance in general—contributed to the Asian crisis of 1997–1998.[22]

---

[20]In the United States, the SEC does *not* have the power to deny share issues. Its mandate is only to ensure that investors are given adequate information.

[21]M. Bertrand, P. Mehta, and S. Mullainathan, "Ferreting out Tunneling: An Application to Indian Business Groups," *Quarterly Journal of Economics* 117 (February 2002), pp. 121–148.

[22]S. Johnson, P. Boone, A. Breach, and E. Friedman, "Corporate Governance in the Asian Financial Crisis," *Journal of Financial Economics* 58 (October/November 2000), pp. 141–186.

A good financial system appears to accelerate economic growth.[23] In fact, at least rudimentary finance may be necessary for any growth at all. Raghu Rajan and Luigi Zingales give the example of a bamboo-stool maker in Bangladesh, who needed 22 cents to buy the raw materials for each stool. Unfortunately, she did not have the 22 cents and had to borrow it from middlemen. She was forced to sell the stools back to the lenders in repayment for the loans and was left with only 2 cents' profit. Because of a lack of finance, she was never able to break out of this cycle of poverty. In contrast, they give the example of Kevin Taweel and Jim Ellis, two Stanford MBAs, who were able to purchase their own business soon after graduating. They had insufficient capital of their own but were able to raise seed funding to search for the right acquisition, and then additional funding to complete it.[24] Taweel and Ellis were the beneficiaries of a modern financial system, including a sophisticated private-equity market.

It is easy to understand the connection between financial and economic development by considering a very simple financial decision. Suppose you must decide whether to extend credit to a small business. If you are in the United States, you can almost instantaneously pull down a Dun and Bradstreet report via the Internet on any one of several million businesses. This report will show the company's financial statements, the average size of its bank balances, and whether it pays its bills on time. You will also receive an overall credit score for the company. Such widely available credit information reduces the cost of lending and increases the availability of credit. It also means that no one lender has a monopoly of information, which increases competition among suppliers of credit and reduces the costs to borrowers. In contrast, good credit information is not readily available in most developing economies, and lenders to small businesses are both few and expensive.

Of course, finance matters. But does the nature of a country's financial system matter as long as it is advanced? Does it matter whether a developed country has a market-based or bank-based system? Both types are effective, but each has potential advantages.

Risk and Short-Termism

If you look back to Figure 33.2, you will see that in different countries, the amount of risk borne by households in their financial portfolios varies significantly. At one extreme is Japan, where households hold more than half of their financial assets in bank accounts. Much of the remainder is in insurance and pension funds that, in Japan, mainly make fixed payments and are not linked to the stock market. Only a small proportion of household portfolios are linked to the stock market and to the business risk of Japanese corporations. European households also have relatively little direct exposure to the risks of the corporate sector. At the other extreme, households in the United States have large investments in shares and mutual funds.

Of course, someone has to bear business risks. The risks that are not borne directly by households are passed on to banks and other financial institutions and finally to the government. In most countries, the government guarantees bank deposits either explicitly or implicitly. If the banks get into trouble, the government steps in and society as a whole bears the burden. This is what happened in the crisis of 2007–2009.[25]

---

[23]R. Levine, "Financial Development and Economic Growth: Views and Agenda," *Journal of Economic Literature* 35 (1997), pp. 688–726; and R. Rajan and L. Zingales, "Financial Dependence and Growth," *American Economic Review* 88 (1998), pp. 559–586.

[24]R. Rajan and L. Zingales, *Saving Capitalism from the Capitalists* (New York: Crown Business, 2003), pp. 4–8.

[25]Another possibility is that banks that take a long-run view and are not subject to intense competition can smooth risk across different generations by building up reserves when returns are high and running them down when returns are low. Competition from financial markets prevents this type of intergenerational risk sharing. Generations with high returns want to receive their full returns and will not be willing to have reserves built up. See F. Allen and D. Gale, "Financial Markets, Intermediaries, and Intertemporal Smoothing," *Journal of Political Economy* 105 (June 1997), pp. 523–546.

Some people argue that firms are free to "invest for the long run" in bank-based systems where financial institutions absorb business risks and few individuals invest directly in the stock market. The close ties of Japanese and German companies to banks are supposed to prevent the dreaded disease of *short-termism*. Firms in the United States and United Kingdom are supposedly held captive by shareholders' demands for quick payoffs and therefore have to deliver quick earnings growth at the expense of long-term competitive advantage. Many found this argument persuasive in the late 1980s when the Japanese and German economies were especially robust.[26] When market-based economies surged ahead in the 1990s, views changed accordingly. If short-termism is a problem in market-based economies, why not provide incentives for shareholders to hold on to their shares? France, for example, already has adopted a rule that gives extra voting rights to long-term shareholders. The danger is that disenfranchising new investors may serve to entrench incompetent managers.

Growth Industries and Declining Industries

Market-based systems seem to be particularly successful in developing brand-new industries. For example, railways were first developed in the United Kingdom in the nineteenth century, financed largely through the London Stock Exchange. In the twentieth century, the United States led development of mass production in the automobile industry, even though the automobile was invented in Germany. The commercial aircraft industry was also mainly developed in the United States, as was the computer industry after World War II, and more recently the biotechnology and Internet industries.[27] On the other hand, Germany and Japan, two countries with bank-based financial systems, have sustained their competitive advantages in established industries, such as automobiles.

Why are financial markets better at fostering innovative industries?[28] When new products or processes are discovered, there is a wide diversity of opinion about the prospects for a new industry and the best way to develop it. Financial markets accommodate this diversity, allowing young, ambitious companies to search out like-minded investors to fund their growth. This is less likely when financing has to come through a few major banks.

Market-based systems also seem to be more effective at forcing companies in declining industries to shrink and release capital.[29] When a company cannot earn its cost of capital and further growth would destroy value, stock price drops, and the drop sends a clear negative signal. But in bank-based financial systems, uneconomic firms are often bailed out. When Mazda faltered in the 1970s, Sumitomo Bank guaranteed Mazda's debts and orchestrated a rescue, in part by exhorting employees within its keiretsu to purchase Mazda cars. Sumitomo Bank had an incentive to undertake the rescue because it knew that it would keep Mazda's business when it recovered. In the 1990s, Japanese banks continued to lend to "zombie" firms long after it became clear that prospects for their recovery were hopeless. For example, a coalition of banks kept the Japanese retailer Sogo afloat for years, despite clear evidence of insolvency. When Sogo finally failed in 2000, its debts had accumulated to ¥1.9 trillion.[30]

---

[26]See M. Porter, "Capital Disadvantage: America's Failing Capital Investment System," *Harvard Business Review,* September/October 1992, pp. 65–82.

[27]There are counterexamples, such as the development of the chemical industry on a large scale in nineteenth-century Germany.

[28]See F. Allen and D. Gale, "Diversity of Opinion and the Financing of New Technologies," *Journal of Financial Intermediation* 8 (January 1999), pp. 68–89.

[29]See R. Rajan and L. Zingales, "Banks and Markets: The Changing Character of European Finance," in V. Gaspar, P. Hartmann, O. Sleijpen, eds., *The Transformation of the European Financial System,* Second ECB Central Banking Conference, October 2002, Frankfurt, Germany (Frankfurt: European Central Bank, 2003), pp. 123–167.

[30]T. Hoshi and A. Kashyap, "Japan's Financial Crisis and Economic Stagnation," *Journal of Economic Perspectives* 18 (Winter 2004), pp. 3–26.

Transparency and Governance

Despite all these advantages of market-based systems, serious accidents happen. Think of the many sudden, costly corporate meltdowns after the telecom and dot-com boom of the late 1990s. In the last chapter, we noted the $100 billion bankruptcy of WorldCom (reorganized as MCI and now part of Verizon). But the most notorious meltdown was Enron, which failed in late 2001.

Enron started as a gas pipeline company, but expanded rapidly into trading energy and commodities, and made large investments in electricity generation, broadband communications, and water companies. By the end of 2000, its total stock market value was about $60 billion. A year later, it was bankrupt. But that $60 billion wasn't really lost when Enron failed because most of that value wasn't there in the first place. By late 2001, Enron was in many ways an empty shell. Its stock price was supported more by investors' enthusiasm than by profitable operating businesses. The company had also accumulated large hidden debts. For example, Enron borrowed aggressively through *special-purpose entities* (SPEs). The SPE debts were not reported on its balance sheet, even though many of the SPEs did not meet the requirements for off-balance-sheet accounting. (The fall of Enron also brought down its accounting firm, Arthur Andersen.)

The bad news started to leak out in the last months of 2001. In October, Enron announced a $1 billion write-down of its water and broadband businesses. In November, it consolidated its SPEs retroactively, which increased the debt on its balance sheet by $658 million and reduced past earnings by $591 million.[31] Its public debt was downgraded to junk ratings on November 28, and on December 2, it filed for bankruptcy.

Enron demonstrated the importance of *transparency* in market-based financial systems. If a firm is transparent to outside investors—if the investors can see its true profitability and prospects—then problems will show up right away in a falling stock price. That, in turn, generates extra scrutiny from security analysts, bond rating agencies, and investors. It may also lead to a takeover.

With transparency, corporate troubles generally lead to corrective action. But the top management of a troubled opaque company may be able to maintain its stock price and postpone the discipline of the market. Market discipline caught up with Enron only a month or two before bankruptcy.

Opaqueness is not so dangerous in a bank-based system. Firms will have long-standing relationships with banks, which can monitor the firm closely and urge it to staunch losses or to cancel excessively risky strategies. But no financial system can avoid occasional corporate meltdowns.

Parmalat, the Italian food company, appeared to be a solidly profitable firm with good growth prospects. It had expanded around the world, and by 2003 was operating in 30 countries with 36,000 employees. It reported about €2 billion in debt but also claimed to hold large portfolios of cash and short-term liquid securities. But doubts about the company's financial strength began to accumulate. On December 19, 2003, it was revealed that a €3.9 billion bank deposit reported by Parmalat had never existed. Parmalat's stock price fell by 80% in two weeks, and it was placed in administration (the Italian bankruptcy process) on December 24. Investors learned later that Parmalat's true debts exceeded €14 billion, that additional billions of euros of asset value had disappeared into a black hole, and that its sales and earnings had been overstated.

It's nice to dream of a financial system that would completely protect investors against nasty surprises like Enron and Parmalat. Complete protection of investors is impossible, however. In fact, complete protection would be unwise and inefficient even if it were feasible. Why? Because outside investors cannot know everything that managers are doing or why they are doing it. Laws and regulations can specify what managers can't do but can't tell them what

---

[31] Enron faced many further financial problems. For example, it told investors that it had hedged business risks in SPE transactions but failed to say that many of the SPEs were backed up by pledges of Enron shares. When Enron's stock price fell, the hedges unraveled. See P. Healy and K. Palepu, "The Fall of Enron," *Journal of Economic Perspectives* 17 (Spring 2003), pp. 3–26.

they should do. Therefore, managers have to be given discretion to act in response to unanticipated problems and opportunities.

Once managers have discretion, they will consider their self-interest as well as investors' interests. Agency problems are inevitable. The best a financial system can do is to protect investors reasonably well and to try to keep managers' and investors' interests congruent. We have discussed agency problems at several points in this book, but it won't hurt to reiterate the mechanisms that keep these problems under control:

- Laws and regulations that protect outside investors from self-dealing by insiders.
- Disclosure requirements and accounting standards that keep public firms reasonably transparent.
- Monitoring by banks and other financial intermediaries.
- Monitoring by boards of directors.
- The threat of takeover (although takeovers are very rare in some countries).
- Compensation tied to earnings and stock price.

In this chapter, we have stressed the importance of investor protection for the development of financial markets. But don't assume that more protection for investors is always a good thing. A corporation is a kind of partnership between outside investors and the managers and employees who operate the firm. The managers and employees are investors, too: They commit human capital instead of financial capital. A successful firm requires co-investment of human and financial capital. If you give the financial capital too much power, the human capital won't show up—or if it does show up, it won't be properly motivated.[32]

---

[32]It is difficult to observe effort and the value of human capital and, therefore, difficult to set up compensation schemes that reward effort and human capital appropriately. Thus, it can be better to allow managers some leeway to act in their own interests to preserve their incentives. Stockholders can provide this leeway by relaxing some of their rights and committing not to interfere if managers and employees capture private benefits when the firm is successful. How to commit? One way is to take the firm public. Direct intervention by public stockholders in the operation of the firm is difficult and, therefore, rare. See M. Burkart, D. Gromb, and F. Panunzi, "Large Shareholders, Monitoring, and the Value of the Firm," *Quarterly Journal of Economics* 112 (1997), pp. 693–728; S. C. Myers, "Outside Equity," *Journal of Finance* 55 (June 2000), pp. 1005–1037; and S. C. Myers, "Financial Architecture," *European Financial Management* 5 (July 1999), pp. 133–142.

SUMMARY

It's customary to distinguish market-based and bank-based financial systems. The United States has a market-based system because it has large stock and bond markets. The United Kingdom also has a market-based system: Its bond market is less important, but the UK stock market plays a crucial role in corporate finance and governance. Germany and Japan have bank-based systems because most debt financing comes from banks, and these countries' stock markets are less important.

Of course, the simple distinction between banks and markets is far from the end of the story. For example:

- UK households tend to hold shares indirectly, through equity-linked insurance and pensions. Direct investment in shares is much less common than in the United States.
- Japanese households bear relatively little equity risk. Most of their savings goes into bank accounts and insurance policies.
- In Europe, large blocks of a company's stock are often held by other corporations.
- In Japan, companies rely heavily on trade-credit financing, that is, on accounts payable to other companies.

In Japan and Germany, the role of banks goes beyond just lending money. The largest Japanese banks are the hubs of *keiretsus,* large, cooperative groups of firms. Each keiretsu is held together by long-standing ties to the main bank and by extensive cross-shareholdings within group companies. German banks also have traditionally had long-standing ties to their corporate customers (the *hausbank* system). The banks also exercise influence by voting shares held for other investors.

Ownership of large, public corporations in the United States and United Kingdom is pretty simple: There is one class of shares, which trade actively, and ownership is dispersed. In Japan, there is usually one class of shares, but a significant fraction of the shares is locked up in cross-shareholdings within keiretsus, although this fraction has decreased since the mid-1990s. Japanese stockholders have little say in corporate governance. European stockholders likewise have little say, given the concentration of ownership by banks and other corporations.

In the United States and United Kingdom, the law puts shareholders' interests first. Managers and boards of directors have a fiduciary duty to shareholders. But in Germany, the management board, which runs the business, answers to a supervisory board, which represents all employees as well as investors. The company as a whole is supposed to come first.

Outside the largest developed economies, a different pattern of ownership emerges. Groups of companies are controlled by families and sometimes by the state. Control is maintained by cross-shareholdings, pyramids, and issues of shares with extra voting rights to the controlling investors.

Wealthy families control large fractions of the corporate sector in many developing economies. These family groups operate as conglomerates. Conglomerates are a declining species in the United States, but a conglomerate's internal capital market can make sense where financial markets and institutions are not well-developed. The conglomerates' scale and scope may also provide political power, which can add value in countries where the government tries to manage the economy or where laws and regulations are enforced erratically.

Concentrated family control can be a good thing if it is used to force managers to run a tight ship and focus on value-maximizing investments. But concentration of control can also open the door to tunneling of resources out of the firm at the expense of minority investors.

Protection for outside investors varies greatly around the world. Where protection is good, market-based systems flourish. These systems have certain advantages: They appear to foster innovation and to encourage the release of capital from declining industries. On the other hand, market-based systems may end up investing too much in trendy innovations, as the collapse of the dot-com and telecom boom has illustrated. Bank-based systems may be better-suited to established industries. These systems also help shield individuals from direct exposure to stock market risk.

Market-based systems work only when public firms are reasonably transparent to investors. When they are opaque, like Enron, occasional meltdowns can be expected. Bank-based financial systems may have an advantage in monitoring and controlling opaque firms. The banks have long-standing relationships with their corporate customers and, therefore, have better information than outside investors.

FURTHER READING

The following studies survey or compare financial systems:

F. Allen and D. Gale, *Comparing Financial Systems* (Cambridge, MA: MIT Press, 2000).

M. Aoki, G. Jackson, and H. Miyajima, *Corporate Governance in Japan* (Oxford, UK: Oxford University Press, 2007).

J. P. Krahnen and R. H. Schmidt, eds., *The German Financial System* (Oxford, UK: Oxford University Press, 2004).

R. La Porta, F. Lopez-de-Silanes, and A. Shleifer, "Corporate Ownership around the World," *Journal of Finance* 54 (April 1999), pp. 471–517.

For excellent discussions of corporate governance, see:

M. Becht, P. Bolton, and A. Röell, "Corporate Governance and Control" in G. Constantinides, M. Harris, and R. Stulz, eds., *Handbook of the Economics of Finance* (Amsterdam: North-Holland, 2003), pp. 1–109.

R. Morck and B. Yeung, "Never Waste a Good Crisis: An Historical Perspective on Comparative Corporate Governance," *Annual Review of Financial Economics* 1 (2009), pp. 145–179.

A. Shleifer and R. W. Vishny, "A Survey of Corporate Governance," *Journal of Finance* 52 (June 1997), pp. 737–783.

For discussions of the role of law, politics, and finance see:

R. LaPorta, F. Lopez-de-Silanes, and A. Shleifer, "The Economic Consequences of Legal Origins," *Journal of Economic Literature* 46 (2008), pp. 285–332.

R. Rajan and L. Zingales, *Saving Capitalism from the Capitalists* (New York: Crown Business, 2003).

For the evidence on why finance matters for growth, see:

R. Levine, "Financial Development and Economic Growth: Views and Agenda," *Journal of Economic Literature* 35 (1997), pp. 688–726.

R. Rajan and L. Zingales, "Financial Dependence and Growth," *American Economic Review* 88 (June 1998), pp. 559–586.

Finally, if you'd like to read about corporate governance gone wrong . . .

P. Healy and K. Palepu, "The Fall of Enron," *Journal of Economic Perspectives* 17 (Spring 2003), pp. 3–26.

S. Johnson, R. La Porta, F. Lopez-de-Silanes, and A. Shleifer, "Tunneling," *American Economic Review* 90 (May 2000), pp. 22–27.

PROBLEM SETS

 **Select problems are available in McGraw-Hill's *Connect*. Please see the preface for more information.**

1. **Financial markets and institutions** Which major countries have

   a. The largest stock markets?

   b. The largest bond markets?

   c. The smallest direct holdings of shares by individual investors?

   d. The largest holdings of bank deposits by individual investors?

   e. The largest holdings of shares by other corporations?

   f. The largest use of trade credit for financing?

   In each case, define "largest" or "smallest" as total value relative to GDP.

2. **Financial markets and institutions*** True/ false?

   a. Direct holdings of equity by households are larger in Japan than in the United States.

   b. Bank financing of corporations is relatively important in Japan and continental Europe.

   c. Intercompany loans and trade credit are particularly important in the United States.

3. **Financial markets and institutions** What is a keiretsu? Give a brief description. What are some of their advantages and disadvantages?

4. **Financial markets and institutions** Banks are not the only financial intermediary from which corporations can obtain financing. What are the other intermediaries? How much financing do they supply, relative to banks, in the United Kingdom, Germany, and Japan?

5. **Financial markets and institutions** Why may market-based financial systems be better in supporting innovation and in releasing capital from declining industries?

6. **Company objectives** Generally in most Anglo-Saxon economies, managers have an obligation to act in the interests of shareholders. In other countries, they may have wider obligations to society as a whole. What are the pros and cons of the two sets of obligations?

7. **Company ownership*** True/false?

   a. In China, networks of companies are known as keiretsus.

   b. Dual-class equity prevents any one group of shareholders from maintaining control.

   c. Large firms in Germany have two boards of directors.

   d. Opaqueness is particularly dangerous in market-based systems.

   e. "Tunneling" refers to the practice of transferring resources out of the company to a controlling shareholder.

8. **Company ownership** It is suggested that family control allows the firm to focus on the long-term interests of the firm. What do you think are the offsetting disadvantages of family ownership?

9. **Company ownership** What is meant by dual-class equity? Do you think it should be allowed or outlawed?

10. **Company ownership** Do large blockholders increase company value? Does your answer depend on the structure of the financial system?

11. **Pyramids** Suppose that a shareholder can gain effective control of a company with 30% of the shares. Explain how a shareholder might gain control of company Z by setting up a holding company X^2 that holds shares in a second holding company X, which in turn holds shares in Z.

12. **Pyramids** Why are pyramids common in many countries but not in the United States or United Kingdom?

13. **Corporate governance** Do Japanese investors play an important role in corporate financial policy and governance? If not, could they?

14. **Corporate governance** German banks often control a large fraction of the shareholder votes for German businesses. How do they get that voting power?

15. **Corporate governance** What is meant by the German system of *codetermination*?

16. **Corporate governance** What is tunneling? Why does the threat of tunneling impede the development of financial markets?

17. **Corporate governance** Agency problems are inevitable. That is, we can never expect managers to give 100% weight to shareholders' interests and none to their own.

    a. Why not?

    b. List the mechanisms that are used around the world to keep agency problems under control.

18. **Corporate governance** Why is transparency important in a market-based financial system? Why is it less important in a bank-based system?

CHAPTER

34

Conclusion: What We Do and Do Not Know about Finance

It is time to sign off. Let us finish by thinking about some of the things that we do and do not know about finance.

34-1 What We Do Know: The Seven Most Important Ideas in Finance

What would you say if you were asked to name the seven most important ideas in finance? Here is our list.

1. Net Present Value

When you wish to know the value of a used car, you look at prices in the secondhand car market. Similarly, when you wish to know the value of a future cash flow, you look at prices quoted in the capital markets, where claims to future cash flows are traded (remember, those highly paid investment bankers are just secondhand cash-flow dealers). If you can buy cash flows for your shareholders at a cheaper price than they would have to pay in the capital market, you have increased the value of their investment.

This is the simple idea behind *net present value* (NPV). When we calculate an investment project's NPV, we are asking whether the project is worth more than it costs. We are estimating its value by calculating what its cash flows would be worth if a claim on them were offered separately to investors and traded in the capital markets.

That is why we calculate NPV by discounting future cash flows at the opportunity cost of capital—that is, at the expected rate of return offered by securities having the same degree of risk as the project. In well-functioning capital markets, all equivalent-risk assets are priced to offer the same expected return. By discounting at the opportunity cost of capital, we calculate the price at which investors in the project could expect to earn that rate of return.

Like most good ideas, the net present value rule is "obvious when you think about it." But notice what an important idea it is. The NPV rule allows thousands of shareholders, who may have vastly different levels of wealth and attitudes toward risk, to participate in the same enterprise and to delegate its operation to a professional manager. They give the manager one simple instruction: "Maximize net present value."

2. The Capital Asset Pricing Model

Some people say that modern finance is all about the capital asset pricing model. That's nonsense. If the capital asset pricing model had never been invented, our advice to financial managers would be essentially the same. The attraction of the model is that it gives us a manageable way of thinking about the required return on a risky investment.

Again, it is an attractively simple idea. There are two kinds of risk: risks that you can diversify away and those that you can't. You can measure the *nondiversifiable,* or *market,* risk of an investment by the extent to which the value of the investment is affected by a change in the *aggregate* value of all the assets in the economy. This is called the *beta* of the investment. The only risks that people care about are the ones that they can't get rid of—the nondiversifiable ones. This is why the required return on an asset increases in line with its beta.

Many people are worried by some of the rather strong assumptions behind the capital asset pricing model, or they are concerned about the difficulties of estimating a project's beta. They are right to be worried about these things. In 10 or 20 years' time, we may have much better theories than we do now.[1] But we will be extremely surprised if those future theories do not still insist on the crucial distinction between diversifiable and nondiversifiable risks—and that, after all, is the main idea underlying the capital asset pricing model.

3. Efficient Capital Markets

The third fundamental idea is that security prices accurately reflect available information and respond rapidly to new information as soon as it becomes available. This *efficient-market theory* comes in three flavors, corresponding to different definitions of "available information." The weak form (or random-walk theory) says that prices reflect all the information in past prices. The semistrong form says that prices reflect all publicly available information, and the strong form holds that prices reflect all acquirable information.

Don't misunderstand the efficient-market idea. It doesn't say that there are no taxes or costs; it doesn't say that there aren't some clever people and some stupid ones. It merely implies that competition in capital markets is very tough—there are no money machines or arbitrage opportunities, and security prices reflect the true underlying values of assets.

Extensive empirical testing of the efficient-market hypothesis began around 1970. By 2018, after almost 50 years of work, the tests have uncovered dozens of statistically significant anomalies. Sorry, but this work does *not* translate into dozens of ways to make easy money. Superior returns are elusive. For example, only a few mutual fund managers can generate superior returns for a few years in a row, and then only in small amounts.[2] Statisticians can beat the market, but real investors have a much harder time of it. And on that essential matter there is now widespread agreement.[3]

4. Value Additivity and the Law of Conservation of Value

The principle of *value additivity* states that the value of the whole is equal to the sum of the values of the parts. It is sometimes called the *law of the conservation of value.*

When we appraise a project that produces a succession of cash flows, we always assume that values add up. In other words, we assume

$$\text{PV(project)} = \text{PV}(C_1) + \text{PV}(C_2) + \cdots + \text{PV}(C_t)$$

$$= \frac{C_1}{1+r} + \frac{C_2}{(1+r)^2} + \cdots + \frac{C_t}{(1+r)^t}$$

---

[1] We must confess that we made this prediction 35 years ago in the first edition of this book. Sooner or later we will be right.

[2] See, for example, R. Kosowski, A. Timmermann, R. Wermers, and H. White, "Can Mutual Fund 'Stars' Really Pick Stocks? New Evidence from a Bootstrap Analysis," *Journal of Finance* 61 (December 2006), pp. 2551–2595.

[3] Some years ago, a young, upwardly mobile investment manager boasted to one of the authors that if he could not beat the market by 25% every year, he would shoot himself. Few people today would say that with a straight face. Even fewer would be alive tomorrow.

We similarly assume that the sum of the present values of projects A and B equals the present value of a composite project AB.[4] But value additivity also means that you can't increase value by putting two whole companies together unless you thereby increase the total cash flow. In other words, there are no benefits to mergers solely for diversification.

5. Capital Structure Theory

If the law of the conservation of value works when you add up cash flows, it must also work when you subtract them.[5] Therefore, financing decisions that simply divide up operating cash flows don't increase overall firm value. This is the basic idea behind Modigliani and Miller's famous proposition 1: In perfect markets changes in capital structure do not affect value. As long as the *total* cash flow generated by the firm's assets is unchanged by capital structure, value is independent of capital structure. The value of the whole pie does not depend on how it is sliced.

Of course, MM's proposition is not The Answer, but it does tell us where to look for reasons why capital structure decisions may matter. Taxes are one possibility. Debt provides a corporate interest tax shield, and this tax shield may more than compensate for any extra personal tax that the investor has to pay on debt interest. Also, high debt levels may spur managers to work harder and to run a tighter ship. But debt has its drawbacks if it leads to costly financial distress.

6. Option Theory

In everyday conversation, we often use the word "option" as synonymous with "choice" or "alternative"; thus, we speak of someone as "having a number of options." In finance, *option* refers specifically to the opportunity to trade in the future on terms that are fixed today. Smart managers know that it is often worth paying today for the option to buy or sell an asset tomorrow.

Since options are so important, the financial manager needs to know how to value them. Finance experts always knew the relevant variables—the exercise price and the exercise date of the option, the risk of the underlying asset, and the rate of interest. But it was Black and Scholes who first showed how these can be put together in a usable formula.

The Black–Scholes formula was developed for simple call options and does not directly apply to the more complicated options often encountered in corporate finance. But Black and Scholes's most basic ideas—for example, the risk-neutral valuation method implied by their formula—work even where the formula doesn't. Valuing the real options described in Chapter 22 may require extra number crunching but no extra concepts.

7. Agency Theory

A modern corporation is a team effort involving a number of players, such as managers, employees, shareholders, and bondholders. For a long time, economists used to assume without question that all these players acted for the common good, but in the last 30 years, they have had a lot more to say about the possible conflicts of interest and how companies attempt to overcome such conflicts. These ideas are known collectively as *agency theory*.

Consider, for example, the relationship between the shareholders and the managers. The shareholders (the *principals*) want managers (their *agents*) to maximize firm value. In the

---

[4]That is, if

$$PV(A) = PV[C_1(A)] + PV[C_2(A)] + \cdots + PV[C_t(A)]$$
$$PV(B) = PV[C_1(B)] + PV[C_2(B)] + \cdots + PV[C_t(B)]$$

and if for each period t, $C_t(AB) = C_t(A) + C_t(B)$, then

$$PV(AB) = PV(A) + PV(B)$$

[5]If you start with the cash flow $C_t(AB)$ and split it into two pieces, $C_t(A)$ and $C_t(B)$, then total value is unchanged. In other words, $PV[C_t(A)] + PV[C_t(B)] = PV[C_t(AB)]$. See Footnote 4.

United States, the ownership of many major corporations is widely dispersed, and no single shareholder can check on the managers or reprimand those who are slacking. So, to encourage managers to pull their weight, firms seek to tie the managers' compensation to the value that they have added. For those managers who persistently neglect shareholders' interests, there is the threat that their firm will be taken over and they will be turfed out.

Some corporations are owned by a few major shareholders, and therefore, there is less distance between ownership and control. For example, the families, companies, and banks that hold or control large stakes in many German companies can review top management's plans and decisions as insiders. In most cases, they have the power to force changes as necessary. However, hostile takeovers in Germany are rare.

We discussed the problems of management incentives and corporate control in Chapters 12, 14, 32, and 33, but they were not the only places in the book where agency issues arose. For example, in Chapters 18 and 24, we looked at some of the conflicts that arise between shareholders and bondholders, and we described how loan agreements try to anticipate and minimize these conflicts.

Are these seven ideas exciting theories or plain common sense? Call them what you will, they are basic to the financial manager's job. If, by reading this book, you really understand these ideas and know how to apply them, you have learned a great deal.

34-2   What We Do Not Know: 10 Unsolved Problems in Finance

Since the unknown is never exhausted, the list of what we do not know about finance could go on forever. But, following Brealey, Myers, and Allen's Third Law (see Section 29-5), we list and briefly discuss 10 unsolved problems that seem ripe for productive research.

1. What Determines Project Risk and Present Value?

A good capital investment is one that has a positive NPV. We have talked at some length about how to calculate NPV, but we have given you very little guidance about how to find positive-NPV projects, except to say in Section 11-2 that projects have positive NPVs when the firm can earn economic rents. But why do some companies earn economic rents while others in the same industry do not? Are the rents merely windfall gains, or can they be anticipated and planned for? What is their source, and how long do they persist before competition destroys them? Very little is known about any of these important questions.

Here is a related question: Why are some real assets risky and others relatively safe? In Section 9-3, we suggested a few reasons for differences in project betas—differences in operating leverage, for example, or in the extent to which a project's cash flows respond to the performance of the national economy. These are useful clues, but we have, as yet, no general procedure for estimating project betas. Assessing project risk is therefore still largely a seat-of-the-pants matter.

2. Risk and Return—What Have We Missed?

In 1848, John Stuart Mill wrote, "Happily there is nothing in the laws of value which remains for the present or any future writer to clear up; the theory is complete." Economists today are not so sure about that. For example, the capital asset pricing model is an enormous step toward understanding the effect of risk on the value of an asset, but there are many puzzles left, some statistical and some theoretical.

The statistical problems arise because the capital asset pricing model is hard to prove or disprove conclusively. It appears that average returns from low-beta stocks are too high (that is, higher than the capital asset pricing model predicts) and that those from high-beta stocks are too low; but this could be a problem with the way that the tests are conducted and not with the model itself.[6] We also described the puzzling discovery by Fama and French that expected returns appear to be related to the firm's size and to the ratio of the book value of the stock to its market value. Nobody understands why this should be so; perhaps these variables are related to variable *x,* that mysterious second risk variable that investors may rationally take into account in pricing shares.[7]

Meanwhile, scholars toil on the theoretical front. We discussed some of their work in Section 8-4. But just for fun, here is another example: Suppose that you love fine wine. It may make sense for you to buy shares in a grand cru chateau, even if doing so soaks up a large fraction of your personal wealth and leaves you with a relatively undiversified portfolio. However, you are *hedged* against a rise in the price of fine wine: Your hobby will cost you more in a bull market for wine, but your stake in the chateau will make you correspondingly richer. Thus, you are holding a relatively undiversified portfolio for a good reason. We would not expect you to demand a premium for bearing that portfolio's undiversifiable risk.

In general, if two people have different tastes, it may make sense for them to hold different portfolios. You may hedge your consumption needs with an investment in wine making, whereas somebody else may do better to invest in a chain of ice cream parlors. The capital asset pricing model isn't rich enough to deal with such a world. It assumes that all investors have similar tastes: The hedging motive does not enter, and therefore they hold the same portfolio of risky assets.

Merton has extended the capital asset pricing model to accommodate the hedging motive.[8] If enough investors are attempting to hedge against the same thing, the model implies a more complicated risk–return relationship. However, it is not yet clear who is hedging against what, and so the model remains difficult to test.

So, the capital asset pricing model survives not from a lack of competition but from a surfeit. There are too many plausible alternative risk measures, and so far, no consensus exists on the right course to plot if we abandon beta.

In the meantime, we must recognize the capital asset pricing model for what it is: an incomplete but extremely useful way of linking risk and return. Recognize too that the model's most basic message, that diversifiable risk doesn't matter, is accepted by nearly everyone.

3. How Important Are the Exceptions to the Efficient-Market Theory?

The efficient-market theory is strong, but no theory is perfect; there must be exceptions.

Now some of the apparent exceptions could simply be coincidences, for the more that researchers study stock performance, the more strange coincidences they are likely to find. For example, there is evidence that daily returns around new moons have been roughly double those around full moons.[9] It seems difficult to believe that this is anything other than a chance relationship—fun to read about but not a concern for serious investors or financial managers. But not all exceptions can be dismissed so easily. For example, the stocks of firms that announce unexpectedly good earnings continue to perform well for a couple of months after the announcement date. Some scholars believe that this may mean that the stock market is inefficient and that investors have consistently been slow to react to earnings announcements. Of course, we can't

---

[6]See R. Roll, "A Critique of the Asset Pricing Theory's Tests: Part 1: On Past and Potential Testability of the Theory," *Journal of Financial Economics* 4 (March 1977), pp. 129–176; and, for a critique of the critique, see D. Mayers and E. M. Rice, "Measuring Portfolio Performance and the Empirical Content of Asset Pricing Models," *Journal of Financial Economics* 7 (March 1979), pp. 3–28.

[7]Fama and French point out that small firms, and firms with high book-to-market ratios, are also low-profitability firms. Such firms may suffer more in downturns in the economy. Thus size and book-to-market measures may be proxies for exposure to business-cycle risk. See E. F. Fama and K. R. French, "Size and Book-to-Market Factors in Earnings and Returns," *Journal of Finance* 50 (March 1995), pp. 131–155.

[8]See R. Merton, "An Intertemporal Capital Asset Pricing Model," *Econometrica* 41 (1973), pp. 867–887.

[9]K. Yuan, L. Zheng, and Q. Zhu, "Are Investors Moonstruck? Lunar Phases and Stock Returns," *Journal of Empirical Finance* 13 (January 2006), pp. 1–23.

expect investors never to make mistakes. If they have been slow to react in the past, perhaps they will learn from this mistake and price the stocks more efficiently in the future.

Some researchers believe that the efficient-market hypothesis ignores important aspects of human behavior. For example, psychologists find that people tend to place too much emphasis on recent events when they are predicting the future. If so, we may find that investors are liable to overreact to new information. It will be interesting to see how far such behavioral observations can help us to understand apparent anomalies.

During the dot-com boom of the late 1990s, stock prices rose to astronomic levels. The Nasdaq Composite Index rose 580% from the beginning of 1995 to its peak in March 2000 and then fell by nearly 80%. This is not the only occasion that asset prices have reached unsustainable levels. In the late 1980s, there was a surge in the prices of Japanese stock and real estate. In 1989, at the peak of the real estate boom, choice properties in Tokyo's Ginza district were selling for about $1 million a square foot. Over the next 17 years, Japanese real estate prices fell by 70%.[10]

Maybe such extreme price movements can be explained by standard valuation techniques. However, others argue that stock prices are liable to speculative bubbles, where investors are caught up in a scatty whirl of irrational exuberance.[11] Now that may be true of your Uncle Harry or Aunt Hetty, but why don't hard-headed professional investors bail out of the overpriced stocks? Perhaps they would do so if it was their money at stake, but maybe there is an agency problem that stems from the way that their performance is measured and rewarded that encourages them to run with the herd.[12] (Remember the remark by the CEO of Citigroup: "As long as the music is playing, you've got to get up and dance.")

These are important questions. Much more research is needed before we have a full understanding of why asset prices sometimes get so out of line with what appears to be their discounted future payoffs.

4. Is Management an Off-Balance-Sheet Liability?

Closed-end funds are firms whose only asset is a portfolio of common stocks. One might think that if you knew the value of these common stocks, you would also know the value of the firm. However, this is not the case. The stock of the closed-end fund often sells for substantially less than the value of the fund's portfolio.[13]

All this might not matter much except that it could be just the tip of the iceberg. For example, real estate stocks appear to sell for less than the market values of the firms' net assets. In the late 1970s and early 1980s, the market values of many large oil companies were less than the market values of their oil reserves. Analysts joked that you could buy oil cheaper on Wall Street than in West Texas.

All these are special cases in which it was possible to compare the market value of the whole firm with the values of its separate assets. But perhaps if we could observe the values of other firms' separate parts, we might find that the value of the whole was often less than the sum of the values of the parts.

Whenever firms calculate the net present value of a project, they implicitly assume that the value of the whole project is simply the sum of the values of all the years' cash flows. We

---

[10]See W. Ziemba and S. Schwartz, *Invest Japan* (Chicago, IL: Probus, 1992), p. 109.

[11]See C. Kindleberger, *Manias, Panics, and Crashes: A History of Financial Crises,* 4th ed. (New York: Wiley, 2000); and R. Shiller, *Irrational Exuberance* (Princeton, NJ: Princeton University Press, 2000).

[12]Investment managers may reason that if the stocks continue to do well, they will benefit from increased business in the future; on the other hand, if the stocks do badly, it is the customers who incur the losses and the worst that can happen to the managers is that they have to find new jobs. See F. Allen, "Do Financial Institutions Matter?" *Journal of Finance* 56 (August 2001), pp. 1165–1175.

[13]There are relatively few closed-end funds. Most mutual funds are *open-end*. This means that they stand ready to buy or sell additional shares at a price equal to the fund's net asset value per share. Therefore the share price of an open-end fund always equals net asset value.

referred to this earlier as the law of the conservation of value. If we cannot rely on that law, the tip of the iceberg could turn out to be a hot potato.

We don't understand why closed-end investment companies or any of the other firms sell at a discount on the market values of their assets. One explanation is that the value added by the firm's management is less than the cost of the management. That is why we suggest that management may be an off-balance-sheet liability. For example, the discount of oil company shares from oil-in-the-ground value can be explained if investors expected the profits from oil production to be frittered away in negative-NPV investments and bureaucratic excess. The present value of growth opportunities (PVGO) was negative!

We do not mean to portray managers as leeches soaking up cash flows meant for investors. Managers commit their human capital to the firm and rightfully expect a reasonable cash return on these personal investments. If investors extract too great a share of the firm's cash flow, the personal investments are discouraged, and the long-run health and growth of the firm can be damaged.

In most firms, managers and employees co-invest with stockholders and creditors—human capital from the insiders and financial capital from outside investors. So far we know very little about how this co-investment works.

5. How Can We Explain the Success of New Securities and New Markets?

In the last 50 years, companies and the securities exchanges have created an enormous number of new securities: options, futures, options on futures; zero-coupon bonds, floating-rate bonds; bonds with collars and caps, asset-backed bonds; catastrophe bonds; . . . the list is endless. In some cases, it is easy to explain the success of new markets or securities; perhaps they allow investors to insure themselves against new risks, or they result from a change in tax or in regulation. Sometimes a market develops because of a change in the costs of issuing or trading different securities. But there are many successful innovations that cannot be explained so easily. Why do investment bankers continue to invent, and successfully sell, complex new securities that outstrip our ability to value them? The truth is we don't understand why some innovations in markets succeed and others never get off the ground.

And then there are the innovations that do get off the ground but crash later, including many of the complex and overrated securities backed by subprime mortgages. Subprime mortgages are not intrinsically bad, of course: They may be the only route to home ownership for some worthy people. But subprime loans also put many homeowners in nasty traps when house prices fell and jobs were lost. Securities based on subprime mortgages caused enormous losses in the banking industry. A number of new securities and derivatives went out of favor during the crisis. It will be interesting to see which will remain permanently consigned to the dustbin and which will be dusted off and recover their usefulness.

6. How Can We Resolve the Payout Controversy?

We spent all of Chapter 16 on payout policy without being able to resolve the payout controversy. Many people believe dividends are good; others point out that dividends attract more tax, and therefore, it is better for firms to repurchase stock; and still others believe that as long as the firm's investment decisions are unaffected, the payout decision is irrelevant.

Perhaps the problem is that we are asking the wrong question. Instead of inquiring whether dividends are good or bad, perhaps we should be asking *when* it makes sense to pay high or low dividends. For example, investors in mature firms with few investment opportunities may welcome the financial discipline imposed by a high dividend payout. For younger firms or firms with a temporary cash surplus, the tax advantage of stock repurchase may be more influential. But we don't know enough yet about how payout policy should vary from firm to firm.

The way that companies distribute cash has been changing. An increasing number of companies do not pay any dividends, while the volume of stock repurchases has mushroomed. This may partly reflect the growth in the proportion of small high-growth firms with lots of investment opportunities, but this does not appear to be the complete explanation. Understanding these shifts in company payout policy may also help us to understand how that policy affects firm value.

7. What Risks Should a Firm Take?

Firms need to manage risk. In many cases this simply means having contingency plans in case there is a threat to the supply of raw materials or the loss of an important market. But in other cases there are actions that the firm can take to protect itself. For example,

- When a firm expands production, managers often reduce the cost of failure by building in the option to alter the product mix or to bail out of the project altogether.
- By reducing the firm's borrowing, managers can spread operating risks over a larger equity base.
- Most businesses take out insurance against a variety of specific hazards.
- Managers often use futures or other derivatives to protect against adverse movements in commodity prices, interest rates, and exchange rates.

All these actions reduce risk. But less risk can't always be better. The point of risk management is not to reduce risk but to add value. We wish we could give general guidance on what bets the firm should place and what the *appropriate* level of risk is.

In practice, risk management decisions interact in complicated ways. For example, firms that are hedged against commodity price fluctuations may be able to afford more debt than those that are not hedged. Hedging can make sense if it allows the firm to take greater advantage of interest tax shields, provided the costs of hedging are sufficiently low.

How can a company set a risk management strategy that adds up to a sensible whole?

8. What Is the Value of Liquidity?

Unlike Treasury bills, cash pays no interest. On the other hand, cash provides more liquidity than Treasury bills. People who hold cash must believe that this additional liquidity offsets the loss of interest. In equilibrium, the marginal value of the additional liquidity must equal the interest rate on bills.

Now what can we say about corporate holdings of cash? It is wrong to ignore the liquidity gain and to say that the cost of holding cash is the lost interest. This would imply that cash always has a *negative* NPV. It is equally foolish to say that because the marginal value of liquidity is equal to the loss of interest, it doesn't matter how much cash the firm holds. This would imply that cash always has a *zero* NPV. We know that the marginal value of cash to a holder declines with the size of the cash holding, but we don't really understand how to value the liquidity service of cash, and therefore, we can't say how much cash is enough or how readily the firm should be able to raise it. To complicate matters further, we note that cash can be raised on short notice by borrowing or by issuing other new securities, as well as by selling assets. The financial manager with a $100 million unused line of credit may sleep just as soundly as one whose firm holds $100 million in marketable securities. In our chapters on working capital management, we largely finessed these questions by presenting models that are really too simple or by speaking vaguely of the need to ensure an "adequate" liquidity reserve.

Here is another problem. You are a partner in a private-equity firm contemplating a major new investment. You have a forecast of the future cash flows and an estimate of the return that investors would require from the business *if it were a publicly traded company*. But how much extra return do you need to compensate for the fact that the stock cannot be traded? An addition of 1 or 2 percentage points to the discount rate can make a huge difference to the estimated value.

The crisis of 2007–2009 has again demonstrated that investors seem to value liquidity much more highly at some times than at others. Despite massive injections of liquidity by central banks, many financial markets effectively dried up. For example, banks became increasingly reluctant to lend to one another on an unsecured basis and would do so only at a large premium. In the spring of 2007, the spread between LIBOR and the interest rate on Treasury bills (the TED spread) was .4%. By October 2008, the market for unsecured lending between banks had largely disappeared, and LIBOR was being quoted at more than 4.6% above the Treasury bill rate.[14]

Financial markets work well most of the time, but we don't understand well why they sometimes shut down or clog up, and we can offer relatively little advice to managers as to how to respond.

9. How Can We Explain Merger Waves?

Of course, there are many plausible motives for merging. If you single out a *particular* merger, it is usually possible to think up a reason that merger could make sense. But that leaves us with a special hypothesis for each merger. What we need is a general hypothesis to explain merger waves. For example, everybody seemed to be merging in 1998–2000 and again in 2006–2007, but in the intervening years, mergers went out of fashion.

There are other instances of apparent financial fashions. For example, from time to time, there are hot new-issue periods when there seem to be an insatiable supply of speculative new issues and an equally insatiable demand for them. We don't understand why hard-headed businessmen sometimes seem to behave like a flock of sheep, but the following story may contain the seeds of an explanation.

It is early evening and George is trying to decide between two restaurants, the Hungry Horse and the Golden Trough. Both are empty and, because there seems to be little reason to prefer one to the other, George tosses a coin and opts for the Hungry Horse. Shortly afterward, Georgina pauses outside the two restaurants. She somewhat prefers the Golden Trough, but observing George inside the Hungry Horse while the other restaurant is empty, she decides that George may know something that she doesn't, and therefore, the rational decision is to copy George. Fred is the third person to arrive. He sees that George and Georgina have both chosen the Hungry Horse and, putting aside his own judgment, decides to go with the flow. And so it is with subsequent diners, who simply look at the packed tables in the one restaurant and the empty tables elsewhere and draw the obvious conclusions. Each diner behaves fully rationally in balancing his or her own views with the revealed preferences of the other diners. Yet the popularity of the Hungry Horse owed much to the toss of George's coin. If Georgina had been the first to arrive or if all diners could have pooled their information before coming to a decision, the Hungry Horse might not have scooped the jackpot.

Economists refer to this imitative behavior as a *cascade*.[15] It remains to be seen how far cascades or some alternative theory can help to explain financial fashions.

10. Why Are Financial Systems So Prone to Crisis?

The crisis that started in 2007 was an unwelcome reminder of the fragility of financial systems. One moment, everything seems to be going fine; the next moment, markets crash, banks

---

[14]See M. Brunnermeier, "Deciphering the Liquidity and Credit Crunch 2007–2008," *Journal of Economic Perspectives* 23 (Winter 2009), pp. 77–100.

[15]For an introduction to cascades, see S. Bikhchandani, D. Hirshleifer, and I. Welch, "Learning from the Behavior of Others: Conformity, Fads, and Informational Cascades," *Journal of Economic Perspectives* 12 (Summer 1998), pp. 131–170.

fail; and before long, the economy is in recession. Carmen Reinhart and Kenneth Rogoff have documented the effects of banking crises in many countries.[16] They find that systemic banking crises are typically preceded by credit booms and asset price bubbles. When the bubbles burst, housing prices drop, on average, by 35% and stock prices fall by 55%. Output falls by 9% over the following two years, and unemployment rises by 7% over a period of four years. Central government debt nearly doubles compared with its pre-crisis level.

At the start of 2010, the increased government debt in Greece and a number of other periphery eurozone countries caused the financial crisis to change into a sovereign debt crisis. First Greece, and later Ireland and Portugal, required a bailout from the IMF and other eurozone countries. Spain and Italy also needed to arrange government bailouts for their banks. In 2012, Greece finally defaulted on its government debt, and it has continued to lurch from one crisis to the next.

Our understanding of these financial crises is limited. We need to know what causes them, how they can be prevented, and how they can be managed when they do occur. We reviewed the roots of the latest crisis in Chapter 14. But crisis prevention will have to incorporate principles and practices that we discussed in other chapters, such as the importance of good governance systems, well-constructed compensation schemes, and efficient risk management. The interaction of politics and economics at such times is particularly important but poorly appreciated. Understanding financial crises will occupy economists and financial regulators for many years to come.[17] Let's hope they figure out the last one before the next one knocks on the door.

34-3 A Final Word

That concludes our list of unsolved problems. We have given you the 10 uppermost in our minds. If there are others that you find more interesting and challenging, by all means construct your own list and start thinking about it.

It will take years for our 10 problems to be finally solved and replaced with a fresh list. In the meantime, we invite you to go on to study further what we *already* know about finance. We also invite you to apply what you have learned from reading this book.

Now that the book is done, we sympathize with Huckleberry Finn. At the end of his book he says:

> So there ain't nothing more to write, and I am rotten glad of it, because if I'd a' knowed what a trouble it was to make a book I wouldn't a' tackled it, and I ain't a' going to no more.

---

[16] See C. Reinhart and K. Rogoff, "The Aftermath of Financial Crises," *American Economic Review* 99 (May 2009), pp. 466–472.
[17] For a review of the current literature on financial crises, see F. Allen, A. Babus, and E. Carletti, "Financial Crises: Theory and Evidence," *Annual Review of Financial Economics* 1 (2009), pp. 97–116.

Answers to Select Problems

CHAPTER 1

2. a. Financial; b. financial; c. real; d. real; e. real; f. financial; g. real; h. financial

4. c; d

6. a

CHAPTER 2

7. a. $179.08; b. $320.71; c. $148.02; d. $219.11

13. $23,696

17. −$14.67

21. a. 10.50%; b. 0.819; c. 0.905 + 0.819 = 1.724; d. 2.465; e. 2.465 − 1.724 = 0.741

22. PV of payments to Kangaroo is $8,938, which makes it a better deal than Turtle's.

31. a. $402,265;

b.

		Figures in 000's			
Year	Beginning-of-Year Balance	Total Year-End Payment	Interest	Amortization of Loan	End-of-Year Balance
1	$402.265	$70	$32.18	$37.82	$364.45
2	364.45	70	29.16	40.84	323.60
3	323.60	70	25.89	44.11	279.49
4	279.49	70	22.36	47.64	231.85
5	231.85	70	18.55	51.45	180.40
6	180.40	70	14.43	55.57	124.83
7	124.83	70	9.99	60.01	64.81
8	64.81	70	5.19	64.81	0.00

39. You should prefer the continuously compounded investment:

	Future Value of $1		
Interest	Year 1	Year 5	Year 20
12% annual	$1.1200	$1.7623	$9.6463
11.71% semiannual	1.1204	1.7657	9.7193
11.50% continuous	1.1219	1.7771	9.9742

CHAPTER 3

1. (a) Does not change; (b) price falls; (c) yield rises

4. PV = $5/1.06 + 5/1.06^2 + 5/1.06^3 + \cdots + 5/1.06^9 + 105/1.06^{10} = 92.64$

9. a. PV today = $8/1.06 + 8/1.06^2 + 8/1.06^3 + 8/1.06^4 + 108/1.06^5 = 108.425$

b. PV year 1 = $8/1.06 + 8/1.06^2 + 8/1.06^3 + 108/1.06^4 = 106.93$

c. Return = $(8 + 106.930)/108.425 − 1 = .06$, or 6%

d. If the yield over any period does not change, the return on the bond is equal to the yield.

11. a. False. Duration depends on the coupon as well as the maturity.

b. False. Given the yield to maturity, volatility is proportional to duration.

c. True. A lower coupon rate means longer duration and therefore higher volatility.

d. False. A higher interest rate reduces the relative present value of (distant) principal repayments.

24. a. $d_1 = .9524$; $d_2 = .9002$; $d_3 = .8468$; $d_4 = .7951$; $d_5 = .7473$

b. i. PV = $50(d_1 + d_2) + $1,000d_2 = 992.79; ii. PV = $50(d_1 + d_2 + d_3 + d_4 + d_5) + $1,000d_5 = 959.34; iii. PV = $100((d_1 + d_2 + d_3 + d_4 + d_5) + $1,000d_5 = 1171.43

26. a. $r_2 = 5.00\%$, $r_3 = 5.20\%$, $r_4 = 5.25\%$, $r_5 = 5.3\%$

b. Upward sloping

c. Since the yield on the coupon bond reflects partly the spot rates for the years 2021 to 2023, it will be higher than the yield on the 2020 strip.

30. a. Total nominal return = $1.08^2 − 1 = .1664$, or 16.64%; total real return = $(1.08/1.03 × 1.08/1.05) − 1 = .0785$, or 7.85%

b. Total real return = $1.08^2 − 1 = .1664$, or 16.64%; total nominal return = $1.08^2 × 1.03 × 1.05 − 1 = .2615$, or 26.15%

CHAPTER 4

3. a. $103

b. $103.8

c. Yes. Ask prices are already below $105 limit.

8. $(5 + 110)/1.08 = \$106.48$

10. $10/(.08 - .05) = \$333.33$

13. a. A. $\$1/\$2 = .5$; B. $\$1/\$1.5 = .67$

b. A. $(1 - .5)15\% = 7.5\%$; B. $(1 - .67)10 = 3.3\%$

c. $PV_A = \$1/(.15 - .075) = \$13.33$; $PV_B = \$1/(.15 - .033) = \$8.55$

18. If $r = 10\%$,

$PV_A = \$10/.10 = \$100$

$PV_B = \$5/(.10 - .04) = \$83.33$

$PV_C = 5/1.1 + 6/1.1^2 + 7.2/1.1^3 + 8.64/1.1^4 + 10.37/1.1^5 + 12.44/1.1^6 + (12.44/.1)/1.1^6 = \$104.51$

C is the most valuable.

If $r = 7\%$,

$PV_A = \$10/.07 = \$142.86$

$PV_B = \$5/(.07 - .04) = \$166.67$

$PV_C = 5/1.07 + 6/1.07^2 + 7.2/1.07^3 + 8.64/1.07^4 + 10.37/1.07^5 + 12.44/1.07^6 + (12.44/.07)/1.07^6 = \$156.50$

B is the most valuable.

31. a. $PV = 0/1.09 + 1/1.09^2 + 2/1.09^3 + 2.3/1.09^4 + 2.6/1.09^5 + (2.6/.09)/1.09^5 = \$24.48$ million

b. $24.48/12 = \$2.04$

c. $r = (P_1 + DIV_1)/P_0 - 1$. $r_{2020} = (0 + 26.68)/24.48 - 1 = .09$; $r_{2021} = (1 + 28.09)/26.68 - 1 = .09$; $r_{2022} = (2 + 28.61)/28.09 - 1 = .09$; $r_{2023} = (2.3 + 28.89)/28.61 - 1 = .09$; $r_{2024} = (2.6 + 28.89)/28.89 - 1 = .09$

CHAPTER 5

1. a. $A = 3$ years, $B = 2$ years, $C = 3$ years

b. B

c. A, B, and C

d. $NPV_A = -\$1,011$; $NPV_B = \$3,378$; $NPV_C = \$2,405$

e. True

f. It will accept no negative-NPV projects but will reject some with positive NPVs.

5. a. $\$15,750$ ($r = 0$); $\$4,250$ ($r = 50\%$); $\$0$ ($r = 100\%$)

b. 100%

8. a. Two

b. -50% and $+50\%$

c. Yes, NPV = $\$14.58$ (NPV is positive for any r between the two IRRS)

9. a. The IRR on Beta is higher than the cost of capital. The incremental cash flows on Alpha are Year 0: $-200,000$, Year 1: $+110,000$, Year 2: $121,000$. The

IRR on these incremental flows is 10%, which is also higher than the cost of capital. Alpha should therefore be preferred to Beta.

16. a. 1, 2, 4, and 6

CHAPTER 6

1. a, b, d, g, h

3. a. False; b. false; c. false

9.

	2019	2020	2021	2022	2023
Net working capital	50,000	230,000	305,000	250,000	0
Cash flows		−50,000	−180,000	−75,000	+55,000	+250,000

10.

	$ millions				
Year	0	1	2	3	4	5
1 Investment cash flow	−6					0.375
2 Sales		2	2.4	4	4	2.4
3 Production costs		0.5	0.6	1.0	1.0	0.6
4 Depreciation (Investment/5)		1.2	1.2	1.2	1.2	1.2
5 Pretax profit (2 − 3 − 4)		0.3	0.6	1.8	1.8	0.6
6 Tax (.25 × 5)		0.075	0.15	0.45	0.45	0.15
7 Net profit (5 − 6)		0.225	0.45	1.35	1.35	0.45
8 Operating cash flow (4 + 7)	0	1.425	1.65	2.55	2.55	1.65
9 Working capital	0.2	0.24	0.4	0.4	0.24	0
10 Cash flow from working capital	−0.2	−0.04	−0.16	0	0.16	0.24
11 Total cash flow (1 + 8 + 10)	−6.2	1.385	1.49	2.55	2.71	2.265
12 PV	−6.2	1.24	1.19	1.82	1.72	1.29
NPV =	1.05					

Salvage value is net of tax

21. 25-year annuity factor = 14.094

Equivalent annual cost = $1,500,000/14.094 + 200,000 = \$306,429$

29. 1. *Sell the new machine:* Receive the cash flow from the sale of the new machine, pay up-front cost of overhaul of old machine, pay the costs for five years of operating the old machine, and receive the proceeds from the sale of the old machine at the end of year 5. PV of costs = $59,492.

2. *Sell the old machine:* Receive the cash flow from the sale of the old machine, pay the costs for 10 years of operating the new machine, pay the year 5 overhaul cost, and receive the proceeds from selling the new machine at the end of year 10. PV of costs = $93,376.

Equivalent annual cost of selling new machine = 59,492/5-year annuity factor = $16,504.

Equivalent annual cost of selling old machine = 93,376/10-year annuity factor = $16,526.

Therefore, (by a small margin) sell new machine.

CHAPTER 7

3.   a. $150 \times (.9 + 1.2 + 1.5)/3 = \$180$

b.   20%

c.   Correctly ($180/1.2 = $150)

d. $(.9 \times 1.2 \times 1.5)(1/3) - 1 = .174$ or 17.4%

e.   Overestimate

4.

Year	Real Return (%)	Risk Premium (%)
1929	−14.33	−19.3
1930	−23.72	−30.7
1931	−38.01	−45.0
1932	.45	−10.9
1933	56.52	57.0
Average	−3.82	−9.8

12.   a. $sA^2 = 47.48$, $sA = 6.89\%$; $sB^2 = 23.23$, $sB = 4.82\%$
A is more risky.

b.   Portfolio returns are 11%, −1%, 4.5%, 10%, −1%, 4%, −2.5%, −5%
$sP^2 = 30.06$, $sP = 5.48\%$

c.   Risk is less than half way between the risk of A and B.

14.   a. False; b. true; c. false; d. false; e. false;f. false; g. false; h. true; i. true; j. false

20.   a. $sP^2 = (.60^2 \times .10^2) + (.40^2 \times .20^2) + 2(.60 \times .40 \times 1 \times .10 \times .20) = .0196$; $sP = .140$

b. $sP^2 = (.60^2 \times .10^2) + (.40^2 \times .20^2) + 2(.60 \times .40 \times .50 \times .10 \times .20) = .0148$; $sP = .122$

c. $sP^2 = (.60^2 \times .10^2) + (.40^2 \times .20^2) + 2(.60 \times .40 \times 0 \times .10 \times .20) = .010$; $sP = .100$

21. $\beta A = 1.0$

$\beta B = 2.0$

$\beta C = 1.5$

$\beta D = 0$

$\beta E = -1.0$

CHAPTER 8

3.   a.   See Figure 1.

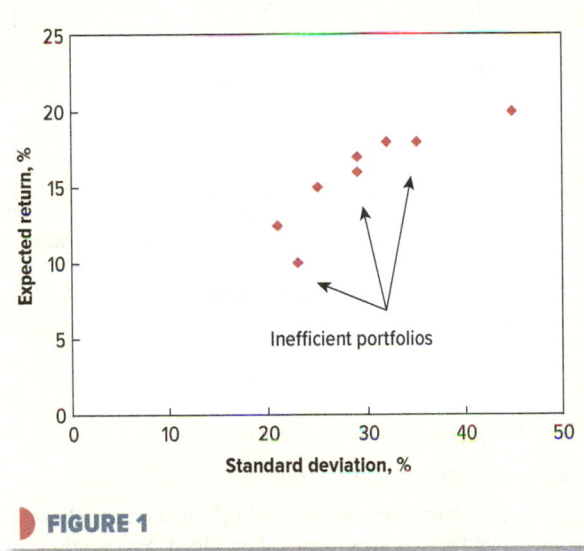

▶ **FIGURE 1**

b.   Portfolios A, D, and G. B has a higher expected return than A and lower risk. Splitting one's money evenly between C and E gives the same expected return as D and lower risk. F has a same expected return as G and lower risk.

c.   F has a Sharpe ratio of $(18 - 12)/32 = .1875$.

d.   15% (portfolio C)

e.   16.7% (invest (25/32) of wealth in portfolio F, which has the highest Sharpe ratio) and lend the remainder.

6.   a.   Expected return = $.6 \times 15 + .4 \times 20 = 17\%$
Standard deviation = $(.6 \times 20)^2 + (.4 \times 22)^2 + (2 \times .6 \times .4 \times .5 \times 20 \times 22) = 18.1\%$

b.   If $\rho = 0$, standard deviation = 14.9%
If $\rho = -.5$, standard deviation = 10.8%

c.   Better (it has a higher return and lower standard deviation)

7. (a) 7%; (b) 27% with perfect positive correlation; 1% with perfect negative correlation; 19.1% with no correlation; (c) see Figure 2; (d) no, measure risk by beta, not by standard deviation.

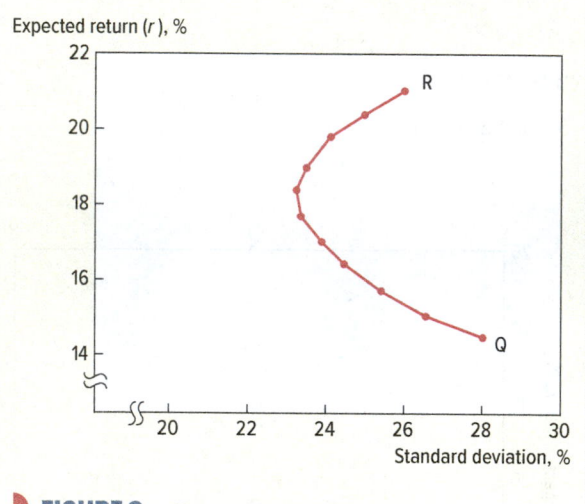

> **FIGURE 2**   Chapter 8, Problem 7(c).

9. Sharpe ratio = 7.7/19.9 = .387.

11. a. $4 \times .82 + .6 \times .10 = .39$

b. Not unless you had special information to believe that these shares were undervalued. You would do better to construct a fully diversified portfolio with a beta of .39 by investing 39% of your money in the market portfolio and the balance in risk-free securities.

c. Your portfolio would have a beta of $.4 \times .1.26 + .6 \times .1.47 = 1.39$. You could construct a fully diversified portfolio with this beta by borrowing 39% of your wealth and investing this and all your own money in the market portfolio.

12. a. False (required return depends on market risk not total variability); b. false (expected return would equal the interest rate); c. false (beta = $.33 \times 0 + .67 \times 1.0 = .67$); d. true; e. true

21. $r_{Ford} = 2 + (1.24 \times 7) - (0.07 \times 3.2) + (0.28 \times 4.9) = 11.8\%$

$r_{Walmart} = 2 + (0.41 \times 7) - (0.47 \times 3.2) - (0.25 \times 4.9) = 2.1\%$

$r_{Citi} = 2 + (1.52 \times 7) - (0.01 \times 3.2) + (0.85 \times 4.9) = 16.8\%$

$r_{Apple} = 2 + (1.25 \times 7) - (0.67 \times 3.2) - (0.72 \times 4.9) = 5.1\%$

CHAPTER 9

2. a. False; b. false; c. true

7. WACC = $.4 \times (1 - .20) \times 10 + .6 \times (10 + .5 \times 8) = 11.6\%$

11. a. 12% of Sun Life's risk was market risk and 88% was specific risk; 6% of Loblaw's risk was market risk and 94% was specific.

b. The variance was $18.7^2 = 349.69$; specific variance $= .88 \times 349.69 = 307.73$

c. Confidence interval = $.63 \pm 2 \times .33$

d. $5 + .86 \times (12 - 5) = 11.0\%$

e. $5 + .86 \times (20 - 5) = 17.9\%$

14. Beta of assets = $.5 \times .15 + .5 \times 1.25 = .70$

20. a. $(.2 \times \$0) + (.4 \times .8 \times 1,000 \times \$100) + (.6 \times .8 \times 5,000 \times \$100) = \$272,000$ per day, or \$99.28 million a year.

b. The possibility of a dry hole is a diversifiable risk and should not affect the discount rate. This possibility affects forecasted cash flows, as seen in part a. The appropriate discount rate for the project is the oil company's normal cost of capital.

21. a. PV = $110/1.1 + 121/1.1^2 = 200$.

b. $CEQ_1 = 105$ (i.e., $105/1.05 = 100$); $CEQ_2 = 110.25$ (i.e., $110.25/1.05^2 = 100$).

c. Year 1 ratio = $105/110 = .9545$; Year 2 ratio = $110.25/121 = .9112 = .9545^2$.

CHAPTER 10

1. a. 1. a. Scenario analysis; b. real option; c. sensitivity analysis; d. operating leverage; e. decision tree; f. tornado diagram; g. break-even analysis; h. Monte Carlo simulation

7. a. Cash flow increases from 2.37 to \$2.77 million.

b. Cash flow declines from 2.37 to \$1.19 million.

19. a. Profits increase by 40% from \$500 to \$700.

b. DOL = $1 + 1500/500 = 4$.

24. a. Average sales price = \$36; average cash flow = $10,000(36 - 32) - 40,000 = \$0$

b. If the sales price is \$48, the company keeps the mine open. Cash flow = $10,000(48 - 32) - 40,000 = \$120,000$.

If the sales price is \$24, the company closes the mine. Cash flow = $-\$40,000$.

The option to close increases the average cash flow to $(120,000 - 40,000)/2 = \$40,000$.

27.

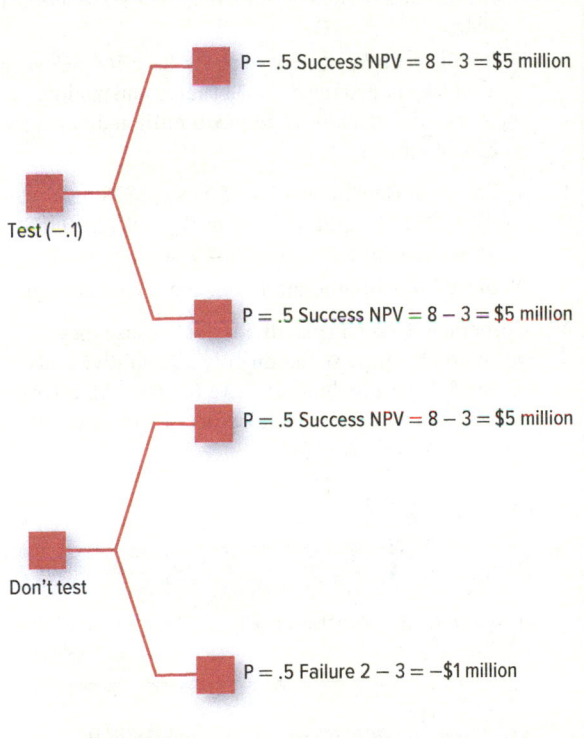

If you test, NPV = −.1 + .5(5 + 0) = $2.4 million
If you don't test, NPV = .5(5 − 1) = $2 million
It pays to test.

CHAPTER 11

1. (a) False; (b) true; (c) true

10. a. You are guaranteed to receive 10,000 × $5,500 = $55,000,000 at year-end. It, therefore, has a PV of 55,000,000/1.02 = $53,922,000.

b. The expected return on copper is 2 + 1.2 × (8 − 2) = 9.2%. The expected price is 1.092 × $5,392 = $5,888. The certainty-equivalent price is $5,500. You would be indifferent between receiving a certain $5,500 and a risky $5,888.

15. (a) False; (b) true; (c) true; (d) false

CHAPTER 12

1. a. The loss in value that arises when an agent (e.g., a manager) acts in his own interests rather than trying to maximize NPV.

b. Benefits that accrue to an individual in the firm rather than to shareholders as a whole.

c. A manager's attempt to build a large company even if value is sacrificed.

d. A manager's preference for projects that demand his or her special skills.

e. Shareholders partly rely on other bodies such as the directors or the firm's lenders to monitor managers.

4. a. True; b. true; c. false; d. true

13.

	1	2	3
Cash flow	0	78.55	78.55
PV at start of year	100.00	120.00	65.46
PV at end of year	120.00	65.46	0
Economic depreciation	−20.00	+54.55	+65.46
Cash flow	0	78.55	78.55
Economic income	20.00	24.00	13.11

15. ROI = 1.6/20 = .08 , or 8%
Net ROI = 8 − 11.5 = −3.5%
EVA = 1.6 − .115 × 20 = −$0.7

19. EVA = 1.2 − .15 × (4 + 2 + 8) = −$0.9 million

CHAPTER 13

2. a. False; b. false; c. true; d. false

8. This does present some possible evidence against the efficient capital market hypothesis. One key to market efficiency is the high level of competition among participants in the market. For small stocks, the level of competition is relatively low because, for reasons such as transaction costs, major market participants (e.g., mutual funds and pension funds) mainly hold the securities of larger, well-known companies. Thus, it is plausible that the market for small stocks is fundamentally different from the market for larger stocks and, hence, that the small-firm effect is simply a reflection of market inefficiency. However, another explanation is that firms with small market capitalization may contain some type of as-yet-unidentified additional risk that is not measured in the studies.

9. a. Not an inefficiency. Investors correctly take tax into account when valuing securities.

b. Contradicts strong form (though it is illegal for managers to use inside information).

c. Not an inefficiency. Investors correctly take forecasts of future profits into account when valuing securities.

d. Contradicts the weak form and appears to offer profit opportunities.

e. Not an inefficiency. Investors are able to spot possible acquisition candidates.

f. Contradicts the semi-strong form.

g. Not an inefficiency.

14. a. False; b. false (though the attempt to pick stocks may be a mug's game); c. false; d. true

15. Expected return $= -0.2 + 1.45 \times 5 = 7.05\%$; abnormal return $= 6 = 7.05 = -1.05\%$

CHAPTER 14

1. a. Subordinated; b. floating rate; c. convertible; d. warrant; e. common stock, preferred stock

4. a. False; b. true; c. false; d. false

8. a. $(760 - 100)(1 - .21) = \$521.4$ thousand; b. $760 \times (1 - .21) - 80 = \$520.4$ thousand.

9. a. and b. Increase. c. reduces value

12. a. False; b. false; c. true; d. true

CHAPTER 15

1. aB; bA; cD; dC.

5. a. $\$400,000/.4 = \$1,000,000$

b. $\$1,000,000/25,000 = \$40$

10. a. 135,000 shares

b. Primary offering = 500,000 shares; secondary offering = 400,000 shares

c. $\$105/\$80 - 1 = .3125$, or 31.25%, roughly double the average level of IPO underpricing

d. Underwriting fee = $\$5,040,000$; administrative costs = $\$820,000$; underpricing = $900,000 \times (\$105 - 80) = \$22,500,000$; total cost = $\$28,360,000$

19. a. Further sale of an already publicly traded stock

b. U.S. bond issue by a foreign corporation

c. Bond issue by an industrial company

d. Bond issue by a large industrial company

CHAPTER 16

1. a. A1 Declaration date; A2 last with-dividend date; A3 ex-dividend date; A4 record date; A5 payment date

b. On November 8, the ex-dividend date

c. $(.89 \times 4)/\$86 = .0414$, or 4.14%

d. $(.89 \times 4)/\$6.90 = .5159$ or 51.59%

e. The price would fall to $86/1.10 = \$78.18$

12. a. There will still be 1 million shares and the stock price will fall to $10. Shareholders' wealth, including the cash dividend, will equal $10 + 2 = \$12$ per share.

b. It will spend $2 million to repurchase 166,667 shares at $12 each, leaving 833,333 shares outstanding. Stock price remains at $12 ($10 million divided by 833,333 shares).

17. a. Free cash flow in year $1 = .5 \times 56 = \$28$ million. PV $= 28/(.12 - .05) = \$400$ million. With 10 million shares stock price = 400/10 = $40.

b. In well-functioning markets it should not change.

25. Corporations prefer cash dividends because they pay corporate income tax on only 50% of dividends received, lowering their effective tax rate. All others are indifferent (assuming capital gains cannot be deferred).

CHAPTER 17

1.

	Market Value
Common stock (8 million shares at $2)	$16,000,000
Short-term loans	$2,000,000

Ms. Kraft owns .625% of the firm, which will increase common stock to $17 million and cut short-term debt. Ms. Kraft can offset this by (a) borrowing $6,250, and (b) buying that much more Copperhead stock.

3. a.

	Outcomes			
Operating income ($)	500	1,000	1,500	2,000
Interest ($)	250	250	250	250
Equity earnings ($)	250	750	1,250	1,750
Earnings per share ($)	.33	1.00	1.67	2.33
Return on shares (%)	3.33	10.00	16.67	23.33

b. New debt ratio $= D/V = 2,500/10,000 = .25$

Beta assets $= (D/V)$beta debt $+ (E/V)$beta equity

$0.8 = .25 \times 0 + .75 \times$ beta equity

Beta equity $= .8/.75 = 1.07$

7. a. Unchanged

b. 16 million

c. $250 million

d. .64

e. No one

17. $r_E = 22.0$ $r_D = 12\%$ $r_A = 17.0$
$\beta_E = 1.5$ $\beta_D = .25$ $\beta_A = .875$
$r_f = 10\%$ $r_m = 18\%$ $D/V = 0.5$

20. a. $r_E = r_A + (r_A - r_D)(D/E) = .14 + (.14 - .095) \times (45/55)$
$r_E = .1768$, or 17.68%
b. WACC $= r_D(1 - T_c)(D/V) + r_E(D/E) = .095 \times$
$(1 - .40) \times .45 + .1768 \times .55 = .1229$, or 12.29%

CHAPTER 18

2. a. $(.3 \times .08 \times \$1,000)/1.08 = \$22.22$
b. $(.3 \times .08 \times \$1,000) \times (1/1.08 + 1/1.08^2 + 1/1.08^3 +$
$1/1.08^4 + 1/1.08^5) = \$95.83$
c. $.3 \times 1,000 = \$300$

6. Firms are less likely to be able to receive an interest tax shield if they are more likely to make a loss. Therefore, firms with low or fluctuating profits should borrow less.

12. a. True; b. true; c. false (the interest rate on the debt will reflect the probability of bankruptcy)

14. a. Shareholders' gain; b. bondholders' gain; c. existing bondholders' loss; d. bondholders' and shareholders' gain; e. shareholders' gain.

17. a. Bondholders' gain because the covenants prevent management from playing games at the bondholders' expense.
b. Shareholders benefit from the lower interest rate that comes from reassuring bondholders that games will not be played at their expense. The company is more likely to issue the bond with standard restrictions.

21. a. A preference for internal finance and for debt if external finance is necessary; b. the least profitable firms will generate the least cash.

23. a. True; b. false; c. true

CHAPTER 19

3. Market values of debt and equity are:
$D = .9 \times 75 = \$67.5$ million
$E = 42 \times 2.5 = \$105$ million
$D/V = .39$ and WACC $= .09(1 - .21).391 + .18(.609) =$
$.1374$, or 13.74%

4. Step 1: Opportunity cost of capital $= r_D D/V + r_E E/V =$
$9 \times .391 + 18 \times .609 = 14.48\%$
Step 2: $r_E = r + (r - r_D)D/E = 14.48 + (14.48 - 8.6)$
$(15/85) = 15.52\%$
Step 3: New WACC $= r_D(1 - T_c)D/V + r_E(E/V) =$
$8.6(1 - .29).15 + 15.52(.85) = 14.21\%$

13. a. $-.15 \times 500,000 = -\$75,000$
b. $\$76,000$

CHAPTER 20

1. Call; exercise; put; European

2. a. Call seller; b. call buyer

6. a. Exercise price; b. stock price

8. a. See Figure 20.1.
b. Put-call parity states that $S + P = C + PV(EX)$. Therefore, $C - P = S - PV(EX) = 100 - 100/1.10 = \$9.09$.

20. a. $S + P = C + PV(EX)$. Therefore, $P = C + PV(EX) - S = 10.18 + 145/1.01^{.67} - 145 = \$9.22$.

22. a. Up; b. down; c. up; d. up; e. down; f. down

28. a. A 6-month Wombat call sells for less than a 3-month call with the same exercise price. Buy 6-month call and sell 3-month. This gives you a positive inflow of $1 and a "free" call option for months 3 to 6.
b. The cost of a Ragwort stock and put is greater than the cost of a Ragwort call plus the present value of the exercise price. Buy call and invest PV(EX) in risk-free loan, and sell stock and put option to earn a risk-free profit of $20.3.
c. The cost of a Ragwort put plus the exercise price is greater than the stock price. Buy stock and put option for $90 and exercise put to sell stock for $100.

CHAPTER 21

1. a. Delta $= 100/(200 - 50) = .667$
b.

	Current Cash Flow	Possible Future Cash Flows	
Buy call	−36.36	0	+100
equals buy .667 shares	−66.67	+33.33	+133.33
and borrow PV(33.33)	+30.30	−33.33	−33.33
	−36.36	0	+100

c. $(p \times 100) + (1 - p)(-50) = 10, p = .4$
d. Value of call $= \dfrac{(.4 \times 100) + (.6 \times 0)}{1.10} = 36.36$
e. No. The true probability of a price rise is almost certainly higher than the risk-neutral probability, but it does not help to value the option.

5. The possible stock prices and risk-neutral probabilities are unchanged from Fig. 21.2. Option payoffs at month 6 are in parentheses:

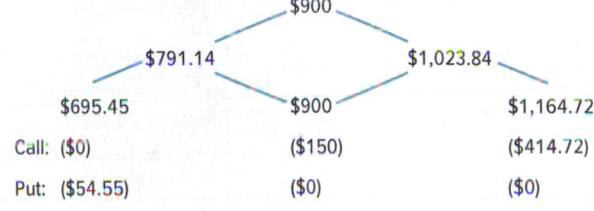

If stock price increases in the first period, expected risk-neutral payoff to call = .4774 × 414.72 + .5226 × 150.00 = 276.38, with PV of 275.69. If stock price falls, expected risk-neutral payoff = .4774 × 150.00 + .5226 × 0 = 71.61, with PV = 71.43.

Calculate value today. Expected risk-neutral value = .4774 × 275.69 + .5226 × 71.43 = 168.94, with PV = call value = $168.52.

The put is worthless if stock price increases in first period. If price falls, expected risk neutral payoff is .4774 × 0 + .5226 × 54.55 = 28.51, with PV = 28.44. Expected risk-neutral value today =.4774 × 0 + .5226 × 28.44 = 14.86, with PV = put value = $14.82.

9. a. No, the maximum delta for a call is 1.0 when the option is certain to be exercised.

   b. No, the minimum delta for a call is 0 if there is no chance of exercise.

   c. Call delta increases if the stock price rises.

   d. Call delta increases if the standard deviation of the stock returns increases.

11. a. PV Call = $8.77

   b. (i) 12.70; (ii) 10.67; (iii) 5.22; (iv) 15.79; (v) 9.20

   c. Increasing the exercise price

15. a. You are investing $781.48 in the stock and −$615.98 in the loan. Therefore, the beta of the option is

   β_{option} = (−615.98 × 0 + 781.48 × 1.50)/(−615.98 + 781.48) = 7.08

   With a lower exercise price the risk of the option falls.

   b. You are now investing 728.20 in the stock and −543.05 in the loan. Therefore, the beta of the option is

   β_{option} = (−543.05 × 0 + 728.20 × 1.50)/(−543.05 + 728.20) = 5.90

   With a longer maturity, the risk of the option also falls.

CHAPTER 22

6. a. Increase value; b. increase value; c. reduce value

8. a. If you wait, you may decide that development is not worth the costs or that there are alternative better ways to develop the land.

   b. The advantage of waiting may not compensate for the lost income.

14. Gas turbines can be started up on short notice when spark spreads are high. The turbines' value comes from flexibility in production.

16. Asset value (S) = 1.7; exercise price (EX) = 2; interest rate (r_f) = 12%; maturity (t) = 1; standard deviation (s) = 15%; value of call = .0669, or $66,881

CHAPTER 23

2. a. 0.52%; b. 1.65%; c. 118.39 − 103.88 = 14.51%

5. a. Increase; b. increase; c. increase

10. Probability of bankruptcy a. rises; b. falls; c. falls; d. falls; e. falls; f. falls; g. rises.

11. a. PV(firm assets); b. face value of debt; c. maturity of debt; e. interest rate; f. volatility of firm assets

CHAPTER 24

4. (a) High-grade; (b) railroads; (c) asset-backed security

8. First mortgage bonds, $250 million
   Senior debentures, $50 million
   Subordinated debentures, $0

17. a. $1,000/$47 = 21.28; b. $1,000/50 = $20.00; c. 21.28 × 41.50 = 88.298%; d. $650/21.28 = $30.55; e. no; f. ($910 − $650)/21.28 = $12.22; g. $47/$41.50 − 1 = .1325, or 13.25%

22. Ab; Bf; Cd; Dc; Ee; Fa

24. Revolving credit; commitment fee; floating lien; warehouse receipt; unsecured; commercial paper; medium-term note

CHAPTER 25

1. aE; bC; cA; dB; eD; fG; gF

5. a. True; b. false; c. false; d. true; e. true; f. true; g. true

7.

	0	1	2	3	4	5	6
Initial cost	−3,000						
After-tax admin cost		−316	−316	−316	−316	−316	−316
Dep'n tax shield	630						
Total	−2,370	−316	−316	−316	−316	−316	−316
PV at 9% = −3,788							
Pre-tax break-even rent	980.6	980.6	980.6	980.6	980.6	980.6	
After-tax break-even rent[a]	774.7	774.7	774.7	774.7	774.7	774.7	
PV at 9% = 3,788							

[a] The after-tax break-even rents are an annuity-due with a present value equal to PV costs

CHAPTER 26

1. a. Price paid for immediate delivery.

   b. Forward contracts are contracts to buy or sell at a specified future date at a specified price. Futures differ from forwards in two main ways. They are traded on an exchange and they are marked to market.

   c. Investors who are long have agreed to buy the asset. Investors who are short have contracted to sell.

   d. The risk that arises because the price of the asset used to hedge is not perfectly correlated with that of the asset that is being hedged.

   e. Profits and losses on a position are settled on a regular basis (e.g., daily).

   f. The advantage from owning the commodity rather than the promise of future delivery *less* the cost of storing the commodity.

6. a. True; b. false; c. true; d. true

8. She is asking you to pay money because your sale is showing a loss.

10. $F = S(1 + r_f - y)^t = \$A6,001(1 + .018 - .044)^{.5} =$ $\$A5,922$, which is slightly less than the quoted futures price.

25. Sell short $1.2 million of the market portfolio. In practice, rather than "sell the market," you would sell futures on $1.2 million of the market index.

31. a. Durations: A = 1.95 years; B = 1 year; C = 2.74 years

   b. Proportion in B × duration of B + (1 − proportion in B) × duration of C = duration of A. Therefore, $\text{propn}_B \times 1 + (1 - \text{propn}_B) \times 2.74 = 1.95$. To hedge investment in A, sell $4.54 million of B and $5.46 million of C.

   c. Similarly, $\text{propn}_A \times 1.95 + \text{propn}_C \times 2.74 = 1$. To hedge investment in B, sell $22.0 million of A and buy $12.0 million of C.

32. Basis risk is the residual risk in an imperfect hedge.

   a. Disney stock is imperfectly correlated with market. Significant basis risk.

   b. Value of farmer's corn may be highly but not perfectly correlated with that of the corn in the futures contract. Limited basis risk.

   c. Hedging currency risk involves no basis risk.

CHAPTER 27

1. a. JPY112.61

   b. JPY111.94 = USD1

   c. Yen is at a premium (dollar is at a discount)

   d. (112.61/109.99) − 1 = .0238 or 2.38%

   e. $1 + r_¥ = (112.61/109.99)1.025 = 1.0012$. $r_¥ = .12\%$

   f. JPY111.94 = USD1

   g. (1 + 3-month Japanese inflation) = (111.94/112.61) × (1 + U.S. 3-month inflation) = .9941 × (1 + U.S. 3-month inflation)

13. a. MXN500,000/19.131 = USD 26,136

   b. $r_{peso} = 550,000/500,000 - 1 = .1$, or 10%; $r\$ = (550,000/20)/26,136 - 1 = .052$, or 5.2%

   c. She has made an exchange profit. Although the peso has depreciated, it has fallen less than the forward rate would suggest. If she had hedged by selling 550,000 pesos forward, she would have earned a dollar return of only $(550,000/20.371)/26,136 - 1 = .033$, or 3.3%.

14. b.

21. a. $\text{NPV}_€ = -80 + 10/1.06 + \ldots = €6.61$ million, which is equivalent to 6.61 × 1.2 = $7.94 million.

   b. Forward rates and dollar cash flows are:

			Years	
	0	1	2	3-6
Forward rates	1.2	1.2 × 1.08/1.06 = 1.223	1.223 × 1.08/1.06 = 1.246	etc.
Dollar cash flows	−80 × 1.2 = −96	10 × 1.223 = 12.23	20 × 1.246 = 24.91	etc.

   NPV = −96 + 12.23/1.08 + . . . = $7.94 million

   c. It doesn't. The company can always hedge against a fall in the euro.

CHAPTER 28

3. a. $2,960 \times \$106 - \$77,869 = \$235,891$ million

   b. $2,960 \times \$106/\$77,869 = 4.03$

   c. EVA = $(.65 \times \$2,178 + \$10,523) - .05 \times (\$42,018 + \$77,798) = \$5,948$ million

   d. ROC = $(.65 \times \$2,178 + \$10,523)/(\$42,018 + \$77,798) = 9.96\%$

5. a. 6.00%; b. 2.39%; c. 2.52; d. 8.67; e. .47; f. .76; g. .16

9.

Balance Sheet ($ in millions)		
	December 2018	**December 2017**
Cash	11	20
Accounts receivable	44	34
Inventory	22	26
Total current assets	77	80
Fixed assets (net)	38	25
Total	115	105
Notes payable	25	20
Accounts payable	30	35
Total current liabilities	55	55
Long-term debt	24	20
Equity	36	30
Total	115	105

Income Statement ($ in millions)	
Sales	195.00
Cost of goods sold	120.00
Selling, general, and administrative expenses	10
Depreciation	20
EBIT	45.00
Interest	5.63
Earnings before tax	39.38
Tax	15.75
Earnings available for common stock	23.63

CHAPTER 29

4.

	Cash	Working Capital
a.	$10 million decline	$10 million decline
b.	$2,500 increase	Unchanged
c.	$50,000 decline	Unchanged
d.	Unchanged	$10 million increase
e.	Unchanged	Unchanged
f.	$5 million increase	Unchanged

6. a. Cash cycle lengthens; b. cycle shortens; c. cycle lengthens; d. cycle shortens; e. cycle lengthens

8.

	Month 1	Month 2	Month 3	Month 4
Receivables at start of period				
Cash sales	15	24	18	14
Sales on credit	100	120	90	70
Collections on credit sales:				
Sales in current period	50	60	45	35
Sales in last period		30	36	27
Sales in last period but one			20	24
Total collections			101	86
Cash sales + collections			*119*	*100*

22. a. $2,900 (sales = $1,100 = 40% of average assets of £2,750)

    b. $225 (net income = $150; retained earnings = $75; growth in assets = $300)

    c. 25% (equity = $2,100 + $75; net assets = $2,900)

25. a. Internal growth rate = plowback ratio × return on equity × equity/net assets = $.5 \times 500/1,800 \times 1,800/2,700 = .0926$, or 9.26%

    b. Sustainable growth rate = plowback ratio × return on equity = $.5 \times 500/1,800 = .139$, or 13.9%

CHAPTER 30

2. a. False; b. true; c. false; d. false; e. false; f. true

3. a. False; b. true; c. true; d. false

8. a. 2% discount if payment within 30 days. Otherwise, full amount within 60 days.

   b. 2% discount if payment within 5 days of end of month. Otherwise, full payment within 30 days.

   c. Cash on delivery

13. No. If Branding accepts, it loses the $40 production cost on each unit and receives revenues with a PV of $50/1.1^{.5}$ with a probability of .75. PV of order is, therefore, $-40 + .75 \times 50/1.1^{.5} = -\$4.25$.

22. a. False; b. false; c. true; d. true; e. true

28. Effective yield on 3-month bill = $(100/97.5)^4 - 1 = .1066$, or 10.66%

    Effective yield on 6-month bill = $(100/95)^2 - 1 = .1080$, or 10.80%

CHAPTER 31

1. a. True; b. false; c. false; d. true; e. false (they may produce gains, but "large" is stretching it); f. false; g. true

3. a. Horizontal; b. conglomerate; c. vertical; d. conglomerate

8. a.

	World Enterprises	Wheelrim and Axle	Merged Firm
Earnings per share	$2.00	$2.50	$2.67
Price per share	$40	$25	34.33
Price–earnings ratio	20	10	12.86
Number of shares	100,000	200,000	262,172
Total earnings	$200,000	$500,000	$700,000
Total market value	$4,000,000	$5,000,000	$9,000,000

 b. $162.17/200 = .81$

 c. $162,172 \times \$34.33 - \$5,000,000 = \$567,000$

 d. $100,000 \times \$34.33 - 4,000,000 = -\$567,000$

11. a. NPV $= \$15,000 - 2,000 \times (\$20 - \$17.50) = \$10,000$

 b. $\$50 + \$10,000/3,000 = \$53.33$

 c. $20

 d. Gobi shareholders gain $\$10,000/(3,000 \times \$50) = .067$, or 6.7%. Universal shareholders gain $\$2.5/\$17.50 = .143$ or 14.3%.

 e. Gobi issues $.4 \times 2,000 = 800$ shares. Value of merged firm $= 3,000 \times \$50 + 2,000 \times \$17.50 +$

$15,000 = \$200,000$. Price per share $= \$200,000/(3,000 + 800) = \$52.63$.

 f. Cost $= (800 \times \$52.63) - (2,000 \times \$17.50) = \$7,105$. NPV $= \$15,000 - \$7,105 = \$7,895$. Cost in this case depends on the value of the merged company.

CHAPTER 32

1. a. Purchase of a business using mostly debt financing. The company goes private. Management is given a substantial equity stake.

 b. An LBO undertaken by management.

 c. A parent company creates a new company with part of its assets and operations. Shares in the new business are distributed to the parent's stockholders.

 d. Like a spin-off, but shares in the new business are sold to investors.

 e. Sale of specific assets rather than entire firm.

 f. A government-owned business is sold to private investors.

 g. A company moves to a much higher debt ratio. Proceeds of additional borrowing are paid out to stockholders.

2. a. True; b. false; c. true; d. false; e. true; f. true

11. a. True; b. false; c. false; d. true

16. a. False; b. true; c. true; d. false

CHAPTER 33

2. a. False; b. true; c. false

7. a. False; b. false; c. true; d. true; e. true

A

Adjusted present value (APV) *Net present value* of an asset if financed solely by equity plus the *present value* of any financing side effects.

Agency costs Costs that arise when an agent (e.g., a manager) does not act solely in the interests of the principal (e.g., the shareholder).

Annual percentage rate (APR) The interest rate per period (e.g., per month) multiplied by the number of periods in a year.

Annuity Investment that produces a level stream of cash flows for a limited number of periods.

Annuity due *Annuity* whose payments occur at the start of each period.

Annuity factor *Present value* of $1 paid for each of *t* periods.

APR *Annual percentage rate.*

APT *Arbitrage pricing theory.*

APV *Adjusted present value.*

Arbitrage Purchase of one security and simultaneous sale of another to give a risk-free profit. Often used loosely to describe the taking of offsetting positions in related securities, e.g., at the time of a takeover bid.

Arbitrage pricing theory (APT) Model in which expected returns increase linearly with an asset's sensitivity to a small number of pervasive factors.

Asked price (offered price) Price at which a dealer is willing to sell (cf. *bid price*).

Asset beta The *beta* of the firm if it were unlevered.

Automated Clearing House (ACH) Private electronic system run by banks for high-volume, low-value payments.

B

Banker's acceptance (BA) Written demand that has been accepted by a bank to pay a given sum at a future date (cf. *trade acceptance*).

Basis risk Residual risk that results when the two sides of a hedge do not move exactly together.

Beta Measure of *market risk*.

Binomial method Method for valuing *options* that assumes there are only two possible changes in the asset price in any one period.

Bridge loan Short-term loan to provide temporary financing until more permanent financing is arranged.

C

Call option Option to buy an asset at a specified exercise price on or before a specified exercise date (cf. *put option*).

CAPEX Capital expenditure.

Capital asset pricing model (CAPM) Model in which expected returns increase linearly with an asset's *beta*.

Capital budget List of planned investment projects, usually prepared annually.

Capital lease *Financial lease.*

Capital structure Mix of different securities issued by a firm.

CAPM *Capital asset pricing model.*

Carve-out Public offering of shares in a subsidiary.

Certainty equivalent A certain cash flow that has the same present value as a specified risky cash flow.

Closed-end fund Company whose assets consist of investments in a number of industrial and commercial companies.

Commercial draft (bill of exchange) Demand for payment.

Commercial paper (CP) Unsecured *notes* issued by companies and maturing within nine months.

Company cost of capital The expected return on a portfolio of all the firm's securities.

Compound interest Reinvestment of each interest payment on money invested to earn more interest (cf. *simple interest*).

Concentration account If the firm's customers make payments to a regional collection center, the deposits can be automatically transferred to a centralized concentration account.

Conglomerate merger *Merger* between two companies in unrelated businesses (cf. *horizontal merger, vertical merger*).

Consumer credit Bills awaiting payment from final customer to a company.

Conversion price *Par value* of a *convertible bond* divided by the number of shares into which it may be exchanged.

Conversion ratio Number of shares for which a *convertible bond* may be exchanged.

Convertible bond *Bond* that may be converted into another security at the holder's option. Similarly convertible *preferred stock.*

Corporation A business that is legally separate from its owners.

Cost of (equity) capital *Opportunity cost of capital.*

Coupon   (1) Specifically, an attachment to the certificate of a *bearer security* that must be surrendered to collect interest payment; (2) more generally, interest payment on debt.

Covariance   Measure of the co-movement between two variables.

D

DCF   *Discounted cash flow.*

Death-spiral convertible   *Convertible bond* exchangeable for shares with a specified market value.

Debenture   Unsecured *bond*.

Decision tree   Method of representing alternative sequential decisions and the possible outcomes from these decisions.

Degree of operating leverage (DOL)   The percentage change in profits for a 1% change in sales.

Direct lease   *Lease* in which the *lessor* purchases new equipment from the manufacturer and leases it to the *lessee* (cf. *sale and lease-back*).

Discount factor   *Present value* of $1 received at a stated future date.

Discounted cash flow (DCF)   Future cash flows multiplied by *discount factors* to obtain *present value*.

Dividend discount model   Model showing that the value of a share is equal to the discounted value of future *dividends*.

Dividend yield   Annual *dividend* divided by share price.

Du Pont formula   Formula expressing relationship between return on assets, sales-to-assets, profit margin, and measures of leverage.

Duration   The average number of years to an asset's *discounted cash flows*.

E

Economic depreciation   Decline in *present value* of an asset.

Economic income   Cash flow plus change in *present value*.

Economic value added (EVA)   A measure of *residual income* implemented by the consulting firm Stern Stewart.

Efficient portfolio   Portfolio that offers the lowest risk (*standard deviation*) for its *expected return* and the highest expected return for its level of risk.

Equipment trust certificate   Form of *secured debt* generally used to finance railroad equipment. The trustee retains ownership of the equipment until the debt is repaid.

ETF   *Exchange-traded fund.*

Eurobond   (1) Bond that is denominated in one country's currency but marketed internationally outside that country. (2) Also used to refer to suggested sovereign bond issues that would be guaranteed by all Eurozone governments.

EVA   *Economic value added.*

Evergreen credit   *Revolving credit* without maturity.

Exchange-traded fund (ETF)   A stock designed to track a stock market index.

Expectations theory   Theory that *forward interest rate* (*forward exchange rate*) equals expected *spot rate*.

F

Face value   *Principal.*

Factor   (1) A common influence on security prices (e.g., the level of interest rates or oil prices); (2) a business providing *factoring*.

Financial assets   Claims on *real assets*.

Financial engineering   Combining or dividing existing instruments to create new financial products.

Financial intermediary   An organization that raises money from many investors and provides financing to individuals, corporations, and other organizations.

Financial lease (capital lease, full-payout lease)   Long-term, noncancelable lease (cf. *operating lease*).

Financial leverage (gearing)   Use of debt to increase the *expected return* on *equity*. Financial leverage is measured by the ratio of debt to debt plus equity (cf. *operating leverage*).

Financial markets   Markets in which securities are issued and traded.

Floating-price convertible   *Death-spiral convertible.*

Forward contract   Agreement to buy or sell an asset in the future at an agreed-upon price.

Forward exchange rate   Exchange rate fixed today for exchanging currency at some future date (cf. *spot exchange rate*).

Forward price   Agreed-upon price for a *forward contract*.

Free cash flow (FCF)   Cash not required for operations or for reinvestment.

Full-payout lease   *Financial lease.*

Full-service lease (rental lease)   *Lease* in which the *lessor* promises to maintain and insure the equipment (cf. *net lease*).

Futures contract   A contract to buy a commodity or security on a future date at a price that is fixed today. Unlike forward contracts, futures are traded on organized exchanges and are *marked to market* daily.

Futures exchange   Exchange where *futures contracts* are traded.

G

Generally accepted accounting principles (GAAP)   Procedures for preparing financial statements.

H

Hedge fund   An investment fund charging a performance fee and open to a limited range of investors. Funds often follow complex strategies including *short sales*.

Hedge ratio (delta, option delta)   The number of shares to buy for each *option* sold to create a safe position; more generally, the number of units of an asset that should be bought to hedge one unit of a liability.

High-yield bond   *Junk bond*.

Horizontal merger   *Merger* between two companies that manufacture similar products (cf. *vertical merger, conglomerate merger*).

I

Indenture   Formal agreement, e.g., establishing the terms of a *bond* issue.

Initial public offering (IPO)   A company's first public issue of *common stock*.

Internal rate of return (IRR)   *Discount rate* at which investment has zero *net present value*.

IPO   *Initial public offering*.

J

Junk bond (high-yield bond)   Debt that is rated below an *investment-grade bond*.

K

Keiretsu   A network of Japanese companies organized around a major bank.

L

Lease   Long-term rental agreement.

Lessee   User of a leased asset (cf. *lessor*).

Lessor   Owner of a leased asset (cf. *lessee*).

Leveraged buyout (LBO)   Acquisition in which (1) a large part of the purchase price is debt-financed and (2) the remaining *equity* is privately held by a small group of investors.

Leveraged lease   *Lease* in which the *lessor* finances part of the cost of the asset by an issue of debt secured by the asset and the lease payments.

Limited liability   Limitation of a shareholder's losses to the amount invested.

Liquidity   Ability to sell an asset on short notice at close to the market price.

Lockbox system   Form of *concentration banking*. Customers send payments to a post office box. A local bank collects and processes the checks and transfers surplus funds to the company's principal bank.

London interbank offered rate (LIBOR)   The interest rate at which major international banks in London borrow from each other. (LIBID is London interbank bid rate; LIMEAN is mean of bid and offered rate.)

M

Management buyout (MBO)   *Leveraged buyout* whereby the acquiring group is led by the firm's management.

Margin   Cash or securities set aside by an investor as evidence that he or she can honor a commitment.

Marked to market   An arrangement whereby the profits or losses on a *futures* contract are settled up each day.

Market capitalization   Market value of *outstanding share capital*.

Market capitalization rate   *Expected return* on a security.

Market risk (systematic risk)   Risk that cannot be diversified away.

Market value added   Difference between market value and book value of firm's *equity*.

Market-to-book ratio   Ratio of market value to book value of firm's *equity*.

MBO   *Management buyout*.

Medium-term note (MTN)   Debt with a typical maturity of 1 to 10 years offered regularly by a company using the same procedure as *commercial paper*.

Money market   Market for short-term safe investments.

Monte Carlo simulation   Method for calculating the probability distribution of possible outcomes, e.g., from a project.

Mortgage bond   *Bond* secured against plant and equipment.

Mutual fund   Managed investment fund whose shares are sold to investors.

Mutually exclusive projects   Two projects that cannot both be undertaken.

N

Negotiable certificate of deposit (CD)   A certificate for a time deposit of $1 million or more that can be sold before maturity.

Net lease   *Lease* in which the *lessee* promises to maintain and insure the equipment (cf. *full-service lease*).

Net present value (NPV)   A project's net contribution to wealth—*present value* minus initial investment.

Net working capital   *Current assets* minus *current liabilities*.

Note   Unsecured debt with a maturity of up to 10 years.

O

Operating lease   Short-term, cancelable *lease* (cf. *financial lease*).

Operating profit margin   After-tax operating income as a percentage of sales.

Opportunity cost of capital (hurdle rate, cost of capital)   *Expected return* that is foregone by investing in a project rather than in comparable financial securities.

P

Payback period   Time until the cumulative cash flow equals the initial investment.

Payback rule   Requirement that project should recover its initial investment within a specified time.

Payout ratio   *Dividend* as a proportion of earnings per share.

Pension fund   Investment plan set up by an employer to provide for employees' retirement.

Perpetuity   Investment offering a level stream of cash flows in perpetuity (cf. *consol*).

Preferred stock   Stock that takes priority over common stock in regard to *dividends*. Dividends may not be paid on *common stock* unless the dividend is paid on all preferred stock (cf. *cumulative preferred stock*). The dividend rate on preferred is usually fixed at time of issue.

Present value (PV)   Discounted value of future cash flows.

Principal   Amount of debt that must be repaid.

Private equity   *Equity* that is not publicly traded and that is used to finance business start-ups, *leveraged buyouts,* etc.

Privatization   Sale of a government-owned company to private investors.

Profitability index   Ratio of a project's *NPV* to the initial investment.

Project finance   Debt that is largely a claim against the cash flows from a particular project rather than against the firm as a whole.

Prospectus   Summary of the *registration* statement providing information on an issue of securities.

Put option   *Option* to sell an asset at a specified *exercise price* on or before a specified exercise date (cf. *call option*).

Put-call parity   The relationship between the prices of European *put* and *call options*.

PVGO   *Present value of growth opportunities.*

R

Rate of return   Total income and capital appreciation per period per dollar invested.

Real assets   *Tangible assets* and *intangible assets* used to carry on business (cf. *financial assets*).

Real option   The flexibility to modify, postpone, expand, or abandon a project.

Registration statement   A detailed document prepared for the Securities and Exchange Commission that presents information about a firm's proposed financing and the firm's history, existing business, and plans for the future.

Rental lease   *Full-service lease.*

Replicating portfolio   Package of assets whose returns exactly replicate those of an *option*.

Return on assets (ROA)   After-tax operating income as a percentage of total assets.

Return on capital (ROC)   After-tax operating income as a percentage of long-term capital.

Return on equity (ROE)   Usually, equity earnings as a proportion of the book value of equity.

Revolving credit   Legally assured *line of credit* with a bank.

ROE   *Return on equity.*

S

Sale and lease-back   Sale of an existing asset to a financial institution that then *leases* it back to the user (cf. *direct lease*).

Scenario analysis   Analysis of the profitability of a project under alternative economic scenarios.

Securities   Claims on *real assets.*

Security market line (SML)   Line representing the relationship between *expected return* and *market risk.*

Self-liquidating loan   Loan to finance *current assets.* The sale of the current assets provides the cash to repay the loan.

Specific risk (residual risk, unique risk, unsystematic risk)   Risk that can be eliminated by diversification.

Spin-off   Distribution of shares in a subsidiary to the company's shareholders so that they hold shares separately in the two firms.

Spot exchange rate   Exchange rate on currency for immediate delivery (cf. *forward exchange rate*).

Spot price   Price of asset for immediate delivery (in contrast to forward or futures price).

Spot rate   Interest rate fixed today on a loan that is made today (cf. *forward interest rate*).

Standard deviation   Square root of the *variance*—a measure of variability.

Stripped bond (strip)   *Bond* that is subdivided into a series of *zero-coupon bonds.*

T

Term loan   Medium-term, privately placed loan, usually made by a bank.

Term structure of interest rates   Relationship between interest rates on loans of different maturities (cf. *yield curve*).

Trade acceptance   Written demand that has been accepted by an industrial company to pay a given sum at a future date (cf. *banker's acceptance*).

Trade credit   *Accounts receivable.*

Trust deed   Agreement between trustee and borrower setting out terms of a *bond*.

V

Variance   Mean squared deviation from the expected value; a measure of variability.

Vertical merger   *Merger* between a supplier and its customer (cf. *horizontal merger, conglomerate merger*).

W

WACC   *Weighted-average cost of capital.*

Warrant   Long-term *call option* issued by a company.

Weighted-average cost of capital (WACC)   *Expected return* on a portfolio of all the firm's securities. Used as *hurdle rate* for capital investment.

Working capital   *Current assets* less *current liabilities.* The term is commonly used as synonymous with *net working capital*.

Y

Yield to maturity   *Internal rate of return* on a bond.

Index

Note: Italicized page numbers indicate figures and tables; page numbers followed by *n* indicate notes.

A

A. M. Best, *622n*
Abandonment option, 268–269, *270,* 597–599, *599*
Abbott Laboratories, 817, *874*
AbbVie, 426, *874*
Abe, Shinzo, 894
Abnormal returns, 344–345, 344*n, 345*
ABS (asset-backed securities), 631, 635–636, *645,* 651
Absolute priority, 486–487
Absolute risk, 230
Accelerated depreciation, 142, 143, 148–150, 676, 775*n*
Accenture, 139
Accounting income, 136–137
Accounting rates of return, 751–752
Accounting standards, 666–667, 744–745, 845–846
Accounts payable, 138, 779
Accounts receivable period, 776–778
Accrued interest, 49*n,* 634
Acharya, V. V., 636*n*
ACH (Automated Clearing House), 814, 814*n*
Acid-test ratio, 759
Ackman, Bill, 849
Acquire option, 602
Acquisitions. *See* Mergers and acquisitions
Actavis, 847, 850
Actelion, *830*
Active investing, 185
Activist investors, 11, 315–316, 371
Adaro Power, 661
Adecco, *730*
Adjusted present value (APV), 524–529
    for business valuation, 526–528, *527*
    calculation of, 524
    debt capacity and, 524, 529
    for international investments, 528–529
    issue costs and, 525, 526
    leases and, 674
Admati, A. R., 465*n*
Administrative costs, 665, 688
ADT, *864*
Adverse selection risk, 688
Aetna, *830*
After-sales cash flow, 139
After-tax WACC, 232, 235–236, 467–468, *468,* 508–512, 529–530
Agency costs
    of borrowing, 490–492
    elements of, 12
    reduction of, 314, 384

risk management and, 686
subprime mortgages and, 314
Agency for International Development, 819*n*
Agency problems, 311–331
    compensation plans, 316–323, *317–318*
    corporate governance and, 12–13, 911–912
    costs (*See* Agency costs)
    monitoring, 314–316
    overview, 311–312
    performance measurement, 323–331
    risk management and, 686
    risk taking and, 313–314
    short-termism, 321–323
    subprime mortgages and, 314, 353
    transparency and, 904–905
Agency securities, 819
Agency theory, 911–912
Agents vs. principals, *12,* 911–912
Aggarwal, R. K., 877*n*
Aghion, P., 882*n*
Agrawal, A., 850*n*
Agricultural Bank of China, *179,* 396
Ahold Delhaize, *3*
AIG (American International Group), 52, 315, 385, 617–618, *750*
Airbnb, 397, 398, 706
Airbus, *602,* 602–604
Air India, 877
Aivasian, V., 498*n*
Akers Biosciences, *409*
Alabama Power, 67
Aldi, 398*n*
Alibaba Group, 5, 396, *409*
Allen, Franklin, 174, 241*n,* 286, 353*n,* 789, 889*n,* 902–903*n,* 912, 914*n,* 918*n*
Allergen, 144, 849–850
Allied Crude Vegetable Oil Refining Corporation, 650
Allied Irish Bank, 385
Allocated overhead costs, 140
All-or-none underwriting, 401*n*
Alpert, M., 286*n*
Alphabet, 95, 144, 395, 427, 607, 816
Alpha (α), 344
Alpine bonds, 640
Alstom, *830*
Altinkilic, O., 409–410*n*
Altman, Edward I., 486*n,* 624*n,* 626, 626*n,* 866*n*
Altria, *874*
Amazon
    betas for stock, *186, 207*
    binomial method of option pricing and, 568–572, *569–572*
    Black–Scholes option pricing model and, 574–577, *576*
    call options on, 543–545, *544*
    equity finance and, 607
    mergers involving, *830*

option equivalents and, 564–567
payoffs from buying/selling stock, 547, *547,* 550
portfolio risk and, 181–183
put option valuation, 567–568
rate of return on stock, *180,* 181, 186, *187, 200, 202*
selling calls and puts, 545, *546*
standard deviation of stock returns, *179*
stock option valuation, 554, *555*
as zero-dividend company, 86, 427
AMC Entertainment Holdings, *409*
American Airlines, 302, 376, 617, 621, 666
American Association of Individual Investors, 350, *351*
American International Group. *See* AIG
American Jobs Creation Act of 2004, 676*n*
American options, 543, 567*n,* 580–582
American States Water, *89*
American Water Works, *89*
Aminadav, G., 899*n*
Amortization, 32, *32–33,* 143
Anadarko, *81*
Anders, C., 865*n*
Andrade, G., 486, 486*n,* 844, 844*n,* 852, 852–854*n,* 854
Android, 302
Angel investors, 393
Anglo-Irish Bank, 878*n*
Annual coupon, 47–48, 632
Annual percentage rate (APR), 36, 36*n*
Annuities, 29–36
    annual payment calculation, 31–32, *32*
    annuities due valuation, 31
    defined, 29
    formula for, 39*n*
    future value of, 33–34
    growing, 34, *35,* 35*n*
    level vs. declining, 668*n*
    lottery winnings, 35–36
    present value of, *29,* 29–30
Annuities due, 31
Annuity factor, 29
Anomalies, 338, 347
Anthony, R., 324*n*
Anti-Tax Avoidance Directive (European Union), 476*n*
Antitrust law, 844–845
Aoki, M., 894*n*
AOL, 358, 832, 846
Apache, *81*
Apollo Management, *864*
Apple Inc.
    cash holdings and marketable securities, 441–443, *442*
    competitive advantage of, 302
    foreign profits of, 144
    initial public offering, 399*n*
    liquidity of, 772

Apple Inc.—*Cont.*
    marketable securities and, 816
    performance measurement, 748,
        748, 750
    tax avoidance by, 12
    venture capital and, 395
Appropriation requests, 285, 286
APR (annual percentage rate), 36, 36*n*
APT (arbitrage pricing theory), 213–217
APV. *See* Adjusted present value
Aqua America, 88–89, *89*
Aramark, 397
Arbitrage
    defined, 59, 351
    limits to, 351–353
    market efficiency and, 351–353
    money machines and, 59, 722
    risk, 852*n*
    risk-neutral option valuation
        and, 565–567
Arbitrage pricing theory (APT),
    213–217
Arcelor, 852
Archipelago, 79*n*
Argentina, default on debt, 69, 618*n*
Arithmetic average of returns,
    169–170, 170*n*
Arnault, Bernard, 900
Arrangers, 649
Arthur Andersen, 904
Articles of incorporation, 5
Ashanti Goldfields, 685*n*
Asian (average) options, 582
Asked price, 49
Asquith, Paul A., 354*n*, 490*n*, 639, 639*n*
Asset-backed securities (ABS), 631, 635–636,
    645, 651
Asset betas, 236–239
Asset price bubbles, 918
Asset restructuring, *851*
Assets
    current, 746, 771–772
    financial, 2
    human, 832
    intangible, 20, 81, 135–136, 846
    long-lived, 153–155, 244–246
    real, 2, 19
    return on, 98, 323*n*, 751–752, 754–756
    short-lived, 153–155
    short-term, 138*n*
    strategic, 292
    tangible, 20, 498, 845
Asset sales, 876–877
Asset stripping, 11
Asset turnover ratio, 753, 755, *755–756*
Assignment loan sales, 649*n*
Astra Zeneca, *81*
Asymmetric information, 495–497,
    843–844
As-you-like-it (chooser) options, 582
AT&T, *830,* 831, *873,* 873–874
At-the-money options, 577*n*
Auction markets, 79
Auction-rate preferred stock, 821–822
Auditors, 315
Auerbach, A. J., 854*n*

Australia
    corporate tax rate in, *142*
    elimination of tax penalty on dividends in,
        438
    imputation tax system in, 439–440, 495*n*
Autocorrelation coefficient, 341*n*
Automated Clearing House (ACH), 814, 814*n*
Automatic debit, 814
Autonomy, 3

B

Babus, A., 918*n*
Bachelier, Louis, 340*n*
Backdating, 579
Bait and switch game, 490
Baker, G. P., 872, 872*n*
Baker, M., 351*n*, 436*n*, 499*n*
Baker Hughes, 844
Balance sheets
    debt ratios on, 367, *367, 475,* 523*n*
    elements of, 745–747, *746*
    tracing cash flow with, 773, *774*
Balloon payments, 647
Banco Central Hispanico, 836
Banco Santander, 836
Bandler, J., 579*n*
Bankers' acceptances (BAs), 808, *820,* 821
Bankers Trust, 355
Bank holding companies, 651*n*
Bank loans, 2, 31–32, 647–650, 781
Bank of America
    acquisitions by, 836, *836*
    Countrywide and, 832
    investment banking options at, 382
    Merrill Lynch and, 319, 382*n*, 385
    performance measurement, 748, *750*
    stock holdings for, 377, 378, 378*n*, 381
    in subprime mortgage crisis, 314
    underwriting and, *401*
Bank of International Settlements, 706*n*
Bankruptcy, 878–883
    alternative procedures, 882
    case study, 883
    chapter 7, 878
    chapter 11, 878–881
    control rights and, 370
    costs of, 483–487, *484–485*
    largest bankruptcies, *878*
    leases and, 665
    workouts, 881–882
Bankruptcy Reform Act of 1978, 878, 879*n*
Banks. *See also specific banks*
    borrowing and lending through, 381–382
    commercial, 381, 381*n*, 382
    concentration accounts at, 815
    consolidation of, 835–836, *836*
    in corporate financing, 381–382
    in direct payment, 814
    in financial markets, 888–892
    as intermediaries, 381–382
    international, 815
    investment, 381–382, 403
    loans from, 2, 31–32, 647–650
    Modigliani–Miller propositions and, 465

    multicurrency accounts, 815
    paying for services of, 815–816
    payment mechanisms and, 382
    time deposits and certificates of deposit,
        820, 821
Banque Paribas, 836
Barberis, N., 213*n*, 350*n*
Barclays, *401*
Baring Brothers, 313*n*, 706
Barrier options, 582
Barro, R., 683*n*
BAs (bankers' acceptances), 808, *820,* 821
Basel III Accord, 465
BASF, 644
Basis risk, 693, 703–705
Baskin, J., 870*n*
BATS Exchange, *78,* 78–79
Bausch & Lomb, 301
Bautista, A. J., 674*n*
Bayer, *830*
Bayerische Vereinsbank, 836
BBVA, 646
BC Partners, *864*
Bearer bonds, 47*n*, 634
Bear Stearns, 385, 636
Beaver, William H., 625*n*
Bebchuk, L. A., 882*n*, 899*n*
Behavioral finance.
    dividend payments in, 428–430,
        429, 437
    limits to arbitrage and, 351–353
    market efficiency and, 349–353
    market timing and, 499
    sentiment in, 350–351, *351*
    signaling and, 392, 428, 430
Bell Laboratories, 873
Benartzi, L., 213*n*
Benefit-cost ratio, 123*n*
Benmelech, E., 666*n*
Benveniste, L. M., 406*n*
Berger, P., 872*n*
Bergman, N. K., 666*n*
Berk, J., 347*n*
Berkshire Hathaway, 12*n*, 293*n*, 302, 427,
    854*n*
Berle, A. A., 370, 370*n*
Bermuda options, 582
Berndt, A., 617*n*
Bertelsmann, 398*n*
Bertrand, M., 313*n*, 321, 321*n*, 499, 499*n*,
    901, 902*n*
Best-efforts underwriting, 401
Beta (β)
    asset, 236–239
    calculation of, 188, 188*n*, *189*
    capital asset pricing model, 210–211, *211*
    cash-flow, 237
    changes in capital structure and, 462–463
    defined, 186
    earnings, 237
    estimation of, 232–234, 232*n*, *233–234*,
        234*n*
    fixed-cost, 238–239
    industry, 234, *234*
    market model and, 344, 344*n*
    market risk and, 186, *186–187*, 910

portfolio, 234, *234,* 236
portfolio risk and, 186–188, *188–189,*
    205–206, *206*
project, *230,* 238
relevering, 522, 523*n*
unlevering, 522, 523*n,* 593*n*
BeyondSpring, *409*
Bhagat, S., 876*n*
Bhandari, J. S., 879*n*
Bharath, S. T., 881*n*
BHP Billiton, 82, 95, *179,* 876
Bias
    in accounting measures of performance,
        326–331
    conservatism bias, 350
    in forecasts, 285–286
    overconfidence bias, 285–286, 286*n,* 350
Big Mac Index, 725, *725*
Big-ticket leases, 676–677
Bikhchandani, S., 917*n*
Binary options, 582
Binomial method of option pricing, 568–573
    Black–Scholes model and, 577
    decision trees and, 572–573
    defined, 568
    general method, 571–572
    justification for use, 606
    overview, 568–570
    risk-neutrality and, *595,* 595–596
    two-step method, 570–571
Bizjak, J. M., 316*n*
Black, B., 395*n*
Black, Fischer, 210–211*n,* 564, 564*n,* 574–580,
    574*n*
BlackBerry, 302
Black Monday (1987), 178, 581*n*
Black–Scholes option pricing model, 573–580
    application of, 574–580, *578*
    binomial method and, 577
    development of, 574, 911
    for executive stock options, 577, *578*
    for follow-on investment opportunities,
        591–593
    for implied volatilities evaluation, 578–
        580, *579*
    justification for use, 606
    overview, 573–574
    for portfolio insurance valuation, 578
    for research and development, 604–605
    risk of options and, 576
    for warrant valuation, 577–578
Blackstone Group, *864,* 869, 870, *870*
"Black swans," 200*n*
Blitzen Computers case study, 542, 590–594,
    591–592, 594
Blockchains, 14
Bloomberg, 228
Blue-sky laws, 399
BNP, 836
Board of directors
    articles of incorporation on, 5
    compensation committee, 316
    control rights and, 370, 892–901
    European, 896
    monitoring function of, 314–315
    staggered (classified), 370–371, *851*

venture capital and, 392*n*
voting procedures and, 370–371
Bodie, Zvi, 331*n,* 376*n*
Boeing, *78,* 78–80, 139–140, 267, 426
Bohr, Niels, 13
Bond covenants, 637–639, *638*
Bond ratings, 808
    equipment trust certificates and, 635
    financial crisis and, 385
    probability of default and, 622–623,
        623–624
    sources for, 67, *68*
Bonds, 46–70. *See also* Debt financing; Debt
    policy
    alpine, 640
    bearer, 47*n,* 634
    catastrophe, *645,* 688
    convertible, 375–376, *410,* 641–645
    corporate (*See* Corporate bonds)
    coupon, 47–50, 47*n,* 632
    discounted, 48
    duration of, 52–56, *53–54,* 54–56*n*
    eurobonds, 375, 409, 640
    face value of, 47, 48
    foreign, 408–409
    global bonds, 409, 640
    holdings issued in U.S., 374, *374*
    indexed, 64, 64*n*
    inflation and, 61–67, *62–63, 66*
    innovation in bond market, *645,* 645–646
    interest rates and, 48, *50–52,* 50–54,
        62–67, *65*
    international, 375, 408–409, 640
    long-term, 632–640
    overview, 46
    present value of, 47–50
    principal, 47
    rate of return on, 51–52
    rating (*See* Bond ratings)
    registered, 47*n,* 634
    risk of, 177*n*
    samurai, 640
    sovereign bonds, 68–70
    spreadsheet functions for valuation of, 55
    stripped, 58, *59,* 62
    term structure of interest rates and, 56–61
    Treasury (*See* Treasury bonds)
    valuation of, 47–50, 641–644
    volatility of, 54
    yankee, 640
    yield to maturity, 48, 49, 115*n*
Bond–warrant packages, 644–645
Bon-Ton Department Stores, 519
Bonus depreciation, 143, 149
Bookbuilding method, 406
Book rate of return, 111–112, 121, 751
Bookrunners, 400*n*
Book-to-market effect, 212, *212,* 212*n,*
    215–217
Book value, 80–81, 80*n*
Boone, P., 901, 901*n*
Booth, L., 498*n*
Bootstrap game, 838, *838*
BorgWarner, 316
Borrowing. *See* Lenders and lending
Bowie, David, 636

Boycko, M., 877*n*
BP, *179, 187,* 373
BPI, 661
Bradley, M., 99*n,* 650*n*
Branson, Richard, 237
Brau, J. C., 397*n*
Brav, A., 316*n,* 429*n*
Brazil, corporate tax rate in, *142*
Breach, A., 901, 901*n*
Break-even analysis, 150, 262–263, *262–263*
Break-even points, 262–263, *263*
Brealey, Richard A., 174, 241*n,* 286, 789, 912
Brennan, Michael J., 599*n*
Brickley, A., 852*n*
Bridge loans, 381*n,* 647
Bristol Myers, 834
British American Tobacco, *830*
British Salt, 831
Brunnermeier, M., 349*n,* 917*n*
Bubbles
    Chinese warrant, 580
    dot.com stocks, 349, 350, 358, 384, 401
    in Japan, 349, 350
    market efficiency and, 348–349
    price bubbles, 918
    subprime mortgage crisis, 353
Budget Control Act of 2010, 69
Buffett, Warren, 12*n,* 28, 293, 302, 302*n,* 706,
    854
Bullet payments, 647
Bulow, J. I., 577*n*
Burch, T. R., 875*n*
Burkart, M., 905*n*
Burroughs, 302
Burroughs, B., 865*n*
Bush, George W., 385*n*
Businesses. *See* Corporations
Business plans, 392
Business valuation process, 512–517
    adjusted present value in, 526–528, *527*
    discounted cash flow in, 95–100, *96*
    flow-to-equity method in, 516–517
    free cash flow in, 96, *96,* 99–100, 512–
        514, *515*
    horizon value in, 96–99, 514–516
Busse, J. A., 344*n*
Butler, G. F., 602–603*n*
Bylaws, corporate, 5*n*

C

Cable, 719*n*
CAC, 693–694
California Public Employee Retirement
    System (CALPERS), 579
California State Teachers' Retirement System
    (CSTRS), 11
California Water, *89*
Call options
    American, 543
    American calls, 580–582
    defined, 543
    European calls, 543, 580–582
    position diagrams and, 543–545, *544*
    price determinants for, *556*

Call options—*Cont.*
  relationship between put prices and, 568, 621
  selling/writing, 545, *546*
  valuation of, 564–567, 574–576
Call provisions, 637
CALPERS (California Public Employee Retirement System), 579
Calpine, *864, 878*
Campa, J. M., 872*n*
Campbell, J. Y., 239*n*, 624*n*
Canada
  corporate tax rate in, 142, *142*
  interest payments in, 48*n*
Canadian Pacific Railway, 78, *81, 234,* 292*n*, 519
Cancellation options, 665, 669
Capital, defined, 4
Capital asset pricing model (CAPM), 206–217
  alternatives to, 213–217, 232*n*
  assumptions of, 213, 910
  beta and, 210–211, *211*
  capital structure and, 462
  certainty-equivalent form of, 243*n*
  comparison with arbitrage pricing theory, 215
  cost of equity capital and, 232–236, 530
  defined, 206
  estimates of expected returns in, 206–207
  review of, 207–208
  risk and return in, 912–913
  security market line and, 206, *208,* 208–209, *210*
  as short-term model, 235
  tests of, 209–213
  validity and role of, 209–213
Capital budgeting
  capital rationing in, 123–126, 203, 286
  defined, 2
  in long-term financial planning, 784
  market values in, 287–292, *289*
  Monte Carlo simulation in, 264–266
  postaudits in, 287
  process overview, 284–285
  project authorizations and, 285–286
Capital constraints, 125
Capital expenditures
  calculation of, 136
  defined, 2
  depreciation of, 111
  forecasting, 779
  leases and, 666
  in net present value analysis, 136–137
Capital gains taxes, 437–440
Capitalia, 836
Capital investments, 2–3, 111, 144, 145. *See also* Capital budgeting; Investment decisions
Capital leases. *See* Financial leases
Capital markets. *See* Financial markets
Capital rationing, 123–126
  defined, 123
  hard, 125–126

  in investment decisions, 286
  linear programming in, 124–125, 203
  profitability index in, 123–124
  quadratic programming in, 203
  soft, 125
  uses of, 124–126
Capital structure. *See also* Debt
  changes in, 462–463
  defined, 4, 451
  Modigliani–Miller approach to, 431, 453–454, 911
  recasting, 477–478, *477–478*
  theory of optimal, 500–501
  trade-off theory of, 483, *483,* 493–495, 498–499
CAPM. *See* Capital asset pricing model
Caps, 633
Caput options, 582
Cargill, 397
Carhart, Mark M., 343*n*, 347*n*
Carletti, E., 918*n*
Carlyle Group, *864*
Carried interest, 394, 869
Carow, K. A., 645*n*
Carry-forwards, 143
Carry trades, 728
Carve-outs, 875–876
Cascades, 917
Cash before delivery (CBD), 807
Cash budgeting, 778–780, *779–780*
Cash coverage ratio, 757
Cash cycle, 776–778, *777*
Cash discounts, 807
Cash flow
  after-sales, 139
  certainty-equivalent, 243, 243*n*, 291
  in corporations, 7, *7*
  debt-equivalent, 539–540
  discounted (*See* Discounted cash flow (DCF))
  equivalent annual, 154–155
  forecasting (*See* Cash flow forecasts)
  free, 96, *96,* 99–100
  incremental, 119*n*, 120, 138–140
  in Monte Carlo simulation, 264–266
  in net present value analysis, 26–27, 111–112, 136–142
  nominal, 62–63, 538–541
  operating, 145–146, 147*n*
  real, 62–63
  reinvestment of, 4
  salvage value and, 144
  surplus funds, 834–835
  tracing changes in cash, 773–778
Cash-flow beta, 237
Cash-flow forecasts
  errors in, 293
  with multiple cash flow, 26–27
  net present value and, 110, 138, 145–148, *146*
  in sensitivity analysis, *258,* 258–259
  sources of cash, 778–779, *779*
  uses of cash, 779, *780*
Cash-flow rights, 369–372, 393
Cash-flow statement, 773–775, *774*
Cash in and run game, 489–490

Cash management, 812–816
  in collections, 778–779, 814–815
  in disbursement, 779, 812–814, *813*
  international, 815
  money-market investments and, 379, 817–822
Cash on delivery (COD), 807
Cash-or-nothing options, 582
Cash ratio, 759
Catastrophe bonds, *645,* 688
Cathay Pacific, 315
CBD (cash before delivery), 807
CBOE (Chicago Board Options Exchange), 543*n*, 578, 581
CBOE Futures Exchange, 692
CBOT (Chicago Board of Trade), *691–692,* 691*n*, 692
CBS, *750*
CD&A (Compensation Discussion and Analysis), 316–317
CDOs (collateralized debt obligations), 636, 636*n*
CDs (certificates of deposit), *820,* 821
CEOs. *See* Chief executive officers
Cerberus Capital Management, 832, 864, 869, 883
Certainty-equivalent cash flow, 243, 243*n*, 291
Certainty equivalents, 242–246
  long-lived assets and, 244–246
  overview, 242
  risk-neutral method and, 606
  valuation by, 243, *244,* 291, 567
Certificates of deposit (CDs), *820,* 821
CFOs (chief financial officers), 312, 322, 411
Chain letter game, 838
Chandler, A., 870*n*
Chapter 7 bankruptcy, 878
Chapter 11 bankruptcy, 878–881
Chava, S., 638*n*
Chavez, Hugo, 878
Check Clearing for the 21st Century Act (Check 21), 814
Check conversion, 814–815
Chen, C. R., 865*n*, 866, 866*n*
Chen, H. C., 402, 402*n*
Chevron Corp., 433, 871
Chicago Board of Trade (CBOT), *691–692,* 691*n*, 692
Chicago Board Options Exchange (CBOE), 543*n*, 578, 581
Chicago Mercantile Exchange (CME), *691–692,* 691*n*, 692
Chief executive officers (CEOs)
  agent–principal roles of, 312
  compensation for, *317–318,* 317–319
  earnings targets and, 321–322
  influence on market reaction to stock issues, 411
  monitoring of, 315
  ownership of common stock by, 369
  replacement of, 315
Chief financial officers (CFOs), 312, 322, 411
Childs, P. D., 596–597*n*
Chile, short-term capital inflows, 529
China
  corporate tax rate in, *142*
  initial public offerings in, 396
  privatizations, 877

China Eastern Airlines, 78
China National Chemical, *830,* 852
CHIPS, 814, 814*n*
Chiquita Brands, 852
Chooser (as-you-like-it) options, 582
Christian Dior, 900
Chrysler, 487, 501, 832, 834, 864, 867, *878,* 881–883
Chui, M., 889–891*n*
Cingular Wireless, 873
Cisco Systems, 426, 772, 817
Citicorp, 873
Citigroup, 313, 382, *401,* 649
Claessens, S., 368, 368*n*
Class A stocks, 900
Class B stocks, 900
Classified board defense, *851*
Classified (staggered) boards, 370–371
Clayton, J., 236*n*
Clayton Act of 1914, 844
Clean (flat) price, 49*n*
Closed-end mutual funds, 80*n,* 379, 914, 914*n*
Closely held corporations, 5
Close-to-the-money projects, 121*n*
CME (Chicago Mercantile Exchange), *691–692,* 691*n,* 692
CME Group, 691*n*
CNBC, 344
Coca-Cola
  arbitrage pricing theory and, 214
  betas for stock, *186,* 207, *207*
  compensation plans from, 316*n*
  market efficiency and, 348
  performance measurement, *748,* 749, *750*
  rate of return on stock, *202,* 203
  standard deviation of stock returns, *179*
COD (cash on delivery), 807
Codetermination, in Germany, 896
Coffee, J. C., Jr., 854*n*
Colak, G., 875*n*
Collars, 633
Collateral, 352*n,* 375, 635, 649
Collateralized debt obligations (CDOs), 636, 636*n*
Collateral trust bonds, 635
Collections, 811–812, 814–815
Comcast, *830*
COMEX (Commodity Exchange Division of NYMEX), *691,* 691*n*
Comment, R., 430, 430*n*
Commercial banks, 381, 381*n,* 382
Commercial drafts, 807
Commercial paper (CP), 631, 650–652, *820,* 821
Commerzbank, 836
Commit now option, 602
Commodity Exchange Division of NYMEX (COMEX), *691,* 691*n*
Commodity futures contracts, 695–696
Commodity price risk, 687
Common stock, 77–100. *See also* Equity financing; Portfolio risk
  betas for, *186–187*
  classes of, 900
  combining into portfolios, 200, 202–203

cost of equity capital estimations and, 87–92
dividends (*See* Dividends)
expected returns on, 234–235
growth stock, 92, 212, *212*
historical performance of, 168, *168,* 171–174, *172–173, 175*
income stock, 92
IPOs and (*See* Initial public offerings)
new issues of (*See* New issues of stock)
options (*See* Stock options)
overview, 77
ownership of, *369,* 369–370
price of (*See* Stock price)
rate of return on, 169, *169,* 174, *175*
repurchase of (*See* Stock repurchases)
risk in, 168, 205
security sales and, 408–413
standard deviation of market returns, 177–178, *177–179*
trading of, 78–80
trusts and, 373
valuation of, 80–87
value stocks, 212, *212*
variability of, 177
voting procedures and, 370–371
Companies. *See* Corporations
Company cost of capital, 228–246. *See also* Weighted-average cost of capital (WACC)
  certainty equivalents and, 242–246
  cost of equity and, 232–236
  debt and, 231–232
  defined, 229
  expected return and, 458
  overview, 228
  perfect pitch and, 230–231
  project risk and, 230, 236–242
  projects costs and, 229–230
Comparables, *81,* 81–82, 236–237, 593
Compensating balances, 816
Compensation committees, 316
Compensation Discussion and Analysis (CD&A), 316–317
Compensation plans. *See also* Incentives; Stock options
  for financial managers, 312, 313, 316–323, *317–318,* 384
  golden parachutes, 851
  pay-for-performance standards, 317, 320
  performance measurement and, 323–331
Competitive advantage. *See also* Leverage
  in capital budgeting, 285
  case study on, 295–302
  economic rents and, 292–295, *294–295*
  efficient-market hypothesis and, 341–342
  in real option analysis, 607–608
  sources of, 292
Complementary resources, of merger candidates, 834
Compound annual returns, 169–170
Compound calls, 605
Compound interest, 21, *21,* 37, 39
Compound options, 582, 620
Concentration accounts, 815
Confidence intervals, 234

Conglomerate mergers, 831, 861–862
Conglomerates, 237, *870,* 870–873, *872,* 901
Connecticut Water, *89*
Conoco, *750*
ConocoPhilips, *874*
Conrad, Joseph, 735*n*
Conseco, *878*
Conservatism bias, 350
Consistency, 540–541, 785
Consolidated Edison, *179, 186, 202, 203, 207,* 232–234, *233*
Consolidation trend, 835–836
Consols, 28
Constant-growth formulas
  dangers of, 89–92
  in horizon value estimations, 97–99
  market efficiency and, 348
Consumer credit, 806
Consumer price index (CPI), 62
Contingency planning, 784–785
Contingent convertible bonds (cocos), *645,* 646
Continuous compounding, 37, 39
Continuous payments, 37*n*
Control Data, 302
Control rights, 369–370, 393, 892–901
Convenience yield, 290*n,* 695, *696*
Convergence trading, 352
Conversion price, 641
Conversion ratio, 641
Convertible bonds, 375–376, *410,* 641–645
Cooper, I. A., 170*n*
Cooper, M., 349*n*
Cootner, P. H., 340*n*
Cornell, B., 239*n*
Cornelli, F., 406*n*
Cornett, M. M., 411, 411*n*
Corporate bonds. *See also* Debt financing; Debt policy
  bond covenants, 637–639, *638*
  bond terms, 632–634
  call provisions and, 637
  characteristics of, 2
  convertible, 375–376, 641–645
  default risk and, 67–70, 236*n*
  domestic and foreign, 375, 408–409, 640
  indentures, 634
  junk, 616, 622, *623,* 866
  liquidity of, 68*n*
  private placements, 413, 639–640
  puttable, 637
  ratings for, 622–623
  security and seniority and, 634–635, *635*
  sinking funds and, 637
  types of, 634–635, *645*
  yields on, 67–68, *68,* 614–618, *616*
Corporate financing, 365–386. *See also* Financial planning; Financing decisions
  bonds (*See* Corporate bonds)
  debt in, 367–368, *367–368,* 374–377
  financial institutions in, 381–382, 888–892
  financial markets and intermediaries in, 377–386
  fusion and fission in, 873–878
  internal funds in, 366–367
  IPOs (*See* Initial public offerings)
  patterns of, 365–368

Corporate financing—*Cont.*
  security sales and, 408–413
  stock, 369–373 (*See also* Common stock)
  venture capital, 391–395, *394–395*
Corporate governance, 892–901. *See also*
  Ownership and control
  agency problems and, 12–13, 911–912
  board of directors and (*See* Board of
    directors)
  differences in, 902–905
  financial markets and institutions in,
    888–892
  managerial role in (*See* Financial
    managers)
  payout policy and, 443
Corporate raiders, 11
Corporate taxation
  deductibility of interest in, *476,* 476–479
  depreciation rules in, 143, 148–149
  disadvantages of, 6
  international comparisons, 142, *142*
  investment decisions and, 148–149
  rate of, 480–482
  reform measures, 143–144
  territorial vs. worldwide, 144
Corporate venturers, 394
Corporations. *See also* Corporate financing;
  Shareholders
  bonds (*See* Corporate bonds)
  cash flow in, 7, *7,* 377, *377*
  closely held, 5
  defined, 5
  financial goals of, 7–10, 18–19
  governance of (*See* Corporate governance)
  ownership of (*See* Ownership and control)
  professional, 6
  public (*See* Public companies)
  restructuring by (*See* Restructuring)
  stock (*See* Common stock)
  taxation of (*See* Corporate taxation)
  terminology considerations, 2*n*
  value maximization in, 7–10, 18–19, 312
Corus Steel, 831, 852
Cost of capital. *See* Opportunity cost of capital
Cost of equity capital. *See also* Company cost
  of capital; Opportunity cost of capital
  in CAPM model, 232–236, 530
  defined, 83
  estimation of, 87–92
  leverage and, 459–462
  measurement of, 232–236
Costs
  administrative, 665, 688
  agency (*See* Agency costs)
  of bankruptcy, 483–487, *484–485*
  of debt, 231–232
  equivalent annual, 153–154
  of excess capacity, 156
  of general cash offers, 409–410
  of new issues of stock, 402
  of new projects, 156
  overhead, 140
  sunk, 140
  transaction, 665
Counterparty risk, 690
Countrywide, 832

Coupons (bond), 47–50, 47*n,* 632
Coval, J. D., 636*n*
Covariance, 182–183, 182*n,* 188, *189*
Cowgill, B., 357*n*
Coy, P., 602*n*
CP (commercial paper), 631, 650–652,
  820, 821
CPI (consumer price index), 62
Crash of 1929, 11, 210*n*
Credit analysis, 808
Credit decision, 808–811, *809–810*
Credit default swaps, 617–618, 701
Credit events, 618
Credit insurance, 811*n*
Credit-linked bonds, *645*
Credit management, 806–812, *809–810*
  collection policy in, 811–812
  credit analysis in, 808
  credit decision in, 808–811, *809–810*
  overview, 806–807
  promise to pay and, 807–808
  terms of sale in, 807
Credit risk, 618–622, 637, 649. *See also* Bond
  ratings
Credit scoring systems, 624
Credit Suisse, *401*
Cross-border leasing, 676, 676*n*
Cross-border mergers, 830, 845, 847
Crowdfunding, 394, 396
CSTRS (California State Teachers' Retirement
  System), 11
CSX, *81, 234, 234*–236, 315
Cummins, J. D., 688*n*
Cummins Inc., 347, 802–804, *803*
Cumulative capital requirements, 771, *771*
Cumulative preferred stock, 373
Currency futures market, 719
Currency risk, 728–731
Currency swaps, *700,* 701, 701*n*
Current assets, 746, 771–772
Current liabilities, 518, 746
Current ratio, 759
Current yield, 48
Cusatis, P. J., 875*n*
Cutoff date, in payback period, 112–114
Cutrale-Safra, 852
CVS Health, *830*
Cyclicality, asset beta and, 237

D

Dabora, E., 345*n*
Daimler AG, 894
Daimler-Benz, 832, 894, *895*
DaimlerChrysler, 864
Dakota, Minnesota & Eastern Railroad, 292*n*
Daley, L. V., 875*n*
Dalian Commodity Exchange (China), *691*
Daniel, K., 350*n*
Danone, 845
Data mining/data snooping, 212
Davis, S. J., 867*n*
Davydenko, S. A., 882, 882*n*
DBRS, 622*n*
DCF. *See* Discounted cash flow

Dealer markets, 79
DeAngelo, H., 441*n,* 495, 495*n*
DeAngelo, L., 441*n*
Death bonds, 646
Death-spiral, 645
Debentures, 634
Debt capacity, 511–513, 523*n,* 524,
  529–530, 541
Debt covenants, 637–639, *638,* 650
Debt–equity ratio (D/E), 458–460, *460–461,*
  520–521
Debt-equivalent cash flow, 539–540
Debt financing, 631–662. *See also* Debt policy
  asset-backed securities and, 631, 635–636,
    645, 651
  bank loans, 647–650
  bonds (*See* Bonds)
  in company cost capital, 231–232
  corporate, 367–368, *367–368,* 374–377
  debt ratios, 367–368, *367–368, 475,*
    497–498, 523*n,* 756–757
  in disguise, 376
  fixed-rate vs. floating, 375
  forms of, 374–376
  government loan guarantees and, 621–622
  international security issues in, 408–409
  long-term (*See* Long-term debt financing)
  medium-term notes and, 631, 652, *820, 821*
  overview, 631–632, *632*
  private placements and, 413, 639–640
  project finance loans, 660–662
  security sales and, 408–413
  short-term (*See* Short-term debt financing)
  yields on corporate debt and, 614–618
Debtor in possession (DIP), 861
Debt policy
  after-tax WACC and, 467–468, *468*
  agency costs and, 490–492
  asymmetric information and, 495–497
  bankruptcy costs and, 483–487, *484–485*
  costs of financial distress and, 482–495
  effect of leverage in competitive tax-free
    economy, 452–457
  financial risk and expected returns,
    457–464
  financial slack and, 499–500
  interest tax shields and stockholders'
    equity, 477
  law of conservation of value and, 454–459
  overview, 451
  pecking order of financing choices and,
    495–501
  taxation and, 476–482
  trade-off theory of capital structure and,
    483, *483,* 493–495
Debt ratios, 367–368, *367–368, 475,* 497–498,
  523*n,* 756–757
Decision trees, 267–274
  abandonment option and, 268–269, *270*
  binomial method of option pricing and,
    572–573
  example of use, 271–273, *272*
  expansion option and, 267–268, *268*
  investment option and, 267–268, *604,*
    604–605
  pro and con, 273–274

production option and, 269
timing options and, 269–270
Declining annuities, 668n
Declining industries, 903
D/E (debt–equity ratio), 458–460, *460–461*, 520–521
Deep-in-the-money projects, 121n
Deere, 663
Default option, 618–622, 637
Default puts, 619–620
Default risk. *See also* Bankruptcy
    corporate bonds and, 67–70, 236n
    credit ratings and, 67, 618, 622–623, *623–624*
    credit scoring systems and, 624
    money-market investments and, 818
    predicting probability of default, 624–627
    sovereign bonds and, 68–70
    statistical models of, 624–626, *625*
    structural models of, 626–627, *627*
Deferred taxes, 517n
Defined-benefit pension plans, 380n, 714–715, *715*
Defined-contribution pension plans, 380, 380n, 715n
Deflation, 62, 64n
DeGeorge, F., 322, 322n
Degree of operating leverage (DOL), 238n, 263, 263n
Degrees of freedom, 174n
De Jong, A., 345n
Dell, Michael, 397
Dell Technologies, 397, 476, 806
Delphi, 834, 879
Delta Air Lines, 302
DeMarzo, P. M., 465n
Demirguc-Kunt, A., 498n
Denis, D. J., 426n, 639n, 647n
Depreciation
    accelerated, 142, 143, 148–150, 676, 775n
    biases in calculating returns, 328
    bonus, 143, 149
    of capital expenditures, 111
    double-declining-balance method of, 148–149, 149n
    economic, 328–331, *329*
    investment decisions and, 148–149
    net present value and, 137, 142, 149, *149*
    salvage value and, 668
    straight-line, 142, 143, 150
    tax shields and, 148–149, 540, 668, 670–671
Derivatives, 687, 690–702. *See also* Forward contracts; Futures contracts; Options; Swaps
Descartes, René, 117n
Deutsche Bank, 78, *401*, 412, 412n, 833, 894, 896, 898
Deutsche Börse, 79
Deutsche Telecom, 646
Devon Energy, *81*, 82, 82n
Diamond, D., 375n
DIAMONDS, 380
Diet deals, 866
Digital options, 582
Dill, D. A., 674n

Dilution, in convertible bond valuation, 644
Dimitrov, O., 349n
Dimon, James, 430
Dimson, E., 62–63n, 63n, 66n, 167, 167–169n, 171–172, 172n, 175n, 177n, 727n
DIP (debtor in possession), 861
Direct debit, 814
Direct deposit, 814
Direct leases, 664
Directors. *See* Board of directors
Direct payment, 814
Direct quote, 718–719
Direct TV, 874
Dirksen, Everett, 631n
Dirty (full) price, 49n
Disbursements, management of, 779, 812–814, *813*
Discounted bonds, 48
Discounted cash flow (DCF)
    business valuation by, 95–100, *96*
    in common stock valuation, 82, 83, 85, 87–92
    dangers of constant-growth formula, 89–92
    formula for, 26, 85n
    models with two or more stages of growth, 90–92
    problems in option pricing, 564
    rate of return and (*See* Internal rate of return (IRR))
    in real option valuation, 608
    safe and nominal, 538–541
    in setting water, gas, and electricity prices, 87–89, *89*
    spreadsheet functions for, 38–39
    stock repurchases and, 433–434
Discounted-cash-flow rate of return. *See* Internal rate of return (IRR)
Discounted payback measure, 113–114
Discount factor, 22, 58–59
Discount rates. *See also* Opportunity cost of capital
    avoiding fudge factors in, 241–242, 286n
    for international projects, 242
    in present value formula, 22
    risk-adjusted, 243–246
    single, 244–246
    WACC in adjustment of, 529–531
Discriminatory auctions, 407
Disinvestment, 312
Disney, *830*
Dittmann, I., 896, 896n
Dittmar, A. K., 875n
Diversifiable risk. *See* Specific risk
Diversification
    arbitrage pricing theory and, 214–215
    internal, 901
    limits to, 184–185
    market risk and, 178–181, *180–181*
    mergers and, 836–837
    portfolio risk and, 174–181, *179*
    value additivity and, 189–190
Divestitures, 876
Dividend discount model. *See* Discounted cash flow (DCF)
Dividend reinvestment plans (DRIPs), 427
Dividends. *See also* Payout policy

in convertible bond valuation, 643
free cash flow as, 99–100
information content of, 428–430, *429*
irrelevance of, 431, 434, 436
in option pricing, 581–582
payout ratio and, 88, 436
preferred stock and, 373
regular cash dividends, 427
share issues and, 434–436
special, 427
stock dividends, 428, 428n
stock price and, 83–87
taxation of capital gains vs., 437–440
Dividends per share, 86n
Dividend yield, 79, 87, 172–173, *173*
Dixit, A. K., 599n
Djankov, S., 368, 368n, 892n
Dr Pepper Snapple, *830*
Doherty, N. A., 688n
DOL (degree of operating leverage), 238n, 263, 263n
Dollar loans, 720
Dot.com bubble, 349, 350, 358, 384, 401
Double-declining-balance depreciation, 148–149, 149n
Double-dipping, 676
Douglas, R., 617n
Dow Chemical, 315, *830*, 845, 875
Dow Jones Industrial Average, 80, *178,* 380
DP World, 845
Dresdner Bank, 836
Dresdner Kleinwort, 401
Drexel Burnham, 866
DRIPs (dividend reinvestment plans), 427
Dropbox, 398
Du, W., 723–724, 724n
Dual-class equity, 900, *900*
Dual-class shares, 371–372
Due diligence, 401
Duffie, D., 617n
Dun and Bradstreet, 808, 902
DuPont, 315, *830*, 845, 875
Du Pont formula, 754–755
Durand, David, 453n
Duration hedging, 703, 703n
Duration of bonds, 52–56, *53–54*, 54–56n
Dutch auction, 428
Dyck, A., 347n

E

Earnings before interest, taxes, depreciation, and amortization (EBITDA), 82n, 97n, 143, 476, 479, 528
Earnings before interest and taxes (EBIT), 82n, 97n, 143, 476, 479, 528, 747, 757
Earnings beta, 237
Earnings per share (EPS)
    earnings targets, 321–322
    examples of, 79
    financial leverage and, 457–458, *459*
    forecasting, 321–322
    mergers and, 837–838, *837–838*
    stock price and, 79, 82, 82n, 92–95
    in valuation by comparables, 82

Earnings–price ratio, 93–94
Easterbrook, F., 437n
Eastern Airlines, 486, 880
Eastman Kodak, 81
eBay, 402, 405, 874
EBIT. See Earnings before interest and taxes
EBITDA. See Earnings before interest, taxes, depreciation, and amortization
EBPP (electronic bill presentation and payment), 813
Eckbo, B. E., 344n
ECNs (electronic communication networks), 78
Economic depreciation, 328–331, 329
Economic disasters, 683, 684
Economic exposure, 730–731
Economic income, 328
Economic order quantity (EOQ), 805, 805n
Economic profit (EP), 325
Economic rents
    case study on, 295–302
    competitive advantage and, 292–295, 294–295
    defined, 292
Economic value added (EVA), 324–331
    biases in, 326–331, 327, 329–330
    calculation of, 324–325, 750
    defined, 749
    origins of, 324n
    problems with, 752
    pros and cons of, 325–326
Economies of scale, 292, 833–834
Ecuador, refusal to pay debts, 69n
EDF (Electricité de France), 877
Edmans, Alex, 370n, 550n, 898, 898n
Effective annual interest rate, 36
Efficiency analysis, 752–754
Efficient-market hypothesis, 340–358
    behavioral finance and, 349–353
    bubbles and, 348–349
    competition and, 341–342
    evidence for, 342–348
    exceptions to, 913–914
    forms of market efficiency, 340, 910
    information effect in, 341–344, 347–348, 354
    lessons of market efficiency, 354–356, 358
    mispricing and, 338, 352, 353, 356, 358
    random walks and, 340–343, 342–343, 555n
    semistrong efficiency and, 340, 343–345, 345, 910
    strong efficiency and, 340, 345–348, 346, 910
    weak market efficiency and, 340, 342–343, 343, 354, 910
Efficient portfolios, 202–203, 203–208, 213
Egan-Jones Ratings, 622n
Ehrbar, A., 325, 325n
Eichholtz, P., 236n
Eight O'Clock Coffee, 831
Einstein, Albert, 340n
Electricité de France (EDF), 877
Electronic bill presentation and payment (EBPP), 813
Electronic communication networks (ECNs), 78

Ellis, Jim, 902
Ellis, K., 399n
Ellison, Larry, 320, 577
Embedded options, 542
EMC, 476
Emigrant Mercantile Bank, 381
Empire building, 312
EMU (European Monetary Union), 718n, 818
Energy Capital, 864
Energy Future Holdings, 5, 878, 882
Enriques, L., 896n
Enron, 376, 397, 485, 493, 623, 632, 878, 904
Entergy, 321, 802, 804
Entrenching investment, 312
EOG Resources, 81
E.ON, 874, 876
EOQ (economic order quantity), 805, 805n
EPA (U.S. Environmental Protection Agency), 343
EP (economic profit), 325
EPS. See Earnings per share
Equifax, 624n, 808n
Equipment trust certificates, 635
Equity financing
    in disguise, 373
    in financial distress situations, 489
    international security issues in, 408–409
    IPOs (See Initial public offerings)
    methods of, 4
    in partnerships, 373
    preferred stock and, 373
    rights issues in, 412–413
    security sales and, 408–413
    stock (See Common stock)
    trusts and, 373
    venture capital and, 391–395, 394–395
Equity investors, 4
Equity-linked bonds, 645
Equity premium puzzle, 171n
Equivalent annual cash flow, 154–155
Equivalent annual cost, 153–154, 667
Equivalent formula, 30n
Equivalent loans, 673
Erb, C., 734n
Erturk, I., 465n
Erwin, G.R.
Essilor, 830
ETFs (exchange-traded funds), 80, 185, 369, 380
Ethical considerations, 11–12
Eurex Exchange, 692
Euribor, 818
Eurobonds, 375, 409, 640
Eurocurrency, 375
Eurodollars, 818
Euro interbank offered rate, 818
Euronext exchange, 78, 79n, 691n, 694
European Central Bank, 70
European Monetary Union (EMU), 718n, 818
European options, 543, 568, 580–582
Euros, 375, 718n
Eurozone debt, 70
EVA. See Economic value added
EVA Dimensions, 748, 752
Event risks, 639
Event studies, 344
Evergreen credit, 647

Excess capacity costs, 156
Exchange rates, 720–723, 726–728. See also Foreign exchange markets
Exchange-traded funds (ETFs), 80, 185, 369, 380
Executive stock options, 577, 578
Exelon Corporation, 347
Exercise price, 543
Exotic securities, 466
Expansion option
    decision trees and, 267, 267–268
    exploitation of new technology and, 295–302
    follow-on investment opportunities, 590–594
    net present value and, 293, 295, 297–301, 299
Expectations theory of exchange rates, 721
Expectations theory of forward rates, 724
Expectations theory of term structure, 60–61
Expected returns, 206–207, 234–235, 457–464
Experian, 624n, 808n
Export-Import Bank, 811n
External financing, 497, 789, 789–790
Exxon Mobil
    arbitrage pricing theory and, 214
    betas for stock, 186, 207
    investment and financing decisions by, 2, 3, 7
    rate of return on stock, 202
    risk shifting game and, 489
    standard deviation of stock returns, 179, 203
    stock holdings for, 377, 378n
Ezzell, J., 523n

F

Facebook, 2, 3, 371, 900
Face value of bonds, 47, 48
Factoring, 811
Fair Isaac and Company, 808n
Fair market rent, 289, 289n
Fair price defense, 851
Fallen angels, 622
Fama, Eugene F., 172n, 212n, 215–217, 215n, 216, 347n, 494n, 499n, 724n, 913, 913n
Fama–French three-factor model, 215–217, 215n, 216, 291, 344n
Family control, 898–899, 898–899
Fanjul, G., 866n
Fannie Mae. See Federal National Mortgage Association
Farm Credit Financial Assistance Corporation, 819n
Farre-Mensa, J., 439n
FASB (Financial Accounting Standards Board), 666–667, 845
Fawcett, S. E., 397n
FCF. See Free cash flow
FCIA (Foreign Credit Insurance Association), 811n
FCX, 140
FDA (U.S. Food and Drug Administration), 271–273, 607
Federal agency securities, 819

Federal Deposit Insurance Corporation
(FDIC), 622
Federal Family Education Loan (FFEL), 622
Federal funds rate, 648*n*
Federal Home Loan Mortgage Corporation
(Freddie Mac), 52, 353, 385, 819, 878
Federal National Mortgage Association
(Fannie Mae), 52, 353, 385, 819, 878
*Federal Power Commission v. Hope Natural
Gas Company* (1944), 87*n*
Federal Reserve Bank of New York, 352
Fedwire, 814, 814*n*
Feldhütter, P., 620*n*
Ferguson, M., 617*n*
Fernandez, P., 171*n*
Fernández Acín, I., 171*n*
Ferrari, *874, 876*
FFEL (Federal Family Education Loan), 622
Fiat, 487, 864
Fiat Chrysler, *3, 874, 876*
FICO scores, 624*n*, 808*n*
Fidelity Investments, 379
Fiduciary duty, 893
Financial Accounting Standards Board
(FASB), 666–667, 845
Financial analysis, 743–762
Du Pont formula for, 754–755
efficiency measurement, 752–754
financial ratios in, 743–744, *744*
financial statements in, 744–747, *746–747*
interpretation of financial ratios in,
760–761, *762*
leverage measurement, 756–758
of liquidity, 758–759
performance measurement, 748–752
return on assets analysis, 754–756
Financial assets, 2. *See also* Marketable
securities
Financial crisis (2007–2009)
liquidity value during, 917
origins of, 384, 917–918
standard deviation of stock market returns
in, 178
stock options during, 321
subprime mortgages and, 314, 353,
384–385, 617, 636
Financial distress, 482–495. *See also*
Bankruptcy
asset types and, 492–493
bait and switch game and, 490
cash in and run game and, 489–490
equity financing in, 489
incentives and, 487–488
leases and, 665–666
overview, 482–483
playing for time game and, 490
risk management and, 685–686
risk shifting game and, 488–489
trade-off theory of capital structure and,
483, *483,* 498–499
without bankruptcy, 487
Financial engineering, 551–552
Financial institutions, 381–382. *See also* Banks
Financial intermediaries
banks as, 381–382
corporate equity holdings by, 369, *369*

defined, 378
financial assets of, 378, *379*
role of, 378, 378*n,* 382–386
Financial leases, 669–676
advantages of, 669, 674
defined, 664, 756*n*
example of, 670, *670*
international, 676
net value of, 672–673, *673*
ownership of leased asset, 671
requirements for, 666
taxation and, 671–672
Financial leverage
cautions regarding, 464–467
cost of equity capital and, 459–462
defined, 452, 756
effect in competitive tax-free economy,
452–457
expected stream of earnings per share and,
457–458, *459*
leverage ratios, 756, 758
measurement of, 756–758
Modigliani–Miller propositions and, 453–454
off-balance-sheet, 607
return on equity and, 758
volatility and, 313*n*
Financial managers
agency problems and, 12–13, 911–912
CEOs (*See* Chief executive officers)
CFOs (*See* Chief financial officers)
compensation and incentive plans for, 312,
313, 316–323, *317–318,* 384
ethical considerations for, 11–12
lessons of market efficiency for, 354–356,
358
monitoring of, 312, 314–316
as off-balance-sheet liabilities, 914–915
risk identification by, 5
role of, 7
separation of ownership and control and,
6, 12, 848, 892–901
value maximization by, 7–10
Financial markets. *See also* International
finance
current vs. future consumption
reconciliation in, 18, *18*
defined, 378
financial institutions in, 381–382, 888–892
historical data on, 167–174
imperfections and opportunities in,
466–467
information effect in, 383–384
international capital markets, 888–892,
889–891
investor protection and, 892
IPOs in (*See* Initial public offerings)
pooling risk and, 383, 687–688
role of, 382–386
success of new markets, 915
well-functioning, 8, 8*n*
Financial planning, 770–790. *See also*
Financing decisions
cash budgeting in, 778–780, *779–780*
consistency in, 785
growth and external financing in, *789,*
789–790

long-term, 770–773, 784–789
short-term, 664, 770–773, 778–784
tracing changes in cash, 773–778
Financial ratios, 743–744, *744,* 760–761, *762*
Financial risk. *See* Risk
Financial slack, 499–501
Financial statements. *See also* Balance sheets
income, 323, *324,* 747, *747, 773, 773*
in merger analysis, 845, *846*
standards for, 744–745
statement of cash flows, 773–775, *774*
Financial structure. *See* Capital structure
Financière Agache, 900
Financing decisions. *See also* Financial
planning
adjusted present value in, 524–529
business valuation process and, 512–517
corporate (*See* Corporate financing)
debt (*See* Debt financing)
defined, 2
equity (*See* Equity financing)
examples of, *3,* 4–5
investment decisions vs., 4–5, 141, 147,
338–340
long-term (*See* Long-term debt financing)
mergers and, 838–839
short-term (*See* Short-term debt financing)
WACC in, 508–512, 529–531
Fintech, 14
Firms. *See* Corporations
First-stage financing, 392
Fisher, F., 539*n*
Fisher, Irving, 65, 723*n*
Fisher Scientific, 876
Fitch credit ratings, 67, 622, 651*n*
Fixed-cost beta, 238–239
Fixed-income market, 48
Fixed-rate debt, 375
Flat (clean) price, 49*n*
Fledgling Electronics, 83–85, *85, 94–95*
Flexible production and procurement,
600–604, *601–603*
Floating lien, 649
Floating-price convertibles, 645
Floating-rate debt, 375, 617, 617*n,* 698–699
Floating-rate notes, 633
Flooring charge, 650*n*
Floor interest rate, 633
Flow-to-equity method of valuing companies,
516–517
Floyd, E., 426*n*
Folgers, 356
Follow-on investment opportunities,
590–594
Forcing conversion, 642
Ford, Henry, 893, 893*n*
Ford Motor Company
CEOs of, 315, 319
commercial paper and, 651
discounted cash flow and, 38
financial slack and, 500, 501
gross underwriting spreads for, *409*
outsourcing by, 834
overseas operations, 735
ownership of, 900
shareholders and, 893

Forecasts
  biased, 285–286
  cash flow (*See* Cash flow forecasts)
  earnings per share, 321–322
  errors in, 266*n*, 287, 293
  market values in, 287–292
  optimistic, *241*, 241–242
  prediction markets, 357
  product sales, 139
  risk premiums, 171*n*
  unbiased, 240
Foreign bonds, 375, 408–409, 640
Foreign Credit Insurance Association (FCIA), 811*n*
Foreign currency debt, 69
Foreign exchange markets, 717–734
  exchange rates and interest rates in, 720–721
  forward premium and spot rate changes in, 721–722
  hedging currency risk in, 728–731
  inflation and exchange rates in, 722–723
  interest rates and inflation in, 723, *728*
  international investment decisions in, 731–734
  overview, 717–719
  purchasing power parity in, 722, 722*n*, 724–726, *726*
  real vs. nominal exchange rates in, 726–728, 726*n*, *727*
Forelle, C., 579*n*
Fortis, 385
Forward contracts, 690, 697, *698*, 719
Forward exchange rates, *718*, 719
Forward interest rate, 697
Forward market, 719
Forward premium, 719, 721–722
Forward prices, 690
Forward rate, expectations theory of, 724
Forward rate of interest, 60*n*
France
  corporate tax rate in, *142*
  government bonds in, 47–48, 47*n*
  interest rates in, 36
  nominal vs. real exchange rates in, 726, *727*
  ownership and control in, 896
  tax vs. shareholder books in, 150*n*
Frank, M., 499*n*
Franks, J. R., 486, 486*n*, 674*n*, 844*n*, *878*, 881–882*n*, 882, 895*n*
FRAs (forward rate agreements), 697
Fraud, 12
Fraudulent conveyance, 490*n*
Freddie Mac. *See* Federal Home Loan Mortgage Corporation
Free cash flow (FCF)
  in business valuation, 96, *96*, 99–100, 512–514, *515*
  financial slack and, 500
  as motive for takeovers, 835
Free-cash-flow problem, 312
Freeport-McMoran, *67*, *750*
Free-rider problem, 370
French, Kenneth R., 172*n*, 212*n*, 215–217, 215*n*, *216*, 347*n*, 349*n*, 494*n*, 499*n*, 913, 913*n*

Friedman, E., 901, 901*n*
Frontier Communications, 614–615
Froot, K. A., 345*n*, 688*n*, 724*n*
Frydman, C., 317*n*
FTC (U.S. Federal Trade Commission), 844
Full (dirty) price, 49*n*
Full-payout leases. *See* Financial leases
Full-service leases, 664
Fürstenberg, Carl, 897*n*
Futures contracts
  commodity, 695–696
  hedging with, 691–696
  mechanics of trading, 692–693
  standardization of, 719
  trading and pricing, 693–694
  valuing, 694
Futures exchanges, 691, *691–692*
Futures markets, 291–292, 686, 696*n*, 704, 719
Future value
  of annuities, 33–34
  calculation of, 20–21
  of stock, 84–87, *85–86*

G

GAAP (generally accepted accounting principles), 80, 315, 745
Gabaix, X., 319*n*, 550*n*
Gabor, D., 465*n*
Gadanecz, B., 649*n*
Galai, D., 839*n*
Gale, D., 902–903*n*
Gambling for redemption, 313, 313*n*, 686*n*
Gao, P., 651*n*
Gao, X., 398, 398*n*
Gaspar, V., 903*n*
Gates, Bill, 28
Gavazza, A., 669*n*
GE. *See* General Electric
Gearing. *See* Financial leverage
GE Capital Aviation Services, 663
Geely, 852
Geithner, Tim, 69
Geltner, D., 236*n*
General cash offers, 408–410
General Electric (GE), 80, 80*n*, 139, 302, 322*n*, 844
General Growth Properties, *878*
Generally accepted accounting principles (GAAP), 80, 315, 745
General Motors (GM)
  bankruptcy by, 501, *878*, 881
  commercial paper and, 651
  dividends and, 430
  outsourcing by, 834, 879
  pension deficit, 632
  sale of stock, 396
General partnerships, 868–869
General Services Administration (GSA), 819*n*
Genesee & Wyoming, *234*
Geometric average return, 170*n*
Germany
  agency problems in, 912
  CEO compensation in, 317, *317*

corporate taxation in, *142*, 151
  economic stability in, 177
  growth and declining industries in, 903
  interest rates in, 36, 66, *66*
  mergers and, 832
  net present value calculations in, 151
  ownership and control in, 894–896, *895*
  private companies in, 398, 398*n*
  short-termism in, 903
  Zinsschranke rule in, 476*n*
Gertner, R., 875*n*
Gilligan, Thomas W., 665*n*
Gilson, R., 395*n*
Ginnie Mae (Government National Mortgage Association), 819*n*
Glass Lewis, 317
GlaxoSmithKline, 2, *3*
Global bonds, 409, 640
Global Crossing, *878*
Global markets. *See* International finance
GM. *See* General Motors
Goetzmann, W. N., 171*n*
Going-concern value, 80
Going dark, 397*n*
Gold, 290–291*n*, 290–292, 684–685, 685*n*, 687
Golden parachutes, 851
Goldman Sachs, 6, 382, 382*n*, *401*, 649
Goldreich, D., 406–407*n*
Gompers, P. A., 392*n*, 850*n*
Goodhart, C., 465*n*
Goodwill, 846
Google
  equity finance and, 493
  foreign profits, 817
  IPOs and, 406, 406*n*
  ownership of, 900
  parent company of, 95
  prediction markets and, 357
  venture capital and, 395
Goolsbee, A. D., 883*n*
Gordon, M. J., 87*n*
Gorgon natural gas field, 3–4
Gornall, W., 392*n*, 395, 395*n*
Goujon, Jean, 900
Governance. *See* Corporate governance; Ownership and control
Government bonds. *See* Treasury bonds
Government National Mortgage Association (Ginnie Mae), 819*n*
Government regulation, 646. *See also specific laws and government agencies*
Government sponsored enterprises (GSEs), 819, *820*
Goyal, V., 499*n*
Graham, John R., 111*n*, 209*n*, 322, 322*n*, 429*n*, 436*n*, 438*n*, 494–495*n*, 495, 642, 643*n*, 665*n*, 685*n*, 771*n*
Gray market, 404*n*
Great Depression, 62, 353, 892
Greece, sovereign debt crisis in, 70, 385–386, 618, 918
Green, T. C., 344*n*
Greenshoe option, 400
Greenspan, Alan, 351*n*
Grinstein, Y., 438*n*

Gromb, D., 905n
Grossman, S. J., 347n
Groupe Arnault SAS, 900
Growth industries, 302, 903
Growth rates, 790
Growth stocks, 92, 212, *212*
Growth-Tech Inc., *90,* 90–91, 96
Gruber, M. J., 347n
Grullon, G., 429n
GSA (General Services Administration), 819n
GSEs (government sponsored enterprises), 819, *820*
Guiso, L., 10n
Gulf & Western Industries, *870*

H

Hall, B. H., 854n
Halliburton, 844
Haltiwanger, R. S., 867n
Hamada, R. S., 524n
Handelsbanken, 315
Hansen, Robert S., 402n, 409–410n
Hard rationing, 125–126
Harford, J., 853n
Harper, J. T., 877n
Harris, R. S., 395n, 734n, 844n
Hart, O., 369n, 882n
Hartman, P., 889n, 903n
Hart–Scott–Rodino Antitrust Act of 1976, 844, 844n
Harvey, Campbell R., 111n, 209n, 322, 322n, 429n, 494n, 642, 643n, 734n, 771n
Haushalter, G. David, 687, 687n
HBOS, 401, 412
Healy, Paul M., 429, 429n, 854, 854n, 904n
Hedge funds, 352–353, 380, 636
Hedge ratio, 565, 703–705, *705*
Hedging
    commodity price risk, 687
    currency risk, 687, 728–731
    defined, 690
    fuel costs, 689, 692–693
    futures contracts, 691–696
    interest rate risk, 687
    setting up hedge, 702–705
    as zero-sum game, 684
Heineken, *187*
Heinz, 833
Hellman, T., 394n
Hellman & Friedman, *864*
Hellwig, F., 465n
Hellwig, M., 897n
Helmsley Iron, 117–118, *118*
Helyar, J., 865n
Hendel, Igal, 665n
Herman Miller Corporation, 325
Hershey, 355n, 542
Hewlett-Packard (HP), 3, 542, 601–602, 602n, 853, *874*
Higgins, R. C., 839n
High-frequency trading, 343n
High-yield bonds, 622
Hilscher, J., 624n
Hirshleifer, D., 350n, 917n

Historical data
    on capital markets, 167–174
    on CEO compensation, *317–318,* 317–319, 317n
    for cost of capital evaluations, 170–174
    on inflation, 62, *62–63,* 66
    on mergers, *831,* 853
    on rate of return, 169, *169,* 174, *175*
    on Treasury bond interest rates, 50, *50*
Hodges, Stewart D., 295n, 674n
Holcim, *730*
Holderness, Clifford, 370, 370n
Holstein Oil, 81
Home Depot
    efficiency analysis for, 752–754
    financial ratios for, 760–761, *760–761*
    financial statements for, *745–746,* 745–747
    leverage measurement, 756–758
    liquidity analysis for, 759
    performance measurement, 748–752
    return on assets analysis for, 754–755
    severance package received by, 319
Honeywell, 302, 844
Horizontal mergers, 831
Horizon value, 96–99, 514–516
Hoshi, T., 893, 893n, 903n
Host Marriott, 639
Hotchkiss, E. S., 626n, 880n
Household portfolios, 889, *890*
Houston, J. F., 836n
HP. *See* Hewlett-Packard
HR Ratings de Mexico, 622n
HSBC, 664, 664n
Huang, M., 311n, 350n
Hudson's Bay Company, 6
Human assets, 832
Hurdle rate. *See* Opportunity cost of capital
Hyperinflation, 62
Hypobank, 836
Hypo Group, 385
Hypo Real Estate, 878n
Hyundai, 901

I

IASB (International Accounting Standards Board), 745
IBES, 88n
IBFs (international banking facilities), 819
IBM
    book ratio debt, 495
    compensation plans from, 316n
    competitive advantage of, 302
    daily returns on stock, 198, *199*
    discount rates for international projects, 242
    leasing by, 663
    option to default, 619
    rate of return on stock, 109
    stock holdings in, 64n
    total return swap and, *702*
Icahn, Carl, 315
ICE Benchmark Administration, 648
ICE (Intercontinental Exchange), *691–692,* 691n

Ichor Holdings, *409*
IFC (International Finance Corporation), 661
IFM Therapeutics, 834
IFRS (International Financial Reporting Standards), 745
IIGF (Indonesia Infrastructure Guarantee Fund), 661
Ikenberry, D., 430n
IMF (International Monetary Fund), 70, 386, 918
Implied volatilities, 578–580, *579*
Imputation tax system, 439–440, *439–440,* 495n
Incentives. *See also* Stock options
    economics of, 319–321
    financial distress and, 487–488
    for financial managers, 312, 317, *318,* 319–321, 384
    leveraged buyouts and, 867
    payout policy and, 437
Incidental effects, 138
Income statements
    elements of, 747, *747*
    simplified, 323, *324*
    tracing cash flow with, 773, *773*
Income stocks, 92
Incomplete contracts, 369n
Incremental cash flow, 119n, 120, 138–140
Incremental net present value, 138–139
Incurrence covenants, 650
Indentures, 634
Indexed bonds, 64, 64n
Index funds, 185, 347, 379
Index futures, 694
India, corporate tax rate in, *142*
Indirect quote, 718
Indonesia Infrastructure Guarantee Fund (IIGF), 661
Industrial and Commercial Bank (China), *187,* 877
Industry beta, 234, *234*
Industry consolidation, 835–836
Industry structure, elements of, 292–293
Inefficiencies, elimination of, 835
Inflation
    bonds and, 61–67, *62–63,* 66
    consumer price index as measure of, 62
    equivalent annual cash flow and, 154–155
    exchange rates and, 722–723
    historical data on, 62, *62–63,* 66
    hyperinflation, 62
    interest rates and, 62–67, 723, *728*
    international comparisons, 62, *63,* 66, *66*
    in net present value analysis, 140–141
    in term structure of interest rates, 61
Inflation swaps, 701
Informatica, *864*
Information asymmetries, 495–497, 843–844
Information effect. *See also* Signaling
    in efficient-market hypothesis, 341–344, 347–348, 354
    in financial markets, 383–384
    investor response to, 344–345, *345,* 345n
    market reaction to stock issues and, 410–411
    mergers and, 843–844, 853–854

Information effect—Cont.
  of payout policy, 428–430, 429
  in semistrong form of market
      efficiency, 910
  of stock repurchase plans, 430
  in strong form of market efficiency, 910
  in weak form of market efficiency, 910
Information memos, 649
ING, 385
Initial public offerings (IPOs), 396–407
  advantages and disadvantages of,
      396–398
  alternative issue procedures for, 406–407
  arranging, 399
  costs of, 410
  hot new-issue periods and, 405–406
  international, 396, 403, 404
  long-run performance of IPO stocks, 406
  mini, 396
  motivations for, 396, 397
  steps for, 407
  underpricing of, 402–405
  underwriters of, 399–401, 401
  winner's curse and, 403, 404n, 407n
Installment plan costing, 30, 31
Institutional investors, 400, 413
Insurance, 578, 687–688, 811n
Insurance companies, 382, 383
Intangible assets, 20, 81, 135–136, 846
Intel, 135, 300, 394, 395, 772
Intercompany loans, 891, 891
Intercontinental Exchange (ICE), 79n,
  691–692, 691n
Interest and interest rates
  accrued, 49n, 634
  on bank loans, 648
  bond prices and, 48, 50–52, 50–54,
      62–67, 65
  bond terms and, 632–634
  carried, 394, 869
  compound, 21, 21, 37, 39
  deductions for, 143
  exchange rates and, 720–721
  Fisher's theory of, 65, 723n
  forward, 60n, 697
  inflation and, 62–67, 723, 728
  on money-market investments, 817
  nominal, 63–67, 65
  option value and, 553–556, 556
  prejudgment interest awards, 539–540
  real, 63–65, 64n, 65
  risk-free, 548n
  term structure of, 56–61
  on Treasury bills, 171
  on Treasury bonds, 50–51, 50–52
Interest coverage, 757
Interest rate parity theory, 721, 723–724
Interest rate risk, 56, 687, 702–703, 704
Interest rate swaps, 698–700
Interest tax shields, 143, 476–479, 477n, 478,
  479n, 493–495, 498
Intermagnetics, 834n
Intermediaries. See Financial intermediaries
Internal capital market, 870–873
Internal diversification, 901
Internal funds, 366–367

Internal growth rate, 790
Internal rate of return (IRR), 114–122
  calculation of, 115–116
  defined, 115
  in lending or borrowing, 116–117
  leveraged leases and, 677n
  modified, 118n
  multiple rates of return, 117–118,
      118, 118n
  for mutually exclusive projects,
      118–120, 120
  net present value and, 115–121, 116, 118
  opportunity cost of capital and, 120–121
  overview, 114
  pitfalls of, 116–121
  rule for, 116
  spreadsheet functions for, 122
  on venture capital funds, 395, 395
Internal Revenue Service (IRS), 150, 438n,
  517n, 671–672, 671n, 817
International Accounting Standards Board
  (IASB), 745
International banking facilities (IBFs), 819
International finance, 867–885. See also
  Foreign exchange markets; specific
  countries
  accounting standards, 745
  adjusted present value in, 528–529
  banks in, 815
  betas for selected stocks, 187
  bonds in, 375, 640
  bubbles in, 349
  cash management, 815
  CEO compensation, 317, 317
  comparisons across countries, 888–892,
      889–891
  conglomerates, 901
  corporate names, 5n
  corporate tax rates, 142, 142
  cross-border mergers, 830, 845, 847
  debt ratios, 368, 368
  defaulting debt, 615
  discount rates for international
      projects, 242
  dual-class equity, 372, 900, 900
  financial markets and institutions,
      888–892
  imputation tax systems, 439–440,
      439–440, 495n
  inflation rates across countries, 62, 63, 66,
      66, 728, 728
  initial public offerings, 396, 403, 404
  interest payments, 48n
  interest rates, 36
  international money market, 818–819
  leases in, 676, 676n
  market risk premium, 171–172, 172
  mergers, 830, 845, 851–852
  net present value, 151
  ownership and control, 892–901
  percentage of equity owned by
      shareholders, 370, 371
  perpetuities in, 28–29
  privatization in, 877–878
  put options, 689, 689
  risk in (See International risk)

  security issues, 408–409
  sovereign debt, 68–70, 385–386
  standard deviation of stock market returns,
      177, 177–178, 179
  taxation of multinational companies,
      11–12
International Finance Corporation (IFC), 661
International Financial Reporting Standards
  (IFRS), 745
International Fisher effect, 723n
International Monetary Fund (IMF), 70,
  386, 918
International risk
  currency risk, 728–731
  exchange risk, 731–734
  political risk, 734–736, 735
International Securities Exchange (ISE), 543n
International Swaps and Derivatives
  Association (ISDA), 617n, 618, 698n
Internet bubble, 349, 350, 358, 384, 401
Intrepid Potash, 409
Inventory management, 804–806, 805
Inventory period, 776–778
Inventory turnover, 753
Inversions, 144
Investment banks, 381–382, 403
Investment decisions. See also Capital
  budgeting; Project finance
  book rate of return in, 111–112, 121
  capital rationing in, 286
  corporate taxation and, 148–149
  defined, 2
  depreciation and, 148–149
  examples of, 2–4, 3
  excess capacity costs and, 156
  financing decisions vs., 4–5, 141, 147,
      338–340
  foreign exchange risk and, 731–734
  for gold, 290–291n, 290–292
  internal rate of return in, 114–122
  long-lived vs. short-lived assets, 153–155
  market value in, 287–292, 289
  methods for evaluation of, 110, 111
  monitoring, 314
  net present value and (See Net present
      value (NPV))
  payback period and, 112–114, 121
  present value analysis for, 22–24, 23
  for real estate, 288–290, 289
  replacement decisions, 155
  resource limitations and, 122–126
  robo advisors for, 14
  timing considerations in, 152–153
  trade-offs in, 9, 9–10, 109, 110
Investment funds, 378–381. See also specific
  types of funds
Investment-grade bonds, 622
Investment option
  decision trees and, 267–268, 604,
      604–605
  exploitation of new technology and,
      295–302
  follow-on opportunities, 590–594
Invitation Homes, 409
Involuntary issuers, 411n
Iowa Electronic Markets, 357

IPOs. *See* Initial public offerings
Ireland
    bailout for, 918
    corporate tax rate in, *142*, 144
Iridium Communications Inc., 3, *3n*
IRR. *See* Internal rate of return
Irrational exuberance, 351*n*
IRS. *See* Internal Revenue Service
ISDA (International Swaps and Derivatives
    Association), 617*n*, 618, 698*n*
ISE (International Securities Exchange), 543*n*
Ishii, J. L., 850*n*
ISS, 317
Italy
    economic stability in, 177
    nominal vs. real exchange rates in, 726, *727*
Itochu Corporation, 661
ITT, 870, *870*

J

J. B. Hunt, 802, 804
JAB, *864*
Jackson, G., 894*n*
Jacquier, E., 170*n*
Jaguar Land Rover, 831, 852
James, C. M., 836*n*
James Webb Space Telescope, 140
Japan
    bubbles in, 349, 350
    CEO compensation in, 317, *317*
    corporate tax rate in, *142*
    economic stability in, 177
    foreign bonds in, 640
    interest payments in, 48*n*
    mergers and, 833
    ownership and control in, 893–894, 903
    short-termism in, 903
    tax reform in, 438–439
    tax vs. shareholder books in, 150*n*
Japan Bank for International Cooperation
    (JBIC), 661
Japan Credit Rating, 622*n*
Japan Exchange Group, *692*
Jarmin, R. S., 867*n*
Jarrell, G., 99*n*, 430, 430*n*, 852*n*
Jegadeesh, N., 343*n*
Jenkinson, T., 395*n*
Jensen, Michael C., 312, 312*n*, 437*n*, 500,
    500*n*, 852*n*, 866*n*, 882, 882*n*
Jenter, D., 550*n*
Jiang, W., 316*n*
Jin, L., 376*n*
Jobs, Steve, 442
JOBS (Jumpstart Our Business Startups) Act
    of 2016, 396, 398
John Bean Technologies, *409*
Johnson, E. J., 350*n*
Johnson, Ross, 865, 866
Johnson, S., 372*n*, 901, 901*n*
Johnson & Johnson
    betas for stock, *186, 207*
    capital structure and, 477–478,
        477–478, 494
    company cost of capital, *229–230, 230*

competitive advantage for, 301
corporate bonds for, 67, *67*
foreign profits, 817
mergers involving, *830*
performance measurement, 748, *748,
    749, 750*
pure plays and, 237
rate of return on stock, 202, *202*
standard deviation of stock returns, *179,* 203
valuation of stock, *81, 82*
Jorion, P., 171*n*
Jounce Therapeutics, *409*
JPMorgan Chase, 381, 385, *401,* 429, 430, 649
JP Morgan Money Market Fund, 379
J-Power, 661
Jump risks, 688
Jumpstart Our Business Startups (JOBS) Act
    of 2016, 396, 398
Jung, K., 410*n*
Junior debt, 375, 638
Junk bonds, 616, 622, *623,* 866
Jurek, J., 636*n*
Just-in-time approach, 806

K

Kadant Inc., 876
Kahneman, D., 286*n*, 349–350*n*
Kane, A., 170*n*
Kaneko, T., 407*n*
Kansas City Southern Railroad, *81, 234,* 519
Kaplan, S. N., 319*n*, 392*n*, 394–395*n*, 486,
    486*n*, 527–528, 528*n*, 866–867*n*, 867
Kashyap, A., 893, 893*n*, 903*n*
Kay, John A., 292, 292*n*, 327*n*
Kedia, S., 872*n*
Keiretsu, 893–894, 903
Keller, M. R., 602–603*n*
Kendall, Maurice G., 340–342, 340*n*
Kershaw, Clayton, 319
Keurig Green Mountain, *830, 864*
Keysight Technologies, *409*
K.G.R. (Ökologische Naturdüngemittel
    GmbH), 151
Kickstarter, 396
Kim, Y-C., 410*n*
Kindleberger, C., 914*n*
Kiska, Wendy, 622
Knoeber, C. R., 850*n*
Koch Industries, 397
Kohlberg, Kravis, Roberts (KKR),
    864–865, 869
Kosowski, R., 347*n*, 910*n*
Kothari, S. P., 344*n*
Kozlowski, Dennis, 12
KPMG, 80
Kraakman, R., 899*n*
Kraft Foods, 833, *874*
Krigman, L., 399*n*
Kroll Bond Rating, 622*n*
Krueger, A. B., 883*n*
Kulatilaka, N., 600*n*
Kumar, A., 436*n*, 438*n*
Kumar, P., 638*n*
Kuroki, F., 894*n*

L

LafargeHolcim, 315
Lakonishok, J., 430*n*
Lamont, O. A., 871, 871*n*, 875*n*
Landier, A., 319*n*
Landsbanki, 878*n*
La Porta, R., 370*n*, 443*n*, 892, 892*n*, 898, 898*n*
Law of conservation of value, 454–459,
    910–911
Law of one price, 13*n, 57, 57–58,* 617, 722*n*
Lazard, 382
LBOs. *See* Leveraged buyouts
Leary, M. T., 495, 495*n*, 665*n*
Leases, 663–677
    cancellation options for, 669
    characteristics of, 663–664
    debt financing and, 376
    financial leases (*See* Financial leases)
    leveraged, 664, 676–677, *677,* 677*n*
    as off-balance-sheet financing, 666–667
    operating, 664, *667,* 667–669
    reasons for leasing, 664–667
    in theory of optimal capital structure, 500
Lee, D. S., 430*n*
Leeson, Nick, 313*n,* 706
Lehman Brothers, 5, 52, 385, 467*n,* 485, 651,
    817, 878
Lemmon, M. L., 316*n*, 495*n*, 499*n*
"Lemons" problem, leasing and, 665*n*
Lenders and lending. *See also* Debt financing;
    Leases
    agency costs of, 490–492
    assurances made to, 375
    bank loans, 2, 31–32, 647–650
    internal rate of return and, 116–117
    monitoring function of, 315
    peer-to-peer, 14, 383*n*
    in portfolio theory, *204,* 204–205
    project finance loans, 660–662
    role in financial markets, 383
    short-term sources of, 783
Lending Club, 14, 383*n*
Lenovo, 2, *3,* 852
Le Peigne, 900
Lerner, J., 867*n*
Lessee (user), 663
Lessor (owner), 663
Lev, B., 238*n*
Level annuities, 668*n*
Leverage. *See also* Competitive advantage
    cost of equity capital and, 459–462
    financial (*See* Financial leverage)
    hidden, 463–464
    operating, 237–239, *263, 263,* 263*n*
Leveraged buyouts (LBOs), 863–868
    adjusted present value and, 527–528
    debt ratios and, 757
    examples, *864,* 864–866
    financial distress and, 490
    incentives and, 867
    junk bonds and, 866
    stakeholders in, 866
    taxation and, 866
Leveraged leases, 664, 676–677, *677,* 677*n*

Leveraged restructurings, 867–868
Leverage ratios, 756–758
Levered equity, 452, 459
Levi, Y., 519n
Levine, R., 902n
Lewellen, W. G., 839n
Lewis, C. M., 643n
Lewis, M., 343n
Li, N., 426n
Liabilities
    current, 518, 746
    off-balance-sheet, 607, 666–667, 914–915
    short-term, 138n
Liability restructuring, 851
LIBOR. See London Interbank Offered Rate
Lichtenberg, F., 854n
Lie, E., 579n
Life cycle of firm, payout policy and, 441–443
LIFFE, 691n
Limited liability, 5, 483, 484, 618–620
Limited liability companies (LLCs), 6
Limited liability partnerships (LLPs), 6
Limited partnerships, 6, 373, 394, 868–869
Limit orders, 78
Lindt & Sprüngli, 730
Linear programming (LP), 124–125, 203
LinkedIn, 900
Lins, K. V., 347n
Lintner, John, 206, 206n, 431n
Liquidation value, 81, 516
Liquidity
    of corporate bonds, 68n
    of current assets, 771–772
    measurement of, 758–759
    value of, 916–917
Liquidity ratios, 758–759
Liquid yield option notes (LYONs), 645
Litton Industries, 870
Litzenberger, R. H., 439n
Lizzeri, Alessandro, 665n
Ljungqvist, A., 406n
LLCs (limited liability companies), 6
LLPs (limited liability partnerships), 6
LME (London Metal Exchange), 691
Lo, A., 439n
Loan covenants, 650
Loans. See Bank loans; Lenders and lending
Lockbox systems, 815
Loeb, Daniel, 315, 371
Lognormal distributions, 200n
London Interbank Offered Rate (LIBOR), 375, 633, 648, 648–649, 697n, 698–702, 818
London Metal Exchange (LME), 691
London Stock Exchange, 78, 79, 903
Longevity bonds, 645
Long-lived assets, 153–155, 244–246
Long Term Capital Management (LTCM), 352–353
Long-term debt financing, 632–640
    asset-backed securities and, 631, 635–636, 645, 651
    bond terms in, 632–634
    call provisions in, 637
    contingency planning, 784–785
    debt covenants and, 637–639, 638
    foreign bonds and eurobonds, 640

private placements and, 639–640
    security and seniority in, 634–635, 635
    short-term debt financing vs., 374–375
Long-term financial planning
    contingency planning, 784–785
    example of, 785–788, 786–787
    selection of plan, 788–789
    short-term financial planning vs., 770–773, 771–772
Lookback options, 582
Loomis, C., 302n
Lopez-de-Silanes, F., 370n, 443n, 892, 892n, 898, 898n
LoPucki, Lynn, 882n
Los Angeles Dodgers, 319
Loss of a degree of freedom, 174n
Lottery winnings, 35–36
Loughran, T., 404–405n, 405
Lowenstein, J., 854n
Lowe's, 760–761, 761
Lowry, M., 406n
LP (linear programming), 124–125, 203
LTCM (Long Term Capital Management), 352–353
LTV, 870
Lu, Qi, 358n
Lucas, Deborah, 622
Lucent Technologies, 873
Lufthansa, 376
Luxottica, 830
LVMH, 179, 187, 899–900
Lyondell Chemical Company, 878
LYONs (liquid yield option notes), 645

M

Macaulay duration, 53, 56n
MacKie-Mason, J., 494n
MacKinlay, A. C., 344n
Macquarie Bank, 382
MACRS (modified accelerated cost recovery system), 143, 149, 149n
Macy's, 802, 804
Maddaloni, A., 889n
Madoff, Bernard, 12, 12n
Maintenance covenants, 650
Majd, S., 598n
Majluf, N. S., 411n
Maksimovic, V., 498n, 876, 876n
Malkiel, B. G., 347n
Malmendier, U., 854n
Management buyouts (MBOs), 863–864, 867
Managers. See Financial managers
Mandelker, G. N., 238n
Marathon, 81, 82
Margin, in futures trading, 692–693
Marginal tax rate, 520
Margrabe, W., 593n
Marked to market futures contracts, 692
Marketable securities, 816–822. See also specific types of securities
    investment choices, 817
    money-market investments, 817–822, 820

as short-term assets, 138n
    tax strategies for, 816–817
Market–book ratios, 97
Market capitalization, 4, 79, 748
Market capitalization rate, 83, 88. See also Cost of equity capital
Market efficiency. See Efficient-market hypothesis
Market factor, in three-factor model, 216–217
Market for corporate control, 848
Market model, 344, 344n
Market orders, 78, 79
Market portfolio, 170–171, 210n
Market prices, trust in, 354–355
Market risk
    beta and, 186, 186–187, 910
    defined, 181
    diversification and, 178–181, 180–181
    estimation of, 247–248
    measurement of, 910
    spreadsheet functions for, 247–248
    terminology considerations, 181n
Market risk premium
    defined, 205
    estimation of, 171n
    expected, 172
    historical data on, 171
    international comparisons, 171–172, 172
    in three-factor model, 216
Markets. See Financial markets
Market timing, 499
Market-to-book ratio, 748–749, 748n
Market value, 287–292, 289, 619, 637
Market value added, 81, 748, 748n, 749
Market Volatility Index (VIX), 578–581, 579
Markowitz, Harry M., 198, 198n, 203
Marks and Spencer, 315, 341, 342
Marriott Corporation, 639
Marsh, P. R., 62–63n, 66n, 167, 167–169n, 171–172, 172n, 175n, 177n, 354n, 727n
Mars Inc., 397
Marston, F. C., 734n
Martin, K. J., 835, 835n
Marvin Enterprises case study
    alternative expansion plans in, 299, 299–300
    cost structure of old and new technologies in, 296, 296
    demand curve and price reductions in, 295, 296
    initial public offerings and, 399–402
    lessons from, 300–302
    price forecasting in, 297–298
    prospectus in, 421–424
    stock value in, 300
    value of new expansion in, 298–299
    venture capital and, 391–393
Massa, M., 412n
Mastercard, 426
Master limited partnerships, 373
Masulis, R. W., 839n
Matthews, J., 636n
Mauer, D. C., 771n
Maug, E., 896, 896n
Maxwell House, 356
Mayer, C., 889n, 895n

Mayers, D., 913n
Mazda, 903
MBOs (management buyouts), 863–864, 867
MBSs. *See* Mortgage-backed securities
McCardle, K. F., 855, 855n
McConnell, J. J., 645n, 669n, 835, 835n
McDonald's, 2, *3*, 749n
McGuire, William, 579
MCI, 904
McKinnell, Henry, 319
McKinsey & Company, 325
McLiesh, C., 892n
McNichols, Maureen F., 625n
Means, G. C., 370, 370n
Medium-term notes (MTNs), 631, 652, *820*, 821
Megginson, W., 878n
Mehra, R., 171n
Mehrotra, V., 875n
Mehta, P., 901, 902n
Mei, J., 239n
Mercedes Automobil Holding, 894
Mercedes-Benz, 864
Merck, *81*, 135–136, 733
Mergers and acquisitions, 831–892
    accounting for, 845–846, *846*
    antitrust law and, 844–845
    conglomerate mergers and value
        additivity, 861–862
    corporate taxation and, 144
    estimating gains and costs of, 839–844,
        852–853
    examples of, *830*
    form of acquisition, 845
    mechanics of, 844–847
    motives for, 831–839
    profitability of, 854–855
    synergies in, 832–833
    takeover battles and tactics,
        847–853, *851*
    tax consequences of, 846–847
    types, 831
    waves of, *831*, 853, 917
Merrill Lynch, 314, 319, 382n, 385
Merton, Robert C., 376n, 439n, 574n, 626,
    626–627n, 913, 913n
Merton model of default risk, 626–627
Metrick, A., 850n, 869n
Mexico, put options and oil prices in, *689*, *689*
Mezzanine financing, 393, 393n
Michaely, R., 399n, 406n, 429n, 438–439n
Microsoft
    betas for stock, 232–234, *233*
    equity financing by, 493
    financing decisions by, 4
    foreign profits, 144, 816
    gross underwriting spreads for, *409*
    performance measurement, 748, *748*, *750*
    random walk hypothesis and, 341, *342*
    return on capital, 751
    venture capital and, 395
Middlesex Water, *89*
Mihov, V. T., 639n, 647n
Mikkelson, W. H., 430n
Miles, J. A., 523n, 875n
Mill, John Stuart, 912

Miller, Merton H., 431–432, 431n, 439n, 453n,
    479n, 481, 481n, 523n, 646, 685
Miller, N. G., 236n
Miller, S. C., 649n
Mini IPOs, 396
Minority shareholders, 372
Miranda, J., 867n
Miranti, P. J., Jr., 870n
MIRR (modified internal rate of return), 118n
Mishra, D. R., 734n
Mitchell, M., 844, 844n, 852, 852–854n, 854
Mitsubishi Estate Company, 492n
Mittal Steel, 852
Mittelstand, 398
Miyajima, H., 894n
Mizuho Bank, 649, 833, 833n
MM approach. *See* Modigliani–Miller
    approach
Modified accelerated cost recovery system
    (MACRS), 143, 149, 149n
Modified duration, 54, 54–55n
Modified internal rate of return (MIRR), 118n
Modigliani, F., 431–432, 431n, 453n, 479n,
    523n, 685
Modigliani–Miller (MM) approach
    banks and, 465
    to capital structure, 453–454, 911
    guidelines for use, 523–524
    law of conservation of value and, 454–459
    to payout policy, 431–432, 441, 451
    taxation in, 479
Moeller, S. B., 854n
Mohan, N., 865n, 866, 866n
Momentum, 343, 343n
Mondelez International, 316, *874*
Money, time value of, 20, 110
Money machines, 58–59, 722
Money market, 817
Money-market investments, 379, 467n,
    817–822, *820*
Monoline insurers, 617
Monopolies, 844
Monsanto, *830*
Monte Carlo simulation, 264–266
Montgomery, C., 872, 872n
Moody's
    bond ratings, 67, *68*, 622
    commercial paper ratings, 651n
    credit ratings, 808
Moore, J., 882n
Moral hazard risk, 688
Moretti, E., 854n
Morgan Stanley, 6, 382, 382n, 401, *401*, 408
Morningstar Credit Ratings, 622n
Mortality bonds, *645*, 646
Mortgage-backed securities (MBSs), 11, 314,
    353, 385, 617, 636, 915
Mortgage bonds, 634–635
Mortgage payment calculation, 32, *33*
Mortgages. *See* Subprime mortgages
Motorola, *874*
MTNs (medium-term notes), 631, 652, *820*, 821
Mulally, Alan, 501
Mulesoft, *409*
Mullainathan, S., 313n, 321, 321n, 901, 902n
Mullins, David W., Jr., 354n

Multi Commodity Exchange (India), *691*
Multiplan, *864*
Müntegering, Franz, 866n
Murphy, T., 806n
Mutual funds, 80n, 185, 378–380, 914, 914n
Mutually exclusive projects, 118–120, *120*,
    151–156
Myers, Stewart C., 174, 241n, 286, 411n, 499n,
    524n, 598n, 607n, 674n, 694n, 789, 838n,
    905n, 912

N

Nagel, S., 436n
"Naked" call options, 230n
Nanda, V., 406n, 875n
Nardelli, Robert, 319
Nasdaq Composite Index, 349, 914
Nasdaq Futures, *691*
Nasdaq (National Association of Securities
    Dealers Automated Quotations System),
    78–79, 185, 580
Nasdaq 100 index, 380
Nationalization, 877–878
Nationally recognized statistical rating
    organizations (NRSOs), 622n
Naveen, L., 316n
Navistar, 315
NCR, 302, 873
Negative pledge clause, 634, 638
Negotiable certificates of deposit, *820*, 821
Nenova, Tatiana, 368, 368n, 372, 372n, 900
Nestlé, *179*, *187*, 316, 355n, 371, 730, *730*
Net convenience yield, 695, *696*
Net leases, 664
Net operating profit after tax (NOPAT), 751n
Net present value (NPV), 135–156
    alternatives to, 110
    book rate of return vs., 111–112
    break-even analysis and, 262
    calculation of, 24, *24*, 108–109, 148
    capital expenditures and, 136–137
    cash flow and, 26–27, 111–112, 136–142
    defined, 24n, 108
    depreciation and, 137, 142, 149, *149*
    earnings targets and, 322
    excess capacity costs and, 156
    expansion option and, 293, 295,
        297–301, *299*
    financing vs. investment decisions and,
        141, 147, 338–340
    of follow-on investment opportunities,
        591–594
    forecast bias and, 286
    incremental, 138–139
    inflation and, 140–141
    internal rate of return and, 115–121,
        116, *118*
    leases and, 672–674
    long-lived vs. short-lived assets and,
        153–155
    market value and, 288, 290–291
    of multiple cash flow, 26–27, *27*
    opportunity cost of capital and, 110–113,
        139–140

Net present value (NPV)—*Cont.*
  overinvestment and, 312
  payback period vs., 112–114
  production option and, *603*, 603–604
  project analysis with, 150
  project risk and, 912
  project selection and, 151–156
  properties of, 110–111
  replacement decisions and, 155
  rule for, 26, 135–142, 909
  sensitivity analysis and, 150, 259–260,
    259–260
  taxation and, 138, 142, 149
  timing decisions and, 152–153
  working capital and, 137–138, 138*n*
  for worldwide companies and
    currencies, 151
Net return on investment, 324
Netter, J. M., 852*n*, 878*n*
Net working capital. *See* Working capital
Net-working-capital-to-total-assets, 759
Neuberger, Anthony J., 292*n*, 309*n*
Neuer Markt, 914
New issues of stock. *See also* Initial public
    offerings (IPOs)
  auctions for, 407
  costs of, 402
  efficient-market hypothesis
    and, 340–348
  hot new-issue periods, 405–406
  primary issues, 378, 396
  secondary issues, 396, 408–413
Newmont Mining, *179*, 186, *186*, 202, *202*,
    206, *207*
New projects. *See also* Capital budgeting
  additional costs associated with, 156
  incidental effects of, 138
  operating cash flow from, 145
New York Mercantile Exchange (NYMEX),
    691–692, 691*n*, 692, 693
New York Stock Exchange (NYSE), 5, 7,
    78–79, 79*n*, 185, 316, 373
Ng, C. K., 807*n*
NGL Energy, 67
Nifty Fifty growth stocks, 81
Nikkei 225 Index, 349
NINJA loans, 385
Nippon Telegraph and Telephone (NTT), 877
Nissan, 894, 896
No-arbitrage condition, 13*n*
Nokia, 302
Nominal cash flow, 62–63, 538–541
Nominal exchange rates, 726–728, 726*n*, 727
Nominal rate of interest, 63–67, 65
Nominal returns, 723
Nomura, 382
Nondiversifiable risk. *See* Market risk
Non-negotiable time deposits, *820*
Nonrecourse debt, 676
NOPAT (net operating profit after tax), 751*n*
Norfolk Southern, *81, 234*
Northern Rock, 878*n*
Notes
  defined, 634
  floating rate, 633
  medium-term, 631, 652, *820, 821*

Treasury, 48, 49
  yield-curve, *645*
Notional principal, 699, 700
Notional value, 699
Novartis, *81, 428, 730*
NPV. *See* Net present value
NRSOs (nationally recognized statistical
    rating organizations), 622*n*
NTT (Nippon Telegraph and Telephone), 877
NXP Semiconductors, *830*
NYMEX (New York Mercantile Exchange),
    691–692, 691*n*, 692, 693
NYSE. *See* New York Stock Exchange
NYSE Euronext, 691*n*

O

OATs (Obligations Assimilables du Trésor),
    47–48, 47*n*
Obama, Barack, 69, 357, 396
O'Brien, T. J., 734*n*
Ofek, E., 349*n*, 872*n*
Off-balance-sheet liabilities, 607, 666–667,
    914–915
Offering price, 402
O'Hara, M., 399*n*
Omidyar, Pierre, 405
Onji, K., 439*n*
Open accounts, 807
Open-end mutual funds, 80*n*, 379, 914*n*
Operating cash flow, 145–146, 147*n*
Operating cycle, 776–778
Operating expenses, 111
Operating leases, 664, *667*, 667–669
Operating leverage, 237–239, 263, *263*, 263*n*
Operating profit margin, 754
Opler, Tim, 772, 772*n*
Opportunity cost of capital. *See also* Discount
    rate
  arithmetic average as measure of, 170, 170*n*
  calculation of, 23
  company (*See* Company cost of capital)
  defined, 10, 83
  discounted cash flow and, 95
  financing decisions and, 339
  forecast bias and, 286
  historical evidence for evaluation of,
    170–174
  internal rate of return and, 120–121
  for international investments, 733–734
  net present value and, 110–113, 139–140
  present value and, 27
  project, 229–232
  as standard of profitability, 116
  use of capital and, 229
Optimal capital structure theory, 500–501
Optimistic forecasts, *241*, 241–242
Optimization models, 784
Option ARM loans, 384*n*
Option delta, 565, 567, 567*n*, 570
Option equivalents, 564–567
Option pricing models, 563–580
  binomial method, 568–573, 595–596, 606
  Black–Scholes, 573–580, 591–593,
    604–606, 911

for call options, 564–567, 574–576
  dividends in, 581–582
  government financial guarantees, 621–622
  overview, 563
  risk and, 556, 565–567, 576
  simple option-valuation model, 564–568,
    607–608
  stock value and, *552, 552–557, 555*
Options, 542–552. *See also* Option pricing
    models
  abandonment (*See* Abandonment option)
  call (*See* Call options)
  in disguise, 542
  embedded, 542
  expansion (*See* Expansion option)
  investment (*See* Investment option)
  production, 269
  put (*See* Put options)
  real (*See* Real options)
  reducing risk with, 689
  spotting, 550–552, *551*
  stock (*See* Stock options)
  strategies for use, 547–552, *548–549*
  timing, 269–270
  types of, 580–582
Option theory, 911
Option valuation. *See* Option pricing models
Oracle Corporation, 320, 577, 577*n*
Original issue discount bonds, 633*n*
Orihara, M., 439*n*
Osobov, I., 426*n*
OTC (over-the-counter) markets, 378
Outland Steel, 728–730
Out-of-the-money options, 593
Outsourcing, 834
Overconfidence bias, 285–286, 286*n*, 350
Overhead costs, 140
Overinvestment, 312
Over-the-counter (OTC) markets, 378
Owens Corning, 577–578, 578*n*
Ownership and control. *See also* Board of
    directors; Corporate governance
  of common stock, *369*, 369–370
  of conglomerates, 901
  dual-class equity in, 900
  dual-class shares in, 371–372
  family in, 898–899, *898–899*
  in France, 896
  in Germany, 894–896, *895*
  in Japan, 893–894
  of leased assets, 671
  pyramids in, 899–900
  risk and short-termism and, 902–903
  separation of, 5–6, 12, 848, 892–901
  transparency and, 904–905

P

Pacific Gas and Electric, 651, *878*
Palepu, Krishna G., 429, 429*n*, 854, 854*n*,
    904*n*
Palm, 875, 876
Panchapegesan, V., 881*n*
P&O, 845
Panunzi, F., 905*n*

Papaioannou, E., 899*n*
Paramount, 851
Parmalat, 904
Partch, M. M., 430*n*
Participation loans sales, 649*n*
Partnerships, 6, 373, 394
Partnoy, F., 316*n*
Passive investing, 185
Pastor, L., 406*n*
Patel, J., 322, 322*n*
Patrick, H., 894*n*
Pattenden, K., 438*n*
Paulson, John, 11, 11*n*, 353*n*
Payback period, 112–114, 121
Payback rule, 112–113
Pay-for-performance standards, 317, 320
Pay-in-kind bonds (PIKs), *645*
Payment mechanisms, 14, 382–383
Payout fixed by contract, 539
Payout policy, 425–443
    in capital structure and tax-free economy,
        452–457
    controversy concerning, 431–436, 915–916
    corporate governance and, 443
    decisions regarding, 4
    facts regarding, 426–428
    information effect and, 428–430, *429*
    leftist position on, 437–440
    life cycle of the firm and, 441–443
    methods of paying dividends, 427–428
    Modigliani–Miller approach to, 431–432,
        441, 451
    overview, 425
    rightist position on, 436–437
    stock repurchases and, 433–434
Payout ratios, 88, 436
PayPal, *874*
PBGC (Pension Benefit Guarantee
    Corporation), 621–622, 879
P/B (price-to-book) ratio, 82
PCs (professional corporations), 6
Pecking order of financing choices, 495–501
    asymmetric information and, 495–497
    financial slack and, 499–501
    implications of, 497–498
    trade-off theory vs., 498–499
Peer-to-peer (P2P) lending, 14, 383*n*
PEFCO (Private Export Funding Corporation),
    819*n*
Peltz, Nelson, 315, 848
Pemex, 689
Pension Benefit Guarantee Corporation
    (PBGC), 621–622, 879
Pension funds, 369, 376, 380, 394, 438,
    621–622, 715*n*
P/E (price-earnings) ratio, 79, 82, 82*n*, 97
PepsiCo, 348, 845
Percentage of sales model, 788
Performance measurement, 323–331, 748–752
Performance shares, 321
Periodic review system, 806*n*
Perks, 312, 312*n*, 314
Permira, *864*
Perpetuities
    growing, 34, *35*, 35*n*, 87
    present value of, 28–29, *29*

Pershin, V., 171*n*
Pershing Square, 849–850
Peso loans, 720
Peters, F., 854*n*
Peterson, M. A., 812*n*
PetSmart, *864*
Pettway, R., 407*n*
Pfizer, *81*, 144, 300, 319, 427, *427*, 817
Pfleiderer, P., 465*n*
Phaup, Marvin, 622
Philip Morris International, *874*
Philips Electronics, 341, *342*, 834*n*
Phillips, G., 876, 876*n*
Phillips 66, *874*
Phoenix Corp., *91*, 91–92
PIKs (pay-in-kind bonds), *645*
Pindyck, R. S., 599*n*
Pinkowitz, L., 772–773*n*, 773
Piraeus, 877
Plains All American Pipeline LP, 373
Playing for time game, 490
PLCCs (professional limited liability
    companies), 6
PLN, 661
Poison pill defense, 849–851, *851*
Poison put defense, *851*
Political risk, 734–736, *735*
Pomorski, L., 347*n*
Ponzi, Charles, 12*n*
Ponzi schemes, 12, 12*n*
Pooling risk, 383, 687–688
Porsche, 352
Porter, Michael E., 292–293, 903*n*
Portfolio beta, 234, *234*, 236
Portfolio insurance, 578
Portfolio risk, 174–189
    beta and, 186–188, *188–189,* 205–206, *206*
    calculation of, 181–185, *182, 184*
    covariance and, 182–183, 182*n*
    diversification and, 174–181, *179*
    individual securities and, 185–188
    relationship between return and, 205–207
    standard deviation in, 174–176, 187
    variability of, 176–178
    variance in, 174–176
Portfolio theory, 198–205
    birth of, 198–205
    combining stocks into portfolios, 200,
        202–203
    efficient portfolios in, *202–203,* 203–208,
        213
    lending and borrowing in, *204,* 204–205
    standard deviation in, 198, 200, *201–203,*
        203–205, 204*n*
Portfolio values, 168*n*
Portugal
    bailout for, 918
    market risk premium in, 172, *172*
    standard deviation of stock market returns
        in, 177
Position diagrams, 543–545, *544*
Postaudits, 287
Postbank, 877
Poterba, J. M., 349*n*
Powell, Jerome, 319
Powers, E., 875*n*

Prediction markets, 357
Preferred stock, 373, 392, 821–822
Prejudgment interest awards, 539–540
Premium (bonds), 48
Present value of growth opportunities (PVGO),
    93–94, 98–99, 268, 321, 322*n*
Present value (PV), 21–30
    adjusted (*See* Adjusted present value
        (APV))
    of annuities, *29,* 29–30
    of bonds, 47–50
    calculation of, 21–22, *23,* 28*n*
    defined, 24*n,* 108
    of investment opportunities, 22–24, *23*
    in Monte Carlo simulation, 266
    of multiple cash flow, 26–27
    net (*See* Net present value (NPV))
    opportunity cost of capital and, 27
    of perpetuities, 28–29, *29*
    rate of return and, 25–26
    risk and, 24–25
    of stock, 83–84, *85–86*
President's Council on Jobs and
    Competitiveness, 398
Price bubbles, 918
Price discovery, 696*n*
Price-earnings (P/E) ratio, 79, 82, 82*n,* 97
Price-to-book (P/B) ratio, 82
Primary issues of stock, 378, 396. *See also*
    Initial public offerings (IPOs)
Primary markets, 78
Prince, Charles, 313
Principal (bonds), 47
Principals vs. agents, 12, 911–912
Private benefits, 312, 312*n,* 371–372
Private companies, 398, 398*n*
Private equity investing, 394, 863,
    868–873, *872*
Private Export Funding Corporation
    (PEFCO), 819*n*
Private placements, 413, 639–640
Privatization, 877–878
Privileged subscription issues, 412–413
Probabilities, beliefs about, 350
Procter & Gamble, 2, *3,* 4, 7, 315, 355, 848
Procurement, 601
Production option, 269, 600–604, *601–603*
Product sales forecasts, 139
Professional corporations (PCs), 6
Professional limited liability companies
    (PLCCs), 6
Profitability index, 110, 123–124, 123*n*
Profitability measures
    biases in, 326–331
    economic value added, 324–331
    internal rate of return, 115–116
    net return on investment, 324
Profit diagrams, *546,* 546–547, 547*n*
Profit margin, 754
Profit maximization, 810
Progress payments, 807
Project analysis, 257–274
    break-even analysis in, 262–263, *262–263*
    decision trees in, 267–274
    Monte Carlo simulation in, 264–266
    net present value in, 150

Project analysis—*Cont.*
  overview, 257
  postaudits in, 287
  real options in, 266–274
  scenario analysis in, *261,* 261–262
  sensitivity analysis in, 258–261
  WACC in, 510
Project authorizations, 285–286
Project beta, *230,* 238
Project cost of capital, 229–232
Project finance
  adjusted present value for international investments, 528–529
  appropriation requests, 285, 286
  common features of, 660
  defined, 660
  discount rates for international projects, 242
  example of, 661
  role of, 660–661
Project life, abandonment value and, 598
Project risk, 230, 236–242, 912
Proposition 1 (Modigliani–Miller), 454–459, *455–457,* 462, 466–468, 477–479, 521
Proposition 2 (Modigliani–Miller), 458–462, *460–461,* 464, 467, 521
Prospect theory, 349, 349*n*
Prospectus, 399, 400, 409, 421–424
Prosper, 383*n*
Protective put, 547*n*
Prowse, S., 896*n*
Proxy contests, 371, 848
PRS Group, Inc., 734, 735*n*
Prudhoe Bay Royalty Trust, 373
PSEG, *67*
Public companies
  defined, 5
  dispersal of ownership in, 370
  ownership and control in, 5–6
  security sales by, 408–413
Purchase method of merger accounting, 845, *846*
Purchase option, *602–603,* 602–604
Purchasing power parity, 722, 722*n,* 724–726, *726,* 730*n*
Pure discount bonds, 633*n*
Pure plays, 237
Puri, M., 394*n*
Put–call parity, 549–550, 549*n*
Put options
  relationship between call prices and, 568, 621
  in risk reduction, 689
  selling, 545, *546*
  valuation of, 567–568
Puttable bonds, 637
PV. *See* Present value
PVGO. *See* Present value of growth opportunities
Pyramids, 899–900

Q

QQQs, 380
Quadratic programming, 203
Qualcomm, *830*

Qualified institutional buyers, 413
Qualified opinions, 315
Quatar Petroleum, 871*n*
QUBES, 380
Quick ratio, 759
Quiet period, 399*n*
Quinenco, 901
Quorum Health, 67, *67*
Quoted annual interest rate, 36
QVC, 851

R

Raiders, corporate, 11
Raiffa, H., 286*n*
Rainbow options, 582
Rajan, Raghu G., 312*n,* 498, 498*n,* 812*n,* 892, 892*n,* 902, 902–903*n*
Rajgopal, S., 322, 322*n*
Ramaswamy, K., 439*n*
R&D. *See* Research and development
Random walk hypothesis, 340–343, *342–343,* 555*n,* 910
Rate of return. *See also specific types of return*
  accounting, 751–752
  arithmetic average of, 169–170, 170*n*
  on bonds, 51–52
  book, 111–112, 121, 751
  compound annual, 169–170
  historical data on, 169, *169,* 174, *175*
  internal (*See* Internal rate of return (IRR))
  on levered equity, 459
  present value and, 25–26
Rate of return rule, 26
Rau, P. R., 349*n*
Rauh, J. D., 319*n*
Ravenscroft, D. J., 854, 854*n*
Ravid, S. A., 882*n*
RCA, 302
Read, J. A., Jr., 607*n,* 694*n*
Real assets, 2, 19
Real cash flow, 62–63
Real estate
  investment decisions for, 288–290, *289*
  optimal timing for development of, 596–597, *597*
Real estate investment trusts (REITs), 236, 236*n,* 373, 492*n*
Real exchange rates, 726–728, 726*n, 727*
Real options, 590–608
  abandonment option, 268–269, *270,* 597–599, *599*
  conceptual problems regarding, 606
  decision trees and, 267–274
  default option, 618–622, 637
  default risk, 615, 619, 620
  defined, 267
  expansion (*See* Expansion option)
  investment (*See* Investment option)
  practical challenges in application of, 607–608
  production option, 269, 600–604, *601–603*
  in project analysis, 266–274
  purchase option, *602–603,* 602–604

  taxation and, 606–607
  timing options, 269–270, 594–597
  valuation of, 606–608
Real rate of interest, 63–65, 64*n, 65*
Real-time, gross settlement systems, 814*n*
Rebalancing debt, 522–523
Receivables turnover, 753–754
Red herring, 400*n*
Registered bonds, 47*n,* 634
Registration statements, 399
Regular cash dividends, 427
Reinhart, Carmen M., 918, 918*n*
REITs (real estate investment trusts), 236, 236*n,* 373, 492*n*
Relational Investors, 11
Relative risk, 230
Relative tax advantage of debt, 480–481
Relevering beta, 522, 523*n*
Renault, 896
Rental leases, 664
Reorder point (two-bin) system, 806*n*
Replacement decisions, 155
Replicating portfolio, 565
Repurchase agreements (repos), *820,* 821
Repurchase programs. *See* Stock repurchases
Research and development (R&D), 2, 135, 143, 150, 271–273, *272,* 604–605
Reserve Primary Fund, 467*n,* 817
Residual claims, 369
Residual income measures, 324–325, 324*n*
Residual risk. *See* Specific risk
Restricted shares, 320–321
Restricted voting rights defense, *851*
Restructuring, 863–883
  asset/liability, *851*
  asset sales and, 876–877
  of AT&T, 873–874
  bankruptcy, 878–883
  carve-outs, 875–876
  leveraged buyouts and, 863–868
  leveraged restructurings, 867–868
  private equity, 868–873
  privatization and nationalization, 877–878
  spin-offs, *874,* 874–875
  as takeover defense, *851*
Return on assets (ROA), 98, 323*n,* 751–752, 754–756
Return on capital (ROC), 323*n,* 750, 751, 751*n*
Return on equity (ROE), 88, 90–91, 751, 758
Return on investment (ROI), 323–324, 326–331, *327, 330,* 751*n*
Revenue adequacy, 89–90
Reverse floaters (yield-curve notes), 645
Reverse repos, 821
Reverse stock splits, 372, 372*n*
Revlon, 849*n*
Revolving line of credit, 631, 647
Reynolds American, *830*
Rhee, S. G., 238*n*
Rhie, Jung-Wu, 625*n*
Rice, E. M., 913*n*
Richardson, M. W., 349*n,* 636*n*
Richemont, *730,* 730–731
Riddiough, T. J., 596–597*n*
Rieker, M., 430*n*
Rights issues, 401*n,* 412–413

Right to default, 483
Rio Tinto, 341, *342*
Risk. *See also* Risk management
    absolute, 230
    agency problems and, 313–314
    attitudes toward, 349–350
    of bonds, 177*n*
    in capital asset pricing model, 206–207
    in common stock, 168, 205
    counterparty, 690
    default (*See* Default risk)
    expected returns and, 457–464
    of foreign investment, 242
    identification by financial managers, 5
    international (*See* International risk)
    market (*See* Market risk)
    option pricing and, 556, 565–567, 576
    political, 734–736, *735*
    pooling, 383, 687–688
    portfolio (*See* Portfolio risk)
    present value and, 24–25
    project, 230, 236–242, 912
    relative, 230
    return and, 205–207, *206–207,* 912–913
    short-termism and, 902–903
    specific, 181, 181*n*, 187, 239–241
    stock, 247–248
    in term structure of interest rates, 61
    in Treasury bills, 167–168, 205
    in Treasury bonds, 168
Risk-adjusted discount rate, 243–246
Risk arbitrage, 852*n*
Risk-averse shareholders, 8
Risk class, 83
Risk-free rate of interest, 548*n*
Risk management, 683–707
    agency costs, 686
    derivatives in, 687, 690–702
    evidence on, 687
    financial distress and, 685–686
    forward contracts and, 690
    futures contracts and, 691–696
    hedging and, 702–705
    insurance and, 687–688
    international risk in
        (*See* International risk)
    options in, 689
    overview, 683
    reasons for, 684–687
    speculation and, 705–707
    strategies for, 916
    swaps and, 697–702
Risk-neutral option valuation, 565–567,
    595–596, 606
Risk premium
    defined, 171*n*, 205*n*
    dividend yields and, 173
    expected, 172
    forecasting, 171*n*
    historical data on, 171
    market (*See* Market risk premium)
    rate of return and, 169, *169*
    in Sharpe ratio, 205
    standard deviation of, 169*n*
Risk shifting game, 488–489
Risk-tolerant shareholders, 8

Ritter, J. R., 398, 398*n,* 402, 402*n,* 404–405*n,*
    405, *405*
Ritz Carlton, 831
RJR Nabisco, 490, 490*n,* 863–866
Road shows, 400
ROA (return on assets), 98, 323*n,* 751–752,
    754–756
Robert Bosch, 896
Roberts, M. R., 495, 495*n,* 647*n,* 650*n*
Robo advisors, 14
Roche, 731–733
Rockefeller Center Properties, 492*n*
Rockwell Collins, *830*
ROC (return on capital), 323*n,* 750, 751, 751*n*
Roe, M., 883*n*
ROE (return on equity), 88, 90–91, 751, 758
Rogalski, R. J., 643*n*
Rogoff, Kenneth, 918, 918*n*
ROI. *See* Return on investment
Rolfe, David A., 442
Roll, Richard, 495, 495*n,* 913*n*
Rolling options, 604
Romaine, C., 539*n*
Romney, Mitt, 357
Rose-Ackerman, S., 854*n*
Rosenthal, L., 345*n*
Ross, Stephen, 213
Rossi, S., 429*n*
Royal Bank of Canada, *401*
Royal Bank of Scotland, 385
Royal Dutch Shell, 78, 345, *346,* 352, 425, 871*n*
Royal Mail, 877
Royal Statistical Society, 340
Ruback, Richard S., 527–528, 528*n,* 852*n,* 854,
    854*n,* 866, 866*n*
Rule 144A (SEC), 413, 640
Rule 10b-18 (SEC), 428*n*
Rule of signs (Descartes), 117*n*
Russian debt default (1998), 69–70, 352, 352*n,*
    618*n*
RWE, 876
Rydqvist, K., 404*n*
Ryngaert, M. D., 836*n*

S

Sacconaghi, A. M., 442
Saks, R., 317*n*
Sale and lease-back arrangements, 664
Salix Pharmaceuticals, 850
Salvage value
    cash flow and, 144
    depreciation and, 668
    leases and, 668
    in net present value analysis, 140
    in replacement decisions, 155
Samsung, *179, 187,* 901
Samurai bonds, 640
S&P. *See* Standard & Poor's
Santos, T., 311*n,* 350*n*
Sapienza, P., 10*n*
Sarbanes–Oxley (SOX) Act of 2002, 314, 397,
    398, 443, 869
Savings banks, 381*n*
Savor, Pavel, 358*n*

SBA (Small Business Administration),
    622, 819*n*
SBC Communications, Inc., 873–874
Scenario analysis, 150, *261,* 261–262, 593*n*
Schaefer, S. M., 620*n*
Schall, L. D., 839*n*
Schallheim, J. S., 669*n*
Scharfstein, D., *874,* 893, 893*n*
Scherer, F. M., 854, 854*n*
Schlingemann, F. P., 854*n*
Schmalz, M., 439*n*
Schneider, C., 896, 896*n*
Schoar, A., 499, 499*n*
Scholes, Myron S., 427*n,* 439*n,* 564, 564*n,*
    574–580, 574*n*
Schreffler, R., 806*n*
Schultze, George J., 883*n*
Schwartz, E. S., 292*n,* 599*n*
Schwartz, S. L., 349, 349*n,* 914*n*
Schwarz Gruppe, 398*n*
SCOR, 646
Sealed Air Corporation, 867
Seasoned equity offerings (SEOs),
    410, 412
SEC. *See* U.S. Securities and Exchange
    Commission
Secondary issues of stock, 396, 408–413
Secondary markets, 78
Secondary transactions, 378
Second-stage financing, 393
Secured debt, 375, 634–635, *635*
Securities. *See also specific types*
    of securities
    asset-backed, 631, 635–636, *645*
    defined, 2
    exotic, 466
    marketable, 138*n,* 816, 816–822, *820*
    mortgage-backed, 11, 314, 353, 385, 617,
        636, 915
    portfolio risk and, 185–188
    success of new markets, 915
Securities Act of 1933, 399*n*
Securitization, defined, 636
Security market line, 206, *208,*
    208–209, *210*
Security sales, 408–413
    costs, *409,* 409–410
    general cash offers in, 408–410
    international issues in, 408–409
    market reaction to stock issues, 410–411
    rights issues in, 412–413
    underwriters of, 408–409, *409*
Self-liquidating loans, 647
Semiannual coupons, 48–50, 632
Semistrong market efficiency, 340, 343–345,
    345, 910
Semyrhamis, 900
Senior debt, 375, 634–635, *635,* 638
Sensitivity analysis
    in arbitrage pricing theory, 214
    defined, 258
    limits to, 260–261
    net present value and, 150, 259–260,
        259–260
    in three-factor model, 216–217
    value of information in, 259–260

Sentiment, in behavioral finance, 350–351, *351*
SEOs (seasoned equity offerings), *410*, 412
Separation of ownership and control, 5–6, 12, 848, 892–901
Seward, J. K., 643*n*
SGX (Singapore Exchange), *692*
Shanghai Futures Exchange, *691*
Shapiro, E., 87*n*
Shareholders
    agency problems and, 12–13, 911–912
    as equity investors, 4
    interest tax shields and value of equity, 477
    limited liability of, 5
    minority, 372
    monitoring function of, 315–316
    percentage of equity owned by, 370, *371*
    risk-averse vs. risk-tolerant, 8
    separation of ownership and control and, 5–6, 12, 848, 892–901
    stakeholders vs., *897*, 897–898
    terminology considerations, 2*n*
    value maximization for, 7–10, 18–19
Share repurchases. *See* Stock repurchases
Shark-repellent charter amendments, 850, *851*
Sharpe, William F., 206, 206*n*
Sharpe ratio, 205
Shaw, W. H., 399*n*
Shefrin, H., 437*n*
Sheifer, A., 898, 898*n*
Shelf registration, 408
Shell Transport & Trading, 78, *346*, 352
Shenzhen Stock Exchange, 580
Shiller, Robert J., 351*n*, 914*n*
Ship Finance International, *409*
Shivdasani, A., 875*n*
Shleifer, A., 312*n*, 370*n*, 443*n*, 874, 876–877*n*, 892, 892*n*
Short-lived assets, 153–155
Short selling, 11, 11*n*, 352, 352*n*
Short squeeze, 352
Short-term assets, 138*n*
Short-term debt financing
    bank loans, 783
    commercial paper, 631, 650–652, *820*, 821
    long-term debt financing vs., 374–375
    stretching payables, 783
    WACC and, 518
Short-term financial planning
    cash budgeting, 778–780, *779–780*
    leases in, 664
    long-term financial planning vs., 770–773, *771–772*
    models of, 784
    plan development and evaluation, 780–784
Short-termism, 321–323, 869, 902–903
Short-term liabilities, 138*n*
Short-term tax-exempts, 819–820
Shoven, J. B., 577*n*
Shue, Kelly, 313*n*
Shumway, T., 624*n*
Shyam-Sunder, L., 411*n*, 499*n*
"Siamese twins," 345, 345*n*
Sidel, R., 430*n*
Siegel, D. R., 430*n*, 854*n*

Siemens, *179, 187,* 428, *830*
Sight drafts, 807
Signaling, 392, 428, 430. *See also* Information effect
Simons, James, 380*n*
Singapore Exchange (SGX), *692*
Singer, Paul, 315
Singh, R., 406*n*
Sinking funds, 637
Sivakumar, R., 875*n*
SIVs (structured investment vehicles), 651, 758–759
Size factor, in three-factor model, 216–217
SJW Corp., *89*
Skeel, D., 883*n*
Skinner, Douglas J., 426*n*, 441*n*, 442
Sky, *830*
Slovic, P., 286*n*
Small Business Administration (SBA), 622, 819*n*
Small businesses, 6
Small-firm effect, 215, 216
Smit, H., 607*n*
Smith, Clifford W., Jr., 685*n*
Smith, J. K., 807*n*
Smith, R. L., 807*n*
Société Générale, 706
Softbank, 5
Soft rationing, 125
Sogo, 903
Sole proprietorships, 6
Solera, *864*
Sony, 78, 138, *179, 187*
Southern California Edison, 651
Southwest Airlines
    betas for stock, *186, 207*
    portfolio risk and, 181–183
    profitability of, 302
    rate of return on stock, *180,* 181, 200, *202*
    standard deviation of stock returns, *179*
Southwestern Bell, 874
Sovereign bonds, 68–70
SOX Act. *See* Sarbanes–Oxley Act of 2002
Spark spread, 600
SPDRs (Standard & Poor's Depository Receipts), 380
Special dividends, 427
Special-purpose entities (SPEs), 376, 493, 632, 676–677, 904
Specific risk, 181, 181*n*, 187, 239–241
Speculation, 705–707
Spindt, P. A., 406*n*
Spinning, 401, 403
Spin-offs, *874,* 874–875
Spitzer, Eliot, 403
Split-ups, 874
Spot prices, 690, 695–696
Spot rate
    defined, 56
    of exchange, *718,* 719
    forward premium and, 721–722
    law of one price and, 57–58, 722*n*
Spread
    IPOs, 402
    spark, 600

statistical measure os, 174
    underwriting, 402, 402*n*, 409, *409*
    yield, 67–68, *68,* 616, 616–618
Spreadsheet functions
    bond valuation, 55
    discounted cash flow, 38–39
    internal rate of return, 122
    market risk estimation, 247–248
    stock risk estimation, 247–248
Stafford, E., 636*n*, 844, 844*n*, 852, 852–854*n*, 854
Staggered board defense, *851*
Staggered (classified) boards, 370–371
Stakeholders vs. shareholders, *897*, 897–898
Standard deviation
    calculation of, 174–176, *176*
    defined, 174
    in portfolio risk, 174–176, 187
    in portfolio theory, 198, 200, *201–203*, 203–205, 204*n*
    of risk premium, 169*n*
    in Sharpe ratio, 205
    of stock market returns, 177–178, *177–179*
Standard error, 169*n*, 234
Standard of profitability, 116
Standard & Poor's (S&P)
    bond ratings, 67–69, *68,* 622
    commercial paper ratings, 651*n*
    Composite Index, 170, 185, 348, 379, 579–580
    credit ratings, 808
    Depository Receipts, 380
    500 Index, 80, 317, *318,* 347, 581
Standards, accounting, 666–667, 744–745, 845–846
Starbucks, 11–12
Statement of cash flows, 773–775, *774*
Statistical models of default risk, 624–626, *625*
Statman, M., 437*n*
Staunton, M., 62–63*n*, 66*n*, 167, 167–169*n*, 171–172, 172*n*, 175*n*, 177*n*, 727*n*
STB (U.S. Surface Transportation Board), 89–90, 90*n*
Stein, Jeremy C., 358*n*, 643*n*
Step-up bonds, *645*
Stern Stewart, 324*n*
Stertz, Bradley A., 832*n*
Stigler, George, 495
Stiglin, L., 866*n*
Stiglitz, J. E., 347*n*
Stillwell Financial, 519
Stock, common. *See* Common stock
Stock, preferred. *See* Preferred stock
Stock dividends, 428, 428*n*
Stockholders. *See* Shareholders
Stock options. *See also* Option pricing models
    Black–Scholes model for valuing, 573–580, 911
    call (*See* Call options)
    executive, 577, *578*
    incentives created by, 313, 320
    payout policy and, 437
    profit diagrams and, *546,* 546–547, 547*n*
    put (*See* Put options)

strategies for use, 547–552, *548–549*
taxation on, 320
types of, 580–582
valuation of, *552,* 552–557, *555*
Stock price
    anticipation of merger and, 841–842, 853–854
    dividends and, 83–87
    earnings per share and, 79, 82, 82*n,* 92–95
    future, 84–87, *85–86*
    lognormal distribution of, *573,* 573–574
    market reaction to stock issues and, 410–411
    momentum and, 343
    option values and, *552,* 552–557, *555*
    present, 83–84, *85–86*
Stock repurchases
    discounted cash flow and, 433–434
    free cash flow as, 99–100
    growth in, 366
    information content of, 430
    irrelevance of, 431, 434, 436
    methods for, 428
Stock risk, 247–248
Stock splits, 372, 372*n,* 428*n*
Stohs, M. H., 771*n*
Stonier, J. E., 602*n*
Stored-value cards, 813
Straight-line depreciation, 142, 143, 150
Strategic assets, 292
Strebulaev, I. A., 392*n,* 395, 395*n*
Stretching payables, 781
Strike price, 543
Stripped bonds, 58, *59,* 62
Stromberg, P., 394*n,* 882*n*
Strong market efficiency, 340, 345–348, *346,* 910
Structural models of default risk, 626–627, *627*
Structured investment vehicles (SIVs), 651, 758–759
Stulz, R. M., 410*n,* 734*n,* 772*n,* 854*n*
Subordinated debt, 375
Subprime mortgages, 314, 353, 384–385, 617, 636, 915
Sufi, A., 647*n,* 649*n*
Sumitomo Bank, 903
Sundgren, S., 882*n*
Sunk-cost fallacy, 140
Supermajorities, 371, 850, *851*
Surplus funds, 834–835
Sussman, O., 486, 486*n*
Sustainable growth rate, 790
Swaminathan, B., 429*n*
Swaps, 697–702
    credit default, 617–618, 701
    currency, *700,* 701, 701*n*
    inflation, 701
    interest rate, 698–700
    overview, 697–698
    total return, 702
Swatch Group, 5, *730,* 730–731
Sweeps, 650
Swiss Bank Corp., 836
Swiss Re, 730, *730*
Switzerland

economic and transaction exposure in, 730–731, *731*
    foreign bonds in, 640
    market risk premium in, 172, *172*
Syndicated loans, 648–649, 649*n*
Syndicate of underwriters, 408
Synergies, 832–833
Syngenta, *830*
Systematic risk. *See* Market risk
Szilagyi, J., 624*n*

T

Takeover premium, 344–345
Takeovers, 313*n,* 316, 345, 847–853. *See also* Mergers and acquisitions
Tangible assets, 20, 498, 845
Target, 722
TARP (Troubled Asset Relief Program), 430
Tata Group, 831, 852, 901
Tata Motors, 78, *179, 187*
Tauron Polska Energia, 877
Taweel, Kevin, 902
Taxation
    avoidance of, 11–12
    in bond market, 646
    of bond–warrant packages, 644
    of capital gains vs. cash dividends, 437–440
    corporate (*See* Corporate taxation)
    debt policy and, 476–482
    deferred, 517*n*
    equivalent annual cash flow and, 155
    financial leases and, 671–672
    imputation tax system, 439–440, *439–440,* 495*n*
    of individuals, *480,* 480–482, 481*n*
    leveraged buyouts and, 866
    marginal tax rate, 520
    marketable securities and, 816–817
    in mergers and acquisitions, 846–847
    in net present value analysis, 138, 142, 149
    of partnerships, 6, 373
    real options and, 606–607
    on REITs, 373
    on stock options, 320
    tax inversion, 847
Tax Cuts and Jobs Act of 2017, 143, 143*n,* 149, 150, 479, 494, 666
Tax-exempt municipal notes, 819–820
Tax shields
    depreciation, 148–149, 540, 668, 670–671
    interest, 143, 476–479, 477*n,* *478,* 479*n,* 493–495, 498
    leases and, 665, 668, 668*n,* 670–673
Team Health Holdings, *864*
Technological change
    equivalent annual cash flow and, 154–155
    exploitation for competitive advantage, 295–302
    fintech and, 14
TED spread, 648, *648*
Tehranian, H., 411, 411*n*

Telefonica Brasil, 78
Temporary abandonment, 598–599
Tender offer, 428
Tender offers, 848–849
10-K filings, 316, 744
Tenneco, *870*
10-Q filings, 744
Tepco, 878
Tepper, A., 723–724, 724*n*
Term loans, 647
Terms of sale, 807
Term structure of interest rates, 56–61
    defined, 56
    discount factor and, 58–59
    expectations theory of, 60–61
    inflation in, 61
    law of one price and, *57,* 57–58
    measurement of, 58
    patterns of, 56, *56*
    risk in, 61
Territorial corporate taxation, 144
Tesco, 315
Tesla Motors
    betas for stock, *186, 207*
    convertible bonds, *641,* 641–642
    investment decisions by, *3,* 9–10
    rate of return on stock, *202, 203*
    standard deviation of stock returns, *179*
Tetley Tea, 852
Tetlow, R. S., 870*n*
Texaco, *878*
TFX (Tokyo Financial Futures Exchange), *692*
Thaler, R. H., 213*n,* 350*n,* 724*n,* 875*n*
Thermo Electron, 876
Thomas, R., 316*n*
Thorburn, Karin, 486*n*
3Com, 875
3Doodler, 396
Three-factor model, 215–217, 215*n,* *216,* 291, 344*n*
3Par, 853
Time deposits, *820,* 821
Time drafts, 807
Times-interest-earned ratio, 757, 757*n*
Time to maturity, option value and, 553–556, *556*
Time value of money, 20, 110
Time Warner, 358, *830,* 831, 832, 874
Timing decisions, 152–153
Timing options, 269–270, 594–597
Timken Co., 11
Timmerman, A., 347*n,* 910*n*
TIPS (Treasury Inflation-Protected Securities), 64, 64*n,* *65*
Titman, S., 343*n,* 844*n*
Tokyo Commodity Exchange, *691*
Tokyo Financial Futures Exchange (TFX), *692*
Tokyo Gas, 833
Tokyo Grain Exchange, *691*
Tokyo Stock Exchange (TSE), 79, 894
"Too big to fail" mentality, 353
Toronto Dominion Bank, *179, 187*

Torous, W. N., 881*n*
Toshiba, 315
Total capitalization, 518, 749
Total expected profit, 809
Total return payer, 702
Total return receiver, 702
Total return swaps, 702
Townsend, Richard, 313*n*
Toyota, 229, 319, 428, 806
TPG Capital, 864
Trade acceptances, 808
Trade credit, 806, 891, *891*
Trade-off theory of capital structure, 483, *483*, 493–495, 498–499
Trade sales, 869
Tranches, 636
Transaction costs in leases, 665
Transaction exposure, 730–731
Transfer of value, 434–436, *435–436*
Transparency, 904–905
TransUnion, 624*n*, 808*n*
Trans World Airlines (TWA), 302*n*, 666
The Travelers Companies, *179, 186, 202, 207*
Travlos, N., 827*n*
Treasury bills
    defined, 48
    features of, 819, *820*
    historical performance of, 168, *168*
    interest rate on, 171
    rate of return on, 169, *169*
    risk in, 167–168, 205
    trading of, 49
    variability of, 177
Treasury bonds
    duration of, 54, *54*
    historical performance of, 168, *168*
    indexed, 64, 64*n*
    interest payments on, 48
    interest rates on, *50–51, 50–52*
    price quotes for, 49, *49*
    rate of return on, 169, *169*
    risk in, 168
    stripped, 58, *59*, 62
    variability of, 177
    yield spreads on, 67–68, *68*, 616, *616*
    yield to maturity for, 49, 50
Treasury Inflation-Protected Securities (TIPS), 64, 64*n*, 65
Treasury notes, 48, 49
Treynor, Jack, 206, 206*n*
Triantis, A. J., 596–597*n*, 899*n*
Trigeorgis, L., 607*n*
Troubled Asset Relief Program (TARP), 430
Trust deed, 634
Trusts, 373. *See also* Real estate investment trusts (REITs)
Truth-in-lending laws, 36*n*
TSE (Tokyo Stock Exchange), 79, 894
Tufano, Peter, 687, 687*n*
Tufts Center for the Study of Drug Development, 271*n*
Tunneling, 372, 901
Tversky, L. A., 286*n*, 349*n*
TWA (Trans World Airlines), 302*n*, 666

21st Century Fox, *830*
Twite, G., 438*n*
Twitter, 542
Two-bin (reorder point) system, 806*n*
Two-step binomial method, 570–571
TXU, 4–5, 864, 867
Tyco, 12

U

UAL, *878*
UAW (United Auto Workers), 879
Uber, 398
UBS, 385, 706, 836
Unbiased forecasts, 240
Underwriters, 381, 399–401, *401*, 408–409
Undiversifiable risk. *See* Market risk
Unicredit, 836
Uniform-price auctions, 407
Union Pacific, *81*, 81–82, 82*n*, 234
Uniper, *874*
Unique risk. *See* Specific risk
United Airlines, 302
United Auto Workers (UAW), 879
United Health Group Inc., 579
United Kingdom
    corporate tax rate in, 142, *142*
    electricity prices in, 600–601, *601*
    financial system in, 888–892, *889–891*
    forward currency market in, 724, *724*
    interest payments in, 48*n*
    interest rates in, 36, 66, *66*
    nominal vs. real exchange rates in, 726, *727*
United States
    bankruptcy regulation in, 878–883
    betas for selected stocks, *186*
    bond holdings issued in, 374, *374*
    CEO compensation in, *317–318*, 317–319
    corporate taxation in, *142*, 142–144
    deficit crisis of 2010, 69
    dividend yields in, 172–173, *173*
    financial system in, 888–892, *889–891*
    historical performance of capital markets in, 167–174, *168, 173, 175*
    inflation in, 62, *62–63*, 66, *66*
    interest rates in, 36
    IPOs in (*See* Initial public offerings)
    market risk premium in, 172, *172*
    merger waves in, *831*, 853
    payout policy in, *426*, 426–427
    ratio of cash to assets in, 772, *772*
    semiannual coupons and bond prices in, 48–50
    sources of funds for nonfinancial corporations, 365–366, *366*
    standard deviation of stocks in, 178, *178–179*
    stock market returns in, 168, *168*, 172, *173*, 174, *175*
    truth-in-lending laws in, 36*n*
    venture capital financing in, 393–395, *394*
    working capital composition for corporations, *801–803*, 801–804

United Technologies, *409, 830*
UNIVAC, 302
Unlevering beta, 522, 523*n*, 593*n*
Unsecured debt, 634
Unsystematic risk. *See* Specific risk
UPS, 267, *267*
Ursua, J. F., 683*n*
U.S. Bank National Association, 634
U.S. Department of Justice, 402*n*, 844–845, 874
U.S. Department of Veterans' Affairs, 819*n*
U.S. Environmental Protection Agency (EPA), 343
U.S. Federal Reserve, 384, 385, 636
U.S. Federal Trade Commission (FTC), 844
U.S. Food and Drug Administration (FDA), 271–273, 607
U.S. Nuclear Regulatory Commission, 3
U.S. Robotics, 875
U.S. Securities and Exchange Commission (SEC)
    accounting and reporting standards, 744–745
    approval of IPOs by, 399
    on compensation committee guidelines, 316
    on Mini IPOs, 396
    proposed Rule 14a-11, 371*n*
    role in reorganizations, 880
    Rule 144A, 413, 640
    Rule 10b-18, 428*n*
    on well-known seasoned issuers, 408*n*
U.S. Steel, *179, 186, 202*, 206, *207*, 232–234, *233*, 234*n*
U.S. Supreme Court, 87*n*
U.S. Surface Transportation Board (STB), 89–90, 90*n*

V

Vale, *3*
Valeant, 849–850
Va Linux, 401, 402*n*
Valuation. *See also* Option pricing models
    of abandonment option, 598
    of annuities, *29*, 29–31, 33–34
    of bonds, 47–50, 641–644
    of businesses (*See* Business valuation process)
    by certainty equivalents, 243, *244*, 567
    of common stock, 80–87
    by comparables, *81*, 81–82
    consistency in, 540–541
    of financial leases, 669–675
    future (*See* Future value)
    of liquidity, 916–917
    present (*See* Present value (PV))
    of real options, 606–608
    of stock options, 552, *552–557, 555*
    of warrants, 577–578
Valuation horizon, 96–99, 514–516
Value additivity
    assumptions regarding, 910–911
    defined, 189–190
    diversification and, 189–190

economic value added, 324–331
  law of conservation of value and, 454
  mergers and, 837, 861–862
Value Line, 88*n*
Value maximization, 7–10, 18–19, 312
Value stocks, 212, *212*
Van Binsbergen, J. H., 347*n*
Van Dijk, Mathijs, 345–346*n*
Vanguard 500 Index Fund, 347, 379
Vanguard Total Stock Market index, 380
VantageScore scoring system, 624*n*
Variability, 176–181
Variable-rate demand notes (VRDNs), 820–821
Variance
  calculation of, 174–176, *176*
  defined, 174
  in portfolio risk, 174–176
VEBA (Voluntary Employees' Beneficiary Association), 883
Venture capital, 391–395, *394–395*
Verdelhan, A., 723–724, 724*n*
Veritas, *864*
Verizon, 784, 785, 904
Vermaelen, T., 412*n*, 430*n*
Veronesi, P., 406*n*
Vertical mergers, 831, 833–834
Vestergaard, J., 465*n*
Viacom, 851
Viasys Health Care, 876
Villalonga, B., 872*n*
Violations of absolute priority, 883
Virgin Atlantic, 237
Virgin Rail Group, 237
Vishny, R. W., 312*n*, 443*n*, 876–877*n*, 892, 892*n*
Viskanta, T., 734*n*
Vista Equity Partners, *864*
Viswanathan, S., 855, 855*n*
VIX (Market Volatility Index), 578–581, *579*
Vlasic, Bill, 832*n*
Volatility. *See also* Beta
  of bonds, 54
  financial leverage and, 313*n*
  implied, 578–580, *579*
  option value and, 556–557, *556–557*
  of stock market, 178
Volcker, Paul, 50
Volkova, E., 406*n*
Volkswagen (VW), 5, 10, 343–344, 352, 785
Volpin, P., 896*n*
Voluntary Employees' Beneficiary Association (VEBA), 883
Volvo, 852
Voting rights, 370–371, 373, *851*
VRDNs (variable-rate demand notes), 820–821
Vulture funds, 380
VW. *See* Volkswagen

W

WACC. *See* Weighted-average cost of capital
Wait and decide option, 602, 603
Waiting period defense, *851*

Wald, J. K., 494*n*
"Wall Street Walk," 11, 316
Walmart
  corporate bonds for, *67*
  investment decisions by, 3
  performance measurement, 748, *748, 750*
  purchasing power parity and, 722
Warga, A., 638*n*
Warner, J. B., 344*n*, 486*n*
Warner-Chilcott, 847
Warrants
  bond–warrant packages, 644–645
  defined, 376
  valuation of, 577–578
Washington Mutual, 878
Washington Public Power Supply System (WPPSS), 819*n*
Weak market efficiency, 340, 342–343, *343,* 354, 910
Weber, M., 429*n*
Weighted-average cost of capital (WACC).
  See also Company cost of capital
  accounting rates of return and, 751
  adjusting when debt ratio and business risk differs, 520–521, *521*
  after-tax, 232, 235–236, 467–468, *468,* 508–512, 529–530
  application of, 517–524, 529–531
  assumptions regarding, 511
  calculation of, 508–509
  defined, 231
  expected returns and, 458
  flow-to-equity valuation method vs., 516–517
  mistakes in use of, 511–512
  in project valuation, 510
  rebalancing debt and, 522–523
  in unlevering and relevering betas, 522, *523n*
Weiss, Lawrence A., 486, 486*n*, 879–880*n*
Welch, I., 519*n*, 917*n*
Well-known seasoned issuers (WKSIs), 408*n*
Wells Fargo, 315, *401*
Wermers, R., 347*n*, 910*n*
Werner, I., 881*n*
Western Electric, 873
West Japan Railway Company, 877
WestLb, 385
Whaley, R. E., 581*n*
White, H., 347*n*, 910*n*
White, M. J., 879*n*
Whited, T. M., 875*n*
Whole Foods, *830*
Williams, J. B., 87*n*, 431*n*, 453*n*
Williams Act of 1968, 849, 849*n*, 852
Williamson, R., 772–773*n*, 773
Wilshire 5000 Index, 345, *346*
Wingfield, N., 442*n*
Winner's curse, 403, 404*n*, 407*n*
Wizman, Thierry, 639, 639*n*
WKSIs (well-known seasoned issuers), 408*n*
WobbleWorks, 396
Wolfson, M. A., 427*n*

Womack, K. L., 399*n*
Woolridge, J. R., 875*n*
Working capital. *See also* Working capital management
  in cash budgeting, 778–780, *779–780*
  in cash cycle, 778
  cash flow and, 775
  composition of, *801–803,* 801–804
  defined, 137, 323*n*, 747, 801
  investment in, 137–138, 138*n*, 145, 147
  in net present value analysis, 137–138
Working capital management, 804–822. *See also* Working capital
  cash management and, 812–816, *813–814*
  credit management and, 806–812, *809–810*
  inventories in, 804–806, *805*
  marketable securities in, *816,* 816–822, *820*
Workouts, 881–882
World Bank, 660, 661, 736
WorldCom, 397, *878,* 904
Worldwide corporate taxation, 144
WPPSS (Washington Public Power Supply System), 819*n*
Wruck, K. H., 486*n*, 867*n*, 880*n*
Wulf, J., 312*n*
WuLiangYe Corporation, 580
Wurgler, J., 351*n*, 436*n*, 499*n*

X

Xiong, Wei, 580*n*
Xu, M., 412*n*

Y

Yahoo!, 349
Yahoo! Finance, 79, 79*n*, 228, 544*n*
Yankee bonds, 640
Yasuda, A., 869*n*
Yermack, D., 579*n*
Yield
  convenience, 290*n*, 695, *696*
  on corporate bonds, 67–68, *68,* 614–618, *616*
  on corporate debt, 614–618
  current, 48
  dividend, 79, 87, 172–173, *173*
  to maturity, 48–50, 115*n*
  on money-market investments, 817
Yield curve, 58
Yield-curve notes, *645*
Yield spreads, 67–68, *68,* 616, 616–618
York Water Co., *89*
Yoshimori, M., 897*n*
Yu, Jialin, 580*n*
Yuan, K., 913*n*
Yun, H., 651*n*

Z

Zeckhauser, R., 322, 322n
Zender, J. F., 495n, 499n
Zero-coupon bonds, 633n
Zero-maintenance hedging, 702–703
Zero-stage investment, 391–392

Zero-sum games, 684, 684n
Zheng, L., 913n
Zhengzhou Commodity Exchange, *691*
Zhu, Q., 913n
Zhu, Z., 398, 398n
Ziemba, W. T., 349, 349n, 914n

Zingales, Luigi, 10n, 487, 487n, 498, 498n,
    892, 892n, 902, 902–903n
Zinsschranke rule, 476n
Zitzewitz, E., 357n
Z-score model of default risk, 624n, 626
Zuckerman, G., 11n